W9-BZS-602

WESTERN
HIGHLANDS
AND ISLANDS

CENTRAL
AND EASTERN

SOUTHERN
AND BORDERS

NORTHERN
IRELAND

NORTHUMBRIA

CUMBRIA

ISLE
OF MAN

YORKSHIRE
AND
HUMBERSIDE

NORTH-
WEST

EAST
MIDLANDS

WALES

HEART
OF ENGLAND

EAST
ANGLIA

THAMES AND
CHILTERNS

LONDON

SOUTH
OF
ENGLAND

SOUTH-EAST

WEST   COUNTRY

CHANNEL
ISLANDS

Scale
0   50 km
0   50 miles

THE HACHETTE GUIDE TO GREAT BRITAIN

Special thanks to :

- The British Tourist Authority
- Regional and local Tourist Authorities

Original work conceived under the direction of Adélaïde Barbey and the Guides Bleus.

Direction : Adélaïde Barbey

Executive Editor : Marie-Pierre Levallois

Editors : Michael Raeburn and Isabelle Jendron

Contributors : Monique Allouche, Charlotte Atkins, Brigid Avison, Alan Blackwood, Emmanuelle Bourdet, Ann Bridges, Wendy Brown, Duncan Brewer, Thelma Clinton, Roderic Donovan, Georgeanne Downes, Peter McGreg Eadie, Julia Engelhardt, Jennifer Gordon, Ann F. Hill, Katharine Holme, Sarah Jones, Sylvie Lasserre, Barba Littlewood, David Lorking, Kenneth E. Lowther, Marilyn McCully, Sheila Mooney Mall, Angela Murphy, Ro Patching, Diana Phillips, Jeanette Rajadel, Alexandra Tufts-Simon, John Tyler Tuttle, Christine Vincent.

Paste-up : Irène de Moucheron

Cartography : Hachette-Guides Bleus (René Pineau, Alain Mirande) and B.T.A.

Illustrations : Trevor Vincent

Production : Gérard Piassale, Françoise Jolivot

Editorial computing : Catherine Julhe, M.C.P. Orléans, Tadia

Photocomposition : M.C.P. Orléans

Manufactured in France by Maulde et Renou Aisne and Reliure Brun

First American Edition

© 1988 by Hachette and Random House, Inc.

© British Tourist Authority for maps, 1988

ISBN : 0-394-57044-8

ISSN: 0895-3767

THE HACHETTE GUIDE
TO
GREAT BRITAIN

PANTHEON BOOKS
NEW YORK

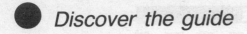

Discover the guide

The Hachette Guides collection is growing. After the Guides to France and Italy, now it's time to take inventory of the scenic beauties, tourist sites and monuments, and all the leisure activities to be enjoyed in Great Britain. So that your holiday will be a memorable one, we've come up with 3,500 hotels and restaurants, 2,000 inns and pubs, 3,000 ideas for your leisure hours. Castles, museums, historic sites and folk festivals throughout Great Britain are yours to discover in these pages.

A thorough tourist guide, the Guide to Great Britain also offers:
● maps of exceptionally high quality produced by the Hachette Guides Bleus and the B.T.A. (British Tourist Authority);
● for each region, sites not to be missed, as well as a choice of tourist itineraries, selected for their scenic or cultural interest;
● a selection of delightful stopovers: the most pleasant hotels are marked with a blue dot; red dots indicate gourmet restaurants or, more simply, establishments which represent excellent value for money;
● solutions to your basic problems in our Practical Holiday Guide.

So take along the Hachette Guide to Great Britain, whether you're traveling as a couple, a family, or by yourself, and discover the many faces of England, Scotland, Wales and Northern Ireland.

The Editors

Symbols and abbreviations

● Maps and places of interest

★ interesting
★★ remarkable
★★★ exceptional

Regional maps: towns and sites marked in red are worth a detour. Places set off in a frame are not to be missed.

City maps: legends are noted on each map.

Careful! Maps and diagrams vary in scale. The scale is always indicated by a calibration.

An arrow (→) refers to another entry.

● Practical information

Cities and towns

☎ telephone code
ⓘ tourist information office
🚂 train station
🚌 bus station
✈ airport

🚢 boat line
⋏ campground
♨ spa
⛷ ski area

♥ editor's choice (establishments that particularly caught the fancy of our editorial team)

Hotels and restaurants

★ simple
★★ simple and comfortable
★★★ very comfortable
★★★★ first-class hotel
● Recommended hotel
● Recommended restaurant (gourmet food or good value for money)

Abbreviations

(A.N.C.)	Anchor Hotels	(I.N.C.)	Inter-Continental Hotels	(Q.M.H.)	Queens Moat Houses
(B.W.)	Best Western Hotels	(I.N.H.)	Inter Hotels	(R.C.)	Relais et Châteaux
(E.D.W.)	Edwardian Hotels	(L.A.D.)	Ladbroke Hotels	(T.H.F.)	Trusthouse Forte Hotels
(F.O.R.)	Forestale Hotels	(M.C.H.)	Mount Charlotte Hotels		

Amenities

Tx telex
Ⓟ parking
view
park or garden

quiet
access for the handicapped
music
no pets

pool
tennis
golf
horseback riding

Prices

Prices are noted at the end of each entry. Remember, they are estimates, not firm and definite tariffs. Check current prices before you reserve your room or a table.

Hotels: Average price for a double room with bath, including tax, not including breakfast.

Restaurants: Average price for an à la carte meal, including tax.

Principal credit cards accepted :
AC Access/Eurocard
AM American Express
DI Diners Club
BA Barclaycard/Visa

● Contents

4-5   *Discover the Guide*
  ● Symbols and abbreviations

7   *How to use the guide*

8   *Tourist itineraries*

9   *The many faces of England*
History — art — climate — the people

29   *Practical holiday guide*
Basic information for your trip

61   *The regions of Great Britain*
Region by region, all localities are listed in alphabetical order. The descriptions of cultural treasures are followed by useful addresses: hotels, restaurants, pubs, campgrounds, bed and breakfasts, leisure activities. Watch for the addresses marked with a ♥ : they're the editors' favourites (shops, antiques, tea rooms...).

703   *Index*
Key to the *Guide,* this is where you will find all the sites, cities and towns described in the text, with their page numbers.

● *How to use the Guide*

The 19 regions: For touring purposes, we have divided Great Britain into 19 different regions, including London, Wales, Scotland, Northern Ireland and the Channel Islands. All 19 are listed on the inside cover, with the counties they encompass and the appropriate page reference. For each region, the Guide provides a brief presentation of the area's geography, history, economy and sites of interest, a regional map, a county map and useful addresses for obtaining further information, for taking courses or for practicing your favourite sport. All the localities in a given region are arranged in alphabetical order and by degree of historic or scenic importance (★ to ★★★). Each site mentioned has a reference to help you locate it on the regional map.

Hotels: Great Britain does not employ an official rating system for hotels. Our classification gives from one to four stars, the higher number going to hotels which offer their guests a warm welcome, a pleasant decor, adequate amenities and good value for money. From country inns to luxurious hotels, the most pleasant establishments are marked with a blue dot. Those places which do not permit children under a certain age are duly indicated.

Restaurants: Only good quality establishments are listed in the Guide, be they modest inns or renowned restaurants. In addition to the food, comfort and service have been taken into consideration. Red dots indicate places offering carefully prepared cuisine and good value for money.

Inns and pubs: A cordial atmosphere, an attractive decor, good beer: these are the criteria we used for selecting the pubs listed here. The Guide's friendly inns are all small (3 to 15 rooms), and serve good, home-style food.

Recommended: The best addresses for amusement, shopping, antiques, handicrafts, golf, horseback riding... cozy bed and breakfasts, picturesque farmhouses that offer quiet and a friendly welcome, and the editors' choices.

For more information: The many faces of England; an illustrated overview of England from prehistoric times to the present: history, art, culture and a look at the climate and people of Great Britain.

And for the best holiday ever: Practical holiday guide: A wealth of practical advice under several headings: Information — Calendar, events — Traveling in Britain — Accommodation — Eating and drinking — Sporting Holidays.

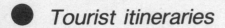

Tourist itineraries

Throughout the guide, tourist itineraries are recommended. You will find them on the pages indicated below.

Cumbria

132 Solway round trip
140 Ravenglass to Eskdale excursion
143 Windermere environs

East Anglia

158 Cambridge villages round trip
174 Norfolk Broads
179 Suffolk wool towns

East Midlands

205 Lincolnshire Wolds
215 Northern Peak District

Heart of England

237 The Shropshire hills
241 Vale of Evesham villages
249 North Staffordshire moors
260 North Cotswolds villages

Northern Ireland

274 Ards Peninsula
282 Lower Lough Erne

Northumbria

296 Allendales
298 South Tweed Valley

North-West

329 From Lancaster through Trough of Bowland
340 Ribble Valley and Forest of Pendle

Central and Eastern Scotland

365 Round trip from Pitlochry

Southern Scotland

391 Galloway Forest Park

Western Scotland, Highlands and Islands

401 Round trip from Bonar Bridge
416 Loch Ness
417 Round trip to Moidart

South East

467 North Downs
473 South Downs
477 The Weald

South of England

495 Isle of Wight
497 New Forest

Thames and Chilterns

517 Thames Valley villages
521 North Oxfordshire villages
527 The Chiltern hills
544 Villages of the Windrush & Upper Thames

Wales

560 Black Mountains
568 Gower Peninsula
572 Snowdon Mountain
577 Llyn Brianne Dam round trip

West Country

598 Taw valley
601 Avon valley
609 Eastern Dartmoor
617 Exmoor National Park
624 Lizard Peninsula
631 Marlborough Downs
636 Penwith Peninsula
641 Nadder and Wylye valleys
655 Around Wadebridge

Yorkshire, Humberside

683 North York moors
683 Cleveland hills
694 Upper Nidderdale

The many faces of England

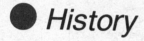

History

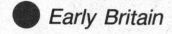

Early Britain

Stone Age man

Britain was not always cut off from the continental mainland. When the early hunters of the Stone Age wandered into the country, they came over a land-bridge to a region that was probably a windswept, treeless desert. As the Ice Age retreated, however, around 10,000 B.C., trees began to grow, and by about 5,000 B.C. — by which time Britain had become separated from the Continent — the countryside was probably covered by a dense, deciduous forest. Not surprisingly, perhaps, **Stone Age man** made little impression on the landscape, and it was not until around 3,500 B.C., when the first farmers arrived from France and Belgium, bringing with them barley and wheat, and probably sheep and cattle by now domesticated, that changes to the land's appearance began to occur. With their axes of polished stone, they started to clear areas of woodland and till the soil. The flints needed for their axes and knives, as well as pottery, jet and possibly salt, were taken along tracks such as the Ridge-way in Berkshire and the Icknield Way, running some 190 miles from the Wash almost to **Stonehenge**. This was Europe's most impressive megalithic monument, begun in 1,300 B.C. During this period more immigrants, known from their pottery as the Beaker Folk, arrived from the Rhineland. They knew how to work copper, gold and tin, and soon weaving was also developed. So the Bronze Age dawned, around 2,000 B.C.

Stonehenge

Prehistoric and early Christian sites

At this time, the climate of Britain was becoming warmer and drier, and the Beaker Folk, continuing a process that had already begun more than a thousand years before, cleared the southern downlands of England, which they divided into small square fields, roughly an acre each. Though now incorporated into larger fields, the outlines are still visible in part of Dorset, for example. They then moved on to areas of virgin forest, and Dartmoor was cleared of trees and divided up into fields, separated by stone walls. The stones taken from the soil that were not used for the walls were assembled into heaps or cairns which, along with the stone walls, are such a feature of the hills and moors of Britain. At Grimspound, on Dartmoor, we may still see the site of what was once a farming community of some twenty or thirty circular stone huts, and contained within one outer stone wall, indicating that some form of defense was necessary.

The unfortunate effect of this dual process of tree felling and pasture grazing was that erosion developed on a large scale; as the climate became colder and wetter around 1,200 B.C., moss took over from grass, creating what are still amongst the wildest and most barren areas of Britain.

The Iron Age: The Celts

The Iron Age was ushered in by the arrival, about 650 B.C., of the **Celts**. They were a warlike race, with a distinct warrior class and chieftains who laid claims to territories. They were also excellent horsemen and had chariots and iron swords, and made special armour for their horses. At the same time they were efficient farmers and knew how to raise stock and practise crop rota-

tion. A second wave arrived in about 300 B.C., from Northern France and Brittany, where the La Tene culture flourished. Metalwork was developed to a high degree of sophistication with raised curvilinear patterns based on plant motifs, inset with polished gems. Pottery too became an accomplished art form. The hill forts that were built in the centuries preceding the Roman Conquest demonstrate a considerable engineering skill, an ability to move thousands of tons of soil and erect vast numbers of wooden posts. The Celtic religion was concerned with placating the forces of nature. Magical rites were performed at sacred groves and springs, with festivals keyed to the seasons of the agricultural year. By the time that Belgic tribes came to Britain in two waves around 150 B.C. and 60 B.C., the Celtic people were developing an efficient system of agriculture. Copper and tin were being mined, woolen textiles were renowned and leatherwork extensively practised. Small lowland townships began to replace the earlier hill forts as centres of commerce, representing the headquarters of individual rulers. Some were prosperous enough to import for their personal use luxury goods from the Mediterranean such as silver vessels and fine tableware. There are signs too of the beginnings of literacy, since the first coins bore Latin inscriptions. Although Britain was still a country of rural peasants, society was becoming increasingly complex, local leaders competing with one another for territory and prestige, local groups becoming larger and more widespread. It was around this time that towns such as Colchester, St. Alban's and Winchester were built.

Roman Britain

This then was the society with which Rome was confronted when **Julius Caesar** invaded Britain in 55 and 54 B.C., his stated reason being that the Belgic tribes in Britain were supporting their neighbours in Gaul and helping to stiffen resistance there. Julius Caesar, however, did not establish a permanent Roman presence in England and it was with the invasion of the **Emperor Claudius** in A.D. 43 that Britain became a province of the Roman Empire. Within four years the new rulers had occupied most of Britain south of the River Trent and east of the Severn. Existing towns, such as Colchester and St. Alban's were expanded, and less permanent sites such as London and Dorchester were developed. There was a serious challenge to Rome in A.D. 61 when **Boudicca**, Queen of the **iceni**, led a particularly fierce revolt, but soon a relative peace was restored, villas were built and, within twenty years, the basic pattern of Roman roads in Britain was established. A major change was made to the landscape when drainage of the Fens created new farmland. With easier communications and better means of transport, the legions pacified Wales, and **Agricola** embarked on his conquest of Scotland. The northern tribes retaliated fiercely and, between 122 and 128 **Hadrian's Wall** was built from the Tyne to the Solway Firth to hold them back. The Romans nevertheless pushed north into Scotland, and in 141 built the **Antonine Wall** across the narrow part of the country between the Forth and the Clyde, but in 163 that wall was abandoned, and they retreated to Hadrian's Wall maintaining this as their northern frontier.

The Romans occupied Britain for almost four hundred years, linking the country by an elaborate road system and guarding it with a skilful disposition of a vast number of forts and fortlets. **Hadrian's Wall** held back incursions from the bellicose Caledonians, and Wales, although conquered by the late 80s, was held in check by the establishment of military strongholds at Carleon and Chester. In general, the Romans used force of arms only when absolutely necessary. A rebellious local ruler would be firmly suppressed, but expediency was preferred, goods and services in exchange for protection. Indeed, when Suetonius put down the **Boudiccan revolt** with exceptional severity he was hastily recalled to Rome.

The lifestyle of the ordinary inhabitants probably changed little, but the life of the townspeople altered dramatically and not just because they were able to see the efficient Roman civil service in action. Cities such as Colchester, St. Alban's, Bath and London had a forum, baths, temples, stadia and, of course, shops. Christianity, after it had become officially tolerated, also found more support in the towns, country districts clinging to the native Celtic rites.

Christianity reaches Britain

The Romans finally withdrew from Britain in 407, when the Emperor Honorius told the British to look to their own defenses against the marauding Germanic peoples. Saxon pirates had raided Southeast England as early as 275, and in 377 Picts, Scots and Saxons combined to challenge the power of Rome in

300,000 BC	Britain part of Continent
10,000 BC	Milder Climate. Britain covered in coniferous forests
5,000 BC	Britain now an island cut off from Continent
3,000 BC	First farmers from Flanders and France
2,750 BC	Stonehenge Beaker Folk, so-called from their pottery
2,000 BC	Bronze Age
650 BC	Iron Age Celts arrive
55-54 BC	Roman invasions under Julius Caesar
43 BC	Roman colonization of Britain under reign of Emperor Claudius
AD 122	Agricola incursion into Scotland
128	Romans build Hadrian's wall across Northern England
407	Romans depart
5th & 6th Centuries	Invasions of Jutes, Angles and Saxons
597	St. Augustine of Canterbury brings Christianity to England
8th Century	Danish settlements in North of England
827	Egbert, King of Wessex becomes first king of England
897-899	Alfred the Great
1016-1035	Canute the Great
1042	Edward the Confessor
1066	Harold King of England. Norman invasion under William the Conqueror

Britain. Now, with the Romans gone, invading Germanic peoples — Angles and Saxons from the northwest of Germany — gradually took over the country. Meanwhile Christianity, no longer outlawed in the Roman Empire, had reached Britain, and the Saxons who had settled in Kent and East Anglia began to push inland, driving the Christian Britons before them into Wales and the peninsula of Devon and Cornwall. Thus it was that Christianity went from Wales to Ireland, and from Devon to Germany, with **St. Patrick** and **St. Boniface** respectively. From Ireland **St. Columba** took the faith to Scotland, and while the flame flickered and went out in the south of Britain, so it was that Christianity prospered in the two island powerhouses of **Iona**, off the southwestern coast of Scotland, and **Lindisfarne**, off the coast of Northumbria. Of the Roman presence, the roads, the Wall, some of the fortresses, the towns and the villas remained and indeed, some of Britain's most attractive towns and cities prove to be Roman in origin. But so strong was the impact of the incoming peoples that the Roman influence on British law, institutions and language was considerably diminished.

Northumbrian stone cross

St. Augustine of Canterbury came to Britain from Rome to convert the pagans of Southern England to Christianity. At Canterbury in Kent, he founded what was to become the heart of the faith in Britain, but eventually there had to be agreement with the northern Church. By the **Synod of Whitby** in 664, the Roman influence was accepted as superior to that of the Celtic tradition.

The Germanic tribes invade

The occupation of Britain by Germanic tribes was a process that took nearly three centuries, but by the 7th Century Anglo-Saxon kings ruled all of modern England, apart from Cornwall. Amongst important contributions to British society, the Anglo-Saxons were responsible for a system of law codes in which there was a very carefully ordered hierarchy of social status, justice being meted out according to the status of the individual. At the top is the king, then comes his servant, the great lord and, at the bottom, the slave. Opportunities, though carefully designated, were extremely unequal. In the 9th Century there was a new wave of invaders — the Vikings who sacked Lindisfarne in 793. They had settled in the Orkneys and Shetland and they invaded East Anglia, advancing into Mercia and north into Northumbria. It was Alfred, King of Wessex, who eventually made a treaty with them, restricting them to the Danelaw, which comprised much of central and eastern England. The initial strength of the Vikings, who sought and took the wealth of the Anglo-Saxon kingdoms, lay in their mobility. Once settled, they became the prey to skilful manoeuvres of King Alfred and his successors, so that ultimately the Kings of Wessex became the Kings of England. A second period of Viking raids, this time restricted to Danes, was better equipped and organized, and in 1016, a Danish king, Cnut, assumed the throne. Eventually it was a descendant of one of those Vikings or Norsemen

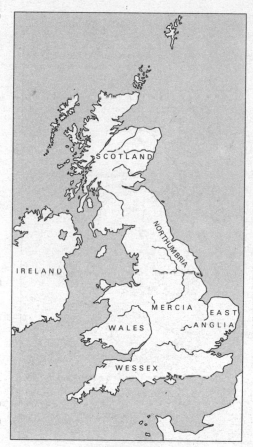

Old kingdoms

who settled in France, across the English Channel, in the person of the Duke of Normandy, **William the Conqueror**, who invaded Britain for the last time, defeating Harold at the **Battle of Hastings**, and laying the foundations of the country as we know it.

 # The Middle Ages

Norman Britain

With the Norman Conquest, the continuous development of British social, artistic and cultural tradition began. The monuments, cities, towns and villages that visitors are most likely to see about them will probably be post-Conquest, although earlier influences had a vital effect on the way buildings were placed, or towns and villages developed, and there are some remarkable survivals in terms of artifacts and isolated buildings from earlier times. Until the advent of the motorways, Britain's road system, for example, was still in many places heavily indebted to the Romans. In Kent, the motorway builders found no better route for the **M2** than that chosen by the Romans, so they put their roads parallel to it. Then the division of the countryside into fields, in some places, was made in Anglo-Saxon times, and several villages owe their layout to the Saxons — either 'street' villages strung out along the sides of a single street, with a church at one end, or the more picturesque 'green' villages built around a green with its church and, sometimes, a well.

1. Cambridge
2. Bury St Edmunds
3. Framlingham

Kirkwall

Elgin

Dunvegan

Eilean
Donan

Iona

Dunblane

St Andrews

Dunfermline

Edinburgh

Glasgow

Lindisfarne

Melrose

Hexham

Richmond
Rievaulx

Fountains

York

Beverley

Beaumaris

Holywell

Conwy

Chester

Lincoln

Caernarfon

Castle
Rising

Harlech

Peterborough

Norwich

Lichfield

Stokesay

Warwick

Ely

2 3

Worcester

Chipping
Campden

1

Hereford

Lavenham

Goodrich

Tewkesbury

St David's

Gloucester

St Albans

Tintern

London

Bristol Oxford

Rochester

Pembroke

Bath Windsor

Wells

Canterbury

Salisbury

Dover

Winchester

Bodiam

Exeter

Sherborne

Chichester

Christchurch

Medieval sites

Romanesque style

It is, however, the powerful Norman buildings that more readily command attention; the castles, churches and cathedrals, built in the **Romanesque style** they brought with them, and known in Britain, therefore, as **Norman**. The castles were built to protect the Normans' new domain, catalogued in the **Domesday Book** in 1086, and their massive keeps may still be seen at **Dover, Rochester, Richmond** in Yorkshire or, the earliest of all, the **White Tower** of the Tower of London. It is the ecclesiastical buildings, however, that are among the richest gifts of the Normans to the British heritage, most of them dating from the last decades of the 11th Century. **Canterbury** was begun in about 1070, though a fire destroyed much of the Norman church in 1174, four years after the murder of **Thomas Becket**. However, the crypt, the largest in England, has survived, and its sturdy columns, groin vaulting and richly carved capitals are a powerful testimony to the skill of the first Romanesque builders and craftsmen in this country. Another example can be found at **Worcester**, where the Norman crypt, begun in 1084, survives beneath the later cathedral.

Winchester was especially significant for the Normans, because the city had been the capital of England. In fact, William I was crowned there, as well as in Westminster Abbey. He therefore ordered the Saxon building to be replaced in 1079, and the new cathedral, at 556 ft, is the longest in Europe. A much better idea of the effect of a Romanesque cathedral in its ensemble, however, is found at **Durham**, begun in 1093, and one of the world's supreme achievements in that style. It has the earliest flying buttresses (1133) in England, and was the first building in Europe to have ribbed vaulting throughout, as well as being one of

the earliest to have pointed transverse arches in the nave. However, the effect remains supremely Romanesque, distinct from the Gothic that was to follow. The cathedral was originally the church of a Benedictine abbey, and most of the monastic buildings have survived, adding to the interest of the place. With its adjacent bishop's palace, now part of the university, **Durham** is a rewarding place to visit. Similar Benedictine foundations, with magnificent long naves, are at **Peterborough**, begun in 1177, and **Norwich**, about 1121, though the east end was begun in the previous century.

The Gothic style: Early English

Gothic architecture developed in France about 1140, and was brought to England largely by the **Cistercians** and **William of Sens**, who was charged with the rebuilding of the east end of Canterbury after the fire of 1174. But whereas there is something rather graceless in the new work at Canterbury, a native style soon began to develop, known as Early English, which one sees in the nave and transepts of **Wells Cathedral**, begun in 1180, and its magnificent west facade, containing some 400 stone figures, completed a century later. A similar development occurred in two eastern cathedrals — at Peterborough, where the west front is conceived as a vast screen, pierced with three tall arches 81 ft tall, and at **Lincoln**, which was begun in 1072, though an earthquake of 1185 (a rare event in Britain) destroyed all but the west front and two west towers. A Cistercian, **Hugh of Avalon**, was appointed bishop by Henry II, and started rebuilding the cathedral in 1192. Some of the finest Early English architecture is to be seen in the choir and transept at Lincoln, and the nave demonstrates well the fact that when the Gothic style came to England the emphasis tended, unlike France, to be on length rather than height, so that, at just 102 ft, the nave vault of **Westminster Abbey**, begun by **Henry III** in 1245, is the highest in England. Perhaps the purest expression of the Early English is found at **Salisbury**, begun in 1220, five years after the signing of **Magna Carta**, which formed the basis of English civil liberty. The only Gothic cathedral built in England on a totally new site, Salisbury was completed in just over forty years, apart from its tower and spire which, at 404 ft, is the tallest medieval stone spire in the world. The fourteenth-century spire at Lincoln reached 524 ft, but was blown down in 1548. Even so, the central tower, at 271 ft, is still the tallest cathedral tower in England.

The Gothic style: Decorated

In ecclesiastic architecture the Gothic style developed subsequently in England first as **Decorated** (about 1250-1370). As the names imply, these styles were an elaboration of the elements of Gothic, assisted by the very favourable conditions prevalent in England with its eminently suitable limestone readily avail-

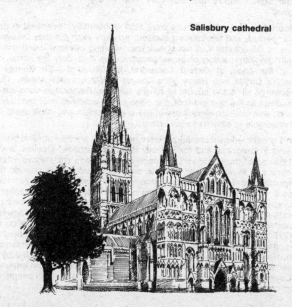

Salisbury cathedral

1066	Romanesque style of architecture
1067	Tower of London built
1075	Winchester Cathedral built
1084	Worcester Cathedral built
1085	Doomsday Book
1093	Durham Cathedral built
1121	Norwich Cathedral built
1154-1189	Henry II Plantagenet and Eleanor of Aquitaine
1176	Murder of Thomas Becket
1175	Gothic Style of Architecture
1214-1294	Roger Bacon, philosopher
1215	Magna Carta
1220	Salisbury Cathedral built
1245	Westminster Abbey built
1250	Gothic Decorated Style
1275	Exeter Cathedral built
1322	Ely Cathedral built
1327-1377	Edward III
1338-1453	Hundred Years' War
1340-1400	Geoffrey Chaucer poet
1346	Battle of Crécy
1347	Capture of Calais
1348-1349	Black Death
1356	Battle of Poitiers
1377-1399	Richard II (murdered)

able, and a seemingly inexhaustible supply of oak for timber. Moreover, in the earlier period the country was prosperous and the Church wealthy. Until the **Black Death** of 1348-49, when it is estimated that between one third and half the population perished, Gothic architecture saw a remarkable flowering in England. The best example of the Decorated style is to be found at **Exeter Cathedral**, begun in about 1275, though the nave was not completed until almost a century later. A marvelous tierceron vault runs for 300 ft along the entire length of nave and choir, thus extending the Early English idea of completeness of ensemble. The octagonal chapter house at Wells, with its soaring vaulted roof, whose thirty-two ribs spring from a central pillar, also dates from this period, as well as the octagon of **Ely Cathedral**, the only Gothic 'dome', which was the response of the architects to the collapse of the Norman tower in 1322. Another Decorated octagonal chapter house even more daring than that at Wells is at **York**, built between 1260 and 1300. It is fifty-eight ft in diameter, and the roof soars up with no central support at all. This is only one of the glories of York, however, for the **Minster** is the largest medieval church in England, housing some of the country's finest medieval stained glass. The city, too, is a fascinating palimpsest of civilization in Britain, with interesting Roman and Viking remains upon which the medieval town was superimposed. There are also important Georgian and Victorian elements, making York a prime example of a British provincial city.

The Gothic style: Perpendicular

In the perpendicular period more towers were built. Especially notable is that at **Canterbury Cathedral** known as **Bell Harry** (1480), one of the finest of its type, and the chapter house has a barrel-vaulted timber roof that is surpassed only by the hammer-beam roof of Westminster Hall, where England's first parliament met in 1265. Roofs were one of the chief glories of this period, and some magnificent timber examples are to be found in East Anglia, where the wool trade gave support to the building of beautiful parish churches. The angel roof at **St. Wendreda**, March, Cambridgeshire, dating from about 1500, is a fine example of a double hammer-beam roof.

The parish churches of Britain are always worth visiting, for they present, on a small scale, the full range of architectural styles and local variants. Apart from the buildings themselves, the monuments they contain are also of great interest, the inscriptions providing a detailed social history of the place. Those who wish to trace ancestors can consult tombstones and parish registers (though, for safety, most of the latter are now preserved elsewhere). A glance at the list of incumbents of the parish will reveal much about local religious history and the succession of architectural styles, and variations from county to county provide endless opportunities for study. Despite the depredations of the Reformation in the 16th Century and the Civil War in the 17th, a remarkable number survive.

As well as roofs of wood, stone vaults were also wonderfully developed in the **Perpendicular period**, and fan-vaulting evolved. An early example may be seen in the cloister of Gloucester Cathedral, but later vaulting became much more elaborate with the introduction of stone pendants, as if to defy the force of gravity, as in the choir of **Oxford Cathedral**, the choir of   **St. George's Chapel**, Windsor Castle and **Henry VII's Chapel** in Westminster Abbey. The most impressive of all is the chapel of **King's College**, Cambridge completed in 1515. In addition to the soaring roof, the glass of the windows is of outstanding quality and, with the rich woodwork of the organ screen and choir stalls, a magnificent ensemble is offered to the visitors.

While Britain's great medieval cathedrals were being built, another parallel building activity was in progress and for a vastly different purpose. Castles were ubiquitous features of the medieval landscape and hundreds still survive, often in a ruined state and in remote and romantic settings. Castles were needed for the twin purposes of defense and fiscal administration, and during the Norman period, stone keeps were erected across the country with remarkable rapidity. Later, the single stone tower with outer earthwork defenses was followed by more elaborate edifices consisting of curtain walls with regularly spaced towers and a gatehouse. But the great castle-building period belongs to the reign of **Edward I** (1272-1307), when a powerful chain of sixteen fortresses was built in North Wales, the most important being **Flint, Rhuddland, Conwy, Caernarvon** and **Harlech**. Here, the massive towers and gatehouses were surrounded by a second, lower wall, also equipped with towers, sometimes with a moat beyond. Of these, Caernarvon is the best preserved, presenting a potent image of strength and majesty, with the sea to one side and the town beyond.

Bodiam castle

Secular architecture

Secular architecture of a gentler kind is best represented in the university cities of Oxford and Cambridge; the colleges there span almost every period from their foundation in the 12th and early 13th Centuries to the present day. The Old Court of **Corpus Christi College**, Cambridge, is a wonderful example of domestic architecture of the period, while **Merton College**, Oxford, founded in 1274, has the oldest library in England (1371). In general, all the colleges that together comprise the university have a chapel, library and a hall where the members of the foundation take their meals together. The college hall may often contain a succession of portraits of its distinguished scholars across the centuries that are of both historical and artistic interest. Having usually started out as charitable institutions to provide education for the needy, the individual colleges became rich through endowments and, by the time the monasteries were dissolved by **Henry VIII** in the 16th Century, the Church had lost its monopoly of education, and the universities were all placed to continue as the centres of the nation's intellectual life. For this reason, until the establishment of other universities in the 19th Century, the colleges of Oxford and Cambridge, and in Scotland those of the universities of St. Andrews, Edinburgh, Glasgow and Aberdeen have played an extremely important role in the history of the nation. Strangely, however, the first great poet of the English language, **Geoffrey Chaucer** (1340-1400), was not a university man.

 # Reformation and Renaissance

Dissolution of the monasteries

The 16th Century, which saw the establishment of the reformed Church of England, was a period of dynamic development for Britain. After the dynastic struggles of the **Hundred Years War** with France (1338-1453), the country had been racked by the **War of the Roses** (1455-85) between the rival royal houses of York and Lancaster, a conflict that was only resolved with the establishment of the Tudor dynasty under **Henry VIII**. The 16th Century in Britain was the century of the Tudors, epitomized by **Henry VIII** and **Elizabeth I**. Henry VIII declared himself head of the **English Church** in 1534, began the **Dissolution of the monasteries** in 1536, the same year in which Wales was annexed to England by an Act of Union. His daughter **Mary** attempted to restore Roman Catholicism during her brief reign (1553-58) but failed. Under her sister, Good Queen Bess, as she became affectionately known, Britain saw a remarkable flourishing of exploration: **Francis Drake** began his voyage round the world in 1577, and the beginnings of an overseas empire were established. At the same time there was a surge of artistic activity in music, literature, drama, painting and a renewed emphasis on learning. In short, the waves of the Renaissance, which had

1399-1413	Henry IV
1413-1422	Henry V
1415	Battle of Agincourt
1422-1491	William Caxton, printer
1450	Gothic Perpendicular Style
1453	All France lost
1455-1485	War of the Roses
1460-1529	John Skelton poet
died 1470	Sir Thomas Malory (Morte d'Arthur)
1478-1535	Sir Thomas More (Utopia)
1480	Canterbury Cathedral Tower built
1483-1485	Richard III killed Battle of Bosworth
1485-1509	Henry VII Tudor
1500	St. Wendreda Church, March, built
1509-1547	Henry VIII
1534	Henry declares himself Head of English Church; Reformation
1536	Dissolution of the monasteries; Wales annexed
1540	Thomas Cromwell executed
1543-1623	William Byrd musician
1544	War with France
1546	War with Scotland
1550	Gloucester Cathedral Tower built in Perpendicular Style
1552-1618	Sir Walter Raleigh
1552-1599	Edmund Spenser poet

1553-1558 Mary I, married to Philip II of Spain, becomes Queen of England

1554-1607 John Lyly dramatist

1555-1556 Burning of Latimer and Cranmer

1558 Longleat Historic House built. Calais lost

1558-1603 Elizabeth I

1558-1595 Thomas Kyd dramatist

1560-1592 Robert Green dramatist

1561-1626 Francis Bacon philosopher and statesman

1564-1593 Christopher Marlowe dramatist

1564-1616 William Shakespeare dramatist

1570-1632 Thomas Dekker dramatist

1572-1637 Ben Johnson dramatist

1572 Drake's voyage round the world

1573-1631 John Donne poet

1573-1632 Ingo Jones architect

1577-1640 Robert Burton philosopher and man of letters

1578-1657 William Harvey physician

1580-1640 John Webster dramatist

1583-1640 Philip Massinger dramatist

1583-1625 Orlando Gibbons musician

1586-1640 John Ford dramatist

1596 Mary Queen of Scots executed

1587 Drake attacks Cadiz

1588 Defeat of Spanish Armada

Stately homes and castles

flowed across most of the rest of Europe, finally reached the shores of Britain, somewhat late in the day, but nevertheless at a period when the country was best placed to absorb them. One must not forget, however, that the **Scottish Court**, because of its close ties with France, reached a high level of sophistication, and its music in particular was of a rich and varied nature.

Notable landscape changes

By 1600, London, with its 200,000 inhabitants had become the largest city in Europe and one of the major financial centres in the world. **William Shakespeare** (1564-1616) was writing his major tragedies, and composers such as **William Byrd** (1543-1623) and **Orlando Gibbons** (1583-1625) brought British music to heights it had not experienced since the days of **John Dunstable** (d.1453). In **Nicholas Hilliard** (1547-1619), we find the first English painter whose life and work are documented, and who left such remarkable records for us of the people of his age.

Throughout the Middle Ages and the 16th Century the British landscape altered very little. The most notable changes would have been the ruins of some of the monastic buildings and the rise of the new homes of the ruling classes, often taken from those same monastic buildings, which they treated as some handy, ready-made quarry. Though there is cause for regret in the destruction of some of the monasteries, such as **Fountains Abbey** in Yorkshire, and the dispossession of many of the inmates, nevertheless most of them seem to have been readily absorbed into society and, in most cases, especially the cathedral foundations, the transfer of authority was purely an administrative one, from an abbot

and/or prior to a diocesan bishop, with a chapter consisting of a dean and canons responsible for the administration of the buildings and estates. In some of the remote parishes, one priest might well survive all the changes within the church, as at **St. Gerrans** in Cornwall, where the same man was in charge from 1547 until 1581. In many cases, the fabric of the buildings was never seriously harmed, though some ancient shrines, such as that of St. Thomas Becket at Canterbury, were despoiled or destroyed.

The confiscated wealth and estates of the monasteries had provided Henry VIII with means of rewarding his followers at a minimum of cost to himself, and was one that his Protestant daughter Elizabeth readily adopted, though she also made use of other sources of revenue, such as the awarding of monopolies in trade and manufacturing, indicating that by now they had become lucrative. In this way were laid the foundations of the wealth and influence of many of the great aristocratic families of Britain, such as that of Duke of Devonshire at **Chatworth** or the Marquess of Bath at **Longleat**. Unfortified Longleat was only one of the many Elizabethan mansions — **Hardwick Hall**, with its enormous windows, was another — that were made possible not only by the wealth conferred on their owners, but because the country was at peace internally, and so the need for the old fortified houses diminished. One sees this strikingly at **Kenilworth Castle**, Warwickshire, where the medieval keep and hall of John of Gaunt's castle, a gift from the queen to her favorite, **Robert Dudley**, Earl of Leicester, were suddenly extended by the addition of an immense wing with large windows, which the latter hastily threw up when the queen was to stay with him in 1575. Patronage of one sort or another, which had been the basis of feudal society and had been closely linked to the manorial landed system, was an important aspect of the way in which Elizabethan society was organized, and demonstrates the extent to which the medieval system had survived.

Hardwick Hall

Elizabeth I brought her country safely to the threshold of modern times, but failed to anticipate the one great problem of the next century, the inevitable rise of the power of parliament, thus storing up for her successors, the Stuarts, trouble with which they were hopelessly ill-equipped to deal. Moreover, the rise of the middle classes was a phenomenon with which the remains of a basically feudal society had no means of dealing, either. The 17th Century was to be one of domestic turmoil for Britain.

The Stuarts and the Civil War

After the death of Elizabeth I in 1603, the throne of England passed to James VI of Scotland, son of **Mary Queen of Scots**, who for so long had been a thorn in Elizabeth's side, and whom she ultimately had executed in 1587. With the accession of James as **James I of England**, the kingdoms of England and Scotland came under one sovereign. A formal Act of Union between the two countries did not come until 1707, however, when one Parliament was instituted, although Scotland has still largely preserved her own legal and educational systems. Under James I and his son **Charles I**, artistic life continued to thrive in Britain,

1588-1679 Thomas Hobbes philosopher (Leviathan)

1591-1674 Robert Herrick poet

1593-1633 George Herbert poet

1600 London has 200,000 inhabitants

1603 Death of Queen Elizabeth

1603-1625 James VI of Scotland becomes James I of England, Foundation of Great Britain by union of Scotland and England

1605 Gunpowder plot

1607 Plantation of Ulster (Ireland)

1608-1674 John Milton poet

1621-1678 Andrew Marvell poet

1624 War with France

1625-1649 Charles I

1627-1691 Robert Boyle philosopher chemist and

1629-1640 Charles I rules without Parliament

1632-1704 John Locke philosopher

1632-1722 Christopher Wren architect

1633-1703 Samuel Pepys diarist

1640-1689 Aphra Behn woman dramatist and novelist

1642 Charles I raises royal standard at Nottingham

1643-1724 Sir Isaac Newton mathematician and scientist

1643-1645 Battles of Marston Moor and Naseby. Charles I defeated by Parliamentarians

and intellectual life too, and there is truth in the paradox that James was called 'the wisest fool in Christendom'. In the realms of music, literature, painting and architecture, the spirit of the previous century largely continued to inspire developments, to the extent that a house like **Blickling Hall** in Norfolk, though built around 1620, with a magnificent plaster ceiling in its long gallery, has clear affinities with houses of the previous century and even earlier. In the work of the architect Inigo Jones, however, Britain experienced a dramatic new style, evident in his three surviving buildings, the **Queen's House** at Greenwich (begun in 1616), the **Banqueting House**, Whitehall (1619-22) and the **Queen's Chapel**, St. James's Palace (1627). At Wilton House, Jones designed the magnificent **Double Cube Room** to display the Earl of Pembroke's Van Dyck portraits, and the fact that a Rubens ceiling adorns the Banqueting House in Whitehall gives some indication of the new height to which painting in Britain now aspired.

There were, however, other forces at work, and people who burned with religious conviction, unwilling to subscribe to the Stuart connection of monarchy. In Henrietta Maria of France, Charles had a foreign, Roman Catholic wife and, in defiance of custom, he ruled without Parliament from 1629 until 1640. Conflict was inevitable. Some who did not approve, like the Pilgrim Fathers, had left for a New World in 1620. Others preferred to stay and fight. In 1642, on 22 August, **Charles I** raised his standard at Nottingham, and the Civil War began. There were battles against the Parliamentary forces, under the general leadership of **Oliver Cromwell**, at **Edgehill** (1642), two at **Newbury** (1643 and 44), **Marston Moor** (1644) and **Naseby** (1645). Bristol and Gloucester were besieged. For a time, the king made Oxford the seat of his court. The capture of Colchester on 28 August 1648 by the Parliamentarians put an end to this phase of the war. Charles was executed on 30 January 1649, and Cromwell, as Lord Protector, ruled England until his death in 1658, ironically mostly without the help of Parliament. His son **Richard** was named to succeed him, but by this time the British had had enough of the Puritan way of life and, in 1660, welcomed back **Charles II**, who had taken refuge in France after an unsuccessful attempt to take the throne, with a Scots army, at the Battle of Worcester in 1651. It was after this battle that he took refuge in an oak tree, thus giving the name of the Royal Oak to hundreds of pubs in later years. Through his illegitimate sons, Charles II gave the British aristocracy a new lease on life by creating for them the dukedoms of Monmouth, Southampton, Grafton, Richmond and St. Albans.

The Restoration

Cultural life, which had been in a vacuum during the interregnum, now flourished once more, and the **Fire of London** in 1666, devastating though it was, gave scope to Britain's most celebrated architect, **Sir Christopher Wren** (1632-1723) to endow London with what is still one of its most famous landmarks, **St. Paul's Cathedral** (1675-1710), as well as 51 City churches which, when not personally designed by him, were under his direction. The steeples, especially, display an astonishing virtuosity. **St. Stephen**, Walbrook, is important as a predecessor to St. Paul's and, as general examples of Wren's masterly designs and planning on some awkward sites, one may mention **St. Lawrence Jewry, St. Mary-le-Bow** and **St. Clement Danes**. Examples of Wren's secular work in or near London include the Royal Hospital, Chelsea, Kensington Palace, Hampton Court (south and east wings) and Greenwich Palace, though the King Charles block there, begun in 1665, was the work of John Webb, a pupil of Inigo Jones, thus demonstrating that earlier architectural traditions had survived the upheavals of the Civil War. In fact, Webb drew for his inspiration on Jones' plans for a new palace at Whitehall, of which the Banqueting House was only a fragment.

As a reaction against the Puritan ethos, the Restoration theatre tended to be somewhat bawdy and libertine in outlook, though in the classical tradition of poetry one sees a more direct strand uniting **John Milton** (1608-74) to **John Dryden** (1631-1700), and **Alexander Pope** (1688-1744), whilst in the realm of music, despite the king's importation of French elements absorbed during his exile in Paris, **Henry Purcell** (1659-95) stands far above any of his contemporaries, and it was a tragedy for British music that he should have died so young. With his demise, there was to be no comparable native talent for almost two centuries, and although in **Handel** (1685-1759) the new Hanoverian regime was to find a devoted musician of truly international status, who was taken firmly to its heart by the country of his adoption, the fact remains that British music experienced a serious setback. Court painting is best represented by Van Dyck and Lely, though neither was English. Among indigenous painters, mention should be made of the perceptive miniaturist work of Samuel Coope, a Londoner.

Timeline (left margin):

- 1649-1660 — England becomes a Commonwealth and Protectorate
- 1649 — Charles I executed
- 1650-1722 — John Churchill, 1st Duke of Marlborough, soldier
- 1651 — Battle of Worcester : Charles II defeated by Cromwell
- 1652 — War with Holland
- 1653 — Oliver Cromwell Protector
- 1656-1742 — Edmund Halley astronomer
- 1656 — War with Spain
- 1658 — Death of Cromwell
- 1658-1695 — Henry Purcell musician
- 1660-1685 — Restauration, Charles II
- 1660-1731 — Daniel Defoe novelist
- 1661-1736 — Nicholas Hawksmoor architect
- 1665 — Great Plague
- 1666 — Fire of London
- 1670-1729 — William Congreve dramatist
- 1672-1729 — Richard Steele essayist
- 1672-1719 — Joseph Addison essayist
- 1675-1710 — St. Paul's Cathedral built by Wren
- 1678 — Popish plot
- 1685-1688 — James II
- 1685 — Monmouth's rebellion defeated at Sedgemoor
- 1685-1753 — George Berkeley philosopher
- 1688-1744 — Alexander Pope poet
- 1688 — Chatsworth House (Historic Mansion) built

The Glorious Revolution

Political and religious difficulties were prevented from breaking out into new conflict when, through the Glorious Revolution of 1688, the Catholic **James II** gave up the throne in favour of his Protestant daughter Mary and her husband **William of Orange**, who ruled as joint sovereigns. The social and commercial life of the country continued to thrive, and in 1694 the Bank of England began to circulate paper money for the first time. Coffee and tea became popular beverages, and Chinese porcelain was imported, eventually inspiring the foundation of Britain's own porcelain industry. Almost imperceptibly the Industrial Revolution, not usually defined as having begun until the middle of the 18th Century, was on its way for, at the turn of the century, in 1705, **Thomas Newcomen's** steam pump for coal mining was in operation and, four years later, **Abraham Darby's** method of using coke for iron smelting. Both were to have profound effects on future industrial development.

The 18th Century

Baroque style

The new century saw some of the greatest changes to the British landscape since the Middle Ages and beyond. The introduction of a four-year crop rotation farming system involved the conversion of open fields into individual square fields of roughly ten acres each, enclosed by hedges or walls. Vast tracts of land were thus enclosed in England, whereas in Scotland the reverse happened, and existing tenant farmers there were evicted in order to make way for sheep grazing. When landowners wished to extend or improve their private parks in England, they adopted the same method, and sometimes entire villages were destroyed so as not to spoil the view. Once more the aristocracy were building on a vast scale.

In the footsteps of Wren followed architects such as **Nicholas Hawksmoor** (1661-1736), who added the towers to Westminster Abbey, thus showing sympathy with the much earlier Gothic, and **Sir John Vanbrugh** (1664-1726). The two men worked together on **Castle Howard** in Yorkshire (1701) and **Blenheim Palace**, Oxfordshire (1705), which is the nearest to a British Baroque style, though Thomas Archer (1668-1743) went to Rome, and his St. John's Church, Smith Square in Westminster (1713-29) is a fruit of that visit. James Gibbs (1682-1754) also trained in Rome and gave to London two of its best-known churches, **St. Mary-le-Strand** (1714-17) and **St. Martin-in-the-Fields** (1721-26), though one of his most imaginative buildings, the Radcliffe Camera (1737-49), is in Oxford, and he also worked in Cambridge.

Palladianism

Alongside the tendency towards the Baroque style at this time went a revival of interest in Palladianism, seen earlier in the work of Inigo Jones. The architect **Campbell** began **Burlington House**, Piccadilly, in 1715, and **Stourhead** in Wiltshire around 1720. The Earl of Burlington himself set to work at **Chiswick House** (1726), which he built in collaboration with his protégé William Kent (1685-1748). Together they also began **Holkham Hall** in Norfolk (1734) for Thomas Coke, Earl of Leicester. Kent also designed gardens, for example, at **Chiswick House** and **Rousham Park**, Oxfordshire, and from now on the gardens and general setting of a house became almost as important an element as the

The Palladian bridge
at Wilton House

1688	Glorious Revolution, James II flees. William of Orange arrives in England
1689-1694	William & Mary
1689-1761	Samuel Richardson novelist
1690	Battle of the Boyne. James II Catholic defeated by Protestant Orange forces in Northern Ireland
1692	Massacre of Glencoe, Scotland
1694-1702	William reigns alone
1697-1764	William Hogarth painter and engraver
1701-1713	War of Spanish Succession
1702	Queen Anne
1704	Marlborough defeats French and Bavarians at Blenheim
1705	Early stages of Industrial Revolution
1705	Thomas Newcomen's steam pump
1705	Baroque Style Blenheim House built
1707-1754	Henry Fielding novelist
1709-1784	Samuel Johnson poet
1711-1776	David Hume philosopher
1714-1727	George I
1715	Palladian Style Burlington House, Piccadilly, built
1721-1771	Tobias George Smollett novelist
1723-1792	Joshua Reynolds portrait painter
1726	Chiswick House built (Palladian)
1727-1788	Thomas Gainsborough painter
1727-1760	George II
1728-1792	Robert Adam architect

1730-1819 James Watt engineer (Watt's steam engine)

1739-1748 Jacobite Rebellion in Scotland

1740-1795 James Boswell biographer

1751-1816 Richard Brinsley Sheridan dramatist

1752-1835 John Nash, architect

1756-1823 Henry Raeburn portrait painter

1756-1763 Seven years war with France

1757-1817 William Blake poet

1759-1796 Robert Burns poet

1769-1797 Mary Godwin writer

1760-1820 George III

1763 Peace of Paris

1769-1830 Thomas Lawrence painter

1770-1850 William Wordsworth poet

1771-1832 Sir Walter Scott novelist

1772-1834 Samuel Taylor Coleridge poet, philosopher and critic

1773 Boston Tea Party (U.S)

1774 First Congress of American Colonies

1775-1864 Walter Savage Landor poet

1775-1851 Joseph Turner painter

1775-1817 Jane Austen novelist

1775-1834 Charles Lamb essayist

1775 War of American Independence (Lexington)

1776 Somerset House built by Chambers

house itself. One sees this supremely at Stourhead, of course, and at **Stowe House**, Buckinghamshire. It is only fair to add that the interest of the aristocracy in architecture had also a political motivation, since the cause of Palladianism tended to be taken up by the Whig party as an act of defiance to the old Jacobite Tories, who were discredited after the death of Queen Anne in 1714. But Palladianism was not confined to the estates of the aristocracy. Taking their inspiration from the way in which Lord Burlington had laid out Mayfair as a series of squares connected with regular streets of elegant terraced houses, **John Wood** (1705-54) and his son turned Bath into one of the most elegant resorts in Europe. **Queen Square** (begun 1728), **The Circus** (1754-70) and the **Royal Crescent** (begun 1767) are the best examples of their work there. By 1740 sash windows had been introduced, and wallpaper was used in fashionable houses. In 1753, **Thomas Chippendale** opened his furniture shop in London. It was indeed an age of elegance and improved comfort.

Neoclassicism

The two streams of Baroque and Palladianism in British architecture came together in Neoclassicism, in the second half of the 18th Century, in the work of William Chambers (1723-96) and Robert Adam (1728-92). Somerset House in London (begun 1776) is one of Chamber's best-known works, reflecting a French influence, whilst Adam worked on numerous projects, often remodeling existing houses of much earlier times, such as **Osterley Park**, Middlesex, and **Syon House**, Isleworth, or taking up the work of others, as at Kedleston Hall in Derbyshire. In his interiors he drew his inspiration from Etruscan, Pompeiian and Grecian sources, as well as from more recent architects such as Vanbrugh and Burlington. Essentially, however, Neoclassicism was the concept of the ensemble, which concerned itself not only with the general appearance, but also with the execution, down to details as small as door furniture, and their integration into the whole. This drew together not only skilled craftsmen, such as **Matthew Boulton**, but also artists such as **Angelica Kauffmann**. Nor was it a phenomenon restricted to Adam. William Kent also designed furniture and gardens. The ubiquitous **'Capability' Brown**, who developed Kent's ideas after 1750, was responsible for many of the beautiful landscaped parks and gardens we enjoy today. The taste for the Gothic novel, parodied by Jane Austen in Northanger Abbey, is paralleled in architecture by Horace Walpole's house at Strawberry Hill, Twickenham (1748), complete with fan-vaulting, and by Wyatt's Gothic fantasy, Fonthill Abbey (1796), now vanished.

Painting

In painting, this was supremely the age of the portrait, with **Reynolds** (1723-92), **Gainsborough** (1727-88) and **Romney** (1734-1802), many of whose works still hang in the houses of the families for whom and of whom they were painted. **William Hogarth** (1697-1764) observed with a satiric eye the daily life of all classes of society, and **Georges Stubbs** (1724-1806), the greatest painter of animals, brought a new realism and drama to his racing scenes. The theatre flourished as never before, where the somewhat licentious and jaded taste of the Restoration had been transformed almost single-handedly by the first great British actor-manager, **David Garrick** (1717-79), who virtually rediscovered Shakespeare for the public. From this time, Stratford-upon-Avon in Warwickshire became a place of Shakespearean pilgrimage. Under Garrick's encouragement, the comedy of manners flourished, an important element in the history of British theatre, with the plays of such writers as **Oliver Goldsmith** (1728-74) and **Richard Sheridan** (1751-1816), Garrick's successor at Drury Lane. This period also saw the rise of the British novel, with **Daniel Defoe** (1660-1731), **Samuel Richardson** (1689-1761), **Henry Fielding** (1707-54), **Lawrence Sterne** (1713-68), **Tobias Smollett** (1721-71), **Fanny Burney** (1752-1840) and **Jane Austen** (1775-1817).

 The 19th Century

The Victorian Age

Although the 19th Century is dominated by the Victorian Age, it must be remembered that in 1800 George III was on the throne, Napoleon had still to be defeated, and the first passenger railway was a quarter of a century distant. The victories at **Trafalgar** (1805) and **Waterloo** (1815) created a mood of euphoria in

The Houses of Parliament, in Westminster

Britain, emphasized by the presence of the Prince Regent as leader of an extravagant society. The Regency period has been described as the 'Age of Elegance', and that elegance is exemplified in the terraces, crescents and villas designed by **John Nash** (1752-1835), the prince's favourite architect. Central London was transformed with an architectural scheme that stretched from **Regent's Park** to the **The Mall**. But perhaps the frivolous mood is best represented by the **Royal Pavilion** at Brighton, fashioned by Nash into an exotic confection, with Chinese interiors, Indian domes, minarets and Gothic windows. Significantly, the palm-tree columns of the Great Kitchen are made not of stone but of cast iron surmounted by fronds of sheet copper — functionalism was on its way. And the development of Brighton as a resort also indicated that fashionable society had now discovered the sea as a source of refreshment and relaxation, so setting the pattern for a large proportion of British vacations for the next 150 years, as the middle classes copied the aristocracy, and the advent of the railways made access to the seaside easier.

It was Queen Victoria who took Scotland to her heart, but it was the **Prince Regent**, under the influence of the novelist **Sir Walter Scott** (1771-1832), who rediscovered it for the English, and along with it the poems of **Robert Burns** (1759-96) and much of the romantic content of Scott's own works. In the paintings of **Turner** (1775-1851) and **Constable** (1776-1837), a romantic, even impressionistic, view of the British countryside and coastline were presented to the viewer at the very moment industry was taking them over, and a new spirit was abroad in portraiture in the works of **Henry Raeburn** (1756-1823) and **Thomas Lawrence** (1769-1830). In poetry, the work of **Wordsworth** (1770-1850) gave way to **Byron** (1788-1824), though it was **Tennyson** (1809-92) who was the acknowledged poet of Victorian England, much as with the novel, the works of the **Brontes** (Charlotte 1816-55, Emily 1818-48, Anne 1820-49) were overshadowed by the much more prolific **Charles Dickens** (1812-70). Social satire is delightfully represented by **Thackeray's** *Vanity Fair* (1848), while the novels of **George Eliot** (1819-80) and **Anthony Trollope** (1815-82) were equally popular.

The Industrial Revolution

The 19th Century saw a vast change in the face of Britain, created by the two interdependent phenomena of the Industrial Revolution and the growth in communications. Between 1750 and 1800 the population had increased by 150 percent, and one-third of the nation came to live in towns. By 1901, it had reached 32 million, and two-thirds of the nation now lived in towns. The Industrial Revolution had been gathering momentum for some time during the previous century, and the invention of the steam engine, requiring large quantities of coal, created an immense impact as new mining areas developed in Wales, the North of England and lowland Scotland.

The latter part of the 18th Century had been the age of canals, which at first followed the contours of the land, but a second generation of canal builders became more adventurous, and **Thomas Telford** (1757-1834) built the **Pontcy-**

1776-1837   John Constable painter

1776   American Declaration of Independence

1777   Britain defeated in U.S. at Battle of Saratoga

1778   France declares war on Britain

1779   British capitulation in U.S. at Yorktown

1781-1848   James Stephenson engineer and inventor

1783   Independence of U.S. Colonies recognized at Peace of Versailles

1788-1824   George Gordon Byron poet

1791-1867   Michael Faraday electrician and chemist, natural philosopher

1792-1822   Percy Bysshe Shelley poet

1793-1815   War with France

1795-1821   John Keats poet

1795-1860   Charles Barry architect

1795-1881   Thomas Carlyle historian and essayist

1797-1851   Mary Shelley novelist

1801   Symington's steamboat Charlotte Dundas fitted with one of Watt's engines

1801-1890   Cardinal J.H. Newman theologian

1802   Treaty of Amiens

1803-1814   War with France

1803-1849   Thomas Lovell Beddoes poet

1805   Trafalgar

1806-1861   Elizabeth Barrett Browning poetess

1808-1892 Cardinal H.E. Manning theologian
1809-1882 Charles Darwin naturalist
1809-1892 Alfred Tennyson poet
1811-1863 William Makepeace Thackeray novelist
1812-1870 Charles Dickens novelist
1815-1882 Anthony Trollope novelist
1816-1855 Charlotte Bronte novelist
1818-1848 Emily Bronte novelist
1819-1880 George Eliot novelist
1819-1900 John Ruskin writer on Art, Economics
1820-1849 Anne Bronte novelist
1820-1903 Herbert Spencer philosopher
1820-1830 George IV
1824 Trade Unions legalized
1824-1881 George Edmund Street architect
1824 Stephenson's 'Rocket' (railway engine)
1825-1895 Thomas H. Huxley scientist
1825 First steam-hauled passenger train
1827-1910 Holman Hunt painter
1828-1909 George Meredith novelist
1828-1882 Dante Gabriele Rossetti poet and painter
1829-1896 John Everett Millais painter
1829 Catholic Emancipation
1830-1837 William IV
1830-1905 Alfred Waterhouse architect

19th and 20th C. historic houses and sites

syllte Aqueduct, completed in 1805 — the year of the Battle of Trafalgar — 1,000 ft long, to carry the Ellesmere Canal across the River Dee in Wales, thus demonstrating the potential of cast iron for large-scale engineering and architectural projects, though the first cast-iron bridge had already been built at Coalbrookdale in Salop as early as 1779. There are still many canals in existence, and some have been restored, offering a delightful form of vacation for those with sufficient time to spend, and often passing through some of the most unspoilt parts of Britain. John McAdam had begun his experiments in road surfacing in 1743 and, after the canals came the new roads, often requiring new bridges. In 1826 **Telford** built the **Menai Suspension Bridge**, linking the island of Anglesey to the mainland and, in 1836, **Brunel** designed the **Clifton Suspension Bridge** spanning 702 ft across the Avon Gorge at Bristol, but not completed until 1864, five years after his death. The name of **George Stephenson** is inextricably linked with the railways, and it was the advent of the train that put an end to the canal boom in Britain. In 1825 the **world's first steam-hauled passenger railway** opened between **Stockton and Darlington**, drawn by Stephenson's famous 'Rocket', and by 1850 some 6,600 miles of railway tracks had been laid in Britain, and with them came cuttings and tunnels, viaducts and embankments. Not until the building of motorways in the present century was such an impression to be made upon the landscape.

Victorian architecture

With the increase in trade and communications came a spate of building — mills, docks, warehouses, railway stations and hotels, and the growth of the new towns such as Birmingham and Manchester, Leeds and Bradford required

new housing and appropriate civic building to reflect the new prosperity. The architecture of the Victorian Age still dominates Britain's towns and cities, and so powerful has been its presence that it has taken over a century for us to be able to look at it with dispassion, understanding and finally affection. Basically there are two parallel growths — the **docks, mills and warehouses** which are massive, but essentially functional and simple, and the **civic monuments** which are not. The former have always been easier to appreciate, the latter have been subject to violent reaction and perhaps only now can be fully appreciated. It is the seriousness with which the whole matter was approached that explains a great deal about their appearance and our reaction to it.

Lloyds building in London

The battle of the styles

Style was thought to represent specific things — the Classical reflecting civic virtue and the Gothic Christian ideals or moral earnestness. The famous **'battle of the styles'** was won in the case of the Foreign Office, and with Palmerston's insistence, by the Classical lobby, while **Barry's Houses of Parliament** are Gothic, particularly in the detailing which was all the work of A.W.N. Pugin. The outstanding architects of the Victorian period can now be seen to have produced some of the most exciting designs in the whole history of architecture. **Augustus Welby Northmore Pugin** (1812-52) is best remembered for his work at Westminster which is Gothic revival at its purest — scholarly, rational, authentic. His church of **St. Giles** at Cheadle in Staffordshire should also be mentioned as well as **St. Chad's**, Birmingham. The work of **William Butterfield** (1814-1900) at **All Saints**, Margaret Street, London and at **Keble** College in Oxford is both colourful and strikingly self-confident. **George Edmund Street** (1824-81) built the **Law Courts** in the Strand, London, which go back in inspiration to the 13th Century, but are also a prime example of what we now call town planning. Equally, his parish churches such as **St. James's Kingston** in Dorset, possess a symmetry and elegance that contradict more than any other the old-fashioned view of Victorian churches as being 'heavy and fussy.' Finally there is **Alfred Waterhouse** (1830-1905), whose **Natural History Museum** in Kensington, London, is in the Romanesque style — a totally harmonious building that has recently been cleaned to reveal the marvelous honey-coloured brickwork. But apart from these giant figures, and apart from innovators such as **Joseph Paxton** of Crystal Palace fame, we should look as well to the work of the ordinary speculative builder of the 19th Century. In any town or city you will find interesting terraces and squares put up quite cheaply and anonymously for ordinary households. Built in many styles and in stucco or brick, with a nicely judged use of ornament, these houses possess real quality and charm. In spite of the immense self-confidence of the Victorian age, there was in many areas of art and craft a hankering after a distant past, sometimes as a reaction to the increasing mechanization of production methods.

The pre-Raphaelites

The pre-Raphaelite Brotherhood, founded in 1848 with **John Everett Millais** (1829-96), **William Holman Hunt** (1827-1910) and **Dante Gabriel Rossetti** (1828-82) as its principal members, looked back, not to Raphael who was too

1832   Reform Act passed

1832-1898   Lewis Carroll author

1833-1898   Edward Burne-Jones painter

1834-1896   William Morris poet and artist

1836   Houses of Parliament built by Charles Barry

1837-1901   Queen Victoria

1840-1928   Thomas Hardy novelist

1840   Penny postage stamp

1842   Chartist Riots

1846   Repeal of the Corn Laws

1848   Pre-Raphaelite Brotherhood of Painters founded

1849-1945   Andrew Fleming physician (penicillin)

1850   6600 miles of railways in Britain

1851   Great Exhibition

1854   Crimean War

1854-1900   Oscar Wilde poet and dramatist

1857-1934   Edward Elgar composer

1857   First Atlantic cable laid

1860-1942   Walter Richard Sickert painter

1862-1934   Frederick Delius composer

1865-1936   Rudyard Kipling novelist

1871-1937   Ernest Rutherford physicist

1872-1898   Aubrey Beardsley illustrator

1877   Queen Victoria proclaimed Empress of India

1885-1930   D.H. Lawrence novelist

1888-1965   T.S. Eliot poet

1888-1935 — T.E. Lawrence historian (Lawrence of Arabia)

1894-1963 — Aldous Huxley novelist

1899-1902 — Boer War

1901 — Death of Queen Victoria

1901 — Population of Britain 30 million

1901-1910 — Edward VII

1903-1966 — Evelyn Waugh novelist

1904 — Entente Cordiale

1910-1936 — George V

1910 — Liberal Government (Prime Minister Herbert Asquith)

1914-1918 — World War I

1916 — Uprising in Ireland

1916 — David Lloyd George succeeds Asquith as Prime Minister

1921 — Ireland (excluding North) granted Home Rule

1922 — Andrew Bonar Law Prime Minister (Conservative government)

1923 — Stanley Baldwin replaces Bonar Law as Prime Minister

1926 — General Strike

1929 — Two million unemployed

1929 — Labour Government (Ramsay McDonald Prime Minister)

1935 — Conservative Government under Stanley Baldwin

1937 — Neville Chamberlain replaces Stanley Baldwin as Prime Minister

1939-1945 — World War II

classical, but to primitive Italian painting for their inspiration. They found the fashionable 'history' painting of their own period to be sterile and stated their wish to disregard academic rules and return to nature. At the same time **John Ruskin** (1819-1900) was extolling the virtues of the medieval guild system and praising Gothic for its 'naturalness.' **William Morris**, the moving force behind the **Arts and Crafts Movement**, sought to raise the crafts of pottery, weaving, printing and metalwork to the level of fine art that they had enjoyed in the Middle Ages. There was a genuine fear of the dangers of mass production and the stereotype, and the influence particularly of Ruskin and Morris was far-reaching. That was one side of the coin. On the other was the **Great Exhibition** of 1851, a phenomenally ambitious affair visited by thousands of people every day, in which were assembled the oddest and grandest and most outlandish collection of exhibits ever put together, from Egyptian colossi to stuffed mice.

In 1901 Queen Victoria died and there was a genuine feeling throughout the land that this was the end of an era. The century in which Britain led the world, possessing an empire upon which 'the sun never sets' was over. Victorian high-mindedness and upholstered comfort would gradually fade, and a new spirit would take their place.

 # The people of Britain

Successive waves of invaders

If one had to define who the British people were, one sees that successive waves of invaders contributed to the race, down to the Norman Conquest, with the original inhabitants pushed to Scotland, Wales and the peninsula of Devon and Cornwall. It is no coincidence that **Gaelic, Welsh**, and less strongly, **Cornish**, survived as individual languages for centuries, and today — especially as far as Welsh is concerned — still give a sense of national identity. For although Britain with Ulster constitutes the United Kingdom of Great Britain and Northern Ireland, one must not forget that the constituent parts of that kingdom are in fact individual countries, and even within England, extremely powerful regional differences obtain. In many cases this is born of a marriage between the people and the very land itself.

Regional differences

For centuries, rivers were considerable barriers to freedom of movement, so that those living north or south of the Tyne, the Wear or the Humber regarded themselves primarily as inhabitants of their respective counties of Northumberland, Durham, Yorkshire or Lincolnshire. Similarly those in Yorkshire, on the eastern side of the Pennines, still feel themselves to be very different from those on the western side in Lancashire. And there are even more pronounced differences. As one crosses the Tamar, for example, from Devon into Cornwall, not only does the soil actually change colour from a rich red to more muted greys and black, but the landscape itself becomes bleaker, until the traveler drops down into the valleys and inlets where some of the ancient settlements survive almost unchanged. But in keeping with the harsher existence in Cornwall by comparison with Devon the people tend to be more reserved, less easy of access.

Cornwall offers an illustration of the way in which many aspects of life have been changing inexorably over hundreds of years. A once relatively thickly populated county in the reign of **Elizabeth I**, it returned forty-two members to Parliament at a time the whole of Essex returned four. Now closures of mines and the decline of the fishing industry have obliged the young to move elsewhere, and the people who remain turn to the tourist industry for their livelihood.

The same is true of the traditional manufacturing areas of the Midlands and the northeast and northwest. What was always regarded as the core of Britain's commercial prosperity, the wool and cotton industries of Yorkshire and Lancashire, the coal mines, shipbuilding yards and blast furnaces of Wales, the northeast and central Scotland, are in decline, and even a more recent implant, such as the car industry in the Midlands, is undergoing radical reorganization.

Second demographic upheaval

The conversion of English society during the 18th Century from rural to urban, with its concomitant drift from the country to the towns and cities, is now seeing a **second demographic upheaval** as employment prospects draw people to the flourishing Southeast. As the earlier urban centres decline, there is a tendency for members of the old British Empire to settle there, creating large communities from the **Caribbean** and the **Indian subcontinent**, as well as the **Far East**, adding colour to contemporary society, and bringing new folk festivals such as the **Chinese New Year** celebrations and the essentially Caribbean Notting Hill Carnival to the streets of London. For centuries, Britain has provided a haven for oppressed peoples, whether it be the **Protestant Huguenots** from 17th Century France or the more recent fugitives from Fascist and Communist persecution in Europe. Such peoples have enriched their new home with their own individual customs and cultural heritage. It seems that the soil of Britain has a special quality in that newcomers find it easy to put down roots here and to blend harmoniously with the indigenous stock. But while Britain possesses this infinite capacity to assimilate others it does not rob them of their individuality. That is the country's strength.

Patterns of change and continuity

We have seen that the British people are made up of many strands. **Armed invaders** imposed their will on the native population, then blended with it, and victims of oppression in later periods brought further elements to add to the rich mixture. But while the centuries have witnessed great changes, there are also patterns of continuity, and these parallel forces are reflected in the cities on the one hand and the countryside on the other. The cities are genuinely cosmopolitan, with a colourful mix of people of widely differing origins. Yet in the countryside, village life has continued virtually unchanged. Local families still trace their roots back for many generations. Regional accents of speech and local dialect words still survive in agricultural communities. The village remains, with its parish church, pub and cricket grounds. Picturesque, rural Britain has mercifully survived and is now consciously being preserved, both by its inhabitants and by conservation groups. Local crafts are seeing a renewal as the realization grows that handmade, local, individual products are not only more attractive and more varied but increasingly marketable.

The land presents striking contrasts both in its physical appearance and in the nature of its inhabitants. It is not possible to say that this region or that city is typical. The totality, in all its manifestations, represents the British people and the British way of life.

The Climate

Regional differences

Britain is not only a country of individual nations, but of individual regions differing from their neighbours for reasons that may be ethnic, historical, geographic or economic. The basic geology and climate of the country has also played a decisive role, determining not only the original distribution of the population, but their activities, produce, architecture, and even their clothing and diet. Generally speaking, the west and north of the country are hilly, even mountainous in places, whilst the south and east are more flat. (Naturally this is only a broad generalization, since there is a succession of **Downs** to the south and west of London, and to the north and west first the **Chiltern Hills** and then the **Cotswolds**, providing attractive countryside for the visitor).

The British weather is a major topic of conversation amongst the inhabitants, if only because it is one of the few subjects guaranteed to find a response in almost anyone one meets. For the bewildered visitor, however, it may well be a matter for congratulation or despair, depending on the circumstances. Certainly the British climate has great variety, and the golden rule is be prepared. Bring a sweater with you, a light raincoat and comfortable walking shoes. But bear in mind that a day dawning overcast may well become hot and sunny an hour or two later.

1940 — Winston Churchill forms a Coalition government

1945 — First post-war government, Labour under Clement Attlee

1950 — Korean War

1951 — Conservative government under Winston Churchill

1952 — Death of George V.; Queen Elizabeth II; First British Atomic Bomb exploded at Wᵒmera (Australia)

1953 — Queen Elizabeth Coronation

1955 — Eden succeeds Churchill as Prime Minister

1956 — Anglo-French Suez Expedition fiasco. Eden resigns

1957 — Conservative government under Macmillan

1960 — Process of de-colonization begins world wide

1963 — Alexander Douglas Home replaces Macmillan who resigns

1964 — Harold Wilson Labour Government

1970 — Tory government under Edward Heath

1973 — Britain joins the Common Market

1976 — Labour Government under James Callaghan

1979 — Margaret Thatcher first woman to be Prime Minister of Britain heads Tory government

1982 — Falkland War

1983-1987 — Margaret Thatcher's government re-elected

Driest season

Situated as it is between the **Atlantic Ocean** and the land mass of **Europe**, Britain is inevitably very much affected by conditions at either side. If the wind blows from the west, at any time of the year, it brings the comparatively mild atmosphere of the ocean. If the wind blows from the east, however, it may bring very different conditions, depending on the season. Because the east wind comes to Britain after crossing a huge land mass that heats and cools more rapidly than the sea, then in summer it may bring a heatwave from Europe, whereas in winter it may bring a bitterly sharp cold. It is perhaps, the apparent unpredictability of the weather that visitors find so perplexing, but there are patterns and, to a certain extent, the weather may be forecast. What happens over the Atlantic Ocean, for example, is that cold air coming south from the **Arctic** tends to meet air, laden with moisture, moving north from the tropics. When they meet, pockets of low air pressure, known as depressions, are formed, which then move east or northeast across the ocean, and either skirt the coasts of Britain or cross directly over it. The result is usually a spell of mild, wet and windy weather, followed fairly quickly by a warm but dull period, or cool, squally weather. On the other hand, an area of high pressure, with its centre above the Azores, will extend northwards, and then a much more settled period of weather sets in, giving clear, sunny days.

Although, traditionally, **April** is a showery month, spring is usually the driest season of the year in Britain. If the weather is cold at this time of year, then it is rare for it to last much beyond the middle of the month, and then there may well be a pleasantly warm spell ahead. Many British people who holiday at home at this time of the year tend to make for the west coast or the south-west, since they are less likely to experience wintery east or north winds there. Spring flowers and the first green leaves are a welcome sight in south Devon and sheltered areas of Cornwall, and in some parts the grass remains a vivid green all the year round through lack of frost. By late spring one may expect temperatures during the day of 21-24 (deg) C over much of the country. During **May** and **June** daytime temperatures tend to be 5-9 (deg) C warmer on the coast than at sea, and even higher along the east coast, which creates alternating on-shore and off-shore breezes, ideal conditions for those who enjoy sailing or coastal walks and sea air.

Sunniest months

July and August are usually the sunniest months in Britain, though it has to be an exceptional year for it ever to get oppressively hot. June is the month that sees many of the highlights of the social season, as well as ceremonial occasions such as the **Trooping the Colour** on the Queen's official birthday. In the south of England there is an average of eight hours sunshine a day, reducing to about five in the north of Scotland. Also, often considered the sunniest months, July and August tend to be rainy because the depressions from the Atlantic come closer to Britain at this time of year, and because the air, as it gets warmer, holds more moisture. In such circumstances, during a period of changeable weather, the flat seaboard areas are inclined to have less rain than areas further inland, especially on or near high ground, though the lee of the high ground may remain dry and sunny. Thus eastern Wales and the Welsh borders may well stay dry when the western side of the country receives the rain carried by winds from the southwest. Similarly, in southwest England, if the wind is coming from the north, then south of Dartmoor the sun may well be shining. Britain often enjoys long spells of warm dry weather that continue into **September**. For those taking a holiday by the sea, the advantage is that the water is still warm because of the heat that it has stored up during the earlier part of the summer. That is why resorts on the east coast are attractive at this time of the year, since winds usually blow from the southwest, and have deposited a good deal of their moisture as they crossed the rest of the country. As the autumn draws on, however, the winds move round to the west and northwest, and so the weather becomes unsettled. Even so, it is a very pleasant time of the year to see the countryside. Many of the vacationers have departed, leaving the resorts quiet and uncrowded, and the air may be wonderfully clear when it is sunny. Inland, the countryside is very beautiful as the leaves acquire the red and gold tints of autumn, and there may even be a first frost to enhance the effect. These crisp autumn days are ideal for seeing Britain, either the towns and cities or its countryside, especially for those who like walking. For those who enjoy **winter sports**, centres have been developed in Scotland where these may be pursued. Then the rugged landscape is rendered even more majestic by the coating of snow.

Practical holiday guide ●

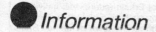

● Information

British Tourist Authority (BTA)

Tourism is now Britain's biggest growth industry. The **British Tourist Authority**, represented in many cities abroad, is the single source of information on all aspects of Britain for the traveler preparing a visit.

In addition to promoting tourism to Britain from overseas, the BTA's responsibilities are to advise the government on tourism matters affecting Britain as a whole and to encourage the provision and improvement of tourist amenities and facilities in Britain.

Located at Thames Tower, Black's Road, London W6 9EL (☎ 01-846 9000), the BTA works in close cooperation with the four **National Tourist Boards** — England, Scotland, Wales and Northern Ireland — as well as with the **Regional Tourist Boards, local government authorities** and other principal **tourism organizations**.

BTA

The BTA's overseas offices work closely with all tourist interests in the territories for which they are responsible, including leading travel agents and tour operators. The overseas offices are provided with a wide range of professional, technical and creative services by BTA staff in London. Services offered abroad include the distribution of numerous free leaflets and information on a wide range of subjects including suggested travel itineraries, methods of travel, useful addresses, accommodation, tourist attractions and events.

Tourism organizations

● **British Tourist Authority offices abroad:**

Information

Australia and New Zealand: Associated Midland House, 171 Clarence Street, Sydney, NSW 2000 (☎ 010 61 2 29 8627).
Belgium and Luxembourg: 52 Rue de la Montagne/Bergstraat, Brussels 1000 (☎ 010 32 2 511 43 90).
Canada: Suite 600, 94 Cumberland Street, Toronto, Ont. M5R 3N3 (☎ 010 1 416 961 8124/925 6326).
Denmark: Montergade 3, 1116 Copenhagen K (☎ 010 45 1 12 07 93).
France: 65 rue Pierre Charron, 75008 Paris (☎ 010 42 89 11 11).
West Germany: 6000 Frankfurt 1, Neue Mainzer Strasse 22 (☎ 010 49 69 23 8075011).
Holland: Aurora Gebouw 5E, Stadhouderskade 2, 1054 ES Amsterdam (☎ 010 91 85 50 51).
Italy: Via S. Eufemia 5, 00187 Rome (☎ 010 39 6 678 55 48).
Japan: 246 Tokyo Club Building, 3-2-6 Kasumigaseki, Chiyoda-ku, Tokyo 100 (☎ 010 81 3 581 3603).
Mexico: Edificio Alber, Paseo de la Reforma 332-5, Piso 06600 Mexico DF (☎ 010 525 533 6375).
Norway: Fridtiof Nansens Plass, 0160 Oslo 1 (☎ 010 47 2 41 18 49).
Singapore: 14 Collyer Quay 05-03, Singapore Rubber House, Singapore 0104 (☎ 010 65 2242966/7).

Spain and Portugal: Torre de Madrid 6/4, Plaza de Espana, 28008 Madrid (☎ 010 34 1 241 13 96).
Sweden and Finland: Malmskillnadsgatan 42, Box 7293, s -103 90 Stockholm 40 (☎ 010 46 8 21 24 44).
Switzerland: Limmatquai 78, 8001 Zurich (☎ 010 41 1 47 42 77/97).
USA: 3rd floor, 40 West 57th Street, New York NY 10019 (☎ 010 1 212 581 4700); 350 S. Figueroa Street, Los Angeles, California 90017 (☎ 010 1 213 628 3525); John Hancock Centre, 875 North Michigan Avenue, Chicago III 60611 (☎ 010 1 312 787 0490); Cedar Marple Plaza, Suite 2305, Cedar Springs Road, Lock Box 346, Dallas, Texas 75201 (☎ 010 1 214 720 4040).

● **National Tourist Offices:**
English Tourist Board, Thames Tower, Black's Road, Hammersmith, London W6 9EL (☎ 01-846 9000).
Scottish Tourist Board, 23 Ravelston Terrace, Edinburgh EH4 3EU (☎ 031-332 2433).
Welsh Tourist Board, Brunel House, 2 Fitzalan Road, Cardiff CF2 1UY (☎ 0222-499909).
Northern Ireland Tourist Board, River House, 48 High Street, Belfast BT1 2DS (☎ 0232 231221).

● **Regional Tourist Boards:**
The Regional Tourist Boards are subdivided into 'local' **tourist information centres** (TICs) which can provide detailed and often 'off-beat' information about the town or village in which they are situated. There are more than 700 throughout Great Britain (addresses: individual town sections). Most TICs are in town centres, often in places such as a historic building, a library or a specially designed trailer, and signposted throughout the town by an 'ic'. Staff should be able to answer any queries regarding local attractions and can supply written details of local events. Many centres will make an accommodation reservation for the same night in their locality (at a marginal cost) and several centres operate the *Book-a-Bed-Ahead Service* (BABA) which can, for a small fee, make a reservation for accommodation in any other town that also operates the service, for the same or next night.
● **The London Tourist Information Centre** (serving the Greater London Area) is on the forecourt of Victoria Station, London SW1, with a telephone information service on 01-730 3488, Mon. to Fri., 9am-5:30 pm (automatic system — hold until a receptionist answers). Written inquiries to: **LVCB**, Central Information Unit, 26 Grosvenor Gardens, London SW1W ODU.
● **British Travel Centre,** Rex House, 4-12 Lower Regent Street, London SW1 (☎ 01-730 3400). Telephone service is open Mon. to Fri., 9am-6:30pm; Sat., 10am-5pm; closed Sun. The centre is open Mon. to Fri., 9am-6:30pm; Sat., 10am-6pm and Sun., 10am-4pm for tourist information and leaflets, on air, rail, bus and car travel; sightseeing tours; accommodation; theatre seats; money exchange; gift and book shops; and displays of forthcoming attractions in Britain.

Getting to Britain

Air travel Most major airlines serve **London Heathrow** (LHR — the world's busiest international airport) or **Gatwick** (GTW). As well as the regular all-year-round services to these two airports, scheduled flights also operate from many parts of the world direct to Britain's other international airports — **Edinburgh, Glasgow, Luton, Birmingham, Manchester, Bristol, Cardiff** and **Belfast**. Where there is no direct service to the area you wish to visit, you can usually transfer to a domestic service that will take you to your destination or within easy reach of it. Airlines sell seats at a wide variety of prices subject to various pre-conditions. The cheaper the ticket, the more restrictions and qualifications are applied both before and after the flight.

From USA In the USA, direct flights to Great Britain are available from Atlanta, Boston, Chicago, Dallas/Fort Worth, Los Angeles, New York and San Francisco, among others. Airlines offering regularly scheduled flights from the USA to Great Britain, the majority on a daily basis, are: Air India, Air New Zealand, American Airlines, British Airways, British Caledonian, Continental, Delta, El Al, Kuwait Airways, Northwest Orient, Pan Am, TWA, Virgin Atlantic and World. All scheduled flights land at London Heathrow, Gatwick, Manchester International or Prestwick. There are several fare categories offered by scheduled carriers from the USA to Great Britain: 1st class, business, economy and advance purchase excursion (APEX).

● **Concorde:** a luxurious, supersonic jet flown by British Airways. It only flies from New York, Washington DC and Miami except on special charters. Information can be obtained from most travel agents or British Airways offices.
● **Virgin Atlantic:** a carrier well known for low-cost transatlantic flights (Newark-London Gatwick twice weekly off-season, daily in summer). Information and reservations: ☎ 201 623 0500 or call 800 555 1212 for the airline's toll-free number for your area.

● **Passenger service information:** Information on flights serving specific international airports is available at the following numbers: London (Heathrow): 01-759 4321; (Gatwick): 0293 28822 or 01-668 4211; Glasgow: 041-887 1111; Edinburgh: 031-333 1000; Luton: 0582 31231; Birmingham: 021-767 5511; Manchester: 061-489 3000; Bristol: 0275 87 4441; Cardiff: 0446 711211; Belfast: 0232 229271.

● **Sky Guide:** Up-to-the-minute flight information 'direct' from the seven major airports and a number of the smaller regional airports is available on Prestel through American Express. Key ★2691 for details.

● **Air Taxis:** Information concerning Air Taxi charter throughout the UK can be obtained from the *Air Transport Operators' Association* (☎ 0428 4804).

● **British Airways offices in Britain:** head office: PO Box 10, Heathrow Airport London, Hounslow, Middlesex TW6 2JA (☎ 01-759 5511); BA Gatwick: ☎ 0293 518033.

● **British Airways offices in the USA:** New York: 212 687 1600; Chicago: 312 332 7744; Los Angeles: 213 272 8866; Washington DC: 207 393 5300.

[margin: **Information**]

● Aer Lingus: 01-734 1212; Aeroflot: 01-493 7436; Air Canada: 01-759 2636; Air France: 01-499 9511; Air India: 01-491 7979; Air New Zealand: 01-930 3434; Air Portugal: 01-828 0262; Alitalia: 01-602 7111; American Airlines: 01-834 5151; Austrian Airlines: 01-439 0741; British Caledonian: 01-668 4222; Cathay Pacific: 01-930 7878; Delta Airlines: 01-668-0935; Eastern: 0223 517 622; Egyptair: 01-734 2395; El Al: 01-437 9255; Finnair: 01-408 1222; Gulf Air: 01-409 0191; Japan Airlines: 01-408 1000; KLM: 01-750 9000; Lufthansa: 01-408 0442; Malaysian Airlines: 01-491 4542; Middle East Airlines: 01-493 5681; Northwest: 01-629 5353; Olympic: 01-846 9080; Pan Am: 01-409 0688; Qantas: 01-748 5050; Royal Air Maroc: 01-439 8859; Sabena: 01-437 6950; SAS: 01-734 9841; Singapore: 01-439 8111; Swissair: 01-439 4144; TAP: 01-734 4282; TWA: 01-636 4090; Varig Brazilian Airlines: 01-029 5824; Virgin Atlantic: 0293 38222; World: 01-434 3252.

[margin: **Other airline reservations in London**]

Although it may be more convenient for some visitors to fly direct to a provincial airport, by far the most popular are London's Heathrow and Gatwick. Both are linked to central London by frequent public transport services. London Heathrow is 15 miles west of central London, linked by bus and subway (with one underground stop for Heathrow's Terminals 1, 2 and 3, another for Terminal 4). Heathrow lies at the end of the Piccadilly line and the journey to central London takes approximately 45 minutes.

London Transport operates three **Express Airbus** services (☎ 01-222 1234 5am-11pm, 6:45am on Sun.) that run at approximately 10-minute intervals connecting Heathrow to three of London's main railway stations — Victoria (A1), Paddington (A2) and Euston (A3). Journey time is approximately 40 minutes. All the major hotel areas in central London are served and the three routes offer 18 pick-up points.

Car rental is available at Heathrow, as are taxis, the most expensive form of public transport. Gatwick is a mainline 30-minute train ride from Victoria. Trains run every 15 minutes between 6am and midnight (once an hour throughout the night).

[margin: **Arrival in Britain**]

The most luxurious transatlantic ship is Cunard's Queen Elizabeth II which operates between New York and Southampton (occasionally via Cherbourg in northern France) between April and December. Cunard air/sea packages, combining a one-way crossing with a return flight on Concorde, are also available in conjunction with British Airways. Information: USA: Cunard, 555 Fifth Avenue, New York NY 10017 (☎ (212) 661 7777/(800) 221 4770); London: The Cunard Steam-Ship Company Ltd, 30-35 Pall Mall, London W1Y 5LS (☎ 01 491 3930).

[margin: **QE2**]

Some ten ferry companies (plus one hydrofoil and two hovercraft services) operate a total of 32 services linking Britain to the rest of Europe. The majority carry cars, campers, trailers, caravans, motorcycles and bicycles, as well as passengers. The two major ferry companies, **Sealink/British Ferries** and **P. and O.**, plus **Hoverspeed**, run a virtual shuttle service at ten-minute intervals during the summertime rush hours. Journey times vary from the speedy half-hour hovercraft trip across the English Channel to the 24-hour and longer, more leisurely North Sea crossing in one of the larger cruise-style ships. About a third of the total cross-Channel traffic is via Dover-Calais, the shortest, quickest, most popular ferry route (1 hour 30 minutes). Considerable savings can often be made by traveling off-season or choosing a mid-week sailing during the summer.

There are frequent rail and bus services linking the ports with London and other cities and towns.

[margin: **Ferries**]

● Information and reservations can be obtained from most travel agents or directly from the ferry companies: **Brittany Ferries,** The Brittany Centre, Wharf Road, Portsmouth, Hampshire PO2 8RU (☎ 0705 827701) (Plymouth/Roscoff, St. Malo, Santander).

● **Sealink British Ferries,** PO Box 29, London SW1V 1JX (☎ 01-834 8122) (Folkestone/Boulogne, Dover/Calais, Portsmouth/Cherbourg, Weymouth/Cherbourg, Harwich/Hook of Holland) (inquiries and reservations in most major British Rail booking offices).

● **P. and O.,** Enterprise House, Channel View Road, Dover, Kent CT17 9TJ (☎ 0304 203388) (Dover/Zeebrugge, Felixstowe/Zeebrugge, Dover/Boulogne, Dover/Calais, Portsmouth/Cherbourg, Portsmouth/Le Havre).

[margin: **Information**]

● **Hoverspeed UK Ltd,** Maybrook House, Queens Gardens, Dover CT17 9UQ (☎ 0304 240241 and 02 554 7061) (Dover/Ostend, Dover/Calais).
● **DFDS Seaways,** Parkeston Quay, Harwich, Essex CO12 4SY (☎ 0255 508933) (Harwich/Esjberg, Esjberg/Newcastle, Harwich/Hamburg, Harwich/Gothenburg, Newcastle/Gothenburg).
● **Fred Olsen Lines,** Victoria Plaza 111 Buckingham Palace Road, London SW1W OSP (☎ 01-630 0033) (Harwich/Kristiansand, Harwich/Oslo, Hirthals/Harwich).
● **Sally Line,** 81 Piccadilly, London W1 (☎ 01-409 2240) (Ramsgate/Dunkirk).

Rail   Britain is linked into Europe's extensive, fast rail system which links with main passenger ferry services across the Channel and hence to London. Reduced fares are available for students and senior citizens.
BR Inter City Europe passenger information: ☎ 01-834 2345. All calls are answered in strict rotation (section on rail travel).

Customs, passports and visas

Passports   Entry requirements for Britain vary according to the nationality of the visitor and the length
and visas   and purpose of the trip. On arrival you must produce a valid national passport or other document satisfactorily establishing your identity and nationality. You do not need a visa if you are a citizen of the Commonwealth (including Australia, Canada and New Zealand), the Republic of South Africa or the USA. If you are not a citizen of an EEC country, you may be asked to complete a landing card before you pass through passport control. The immigration officer will place an endorsement in your passport that will probably impose a time limit on your stay. Other conditions may restrict your freedom to take employment or require you to register with the police.

Information   Should you wish to extend your stay or seek a variation of any conditions attached to it, write, before the expiry date of your permitted stay, to the Under Secretary of State, Home Office, Immigration Department, Lunar House, Wellesley Road, Croydon CR9 2BY, Surrey (☎ 01-686 0688), enclosing your passport or national identity card and form IS120 if these were your entry documents.

Customs   A colour-coded customs method is employed at most ports and airports in Britain. Go through the Red Channel if you have goods to declare (or if you are unsure of importation restrictions), or the Green Channel (which is subject to spot-checks by a customs officer) if you have nothing to declare. Visitors arriving in cars can obtain red or green windscreen (windshield) stickers on the boat. Where this system is not in operation, report to the customs officer in the baggage hall.
Visitors to Britain may leave with limited amounts of alcoholic drink, tobacco, perfumes and gifts free of import duty. Visitors from EEC countries are subject to two distinct allowance rates: (a) for goods obtained duty and tax free in the EEC, or duty and tax free on a ship or an aircraft, or goods obtained outside the EEC and (b) for goods obtained duty and tax paid within the EEC. Details of these allowances are available at most ports of entry to Britain.
Restrictions are enforced regarding importation of certain specialized goods, including controlled drugs; firearms; fireworks and ammunition; counterfeit coins; meat and poultry and most of their products (cooked or uncooked), including eggs and milk; animals and birds. Licenses can be granted for the importation of firearms, animals and birds.
Goods requiring a license for export include the following: controlled drugs, firearms and ammunition, most animals and birds and certain goods derived from protected species (e.g., furskins and ivory). You must declare anything you intend to leave or sell in Britain.

VAT   Tax relief: In Britain, except in the Channel Islands, Value Added Tax (VAT) is charged on most goods at a standard rate of 15 percent (at time of going to press). It is also charged at the standard rate on services you may receive, for example in hotels, restaurants and on car rental. VAT on services may not be reclaimed, but visitors can take advantage of the *Retail Export Scheme,* whereby they can reclaim VAT on goods purchased for export. *NB:* Not all shops operate the scheme, and there is often a minimum purchase price, as well as minimum values which apply to travelers from EEC countries. Shops operating the scheme will ask to see your passport before completing the VAT form. This form must be presented, with the goods, to the customs office at the point of departure from Britain (or to customs at the point of importation into an EEC country if you qualify as a Community traveler), within three months of purchase. After the customs officer has certified the form it should be returned to the shopkeeper, who will then send you the VAT refund, from which a small administration fee may be deducted.
English Customs Information Centre: HM Customs and Excise, Dorset House, Stamford Street, London SE1 9PS (☎ 01-928 0533).

Money

You may bring in sterling notes, foreign currency notes, travelers' checks, letter of credit, etc. in any currency and up to any amount. There is no restriction on the value of travelers' checks you can change.

The British money system is based on decimalization. There are one hundred **pence** to each **pound** sterling. Notes are issued to the value of £50, £20, £10 and £5. Coins are issued to the value of £1, 50p, 20p, 10p, 5p, 2p, and 1p. In Scotland, Northern Ireland, the Channel Islands and the Isle of Man, local bank notes are widely used, as well as the national bank notes. These are different in design and colour, but are of exactly the same value. If necessary, you can exchange them for normal Bank of England notes at any bank in England and Wales. There is no handling charge.

Banks

You will get the best rate of exchange at any branch of the main British clearing banks: Barclays, Lloyds, Midland and National Westminster. Banks are open Mon. to Fri. from 9:30am to 3:30pm, except Scotland where they close for one hour at lunchtime. At weekends and on public holidays you can go to one of the money exchanges at the airports or in central London and other major cities, or you can change travelers' checks at big travel agents such as Thomas Cook (they have more than 200 offices throughout the country) or at the larger hotels and some department stores. Non-bank commission charges vary considerably.

Information

Barclays, 54 Lombard Street, London EC3P 3AH (☎ 01-283 2161); Lloyds, 71 Lombard Street, London EC3 (☎ 01-626 1500); Midland, Poultry, London EC2 (☎ 01-606 9911); National Westminster, 41 Lothbury, London EC2P 2BP (☎ 01-726 1000).

Major exchange offices

London: Eurochange Bureaux Ltd (open 7 days a week), 95 Buckingham Palace Road, London SW1 (☎ 01-828 4953); offices at the following underground stations: Knightsbridge, Gloucester Road, Tottenham Court Road, Kings Cross and Embankment; Deak International (open 7 days a week), 22 Leinster Terrace, London W2 (☎ 01-402 5128); offices at 15 Shaftesbury Avenue, London W1; 237 Oxford Street, London W1; 2 London Street, Paddington W2; 2 Pembridge Road, London W2; and in Kings Cross and Liverpool Street stations; Thomas Cook Head Office, 45 Berkeley Street, London W1 (☎ 01-499 4000); Heathrow Airport: Barclays and Midland Banks (open 7 days a week, one 24 hours); Gatwick Airport: Lloyds and Midland Banks (open 24 hours, 7 days a week); Glasgow Airport: Clydesdale Bank (open 7 days a week).

Credit cards

The Visa card is by far the most widely accepted credit card in Britain. Diners Club, Access/Eurocard/Mastercharge and American Express cards are less widely accepted, although these organizations do have very extensive British networks. (The American Express organization, 6 Haymarket, London SW1 (☎ 01-930 4411) also provides a wide range of banking, credit card, travel and other services for visitors.)

★ In case of loss: Visa: (☎ 0604 21288); American Express: (☎ 0273 696933/01-551 1111); Diners Club: (☎ 0252 516261); Access/Eurocard/Mastercharge: (☎ 01-636 7878).

Emergencies

Medical

If a traveler becomes ill in Britain, or if an existing condition worsens to the extent that treatment cannot be delayed until he or she returns home, he or she is entitled to free *National Health Service* (NHS) treatment including treatment at NHS Accident and Emergency departments of hospitals. Emergency dental treatment can be obtained in the same way. If, however, it is necessary to stay overnight or longer in a hospital, you will probably be asked to pay. You are therefore strongly advised to take out adequate insurance coverage before traveling to Britain (consult your broker or travel agent for a suitable policy). The telephone operator (dial 100) will give you the telephone number and address of the local NHS doctor's surgery, or you can go to the casualty department of any general hospital.

In cases of emergency, dial 999 (the free nationwide emergency number) and ask for either 'Fire', 'Police' or 'Ambulance'. State that you are a foreign tourist, the nature of your problem and your location.

Pharmacies

In every town or city district at least one pharmacy remains open for one hour on Sundays and public holidays. The local police station will have a list of pharmacies providing this service. London: 50 Willesden Lane, NW6 (☎ 01-624 8000) (24 hours daily).

Post and telephone

The postal system in Britain is run by the state-controlled *Post Office,* while the telephone system is now owned and run by a private organization, *British Telecom.*

Post
Post offices, generally, are open from 9am-5:30pm from Mon. to Fri., 9am-12:30pm on Sat., although smaller town and village offices sometimes close for lunch. Stamps can normally only be bought at post offices although they can sometimes be bought from a machine outside larger branches. There are no collections on Sundays and the final weekend collection is usually about midday on Saturdays. The largest post office, **open 24 hours daily,** is in St. Martin's-le-Grand, London EC1 (☎ 01-432 1234). Telephone directories from all over the world can be consulted there. The main post office in each city or town handles **poste restante** and letters can be collected (for a small fee) upon production of proof of identity.

Telephone
Most public telephone booths are now made of smoked glass and have the yellow British Telecom insignia (though the old telephone boxes survive in some areas). Many public buildings, post offices, pubs and shops have payphones inside. There are three types of payphone: 1) dial coinbox, operated by 5p and 10p coins; 2) push-button coinbox, suitable for calls to most places in Western Europe and a few other countries, which accept 2p, 10p and 50p coins (minimum 6p); 3) cardphones, becoming more widely available. Cardphones are clearly marked — to use them you must buy a special card available from post offices and certain shops near cardphones. You may then make any number of calls in a cardphone up to the value of the card, without needing cash.

Telephone rates
National charges: Different types of calls cost different amounts, depending on when and to where you make them. There are three call rates that relate to different times of the day and week: peak rate is between 9am-1pm, Mon. to Fri.; standard rate is between 8am-9am and between 1pm-6pm, Mon. to Fri.; cheap rate is between 6pm-8am, Mon. to Fri. and all day and night at weekends.
International Direct Dialing (IDD) charges: Direct dialing is possible to anywhere within Great Britain and to most countries overseas if dialing from London. There are a lot of digits involved once you start dialing overseas, but by avoiding operator-assisted calls, costs are cut considerably and rates are reasonable. On IDD calls you pay only for the length of time you are connected. The cost of an IDD call varies depending on which Charge Band the country you are calling is in and the time of day. An IDD cheap rate is available to most countries, which differs in time from national call rates. Avoid calls through hotel switchboards — as much as 300-400 percent of the phone charge can be added to the bill by the individual hotel.

Codes
There are three types of dialing code — local, national and international. Local codes apply to your local call area (details are in the British Telecom code book supplied with all private and public telephones). All areas, down to the smallest village, have their own national (STD) code which is fixed. It usually begins with the number 0 and must always be dialed at the beginning of a call from virtually anywhere in the UK, and from overseas minus the 0. In certain cases, local area codes may apply for calls to nearby exchanges.
Attended call bureaus: These are located in a very few main post offices. The caller pays in advance and an attendant connects the call. Charges are by the minute. New style bureaus can be found in a few places where you dial your own call to any of over 100 countries throughout the world and pay only for the time you have used. Central London Bureau: 1 Broadway, Victoria, London SW1, plus in Oxford, Cambridge, London Heathrow and Gatwick airports and (during the summer) in Chester, Perth and Fort William, Scotland.
Free calls: The most important, in addition to the emergency 999 numbers, is the operator (dial 100). For free directory inquiries, dial 142 for a London number and 192 for numbers outside London. International directory inquiry numbers are listed in the BT code book under the names of the individual countries.

The disabled

The severely handicapped should contact one of the various specialist organizations such as **RADAR** (Royal Association for Disability and Rehabilitation) before planning a vacation in Britain. For those with minor handicaps, a few advance inquiries should ensure a trouble-free vacation.

Hotels
Most hotels and restaurants are happy to accommodate handicapped guests, though not all are suitable for the severely disabled or people restricted to a wheelchair. The wheelchair

symbol in this guide indicates hotels that are accessible to disabled people; however, specific requirements should be checked in advance. Suitable rooms may be limited, early booking is advisable.

The BTA can provide up-to-date lists of the facilities offered by various hotel networks as well as details of associations that arrange vacations to a variety of destinations in Britain. There are also specially adapted hotels, vacation homes or self-catering accommodation. Regional tourist offices may also be able to provide useful information in this respect.

● **RADAR,** 25 Mortimer Street, London W1N 8AB (☎ 01-637 5400): provides vacation information and advice for physically handicapped people and publishes an annual guide, *Holidays for Disabled People*, costing £2 and available from leading bookshops. **Information**

● **Holiday Care Service,** 2 Old Bank Chambers, Station Road, Horley, Surrey RH6 9HW (☎ 0293 774535): provides vacation information for disabled and elderly people, single parents and others with special needs.

● **Age Concern,** Bernard Sunley House, 60 Pitcairn Road, Mitcham, Surrey CR4 3LL (☎ 01-640 5431): produces a booklet, *Your Holidays in Retirement*, designed to help the elderly and disabled plan their vacation.

● **The British Nursing Association,** 443 Oxford Street, London W1N 0HQ (☎ 01-629 9030): 50 branches in Great Britain and is able to provide trained nurses in most instances for escorting, visiting, staying throughout the night or just to be 'on call'. Fees are negotiated through individual branches.

● *Door to Door* is a useful publication covering all transport services for the disabled, available from the **Department of Transport,** Freepost, Ruislip, Middlesex HA4 0BR.

● **The National Trust** publishes a free booklet *Facilities for the Disabled and Visually Handicapped,* for use in conjunction with their *Properties Open* booklet and with the general information contained in the BTA's free *Britain for the Disabled* booklet.

Children and young people

The ideal vacations for those traveling with young children are self-catering, where children are able to run riot with no embarrassment caused to parents and where there are no strict regulations, e.g., mealtimes. A large number of Britain's hotels and restaurants, however, now have special facilities such as gardens, cots in bedrooms, high chairs in dining rooms, a babysitting service and special mealtimes for children. Many hotels do not charge for children if they are staying in the same room as their parents. Some restaurants have restrictions on very young babies, while others supply high chairs and have a special children's menu. The *Peaudouce Family Welcome Guide* outlines establishments in Britain where special efforts have been made by proprietors to make families feel welcome.

Booking in advance, especially on major airlines, may be necessary if traveling with small children, but a number of major scheduled airlines offer package deals and special rates. This can be more difficult with chartered planes. Children under two years flying from the USA to Europe do so at 10 percent of the full fare paid by an accompanying adult as long as the child sits on the parent's lap. A second child under two years without a second adult flies at the same fare applicable for a child of two to eleven years (usually half the adult economy fare). If given advance warning, most airlines will provide special infant seats and children's meals. **Travel**

On trains, adults holding Family or Senior Citizen railcards can take up to four children for £1 each. Children under 16 travel at half price, and under fives go free.

On National Express buses, children aged from five to seventeen are charged a discounted fare (anything from two-thirds to half the normal fare). One child under five not occupying a seat may travel free, if accompanied by an adult fare-paying passenger. On Scotland to London services, adult fares are charged from the sixteenth birthdays.

Stations, airports and other public places that have nurseries or mothers' rooms are clearly marked.

Britain offers a wide variety of inexpensive accommodation suitable for young people. There are youth hostels, university, college and school residences, hostels run by the Young Men's and Young Women's Christian Associations (YMCAs and YWCAs), student and budget hotels and all kinds of other possibilities. Members of the Youth Hostel Association can stay at any hostel in Britain. (See also p. 46.) **Youth hostels**

● Buy an international membership card from **YHA Services**, 14 Southampton Street, London WC2. **Information**

● **YHA National Office,** Trevelyan House, 8 St. Stephen's Hill, St. Albans, Hertfordshire.
● **YHANI National Office** (Northern Ireland), 56 Bradbury Place, Belfast BT7 2RU.
● **YHS National Office** (Scotland), 7 Glebe Crescent, Stirling, Central FK8 2JA.

● **YMCA Britain,** National Council of YMCAs, 640 Forest Road, Walthamstow, London EI7 3DZ.
● **YWCA London Accommodation and Advisory Service,** 16 Great Russell Street, London WC1B 3LR.
● **Student Accommodation Services,** 67 Wigmore Street, London W1H 9LG (☎ 01-935 9979) find private homes (from £38 per week for bed and breakfast), hostels (from £10 per week), hotels (most in the medium price range from £18 per week) and halls of residence for summer and Easter vacations only (from £10 per week including Continental breakfast). They offer a wide choice of private homes in the inner London suburbs.
● **International Students House,** 229 Great Portland Street, London W1 (☎ 01-631 3223) is open 10am-11pm daily, a hostel with three and four-bedrooms specifically for last-minute bookings. The association publishes a free list of hostels in London and, for approximately 50p, will phone to help people who are not fluent in English.

Youth activities

In addition to the traditional international organizations, such as the scouting movement or the YHA, a number of less well-known associations offer constructive vacations built around subjects ranging from computers and pottery to pony-trekking and wind surfing (considerable youth-oriented information is contained under the relevant subject headings of this guide).
— **PGL Young Adventure Holidays,** 107 Station Street, Ross on Wye, Hereford HR9 7AH (☎ 0989 64211): run a number of centres for families and unaccompanied children aged between six and eighteen. Details of their courses and the activities offered are available from most travel agents or from PGL direct.
— **Outward Bound Eskdale,** Eskdale Green, Cumbria CA19 1TE (☎ 09403 281): run 20 night outward bound courses throughout the year, and 6 night courses for adults. Activities include canoeing, camping, rock climbing, orienteering and fell walking. Designed for young people aged 16-20.
— **Camp Beaumont,** Corpus Christi House, 9 West Street, Godmanchester, Cambridgeshire (☎ 0480 56123): was the first centre in Britain to introduce day camps. Prices start at £90 per week on a daily basis, £142 for a residential week.
— **Dolphin Activity Holidays,** 68 Churchway, London NW1 1LT (☎ 01-387 5602): organize 17 day centres and 11 residential one-week vacations throughout England during Easter and summer school vacations, for children aged 5-16.
— **Young Leisure Activity Holidays,** PO Box 99, Tunbridge Wells TN1 2EL (☎ 0892 31504): run courses for children and teenagers.

Information

The National Youth Bureau, 17-23 Albion Street, Leicester 1EI 6GD (☎ 0533 554775) provides a national resource centre for information, publications, training, research and development in the broad field of the social education of young people.

Student discounts

Exploring Britain need not be expensive, and a student or youth identity card (discount cards below) entitles the young visitor to a whole range of discounts on admission fees (cinema, theatre, art galleries, etc.), shopping and travel. Check your card's validity before leaving for Britain.
● **Museums:** The larger museums do charge a fee for admission to major special exhibitions, so take a student or youth identity card which will entitle you to reduction on any charges.
● **Theatre:** Theatre tickets unsold immediately before the performance are sometimes available at reduced rates; check with the box office for possible availability of these standby tickets. Many are only on offer to students and in London, theatres operating the **Student Standby Scheme** are indicated by the (S) symbol in the printed theatre listing. Student identity cards are necessary.

Discount cards in Britain

● **Student Coach Card:** available to students over 17 years, if in full-time study; allows one-third off the normal coach fare. Price: £2.90. Available from Victoria Coach Station, London SW1 and National Express agents.
● **Irish Overlander:** allows unlimited travel by scheduled road and rail services throughout Ireland. Price: £82.40 adult, £41.20 child under 14 years, valid for 15 days. Available from Ulsterbus Ltd, 10 Glengall Street, Belfast BT12 5AB (☎ 0232 220011).
● **Freedom of Scotland:** allows unlimited travel on scheduled rail services within Scotland for 7 to 14 days. Price: £38 or £55. Available from British Rail stations, at least 7 days in advance.
● **Countdown:** issued together with special offer vouchers giving up to 50 percent discount on entry to places of interest (museums, galleries, etc.) and entitles the holder to a 10 percent discount for cash payment in many shops, restaurants, discotheques and nightclubs. Valid for 3 months, price £5. Available from Countdown Ltd, 88-92 Earls Court Road, London W8 (☎ 01-938 1041).
● **National Student Discount Card:** should be purchased before arrival in Britain. Details of concessions are supplied with the card, and include discount on clothes, records, hairdressing, accommodation and car rental. Available by post from NSDS, PO Box 190, London WC1. Price: £2.99.

Calendar, events

Calendar

The British celebrate the coming of spring and high summer with a number of traditional fairs and festivals — from small, local events dating back to medieval times to the big music and arts festivals that are now world-famous (e.g., those held in Edinburgh, Bath, Cambridge and Canterbury). There are a number of traditional celebrations (many of them religious) that are held on the same day every year; the dates of others vary. One of the most famous annual events takes place on the Saturday nearest 11 June in London when the Queen takes the salute at the ceremony of **Trooping the Colour** in Whitehall, London. The **Lord Mayor's Show** is a huge attraction on the second Saturday in November, when London's new Lord Mayor rides through the streets in a golden coach.

Religious Events

Christmas is the most widely enjoyed religious festival in Britain. The nativity is celebrated in all churches and there are a series of carol concerts in churches across the country during the week preceding 25 December, including the world-famous service at King's College, Cambridge and those held in St. Paul's Cathedral and Westminster Abbey in London. **Christmas Eve, Christmas Day, Boxing Day** (26 December) and **New Year's Day** are all Bank Holidays, when the majority of shops and services are closed. Shops re-open on 2 January and huge bargains are available when large stores begin the 'sales' of their winter stock on that day or soon after.   **Christmas**

Easter is a 3-day holiday for most Britons. They celebrate Good Friday (two days before Easter Sunday) with spicy hot-cross buns, served with butter. Good Friday, Easter Sunday and Easter Monday are Bank Holidays. Many local fairs take place on Easter Monday, and there is a colourful Easter Parade in Battersea Park, London.   **Easter**

The last day of October is **Halloween** (All Hallows' Eve), when witches' hats are donned and pumpkin lanterns lit, a custom originating in Celtic times when fires were made to drive away witches. On Nov. 5, **Guy Fawkes' Day,** the whole country lights up bonfires and there are large community firework displays to commemorate the failure of Fawkes.   **Halloween**

Major festivals

Trooping the Colour, the Queen's Official Birthday Parade (Sat. nearest 11 Jun.); **Battle of Flowers,** Jersey (13 Aug.); **Royal Highland Show,** Edinburgh (21-24 Jun.); **Royal Tournament,** Earls Court, London (13-31 Jun.); **Edinburgh Military Tattoo** (14 Aug.-5 Sep.); **Blackpool Illuminations** (4 Sep.-1 Nov.).   **Traditional**

Jorvik Viking Festival (24-28 Feb.); **St. Andrews** (12-21 Feb.); **Chelsea Antiques Fair** (10-21 Mar.); **Edinburgh Folk Festival** (28 Mar.-6 Apr.); **Scottish Antiques Fair,** Edinburgh (2-4 Apr.); **Harrogate International Youth Music Festival** (15-22 Apr.); **Glyndebourne Festival Opera Season** (May to Aug.); **Bath Festival** (22 May-7 Jun.); **Robert Burns Festival,** Ayr and other locations (6-14 Jun.); **Grosvenor House Antiques Fair,** London (10-20 Jun.); **Aldeburgh Festival of Music and the Arts** (12-28 Jun.); **Cheltenham International Festival** (4-19 Jul.); **City of London Festival** (5-25 Jul.); **Llangollen International Musical Eisteddfod** (7-12 Jul.); **Edinburgh Festival Fringe and International Festival** (9-31 Aug.); **Edinburgh Film** (8-22 Aug.); **Swansea Musical** (28 Sep.-17 Oct.); **Belfast Arts** (10-28 Nov.).   **Music and the arts**

Most famous of all surviving English ritual ceremonial dances is **morris dancing:** six men dance on a village green or outside a pub on a summer's day, dressed in white trousers and shirts; bells are tied below their knees and they carry white handkerchiefs. They are accompanied by a fiddle or accordion. Spring is the season traditionally associated with **maypole dancing** with ribbons and garlands. The first Monday in May is a Bank Holiday. Spring Bank Holiday (the last Monday in May) is the time for traditional Whitsuntide events, including country fairs, 'miracle plays' and more morris dancing.   **Traditional dance**

Theatre   **Shakespeare Theatre** season, Stratford-upon-Avon (Mar.-Jan.); **Pitlochry** season (May-Oct.); **Chichester Festival Theatre** season (May-Sep.); **Open Air Theatre,** Regents Park, London (May-Sep.).

Information   Details of festivals are available either from the **London Visitor and Convention Bureau** (☎ 01-730 3488) or from individual tourist information centres. The BTA publish *Britain For All Seasons*, which includes a list of major events held in Britain throughout the year (available free from overseas offices and tourist information centres in Britain). In Britain and Ireland the *Welcomes* are monthly magazines published by the respective tourist boards and on sale in bookshops.

Sporting events

Great Britain offers sporting events of every type the year round; BTA can provide up-to-date information.
Boating London International Boat Show (7-18 Jan.). Oxford and Cambridge Boat Race (Mar./Apr.). Henley Regatta (Jul.). Southampton International Boat Show (18-26 Sep.).
Cricket Test Matches draw the crowds from mid-Jun. to mid-Aug.
Dog show Crufts Dog Show, London (13-15 Feb.).
Fishing Freshwater trout season begins in mid-Mar. and runs until the end of Sep. Sea-trout fishing is at its best in Aug.
Football Football (soccer) season is in full swing throughout the spring, until the beginning of May, with exciting games to be seen all over the country on Sat. afternoons, as well as some weekday evenings.
Golf Conditions are good on hundreds of golf courses from mid-Mar. until the end of Sep. Golf Walker Cup, Berkshire (27-28 May).
Horses From mid-Mar. until the end of Sep. there are flat-race meetings for horseracing fans; the steeplechase season begins early in Aug. Grand National Racing, Aintree (2-4 Apr.). Badminton Horse Trials (9-12 Apr.). The Derby Horse Races, Epsom, Surrey (3-6 Jun.). Royal Ascot Horse Racing (16-19 Jun.). Horse of the Year Show (4-10 Oct.).
Hunting 'Glorious Twelfth' of Aug. marks the opening of Scotland's grouse-shooting season.
Motorcycling TT Motorcycle Races, Isle of Man (17-22 Apr.).
Motor-racing Circuit of Ireland International Motor Rally (17-22 Apr.). British Grand Prix, Silverstone (12 Jul.). London to Brighton Veteran Car Run (1 Nov.).
Sailing Cowes Week, Isle of Wight (1-9 Aug.).
Tennis Wimbledon Tennis Championships (23 Jun.-6 Jul.).

 Traveling in Britain

Driving and car rental

The rule to follow when driving in Britain is to drive on the left and overtake on the right. Unlike some European countries, there is **no automatic priority for traffic approaching junctions from the left.** Priority is indicated by road markings, usually by a white line and a sign showing that you should stop, or slow down and 'give way'. The speed limit is **30 mph** (miles per hour) in towns and cities unless you see a sign showing **40** or **50.** On country roads do not exceed **60** mph. On highways and dual carriageway trunk roads there is a maximum speed limit of **70** mph. It is now compulsory to wear front seat belts in Britain.

Breakdown   The best provision to make before coming to Britain is to join one of the motoring organizations affiliated to the two major British ones, the AA and the RAC (below for addresses). On arrival in Britain, their offices will inform you of the services extended to affiliated and non-affiliated members. All highways have **roadside telephones** and, if you break down, a call will bring fast help from either organization. On other roads, you can call from an ordinary telephone box. Alternatively, ask for an emergency repair garage, but it will cost more.

Insurance   When renting a vehicle you will be required to complete an insurance proposal form and it is important to assess, at that time, your maximum liability for damage to the rented vehicle and whether you have the option to have this covered by payment of an additional fee (a **collision damage waiver**). It is important to remember, too, that the insurance coverage is

- • Airports
- • <u>Air and seaports</u>
- • Seaports

Lerwick

Stromness
Thurso
Stornoway
Ullapool
<u>Aberdeen</u>
Oban
Glasgow
Edinburgh
Prestwick
Newcastle-
upon-Tyne
Larne
<u>Belfast</u>
Stranraer
Tees-side
Douglas
Leeds/
Bradford
Hull
Blackpool
<u>Liverpool</u>
Manchester
Humberside
Grimsby
Holyhead
East
Midlands
Norwich
Birmingham
Great
Yarmouth
Fishguard
Felixstowe
Pembroke
Dock
Stansted
Harwich
Cardiff-
Wales
Luton
Heathrow
Southend
Bristol
Sheerness
Ramsgate
Gatwick
Dover
<u>Southampton</u>
Folkestone
Exeter
Portsmouth
Bournemouth
Newhaven
<u>Plymouth</u>
Weymouth
Penzance

Scale
0   50 km
0   50 miles

St Peter Port
Jersey   St Helier

only operative when you or a driver authorized by the rental company is driving the rented vehicle. There is **no** insurance cover provided by the policy when any other person (even with your permission) is driving the rented vehicle. If you are not insured when you arrive in Britain, the motoring organization (AA or RAC) can usually arrange suitable coverage at your port of entry.

Driving license   The visitor to Britain can use his own valid driving license to drive in Britain for up to 12 months from the date of his last entry into the country. Alternatively a current **international driving permit** may be used.

Information   The BTA publishes a useful booklet on vehicle rental with information about companies in Britain that rent self- and chauffeur-driven cars, as well as motor homes, trailer and motor caravans (campers). Operators listed are based at or near sea or air entry points into Britain, or are located in principal railway/bus stations and main tourist centres throughout the country.

Major rental companies
- **Budget Rent A Car,** 89 Wigmore Street, London W1 (☎ 01-935 3518).
- **Godfrey Davis Europcar,** Davis House, Wilton Road, London SW1 (☎ 01-834 8484) is one of Britain's main car rental companies, offering a rail/drive service — they can have a car ready and waiting for you on arrival at any of 73 InterCity railway stations.
- **Swan National,** 305 Chiswick High Road, London W4 (☎ 01-995 4665) have a car rental office based at many of the major bus stations providing a link with the National Express network.
- **Hertz** and **Avis** are also well represented in Britain.
- **British Airways** and **British Caledonian** both operate fly/drive arrangements allowing you to pick up a pre-booked rental car at the airport on your arrival.
- **Automobile Association** (AA), Fanum House, Basingstoke, Hants RG21 2EA (☎ 0256 20123, for 24-hour service ☎ 01-954 7373).
- **Royal Automobile Club** (RAC), 49 Pall Mall, London SW1Y 5JG (☎ 01-839 7050, for 24-hour service ☎ 01-681 3611 or Dover (0304) 204153).

Britain by plane

Within Britain there is a vast network of domestic air routes, with scheduled flights connecting major cities and islands. For speedy, no-fuss flights, **British Airways** operate shuttle flights between London and Edinburgh, Glasgow, Manchester and Belfast. Passengers on these flights need check in only ten minutes before departure (20 minutes for flights to Belfast).

Discount fares   A wide range of discount fares is available. Most scheduled airlines offer standby fares, usually restricted to 'off-peak' flights on weekdays and on flights at weekends, and on many, children under two years may travel free. On British Airways flights, senior citizens are entitled to 30 percent discount on the full economy round-trip (return) fare (minimum stay 6 nights). For **British Caledonian** flights, there are considerable discounts offered on round-trip fares; London to Edinburgh, Glasgow, Manchester, etc.

Sightseeing trips   Visitors interested in helicopter or small aircraft sightseeing trips of Britain should make enquiries at local airports (see yellow pages or local tourist information centre where staff should have details of any such flights or charters available in their immediate area). All travel agents can provide details.

Information   — Airship trips of the London area are available through **Airship Industries,** Bond Corporation House, 347-353 Chiswick High Road, London W4 4HS (☎ 01-995 7811). Reservations may be made by telephone or through the **London Visitor and Convention Bureau,** but heavy demand has resulted in a huge waiting list. Each trip takes three to four passengers, lasts one-and-a-half hours and costs approximately £100. The Skyship 600, a larger version of the Skyship 500 currently in operation, is due to be launched in 1987. This new model will hold up to ten passengers.
— **Tempus Aviation Ltd,** Grove House, 628 London Road, Colnbrook, Buckinghamshire SL3 8QA (☎ 02812 4750 between 9:30am-2:30pm) offer scenic flights over London in small aircraft that cost £42 including transport from a hotel and return. Price includes a conducted tour of historic aircraft kept at Booker Airfield, near High Wycombe, Buckinghamshire.
— Fifteen-minute helicopter sightseeing tours of London are available from **Air Taxis, Charter and Freight,** Westland Heliport, Lombard Road, London SW11 3RE (☎ 01-228 0181). Trips include panoramic views over the capital from heights of up to 2,000 feet and cost £35.

Britain by train

Travel by **British Rail** is fast, comfortable and easy. On the **InterCity network,** services operate frequently and at speeds up to 125 mph (200 kph). InterCity has 125 services which link London, South Wales, the West Country, the Northeast of England and Scotland's East Coast and offer comfort, relaxation and shortened journey times between cities and major towns, linking London to Edinburgh, for example, in only 4.5 hours.

On most long-distance trains, seats can be reserved in advance, but it is not compulsory except on a very limited number of services, in order to prevent overcrowding. Seat reservation is recommended on popular routes during vacation periods.

Connecting with InterCity is a network of local and cross-country lines. Many are scenic and attractive in themselves such as Inverness to Kyle of Lochalsh in Scotland and Aberystwyth to Pwllheli in Wales. Most trains have both first- and second-class (economy) carriages and InterCity trains usually have a restaurant and/or buffet car where hot meals or light snacks and drinks are served.

Sleepers

Overnight sleeping car trains are an ideal way to gain a day and save on hotel charges. On sleepers the supplementary charge is £15 per journey, for first and second class. Reservations should be made well in advance. Travelers to the West and North of England and Scotland can take advantage of **Motorail,** the car-carrying train service — while you sleep, your car is conveyed in another section of the train. The service operates from London to major towns in Scotland and to Northwest, Northeast and Southwest England. Avoid London by joining sleepers at Watford, Stevenage or Reading.

Information: From Euston: ☎ 01-387 7070; from Kings Cross: ☎ 01-278 2477; from Paddington: ☎ 01-262 6767.

Rail fares

Return tickets cost double the price of single (one-way) tickets, except for day excursions and city saver fares. One way of economizing is to travel outside the rush hour. The **Cheap Day Return** saves about one-third the normal fare on a day's outing if you depart after the morning rush hour. The Eurailpass is not valid for travel in Great Britain, while the **BritRail Pass** caters specifically to the overseas visitor to Britain but is only sold overseas. It offers unlimited rail travel in England, Scotland and Wales, and first- or second-class passes are available for 8, 15, 22 days or one month. Children aged between 5 and 15 years pay half-fare and for young people aged between 16 and 25 years there is a **Student Rail Card** (second class only). Details are available from **Britrail Travel International** offices in Europe and North America or main railway stations in Europe. The **BritRail Seapass** offers the same facilities as the BritRail pass plus a round trip between London and Ireland by rail and Sealink/British Ferries ship. (For telephone numbers of main inquiry offices: gazetteer sections.)

On Britain's rail network, there are three types of rail fares: **Standard, Cheap Day** and **Saver.** The Standard ticket is available on any train, any day, first or second class, with 3 days' validity. The Standard Return, at double the Standard Single, is valid for 3 months.

Monthly return tickets (traveling out on the day and returning within one calendar month) are available on InterCity between most British Rail stations near London.

InterCity Savers operate on the InterCity network between London and the provinces, and are the cheapest way to travel by train over longer distances. Certain time restrictions exist on weekdays, and tickets are only available for second-class travel.

Travel first or second class. Second class is perfectly comfortable although first-class seats are wider and accommodation more spacious. There is a yellow strip above first-class carriage windows, and a red strip on those of the restaurant and buffet car.

Seats can be reserved for £1 from many British Rail stations or ☎ 01-388 6061 (quote a credit card number).

Railcards

Railcards can save customers just over one-third the Saver price. Categories of railcard available:

— Young Persons (under 24 years) and Students.
— Family (for groups traveling with children).
— Senior Citizen (over 60 years).
— Annual Season Ticket Holder.
— Disabled Persons.

The disabled

The **Disabled Persons Railcard** is for permanently and severely disabled travelers. Signs with purple backgrounds at stations indicate the location of special facilities. Details of individual train services and reservation facilities are given in passenger timetables. Always book in advance to allow special arrangements to be made.

Sleeper Supplements for overnight berths on InterCity cost £15. Many sleeper trains also offer the Motorail service — drive on, sleep overnight in a train cabin, drive off the next morning: London to Aberdeen, Edinburgh, Inverness, Penzance, Stirling and between Crewe and Inverness, plus the daytime London to Carlisle. Brochures are available from British Rail stations, rail-appointed travel agents or phone: ☎ 01-387 8541. Railcard holders pay the £15 sleeper supplement but save 34 percent on Saver fares.

Children under 16 years travel half price. Under 5s travel free. Adults holding Family or Senior Citizen Railcards can take up to four children for £1 each.

The **One Day Capitalcard** combines British Rail and London Transport services and allows unlimited use of train, underground and bus services in London for one day. Cost: £2.50 for inner London travel. Travelers from outside London can buy a card for 80p more than the cost of a Cheap Day Return ticket to London. Available from London Underground and most British Rail stations throughout the country.

Britainshrinkers are fully escorted all-day tours of Britain by rail or bus. Special reductions are offered if passengers use a BritRail Pass as the travel ticket.

InterCity Ireland: the ticket cost covers ferry crossings on Sealink British Ferries, B & I Line, Belfast Car Ferries, British Railways and Northern Ireland Railways. Crossings are from Fishguard, Holyhead, Liverpool or Stranraer.

An inclusive ticket allows passengers to travel from London stations via Harwich to the Hook of Holland, Dover to Calais, Folkestone to Boulogne, Newhaven to Dieppe. Depending on the route, sea crossings are by ferry, hovercraft or jetfoil service. Duty free facilities are available on them all. On the Continent, link up with the InterCity Europe rail network which travels through Europe quickly and comfortably.

Reservations should be made at any Rail Travel Centre or travel agent (there are 200 rail-appointed travel agents in London alone). All tickets and train transactions can be made using credit cards: Access, American Express, Travel Key or Visa.

Information
- **London Transport:** ☎ 01-222 1234.
- **Motorail:** ☎ 01-387 8541.
- **Sleeper services:** ☎ 01-388 6061 (Euston), ☎ 01-278 2411 (Kings Cross), ☎ 01-723 7681 (Paddington).
- **Travel Centres:** 14 Kingsgate Parade, Victoria Street, London SW1; 407 Oxford Street, London W1; British Travel Centre, 12 Regent Street, London SW1 (the principal centre, open 9am-5pm, Mon. to Fri.). There are centres at the following London mainline stations: Cannon Street, Charing Cross, Euston, Kings Cross, London Bridge, Paddington, St. Pancras, Victoria, Waterloo.

British Rail British Rail has offices in Europe and BritRail Travel offices in North America (New York, Ohio, Los Angeles, Toronto, Vancouver and Dallas). Most can provide tickets for rail travel in Britain, Continental and Irish ferry crossings and can make seat and sleeper reservations.

Ferry services

Most ferry services have connecting passenger trains or buses. Scheduled ferry services make even the remotest of Britain's islands accessible. There are drive-on car ferries as well as passenger-only ferries to most of the larger Scottish Isles, the Channel Islands, Isle of Man and Isles of Scilly. **Sealink British Ferries**, **Belfast Car Ferries Ltd, P. and O.** and **B & I Line** operate to Northern Ireland. Space for cars should generally be booked in advance, especially during vacation periods. All details are available from High Street travel agents.

Bus/coach

Britain's long-distance bus network reaches all major towns and is an extremely economical means of travel. **National Bus Company Ltd** (NBC) is by far the biggest company, operating a network of National Express buses throughout England and Wales, while the major bus companies in Scotland come under the heading of the **Scottish Bus Group,** and in Northern Ireland, **Ulsterbus.** Since deregulation, a number of smaller, private companies have been established which means that cut-price fares are often available.

Purchase of the **NBC BritExpress Card** entitles travelers to one-third off standard fares for any number of journeys taken during 30 consecutive days on all National Express bus services in England and Wales, selected services to and within Scotland, and some other services of associated companies. The card is available from certain travel agents or, upon presentation of a valid passport, at the **National Travel Office**.

For visitors staying in London, the **London Explorer** ticket gives unlimited travel on almost all the London bus and subway (underground) system for a period of one, three, four or

seven days. The ticket includes one return journey by underground or Airbus between London (Heathrow) Airport and central London — and there are discounts on tours and admission to places of interest. Available from certain travel agents overseas (including **BritRail Travel International** offices in North America) or any underground station or London Transport Information Centre.

Information

- **London Transport Information Centre,** 55 Broadway, London SW1 (☎ 01-222 1234).
- **The National Travel Office,** Victoria Coach Station, London SW1 (☎ 01-730 0202) supplies information and timetables and handles all bus and coach bookings. If you are planning a tour, rather than an A to B journey, a large percentage of travel agencies can make bus bookings. Alternatively, book directly with the bus company. Look in the yellow pages telephone directory for local companies, contact the tourist information office nearest you, or ring National Express who will do credit card bookings for passengers five (or more) days in advance of travel.

The following companies operate bus tours of Great Britain:
- **Evans Tours,** 27 Cockspur Street, Trafalgar Square, London SW1Y 5BT (☎ 01-930 2377).
- **Grey-Green,** 55 Stamford Hill, London NI6 5TD (☎ 01-800 8010).
- **London Crusader,** Dept. DOL, Western House, Argyll Street, 237-239; Oxford Street, London W1R 1AB (☎ 01-437 0124).
- **Road 'n' Rail Tours,** 10 Queen Street, London W1X 7PD (☎ 01-499 5569).
- **Venture Tours,** Harrow Coach Station, Pinner Road, Harrow, Middlesex (☎ 01-427 0101).
- **National Express Tourist Trail** (details from any travel agent).

Accommodation

Hotels

Hotels range from the small, old-fashioned, family-run type to huge modern buildings offering every amenity from shops to saunas. There is an ever-increasing number of motels, mostly located outside cities, that offer hotel-type rooms, or alternatively separate chalets, but all with plenty of space for parking the car close to your room. At the top end of the London market are the outstanding older style hotels — the Savoy, Claridges, the Dorchester — most very central but expensive. There are hundreds of less formal hotels providing excellent accommodation on a smaller scale. Some of the best, and the most convenient for getting into central London, are in Bayswater and Kensington — north and south of Hyde Park respectively.

The large hotel chains and groups (Grand Metropolitan, Trusthouse Forte, Best Western, Embassy and others) not only offer a good standard of accommodation but also centralized booking facilities — which can usually be tapped through travel agents in your home town, or through your nearest BTA office.

If you want to make a firm reservation, which is highly advisable during July and August, you can do it from home, through a travel agent or through a TIC **'Book A Bed Ahead Scheme'** (known as the 'Bed Booking Service' in Wales). They charge a booking fee of about £1.25 in England (excluding London) and nothing at all in Wales or Northern Ireland. Scottish centres ask for a deposit which is returnable when your hotel bill is paid. The same applies to the two London centres that operate this scheme — Victoria Station and Heathrow Airport — here you are charged £5, £4 of which is returnable when your hotel bill is paid.

Reservations

Short off-season bargain breaks, some combined with specific activities, are offered by most major hotel chains in their enthusiasm to extend the short summer peak season and to fill weekend beds left vacant by the weekday businessman.

Bargain breaks

- **Inter-Hotel's Time Away program** covers over 60 privately owned hotels throughout Britain. From £20 per person including 2 nights' accommodation and full breakfast. Children under 14 years free. 35 Hogarth Road, London SW5 0QH (☎ 01-373 3241).
- **Superbreak Mini Holidays** start at £28 per person including full breakfast. Half board available in many of their 161 hotels and rail-inclusive packages at £148. Their **Sneak A Week** holidays offer 7 nights for the price of 6 at 42 country and seaside hotels (☎ 01-278 9646).
- **Holiday Inn Weekender** programs at their luxurious, modern hotels start at £24.50 per person and can be tailored to individual requirements. 10-12 New College Parade, Finchley Road, London NW3 5EP (☎ 01-772 7755).
- **A Best Western Hotels Getaway Break** (mid-week or weekend) is a minimum of 2 nights' accommodation. Prices start at £22.50 per person per night and include full board and service and discount on rail travel. Special interest breaks include golf, shooting, hot-air balloon-

Information

ing and skiing. London breaks can include theatre tickets and sightseeing trips. Interchange House, 26 Kew Road, Richmond, Surrey TW9 2NA (☎ 01-940 9766) (open Saturday mornings). Glasgow office: 5th floor, Gordon Chambers, 90 Mitchell Street, Glasgow G1 3NQ (☎ 041-204 1794).

● **Trusthouse Forte Hotels** operate leisure breaks and special interest and activity breaks at hotels around Britain. Packages can be rail-inclusive or bus-inclusive between 2 Apr. and 2 Nov., with weekend rail fare savings greater than mid-week. Prices vary for each hotel by the month but start at £25 per person per night full board. A Saturday night must be included in a London break. 11 hotels are particularly suitable for families. 24-30 New Street, Aylesbury, Buckinghamshire HP20 2NW (☎ 01-567 3444) (open 7 days a week).

● **Embassy Hushaway breaks** are year-round and include bed and breakfast, Christmas, rail-inclusive and Downtown Rail breaks, from £16.50 per person per night. Reservation Centre, PO Box 671, London SW7 5JQ (☎ 0345 581 811).

● **London-based breaks** are by far the most popular — **Capital Breaks** is a London mini-vacation company operating from a selection of 15 city hotels. A Capital Break includes a return rail ticket, two nights' accommodation, full breakfast, a 3-day London Explorer pass entitling unlimited bus and underground travel, free places for children and discounts on sightseeing tours and restaurants. Prices start at £57 per person for 2 nights, although one-night stopovers are available. Freepost, London NW7 2BR (☎ 01-581 1414 for brochure or call free for reservations on ☎ 0800 18 11 11).

● **Keith Prowse** operate their own **Londoners** program which includes tickets for one theatre show of your choice, two nights in a West End hotel and a meal for about £40 (rail fares or car rental are extra but can be arranged through Keith Prowse at discount rates). At the other end of the scale their **Post and Pampered break** covers best theatre seats, a 5 star hotel and a meal in a top restaurant. Banda House, Cambridge Grove, London W6 (☎ 01-741 7441).

All mini-breaks can be booked either through a local travel agent (who can supply brochures for all tour operators), through the tour operator or the hotels direct. If rail tickets are required, book at least five days in advance. Bookings from abroad can be made through BTA overseas offices.

Alternative accommodation

Bed and Breakfasts

An alternative means of accommodation if traveling around Britain is the traditional boarding house or Bed and Breakfast (B.B.) establishment. More and more, private individuals are converting their own homes into B.B.s. They are usually quite small residential properties, some taking only six or eight guests. Unlike hotels and inns, they do not normally have a license to sell alcohol. There may be just one set menu in the evening and meal times are often rigid. Look for the Bed and Breakfast signs displayed outside. Prices start at as little as £4.50 per person and include a cooked breakfast.

Guesthouses

Guesthouses, found mainly in seaside towns and other tourist centres, are slightly more expensive than B.B.s, but have more bedrooms and bathrooms. Useful publications are the Automobile Association's *Guesthouses, Farmhouses and Inns*, and BTA's *Farmhouses, Bed and Breakfast, Inns and Hostels* and *Stay at an Inn*.

Inns

There are few country towns and villages without a good inn, most full of character with home-cooking, roaring log fires and locally brewed 'real' ale. Some working farms also offer accommodation, based as they are in tranquil, idyllic countryside serving up traditional farmhouse cooking.

Information

● **BTA Commended book** (£2.75): This lists hotels, guesthouses and restaurants in country areas that have been commended by the BTA for their particularly high standards of service, food and hospitality.

● **Go-As-You-Please:** Some organizations sell a book of vouchers for hotels in their group, the advantage being that you know in advance how much your accommodation will cost. The scheme supplies a list of hotels where vouchers are accepted. Details are available from travel agents.

● **Farm Holiday Bureau,** National Agricultural Centre, Stoneleigh, Kenilworth, Warwickshire, supplies information for visitors wanting farm accommodation (☎ 0203 555100). The bureau publishes a book, *Farm Holidays in Britain*.

● **Scottish Farmhouse Holidays,** (☎ 0337 30451).

● **Country Farm Holidays,** Shaw Mews, Shaw Street, Worcester WR1 3QQ (☎ 0905 613744).

Landmark Trust

The Landmark Trust is a non-profit organization that has bought and restored about sixty buildings of historical importance, most of which have long outlived their original function. Rather than merely preserving the buildings as museum pieces for visitors, the Trust rents

them to travelers. Each year about ten thousand people can enjoy holidays in properties that are, if nothing else, far removed in shape, style and situation from their normal homes. The properties are mainly found in rural settings. The most eccentric structure is **The Pineapple** (Airth, Stirlingshire, Scotland), built in the eighteenth century as fancy Scottish summer house for the Earl of Dunmore to celebrate his success in growing hothouse pineapples. Trust properties contain basic comforts, and rents are very low. Despite infrequent advertising, however, the landmarks are generally booked well in advance. A handbook that lists all the properties, each one photographed, shown in plan form, and indicated on a map, together with full booking details and prices, can be obtained by sending a stamped addressed envelope to The Landmark Trust, Shottesbrooke, Maidenhead, Berkshire. Before sending a deposit for accommodation, telephone ☎ 062 882 5925 to check the availability of a specific landmark and to discuss alternatives if your first choice is not available.

British universities and colleges offer good value, low cost accommodation at over 50 locations during the summer and other student vacation periods.

University accommodation

The British Universities Accommodation Consortium Ltd, Box C85, University Park, Nottingham NG7 2RD; **Higher Education Accommodation Consortium,** 36 Collegiate Crescent, Sheffield S10 2BT.

Information

Self-Catering

City apartments, country cottages, converted farmhouse barns, Scottish crofts, forest cabins, seaside chalets, trailers, caravans and tents can all be rented as self-catering units. Many agencies and individual owners are listed in free BTA guides called *Holiday Homes* (for London, there is a similar publication entitled *Apartments in London*). Generally, all household requisites are supplied and a deposit is payable before occupying the premises.

Information

● *Scotland Self-Catering Accommodation 1987* produced by the **Scottish Tourist Board** (£2.97).
● *All the Places to Stay 1987* produced by the **Northern Ireland Tourist Board** (£2.95).
● *The Good Holiday Cottage Guide* is an annual guide to self-catering cottages and agencies throughout England, Scotland and Wales.

Book self-catering units direct or through the growing number of agencies now established throughout Britain:
● **Classic Cottages,** Worval House, Garras, Helston, Cornwall TR12 6LP (☎ 032622 751 or 755) have one of the best agency reputations in the country — their 200 cottages adhere to strict standards, all within an hour's drive of Helston.
● **Character Cottages,** 34 Fore Street, Sidmouth, Devon (☎ 03955 77001) let a range of accommodation from Olde Worlde cottages to compact, modern flats. Long weekend breaks and part-week holidays are available at short notice.
● **Cabin Holidays Ltd,** Bull Plain, Hertford SG14 1DY (☎ 0992 553535) have 10 cabins on the rugged, beautiful Scottish Isle of Skye, a selection of other sites elsewhere in Scotland and a few in England and Wales.
● **English Country Cottages,** Claypit Lane, Fakenham, Norfolk NR21 8AS (☎ 0328 51155, 'dial-a-brochure' on 0328 4041) is closely linked with Norfolk and East Anglia but is now a highly efficient organization with cottages in every corner of Britain (approximately 200 in East Anglia).
● **Country Farm Holidays,** Shaw Street, Worcester (☎ 0905 613744) have a selection of 60 farmhouse holidays all at £9.95 for bed and breakfast. They also operate **Country Rover** touring holidays based on 450 farmhouses throughout Britain, giving visitors the freedom to roam Britain staying overnight at any of the 450 farmhouses participating in the scheme. Every farm will exchange a Country Rover Voucher for one night's bed and breakfast and a free telephone call to book the next night's accommodation (available from travel agents or Country Farm Holidays).

Camping and trailers

Britain has approximately 5,000 licensed sites to choose from — most open from Easter through October. Unlike the requirements of some countries, campers do not have to produce an identity card or complete any forms. If you have not booked a pitch in advance it is advisable to look for a site as early in the day as possible. During the peak summer months

(Jul.-Sep.) many sites, particularly those by the coast or lakes, fill up quickly, so be prepared to travel a few miles inland or seek help from tourist advisory services.

Equipment rental　It is probably more convenient to rent a trailer or motorvan since rental charges are comparable to the cost of bringing a trailer or heavy tent to Britain. Motor homes are well-equipped with all conveniences for cooking and sleeping, and there is normally temporary membership in a motoring organization. Rental prices vary according to the length of the rental, size of the vehicle and time of year, but it costs approximately £180 to rent a luxury 5/6 berth vehicle for one week, and £4 for a camping park pitch per night.

The establishments listed below rent trailers, motor caravans, tents and camping equipment. Prices vary according to the size of van, the length of rental and time of year. It is always wise to book well in advance. If a towing bracket is fitted to the car before leaving for Britain, the bracket should have a coupling ball bolted on, allowing for height adjustment, i.e., not integral.

● **Arthur Fitt Caravans,** Sweechbridge Road, Hillborough, Herne Bay, Kent CT6 6TE (☎ 0227 373848).
● **Trailer Services,** 16 Palace Gates Road, London N22 4BN (☎ 01-889 4242).
High street outdoor centres and sports shops sometimes rent camping and trailer equipment — see yellow pages telephone directory for nearest dealer.

Information　● **Motor Caravanners' Club Ltd,** 52 Wolseley Road, London N8 8RP (☎ 01-340 5865).
● **National Caravan Council Ltd,** Catherine House, Victoria Road, Aldershop, Hants GU11 1SS (☎ 0252 318251).
● **Tourist Boards** have a voluntary register of camp sites.
● **Camping and Caravanning Advisory Services** offer more specialized help and advise on the availability of sites during the July and August peak, though some are open throughout the vacation period. Services operate in the following areas: Lake District (☎ 09662 5515); Norwich (☎ 0603 20679); London, Platform 15, London Victoria Station; Hampshire, Dorset and the Isle of Wight (☎ 0703 611688); Devon (☎ 0392 79088); Cornwall (☎ 0872 74057, Sat. only).
● **Camping in London:** It is not easy to camp in London, and preferable to find a site on the outskirts. The following are the only town sites: **Co-operative Woods Caravan Club Site,** Federation Road, Abbey Wood, Greenwich, London SE2 OLS (☎ 01-310 2233)(open Jan.-Dec.). **Hackney Camping,** Millfields Road, Hackney, London E5 (☎ 01-985 2071) (open Jun.-Aug.). **Lee Valley Park,** Picketts Lock Lane, Edmonton, London N9 OAS (☎ 01-803 4756) (open Jan.-Dec.). **Lee Valley Park,** Eastway Cycle Circuit, Temple Mills Lane, Newham, London E15 2EN (☎ 01-534 6085) (open Apr.-Sep.); **Sewardstone Caravan Park,** Sewardstone Road, Chingford, London E4 7RA (☎ 01-529 5689) (open Apr.-Oct.).

Youth hostels

There are over 250 youth hostels in England and Wales provided by the **Youth Hostels Association,** Trevelyan House, St. Albans, Herts AL1 2DY (☎ 0727 55215); 14 Southampton Street, London WC2 (☎ 01-240 3158). Extremely cheap self-catering accommodation is available in a wide range of buildings. Youth hostels are open to members (usually travelers on the move, e.g. the walker or cyclist). An international membership card can be obtained from the Youth Hostels Association.

Conditions　Members can stay in any of the 5,000 hostels in Britain and abroad. The 260 hostels in Britain are spread throughout cities, towns, the seaside, National Parks and long-distance footpaths. Renowned for being economical and friendly, hostel membership offers discounts on local attractions, a quarterly magazine and special rates on travel and insurance.

Hostels attract cyclists, walkers and motorists — most hostels have a parking lot in the grounds or nearby where a vehicle can be left for unlimited periods. The head office supplies details of **YHA Adventure Holidays** combining relaxation with acquisition of new skills, e.g. watersports. Campers can erect their own tents in the grounds of certain hostels, and are charged half the senior overnight fee. A copy of the camping code is available from the head office.

Information　*Youth Hostel Association handbook,* available from bookshops (£1.50).

Membership cards are also valid at the following:
● **Scotland YHA,** 7 Glebe Crescent, Stirling FK8 2JA (☎ 0786 72821) (80 hostels).
● **YHA of Northern Ireland,** 56 Bradbury Place, Belfast BT7 2RU (☎ 0232 324733).
Children over 12 years are welcome, 9 - 12 years must be accompanied by a parent or a member over 18 years, and if under 9 years, by a parent of the same sex. Family dormitories must be booked in advance, as must parties of mentally handicapped visitors.

Vacation Centres

Vacation camps are now known as centres or 'villages' of chalets. Situated at various resorts around Britain, a vacation at one of the camps (at Christmas, Easter or during the summer season) consists either of full board accommodation, or is at a self-catering centre with fully equipped modern chalets, supermarket, cafes or restaurants on site, free sports facilities and a full program of entertainment.

National Association of Holiday Centres Ltd, 11 Bolton Street, Piccadilly, London W1Y 8AU (☎ 01-499 8000).   **Information**

Eating and drinking

Cuisine

The visitor to Britain is often unaware of the true wealth of the country's home-produced food and drink and the variety of traditional recipes. Most areas are famous for the excellence of a particular dish. Specialties include **gingerbread** and **mint cake** from Cumbria; **salmon** from the Scottish borders; **shrimps** from Morecambe Bay; **'Singin Hinnies' griddle scones, Stottie Cake** (a huge, round, flat loaf filled with cheese, ham, tongue or chicken) and **Lindisfarne Mead** from Northumbria; **baps** and **barm cakes** from the northwest; first-class **beef, Yorkshire pudding** and **gravy** from the Yorkshire Dales; **salmon** and **trout** from the Severn Valley; **black puddings, sage sausages, Stilton cheese, Bakewell tarts** from the East Midlands; **Game Pie** from Oxfordshire; **fish** and **shellfish** from East Anglia; **Suffolk smoked hams,** and finally **cider, Cornish pasties, scones with jam and clotted creams,** and **Cheddar cheese** from the West Country. The best guides to where to find traditional British dishes and local specialties are those published by the tourist boards. *A Taste of England, A Taste of Scotland* and *A Taste of Wales* list restaurants, pubs and hotels where you will find at least one traditional item on the menu.   **British specialties**

Restaurants

Britain's restaurants reflect the highly cosmopolitan nature of its population. There are scores of **Indian, Chinese, Greek** and **Italian** restaurants throughout the country, often in small, out-of-the-way places, and built to serve the needs of the local immigrant community. The large cities have even wider international choices, including a growing trend in American-style fast-food establishments. British food and drink is far better in quality than it is reputed to be, and vegetarian and wholefood restaurants are a common sight in the High Street. The range and choice of where you can eat is wider than ever: in price, ambiance and type of food, there's something to suit all tastes.   **Wide variety**

Hotel restaurants can be relied on for quality cuisine and are nearly always open to non-residents, although opening times may be restricted. For residents the price of dinner and Continental/English breakfast is usually included in the overall accommodation price.   **Hotel restaurants**

London, at the hub of international transport, is able to fill her shops (and consequently the kitchens of her restaurants and hotels) with fresh food from all over the world and excels in a vast range of pubs, wine bars, more casual bistro-style eating houses, restaurants and hotels. The big city attracts the finest of the world's chefs from such corners of the globe as Korea, the Caribbean, Indonesia, Poland, Turkey, Greece and Thailand, as well as the more popular France and Italy. Chefs bring their own particular styles to cooking, none more popular today in Britain's top restaurants than *nouvelle cuisine,* where quantity is outweighed by quality and presentation.   **London**

Fish plays an important part in the British menu, as both fishermen and chefs take advantage of the island's long coastline and variety of catch. One of the best-known dishes is **fish and chips** (fish cooked in batter with fried potato chips), the local 'chippie' being almost as much an institution as the local pub. You can either sample its fare on the spot or take it away in its wrapping — traditionally yesterday's newspaper. Fishing ports dotted around   **Fish**

the country catch their own specialties: North Sea fishing boats (cobles) net cod, haddock and whiting, the Isle of Man and Loch Fyne in Scotland are the traditional homes of kippers (smoked herring), the Scottish borders and the River Tweed offer salmon, scampi, crab and shrimps, while shellfish are equally popular in East Anglian ports, along with cockles, crabs, mussels and whelks sold in fish shops and at market stalls throughout the country. Down on the South Coast, Margate, Ramsgate and Hastings operate small fishing fleets, while in Devon and Cornwall the traditional industry is fishing, the pubs and restaurant menus offering crab, pollock, mackerel, pilchards, plaice, sole (including the expensive specialty, Dover sole), dabs, whiting, sprats, prawns and shrimps.

Breakfast Fish for breakfast often comes as a surprise to the unsuspecting overseas visitor, but so does the rest of the menu. Hotel and guesthouse menus often extend to three or four courses: in Scotland one of these is porridge oats cooked with a pinch of salt, and eaten with sugar and cream. Throughout Britain the next course is bacon and eggs which make an excellent start to the day, followed by toasted bread and marmalade or jam, all washed down with a cup of coffee or tea.

Roast meat and poultry The traditional roast meat is served as Sunday lunch in British homes, but can also be found in restaurants and pubs. The meat, whether it is beef served with horseradish sauce, lamb with mint sauce or pork with apple sauce, is usually accompanied by potatoes and a selection of home-grown vegetables including carrots, cabbage, spinach, brussels sprouts, celery and parsnips.
Britain is also famous for its game and poultry — pheasant, partridge, grouse, duck, chicken and turkey may be found roasted or in pies all over the country.

Puddings British puddings are an institution in themselves — rural areas abound with jam roly-polys, spotted dick, treacle puddings (all made with suet), and apple, plum, gooseberry and cherry tarts and pies. In London restaurants most puddings are cold and highly decorated gateaux, trifles and mousses. At Christmas, the traditional Christmas pudding has usually been made months in advance and is filled with dried fruit, soaked in brandy and then set alight as it is brought to the table.

Tea As Mediterranean countries have their siesta, so England grinds to a halt for the 'cuppa' or afternoon tea at around 4pm. The English Tourist Board's *Stop for Tea* is a guide to the numerous towns with places in which you can take afternoon tea; this is accompanied by scones, cream and jam, hot buttered crumpets, biscuits, homemade cakes and even cucumber sandwiches. Many traditional cakes and buns, such as Chelsea and Bath buns, Eccles cakes and Bakewell tarts take their names from the towns where they originated, and in some cases have been made for over 300 years.

Cheeses British cheeses include tangy Stilton and simple but strong 'hard' cheeses such as Cheddar, Cheshire and Double Gloucester. Stronger cheeses produced in Britain included red Leicester and white Derby, which is sometimes veined with green by the addition of sage. These and the newer 'mixed' cheeses with port wine or herbs added are on sale in supermarkets with delicatessen stands or specialist food shops.

Wine Vineyards have existed in Britain since Roman times. Today, there are over 150 vineyards open to the public in 17 counties, stretching across Southern Britain from Dyfed in Wales and Cornwall in the southwest of England to Kent and Essex in the east. Several offer tours of the vineyard and the museum if they have one, and always offer a few tastings. Between 800 and 1,000 acres of vineyards are under cultivation, producing up to 750,000 bottles. Most English wines are white, and Germanic in flavour. As there is not a sufficient acreage available for grape-growing, wine is reasonably priced table wine rather than *vin ordinaire*. Britain's biggest wine event, featuring wine from all over the globe, is the **World Wine Fair**, held in Bristol each July. Special events including concerts, wine tastings, film shows and lectures are normally arranged during the fair.

Pubs

The British pub (public house) is a unique institution, and in smaller towns and villages the local pub is usually the hub of social life. Over the centuries pubs have provided refreshment and shelter for the traveler and cheap accommodation is still available at many. Pubs offer a range of up to twenty different beers, on draught or bottled. A wealth of regional brews has developed over the centuries, as ale does not travel well.

Beers All brews are based on the essential ingredient of hops, originally introduced in the 15th Century by Flemish weavers. Today large-scale brewing is a massive industry, and beer is the generic name for all brews — milds, bitters, stouts, lagers, brown ales, pale ales and over 100 others. Cider, a drink made from crushed apples or pears, was originally popular

mainly in the West Country (where extra-strong farmhouse 'scrumpy' is still served) and is now available everywhere on draught. The most popular way of drinking beer is in pints or half-pints of draught ale (though lager has become as popular).

Cask-conditioned ales stand apart as 'real' ales, brewed in their casks and considered more authentic. Spirits, vermouths, brandies, rum and soft drinks are also on sale in pubs; wines are available by the glass or bottle, and all but the latter sold in 'measures'.

Hints

Pubs are open on weekdays roughly between 11am-10:30pm (11pm in London, and many other places on Fridays and Saturdays). On Sunday they are open for a shorter time, and in Northern Ireland and some parts of Wales remain closed. In Scotland, the new Licensing Act which provides for Sunday opening has taken effect, but you will still find some pubs closed all day. Patrons must be 18 years old to buy or consume alcoholic drinks in a bar, and 16 years old to buy cigarettes. Children of 14 years and over may be admitted legally to a bar and may buy non-alcoholic drinks, and where licensed premises have a room set aside from the bar for the service of meals, children of 16 may purchase certain alcoholic drinks for consumption with a meal. Children of all ages may be admitted to a licensed restaurant, so while they may not be allowed into a bar, they may be welcomed in an adjoining room where food is being served, or into the beer garden in summer.

Some clubs, restaurants and hotels have special licenses that allow them to serve drinks into the early hours of the morning, but unlicensed premises, such as cafés, cannot serve alcohol at any time. At clubs and hotels with a residential license, residents and their friends can be served with alcoholic drinks at any hour.

Food

The majority of pubs serve food ranging from bar snacks and 'meals in a basket' to bangers and mash (sausages and mashed potato), bubble and squeak (cabbage and pre-mashed potato, chopped and fried), Scotch eggs (hard-boiled eggs rolled in sausage meat and breadcrumbs) and shepherds pie (minced beef covered with mashed potato and lightly browned). These are served between licensing hours only. The growing British trend for eating while drinking coupled with demand for music and comfortable surroundings has led to the opening of numerous wine bars particularly in the more affluent areas of the southeast. Here the customer finds a choice of reasonably priced house wines to buy by the glass or bottle, accompanied by such food as cheese, quiches, pâté, salads and pies, and often live music performances.

Vacation themes

Wildlife

Since the most spectacular scenery is often remote, walking is often the only way of discovering Britain's most beautiful rural assets. In England and Wales alone there are more than 100,000 miles of public footpaths, all marked by red dots or dashes on the *Ordnance Survey 'Landranger'* series of 1:50,000 scale topographical maps. The **ten National Parks** that cover some nine percent of England and Wales encompass some of the country's most magnificent scenery, a blend of mountain and moorland, downland and heathland, cliffs and seashore, all offering plenty of great escape potential. (Although designated 'National' the land is not necessarily state owned.)

Most of Britain's countryside and abundant wildlife, from the wild and rugged mountains of Snowdonia to the winding country lanes of Devon, are accessible to the traveler, due to the work of organizations such as the **Royal Society for the Protection of Birds** (RSPB), the **National Trust** and the **Wildfowl Trust and Nature Conservancy Council**. A number of safari and wildlife parks are open to the public where Britain's birds and animals can be seen in their natural state. Visitors can only drive through many of these parks, either in a bus or in a private car that allows safe observation at close quarters: remember that doors and windows must be kept tightly shut and some establishments do not allow soft-top cars. Most make provision for physically handicapped visitors. Pets are usually prohibited, but some have kennels where dogs can be kept. Safari parks are often situated in the grounds of historic houses.

Information

● **Whipsnade Park Zoo:** 50 acres housing some 2,000 animals from all over the world, including white rhinos, gnus, wolves, hippopotami, cheetahs and dolphins. Three parking lots, steam railway, café and picnic area. Dogs not allowed. Open every day except Christmas Day, 10am-7pm (or sunset if earlier). Whipsnade, Dunstable LU6 2LF, Bedfordshire (☎ 0582 872171).

● **Woburn Wild Animal Kingdom:** One of Europe's largest drive-through game reserves, containing a wide variety of wild animals living in relative freedom. Mostly African exhibits

including giraffes, tigers, lions, white rhinos, elephants. Open every day, 10am-5pm, closing earlier in winter. Woburn Park, Woburn, Milton Keynes MK17 9QN (☎ 052525 246).

● **Windsor Safari Park:** See the majority of animals at this 150-acre park either from your car or from a safari train, as the lions, giraffes, llamas, ostriches, zebras, flamingoes and others roam free. Open 31 Mar.-31 Dec., 10am-7pm (or dusk if earlier), last admission 5pm. Windsor SL4 4AY (☎ 95 869841).

● **Lowther Wildlife Country Park:** 150 acres, specializing in deer. Open 8 Apr.-14 Oct. daily, 10am till dusk. Hackthorpe, nr Penrith, Cumbria CA10 2HG (☎ 09312 523).

● **Dartmouth Wildlife Park:** Over 100 species of mainly British and European mammals and birds kept in near natural conditions. Open every day, 10am till dusk. Sparkwell, nr Plymouth, Devon PL7 5DG (☎ 075 537 209).

● **Mole Hall Wildlife Park:** Woolly monkeys, Canadian otters, Arctic foxes, pheasants and peafowl among the exhibits. Open daily (except Christmas Day), 10:30am-6pm. Widdington, Newport, nr Saffron Walden CB11 3SS, Essex (☎ 0799 40400).

● **Curraghs Wildlife Park:** 26-acre park with waterfowl, various birds and animals world-wide. Open 13 Apr.-30 Sep., 10am-6pm. Ballaugh, Isle of Man (☎ 062489 7323).

● **Knowsley Safari Park:** 450 acres make up six game reserves, where African and other animals are kept in near natural surroundings. Open 1 Apr.-31 Oct., 10am-5pm. Rest of year if good weather, 10am-3pm. Prescot L34 4AN, Merseyside (☎ 051 4262167).

● **The Wildfowl Trust** is the central body involved in preserving extinct or endangered species. It maintains major collections and wild refuges at the following centres. Slimbridge: Slimbridge, Gloucester GL2 7BT (☎ 045 389 333); Martin Mere: Burscough, nr Omskirk, Lancashire L40 OTA (☎ 0704 895181); Washington: Wildfowl Trust, Waterfowl Park, District 15, Washington, Tyne and Wear NE38 8LE (☎ 091 4165454); Arundel: Mill Road, Arundel, W. Sussex BN18 9PB (☎ 0903 883355); Peakirk: The Waterfowl Gardens, Peakirk, Peterborough PE6 7NP (☎ 0733 252271); Caerlaverock: Eastpark Farm, Caerlaverock, Dumfriesshire DG1 4RS (☎ 038777 200).

Birdwatching

Since Britain has such an active conservation movement and a great variety of habitat, the opportunities for birdwatching are plentiful, and the country can boast a large number of resident species and summer visitors. **The RSPB** has nearly half a million members and owns or cares for a large number of nesting sites and reserves in many parts of the country. While many birds have adapted well to modern conditions, rarer species have been confined to the more remote areas. The Highlands of Scotland contain the Golden Eagle and the recently re-introduced Osprey, a fish-eagle that has begun to nest regularly round Aviemore. Britain has a large number of native birds of prey; kestrels are a familiar sight hovering beside the country's highways.

Waders and other seabirds are common all around the coast, but are in particular abundance in reserves around the Wash and in the Severn Estuary, where the **Wildfowl Trust** (at Slimbridge) is a big attraction for those who want to observe geese, swans and ducks. Exotic wildfowl, even pelicans, can be found in such unlikely places as the centre of London, for example in Regent's Park and St. James's Park. Cley-next-the-Sea in Norfolk is probably the most famous spot from which to watch waders, wildfowl and other water birds. Publicly maintained hides are provided by the **National Trust**.

Birdwatching is a popular vacation option for many activity vacation companies in the UK and many of the country's activity centres co-operate closely with the local RSPB reserve when offering birdwatching vacations to their guests. Here, visitors can observe nesting species from carefully sited hides and benefit from the knowledge of experienced local ornithologists. All wild birds are protected by the law, and it is an offence to kill, injure or take any from their natural habitat, to steal a nest egg, to disturb certain birds while nesting and to possess a wild bird not killed previously or taken legally.

Information   ● **Royal Society for the Protection of Birds**, The Lodge, Sandy, Bedfordshire SG19 2DL (☎ 0767 80551).

● **The Field Studies Council**, Preston, Montford, Shropshire SY4 1HW (☎ 0743 850674) runs about 36 courses in Bird Ecology at nine centres throughout the country.

● **Ornitholidays**, 1-3 Victoria Drive, Bognor Regis, West Sussex (☎ 0243 821230).

Hints   The key to the country's public footpath network where superb birdwatching is accessible is the *Ordnance Survey 1:50000 Landranger map series*, on which public rights of way are marked with a dotted magenta line. Be aware of public rights of way before planning a route. The law in Scotland is more lax and you are generally free to wander at will on the moors and mountains.

National Park
Forest Parks and Areas
of outstanding beauty

SHETLAND

ORKNEY

HEBRIDES

NORTHWEST HIGHLANDS

Glen
More

GRAMPIAN MTS

Argyll   Queen
          Elizabeth

Galloway   The
            Border

Mountains
of Antrim   Northumberland

Binevenagh Mt.

Sperrin
Mts

Lough   Lake   Yorkshire
Erne   District   Dales
                                          PENNINE
Strangford   North York
Lough   Moors
          Slieve
          Gullion   Mourne
                     Mountains   Forest of
                                            Bowland   CHAIN

Anglesey   Lincolnshire
                                          Peak   Wolds
                                          District
          Lleyn   Norfolk
                     Snowdonia   Coast
                              CAMBRIAN MTS   Cannock
                                              Chase
                                                        Suffolk Coast
                                          Shropshire   and Heaths
                                          Hills
          Pembrokeshire   Dedham Vale
          Coast   Malvern Hills
                     Brecon
                     Beacons   The
                     Gower   Cotswolds   The Chilterns
                              Dean Forest and   North
                              Wye Valley   Wessex   Surrey
                                                 Downs   Hills
          North   Kent
          Devon   Mendip   Downs
                             Hills
                     Quantock   East Hampshire   Sussex Downs
                     Hills   New Forest
          Exmoor   East Devon
          Dartmoor   Chichester
                              Dorset   Harbour
          Cornwall
                                        Isle of
                                        Wight
                     South Devon

Scale
0   50 km

0   50 miles

Always try to follow the **Countryside Code** which loosely means that you stick to public rights of way and respect the owner of the land you are on, i.e., do not drop litter, and always close gates behind you, whether or not the field contains animals.

Castles and historic homes

Open to View is a bargain ticket that provides unlimited entry to over 500 castles, stately homes, historic sites and gardens in Britain. Holders also get reduced-price entry into many museums and discounts at museum shops. The ticket is valid for one month, and is half price for children under 16. It is available from **BritRail Travel International** in the USA and Canada, **Thomas Cook Travel** in Australia, and *TAANZ*-bonded travel agents in New Zealand. Many Open-to-View properties are open all year, although opening hours are reduced between October and March.

Other orga-
nizations
- **The Countryside Commission,** John Dower House, Crescent Place, Cheltenham, Gloucestershire GL50 3RA (☎ 0242 521381).
- **Forestry Commission,** 231 Costorphine Road, Edinburgh EH12 7AT (☎ 031 334 0303). There is no other country with such a high proportion of historic houses regularly open to the public. The **National Trust**, the **National Trust of Scotland** and the **National Trust of Northern Ireland** have been able to accept baronial country houses and estates in settlement of taxes while the **National Heritage Fund** supply invaluable endowments, ensuring that only a fraction of Britain's heritage is annually destroyed. Many houses are still inhabited by descendents of the original owners, but open their doors and gardens to the public (sometimes at no charge) throughout the year.

Antiques and crafts

Britain is one of the best countries in which to collect antiques. London's **Portobello** and **Bermondsey Street Markets** are mainly for specialists; amateurs should head for well-established shops and antique markets where reputable shops are grouped together.

Hints May and June are the best months for viewing and buying art and antiques in Britain, with a concentration of events overlapping throughout the country. These include **Bath Contemporary Art Fair**, **Bath Festival**, **London's International Contemporary Art Fair** and **Fine Art and Antiques Fair**, **Summer Exhibition at the Royal Academy** and the **Grosvenor House Antiques Fair**, who arrange the despatch of objects to anywhere in the world.

Dealers in antiques and crafts range from flea market stall holders with piles of bargains to wade through to auction houses (such as the famous **Sotheby's** and **Christie's** which have viewing days prior to the actual auction). Then there are the antique shops and antique fairs that often bring many dealers and their wares together in one place. In shops, ethical standards are high. London and Bath have the highest concentration, Bath having five dozen shops, with over 40 at the **Great Western Antique Centre**.

Recom-
mended
London
shops
- **Partridge**, 144 New Bond Street, London W1 stocks many pieces of museum quality, 18th-Century furniture, English sporting prints, Italian paintings and Renaissance bronzes.
- **Mallett and Son**, 40 New Bond Street, London W1.
- **Christopher Gibbs**, 118 New Bond Street, London W1.
- **Harvey's Auctions**, 14 Neal Street, London WC2 are very popular and stock a large mixture of very fine pieces.
The **British Antique Dealers' Association**, 20 Rutland Gate, London SW1 1BD (☎ 01-589 4128) ensure that antiques sold to the public through members are genuine, and supply a list of their members. Two comprehensive lists of dealers in Britain are in the *British Art and Antiques Yearbook,* available from **National Magazine House**, 72 Broadwick Street, London W1V 2BP (☎ 01-439 7144), and the *Guide to the Antique Shops of Britain* (£6.95) from the **Antique Collectors Club**, 5 Church Street, Woodbridge, Suffolk IP12 1DS (☎ 03943 5501). The **London and Provincial Antique Dealers' Association** is at 3 Cheval Place, London SW7 1EW (☎ 01-584 7911).

Information

Information on short craft courses and activity vacations is usually available in booklets and pamphlets or even directly from local libraries, colleges of adult/further education, arts centres, local authorities, local tourist boards and travel agents. If you have difficulty in finding information, contact the Information Section (courses), **Crafts Council**, 12 Waterloo Place, London SW1Y 4AU (☎ 01-930 4811). **Contemporary Applied Arts** is at 43 Earlham Street, London WC2 (☎ 01-836 6993). The **Design Council**, 28 Haymarket, London SW1Y 4SU (☎ 01-839 8000) exhibits British crafts. **CoSIRA** (Council for Small Industries in Rural Areas), 141 Castle Street, Salisbury, Wiltshire SP1 3TP (☎ 0722 336255) publishes *Craft Workshops in the Countryside — England and Wales.*

The seaside

When the weather is good, the British coast is second to none. With 7,000 miles to choose from the choices are enormous. Classic sand, sea and sun vacation ingredients are evident in all Britain's lively resorts, picture-postcard harbours and historic coastal towns. The seaside is by far the most popular summer vacation destination in Britain, with approximately 90 resorts strung out along the coastline.

British weather is normally better than the natives admit, but to cope with sudden, summer rain resorts have been investing heavily in providing children's playgrounds, amusement parks, leisure centres, indoor sports complexes and other alternative entertainments so that some are virtually 52-weeks-a-year resorts.

Traditional seaside vacations

The traditional basic ingredients of a British seaside vacation include buckets and spades, tangy salt air, sandy shoes, candy floss, promenades, striped deckchairs grouped around a Punch and Judy Show (live puppet show) on the beach, amusement fairs on the pier, shrimping nets, rock pools, sandcastles and donkey rides. Britain's most popular resorts include **Scarborough** (Yorkshire), **Great Yarmouth** (Norfolk), **Blackpool** (Lancashire), **Clacton-on-Sea** (Essex), **Bridlington** (Yorkshire), **Cromer** (Norfolk), **Barmouth** (Wales), **Criccieth** (Wales), **Gower** (Wales), **Weymouth** (Dorset) and the rocky headlands and huge breakers of **Devon** and **Cornwall**.

Several resorts have companies specializing in short-break packages, which may include special deals in travel arrangements, as well as hotel discounts. Details of where to stay and what to do in Britain's resorts are available from travel agents, from the relevant regional tourist boards or from individual tourist information centres.

Waves is a consortium of four major South Coast resorts — Bournemouth, Brighton, Hastings and Torbay (Reviera) — which offers computer-bookable vacations and therefore enables instant reservations to be made at any travel agent using the Prestel system.

A number of islands off Britain's coast are popular with vacationers and all are within easy access of the mainland, linked by regular flight/ferry services (details from travel agents) — **Isle of Wight** (a few miles off the South Coast), the **Channel Islands** (nearer to France, but nevertheless British), the **Isle of Man** (midway between Lancashire and Northern Ireland in the Irish Sea), the **Isles of Scilly** (more than 100 islands in the Atlantic Ocean some 28 miles southwest of Land's End, Cornwall) and the **Scottish Isles** (comprising the **Western Isles**, the **Orkneys** and **Shetlands**).

Northern Ireland

Many visitors to Britain extend their tour to include Northern Ireland. There you can drive on uncrowded roads, cruise along the waterways, fish in huge lakes and study abundant wildlife. It is also ideal country for riding and camping. Belfast is easily accessible from England, Scotland and Wales by sea, as ferry services operate from several ports on the West Coast. Air services to Belfast operate from London and other domestic airports.

Information

● **British Travel Service**, 54 Ebury Street, London SW1 (☎ 01-730 8986) have an extremely comprehensive brochure of British possibilities with more than 100 hotels in 40 resorts and the promise of free travel anywhere in England and Wales (Scotland has a £6 travel supplement).

● *England's Seaside* is an annual guide published by the **English Tourist Board** and **Hanover Magazines Ltd**. It costs £1.95 and is available from bookshops or by post from: ETB England's Seaside, PO Box 72, Farnham, Surrey GU9 7PS. The guide covers all grades of hotels on England's coast, but all hotels included must have at least 30 percent of their rooms with facilities for sleeping small children, along with plug-in listening devices for young children, or sitting, watching and general minder facilities, childrens' meals and early meal times, toys and games and washing, drying and ironing facilities. Most offer discounts for children, too.

Museums and art galleries

Cities of historical or cultural interest

Britain is home to a vast collection of works of art from all over the world. Although some small percentage of this remains in private hands, the better portion is on display in the nation's great museums, not to mention hundreds of country houses that are as notable for the collections housed within as for their often stunning architecture. (For example, England's **National Portrait Gallery** maintains two collections outside London at **Montacute**, Somerset and at **Beningbrough**, North Yorkshire.)

Britain's museums are usually well designed, with good lighting. Despite recent cutbacks in government support of the arts, admission to most museums and art galleries is free (although a charge may be made for specialist collections and exhibitions, and a few ask for a voluntary donation) and they are open every day except on principal holidays. London's national museums and galleries contain some of the richest treasures in the world and offer a service of advice and scholarly reference. The **British Museum**, the **Victoria and Albert Museum** and other national museums give expert opinion on the age or identity of objects or paintings, but will not give a valuation. Lecture programs are usually offered as well. Most museums and galleries have a shop near the entrance selling pamphlets and booklets on the various collections, postcards, posters and general souvenirs.

Details of exhibitions
Check the daily events listings in local newspapers and tourist information centres. In London, *Time Out* and *City Limits* magazines are the most comprehensive. See *The Shell Guide to Small Country Museums* and *The Good Museum Guide,* both by Kenneth Hudson.

The locations of Britain's principal museums are shown on the map and details can be found in the gazetteer section entries.

Sporting vacations

Aerial sports

The British Hang Gliding Association, Monksilver, Taunton, Somerset have 2,400 hang gliders, and represent 40 clubs and schools. Membership subscription is £7.50 per annum, which includes a copy of *Wings* magazine and insurance.

Hang gliding

All gliding in Britain is organized through clubs. Members learn to fly, look after the glider, drive, winch or tow with a car to launch it. Most clubs have residential accommodation. No pilot licenses are required.
British Gliding Association, Kimberley House, Vaughan Way, Leicester LE1 4SG consists of clubs with 25 members or more. To join a club you must be over 16 years. An annual subscription of £4.90 includes a copy of *Sailplane and Gliding* magazine.
To fly an aeroplane with an engine, you must obtain a private pilot's license (PPL). Contact the *Aircraft Owners' and Pilots' Association*, 50A Cambridge Street, London SW1V 4QQ (☎ 01-834 5631/32).

Gliding

The *British Ballooning and Airship Club*, Kimberley House, Vaughan Way, Leicester LE1 4SG (☎ 0533 51051) represents 40 clubs and 3 schools. Membership costs £6 per annum and includes bi-monthly copies of their magazine *Aerostat*. Training courses are only available through the three schools (Europa, Anglia and Aerial).
Several hotels throughout Britain run Ballooning Weekend breaks. Details from local travel agents.

Hot air ballooning

There are a number of clubs based at airfields throughout the country which charge approximately £60 for one- or two-day courses on the ground and a 'drop' at the end. Follow-up drops then cost £8 to £10, weather permitting. Courses are disciplined — if too long a time period has elapsed between a course and a planned drop, pupils must re-do the course. All equipment is supplied except for sturdy walking shoes with ankle support. No license is required, only basic fitness. *British Parachute Association*, Kimberley House, Vaughan Way, Leicester LE1 4SG (☎ 0533 55778).

Parachuting

Caving/potholing

There are 65 caving clubs in Britain, several connected with universities and polytechnics, e.g., *Oxford University Caving Club, Manchester University Speleological Society, Bradford University Union Potholing Club, Kingston Polytechnic Speleological Society*, and clubs that are based round Derbyshire, Staffordshire, Yorkshire, London (Croydon, Chelsea, Westminster), Kent, Devon, Mendips, Wales and the Severn Valley. For a fully comprehensive list of clubs, contact the *British Cave Research Association*.
There are a number of well-decorated caves open to the public, e.g., **Ingleborough Cave** in Yorkshire and **Wookey Hole** in Somerset, where the River Axe comes up on its subterranean journey through the Mendip Hills. In August, *Craven Pothole Club* uses a power winch to lower visitors into the depths of **Gaping Gile**, Britain's deepest and most celebrated pothole, 340 feet deep and with a cathedral-sized main chamber.

British Caves and Potholes, by P.R. Deakin and D.W. Gill. *Discovering Caves — a guide to Show Caves of Britain*, by Tony and Anne Oldham. *Caves and Potholing in Britain*, by Edmund J. Mason.

Information

Cricket

The highpoints of any cricket season are the **Test Matches** played between England and the various Commonwealth countries such as Australia, India and the West Indies. These are held at various times at the following venues: **Edgbaston** (Birmingham), **Headingley** (Leeds), **Old Trafford** (Manchester), **The Oval**, Kennington, London SW11 (☎ 01-735 4911) and **Lords**, St. John's Wood Road, London NW8 (☎ 01-286 8011). The *National Cricket Association* is

also based at Lords Cricket Ground. In London, both Lords and the Oval, the grounds of the Middlesex Cricket Club and Surrey Cricket Club respectively, are the places to see the best of the capital's cricket. In the rest of the country the main county grounds, usually located in the main city in each county, also offer first-class cricket throughout the summer. In many senses, however, cricket at its best is to be found in the small villages of England, played on the **green** while the spectators lounge around the field in deckchairs clutching glasses of ale and munching their way through picnic hampers.

Cruising and canoeing

Britain's inland waterways and canals are man-made cruising highways, mostly built about 200 years ago as trade arteries of the Industrial Revolution, winding along valleys, climbing hills by locks or burrowing through them in tunnels.

The **British Waterways Board** (address below) owns or manages some 2,000 miles of these waterways from Northern Scotland down to the southwest tip of England. The major part of the system is open to leisure cruising and if you add to this the stretches of canal owned by other bodies, for example the National Trust, plus great river systems like the Thames and the Severn, a network of nearly 3,000 miles emerges, with unlimited exploratory potential.

Rental craft Modern rental craft are like floating self-catering cottages on the inside, usually with good heating, showers, well-equipped kitchens and flush toilets. Along with motor cruisers, the standard type of waterways rental boat, Britain has one of the largest boat rental industries in the world. Boats can usually be as luxurious as the visitor requires. There are five main booking agencies in the vacation boat rental industry, none of which charges the customer any agency or booking fee, taking commission from the boat companies for whom they act as agent.

Information ● **Blakes Holidays,** Wroxham, Norwich NR21 6DH (☎ 06053 2141) provide a free vacation book covering the area of a chosen vacation, and sell a selection of maps, route planners and other publications.
● **Noseasons Holidays Ltd,** Sunway House, Lowestoft, Suffolk NR32 3LT go just about everywhere on everything.
● **Boat Enquiries Ltd,** 43 Botley Road, Oxford OX2 6ED (☎ 0865 727288) also offer vacations in the specialized hotel boat market.
● **Central Booking Agency for Inland Waterways Activities,** 50 Main Street, Thornton, Leicester LE6 1AG (☎ 053021 230).
● **Educational Cruises,** 15 Main Street, Snarestone, Burton-on-Trent, Staffordshire DE12 7DB (☎ 0530 71827).

Locks Some locks are staffed, some you work yourself. Passage is free but it is traditional to tip the lock-keeper.
The Cambs Waterways of the Fenlands consist of 150 miles of notably flat waterway including the Rivers Wissey, Nene, Cam and the Great and Little Ouse. All fenland points are easy to reach by road or rail. Along the way are farms, villages, riverside inns and market towns.

Scotland The Caledonian Canal stretches from Bearly Firth near Inverness through such idyllic landlocked waterways as Loch Ness, Loch Oich, Loch Lochy to Fort William, beyond which cruising is impossible. Alternatively, luxury cruises are available along the Great Glen. Scotland also offers offshore cruising and sailing (for which it is vital that at least one of the crew has had previous experience), small fishing villages, picnic areas, nature reserves and plenty of wildlife.

The Thames The River Thames is 209 miles long from Cirencester in the west to its mouth on the east coast. Its attractions include old villages and pleasant towns, pubs with gardens sloping down to the river, dozens of restaurants and fine hotels. Its subsidiaries, the Rivers Wey, Lee and Medway, are equally enticing and relaxing.

Information **The River Thames Society**, Gresham House, Twickenham Road, Feltham, Middlesex TW13 6HA (☎ 01-894 5811) operate a Thames Information Centre from their office.

The Norfolk Broads consist of 250 cruising miles, all unusually lock-free and ideal for first-time boaters. Northern area: Rivers Bure, Ant and Thurne. Southern area: Rivers Wensum, Yare, Chet and Waveney. To the west one can cruise into the heart of Norwich while to the east the route leads to Lowestoft, England's most easterly town.

Skiff and canoe On the gentle rivers of Britain, the Thames or the Avon, a popular vacation craft is the double-sculling skiff that will take up to six people in perfect comfort and security and can be rented for about £25 for a full day.

On other rivers, such as the Severn or the Wye, the **canoe** comes into its own — the canoeist needs to know something about canoe technique and should wear a life jacket. Canoeing is taught at most activity centres and in many parts of the country.

The BTA produces an *Information Sheet on Water Sports* that gives details on a number of companies offering water sport vacations in Britain. The addresses of companies renting canoes and skiffs can be obtained from the local tourist information office, or often simply by going to the nearest river, where boat rental companies are abundant. The governing body for canoeing in Britain is the **British Canoe Union** (BCU), Flexel House, 45-47 High Street, Addlestone, Weybridge, Surrey KT15 3JV, and canoe courses are offered at the **National Centre for Mountain Activities**, Plas y Brenin, North Wales (☎ 06904 280).
British Waterways Board, Melbury House, Melbury Terrace, London NW1 6JX (☎ 01-262 6711) will provide the public with any necessary information on inland waterways.

Information

Cycling

● **The Cyclist Touring Club**, Cotterell House, 69 Meadrow, Godalming, Surrey GU7 3HS (☎ 04868 7217), the principal organization in Britain for cycling
● **The London Bicycle Company**, 41-42 Floral Street, Covent Garden WC2 (☎ 01-836 2969).
● **Bicycle Association of Great Britain Ltd**, Starley House, Eaton Road, Coventry CV1 2FH (☎ 0203 553838).
● **EACH Cycling Holidays**, The Bookshop, Yoxford, Suffolk (☎ 072877 246) have cycle trips in Devon, Yorkshire, Sussex, Norfolk and Somerset.
● **Scotland Highland Guides**, Aviemore, Inverness, Scotland (☎ 0479 810729) have long weekends or full week cycling vacations around the Highlands, with youth hostel or bed and breakfast accommodation.

Bike rentals, routes, lodging, camping and repairs in various areas are covered by a series of publications available from the magazine *Cycling World,* (£2 from Andrew House, 2A Granville Road, Sidcup, Kent DA14 4BN).

Information

Fishing

Fishing in Britain is divided into **sea-fishing**, **game or sport fishing** (for trout or salmon) and **coarse fishing** for freshwater fish other than trout and salmon. Of these three, coarse fishing is by far the most popular. It is usually necessary to obtain a license to fish in freshwater, since large stretches of water are either reserved for private use or rented out to fishing clubs.
Many hotels offer all the necessary ingredients for a successful fishing vacation: access to water, suitable rods and equipment and useful advice and instruction.
Scotland rightly claims to be one of the world's great rod fishing countries, with the famous **Spey Valley** in Inverness-shire, the **Tweed**, known as the queen of salmon rivers, and the **Osprey Fishing School** at Aviemore. Wales has a vast abundance of lakes and rivers, including the Wye, which is famous also for its salmon, and a long and varied coastline, ideal for sea-fishing.
Sea-fishing is a popular pastime along the British coast and can always be arranged with local fishermen. There is tope, bass, mackerel and even, off the Devon and Cornwall coasts, shark.
For coarse fishing, find the address of the local tackle shop from the yellow pages in the telephone directory and talk to the proprietor who will know all the local waters and will know where a stranger can find a day's fishing. He will also sell you a license and even a few white worms.

● The nearest tourist information office and various BTA publications available from BTA overseas offices and national tourist boards in Britain can supply information.
● **Chalk Farm School of Fly Fishing**, 52B West Street, Alresford, Hampshire (☎ 096273 4864).

Information

Golf

The game of golf began in Scotland where St. Andrews (home of the world-famous Royal and Ancient) is usually credited as the birthplace. Britain has nearly **2,000** golf courses, ranging in standard from a local nine-hole pitch-and-putt course to the championship courses of Turnberry, St. Andrews and Wentworth. English courses tend to be owned by clubs, whereas those in Scotland are often owned by the municipality and open to the general public. Club restrictions usually only apply at weekends when the courses are crowded and therefore reserved for members. To make a reservation, phone the club secretary well in advance for permission to play and advice on green fees. Most golf clubs have a pro-shop where the visitor can hire clubs and shoes, and the larger clubs will have a resident professional who can provide tuition or arrange for a partner.

Several of Britain's hotels either own courses (for example, the world-renowned quartet of courses at Gleneagles in Scotland, and the Cambridgeshire Hotel at Bar Hill, near Cambridge) or have made arrangements for their guests to play on local courses.

The addresses and telephone numbers of golf clubs can be found in the gazetteer section entries. Details can also be obtained from local tourist information centres.

Information
- The publication *Golfing* lists all Britain's courses and is available from the BTA.
- The leading, governing and co-ordinating authority in the game is the **Royal and Ancient Golf Club of St. Andrews**, Fife KY16 9JD, Scotland (☎ 0334 72112).
- **Wentworth Golf Course**, Virginia Water, Surrey (☎ 09904 2201).
- **Cambridgeshire Hotel**, Bar Hill, Cambridgeshire (☎ 0954 80555).
- **Gleneagles Hotel**, Auchterarder, Tayside (☎ 07646 2231).

Hunting

The most common form of hunting in Britain is fox hunting. In recent years the sport has met with a lot of opposition from various ecological and anti-animal cruelty societies, but Boxing Day (Dec. 26) still sees a large number of opening 'meets' up and down the country. The social roots of English fox hunting have always run deeper and broader than those on the Continent. It was originally a royal and aristocratic sport, but the fox soon replaced the more noble deer, allowing a larger section of society to take part. The survival of the sport depends on the participation and tolerance of farmers. There are about 200 packs of foxhounds in Britain, with the more fashionable hunts now over-subscribed and forced to limit membership.

Information
- **British Field Sports Society**, 59 Kennington Road, London SE1 (☎ 01-928 4742).

Riding and Pony Trekking

In any country area, almost every village will have its riding stable or trekking centre, where the experienced rider (having convinced the stables that he is capable of handling a horse competently) can rent a horse or pony and ride off on his own, or where the absolute beginner can either enroll for regular or one-off lessons, or join a group and ride out on a day trek. The pace on a pony trek is gentle and provided the rider is not too heavy, there should be no problem finding a suitable mount. Addresses of local stables are to be found in the nearest tourist information centre or in the yellow pages section of the telephone directory. Charges for day treks vary but are approximately £5 per hour.

A large number of trekking centres are now offering longer vacations of a week or more, with daily treks into the surrounding countryside. Most welcome inexperienced riders and the season usually runs from Easter to October. A variation on pony trekking for more experienced riders is post trekking, which involves a journey on horseback with overnight stops at hotels, or in self-catering accommodation. A week's post trekking on the Isle of Mull in Scotland, for example, is available from the **Erray Riding Centre,** and costs from £162 per week.

Information
- The BTA publish a booklet, *Pony Trekking and Riding*, listing useful addresses.
- **Erray Riding Centre**, Tobermory, Argyll, Scotland (☎ 0688 2052).
- **Lilo Blum Riding School**, 32A Grosvenor Crescent, London SW1 (☎ 01-235 6846).
- **Ponies of Britain** inspects and issues a full descriptive list of over 200 approved Trekking and Riding Holiday Centres free of charge. Ascot Race Course, Ascot, Berkshire SL5 7JN (☎ 0990 25912).

Rock climbing and hill walking

There are a large number of climbing clubs throughout Britain. Main climbs and steepest hills are in the Lake District, North Wales, Derbyshire and the Highlands of Scotland, although cliff climbing around the coast of Cornwall is also popular.

Although British hills are not particularly high, at least by overseas standards, with Ben Nevis at 4,406 ft the highest mountain, they are not to be taken lightly. All walkers entering the hills should, as a minimum, have an Ordnance Survey topographical map, scale 1:50,000 (cost: £2.40) and a compass, be sensibly shod and have a wind- and waterproof jacket. **Hints**

Vacations with instruction on both hill walking and rock climbing can be enjoyed at the **National Centres for Mountaineering Activities**, Plas y Brenin, North Wales, and **Glenmore Lodge**, Aviemore, Scotland. Britain has a large number of activity or adventure centres offering vacation courses. A list can be obtained from the various National Tourist Boards or such specialist publications as *Climber and Rambler* or *The Great Outdoors* available from newsagents.

The **British Mountaineering Council**, Crawford House, Precinct Centre, Booth Street East, Manchester M13 9RZ (☎ 061 273 5835).

Sailing

Britain's enormous variety of options for sailors is inevitable given the opportunities that 7,000 miles of coastline, plus countless rivers, lakes and even gravel-pit reservoirs present. The country is well-endowed with officially recognized sailing schools. More than 600 yachting establishments are recognized by the **Royal Yachting Association**, the sport's governing body. All of them teach elementary dayboat (dinghy) sailing.

● **The National Sailing Centre** (NSC), Arctic Road, Cowes (☎ 0983 295938) offers courses in dinghy and board sailing as well as cruising for all levels of ability. A week's course, inclusive approximately £140 a week, with instruction on a ratio of one to three. Cowes is also host to the annual **Cowes Week regatta**, the sailing event in Britain. **Information**

● **The Island Sailing Club** at Salcombe, deep in the Devon countryside, has over fifty craft ranging from 70-foot ocean-going yachts to their fleet of dinghies. Costs are comparable to the NSC.

● **The Ullswater Sailing School,** Landends, Watermillock, nr Penrith, Cumbria (☎ 085 36438), located in the heart of the Lake District, in Cumbria, is extremely flexible, offering courses ranging from an hour-long introductory lesson to a six-day advanced RYA certified course.

● **Plas y Deri National Outdoor Pursuits Centre for Wales**, Caernarfon, Gwynedd (☎ 0248 070964).

● **The Royal Yachting Association**, Victoria Way, Woking, Surrey (☎ 04862 5022) can supply a list of all their recognized schools.

● **Summer Isles Charters**, Altnaharrie Inn, Ullapool, Wester Ross, Scotland (☎ 085483 230).

● Many boats are available for rental, by the hour, half day, day or week. Several establishments along the coast have yachts available for chartering, with or without a professional skipper.

Stalking and shooting

In Britain, **shooting** means using a shotgun, while **stalking** refers only to hunting deer, and therefore the use of a rifle. **Game** shooting refers to pheasant, partridge or grouse, while **rough** shooting takes in pigeon, hare and rabbit as well. The famous **Glorious Twelfth** denotes the start of the grouse season on August 12th, but there are different open seasons for the various types of game.

All shooting is done on private land, on estates managed specifically for shooting. Many are run in association with a booking agency specializing in shooting vacations, and these are the best contacts. Most shoots are organized in groups of 6 to 8, and agents can usually fit you into a party. In Scotland, the visitor can shoot deer. **Hints**

Insurance is necessary and must be arranged privately if not included in the arrangements made by a tour operator or hotel. Coverage of up to £250,000 is recommended, but premiums are low.

Apart from game shooting, **clay pigeon** shooting is very popular and offered at a number of centres throughout the country.

Information   **The North Wales Shooting School** at Sealand, near Chester, offers practice and instruction on Olympic trap, skeet, sporting, ball trap and down-the-line, at prices from £20 a half day.
● **A & C Sporting Services Ltd**, Hornby, Lancaster have a wide range of shooting available throughout Britain and offer partridge, grouse and duck as well as stalking in the Scottish Highlands.
● **Clay Pigeon Shooting Association**, 107 Epping New Road, Buckhurst Hill, Essex IG9 5TQ (☎ 01-505 6221).
● **British Association for Shooting and Conservation**, National Headquarters, Marford Mill, Rossett, nr Wrexham, Clwyd LL12 OHL, Wales (☎ 0244 570881).
● **Sport in Scotland**, 22 Market Brae, Inverness, Highland IV2 3AB (☎ 0463 222757).
● The BTA produce a booklet, *Hunting and Shooting*.

Tennis

The world-renowned **Wimbledon** tennis fortnight, organized by the **All England Lawn Tennis and Croquet Club** is generally regarded as the world's premier tennis tournament. Visitors interested in attending should make inquiries at the **London Visitor and Convention Bureau** (☎ 01-730 3488) or contact the **Lawn Tennis Association,** Queens Club, Baron's Court, London W14 9EG (☎ 01-385 2366).

Information   The provision of tennis courts in public parks and recreation centres is proceeding in Britain at a rapid pace. Facilities are generally hard courts, but grass courts are available at most tennis clubs and many of the larger hotels have added tennis (or squash) courts to their range of guest facilities. These courts can be rented for a very modest fee, which usually ranges from £1 to £2 for a half hour. Apart from evenings and weekends it is not difficult to find a vacant court, often in the nearest public park. Just turn up, pay and play.

Instruction   Tennis vacations are also popular, offering instruction from professional coaches as the basis for an enjoyable vacation.
● **Beaconsfield School of Lawn Tennis** in Buckinghamshire is open all year round and offers private tuition and group lessons for players of all levels.
● **Windmill Hill Tennis Centre** at Hailsham in Sussex offers residential courses, with expert tuition, video replays to examine and correct technique and an end-of-the-week doubles tournament.

Squash and badminton   Squash and badminton courts can be found in all Britain's leisure centres. Book ahead (usually by the hour or half hour).

Information   ● The BTA publish a useful booklet, *Tennis, Squash and Badminton*, which lists a number of hotels and companies offering suitable facilities. Most hotel directories will list those available.
● **The Vanderbilt Racquet Club,** 31 Sterne Street, London W2 (☎ 01-743 9816) is one of the rare indoor tennis clubs in Britain, and has five courts costing approximately £15 an hour.
● **Squash Racquets Association**, Francis House, Francis Street, London SW1P 1DE (☎ 01-828 3064/7).
● **Badminton Association of England,** National Badminton Centre, Bradwell Road, Loughton Lodge, Milton Keynes MK8 9LA (☎ 0908 568822).

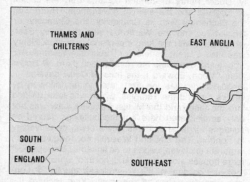

London

▶ A century ago, London was the largest city in the world — capital and principal seaport of the first industrial nation and of a world-wide empire. Londoners called it 'The Smoke', a huge conurbation of industry, railways and houses, notorious for its 'peasoup' fogs. New technologies and the passing of time have changed all that. The old industries, the miles of riverside docks, have gone. So too has the empire they served. The City of London remains a world centre of banking and finance, and upholds traditions already old when Dick Whittington was Lord Mayor. Scarlet-coated guardsmen, household cavalry in gleaming breast-plates and plumed helmets, also keep alive the unique pageantry of the London scene. But today's London has, in other ways, changed almost beyond recognition since the days of the Smoke — a process hastened by WWII bombing and post-war reconstruction. The city is a mecca of the arts and entertainment, an arbiter of fashion, once the prerogative of others. Its famous buildings and monuments have been cleaned of centuries of grime. Its many bridges over the Thames, cleaned and re-painted, have a festive look (while salmon once again swim beneath them). And everywhere, new buildings, whole new civic and commercial centres, have transformed the skyline. □

● Brief regional history

43-410AD

There is no evidence that there was any permanent settlement on the site of the city of London before the second **Roman invasion of 43AD**. London's real history begins in that year, although there was a Celtic village on the site of Heathrow Airport and evidence of pre-Roman habitations along the Thames at Barnes, Hammersmith, Fulham, Wandsworth, Chelsea and Battersea. The construction of a bridge across the Thames fixed the point from which the Roman city grew, and the bridge was necessary for the Roman legions in their pursuit of the rebellious *Catuvellauni*

to their headquarters at Colchester. Once established at the river crossing the settlement quickly became a busy port, trading with continental Europe across the North Sea. A network of roads fanned out from London, the principal ones being Ermine Street (to Lincoln), Stane Street (to Chichester) and Watling Street which, starting at Dover, passed through London on its way north-west to Chester. ● By 60AD, according to Tacitus, London was famous for commerce and crowded with traders. It did not have the status of a *Colonia*, like Lincoln, Gloucester or Colchester, but it was an important commercial centre. ● Although damaged by fire during the Boudiccan Revolt and again in 125AD, the city was substantial by the mid-2ndC with a huge basilica on the site of Leadenhall Market as well as a forum, temples, baths, shops and houses. The military barracks of Cripplegate Fort were built at the north-western edge of the town and by the end of the century a wall of Kentish ragstone had been erected enclosing 325 acres. The four original gates were Aldgate, Bishopsgate, Newgate and Ludgate, whose sites are still crossed by main roads to and from the city. By this time London's population had risen to some 45,000 which it would not achieve again until the 15thC. Remains of the Roman wall can be seen near the Tower of London and the Temple of Mithras is near the Mansion House. There are baths at Cheapside and remains of the forum can be seen near Leadenhall Market. Many Roman artifacts — sculpture, mosaics and metalwork — are now housed in the Museum of London.

410-1065

After the departure of the Romans in 410, London seems to have been abandoned, although it may have provided a temporary haven for Britons retreating before the invaders from the south. Anglo-Saxon farming settlements were plentiful around the original city, which re-emerged into history in 604, when **King Aethelbert** of Kent, having been baptized a Christian by St. Augustine, founded St. Paul's Cathedral and installed Mellitus as bishop there. A subsequent bishop, Eorcenwald, founded the abbeys of Barking and Chertsey; the Church of All Hallows, Barking, dates from about 675. ● In the early 8thC the **Venerable Bede** wrote of London's commercial prosperity, but few details are known of her history until the arrival of the Danes, who raided the city in 839 and returned with a bigger fleet in 851, looting and burning the fragile wooden houses. When **Alfred the Great** made

his treaty with Guthrum, London was part of the Anglo-Saxon kingdom of Mercia, the boundary of the Danelaw lying further east. Alfred occupied the city and saw to its defenses before handing it over to Ethelred of Mercia who had married his daughter Ethelfleda. When the Danes came again in 896 the Londoners were able to repel them. ● London did not become the capital city until after the Norman invasion. **Edgar**, the first king of all England, was crowned at Bath, while the West Saxon kings were usually crowned at Winchester. Canute, however, made London his headquarters, holding court on Thorney Island. It was at Thorney Island that **Edward the Confessor** restored the ancient monastery and endowed the famous abbey church of Westminster which was consecrated in 1065, a few days before his death.

1066-12thC

One of **William the Conqueror's** first acts was to confirm the citizens of London in the rights and privileges which they had enjoyed under Edward I. A further tactical move was to place his fortress, the White Tower, just outside the city walls. The **Tower of London** was to remain a symbol of royal might throughout the centuries, acquiring its most sinister reputation under the Tudors. William did not spend much time in London, being much involved with campaigns in England, Scotland and Wales as well as on the continent. The responsibility for commanding a levy of able-bodied men in times of trouble was assigned to Ralph Baynard, who built himself a fortress, Baynard's Castle, on the river at Blackfriars. Another castle, Mountfichet, lay close by. ● Around London were many villages and hamlets mentioned in the Domesday survey, such as Islington and St. Pancras. Marylebone was called Tyburn, after the stream which flowed toward Westminster, forking to make an island where the abbey stood. At Bermondsey, there was a Cluniac priory and another at Kilburn. Among surviving buildings of the Norman period, the Tower, with St. John's Chapel, London's oldest place of worship, stands supreme. ● William Rufus rebuilt the Palace of Westminster, and the great hall which he founded still stands. The chancel of St. Bartholomew's is a relic of the Augustinian priory established under Henry I. Part of the Temple Church, the crypt of St. John's Gate, Clerkenwell and Old St. Pancras Church also date from the 11th and 12thC. William Fitzstephen, writing in 1174, gives a vivid picture of ordinary life in London, with its cock fights, wrestling, javelin throwing and archery contests. There was horse racing at Smithfield and citizens would go hawking in the Chilterns. ● Until 1209 people crossed the Thames by ferry, the Roman bridge having long since vanished. Finally, after many vicissitudes, **London Bridge** was completed with its chapel, shops and buildings and a drawbridge to admit high-masted vessels. Under **Henry I** London received its first **charter**, by which Londoners, independent of any shire, were given direct access to the king. **Guilds** also began at this time, the goldsmiths' and weavers' being the first. These companies also contributed funds directly to the Crown.

13th-15thC

Until the 13thC, government was wherever the king was and the kings and their retinues traveled endlessly. Under **Henry III** London became truly the capital of England and the seat of government. There was the Exchequer with its Chancellor, the Chancery, or legislature, and the Wardrobe with the Privy Seal, which dealt with the king's personal accounts. Henry was also a great benefactor, rebuilding Westminster Abbey and extending the royal palace there. ● Under Henry's son, Edward I, the **Inns of Court** developed. Lincoln's Inn was the first, later to be followed by Gray's Inn and the Temples, which later divided into the Inner and the Middle Temples. Law was not only administered here but the buildings served as colleges for legal students, there being no university in London. The city and Westminster, originally two separate enclaves, began to be linked as bishops built large houses along the Strand, north of which was the 'convent garden' of the Westminster monks. ● London was the scene of the young King Richard II's confrontation with Wat Tyler and his followers during the dangerous **Peasants' Revolt** of 1381. Tyler's men had crossed the Thames, released prisoners from the Marshalsea and broken into the Tower where they beheaded the Archbishop of Canterbury. Richard's courage in meeting this large army of rebels at Smithfield and listening to their requests was remarkable, and when Tyler was wounded by the mayor, Walworth, the rebels dispersed. Dick Whittington, London's most famous Lord Mayor, served under Richard II, Henry IV and Henry V, becoming very rich with a mansion comparable to a nobleman's house. He gave an immense banquet for Henry V upon his wedding and was among the first to provide conduits of fresh water for the city.

16thC

Around the middle of the 16thC, London experienced a **dramatic growth** of trade and population and between 1530 and 1600 the number of Londoners trebled. With the dissolution of the monasteries, four hospitals were provided to fill their place — St. Bartholomew's, Christ's, Bethlehem (the madhouse known as Bedlam) and Bridewell. Trade was promoted by the establishment of monopolies, such as the Muscovy Company, the Levant Company and the East India Company. The **Royal Exchange** was built in 1566-70 by Sir Thomas Gresham as a meeting place for financiers and merchants. New industries such as silk weaving, glass and pottery making flourished. ● **Henry VIII** began the work of converting York Place into Whitehall Palace and built St. James's Palace across the fields from what is now St. James's Park. Thomas More had a house at Chelsea, where Erasmus was his guest. Noblemen's houses began to appear along the river from Westminster to the city, with gardens down to the water's edge, each with its own watergate. Royal dockyards were built at Deptford and Woolwich. ● The first purpose-built theatre, known simply as 'The Theatre', opened at Shoreditch in 1576. Later the south bank of the river was preferred, although the courtyards of inns, such as that at Southwark, continued to serve as playhouses. Among the new theatres were the 'Rose' particularly associated with Marlowe, the 'Swan' and finally the 'Globe' in which **Shakespeare** had shares and where the plays of Shakespeare, Ben Jonson and Beaumont and Fletcher were performed. Hyde Park became a fashionable venue for the nobility, while Bermondsey was the place where popular festivals and entertainment took

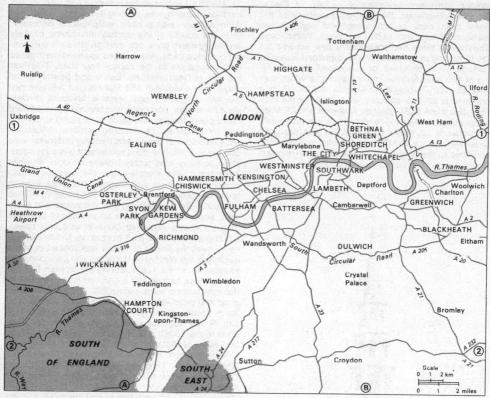

map 1 - Greater London

place, like bear- and bull-baiting. May Day, a public holiday, saw the erection of Maypoles, particularly that at Leadenhall Street, although these were later banned by the Puritans as pagan emblems. John Stow in his Survey of London of 1598 recalls that all the houses on May Day were 'shadowed in green birch, long fennel, St. John's Wort, white lilies and garlands of flowers'. The Midsummer Watch was another popular festival.

17thC

James I was not inclined to show himself to his people or to go on royal progresses as Elizabeth had. Instead, he preferred to isolate himself in his favourite royal palace of **Whitehall** with his dissolute drinking friends, so that the queen soon set up her own establishment at Denmark House. He planned to extend Whitehall on a grandiose scale, but of the grand scheme only the Banqueting House was completed, designed by Inigo Jones and with a painted ceiling by Rubens. Inigo Jones was also responsible for the Italianate piazza at Covent Garden and for St. Paul's Church there. His masterpiece is the superb Queen's House at Greenwich, begun in 1616, demonstrating his mastery of Palladian Classicism. He also designed masques for royal entertainment with elaborate lighting and scenic effects, often in collaboration with Ben Jonson, as in *The Fortunate Isles* of 1625. ● Charles I antagonized Londoners from

the very beginning, particularly when Henrietta Maria filled Somerset House with all her French Catholic friends. Always short of money, he made increasing demands upon the city which the city was increasingly reluctant to pay. From 1629 to 1640 he called no Parliament at all. The results were inevitable. The city was staunchly Parliamentarian, raising nine regiments and 16,000 men, when the **First Civil War** broke out. When, after Edgehill in 1642, Charles returned toward a rebellious London, his path was blocked by trained bands at Turnham Green and he promptly retreated. He tried to blockade London by preventing coal from leaving Newcastle, a Royalist stronghold, giving Londoners a bitterly cold winter. He only returned to London in Jan. 1649 for his trial at Westminster Hall. Spending his last night at St. James's Palace, he walked across the park to Inigo Jones's Banqueting House, before which the scaffold had been erected. He died bravely. ● For the next eleven years London was the capital of a Commonwealth and, although the citizens had supported **Cromwell**, they did not find Puritanism, in practice, much to their liking. All the playhouses were closed, music forbidden in church services and choirs disbanded. Furthermore, the city was still constantly being asked for money. It was with jubilation, therefore, that they welcomed the return of the monarchy in the person of **Charles II**. ● In 1664-5 the **plague**, a frequent invader since the Black Death of 1348, killed 75,000 Londoners. The following year the **great fire** burned from 2 to 5 Sep-

tember, consuming four-fifths of the city. St. Paul's, the Royal Exchange, the guildhall and many of the livery halls were gutted, along with eighty-seven parish churches and 13,000 dwellings. Within days **Christopher Wren** had presented a new scheme for the rebuilding of the city and was appointed Surveyor General. Wren designed, or supervised, the rebuilding of fifty-two churches, all but seven of which survive. St. Mary-le-bow in Cheapside and St. Bride's are famous for their steeples, while many of the interiors, like those of St. Stephen Walbrook and St. Mary Abchurch are rewarding to visit. Wren's masterpiece, of course, is St. Paul's Cathedral. He also designed Greenwich Palace and Chelsea Hospital and provided additions to the palaces at Kensington and Hampton Court. The face of London was transformed.

Steeple of St. Bride's, Fleet Street, 1703.

18thC

The 18thC saw the creation of some of London's most elegant streets and squares. Hanover Square was built in 1715, Cavendish in 1717, Burlington House in 1717-20. St. Martin's-in-the-Fields was designed by James Gibbs, and Nicholas Hawksmoor was responsible for six marvelous churches, like St. Mary Woolnoth in the city. From the 1770s date Portman Square, Bedford Square, Portland Place, Somerset House, the Bank of England, Fitzroy Square and Baker Street. **Robert Adam** was responsible for many town houses and for the Adelphi development in the Strand, the best riverside complex ever seen, now sadly destroyed. He also worked at Osterley House and at Syon, transforming old houses and providing fine Neoclassical interiors. Furniture to adorn the new houses was made at Chippendale's workshop in

St. Martin's Lane or at Hepplewhite's in Cripplegate. Paul de Lamerie was making his finest silver, and John Jackson was printing wallpaper at Battersea. ● In the course of the century merchants, bankers and landowners grew rich through Britain's burgeoning overseas trade. New bridges spanned the Thames and cultural life in the capital flourished. This was the age of Swift, Fielding, Defoe and Sterne, of the playwrights Goldsmith and Sheridan, of Johnson and Boswell. Coffee houses were a favourite rendezvous for writers, politicians and businessmen. Edward Lloyd's was the meeting place of shipping underwriters, for instance. The pleasure gardens of Vauxhall were packed with people and Ranelagh Gardens were opened in 1749, 'the most convenient place for courtships of every kind' wrote Horace Walpole. ● While aristocratic and middle-class life was becoming increasingly refined and elegant, the poor lived in great wretchedness in overcrowded housing with no sanitation. By mid-century, it is estimated that every man, woman and child drank an average of two pints of gin a week — 'Mother Geneva' as it was called. 9,000 children a year died from drink. Crime increased — even the Prince of Wales was robbed in broad daylight in the West End. Hogarth's *Gin Lane* does not exaggerate. In the 1780s, during the **Gordon Riots**, a distillery was sacked and a drunken mob ran amok in the streets for a week before 200 of them were shot dead and order restored. Such were the contrasts of life in a swiftly growing and increasingly self-confident city. ● The **Regency period** could be regarded as a coda to the 18thC, a final flourish of elegance before the dawn of Victorianism. The Prince Regent, later George IV, first employed John Nash to refurbish Carlton House. Later he was to enlarge Buckingham House which became **Buckingham Palace**. But Nash's principal accomplishment was the creation of Regent's Park with its terraces and crescents and the architectural scheme linking Regent's Park to Piccadilly and the Mall to the south. By now, Oxford Street and Fleet Street were lined with elegant shops, lit, after 1812, by gaslight. The streets were full of chaises, carriages and drays in an unending stream. The congested River Thames was provided with docks to make space for the ever-increasing seaborne trade. The West India Dock opened in 1802, the London Dock at Wapping in 1805, the East India a year later. The old coffee houses of the 18thC developed into the gaming houses of the 19thC, like Boodle's and White's. This was the age of the poets Byron, Keats and Shelley and of the painter Thomas Lawrence. Edmund Kean was packing Drury Lane. Sarah Siddons was at Covent Garden. The arbiter of fashion was Beau Brummel.

19thC

Between 1800 and Queen Victoria's death in 1901 the population of London trebled. The rich merchants no longer cared to live in the city of London, and the private houses there were mostly pulled down to make room for ever more warehouses and offices. The age of the commuter had started, to be greatly assisted by the arrival of the **railways** and later of the underground. Many miles of terraced housing were erected for the new clerical class who worked in the city. The numbers of tradesmen, craftsmen, artisans and shopkeepers also increased and, above all, the number of domestic servants. The great buildings of Victo-

rian London were not the town houses but buildings with a much more specific function like the warehouses along the Thames and the great railway terminals like Cubbitt's King's Cross and Brunel's Paddington. ● The new **Houses of Parliament** by Barry and Pugin were completed in 1865, the South Kensington museums were designed in 1851, which was also the date of the Great Exhibition and Paxton's astonishing Crystal Palace. Overcrowding and homelessness in London's East End led to the founding of the Barnardo Homes in 1866 at the same time that William Booth was starting the Salvation Army. Edwin Chadwick, champion of the water closet, was responsible for the Public Health Act of 1848. 1863 saw the arrival of the first **underground** railway and in the 1870s London was criss-crossed with more embankments, bridges and thoroughfares than at any time in her history. The past had to make room for the present.

20thC

Ever more new thoroughfares were built through the centre of London as motorized traffic grew. New hotels, department stores, office blocks and 'mansion' flats were all Edwardian innovations — Harrods was built in 1901-5, Selfridges in 1908, the Ritz Hotel in 1906. **Garden suburbs**, like Hampstead, also date from this time. ● The inter-war years saw the transformation of central London with such buildings as Broadcasting House (1931) and South Africa House (1933). New council estates arose in the suburbs, along with private dwellings in every style from mock-Tudor to mock-Queen Anne. ● The **blitz** destroyed much of London, although St. Paul's miraculously survived, now surrounded with high-rise office buildings like the National Westminster Tower and the high-tech Lloyds Building. The South Bank Arts Complex, begun in 1951 with the Festival Hall, now includes an art gallery, film theatre and the National Theatre. At the **Barbican**, new housing is combined with major cultural facilities. Much has been achieved in the last twenty-five years to preserve the best of London's past and to prevent serious demolitions. The Thames is no longer a sewer as it was in Victorian times but cleaner than it has been for centuries. **Clean Air Acts** have long since banished London's 'peasoup' fogs. The dockland is being intensively developed for residential and office use with widespread restoration of the decaying Victorian warehouses. The city is visited each year by increasing numbers of tourists who can experience nearly 2,000 years of history in the busy streets.

City livery companies

As early as the 1stC AD, a Roman historian described the City of London as a 'busy emporium for trade'. The City, the oldest part of the capital, with its own government (the Corporation) and its own Lord Mayor, has remained busy — though its importance now resides in the fact that it is an international centre for banking, insurance and stockbroking. Although its buildings were largely destroyed by the great fire of 1666, a number of its institutions and traditions date from medieval times. Many of these are connected with its guilds or livery companies.

Guilds were the first workers' organizations in England, and were formed to protect the interests of people practicing a certain trade or craft, and to monitor the way they carried out their business. By the 13th and 14thC, they had become very powerful, and in London were known as livery companies because of the particular dress or 'livery' they wore. The companies also became wealthy enough to finance charities, schools and almshouses for their members as well as churches. In outdoor performances of mystery plays each guild would stage a biblical scene appropriate to its trade — the fishmongers for example, would perform Jonah and the Whale.

There are now ninety-six companies, each with various officials and about 20,000 members. These include the mercers, grocers, drapers, skinners, apothecaries, saddlers and many more. Although membership is now largely an honorary matter, the guilds often give aid to the trades with which they are connected by name and take part in activities related to their trades. For example, the goldsmiths' company is responsible for stamping hallmarks on gold and silver articles. In addition to the main guildhall (the seat of the City of London's government for a thousand years), various livery companies have their own magnificent halls. These may be viewed by the public on certain days, and the companies hold annual banquets there. On these occasions a loving cup of hot mulled wine or of punch is passed from guest to guest: while each person drinks, the men on either side of him stand up until he has finished — this dates from the time when a man holding the cup would be unable to reach for his sword and defend himself if attacked, so his neighbours would act as bodyguards. Each year the livery companies elect a Lord Mayor of London. The new Lord Mayor stages a pageant (the Lord Mayor's Show) on the second Saturday in November. The following Monday there is a lavish banquet at the guildhall, usually attended by the Prime Minister.

▶ BARBICAN*

map 2-D1/Underground: Barbican, Moorgate, St. Paul's. Bus: 5, 55, 4, 63.

The 60-acre site, named after a medieval watchtower, corresponds to the area of London most devastated during WWII. Plans were drawn up soon after for its redevelopment as a combined commercial, residential and recreation centre, but this most ambitious of all post-war London development was only finished in 1981. The most striking feature is the 412-ft. tower blocks, part of the housing scheme.

▶ The **Arts and Conference Centre** (N side), includes a concert hall, exhibition gallery, library, cinema and theatre (London home of the Royal Shakespeare Company). ▶ Next to it is the Guildhall School of Music and Drama; founded in 1880, the school moved into its new premises in 1977. ▶ **London wall** marks the S limit of the site, with sections of the original Roman wall. ▶ At the W end is the **Museum of London** (Tue.-Sat., 10-6; Sun., 2-6), presenting aspects of the city's life from prehistoric times to the present; also houses the Lord Mayor's coach (1757), which takes to the streets once a year in the Lord Mayor's Show. ▶ The 16thC church of **St. Giles Cripplegate** is also within the Barbican complex; John Milton is buried in the churchyard. □

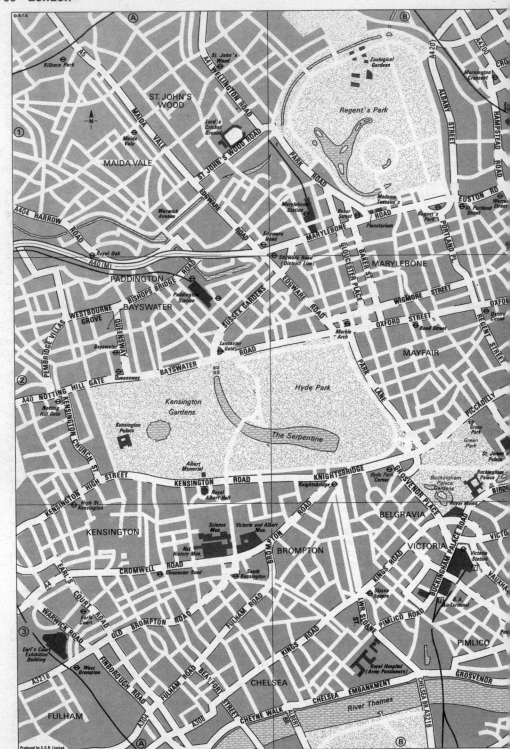

map

Central London

■ Places of Interest
■ Public Buildings
⬛ Information Centre
⊖ Underground Station

▶ **BATTERSEA***

map 1-B1/British Rail: Battersea Park.

For most people, Battersea, facing Chelsea (→), Victoria and Pimlico (→), on the bank of the Thames, means a famous power station, a maze of railway lines around Clapham Junction and grimy Victorian streets. For centuries Battersea was renowned for its market gardens and such local industries as pottery and copperware. The coming of the railways turned it into an industrial suburb. Now its character is changing again.

▶ **Battersea Park**, right by the river, was opened in 1853. It was given a big face-lift for the 1951 Festival of Britain, with a new pleasure garden and works by sculptors Henry Moore and Barbara Hepworth. It is now a popular South London venue for fairs and carnivals. ▶ A short walk W of the park is **Old Battersea House**, a fine late 17thC manor house. ▶ E of park is the monumental **power station**, designed by Sir Giles Gilbert Scott. Built in the 1930s, it no longer functions, but plans are afoot to turn it into a leisure centre. ▶ Close by is the famous Dogs' Home, a canine orphanage. ▶ Further still is the **New Covent Garden** fruit and vegetable market.   □

▶ **BETHNAL GREEN AND SHORE-DITCH**

map 2-B1/Underground: Bethnal Green, Old Street.

Bethnal Green was the poorest district of Victorian London, noted for its Labour Yard, where men broke stones for a bowl of soup. This century's slum clearance and a falling population have changed the area. Neighbouring Shoreditch has theatrical connections. England's first playhouse was erected here in 1576, before being moved and re-erected as the Globe Theatre in Southwark (→). Richard Burbage, actor and friend of Shakespeare, also lived here.

▶ **Bethnal Green Museum of Childhood** (Cambridge Heath Road, E2) has dolls, dolls' houses, puppets and toy theatres *(Mon.-Thu., Sat., 10-6, Sun., 2.30-6)*. ▶ The **Geffrye Museum** (Kingsland Road): former almshouses; displays of English furniture and furnishings from Tudor times onwards, also a reconstructed Georgian street *(Tue.-Sat., 10-5, Sun., 2-5)*. ▶ To the S is **Spitalfields**, East London's fruit, vegetable and flower market. ▶ Facing it is **Christ Church** (Hawksmoor), now being restored *(not regularly open to the public)*.   □

▶ **BLACKHEATH***

map 1-B2/British Rail: Blackheath.

The heath, above Greenwich (→) and the Thames, stands on the historic approach to the capital from Dover and the continent. Henry V was welcomed there after Agincourt, as was Charles II upon his Restoration. The rebel armies of Wat Tyler and Jack Cade gathered there before marching on London. In the 17th and 18thC, the Dover Road made it a notorious place for highwaymen. Residential development in the late 18th and 19thC gives the area its elegant character.

▶ **Colonnade House** and the crescent-shaped **Paragon** (1790) are fine examples of late Georgian domestic building. ▶ Just E of the heath, **Morden College** (1695), attributed to Wren; chapel carvings probably by Grinling Gibbons; large and handsome almshouse group in its own grounds, still a home for the elderly *(visits by appointment only)*.

Nearby

▶ **Charlton House** (Charlton Road) London's best-preserved Jacobean building *(Mon.-Fri., 9-5, wkend by appointment)*. ▶ **Eltham Palace** (off Court Yard, Eltham); 15thC great hall with fine hammer-beam roof *(Apr.-Oct., 10.30-12.15, 2.15-6, Thu., Sun.; Nov.-Mar.: closes at 4)*. ▶ **Severndroog House** (Shooter's Hill), 18thC Gothic folly; local landmark on site of earlier beacon *(not open)*.   □

▶ **BLOOMSBURY***

map 2-C1/Underground: Russell Square, Tottenham Court Road, Euston Square, Goodge Street. Bus: 14, 19, 22, 24, 29, 30, 73.

In the Domesday Book, Bloomsbury was noted for its vineyards. Its real development began in the late 17thC with the creation of Southampton (later Bloomsbury) Square — the first London square so named. Through the 18th and early 19thC, its Georgian and Regency squares made it London's most fashionable area. Early this century it attracted writers and artists who formed the 'Bloomsbury Group'. Today it is the home of London University and related institutions, the British Museum (→) and many publishing houses.

▶ Its garden squares — many named after former estates — include **Bedford** (the best preserved), **Bloomsbury** itself, **Fitzroy** (with work by Robert Adam), **Gordon**, **Russell**, **Tavistock**, **Torrington** and **Woburn**. ▶ Near the **British Museum** (→) is **St. George's Church** (1716), designed by Nicholas Hawksmoor with imposing Classical portico and unusual tower, in the form of a stepped pyramid, crowned by a statue of George I posing as St. George. ▶ In complete contrast is **Congress House** (1958), TUC headquarters, with sculpture by Epstein. ▶ **Senate House** (1932), headquarters of London University, for many years the capital's tallest building. ▶ The **Courtauld Institute Galleries** (Woburn Square) has Renaissance, Impressionist and post-Impressionist paintings including Degas, Manet, Gauguin, Van Gogh, Cezanne *(Mon.-Sat., 10-5, Sun., 2-5)*. ▶ The **Percival David Foundation** (Gordon Square) has Chinese ceramics of eight countries *(Mon., 2-5; Tue.-Fri., 10.30-5; Sat., 10.30-1; Cl. Bank Hols.)*. ▶ **Pollock's Toy Museum** (Scala Street): mainly Victorian toy theatres, dolls and dolls' houses *(Mon.-Sat., 10-5)*. ▶ **Telecom Tower** (1963), formerly Post Office Tower, London's tallest structure (580 ft.) until the 1981 **NatWest Tower** in the City (→). ▶ **University College** (1827), with Classical portico and dome by William Wilkins, architect of the National Gallery (→). ▶ The **Jewish Museum** (Upper Woburn Place; *May-Sep.: Tue.-Fri., 10-4, Sun., 10-12.45; Oct.-Apr.: Tue.-Thu., 10-4,Fri., Sun., 10-12.45)*: ritual objects and antiquities of Jewish life and worship.   □ .

▶ **BRITISH MUSEUM*****

map 2-C1/Gt. Russel Street. Underground: Tottenham Court Road. Bus: 14, 19, 22, 68, 73, 77A, 188.

One of the world's greatest collections of historical treasures, founded 1753. The main part of the present building, with massive south-facing Classical portico and colonnade, was constructed between 1823 and 1847, to designs by Sir Robert Smirke. Later additions include the circular, copper-domed Reading Room (1857) by Sydney Smirke; Edward VII Galleries (1914) and Duveen Gallery (1938). Major bequests include George IV's library of 65,000 volumes and Lord Elgin's Parthenon sculptures.

▶ **Parthenon sculptures** (Elgin Marbles, room 8); **Palace of Nineveh sculptures** (room 21); **Rosetta Stone** and Egyptian monumental sculptures (room 25); ▶ British Library exhibits, including **Magna Carta, Lindisfarne Gospels, Shakespeare First Folio, Gutenberg Bible** (rooms 29-33); Oriental ceramics and sculptures (room 34); **Mildenhall treasures** (room 40); **Sutton Hoo Anglo-Saxon burial ship and treasures** (room 41); **Isle of Lewis chessmen** (room 42); ▶ Clocks and watches (room 44); ▶ Coins and medals (room 50); ▶ Egyptian mummies, tomb paintings, papyri (rooms 60-66) (*Mon.-Sat., 10-5, Sun., 2.30-6; Cl. Bank Hols.*).   □

▶ BUCKINGHAM PALACE*

map 2-B2/Underground: Victoria, St. James's Park. Bus: 11, 24, 29.

Official London residence of the reigning monarch, the palace takes its name from Buckingham House (1715). Bought by George III in 1762, Nash converted it into a royal residence (1820). Much enlarged by Edward Blore (1830-47) for Queen Victoria and her family, there were further renovations and additions by Sir James Pennethorne (1853) and by Sir Aston Webb, who added the East front (facing the Mall →) in 1913. The present building has some 600 rooms, and there is a large garden, with lake, at the back. The royal standard flies over the palace when the monarch is in residence.

▶ The **Queen's Gallery** (Buckingham Palace Road) once the palace chapel, has changing exhibitions from the royal collection of paintings and drawings (*Tue.-Sat., 11-5, Sun., 2-5; Cl. Mon. ex. Bank Hols.*). ▶ The **Royal Mews** (Buckingham Palace Road) by Nash, and separate from the palace, houses the various royal coaches, including the Gold State Coach (1762) used at coronations (*Wed. Thu., 2-4; Cl. Ascot week and during state visits*). ▶ The **Changing of the Guard**, the ceremony usually performed at 11.30 on alternate days in the palace forecourt by detachments of the Brigade of Guards.   □

▶ CEMETERIES*

The city's dead were for a long time buried in the churchyards of local parish churches, but by the 17thC these were overcrowded and a danger to health. New burial grounds were then established near the city limits. These, in turn, were filled, and, during the 19thC many, like Bunhill Fields (→Clerkenwell and Finsbury), were turned into public gardens. At the same time, large new cemeteries were opened on the perimeter of the rapidly growing suburbs. Most of these remain, containing monuments to many famous people and offering remarkable examples of mainly Victorian funeral architecture and imagery.

▶ **Highgate** (1839), best known of London's cemeteries, situated on a slope of the hill, and centered round an Egyptian-style necropolis or circle of catacombs. The old part, with the graves of Michael Faraday, George Eliot, Dante Gabriel Rossetti and John Galsworthy, is being restored after long neglect and vandalism; the new part has the grave and striking monument to Karl Marx. ▶ **Kensal Rise** (1833), with Greek Revival chapel, catacombs and the graves of I.K. Brunel, Leigh Hunt, Thackeray and Trollope; adjoining, Roman Catholic cemetery, with the graves of Francis Thompson and conductor Sir John Barbirolli. ▶ **Brompton** (1840), with large octagonal, domed chapel, Classical Revival catacombs and the graves of George Borrow and suffragette Emmeline Pankhurst. ▶ **City of London Cemetery** (1856), largest municipal cemetery in

Europe, well landscaped and maintained, with imposing monuments to those transferred there from City churchyards. ▶ An unusual addition to London's burial grounds and cemeteries is the **Pets' Cemetery**, on the N side of Kensington Gardens (→), with monuments to pet dogs, cats, monkeys and birds.   □

The great fire of London

One of the city's tallest buildings is the Monument (202 ft.) which was erected in 1677 to commemorate the great fire which caused havoc eleven years before. Only six people died in the blaze, but the old medieval city was burned to the ground over an area of about 400 acres, 80,000 people (more than half of the population) were left homeless and eighty-seven churches and 13,000 houses were destroyed.
The fire started in the house of the royal baker in Pudding Lane very early on Sunday morning on 2 Sep. 1666. There was a strong wind blowing from the east, and the fire burned without stopping until 6 Sep. It spread so quickly and seemed to blaze up in places so far away from the main fire, that many thought it had been started deliberately by Dutch or French enemies or papists (Catholics). The great 17thC diarist Samuel Pepys gave a graphic account of the fire (as he did of the great plague which had swept the capital the previous year) and recorded how he buried his gold and silver valuables in his father-in-law's garden for safekeeping.
Although it caused destruction on a massive scale, the fire was not without its beneficial effects. The architect Christopher Wren drew up a reconstruction plan for the whole of London and, although it was not implemented, Wren was given the job of redesigning St. Paul's Cathedral, which had been destroyed. Wren also designed more than fifty other churches besides, as well as many important public buildings including the Monument, Greenwich Observatory, the Royal Exchange and Chelsea Hospital.
The great cathedral is acknowledged to be his masterpiece, and Wren's tomb bears the inscription: 'Reader, if you would seek his monuments, look around you'.

▶ CHELSEA*

map 2-B3/Underground: Sloane Square. Bus: 11, 14, 19, 22.

In 1520, Sir Thomas More built a country house in the area, followed by Henry VIII. The Porcelain Works of 1745 (closed fifty years later) gave Chelsea an even wider fame. Neat 18th and 19thC streets and squares, the home of many celebrities, plus antique shops and fashion boutiques give Chelsea its charm and chic.

▶ **Cheyne Walk** has 17th, 18th and 19thC houses and gardens facing the Thames. ▶ Standing back from the river is **Chelsea Old Church** (All Saints), with Norman origins; inside are monuments to Sir Thomas More and others, and the only chained books in a London church. ▶ **Carlyle's House** (*Wed.-Sun., Bank Hol. Mon., 11-5*), a Queen Anne house largely preserved as the writer knew it. ▶ By **Chelsea Embankment** is the **Physic Garden** (1676), one of the oldest botanical institutions. ▶ The **Royal Hospital**, founded by Charles II for veteran soldiers (Chelsea Pensioners) and built by Wren (1682); visit the **chapel** and **great hall** (*Mon.-Sat., 10-12, 2-4, Sun., 2-4*) and adjacent **museum** (*Mon.-Fri., 10-12, 2-5, Sat., Sun., 2-4.30*) devoted to the hospital's history; mementoes of

Wellington. ▶ **Ranelagh Gardens** are the scene of the Chelsea Flower Show (*May*). ▶ Close by is the **National Army Museum** (*Mon.-Sat., 10-5.30; Sun., 2-5.30; Cl. Bank Hols.*): British Army relics of five centuries. ▶ **Kings Road**, named after the path taken by Charles II to Nell Gwynne's house in Fulham, has stylish antique shops, boutiques, restaurants and pubs. ▶ **Sloane Square** has the **Royal Court Theatre** and Peter Jones, the architecturally praised 1936 department store. ▶ In Sloane Street is **Holy Trinity** (1888), rich in pre-Raphaelite decoration, with windows by Burne-Jones.   □

▶ **CHISWICK***

map 1-A1/Underground: Turnham Green, Chiswick Park. British Rail: Chiswick, Kew Bridge.

On a bend of the river W of Hammersmith (→), Chiswick remained almost a village until a little over a century ago, when a shipyard and other local industries, plus the railway, brought a rapid rise in population. Many old houses remain and the district has pleasant parks and riverside walks.

▶ **Chiswick Mall** on the river front preserves the village atmosphere with 17th, 18th and 19thC houses. ▶ Round the corner is **St. Nicholas Parish Church** (origins 12thC), where William Hogarth is buried. ▶ Nearby is **Hogarth House** (*Apr.-Sep.: Mon, Wed.-Sat., 11-6, Sun., 2-6; Oct.-Mar.: Mon., Wed.-Sat., 11-4, Sun., 2-4*) with drawings, engravings and other relics of the artist. ▶ Well away from the traffic is **Chiswick House** (*Burlington Lane; mid-Mar. - mid-Oct.: 9.30-6.30; mid-Oct.-mid-Mar.: Wed.-Sun., 9.30-4*), designed as a residence for and by Lord Burlington (1725) in the Classical Revival (Palladian) style, with fine interior decoration by William Kent, who also landscaped the grounds.

Nearby

▶ The **Musical Museum** (High Street, Brentford), a unique collection of mechanical pianos, organs and other instruments, also phonographs and musical boxes (*Mon.-Sat., 10-5, Sun., 2.30-6; Cl. Bank Hols.*). ▶ **Kew Bridge Engines Trust** (Kew Bridge Road, Brentford; *Sat., Sun., Bank Hol. Mon., 11-5*): a museum of early steam engines (sometimes working), traction engines and models.   □

▶ **CHURCHES****

Underground: Chancery Lane, Blackfriars, Barbican, St. Pauls, Mansion House, Bank, Monument, Liverpool Street, Aldgate, Tower Hill. Bus: 6, 9, 11, 15, 22, 25.

Before the Great Fire of 1666 there were 87 City churches. The fire destroyed or badly damaged 76 of them. Fifty-one were rebuilt, many by Wren. Some had gone again by WWII. The war took a further toll. But over thirty remain (some much restored), 23 by Wren.

▶ **St. Andrew Holborn** (Wren), with the tomb of Thomas Coram (→ Holborn and St. Pancras). ▶ **City Temple** (1874). ▶ **St. Bride** has Wren's tallest steeple (226 ft.); WWII bombing revealed Roman remains in the crypt, now a museum. ▶ **St. Dunstan**, Fleet Street. ▶ **St. Benet** (Wren), where Inigo Jones is buried. ▶ **St. Andrew-by-the-Wardrobe** (Wren). ▶ **St. Bartholomew the Great** (1120), London's oldest church, with Norman nave. ▶ **St. Giles Cripplegate** (→ Barbican). ▶ **St. Sepulchre**, a 12thC crusader's church, connected with old Newgate Prison and with music. ▶ **St. Vedast** (Wren): ▶ **St. Martin Ludgate** (Wren). ▶ **St. Mary-le-Bow** (Wren). WWII destroyed the famous bells, but tower and steeple, Wren's finest, survive. Norman crypt. ▶ **St. Michael Paternoster** (Wren): burial place of Richard Whittington, commemorated in

stained glass. ▶ **St. Nicholas Cole Abbey** (Wren). ▶ **St. James Carlickhythe** (Wren). ▶ **St. Mary Aldermary** (Wren). ▶ **St. Stephen Walbrook** (Wren) interior, with dome, anticipates features of St. Paul's; Sir John Vanbrugh's burial place. ▶ **St. Lawrence Jewry** (Wren). ▶ **St. Mary Woolnoth** (Hawksmoor). ▶ **St. Margaret Lothbury** (Wren). ▶ **St. Michael Cornhill** (Wren, Hawksmoor). ▶ **St. Peter-upon-Cornhill** (Wren). ▶ **St. Edmund the King** (Wren). ▶ **St. Mary Abchurch** (Wren): painted dome and reredos by Grinling Gibbons. ▶ **St. Magnus the Martyr** (Wren): Miles Coverdale buried in the tiny churchyard, with relics of Roman wharf and old London Bridge. ▶ **St. Margaret Pattens** (Wren). ▶ **St. Helen Bishopsgate** (14thC): fine monuments, brasses and a memorial window to Shakespeare. ▶ **All Hallows London Wall** (G. Dance). ▶ **St. Botolph Without Bishopsgate** (G. Dance). ▶ **St. Katherine Cree** (17thC): ceiling with livery company coats-of-arms. ▶ **St. Andrew Undershaft** (16thC). ▶ **St. Botolph Aldgate** (G. Dance). ▶ **All Hallows-by-the-Tower** (8th, 17th, 20thC), with fine brasses. ▶ **St. Olave** (15thC).   □

▶ **CITY**

map 2-D2/Underground: Blackfriars, St. Paul's, Bank, Monument, Tower Hill. Bus: 6, 9, 15. British Rail: Blackfriars, Cannon Street, Fenchurch Street, Liverpool Street.

The City of London is the oldest part of the capital, with its own form of government and institutions. The first real chapter of its history is that of Roman township, *Londinium* (*A.D. 50-400*), of which fragments of wall and foundations of various buildings survive. William I (1066) and King John (1215) both granted the City charters giving it a large degree of autonomy. Loans to Edward III and Henry V to fight foreign wars increased its political power and independence. It also grew rich through trade and banking, aided by links with the German Hanseatic League, Italian Lombards, Flemish weavers, French Huguenots. The medieval City spread beyond the Roman walls to occupy an area almost exactly one square mile, and that has remained its limit. Its resident population fell dramatically as the rest of London grew, but it remains a world financial centre and thrives on its traditions.

▶ **Temple Bar**, marking the site of the old gateway, marks the City's limit. South of it is **The Temple** (→). ▶ **Fleet Street** is the home of many national newspapers — note the *Daily Express* building (1932) in Art Deco style. There is also **Prince Henry's Room** (no. 17, *Mon.-Fri., 1.45-5, Sat., 1.45-4.30; Cl. Sun., Bank Hols.*) with Tudor and Jacobean decoration; **Dr. Johnson's House** (*May-Sep.: daily, 11-5.30. Oct.-Apr.: Mon.-Sat., 11-5; Cl. Bank Hols.*), where he compiled his Dictionary; **St. Bride Printing Library** (Bride Lane) with early presses and type displays (*Mon.-Fri., 9.30-5.30*). ▶ Along **Newgate** is the **Central Criminal Court** (*Old Bailey*), with the well-known gilt statue of Justice atop the dome, on the site of old Newgate Prison. ▶ The **National Postal Museum** (*Mon.-Fri., 10-4.30, Sat., 10-4; Cl. Bank Hols.*); mainly 19thC British stamps. Close by is statue to Sir Rowland Hill, founder of the penny post. N of St. Paul's Cathedral (→) is the Barbican (→). ▶ **Bank of England** (The Old Lady of Threadneedle Street), centre of the nation's finances. The earlier building, by Sir John Soane, was largely rebuilt (1921-37). ▶ **Royal Exchange** (1841; *Mon.-Fri., 10-4, Sat., 10-12; Cl. Bank Hols.*), formerly the Stock Exchange; frequent exhibitions. A carillon plays at certain times. ▶ **Mansion House** (1739), official residence of the Lord Mayor. On the front pediment is an allegory of London defeating Envy with Plenty, Father Thames looking on. ▶ The present **Stock Exchange** (1973), Threadneedle Street, has a public gallery and cinema (*Mon.-Fri., 10-3.15; Cl. Bank Hols.*). ▶ **Lloyd's of London**, in its striking new building (1986) by Leadenhall Market, houses the *Lutine Bell*, tra-

Maundy Money and hot cross buns

The word 'maundy' comes from the Latin mandatum meaning 'command', and it is associated with the command Jesus gave his disciples as he symbolically washed their feet before the Last Supper. The command was that they should love one another.

From the time of Edward III in the 14thC, it was the custom for the King of England to wash the feet of poor people in remembrance of that command. Every Maundy Thursday (the day before Good Friday), the feet of London poor people would be cleaned in warm scented water by the Yeomen of the Laundry; the king would then carry out a ceremonial washing and clothing would be distributed. Ever since 1689 the giving of money has become known as Maundy Money. Each person receives specially minted silver pennies equal in value to the age of the king or queen. The money is contained in small leather purses which are distributed by a Yeoman of the Guard. Bunches of sweet-scented flowers and herbs are carried, and the clergy carry linen towels over their shoulders as a reminder of the washing ceremony that used to take place. Since 1953, the ceremony, which used to be held at Westminster Abbey, takes place in cathedrals around the country.

On Good Friday, it is still the custom all over England to eat hot cross buns. Similar buns flavoured with spices and currants or raisins were enjoyed in the 16thC during the period of Lent. At this time all loaves of bread and buns were marked with a cross to ward off evil spirits before being put in the oven. After the Reformation this practice was stopped for all baking except that of the buns eaten on Good Friday, the day commemorating the Crucifixion.

---

ditionally struck for the loss or safe arrival of a ship. ▶ Another new building is the nearby 600-ft. **NatWest Tower** (1981), Britain's tallest. ▶ N of the Bank is the **Guildhall** (→). ▶ Wren's Monument (1671; *May-Sep., 9-5.40, Sun., 2-5.40; Oct.-Apr., 9-3.40; Cl. some Bank Hols.*); a 202-ft. column with viewing platform, commemorating the Great Fire (1666). ▶ By London Bridge (→) is **Fishmonger's Hall** (1841); Imposing city livery company building. ▶ Nearby are the old buildings of **Billingsgate** fish market (1875) and the **Custom House** (1817). ▶ **Trinity Square Gardens**, facing the **Tower of London** (→), includes a section of Roman wall. ▶ Behind is **Trinity House** (1794), which administers the nation's lighthouses. ▶ E is the old **Royal Mint** (1809), just outside the City limits. □

▶ CLERKENWELL AND FINSBURY*

map 2-C1/Underground: Barbican, Faringdon, Old Street, Angel. Bus: 6, 9, 11, 15, 19.

Just N of the City (→), on rising ground, watered by springs and Fleet River, Clerkenwell (Clerk's Well) and neighbouring Finsbury long enjoyed a favoured situation. After the Great Fire (1666), population overspill brought in clockmakers and other craftsmen, while local spas remained popular. The 19thC was a time of slums and industrial unrest — a focal point for the Chartists. Slum clearance and rehousing have transformed the scene, but much Georgian architecture remains.

▶ **Charterhouse Square**, mostly Georgian, with adjacent remains of Charterhouse itself (*Apr.-Jul: Wed., 2.45*): 14thC priory, then a famous school (now moved from London). ▶ By **Smithfield Market** and Square (just within the City), **Cloth Fair**, site of the old Street Bartholomew Fair, with 17thC houses. Next to it the church of **St. Bartholomew the Great** (→Churches). ▶ **St. John's Gate** (off Clerkenwell Road), 16thC gateway to 12thC priory, now a museum (*Tue., Fri., Sat., 10-6*) with relics of the Crusaders' order that founded the priory. ▶ **Clerkenwell Green** has the Karl Marx Memorial Library, where Lenin worked. ▶ **John Wesley's House and Chapel** (*check on opening times*) now a museum for the founder of Methodism who is buried in the chapel yard. ▶ **Bunhill** (Bone Hill) **Fields**, with tombs of Bunyan, Blake, George Fox. ▶ **Eagle pub**, inspiration of a popular old song, has many music-hall prints. ▶ **Sadler's Wells Theatre** (1931), on the site of a spa, pleasure garden and earlier theatre, one-time home of a famous ballet and opera company, now changed into the Royal Ballet (Covent Garden) and English National Opera (Coliseum). □

▶ COVENT GARDEN**

map 2-C2/Underground: Covent Garden. Bus: 6, 9, 11, 15.

Covent (Convent) Garden, on the fringes of Westminster (→), was quite rural until the mid-17thC, when Inigo Jones built his large Italian-style piazza of town houses and church that has largely shaped the area's character and appearance ever since. The 18thC craze for coffee houses and the proximity of two great theatres attracted Garrick, Goldsmith, Sheridan and Pope. Taverns, gaming houses and brothels also gave the area a bad name. The famous vegetable, fruit and flower market, dating from the 17thC, soon grew too big and was never properly managed; it moved to Battersea (→) in 1974.

▶ The Victorian Market Hall in the centre of the cobbled piazza is now an arcade with shops and cafes, plus street entertainers. ▶ On the piazza's W side is **St. Paul's Cathedral**, which Inigo Jones called 'the handsomest barn in England', famous as the setting for the opening of Shaw's *Pygmalion* and the musical *My Fair Lady*. Samuel Butler and Thomas Arne, composer of 'Rule, Britannia', are buried there. ▶ The Flower Market building, on the SE corner, is now the **London Transport Museum** (*daily, 10-6*), housing some of the capital's old buses, trams and trains. ▶ The **Theatre Royal**, Drury Lane (1810), fourth theatre on the site, is one of London's largest and most handsome; it is supposed to be haunted. ▶ The **Royal Opera House** (1857) is also on the site of earlier theatres. Many great singers — Caruso, Melba, Gigli, Tauber, Flagstad — have appeared there. ▶ Facing it is Bow Street police station, reminder of the Bow Street Runners of 1753. ▶ **Lamb and Flag** pub (Rose Street, 1623) is where the poet John Dryden was attacked by footpads. □

▶ DULWICH*

map 1-B2/Underground: West Dulwich, North Dulwich, Forest Hill, Crystal Palace.

This fashionable South London district, once a hunting ground for English kings, remained a village and small spa (Dulwich Wells) until the 19thC. It has, to a large measure, kept its rural character, with 18th and 19thC cottages around the road named Dulwich Village and the only toll gate still operating in the London area.

▶ Standing in its own grounds off College Road is **Dulwich College**, an imposing group of buildings in Victorian Renaissance style. It was founded in 1619, by

Edward Alleyn, impresario and acquaintance of Shakespeare. ▶ Connected with it is the **Picture Gallery** (Sir John Soane, 1814; *check on opening times*), England's oldest public art gallery, with works by Raphael, Rembrandt, Rubens, Van Dyck, Canaletto, Gainsborough, Reynolds. ▶ **Kingswood House**, now a community centre and library, is a local landmark in 19thC Gothic style.

Nearby

▶ The **Horniman Museum**, built in Art Nouveau style, houses a collection of tribal masks, musical instruments and other artifacts gathered by its founder, F.J. Horniman, during his travels as a tea merchant. ▶ **Crystal Palace Park**, Sydenham, named after Joseph Paxton's Crystal Palace Exhibition Hall, moved here from Hyde Park (→) after the Great Exhibition of 1851 and burnt down in 1936. Surviving is a group of model prehistoric monsters grouped round the lake. Today the park is a major sports centre. □

▶ **EALING***

map 1-A1/Underground: Ealing Broadway, Acton Town. British Rail: Ealing Broadway.

Up to the beginning of the 19thC, Ealing was still a rural retreat for the landed gentry. By the end of the century, it prided itself on being 'The Queen of the Suburbs', on account of its good housing, public amenities and transport — qualities still possessed by this large residential W London district.

▶ **Pitshanger Manor**, Walpole Park, converted 1800, by Sir John Soane from an existing manor house. Long used as borough offices, there are plans to open it to the public. ▶ **St. Benedict's** bright Neogothic church (1897) is on the site of a much earlier Benedictine abbey. ▶ **Gunnersbury Park** and **Estate** has an interesting history, including ownership by the Rothschild family. It has a 19thC Gothic folly, orangery and two Regency houses, the larger of which, **Gunnersbury House**, is a museum of local history (*Mar.-Oct.: Mon.-Fri., 9-5, Sat., Sun., Bank Hols., 2-6; Nov.-Feb.: Mon.-Fri., 9-4, Sat., Sun., Bank Hols., 2-4*). □

▶ **GREENWICH***

map 1-B1/British Rail: Greenwich, Maze Hill.

Four miles downstream from Tower Bridge (→) and rising above a broad bend of the river, Greenwich has some of London's finest sights and places of interest. The 15thC Greenwich Palace was a favourite with Tudor royalty, especially with Henry VIII, who was born there. After the Restoration, Charles II put in hard work on the great series of buildings for which Greenwich is now famous. By the 18thC it was also a thriving township — well placed between the Deptford and Woolwich shipyards — attested by the many Queen Anne and Georgian houses that still grace its streets.

▶ **The Royal Naval College**, completed 1726 and formerly the Royal Naval Hospital (*daily ex. Thu., 2.30-5*) stands on the site of the old palace. Mainly the work of Wren, Hawksmoor and Vanbrugh, the whole is best seen from the river. ▶ The magnificent **Painted Hall** is the work of James Thornhill and the place of Nelson's lying-in-state. ▶ Facing it, Wren's chapel, gutted by fire 1779, restored in Neoclassical style. ▶ The two wings of the National Maritime Museum (*Easter-Oct.: Mon.-Sat., 10-6, Sun., 2-5.30; Nov.-Easter: Mon.-Fri., 10-5, Sat., 10-5.30, Sun., 2-5*) commemorate the Battle of Trafalgar and house a

great collection of globes, maps, charts and navigational instruments, model ships and barges, uniforms (including Nelson's), guns and other equipment; also paintings by Canaletto, Hogarth and Reynolds. ▶ Between them, and linked by colonnades, is the **Queen's House** (1635), designed in the Italian Palladian style by Inigo Jones and a part of the museum. ▶ The **Old Royal Observatory** (*Easter-Oct.: Mon.-Sat., 10-6, Sun., 2-5.30; Nov.-Mar.: Mon.-Fri., 10-5, Sat., 10-5.30, Sun., 2-5; Cl. Bank Hols.*) atop the hill of **Greenwich Park**, dates from John Flamsteed's 1675 appointment as the first Astronomer Royal. Flamsteed's House (Wren) and the later Meridian and S buildings (with Planetarium) house telescopes, sun dials, clocks and other astronomical relics. The famous brass meridian line divides the E and W hemispheres. There is also a statue to General Wolfe, a citizen of Greenwich. ▶ On the waterfront, next to the college, are two famous ships: the clipper, *Cutty Sark* (1869), converted into a museum (*Nov.-Mar.: Mon.-Sat., 10.30-5, Sun., 2.30-5; Apr.-Oct.: Mon.-Sat., 10.30-6, Sun., 2.30-6*) and Sir Francis Chichester's yacht *Gipsy Moth IV* (1966). ▶ **Croom's Hill**, running up the E side of the park, has several notable 17th and 18thC houses. ▶ Below it is **St. Alfege**, rebuilt 1718 by Hawksmoor. The composer Thomas Tallis and General Wolfe are buried here. ▶ Above, on the edge of Blackheath (→), with fine **views** over London, is the 18thC **Ranger's House** (*daily, 10-5 ex. Good Fri., Christmas*) displaying Jacobean and Stuart portraits. ▶ West of the park is **Vanbrugh Castle** (1726), a fanciful dwelling the architect and playwright built for himself. ▶ The **Trafalgar Tavern**, **Yacht Tavern** and **Cutty Sark Tavern** all have views of the river. □

▶ **GUILDHALL***

map 2-D2/ off Gresham Street. British Rail: Bank. Bus: 6, 9, 11, 22, 25.

The guildhall is the centre London's civic life. Lord Mayors have been elected there since 1192. It has also seen some famous trials, including that of Archbishop Cranmer (1553). The 15thC building was mostly destroyed by the Great Fire (1666) and rebuilt. It was wrecked again in WWII and later restored. Parts of the 15thC structure, including the crypt, survive.

▶ The **main hall** (*daily, 10-5; Sun. in May-Sep., 2-5; Cl. Bank Hols.*), where the annual Lord Mayor's Banquet is held, contains the coats-of-arms and banners of the twelve great city livery companies, statues to Nelson, Wellington , Churchill and replicas of the large wooden figures of Gog and Magog, mythical founders of pre-Roman London. ▶ The **library** (*Mon.-Sat., 9.30-5; Cl. Bank Hols. and for official functions*), first endowed by Richard Whittington, 1423, has manuscripts, maps and prints relating to the history of the City and of London as a whole. ▶ The **Clock Museum** (*Mon.-Fri., 9.30-5*), the collection of the Worshipful Company of Clockmakers, has over 700 exhibits covering five centuries of horology. □

▶ **HAMMERSMITH AND FULHAM***

map 2-D3/Underground: Hammersmith. Bus: 9, 11, 73. Underground: Putney Bridge. Bus: 14, 22, 30.

Hammersmith has long been a busy place, with coaching inns astride the main road from London to the West. Its high population and continued position as a vital traffic junction have today made it busier than ever; though only a few minutes' walk from the Broadway and the Flyover, the river front is a haven of calm. The life of neighbouring Fulham once cen-

tred round the Palace of the Bishops of London, then grew rapidly as a large Victorian suburb.

▶ Lower Mall and Upper Mall follow the river from Hammersmith Bridge (→Thames Bridges) to Chiswick (→), with 18th and early 19thC houses, once inhabited by such celebrities as artist William Morris. ▶ **St. Paul's Church** by the Broadway dates from 1882, but has interior decoration taken from an earlier church by Wren, and a fine monument to Charles II. ▶ **Fulham Palace**, a 16thC Tudor manor house, was the official residence of the Bishops of London until 1973. Adjoining **Bishops' Park** borders the river and looks across to boating yards on the Putney bank. ▶ Nearby **All Saints Church** was largely rebuilt in the 19thC, but is rich in monuments and brasses, including two from the time of the Civil War; fourteen Bishops of London are buried in the churchyard. ▶ **Fulham Pottery** is commemorated by a 'bottle kiln' preserved on the original site.   □

▶ **HAMPSTEAD AND HIGHGATE***

map 1-B1/Underground: Hampstead. Bus: 24. Underground: Archway. Bus: 19.

Hampstead, climbing steeply towards the heath, was a popular 18thC spa, and with its period houses and

---

London's underground

Despite its name, much of the underground system — certainly when it reaches the outer suburbs — runs above the ground. The first underground, the Metropolitan Railway, was actually little different from the railway in that it used ordinary steam trains. These ran on lines constructed in shallow trenches and then simply roofed over — the so-called 'cut-and cover' method of construction. Nevertheless, at the time it opened, the Metropolitan provided a revolutionary kind of urban transport. On its first day, in 1863, the line carried 30,000 passengers, and extended from Paddington Station in the west to Farringdon Street in the city. With the addition of the District Line, this was to develop into the inner circle. Other lines were built by different companies, and in 1890 the first 'tube' was introduced by the City and South London Railway (later the Northern Line). This was made .by boring through the earth underground, and necessitated elevators to take passengers down to the deeper levels. Electrification further transformed the system, which has continued to develop throughout the present century. In 1933, the whole group of underground railways was united with the bus company to form the London Passenger Transport Board. As the lines extended further into the rural areas surrounding London during the inter-war years, the suburbs developed. During WWII many stations provided shelter against the bombing raids — beds were ranged in rows along the platforms. 20thC improvements to passenger comfort have included sprung upholstered seats, escalators, automatic doors and turnstiles. Recent additions to the service are the Victoria and Jubilee lines and the Piccadilly Line extension which gives travelers the opportunity of going directly from central London to Heathrow Airport.

---

pleasant location has long been North London's most fashionable district, the home of many famous people. Highgate, on the far side of the heath, has retained a little more of its own village atmosphere than bustling Hampstead.

▶ **Hampstead Heath**, London's highest point, with **views** right across the capital; long a refuge at times of crisis — the Black Death, the Plague and the Great Fire. It now attracts large crowds to its Bank Holiday fairs. ▶ Two famous pubs on the heath are **Jack Straw's Castle**, named after a leader of the Peasants' Revolt of 1381, and **The Spaniards Inn and Toll House**, used by the famous highwayman Dick Turpin. ▶ Also on the heath is **Kenwood House** (*Apr.-Sep.: daily, 10-7; Oct., Feb. and Mar.: 10-5; Nov.-Jan.: 10-4*), very fine 18thC mansion, largely the work of Robert Adam, with beautiful interiors and paintings by Rembrandt, Frans Hals, Vermeer, Gainsborough, Romney; summer open-air concerts are given in the grounds. ▶ Just below the heath is **Keats House** (*Mon.-Sat., 10-1 and 2-6, Sun., 2-5*), a Regency dwelling with relics of the poet and his contemporaries. ▶ **Church Walk** is a Georgian enclave, with St. John's parish church of the same period; the artist John Constable is buried there. ▶ Nearby is **Fenton House** (1693) (*Apr.-Oct.: Mon.-Wed., Sat. and Sun., 11-6*), a notable museum of keyboard instruments and porcelain; and **Romney's House** (1797) with distinctive weatherboarding. ▶ Highgate's **Waterlow Park** includes 16th-18thC **Lauderdale House**, home of Nell Gwynne. Next to it is **Highgate Cemetery** (→ Cemeteries).

Nearby

▶ **Alexandra Palace** (Muswell Hill) was built in 1875 to rival the Crystal Palace (→ Dulwich). The world's first television transmission was made from it in 1936; now an exhibition hall.   □

▶ **HAMPTON COURT****

map 1-A2/Underground: Hampton Court.

Hampton Court Palace (*Apr.-Sep.: Mon.-Sat., 9.30-6,Sun., 11-6; Oct.-Mar.: Mon.-Sat., 9.30-5, Sun., 2-5*) was the home of English monarchs from Henry VIII to George II. Begun by Cardinal Wolsey, 1515, it was already the grandest Tudor palace in England when Henry acquired it in 1529 and enlarged it further. In 1689, at the behest of William and Mary, Wren demolished part of it and, working with Grinling Gibbons and others, added a big new wing. Thus the present building, as well as housing many historical and art treasures, is a remarkable marriage of the Tudor and English Renaissance styles.

▶ The **great hall**, one of the finest examples of Tudor construction, is also the oldest surviving English theatre, used by Elizabeth I; 16thC Flemish tapestries. ▶ The **Great Watching Chamber** has a paneled and decorated ceiling and more Flemish tapestries. ▶ The **Cartoon Gallery** was specially designed by Wren and Gibbons to display cartoons by Raphael. ▶ Throughout the apartments there are also paintings by Mantegna, Titian, Giorgione, Veronese, Correggio, Holbein, Van Dyck. ▶ The **Astronomical Clock** (1540) shows the hour, month, date, signs of the zodiac, year and phase of the moon. ▶ The **gardens** include the Broad Walk, surveying the Great Fountain Garden and Long Water; the Great Vine, planted by the landscape artist Capability Brown (1768); the Wilderness and **Maze**. ▶ **Hampton Court Green**, facing the palace, has period houses, including the Old Court House, Wren's home (1706-23). ▶ Nearby **Bushy Park**, formerly a royal hunting reserve, has an avenue of chestnut trees and the Diana fountain, laid out by Wren.   □

▶ HOLBORN AND ST. PANCRAS*

map 2-C2/Underground: Holborn, Chancery Lane. Bus: 22, 25, 68, 77A, 188. Underground: Kings Cross. Bus: 14, 30, 73, 77A.

Holborn (Holebourne, a tributary of the Fleet River), on the edge of the City, grew rapidly in the 17th and 18thC, as a centre of the legal profession and the diamond and silver trades. The area of St. Pancras, further N, was still rural until the coming of the railways, when St. Pancras and Kings Cross stations (→Railway Stations) changed it into an industrial quarter.

▶ **Lincoln's Inn Fields**, one of London's largest squares, has **Sir John Soane's Museum** (*Tue.-Sat., 10-5; Cl. Sun., Bank Hols.*), the architect's home, exactly as he left it, with models and drawings of his work and that of Robert Adam; drawings and etchings by Piranesi, paintings by Hogarth, Canaletto, Reynolds, Turner, and, at the rear (the Crypt), his collection of Egyptian, Greek and Roman antiquities. ▶ Across the square is the **Old Curiosity Shop** (1567), after Dickens' novel of the same name (but not the actual one), selling gifts and curios. ▶ **Lincoln's Inn**, in its own grounds, is one of the legal Inns of Court, with the **old hall** (1492), the **gatehouse** (1518) and **chapel** (1619; *restricted opening hours*). ▶ Chancery Lane has the **Public Records Office Museum** (*Mon.-Fri., 1-4*) with a copy of the Domesday Book and many letters and documents dating back to the 14thC; also the London Silver Vaults (*Mon.-Fri., 9-5.30, Sat., 9-12.30*). ▶ **Staple Inn** with its **hall** (1580) is fronted by timbered houses (1586) that recall London before the Great Fire. ▶ The Victorian **Holborn Viaduct** (just in the City) crosses Farringdon Street, the old course of the Fleet River. ▶ **Hatton Garden**, a street, is London's diamond and jewelry centre. There is also an old charity school (1696) with the figures of two children; in adjoining Ely Place, **St. Ethelreda's Church** with crypt (1251) and fragments of Roman wall. In the connecting passageway is **Ye Olde Mitre** pub (1546). ▶ **Gray's Inn**, another of the Inns of Court, has the **gatehouse** (1688), rebuilt **hall** with Tudor paneling said to come from the wood of a Spanish galleon, and a statue to Sir Francis Bacon, patron of the Inn, who laid out the gardens. ▶ **Bedford Row** and **Doughty Street** are fine Georgian terraces, the latter with **Dickens' House** (*Mon.-Sat., 10-5; Cl. Bank Hols.*), with mementoes of the novelist. ▶ **Coram Fields**, now a children's park, the site of the Foundling Hospital, established by Thomas Coram (1742). The **Thomas Coram Foundation** (*Mon.-Fri., 10-4; Cl. for conferences*) includes items from the hospital's patrons, paintings by Hogarth, a fair copy of Handel's *Messiah* and other scores. ▶ **St. Pancras New Church** (1822), modeled on the Erechtheion and other antique Athenian landmarks. ▶ **St. Pancras Old Church** has Saxon origins and Norman features; Sir John Soane is buried here, in his own mausoleum. □

▶ HOUSES OF PARLIAMENT*

map 2-C3/Underground: Westminster. Bus: 3, 11, 12, 24, 29, 53, 88.

Officially the Palace of Westminster, there being a palace on the site since the time of Edward the Confessor (1042-66). Almost from the start, it was also a place for debate (a parliament) and legislation, by stages becoming the main seat of government, and the scene of such dramatic events as the Gunpowder Plot (1605) and Charles I's demand for five members of the House of Commons (1642), the prelude to Civil War. In 1834 fire destroyed most of the area, and the present Gothic Revival building (1837-60), with 1000 rooms and two miles of corridors, rose in its place

Cockneys

Strictly speaking, the only true cockneys are those Londoners who are born within the sound of Bow Bells. In days gone by, the street traders and other working people in the East End evolved a language of their own which made them unintelligible to outsiders. This 'rhyming slang' as it is known, was developed, it is said, to confuse the police who were always ready to pounce on the market trades for obstruction and other forms of public nuisance. Two or three words would be substituted for the word intended — the only connection being that they rhymed. Thus 'apples and pears' stood for 'stairs', 'Hampstead Heath' for 'teeth' and 'bacon and eggs' for 'legs'. To make matters more confusing, only the first word of the phrase would be used in conversation: so if a man commented on a girl's lovely bacons, he would be referring to her legs, and if he said he'd lost his uncle he would really mean he couldn't find his shirt (from 'Uncle Bert'). 'Hat' was abbreviated to 'titfer' (from 'tit for tat'). While the East End community is not as tightly knit as it was 100 years ago and rhyming slang is no longer quite the private code it once was, many of the words and phrases have been more universally adopted. Many Londoners and others, for example, frequently say that somebody talkative 'rabbits on' without realizing that they are actually using the short form of 'rabbit and pork'. Cockney traders had their own ceremonial dress too. This was quite unlike everyday market wear and consisted of suits of clothes each decorated with thousands of mother-of-pearl buttons, sewn overlapping each other to make patterns. With these costumes the men would wear silk mufflers and the women, enormous ostrich feather hats. Those entitled to sport such finery were called pearly kings and queens and were elected by the different boroughs from among the important members of the street trading community. In the past, these 'kings' and 'queens' did charity work for the old and poor in their areas, and once a year would attend a special harvest festival service in the Old Kent Road. Although the service still takes place (now in St. Martin's-in-the-Fields), there are few 'pearlies' left. However, the Pearly King of the city of London still attends Petticoat Lane market every Sunday.

to designs by Sir Charles Barry and Augustus Welby Pugin. It was damaged in WWII and restored by Sir Giles Gilbert Scott.

▶ The two main external features, best seen from Westminster Bridge or from across the river, are the **Victoria Tower** and the **Clock Tower**, known as **Big Ben** after the bell that strikes every hour. ▶ In **Old Palace Yard** is a statue of Richard I (the Lionheart); facing the Victoria Tower is the **Jewel Tower**, a part of the old palace, and beyond, the **Victoria Tower Gardens**, with a cast of Rodin's *Burghers of Calais* inspired by an event in Anglo-French history. ▶ **Westminster Hall**, with its massive hammer-beam roof (1400) is the major surviving part of the old palace. It has seen royal banquets, the trials of Sir Thomas More, Anne Boleyn, Guy Fawkes and Charles I, the proclamation of Oliver Cromwell as Lord Protector (his statue stands outside), and, in more recent times, the lying-in-state of Sir Winston Churchill. ▶ **St. Stephen's Hall** connects it to the Central Lobby, thence to the House of Commons, with the Speaker's Chair, the Table of the House on which

stands the mace. ▶ The **Royal Entrance**, beneath the Victoria Tower, leads to the most richly decorated apartments: the Robing Room, Royal Gallery and the **House of Lords** with the Throne for State Openings of Parliament and the woolsack for the Lord Chancellor (*access to House of Commons debates by queuing or application to your M.P.; tours of Westminster Hall by application to M.P.*). □

▶ HYDE PARK**

map 2-B2/Underground: Hyde Park Corner, Marble Arch. Bus: 9, 12, 14, 15, 19, 22, 30, 52, 73, 74, 88.

Bordered by Park Lane, Knightsbridge and Bayswater Road, and merging to the W with Kensington Gardens, Hyde Park was first opened to the public in 1637, when it was still on the outskirts of the capital. It has served as military camp and arsenal, duelling ground and haunt of footpads, fashionable carriage and riding venue, and in 1851 as the site of the Great Exhibition (the Crystal Palace). In 1961 it lost some of its land to the widening of Park Lane, but remains London's most accessible and popular open space.

▶ **Hyde Park Corner**, the junction of Park Lane, Knightsbridge and Piccadilly, has WWI memorials to the Royal Artillery and Machine Gun Corps; a statue to the Duke of Wellington; and Decimus Burton's Greek-Corinthian Constitution Arch (1827), crowned by the bronze chariot of Victory, and Greek-Ionic Scree, both originally planned as a royal link between Buckingham Palace (→) and the park. ▶ **Apsley House** (Robert Adam, 1771-1829; *Tue.-Thu., Sat., 10-6, Sun., 2-6; Cl. Bank Hols.*), Wellington's home contains household and military effects, paintings by Correggio, Vermeer, Brueghel, Rubens, Velazquez, Goya; also mementoes of Napoleon. ▶ Facing Apsley House from the park is the **Achilles** statue (1822), cast in bronze from captured French guns, another tribute to Wellington. ▶ **Rotten Row** (*route du roi*) is an equestrian way. William III had lamps hung from the trees — the first English roadway to be lit. ▶ The **Serpentine**, now a boating lake and swimming pool, was created 1730 by damming the Westbourne River. Nearby is the old Powder Magazine (1805). ▶ **Speaker's Corner**, at the junction of Park Lane, Bayswater Road and Oxford Street, designated a place of public debate 1872, is famous for its orators. Across the roadway is Marble Arch (1827), Nash's entrance to Buckingham Palace, moved to its present site 1851. □

▶ IMPERIAL WAR MUSEUM*

map 2-C3/Underground: Lambeth North, Elephant Castle. Bus: 1, 3, 12, 53, 63, 68, 159, 171, 188.

Founded in 1917 and devoted mainly to British Empire and Commonwealth involvement in the two World Wars, the museum is housed in what was part of the Bethlehem Royal Hospital for the Insane (Bedlam). The dome and portico were added in 1838 by Sydney Smirke, architect of the British Museum Reading Room.

▶ WWI Mark V tank, **Sopwith Camel** combat aircraft, 'Ole Bill' London bus troop carrier. ▶ WWII RAF **Spitfire** fighter aircraft, RAF Lancaster bomber fuselage, Italian manned torpedo, German V flying bomb. ▶ **Drawings and paintings** by British war artists: Henry Moore, Paul Nash, John Piper, Laura Knight, Augustus John; in addition, frequent special exhibitions and film shows. The museum also maintains the Cabinet War Rooms (→Whitehall) and *HMS Belfast* (→Thames; *Mon.-Sat., 10-5.30, Sun., 2-5.30*). □

▶ KENSINGTON**

map 2-A3/Underground: Lancaster Gate, High Street Kensington, South Kensington.

Part of the district, on rising ground above the old Thames flood plain, attracted the aristocracy from the 17thC on, their dwellings — Campden House, Holland House, Gore House — remembered in local place names. William and Mary's move to Kensington Palace enhanced its reputation still more. Prosperous urban growth in the 19thC, plus great public buildings and institutions, has maintained Kensington's prestige.

▶ **Kensington Gardens** are a continuation of Hyde Park (→), with the Fountain Garden, Queen Anne's Alcove (Wren), Peter Pan's statue and G.F. Watt's *Physical Energy*. Nearby is the 18thC Round Pond. ▶ Still in Kensington Gardens, the **Serpentine Art Gallery**, once a tea-house, has frequent exhibitions. ▶ The Gothic-Revival **Albert Memorial** (1872) to Queen Victoria's husband Prince Albert, designed by Sir George Gilbert Scott, has figurative ornamental stonework. ▶ Facing it across Kensington Gore is Francis Fowke's massive **Royal Albert Hall** (1870), decorated outside by a frieze around the dome, *The Triumph of Art and Letters*. Inside is seating for 8,000 and a 150-ton organ, the world's largest when installed; home of the famous summer Promenade Concerts. ▶ Grouped around the Albert Hall are the Royal Colleges of Art, of Organists and of Music, and the Imperial College of Science with Italianate tower and dome. ▶ **Kensington Palace** (1690; *Mon.-Sat., 9-5, Sun., 1-5*), on the W edge of the gardens, is part Jacobean but mainly the work of Wren and Hawksmoor, commissioned by William III. Queen Victoria was born there. The King's Staircase has murals by William Kent, and the Gallery paintings by Rubens and Van Dyck; 17th and 18thC furnishings, personal mementoes of Queen Victoria and a collection of court dresses. By the Broad Walk is the Sunken Garden and Orangery. ▶ Just off Kensington High Street is **Kensington Square**, one of the oldest and best preserved, with plaques to famous inhabitants. ▶ Further down the High Street are the **Commonwealth Institute** (1962; *Mon.-Sat., 10-5.30, Sun., 2-5*) with exhibits from 40 Commonwealth countries, plus film, theatre and dance shows; **Leighton House** (1866; *Mon.-Sat., 11-5; Cl. Bank Hols.*), home of the Victorian painter Lord Leighton, with a mosaic Arab Hall and 19thC paintings. ▶ Behind is **Holland Park** and **House** (1606), Jacobean in origin, but bombed in WWII and much restored; setting for open-air plays and concerts. ▶ Situated close together are the **Natural History** (→), **Science** (→) and **Victoria and Albert** (→) Museums; plus the **Geological Museum** (*Mon.-Sat., 10-6, Sun., 2.30-6*), with displays of fossils, gemstones and a piece of the moon. ▶ On Queen's Gate is **Baden Powell House** (*daily 8-10.30 p.m.*) with a memorial exhibition to the founder of the Scout Association. □

▶ KEW GARDENS**

map 1-A1-2/Underground: Kew Gardens. British Rail: Kew Bridge.

The Royal Botanical Gardens, Kew (*winter 10-4 daily, summer 10-8*) grew in size and splendour under royal patronage from the 17thC onward. In 1772 they were landscaped by Lancelot Capability Brown; in 1841, the 300-acre gardens, with over 20,000 species of plant, were given to the nation, both as a park and as a scientific institution.

▶ **Kew Palace**, also known as the Dutch House, a Jacobean mansion by the river, has a 17thC herbal garden. ▶ Other monuments to royal patronage include the **Orangery**, three 18thC Greek-style temples, the **Pagoda**, the

Queen's Cottage, a thatched summerhouse and **King William's Temple**. ▶ The two largest conservatories, both designed by Decimus Burton and the engineer Richard Turner, are the **Palm House** (1844), the finest iron and glass structure of its day, and the **Temperate House** (1860). ▶ The General Museum faces the Palm House across the pond. ▶ The **Japanese Gate** commemorates an exhibition. ▶ The **Marianne North Gallery** has a collection of over 800 botanical paintings by the artist. ▶ Close by is the 225-ft. flagstaff, made from the trunk of a Douglas fir, presented by the government of British Columbia. ▶ **Kew Green**, by the main entrance to the gardens, is graced by Georgian and Regency houses. The interior of St. Anne's (1710-70), like the gardens, has benefitted from royal patronage; Thomas Gainsborough is buried there.   □

▶ **KNIGHTSBRIDGE AND BELGRAVIA***

map 2-B2/Underground: Hyde Park Corner, Victoria, Knightsbridge.

Knightsbridge takes its name from an old bridge over the River Westbourne (→Hyde Park, the Serpentine), where two legendary knights met in combat. Through the 17th and 18thC, both it and adjoining Belgravia were neglected in favour of Kensington (→) to the W. But in the 19thC they grew rapidly, becoming one of London's most exclusive areas, with embassies, institutions, famous shops and department stores.

▶ Facing Hyde Park Corner (→Hyde Park) is the Classical-Revival building of **St. George's Hospital** (1827). ▶ Behind it is elegant **Wilton Crescent**; also **Belgrave Square** (1825-40), one of London's grandest, planned by Thomas Cubitt and George Bavesi in Regency style. A recent addition is a statue to Simon Bolivar. ▶ Neighbouring **Eaton Square** (1826-53), also planned by Cubitt, is really a rectangle divided by the Kings Road. In keeping with its equally grand appearance, it has been the home of three prime ministers: Russell, Baldwin, Chamberlain. **St. Peter's Church** (1824), in the Classical-Revival style harmonizes well. ▶ **Harrods** (1905), one of the world's most famous department stores, with over 13 acres of shop space; interior decoration includes Art Nouveau tiling (main food hall) and Art Deco motifs. ▶ **Brompton Oratory** (1884), named after the Oratory of St. Philip Neri, Rome, was London's main Catholic church until the opening of Westminster Cathedral (→Victoria and Pimlico); in Italian Baroque style, with statues of saints from Siena Cathedral. ▶ Nearby is **All Saints Church** (1846-92), with unusual facade and campanile in the style of an Italian basilica; now Russian Orthodox.   □

▶ **LAMBETH***

map 2-C3/Underground: Waterloo, Oval, Lambeth North. Bus: 12, 53, 68, 188.

Lambeth was marshland until the 18thC, when London began to spread S of the Thames. Its greatest attraction then was the Vauxhall Pleasure Gardens, featured in many period plays, novels and pictures. When the gardens finally disappeared in 1859, the rest of Lambeth was a large South London suburb, supported by such local industries as the Doulton pottery works and the railway into Waterloo (→Railway Stations).

▶ **Lambeth Palace**, the Archbishop of Canterbury's London residence for seven centuries, and for long the only notable building across the river from Westminster (→), with 13thC vaulted crypt, Tudor gatehouse and great hall; used for church functions and not generally open to the public. ▶ Across the road, by St. Thomas's Hospital, is **Albert Embankment**, with a fine view of the Houses of Parliament (→). ▶ Beyond Westminster Bridge is **County Hall** (1919), whose future is currently in doubt after the 1986 abolition of the Greater London Council. ▶ Beyond that again is the South Bank Arts Centre (→). ▶ The **Old Vic Theatre**, Waterloo Road, opened in 1818, was distinguished by its one-time association with the Sadler's Wells opera and ballet companies (→Clerkenwell and Finsbury), and was the first home of the National Theatre (now part of the South Bank complex). ▶ In neighbouring Southwark is the Imperial War Museum (→). ▶ S of Lambeth is the famous Kennington Oval cricket ground.   □

▶ **MADAME TUSSAUD'S AND THE LONDON PLANETARIUM***

map 2-B1/Marylebone Road. Underground: Baker Street. Bus: 30, 74, 159.

Madame Tussaud began her waxworks in Paris during the French Revolution, and opened her first London exhibition in 1835. In 1884, her grandsons moved the exhibition to the present building, where it remains the world's most famous waxworks show. The Planetarium, built on an adjoining WWII bomb site, was opened in 1958.

▶ Madame Tussaud's self-portrait. ▶ The **Grand Hall**: British monarchs, world statesmen, military leaders, writers and artists. ▶ **The Conservatory**: film and TV stars. ▶ **Superstars** from the worlds of sport and popular entertainment. ▶ The **Tableaux**, famous historical scenes, or scenes taken from pictures. ▶ The **Battle of Trafalgar**, on board *HMS Victory* and the Death of Nelson. ▶ The **Chamber of Horrors**: murderers and scenes of crime, instruments of torture and execution. ▶ **The Planetarium** (*daily ex. Christmas, 11-4.30*). ▶ The **Auditorium**, where images of stars, sun, moon, planets are projected onto a multi-dimensional screen. ▶ The **Astronomer's Gallery**, with tableaux, paintings and models tracing the history of astronomy (*Apr.-Sep.: daily, 10-6; Oct.-Mar.: daily ex. Christmas, 10-5.30*).   □

▶ **THE MALL***

map 2-C2/Underground: Charing Cross. Bus: 3, 6, 9, 11, 12, 15, 24, 29, 53, 88, 159.

At the Restoration (1660), The Mall became a popular promenade on the N side of St. James's Park (→). The building of Nash's terraces in the early 19thC added grandeur to the scene, and it was replanned (1910) by Sir Aston Webb as a processional route from Buckingham Palace (→) to Trafalgar Square.

▶ **Admiralty Arch** (1910) marks The Mall's E end. On the S side is the rear of the Admiralty, and the WWII Citadel, a bombproof communications centre; also a statue to explorer Capt.Cook. ▶ On the N side is Nash's **Carlton House Terrace** (1837), last and grandest of his Regency projects. The one-time home of Prime Ministers Palmerston and Gladstone, the terrace now houses various institutions, including the **Institute of Contemporary Arts** (*Tue.-Sun., 12-9*), with gallery, cinema, video library, restaurant; and **The Mall Galleries** (*daily 10-5*); both have changing exhibitions. ▶ Dividing the terrace are the **Duke of York Steps** and **Memorial Column** (1834). ▶ Set back from The Mall is **St. James's Palace** (16thC), Henry VIII's Tudor residence, later modified by Wren, Gibbons, Hawksmoor, Kent; no longer a royal residence, it retains ceremonial functions: newly arrived ambassadors are 'accredited to the Court of St. James'. ▶ Facing it on

Marlborough Road is Inigo Jones' **Queen's Chapel** (1627), built for Charles I's Queen Henrietta Maria, London's earliest Classical-Revival church. ▶ Next to the palace is Nash's **Clarence House** (1825), still a royal residence; then **Lancaster House** (1825), with splendid interior decor, now a government reception and conference centre (*limited public access*). ▶ The Queen Victoria Memorial (1910) marks the W end of The Mall. ▶ **Waterloo Place** (beyond Duke of York Steps) marks the S end of Nash's Regent Street (→), with the **Guards Crimea Memorial**, partly made from captured Russian cannon, and including a statue of Florence Nightingale; also a statue to explorer Capt.Scott. ▶ A commemorative plaque marks General de Gaulle's WWII Free French HQ in Carlton Gardens. ▶ The **Athaneum** (Decimus Burton, 1828), in Classical-Revival style, is London's most distinguished club. ▶ Adjacent is **Pall Mall**, named after a popular 17thC game similar to croquet, the address of other famous clubs. ▶ **St. James's Square** (c. 1670) has the **London Library**, founded 1842 by Thomas Carlyle. The equestrian statue to William III (1808) includes the molehill that caused his fatal riding accident. □

▶ MARKETS*

Many of London's markets were regularized during the 19thC and dignified by handsome halls, galleries and arcades. Some of these, like the famous Billingsgate fish market (→City) have closed, others still flourish, with mainly wholesale but some retail outlets. More lively are the various street markets, trading in a wide variety of commodities, from oranges to antiques. Only the best known are listed here.

▶ **Leadenhall**, a mainly poultry market since the 14thC, on the site of a Roman basilica, housed in a fine Classical-Revival arcade (1881). ▶ **Smithfield**, another 14thC market dealing in cattle, established 1868 as London's premier meat market with extensive new trading halls, originally including a special station linking it with the mainline railway termini. ▶ **Spitalfields**, an old fruit and vegetable market, then one that specialized in silks at the time of Huguenot émigrés, re-opened 1928 for fruit and vegetables. ▶ **New Covent Garden**, or **Nine Elms**, moved to specially built new premises from the original Covent Garden (→) 1974, both London's and Britain's largest fruit, vegetable and flower market. ▶ **Borough**, London's oldest fruit and vegetable market, still operating. ▶ **Petticoat Lane** (Middlesex Street), most famous of London's street markets; in Victorian times it specialized in secondhand clothing; now operates on Sundays, with both clothing and food stalls. ▶ **Berwick Street**, Soho, another well-known street market for food, clothes and other domestic items. ▶ **Portobello Road** began as a Victorian street market, but since WWII has specialized in antiques and general bric-a-brac; Saturday the busiest day. ▶ **Camden Passage**, antique market in the fashionable part of Islington. □

▶ MAYFAIR*

map 2-B2/Underground: Hyde Park Corner, Marble Arch, Oxford Circus. Bus: 3, 6, 7, 12, 15, 30, 53, 74, 88, 159.

A cattle market or fair was held in the vicinity each May until the early 18thC. Residential building first started round the three main squares — Hanover, Berkeley, Grosvenor — moving London's fashionable centre of gravity N and W from Westminster (→) and the Thames (→). Most of Mayfair's great town houses have been replaced by embassies, prestige offices and salesrooms, But its excellent street plan and situation have kept it at the top of the social scale.

Street markets

You can still buy practically everything needed for everyday life (and much else besides) if you know where to look in London's street markets. These have a long and flourishing tradition, dating back to Roman times when London was established, at the lowest crossing point on the River Thames, as a trading post and a port. Numerous London street names indicate the former sites of specialist trading - Bread Street, Ironmonger Lane, Wood Street and Leather Lane tell clearly what used to be sold here. Medieval traders all dealing in one product would group together in guilds in order to protect themselves from excessive trading regulations and traffic.

The product which took up most space was the hay - in enormous quantities - needed to feed London's horses which, until the end of the last century, pulled virtually every kind of transport used in the capital. This was sold not only at Haymarket, but at Whitechapel and Smithfields too. And streets like Cheapside would have been trading centres early in London's history, for the Anglo-Saxon word 'ceap' meant 'market'.

Although many of the markets have changed their location and what they sell, the street trading tradition is still very strong. Some date from only the last ten years or less (the Hampstead Community, Jubilee and Swiss Cottage markets, for instance); some have vanished leaving streets or shops instead (Oxford Street); many sell everything as at Brick Lane, others tend to specialize: Bermondsey, Portobello and Camden Passage for antiques, Columbia Road for plants. Some are open six days a week (Chapel Street and North End Road), others take place once or twice a week (Brick Lane).

Markets have always reflected the character of the surrounding inhabitants, and while Petticoat Lane is a traditionally Jewish area connected with the rag trade (clothes), many of the other East London markets now have a distinctively Asian flavour, while South London's Brixton market offers an exotic range of Caribbean fruits, vegetables, fish and other food unknown elsewhere in London, resounding to the noise of reggae records which are also for sale.

▶ **Park Lane**, running along the E side of Hyde Park (→) has some of London's most famous hotels — Grosvenor House, The Dorchester and the tall London Hilton (1963). A few elegant town houses facing the park remain. ▶ **Curzon Street** has Georgian terraced houses; also Crewe House (1730) in its own grounds; and almost opposite, **Shepherd Market**, named after architect Edward Shepherd, an enclave of small shops, restaurants and pubs. ▶ **The Royal Institution**, Albermarle Street, has the **Michael Faraday Museum** (*Tue.-Thu., 1-4; Cl. Bank Hols.*), a restoration of the scientist's laboratory. ▶ **Berkeley Square** has 18th and 19thC houses on its W side. ▶ The **Church of the Immaculate Conception** (1844), Farm Street, headquarters of the English Jesuits, has a notable Gothic-Revivial interior and high altar by Pugin. ▶ **Grosvenor Chapel** (1739), South Audley Street, is in American colonial style. ▶ **Grosvenor Square** (1731), one of London's largest, was for long its most exclusive address. In WWII no. 20 was General Eisenhower's headquarters, and the American connection remains, with the U.S. Embassy (1959) and statue to President Roosevelt (1948). ▶ **Hanover Square** (1720) E of Bond Street (→), is named after George I, formerly Elector of Hanover. The

Hanover Square Rooms (demolished 1900), on the E side, were London's premier concert hall, where J.C. Bach, Haydn, Paganini and Liszt all performed. ▶ **St. George's Church** (1724), just to the S, has seen many famous weddings — Lady Hamilton, Shelley, Disraeli, George Eliot, Asquith; two cast-iron dogs in the porch are a notable feature.   □

▶ NATIONAL GALLERY*

map 2-C2/Trafalgar Square. Underground: Charing Cross. Bus: 3, 6, 9, 11, 12, 15, 24, 29, 53, 88, 159.

Founded 1824, with a nucleus of 38 pictures, the National Gallery now houses the nation's most valuable collection of over 2000 paintings, from early Italian Renaissance to French post-Impressionism. The building, on the N side of Trafalgar Square, was designed by William Wilkins (1838). There have been several extensions, and another is planned.

▶ Early Italian Renaissance — Duccio, Masaccio, Uccello (*Battle of San Romano*), Piero della Francesca (*Baptism of Christ*), Mantegna, Bellini, Botticelli (rooms 1-6, 10-13). ▶ High Renaissance — Leonardo da Vinci (cartoon, *The Virgin and Child*), Raphael, Michelangelo, Titian (*Bacchus and Ariadne*), Tintoretto, Veronese (rooms 7-9, 14, 30). Early Northern School — Van Eyck, Bosch, Brueghel, Dürer, Holbein (*The Ambassadors*; rooms 23-25). Dutch and Flemish Schools — Frans Hals, Rembrandt (*Self-Portrait*), Vermeer, de Hooch, Rubens (*Portrait, The Straw Hat*), Van Dyck (*Equestrian Portrait of Charles I*; rooms 15-22, 27, 28). ▶ Italian and French Schools, 17th/18thC — Caravaggio, Giordano, Tiepolo, Canaletto, Poussin, Claude (rooms 29, 32-34). Spanish School — El Greco, Velasquez (*The Toilet of Venus*), Murillo, Goya (rooms 41, 42). ▶ British School — Hogarth, Gainsborough, Reynolds, Stubbs, Constable (*The Hay Wain*), Turner (*The Fighting Temeraire*; rooms 35, 36, 38, 39). ▶ French Impressionist and post-Impressionist — Manet, Degas, Cezanne (*Bathers*), Monet, Renoir, Seurat, Van Gogh (*Sunflowers*; rooms 40, 43, 46; *Mon.-Sat., 10-5.30, Sun., 2-5.30; Cl. I Jan., Good Fri., May Day, 24-26 Dec.*).   □

▶ NATIONAL PORTRAIT GALLERY*

map 2-C2/St. Martins Place. Underground: Charing Cross, Leicester Square. Bus: 3, 6, 9, 11,12, 15, 24, 29, 53, 88, 159.

Founded in 1856, the gallery moved to its present building, at the rear of the National Gallery (→), in 1895. It has over 8000 portraits, cartoons and caricatures of famous British men and women, from Tudor times to the present day. There are also many portrait photographs.

▶ Henry VII, Henry VIII, Sir Thomas More by Hobein; Gladstone and Disraeli by Millais; self-portraits by Hogarth, Reynolds, Gainsborough; the Bronte Sisters by brother Branwell; Sir Winston Churchill by Sickert; T.S. Eliot by Epstein (*Mon.-Fri., 10-5, Sat., 10-6, Sun., 2-6; Cl. I Jan., Good Fri., May Day, 24-26 Dec.*).   □

▶ NATURAL HISTORY MUSEUM*

map 2-A3/Cromwell Road. Underground: South Kensington. Bus: 14, 30, 74.

In 1881 the natural history section of the British Museum (→) moved to its new premises in South Kensington. The building, by Alfred Waterhouse, is the most colourful and fanciful of all London's museums. It has accumulated some 40 million specimens (many of them insects), the collection growing annually by about 300,000 specimens.

▶ Ground floor: dinosaurs and their living relatives. Central Hall: fossil mammals; fossil invertebrates and fishes; birds, insects, spiders; whales; human biology; ecology and wildlife in danger. ▶ First floor: Darwin and The Origin of Species ; ▶ Man's place in evolution. ▶ Second floor: British natural history. (*Mon.-Sat., 10-6, Sun., 2.30-6; Cl. I Jan., Good Fri., May Day, 24-26 Dec.*).   □

▶ OSTERLEY HOUSE*

map 1-A1/Thornbury Road. Underground: Osterley.

Set in extensive parkland in West London, Osterley House was originally built by Sir Thomas Gresham, financier to Elizabeth I. It was remodeled several times, most notably by Robert Adam (1763-7), the interior decoration being one of the finest achievements.

▶ The most notable exterior feature is Adam's Greek-Ionic double entrance portico; **entrance hall** with double apse, ceiling with floral scrolls, marble floor; **drawing room**, rich in gilding and other ornamentation, with French Neoclassical sofas and chairs; **library** with furniture and fittings by John Linnell, leading 18thC cabinet-maker; **tapestry room** with Adam motifs, very fine Gobelin tapestries and chairs in matching style (*Apr.-Sep.: Tue.-Sun., 2-6; Oct.-Mar.: Tue.-Sun., 12-4; Cl. I Jan., Good Fri., May Day, 24-26 Dec.*).   □

▶ OXFORD STREET AND BOND STREET

map 2-B2/Underground: Marble Arch, Bond Street, Oxford Circus. Bus: 6, 7, 12, 15, 30, 73, 74, 88, 159.

Oxford Street, dividing Mayfair (→) from Marylebone to the N, was for long known as Tyburn Way, leading to the public place of execution at its W end (now Marble Arch). Though the start of a one-time road to Oxford, it takes its name from the Earl of Oxford, who began its 18thC development. By the end of the 19thC it was London's principal shopping street. Bond Street (Old and New), named after Sir Thomas Bond, 17thC court financier, and the home of William Pitt the Elder, Lord Nelson and Lady Hamilton, is the capital's most exclusive centre for luxury goods and antiques.

▶ Oxford Street's largest department store is **Selfridge's**, built 1909 by American businessman Gordon Selfridge, in massive Greek-Revival style, with clock and figure ('The Queen of Time') over the main entrance; famous for its Christmas window displays. ▶ Two other leading stores are D.H. Evans and John Lewis. ▶ **Sotheby's** (Sotheby Parke Bernet) of New Bond Street, world-famous fine art auctioneers, was founded in 1744, and moved to its present address in 1917; the sculpture over the door is Egyptian (c. 1600 B.C.). ▶ On N side of Oxford Street, **St. Peter's Church**, Vere Street (1721): windows by Burne-Jones. ▶ **Portman Square** (1764) has the **Courtauld Institute of Art** (Robert Adam, 1775). ▶ In **Cavendish Square** (1717) is the **Convent of the Holy Child**, with Epstein's sculpture *Madonna and Child* (1953) over the entrance. ▶ Linking the two squares is Wigmore Street, with the Wigmore (formerly Bechstein) Hall concert room. ▶ Just off Baker Street is Manchester Square and the Wallace Collection (→).   □

▶ PICCADILLY AND HAYMARKET*

map 2-B2/Underground: Green Park, Piccadilly Circus.
Bus: 3, 6, 9, 14, 15, 19, 22, 53, 88, 159.

Piccadilly owes its name to a 17thC dressmaker who grew rich making a type of frilly collar called a 'picadil', and built a house in the vicinity. The thoroughfare, with Green Park on the S side for much of its length, was largely developed by the mid-18thC, with some of London's most palatial homes. Increasing traffic turned it from a residential street into the main commercial artery of London's West End. The Haymarket, a wide street of theatres and cinemas, was once a hay, straw and cattle market. The two thoroughfares encompass the area of St. James's, with its famous clubs.

▶ **Green Park**, with Piccadilly on the N side and Constitution Hill on the S, has seen some famous events, notably the fireworks display celebrating the Peace of Aix-la-Chapelle (1748), for which Handel wrote his Royal Fireworks Music. ▶ By the park's NE corner is the **Ritz Hotel** (1906) in opulent French Empire style. ▶ Running from Piccadilly is **St. James's Street** with some famous London clubs: Boodle's (1765), Brook's (1778) and White's (1788). ▶ **Jermyn Street**, S of and parallel to Piccadilly, has some of London's oldest-established shops. **Piccadilly Arcade** connects the two streets. ▶ The oldest-established shop in Piccadilly itself is **Fortnum and Mason**, founded 1705. ▶ **St. James's Church**, Piccadilly (Wren, 1684) has a large, handsome interior, with reredos, font and organ case by Grinling Gibbons; attached to it is the **London Brass Rubbing Centre** (*Mon.-Sat., 10-6, Sun., 12-6*), with replica brasses from many churches. ▶ On Piccadilly's N side is **Burlington House** (1717 with extensions), home of the Royal Academy, the nation's oldest fine arts society, founded 1768 (*daily 10-6; Cl. Good Fri., Christmas*). Its permanent collection has paintings by Reynolds, Gainsborough, Stubbs, Turner and sculpture by Michelangelo; changing exhibitions throughout the year, including the famous Summer Exhibition. ▶ Behind Burlington House, in Burlington Gardens, is **The Museum of Mankind** (*Mon.-Sat., 10-5, Sun., 2.30-6; Cl. 1 Jan., Good Fri., May Day, 24-27 Dec.*), a branch of the British Museum (→), with ethnic exhibits from around the world. ▶ On the E side of Burlington House is **The Albany** (1774), one of Piccadilly's original residences, the address of many celebrities. ▶ On the other side is **Burlington Arcade** (1819). ▶ **Piccadilly Circus**, at the junction of Piccadilly, Regent Street (→) and Shaftesbury Avenue, is the hub of London's theatreland. Its most famous feature is the fountain and statue of **Eros**, erected 1893 as a memorial to philanthropist Lord Shaftesbury, and recently resited as part of a new traffic scheme. ▶ Neighbouring **Leicester Square**, once a residential precinct with statues ranging from Shakespeare to Charlie Chaplin and several big cinemas. ▶ The **Theatre Royal**, Haymarket (Nash, 1831), with Corinthian-Greek portico, is one of London's most handsome buildings. ▶ Facing it is **Her Majesty's Theatre**, the fourth such building on the site, behind which is the **Royal Opera Arcade** (Nash, 1818), London's earliest shopping arcade.　□

▶ PUBS*

Underground: Blackfriars, St. Paul's, Mansion House, Bank, Monument, Aldgate. Bus: 6, 9, 11, 15.

The City has nearly 200 public houses and wine bars — many catering for the working population and closed at weekends. All are in the tradition of British pubs, often places of strong local character. Some of the best known also enshrine as much of its history.

Coffee houses

An exotic new drink was brought to England in the 17thC: it had arrived in Europe from Arabia and was an infusion of coffee beans. The first coffee house was actually set up in Oxford, but in 1652, London's Cornhill had its own establishment in St. Michael's Alley. Soon there were many coffee houses in the city — along the Strand and Fleet Street. The new drink was supposed to be beneficial to the health — and to cure the effects of too many hours spent in the tavern. It certainly appeared to encourage conversations. In the club-like atmosphere of the coffee houses, men would meet to discuss politics, literature and gossip. Chocolate, imported from the West Indies, was soon drunk in similar surroundings. Distinguished men of the day such as Dr. Johnson, Samuel Pepys, David Garrick, Joseph Addison and Richard Steele frequented such places and in time the coffee and chocolate houses developed their specialist interests from the subjects discussed there. The Tatler magazine, founded by Steele in 1709, first reported 'entertainment' from White's Chocolate House, 'poetry' from Will's Coffee House, and 'foreign and domestic news' from St. James's Coffee House. The Spectator was brought out by Steele and Addison shortly afterwards. Newspapers printed in relatively small quantities were circulated among the coffee and chocolate drinkers, and gradually newspaper offices crowded out the coffee houses in Fleet Street. Business talk at Lloyd's coffee house became a business in itself as Lloyd's became and remained one of the most important names in the world of insurance, and establishments like White's Chocolate House developed into the select gentlemen's clubs they are today.

▶ **Cock Tavern**, Fleet Street, with reminders of Pepys and of its days as a chop house frequented by Dickens. ▶ **Cheshire Cheese**, Fleet Street, largely 17thC oak-beamed building, also with a literary past — Johnson, Boswell, Dickens, Thackeray, Conan Doyle. ▶ Between them is **El Vino's** wine bar, traditional haunt of journalists, where women were not served until 1982. ▶ **Punch Tavern**, with original drawings and cartoons from *Punch* magazine. ▶ **Magpie and Stump**, facing the Central Criminal Court (Old Bailey), with memories of Newgate Prison and public executions. ▶ **Olde Watling**, built by Wren and frequented by him during work on St. Paul's; named after the Roman road on which it stands. ▶ **Samuel Pepys**, in a Thames wharf, with mementoes of the diarist. ▶ **Williamson's Tavern**, 17thC, one-time residence of Lord Mayors, visited by William and Mary, with wrought-iron gates commemorating this; a stone marks the City centre. ▶ **Olde Dr Butler's Head**, restored 17thC; named after a quack physician to James I. ▶ **George and Vulture**, restored 18thC, associated with Dickens' *Pickwick Papers*. ▶ **Jamaica Wine House**, probably also London's first coffee house. ▶ **Square Rigger**, furnished in the style of an 18thC sailing ship. ▶ **Olde Wine Shades**, wine bar founded 1663, with relics of its past. ▶ **Hoop and Grapes**: 13thC foundations, mostly 17thC restored; oldest City pub with many relics.　□

▶ RAILWAY STATIONS*

Britain led the world in railway construction, the first in London being the Greenwich to London Bridge

railway (1836). Soon after, railway companies started building terminus stations linking London with the rest of the country, completely changing the capital's appearance and character in the process. The number of companies and the intense competition between them explain the large number of stations, even for a city of London's size. Some are of outstanding architectural and engineering interest.

▶ **Euston** (1968), London's newest mainline station, but on the site of Robert Stephenson's original 1837 station, and near the historic spot where Richard Tevithick demonstrated his pioneer steam locomotive 'Catch Me Who Can' in 1808. ▶ Near neighbours along the Euston Road are **Kings Cross** (1851), whose handsome structure remains virtually intact, though obscured by the approach, and **St. Pancras**, notable for its arched roof (1866), once the world's widest single span (245 ft.), and for Sir George Gilbert Scott's massive Gothic-Revival hotel and offices (1872). ▶ **Paddington's** splendid triple-arch iron and glass roof (1851) is the work of Isambard Kingdom Brunel; the adjoining hotel (Philip Hardwick, 1854) is equally grand inside. ▶ **Victoria**, long known as 'The Gateway to the Continent', the main rail link between London and the rest of Europe, was the scene of many ceremonial arrivals and departures; adjoining Grosvenor Hotel (1861) is correspondingly opulent. ▶ **Waterloo**, the largest after construction (1900-22), was originally planned to continue across the river into the City. In 1854 there was an adjacent station — long since demolished — serving a fashionable country cemetery, called the Necropolis Station. ▶ Large and busy **Liverpool Street**, **Cannon Street**, with imposing twin towers and above the river, **Blackfriars**, **Holborn Viaduct** and **Fenchurch Street** all penetrate the City. ▶ There are also **Charing Cross**, with another grand Victorian hotel and in the forecourt, a replica of the cross marking the resting place of a queen before burial in Westminster Abbey; **London Bridge**, the oldest in origin; and **Marylebone** (1899). □

▶ REGENT'S PARK**

map 2-B1/Underground: Baker Street, Regent's Park. Bus: 30, 74, 159.

Like most of London's other royal parks, Regent's Park was a hunting reserve. Its transformation dates from 1811, when John Nash, with backing from the Prince Regent (George IV), drew up plans to turn it into a luxurious residential estate or garden suburb. The result is the magnificent group of terraces along much of the park's perimeter, plus Park Crescent, leading to Portland Place and Regent Street (→).

▶ The grandest Regency terraces are **Chester** (1825) and **Cumberland** (1826) on the E side of the park, and **Hanover** (1823) on the W. ▶ Next to Hanover Terrace is the equally striking **Mosque** (1977), with the Islamic Cultural Centre adjoining. ▶ The Inner Circle road was a part of Nash's original plan; it now encloses **Queen Mary's Garden** with fountain, pond, rose garden and restaurant, also the **Open Air Theatre**, first opened in 1933 for summer seasons, mainly of Shakespeare. ▶ Also by the Inner Circle is Bedford College, with an annexe in The Holme (Decimus Burton, 1819). ▶ The boating lake is also a part of Nash's original plan. ▶ The N side of the park is largely given over to the **Zoological Gardens** (*Mar.-Oct.: 9-6, daily; Nov.-Feb.: 10-6; Cl. Christmas*), founded 1826 and expanded from its original 5-acre site to the present 36 acres, with well over 1000 species of mammal, bird, reptile, fish and insect. The Zoological Society of London is a world centre of scientific study and research.

Nearby

▶ Near the park, in Marylebone Road, is Madame Tussaud's and the London Planetarium (→). ▶ In neighbouring Baker Street are the offices of the Abbey National

building society, on the site of what was the home of fictional detective Sherlock Holmes (no. 221B). ▶ By the W side of the park, facing Park Road, is **St. John's Wood Chapel** (Thomas Hardwick, 1813), and beyond that, **Lord's Cricket Ground**, headquarters of the MCC. The **Cricket Memorial Gallery** (*open match days 10.30-5, or by prior appointment*) has the famous Ashes trophy and other cricketing memorabilia. ▶ N of the park, in Regent's Park Road., is **Cecil Sharp House** (*Mon.-Fri., 9.30-5.30*), headquarters of the English Folk Song and Dance Society, with the **Vaughan Williams Memorial Library**. □

▶ REGENT STREET*

map 2-B2/Underground: Oxford Circus, Piccadilly Circus. Bus: 3, 6, 7, 9, 12, 14, 15, 19, 22, 53, 73, 88, 159.

This was part of John Nash's grand design (1811) linking Regent's Park (→), via Portland Place, with Carlton House, the Prince Regent's former palace on The Mall (→), at the same time creating a new NS thoroughfare for fashionable West London. Nash's own colonnaded section, called The Quadrant, was modified in 1848, and more changes were made from then on, until almost the entire street was rebuilt in the 1920s, creating the major shopping centre of today.

▶ At the meeting of Portland Place and Upper Regent Street is **Broadcasting House** (1931), with extensions, the BBC's main administrative and sound broadcasting centre. ▶ Next to it is **All Souls Church**, Langham Place (Nash, 1824), situated at a strategic point in Nash's original plan, and most original in design, with its circular portico and conical spire; bust of the architect by the entrance. ▶ Just S of Oxford Circus is Liberty's department store (1924-6): front section is in Neoclassical style, the slightly earlier part, in adjoining Great Marlborough Street, in mock-Tudor, with oak beams taken from two old sailing ships. Next to it is **Dickens and Jones** department store. ▶ On the N side of The Quadrant is the **Cafe Royal**, founded 1865, frequented by royalty and other celebrities. ▶ Further round The Quadrant are other famous London stores: Austin Reed, Aquascutum, Mappin and Webb (goldsmiths, silversmiths, jewelers). □

▶ RICHMOND**

map 1-A2/Underground: Richmond. British Rail: Richmond. Bus: 65, 71.

Richmond-on-Thames owes its name to Henry VII, who built a palace there, naming it Rychemond, after his estates in Yorkshire. The town prospered, thanks to his palace, its strategic position to other royal homes, at Kew (→), Hampton Court (→) and Windsor, and to its own attractive site. The coming of the railway brought fresh prosperity in the form of residential development. Together with its neighbouring park, it is one of London's most popular recreational areas.

▶ **The Green**, a Tudor jousting ground, retains many fine Georgian houses, notably those in **Maids of Honour Row**. The **Richmond Theatre** (1899) symbolizes the Green's theatrical past, marked by such figures as David Garrick, Edmund Kean and Mrs Siddons. ▶ Nearby are reminders of the **palace** (mostly destroyed during the Civil War), including the **gateway**, with Henry VII's coat-of-arms, the **Wardrobe** building, and the handsomely converted **Trumpeter's House** (once the home of Austrian statesman Metternich). ▶ By the river is **Asgill House** (1760), home of a past Lord Mayor of London. ▶ **Richmond Bridge** (1774),

though widened, retains its charm. ▶ Beyond the railway and Twickenham bridges is Richmond lock and footbridge. ▶ The parish church of **St. Mary Magdalene** is mainly Tudor, with some fine brasses and monuments (including one to Edmund Kean). ▶ **Richmond Hill** commands a splendid view of the river and Petersham meadows, much admired by Turner. **Wick House** (1771) was the home of Joshua Reynolds, who also painted the scene. ▶ **Richmond Park**, enclosed as a hunting reserve by Charles I, is the largest of the royal parks (2470 acres), noted for its deer and other wildlife, and for its ancient groves of oak trees. ▶ The **Isabella Plantation** has a profusion of shrubs and flowers. ▶ The top of **Sawyer's Hill**, near Richmond Gate, has a view of St. Paul's and the city of London to the E, and of Windsor Castle to the NW ▶ Two notable buildings in the park are **White Lodge** (1727), now a part of the Royal Ballet School and **Thatched House Lodge** (1670), a royal residence. A third, **Pembroke Lodge**, with surrounding gardens, is a cafeteria restaurant. Buses: 65, 71. ▶ A walk upstream, or a short bus ride, is Ham House (1610; *Apr.-Sep.: Tue.-Sun., 2-6; Oct.-Mar., Tue.-Sun., 12-4*): Jacobean furnishings, paintings, tapestries and gardens laid out in the same period style. □

▶ SCIENCE MUSEUM*
map 2-A3/Underground: South Kensington. Bus: 14, 30, 74.

The collection grew in a haphazard way from the middle of the 19thC, but now comprises Britain's foremost museum of science and industry. The building (1913), designed like a big department store, is ideal for the many large exhibits. An extension, connected with the Imperial College of Science and Technology, houses the museum's library (*Mon.-Sat., 10-5.30; Cl. Bank Hols.*).

▶ Ground floor: **Foucault's Pendulum**, registered the earth's rotation (by the main entrance); motive power, stationary steam engines, steam turbines, hot air, gas and oil engines (galleries 2, 3, 5); rail transport, early steam locomotives, rail equipment, electric traction (galleries 7, 8); road transport, early motor cars, gas-turbine vehicles, motor cycles (galleries 7-10). ▶ First floor: telecommunications (galleries 20, 25); iron and steel (gallery 22); textiles and plastics (galleries 24, 25); gas industry (gallery 26); astronomy, telescopes, terrestrial and celestial globes, orreries (gallery 30). ▶ Second floor: chemistry, history and industries (galleries 41-43, 45); nuclear physics and power (gallery 44); computers (gallery 46). ▶ Third floor: photography and cinematography (gallery 60); electricity and magnetism (gallery 64); aeronautics (gallery 68, 69). ▶ Fourth and fifth floors: Wellcome Museum of History of Medicine (*Mon.-Sat., 10-6, Sun., 2.30-6; Cl. I Jan., Good Fri., May Day, 24-26 Dec.*). □

▶ SOHO*
map 2-C2/Underground: Piccadilly Circus, Leicester Square, Oxford Circus, Tottenham Court Road. Bus: 3, 6, 7, 12, 14, 15, 19, 22, 24, 29, 53, 73, 88, 159.

The name of this most compact and cosmopolitan of all London districts is probably derived from the old hunting cry 'So-Ho', though the area was already quite urban by the 17thC. French Huguenots were among the first to settle there, followed by Italians, Greeks, Chinese and people of many other races and nationalities. From a peak in the 19thC, the resident population has dropped to less than 3000. Most now go there to work, or to seek diversion in its theatres, cinemas, restaurants, nightclubs and sex shops.

The Docklands
London's docks have taken on a new aspect. With the end of Britain's overseas empire, the bombing of World War II and modern means of transport, the once-thriving London docks fell into disrepair. In 1965 a semi-public organization, the London Docklands Development Corporation, was formed to renovate this ancient port on the Thames. This renovation was effected in a grandiose manner. Office buildings, shopping centers, luxury apartments and industrial workspace were designed, and, in order to maintain a sense of the area's character, marinas for pleasure boats were constructed. The Docklands became a city within a city. This new area needed new means of transportation. Accordingly, new roads were laid out, highway links, rail links and boat links were created. The most impressive innovation, however, was the construction of a new airport — right in the center of London. 10 kilometres from the City', London City Airport (Stolport) opened in 1987 and is well-placed to shuttle businessmen to and from the Continent and to other cities in Britain.

▶ **Shaftesbury Avenue** (1886) is noted for its theatres — Apollo, Globe, Lyric, Palace, Queen's Saville. ▶ The **Windmill Theatre**, Great Windmill Street, is famous as the only London theatre to remain open throughout WWII, with its slogan 'We never closed'. ▶ Between Shaftesbury Avenue and Leicester Square, the **Church of Notre Dame de France** (1955), replacing an earlier edifice bombed in WWII, is largely circular, with decoration by Jean Cocteau, including an Aubusson tapestry. ▶ In the vicinity of Golden Square is the **Church of Our Lady of the Assumption**, Warwick Street; also **Carnaby Street** (›). ▶ The **Palladium**, Argyll Street, just off Oxford Circus, is London's chief variety theatre. ▶ Wardour Street and Dean Street are commercial centres of the cinema industry. ▶ **Ronnie Scott's**, Frith Street, is London's premier jazz club. ▶ **Soho Square** (c. 1680) has a statue to Charles II and two churches, **St. Patrick's Roman Catholic Church**, and the **French Protestant Church**, a reminder of Soho's Huguenot past. ▶ On the other side of Charing Cross Road, just outside Soho proper, is the church of **St. Giles-in-the-Fields** (1733), on the site of an earlier church and leper hospital. The Great Plague of 1665 started in the parish. □

▶ SOUTH BANK ARTS CENTRE*
map 2-C2/Underground: Waterloo. Bus: 68, 188.

The genesis of the South Bank, as it is generally known, was the 1951 Festival of Britain, when a semi-derelict industrial area of Lambeth riverside, around Hungerford Railway Bridge and Waterloo Bridge, was chosen for the festival's main exhibition site. A new concert hall, the Royal Festival Hall, was included, and from this the rest of the Arts Centre, unified by a large pedestrian precinct, has grown.

▶ **Royal Festival Hall** (1951, enlarged 1965), with year-round concert and ballet seasons, plus riverside restaurant, cafeterias and bars, bookshop, art exhibitions, and fine panorama of London across the river. ▶ **Queen Elizabeth** and **Purcell Rooms** (1967), complementing the Festival Hall as smaller concert or recital rooms. ▶ **Hayward Gallery** (1968), in the same building complex, stages major art exhibitions. ▶ **National Film Theatre**, beneath Waterloo Bridge, first opened 1951 and enlarged 1970, with two cinemas and a cinema museum in preparation. ▶ On the other side of Waterloo Bridge, the **Nation-**

al Theatre complex (1977) has three theatres: Olivier (the largest), Lyttleton and Cottesloe, plus bookshops, restaurant, cafeterias and striking **views** across the Thames.   ☐

▶ **SOUTHWARK***

map 2-D3/Underground: London Bridge, Borough. British Rail: London Bridge.

Southwark, or South Work, is the oldest part of London S of the Thames, by the main route from the Continent into the City (→) over London Bridge. Hence its many coaching inns. Also, with more space than the City, it became a place of entertainment (Shakespeare's Globe Theatre and the Bear Garden) and of prisons (notably the Clink and Marshalsea). There is still much evidence of this long and colourful past in this bustling S London district today.

▶ **Southwark Cathedral** (St. Saviour's) by the approach to London Bridge. Founded as a priory 1106, most of the edifice dates from the 15thC — London's earliest Gothic church — the square tower being of later date; it became a cathedral only in 1905. The interior is rich in decoration and in **monuments**: wooden effigy of a knight (c. 1275), the memorial to John Gower (friend of the poet Chaucer) and Shakespeare (1912); **Harvard Chapel**, in honour of John Harvard, baptized in the church and founder of America's Harvard University. ▶ Just E of the cathedral is Guy's Hospital, founded 1722, with large modern extensions; the **old operating theatre** in Thomas Street may still be visited (*Mon., Wed., Fri., 12.30-4*). ▶ Under the arches of London Bridge Station is the **London Dungeon** (*Apr.-Sep.: daily 10-5.45; Oct.-Mar.: daily 10-4.30*), a museum of the macabre. ▶ In Borough High Street are reminders of several coaching inns, including the **George Inn** (1676), with surviving galleries and courtyard. ▶ W of the cathedral is **St. Mary Overie's Dock**, containing an old merchant ship; and the remains of Winchester House (c. 1100). ▶ Beyond Clink Street, and traversed by Southwark Bridge, is the area of Bankside, dominated by the power station (1929, Giles Gilbert Scott) now abandoned. ▶ Close by is the site of the Globe Theatre (with plans for its reconstruction) and the **Bear Gardens Museum** (*Tue.-Sat., 10-5.30, Sun., 2-6; Cl. 25-26 Dec., I Jan.*), tracing the history of Elizabethan theatre, with models of the Globe and Cockpit playhouses. ▶ The 18thC **Anchor Inn** has relics of the old Clink Prison. ▶ The **Church of St. George the Martyr** (founded 1122, rebuilt 1736): interesting interior, including memorials to city livery companies and to Dickens' novel *Little Dorrit*, inspired by the nearby Marshalsea debtors' prison.   ☐

▶ **ST. JAMES'S PARK***

map 2-C2/Underground: St. James's Park.

Originally the garden of a leper hospital, St. James's Park is the oldest of London's royal parks and a particular favourite of Charles II who created the lake, famous for its wildfowl. It is a beautiful and tranquil place despite being at the heart of the city.

▶ The **view** from the footbridge across the lake, E to Whitehall (→) and W to Buckingham Palace (→), is one of the most picturesque in London. ▶ At the E end, facing **Horse Guards Parade**, is the **Guards Memorial** (1926). ▶ The park is bordered, on the N side, by The Mall (→), and on the S by **Birdcage Walk** which takes its name from the aviary kept there by Charles II. ▶ By Birdcage Walk are the renovated **Wellington Barracks** (1833) and new **Guards Chapel** (1963). ▶ Just behind Birdcage Walk and the bronze sculpture, *Mother and Child*, by Henry Moore, is **Queen Anne's Gate**, a beautifully preserved enclave of 18thC houses with a statue to the monarch.   ☐

Dick Whittington

The legend of Dick Whittington may be far from the truth, but it was certainly based on a real person who lived in London during the 14thC. According to the story, Dick was a poor boy who came to London to seek his fortune having been told that the streets were paved with gold. He found a job in the house of an Alderman Fitz-Warren, but was so harshly treated by the cook there that he ran away. However, as he walked up Highgate Hill, he heard Bow Bells chiming 'Turn again, Whittington, thrice Mayor of London'. Encouraged by this prophecy, he returned. All he possessed in the world was a cat, but this creature made him a fortune, and he married Alice, daughter of his master.

There was indeed a Richard Whittington who was born around 1358 and died in 1423, no poor boy but the son of Sir William Whittington. Nevertheless, he was apprenticed to Fitz-Warren, a prosperous mercer, and married his daughter. Moreover, he did become Mayor — not just once, nor three times, but four times — as well as being a Member of Parliament. There is no specific record of his cat, but a sculpted stone of him holding a cat was discovered in the foundations of a 15thC house belonging to his family. He had no children, but left his great wealth to charity. During his lifetime he was renowned for his generosity and honesty. He was a member of the mercers' company and attacked bad practice among city merchants; he founded libraries, almshouses, helped individuals in need, restored St. Bartholemew's Hospital, entertained the king and gave him money. A stone set up on Highgate Hill in 1821 marks the spot where the young Richard is supposed to have sat when he heard Bow Bells calling him.

▶ **ST. PAUL'S CATHEDRAL*****

map 2-D2/Underground: St. Paul's, Mansion House. Bus: 6, 9, 11, 15.

The present building owes its existence to the Great Fire of 1666, which destroyed most of the Norman-Gothic cathedral. It was conceived by Sir Christopher Wren as the centrepiece of a new plan for the whole City of London after the fire. Work began on the great Renaissance-style building in 1675, and was finished in 1711, when the last stone in the lantern above the dome was set in place by the 79-year-old architect's son. It was damaged during WWII, but saved from destruction by a special corps of fire-watchers. It has been the setting of many big state occasions, including the funerals of Nelson (1806), Wellington (1852), Sir Winston Churchill (1965) and the Wedding of Prince Charles to Lady Diana Spencer (1981).

▶ The most striking external feature is the **dome**, mounted on its pillared 'drum' and surmounted by the lantern and golden cross, 365 ft. above ground level. ▶ The twin towers on the W front were a last-minute addition by Wren, the S tower with a clock and the bell known as 'Great Tom', the N tower with a peal of bells, which ring each Sunday. ▶ The whole exterior is richly decorated with stone statues and reliefs by Grinling Gibbons and others. ▶ The main interior decoration is the **frescoes** round the vault of the dome, by James Thornhill, the **choir stalls** and **organ case** by Gibbons, wrought-iron **railings**, **gates** and **screens** by French iron-worker Jean Tijou, and the more recent **mosaics** above the choir. ▶ In the nave,

transepts and choir are **monuments** to Nelson, Wellington and John Donne, poet and Dean of old St. Paul's, portrayed in his funeral shroud. ▶ Holman Hunt's painting, *Light of the World*, hangs in the S aisle. ▶ **The American Chapel**, commemorating the dead of WWII, is behind the new High Altar, which commemorates the British Commonwealth dead of two World Wars. ▶ Buried in the **crypt** (*Cl. Sun. and some other days*) is Wren himself; also Nelson and Wellington, whose funeral gun carriage reposes here. There are many other monuments or memorial plaques to famous British men and women. ▶ Access to the internal **Whispering Gallery**, and to the external galleries around the base of the dome and, above it, the **Golden Gallery**, 542 steps from the ground (*Mon.-Sat.: summer 9-6, 5 in winter; Sun.: services only*).

▶ **STRAND, ALDWYCH AND EMBANKMENT***

map 2-C2/Underground: Charing Cross, Aldwych, Embankment. Bus: 3, 6, 9, 11, 12, 15, 23, 29, 53, 68, 88, 159, 188.

The Strand was originally a bridle path along the N side of the Thames. As a link between the City (→) and Westminster (→) — today between Fleet Street and Trafalgar Square — it was important from the 13thC on, first as a place of large houses for the nobility and clergy, and from the 17thC to the present day as an area largely devoted to commerce and entertainment. The Embankment, properly the Victoria Embankment (1864-70), is the main part of the greatest of London's 19thC public works, reclaiming acres of riverside and mud and creating a new N bank for the Thames. It is a vital road link between the City, Westminster, Victoria (→) and Chelsea (→).

▶ By St. Martin's Lane is the church of **St. Martin-in-the-Fields** (James Gibbs, 1724), burial place of Nell Gwynne, highwayman Jack Sheppard, Hogarth, Reynolds and Thomas Chippendale; also associated with charity work and with a London orchestra. ▶ In St. Martin's Lane is **The Coliseum**, home of the English National Opera and **Duke of York's Theatre**. ▶ On the N side of the Strand are the **Adelphi** and **Vaudeville** theatres and Strand Palace Hotel (1930). ▶ On the S side is the **Savoy Hotel**, London's most luxurious when opened by impresario Richard D'Oyly Carte in 1889, with the celebrated Auguste Escoffier as chef. ▶ Adjoining Savoy Theatre (1881, reconstructed 1929), also financed by D'Oyly Carte, saw the first production of most of the Gilbert and Sullivan operettas. ▶ **Savoy Chapel**, chapel of the Royal Victorian Order, dates back to the 16thC, but is mostly of much more recent date. ▶ Savoy Hill, first premises of the BBC, is commemorated by a plaque (no. 2 Savoy Place). ▶ By the E side of Waterloo Bridge (Lancaster Place) is Somerset House (Sir William Chambers, 1776-86), occupied mainly by government offices. On the site of an earlier palace, it is one of London's grandest Classical-Revival buildings, originally with a river frontage, and still with an imposing riverside façade. The E wing (Robert Smirke, 1835) houses King's College, now a part of London University. ▶ In Strand Lane is the so-called Roman Bath, though its authenticity is doubtful. ▶ Aldwych, opened 1905, links Kingsway with the Strand. The Strand and Aldwych theatres and Waldorf Hotel are on the N side. On the S side is Bush House (1935), home of BBC overseas services, flanked by India House and Australia House. ▶ Continuing in the Strand itself, on island sites, are the churches of **St. Mary-le-Strand** (1717) and **St. Clement Danes** (Wren, 1682), largely destroyed in WWII and reconstructed, 1955, as a RAF memorial church. A bronze statue of Dr. Johnson (1910) faces Fleet Street. ▶ Marking the Strand's link with Fleet Street and the City is the **Law Centre** (Royal Courts of Justice, 1874-82), London's last major project in

Gothic-Revival style. The buildings, with over 1000 rooms and four miles of corridor, deal mainly with civil cases; exterior and great hall rich in statuary and other decoration. ▶ The **Victoria Embankment** (the section from Charing Cross Station to Blackfriars), with original decorated seats and lamp standards, is also marked by **Cleopatra's Needle** (erected 1877) and various statues. ▶ In the **Embankment Gardens** is York Watergate (1626), marking the old river bank. ▶ Just E is the **Adelphi Terrace**, the work of Robert Adam and his brothers. Nearby John Adam Street and Adam Street still have period houses. ▶ The **Sherlock Holmes** pub, Northumberland Avenue, has decor inspired by its subject.

▶ **SYON PARK AND HOUSE****
map 1-A1-2/British Rail: Syon Lane.

Syon Park, Brentford, faces Kew Gardens (→) across the Thames. Syon House, on the site of a monastery, dates from the 16thC and has a dramatic, sometimes gruesome, past involving Henry VIII among others. It was largely restyled in the 18thC by Robert Adam, while Lancelot Capability Brown landscaped the park.

▶ The W front of the house, castellated but unadorned, gives no hint of the rich interior : **Red Drawing Room**, with crimson silk walls, has Stuart portraits of royalty by Van Dyck and others; **State Dining Room**, Classically styled with niches, half domes, mirrors, friezes and copies of antique statuary; **Long Gallery**, 136 ft. long, only 14 ft. wide, cleverly designed by Adam to compensate for these proportions. Park includes the **Great Conservatory** (1827) and a **rose garden**; Gardening Centre (*Good Fri.-Oct.: Sun.-Thu., 12-5; Oct.: Sun. only, 12-5*).

▶ **TATE GALLERY***
map 2-C3/Millbank. Underground: Pimlico. Bus: 2, 36, 88, 185.

Built on the site of Millbank Prison, financed by sugar producer Sir Henry Tate and opened 1897, the gallery specializes in British and modern art with many changing exhibitions. The biggest event since its inception was the opening of the Clore Gallery, 1987, a whole new wing eventually bringing together all the works of the Turner Bequest — nearly 300 oil paintings and 19,000 watercolours and drawings.

▶ To the left of the main entrance hall are galleries (2-23) devoted to British art of various periods — Blake, Constable, the pre-Raphaelites, Whistler, Sickert. ▶ To the right of the main entrance are the galleries (30-39) presenting Impressionist, post-Impressionist, Fauvist, Cubist, Surrealist and other recent schools — Monet, Van Gogh, Gauguin, Cezanne, Seurat, Degas, Matisse, Derain, Picasso, Braque, Klee, Max Ernst, Dali, Magritte, Miró, Mondrian, Chagall. ▶ The large central galleries (27, 29) are usually reserved for special exhibitions; other galleries display paintings and sculpture by Bacon, Hockney, Henry Moore, Barbara Hepworth and many other British and foreign 20thC artists (*Mon.-Sat., 10-5.50, Sun., 2-5.50; Cl. I Jan., Good Fri., May Day, 24-26 Dec.*).

▶ **TEMPLE****
map 2-C2/Underground: Temple. Bus: 6, 9, 11, 15.

Situated at the W limit of the City (→), between Fleet Street and the Thames (with access from Fleet Street and Victoria Embankment), the area of the Temple

takes its name from the Knights Templar, the medieval para-military order, who owned the land until the 14thC. It then became the domain of lawyers, and has remained so, forming the Inner and Middle Temple, two of the Inns of Court.

▶ **Temple Church** (*Apr.-Oct.: 10-5 daily; Nov.-Mar.: 10-4.30; open for services only Christmas Day; Cl. 26 Dec.*), built by the Templars, dates from the 12thC, with 19th and 20thC restoration. A blend of Norman and Gothic styles, with a rare circular nave, modeled either on the Church of the Holy Sepulchre or the Dome of the Rock, Jerusalem. Inside are stone effigies of Templar knights, a tiny penitential cell, fine 17thC carved reredos and windows bearing the crests of the Inner and Middle Temples. ▶ **Middle Temple Hall** (14th - 16thC; *Mon.-Fri., 10-12, 3-4.30, Sat., 10-4; Cl. Sun. and Bank Hols.*) has an oak double hammer-beam roof and Tudor furnishings, plus royal portraits and suits of armour and is rich in history. ▶ **King's Bench Walk** (Inner Temple) has terraces built mainly to designs by Wren; playwright Oliver Goldsmith lived at no. 3. ▶ **Inner and Middle Temple** gardens extend to the Victoria Embankment. □

▶ **THE THAMES***

Though small by world standards, the Thames (Roman *Tamesis*) broadens into an estuary through London, being at one time much wider at certain points than it is today. This gives rise to the strong tides, with big variations between high and low water marks. The Thames has been central to London's history, allowing it to prosper as a major seaport until well into this century, when ships became too big for most of its docks and handling facilities. Several of its local tributaries, notably the Fleet (no longer visible), have also played a big part in the city's history and development. From the 12th to the 19thC, control of the Thames was largely in the hands of the City of London. Then came the Thames Conservancy Board, the Port of London Authority and, since 1974, the Thames Water Authority, marking the change from commerce and industry to water conservation and environmental improvement (*regular riverboat services Easter-Sep. from Westminster and Charing Cross Piers, to points downstream as far as Greenwich, and upstream to Hampton Court*).

▶ **Teddington Lock** (1912) marks the river's tidal limit upstream. ▶ Moored by the **Embankment**, between Waterloo and Blackfriars bridges (→Thames Bridges), are two WWI naval sloops, *Wellington* and *Chrysanthemum*, and a WWII frigate, *President*. ▶ Moored by Tower Bridge (→Thames Bridges) is **HMS Belfast** (*access by ferry from Tower Pier or Symon's Wharf, Tooley Street Daily: 11-5.50; Nov.-Mar.: 11-4.30; Cl. 1 Jan., Good Fri., May Day, 24-26 Dec.*), WWII cruiser, a floating extension of the Imperial War Museum (→). ▶ **St. Katherine's Dock**, just beyond Tower Bridge, now restored as a marina and museum of historic river and coastal craft. ▶ The 16thC **'Prospect of Whitby'**, at Wapping, is London's best-known riverside pub, frequented by Pepys, Dickens and other celebrities. ▶ Nearby is Execution Dock, where pirates were hanged up to the beginning of the 19thC. ▶ The **Thames Barrier** (1982) at Woolwich, spanning over 500 yards from bank to bank, is the river's greatest engineering achievement; designed to protect London from flooding by the growing risk of high tides, it has four main steel gates (each weighing 3000 tons), and six smaller ones: when opened — lowered into the water — ships pass over them. □

▶ **THAMES BRIDGES***

From Roman times until the 18thC, London was served by a single bridge over the Thames. Longest standing was the 12thC London Bridge, cluttered with tall houses and a chapel, and constantly menaced by fire and flood, but which survived until the early 19thC. Today thirty-one bridges — road, rail and pedestrian — span the river from Hampton Court upstream, to Tower Bridge.

▶ **Richmond** (1774), a toll bridge well into the 19thC, since widened but retaining its rural character. ▶ Beyond the railway and Twickenham bridges is Richmond footbridge (1890), forming part of lock and sluice gates controlling the tidal flow. ▶ **Hammersmith** (1887), an exuberant Victorian suspension bridge, replacing an earlier one of similar construction. ▶ **Albert** (1873), another decorative suspension bridge. ▶ **Westminster** (1862), replacing the bridge of 1750 that inspired Wordsworth's famous sonnet. ▶ **Hungerford** (1864), best-known of London's railway bridges, also a footbridge; it features in several of Monet's Impressionist paintings of London. ▶ **Waterloo** (1939), biggest of London's bridges, poised high above the river and the Embankment, with a fine view of St. Paul's (→) and the City (→) skyline. ▶ **Blackfriars** (1869), solidly Victorian, of iron and stone. Next to it are the massive cast-iron stanchions of the old railway bridge. ▶ **London** (1973), newest of all the bridges, replacing one of 1831 which, in turn, had replaced the 12thC bridge; the 1831 bridge has been re-erected at Lake Havasu City, Arizona, U.S.A. ▶ **Tower Bridge** (1894), the last before the sea, and one of London's most celebrated landmarks. It is a double bascule or drawbridge, designed to allow shipping into the old Pool of London. The twin Gothic-Revival towers house the bridge machinery and also lifts that originally conveyed pedestrians to a high-level footbridge, since the main bridge was often raised several times a day, now the raising of the bridge is something of an event. □

▶ **TOWER OF LONDON****
map 2-D2/Tower Hill. Underground: Tower Hill. Bus: 15.

The fortress was begun by William the Conqueror soon after the Norman Conquest (1066), both as a symbol of his authority and as a defense against attack from the river. It was added to over the centuries by a succession of monarchs, and used as a royal residence, prison and place of execution (the last prisoner was Rudolf Hess in WWII), treasury and jewel house, mint, armoury, and menagerie. It is now a museum of priceless relics, attended by the Yeomen Warders ('Beefeaters'), originally a royal bodyguard in Tudor uniform. Riverside guns fire salutes on State occasions.

▶ **White Tower** or Keep (1077-97) was the original fortress. It was whitewashed in 1241, hence its name, and the turret cupolas were added in the 14thC. It houses the **Royal Armoury**, one of the greatest collections of arms and armour. St. John's Chapel is a fine example of Norman church architecture. ▶ **The Crown Jewels** (Jewel House) date from the Restoration, most earlier royal regalia having been sold or melted down by Cromwell. They include the **Imperial State Crown**, with 3000 jewels, and the **Royal Sceptre**, containing the Star of Africa, the world's biggest diamond. Also swords of state and other treasures. ▶ **Bloody Tower** (12thC), where Sir Walter Raleigh was incarcerated for 12 years prior to his execution. ▶ **Traitor's Gate** and **St. Thomas's Tower** (14thC), the main entrance from the river, leading to the **Wakefield Tower**. ▶ **Royal Fusiliers Museum, New Armouries** and **Waterloo Barracks** containing arms and other regalia of the regiment, also the Oriental Gallery of arms and

armour from India, Burma, China and Japan. ▶ **Tower Green** was an execution and burial place, numbering among its victims Anne Boleyn and Catherine Howard. (Many more were executed on neighbouring Tower Hill.) The moat was drained and grassed over in the 19thC. ▶ The Yeomen Warders parade each day at 11 a.m., and perform the Ceremony of the Keys each evening at 10 p.m.; (*admission on application only*). ▶ A special feature is the ravens (→; *Mar.-Oct.: Mon.-Sat., 9.30-5.45; Nov.-Feb.: Mon. Sat., 9.30-4.30.*). ◻

Tower of London

The building of Europe's oldest fortress prison was started in the 11thC by William the Conqueror and, in the course of its gory history, it has served as a palace, prison, armoury, and again as a prison during the 20thC world wars. As a royal fortress and state prison it has witnessed many executions, scenes of torture and long periods of incarceration. Many famous people, including Henry VIII's second wife, Anne Boleyn, Thomas More and Lady Jane Grey, have lost their heads here, and Sir Walter Raleigh was imprisoned three times in the Tower — once for twelve years. The last man to be beheaded was Lord Lovat in 1747; but spies during both world wars were shot here and Rudolf Hess was imprisoned at the Tower in 1941.

Walls in the fortress have been inscribed by numerous unfortunate inmates: the name 'Jane' can be seen in two places in the Beauchamp Tower where Lady Jane Grey's young husband, Lord Dudley, was imprisoned before his execution. There are also said to be ghosts. In the White Tower noises of people groaning under torture have been heard, and the headless figure of Anne Boleyn, dressed in white, appears on Tower Green where royalty and nobles were beheaded (commoners met their death outside on Tower Hill). On moonlit nights Walter Raleigh patrols Raleigh's Walk — but if disturbed will instantly disappear. Tower Green is still inhabited by the ominous black ravens, and it is believed that if these leave, the Tower will fall and England will be doomed. About forty Yeoman Warders, dressed in Tudor costume, guard the Tower; every night at half past nine the Chief Warden locks the gates and hands the keys to the Resident Governor — as he has done for the past 700 years.

▶ TWICKENHAM*

map 1-A2/British Rail: St. Margaret, Twickenham, Strawberry Hill, Whitton.

For sportsmen, Twickenham means the international rugby football ground. But this large W London suburb across the Thames from Richmond (→) also has a history and places of notable architectural merit and interest.

▶ **Marble Hill House** (1728; *Mon.-Thu., Sat., Sun., 10-5; Nov.-Jan.: 10-4; Cl. 24-26 Dec.*), a splendid Classical-Revival (Palladian) villa in its own grounds, built by Henrietta Howard, mistress of George II, and frequented by her friend, the poet Alexander Pope; interior and furnishings have been restored as closely as possible to the original. ▶ Next to it, in a riverside garden, **Orleans House Gallery** (*Apr.-Sep.: Tue.-Sat., 1-5.30, Sun., Bank Hols., 2-5.30; Oct.-Mar.: Tue.-Sat.,1-4.30, Sun., Bank Hols., 2-4.30*), the remaining wing of a large 18thC mansion,

once the home of the exiled French Duke of Orléans, later King Louis-Philippe. The gallery shows temporary exhibitions. ▶ Between Marble Hill and Orleans House is **Montpellier Row**, a fine Georgian terrace (1722). ▶ The parish church of **St. Mary the Virgin**; mainly Georgian with medieval tower, has a handsome interior: memorial to Alexander Pope, who is buried here. ▶ **Strawberry Hill** (1776), built by Horace Walpole, son of Prime Minister Sir Robert Walpole and man of letters, in early Gothic-Revival style, with a most fanciful interior; now a theological college (*conducted tours Wed., Sat. on application*). ▶ **Kneller Hall**, built 1711 by court artist Sir Godfrey Kneller, but largely rebuilt 1848 in Neojacobean style; home of the Royal Military School of Music. ◻

▶ VICTORIA AND ALBERT MUSEUM*

map 2-A3/Cromwell Road. Underground: South Kensington. Bus: 14, 30, 74.

The museum, founded 1857 in the wake of the Great Exhibition of 1851 and named after Queen Victoria and her consort, is devoted to fine and applied arts of all countries, styles and periods. The huge collection did not acquire its present home until 1909. The massive building by Sir Aston Webb is surmounted by a tower in the form of an imperial crown.

▶ Lower ground floor: Boiler House project, exhibitions of history, theory and practice of design and consumer products. ▶ Ground floor: Raphael cartoons; dress collection; Indian, Islamic and oriental art; early medieval art and tapestries; Gothic art; Renaissance art; Henry Cole wing of prints, drawings, photographs and paintings; English Renaissance and British art. ▶ First floor: musical instruments; English and continental ironwork; 20thC British art and design; English and continental silver; jewelry; British and continental church plate; tapestries, carpets, lace, embroidery, textiles; stained glass; British art. ▶ Second floor : pottery, ceramics, enamels (*Mon.-Thu., Sat., 10-5.30, Sun., 2.30-5.30; Cl. 1 Jan., Good Fri., May Day, 24-26 Dec.*). ◻

▶ VICTORIA AND PIMLICO*

map 2-B3/Underground: Victoria, Pimlico. Bus: 11, 24, 25, 29.

The low-lying area contained by the bend in the river S of Westminster (→) and Buckingham Palace (→) remained largely neglected until the 19thC. Then the creation of new streets, the extension of Thomas Cubitt's Knightsbridge and Belgravia (→) development, and the building of Victoria Station (→Railway Stations) brought intensive housing and commerce to the two neighbouring districts. Victoria remains largely commercial, while Pimlico is characterized by Victorian terraces and squares.

▶ **Victoria Street**, running from Victoria Station to Parliament Square, is one of London's busiest, with the Victoria Palace variety theatre, the new Army and Navy Stores (rebuilt 1977 as the Army and Navy Victoria), and New Scotland Yard (1967), headquarters of London Metropolitan Police. ▶ Separated from Victoria Street by a small piazza is the Neobyzantine Roman Catholic **Westminster Cathedral** (John Francis Bentley, 1895-1903); the most striking external feature is the 280-ft. domed bell tower or campanile; the building is also exceptionally long (360 ft.), with the widest nave in England. The rich interior decor of marble and mosaics, though impressive, is only half finished: the Stations of the Cross are by designer and sculptor Eric Gill; a giant Rood or Crucifix hangs from the main arch of the nave. ▶ Just S of Victoria Street, in

Greycoat Place, is the restored **Greycoat School** (1701), in Queen Anne style, with wooden figures of a boy and girl in old charity school uniforms. ▶ The surviving building of the **Bluecoat School** (1709), N of Victoria Street, in Caxton Street, is the memorial to another charity school, with the statue of a pupil in blue coat above the door. ▶ Millbank riverfront is marked by the 387-ft. **Millbank Tower** (1963) and the **Tate Gallery** (→). ☐

▶ WALLACE COLLECTION*

map 2-B2/Hertford House, Manchester Square. Underground: Bond Street. Bus: 6, 7, 12, 15, 30, 73, 74, 88, 159.

Hertford House (1777, enlarged 1882), on the N side of Manchester Square, is the home of this major collection of fine art, furnishings, arms and armour, brought together by members of the Hertford family, including Sir Richard Wallace, whose widow bequeathed it to the nation in 1900.

▶ Paintings by Holbein, Titian, Canaletto, Rubens, Rembrandt, Frans Hals (*The Laughing Cavalier*), Velasquez (*Lady with a Fan*), Poussin (*Dance to the Music of Time*), Fragonard (*The Swing*), Watteau, Reynolds, Gainsborough, Lawrence; Sèvres porcelain; Venetian glass; Limoges enamels; 17th and 18thC French furniture and clocks, including pieces for Louis XV and Marie-Antoinette; Renaissance gold and silver work; Medieval to 18thC European arms and armour, also oriental pieces. ☐

▶ WEMBLEY STADIUM AND CONFERENCE CENTRE*

map 1-A1/Underground, British Rail: Wembley Central.

The 13-acre stadium in NW London, built for the British Empire Exhibition of 1923, has since been Britain's premier venue for national and international sporting events, including the 1948 Olympic Games and 1966 World Cup Soccer Football Final. Around it have gathered other major sporting and entertainments facilities, and, most recently, a Conference Centre.

▶ The Wembley Stadium Tour (*10, 11, 12, 2, 5, also 4 in the summer, Thu., Christmas and days of big events*) takes visitors round the 100,000-capacity stadium, including the dressing rooms, famous Player's Tunnel and Royal Box. ▶ **Wembley Arena** (formerly 1934 Empire Pool) stages ice shows, ice hockey, boxing, gymnastics and many other sporting events, also pop concerts. ▶ The **International Conference Centre** (1977), with large auditorium also used as a concert hall. ☐

▶ WESTMINSTER*

map 2-C3/Underground: Westminster. Bus: 3, 11, 12, 24, 25, 29, 53, 88, 159.

The modern City of Westminster is a large administrative area. The district, centred round the site of the old Palace of Westminster and Westminster Abbey (→), is one of the oldest parts of London outside the City (→) itself. Despite the palace and abbey, it was quite a disreputable area up to the 19thC, when the present Houses of Parliament (→) were built and adjacent Parliament Square laid out, giving it today's dignified atmosphere.

▶ At the corner· of Westminster Bridge and Victoria Embankment is the bronze **statue** of Queen Boudicca and daughters in a war chariot (1855). ▶ By the **Embankment** is the imposing **Norman Shaw Building** (1906), named

after its architect, formerly New Scotland Yard and headquarters of London's Metropolitan Police. ▶ **Parliament Square** (1868), bordered by the Houses of Parliament and Westminster Abbey, has statues to British Prime Ministers Lord Palmerston, Canning, Peel, Disraeli and Sir Winston Churchill (1973), also to President Lincoln and Field Marshal Smuts (Epstein, 1958). ▶ In the shadow of Westminster Abbey is **St. Margaret's**, parish church of the House of Commons dating from the 15thC, with 19thC restorations by Sir Giles Gilbert Scott; it has Tudor monuments and some fine stained glass; Samuel Pepys, John Milton, Sir Walter Raleigh and Admiral Blake are buried here. ▶ W of Parliament Square is the large **Methodist Central Hall** (1905), used for public gatherings, and the new Conference Centre (1985). ▶ The corner of Victoria Street and Great Smith Street marks the site of William Caxton's first British **printing press** (1476). ▶ Just behind, approached through a gateway from Broad Sanctuary, is **Dean's Yard**, with **Church House**, used during WWII by both houses of parliament, **Westminster Abbey Choir School**, and, through another gateway, historic **Westminster School**. ▶ A few minutes' walk away is **Smith Square** (1726), with national headquarters of the Conservative and Labour (Transport House) parties. In the middle of the square is the Baroque **St. John's Church** (Thomas Archer, 1714), restored after WWII bombing and now a public hall, much used for concerts. ☐

▶ WESTMINSTER ABBEY*

map 2-C3/Underground: Westminster. Bus: 3, 11, 12, 24, 25, 29, 53, 88, 159.

Edward the Confessor's abbey of 1042-66 was largely replaced by Henry III, whose 13thC Gothic edifice represents the bulk of the present abbey, with two major additions in the shape of Henry VII's Chapel (1503) and Nicholas Hawksmoor's twin W towers (1735). It has seen the coronation of every English or British monarch since William I in 1066. Many of the nation's most famous men and women are either buried within its precincts or are commemorated here.

▶ Facing the W entrance, in the centre of the nave, is the **Tomb of the Unknown Soldier**, commemorating the dead of WWI. Next to it is a commemorative **plaque** to Sir Winston Churchill and nearby, another to President Roosevelt. ▶ The **nave** is noted for its Gothic vaulting; organ, choir stalls and screen are 18th and 19thC respectively. ▶ Beyond the choir and Sanctuary is **Edward the Confessor's Chapel**, containing Edward's shrine and the tombs of eight other kings and queens. ▶ This chapel also houses the 13thC oak **Coronation Chair** with, beneath it, the **Stone of Scone** (ancient Scottish coronation stone taken by Edward I). It has been used for every coronation since 1308, for which ceremonies it is moved round the 15thC stone screen, to face the Sanctuary. ▶ Beyond Edward the Confessor's Chapel is that of Henry VII, with magnificent Perpendicular fan **vaulting**, and the tombs of Henry VII himself, Elizabeth I, Mary Queen of Scots and other royal personages. ▶ The **Battle of Britain Chapel** at the far end (founded 1947) includes the tombs of RAF leaders Lords Trenchard and Dowding. ▶ **Poet's Corner**, in the S transept, has the tombs of Chaucer, Jonson (buried upright), Dryden, Johnson, Sheridan, Browning, Tennyson and memorials to Shakespeare, Blake, Milton, Keats, Shelley, Byron, Wordsworth, Dickens, Hardy, Kipling and, alone among composers, Handel. ▶ Others buried in the abbey or commemorated are, among scientists and inventors, Michael Faraday, Lords Rutherford and Lister, Robert Stephenson, James Watt; and Prime Ministers Pitt the Elder and Younger, Palmerston, Disraeli, Gladstone, Asquith, Lloyd George, Attlee. ▶ The 13thC **Chapter House** has Gothic vaulting, fine tiled floor and 13th and 14thC sculptures and paintings. ▶ The 13th and14thC **cloisters** have a brass rubbing centre. ▶ The abbey **museum** (*separate entrance and admission charge*) has

wooden or wax funeral effigies of several monarchs, Henry V's shield and helmet from Agincourt and other treasures (*nave and cloisters open weekdays 8-6, Wed., 8-7.45; other parts of the abbey: Mon.-Fri., 9-4.45, Sat., 9-2.45, 3.45-5.45; Sun. open to visitors between services*). □

▶ WHITECHAPEL*

map 2-D2/Underground: Aldgate East, Whitechapel.

Bordering the City (→) to the E, Whitechapel was once noted for coaching inns and markets by the main road from the E coast, and for heavy industries serving the City and nearby docks. Poverty and overcrowding were at their worst in the 19thC, with a large, mainly Jewish immigrant population; notoriety was added by the murders of Jack the Ripper. It remains a place of bustling local industry and commerce, a vital part of London's East End.

▶ **Whitechapel Art Gallery** 1897 (*Tue.-Sun., 11-5.50, Tue., Thu., 11-7.50*), a striking building in Art Nouveau style, has changing exhibitions through the year, mainly of modern art. ▶ **Petticoat Lane** (Middlesex Street): Sunday market is the most famous of all London's street markets (→ Markets). ▶ **Whitechapel Bell Foundry**, founded 1420, a distinguished survivor of the district's old industries; among the bells cast were those for Westminster Abbey (→) and Big Ben (→ Houses of Parliament). ▶ **Trinity Almshouses** (1695), Mile End Road, originally built for retired seamen or their widows, with a handsome chapel at one end. ▶ **St. George-in-the-East** (Hawksmoor, 1714), an imposing church in English Renaissance style, bombed in WWII but restored, with windows by Sir Joshua Reynolds. □

▶ WHITEHALL*

map 2-C2/Underground: Westminster, Charing Cross. Bus: 3, 11, 12, 24, 25, 29, 53, 88, 159.

The thoroughfare of Whitehall, running from Trafalgar Square to Parliament Square, takes its name from the former royal palace, burned down in 1698. Soon after, Whitehall itself was widened and flanked by the ministeries and other major government offices that have shaped its character to the present time.

▶ **Trafalgar Square** was planned by Nash and modeled by Sir Charles Barry, 1840. With the National Gallery (→) on its N side, its most famous feature is **Nelson's Column** (1839), the 17-ft. figure of the admiral being added four years later; the bronze reliefs round its base, cast from captured cannon, celebrate his victories. The **lions** are by Landseer. There are other statues in the square to George IV and General Napier and, just to the S, facing Whitehall, an equestrian statue of Charles I. ▶ The Palladian-style **Horse Guards** building (William Kent, 1745) is presided over by sentries of the Horse Guards cavalry regiments, who parade each day (*11a.m., 10a.m., Sun., 4p.m.*). On the far side is **Horse Guards Parade**, flanked to the N by the **Admiralty Building**, and to the S by the rear of Downing Street, where the Trooping of the Colour ceremony takes place each June. There are **statues** to Field Marshals Kitchener, Wolseley and Roberts, and the **Cadiz Memorial**, a huge French mortar mounted on a cast-iron dragon, captured during the Peninsular War (1812). ▶ Opposite the Horse Guards, in Whitehall, is the Renaissance-style **Banqueting House** (*Tue.-Sat., 10-5.30, Sun., 2-5.30; Cl. I Jan., Good Fri., 24-26 Dec., Bank Hols.*), built by Iñigo Jones, 1619, for James I, and the only surviving part of Whitehall Palace. Charles I commissioned the painted **ceiling** by Rubens, and was executed outside in 1649. ▶ **No. 10 Downing Street** has been the official home of prime ministers since 1731; the Cabinet regularly meets

here. **No. 11** is the home of the chancellor of the exchequer. ▶ At the far end of King Charles Street (between the buildings of the Foreign and Home offices) are the WWII underground **Cabinet War Rooms** (*Tue.-Sun., 10-5.50; Cl. I Jan., Good Fri., May Day, 24-26 Dec., Mon.*), preserved exactly as they were when used by Churchill and his wartime government. ▶ Back in Whitehall stands the **Cenotaph** (Sir Edwin Lutyens, 1919), a national memorial to the dead of two World Wars, and focal point for an annual service of Remembrance on the nearest Sunday to WWI Armistice Day (*II Nov.026*). ▶ Nearby are **statues** to Field Marshals Earl Haig and Viscount Montgomery of Alamein. □

▶ WIMBLEDON*

map 1-A2/Underground, British Rail: Wimbledon.

This South London district has a long history, centred round the High Street at the top of Wimbledon Hill, though little of historical interest remains. Its great fame comes from its international tennis championships, while its attraction for many Londoners is the Common, one of the capital's largest open spaces.

▶ The **All England Lawn Tennis and Croquet Club** was founded 1869, and its annual tennis championships are a world sporting event. The associated **Lawn Tennis Museum** (*Tue.-Sat., 11-5, Sun.,2-5; Cl. Mon., Bank Hols; open only to spectators during the championship fortnight in June*) has many historical relics of the game. ▶ **Wimbledon Common**, over 1000 acres of largely natural heathland, includes a **Wind Flour Mill** (1817), handsomely restored, with a small museum of agricultural relics. □

Frost fairs

A number of exceptionally severe winters have had a memorable effect on London's River Thames. On several recorded occasions, part of the river has frozen solid and Londoners have taken advantage of this to turn it into a sort of pleasure ground. During the winter of 1564, the Thames was more crowded with people than any street in the city, and lively games of football took place there. In 1684, the diarist John Evelyn recorded how all sorts of booths were arranged in 'streets' upon the ice, and visitors (including King Charles II) could have their names printed on special cards by an enterprising entrepreneur who had set up a press there. During the winter of 1715-16, the river was thickly frozen for a distance of several miles, and entertainments to be enjoyed included the roasting of a whole ox on the ice. For weeks, in Jan. 1740, people lived in temporary 'towns' on the frozen water; while at the 'frost fair' of 1814, a sheep was cooked and sold in slices as 'Lapland mutton'. On this occasion there were musicians to accompany dancing, merry-go-rounds and skittle games. The ice, which was solid between London and Blackfriars bridges, lasted for nearly a week; unfortunately the thaw, when it came, was sudden. Some of the traders, reluctant to lose customers, stayed longer than was wise; three people were drowned, vast numbers got soaked, and a strange assortment of tents, merry-go-rounds and printing presses could be seen stranded on blocks of ice which floated down the river. In 1832, old London Bridge, with its narrow arches, was replaced by a new bridge which allowed the water to flow more freely: the Thames never again froze in the same way.

Practical information

⬛*London Visitor and Convention Bureau*: 26 Grosvenor Gardens, SW1, ☎ 730 3488, open Mon. to Fri., 9 to 5.30, written and telephone inquiries only. *London Tourist Information Centre*, Victoria Station Forecourt, SW1, open daily, 9 to 8.30, till 10 Jul. and Aug. (bookshop closes at 8, book for guided tours before 7.30). *Selfridges Department Store* (ground floor), Oxford Street, W1, open 9 to 6 Mon. to Sat. except Thu., 9 to 7.30. *Harrods Department Store* (fourth floor), Brompton Road, SW1, open 9 to 5, Mon. to Fri., 9.30 to 5, Wed., 9 to 6, Sat. *Heathrow Central Underground Station*, open daily 9 to 6. *Tower of London* (west gate), EC3, open 10 to 6, Mon. to Sat., 10.15 to 6, Sun. *London Information Centre*, 25 Shaftesbury Avenue, W1, ☎ 730 3488. *Piccadilly Circus Underground Station*, multilingual information staff, bookshop, direct no-fee ticket booking for Royal Festival Hall, open 10 to 8 daily.

Embassies and consulates: *American Embassy*, 24 Grosvenor Square, W1, ☎ 499 9000; *French Embassy*, 58 Knightsbridge, SW1, ☎ 235 8080; *Canadian High Commission*, Mcdonald House, 38 Grosvenor Street, W1, ☎ 629 9492; *Irish Embassy*, 17 Grosvenor Place, SW1, ☎ 235 2171.

Further information: the most detailed sources of information for the visitor are the weeklies *Time Out*, *City Limits* and *What's On in London*, which come out on Wed. and are sold at all newsagents and newsstands. These publications provide full information on theatres, shows, cinemas, concerts, exhibitions, festivals, TV, radio, children's activities, etc., along with practical information compiled for Londoners as much as for visitors.

Emergency: medical emergency treatment is free. Dial 999 and ask for an ambulance. *Capital Helpline*, ☎ 388 7575, is open Mon. to Fri. 9.30 to 5.30 to direct callers to specialists who can help with their problem. *The Samaritans*, St. Stephen's, 39 Walbrook Road, EC4, ☎ 283 3400, open 24 hours a day to the depressed and suicidal. *Teledate*, ☎ 200 0200, a 24-hour service with details of all emergency services. *Pharmacy*: Wayman Freed, 45 Golders Green Road, NW11, ☎ 455 4351, open 9.30 to midnight daily. *Dental Emergency Care*, ☎ 677 6363/584 1008, 24 hours a day. *Lost Property*: inform local police station. London Transport operates a 24-hour recorded message for lost property, ☎ 486 2496.

Guided tours: *London Transport*, ☎ 222 1234 operates half and full day tours from Victoria Coach Station, Buckingham Palace Road. Advance booking at any London Travel Enquiry office (no phone bookings). *Culture Bus*, ☎ 629 4999, covers twenty boarding points where passengers can get on or off as they please. Daily every 20 min. from 9 to 6.30, first stop Baker Street tube station, bus stop D. Weekly information sheets as mentioned above and local newspapers give details of the numerous independent lecturers and walking tour associations available.

Audio guide: *Tours by Tape*, 77 Wells Street, W1, ☎ 580 9088.

Post office: *Central Post Office*, Trafalgar Square, 24 William IV Street, WC2, ☎ 930 9580, open 24 hours a day.

Banks: open daily except Sat., Sun. and bank holidays. Principal clearing banks (National Westminster, Midland, Barclays, Lloyds) have foreign departments that cash travelers checks during banking hours: 9.30 to 3.30 Mon. to Fri. Certain branches are open 9.30 to noon or 12.30 Sat.

Foreign exchange offices: the following exchange bureaux are open 24 hours a day, 7 days a week: *Chequepoint*, 548 Oxford Street, W1, ☎ 723 2646; *Erskine*, 15 Shaftesbury Avenue, W1, ☎ 734 1400; *Lenlyn*, Victoria British Rail Station, SW1, ☎ 828 8367; Heathrow and Gatwick airports both have 24-hour banks. *American Express*, 6 Haymarket, SW1, ☎ 930 4411; *Thomas Cook*, 45 Berkeley Street, W1, ☎ 499 4000.

British Rail: *British Rail Travel Centre* (24 hours, multilingual): 12 Lower Regent Street, SW1. Open 9 to 6.30, Mon. to Sat., 10 to 4 Sun. Charing Cross, ☎ 928 5100; Euston, ☎ 387 7070; Holborn Viaduct, ☎ 928 5100; King's Cross, ☎ 278 2477; Liverpool Street, ☎ 283 7171; London Bridge, ☎ 928 5100; Marylebone, ☎ 387 7070; Paddington, ☎ 262 6767; Victoria, ☎ 928 5100; Waterloo, ☎ 928 5100. *Intercity general inquiries*: ☎ 834 2345. For all the above, a central stacking system insures that all phone calls are answered in strict rotation, so be patient and wait for a reply.

Airports: *London Heathrow*, 15 m W, ☎ 759 4321; *British Airways* information, ticket sales and bookings, ☎ 370 5411; access: terminal of Piccadilly Underground line (stop one before the last for Terminal 4, last stop for Terminals 1, 2 and 3). 45 min. tube from London centre every 5 min., 20 hours a day. *Airbuses*: two routes to Heathrow, picking up at 13 points throughout the main hotel areas of Central London. *Gatwick*, ☎ 668 4211, 30 min. from Victoria Station by British Rail Gatwick Express (every 15 min., 5.30 a.m. to 11 p.m., hourly service throughout the night). Combined Gatwick Express/Underground tickets available from any underground station. *London City Airport (Stolport)*, Connaught Road, Silver Town, London E16 2PX, ☎ 474 5555. Access: Silver Town Station.

Underground (tube): London Regional Transport controls both *red* buses and underground trains. ☎ 222 1234 for their 24 hour a day travel information service (English only). The first trains run from 6 or 6.30 (later on Sun.), and the last at approximately midnight. Under 14 years old reduced fares, and 14 and 15 years old reduced fares with a child-rate photocard (available from post offices in London area). Under 5's travel free. Free maps of tube and bus services and a huge number of ever-changing leaflets describing various fares and special passes are available from underground and bus stations.

Bus service: controlled by London Regional Transport. The map of the city bus network is posted on tube station platforms, bus shelters and main bus stations. Individual bus routes are detailed at bus shelters. Fares on both tube and bus are computed according to stages and zones, therefore a short bus ride crossing three fare zones will cost the same or more than a much longer ride in a single zone. *Tourist passes. The London Explorer* pass allows unlimited travel on all London's red buses (except structured sightseeing tours) and almost all the underground (including Heathrow by Airbus or tube) for 1, 2, 3, 4 or 7 days. Special prices for those under 16. Ideal for longer excursions into London's hinterland. The *Capitalcard* costs £2.50 (£1.25 if under 16) and offers unlimited off-peak travel (i.e., after 9.30 Mon. to Fri.) for the day throughout London by train, underground or bus. Available from British Rail and underground stations. **London By Bus**: book for escorted coach tours of London sights at any London Regional Transport station or the LVCB information centre, Victoria Coach Station, Wilton Road, SW1, or at selected travel agents.

Taxis: London black cabs are rated the best in the world. Any cab with its yellow 'for hire' sign lit should stop if you flag it, and provided your journey is under six miles and within the London borders, the cab must take you where you want to go. *Radio Taxis*, ☎ 272 0272/272 3030/253 5000, 24 hours a day. *Minicabs: Addison Lee*, ☎ 720 2161; *Abbey Car Hire*, ☎ 727 2637. Many others listed in yellow pages.

Driving in London: do not use your car in London unless it is absolutely necessary; traffic is extremely dense, with numerous traffic jams. Parking places must nearly always be paid for, either at parking meters or at one of the National Car Parks throughout the city. *Cavendish Square*, ☎ 629 6968; *Piccadilly Circus*, Brewer Street, W1, ☎ 734 9497. For cheaper parking, the *NCP* at the National Theatre, Southbank, SE1, ☎ 928 3940. Free list of locations from NCP, 21 Bryanston Street, W1, ☎ 499 7050. The north and south circular ringroads of London are easily accessible from the centre and link up to all major motorways around London.

Car-rental: *Budget*: Central bookings, ☎ 935 3518; British Rail King's Cross, ☎ 833 0972; NCP car park, Victoria, Semley Place, SW1, ☎ 730 5233. *Avis*: 68 North Row, W1, ☎ 848 8733; Gatwick Airport, ☎ 0293 29721; Heathrow Airport, Hounslow, Middlesex, ☎ 897 9321. *Godfrey Davis Rail Drive* : Kings Cross, ☎ 834 8484; Paddington, ☎ 262 5655; Heathrow Airport, ☎ 897 0811. *Hertz*: Heathrow Airport, ☎ 897 9849; 1272, London Road, ☎ 679 1799.

Excursions on the Thames: upstream: boats leave from Westminster Pier, opposite Big Ben and travel upstream to Kew every 30 min., 10.30 to 3.30. Trips upstream to Hampton Court leave at 10, 10.30, 11.30 and 12, ☎ 930 4721. **Downstream**: boats leave Westminster Pier to the Tower of London (20 min. journey) every 20 min. 10.30 - 4 and to Greenwich (45 min. journey) every 20 min. 10.30 - 4. Three-hour round-

trip cruises to the Thames Flood Barrier from Westminster Pier at 10 and 1.30. One-hour cruises every 30 min. 11.30 - 5.

On the Regent Canal: *Zoo Waterbus* departs from Little Venice, Warwick Avenue/Camden Town tubes, ☎ 482 2550; *Jason's Trip* cruise along the canal, Camden Town tube, ☎ 286 3428. Riverboat Information Service, ☎ 730 4812.

Aerial views of London: *UK Air Taxis*, Westland Heliport, Lombard Road, SW11, ☎ 228 9114. Main line station Clapham Junction. *Tempus Aviation*, Grove House, 628 London Road, Colnbrook, Buckinghamshire, ☎ 028 12 4750.

Weather forecast: ☎ 836 4311.

Theatre: West End: *Aldwych*, WC2, ☎ 836 6404, London home of the Royal Shakespeare Company with plays often directly from Stratford-upon-Avon; *Barbican*, EC2, ☎ 628 8795; *National*, South Bank, SE1, ☎ 928 2252; *Palace*, Shaftesbury Avenue, W1, ☎ 437 8327; *Old Vic*, Waterloo Road, SE1, ☎ 928 7616; *Open Air*, Regent's Park, NW1, ☎ 486 2431; *Drury Lane*, Theatre Royal, Catherine Street, WC2, ☎ 836 8108. **Fringe**: *Albany*, Creek Road, SE8, ☎ 692 0765; *ICA*, Nash House, 12 Carlton House Terrace, SW1, ☎ 930 6393; *Riverside Studios*, Crisp Road, W6, ☎ 748 3354; *Tricycle*, 269 Kilburn High Road, NW6, ☎ 328 8626; *The Little Angel*, marionette theatre for children, 14 Dagmar Passage, Cross Street, N1, ☎ 226 1787. **Theatre ticket agencies**: charge up to 20 % commission but can usually secure tickets advertised as 'sold out' both before and on the same day as a performance: first call ☎ 240 7200, 24 hours a day, for credit card bookings (£1.75 per ticket). *Keith Prowse*, 44 Shaftesbury Avenue, W1, ☎ 437 8976; *SWET Ticket Booth*, southwest corner of Leicester Square, WC2, 2.30-6.30; *Premier Box Office*, 188 Shaftesbury Avenue, W1, ☎ 240 2245/7. Same-day reduced price seats sold at most theatres. Most major hotels also have booking offices in the lobby.

Concert halls: *Barbican Hall*, Barbican Centre, EC2, ☎ 628 8795, 638 8891. *Royal Albert Hall*: Kensington Grove, SW7, ☎ 589 8212, 589 9465. *Royal Festival Hall, Queen Elizabeth Hall* and the *Purcell Room* at the South Bank Arts Centre, SE1, ☎ 928 3191, 928 8000. Open-air concerts are given in the summer by the lake at *Crystal Palace*, in Holland Park, Kensington, W8, and at *Kenwood*, Hampstead, N6.

Art galleries: *Barbican*, Barbican Centre for Arts and Conferences, EC2, ☎ 638 4141, for thematic, non-specialized exhibitions; *British Library*, Great Russell Street, WC1, ☎ 636 1544, permanent exhibition of national collection of books and manuscripts, plus temporary exhibitions, lectures and audio-visual programs; *Crafts Council Galleries*, 12 Waterloo Place, SW1, ☎ 930 4811; *Christie's Contemporary Art*, 8 Dover Street, W1, ☎ 499 6701, a commercial gallery with continuous exhibitions by its artists; *Fisher Fine Art*, 30 King Street, St. James, SW1, ☎ 839 3942, exhibitions of 20thC European artists and British real-

ists every 4 to 6 weeks; *Hayward*, Belverdere Road, SE1, ☎ 938 3144, the main platform for the British Arts Council with five interconnected galleries and three sculpture courts; *Institute of Contemporary Arts*, Nash House, 12 Carlton House Terrace, SW1, ☎ 930 0493, platform for all new developments in art, with twenty-four exhibitions annually held in its three galleries; *Marlborough Fine Art*, 6 Albemarle Street, W1, ☎ 629 5161, Impressionist and 20thC art; *National*, Trafalgar Square, WC2, ☎ 839 3321, frequent exhibitions of 'the country's greatest collection of European paintings'; *Royal Academy of Arts*, Piccadilly, W1, ☎ 734 9052, mounts large shows arranged months in advance and extremely popular; *Tate*, Millbank, SW1, ☎ 821 1313, British collection, 1500-1900, modern collection of works by later 19th and 20thC artists; *Waddington*, 2, 4, 31 and 34 Cork Street, W1, ☎ 439 1866, specializing in painting and sculpture; *Anthony d'Offay*, 9 and 23 Dering Street, W1, ☎ 629 1578, a private gallery with 10-12 exhibitions annually of British and international contemporary art.

Antiques: There is a huge amount of 18th and 19thC furniture, china and *objets d'art* available throughout London. By far the best places for hunting are Portobello and Camden Passage markets (→ *markets* below) and the Chelsea Antiques Fair, Chelsea Old Town Hall, Kings Road, SW3, ☎ 937 5464, usually held in Mar. and Sep. Many antique shops also deal in silverware and jewelry, particularly those in the Burlington Arcade, SW1. *Antique shops*: T. Crowther, 282 North End Road, SW6, ☎ 385 1375; *Jeremy*, 255 Kings Road, SW3, ☎ 352 0644; *Pelham Galleries*, 163 and 165 Fulham Road, SW3, ☎ 589 2686; *Barrett Street Antique Supermarket*, W1, ☎ 493 5833; *Gray's Antique Market*, Davies Street, W1, over 100 stalls with wide range of antiques; *Chelsea Antique Market*, Kings Road, SW3. *Jewelry and silver*: Bentley, 65 New Bond Street, W1, ☎ 629 0651; *Bond Street Silver Galleries*, 111-112 New Bond Street, W1, ☎ 493 6180; *Collingwood*, 46 Conduit Street, W1, ☎ 734 2656; *Garrard*, 112 Regent Street, W1, ☎ 734 7020, jewelers to the Queen; *S.J. Phillips*, 139 New Bond Street, W1, ☎ 629 6261.

Auction rooms: *Christie's (South Kensington) Ltd., Art and Antiques*, 85 Old Brompton Road, SW7, ☎ 581 2231; *Christie's Fine Art*, 8 King Street, SW1, ☎ 839 9060, open Mon. to Fri. 9.30 to 4.45; *Phillips*, 7 Blenheim Street, W1, ☎ 629 6602, open 8.30 to 5, Mon. to Fri., 8.30 to 12, Sat.; *Sotheby's*, 34-35 New Bond Street, W1, ☎ 493 8080 and 19 Motcomb Street, SW1, ☎ 235 4311.

Markets: *Bermondsey*, SE1, antiques and bric-a-brac, Fri. from 5 a.m.; *Berwick Street*, W1, Mon. to Sat. for fruit and vegetables; *Brick Lane*, huge flea market on Sun. morning; *Camden Lock*, NW1, Sat. and Sun. for crafts, antiques, bric-a-brac, second-hand and new clothing; *Camden Passage*, NW1, for expensive antiques: 8-4, Tue., Wed., Sat., 9-5, Thu., Fri.; *Columbia Road*, Shoreditch, E2, Sun. morning for flowers and plants; *Electric Avenue*, Brixton, SW9, Mon., Tue., Thu., Fri., Sat. all day, Wed. (mornings only) for second-hand clothing and Afro-Caribbean foods; *Greenwich Antiques Market*, Greenwich High Road, SE10, Sat. and Sun. for antiques; *Kensington Market*,

Kensington High Street, W8, Mon. to Sat. for modern and unusual clothing; *Leather Lane*, EC1, Mon. to Fri. for fruits and vegetables, plants, clothing; *London Silver Vaults*, Chancery Lane, WC2, Mon. to Fri. and Sat. mornings for antique and modern silver; *Petticoat Lane*, Middlesex Street, EC1, Sun. mornings for general goods; *Portobello Road*, W11, Mon. to Sat. for general goods, Mon.-Thu. bric-a-brac, Fri.-Sat. flea market, Sat. antiques; *Shepherd's Bush*, W12, Mon. to Wed., Fri. and Sat., Thu. mornings for general goods; *Wembley*, Wembley Stadium Car Park, Middlesex, Sun. mornings for clothing, jewelry, food, bric-a-brac. London's *wholesale* markets are almost institutions in themselves, well worth a visit for the lively atmosphere, the range of fresh poultry, game, flowers and fish on display and the continual bartering. Since they are primarily there to serve retailers, hoteliers and restaurateurs who want fresh produce, the markets begin very early (4 a.m. onwards) and are all closed by midday: *Billingsgate*, North Quay, West India Dock Road, E14, Tue. to Sat., London's principal fish market; *New Covent Garden*, Nine Elms, SW5, Mon. to Fri., Sat. 4 to 9 a.m., London's principal fruit and vegetable market, with flowers on Sat.; *Smithfield*, EC1, Mon. to Fri., for meat, poultry and game; *Spitalfields*, E1, Mon. to Fri., Sat. 4.30 to 9 a.m. for fruit, vegetables and flowers.

Clubs, discothèques: *Stringfellows*: where you can rub shoulders with the rich and famous on Peter Stringfellows' glittering dance floor. First class nouvelle cuisine restaurant. 16/19 Upper St. Martin's Lane, WC2, ☎ 240 5534. *Ronnie Scott's*: to be upstairs at Ronnie Scott's, listening either to the man himself or one of his guest jazz bands, is to have made it. 47 Frith Street, W1, ☎ 439 0747. *The Empire Ballroom*: live disco bands, top UK disc jockeys, a light entertainment show and six bars. Leicester Square, WC2, ☎ 437 1446. *The Hippodrome*: a sophisticated nightclub with a laser floor show. Hippodrome Corner, Leicester Square, WC2, ☎ 437 4311. *Xenon*: lavishly equipped with a cocktail bar and hydraulic stage with waterfalls and fountains. 196 Piccadilly, W1, ☎ 734 9344. *100 Club*: a haven for jazz enthusiasts, attracting such names as Acker Bilk and his Paramount Jazz Band, Ken Colyer's All Star Jazz Men and Max Collie's Rhythm Aces. 100 Oxford Street, W1, ☎ 636 0933.

Riding: *Lilo Blum*, 32 Grosvenor Crescent Mews, SW1, ☎ 235 6846, includes rides in Hyde Park; *Bathurst Riding Stables*, 63 Bathurst Mews, W2, ☎ 723 2813; *Fir Tree Farm*, Woodlands Road, Little Bookham, Leatherhead, Surrey, ☎ Bookham 58712; *Roehampton Gate Riding and Livery Stables*, Priory Lane, SW16, adjacent to Richmond Park, ☎ 876 7089.

Cycling: more and more people are taking to the road on bicycles in London, both for economy and health reasons. *The London Cycling Campaign*, ☎ 928 7220, has been set up to provide cyclists with advice and information, and bicycles are available for rent from the following firms: *Bell Street Bikes*, 73 Bell Street, NW1, ☎ 724 0456; *London Bicycle Company*, 'Rent A Bike', 41 Floral Street, WC2, ☎ 240 3211; they also organize cycling holidays from Kensington Barracks,

Kensington Church Street, W8, ☎ 937 0726; *Bicycle Revival*, 17-19 Elizabeth Street, SW1, ☎ 730 6716.

Golf: many membership courses will extend guest facilities to members of comparable clubs from overseas. *Brent Valley Golf Course*, Church Road, Hanwell, W7, ☎ 567 1287, an 18-hole course in Brent River Park; *Richmond Park*, Roehampton Gate, SW15, ☎ 876 3205, two 18-hole parkland courses with advanced booking necessary at weekends; *Royal Mid Surrey*, Old Deer Park, Twickenham Road, Richmond, TW9 2SB, ☎ 940 1894, two 18-hole parkland courses open Mon. to Fri. Players must be members of recognized clubs and hold a handicap certificate; *South Herts*, Links Drive, Totteridge, N20, ☎ 445 2035, an 18-hole parkland course, open Mon. to Fri. Players must be members of recognized clubs. Municipal courses where it is not necessary to be a member: *Twickenham*, Staines Road, Twickenham, Middlesex, ☎ 979 6946, 9 hole; *Royal Epping Forest*, Forest Approach, Station Road, Chingford, Essex, ☎ 529 1039, 18 hole; *Home Park*, Hampton Wick, Kingston-upon-Thames, Surrey, ☎ 977 6645, 18-hole.

London events: **January**: *International Boat Show*; *West London Antiques Fair*; *Holiday on Ice*, Wembley Arena; *Brent Festival of Music and Dance*; *Benson and Hedges Masters Snooker Tournament*. **February**: *International Food and Drink Exhibition*; *Crufts Dogs Show*; *Stratford and East London Music Festival*; *Chinese New Year*, Soho. **March**: *Chelsea Antiques Fair*; *London International Opera Festival*; *British Designer Show*; *London Photograph Fair*; *Devizes to Westminster International Canoe Race*; *Oxford v. Cambridge University Boat Race*, Putney to Mortlake; *International Festival of Country Music*; *Easter Parade*, Battersea Park; *Daily Mail Ideal Home Exhibition*. **April**: *London Book Fair*; *London Drinker Beer Festival*; *Champions All International Gymnastics*; *Craft Fair*; *London Marathon*; *Milk Cup Football Final*; *FA Vase Final*; *Easter Parade*, Battersea Park; *London Harness Horse Parade*, Regent Park. **May**: *Rugby League Challenge Cup Final*; *Historic Commercial Vehicle Run*, Battersea Park to Brighton; *Royal Windsor Horse Trials*; *FA Cup Final*; *Chelsea Flower Show*; *International Contemporary Art Fair, Fine Art and Antiques Fair*, Olympia; *Greenwich Festival*; *Royal Academy of Arts Summer Exhibition*; *London Marathon*, Greenwich to Westminster. **June**: *Horse Guards Parade 'Beating the Retreat'*; *Derby Day Horse Racing at Epsom*; *Stella Artois Tennis Championships*; *Grosvenor House Antiques Fair*; *Trooping the Colour*; *All England Club Lawn Tennis Championships*, Wimbledon; *Metropolitan Police Horse Show*; *London to Brighton Bicycle Ride*; *Putney Show*, Putney Lower Common. **July**: *Festival of the City of London*; *Berkeley Square Charity Ball*; *Royal Tournament*, Earl's Court; *Richmond Festival*; *Henry Wood Promenade Concerts (Proms)*; *Finchley Carnival*; *Chelsea Village Fair*; *Swan Upping*, River Thames; *Doggetts Coat and Badge Race*, Tower Bridge to Chelsea. **August**: *West London Antiques Fair*; *Greater London Horse Show*; *Greenwich Clipper Weeks*; *Notting Hill Caribbean Carnival*. **September**: *Chelsea Antiques Fair*; *Battle of Britain Service*; *Sunday Times Fun Run*, Hyde Park; *Punch and Judy Festival*, Covent Garden Piazza. **October**: *National Brass Band Championships*; *Horse of the Year Show*; *Chelsea Crafts Fair*; *Trafalgar Day Parade by Sea Cadets*; *International Bike Show*. **November**: *London to Brighton Veteran Car Run*; *Kensington Antiques Fair*; *Caravan Camping Holiday Show*, Earl's Court; *Lord Mayor's Show*; *London Craft Fair*; *Daily Mail International Ski Show*; *Benson and Hedges Tennis Championships*; *World Travel Market*. **December**: *Olympia International Showjumping Championships*; *Christmas Lights and Trees*, Oxford Street and Regent Street.

The Gunpowder Plot

The years following the establishment of the Church of England under Henry VIII saw much conflict between English Protestants and Catholics. During the reign of Henry's daughter Mary Tudor, Catholicism was briefly restored, and over 300 Protestants were put to death. But for most of the next 150 years Catholics were regarded as public enemies and could be severely punished for not attending the Anglican Church. There were a number of Catholic uprisings, including a 1586 conspiracy to murder Elizabeth I and put Catholic Mary Queen of Scots in her place. But the most famous plot of all was the 1605 scheme to blow up the Houses of Parliament.

This was to have taken place on 5 Nov., at the state opening of Parliament, and was intended to kill the king, his ministers and all the members of both Houses of Parliament. The plot was organized by Robert Catesby, but it was Guy Fawkes who was to set off the explosion. The conspirators rented a building next to the House of Lords in Dec. 1604, and began tunneling through the cellars. After eleven months they had reached the vaults of Parliament and managed to store thirty-six barrels of gunpowder. However, the plot was betrayed when an anonymous letter was sent to one of the peers. A search was made, and Guy Fawkes was discovered with his lantern, matches and tinderbox. (The plan had been for him to light the explosive with a slow-burning fuse and then to escape in a boat waiting on the Thames.) Fawkes was arrested and later tortured and executed — along with those other conspirators who had not been killed while attempting to escape. Ever since then, festivities have taken place on 5 Nov. in his name. On Guy Fawkes or Bonfire Night, 'Guys' or effigies of Fawkes are burned on bonfires throughout the country and fireworks are lit. Children prop up Guys they have made in the streets, and beg passers-by for 'a penny for the Guy', and before every annual state opening, the cellars of the Houses of Parliament are searched.

Accommodation: *London Homes*, P.O. Box 730, London, SW6, 2QN, ☎ 748 4947. London Homes has gathered close to 80 addresses for reasonably priced places to stay, all located near underground stations. Prices are less than £10 a night per person, including breakfast. For a longer stay, it is possible to rent an apartment (minimum stay: two weeks) starting at £70 a week.

Room and board with a London resident: *London Homestead Services* has 250 houses in its scheme,

each offering home comforts and breakfast. Prices start at £10 per person per night at all properties 20 to 30 min. traveling time from Piccadilly. Minimum stay 3 nights. 154 Warwick Road, Kensington, W14, 8PS, ☎ 602 9851, 9 to 5.30.

Lodging for young people: *Y.H.A.*, Trevelyan House, 8 St. Stephen's Hill, St. Albans, Hertshire, AL1 2DY, ☎ 0727 55215; *Y.M.C.A.* Accommodation Service, 16 Russell Street, WC1, ☎ 636 4363; *Student Accommodation Services*, 44 Langham Street, W1, ☎ 637 3250.

 Central London

BATTERSEA

map 1-B1

Restaurants:
♦ *Di's Larder*, 62 Lavender Hill, ☎ (01) 223 4618 Ⓟ 🕭 🍽 Cl. 2 wks. Aug., Bank Hols., eves., Sun. Vegetarian cuisine. £4.50.
♦ *Jason's Taverna*, 50 Battersea Park Road, ☎ (01) 622 6998 Ⓟ 𝄁 🍽 Cl. 1st, 2nd wks. Aug., Bank Hols., lunch, Sun. Greek cuisine. Book. £8.50.
♦ *La Preferita*, 163 Lavender Hill, ☎ (01) 223 1046, AC AM BA DI 𝄁 🍽 Cl. 26-30 Dec., Sun. Italian cuisine. Book. £12.
♦ *Ormes*, 245 Lavender Hill, ☎ (01) 228 9824, AC AM BA DI Lunch not served. Cl. Sun. Fish dishes.
♦ *Pollyanna's*, 2 Battersea Rise, ☎ (01) 228 0316, AC AM BA Lunch not served Mon.-Sat. No dinner Sun. Cl. 24-27 Dec. and 1 Jan. £16.

BAYSWATER

map 2-A2

Hotels:
★★★★ *Royal Lancaster* (Rank), Lancaster Terrace, W2 2TY, ☎ (01) 262 6737, Tx 24822, AC AM BA DI, 435 rm. Ⓟ ≼ 🕭 🍽 £143. Rest. ♦ £17.50.
★★★ *Central Park*, Queensborough Terrace, W2 3SS, ☎ (01) 229 2424, Tx 27342, AC BA AM DI, 287 rm. Ⓟ £66. Rest. ♦ £9.
★★★ *London Embassy* (Embassy), 150 Bayswater Road, W2 4RT, ☎ (01) 229 1212, Tx 27727, AC AM BA DI, 192 rm. Ⓟ 🕭 £85. Rest. ♦ £12.
★★★ *Park Court* (M.C.H.), 75 Lancaster Gate, W2 3NR, ☎ (01) 402 4272, Tx 23922, AC AM BA DI, 412 rm. 𝄟 🍽 £69. Rest. ♦ £10.
★★★ *Pembridge Court*, 34 Pembridge Gardens, W2 4DX, ☎ (01) 229 9977, Tx 298363, AC BA AM DI, 35 rm. Ⓟ £65. Rest. ♦ Cl. Sun., Bank Hols. £11.
★★★ *White's* (M.C.), Lancaster Gate, W2 3NR, ☎ (01) 262 2711, Tx 24771, AC AM BA DI, 61 rm. Ⓟ £126. Rest. ♦ £26.
★★ *Coburg* (B.W.), 129 Bayswater Road, W2 4RJ, ☎ (01) 229 3654, Tx 268235, AC AM BA DI, 125 rm. £69. Rest. ♦ Cl. Christmas wk. £12.
★★ *Hospitality Inn* (M.C.H.), 104 Bayswater Road, W2 3HL, ☎ (01) 262 4461, Tx 22667, AC AM BA DI, 175 rm. Ⓟ ≼ £85. Rest. ♦ £11.
★★ *Mornington* (B.W.), 12 Lancaster Gate, W2 3LG, ☎ (01) 262 7361, Tx 24281, AC AM BA DI, 65 rm. £73.
★ *Allandale*, 3 Devonshire Terrace, W2 3DN, ☎ (01) 723 8311, AC BA DI, 20 rm. 🍽 £37.

Restaurants:
● ♦ *Kalamara's*, 76-78 Inverness Mews, ☎ (01) 727 9122, AC AM BA DI 𝄟 𝄁 🍽 Cl. lunch, Christmas eve., Bank Hols., Sun. Seafood in Greek pastry. Book. £14.50.
♦ *Al Khayam*, 27-29 Westbourne Grove, ☎ (01) 727 2556 𝄁 🍽 Cl. Christmas. Indian cuisine. Book. £16.
♦ *Bali*, 101 Edgware Road, ☎ (01) 723 3303, AC AM BA DI.
♦ *Bombay Palace*, 2 Hyde Park Square, ☎ (01) 723 8855, AC AM BA DI £13.
♦ *Concordia*, 29-31 Craven Road, ☎ (01) 402 4985, AC AM BA DI Cl. Sun., Bank Hols. £23.
♦ *Fortuna Cookie*, 1 Queensway, ☎ (01) 727 7260.
♦ *Ganges*, 101 Praed Street, ☎ (01) 262 3835, AC AM BA DI Cl. 25-26 Dec. £12.
♦ *Green Jade*, 29-31 Porchester Road, ☎ (01) 229 7221, AC AM BA DI Cl. Sun. lunch.
♦ *Le Mange Tout*, 34 Sussex Place, ☎ (01) 723 1199, AC AM BA DI Cl. Sat. lunch, Christmas, Bank Hols. £19.
♦ *Maharajah*, 50 Queensway, ☎ (01) 727 1135 £13.
♦ *San Marino*, 26 Sussex Place, ☎ (01) 723 8395, AC AM BA DI Cl. Sun., Bank Hols. £18.

Inn or Pub:
Victoria (Charringtons), 10A Strathearn Place, ☎ (01) 262 5696.

Recommended
Cafe: *Pierre Pechon*, 127 Queensway, ☎ (01) 229 0746, choice of over 100 cakes and pastries.
Shopping: *Themes and Variations*, 231 Wesbourne Grove, ☎ (01) 727 5531, Art Deco, fifties furniture and gallery.

BELGRAVIA

map 2-B2-3

Hotels:
● ★★★★ *Berkeley* (Savoy), Wilton Place, SW1X 7RL, ☎ (01) 235 6000, Tx 919252, AC AM BA DI, 160 rm. Ⓟ 🕭 🍽 ▭ £195. Rest. ♦ Cl. Sat., Sun, Bank Hols. and Aug. £30.
★★★★ *Hyatt Carlton Tower* (Hyatt), 2 Cadogan Place, SW1X 9PY, ☎ (01) 235 5411, Tx 21944, AC AM BA DI, 228 rm. Ⓟ 🍽 £224. Rest. ● ♦ *Chelsea Room*, Cl. 3 days Christmas. £37.
★★★★ *Hyde Park* (T.H.F.), 66 Knightsbridge, SW1Y 7LA, ☎ (01) 235 2000, Tx 262057, AC AM BA DI, 179 rm. ≼ £176. Rest. ♦ *Park Room* 𝄁 Roast rib of beef. £21.
★★★★ *Lowndes Thistle* (Thistle), 19 Lowndes Street, SW1X 9ES, ☎ (01) 235 6020, Tx 919065, AC AM BA DI, 79 rm. £149. Rest. ♦ £18.
★★★★ *Sheraton Park Tower*, 101 Knightsbridge, SW1X 7RN, ☎ (01) 235 8050, Tx 917222, AC AM BA DI, 295 rm. Ⓟ 🍽 Rest. ♦ 𝄁 £20.
● ★★★ *Capital*, 22-24 Basil Street, SW3 1AT, ☎ (01) 589 5171, Tx 919042, AC AM BA DI, 60 rm. Ⓟ £151. Rest. ● ♦ Mousseline of scallops with sea-urchin cream, rack of lamb. £21.
★★★ *Belgravia Sheraton*, 20 Chesham Place, SW1X 8HQ, ☎ (01) 235 6040, Tx 919020, AC AM BA DI, 89 rm. 🍽 £158. Rest. ♦ Cl. Sat. lunch. £20.
★★ *Basil Street*, SW3 1AH, ☎ (01) 581 3311, Tx 28379, AC AM BA DI, 94 rm. £99. Rest. ♦ *Dining Room* 𝄁 Roast beef carved from the trolley. £18.

Restaurants:
● ♦ *Ports*, 11 Beauchamp Place, ☎ (01) 581 3837, AC AM BA DI 𝄁 🍽 Sun. and Bank Hols. Portuguese dishes, seafood. Book. £17.
● ♦ *Salloos*, 62-64 Kinnerton Street, ☎ (01) 235 4444, AC AM BA DI Cl. Sun. and Bank Hols. Indian cheese soufflé. £25.
● ♦ *San Lorenzo*, 22 Beauchamp Place, ☎ (01) 584 1074 ≼ 𝄁 Cl. Christmas, Easter, Sun. Italian cuisine. Book. £17.
♦ *Dumpling House*, 9 Beauchamp Place, ☎ (01) 589 8240, AC AM BA DI 🍽 Cl. 25-26 Dec. Peking duck, king prawns. £8.50.

◆ *La Fantaisie Brasserie*, 14 Knightsbridge Green, ☎ (01) 589 0509, AC AM BA DI ⚲ ♪ ✻ Cl. Bank Hols., Sun. Book. £16.

◆ *Maroush II*, 38 Beauchamp Place, ☎ (01) 581 5434, AC AM BA DI ⚲ ♪ ✻ Cl. Christmas. Middle Eastern cuisine. Book. £17.50.

◆ *Ménage à Trois*, 15 Beauchamp Place, ☎ (01) 589 4252, AC AM BA DI ♪ Cl. Christmas, Sun. Mousse with caviar, smoked salmon and scallops. Book. £30.

◆ *Mes Amis*, 31 Basil Street, ☎ (01) 584 4484, AC AM DA DI £18.

◆ *Motcombs*, 26 Motcomb Street, ☎ (01) 235 6382, AC AM BA DI Cl. Sun. £16.

◆ *San Martino*, 103 Walton Street, ☎ (01) 589 3833, AC AM BA DI ℙ ⚲ ♿ ✻ Cl. Christmas, Easter, Bank Hols., Sun. Pasta dishes. Book. £10.

◆ *San Ruffillo*, 8 Harriet Street, ☎ (01) 235 3969, AC AM BA DI Cl. Sun. and Bank Hols. £15.

◆ *Tent*, 15 Eccleston Street, ☎ (01) 730 6922, AC AM BA Cl. Sat. £12.

Inns or Pubs:

Antelope (Benskins), 22 Eaton Terrace, ☎ (01) 730 7781.

Grenadier (Watneys), 18 Wilton Row, ☎ (01) 235 3074, AC AM BA DI ✻ Traditional English food in restaurant. £18.

Nag's Head (Benskins and Burton), 53 Kinnerton Street, ☎ (01) 235 1135 £4.

Recommended

Café: Bendicks, 195 Sloane Street, ☎ (01) 235 4749, coffee, tea and gateaux.

Shopping: *Bertjerman and Barton*, 43 Elizabeth Street, new boutique of famed teas and teapots;*Fogal*, 51 Brompton Road, sophisticated stockings;*Harvey Nichol's*, Knightsbridge, Lady Di's favourite store;*Max Pike's*, 4 Eccleston Street, bathroom accessories;*Mostly Smoked*, 47 Elizabeth Street, specialized in smoked fish;*Scotch House*, 2 Brompton Road, Scotch classics.

Teashop: *Fouquet of Paris*, 58 Beauchamp Place, Knightsbridge, ☎ (01) 581 5540, homemade chocolate, teas, coffees, champagnes and jams.

Wine bar: *Carriages*, 43 Buckingham Palace Road, ☎ (01) 434 8871, upmarket wine list.

BLOOMSBURY

map 2-BC1

Hotels:

★★★★ *Kenilworth* (E.D.W.), 97 Great Russell Street, WC1B 3LB, ☎ (01) 637 3477, Tx 25842, AC AM BA DI, 180 rm. ✻ £90. Rest. ◆ £17.

★★★★ *Regent Crest* (Crest), Carburton Street, W1P 8EE, ☎ (01) 388 2300, Tx 22453, AC AM BA DI, 322 rm. ℙ ✻ £95. Rest. ◆ £16.

★★★ *Bedford Corner* (Aquarius), Bayley Street, WC1B 3HD, ☎ (01) 580 7766, Tx 296464, AC AM BA DI, 88 rm. £77. Rest. ◆ ♪ Cl. 24 Dec.-1 Jan. £15.

★★★ *Berners*, 10 Berners Street, W1A 3BE, ☎ (01) 636 1629, Tx 25759, AC AM BA DI, 234 rm. ♿ ✻ £115. Rest. ◆ £14.

★★★ *Bloomsbury Crest*, Coram Street, WC1N 1HT, ☎ (01) 837 1200, Tx 22113, AC AM BA DI, 250 rm. ℙ £85. Rest. ◆ £12.

★★★ *Grafton* (E.D.W.), 130 Tottenham Court Road, W1P 9HP, ☎ (01) 388 4131, Tx 297234, AC AM BA DI, 178 rm. ✻ £94. Rest. ◆ £11.

★★★ *Kennedy* (M.C.H.), 43 Cardington Street, NW1 2LP, ☎ (01) 387 4400, Tx 28250, AC AM BA DI, 320 rm. ℙ ✻ £65. Rest. ◆ £11.

★★★ *Kingsley* (M.C.H.), Bloomsbury Way, WC1A 2SD, ☎ (01) 242 5881, Tx 21157, AC AM BA DI, 146 rm. £80. Rest. ◆ Cl. Sat. and Sun. £14.

★★★ *Royal Scot* (M.C.H.), 100 Kings Cross Road, WC1X 9DT, ☎ (01) 278 2434, Tx 27657, AC AM BA DI, 349 rm. ℙ £65. Rest. ◆ ♪ £10.

★★★ *Russell* (T.H.F.), Russell Square, WC1B 5BE, ☎ (01) 837 6470, Tx 24615, AC AM BA DI, 318 rm. £89. Rest. ◆ £16.

★★★ *St. George's* (T.H.F.), Langham Place, W1N 8QS, ☎ (01) 580 0111, Tx 27274, AC AM BA DI, 85 rm. £120. Rest. ◆ £19.

★★ *Bonnington*, 92 Southampton Row, WC1B 4BH, ☎ (01) 242 2828, Tx 261591, AC AM BA DI, 242 rm. ♿ £68. Rest. ◆ £10.

★★ *Royal National* (Imperial London), Bedford Way, WC1H 0DG, ☎ (01) 637 2488, Tx 21822, AC AM BA DI, 1028 rm. ℙ ♿ ✻ £50. Rest. ◆ ♪ ♿ £11.

★ *Crichton*, 36 Bedford Place, WC1B 5JR, ☎ (01) 637 3955, Tx 22353, AC AM BA DI, 64 rm. Listed building. £33.

Restaurants:

● ◆ *Porte de la Cité*, 65 Theobalds Road, ☎ (01) 242 1154, AC AM BA DI ✻ Cl. Christmas, Easter, Bank Hols., eves., Sat. and Sun. Supreme de poulet. Book. £16.50.

● ◆ *Rue St. Jacques*, 5 Charlotte Street, ☎ (01) 637 0222, AC AM BA DI ♪ ♿ ✻ Cl. Sat. lunch., Sun., Easter, Bank Hols, 24 Dec.-5 Jan. Book. £32.

● ◆ *White Tower*, 1 Percy Street, ☎ (01) 636 8141, AC AM BA DI ✻ Cl. 3 wks. Aug., 1 wk. Christmas, Bank Hols., Sat., Sun. Greek dishes, roast duckling. Book. £20.

◆ *Aunties*, 126 Cleveland Street, ☎ (01) 387 1548, AC AM BA DI No lunch Sat. Cl. Sun., 25-26 Dec., 1 Jan. and Bank Hols. £16.

◆ *Cranks*, Tottenham Street, ☎ (01) 631 3912 ♪ ✻ Cl. Bank Hols., Sun. Health food breakfast, quiche, flans, pizza, salads. £7.

◆ *Elephants and Butterflies*, 67 Charlotte Street, ☎ (01) 580 1732, AC AM BA DI ♪ ✻ Cl. Bank Hols., Sat. lunch., Sun. Vegetarian cuisine. Organic ingredients. Book. £9.50.

◆ *Gonbei*, 151 Kings Cross Road, ☎ (01) 278 0619 ♪ ✻ Cl. Sun., 25 Dec.- 1 Jan. Japanese dishes. Sushi. Book. £13.

◆ *Hare Krishna Curry House*, 1 Hanway Street, ☎ (01) 636 5262, AC AM BA DI ⚲ ♪ ♿ ✻ Cl. Sun. Hindu vegetarian dishes. £6.

◆ *Lai Qila*, 117 Tottenham Court Road, ☎ (01) 387 4570, AC AM BA DI Cl. 25-26 Dec. £14.

◆ *Les Halles*, 57 Theobalds Road, ☎ (01) 242 6761, AC AM BA DI No lunch Sat. Cl. Sun. and Bank Hols. £25.

◆ *Little Akropolis*, 10 Charlotte Street, ☎ (01) 636 8198, AC AM BA DI No lunch Sat. Cl. Sun. and Bank Hols. Greek cuisine. £10.

◆ *L'Etoile*, 30 Charlotte Street, ☎ (01) 636 7189, AC AM BA DI ✻ Cl. Aug., Bank Hols. French cuisine. Book. £30.

◆ *Mandeer*, 21 Hanway Place, ☎ (01) 323 0660, AC AM BA DI ⚲ ♪ ✻ Cl. Bank Hols., Christmas, Sun. Indian vegetarian dishes. Book. £10.

◆ *Mr Kai*, 50 Woburn Place, ☎ (01) 580 1188, AC AM BA DI Cl. 25-26 Dec., 1 Jan. and Bank Hols. £21.

◆ *The Greenhouse*, 16 Chenies Street, ☎ (01) 637 8038 ♪ ✻ Cl. 24 Dec.-1 Jan., Sun. Wholefood and vegetarian dishes. £4.50.

◆ *Winstons Eating House*, 24 Coptic Street, ☎ (01) 580 3422, AM AC BA DI No lunch Sat. No dinner Sun. Cl. Christmas, New Year and Bank Hols.

Inns or Pubs:

Museum Tavern, 49 Great Russell Street, ☎ (01) 242 8987, BA DI Cream teas Mon.-Sat.

Lamb (Youngs), 94 Lambs Conduit Street, ☎ (01) 405 0713.

Recommended

Bicycles: *Condor cycles*, 144 Grays Inn Road, the cream of the crop, possible to make your own bicycle.

Bookshop: *Bloomsbury Rare Books*, 29 Museum Street, an agreeable disorder of rare books.

Shoes: *Sacha*, 351 New Oxford Street, ☎ (01) 499 7272, fashionable shoes for women.

♥ *prints:* *The Print Room*, 37 Museum Street, enchanting prints, principally on natural history; *umbrellas:* *James Smith and Son*, 53 New Oxford Street, umbrellas since 1830.

CHELSEA

map 2-B3

Hotels:
★★★★ *Holiday Inn*, 17-25 Sloane Street, SW1X 9NU, ☎ (01) 235 4377, Tx 919111, AC AM BA DI, 202 rm. ♨ ▣ £118. Rest. ♦ £17.
★★ *Willet*, 32 Sloane Gardens, SW1V 8DJ, ☎ (01) 730 0634, 17 rm. ♨ £37.50.
★ *Fenja*, 69 Cadogan Gardens, SW3 2RB, ☎ (01) 589 1183, AC AM BA DI, 18 rm. ♨

Restaurants:
● ♦ *Beccofino*, 100 Draycott Avenue, ☎ (01) 584 3600, AC AM BA ♪ ♨ Cl. Bank Hols., Sun. Book. £20.
● ♦ *Dans*, 119 Sydney Street, ☎ (01) 352 2718, AC AM BA DI Cl. Sat., Sun., Bank Hols. and 1 wk. Christmas. £15.
● ♦ *English Garden*, 10 Lincoln Street, ☎ (01) 584 7272, AC AM BA DI ♪ ♨ Cl. 25-26 Dec. Quail egg patty. Book. £28.50.
● ♦ *English House*, 3 Milner Street, ☎ (01) 584 3002, AM BA DI AC ♧ ♨ Cl. 25-26 Dec. Lamb in salt crust. Book. £24.
● ♦ *Gavvers*, 61 Lower Sloane Street, ☎ (01) 730 5983, AM DI No lunch. Cl. Sun. and Bank Hols. £18.
● ♦ *Ma Cuisine*, 113 Walton Street, ☎ (01) 584 7585, AM DI Cl. 14 Jul.-14 Aug., Sat., Sun., Christmas, 1 Jan., 1 wk. Easter. £17.
● ♦ *Ponte Nuovo*, 126 Fulham Road, ☎ (01) 370 6656, AC AM BA DI ∭ ♨ Cl. Bank Hols. Linguine al cartoccio. Book. £16.
● ♦ *San Frediano*, 62 Fulham Road, ☎ (01) 584 8375, AC BA DI ♨ Cl. Sun. Book. £16.
● ♦ *St. Quentin*, 243 Brompton Road, ☎ (01) 589 8005, AC AM BA DI ♨ Cl. 1 wk. Christmas. Feuilletés d'escargots. Book. £20.
● ♦ *Tante Claire*, 68 Royal Hospital Road, ☎ (01) 352 6045, AM DI ♨ Cl. 1 wk. Christmas, 1 wk. Easter, 3 wks. Aug., Sat., Sun. Galette de foie gras. Book. £36.
● ♦ *Waltons*, 121 Walton Street, ☎ (01) 584 0204, AC AM BA DI Cl. Bank Hols. 'Moneybag' of chicken and asparagus. Book. £29.
♦ *Avoirdupois*, 334 Kings Road, ☎ (01) 352 6151, AC AM BA DI.
♦ *Choy's*, 172 Kings Road, ☎ (01) 352 9085, AC AM BA DI £20.
♦ *Daphne's*, 112 Draycott Avenue, ☎ (01) 589 4257, AC AM BA DI ♨ Cl. Sun., Bank Hols. No lunch. £18.50.
♦ *Don Luigi's*, 316 Kings Road, ☎ (01) 730 3023.
♦ *Eleven Park Walk*, 11 Park Walk, ☎ (01) 352 3449, AC AM DI £21.
♦ *Good Earth*, 233 Brompton Road, ☎ (01) 584 3658 Cl. 24-27 Dec.
♦ *Good Earth*, 91 Kings Road, ☎ (01) 352 9231, AC AM BA DI Cl. 24-27 Dec. £17.
♦ *La Brasserie*, 272 Brompton Road, ☎ (01) 584 1668, AM AC BA DI ♪ ♨ Cl. 25-26 Dec. Book. £12.50.
♦ *Le Français*, 259 Fulham Road, ☎ (01) 352 4748, AM BA ♨ Cl. Christmas, Sun. French regional cuisine. Book. £23.
♦ *Le Suquet*, 104 Draycott Avenue, ☎ (01) 581 1785, AM ♨ Cl. 25 Dec.-4 Jan. Seafood. Book. £40.
♦ *Mario*, 260-262A Brompton Road, ☎ (01) 584 1724, AC AM BA DI Cl. Bank Hols. £14.
♦ *Meridiana*, 169 Fulham Road, ☎ (01) 589 8815, AC AM BA DI ∭ ♪ ♨ Homemade gnocchi. Book. £22.
♦ *Monkeys*, 1 Cale Street, Chelsea Green, ☎ (01) 352 4711 ♨ Cl. 25-26 Dec., 1 wk. Feb., 3 wks. Aug. Game meats. Book. £15.
♦ *Poissonnerie de l'Avenue*, 82 Sloane Avenue, ☎ (01) 589 2457, AC AM BA DI ♧ ♨ Cl. Bank Hols., Sun., 24 Dec. - 2 Jan. Seafood. Book. £18.
♦ *Tandoori*, 153 Fulham Road, ☎ (01) 589 7749, AC AM BA DI ▣ ♧ ♪ ♨ Cl. 25-26 Dec. King prawn, bhuna, masala. Book. £16.
♦ *Thierry's*, 342 Kings Road, ☎ (01) 352 3365, AM BA DI ♪ Cl. last 2 wks. Aug., Bank Hols., Sun., Christmas, Easter. French cuisine. Rack of lamb. Book. £15.

♦ *Toto*, Walton House, Walton Street, ☎ (01) 589 0075, AC AM BA Cl. Easter and 4 days Christmas. £21.
♦ *Zen Chinese*, Chelsea Cloisters, Sloane Avenue, ☎ (01) 589 1781, AC AM BA DI Cl. 25-27 Dec. Old Buddhist dishes. £13.

Inns or Pubs:
Cross Keys (Courage), Lawrence Street. Bar food.
Henry J Bean's, 195-197 Kings Road, ☎ (01) 352 9255 ∭ ♧ £8.

Recommended
Antique market: *Antiquarius*, 135 Kings Road, covered market with good coffee shop.
Gallery: *Chenil Galleries*, 181 Kings Road, for lovers of Art Deco and Art Nouveau, good cafeteria.
Fashion: *Reiss*, 114 Kings Road, American sportswear; *Stephen King*, 315 Kings Road.
Shoes: *Zapata Shoes Co.*, 49-51 Old Church Street.

CITY

map 2-CD2
▯ City of London information, St. Paul's Churchyard, ☎ 606 3030.

Hotels:
★★★★ *Tower Thistle* (Thistle), St. Katharine's Way, Tower Hamlets, E1 9LD, ☎ (01) 481 2575, Tx 885934, AC AM BA DI, 826 rm. ℙ £112. Rest. ♦ £20.
★★★ *Great Eastern* (Compass), Liverpool Street, EC2M 7QN, ☎ (01) 283 4363, Tx 886812, AC AM BA DI, 163 rm. £75. Rest. ♦ *City Eates* ♪ Cl. 24 Dec.-2 Jan. Carvery. £9.

Restaurants:
● ♦ *Hana Guruma*, 49 Bow Lane, ☎ (01) 236 6451, AC AM BA DI ♪ ♧ ♨ Cl. Christmas, 1 Jan., Sat., Sun. Yakitori bar. Book. £13.
● ♦ *Le Poulbot*, 45 Cheapside, ☎ (01) 236 4379, AC AM BA DI ♨ Cl. Christmas, 1 Jan., Bank Hols., dinner, Sat., Sun. French cuisine. No children under 4. Book. £25.50.
♦ *Baron of Beef*, Gresham Street, ☎ (01) 606 6961, AC AM BA DI ♧ ♪ ♨ Cl. Sat., Sun. Sirloin of beef, summer pudding. Book. £30.
♦ *Cafe St. Pierre*, 29 Clerkenwell Green, ☎ (01) 251 6606, AC AM BA DI Cl. Sat., Sun., 24 Dec.- 2 Jan., Bank Hols £17.
♦ *Corney Barrow*, 118 Moorgate, ☎ (01) 628 2898, AC AM BA DI ♪ ♨ Cl. Christmas, 1 Jan., Easter, Bank Hols., Sat., Sun. Anglo-French cuisine. Book. £32.
♦ *Ginnan*, 5 Cathedral Place, ☎ (01) 236 4120 AC AM BA DI ♪ ♨ Cl. Bank Hols., Sat. eve., Sun. Japanese cuisine. £18.
♦ *La Bastille*, 116 Newgate Street, ☎ (01) 600 1134, AC AM BA DI Cl. dinner, 1 wk. Aug., 2 wks. Dec. £18.
♦ *Le Gamin*, 32 Old Bailey, ☎ (01) 236 7931, AC AM BA DI Cl. dinner, Sat., Sun., Bank Hols. Book. £19.
♦ *Oscar's Brasserie*, Temple Chambers, Temple Avenue, ☎ (01) 353 6272, AC AM BA DI ♢ ♧ ♪ ♨ Cl. last 3 wks. Aug., last wk. Dec., Bank Hols., Sat., Sun. Turbot marinière, fillet of lamb. Book. £15.
♦ *Shares*, 12-13 Lime Street, ☎ (01) 623 1843 Cl. dinner, Bank Hols. £24.
♦ *The Nosherie*, 12-13 Greville Street, ☎ (01) 242 1591 ♨ Cl. Sat., Sun. Jewish cuisine. Salt beef, cheese blintzes. £7.
♦ *Wheeler's*, 33 Foster Lane, ☎ (01) 606 0896, AC AM BA DI ♪ ♨ Cl. Sat., Sun., Mon.-Fri. eve. Fish and seafood. £22.50.

Inns or Pubs:
Black Friar, 174 Queen Victoria Street, ☎ (01) 236 5650. Opulent Art Nouveau and Edwardian decor. Home-cooked lunch ex. Sat.-Sun.
Chiswell Vaults (Whitbreads), Chiswell Street, ☎ (01) 588 5733.
Cock Tavern, The Poultry Market, Central Markets, ☎ (01) 248 2918, AC AM BA DI Breakfast, lunch, snacks eve. £7.50.
Dirty Dick's, 202 Bishopgate, ☎ (01) 283 5888, BA DI.

Fox Anchor (Inde Coope), 115 Chartershouse Street, ☎ (01) 253 4838 ℗ & Breakfast, lunches. £6.50.
Hand Shears (Courage), 1 Middle Street, ☎ (01) 600 0257.
Old Bell Tavern, 95 Fleet Street, ☎ (01) 583 0070.
Old Dr. Butler's Head, Masons Avenue, ☎ (01) 606 3504, BA DI.
Old Wine Shades, 6 Martin Lane.
Olde Chesire Cheese, 145 Fleet Street, ☎ (01) 353 6170 Traditional English menu. £9.
Olde Mitre (Allied), Ely Court, Hatton Garden, ☎ (01) 405 4751 3 rm.
Olde Watling (Vintage), 29 Watling Street, ☎ (01) 248 6235, BA DI.
Printer's Devil (Whitbreads), 98 Fetter Lane, ☎ (01) 242 2239.
Samuel Pepys (Toby-Bass), Brooks Wharf, Upper Thames Street, ☎ (01) 248 3048, AC AM BA DI ≮ £10.50.
Three Compasses (Trumans), 66 Cowcross Street, ☎ (01) 253 3368.
Windmill (Charringtons), 27 Tabernacle Street, ☎ (01) 638 2603. & £6.

Recommended
Silver: *London Silver Vaults*, incredible number of booths selling antiques, modern silver.
♥ shoes: *Church's English Shoes*, 90 Poultry Street.

EMBANKMENT

map 2-C2
Hotels:
● ★★★★ **Savoy**, The Strand, WC2R 0EU, ☎ (01) 836 4343, Tx 24234, AC AM BA DI, 200 rm. ℗ ≮ ✀ £220. Rest. ● ♦ **River**, £26.
★★★★ **Howard** (Barclays), 12 Temple Place, WC2 2PR, ☎ (01) 836 3555, Tx 268047, AC AM BA DI, 141 rm. ℗ ≮ ✀ £190 Rest. ♦ **Quai d'Or** ♪ 'Fillets of sole isle de France'. £30.
★★★★ **Waldorf** (T.H.F.), Aldwych, WC2B 4DD, ☎ (01) 836 2400, Tx 24574, AC AM BA DI, 312 rm. £110. Rest. ♦ Cl. Sat. lunch, Sun. and Bank Hols. Hotel Cl. 24 Dec., 1 Jan. £21.
★★★ **Charing Cross**, P.O. Box 99, The Strand, WC2N 5HX, ☎ (01) 839 7282, Tx 261101, AC AM BA DI, 219 rm. ℗ £85. Rest. ♦ ♪ Cl. 1 wk. Christmas. £12.
★★★ **Royal Horseguards** (Thistle), Whitehall Court, SW1A 2EJ, ☎ (01) 839 3400, Tx 917096, AC AM BA DI, 284 rm. ≮ ✀ £135. Rest. ♦ £22.
★★★ **Strand Palace** (T.H.F.), The Strand, WC2R 0JJ, ☎ (01) 836 8080, Tx 24208, AC AM BA DI, 775 rm. £81. Rest. ♦ £16.

Restaurants:
● ♦ **Simpsons**, 100 The Strand, ☎ (01) 836 9112, AC AM BA DI ✀ Cl. Christmas, Easter, Sun., Bank Hols. 3 rm. Roast sirloin of beef. Book. £18.
♦ **Azami**, 13-15 West Street, ☎ (01) 240 0634.
♦ **Cafe Pelican**, 45 St. Martin's Lane, ☎ (01) 379 0309, AC AM BA DI ₪ ♪ ✀ Cl. 25-26 Dec. Book. £18.
♦ **Cranks**, Unit 11, The Market, Covent Garden, ☎ (01) 379 6508 ✀ Cl. Bank Hols., Sun. Book. £8.
♦ **Flounders**, 19 Tavistock Street, ☎ (01) 836 3925 Seafood.
♦ **Food for Thought**, 31 Neal Street, Covent Garden, ☎ (01) 836 0239 ✀ Cl. last wk. Dec.-1st wk. Jan., Bank Hols., Sat., Sun. £5.50.
♦ **Laguna**, 50 St. Martin's Lane, ☎ (01) 836 0960, AC AM BA DI Cl. Sun. and Bank Hols. £13.50.
♦ **Le Cafe du Jardin**, 28 Wellington Street, ☎ (01) 836 8769, AC AM BA DI Cl. Sat. lunch, Sun. and Christmas.
♦ **P S Hispaniola**, River Thames, ☎ (01) 839 3011, AC BA DI Cl. 25 Dec.- 1 Jan. No lunch Sat. Restaurant is on board a boat. £18.
♦ **Sheekey's**, 29-31 St. Martin's Court, ☎ (01) 240 2565, AC AM BA DI ✀ Cl. Christmas, Easter, Bank Hols., Sat. lunch, Sun. Dish of the day. £12.

♦ **Shuttleworth's of Aldwych**, 1 Aldwych, ☎ (01) 836 3346, AC AM BA DI ♪ ✀ Cl. Bank Hols., Sat. lunch, Sun. Game meats. Scotch steaks. Book. £14.50.
♦ **Taste of India**, 25 Catherine Street, ☎ (01) 836 6591, AC AM BA DI ≮ ◿ & ✀ Book. £17.
♦ **Thomas de Quincey's**, 36 Tavistock Street, ☎ (01) 240 3972, AC AM BA DI No lunch Sat., Cl. Sun., Bank Hols., 3 wks. Aug. £30.

Inns or Pubs:
Lamb & Flag (Courage), 33 Rose Street, Covent Garden, ☎ (01) 836 4108 Bar food with cheese specialities. £2.50.
Punch & Judy (Courage), The Market.
Seven Stars (Courage), 53 Carey Street, ☎ (01) 242 8521.
Sherlock Holmes (Whitbreads), 10 Northumberland Street, ☎ (01) 930 2644.

FINSBURY

map 2-CD1
Hotel:
★★★ **London Ryan** (M.C.), Gwynne Place, Kings Cross Road, WCIX 9QN, ☎ (01) 278 2480, Tx 27728, AC AM BA DI, 213 rm. ℗ ✀ £60. Rest. ♦ £10.

Inn or Pub:
Pheasant Firkin (Bruce's), 166 Goswell Road, ☎ (01) 253 7429.

FULHAM

map 2-A3
Restaurants:
● ♦ **Le Gastronome**, 309 New Kings Road, ☎ (01) 731 6993, AC AM BA DI ♪ ✀ Cl. 25 Dec.-1 Jan., Bank Hols., Sat. lunch, Sun. Desserts. Book. £18.
● ♦ **L'Hippocampe**, 131 Munster Road, ☎ (01) 736 5588, AC AM BA ℗ Cl. Sat. lunch, Sun., 24 Dec.-31 Jan. £21.
● ♦ **Perfumed Conservatory**, 182 Wandswth Br. Road, ☎ (01) 731 0732, AC AM BA Cl. Sun., Mon., 1 wk. Christmas and Bank Hols. £20.
♦ **Barbarella**, 428 Fulham Road, ☎ (01) 385 9434, AC AM BA DI ♪ ✀ Cl. Bank Hols., Sun. Book. £17.
♦ **Hiders**, 755 Fulham Road, ☎ (01) 736 2331, AC AM BA ✀ Cl. 2 wks. Aug., Sat. lunch, Sun., 25 Dec.-1 Jan., Bank Hols. French cuisine. Crab terrine. Noisette of lamb. Book. £14.50.
♦ **The Garden**, 616 Fulham Road, ☎ (01) 736 6056, AC AM BA DI ♪ Cl. 2-3 wks. Aug., Bank Hols., Sun. Chicken and artichoke pies. Vegetarian dishes. Book. £12.
♦ **Trencherman**, 271 New Kings Road, ☎ (01) 736 4988, AM BA Brench provincial.
♦ **Windmill Restaurant**, 486 Fulham Road, ☎ (01) 385 1570 ♪ & ✀ Vegetarian cuisine.

Inns or Pubs:
Ferret Firkin (Bruce's), 114 Lots Road, ☎ (01) 352 6645.
King's Head, Eight Bells (Whitbread), 50 Cheyne Walk, ☎ (01) 352 1820, AC AM BA DI & Gourmet pies and salads, hot meals and pub food. £5.50.
White Horse (Vintage), 1 Parsons Green, ☎ (01) 736 2115. Breakfast Sat.-Sun. and famous bar meals. £5.

Recommended
♥ *Joseph*, 268 Brompton Road, new line of clothes; *Whittays*, 111 Fulham Road, dozens of varieties of coffee and tea.

HOLBORN

map 2-C2
Hotel:
★★★ **Drury Lane Moat** (Q.M.H.), Drury Lane, WC2B 5RE, ☎ (01) 836 6666, Tx 8811395, AC AM BA DI, 128 rm. ℗ ✀ £99. Rest. ♦ £17.

Inn or Pub:
Princess Louise (Vaux), 208 High Holborn, ☎ (01) 405 8816.

KENSINGTON

map 2-A2-3

Hotels:

★★★★ ***Blakes***, 33 Roland Gardens, SW7 3PF, ☎ (01) 370 6701, Tx 8813500, AC AM BA DI, 50 rm. ✗ £165. Rest. ◆ ♪ Cl. 25-26 Dec. Roast rack of English lamb with rosemary. £33.50.

★★★★ ***Gloucester*** (Rank), 4 Harrington Gardens, SW7 4LH, ☎ (01) 373 6030, Tx 917505, AC AM BA DI, 531 rm. Ⓟ ♿ ✗ £126. Rest. ◆ £26.

★★★★ ***Hilton Kensington***, 179 Holland Park Avenue, Notting Hill, W11 4UL, ☎ (01) 603 3355, Tx 919763, AC AM BA DI, 606 rm. Ⓟ ♿ ✗ £120. Rest. ◆ ***Market***, £21.

★★★★ ***London Tara*** (B.W.), Scarsdale Place, Wrights Lane, W8 5SR, ☎ (01) 937 7211, Tx 918834, AC AM BA DI, 830 rm. Ⓟ ♿ ✗ £80. Rest. ◆ ***Poachers*** ♪ ♿ £20.

★★★★ ***Portobello***, 22 Stanley Gardens, Notting Hill, W11 2NG, ☎ (01) 727 2777, Tx 21879, AC AM BA DI, 25 rm. £103. Rest. ◆ Cl. 24 Dec.-2 Jan. Residents only. £15.

★★★★ ***Royal Garden*** (Rank), Kensington High Street, W8 4PT, ☎ (01) 937 8000, Tx 263151, AC AM BA DI, 395 rm. Ⓟ ⚟ ✗ £150. Rest. ◆ ***Royal Roof***, Cl. Sat. lunch, Sun., Bank Hols., lunch, 3 wks. Aug. £23.

★★★ ***Alexander*** (B.M.H.), 9 Sumner Place, SW7 3EE, ☎ (01) 581 1591, Tx 917133, AC AM BA DI, 38 rm. Ⓟ ≋ ✗ £84. Rest. ◆ £11.50.

★★★ ***Baileys***, 140 Gloucester Road, SW7 4QH, ☎ (01) 373 6000, Tx 264221, AC AM BA DI, 158 rm. ✗ £78. Rest. ◆ ***Bombay Brasserie*** ♪ Cl. 26-28 Dec. Indian cuisine. £20.

★★★ ***Barkston***, Barkston Gardens, Earl's Court, SW5 0EW, ☎ (01) 373 7851, Tx 8953154, AC AM BA DI, 77 rm. £52.50. Rest. ◆ ♪ £10.

★★★ ***Eden Plaza***, 68 Queen's Gate, SW7 5JT, ☎ (01) 370 6111, Tx 916228, AC AM BA DI, 65 rm. £60. Rest. ◆ ♪ £9.50.

★★★ ***Forum*** (Forum), 97 Cromwell Road, SW7 4DN, ☎ (01) 370 5757, Tx 919663, AC AM BA DI, 907 rm. Ⓟ £84. Rest. ◆ £12.

★★★ ***Gore*** (B.W.), 189 Queen's Gate, SW7 5EX, ☎ (01) 584 6601, Tx 296244, AO AM BA DI, 57 rm. ✗ £110. Rest. ◆ Cl. Sat. £16.

★★★ ***John Howard***, 4 Queen's Gate, SW7 5EH, ☎ (01) 581 3011, Tx 8813397, AC AM BA DI, 40 rm. ✗ £108. Rest. ◆ ♪ Mousse de langouste aux perles de la Caspienne. £23.

★★★ ***Kensington Close*** (T.H.F.), Wrights Lane, W8 5SP, ☎ (01) 937 8170, Tx 23914, AC AM BA DI, 537 rm. Ⓟ ≋ ▭ Amenities include gym., coffee shop £75. Rest. ◆ £17.

★★★ ***Kensington Thistle***, De Vere Gardens, W8 5AF, ☎ (01) 937 8121, Tx 262422, AC AM BA DI, 298 rm. ✗ £107. Rest. ◆ ♪ Cl. Sun. £18.

★★★ ***London International*** (S.W.A.), 147C Cromwell Road, Earl's Court, SW5 0TH, ☎ (01) 370 4200, Tx 27260, AC AM BA DI, 415 rm. Ⓟ Constructed in air space over District Line on a steel concrete bridge. £68. Rest. ◆ £25.

★★★ ***Regency*** (Sarova), 100-105 Queen's Gate, SW7 5AG, ☎ (01) 370 4595, Tx 267594, AC AM BA DI, 188 rm. ✗ £87. Rest. ◆ £12.

★★★ ***Rembrandt*** (Sarova), Thurloe Place, SW7 2RS, ☎ (01) 589 8100, Tx 295828, AC AM BA DI, 200 rm. ✗ ▭ £90. Rest. ◆ £15.

★★★ ***Vanderbilt*** (E.D.W.), 76 Cromwell Road, SW7 5BT, ☎ (01) 589 2424, Tx 919867, AC AM BA DI, 230 rm. £84. Rest. ◆ ♪ £9.50.

★★ ***Hogarth*** (I.N.H.), Hogarth Road, Earl's Court, SW5 0QQ, ☎ (01) 370 6831, Tx 8591994, AC AM BA DI, 88 rm. Ⓟ ✗ £50. Rest. ◆ £9.50.

★★ ***Lexham***, 32-38 Lexham Gardens, W8 5JU, ☎ (01) 373 6471, Tx 268141, AC BA, 60 rm. ≋ ✗ £39. Rest. ◆ ♪ Cl. Christmas wk. £7.50.

★★ ***Number Sixteen***, 15-17 Sumner Place, SW7 3EG, ☎ (01) 589 5232, Tx 266638, AC AM BA DI, 32 rm. ≋ ✗ £85.

★★ ***Town House***, 44-48 West Cromwell Road, Earl's Court, SW5 9QL, ☎ (01) 373 4546, Tx 918554, AC AM BA DI, 47 rm. ✗ £55.

★ ***Embassy House*** (Embassy), 31 Queen's Gate, SW7 5JA, ☎ (01) 584 7222, Tx 8813387, AC AM BA DI, 70 rm. £66. Rest. ◆ Cl. lunch Sat. and Sun. £10.

Restaurants:

● ◆ ***Bahn Thai***, 35 Marloes Road, ☎ (01) 937 9960, AC AM DI ⛱ ♪ ✗ Cl. 2 wks. Aug., 2 wks. Christmas. Thai cuisine. Book. £12.

● ◆ ***Chanterelle***, 119 Old Brompton Road, ☎ (01) 373 5522, AC AM BA DI ✗ Cl. 4 days Christmas. Book. £13.

● ◆ ***Clarke's***, 124 Kensington Church Street, ☎ (01) 221 9225, AC BA Cl. Sat., Sun., 3 wks. Aug., 10 days Christmas, 1 wk. Easter. Char grills. Book. £19.

● ◆ ***Hilaire***, 68 Old Brompton Road, ☎ (01) 584 8993, AC AM BA DI ✗ Cl. Bank Hols., Sat. lunch, Sun. Book. £23.

● ◆ ***Kensington Tandoori***, 1 Abingdon Road, ☎ (01) 937 6182, AC AM BA DI.

● ◆ ***La Ruelle***, 14 Wrights Lane, ☎ (01) 937 8525, AC AM BA DI Cl. Sat., Sun., Bank Hols. No children under 12. £29.

● ◆ ***Read's***, 152 Old Brompton Road, ☎ (01) 373 2445, AC AM BA DI ≋ ✗ Cl. Christmas, Bank Hols., Sun. dinner. Anglo-french cuisine. Book. £30.

● ◆ ***Tiger Lee***, 251 Old Brompton Road, Earl's Court, ☎ (01) 370 2323, AM BA DI AC ♿ ✗ Cl. Christmas, lunch. Lobster, crispy duck. Book. £22.

◆ ***Bombay Brasserie***, Courtfield Close, 140 Gloucester Road, ☎ (01) 370 4040, AC AM BA DI £20.

◆ ***Cap's***, 64 Pembridge Road, ☎ (01) 229 5177, AC AM BA DI ♪ ✗ Cl. Bank Hols., Sun., lunch. 29 rm. Book. £11.

◆ ***Chez Moi***, 1 Addison Avenue, ☎ (01) 603 8267, AC AM BA DI ⛱ ✗ Cl. 2 wks. Aug., Christmas, lunch, Sun. Rack of lamb. Book. £21.

◆ ***Crystal Palace***, 10 Hogarth Place, Hogarth Road, Earl's Court, ☎ (01) 373 0754, AC AM BA DI ⛱ ♪ ✗ Cl. Bank Hols. Peking, Szechuan. £12.50.

◆ ***Daquise***, 20 Thurloe Street, ☎ (01) 589 6117 ✗ Cl. 25-26 Dec. 2 rm. Polish and Russian main dishes. £7.

◆ ***Franco Ovest***, 3 Russell Gardens, ☎ (01) 602 1242, AC AM BA DI Cl. Sat. lunch, Sun. Italian. £18.

◆ ***Golden Chopsticks***, 1 Harrington Road, ☎ (01) 584 0855 ⛱ ♪ ♿ ✗ Cl. Christmas. Book. £13.

◆ ***Hiroko of Kensington***, 179 Holland Park Avenue, ☎ (01) 603 5003, AC AM BA DI Cl. Mon. lunch, 25-26 Dec., 1-4 Jan., Bank Hols. Japanese cuisine. £20.

◆ ***Holland Street***, 33C Holland Street, ☎ (01) 937 3224, AC BA ✗ Cl. Aug., Bank Hols., Sat. lunch, Sun. eve. Chicken breast stuffed with spinach and Stilton cheese. Book. £14.

◆ ***I Ching***, 40 Earl's Court Road, ☎ (01) 937 7047.

◆ ***Il Barbino***, 32 Kensington Church Street, ☎ (01) 937 8752, AC AM BA DI Cl. Sat. lunch, Sun. £11.

◆ ***Julie's***, 135 Portland Road, Holland Park, ☎ (01) 727 4585, AC AM BA DI ≋ ⛱ ♪ ✗ Cl. 4 days Christmas, Easter, Aug., Bank Hols. Cotswold duck with peaches, port and cherries. Book. £20.

◆ ***La Paesana***, 30 Uxbridge Street, ☎ (01) 229 4332, AC BA DI ⛱ ♪ ✗ Cl. Bank Hols., Sun., 17-20 Apr., 25-26 Dec. Italian cuisine Book. £13.

◆ ***La Pomme d'Amour***, 128 Holland Park Avenue, ☎ (01) 229 8532, AC AM BA DI ≋ ⛱ ♿ ✗ Cl. Bank Hols., Sat. lunch, Sun. Caneton au poivre vert et ananas. Book. £23.

◆ ***La Residence***, 148 Holland Park Avenue, ☎ (01) 221 6090, AC AM BA DI Cl. Sat. lunch, Mon. and Bank Hols. £13.

◆ ***Le Crocodile***, 38C/D Kensington Church Street, ☎ (01) 938 2501, AC AM BA DI ♪ ♿ ✗ Cl. Sat. lunch, Sun. Boudin de fruits de mer au riz sauvage. Book. £22.

◆ ***Le Quai St. Pierre***, 7 Stratford Road, ☎ (01) 937 6388, AM DI Cl. Mon. lunch and Sun.

♦ **Leith's**, 92 Kensington Park Road, ☎ (01) 229 4481, AC AM BA DI ⅋ Cl. Christmas 4 days, Bank Hols. Brill fillet stuffed with crab mousseline, lobster sauce. Book. £27.
♦ **Lilly's**, 6 Clarendon Road, ☎ (01) 727 9359, AC AM BA DI ⅋ ♪ ⅋ Cl. 1 wk. Christmas. Supreme of halibut with mango banana. Book. £15.
♦ **L'Aquitaine**, 158 Old Brompton Road, Earl's Court, ☎ (01) 373 9918, AC AM BA DI ♪ ⅋ Cl. Sun. Confit de canard à la crème de flageolets. Book. £19.
♦ **L'Artiste Affamé**, 243 Old Brompton Road, Earl's Court, ☎ (01) 373 1659, AC AM BA DI Cl. Sun., 24-26 Dec., Bank Hols.
♦ **L'Artiste Assoiffé**, 122 Kensington Park Road, ☎ (01) 727 4714, AC AM BA DI Ⓟ ♪ Cl. Sun. Crab mango. Book. £12.
♦ **Maggie Jones**, Church Street, 6 Old Court Place, ☎ (01) 937 6462, AC AM BA DI Cl. lunch Sun.
♦ **Malabar**, 27 Uxbridge Street, ☎ (01) 727 8800, AC BA ⅋ Cl. last 2 wks. Aug., 25-27 Dec. Indian cuisine. Devilled Kaleja (chicken livers). Book. £15.
♦ **Mama San**, 11 Russell Gardens, ☎ (01) 602 0312.
♦ **Mandarin**, 197C High Street, ☎ (01) 937 1551, AC AM BA DI ⅋ Cl. 24-25 Dec. Peking duck. Crispy beef. Book. £22.
♦ **Memories of India**, 18 Gloucester Road, ☎ (01) 589 6450, AC AM BA DI Ⓟ ⁘ ♪ ⅋ Cl. 25-26 Dec. King prawn Mahala. Book. £11.50.
♦ **Michel**, 343 Kensington High Street, ☎ (01) 603 3613, AC AM BA DI ⅋ French cuisine. Book. £19.
♦ **Monsieur Thompsons**, 29 Kensington Park Road, ☎ (01) 727 9957.
♦ **Montpeliano**, 13 Montpelier Street, ☎ (01) 589 0032 Cl. Sun., Christmas, Bank Hols.
♦ **New Lotus Garden**, 257 Old Brompton Road, Earl's Court, ☎ (01) 370 4450, AM AC BA DI Pekinese.
♦ **New Singapore Mandarin**, 120-122 Holland Park Avenue, ☎ (01) 727 6341, AM BA DI ⅋ ♪ ⅋ Cl. Christmas. Book. £12.
♦ **Phoenicia**, 11-13 Abingdon Road, ☎ (01) 937 0120, AC AM BA DI ⅋ ♪ ⅋ Cl. 25-26 Dec. Lebanese dishes. Tabouleh. Book. £12.50.
♦ **Pontevecchio**, 254-258 Old Brompton Road, Earl's Court, ☎ (01) 373 9082, AC AM BA DI ⅋ Cl. Bank Hols. Italian cuisine. Book. £16.
♦ **Pun Chinese Cuisine**, 53 Old Brompton Road, ☎ (01) 225 1609, AC AM BA DI ⅋ Cl. 25-26 Dec. Book. £17.
♦ **Restaurant 192**, 192 Kensington Park Road, ☎ (01) 229 0482, AC AM BA DI Cl. lunch Sun. £17.
♦ **Sailing Junk**, 59 Melrose Road, ☎ (01) 937 2589, AC AM BA DI Cl. lunch, 25-26 Dec., Good Fri. £14.50.
♦ **Siam**, 12 St. Alban's Grove, ☎ (01) 937 8765, AC AM BA DI ⅋ ♪ ⅋ Cl. lunch Mon. and Sat. Siam baked platter. Book. £15.75.
♦ **The Ark**, 36 Kensington Street, ☎ (01) 937 4294, AC AM BA DI ⅋ Cl. Sun. lunch., 4 days Christmas, 4 days Easter. Rack of lamb, steak and kidney pie. Book. £10.
♦ **Topo d'oro**, 38 Uxbridge Street, ☎ (01) 727 5813, AC AM BA DI Ⓟ ♪ ⅋ Cl. 25-26 Dec. Book. £15.
♦ **Trattoo**, 2 Abingdon Road, ☎ (01) 937 4448, AC AM BA DI Cl. Easter and Christmas. Italian. £14.

Inns or Pubs:
Anglesea Arms, 15 Selwood Terrace.
Frog Firkin (Bruce's), 41 Tavistock Crescent, Westbourne Park, ☎ (01) 727 4250 ⌂⌂⌂
Narrow Boat (Fullers), 346 Ladbroke Grove ⅋ ⌂⌂⌂
Scarsdale Arms (Watneys), 23 Edwardes Square, ☎ (01) 937 4513 ⌂⌂⌂
Windsor Castle (Charringtons), 114 Campden Hill Road, ☎ (01) 727 8491, BA ⌂⌂⌂ £4.

Recommended
Antique market: Portobello Road, most famous in the world, open Sat. 7-5.
Bookshop: *Waterstone and Co. Ltd.*, 135 Kensington High Street.
Tearoom: *Julie's*, 137 Portland Road, ☎ (01) 727 7987, open until 7 p.m.; *Muffin Man*, Wrights Lane, ☎ (01) 937 6652, open until 7 p.m.

♥ **Hyper Hyper**, Kensington High Street, three floors of booths of jewelry, clothes made by students.

LAMBETH

map 2-C3
Hotel:
★★ **London Park** (Consort), Brook Drive, SE11 4QU, ☎ (01) 735 9191, Tx 919161, AC AM BA DI, 388 rm. Ⓟ £47. Rest. ♦ £8.

Restaurants:
● ♦ **Chez Nico**, 129 Queenstown Road, ☎ (01) 720 6960, AC BA DI Cl. Sun., Mon., 3 wks. in summer, 1 wk. Christmas, Sat. lunch. Book. £30.
● ♦ **L'Arlequin**, 123 Queenstown Road, ☎ (01) 622 0555, AC AM BA DI Cl. Sat., Sun., Bank Hols., 1 wk. Christmas, 3 wks. Aug. Challand duck with foie gras. Ris de veau et homard. Book. £40.
♦ **Alonso's**, 32 Queenstown Road, ☎ (01) 720 5986, AC AM BA DI Cl. Sat. lunch and Sun. £18.
♦ **Lampwicks**, 24 Queenstown Road, ☎ (01) 622 7800, AM AC BA DI Cl. Sun., Mon., 2 wks. Christmas, last 2 wks. Aug.

MAIDA VALE

map 2-A1
Hotel:
★★★ **Colonnade**, 2 Warrington Crescent, W9 1ER, ☎ (01) 289 2167, Tx 298930, AC AM BA DI, 51 rm. Ⓟ £82. Rest. ♦ Cl. Fri. and Sat. £13.

Restaurant:
♦ **Didier**, 5 Warwick Place, ☎ (01) 286 7484, AC AM BA ⅋ ⅋ ⅋ Cl. Bank Hols., Sat., Sun. Book. £15.

MARYLEBONE

map 2-B1-2
Hotels:
★★★★ **Churchill**, 30 Portman Square, W1A 4ZX, ☎ (01) 486 5800, Tx 264831, AC AM BA DI, 489 rm. Ⓟ ⅋ ⅋ ⅋ £162. Rest. ♦ £32.
★★★★ **Cumberland** (T.H.F.), Marble Arch, W1A 4RF, ☎ (01) 262 1234, Tx 22215, AC AM BA DI, 905 rm. ⅋ ⅋ £110. Rest. ♦ **Wyvern** ♪ ⅋ Cl. 26 Dec., 1 Jan. £19.
★★★★ **Marble Arch** (Holiday Inn), 134 George Street, W1H 6DN, ☎ (01) 723 1277, Tx 27983, AC AM BA DI, 241 rm. Ⓟ ⅋ ⊟ £130. Rest. ♦ **La Bibliothèque** ⅋ Cl. lunch, Sun., Bank Hols. Steak 'Lucien', scampi maître d'hôtel. £20.
★★★★ **Mount Royal** (M.C.H.), Bryanston Street, W1A 4UR, ☎ (01) 629 8040, Tx 23355, AC AM BA DI, 700 rm. Amenities: coffee shop, shopping arcade. £76. Rest. ♦ £12.
★★★★ **Portman Inter-Cont** (I.N.C.), 22 Portman Square, W1H 9FL, ☎ (01) 486 5844, Tx 261526, AC AM BA DI, 276 rm. Ⓟ ⅋ ⁘ Modern brick hotel. Amenities: coffee shop, air conditioning, theatre desk, secretarial agency. £150. Rest. ♦ £25.
★★★★ **Selfridge** (Thistle), 400 Orchard Street, W1H 0JS, ☎ (01) 408 2080, Tx 22361, AC AM BA DI, 298 rm. Ⓟ ⅋ ⅋ Modern hotel behind the Oxford Street store of the same name. Air conditioning. Restaurants and coffee shop. £165. Rest. ♦ £25.
★★★★ **White House** (Rank), Regent's Park, NW1 3UP, ☎ (01) 387 1200, Tx 24111, AC AM BA DI, 580 rm. £100. Rest. ♦ ♪ Cl. Sat. lunch, Sun., Bank Hols. £22.
★★★ **Bryanston Court**, 56-60 Great Cumberland Place, W1H 7FD, ☎ (01) 262 3141, Tx 262076, AC AM BA DI, 56 rm. ♦ £63. Rest. ♦ £14.
★★★ **Clifton Ford**, 47 Welbeck Street, W1M 8DN, ☎ (01) 486 6600, Tx 22569, AC AM BA DI, 220 rm. Ⓟ £99. Rest. ♦ Roast rib of beef from the trolley. £18.

★★★ **Concorde**, 50 Great Cumberland Place, W1H 7FD, ☎ (01) 402 6169, Tx 262076, AC AM BA DI, 28 rm. ⬥ £50. Rest. ♦ ↓ Cl. Sat., Sun. £13.

★★★ **Durrants**, 26-32 George Street, W1H 6BJ, ☎ (01) 935 8131, Tx 894919, AC AM BA DI, 102 rm. ⬥ Georgian building built 1789. £81. Rest. ♦ £17.

★★★ **Harewood**, Harewood Row, Regent's Park, NW1 6SE, ☎ (01) 262 2707, Tx 297225, AC AM BA DI, 93 rm. ⬥ £70. Rest. ♦ **Street Cars** ↓ Grill only. £9.

★★★ **Londoner** (Sarova), 57-59 Welbeck Street, W1M 8HS, ☎ (01) 935 4442, Tx 894630, AC AM BA DI, 142 rm. ⬥ £90. Rest. ♦ ↓ Cl. Sat., Sun. lunch. £11.

★★★ **Mandeville**, Mandeville Place, W1M 6BE, ☎ (01) 935 5599, Tx 269487, AC AM BA DI, 164 rm. £94.50. Rest. ♦ £16.

★★★ **Montcalm**, Great Cumberland Place, W1A 2LF, ☎ (01) 402 4288, Tx 28710, AC AM BA DI, 116 rm. £150. Rest. ♦ **La Varenne** ↓ Veal kidneys with wild mushrooms. £25.

★★★ **Mostyn** (Sarova), Portman Street, W1H 0DE, ☎ (01) 935 2361, Tx 27656, AC AM BA DI, 123 rm. Parts date back 200 years. Adam ceilings in restaurant. £90. Rest. ♦ £10.

★★★ **Stratford Court** (E.D.W.), 350 Oxford Street, W1N 0BY, ☎ (01) 629 7474, Tx 22270, AC AM BA DI, 138 rm. ⬥ £94. Rest. ♦ ↓ Coffee shop and carvery. £10.

★ **Hallam**, 12 Hallam Street, W1N 5LJ, ☎ (01) 580 1166, AC AM BA DI, 23 rm. ⬥ £53.

★ **Portman Court**, 30 Seymour Street, 5WD W1H, ☎ (01) 402 5401, AC AM BA DI, 30 rm. ⬥ £47.

Restaurants:

● ♦ **Langan's Bistro**, 26 Devonshire Street, ☎ (01) 935 4531, AM ⬥ ⬥ Cl. Christmas, Bank Hols., Sat. lunch, Sun. French cuisine. Chocolate pudding. Book. £25.

● ♦ **Le Muscadet**, 25 Paddington Street, ☎ (01) 935 2883, AC BA ↓ ⬥ Cl. Sun., 1-21 Aug., 2 wks. Christmas, Bank Hols., Sat. lunch. Book. £13.

● ♦ **Odin's**, 27 Devonshire Street, ☎ (01) 935 7296, AM ⬥ Cl. Christmas, 1 Jan., Sat. lunch. Sun. Anglo-French. Book. £25.

♦ **Asuka**, Berkeley Arcade, 209A Baker Street, ☎ (01) 486 5026, AC AM BA DI Cl. Sat. lunch, Sun., 24 Dec.- 5 Jan. Japanese cuisine. £40.

♦ **Biagi's**, 39 Upper Berkeley Street, ☎ (01) 723 0394, AC AM BA DI ⬥ Cl. Bank Hols. Italian cuisine. Book. £12.

♦ **Caravan Serai**, 50 Paddington Street, ☎ (01) 935 1208, AC AM BA DI ⬟ ⬥ ↓ ⬥ Cl. Sun. lunch. Middle-Eastern cuisine. Ashak. Book. £8.

♦ **Chaopraya**, 22 St. Christopher's Place, ☎ (01) 486 0777, AC AM BA DI Cl. Sat. lunch, Sun. and Bank Hols. Thai cuisine. £15.

♦ **Defune**, 61 Blandford Street, ☎ (01) 935 8311, AM DI ⬟ ↓ ⬥ Cl. 10 days Dec., Bank Hols., Sun. Japanese cuisine. Sushi, sashimi. Book. £23.

♦ **Del Monico's**, 114 Crawford Street, ☎ (01) 935 5736, AC AM BA DI ↓ ⬥ Cl. 25-26 Dec., 1 Jan., Sun. Italian cuisine. Book. £16.50.

♦ **Gaylord**, 79 Mortimer Street, ☎ (01) 580 3615, AC AM BA DI ⬟ ⬥ ↓ ⬥ Indian and Pakistani cuisine. Book. £12.

♦ **Geneviève**, 13 Thayer Street, ☎ (01) 935 5023, AC AM BA DI ⬟ ⬥ ⬥ Cl. Bank Hols., Sat., Sun. French cuisine. Guinea fowl in pastry with ginger sauce. Book. £11.50.

♦ **Kerzenstuberl**, 9 St. Christopher's Place, ☎ (01) 486 3196, AC AM BA DI Cl. Sat. lunch, Sun., Christmas, Bank Hols., 3 Aug.- 3 Sep. Austrian cuisine. £20.

♦ **La Pavona**, 5-7 Blandford Street, ☎ (01) 486 9696 Italian cuisine.

♦ **Masako**, 6-8 St. Christopher's Place, ☎ (01) 935 1579, AM AC BA DI Cl. Sun., Christmas, 3 days New Year, Easter, Bank Hols. Japanese cuisine.

♦ **Raw Deal**, York Street, ☎ (01) 262 4841 ⬟ ↓ ⬥ Cl. Bank Hols., Sun. Vegetarian cuisine. £5.

♦ **Sidi Bou Said**, 9 Seymour Place, ☎ (01) 402 9930, AC AM BA ↓ ⬥ Cl. Sun. Couscous. Book. £8.

♦ **Topkapi**, 25 Marylebone High Street, ☎ (01) 486 1872, AC AM BA DI ⬟ ↓ ⬟ ⬥ Cl. 25-26 Dec. Middle-Eastern cuisine. Lamb kebab. Book. £9.

♦ **Viceroy of India**, 3 Glentworth Street, ☎ (01) 486 3401, AC AM BA DI ↓ ⬥ Cl. Christmas. Indian cuisine-Bataire masala (quail). Book. £11.

Inn or Pub:
George, 55 Great Portland Street, ☎ (01) 636 0863.
Nag's Head (Mc Muller), 10 James Street, ☎ (01) 836 4678.

Recommended
Bed and breakfast: **Merryfield House**, 42 York Street, ☎ (01) 935 8326. £32 double; B. & B.
Gallery: **Diorama**, 18 Park Square East, ☎ (01) 487 2896, where unknown artists can get their first break.
Tearoom: **Maison Sagne**, 105 Marylebone High Street, ☎ (01) 935 6240, since 1921, Italian style decor.
Wine bar: **Crawfords**, 10-11 Crawford Street, ☎ (01) 486 0506, cold buffets available from £3.95, popular and agreeable.
♥ **Ixi**, 14-15 Stratford Place, St. Christopher's Place, casual sportswear; **Miss Selfridge**, 400 Oxford Street, satisfy your wildest dreams cheaply; **Nicole Fahri**, 26 St. Christopher's Place, elegant, conservative clothes for business women; **Squash**, 29 St. Christopher's Place, reasonably priced fashion for the young; **W. H. Models**, 11 Cavendish Mews, Ali Baba's cave for model-lovers.

MAYFAIR

map 2-B2

▣ London Transport travel information at Selfridges Department Store, Oxford Street.
Car-rental: Avis, 68 North Row, ☎ 629 7811.

Hotels:
● ★★★★ **Athenaeum** (Rank), 116 Piccadilly, W1V 0BJ, ☎ (01) 499 3464, Tx 261589, AC AM BA DI, 112 rm. ⬥ £165. Rest. ♦ £24.

● ★★★★ **Brown's** (T.H.F.), Albemarle Street, W1A 4SW, ☎ (01) 493 6020, Tx 28686, AC AM BA DI, 125 rm. £155. Rest. ♦ **L'Aperitif**, £24.

● ★★★★ **Claridge's**, Brook Street, W1A 2JQ, ☎ (01) 629 8860, Tx 21872, AC AM BA DI, 205 rm. ⬟ ⬥ £195. Rest. ♦ Cl. Sat., Bank Hols. £30.

● ★★★★ **Connaught** (Savoy), 16 Carlos Place, W1Y 6AL, ☎ (01) 499 7070, AC, 90 rm. ⬥ £140. Rest. ● ♦ £35.

● ★★★★ **Dorchester**, 53 Park Lane, W1A 2HJ, ☎ (01) 629 8888, Tx 887704, AC AM BA DI, 280 rm. ▣ ⬟ ⬥ £185. Rest. ● ♦ **Terrace Room**, Cl. Sun. £38.

● ★★★★ **Intercontinental** (I.N.C.), 1 Hamilton Place, Hyde Park Corner, W1V 0QY, ☎ (01) 409 3131, Tx 25853, AC AM BA DI, 490 rm. ▣ ⬥ £190. Rest. ● ♦ **Le Soufflé** ↓ Cl. Sat. lunch. Savoury and sweet soufflés, veal mignon and sweetbreads. £20.

★★★★ **Britannia** (I.N.C.), Grosvenor Square, W1A 3AN, ☎ (01) 629 9400, Tx 23941, AC AM BA DI, 356 rm. ▣ ⬥ Amenities include coffee shop, shopping arcade. £136. Rest. ♦ **Best of Both Worlds**, £20.

★★★★ **Chesterfield** (I.N.C.), 35 Charles Street, W1X 8LX, ☎ 491 2622, Tx 269394, AC AM BA DI, 114 rm. ⬥ £115. Rest. ♦ £20.

★★★★ **Grosvenor House** (T.H.F.), Park Lane, W1A 3AA, ☎ (01) 499 6363, Tx 24871, AC AM BA DI, 472 rm. ▣ ⬥ ▢ Once the home of the Grosvenor family. Designed by Edwin Lutgens. Recently modernized. Largest ballroom in Europe. £170. Rest. ♦ Cl. Sat. lunch, Sun. and Bank Hols. £40.

★★★★ **Inn on the Park**, Hamilton Place, Park Lane, W1A 1AZ, ☎ (01) 499 0888, Tx 22771, AC AM BA DI, 228 rm. ▣ ⬟ £200. Rest. ♦ **Lanes and Four Seasons**, £30.

★★★★ **London Hilton**, 22 Park Lane, W1A 2HH, ☎ (01) 493 8000, Tx 24873, AC AM BA DI, 501 rm. ▣ ⬥ £190. Rest. ♦ **British Harvest** ↓ ⬟ £34.

★★★★ **May Fair** (I.N.C.), Stratton Street, W1A 2AN, ☎ (01) 629 7777, Tx 262526, AC AM BA DI, 322 rm. ⬥ £177. Rest. ♦ **Le Chateaubriand** ↓ Cl. Sat. lunch. £25.

★★★★ *Mayfair* (Holiday Inn), Berkeley Street, W1X 6NE, ☎ (01) 493 8282, Tx 24561, AC AM BA DI, 185 rm. P ☒ Restaurant. air conditioning. £133. Rest. ♦ £35.
★★★★ *New Piccadilly* (Gleneagles), Piccadilly, Westminster, W1V 0BH, ☎ (01) 734 8000, Tx 25795, AC AM BA DI, 290 rm. ☜ ☐ £165. Rest. ♦ £20.
★★★★ *Park Lane*, Piccadilly, W1Y 8BX, ☎ (01) 499 6321, Tx 21533, AC AM BA DI, 32 rm. P Art Deco ballroom of outstanding interest. Tea time pianist. £140. Rest. ♦ *Bracewells*, £20.
★★★★ *Westbury* (T.H.F.), New Bond Street, W1A 4UH, ☎ (01) 629 7755, Tx 24378, AC AM BA DI, 242 rm. ♿ £132. Rest. ♦ ♪ £26.
★★★ *London Marriott* (Marriott), Grosvenor Square, W1A 4AW, ☎ (01) 493 1232, Tx 268101, AC AM BA DI, 228 rm. P ♿ coffee shop. £160. Rest. ♦ *Diplomat*, £25.
★★★ *Washington* (Sarova), Curzon Street, W1Y 8DT, ☎ (01) 499 7030, Tx 24540, AC AM BA DI, 164 rm. ☜ £90. Rest. ♦ £20.
★★ *Ladbroke Curzon* (L.A.D.), Stanhope Row, Park Lane, W1Y 7HE, ☎ (01) 493 7222, Tx 24665, AC AM BA DI, 7rm. P £110.

Restaurants:
● ♦ *Al Hamra*, 31-33 Shepherd Market, ☎ (01) 493 1954, AC AM BA DI ◕ ♪ ♿ ☜ Cl. 25 Dec.- 1 Jan. Lebanese cuisine. Kibben, vamla. Book. £12.
● ♦ *Greenhouse*, 27A Hay's Mews, ☎ (01) 499 3331, AC AM BA DI ☜ Cl. 25 Dec.-1 Jan., Bank Hols., Sat. lunch, Sun. Roast rack of lamb. Book. £27.
● ♦ *Ho-Ho*, 29 Maddox Street, ☎ (01) 493 1228, AC AM BA DI ♪ ☜ Cl. Sun. Chinese cuisine. Steamed scallops. No children under 6. Book. £23.
● ♦ *Langan's Brasserie*, Stratton Street, ☎ (01) 491 8822, AC AM BA DI ♪ ☜ Cl. Christmas, Easter, Bank Hols., Sat. lunch, Sun. Grilled sea bass with herb butter sauce. Book. £17.
● ♦ *Le Gavroche*, 43 Upper Brook Street, ☎ (01) 408 0881, AC AM BA DI ☜ Cl. Bank Hols., Sat., Sun.,24 Dec.-1 Jan. Caneton Gavroche, l'Assiette du chef, soufflé suisse. No children under 6. Book. £40.
● ♦ *One Two Three*, 27 Davies Street, ☎ (01) 409 0750, AC AM BA DI ♪ ☜ Cl. Christmas, 1 Jan., Sat., Sun. Japanese cuisine. Book. £30.
♦ *Champagne Exchange*, 17C Curzon Street, ☎ (01) 493 4490, AC AM BA DI ♪ Cl. Sat., Sun. lunch. Caviar, smoked fish, shellfish. Book. £25.
♦ *Gaylord*, 16 Albermarle Street, ☎ (01) 580 3615, AC AM BA DI ◕ ♪ ☜ Cl. 25-26 Dec. Indian and Pakistani dishes. £10.
♦ *Golden Carp*, 8A Mount Street, ☎ (01) 499 3385, AC AM BA DI ♪ ☜ Cl. Bank Hols., Sat. lunch, Sun. £17.
♦ *Guinea Grill*, 26 Bruton Place, ☎ (01) 499 1210, AC AM BA DI ◕ ♪ ☜ Cl. Sat. lunch, Sun. Steaks. Book. £30.
♦ *Hard Rock Cafe*, 150 Old Park Lane, ☎ (01) 629 0382 ☜ Hamburgers, chips and salads, smoked pork. £8.
♦ *Ikeda*, 30 Brook Street, ☎ (01) 629 2730, AC AM BA DI Cl. Sat., Sun. Japanese cuisine. £30.
♦ *Justin de Blank*, 54 Duke Street, ☎ (01) 629 3174 ☜ Cl. Bank Hols., Sat. eve., Sun. Anglo-French cuisine. Lamb and aubergine casserole. £10.
♦ *Library*, 115 Mount Street, ☎ (01) 499 1745, AC AM BA DI Cl. Sat., Sun., Christmas, 1 Jan. £16.
♦ *Marquis*, 121A Mount Street, ☎ (01) 499 1256, AC AM BA DI ☜ Cl. Bank Hols., Sun. International cuisine. Game in season. Book. £13.
♦ *Mirabelle*, 56 Curzon Street, ☎ (01) 499 4636 ♨
♦ *Miyama*, 38 Clarges Street, ☎ (01) 499 2443, AC AM BA DI ♪ ☜ Cl. Easter, Bank Hols., Sat. lunch, Sun, 25 Dec.-1 Jan. Teppan-Yaki. Book. £30.
♦ *Mr Kai of Mayfair*, 65 South Audley Street, ☎ (01) 493 8988, AC BA DI ◕ ♪ ☜ Cl. 25-26 Dec., Bank Hols. Chinese cuisine. Peking duck. Book. £28.
♦ *Ninety Park Lane*, 90 Park Lane, ☎ (01) 409 1290, AC AM BA DI P ♪ ☜ Cl. Bank Hols., Sat. lunch, Sun. 325 rms. No children under 6. Book. £42.
♦ *Relais des Amis*, 17B Curzon Street, ☎ (01) 499 7595, AC AM BA DI £19.

♦ *Scotts*, 20 Mount Street, ☎ (01) 629 5248, AC AM BA DI P ◕ ☜ Cl. Christmas, Easter, Bank Hols., Sun. lunch. Fish. Supreme de turbotin teymour. Book. £35.
♦ *Shogun*, Adams Row, ☎ (01) 493 1255 Japanese cuisine.
♦ *Tandoori of Mayfair*, 37A Curzon Street, ☎ (01) 629 0600, AC AM BA DI ♨ ♪ ☜ Cl. 25-26 Dec. Fish tikka, Sah boti. Book. £14.
♦ *The Magic Moment*, 233 Regent Street, ☎ (01) 734 2251, AC AM BA DI ♪ ☜ Clam chowder, chargrilled prime rib. Book. £14.
♦ *Tiberio*, 22 Queen Street, ☎ (01) 629 3561, AC AM BA DI Cl. Sat. lunch and Sun. Italian dishes. £25.
♦ *Trader Vic's*, London Hilton, 22 Park Lane, ☎ (01) 493 7586, AC AM BA DI Cl. Sat. lunch, Christmas. Polynesian cuisine. £37.
♦ *Trattoria Fiori*, 87-88 Mount Street, ☎ (01) 499 1447, AC AM BA DI Cl. Sun., Bank Hols. Italian dishes. £26.

Inns or Pubs:
Audley (Clifton), 41 Mount Street, ☎ (01) 499 1843, AC AM BA DI Bar and restaurant food. £10.
Bunch of Grapes, 16 Shepherd Market, ☎ (01) 629 4989 ♿ Lunches: set price for unlimited quantity. £8.
Guinea, 30 Bruton Street, ☎ (01) 499 1210, AC AM BA DI Grill-room restaurant. £20.
Red Lion (Watneys), 1 Waverton Street, ☎ (01) 499 1307 Bar food and restaurant

Recommended
Bookshop: *Hatchards*, 187 Piccadilly, ☎ (01) 437 3924.
Confectioners: *Charbonnel et Walker*, 2 Knight's Arcade, Brompton Road, ☎ (01) 581 3117, set up by Edward VII (then Prince of Wales);*Prestat*, 40 South Molton Street, ☎ (01) 629 4838, wide range of handmade truffles, fudge, Turkish delights.
Fashion: *Aquascutum*, 100 Regent Street, classic high quality for men;*Browns*, 23/27 South Molton Street, European style, high prices;*H. Huntsman and Sons*, 3 Burlington Arcade, ☎ (01) 734 7441, classic clothes for men;*Hawes Curtis*, 8 Burlington Gardens, favourite shirtmaker of Prince Charles;*James Drew*, 3 Burlington Arcade, ☎ (01) 493 0714, classic women's clothes;*N. Pealm*, 37 Burlington Arcade, great assortment of cashmeres;*Nutters of Saville Row*, 11 Saville Row, ☎ (01) 437 6850, classic clothes for men;*Swaine Adenyard Brigg*, 185 Piccadilly, chic outdoor clothes;*W . Bill*, 93 New Bond Street, real shetland sweaters.
Jewelers: *Asprey's*, 166 New Bond Street, silver and gold.
Shopping: *Hamley's*, 200 Regent Street, toystore for children and adults.
Tearoom: *Richoux*, 41 South Audley Square, ☎ (01) 629 5228, Victorian atmosphere;*The Palm Court Room*, The Ritz, Piccadilly, ☎ (01) 493 8181, tea dances held in this ornate-ceilinged room with fountain.
♥ shoes: *Church and Co.*, 58-59 Burlington Arcade, ☎ (01) 493 8307;*Maxwell's*, 11 Saville Row, ☎ (01) 734 9714, shoes for men; *Russell and Bromley*, 24 New Bond Street, ☎ (01) 629 6903.

PADDINGTON

map 2-A2
Car-rental: Godfrey Davis Rail Drive, Paddington Station, ☎ 262 5655.

Hotel:
★★★★ *London Metropole*, Edgware Road, W2 1JU, ☎ (01) 402 4141, Tx 23711, AC AM BA DI, 586 rm. P ☽ ☜ Coffee shop. £90. Rest. ♦ £19.

Restaurants:
● ♦ *Maroush*, 21 Edgware Road, ☎ (01) 723 0773, AC AM BA DI ♪ ☜ Cl. Christmas. Middle-Eastern cuisine. Book. £11.
♦ *Canaletto da Leo*, 451 Edgware Road, ☎ (01) 262 7027 Cl. Sat. lunch, Sun. Italian cuisine. £16.

♦ *Knoodles*, 30 Connaught Street, ☎ (01) 262 9623, AC AM BA DI ⟨symbols⟩ Cl. Bank Hols., Sun. International cuisine. Homemade pasta dishes. Book. £11.50.
♦ *Trat-West*, 43 Edgware Road, ☎ (01) 723 8203, AC AM BA DI Cl. Sun., Easter, Christmas. Italian cuisine.
♦ *Veronica's Chez Franco*, 3 Hereford Road, ☎ (01) 229 5079, AC AM BA DI Cl. Sat. lunch, Sun., Bank Hols.

PIMLICO

map 2-B3

ⓘ BA Terminal, Buckingham Palace Road.

Hotel:
★ *Elizabeth*, 37 Eccleston Square, SW1V 1PB, ☎ (01) 828 6812, 25 rm. ⟨symbols⟩ £52.

Restaurants:
● ♦ *Pomegranates*, 94 Grosvenor Road, ☎ (01) 828 6560, AC AM BA DI ⟨symbols⟩ Cl. Bank Hols., Sat. lunch, Sun. Jamaican curried goat, gravlax. Book. £25.
♦ *Hunan*, 51 Pimlico Road, ☎ (01) 730 5712 £12.
♦ *La Fontana*, 101 Pimlico Road, ☎ (01) 730 6630, AM BA DI ⟨symbols⟩ Cl. Bank Hols. International cuisine. Book. £16.

Inn or Pub:
Orange Brewery, 37 Pimlico Road, ☎ (01) 730 5378, AM DI.

Recommended
♥ *Mr Fish*, 52 Pimlico Road, clothes from the sixties.

SOHO

map 2-C2

ⓘ London Transport travel information, Oxford Circus, Piccadilly Circus; British Travel Centre, 12 Lower Regent Street.

Restaurants:
● ♦ *Gay Hussar*, 2 Greek Street, ☎ (01) 437 0973 ⟨symbols⟩ Cl. Bank Hols., Sun. Hungarian dishes. Book. £21.
● ♦ *New World*, 1 Gerrard Place, ☎ (01) 734 0677, AC AM BA DI ⟨symbols⟩ Cl. Christmas. Lobster with chilli black bean sauce. £7.
● ♦ *Poon's*, 4 Leicester Street, ☎ (01) 437 1528 Ⓟ ⟨symbols⟩ Cl. Christmas, Sun. Deep-fried squid with chopped garlic, wind-dried food mix, Cantonese dishes. Book. £25.
● ♦ *Red Fort*, 77 Dean Street, ☎ (01) 437 2525, AC AM BA DI ⟨symbols⟩ Cl. 25-26 Dec., 1 Jan. Indian cuisine. Tandoori quails. Book. £13.
● ♦ *Soho Brasserie*, 23-25 Old Compton Street, ☎ (01) 439 9301, AC AM BA DI ⟨symbols⟩ Cl. Sun. French cuisine. Magret de canard in sherry vinegar sauce. Book. £13.
♦ *Arirang*, 31 Poland Street, ☎ (01) 437 6633, AC AM BA DI Cl. Sun., Easter Mon., Christmas.
♦ *Au Jardin Des Gourmets*, 5 Greek Street, ☎ (01) 437 1816, AC AM BA DI ⟨symbols⟩ Cl. Sat. lunch, Sun. eve., Christmas, Easter, Bank Hols. 2 rms. French cuisine. Fricassée de poissons au safran. Book. £28.
♦ *Beotys*, 79 St. Martin's Lane, ☎ (01) 836 8768, AC AM BA DI ⟨symbols⟩ Cl. Bank Hols., Sun. Greek dishes. Book. £15.50.
♦ *Brewer Street Buttery*, 56 Brewer Street, ☎ (01) 437 7695 ⟨symbols⟩ Cl. Bank Hols., Sat., Sun. 1 rm. Polish cuisine. Pieroshki, bigos. £5.25.
♦ *Cafe Royal (Grill Room)*, 68 Regent Street, ☎ (01) 439 6320, AC AM BA DI ⟨symbols⟩ Cl. Sun. £30.
♦ *Chesa (Swiss Centre)*, 10 Wardour Street, ☎ (01) 734 1291, AC AM BA DI Ⓟ ⟨symbols⟩ Cl. 25-26 Dec. Fondue, air-cured meats, bratwurst, chocolate mocca, orange mousse. Book. £24.
♦ *Chiang Mai*, 48 Frith Street, ☎ (01) 437 7444, AC AM BA Thai. £10.
♦ *Cork Bottle Wine Bar*, 44-46 Cranbourn Street, ☎ (01) 734 7807, AC BA DI ⟨symbols⟩ Cl. 25-26 Dec., 1 Jan. Raised creamy ham and cheese pie. £7.

♦ *Country Life Vegetarian Buffet*, 123 Regent Street, ☎ (01) 434 2922 ⟨symbols⟩ Cl. Bank Hols., Sat., Sun. Vegetarian cuisine. £3.50.
♦ *Cranks*, 8 Marshall Street, ☎ (01) 437 9431, AC AM BA DI ⟨symbols⟩ Cl. Bank Hols., Sun. Vegetarian cuisine. £8.
♦ *Desaru*, 60-62 Old Compton Street, ☎ (01) 734 4379, AC AM BA DI ⟨symbols⟩ Cl. 25-26 Dec., 1 Jan. Indonesian and Malaysian cuisine. Book. £12.
♦ *Estoril da Luigi e Roberto*, 3 Denman Street, ☎ (01) 437 8700, AC AM BA DI ⟨symbols⟩ Venison. Book. £15.
♦ *Frith's*, 14 Frith Street, ☎ (01) 439 3370, AC AM BA DI ⟨symbols⟩ Cl. Bank Hol. eve., Sat. lunch, Sun. Salmon trout with bread and orange sauce. Book. £18.
♦ *Fuji*, 36 Brewer Street, ☎ (01) 734 0957, AC AM BA DI Cl. lunch Sat., Sun., 2 wks. Christmas. Japanese dishes. £26.
♦ *Fung Shing*, 15 Lisle Street, ☎ (01) 437 1539, AC AM BA DI £14.
♦ *Gallery Rendezvous*, 53-55 Beak Street, ☎ (01) 734 0445, AC AM BA DI ⟨symbols⟩ Cl. Christmas, 1 Jan. 3 rms. Chinese cuisine. Barbecued Peking duck. Book. £12.
♦ *Grahame's Seafare*, 38 Poland Street, ☎ (01) 437 3788, BA ⟨symbols⟩ Cl. last wk. Dec., 1st wk. Jan. Jewish style. Halibut with egg lemon sauce. Book. £8.
♦ *Han Kuk Hoe Kwan*, 2 Lowndes Court, Carnaby Street, ☎ (01) 437 3313, AC AM BA DI ⟨symbols⟩ Cl. 3 days Christmas, 1 Jan., Sun. Bulgoggi — thin sliced beef. Book. £26.
♦ *Il Passetto*, 230 Shaftesbury Avenue, ☎ (01) 836 9391, AC AM BA DI Cl. Sun. £21.
♦ *Joy King Lau*, 3 Leicester Square, ☎ (01) 437 1132 £19.
♦ *Kaya*, 22 Dean Street, ☎ (01) 437 6630, AC AM BA DI Cl. lunch Sat. and Sun. £22.
♦ *La Bastide*, 50 Greek Street, ☎ (01) 734 3300, AC AM BA DI ⟨symbols⟩ Cl. Bank Hols., Sat. lunch, Sun. Salmon with sorrel sauce. Book. £17.
♦ *La Corée Korean*, 56 St. Giles High Street, ☎ (01) 836 7235, AC AM BA Cl. Sun., Bank Hols., 3 days Christmas, 2 days New Year.
♦ *La Cucaracha*, 12 Greek Street, ☎ (01) 734 2253, AC AM BA DI Cl. Christmas.
♦ *Lee Ho Fook*, 15 Gerrard Street, ☎ (01) 734 9578, AC AM BA DI ⟨symbols⟩ Cl. Christmas, 1 Jan. Duck. £11.
♦ *Leoni's Quo Vadis*, 26-29 Dean Street, ☎ (01) 437 9585, AC AM BA DI Cl. Sat. and Sun. lunch, Christmas, 1 Jan. £19.
♦ *L'Escargot*, 48 Greek Street, ☎ (01) 437 2679, AC AM BA DI ⟨symbols⟩ Cl. Christmas, 1 Jan., Bank Hols., Sat. lunch, Sun. Book. £20.
♦ *Mayflower*, 66-70 Shaftesbury Avenue, ☎ (01) 734 9027, AC AM BA DI.
♦ *Melati*, 21 Great Windmill Street, ☎ (01) 437 2745, AC AM BA DI ⟨symbols⟩ Cl. Christmas. Malaysian dishes. Satay, Singapore laksa. Book. £10.
♦ *Nuthouse*, 26 Kingly Street, ☎ (01) 437 9471 ⟨symbols⟩ Cl. Sun. Vegetarian cuisine. £4.
♦ *Old Budapest*, 6 Greek Street, ☎ (01) 437 2006, AC AM BA ⟨symbols⟩ Cl. Christmas, Sun., Bank Hols. Smoked goose, red cabbage, Pungen beans. Book. £15.
♦ *Pizza Express*, 29 Wardour Street, ☎ (01) 437 7215, AC ⟨symbols⟩ Pizza veneziana. £4.25.
♦ *Rugantino*, 26 Romilly Street, ☎ (01) 437 5302, AC AM BA DI ⟨symbols⟩ Cl. Sat. lunch, Sun. Italian cuisine sea bass in pernod and fennel-seed sauce. £14.
♦ *Saigon*, 45 Frith Street, ☎ (01) 437 7109, AM BA DI ⟨symbols⟩ Cl. Bank Hols., Sun. SE Asian dishes. Vietnamese barbecued beef. Book. £15.
♦ *The Diamond*, 23 Lisle Street, ☎ (01) 437 2517.
♦ *Wheeler's*, 19 Old Compton Street, ☎ (01) 437 2706, AC AM BA DI ⟨symbols⟩ Fish and seafood. Book. £22.50.
♦ *Wong Kei*, 41-43 Wardour Street, ☎ (01) 437 3271 ⟨symbols⟩ Cl. Christmas. Soya chicken. £5.

Inn or Pub:
Salisbury, 90 St. Martin's Lane, ☎ (01) 836 5863.

Recommended
Fashion: *Marvelette*, 4 Rupert Court, ☎ (01) 436 9656, the best for secondhand 1940s and 1950s clothes; *Powell and Co.*, 11 Archer Street, ☎ (01) 734 5051, modern vision of 1960s suits.

Nightclub: *Reptile House*, 146 Charing Cross Road, ☎ (01) 240 2261, on Sat. at the Wispers, from 10.30 p.m. to 3 a.m.;*Sacrosanct*, Shaftesbury Avenue, ☎ (01) 734 2017, on Tue. at Shaftesbury's from 10.30 p.m. to 3 a.m.;*The 100 Club*, 100 Oxford Street, ☎ (01) 636 0933, the best jazz club in London, from 7.30 p.m. till after 12 midnight;*The Marquee*, 90 Wardour Street, ☎ (01) 437 6603, most famous rock'n roll place in Europe since 1950;*Whisky a Go-Go*, 35 Wardour Street, ☎ (01) 437 5534, on Tue. at the Wag from 10.30 p.m. to 3 a.m.

Tearoom. *Maison Bertaux*, 44 Old Compton Street, ☎ (01) 437 6007, since 1871, a popular little tearoom overlooking Soho;*Patisserie Valerie*, 44 Old Compton Street, ☎ (01) 437 3466, a tiny Belgian cafe serving coffee, tea, brioches pastries.

Wine bar: *Shampers*, 4 Kingly Street, ☎ (01) 437 1692, best bargains here are Australian and New Zealand wines.

SOUTHWARK

map 2-CD2-3

Restaurants:

● ♦ *Mabileau*, 61 The Cut, ☎ (01) 928 8645, AC AM BA DI ♪ ℀ Cl. Christmas, 1 Jan., Sat. lunch, Sun. French cuisine. Book. £18.

● ♦ *RSJ*, 13A Coin Street, ☎ (01) 928 4554 ♪ ℀ Cl. 2 days Christmas, Bank Hols., Sat. lunch, Sun. Fresh salmon with saffron cream sauce. Book. £16.

♦ *Dining Room*, Winchester Walk, off Cathedral Street, ☎ (01) 407 0337 Cl. Sat., Sun., Mon. Vegetarian. £11.

♦ *South of the Border*, Joan Street, ☎ (01) 928 6374, AC AM BA DI Ⓟ ∰ ◿ ♪ ℀ Cl. Sat. lunch. Australasian, Indonesian, South Pacific cuisine. Book. £16.

Inns or Pubs:

Anchor (Courage), 1 Bankside, ☎ (01) 407 1577, AC AM BA DI Ⓟ ≼ ∰ Restaurant and barbecue food. £13.

Founders Arms (Youngs), 52 Hopton Street, Bankside, ☎ (01) 928 1899, AC BA Ⓟ ≼ ∰ ♿ £7.

George Inn (Whitbread Fremling), 77 Borough High Street, ☎ (01) 407 2056, AC AM BA DI ℀ The last of London's galleried coaching inns. £11.50.

Goose Firkin (Bruce's), 47 Borough Road, ☎ (01) 403 3590.

Hole in the Wall, 5 Mepham Street.

Market Porter, 9 Stoney Street, ☎ (01) 407 2495, AC BA ℀ Pub food and restaurant. £8.

Recommended

Garden: *Dulwich Park*, a rock garden, sculpture by Hepworth.

Wine bar: *Bar du Musée*, 17 Nelson Road, serves imaginative hot and cold dishes with wine.

ST. GILES

map 2-C2

Restaurants:

● ♦ *Boulestin*, 1A Henrietta Street, ☎ (01) 836 7061, AC AM BA DI ℀ Cl. last 3 wks. Aug., 1 wk. Christmas, Bank Hols. French cuisine. Pigeon and mushrooms. Book. £30.

● ♦ *Inigo Jones*, 14 Garrick Street, ☎ (01) 836 6456, AC AM BA DI ◿ ℀ Cl. Bank Hols., Sat. lunch, Sun. French cuisine. Book. £40.

● ♦ *Neal Street*, 26 Neal Street, ☎ (01) 836 8368, AC AM BA DI ℀ Cl. 25 Dec.-2 Jan., Sat., Sun., and Bank Hols. Truffles in season, wine-mushroom soup. Book. £28.

● ♦ *Poons of Covent Garden*, 41 King Street, ☎ (01) 240 1743, AC BA DI ℀ Cl. Sun., 24-27 Dec. Lap yuck soom, Kam. Ling duck. Book. £17.50.

● ♦ *Tourment d'Amour*, 19 New Row, ☎ (01) 240 5348, AC AM BA DI ♪ ℀ Cl. 2 wks. Christmas, Bank Hols., Sat. lunch, Sun. No children under 10. Book. £21.

♦ *Chez Solange*, 35 Cranbourne Street, ☎ (01) 836 0542, AC AM BA DI ♪ ℀ Book. £18.

♦ *Frères Jacques*, 38 Long Acre, ☎ (01) 836 7823, AC AM BA DI Seafood. £19.

♦ *Grimes*, 6 Garrick Street, ☎ (01) 836 7008, AC AM BA DI ♪ Cl. Sat. lunch, Sun. Fish. Colchester oysters. Book. £15.

♦ *Interlude de Tabaillau*, 7-8 Bow Street, ☎ (01) 379 6473, AC AM BA DI Cl. 15 Aug. 7 Sep. Sun., Bank Hols., 2 wks. Christmas, 10 days Easter.

♦ *La Provence*, 8 Mays Court, ☎ (01) 836 9180, AC AM BA DI ♪ ℀ Cl. Sat. lunch, Sun. Supreme de volaille aux framboises. Book. £16.

♦ *Last Days of The Raj*, 22 Drury Lane, ☎ (01) 836 1628, AC AM BA DI.

♦ *Le Cafe des Amis du Vin*, 11-14 Hanover Place, ☎ (01) 379 3444, AC AM BA DI Cl. Sun. and Christmas.

♦ *L'Opera*, 32 Great Queen Street, ☎ (01) 405 9020, AC AM BA DI ◿ ♪ ℀ Cl. Bank Hols., Sat. lunch, Sun. French cuisine. Book. £22.

♦ *Magno's Brasserie*, 65A Long Acre, ☎ (01) 836 6077, AC AM BA DI Cl. Sat. lunch, Sun. and 24 Dec.- 2 Jan. £19.

♦ *Mon Plaisir*, 21 Monmouth Street, ☎ (01) 836 7243, AC AM BA Cl. Sat. lunch, Sun. and Bank Hols. £14.

♦ *Plummers*, 33 King Street, ☎ (01) 240 2534, AC AM BA DI ♪ ℀ Cl. Sat. lunch, Sun. British dishes. Clam chowder, salmon pie. Book. £13.

♦ *Rules*, 35 Maiden Lane, ☎ (01) 836 5314, AC AM BA DI ◿ ℀ Cl. 24 Dec.-1 Jan., Bank Hols., Sun. Book. £16.

Recommended

Fashion: *Colin Swift*, 48 Monmouth Street, superb display of fashion and women's hats;*S. Fischer*, 18 The Market, classic shoes, all colours, cableknit sweaters for men;*The Scottish Merchant*, 16 New Row, handknitted sweaters;*Westaway and Westaway*, 62-65 Great Russell Street, huge selection of woolens in many colours;*Whistles*, 20 The Market, feminine and casual.

Nightclub: *Ascension*, 14 Leicester Square, ☎ (01) 734 4111, Thu., from 10.30 to 3 a.m. £4.

Shopping: *World*, 27 Litchfield Street, ☎ 379 5588, boutique with clothes, hats, jewels from around the world.

Wine bar: *Bar des Amis*, 11-14 Hanover Place, ☎ (01) 379 3444, a popular basement bar Cl. Sun., £5, wide range of wines.

♥ kite: *The Kite Shop*, 69 Neal Street, wide variety; natural foods: *Neal's Yard Wholefood Warehouse*, 21-23 Short Gardens, jams, honey, wholewheat.

ST. JAMES'S

map 2-BC2

① London Transport travel information, St. James's Park.

Hotels:

● ★★★★ *Dukes* (Prestige), 35 St. James's Place, SW1A 1NY, ☎ (01) 491 4840, Tx 28283, AC AM BA DI, 51 rm. ◿ £160. Rest. ♦ Chicory parcels filled with brill on light red wine sauce. £30.

★★★★ *Cavendish* (T.H.F.), Jermyn Street, SW1Y 6JF, ☎ (01) 930 2111, Tx 263187, AC AM BA DI, 253 rm. Ⓟ £125. Rest. ♦ £24.

★★★★ *Ritz*, Piccadilly, W1V 9DG, ☎ (01) 493 8181, Tx 267200, AC AM BA DI, 128 rm. ℀ £200. Rest. ♦ ♪ Skewered Oban scampi in fish mousse on saffron sauce. £35.

★★★ *Pastoria*, St. Martin's Street, WC2H 7HL, ☎ (01) 930 8641, Tx 25538, AC AM BA DI, 52 rm. ℀ £82.

★★★ *Royal Trafalgar* (Thistle), Whitcomb Street, WC2H 7HG, ☎ (01) 930 4477, Tx 298564, AC AM BA DI, 108 rm. £107. Rest. ♦ ♪ £15.

Restaurants:

● ♦ *Green's*, 36 Duke Street, ☎ (01) 930 4566, AC AM BA DI ♪ ℀ Cl. Sat., Sun. Fish cakes, English puddings. Book. £16.

● ♦ *Suntory*, 72-73 St. James's Street, ☎ (01) 409 0201, AC AM BA DI ℀ Cl. Bank Hols. Japanese cuisine. Teppan-yaki, Shabu-shabu. Book. £32.50.

♦ *Le Caprice*, Arlington House, Arlington Road, ☎ (01) 629 2239, AC AM BA DI ♪ ❦ Cl. 24 Dec.- 2 Jan., Sat. lunch. Noisettes d'agneau bergère. Book. £16.
♦ *Maxim's de Paris*, 32 Panton Street, ☎ (01) 839 4809.

Inns or Pubs:
Red Lion (Watney Combe Reid), 23 Crown Passage, ☎ (01) 930 8067, £6.
Two Chairmen (Courage), 1 Warwick House Street, ☎ (01) 930 1166.

Recommended
Bookshops: *Design Centre*, 28 Haymarket, excellent selection on design;*Foyle's*, 119 Charing Cross Road, the widest choice in London.
Fashion: *James Lock*, 6 St. James's Street, renowned hatmaker.
Nightclub: *BPM*, Hungerford Lane, off Grosvenor Street, from 10:30 p.m.-3 a.m. on Thu. at the Sanctuary.
Shoes: *Lobbs*, 9 St. James's Street, since 1700, famous bootmaker.
Shopping: *Burberry's*, 18 Haymarket, raincoats.

ST. JOHN'S WOOD

map 2-A1
ⓘ Clerkenwell Heritage Centre, 33-35 St. John's Square, ☎ 250 1039.

Hotel:
★★★★ *Ladbroke Westmoreland*, 18 Lodge Road, NW8 7JT, ☎ (01) 722 7722, Tx 23101, AC AM BA DI, 347 rm. ℗ £108. Rest. ♦ £14.

Restaurants:
● ♦ *Au Bois St. Jean*, 122 High Street, ☎ (01) 722 0400, AC BA ♪ ❦ Cl. Christmas, Easter, Sat. lunch. Avocat Cannoise. Book. £15.
♦ *Don Pepe*, 99 Frampton Street, ☎ (01) 262 3834, AC AM BA DI ℗ ♪ ❦ Cl. 24-25 Dec. Spanish food. Merluza a la Gallega. £15.
♦ *Fortuna Garden*, 128 Allitsen Road, ☎ (01) 586 2391, AC AM BA DI Peking cuisine.
♦ *Lords Rendezvous*, 24 Finchley Road, ☎ (01) 722 4750, AM AC BA DI ❦ Cl. 25-26 Dec. Chinese. Book. £25.
♦ *L'Aventure*, 3 Blenheim Terrace, ☎ (01) 624 6232, AM Cl. lunch Sat., dinner Sun.
♦ *Oslo Court*, Prince Albert Road, ☎ (01) 722 8795, AC AM BA DI Cl. dinner Sun.

Inns or Pubs:
Crockers (Vaux), 24 Aberdeen Place.
Clifton (Taylor Walker), 96 Clifton Hill, ☎ (01) 624 5233, AC BA ♨ Country Food menu. £8.

ST. PANCRAS

map 2-C1
ⓘ London Transport travel information, Kings Cross/St. Pancras Underground.
Car-rental: Budget, British Rail Kings Cross, ☎ 833 0972.

Hotels:
★★★ *New Ambassadors*, 12 Upper Woburn Place, WC1H 0JH, ☎ (01) 387 1456, Tx 267074, AC AM BA DI, 101 rm. ❦ £45. Rest. ♦ ♪ £7.50.
★★ *Great Northern* (Compass), Kings Cross, N1 9AN, ☎ (01) 837 5454, Tx 299041, AC AM BA DI, 87 rm. ℗ £75. Rest. ♦ ♪ Cl. 25 Dec.-1 Jan. Prime roast beef, traditional steak,and kidney pie. £9.

STOCKWELL

map 2-C3 off map
Restaurant:
♦ *Twenty Trinity Gardens*, 20 Trinity Gardens, ☎ (01) 733 8838, BA ℗ ♧ ♪ ❦ Cl. Christmas, 1 Jan., Sun. and Sat. lunch. Book. £15.

VICTORIA

map 2-B2-3
ⓘ London Transport travel information, Victoria Station forecourt; Victoria Underground, ☎ 222 1234.
Car-rental: Budget, Victoria NCP car park, Semley Place ☎ 730 5233; Hertz, Victoria coach station, ☎ 730 8323.

Hotels:
● ★★★★ *Goring*, 15 Beeston Place, Grosvenor Gardens, SW1W 0JW, ☎ (01) 834 8211, Tx 919166, AC AM BA DI, 100 rm. ℗ ❦ First hotel in the world to have central heating and a private bath for each bedroom. £129. Rest. ♦ ♪ £18.
★★★ *Royal Westminster* (Thistle), 49 Buckingham Palace Road, SW1W 0QT, ☎ (01) 834 1821, Tx 916821, AC AM BA DI, 134 rm. £149. Rest. ♦ £23.
★★★ *St. Ermin's* (Stakis), Caxton Street, SW1H 0QW, ☎ (01) 222 7888, Tx 917731, AC AM BA DI, 296 rm. ℗ £104. Rest. ♦ *Carvery*, £13.
★★★ *St. James Court*, Buckingham Gate, SW1E 6AF, ☎ (01) 834 6655, Tx 919557, AC AM BA DI, 400 rm. ℗ £155. Rest. ♦ ♪ Fillet of salmon with aubergines. £26.
★★ *Hamilton House*, 60 Warwick Way, SW1V 1SA, ☎ (01) 821 7113, Tx 28604, AC AM BA, 41 rm. £47. Rest. ♦ ♪ £6.50.
★★ *Rubens* (Sarova), 39-41 Buckingham Palace Road, SW1W 0PS, ☎ (01) 834 6600, Tx 916757, AC AM BA DI, 172 rm. £98. Rest. ♦ £12.

Restaurants:
● ♦ *Ciboure*, 21 Eccleston Street, ☎ (01) 730 2505, AC AM BA DI ❦ Cl. 1 wk. Christmas, Sat. lunch, Sun. French cuisine. Leek mushroom mousse, scallops. No children under 10. Book. £25.
● ♦ *Ken Lo's Memories of China*, 67 Ebury Street, ☎ (01) 730 7734, AC AM BA DI ❦ Cl. Bank Hols., Sun., Peking duck. Book. £26.
● ♦ *Le Mazarin*, 30 Winchester Street, ☎ (01) 828 3366, AC DI AM ♨ ♪ Cl. Christmas, Bank Hols., Sun. Book. £22.
● ♦ *Mijanou*, 143 Ebury Street, ☎ (01) 730 4099, AC AM DI ♨ ❦ Cl. Sat., Sun., 3 wks. Aug., 2 wks. Christmas, 1 wk. Easter. French cuisine. Cailles au riz sauvage. Book. £17.
● ♦ *Simply Nico*, 48 A Rochester Row, ☎ (01) 630 8061, AC AM BA DI Cl. Sat., Sun., 3 wks Aug and 1 wk Christmas. French rest. Book. £30.
♦ *Bumbles*, 16 Buckingham Palace Road, ☎ (01) 828 2903, AC AM BA DI Cl. Sat. lunch, Sun., Bank Hols. Scotch rump steak. Book. £14.
♦ *Dolphin Brasserie*, Rodney House, Dolphin Square, Chichester Street, ☎ (01) 828 3207, AM AC BA DI £19.
♦ *Eatons*, 49 Elizabeth Street, ☎ (01) 730 0074, AC AM BA DI ♪ ❦ Cl. Sat., Sun. and Bank Hols. French cuisine. Smoked salmon, fresh herrings. Book. £17.
♦ *Gran Paradiso*, 52 Wilton Road, ☎ (01) 828 5818, AC AM BA DI Cl. Sat. lunch, Sun., Bank Hols. £13.
♦ *La Poule au Pot*, 231 Ebury Street, ☎ (01) 730 7763, AC AM BA DI Lunch not served Sat. Cl. Sun.
♦ *Methuselah's*, 29 Victoria Street, ☎ (01) 222 0424, AC AM BA DI ♪ ♧ ❦ Cl. Bank Hols., Sat., Sun. Book.
♦ *Mimmo d'Ischia*, 61 Elizabeth Street, ☎ (01) 730 5406 £14.
♦ *Santini*, 29 Ebury Street, ☎ (01) 730 4094, AC AM BA DI Cl. lunch Sat. and Sun. £19.

◆ *Villa Medici*, 35 Belgrave Road, ☎ (01) 828 3613, AC AM BA DI Cl. Sat. lunch, Sun. and Bank Hols. £14.

Inns or Pubs:
Buckingham Arms (Youngs), 62 Petty France, ☎ (01) 2223386 Lunchtime snacks.
Albert (Host), 52 Victoria Street, ☎ (01) 2225577.

WEST BROMPTON

map 2-A3

ⓘ London Transport travel information at Harrods Department Store (4th floor), Brompton Road.

Restaurants:
● ◆ *Bagatelle*, 5 Langton Street, ☎ (01) 351 4185, AC AM BA DI ⚹ Cl. Bank Hols., Sun. and 1 wk. Christmas. Rack of lamb with mustard sauce. Book. £21.
● ◆ *La Croisette*, 168 Ifield Road, ☎ (01) 3733694, AM ⚹ Cl. Mon., Tue. lunch, 2 wks. Christmas. Seabass. Book. £21.
● ◆ *L'Olivier*, 116 Finborough Road, ☎ (01) 370 4183, AC AM BA DI 𝔐 ♪ ⚹ Cl. Sun., 2 wks. Christmas. Book. £25.
◆ *Brinkley's*, 47 Hollywood Road, ☎ (01) 351 1683, AC AM BA DI Cl. Sun., lunch. £14.
◆ *Chelsea Wharf*, Lots Road, ☎ (01) 351 0861, AC AM BA DI No lunch Mon. Cl. Bank Hols.
◆ *Nikita's*, 65 Ifield Road, ☎ (01) 352 6326, AC AM BA DI Cl. Sun., Christmas and Bank Hols. Russian. £21.
◆ *September*, 457 Fulham Road, ☎ (01) 352 0206, AC AM BA DI Cl. Sun., no lunch. £14.50.
◆ *T'ang*, 294 Fulham Road, ☎ (01) 351 2599 Oriental.

WESTMINSTER

map 2-BC3

Restaurants:
◆ *Kundan*, 3 Horseferry Road, ☎ (01) 834 3434, AC AM BA DI ⚶ ♪ ⚹ Cl. Bank Hols., Sun. Indian cuisine. Book. £14.50.
◆ *Lockets*, Marsham Street, ☎ (01) 834 9552, AC AM BA DI Cl. Sat. lunch, Sun. and Bank Hols. £16.
◆ *L'Amico*, 44 Horseferry Road, ☎ (01) 222 4680, AC AM BA DI Cl. Sat. and Sun. No children under 4. £16.
◆ *Tate Gallery*, Millbank Embankment, ☎ (01) 834 6754 ⚹ Cl.24-26 Dec., 1 Jan., Sun., 1 May and Good Fri. British dishes. Book. £19.

Inn or Pub:
St. Stephen's Tavern (Whitbreads), 10 Bridge Street, ☎ (01) 9303230 ⚹ Homemade soups and salads.

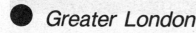

Greater London

EAST

map 1-B1

⚓ at Chingford, *Sewardstone C.P.*, Sewardstone Road (242 pl), ☎ (01) 529 5689; at Newham, *Lee Valley Park*, Eastway Cycle Circuit, Temple Mill Lane (20 pl), ☎ (01) 534 6085.

BETHNAL GREEN

Restaurant:
◆ *The Cherry Orchard*, 241-245 Globe Road, ☎ (01) 980 6678 𝔐 ♪ ♿ ⚹ Cl. 1 wk. Aug., Christmas, 1 Jan. Vegetarian cuisine. £4.50.

HACKNEY

Restaurant:
◆ *Seashell*, 424-426 Kingsland Road, ☎ (01) 254 6152 ℗ ♪ Cl. 10 days Christmas, Sun., Mon. £5.

HOMERTON

Inn or Pub:
Falcon Firkin (Bruce's), 274 Victoria Park Road, ☎ (01) 985 0693 ℗ 𝔐 ♿

HORNCHURCH

Hotel:
★★ *Ladbroke* (Ladbroke), Southend Arterial Road, RM11 3UJ (B1 off map), ☎ Ingrebourne (040 23) 46789, Tx 897315, AC AM BA DI, 135 rm. ℗ 𝔐 ♿ £66.50. Rest. ◆ £11.

PLAISTOW

Inn or Pub:
Black Lion (Imperial), 59 High Street, ☎ (01) 4722351. Steak and kidney pudding, fish and chips. £3.

POPLAR

Restaurants:
◆ *Good Friends*, 139 Salmon Lane, ☎ (01) 987 5541, AC AM BA DI. Cl. 25-26 Dec. £13.
◆ *New Friends*, 53 West India Dock Road, ☎ (01) 987 1139, AC AM BA DI ♪ ⚹ Cl. Christmas. Suckling pig. Book. £8.

Inn or Pub:
Grapes (Taylor Walker), 76 Narrow Street, Limehouse, ☎ (01) 9874396 ⚶ Seafood specialties.

SOUTH WOODFORD

Restaurant:
◆ *Ho-Ho*, 20 High Road, ☎ (01) 989 1041, AC AM BA DI ℗ ⚶ ♪ ⚹ Cl. 25-26 Dec. Scallops, prawns and squid in spicy sauce. Book. £16.

ST. KATHARINE'S DOCK

Inn or Pub:
Dickens Inn (Courage), St. Katharine's Way, ☎ (01) 488 1226, AC AM BA DI. £12.50.

STEPNEY

Restaurant:
◆ *Blooms*, 90 Whitechapel High Street, ☎ (01) 247 6001, AC BA. Cl. Sat., no dinner Fri. Kosher.

Inn or Pub:
Hollands, 9 Exmouth Street, ☎ (01) 790 3057.

WAPPING

Inn or Pub:
Prospect of Whitby (Watneys), Wapping Wall, ☎ (01) 481 1095. Restaurant and bar food. £15.

WHITECHAPEL

Inn or Pub:
Grave Maurice (Trumans), 265 Whitechapel Road.

Recommended
Antique market: *Petticoat Lane*, Sun. only.

WOODFORD GREEN

Hotel:
★★★ *Woodford Moat House* (Q.M.H.), Oak Hill, IG8 9NY, ☎ (01) 505 4511, Tx 264428, AC AM BA DI, 99 rm. ℗ 𝔐 ↲ £58. Rest. ◆ ♪ Cl. 25 Dec. eve. £13.

NORTH

map 1-A-B1

Car-rental: Europcar, Old Oak Motor Co. Ltd., 79 Windmill Road, ☎ (01) 3665907.

⚓ at Edmonton, *Lee Valley Park*, Picketts Lock Lane (125 pl), ☎ (01) 803 4756.

ENFIELD

Hotels:
★★★ *Holtwhites*, 92 Chase Side, EN2 OQN (B1 off map), ☎ (01) 363 0124, Tx 299670, AM BA AC DI, 28 rm. Ⓟ £65. Rest. ◆ ♪ £18.
★★★ *Royal Chace*, 162 The Ridgeway, EN2 8AR (B1 off map), ☎ (01) 366 6500, Tx 266628, AC AM BA DI, 93 rm. Ⓟ ≼ ⅏ ⅋ ⅏ ⊡ £54. Rest. ◆ £10.

Recommended
Golf course: Enfield Municipal, Beggars Hollow, ☎ (01) 363 4454.

FINCHLEY

Restaurant:
◆ *Fogareiro*, 16-18 Hendon Lane (A1 off map), ☎ (01) 346 0315, AC AM BA DI. Cl. Sun. Seafood.

Inn or Pub:
Old White Lion (Vintage), Great North Road, ☎ (01) 444 0554 Ⓟ ⅏ ⅋ ⅏ £3.50.

Recommended
Golf course: Nether Court, Frith Lane, ☎ (01) 346 2436.

HADLEY WOOD

Hotel:
★★★ *West Lodge*, Cockfosters Road, EN4 OPY (A1 off map), ☎ (01) 440 8311, Tx 24734, AC BA AM DI, 52 rm. Ⓟ ⅏ ⊿ Hunting lodge, parts of which date from 1547, standing in 34 acres. £75. Rest. ◆ £12.

HIGHGATE

Restaurants:
● ◆ *One Hampstead Lane*, 1 Hampstead Lane, ☎ (01) 340 4444, AC AM BA DI ⅏ ♪ ⅏ Cl. Tue.-Fri. lunch, Mon., Sun. eve. French cuisine. Three fillets of meat in cream & wine sauce. Salmon with champagne sauce. £16.
◆ *Bayleaf Tandoori*, 2 North Hill, ☎ (01) 340 1719. £11.
◆ *San Carlo*, 2 High Street, ☎ (01) 340 5823, AC AM BA DI Ⓟ ⅏ ⅏ ♪ ⅏ Cl. Bank Hols., Mon. Italian cuisine. Book. £18.

Inn or Pub:
Flask (Ind Coope), 77 Highgate West Hill, ☎ (01) 340 3969.

HOLLOWAY

Inn or Pub:
Flounder Firkin (Bruce's), 54 Holloway Road, ☎ (01) 609 9574.

HORNSEY

Restaurant:
◆ *M'sieur Frog's Bistro*, 36 The High Street (B1 off map), ☎ (01) 340 2116, AM BA ⅏ Cl. 3 wks. Aug., 1 wk. Christmas, lunch. Book. £14.

ISLINGTON

Restaurants:
● ◆ *Anna's Place*, 90 Mildmay Park, Canonbury, ☎ (01) 249 9379 ⅏ ⅏ ♪ ⅏ Cl. 2 wks. Christmas, Easter, Aug., Sun., Mon. Swedish. Book. £15.
◆ *Frederick's*, Camden Passage, ☎ (01) 359 2888, AC AM BA DI ≼ ⅏ ♪ ⅏ Cl. 26 Dec., 1 Jan., Bank Hols., Sun. Book. £19.
◆ *Hodja Nasreddin*, 53 Newington Green Road, ☎ (01) 226 7757, AC AM BA DI ♪ ⅏ Cl. Christmas. Book. £6.
◆ *Mr. Bumbles*, 23 Islington Green, ☎ (01) 354 1952, AC AM BA DI. Cl. Mon. Greek. £10.
◆ *M'sieur Frog*, 31A Essex Road, ☎ (01) 226 3495, AC BA. Lunch not served. Cl. Sun., 1 wk. Christmas, 3 wks. Aug. £18.
◆ *Portofino*, 39 Camden Passage, ☎ (01) 226 0884, AC AM BA DI ⅏ ♪ ⅏ Cl. Christmas, Easter, Bank Hols., Sun. Book. £16.
◆ *Upper Street Fish Shop*, 324 Upper Street, ☎ (01) 359 1401 ⅏ Cl. 2 wks. Christmas, Bank Hols., Sun. Poached halibut with herb sauce. £6.

Inns or Pubs:
Compton Arms, 4 Compton Avenue, Canonbury Lane, Canonbury.
Eagle Tavern (Charrington), 12 Shepherdess Walk, ☎ (01) 253 4715 Ⓟ ⅏ ⅋ £5.
Hemingford Arms, 158 Hemingford Road, Barnsbury, ☎ (01) 607 2861 ⅋ ⅏ Home-cooked food. £5.
Island Queen (Charringtons), Noel Road (B1 off map), ☎ (01) 359 7586. Lunchtime food bar and restaurant Thu.-Sat. eve. £4.
Slug & Lettuce (Watney Combe Reid), 1 Islington Green, ☎ (01) 226 3864. Full range of hot and cold meals. £9.
Waterside Inn (Hoskins), 82 York Way, Kings Cross, ☎ (01) 837 7118 ≼ ⅏ ⅋ Buffet menu. £6.

Recommended
♥ *Strike One*, 15 Camden Passage, ☎ (01) 226 9709, wide choice of beautiful antique clocks.

SOUTHGATE

Restaurant:
◆ *L'Oiseau Noir*, 163 Bramley Road, ☎ (01) 367 1100, AC AM BA DI. Cl. Sun. eve., Mon. £19.

STOKE NEWINGTON

Restaurant:
◆ *Eleganza*, 70 High Street, ☎ (01) 254 1950, AC AM BA DI. Cl. lunch Sun. No children under 4. £15.

WINCHMORE HILL

Restaurant:
◆ *Dragon Garden*, 869 Green Lane, ☎ (01) 360 9125.

Inn or Pub:
Green Dragon (Courage), 889 Green Lane (B1 off map), ☎ (01) 360 2374 Ⓟ ⅏ ⅋ Food at lunchtime. £5.

NORTH EAST

map 1-B1

ILFORD

Restaurants:
◆ *Da Umberto*, 361 Ley Street, ☎ (01) 553 5763, AC BA ♪ ⅏ 3 wks. Aug., Bank Hols., Sat. lunch, Sun. Boeuf Napoleon. Book. £15.
◆ *Mandarin Palace*, 559 Cranbrook Road, ☎ (01) 550 7661, AC AM BA DI. Peking and Canton cuisine. £20.

LEYTONSTONE

Restaurant:
◆ *Trattoria Parmigiana*, 715 High Road, ☎ (01) 539 1700, AC AM BA DI. Cl. Sun. £15.

NORTH WEST

map 1-A-B1

CAMDEN TOWN

Restaurants:
● ◆ *Le Bistroquet*, 273-275 Camden High Street, ☎ (01) 267 4895, AM BA DI ⅏ ♪ ⅏ Cl. 25-27 Dec. Special café section for drinking, snacks. Book. £12.
● ◆ *Lemonia*, 154 Regent's Park Road, ☎ (01) 586 7454 ⅏ ⅋ ♪ ⅏ Cl. 1st 2 wks. Aug., 3 days Christmas, Bank Hols. Greek cuisine. Book. £7.
◆ *Daphne*, 83 Bayham Street, ☎ (01) 267 7322, AC ⅏ ♪ ⅋ ⅏ Cl. Sun. Greek cuisine, Xifias swordfish. £5.50.
◆ *Koto*, 75 Parkway, ☎ (01) 482 2036, AC AM BA DI ⅋ ♪ ⅋ ⅏ Cl. Sun. Japanese cuisine, yose nabe, sushi, char-coal-grilled swordfish. Book. £23.
◆ *Nontas*, 16 Camden High Street, ☎ (01) 387 4579, AC AM DI ♪ ⅏ Cl. Bank Hols., Christmas, Sun. Greek cuisine, meze: 14 different dishes. Book. £6.

♦ **Odette's**, 130 Regent's Park Road, ☎ (01) 586 5486, AC AM BA DI 🅿 ⚘ ⚘ International cuisine, roulade of salmon & brill, parfait of scallops. Book. £15.

Recommended

♥ bookshop: *Compendium*, 234 Camden High Street, ☎ (01) 485944; market: *Camden Lock*, Chalk Farm Road, silver, jewelry, objets d'art.

CRICKLEWOOD

Restaurant:

● ♦ **Quincy's '84**, 675 Finchley Road, ☎ (01) 794 8499, AC BA ⚘ Cl. 3 wks. from 24 Dec., Mon. Book. £15.

GOLDERS GREEN

Restaurants:

♦ **Il Cavaliere**, 14 North End Road, ☎ (01) 455 3849, AC AM BA DI 🅿 ♪ ⚘ Cl. 2 wks. summer, Mon. Linguine al frutti di' mare. Book. £10.50.

♦ **La Madrague**, 816 Finchley Road, ☎ (01) 455 8853, AM BA 🅿 ⚘ ♪ ⚘ Cl. 3 wks. Jan., Bank Hols., Sun. Civet de canard aux olives. Book. £11.

♦ **Luigi's Belmont**, 2-4 Belmont Parade, Finchley Road, ☎ (01) 455 0210, AC AM BA DI. Cl. Mon., Christmas, Good Fri. £14.

♦ **Peking Duck**, 30 Temple Fortune Parade, Finchley Road, ☎ (01) 455 9444, AC AM BA DI ♪ ⚘ Cl. 25-26 Dec., Tue. Book. £12.

HAMPSTEAD

Hotels:

★★★★ **Holiday Inn Swiss**, 128 King Henry's Road, NW3 3ST, ☎ (01) 7227711, Tx 267396, AC AM BA DI, 291 rm. 🅿 ⚘ 🖼 ⏎ £120. Rest. ♦ ♪ ⚘ Surf and turf. £16.50.

★★★ **Charles Bernard**, 5 Frognal, NW3 6AL, ☎ (01) 794 0101, Tx 23560, AC AM BA DI, 57 rm. 🅿 £64. Rest. ♦ £10.

★★★ **Ladbroke Clive** (Ladbroke), Primrose Hill Road, NW3 3NA, ☎ (01) 586 2233, Tx 22759, AC AM BA DI, 84 rm. 🅿 £86. Rest. ♦ Cl. Sat. lunch. £11.

★★★ **Swiss Cottage**, 4 Adamson Road, NW3 3HP, ☎ (01) 722 2281, Tx 297232, AC AM BA DI, 64 rm. 🅿 ⚘ £73. Rest. ♦ £12.

★★ **Post House** (T.H.F.), 215 Haverstock Hill, NW3 4RB, ☎ (01) 794 8121, Tx 262494, AC AM BA DI, 140 rm. 🅿 ⚘ £78. Rest. ♦ £10.

★ **Sandringham**, 3 Holford Road, NW3 1AD, ☎ (01) 435 1569, 14 rm. 🅿 ⚘ ⚘ ⚘ £38.

Restaurants:

● ♦ **Keats**, 3 Downshire Hill, ☎ (01) 435 3544, AC AM BA DI ⚘ ⚘ Cl. Sun. and 15-31 Aug. French cuisine, chateaubriand with three sauces. Book. £22.

● ♦ **Peachey's**, 205 Haverstock Hill, ☎ (01) 435 6744, AM BA £DI ♪ ⚘ Cl. 24 Dec.- 2 Jan., Sat. lunch, Sun. eve., 4 days Easter and Bank Hols. French cuisine, beef fillet with anchovies. Book. £15.

♦ **Bunny's**, 9 Pond Street, ☎ (01) 435 1541, AC AM BA. Cl. Mon. Lunch served Sun. only. £17.50.

♦ **Chateaubriand**, 48 Belsize Lane, ☎ (01) 435 4882, AC AM BA DI. Cl. Sun. £19.

♦ **Finches**, 250 Finchley Road, ☎ (01) 435 8622, AC AM BA DI.

♦ **Green Cottage II**, 122A Finchley Road, ☎ (01) 794 3833, AC AM DI ♪ ⚘ Cl. 25-26 Dec., Tue. Chinese vegetarian cuisine. Book. £13.

♦ **Hawelli Tandoori**, 102 Heath Street, ☎ (01) 431 0172, AC AM DI BA. Cl. Christmas. North Indian dishes. Book.

♦ **La Frimousse**, 75 Fairfax Road, ☎ (01) 624 3880, AC AM BA DI. Cl. Sun. No children under 6. £27.

♦ **Lee Ho Fook**, New College Parade, Finchley Road, NW3, ☎ (01) 722 9552, AC AM BA DI. Chinese cuisine. £25.

♦ **Peter's Bistro**, 65 Fairfax Road, ☎ (01) 624 5804, AC AM BA DI. Cl. lunch Sat., dinner Sun. No children under 12. £23.50.

♦ **Sheridans**, 351 West End Lane, ☎ (01) 794 3234, AC AM BA DI ⚘ ♪ ⚘ Cl. last 2 wks. Aug., Jan. 1-14, Mon., lunch Sun. only. Fillet of trout stuffed with prawns & crab. £15.

♦ **The Lantern**, 23 Malvern Road, ☎ (01) 624 1796, BA 🅿 ⚘ ♪ ⚘ Cl. Christmas. International cuisine, pork escalope stuffed with Roquefort and mushroom sauce. Book. £7.

♦ **Viareggio**, 332 West End Lane, ☎ (01) 794 1444, AC AM BA DI ♪ ⚘ Cl. Sun. Book. £12.50.

♦ **Vijay**, 49 Willesden Lane, ☎ (01) 328 1087, AC AM BA DI 🅿 ⚘ ⚘ Cl. 25-26 Dec. South Indian vegetarian dishes. Book. £6.50.

♦ **Villa Bianca**, 1 Perrin's Court, ☎ (01) 435 3131.

♦ **Wakaba**, 31 College Crescent, ☎ (01) 586 7690, AC AM BA DI. Cl. lunch Mon., 4 days Christmas, 4 days Easter, 1 wk. Aug. Japanese cuisine.

Inns or Pubs:

Bull Bush (Ind Coope), North End Way, ☎ (01) 455 3685 🅿 ⚘

Freemasons (Charringtons), Downshire Hill, ☎ (01) 435 2127 ⚘

Holly Bush (Taylor Walker), Holly Mount, ☎ (01) 435 2892 ⚘ £2.

Jack Straw's Castle (Charringtons), North End Way, ☎ (01) 435 8374.

Recommended

Confectioner: *Ackermans*, 9 Goldhurst Terrace, ☎ (01) 624 2742, seventy-five kinds of hand-made chocolate.

Gift shop: *That New Shop*, Perrins Court.

Teashop: *Marine Ices*, 8 Haverstock Hill, ☎ (01) 485 8898, ice cream made without artificial flavours and colours and without animal fat.

♥ Café: *Louis Patisserie*, 32 Heath Street, ☎ (01) 493 9908, Hungarian and Danish pastries and coffee; cheese shop: *Paxton & Whitfield*, 93 Jermyn Street, ☎ (01) 930 0250, 'prince of cheese shops', selling 300 varieties.

HARROW

Hotel:

★★★**Harrow** (Consort), 12-22 Pinner Road, HA1 4HZ (A1 off map), ☎ (01) 427 3435, AC AM BA DI, 95 rm. 🅿 ⚘ £61. Rest. ♦ £12.

HARROW WEALD

Hotel:

★★★ **Grim's Dyke** (B.W.), Old Redding, HA3 68H, ☎ (01) 954 4227, Tx 946240, AC AM BA DI, 48 rm. 🅿 ⚘ ⚘ ⚘ ⚘ Former home of W.S. Gilbert, designed by Norman Shaw. £96.50. Rest. ♦ ♪ Cl. 25-30 Dec. Salmon coulibiac, confit of duckling with chanterelles. £17.50.

HARROW-ON-THE-HILL

Restaurant:

♦ **Old Etonian**, 38 High Street, ☎ (01) 422 8482, AC AM BA DI. Cl. Sat. lunch, Sun., Bank Hols. £16.

HATCH END

Restaurant:

♦ **Swan**, 322 Uxbridge Road (A1 off map), ☎ (01) 428 8821, AC AM BA DI 🅿 ⚘ ♪ ⚘ Peking-style cuisine, grilled dumplings. Book. £21.

HENDON

Hotels:

★★★ **Hendon Hall**, Ashley Lane, NW4 1HF (A1 off map), ☎ (01) 203 3341, Tx 8956088, AC AM BA DI, 52 rm. 🅿 ⚘ A renovated Georgian house. £77. Rest. ♦ £12.

★★ **Travelodge** (T.H.F.), Scratchwood Service Area, M1 Motorway, NW7 3HB (A1 off map), ☎ (01) 906 0611, Tx 8814796, AM AC BA DI, 100 rm. 🅿 ⚘ ⚘ £52.50. Rest. ♦ ♪ ⚘ Cl. lunch. Carvery. £8.

Recommended

Golf course: off Sanders Lane, ☎ (01) 346 6023.

KENTISH TOWN

Restaurant:

♦ **The Bengal Lancer**, 253 Kentish Town Road, ☎ (01) 485 6688, AC AM BA DI ♪ ⚘ Cl. 25-26 Dec. Indian cuisine. Book. £19.

MILL HILL

Restaurants:
♦ *Good Earth*, 143-145 Broadway (A1 off map), ☎ (01) 959 7011, AC AM BA DI. Steamed seabass. Book. £21.
♦ *Hee's*, 27 The Broadway (A1 off map), ☎ (01) 959 7109.
♦ *Taicoon*, 655 Watford Way (A1 off map), ☎ (01) 959 5037.

Inn or Pub:
Railway Tavern (Truman), 129 Hale Lane (A1 off map), ☎ (01) 959 0252 ℗ ⬙ ♿ £3.

Recommended
Golf course: 100 Barnet Way, ☎ (01) 959 2282.

PINNER

Restaurant:
♦ *La Giralda*, 66 Pinner Green (A1 off map), ☎ (01) 868 3429, AC AM BA DI. Cl. Sun., Mon., 3 wks. Aug. £10.

RUISLIP

Hotel:
★★★ *Barn*, West End Road, HA4 6JB, ☎ (089 56) 36057, Tx 892514, AC AM BA, 56 rm. ℗ ⬙ £57. Rest. ♦ ♪ £10.

Recommended
Golf course: Ickerham Road, ☎ (089 56) 32004.

SUDBURY HILL

Inn or Pub:
Black Horse (Taylor Walker), 1018 Harrow Road, ☎ (01) 904 1013 ℗ ⬙ £3.50.

WEMBLEY

Hotel:
★★★ *Ladbroke Int.* (Ladbroke), Empire Way, HA9 8DS, ☎ (01) 902 8839, Tx 24837, AC AM BA DI, 324 rm. ℗ ♿ £70. Rest. ♦ £13.

Restaurants:
♦ *Moghul Brasserie*, 525 High Road (A1 off map), ☎ (01) 903 6967, AC AM BA DI ℗ ≿ ⬙ ⚘ Cl. Christmas. Indian cuisine. Book. £9.
♦ *Woodlands*, 402A High Road, ☎ (01) 902 9869, AC AM BA DI ℗ Cl. Christmas. £9.

Recommended
Bed and breakfast: *Angrador*, 23 Priory Gardens, ☎ (01) 908 2476. £20 double; B. & B.
Golf course: Horsenden Hill, Whitton Avenue, ☎ (01) 902 4555.

WILLESDEN

Restaurants:
♦ *Kuo Yuan*, 217 High Road, ☎ (01) 459 2297 ℗ ⬙ ⚘ Cl. 25-26 Dec., lunch. Pekinese cuisine. Book. £8.
♦ *Sabras*, 263 High Road, ☎ (01) 459 0340, AC AM BA DI ℗ Cl. Mon. Indian and vegetarian cuisine.

SOUTH EAST

map 1-B1-2

⚘ *Co-operative Woods*, The Manager, Federation Road, Abbey Wood (330 pl), ☎ (01) 310 2233.

ABBEY WOOD

Restaurant:
♦ *L'Auberge*, 44 Forest Hill Road, ☎ (01) 299 2211, AC BA ⬙ ⚘ Cl. 3 wks. Aug., Mon. Thin strips of calf's liver sautéed in exotic herbs. Book. £13.50.

BEXLEY

Hotel:
★★★ *Crest*, Black Prince Interchange, Southwold Road, DA5 1ND (B2 off map), ☎ Crayford (0322) 526900, Tx 8956539, AC AM BA DI, 78 rm. ℗ ⬙ ♿ ⚘ £72. Rest. ♦ £16.

Recommended
♥ garden: *Hall Place*, Bourne Road, floral displays and exotic plants.

BLACKHEATH

Hotel:
★★★ *Clarendon*, 8-16 Montpellier Row, SE3 0RL, ☎ (01) 318 4321, Tx 896367, AC AM BA DI, 215 rm. ℗ ⬙ £52. Rest. ♦ ♪ £9.

Inn or Pub:
Royal Standard (Chef Brewer), 44 Vanburgh Park, ☎ (01) 858 1533, AC AM BA DI ℗ ⬙ ♿ £6.50.

Recommended
Bed and breakfast: *The Guest House*, 28 Glenduce Road, ☎ (01) 858 9678. £20 double; B. & B.

BROMLEY

Hotel:
★★★ *Bromley Court* (Consort), Bromley Hill, BR1 4JD, ☎ (01) 464 5011, Tx 896310, AC AM BA DI, 130 rm. ℗ ⬙ £61. Rest. ♦ £10.

Restaurants:
♦ *Capsiano*, 9 Simpson's Road, ☎ (01) 464 8036, AC AM BA. Cl. Sun., Mon., 15 Aug.- 8 Sep. £14.
♦ *Carioca*, 239 High Street, ☎ (01) 460 7130, AC AM BA DI ⬙ ♿ ⚘ Cl. 25-26 Dec. International cuisine. Book. £8.50.
♦ *Peking Diner*, 71 Burnt Ash Lane, ☎ (01) 464 7911. Cl. Sun., Bank Hols. £16.

Recommended
Bed and breakfasts: *Mrs. A.M. McClure*, 97 London Lane, ☎ (01) 464 1092. £16 double; B. & B; Rodway Point, Rodway Road, ☎ (01) 466 6793. £24 double; B. & B.
Golf course: Magpie Hall Lane, ☎ (01) 462 7014.

CAMBERWELL

Inn or Pub:
Phoenix Firkin (Bruce's), 5 Windsor Walk, ☎ (01) 701 8282.

CHISLEHURST

Restaurant:
♦ *Mario*, 53 Chislehurst Road, ☎ (01) 467 1341, AC AM BA DI. Cl. Mon. lunch, Sun., Bank Hols. £13.

CROYDON

ℹ central library, Katherine Street, ☎ (01) 688 3627.
Car-rental: Europcar, Zodiac House, 167 London Road, ☎ (01) 688 2191.

Hotels:
★★★★ *Holiday Inn*, 7 Altyre Road, CR9 5AA, ☎ (01) 680 9200, Tx 8956268, AC AM BA DI, 214 rm. ℗ ♿ ⊠ £85. Rest. ♦ £12.
★★ *Briarley*, 8 Outram Road, CRO 6XE, ☎ (01) 654 1000, Tx 8813271, AC AM BA DI, 25 rm. ℗ ⬙ ✓ £60. Rest. ♦ ♪ Cl. Sun. dinner. £10.
★★ *Central*, 3-5 South Park Hill Road, CR2 7DY, ☎ (01) 688 0840, AC BA, 24 rm. ℗ ⬙ £45. Rest. ♦ £14.

Restaurants:
● ♦ *Hockneys*, 98 High Street, ☎ (01) 688 299, AC AM BA DI ℗ ♪ ⚘ Cl. 2 wks. Aug., Christmas, Sun., Mon. Vegetarian dishes. Book. £8.
♦ *Château Napoleon*, Coombe Lane, ☎ (01) 686 1244, AC AM BA DI ℗ ≿ ⬙ ⬙ ♪ ⚘ Cl. Sun. eve. Fresh home-made pasta and ice creams. Book. £17.
♦ *Kelong*, 1B Selsdon Road, ☎ (01) 688 0726, AC AM BA DI ♪ ⚘ Cl. 1st 2 wks. Aug., Sun. Chili crab. Book. £13.
♦ *Tung Kum*, 205-207 High Street, ☎ (01) 688 0748, AC AM BA DI. Cl. 25-26 Dec., Bank Hols.

Inn or Pub:
Windsor Castle (Toby - Bass), 415 Brighton Road, ☎ (01) 680 4559 ℗ ⬙ ♿ 30 rm. £8.

Recommended
Golf courses: Addington Court, Featherbed Lane, ☎ (01) 657 0281; Cuurdon Court Municipal, ☎ (01) 660 0468.

DULWICH

Inn or Pub:
Crown Greyhound (Taylor Walker), 73 Dulwich Village, ☎ (01) 693 2466 ℗ ⬛ ⁒ Lunches daily, grills Fri.-Sat. eve. £8.50.

FARNBOROUGH

Restaurant:
♦ *L'Umbrello*, 360 Crofton Road, Locks Bottom, ☎ (0689) 52286, AC AM BA DI. Cl. Sun. £14.

Recommended
Golf course: High Elms, High Elms Road (off A21 via Shire Lane), ☎ (06891) 58175.

FOREST HILL

Inn or Pub:
Railway Telegraph (Shepherd Neame), 112 Stansted Road, ☎ (01) 699 6644 ⬛ £5.

GREENWICH

ⓘ Cutty Sark Gardens, near Greenwich Pier, ☎ (01) 858 2668.

Restaurants:
♦ *Le Papillon*, 57 Greenwich Church Street, ☎ (01) 858 2668, AC AM BA DI. Cl. Sat. lunch. Sun. dinner, 25-31 Dec., Bank Hols. £16.
♦ *Mandalay*, 100 Greenwich South Street, ☎ (01) 691 0443, AC BA ⁋ Cl. 25 Dec.-1 Jan., eve. only. Burmese dishes. Book. £11.
♦ *Mean Time*, 47-49 Greenwich Church, ☎ (01) 858 8705, AC AM BA DI. Cl. Sat. lunch, 25-26 Dec., Good Fri. £14.50.
♦ *Mr. Chung*, 166 Trafalgar Road, ☎ (01) 858 4245, AC AM BA DI.
♦ *Spread Eagle*, 2 Stockwell Street, ☎ (01) 853 2333, AC AM BA DI. Cl. Sat. lunch, Sun. dinner, Bank Hols. £16.
♦ *Treasure of China*, 10 Nelson Road, ☎ (01) 858 9884, AC AM BA DI ⁋ ⁒ Cl. 25-26 Dec., Sun. Szechwan prawn. Book. £25.

Inns or Pubs:
Trafalgar Tavern (Host), Park Row, ☎ (01) 858 2507, AC AM BA DI ⁒ Pub food and full restaurant menu. £14.50.
Yacht (Gateway Hosts), Crane Street, ☎ (01) 858 0175 ⅋ ⬛ £3.
⚓ *Co-operative Woods,* Abbey Wood, Federation Wood (330 pl.), ☎ (01) 310 2233.

Recommended
Shopping: *Green Parrot*, 2 Turpin Lane, antiques and gifts.
Teashop: *Jamina Joe*, 279 Creek Road.
Wine bar: *Davy's Wine Vaults*, 165 Greenwich High Road.
▼ market: *Greenwich Market*, Mon.-Fri. fruits and vegetables, Sat.-Sun. antiques, clothes, crafts (open 9-5).

KESTON

Restaurant:
♦ *Giannino's*, 6 Commonside, ☎ (0689) 56410.

LEWISHAM

Car-rental: Budget, 122-132 Lee High Road, ☎ (01) 318 4438.

Restaurant:
♦ *Curry Centre*, 37 Lee High Road, ☎ (01) 852 6544, AC AM BA DI.

Inn or Pub:
Fox Firkin (Bruce's), 316 Lewisham High Street, ☎ (01) 690 8925 ⬛ ⁒

NORWOOD

Restaurant:
♦*Luigi's*, 129 Gipsy Hill, ☎ (01) 670 1843 ℗ ⅋ ⁒ Cl. 3 wks. Aug., Sat. lunch, Sun. Book. £15.

ROTHERHITHE

Restaurant:
♦ *Rogues Kitchen*, St. Marychurch Street, ☎ (01) 237 7452 ⬛ ⅋ ⁋ ⁒ Cl. Christmas, 1 Jan., Sun.-Tue. American cuisine, jambalaya. Book. £10.50.

Inns or Pubs:
Angel, Bermondsey Wall East, ☎ (01) 237 3608, AC AM BA DI ℗ ⊀ ⁒ Bar food and full restaurant menu. £15.
Mayflower (Charringtons), 117 Rotherhithe Street, ☎ (01) 237 4088.
Prince of Orange (Trumans), 118 Lower Road. Jazz Mon.-Fri. eve. and Sat.-Sun. lunchtime.

SANDERSTEAD

Hotel:
★★★★ *Selsdon Park* (B.W.), CR2 8YA (C3 off map), ☎ (01) 657 8811, Tx 945003, AC AM BA DI, 150 rm. ℗ ⬛ ⅋ ⅊ ⌂ ⁋ ☽ 15thC manor house in broad parkland. £100. Rest. ♦ Tournedos farci, suprême de pintade. £19.

Recommended
Golf course: Sedbon Park Hotel, Addington Road, ☎ (01) 657 4129.

ST. MARY CRAY

Hotel:
★ *Mary Rose*, 40-50 High Street, BR5 3NJ (B2 off map), ☎ (0689) 71917, AC AM BA DI, 8 rm. ℗ ⁒ £45. Rest. ♦ ♪ £13.

THORNTON HEATH

Restaurant:
♦ *Mamma Adele*, 23 Brigstock Road, ☎ (01) 683 2233, AC AM BA DI ♪ ⅋ ⁒ Cl. Sun., Sat. lunch. Fresh homemade pasta with smoked salmon, brandy & cream sauce. £13.

Recommended
Bed and breakfast: *Fairview Guest House*, 85 Brigstock Road, ☎ (01) 683 2779. £24 double; B. & B.

SOUTH WEST

map 1-A-B2

BARNES

Restaurants:
● ♦ *Barnaby's*, 39B High Street, ☎ (01) 878 4750, AC AM BA DI ⁒ Cl. Sat.-Mon. lunch, Sep., Bank Hols., 5 days Christmas, Easter. French cuisine, suprême de volaille à l'avocat. Book. £15.
♦ *Il Bellamore*, 5 White Hart Lane, ☎ (01) 876 3335, AC AM BA DI ⊀ ⅋ ♪ ⁒ Cl. 25-26 Dec. Fillet of beef Garibaldi. Book. £12.

Inns or Pubs:
Bull's Head (Youngs), 373 Lonsdale Road, ☎ (01) 876 5241, AC AM BA DI ℗ ⬛ Modern jazz every eve. and Sat.-Sun. lunchtime. £5.50.
Sun Inn (Taylor Walker), 7 Church Road, ☎ (01) 876 5893.

Recommended
Golf course: Richmond Park, Roehampton Gate, ☎ (01) 876 3205.
Riding school: *Roehampton Gate Riding*, Priory Lane, ☎ (01) 876 7089.

KEW

Restaurants:
♦ *Jasper's Bun in the Oven*, 11 Kew Green, ☎ (01) 940 3987, AC AM BA DI. Cl. Bank Hols., Sun., Easter, Christmas. Soft shelled crabs à la Dijonnaise, fillet de boeuf. Book. £15.
♦ *Le Mange Tout*, 3 Royal Park, ☎ (01) 940 9304, AC AM BA DI. Cl. Bank Hols., Sat. lunch, Sun. dinner, 25-26 Dec., 1-2 Jan. £15.

Recommended
▼ teashop: *Maids of Honor*, 288 Kew Road.

KINGSTON

Restaurant:
♦ *Ayudhya*, 14 Kingston Hill, ☎ (01) 549 5984. Thai cuisine.

Inn or Pub:
Wych Elm (Fullers), 93 Elm Road, ☎ (01) 546 3271 Ⓟ
𝔐 £5.50.

Recommended
Bed and breakfast: *Chase Lodge*, 10 Park Road,
Hampton Wick, ☎ (01) 943 1862. £28 double; B. & B.

MORTLAKE

Restaurants:
● ♦ *Crowthers*, 481 Upper Richmond Road, ☎ (01) 876
6372, AC AM ♪ ⚘ Cl. Sun., Mon., Sat lunch, 1 wk. Feb., 2
wks. Aug.-Sep., 25-26 Dec. French cuisine. Book. £18.
♦ *Janine's*, 505 Upper Richmond Road, ☎ (01) 876 5075,
AC AM BA DI ♪ ⚘ Cl. 2 wks. Feb.-Mar., 2 wks. Sep.,
Mon., Tue.-Sat. lunch, Sun. eve. Beef Wellington. £14.50.
♦ *Mr. Lu*, 374 Upper Richmond Road, ☎ (01) 876 2531,
AC AM BA DI ♪ ᵴ ⚘ Cl. 25-26 Dec., Mon. lunch. Peking
cuisine. Book. £12.

Inn or Pub:
Ship, 10 Thames Bank, Riverside, ☎ (01) 876 1439, AC
BA Ⓟ ≮ 𝔐 £6.

NORBURY

Restaurant:
♦ *Malean*, 1585 London Road, ☎ (01) 764 2336, AC AM
BA DI ⚘ Cl. 25-26 Dec., Sun. lunch. Bang-bang chicken.
Book. £10.

PUTNEY

Restaurants:
♦ *Annia's*, 349 Upper Richmond Road, ☎ (01) 876 4456
Cl. Mon.
♦ *Samratt*, 18 Lacy Road, ☎ (01) 788 9110, AC AM BA
DI. Cl. Christmas.
♦ *Wild Thyme*, 96 Felsham Road, ☎ (01) 789 3323, AC
AM BA ⌕ ⚘ Cl. Bank Hols., Sun. French cuisine with
oriental influence. Book. £19.

Inn or Pub:
Green Man (Youngs), Wildcroft Road, Putney Heath, ☎
(01) 788 8096 Ⓟ 𝔐 ᵴ Bar food, barbecue in fine
weather. £5.

Recommended
Bed and breakfast: *Alnwick*, 27 Roehampton Lane,
☎ (01) 878 9449. £20 double; B. & B.

RICHMOND
Ⓘ central library, Little Green, ☎ (01) 940 9125.

Hotels:
★★★ *Petersham*, Nightingale Lane, Richmond Hill, TW10
6RP, ☎ (01) 940 7471, Tx 928556, AC AM BA DI, 56 rm.
Ⓟ ≮ 𝔐 ⚘ £70. Rest. ♦ £16.
★★★ *Richmond Gate*, Richmond Hill, TW10 6RP, ☎ (01)
940 0061, Tx 928556, AC AM BA DI, 50 rm. Ⓟ 𝔐 ⚘ £70.
Rest. ♦ ♪ Cl. Fri. eve, Sat. £13.

Restaurants:
● ♦ *Lichfield's*, 13 Lichfield Terrace, Sheen Road, TW9
IDP, ☎ (01) 940 5236, AC AM ⚘ Cl. 2 wks. Sep., 1 wk.
Christmas, Sun., Mon. Millefeuille of crab with cardamon.
Book. £25.
♦ *Evergreen*, 102-104 Kew Road, ☎ (01) 940 9044, AC
AM BA DI. £13.
♦ *Kew Rendezvous*, 110 Kew Road, ☎ (01) 948 4343, AC
AM BA DI. Cl. 25-26 Dec. £20.
♦ *Madeleine*, 122 Sheen Road, ☎ (01) 948 4445, AM BA
Ⓟ ⌕ ♪ ⚘ Cl. Sep., Sun., Mon. lunch. Chicken stuffed
with crab meat and crab sauce. Book. £13.
♦ *Mrs. Beeton's*, 58 Hill Rise, ☎ (01) 940 9561 ⚘ Cl.
Sun., Mon., Tue. eve. Housewives' commune with differ-
ent chefs each day. Book. £6.50.
♦ *Red Lion*, 18 Red Lion Street, ☎ (01) 940 2371, AC
AM BA DI. Cl. 25-26 Dec. Book. £11.
♦ *The Refectory*, 6 Church Walk, ☎ (01) 940 6264 ≮
𝔐 ⚘ Cl. 25-26 Dec. English regional and traditional
dishes. Book. £10.50.

Inns or Pubs:
Angel Crown (Fullers), 5 Church Court, ☎ (01) 940
1508 ⚘

Inn or Pub:
Orange Tree (Youngs), 45 Kew Road, ☎ (01) 940 0944,
AC AM BA. £6.
White Swan (Courage), Old Palace Lane, ☎ (01) 940
0959 Ⓟ 𝔐 ᵴ

Recommended
Golf courses: Richmond Park, ☎ (01) 876 3205; Royal
Mid-Surrey, Old Deer Park, Twickenham Road,
☎ (01) 940 1894.
♥ skating: *Richmond Ice Rink*, Cleveland Road, East
Twickenham, ☎ (01) 892 3646.

SURBITON

Restaurants:
● ♦ *Chez Max*, 85 Maple Road, ☎ (01) 399 2365, AC
AM BA DI ⚘ Cl. Sat. lunch, Christmas, 1-15 Jan., 1 wk.
summer, Sun., Mon. Book. No children under 6. £21.
♦ *Surbiton Rendezvous*, 110 Ewell Road, ☎ (01) 399
6713, AC AM BA DI. Cl. 25-26 Dec. £17.

SUTTON

Restaurant:
● ♦ *Partners 23*, 23 Stonecot Hill, ☎ (01) 644 7743, AC
AM BA DI ⚘ Cl. 2 wks. Aug., Christmas, 1 Jan., Sun.,
Mon., Sat. lunch. Book. £17.50.

Recommended
Golf course: Oak Sports Centre, Woodmansterne Road,
Carshalton, ☎ (01) 643 8363.

TOOTING

Restaurants:
♦ *Oh Boy*, 843 Garratt Lane, ☎ (01) 947 9760, AC AM
BA DI. Cl. Sun., 15-31 Aug. Book. £13.
♦ *Sree Krishna*, 192-194 Tooting High Street, ☎ (01) 672
4250, AC AM BA ⌕ ♪ ᵴ ⚘ Cl 25-26 Dec. South Indian
dishes, masala dosai. £5.

Recommended
Bed and breakfast: *Mrs. L. Catterall*, 12 Avarn Road,
☎ (01) 767 0584. £19 double; B. & B.

TWICKENHAM
Ⓘ district library, Garfield Road, ☎ (01) 892 0032.

Restaurants:
♦ *Cezanne*, 68 Richmond Road, ☎ (01) 892 3526, AC
AM BA ♪ ⚘ Cl. Bank Hols., Sat. lunch, Sun. Book. £14.
♦ *Quincey's*, 34 Church Street, ☎ (01) 892 6366, AC AM
BA DI. Cl. Sun., Sat. lunch. £14.

Inns or Pubs:
Eel Pie (Badger), 9 Church Street.
White Swan (Watneys) 𝔐 Snacks and hot meals.

Recommended
Golf course: Staines Road, ☎ (01) 976 6946.
♥ garden: *York House*, colourful garden with seasonal
beds.

WANDSWORTH

Inn or Pub:
Brewery Tap (Youngs), 68 High Street, ☎ (01) 870 2894.

Recommended
Cycle rental: *G.W. Stratton Ltd.*, 101 East Hill,
☎ (01) 874 1381.
♥ garden: *Battersea Park*, fine specimen trees on wide
lawns.

WIMBLEDON

Hotel:
★ *Worcester House*, 38 Alwyne Street, SW19 7AE, ☎
(01) 946 1300, AC AM BA DI, 9 rm. ⚘ £49.

Restaurants:
♦ *Les Amoureux*, 156 Merton Hall Road, ☎ (01) 543
0567, AC AM. Cl. lunch. £14.
♦ *San Lorenzo Fuoriporta*, 38 Worple Road Mews, ☎
(01) 946 8463, AC AM BA DI. Cl. Bank Hols. £17.
♦ *Village Restaurant*, 8 High Street, ☎ (01) 947 6477, AC
AM BA ⚘ Cl. 15-31 Aug. Duck with passion fruit, lobster
glazed with shrimp sauce and cucumber. Book. £18.50.

♦ **Village Taverna**, 28 Ridgeway, Wimbledon Village, ☎ (01) 946 4840, AC BA ✗ Cl. Bank Hols., Sun. Souvlaki, kebabs. Book. £8.

Inns or Pubs:
Hand in Hand (Youngs), 7 Crooked Billet, ☎ (01) 946 5720. £3.50.
Rose & Crown (Youngs), 55 High Street ∭

WEST

map 1-A1-2

CHISWICK

Inns or Pubs:
Bull's Head (Host), Strand-on-the-Green, ☎ (01) 994 1204 ≼
City Barge (Courage), Strand-on-the-Green, ☎ (01) 994 2148.

Recommended
Bed and breakfast: *Bedford Park House*, 55 Esmond Road, ☎ (01) 747 0198. £28 double; B. & B.
♥ café: *Carwandine's*, 286 Chiswick High Road; garden: *Chiswick House*, 66 acres laid out in the 1730s.

EALING

Hotels:
★★★ **Carnarvon** (Consort), Ealing Common, W5 3HN, ☎ (01) 992 5399, Tx 935114, AC AM BA DI, 145 rm. ℗ ✗ £66. Rest. ♦ £15.
★★★ **Kenton House**, 5 Hillcrest Road, Hanger Hill, W5 2JL, ☎ (01) 997 8436, Tx 8812544, AC AM BA DI, 51 rm. ℗ ✗ £48. Rest. ♦ Cl. Christmas. Salmon en croûte. £11.
★★ **Montpelier**, 9 Montpelier Avenue, W5 2XP, ☎ (01) 991 1500, AM BA, 9 rm. ℗ ∭ ≼ ✗ £50. Rest. ♦ £11.

Restaurants:
♦ **Gino's**, 4 The Mall, ☎ (01) 567 3681, AC AM BA DI. Cl. Sat. lunch, Sun., Christmas, Bank Hols. £20.
♦ **Maxim**, 153-155 Northfield Avenue, ☎ (01) 567 1719, AC AM BA DI. Cl. Sun. lunch. Chinese cuisine.
♦ **New Leaf**, 35 Bond Street, ☎ (01) 567 2343, AC AM BA. Cl. 25-26 Dec., Sun. lunch. £18.
♦ **Sinar Matahari**, 146 The Broadway, ☎ (01) 567 6821, AM ♪ ✗ Cl. Mon., Sat. lunch. Indonesian dishes, satay, rendang. Book. £13.

HAMMERSMITH

Hotel:
★★★★ **Novotel London**, 1 Shortlands, W6 8DR, ☎ (01) 741 1555, Tx 934539, AC AM BA DI, 640 rm. ℗ ♭ ✗ Businessmen's hotel, good for conferences, includes an exhibition centre; air conditioning. £96. Rest. ♦ £13.

Restaurants:
● ♦ **Light of Nepal**, 268 King Street, ☎ (01) 748 3586, AC AM BA DI ≼ ♤ ✗ Cl. 25-26 Dec. Book. £9.
● ♦ **Shireen**, 270 Uxbridge Road, Shepherd's Bush, ☎ (01) 749 5927, AC AM BA DI ≼ ♤ ♪ ✗ Cl. 25-26 Dec. Book. £11.
♦ **Anarkali**, 303 King Street, ☎ (01) 748 1760, AC AM BA DI. Indian cuisine.
♦ **Aziz**, 116 King Street, ☎ (01) 748 1826, AC AM BA DI. Cl. Sun. and Christmas. £12.
♦ **Balzac Bistro**, 4 Wood Lane, Shepherd's Bush, ☎ (01) 743 6787, AC BA ♤ ♪ ✗ Cl. Christmas 10 days, Sun. Book. £17.
♦ **Paulo's**, 30 Greyhound Road, ☎ (01) 385 9264 ♪ ✗ Cl. 2 wks. Aug., Bank Hols., Sun. Feijao, Vatapa. Book. £11.
♦ **Rajput**, 144 Goldhawk Road, ☎ (01) 740 9036, AC AM BA DI ♪ ✗ Cl. 25-26 Dec. Book. £7.50.

Inns or Pubs:
Black Lion, 2 South Black Lion Lane, ☎ (01) 748 2056 ∭
Dove (Fullers), 19 Upper Mall, ☎ (01) 748 5405 ℗ ≼ ∭
Hot and cold food. £4.

Recommended
♥ cultural centre: *Riverside Studios*, Crisp Road, ☎ (01) 748 3554, exhibitions of painting and sculpture, new plays and films.

HAMPTON COURT

Inn or Pub:
Cardinal Wolsey (Fullers), The Green, Hampton Court Road (A2 off map), ☎ (01) 941 3781 ∭

Recommended
Golf course: Home Park, Hampton Wick, ☎ (01) 997 6645.

HANWELL

Restaurant:
♦ **Happiness Garden**, 22 Boston Parade, ☎ (01) 567 9314.

Recommended
Golf course: Brent Valley Golf Course, Church Road, ☎ (01) 567 1287.

HEATHROW AIRPORT

Ⓘ Heathrow Central Station, London Airport, ☎ (01) 730 3488; London Transport travel information, Heathrow Central Underground.
✈ Heathrow, 15m W via M4 (exit 3) or A4, ☎ (01) 759 4321.
Car-rental: Avis, ☎ (01) 897 9321; Godfrey Davis Rail Drive, ☎ (01) 897 0811.

Hotels:
★★★★ **Excelsior** (T.H.F.), Bath Road, West Drayton, UB7 0DU, ☎ (01) 759 6611, Tx 24525, AC AM BA DI, 609 rm. ℗ ♭ ▭ £86.
★★★★ **Hol. Inn Heathrow**, Stockley Road, West Drayton, UB7 9NA, ☎ West Drayton (0895) 445555, Tx 934518, AC AM BA DI, 400 rm. ℗ ∭ ♭ ▭ ♪ £74. Rest. ♦ ♪ £10.
★★★★ **Sheraton Heathrow**, Bath Road, West Drayton, UB7 OHJ, ☎ (01) 759 2424, Tx 934331, AC AM BA DI, 405 rm. ℗ ∭ ♭ ✗ ▭ £105. Rest. ♦ ♪ £17.
★★★★ **Skyway** (T.H.F.), 140 Bath Road, Hayes, UB3 5AW, ☎ (01) 759 6311, Tx 23935, AC AM BA DI, 411 rm. ℗ ♭ ▭ £76. Rest. ♦ £14.
★★★ **Ariel** (T.H.F.), Bath Road, Hayes, UB3 5AJ, ☎ (01) 759 2552, Tx 21777, AC AM BA DI, 177 rm. ℗ ∭ ♭ ✗ £79. Rest. ♦ ♪ Carvery. £11.
★★★ **Arlington**, Shepiston Lane, Hayes, UB3 1LP, ☎ (01) 573 6162, Tx 935120, AC AM BA DI, 80 rm. ℗ ♭ ✗ £50. Rest. ♦ ♪ Cl. Sat. and Sun. lunch. £9.
★★★ **Berkeley Arms** (Embassy), Bath Road, Cranford, TW5 9QE, ☎ (01) 897 2121, Tx 935728, £AC AM BA DI, 41 rm. ℗ ▭ £85. Rest. ♦ £11.
★★★ **Heathrow Ambassador**, London Road, Colnbrook, SL3 8QB, ☎ Colnbrook (0753) 684001, Tx 847903, AC AM BA DI, 112 rm. ℗ £56.
★★★ **Post House** (T.H.F.), Sipson Road, West Drayton, UB7 0JU, ☎ (01) 759 2323, Tx 934280, AC AM BA DI, 597 rm. ℗ ♭ £80. Rest. ♦ ♪ £12.

HILLINGDON

Ⓘ 22 High Street, Uxbridge.

Hotel:
★★ **Master Brewer**, Western Avenue, Hillingdon Circus, UB10 9NX, ☎ Uxbridge (0895) 51199, Tx 946589, AC AM BA DI, 106 rm. ℗ ∭ £63. Rest. ♦ £10.

HOUNSLOW

Hotels:
★★★★ **Heathrow Penta** (Penta), Bath Road, TW6 2AQ, ☎ (01) 897 6363, Tx 934660, AC AM BA DI, 670 rm. ℗ ≼ ♭ ▭ £97.
★★★ **Master Robert**, 366 Great West Road, TW5 0BD, ☎ (01) 570 6261, AC AM BA DI, 64 rm. ℗ ∭ £63. Rest. ♦ ♪ £10.

Restaurant:
♦ **Hounslow Chinese**, 261-263 Bath Road, ☎ (01) 570 2161, AC AM BA DI. Cl. 25-27 Dec., Sun. lunch.

ISLEWORTH

Recommended
Golf course: Wyke Green, Scyon Lane, ☎ (01) 560 8777.

SOUTHALL

Restaurant:
● ♦ *Brilliant*, 72-74 Western Road, ☎ (01) 574 1928, AC

AM BA DI ⚲ ↕ ⚘ Cl. 3 wks. Aug. Indian cuisine, butter chicken, masala, king prawns. Book. £10.

UXBRIDGE

Restaurant:
♦ *Giovanni's*, Denham Lodge, Oxford Road, ☎ (0895) 31568, AC AM BA DI. Cl. Sat. lunch, Sun. £18.

▶ The Channel Islands are a delightful enigma. Their historical ties and physical closeness to France have given their laws, customs and food a distinctly Gallic flavour. The islands are in fact self-governing although they owe allegiance to the Crown. The Channel Islands' historical connection with France began when they were added to the Duchy of Normandy in AD 933 by Duke William I. This lasted until William the Conqueror won his victory at the Battle of Hastings and had himself crowned William I of England.

The inhabitants of the islands are of Norman stock and although they now speak English, the native tongue used to be Norman-French patois. It can still be heard occasionally in the more remote country parishes. Victor Hugo aptly described the Channel Islands as 'Morceaux de France tombés à la mer et ramassés par l'Angleterre'.

When King John lost the Duchy in 1204 to Philip of France, the Channel Islands remained loyal to the English Crown, despite the constant fear of invasion that can be seen in their castles and Martello towers built to keep Napoleon at bay. During the Second World War, when England was unable to defend the Channel Islands, Hitler's troops marched in in July 1940 and the islands became part of the Atlantic Wall. In May 1945 the Germans left, having surrendered to the Allies.

Ever practical, the Channel Islanders quickly began to build up their tourist industry. In a small area they provide town, countryside or seaside resorts. It is possible to choose from quiet little bays nestling among the cliffs or huge beaches which stretch for miles. Although a popular area, it is always possible to get away from crowds in the Channel Islands. Summers are long in this most southerly section of the British Isles, winters are mild and in early spring the flowers are profuse and beautiful. □

The Channel Islands

Personality of the islanders

The people of the Channel Islands are strong-minded, independent characters, like many who live on small islands. The Jersey people have an expression they direct to any non-islander who criticizes their island - there's a boat in the morning. Each island goes very much its own way and the Jersey people are supposed to be unduly sensitive to any censure of Jersey, the 'Guernsey Donkey', i.e. stubborn in the extreme, is a phrase sometimes bandied about, although not in the hearing of the donkey.
It is also true to say that the islanders are enterprising, hard working and hospitable. They quickly adapt to changing circumstances. Over the centuries when one industry died out another was developed, demonstrating their ability to trim their sails with commendable panache to the prevailing economic wind.
While remaining steadfastly true to the British Crown, they are quick to point out to any patronizing visitor that in 1066, when their Duke became William the Conqueror, he merely added England to his offshore properties. To drive the point home that England is now their oldest possession, citizens on ceremonial occasions propose the royal toast to 'The Queen, our Duke.'

Brief regional history

Prehistory

Human settlement in the Channel Islands began during the Third Ice Age, when the islands were joined to mainland France. Only **Jersey** was inhabited at this time; hand-axes from this period have been identified, and evidence that the now coastal caves were used as habitations. Middle Palaeolithic remains have been found in two caves - La Cotte à la Chèvre and La Cotte de St. Brelade. ● After the last Ice Age, when Jersey had become an island, new settlers who knew how to raise crops and rear stock, arrived in about 4000 BC. They had more sophisticated tools, pottery and personal adornments. ● The most spectacular prehistoric monument is **La Hogue Bie**, near St. Hélier, a passage grave covered by a 40-foot mound with a single tomb chamber and two rectangular side chambers, the walls being made of upright stones. Another example is the **Déhus** in Guernsey, which has four side chambers and seems to have been the burial palce of a distinct community. One of

---

the capstones at Déhus is carved with a female figure, and there is another carved stone in the churchyard at Câtel. ● A hoard of bronze fragments found in Alderney testifies to Bronze-Age settlement of the island. Iron-Age pottery has been excavated on Alderney and Jersey, and an earthwork on the promontory of Le Câtel dates from this period. Hoards of **Celtic** coins have also been found, similar in design to those of Amorica in Brittany.

Roman settlement

Evidence of Roman occupation is slight. There is a Roman building at Pinnacle Rock in Jersey and what may be a Roman fort on Alderney, known as the Nunnery. At Longy Common on Alderney is the site of a Gallo-Roman settlement dating from the 1stC BC.

Saxons and Vikings

After the defeat of the Roman general Syagrius by Clovis, king of the Franks, Roman power in northern France was broken and the Channel Islanders were left to fend for themselves. ● As the Anglo-Saxons spread westwards through England, some of the harrassed **Britons** sought a new life in Brittany. St. Sampson and his followers visited the islands on their way to Brittany and, in 540, St. Marcouf founded a Christian community in Jersey. St. Sampson, now Bishop of Dol in Amorica, returned to form a community in Guernsey and his successor, St. Magloire, built a monastery in Sark, which continued in existence until 1412 when the French evacuated the monks. ● **Viking raiders** established a strong presence in northwest France towards the end of the 9thC and in 911 their leader, Rollo, was granted Normandy. ● By 933 the islands formed part of the **duchy of Normandy**, being organized into a series of feudal fiefs, the Bessin and Cotentin in Guernsey, the Carterets in Jersey, with the customary Norman system of rights and obligations. One office may pre-date the Norman occupation, that of *jurat*, which perhaps derives from the parish headman who adminstered local justice.

The Norman/English connection

There were probably some islanders in the force that accompanied William, 7th Duke of Normandy, to England where, as William the Conqueror, he defeated King Harold at Hastings in 1066. From that time, the Channel Islands have been linked to the **English Crown** and they are the oldest parts of the Commonwealth. ● During the Civil Wars under Stephen, the rights and privileges of the islands were confirmed by his adversary, Geoffrey Plantagenêt. Supporters of Stephen had their estates confiscated, leading to a disproportion of royal lands between Jersey and Guernsey. ● In 1204 the French king, Philippe II, recaptured Normandy, but the Channel Islands remained loyal to the English Crown and King John granted them a continuance of their rights and privileges which were to form the basis of the islands' **constitution and self-governing status**. ● These privileges were again confirmed by Henry III in 1230 and, in 1290, separate Bailiffs were appointed for Jersey and Guernsey to preside over their respective parliaments. These were Crown appointments and have remained so until the present day.

Wars with the French

As threats from France increased, the first castles on the islands were built at Cornet in Guernsey and at Grosnez and Gorey in Jersey. Two groups of militia were also formed. ● The French invaded twice in 1338, taking **Castle Cornet**. Recaptured by the English, it again fell to the French in 1356. Under the treaty of Calais in 1360, the French relinquished all claims to the islands. Nevertheless the French again invaded in 1461, this time capturing the whole of Jersey and remaining in control of the island until 1468. Grosnez Castle in the northwest was destroyed.

The Tudors

In 1483, Pope Sixtus IV issued a Bull which guaranteed the islands' **neutrality** in time of war and ordered that enemy ships and merchandise should be immune from capture. A period of peace and prosperity followed, when the islands developed as trading centres. ● Between 1590 and 1600 **Elizabeth Castle** was built at St. Aubin's Bay, off St. Hélier, by Sir Walter Raleigh, then Governor of Jersey, in honour of Queen Elizabeth. ● During the Reformation, Jersey, mainly Protestant, suffered little, but there was religious persecution of the Catholics of Guernsey. **Huguenot influence** was strong, with Huguenot exiles from France settling here. In 1565, seven Catholic *jurats* were dismissed in Guernsey. By 1570 the Huguenot system of worship was established throughout the Channel Islands, backed by the royal courts.

The Civil Wars

During the English Civil Wars, Jersey supported King Charles, while Guernsey, offended by Charles's suppression of tobacco growing and by his lack of financial support for the island's defenses, declared for Parliament. Parliamentary garrisons were also established on Alderney and Sark to protect them against Royalist raids from Jersey under George Carteret. ● During the Commonwealth, many Jersey Catholics were forced to sell their lands. Military governors were appointed and the islands were heavily taxed. ● The restitution of the monarchy under Charles II was therefore generally welcomed, particularly since he granted all participants an amnesty. Despite resistance, **Anglicanism** replaced the Presbyterian form of worship.

The 18thC

During this period the islands' economy prospered. Privateering was an important source of income during the French wars, and the Newfoundland cod fishing business was profitable. St. Peter Port had been declared a free port, storing large quantities of wines and spirits which were often smuggled into England. ● The new revolutionary ideas from France were attractive to the islanders and led to a more democratic form of government. French émigrés settled here, trebling the population of Jersey. In 1793 a force of 20,000 French gathered at St. Malo with the intention of invading the islands but were thwarted by the British naval blockade.

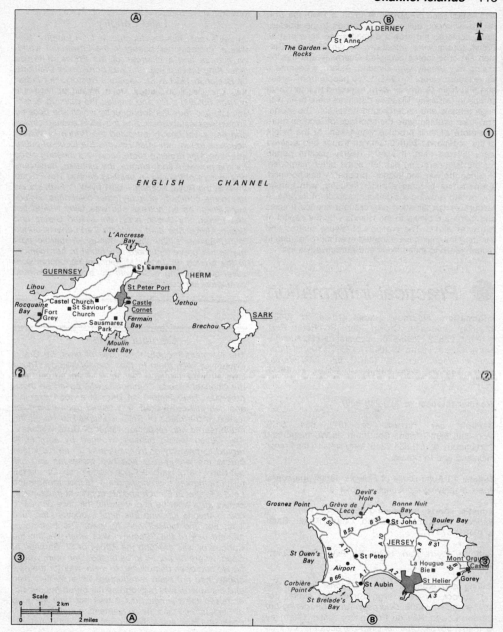

ENGLISH   CHANNEL

ALDERNEY
St Anne
The Garden
Rocks

GUERNSEY
L'Ancresse
Bay
Lihou
St Sampson
HERM
St Peter Port
Rocquaine
Bay
Castel Church
St Saviour's
Church
Jethou
Fort
Grey
Castle
Cornet
Fermain
Bay
Sausmarez
Park
SARK
Brechou
Moulin
Huet Bay

Devil's
Hole
Grosnez Point
Grève de
Lecq
Ronne Nuit
Bay
B 55
B 33
St John
Bouley Bay
B 53
JERSEY
B 31
A 10
St Ouen's
Bay
A 12
B 35
St Peter
La Hougue
Bie
Mont Orgueil
Castle
Airport
A 1
St Helier
A 2
Gorey
Corbière
Point
B 66
St Aubin
A 3
St Brelade's
Bay

Scale
0   1   2 km
0   1   2 miles

The 19thC

Under the threat of a Napoleonic invasion, further measures were taken to improve the islands' defenses. St. Peter Port became an important staging-post on the route to the peninsula and local tradesmen prospered. Strong garrisons were maintained here even after the defeat of France. ● During the 19thC, the shipbuilding industry developed. Trade with Newfoundland and with South America increased.

The export of cattle became a growing source of income and the first glasshouses were built, where grapes and later tomatoes were cultivated.

The 20thC

During **World War I**, Channel Islanders fought with distinction in France. Castle Cornet became a French seaplane base, and a German prisoner-of-war camp

was established on Jersey. ● In June 1940, the British government, believing the islands to be indefensible, declared the area a **demilitarized** zone and all British forces were withdrawn. ● On 30 June, German airborne forces occupied Guernsey and the following day Jersey was invaded. Alderney became a slave labour camp. In 1942, 1,200 people from Jersey and 800 from Guernsey were deported to internment camps in Germany. Massive defenses were built, with huge tunnels and underground hospitals. The islanders' main problem was the shortage of food as more and more of their produce was taken. At the height of the occupation 36,000 German troops and workers were billeted here. It was a deeply **painful period** for the islanders and has left some bitter memories. ● Since the war, the islands' prosperity has boomed. **Tourism** has become a major industry, with tomato and potato growing a significant source of income. A favourable tax situation has brought finance houses and merchant banks to the islands with the capital of many tax exiles. The creation of leisure centres and yachting marinas have attracted even more tourists in recent years to these lively and attractive islands.

 Practical information

Information: Alderney, *States Office*, ☎ (0481) 82 2994; Guernsey, Crown Pier, St. Peter Port, ☎ (0481) 23552 - 23555 for accommodation; *Administrative Office*, Herm, ☎ (0481) 22377; *Tourist Information Office*, Sark, ☎ (0481) 83 2262; *Jersey States Tourism*, Weighbridge, St. Hélier, ☎ (0534) 78000 - 31958.

Weather forecast: ☎ (01) 246 8097.

Sealink car ferries: ☎ (01) 834 8122 Mon.-Sat. 8am-7.15pm. Boat/train via Weymouth and Portsmouth: ☎ (01) 834 2345; ferry links to the French mainland and to Britain.

Events: 13 Aug.: *Battle of Flowers* Jersey (parade of floats displaying thousands of flowers).

Aquatic sports: windsurfing: *Guernsey Windsurfing School*, Violet Lodge, Cobo Coast Road, Câtel, ☎ (0481) 57417.

Golf: St. Pierre Park Hotel, St. Peter Port, Guernsey (9-hole).

Sailing and cruising: sailing: *Channel Islands Sailing School*, Ty-anna, High Street, St. Aubin, Jersey, ☎ (0534) 44306; *Guernsey Yacht Chartering Ltd*, Carlton Lodge, Rue du Presbytère, Câtel, Guernsey, ☎ (0481) 55754; *Channel Craft Services Ltd*, Le Picachon, Le Becquet, Trinity, Jersey, ☎ (0534) 62269.

Lillie Langtry

Jersey's most famous daughter is Lillie Langtry. She was a 'professional' beauty in the Edwardian world, an actress and a mistress of the Prince of Wales (later King Edward VII). She was born Emilie Charlotte Le Breton in 1853 at St. Saviour's Rectory. Her father was the Dean of Jersey. John Millais painted her portrait holding a lily and entitled the painting A Jersey Lily and thus the sobriquet by which she became known was established. She moved in exalted circles and her great beauty attracted the Prince of Wales; needless to say, her affair became the focus of public attention. Her drawing room became a meeting place for the powerful and famous, the painters, musicians and writers of the day. A painting entitled The Private View at the Royal Academy 1881 by W.P. Frith shows her in the company of many other celebrities, including Millais. As an actress she was fairly limited but she toured the British Isles, the United States and South Africa. She died in Monte Carlo and is buried in St. Saviour's churchyard, Jersey. A marble bust marks her grave and there is a tablet to her memory in the church. In Jersey Museum is her magnificent silver-gilt traveling case with its exquisitely-worked containers for cosmetics.

Clameur de Haro

The Normans brought their code of laws, Le Grand Coutumier, with them to the Channel Islands. These laws showed a natural respect for human rights and the Channel Islands Common Law is based on these precepts. The Clameur de Haro is a good example and can still be evoked. It is based upon calling for justice in the name of Rollo (corrupted to Haro), the much feared and respected father of Duke William I. Any citizen feeling himself wronged by another in regard to property or trespass may go on his knees before the wrong-doer and two witnesses and call out Haro! Haro! Haro! A l'aide mon Prince! On me fait tort! ('Someone is wronging me.') He then repeats the Lord's Prayer in French and his opponent must immediately stop what he is doing until the case comes to court. Anyone ignoring this legal injunction, for such it is, will find himself heavily fined. The best-documented use of the 'Clameur' was when William the Conqueror was erecting the Abbey of St. Stephen at Caen, where he hoped to be buried. One man, whose house had been demolished to make way for the new abbey, had not been reimbursed. When William died and his funeral was in progress the bereft householder raised the Clameur and it was not until the King of England had paid the compensation that the funeral could continue and William given a decent burial.

Towns and places

ALDERNEY

pop. 2,068 ☎ 048 182   B1

Alderney is 3 1/4m long and 1 1/4m wide. Most of the residents are from the United Kingdom and settled here after WWII. Alderney was totally evacuated at the outbreak of the war and when the Germans arrived they turned it into a camp for political prisoners and forced labor, many of whom died here. Now the island has a friendly easy-going atmosphere and boasts the longest licensing hours in the British Isles. Politically more democratic than the other Channel Islands, Alderney has an elected president but apart from that, her government is run on similar lines to that of Guernsey and enacts laws relating to local affairs. Alderney has fine bays and sandy beaches, ideal for swimming and for children. It is a naturalist's paradise, having 200 recorded species of birds including goldfinch, hoopoe and golden oriel as well as huge colonies of sea birds.

▶ **St. Anne** is the capital of Alderney and three quarters of the island's population lives there. It is in the centre of the island. The atmosphere of St. Anne is that of an old Norman town, with gaily painted houses and cobbled streets. ▶ The **church of St. Anne** is the finest on the islands. Built of warm Alderney sandstone and white Caen stone, to accommodate both garrison and islanders, it stands against a backdrop of well-spaced trees. ▶ **Connaught Square,** shaded by chestnut trees, has the island's civic buildings situated around it, including **Island Hall,** built 1763, now a library and community centre. ▶ **Le Huret** is the hill running down from Royal Connaught Square. ▶ The **clock tower** is all that is left of the parish church of St. Anne, demolished when the new church was built. ▶ **Alderney Society's Museum:** collection includes important finds from an Iron-Age settlement, Les Huguettes at Longy (*daily, 10.30-12.30*).

Nearby

▶ The rest of the island is best explored by a walk around the coast (*11m*). This can be managed in a day but it is worth taking more time. Many of the footpaths and lanes link the centre to the coast, so a walk can be taken up where it was left off the day before. A good method of transport is by rented bicycle. It is wise to ride around the island in a counter-clockwise direction because the gradient is mainly downhill. ▶ **Fort Albert,** most important in a line of thirteen forts started in 1847 when Britain decided to make Alderney 'the Gibraltar of the Channel Islands.' ▶ **Burhou Island** is uninhabited, except by huge numbers of puffins who nest in the rabbit burrows. Storm petrels, black-backed and herring gulls also nest and breed here. (*Bird watchers may stay overnight. Contact States of Alderney.*) Beyond Burhou: the **Casquets,** a group of treacherous rocks which have claimed many lives. **Ortac Island** lies SW of Burhou, home for hundreds of breeding gannets. ▶ **Alderney Harbour:** in 1847 a huge breakwater was built here to provide a safe anchorage for the British Fleet. It proved a complete failure and had to be breached. ▶ The **Old Harbour** at Braye later became the hub of the granite exporting industry, now used by fishing boats and pleasure craft. The pier is hardly ever used. The bay is the largest in Alderney; sandy beach surrounding a rocky centre, good swimming whatever the tide. ▶ **Essex Castle** (Longy): building was begun in 1546 and abandoned 1554. ▶ **Alderney Lighthouse** (Quèsnard Point): built 1912. The tower stands 106 ft. high, its light has a range of 17m. ▶ **Telegraph Bay** is surrounded by cliffs which are almost perpendicular. Good swimming in bay sheltered from all but southerly winds. Wide sand beach at low

tide. ▶ Further along the cliffs, carpeted with pink thrift is **Val de l'Emauve** where granite rocks form a natural chair. ▶ Nearby is **Trois Vaux Bay** where three valleys meet. Here may be seen the magnificent **Les Etacs** or 'Garden Rocks'. ▶ **Hannaine Bay** has good swimming, strips of sand between rock clumps. ▶ At the NW end of **Clonque Bay** is **Fort Turgis** and a megalith 2m long and 3/4m high. □

Practical information

ℹ️ States Office, ☎ (048 182) 2994.
✈ ☎ (048 182) 2711. Reserv. office, Aurigny Air Services, ☎ (048 182) 2889; air ferries, ☎ (048 182) 2993.
⛴ to France, Torquay (summer only), Jersey, Guernsey, Sark.

ST. ANNE

Restaurants:
◆ *Georgian House*, Victoria Street, ☎ (048 182) 2471, AC BA DI ⌂ ♪ ✿ Cl. 26 Dec. Book. £11.50.
◆ *Nellie Gray's*, Victoria Street, ☎ (048 182) 3333, AC AM BA DI Ⓟ ⌂ ♫ ♪ ✿ Cl. Feb.-Mar. Book. £15.

GOREY **

St. Hélier, 2; St. Aubin, 3 1/2 m
☎ 0534   Jersey B2

Gorey is a pretty village in the N corner of Grouville Bay. It is dominated by the Castle of Mont Orgueil. The Royal Bay of Grouville (the Royal prefix granted by Queen Victoria in 1859) stretches S to La Rocque. There is a sandy beach, safe for swimming. Beyond the beach is the Royal Jersey Golf Course. Along the quayside are attractive old houses, now housing many good restaurants.

▶ Just beyond the village is the **Jersey Pottery,** surrounded by attractive gardens (*all year: Mon.-Sat., 9-5.30*). ▶ The 12thC castle of **Mont Orgueil★★** was practically impregnable before gunpowder. Invaders faced two moats and, to reach the second, had to pass along a path in single file under attack from above. Interior is a fascinating labyrinth of fortifications; tableaux portray scenes such as the defenders of the castle during an attack in 1373 from the French and prisoners who have been incarcerated in the castle (*mid-Mar.-end Oct.: daily, 9.30-5.30*). ▶ **La Hougue Bie★** (Grouville), a tomb built by neolithic man around 3000 BC; 33 ft. entrance tunnel, covered by a 40 ft. mound of earth, limpet shells and rubble, the whole being cruciform; the centre chamber may have been a place of worship with the side rooms used for burial. On top of the mound are two chapels. They are now both covered by the same roof but were built centuries apart. Notre Dame de la Clarté was built in the 12thC and the **Jerusalem Chapel** in the 16thC. ▶ The **Archaeological Museum** (Société Jersiaise) has on display a replica of a magnificent Bronze-Age necklace which must have been worn by a chieftain 3,000 years ago. It contains 26 ounces of gold. The original is at the Jersey Museum in St. Hélier. There is also an Occupation Museum, a Railway Exhibition, a reconstruction of an Old Forge and an Agricultural Museum (*mid-Mar.-end Oct.: Tue.-Sun., 10-5*). ▶ **St. Martin.** The coast line of this parish takes in seven bays as well as several inlets. **St. Catherine's Bay** is sheltered by the huge St. Catherine's Breakwater built at great cost. It is now used by fishermen and yachtsmen and has special barbecue facilities. ▶ **Rozel,** fishing village with small bay much favoured by local lobster fishermen. Picturesque buildings line the quayside. There is an old fort which once housed the local garrison, now hotel and restaurant. The bay faces NE; on a clear day the coast of France can be clearly seen. ▶ There is an attractive walk through

Rozel Valley; at the top of the hill, the oldest mill in Jersey, **Rozel Mill**, first mapped in 1563, can be seen. □

Practical information

Hotels:
★★ *Dolphin*, Gorey Pier, ☎ (0534) 53370, Tx 4192085, AC AM BA, 17 rm. ⌘ £40. Rest. ♦ Cl. Oct.-Mar. £10.
★★ *The Moorings*, Gorey Pier, St. Martin, ☎ (0534) 53633, Tx 4192085, AC BA, 16 rm. £60. Rest. ♦ £15.

Restaurant:
♦ *Galley*, ☎ (0534) 53456, BA DI Ⓟ ≼ ♪ ⅋ ⌘ Cl. 1 Jan.-7 Feb., Mon. Shellfish. Book. £13.

GUERNSEY*

pop. 53,637 ☎ 0481   A2

Guernsey is a triangle with the W coast facing the other islands in the Bailiwick - Herm, Jethou, Sark and Alderney. The two main towns of St. Peter Port and St. Sampson are on this coastline. The hypotenuse runs from Fort Doyle past the golf course on L'Ancresse Common and the sandy beaches from Grand Havre Bay to Vazon Bay down to Pleinmont. The S coast running from the fortifications at Pleinmont to Jerbourg is a region with excellent walking paths that command spectacular views. □

Practical information

ⓘ Crown Pier, St. Peter Port, ☎ (0481) 23552.
✈ La Villiaze, ☎ (0481) 37267.
⛴ to France, Portsmouth, Weymouth and Jersey.
⋏ *La Bailloterie Camp*, Vale, ☎ (0481) 44508.

CASTEL

Hotel:
★★ *De Beauvoir*, Rue Cohu, ☎ (0481) 54750, AC AM BA, 29 rm. Ⓟ ⁂ ⚲ ⅋ ⌘ ⊡ £36. Rest. ♦ ⅋ Cl. Christmas. £6.

COBO BAY

Hotel:
★★ *Cobo Bay*, ☎ (0481) 57102, AC BA, 29 rm. Ⓟ ≼ ⚲ ⅋ ⌘ £26. Rest. ♦ ♪ ⅋ Cl. Feb. Turbot normande, coquille du chef. £7.50.

FERMAIN BAY

Hotel:
★★ *La Favorita*, ☎ (0481) 35666, BA, 30 rm. Ⓟ ≼ ⁂ ⚲ ⅋ ⌘ £45. Rest. ♦ ♪ Cl. 21 Dec.-31 Jan. £6.50.

ST. MARTIN

Hotels:
★★★ *Bella Luce*, La Fosse, ☎ (0481) 38764, 31 rm. Ⓟ ≼ ⁂ ⚲ ⊡ Norman manor house dating from 12thC with 14thC and modern additions. Extensive garden. £58. Rest. ♦ ♪ Cl. late Jan.- early Feb. Duck Montmorency. £13.50.
★★★ *Green Acres*, Les Hubits, ☎ (0481) 35711, AC BA, 48 rm. Ⓟ ⁂ ⚲ ⅋ ⊡ £42. Rest. ♦ ♪ ⅋ £7.50.
★★★ *Le Chalet* (CST), Fermain Lane, ☎ (0481) 35716, AC AM BA DI, 50 rm. Ⓟ ≼ ⁂ ⚲ £48. Rest. ♦ ♪ Cl. 20 Oct.-15 Apr. Austrian specialties. £10.50.
★★★ *St. Margaret's Lodge*, Forest Road, ☎ (0481) 35757, AC AM BA DI, 43 rm. Ⓟ ≼ ⁂ ⅋ ⊡ £44. Rest. ♦ £10.
★★ *La Cloche*, Les Traides, ☎ (0481) 35421, AC AM BA DI, 10 rm. Ⓟ ⁂ ⚲ ⅋ ⊡ £48. Rest. ♦ ⚲ Cl. Oct.-Mar. £9.
★★ *La Trelade*, Forest Road, ☎ (0481) 35454, AC BA, 45 rm. Ⓟ ⁂ ⚲ ⅋ ⊡ £50. Rest. ♦ ♪ £7.50.
★★ *Les Douvres*, La Fosse, ☎ (0481) 38731, AC BA, 21 rm. Ⓟ ≼ ⁂ ⚲ ⌣ £42. Rest. ♦ £12.
★★ *Windmill*, Rue Poudreuse, ☎ (0481) 37402, 18 rm. Ⓟ ⁂ ⅋ ⊡ £42. Rest. ♦ Cl. Oct.-Apr. £7.50.

Inn or Pub:
L'Auberge Divette, La Route de Jerbourg, Jerbourg, ☎ (0481) 38485. £7.

ST. SAVIOUR

Hotels:
★★★ *La Hougue Fouque*, La Bas Courtie, ☎ (0481) 64181, AC BA, 16 rm. Ⓟ ≼ ⁂ ⚲ ⅋ ⅋ ⅊ £45. Rest. ♦ ♪ ⅋ Fillet of Hougue Fouque; fillet de boeuf Rasputin. £8.50.
★★★ *L'Atlantique*, Perelle Bay, ☎ (0481) 64056, AC AM BA DI, 21 rm. Ⓟ ≼ ⁂ ⚲ ⅋ ⊡ £42. Rest. ♦ ♪ £8.50.
★★ *La Girouette Country House*, ☎ (0481) 63269, AC AM BA, 14 rm. ⁂ ⚲ ⅋ £37. Rest. ♦ ⚲ Cl. Oct.-Mar., lunch ex. Sun. £7.

TORTEVAL

Hotel:
★★★ *Imperial*, ☎ (0481) 64044, AC BA, 12 rm. Ⓟ ≼ ⚲ £34. Rest. ♦ ♪ £6.

HERM*

pop. 37 ☎ 0481   Guernsey A2

Part of the Bailiwick of Guernsey, Herm is 1 3/4m long and $1/_2$ m wide and only 20 minutes by boat from St. Peter Port. Since 1949 it has been run as a separate community by the Wood family and remains a beautiful retreat, with tropical and semi-tropical plants, no traffic and only one hotel and one inn and the largest herd of Guernsey cows in the Bailiwick.

▶ **Shell Beach,** running halfway down the island from the NE tip, is composed of over 200 varieties of tiny delicately coloured shells. For thousands of years the sea has constantly renewed these deposits, many of which are normally never seen in the Northern Hemisphere.

Nearby

▶ **Jethou** is a small rocky island 1 1/4m around whose history is closely linked with that of Herm. The **Druid's Stone** by the landing stage marks the entrance to the Fairy Wood and on the S side is **Keitholm Wood**. Both have wonderful displays of bluebells and primroses in the spring (*not open to the public*). □

Practical information
ⓘ administrative office, ☎ (0481) 22377.
⛴ to Guernsey (6 daily), 25 min. or 8 daily (1 hr).

Hotel:
★★ *White House*, ☎ (0481) 22159, AC BA, 30 rm. ≼ ⁂ ⚲ ⅋ ⊡ ⌣ Modern hotel on 600-acre garden. £52.50. Rest. ♦ Cl. Nov.-Mar. £8.50.

JERSEY***

pop. 72,970 ☎ 0534   B3

Jersey is the largest of the Channel Islands measuring 9m from E to W and 5m from N to S. It is a sun trap that slopes from N to S, lying 14m from the French coast. The W coast contains an enormously long sandy beach known as St. Ouen's Bay. The E coast is guarded by the magnificent castle of Mont Orgueil below which lies the little port of Gorey. The N coast consists of rugged cliffs and little bays. The capital, St. Hélier, is on the S coast and is the main shopping centre. □

Practical information

ⓘ Weighbridge, St. Hélier, ☎ (0534) 78000, ☎ (0534) 24779.

✈ States of Jersey Airport, ☎ (0534) 46111.
🚢 to France, Sark, Guernsey, Alderney and Torquay.

ARCHIRONDEL BAY

Hotel:
★★ *Les Arches*, ☎ (0534) 53839, Tx 4192085, AC BA, 54 rm. Ⓟ ∰ ☒ ♪ £33. Rest. ♦ £15.

DEAUMONT

Hotel:
★★ *L'Hermitage*, ☎ (0534) 33314, Tx 4192170, 119 rm. Ⓟ ∰ ℀ ☒ £45. Rest. ♦ Cl. 2 Nov.-15 Mar. £5.50.

BONNE NUIT BAY

Hotel:
★★★ *Cheval Roc*, ☎ (0534) 62865, 45 rm. Ⓟ ⫶ ⟋ ☒ £50. Rest. ♦ .

BOULEY BAY

Hotel:
★ *Water's Edge*, Trinity, ☎ (0534) 62777, Tx 4191462, AC AM BA DI, 56 rm. Ⓟ ⫶ ∰ ⟋ ☒ £69. Rest. ♦ Cl. mid-Oct.-mid-Apr. £12.

HAVRE DES PAS

Hotel:
▲ ▲ *Ommaroo*, ☎ (0534) £0400, Tx 4192226, AM BA DI, 85 rm. Ⓟ ∰ £50. Rest. ♦ £10.

L'ETACQ

Restaurant:
● ♦ *Lobster Pot*, ☎ (0534) 82888, AC AM BA DI Ⓟ ∰ ⟋ ♪ ℀ (13 rm. £65) Lobster. Book. £10.50.

LA HAULE

Hotel:
★★★★ *La Place*, Route du Coin, St. Brelade, ☎ (0534) 44261, Tx 4191462, AC AM BA DI, 42 rm. Ⓟ ⟋ ℀ ☒ £96. Rest. ♦ £9.50.

LA PULENTE

Inn or Pub:
La Pulente Hotel, St. Brelade, ☎ (0534) 41760. £5.

PORTELET BAY

Hotel:
★★★★ *Portelet*, ☎ (0534) 41204, Tx 4192039, AC AM BA DI, 86 rm. Ⓟ ⫶ ∰ ⟋ ℀ ☒ ♪ £59. Rest. ♦ Cl. Oct.-May. £10.

Inn or Pub:
Old Portelet, St. Brelade, ☎ (0534) 41899. £5.

PORTINFER

Hotel:
★ *Le Puits*, Vinchelez, ☎ (0534) 81211, 15 rm. Ⓟ ∰ ℀ ☒ ⟋ £40.

ROZEL BAY

Hotels:
★★★ *Le Couperon de Rozel*, St. Martin, ☎ (0534) 62190, AC AM BA DI, 32 rm. Ⓟ ℀ ☒ £50. Rest. ♦ Cl. mid-Oct.-15 Apr. £11.
★★ *Château La Chaire*, Rozel Valley, ☎ (0534) 63354, AC AM BA DI, 16 rm. Ⓟ ∰ ☒ £55. Rest. ♦ £10.50.

Restaurant:
♦ *Apple Cottage*, ☎ (0534) 61002, AC BA Ⓟ ∰ ⟋ ♪ ♿ ℀ Cl. Jan., Sun. eve., Mon. Sea bass baked with garlic and fennel. Book. £12.

Inn or Pub:
Rozel Bay Inn, St. Martin, ☎ (0534) 63438 £5-£7.

ST. CLEMENT'S BAY

Hotels:
★★★ *Ambassadeur*, Coast Road, ☎ (0534) 24455, Tx 4192296, AC AM BA DI, 41 rm. Ⓟ ⫶ ℀ ☒ £55. Rest. ♦ Cl. Jan.-Mar. £12.
★★★ *Shakespeare*, Samares, Coast Road, ☎ (0534) 51915, AC AM BA DI, 32 rm. Ⓟ £58. Rest. ♦ Cl. Feb., lunch Mon.-Sat. £9.50.

ST. LAWRENCE

Hotel:
● ★★★ *Little Grove*, Rue de Haut, ☎ (0534) 25321, AC AM BA DI, 14 rm. Ⓟ ⫶ ∰ ℀ ☒ £79. Rest. ♦ £15.

ST. SAVIOUR

Hotels:
● ★★★★ *Longueville Manor*, Longueville Road, ☎ (0534) 25501, Tx 4192306, AC AM BA DI, 33 rm. Ⓟ ∰ ☒ ⟋ 𝄆 A 12thC manor house with Norman architecture and a magnificent carved, oak-paneled dining room. £80. Rest. ● ♦ £17.
De France, St. Saviours Road, ☎ (0534) 38990, Tx 4192308, AC AM BA DI, 322 rm. Ⓟ ∰ ☒ ♪ £65. Rest. ♦ £9.

SARK**

pop. 560 ☎ 048 183   Sark A-B2

Sark is $3^1/_2$ m long and $1^1/_2$ m across at its widest point. It is 365 ft. above sea level and has 42m of coastline. In places the cliffs are a sheer drop to sea level. Sark consists of two peninsulas, Great Sark and Little Sark, linked by a narrow isthmus 250 ft. high, known as **La Coupe**. There are three harbours, the main disembarkation for visitors takes place at Maseline Harbour on the E coast. This is also where all stores, fuel and other necessities for the islanders are unloaded. No cars are allowed on Sark, even the local ambulance is drawn by tractor. Transport is by horse and carriage, bicycle or, best of all, on foot. The roads are on a grid system so it is easy to get back to your starting point. Sark has had a feudal constitution since Elizabethan times, the hereditary ruler being known as the Seigneur of Sark. The most striking feature about Sark is the lack of man-made noise. Accordingly, the sounds of bees humming in the hedgerows, bird song and waves lapping against the shore beneath the cliffs take on wonderful clarity. There is an absence of gasoline and diesel fumes, few insecticides are used, so wild flowers abound. During the German Occupation of the Channel Islands the people of Sark refused to be evacuated and perhaps as a result, their way of life has changed very little since pre-war days.

▶ Uphill from **Maseline Harbour** is the commercial centre of the island: picturesque shops and houses and a school where the island's parliament meets. Sark has had a school since 1766. It also has a tiny prison with two cells. ▶ **La Seigneurie**, residence of the Seigneur of Sark, was built in 1565 and enlarged in 1730. It occupies the site of 6thC monastery of St. Magloire. It was considerably updated during the lifetime of the late Dame Sybil Hathaway, Dame of Sark (1927-74). The magnificent wrought-iron **gates** were a wedding present to her. Sheltered gardens with semi-tropical plants (*Wed., Fri., 11-5*). The central path in the walled garden is designed to give a view of the clock on the church tower. ▶ **Le Creux**, built 1570, until Maseline Harbour was constructed, was the only enclosed harbour in the island and probably the world's smallest. Today it is used as a hydrofoil base, for mooring pleasure craft and for fishing. It is approached by a tunnel cut into the cliffs. ▶ **Dixcart Bay** is reached by a path which turns r. at the **Seigneurie Cottages**. Swimming is safe at all tides as the beach shelves gently. Separated from Dixcart Bay by the 'Hog's Back' is **Derrible Bay**, silver stretch of sand at low tide. Here is **Le Creux Derrible**, a cavernous hollow formed by erosion of soft rocks and the subsequent fall of overhanging ground. ▶ **Gouliot** and **Les Boutiques Caves** under the cliffs are worth explor-

ing. They can be reached along cliff paths by people who tolerate heights. It is advisable to go with a guide. Gouliot Caves under the promontory opposite Brechou Island has walls and roof glistening with red, green and yellow anemones, except one cave where they are white. Les Boutiques Caves are reached by a path from **L'Epequerie Common.** ▶ **Brechou Island** off the W coast is one of the forty private farms of Sark, whose owners pay their dues to the Seigneur of Sark. ▶ **La Grande Grève** has good swimming and surfing. ▶ **Little Sark**: the coast is dotted with a number of rock pools ideal for diving. The largest is the Venus Pool, 20 ft. deep and crystal clear. In the 19thC silver was discovered here and silver mines constructed. One shaft is reported to have descended 150m below sea level. The venture failed and the export shipment was lost at sea. ▶ **Sark Lighthouse**, built 1912, stands on Pointe Robert and can be seen on entering Maseline Harbour. Conducted tour and magnificent **views.** Closed to the public when fog horn is working (*daily ex. Sun., 10-5*).   □

Practical information

SARK

ⓘ ☎ (048 183) 2345.

⛴ to France, Jersey, Guernsey and Alderney.

Hotels:

★★★ **Stocks**, ☎ (048 183) 2001, AM BA, 24 rm. ⬟ ⬳ ✿ ▭ ⚬ £60.50. Rest. ◆ Cl. Oct.-mid-Apr. £12.50.

● **Petit Champ**, ☎ (048 183) 2046, AC AM BA DI, 16 rm. ⬟ ⬳ ✿ ▭ £56. Rest. ◆ Cl. Nov.-Apr. Book. £10.50.

Aval du Creux, Harbour Hill, ☎ Via Guernsey (0481 83) 2036, AC AM BA, 13 rm. ≮ ⬟ £52. Rest. ◆ Cl. Oct.-Apr. £9.50.

Dixcart, ☎ (048 183) 2015, AC AM BA, 18 rm. ⬟ £53. Rest. ◆ Cl. Oct.-Apr. £9.50.

Nearby

LITTLE SARK

Hotel:

La Sablonnerie, ☎ (048 183) 2061, AC AM BA, 22 rm. ⬟ ✿ ⚬ £62. Rest. ◆ Cl. Oct.-Apr. £10.

ST. AUBIN

St. Hélier, 4 m
☎ 0534   Jersey B3

In the 18thC St. Aubin rivaled St. Hélier in importance. In 1649 Charles I made a contribution to the building of its pier. By the 18thC St. Aubin was a thriving community but as St. Hélier's harbour grew in size, it attracted the commercial shipping away from St. Aubin where today the harbour is filled with small yachts and pleasure craft.

▶ The **Channel Islands Yacht Club** had Lillie Langtry as its first lady member. ▶ A faithful reconstruction of the Old Market, vital to St. Aubin's economy since 1584, now houses the National Westminster Bank. ▶ The buildings on the Bulwarks - Le Boulevard are very ancient and the **Old Court House**, once the tallest building in Jersey, was where 17thC privateers auctioned off their booty.

Nearby

▶ **St. Brelade's church** has a saddle-back tower and Celtic turret. It is an excellent example of a Norman church; chancel is oldest section with 12thC additions. The materials used were granite boulders taken from the seashore, crushed sea shells and sand boiled in water to make mortar. It is possible to see whole limpet shells embedded in the granite. ▶ **St. Brelade's Bay**, facing S, is divided from Ouaisné Bay by a rocky headland. There is a vast expanse of sand at low tide. Good, safe swimming, wind surfing, water skiing. When tide is low, it is possible to walk across the sand to Ouaisné. ▶ **La Corbière** is probably Celtic in origin, meaning the 'place of the sea birds'

and many ravens are seen flying among the cliffs. Hundreds of ships have met their doom on the rocks below. It was not until 1874 that the lighthouse was built. There is a causeway which can be traversed between half-ebb and half-flood tides; caution is necessary as the tide, when rising, does so very rapidly. The light has a range of 18m; in bad visibility the fog horn sounds for five seconds every minute.   □

Practical information

ST AUBIN

Hotels:

★ **La Tour**, High Street, ☎ (0534) 43770, Tx 4192121, AC AM BA, 21 rm. ℗ ✿ £44. Rest. ◆ Cl. Jan.-Mar., lunch Mon.-Sat. £9.

Old Court House, St. Aubin's Harbour, ☎ (0534) 41156, AC BA, 8 rm. ✿ Some parts date from 1450, but mainly restored in 1611. The inn has a fine restaurant. £60. Rest. ◆ ≮ ⚬ ✿ Cl. Feb. Seafood specialties. Book. £16.

CORBIERE

Hotel:

Le Chalet, ☎ (0534) 41216, AM BA DI, 31 rm. ⬟ ⌁ £65. Rest. ◆ £12.

Restaurant:

◆ **Sea Crest**, Petit Port, St. Brelade, ☎ (0534) 42687, AC AM BA ℗ ⬟ ≮ ✿ Fresh fish. £16.

ST. BRELADE'S BAY

Hotels:

★★★★ **Atlantic** (B.W.H.), La Moye, ☎ (0534) 44101, Tx 4192405, AC AM BA DI, 46 rm. ℗ ⬟ ▭ ⌁ £78. Rest. ◆ Cl. Jan.-7 Mar. £12.

★★★★ **L'Horizon** (Prestige), ☎ (0534) 43101, Tx 4192281, AC AM BA DI, 106 rm. ℗ ≮ ⬙ ✿ ▭ £100. Rest. ◆ £15.75.

★★★★ **St. Brelade's Bay**, ☎ (0534) 46141, AC AM BA DI, 79 rm. ℗ ≮ ⬟ ✿ ▭ ⌁ £80. Rest. ◆ Cl. Oct.-18 Apr. £11.

★★★ **Château Valeuse**, Rue de la Valeuse, ☎ (0534) 43476, AC AM BA, 26 rm. ℗ ≮ ⬟ ✿ ▭ £48. Rest. ◆ Cl. Nov.-Feb. £6.50.

⛺ St. Brelade's Camp, Route des Genêts (300 pl), ☎ (0534) 41398.

ST. HÉLIER**

St. Aubin, 2 m
pop. 29,941 ☎ 0534   Jersey B3

St. Hélier is the administrative capital, the main port and shopping centre of Jersey. Situated on the S coast, it has a beautiful position on a lowlying site, surrounded by hills. St. Hélier was first a fishing village and later a town. For centuries the town was very small but 1815 saw the beginning of much development. Many new thoroughfares, fine crescents and terraces were built to house the new and fashionable residents.

▶ **Royal Square,** originally the market place, is bordered with chestnut trees and has always been the hub of St. Hélier life. In olden times witches were burned, criminals whipped through on their way to the courthouse and the town pillory was placed here. ▶ Two covered markets: the **Central Market★** between Beresford Street and Halkett Place and **Old Market★** or Fish Market just across from Beresford Street; present Central Market was opened 1882. Thirty-seven pillars support the roof and dome; centrepiece is a 15 ft. ornamental fountain with gold fish. Fish Market has local fresh fish and shellfish. ▶ **Parish church:** there are records of original church on this site receiving tithes around 1066 on behalf of William of Normandy; present building is mainly 14thC, granite except the 12thC N and S chapels. The **silver** on display is over 300 years old. ▶ **Jersey Museum** (Pier Road), owned by

Société Jersiaise, founded 1873 to study and conserve cultural and natural history of Jersey (*Mon.-Sat., 10-5*). **Barreau Art Gallery:** a memorial to local artist A.H. Barreau; collection of paintings connected with Jersey or by Jersey artists. **Lillie Langtry Room:** her portraits by Millais and Poynter and personal memorabilia. **Maritime Museum** and **T.B. Davis Room:** items connected with the yacht *Westward* are on first floor, as well as a reconstruction of a Victorian pharmacy. The top floor contains two carefully preserved **Victorian rooms** and a **German Occupation Museum;** basement houses **marine biology room;** room with items connected with Victorian prison life and **natural history room** (*Mon.-Sat., 10-5*). ▶ **Fort Regent,** built 1806-1814 to protect the town against Napoleon. Garrisoned by units of the British Army until 1930, it never saw action until it was occupied by the Germans during WWII. Now one of Europe's largest sports, entertainment and conference centres; concert hall, terraced swimming pool, roller skating facilities, squash courts, aquarium, amusement parks, restaurants, bars, discothèques.

Nearby

▶ **Elizabeth Castle** in St. Aubin's Bay, built late 16th-early 17thC to protect St. Hélier as it grew in commercial importance, on an islet where St. Hélier, son of a Belgian noble, took up residence as a hermit in the 6thC. The castle is reached via causeway exposed at low tide from esplanade in front of Grand Hotel. In summer at high tide the castle can be reached by amphibious craft; introductory exhibition near entrance of castle gives its history; interesting exhibits at the barracks in Lower Ward and inside the Governor's House, where there are historical tableaux of famous people and events that have affected Jersey's history. ☐

Practical information

ⓘ Weighbridge, ☎ (0534) 78000, ☎ (0534) 24779.
Car rental: *Kimgley,* ☎ (0534) 24777; *Zebra,* ☎ (0534) 36556.

Hotels:
★★★★ *De la Plage*, Havre des Pas, ☎ (0534) 23474, Tx 4192328, AC AM BA DI, 96 rm. ℗ ⬦ ⁂ £65. Rest. ◆ Cl. Oct.-mid-Apr. £10.
★★★★ *Grand Hotel*, Esplanade, ☎ (0534) 22301, Tx 4192104, AC AM BA DI, 118 rm. ℗ ▭ £75. Rest. ● ◆ ♪ £10.50.
★★★ *Apollo*, 9 St. Saviour's Road, ☎ (0534) 25441, Tx 4192086, AC AM BA DI, 90 rm. ℗ ▭ £53. Rest. ◆ Cl. Sep.-Apr. £8.
★★★ *Beaufort*, Green Street, ☎ (0534) 32471, Tx 4192160, AC AM BA DI, 54 rm. ℗ ⁂ ▭ £60. Rest. ◆ £8.
★★★ *Pomme d'Or*, The Esplanade, ☎ (0534) 78644, Tx 4192309, AC AM BA DI, 151 rm. ⁂ £54. Rest. ◆ £10.
★★ *Mountview*, New St. John's Road, ☎ (0534) 78887, Tx 4192341, AC BA, 36 rm. ℗ £48. Rest. ◆ Cl. 16 Nov.-19 Mar. £9.
★★ *Royal Yacht*, Weighbridge, ☎ (0534) 20511, Tx 4192085, AC AM BA, 45 rm. ⬦ £43. Rest. ◆ £9.
★★ *Savoy*, Rouge Bouillon, ☎ (0534) 27521, AC, 61 rm. ℗ ⁂ ▭ £45. Rest. ◆ Cl. Nov.-Mar. £8.
★★ *Uplands*, St. Johns Road, ☎ (0534) 70460, 28 rm. ℗ ♨ ▭ £28. Rest. ◆ Cl. Nov.-Apr. £6.50.
Millbrook House, Rue de Trachy, ☎ (0534) 33036, 27 rm. ℗ ♨ ⚲ ⁂ £44. Rest. ◆ Cl. Oct.-May, lunch. £9.

Restaurants:
◆ *La Buca*, The Parade, ☎ (0534) 34283, AC AM BA DI ♪ ♿ ⁂ Cl. 25 Dec.-1 Jan., Wed. Book. £10.50.
◆ *La Capannina*, 67 Halkett Place, ☎ (0534) 34602, AC AM BA DI Cl. Sun. Book. £11.
◆ *Mauro's*, 37 La Notte Street, ☎ (0534) 20147, AC AM BA DI Cl. Sun. 4 Jan.-Feb. £12.

Recommended
Antique shop: *St. Hélier Galleries Ltd.*, Les Ormes, Ville au Bas, ☎ (0534) 82332, paintings and prints.
Cycle rentals: *Doubleday Garage*, 19 Stopford Road, ☎ (0534) 31505; *Lawrence de Gruchy Ltd.*, 46 Don Street, ☎ (0534) 30090.

ST. JOHN

St. Hélier, 2 1/2 m
☎ 0534   Jersey B3

St. John benefits from fine coastal walks and a recreation centre. The centre of this parish is the centre of Jersey. A stone in the garden of **Centre House,** near the Methodist church, marks the place.

▶ Near the main road is the **cemetery of Macpela** where, in the 19thC, many of those who sought refuge in Jersey from strife-torn Europe were buried. It was the custom for the European colony to go en masse to the funeral, marching behind the Red Flag and on many occasions to be addressed by Victor Hugo.

Nearby

▶ **Devil's Hole★** or Le Creux de Vis. This is a huge cave which has been tunneled out over many centuries by the sea to make a natural blow hole. ▶ **Bonne Nuit Bay★** is sheltered by cliffs 400 ft. high and facing N; sand and shingle shore; good swimming for strong swimmers. To the W of the bay is **Frémont Point:** spectacular views. The land on both sides of the road leading away from Bonne Nuit Bay belongs to the National Trust for Jersey. A path has been constructed along the hillside; pleasant walk with beautiful **views.** ▶ **Bouley Bay.** The way to this beach is by a steep winding road down to a granite-walled harbour. The water is deep and clear and the bay is a centre for underwater exploration. The beach is of interest to geologists because of the volcanic rock formation. Swimmers should note that the beach shelves steeply. ▶ **Grève-de-Lecq** is a popular beach of yellow sand reached by a path through a wooded valley. It is quite small, with rock outcrops. The beach shelves cause a strong undertow in heavy seas. ▶ **Grève de Lecq Barracks,** bought by the National Trust for Jersey in 1972; restored to show the grim realities of garrison life. Military equipment, horse-drawn vehicles from 1875, prison cells may be viewed (*Apr.-Sep.: Tue.-Fri., 2-5*).

▶ **Grosnez Point.** Marvelous place to view the sunset and on a clear day views of Herm, Sark, Alderney and the Paternoster Rocks. The ruins of **Grosnez Castle** dominate the NW tip of the island. There are steps and a short path to the lighthouse on Grosnez Point. ▶ **Jersey Zoo** (Trinity, in grounds of Les Angres Manor): the Jersey Wildlife Preservation Trust was formed by Gerald Durrell in 1963; now over 1,200 rare and endangered species, snow leopards, cheetahs, gorillas, as well as pheasants, and a reptile collection. Animals are able to breed here without fear of predators and it is planned to re-populate areas where they have become extinct, or to introduce them to new areas. The star resident is Jumbo the gorilla (*summer: daily, 10-6; winter: 10-4.30*). ☐

ST. PETER

St. Hélier, 5 m
pop. 3,713 ☎ 0534   Jersey B3

Jersey airport is situated here.

▶ **St. Peter church** was in existence before 1066; probably started as a chapel but was designated parish church in a charter signed by William of Normandy; walls of original chapel, made of stones from the beach, are still visible in chancel. The **spire** is the tallest in the Channel Islands; being so near the airport it carries a red light. ▶ **St. Peter's Bunker Museum:** bunker containing range of Occupation relics. Built by forced labour (1942), the Bunker had an important role in guarding the crossroads leading to the airport (*Mar.-Nov.: daily, 10-5*). ▶ **Jersey Motor Museum:** collection of vintage cars, including Rolls-Royce Phantom III used by Field Marshall Montgomery. There is

also a **Jersey Steam Railway** exhibition (*Mar.-Oct.: daily, 10-5*). ▶ **Quetivel Mill:** at one time water mills played a very important part in the life of the community. None of these except the Moulin de Quetivel is now operating; beautifully restored by National Trust for Jersey; demonstrates the process of making stone-ground flour. The flour may be purchased. ▶ Sandy **St. Ouen's Bay** touches three parishes, St. Brelade, St. Peter and St. Ouen, along a 5m stretch of the W coast. Strong Atlantic breakers make for excellent surfing, in a sea that is for experienced swimmers only. There are discothèques, restaurants, a golf range and mini golf along the length of the bay. ▶ St. Lawrence: **German Underground Hospital**, built during WWII by forced labour. It was equipped with operating theatre, dispensary, medical stores and staff quarters. It now houses an exhibition of weapons, documents, newspapers and photographs connected with the Occupation (*daily, 9.30-5.30, last admission 4.30*). ▶ **St. Lawrence Church**, on site of an early Norman chapel, has an interesting legend which tells of a bride-to-be left waiting on her wedding day. When the wedding bells are rung she is said to haunt the nearby lanes in her coach, looking for her errant suitor.   □

Practical information

✈ States of Jersey Airport, ☎ (0534) 46111.
Car rental: *Polar,* ☎ (0534) 24577.

Hotels:
★★ **Greenhill**, Coin Varin, Mont de l'Ecole, ☎ (0534) 81042, Tx 4192249, AC AM BA DI, 18 rm. ℗ ⚏ ⚞ ▱ £82. Rest. ♦ £8.50.
★★ **Mermaid**, Airport Road, ☎ (0534) 41255, AC AM BA DI, 68 rm. ℗ ≼ ⚏ ▱ £60.

ST. PETER PORT*

pop. 15,587 ☎ 0481   Guernsey A2

Considered one of the most attractive harbour capitals in Europe, with buildings ascending from the shore front up the hill. The harbour, yacht marina and esplanade are all reclaimed from the sea and the work is continuous. Despite its development as a tourist centre, the town still keeps some of the character of a fishing village, many houses enjoying fine sea views.

▶ The town's **church of St. Peter** stands by the SE corner of the old harbour. Its fine architecture has earned it the title of 'The Cathedral of the Island'. ▶ Climbing up narrow cobbled streets and flights of steps through the town, look back to breathtaking **views** of Herm, Jethou and Sark. ▶ Granite blocks or *barrières de la ville* still make gateways of old defensive town walls and date from 1700. Guernsey's economy was once based on privateering and smuggling and the cellars where shipments and booty were stored still survive as shops and restaurants along the harbour. Georgian houses recall a building boom in the 18th and 19thC. ▶ The **covered markets** sell local produce. A specialty is the *oreille-de-mer* or sea ear. Only found in Channel Island water, it is a great delicacy, and the shells, which look like mother-of-pearl, are collectors' items. The **French Halles** is the oldest of the markets. The States of Guernsey Dairy has a shop here selling thick golden cream, ice cream, butter and milk from Guernsey cows, the only breed allowed on the island. ▶ The **Royal Court House** (Manor Place), extensively altered after WWII, this is where the sittings of the Royal Court and States are held. Visitors are admitted to the Public Gallery and may visit the Greffe which has housed the island's charters since 1394. ▶ **Guernsey Museum and Art Gallery** is on the hill overlooking St. Peter Port in **Candie Gardens**, miniature botanic gardens with a variety of subtropical plants, trees and shrubs; statue of Victor Hugo and converted Victorian bandstand (refreshments). The museum is organized as a cluster of octagonal pavilions, telling the story of Guernsey from the geological for-

mation of the island to the present. The art gallery houses oil paintings, watercolours and collection of European and Oriental porcelain (*summer: 10.30-5.30; winter: 10.30-4*). ▶ **Hauteville House** in Hauteville at the S end of St. Peter Port was the home in political exile of Victor Hugo, who lived in Guernsey from 1855-70. It is as he left it, furnished at a time when Guernsey shops were laden with the spoils of privateering. From the window of his study you can, on a fine day, see the coastline of France. ▶ The **Guernsey Maritime Trust** headquarters and workrooms at Rue des Fontaines off Victoria Road: the Trust was formed in 1984 to research, record and present the island's maritime heritage. Currently preservation work is being carried out on the remains of an important Gallo-Roman wreck circa 2ndC AD, with the working title *Astérix*, which was raised from the harbour mouth of St. Peter Port in 1985. ▶ **Beau Séjour** is Guernsey's leisure centre: set in parkland overlooking the town with indoor heated swimming-pool, facilities for squash, tennis, badminton, roller skating, as well as bars, restaurants and a cinema. Musicals, plays, pop concerts and discos are regularly advertised in local press. ▶ **St. James★** (College Street), formerly the church of St. James-the-Less, now restored handsomely to its original Regency elegance by local craftsmen. Architecturally one of the most important buildings in Guernsey, its construction in 1818 marked the transition of St. Peter from medieval town to Regency. ▶ 13thC **Castle Cornet★★**, at the end of Castle Pier (*daily, 10.30-6.30*), is the former residence of the Governors of the island and has seen many battles, especially during the frequent troubles with France. During the Civil War (1640-51) the island supported the Roundheads but the Governor was a Royalist and withdrew into the castle with a small troop of men and held it for nine years. The Nazis took possession of it in 1940 and refortified it against invasion before they were defeated in 1945. Housed here are the **Guernsey Militia Museum** and the **Armoury:** suits of armour from the Civil War as well as modern antitank guns. In the Main Guard Museum are eight exhibition rooms, including **German Occupation room**; field equipment, newspaper cuttings and photographs. There is also an **RAF Museum.**

Nearby

▶ **Fermain Bay**, 1¹/₂m from St. Peter Port, lies at the bottom of a thickly-wooded glen. Good swimming with sand at low tide, but beach shelves steeply. In summer there is a boat service (*30 min*) from St. Peter Port to the Bay. S of bay are picturesque cliff walks, well signposted to **Pleinmont Point**. ▶ **Sausmarez Manor** (*S on Fort Road* ¹/₂m). Built on the site of a house erected in Norman times, it is now an interesting mixture of periods. One of the few manor houses in Guernsey open to the public. ▶ The **church of Ste. Mapie du Clatel**, built 12thC on site of an ancient fort. Early in the 19thC, under the whitewash of the N wall were found 13thC frescos and in 1878 a granite statue-menhir, approximately 3,000 years old, was found under the floor of the N chancel, now placed at the N side of the church entrance. ▶ **Sausmarez Park** (Cobo Road) now administrered by the National Trust for Guernsey. ▶ The **Guernsey Folk Museum**, housed in Stable Block, emphasizes past life in Guernsey and includes a traditional kitchen, bedroom, wash-house and dairy, cart room, plough room and tool room. The **Cider Barn** has a magnificent press built 1734. Costume room has authentic costumes from the National Trust's collection (*Mar.-Oct.: 10-5.30*). ▶ **St. Saviour's Church★:** Guernsey's largest country church. The present building dates form the 14th and 15thC. A menhir serves as a gatepost at the NE entrance to the churchyard. ▶ **Fort Grey Museum:** fortress built 1804 against the threat of French invasion. Houses an exhibition of artifacts from ships which have sunk off the coast (*May-Oct.: 10-12.30, 2-6*). ▶ **Rocquaine Bay** (W coast), largest bay in Guernsey, sweeps in a huge curve of 2¹/₂m around l'Erme where stands Martello tower Fort Sausmarez. ▶ Nearby an ancient causeway, only uncovered at certain tides, leads to **Lihou Island**, the smallest of the Channel Islands, 50 acres, 3¹/₂m long. There are

the remains of the ancient priory of Our Lady (1114). The whole island is a wildlife sanctuary. ▶ **Moulin Huet Bay★** (S coast): one of the best beaches on the island and very popular. In the centre of the bay is **Cradle Rock.** Beware of fast incoming tide which makes it dangerous to cross to Petit Port close by. ▶ **St. Peter-in-the Wood Church** is built on a pre-Christian site. Megalithic stones to be found in the walls. The present building is 14th and 15thC. Spiral staircase leads to belfry with two 17thC and one 19thC bell. ▶ **German Underground Hospital,** built by forced labour during WWII. Many of the task force died and were buried in the concrete. ▶ **Pleinmont Point** at the SW corner of Guernsey: romantic scenery, the land gives way to the sea at rugged precipitous cliffs. The ruined castle here is **Pezerie,** built in form of a star. To the W are Les Hanois, very dangerous reefs. The Hanois Lighthouse (1862) has revolving beams with a range of 12m. At bottom of cliff, curious circle of stones with concentric trench is pre-historic in origin and known as 'La Table des Pions' — the Footman's Table. □

Practical information

ℹ Crown Pier, ☎ (0481) 23552.
Car rental: *Avis,* ☎ (0481) 35266; *Hertz,* ☎ (0481) 38008; *A1,* ☎ (0481) 71228; *Airport Garage,* ☎ (0481) 64104.

Hotels:
★★★★ *Duke of Richmond,* Cambridge Park, ☎ (0481) 26221, Tx 4191462, AC AM BA DI, 75 rm. ⌁ ⌂ ▣ ⤵ £63. Rest. ♦ £8.50.
★★★★ *Old Government House,* St. Ann's Place, ☎ (0481) 24921, Tx 4191144, AC AM BA DI, 73 rm. ℗ ⌁ ▥ ▢ Previously the official residence of the Governors of Guernsey. £72. Rest. ♦ ⌂ ♪ Ragout de fruits de mer aioli; Governor's steak. £8.
★★★★ *St. Pierre Park,* Rohais, ☎ (0481) 28282, Tx 4191662, AC AM BA DI, 135 rm. ℗ ⌁ ▥ ⌂ ⅄ ❀ ▢ ∶° ⤵ ⌀ £44. Rest. ♦ ♪ ⌂ £10.50.
● ★★★ *La Frégate,* Les Côtils, ☎ (0481) 24624, AC AM BA DI, 13 rm. ℗ ▥ ⌂ ❀ ⤵ £78. Rest. ● ♦ Timbale de crustacés. £15.50.
★★★ *Royal,* Glategny Esplanade, ☎ (0481) 23921, Tx 4191221, AC AM BA DI, 79 rm. ℗ ⌁ ▢ £62. Rest. ♦ £7.
★★ *Havelet,* Havelet, ☎ (0481) 22199, AC AM BA DI, 33 rm. ℗ ⌁ ▥ ⌂ £45. Rest. ♦ £12.50.
★★ *La Collinette,* St. Jacques, ☎ (0481) 22585, AC AM BA DI, 25 rm. ℗ ⌁ ▥ ⌂ ⌀ £52.50. Rest. ♦ Cl. 24-26 Dec., 31 Dec.- 1 Jan. £12.50.
★★ *Moore's Central,* Pollet Street, ☎ (0481) 24452, AC AM BA DI, 40 rm. £40. Rest. ♦ Cl. Christmas. £8.
★ *Midhurst,* Candie Road, ☎ (0481) 24391, 7 rm. ▥ ❀ Cl. Oct.-Mar. £46.

Restaurants:
♦ *Le Nautique,* Pier Steps, ☎ (0481) 21714, AC AM BA DI ⌁ ♪ ❀ Cl. 3 wks. Jan., Sun. Book. £12.50.
♦ *Nino's,* Lefevre Street, ☎ (0481) 23052, AC AM BA DI Cl. Sun.
♦ *Steak and Stilton,* The Quay, ☎ (0481) 23080, AC AM BA DI Cl. 5 Jan.-Feb. £15.

ST. SAMPSON

St. Peter Port, 1 1/2 m
☎ 0481   Guernsey A2

N of St. Peter Port lies St. Sampson, a prosperous ship building port when wooden sailing ships gave much employment here. Later it was used to take on cargos of granite from the Guernsey quarries. The harbour is built of the local stone and is mainly used to repair small craft.

▶ **St. Sampson's church** (Bulwer Avenue), 12thC building on site of oratory built by St. Sampson, Guernsey's first Christian missionary and the patron saint of Guernsey who arrived here in AD 566. Note roof vaulted with pebbles from the beach ▶ **Vale Castle** guards the N entrance of the harbour. It is pre-Norman and was used as a base to repel a Welsh invasion in 1372. ▶ The **Déhus Dolmen** (King's Road) is near the Channel Island Yacht Marina. (*Electric light switch in wall r. of gate.*) A passage tomb, the second largest in Guernsey, it is 3,000 years old. Note the well-preserved rock carving, referred to as the 'Guardian of the Tomb'. ▶ The church of **St. Michel du Valle** (L'Ancresse Road), consecrated 1117 and built on early Christian site. ▶ **L'Ancresse Bay,** sheltered from E winds, has a wide sandy beach. Lanes across the headland lead to Fort Le Marchant and Fontenelle Bay, with sandy beach and excellent swimming. The entire coastline is fortified with Martello towers. Beyond the bay is the headland of **Chouet** which gives way to the inlet of **Grand Havre.** ▶ **L'Ancresse Common** is the site of Guernsey Golf Course. **Ladies Bay,** parallel to the golf course, has a sandy beach, rarely crowded. At Pembroke End is **La Varde Dolmen,** the largest megalithic tombstone in Guernsey. Recent excavations have uncovered a burial chamber in excellent condition, said to be one of the most interesting finds of this period in Western Europe. □

Practical information

Inn or Pub:
Pony Inn, Petites Capelles Road, ☎ (0481) 44374. £6.50.

Cumbria

▶ This north-western corner of England, bordered by the Irish Sea on the west and the Pennines on the east, has a landscape and character all its own. At the centre is the wild, mountainous area of the Lake District, only some 35 miles square but extraordinary in the wealth and diversity of its natural beauty. Here are found England's largest lakes and highest mountains, the Scafell range, and scenery that changes with each valley, lake and fell. Rugged peaks, cliffs and crags, rounded hills, great expanses of water, numerous tarns, becks and waterfalls are offset by the woodlands and pastures of lakesides and valleys, dotted with farms and a few villages and small towns. Besides its fascination to botanists and geologists, the area has many associations with poets and literary figures, and the former homes of Wordsworth, Ruskin and Beatrix Potter are among those that can be visited.

The Lake District is a National Park, with many sites cared for by the National Trust, but because its magnificent scenic beauty attracts so many walkers, climbers and holidaymakers, it can become overcrowded, which has led to problems of nature conservation. If possible, visit in the spring when the many daffodils are in flower, or in early summer, rather than high summer.

Besides the lakes, Cumbria has much attractive countryside as well as some interesting old towns, villages and historical sites. For centuries, the region was disputed frontier territory and remnants of the western end of Hadrian's Wall lie in the remote borderlands of the north along with many battered castles and fortified houses. The ancient city of Carlisle includes a medieval cathedral among its historic buildings and lies close to the extensive marshlands of the Solway estuary, rich in birdlife. The coastline of cliffs and sandy beaches is marked by a few industrial towns with interesting mining and shipping histories, including Barrow on the fertile Furness peninsula to the south. Wilder countryside is found in the east where the unspoiled valley of the River Eden winds between wooded hills and the steep slopes of the bleak Pennines, with stone-built market towns and isolated villages dating from Roman and Saxon times. □

Brief regional history

Prehistoric Cumbria

Although there is evidence of human habitation in Cumbrian coastal areas from the palaeolithic period, it is for **neolithic developments** that Cumbria becomes of particular interest to archaeologists. As recently as 1947 an important find of polished stone axes was made in **Great Langdale** and subsequently two other sites were discovered nearby. It seems that the Langdale volcanic rock was particularly suitable for cutting and polishing, so much so that neolithic communities had a veritable factory system for the manufacture of these fine cutting edges and exported their wares to other parts of Britain.

● **The Beaker people** also settled the coastal plane and the Eden Valley, but it is to the **Bronze Age** that the Cumbrian stone circles belong. Not as large or as dramatic as Stonehenge, they nevertheless present a compelling sight and testify to considerable engineering ability, since very large stones were somehow transported for substantial distances. The largest is Long Meg and Her Daughters near Little Salkeld. Castlerigg, near Keswick, is the most accessible, while at Swinside the stone circle is to be found high on the fells overlooking the Duddon estuary. ● **Iron-age Celts** came to Cumbria in the 2nd or 3rd century BC, having crossed the Pennines from Yorkshire. They practiced more advanced farming methods and some sophisticated metalwork has survived. Hill-forts have also been discovered in this area and farming settlements revealed by aerial photography.

The Roman occupation

The Roman legions entered Cumbria at some time after AD 71, when the Brigantes were defeated. Under **Agricola**, defense of the territory was strenghtened by a road from Chester through the Lune gorge to Brougham and, by the end of the century, Stanegate was completed linking Carlisle with Corbridge.

● The Roman fort at Galava, near Ambleside, appears to have been occupied until 383. Hardnott fort stands high on the fells above Eskdale, built, as an inscription testifies, to the Emperor Hadrian's First Cohort of Dalmations. On **Hadrian's Wall** there are six forts in the Cumbrian section: Birdoswald, Castlesteads, Stanwix (Carlisle), Burgh-by-Sands, Drumburgh and Bowness-on-Solway, Birdoswald being the best preserved.

Dark-Age Cumbria

After the departure of the Romans, some semblance of a Romanized life continued, particularly in Carlisle, but, as the Picts and Scots descended, old Celtic traditions began to reassert themselves. From the 5thC the **kingdom of Rheged** emerged in the north-west, extending north of the Solway and perhaps as far south as the Ribble. The exploits of the legendary King Urien are celebrated in the poems of the Welsh bard, Taliesin, but, after his death, Rheged became

absorbed into the kingdom of Strathclyde, whose inhabitants were known as **Cymry**, the "compatriots", and from this Celtic word derives both Cumbria and Cymru, the Welsh word for Wales. This association between Cumbria and Wales is further emphasized in Welsh place names in the area.

● St. Mungo, the patron saint of Glasgow, visited Cumbria on a mission some time after 573 and a number of churches are dedicated to him under his other name, **St. Kentigern**. The absence of pagan burial grounds suggests that by the time the Anglian armies arrived, they had already become Christian converts. The powerful Anglo-Saxon kingdom of Northumbria under Aethelfrith (593-617) drove a wedge between the Celtic peoples of Wales and Cumbria, defeating the Cumbrian Celts at the **battle of Chester**, and by the end of the 7thC all of Cumbria was in Northumbrian hands. From this period date some of the finest Anglo-Saxon crosses in Britain, in particular the Bewcastle cross, with its vine scrolls, stylized birds and runic inscriptions. The Ormside bowl, found at Ormside near Appleby, with its intricate repoussé decoration, also testifies to the skill of the local craftsmen.

● The first **Viking settlers** in Cumbria came not directly from Scandinavia but from Ireland and they were not Danish but Norse. Archaeological evidence suggests that Vikings appeared in the Orkneys and Shetlands in the mid-8thC, traveling down the west coast of Scotland and establishing a settlement in the Dublin area. These Norse-Irish people colonized much of Cumbria, as is confirmed by Norse place names right across the area and by Norse words in dialect speech. From this period date a number of carved stone crosses, often combining in their decoration elements from pagan Norse mythology with Christian motifs. Typically Norse are the **"hog-back" tombstones** which survive at such places as Appleby.

New Hall Inn at Bowness - on - Windermere

The Normans

During the century preceding the Norman conquest, the British kingdom of Strathclyde again became powerful and a considerable part of Cumbria came under the control of its northern neighbour. Then, when in 945 King Edmund of Northumbria defeated the king of Strathclyde, Cumbria was handed over to Malcolm I of Scotland. It remained a **part of Scotland** until 1032 when Cnut came to a new arrangement with the Scots, swapping Cumbria for Lothian. Again in 1068 the region was seized by the Scots under Malcolm III, which is why most of the region finds no place in the Domesday survey.

● The *Anglo-Saxon Chronicle* tells how William II marched north with a large army, captured Carlisle and built a castle there. Like the Romans, the Normans saw the Solway as marking the frontier with Scotland. Under Henry I the castle was strengthened, but with the disturbed conditions under Stephen, Scots again invaded and again Carlisle became a Scottish city. The region was to change hands again twice more before in 1216 Henry III brought Cumbria within his realm and it has remained, however precariously, a **part of England** ever since.

● The Normans built **castles** in the Eden Valley and along the coastal plain, at Brougham and Brough and at Appleby. Along the border with Scotland there were castles at Burgh, Liddell, Brampton, Irthington and Naworth. On the coast the two most important defenses were at Cockermouth and Egremont. Within Cumbria there were several large private forests set aside for hunting, Inglewood being an exclusively royal preserve. And the Normans also founded **monasteries** here — St. Bees was a Benedictine house while Furness Abbey was a powerful Cistercian foundation. Apart from Shap, all the Norman monasteries lay outside the mountain area.

Medieval Cumbria

Of all the English kings, **Edward I** can be singled out in the turbulent history of the border area. His determination to impose sovereignty on Scotland had disastrous results on the local population. The Scots laid siege to Carlisle, while Edward besieged Caerlaveroth Castle in Dumfries. After the execution of William Wallace, Robert Bruce was to revive the Wallace tradition and again Carlisle was besieged in 1315; many towns and villages were burned, the churches destroyed, the local treasures carried off. But the most **serious depredations** were to take place in 1322 when a much greater Scottish force poured across the border reaching as far as Preston. The "great raid" caused havoc and massive loss of life.
● Throughout the 14thC there were periods of uneasy peace, but Carlisle was besieged three times in the 1380s and in 1388 Appleby was completely destroyed. The uncertainty which prevailed throughout this period led to the fortification of churches, the building of pele towers and the strengthening even of working farms.

The Tudors

Two factors were to influence the pattern of life in Cumbria during the Tudor period. The first was the **dissolution of the monasteries**, which removed the principal source of benefaction for the poor and needy and the second was the **development of mining**. ● From the 1560s considerable quantities of copper, lead and some silver ore were being produced. Under the terms of the Company of the Mines Royal, one tenth of the proceeds went to the Crown, but this left a sizeable profit for local entrepreneurs. Tunnels and shafts were dug in the Lakeland hills, the ore being transported by packhorse to such places as Brigham, near Keswick, where furnaces and smelting houses were located. Huge quantities of charcoal were needed to fire these furnaces, which led to the purchase of tracts of woodland.

The 17th century

The union of the Crowns in 1603 was a particularly significant event for the English counties lying along the Scottish border, for it brought to an end the protracted border skirmishes which had disturbed the region for so many years. Cumbria could now look forward to a period of **peace** and **prosperity**. New towns could safely be built and a rural middle class, sometimes called the *Statesmen,* acquired position and privilege.

The "Fifteen" and the "Forty-Five"

In 1688 William of Orange was proclaimed king of England as William III. While some of the leading Cumbrian families pledged loyalty to the new king, others, like the Howards of Corby, the Warwicks of Warwick Hall and the Dacres of Lanercost, went into exile with the departure of James II. In 1715 the Highlands rose in support of the Old Pretender and at Penrith a Highland force proclaimed James III king, advancing by way of Appleby, Kendal and Lancas-

ter to Preston where they surrendered to the English without giving battle. ● Much more disruptive from the Cumbrian point of view was the **Jacobite rebellion** of 1745. **Prince Charles Edward Stewart**, "Bonnie Prince Charlie", had landed at Edinburgh in July and by November had led his Highlanders to within a few miles of Carlisle, where he waited for reinforcements from Northumberland. Carlisle was lamentably unprepared for these events and when the city's militia mutinied, the way was clear for Prince Charles to enter Carlisle in triumph, preceded by pipers in full highland dress. The Prince then marched south to Penrith, requisitioning supplies for his onward progress to Lancaster, Preston and Derby. His almost immediate retreat north again was precipitated by the news of the **Duke of Cumberland's** imminent arrival and Charles returned to Carlisle a broken man. Leaving Captain Hamilton there as governor of the city, he fled to Scotland. Cumberland's forces bombarded the town with cannon taken from Whitehaven and subsequently trials and wholesale executions took place, the heads of the victims remaining for years impaled on the city gates. Many rebels were transported overseas. The skirmish at Clifton, where the Highlanders faced the forces of the loyalist Duke of Perth, was the last battle ever to be fought on English soil.

The 18th and 19th centuries: innovation and change

The agricultural revolution of the 18thC was slow in reaching Cumbria. Until the mid-century, farm implements were of the most primitive kind and even wheeled vehicles were rare in the central fells. The introduction of **root crops** was an important innovation, for it meant that livestock could be fed through the winter months, thus avoiding the annual autumn destruction of a high percentage of the herd. Between 1763 and 1800, some 50,000 acres of common land had been enclosed, the dry stone walls becoming a feature of the landscape. The **enclosure policy** caused hardship, but it also made possible an improvement in the breeding of sheep and cattle and the introduction of new breeds. In the 18thC the roads of Cumbria were among the worst in the country, complained of bitterly by the Duke of Cumberland in 1745. The Turnpike Act, under which local improvements could be subsidized by tolls, started to be implemented in the 1750s and 60s and carriers' wagons appeared in the area for the first time. In 1763 the first stage coach made its journey from Kendal to Carlisle.

● As elsewhere in Britain, the railways boosted **industrial and agricultural development**. Whitehaven became an important port and there were shipyards in all the Cumbrian ports. The modern haematite **pig-iron industry** began in the mid-19thC, iron ore being locally mined and transported to blast furnaces at Cleaton Moor, Whitehaven and Workington among other centres. Industrial towns grew in size, particularly Carlisle and Whitehaven. **Tourism** also developed, Windermere becoming a favourite Victorian resort. And the Wordsworth cult began, bringing increasing numbers of visitors to Grasmere.

Epilogue

The beautiful fells and dales of the north-west have been slow to change, and, because of its relative inaccessibility, the Lake District has preserved its traditional character. The Lake District National Park was founded to protect an area of exceptional natural beauty and to maintain farming patterns, while endeavouring also to instruct the ever-growing of summer visitors to respect a unique landscape.

Cumberland rum butter

This sweet mixture of brown sugar, butter and rum, spiced with nutmeg, used to be made for the christening of a baby. Each visitor would eat some of the rum butter spread on oatcakes, bread or biscuits, and it was said that the first woman to taste from the bowl containing the mixture would be the next to become a mother. Alternatively, the bowl would be hidden and local children allowed to eat its contents once they had found it; the empty bowl would then be used to make a collection for the new baby.

Rum butter may also be eaten with Christmas pudding instead of brandy butter, which is made similarly. The pudding traditionally eaten all over Britain with the Christmas meal is a rich combination of dried fruits, nuts, spices, eggs, fat and flour which is steamed for several hours and, once cooked, may be stored for a year or more before eating. In parts of England it is customary for everyone in the family to take a turn in stirring the mixture while it is being made. As they do so they must make a wish. It used to be that, when the pudding was served at table, people would have to bite into their helpings very carefully - to avoid swallowing one of the lucky charms which had been baked into it. Each charm represented a different future: a ring signified marriage within a year; a button, that the recipient would remain a bachelor; and a thimble, that she would be an old maid; a threepenny coin, on the other hand, would be welcomed by all for it foretold wealth.

High Tea

Eating habits in different parts of England vary considerably. The evening meal, for example, may be called "High Tea", "Supper", "Dinner" and can be served as early as 5.30pm or as late as 9pm or after. Country practice - especially on farms - has been for tea to be served around 6pm at the end of the day's work. This may well be followed by a snack just before bedtime.

High Tea is still an important meal in rural parts of England, especially on farms where substantial spreads of cakes and pastries are particularly welcome. There is usually an array of savoury and sweet dishes - always accompanied by a large pot of tea. The meal may start with soup, cold meats, pies or cheese. There will be a plentiful supply of bread, butter and jam, and then a selection of cakes and sweet biscuits or pastries.

A favourite recipe made throughout the north is for parkin or gingerbread. Treacle gives this cake its soft and sticky texture, and ginger its spicy flavour. Parkin is traditionally eaten at Bonfire Night celebrations on 5 November. This used to be the time of an old pagan fire festival, but is now known as Guy Fawkes and commemorates the unsuccessful 17thC plot to burn down the Houses of Parliament.

● Practical information

Information: *Cumbria Tourist Board*, Ashleigh, Holly Road, Windermere, Cumbria LA23 2AQ, ☎ (09662) 4444.

Weather forecast: ☎ (0532) 9092. Lake District Weather: ☎ (09662) 5151.

Ferry: *Sealink UK Ltd*, Evershott House, 163-203 Evershott Street, London NW1 1BG, ☎ (01387) 1234.

Farmhouse holidays: *Farm Holiday Bureau*, NAC, Stoneleigh, Kenilworth, Warwickshire CV8 2LZ, ☎ (0203) 555100.

Self-catering cottages: details and brochures from Jonathan Somervell, *Cumbria and Lakeland Self Caterers Association*, Beaumont, Thornbarrow Road, Windermere, LA23 2DG, ☎ (09662) 5144; *Cottage Life*, Lane Ends Barn, Elterwater, nr. Ambleside, LA22 9HN, ☎ (09667) 292.

Youth hostel: *YHA*, Elleray, Windermere, Cumbria LA23 1AW, ☎ (09662) 2301/2.

Customs and folklore: Jul. Rushbearing (on the 1st Sat.) in Cumbria, a procession of children carrying 'bearings' decorated with flowers and rushes in the shape of crosses.

Events: end of Aug: *Carlisle Great Fair* dating back to 1352, is held for one week: the opening of the market is proclaimed from the steps of the cross in the city centre.

National park: *National Park Visitor Centre*, Brockhole, Windermere LA23 ILJ, ☎ (09662) 6601.

Scenic railway: 7 miles from Ravenglass to Eskdale (Dalegarth station) linking the Cumbrian coast with the head of a mountainous valley; spectacular mountainous ride, 40 minutes uphill, 35 downhill; steam hauled, open all year. Contact: *Ravenglass and Eskdale Railway Co Ltd*, Ravenglass, Cumbria CA18 1SW, ☎ (06577) 266.

Cycling holidays: *Cycleventure*, The Old Mill, Brigsteer, Kendal LA8 8AT, ☎ (04488) 558; *Cyclorama Holidays*, The Grange Hotel, Grange-over-Sands LA11 6EJ, ☎ (04484) 3666; *Rentacamp Leisure Hire*, Spring Gardens, Station Precinct, Windermere LA23 1AH, ☎ (09662) 4786.

Canoeing: numerous lakes for sailing, canoeing and other aquatic sports; inquire *Banerigg Guest House*, Grasmere LA22 9PW, ☎ (09665) 204. Hourly tuition on Lake Grasmere.

Caving and potholing: *Whernside National Park Centre*, Dent, Sedbergh LA10 5RE, ☎ (05875) 213.

Climbing: *Ashley Bank*, Newbiggin on Lune, Kirkby Stephen CA17 4LZ, ☎ (05873) 214; *Brathay Exploration Group*, Brathay Hall, Ambleside LA22 0HP, ☎ (05394) 33942; *Calvert Trust Adventure Centre*, Little Crosthwaite, Underskiddaw, Keswick CA12 4QD, ☎ (07687) 72254; *HF Holidays Ltd*, Derwent Bank, Portinscale, Keswick CA12 5TY, ☎ (07687) 73667; *Outward Bound Eskdale*, Eskdale Green, Holmrook CA19 1TE, ☎ (09403) 281.

Golf: *Wild Boar Hotel*, Crook, Windermere (18-hole); Ulverston (18-hole); Windermere (18-hole).

Orienteering: *Calvert Trust Adventure Centre* (→ Climbing).

Parachuting: *Wild Boar Hotel*, Crook, Windermere LA23 3NF, ☎ (09662) 5225.

Rambling and hiking: *Cyclorama Holidays*, The Grange Hotel, Grange-over-Sands, LA11 6EJ, ☎ (04484) 3666; *Eden Tours*, Appleby CA16 6JP, ☎ (0930) 61685; *Explore Cumbria*, Kirstead, Cartmel LA11 6PR, ☎ (044854) 225; *Mountain Goat*, Victoria Street, Windermere LA23 2DG, ☎ (09662) 5161.

Sailing: *Holiday Fellowship*, Monk Coniston, Coniston LA21 8AQ, ☎ London: (01-203) 0433; *Ullswater Sailing School*, Landends, Watermillock, Penrith CA11 0NB, ☎ (08536) 438.

Skiing: *Helvellyn Youth Hostel*, Greenside, Glenridding, Penrith CA11 0QR, ☎ (08532) 269.

● Towns and places

ALSTON

Brampton, 19; Penrith, 19; London, 279 m
pop. 14,741 ☎ 0498   Cumbria B1

This remote little market town, a crossing point for roads over the Northern Pennines, is set almost 1,000 ft. above sea level and surrounded by wild moorland. The streets of solid, mainly 19thC houses rise steeply from the bank of the South Tyne R., leading to a wide cobbled market place with a small town hall (1857) and rebuilt 12thC church of St. Augustine.

▶ Traces of Roman fort, Whitley Castle, lie NW of town.

Nearby

▶ The **Pennine Way** (→Northumbria) runs N from Alston along the secluded South Tyne Valley and S to attractive hamlet of **Garrigill** (*4m on B6277*); riverside walk to tributary of Ash Gill, before ascending **Cross Fell** (2,930 ft.), the highest summit of the Pennines, and continuing to **Dufton** near Appleby (→), with climbs on W fells of Pennine ridge. The path then swings E through huge stretches of moors on E Pennine slopes to Lune Forest and beautiful Tees Valley in Northumbria (→Middleton-in-Teesdale). ▶ **Nenthead** (*5m E*), remote 19thC mining village claiming to have highest sited buildings in England; wild moors scattered with derelict lead mines where A689 drops into Weardale (→Northumbria).   □

Practical information

ALSTON

ⓘ Railway station, ☎ (0498) 81696.

Hotels:

● ★★ *Lovelady Shield*, Nenthead Road, CA9 3LF, ☎ (0498) 81203, AM DI, 12 rm. 🅿 ⫍ ▦ ◿ ⌁ £46. Rest. ♦ ♪ Cl. mid-Dec.-mid-Mar. Magret de canard, bilberry sauce. £12.

★★ *Lowbyer Manor*, Hexham Road, CA9 3JX, ☎ (0498) 81230, AC AM BA DI, 12 rm. 🅿 ⫍ ▦ ◿ ❀ 400-year-old manor house, which was once the home of the Earls of Derwentwater. £35. Rest. ♦ ♪ ⚬ Cl. 2 wks. between Jan. and Mar. £10.

★ *Hillcrest*, Townfoot, CA9 3RN, ☎ (0498) 81251, 11 rm. 🅿 ⫍ ▦ ◿ ❀ £25. Rest. ♦ . £8.

Restaurant:

● ♦ *High Fell*, ☎ (0498) 81597 🅿 ⫍ ▦ ◿ ♪ ❀ 7 rm. Book. £20.

Inn or Pub:

Angel Inn, Front Street, ☎ (0498) 81363 🅿 ▦ ◿ 3 rm. Soup, sandwiches, grills, fish, salads. £3.

Recommended

Craft workshop: *Gossipgate Gaslight Gallery*, The Butts, ☎ (0498) 81806, display of 40 or more artists and craftspeople.

Guesthouse: *Howhill*, Gorrigil, ☎ (0498) 81519, £17; B. & B.

AMBLESIDE**

Keswick, 17; Windermere, 5; London, 269 m
pop. 2,872 ☎ 0966   Cumbria AB2

The little town of Ambleside is the axis of the NS, EW routes and a popular centre for walking, rock climbing and lakeland excursions. It lies at the foot of Wansfell Pike in the green vale of the R. Rothay, close to N end of Windermere Lake. Loughrigg Fell closes it in on the W, with the lovely Langdales beyond, while to the N rise the summits of the Fairfield range.

▶ Scanty remains of a Roman fort are evidence of Ambleside's long history, though most of the town's grey buildings are 19thC, with some 17thC stone cottages in attractive **Old Ambleside**, the town's upper, E part.
▶ Here also, tiny 17thC **Bridge House**, built on a round arch spanning waters of Stock Ghyll; now information centre. ▶ **Church of St. Mary** (1854) by Sir Gilbert Scott contains memorial chapel to Wordsworth and mural of town's annual rush-bearing ceremony. ▶ Track behind Salutation Hotel leads to **Stock Ghyll Force★**, splendid 120 ft. waterfall, converted old mill on far bank; nearby is path to summit of **Wansfell Pike** (1,581 ft.), giving fine view of Windermere. ▶ **Loughrigg Fell** (1,099 ft.), small plateau ascended from Miller Bridge, with rocky points giving striking views of lake, valleys and woodland. Rothay R skirts Loughrigg and runs past W end of **Borrans Field**, site of Roman fort of *Galava*. ▶ **Waterhead** *(SE)* on lakeside, has boat rental services and steamers running to Bowness and Lakeside at foot of Windermere (→). ▶ W of Waterhead, brief ascent through **Skelghyll Wood** leads to **Jenkin Crag★**, giving splendid view of much of Windermere and spectacular mountain panorama of Langdales and Scafell Pikes.

Nearby

▶ **Stagshaw★** (¹/₂m S): delightful woodland garden set on steep slope overlooking Windermere Lake *(Apr.-Jun.: daily, 10-6.30; Jul.-Oct.: by appt.)*. ▶ **Kirkstone Pass★**, reached by 'The Struggle', very steep 3m road climb E with 19thC inn at summit (1,300 ft.). ▶ Scenic mountain road to Ravenglass (→) via **Wrynose Pass★** (1¹/₂m W); steep climb with Three Shire Stone at summit (1,281 ft.), meeting point of three former counties and start for climbs on **Crinkle Crags** (2,816 ft.) to N and, via Wet Side Edge,

Old Man of Coniston range to S. Road descends along upper valley of R. Duddon, to **Cockley Beck** (*4m W*), and beginning of **Hard Knott Pass★**: narrow, hairpin bends and 1 in 3 gradients; fine views of Eskdale and Sca Fell to NW as road climbs between craggy fell of **Hard Knott** (1,803 ft.) to N and **Harter Fell** (2,129 ft.) to S. Off to r. as Pass begins descent (*6m*) is **Hard Knott Roman fort★**, set on magnificent site overlooking Eskdale, with remains of granaries, HQ buildings and commandant's house.

Excursion to Langdales

▶ Following A593 W: pleasant hamlet of **Clappersgate** (*1m*; 17thC houses), through attractive valley of R. Brathay to **Skelwith Bridge**. After 1m, branch road W leads to **Colwith Bridge** and small waterfall of Colwith Force, where sharp left turn leads into beautiful **Little Langdale Valley★** with **Lingmoor Fell** (1530 ft) to N. Past Little Langdale (5¹/₂m) and Little Langdale Tarn, road forks to l. to **Wrynose Pass** (→). Taking r. fork, road climbs steeply between Lingmoor to E and **Pike of Blisco** (2304 ft) to W; **views★** ahead of **Langdale Pikes** (2323 ft), passing lovely little **Blea Tarn★**, before dropping abruptly into valley of Great Langdale Beck and reaching **Middlefell Place** (*9m*). After 1m on B5343, steep path N leads to **Dungeon Ghyll Force★**, awesome 60ft cascade down narrow, sheer ravine. Starting point for climbs up Langdales, with splendid views N across Borrowdale Fells to Skiddaw from summits of **Pike of Stickle** (2323 ft) and **Harrison Stickle** (2401 ft); large serene pool of Stickle Tarn 1000 ft below. Road continues through **Great Langdale Valley★**; magnificent retrospective views of Langdale Pikes, passing slate quarries on fells around **Chapel Stile** (where hilly branch road leads to Grasmere), **Langdale Estate** holiday centre and 3/4m-long tarn of **Elterwater★**. Loughrigg Tarn lies to E on approach to Skelwith Bridge and junction with A593 back to Ambleside.   □

Practical information

AMBLESIDE

ⓘ Old Courthouse, Church Street, ☎ (0966) 32582. ▭ Windermere, ☎ Windermere (0966) 220397.

Hotels:

● ★★★ *Rothay Manor*, Rothay Bridge, LA22 0EH, ☎ (0966) 33605, AC AM BA DI, 16 rm. 🅿 ▦ ⚬ ❀ £80. Rest. ● ♦ ⚬ Cl. 7 wks. Jan. - Feb. £18.

● ★★ *Holbeck Ghyll*, Holbeck Lane, LA23 1LU, ☎ (0966) 32375, AC, 14 rm. 🅿 ⫍ ▦ ◿ £50. Rest. ♦ Cl. mid-Nov.-Mar. Roast lamb with brandy and rosemary sauce. £10.

★★ *Borrans Park*, Borrans Road, LA22 0EN, ☎ (0966) 33454, AC BA, 13 rm. 🅿 ⫍ ▦ ◿ ⚬ ❀ £40. Rest. ♦ ♪ ⚬ Cl. Christmas. £9.

★★ *Elder Grove*, Old Lake Road, LA22 0DB, ☎ (0966) 32504, AC BA, 14 rm. £34. Rest. ♦ ♪ Cl. Nov.-Feb.. £9.

★★ *White Lion*, Market Place, LA22 9DB, ☎ (0966) 33140, AC BA, 9 rm. 🅿 ⚬ 17thC coaching inn on stage route from Carlisle to London. £30. Rest. ♦ ♪ ⚬ Cl. Christmas, New Year's Day. £8.50.

Restaurant:

♦ *Harvest Vegetarian Restaurant*, Compston Road, ☎ (0966) 33151 ♪ ⚬ Cl. Nov.-Dec., weekdays Jan.-Mar., Thu. Apr.-Jun., Oct. Brazil nut and mushroom roast. £6.50.

⚑ National Trust C.S., Low Wray Farm (200 pl), ☎ (0966) 32810; Skelwith Fold C.P., Skelwith Fold (125 pl), ☎ (0966) 32277; at Langdale, *Greenhowe C.P.* (45 pl), ☎ (096 67) 231.

Recommended

Craft workshop: *Adrian Sankey Glass*, Rothay Road, ☎ (0966) 33039, functional and decorative lead crystal glass.

In preparing for your trip, consult the pages pertaining to the regions. You will find there the description of the region you wish to visit, a brief history and practical information.

Nearby

CLAPPERSGATE, 1 1/2m W on A593

Hotel:
● ★★★ *Nanny Brow*, LA22 9NF, ☎ (0966) 32036, AC BA, 19 rm. ℗ ≷ ▩ ◭ ⌿ £60. Rest. ♦ . £11.

GREAT LANGDALE, 5m W on B5343

Hotels:
★★★ *Pillar Country Club*, LA22 9JB, ☎ (05934) 7302, Tx 65188, AC AM BA DI, 36 rm. ℗ ▩ ◭ ᕣ ❀ ▱ ♫ Modern hotel in 35 acres of woodland, tarns and streams. £69. Rest. ♦ ᕣ Mallard with wild mushroom stuffing. £13.
● ★★ *Langdales*, LA22 9JF, ☎ (09667) 7253, 20 rm. ℗ ≷ ▩ ◭ £28. Rest. ♦ Cl. 5 wks. Jan.-Feb. £3.

Inn or Pub:
Old Dungeon Ghyll Hotel, ☎ Langdale (096 67) 272 ℗ ≷ ▩ ◭ 14 rm. Homemade bread, quiches, pies, casseroles. £9.50.

LITTLE LANGDALE, 5m N off A593

Inn or Pub:
Three Shires, ☎ Langdale (096 67) 215 ℗ ≷ ▩ ◭ ❀ 10 rm. Bar snacks, à la carte menu. £11.50.

SKELWITH BRIDGE, 2 1/2m W on A593

Hotel:
★★ *Skelwith Bridge*, LA22 9NJ, ☎ (0966) 32115, AC BA, 24 rm. ℗ ≷ ▩ ◭ £48. Rest. ♦ ᕣ Open dinner, Sun. lunch. £10.

APPLEBY★★

Penrith, 13; Brough, 8; London, 269 m
pop. 2,344 ☎ 076 83   Cumbria A2

The ancient town of Appleby lies on a loop in the R. Eden, with the Lakeland fells rising to the W and the steep W ridge of the Pennines to the E. Before 1092 it was Scottish and subjected to many border raids, evidence of which remains in the castle overlooking the town. The sloping main street and market square are lined with dignified 18th and 19thC buildings. Appleby makes a convenient base to explore the lovely Eden Valley (→).

▶ On main street of **Boroughgate**, interesting old buildings include: **Moot Hall** (1596); **St. Anne's Hospital**, 17thC almshouses grouped around a courtyard; **St. Lawrence's Church**, with partly-Norman tower and dignified interior including 17thC chancel built by Lady Anne Clifford (d. 1676), last of the powerful local Clifford family: 16thC organ case; monuments. ▶ In Bongate, old part of town on E bank connected by 19thC bridge, is **St. Michael's Church**, dating from Saxon times with Saxon hogback gravestone built into N wall.

Nearby

▶ **Dufton** (*4m NE*), pleasant village at foot of steeply rising Pennines with path to **Pennine Way** (→) and easy climbs on Dufton Pike (1,578 ft.); to N is isolated restored 13thC church shared with **Knock**, where car track leads on to Great Dun Fell (2,780 ft.), a skiing area in winter, with **Milburn Forest** and nature reserve to E and walks over Little Dun Fell (2,761 ft.) and on to flat stony summit of **Cross Fell** (2,930 ft.), highest point on the Pennine ridge.   □

Practical information _____

APPLEBY
ℹ Moot Hall, Boroughgate, ☎ (07683) 51177.
🚃 ☎ Carlisle (0228) 44711.

Hotels:
★★ *Appleby Manor* (BW), Roman Road, CA16 6JD, ☎ (07683) 51571, Tx 64100, AC AM BA DI, 19 rm. ℗ ▩ ᕣ ▱ ♫ £47. Rest. ♦ ♪ ᕣ Beefsteak and oyster pudding. £10.

★★ *Tufton Arms*, Market Square, CA16 6XA, ☎ (07683) 51593, AC BA DI, 18 rm. ℗ £36. Rest. ♦ ♪ Game pie, steak and kidney pie, venison. £9.
★ *Royal Oak Inn*, Bongate, CA16 6UN, ☎ (07683) 1463, AC BA DI AM, 7 rm. ℗ £33. Rest. ♦ ᕣ Cl. Christmas. £9.50.

⚏ at Ormside, *Wild Rose C.P.* (264 pl), ☎ (07683) 51077.

Recommended
Craft workshop: *Clifford House Crafts AJ Designs*, Clifford House, Main Street, Brough, ☎ (093 04) 296, gold and silver jewelry and other local crafts.
Golf course: Brackenber Moor (18 holes), 2m S on A66, ☎ 51432.
Riding schools: Grey Horse Riding Stables, Brough, ☎ (093 04) 651; The Wraes, Drybeck, ☎ (0930) 52313, hacking and trekking, fell, Eden valley and mountains.

Nearby

KIRKBY STEPHEN, 16m S on B6259
ℹ The Bookshop, 22 Market Street, ☎ 71804.

Hotel:
★ *King's Arms*, Market Street, CA17 4QN, ☎ (07683) 71378, AC BA, 9 rm. ℗ ▩ £37. Rest. ♦ Cl. Christmas. £11.50.

ORTON, 0m 3W

Restaurant:
♦ *Gilded Apple*, ☎ (058 74) 345, AC BA ℗ Cl. Mon., Sun. lunch only. No children under 10. £11.50.

⚏ *Tebay C.P.* (70 pl), ☎ (058 74) 482.

RAVENSTONEDALE, 7 1/2m S

Hotels:
● ★★ *Black Swan*, CA17 4NG, ☎ Newbiggin-on-Lune (058 73) 204, AM BA AC, 6 rm. ℗ ▩ ♪ £39. Rest. ♦ Cl. Jan.-Feb., Sun. eve. Medallions of venison with juniper berry and cream sauce. £12.50.
★★ *Fat Lamb*, Cross Bank, CA17 4NG, ☎ Newbiggin-on-Lune (058 73) 242, 9 rm. ℗ ᕣ £34. Rest. ♦ ᕣ Poached salmon with cucumber sauce. £9.

Inn or Pub:
Kings Head, ☎ Newbiggin-on-Lune (058 73) 284, AC BA ℗ ≷ ▩ ◭ ᕣ 5 rm. Bar snacks, à la carte menu. £4.75.

BARROW-IN-FURNESS

Ulverston, 8; Lancaster, 45; London, 280 m
pop. 50,174 ☎ 0229   Cumbria A3

At the top of the Furness peninsula, with the Irish Sea to the W and sandy Morecambe Bay to the E, this once flourishing shipbuilding town grew from a tiny port in the 19thC. Its streets follow the grid plan of 1847-65 laid out by enterprising engineer James Ramsden.

▶ **Museum** (Ramsden Square): devoted to local history and prehistoric finds (*Mon.-Wed., Fri., 10-5, Thu., 10-1, Sat., 10-4; Cl. Sun., Bank Hols.*). ▶ Bridge from docks leads to suburb of Vickerstown on long, narrow **Isle of Walney**, holiday resort with bird preserve at S end, off which lies tiny **Piel Island**; restored ruins of early 14thC castle.

Nearby

▶ **Furness Abbey★** (*1¹/₂m N*), impressive remains of what was one of wealthiest monasteries in the land, founded 1123-4; ruins (12th-15thC) include graceful arches to chapter house and magnificent canopied seats in presbytery (*15 Mar.-15 Oct.: Mon.-Sat., 9.30-6.30, Sun., 2-6.30; 16 Oct.-14 Mar.: Mon.-Sat., 9.30-4, Sun., 2-4*). ▶ **Dalton-in-Furness** (*3¹/₂m N*), ancient, once-important market town where Furness Abbey monks held court, with **castle**, restored 14thC pele tower (*apply locally for admission*); **St. Mary's**, fine late 19thC church on hill behind castle; in

churchyard grave of portrait painter George Romney, born in Dalton 1734. ▶ **Ulverston** (*6m NE*), old market town with traces of industrial boom; around medieval **Market Place** are attractive 18th-19thC buildings and **St. Mary's church**, rebuilt 19thC, including original Norman work and several fine 16th-18thC monuments. To NE is **Hoad Hill** (435 ft.): good views; 20ft-high monument to locally born Sir John Barrow, 19thC explorer and founder of Royal Geographical Society. ▶ **Swarthmoor Hall** (*1m S*), restored 16thC house associated with Quaker founder George Fox (1624-91), who married widow of owner Judge Fell (*15 Mar.-15 Oct.: Mon.-Wed. Sat., 10-12, 2-5*); nearby is Friends' **Meeting House** of 1688. ▶ **Bardsea** (*2m E*): local seaside resort overlooking the beaches of Morecambe Bay. ▶ **Broughton-in-Furness** (*12m N*), small largely-18thC town with handsome Market Square; **St. Mary Magdalene**, restored 19thC church includes late-Norman and 16thC work; **Broughton Tower**, ancient seat of Broughton family, incorporates 14thC pele tower in large 19thC mansion (*private*). ▶ **Millom** (*6m S*), attractive large village with restored 12thC Holy Trinity **church** and ruins of medieval **castle** based around substantial pele tower, now farmhouse; Hodbarrow to S: site of iron ore deposits discovered in 19thC; **Folk Museum**, St. George's Road, includes full-size model of mine from Millom's boom days.   □

Practical information

BARROW-IN-FURNESS
ⓘ Civic Hall, Duke Street, ☎ (0229) 25795.
▰▰▰ ☎ (0229) 20805.
Car rental: *Europcar*, Invincible Motor Co., Holker Street, ☎ (0229) 24554.

Hotel:
★★ *Victoria Park* (Whitbread), Victoria Road, LA14 5JX, ☎ (0229) 21159, AC AM BA DI, 40 rm. Ⓟ ⑩ ⌐ £47. Rest. ♦ ♪ Cl. 1 wk. Christmas. Fresh lobster. £9.

Recommended
Clothes: at Millom, *Schone Leder Mode*, Newton Street/King Street, ☎ (0657) 2761, suede, leather and sheepskin garments made to measure.
Golf course: Barrow Rakesmoore, Hawcoat, ☎ (0229) 25444; Furness, Central Drive, Walney Island, ☎ (0229) 41232.
Craft workshop: *Country Matters*, The Old Bull Pen, ☎ (0657) 2068, comprehensive range of exclusive herbal products.

Nearby
BROUGHTON-IN-FURNESS, 14m N

Hotel:
★★ *Eccle Riggs Manor*, Foxfield Road, LA20 6BN, ☎ (065 76) 398, AC AM BA DI, 13 rm. Ⓟ ⑩ ⌧ ☒ ♧ Victorian mansion standing in 5 acres of parkland. £45. Rest. ♦ ♪ ♿ £10.

DALTON-IN-FURNESS, 2m

Inn or Pub:
Wellington, Market Street, ☎ (0229) 62453 Ⓟ ⌧ 9 rm. Fish and chips. £5.

SANDSIDE, 20m NE on A590

Inn or Pub:
Ship (Scottish Newcastle), ☎ Milnthorpe (044 82) 3113, AC BA Ⓟ ⌧ ⑩ ♧ 6 rm. Ploughman's steaks. £5.

ULVERSTON, 9m N on A590
ⓘ Coronation Hall, County Square, ☎ (0229) 57120.
▰▰▰ ☎ (0229) 20805.

Hotel:
★★ *Virginia House*, Queen Street, LA12 7AF, ☎ (0229) 54844, BA AM, 7 rm. ⑩ ⌧ £35. Rest. ♦ ♪ Cl. Feb., Sun. lunch. £10.

Recommended
Craft workshops: *Cumbria Crystal Ltd*, Lightburn Road, ☎ (0229) 54 400, full lead crystal in clear, uncut form.

BRAMPTON

Carlisle, 9; Hexham, 29; London, 308 m
pop. 4,033 ☎ 069 77   Cumbria B1

A small market town, set on a steep hill in rugged border country. Hadrian's Wall (→) runs just N. Open countryside scattered with tiny villages extends to the Scottish border. The area has associations with Sir Walter Scott, who set many of his novels here.

▶ **Market square** has octagonal **Moot Hall** (1817). ▶ **Church** of St. Martin's★ (1874-8), with a fine tower crowned by a small lead spire and an interior that includes magnificent stained-glass windows designed by William Morris and Edward Burne-Jones.

Nearby

▶ Cross R. Irthing (beautiful Tudor 2-arched bridge) to **Lanercost Priory**★ (*2m ENE*): splendid ruins of 12thC Augustinian priory; the nave of the well-preserved church with its handsome W front is still used as a parish church and remains of monastic buildings include restored Dacre Hall, partly 16thC (*15 Mar.-15 Oct.: Mon.-Sat., 9.30-6.30, Sun., 2-6.30*). The vicarage opposite incorporates a 13thC pele tower. ▶ **Naworth Castle**★ (*3/4m S of Lanercost*), home of Earls of Carlisle, magnificent site above wooded ravine; 14thC, restored in 19thC by Salvin, with an impressive great hall including a huge fireplace and four remarkable heraldic beasts (*May-Sep.: Wed., Sun., also Easter Sun., Bank Hol. Mon.*). ▶ N of Lanercost, extending E to Gilsland on county border and W past Carlisle, are remnants of **Hadrian's Wall** (→Northumbria); small section of wall at attractive village of **Walton** to W, but best parts lie E, well-preserved turret at **Banks East**, milecastle at **Harrow's Scar** and near Gilsland, ruins of Willowford Bridge and large cavalry fort of **Birdoswald**★. ▶ Bleak village of **Upper Denton** (*2m W of Gilsland*) with ancient little **church**★ built with Roman stones and including a Roman arch. ▶ Through lovely border hill country to **Bewcastle** or **Shopford** (*16m NE*), tiny village with isolated 18thC church that includes beautifully carved 14 ft. high Saxon **cross**★ in churchyard; **Irthington** (*4m W*), attractive village on R. Irthing close to Hadrian's Wall; restored church that incorporates Roman stones. ▶ **Talkin Tarn** (*2m S*), small lake forming country park, with sailing facilities. ▶ **Written Rock** (*2m S or ¹/₂ hr walk*): attractive wooded spot by R. Gelt with rock inscribed by Roman soldier in early 3rdC.   □

Practical information

BRAMPTON
ⓘ Moot Hall, Market Square, ☎ (069 77) 3433.
▰▰▰ ☎ Carlisle (0228) 44711.

Hotels:
★★ *Howard Arms*, Front Street, CA8 1NQ, ☎ (069 77) 2357, AC AM BA, 11 rm. Ⓟ £34. Rest. ♦ ♪ ♿. £9.50.
★★ *Sands House*, The Sands, CA8 1UG, ☎ (069 77) 3085, AC AM BA DI, 13 rm. Ⓟ ⑩ ♿ £38. Rest. ♦ ♪ ♿. £7.

Recommended
Craft workshops: *Andru Knitwear*, Low Cross Street, ☎ (069 77) 3927, knitwear. 2m E, *Abbey Mill*, Lanercost, ☎ (069 77) 2638, dolls, toys, quilts, rugs, fabric paintings, puppets.

Nearby

CASTLE CARROCK, 4m

Inn or Pub:
Duke of Cumberland (Marstons), ☎ Hayton (022 870) 341 Ⓟ ⌧ ⑩ ♧ Homemade pies and bar meals. £5.

HALLBANKGATE, 2 3/4m SE on A689

Hotel:
● ★★ *Farlam Hall* (R.C.), CA8 2NG, ☎ Hallbankgate (069 76) 234, AC AM BA, 13 rm. Ⓟ ⌧ ⑩ ♧ ⌧ 17thC

country house standing in 4 acres of garden with lake. £100. Rest. ● ♦ Cl. Feb., 2 wks. Nov. £16.

TALKIN, 3m

Restaurant:
● ♦ *Tarn End*, ☎ (069 77)2340, AC AM BA DI P ⋖ ⋙ ⚲ ⅋ Cl. Mon. lunch, Sun. dinner. 6 rm. £21.

Inn or Pub:
Hare & Hounds, ☎ Brampton (069 77) 3456 P ⋖ ⋙ ⚲ ⅋ 3 rm. Bar meals, à la carte menu. £4.50.

Recommended
Golf course: Talkin Tarn, ☎ (069 77) 2250.

BUTTERMERE**

Keswick, 43; Cockermouth, 10; London, 306 m
pop. 194 ☎ 059 685   Cumbria A2

High craggy fells marked by deep coves and tumbling becks rise abruptly from the shores of this small, narrow lake, connected to the NW by a 3/4m-long stream with Crummock Water, a larger lake closed in by wild, bare fells. Beyond Crummock Water to the W lies lake of Loweswater.

Nearby

▶ From SE, via Borrowdale and Honister Pass, B5829 runs along E shore of **Buttermere** below Buttermere Fell, with **Honister Crag** and summit of **Fleetwith Pike** (2,126 ft.) dominating head of dale; access points to lakeside paths. On W shore rise bold summits of **High Crag** (2,443 ft.), **High Stile** (2,644 ft.) and **Red Pike** (2,479 ft.), with white cataract of **Sour Milk Gill** descending from Bleaberry Tarn; **views**, routes across to Ennerdale (→Cockermouth) and SE to Sca Fell range (→). ▶ At NE end of lake is tiny **Buttermere village**, with superbly positioned little church (1841); **view** over water from Buttermere Howe (1725 ft.) ▶ Opposite village at SW end of Crummock Water, track to splendid **Scale Force**★ waterfall, sheer drop of over 100 ft. ▶ B5289 continues close to E shore of **Crummock Water** below wild and rugged **Whiteless Pike** (2,195 ft.) and **Grassmoor** (2,791 ft.), with various access points. Bare fell of **Mellbreak** (1,670 ft.) rises steeply from shore on W. ▶ Branching SW off B5289, green valley of **Loweswater**; 19thC church in beautiful fell setting; road skirts N shore of lake (1m long) below Darling Fell (1,282 ft.); best views at W end, with crest of **Mellbreak**. ▶ Secondary road from Buttermere village goes NE via Newlands Pass to peaceful **Newlands Vale**, joining A66 at Portinscale E of Keswick (8m). ▶ From pass summit: **Newlands Hause** (1,096 ft.); **view** including Moss Fell waterfall in crags to S; past **Keskadale**, oakwood in fells to N; S branch of road crosses Keskadale Beck to charming hamlet of **Little Town**, home of Beatrix Potter's Mrs. Tiggywinkle; nearby Newlands **church** (rebuilt 19thC); to E rise **Maiden Moor** and **Cat Bells** dotted with derelict lead and copper mines. ▶ Roads rejoin at **Stair** with old mill below Causey Pike, before moving to NW shore of Derwent Water (→).   □

Practical information

BUTTERMERE

Hotel:
★★ *Bridge*, CA13 9UZ, ☎ (059 685) 252, 22 rm. P ⋖ ⚲ £60. Rest. ♦ Cl. Jan. Local salmon. £10.50.

Nearby

BORROWDALE, 9m E on B5289

Hotels:
● ★★★★ *Lodore Swiss*, CA12 5UX, ☎ (059 684) 285, Tx 64305, AM, 72 rm. P ⋖ ⋙ ⚲ ⅋ ⅋ ⊡ ⅋ Originally a 17thC inn, situated in 40 acres of woodland overlooking a lake. £66. Rest. ♦ Cl. Nov.-mid-Mar. £14.
● ★★ *Borrowdale*, CA12 5UY, ☎ (059 684) 224, AC BA,

35 rm. P ⋖ ⋙ ⚲ ⅃ £48. Rest. ♦ Cl. Christmas & Jan. £12.

LOWESWATER, 8m N off B5289

Hotels:
● ★ *Scale Hill*, CA13 9UX, ☎ Lorton (090 085) 232, 14 rm. P ⋖ ⋙ ⚲ ⅃ £50. Rest. ♦ ⅃ Cl. Jan. - Feb. Stuffed local salmon in a pastry case. £10.
★ *Kirkstile Inn*, CA13 0HU, ☎ Lorton (090 085) 219, AC, 10 rm. P ⋖ ⋙ ⚲ £32.50. Rest. ♦ Steak and kidney pie, local smoked trout. £8.75.

ROSTHWAITE, 6m SE on B5289

Hotels:
● ★★ *Hazel Bank*, CA12 5XB, ☎ Borrowdale (059 684) 248, 9 rm. P ⋖ ⋙ ⚲ £44. Rest. ♦ Cl. end Oct.-mid Mar. £8.
★ *Royal Oak*, CA12 5XB, ☎ Borrowdale (059 684) 214, AC, 12 rm. P ⋖ ⅃ Cl. Dec. £42 incl. dinner.

SEATOLLER, 8m SE on B5289

Hotel:
★ *Seatoller House*, Borrowdale CA12 5XN, ☎ Borrowdale (059 684) 218, AC AM BA DI, 9 rm. P ⋖ ⋙ ⚲ Cl. Dec.-Mar. £36.50 incl. dinner

Restaurant:
● ♦ *Yew Tree*, ☎ Borrowdale (059 684) 634 P ⋖ ⋙ ⚲ ⅃ ⅋ Cl. Nov.-mid-Mar., Mon., Sat. lunch. Book. £7.

CARLISLE*

Gretna, 9; Penrith, 19; London, 295 m
pop. 72,206 ☎ 0228   Cumbria A-B1

The county town and largest in Cumbria, Carlisle lies just S of the R. Eden on the tributary rivers of Caldew and Petteril near the Scottish border. It is built on the site of the Roman fort of *Luguvalium* and evidence of its long history as a key border town remains in its medieval **cathedral** and **castle**, old alleyways and several historic buildings.

▶ **Castle**★, started 1092 and frequently attacked and rebuilt, rises steeply above R. Eden; impressive remains include massive 12thC keep housing regimental museum, 13thC outer gatehouse and part of tower (14thC) occupied by Mary Queen of Scots in 1568 (*15 Mar.-15 Oct.: Mon.-Sat., 9.30-6.30, Sun., 2-6.30. 16 Oct.-14 Mar.: Mon.-Sat., 9.30-4, Sun., 2-4*). Road beside W wall (only remnant of old city walls), leads past 15thC tithe barn to scanty remains of priory with 15thC tower. ▶ From Market Place, with 17thC **cross** and **Town Hall** (1717), Castle Street leads to **cathedral**★, dating from 12thC. Present, much smaller building mainly 14thC, including huge E **window**★ with glorious flowing tracery, finest example in England; choir with beautifully carved capitals and delightful 15thC misericords. ▶ **Tullie House** built 1689 with Victorian extensions (Castle Street), now **museum and art gallery** with collections of Roman history of Cumbria including finds from nearby Hadrian's Wall; 19th-20thC British paintings, 18th-19thC English porcelain; costumes, toys and dolls (*Apr.-Sep.: Mon.-Sat., 9-7; Oct.-Mar.: Mon.-Sat., 9-5; also Sun., Bank Hols., Jun.-Aug., 2.30-5*). ▶ Near Market Place: **Guildhall** (Greenmarket), early 15thC half-timbered house with displays of guild, civic and local history (*apply locally for admission*); **St. Cuthbert's** 18thC church (medieval glass).

Nearby

▶ N on A7, over widened **Eden Bridge** (1815) by Robert Smirke to smart suburb of **Stanwick**, site of largest cavalry fort on Hadrian's Wall, through rough border country to **Longtown** (8m N), small market town laid out in late 18thC, reached by 5-arched stone **bridge** across R. Esk; at Arthuret (3/4m S) is long, stately **church** of St. Michael, rebuilt in 17thC. ▶ **Rockcliffe** (4m NW), attractive village at mouth of Eden; **views** N of woods and **Burgh**

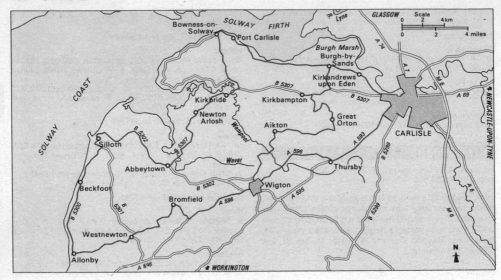

Solway round trip

Marsh across river; **church** rebuilt 19thC has Saxon cross in churchyard. **Castletown House** (*3/4m E*), Georgian country house (*Apr.-Sep.: Wed., Bank Hol. Mon., 2-5*). ▶ **Warwick** and **Warwick Bridge** (*4m E*): attractive villages on R. Eden separated by splendid 3-arched **bridge** (1837) by John Dobson of Newcastle. In Warwick is **Warwick Hall**, Georgian, rebuilt 20thC; to S, little church of **St. Leonard★**: Norman apse and chancel arch. ▶ Busier Warwick Bridge has fine Gothic RC **church** by Pugin (1841) and 19thC Tudor-style mansion, **Holme Eden Hall** (now a nunnery). ▶ **Wetheral** (*1m S*), pretty village set high above W bank of R. Eden; restored **church** of Holy Trinity by riverside containing medieval glass and marble sculpture of young Lady Maria Howard (d. 1789) with her baby, considered Joseph Nollekens' major work. Further S is 15thC gatehouse remaining from Benedictine **priory** founded here in early 12thC. Walk through protected **Wetheral Woods** leads to St. Constantine's cells or Wetheral Safeguards, caves where 6thC Scottish King Constantine is believed to have lived as a hermit. ▶ **Corby Castle** (*S of Great Corby village*) rises splendidly from E bank of R. Eden, a medieval pele tower set in attractive gardens with 18thC grotto and cascade (*grounds sometimes open*).

Solway round trip

▶ Leaving Carlisle on B5307 W, bank NW to Kirkandrews-on-Eden to follow final zigzag course of Hadrian's Wall (virtually no visible remains). ▶ **Burgh-by-Sands** (*6m*), large, smart village on site of Roman fort and one of few examples of fortified border **church★**, dating from 12thC and built of Roman stones. On **Burgh Marsh** to N is 17thC monument to King Edward I who died here in 1307 on his way to fight the Scots. ▶ Continuing W along **Solway Firth** estuary, famed for treacherous fast tides and variety of birdlife: **Port Carlisle** (*11m*), dignified village with attractive disused harbour and traces of canal. ▶ **Bowness** (*13m*), site of large Roman fort at W end of Hadrian's Wall, with Norman **church** built largely of Roman stones and containing fine Norman font. ▶ Continuing around marshlands of Solway headland with shifting sands: **Kirkbride** (*19m*), village at mouth of R. Wampool with Norman church built on hilltop site of Roman fort. Across flat marshes is scattered village of **Newton Arlosh** (*3/4m S*), a 'new town' founded 1305, with restored 14thC fortified

church. ▶ SW to sprawling village of **Abbeytown**, once part of 12thC Cistercian abbey of Holme Cultram; its restored parish church consists of nave of abbey church, including magnificent W doorway. ▶ W to Solway coast and pleasant little 19thC port and seaside resort of **Silloth** (*25m*), with park and promenade by stony beach and **views** across Solway to Scotland. ▶ Follow beautiful coast road S through **Beckfoot** on site of Roman fort, to **Allonby** (*30m*), with fine stretch of sandy beach. ▶ Branch E to long, attractive village of **Westnewton** (*36m*), bisected by a stream, via villages of Langrigg and **Bromfield**, with restored partly-Norman church on ancient site (possibly 2ndC); extensive **views** towards Scotland. To B53023 for **Wigton** (*43m*), small old market town with pleasant 18th-19thC streets and houses. ▶ Return to Carlisle (*50m*) by large residential village of **Thursby** (*A596*) or on minor roads via villages of **Aikton**, **Great Orton** and **Kirkbampton**. ▢

Practical information ───────────

CARLISLE
ℹ️ Old Town Hall, Green Market, ☎ (0228) 25517.
✈ ☎ (0228) 73641.
🚂 ☎ (0228) 44711.
Car rental: *Europcar*, Davidsons Garage, Cecil Street, ☎ (0228) 32849; *Europcar*, Airport, ☎ (0228) 32849.

Hotels:
★★★ *Swallow Hilltop*, London Road, CA1 2PQ, ☎ (0228) 29255, Tx 64292, AC AM BA DI, 110 rm. 🅿 ⊞ & ⊡ £52. Rest. ♦ & ♪ £10.
★★ *Central*, Victoria Viaduct, CA3 8AL, ☎ (0228) 20256, AC AM BA DI, 82rm. 🅿 £38. Rest. ♦ £7.
★ *Pinegrove*, 262 London Road, CA1 2QS, ☎ (0228) 24828, AC BA, 20 rm. 🅿 ⊞ & £38. Rest. ♦ ♪ & Cl. Christmas. £9.

Inns or Pubs:
Beehive Inn (Matthew Brown), Warwick Road, ☎ (0228) 329 23 🅿 Bar snacks, steaks and scampi. £3.50.
Golden Fleece, Ruleholme, ☎ (0228) 736 86 🅿 ⊞ ⊞ ⊡ & Sandwiches, steaks and local fish. £3.

⚓ *Dalston Hall C.P.*, Dalston Road (60 pl) ☎ (0228) 25014; *Orton Grange C.C.S*, Wigton Road (50 pl), ☎ (0228) 710252.

Recommended
Craft workshops: *Glenlivet Weavers,* Eden Valley Woollen Mill, Armathwaite, ☎ (069 92) 406, woven and knitted textiles; *Maurice Mullins-Woodturner Design,* 1 Brickhouse Cottage, Hesket Newmarket, ☎ (069 98) 645, articles in a variety of woods.
Golf course: Aglionby, ☎ (022 872) 303; Stoney Holme, ☎ (0228) 3485.
Guesthouse: *Kenilworth,* 34 Lozenby Terrace, London Road, ☎ (0228) 26179, £17; B. & B.
♥ *John Watt and Son,* 11 Bank Street, ☎ (0228) 21545, Victorian atmospere.

Nearby

CROSBY-ON-EDEN, 4m NE on B6264

Hotel:
● ★★ *Crosby Lodge,* CA6 4QZ, ☎ (022 873) 618, AM BA DI, 11 rm. ℗ ⫢ ⚲ £55. Rest. ♦ Cl. Christmas — end Jan. £16.50.

DALSTON, 3 1/2m S on B5299

Hotel:
★★ *Dalston Hall* (BW), CA5 7JX, ☎ (0228) 710271, AC AM BA DI, 16 rm. ℗ ⁂ ⚲ ✍ ♫ Fortified manor house dating back to the 11thC. £55. Rest. ♦ ♪ ₺ £10.50.

FAUGH, 10m SE off A69

Hotel:
● ★★★ *String of Horses,* Heads Nook, CA4 9EG, ☎ Hayton (022 870) 297, AC AM BA DI, 13 rm. ℗ ⫢ ⚲ ▣ £58. Rest. ♦ ₺ £12.

GAITSGILL, 1/2m

Inn or Pub:
Royal Oak, ☎ (069) 96 422 ℗ ⫢ ⚲ £3.

LONGTOWN, 9m N
ⓘ 21 Swan Street, nr Carlisle ☎ (0228) 791201.

Hotel:
● ★ *Marchbank,* Scotsdyke, CA6 5XP, ☎ (0228) 791325, 6 rm. ℗ ⫢ ⁂ ⚲ ₺ £46. Rest. ● ♦ ♪ ₺ Cl. Nov-Mar. £13.50.

SILLOTH, 28m W on B5302
ⓘ Council Offices, Eden Street, ☎ (0965) 31944.

Hotel:
★★ *Golf,* Criffel Street, CA5 4AB, ☎ (0965) 31438, AC AM DI, 23 rm. £36. Rest. ♦ ♪ Cl. Christmas. £10.

⚿ Stanwix Park Holiday Centre (107 pl), ☎ (0965) 31671; Tanglewood C.P., Causewayhead (31 pl), ☎ (0965) 31253; The Lido Holiday Centre (600 pl), ☎ (0965) 31236.

Recommended
Golf course: ☎ (0965) 31304.

WARWICK ON EDEN, 5m E on A69

Inn or Pub:
Queens Arms, ☎ Wetheral (0228) 60699, AC AM BA DI ℗ ⫢ ⁂ ⚲ 9 rm. Sandwiches, bar snacks, basket meals. £5.50.

WETHERAL, 6 1/2 SE by A6

Restaurant:
♦ *Fantails,* The Green, ☎ (0228) 60239, AC AM BA DI ℗ ⁂ ⚲ ❀ Cl. 1 Jan., Feb., 26 Dec., Sun., Mon. Book. £16.

WIGTON, 5m SW off A595

Hotels:
★ *Greenhill Lodge,* Red Dial, CA7 8LS, ☎ (0965) 43304, AC AM BA DI, 9 rm. ℗ ⫢ ⁂ ⚲ ₺ ♫ £35. Rest. ♦ ₺ Venison. £10.
★ *High Greenrigg House,* CA7 8HD, ☎ (069 98) 430, 8 rm. ℗ ⫢ ⁂ ₺ £34. Rest. ♦ ♪ 1 Nov. - 1 Mar. £9.

Inn or Pub:
Throstles Nest (Marstons), King Street, ☎ (0965) 43139 ₺ Sandwiches, full menu including steaks, scampi. £2.50.

Whitehaven, 14; Keswick, 13; London, 312 m
pop. 7,074 ☎ 0900   Cumbria A2

Pleasant old town with a Norman castle and, at the end of its long, tree-lined main street, the attractive Georgian house where William Wordsworth (→) was born in 1770. The town is on the only road giving access to remote Ennerdale.

▶ **Wordsworth House★** built 1745: 18thC style furniture and personal effects of poet (*Apr.-Oct.: Mon.-Wed., Fri., Sat., 11-4.30(5), Sun., 2-4.30(5); cl. Thur.*). ▶ **Castle** mainly 14thC with traces of Norman work (*open occasionally*).

Nearby

▶ **Papcastle** (*1m NW*), site of Roman fort of *Derventio.* 1¹⁄₂m further N, off A595 - built on old Roman road leading to Carlisle (→) - **Bridekirk,** village with 19thC church built around remains of Norman church containing splendidly carved 12thC font. ▶ **Ennerdale Water★** (*10m SW*), peaceful, less frequented lake (2¹⁄₂m long by ¹⁄₂m wide) used as reservoir; approachable only on foot from **Bowness Point** on N shore, with picnic spots and forest trails; rough walking on S shore, with rugged Angler's Crag near lake foot.   □

Practical information _____

COCKERMOUTH
ⓘ Riverside Car Park, Market Street, ☎ (0900) 822634.

Hotels:
★★ *Trout,* Crown Street, CA13 0EJ, ☎ (0900) 823591, AC BA, 23 rm. ℗ ⫢ ⁂ ⚲ £40. Rest. ♦ ♪ ₺ Cl. Christmas. £12.
★ *Wordsworth,* Main Street, CA13 9JS, ☎ (0900) 822757, AC BA, 18 rm. ℗ ❀ £35. Rest. ♦ ♪ ₺ Cl. Christmas. £8.

⚿ Violet Bank C.P., Simonscale Lane (40 pl), ☎ (0900) 822169; at Bewaldeth, North Lakes C.C.S (195 pl), ☎ (059 681) 510; at Gilcrux, The Beeches C.P. (51 pl), ☎ (0965) 21555; at Lamplugh, Inglenook C.P. (42 pl), ☎ (0946) 861240; at Mealsgate, The Larches C.P. (73 pl), ☎ (09 657) 379.

Recommended
Guesthouse: *Croft,* 68 Challoner Street, ☎ (0900) 822532, near river with fishing. £18 B. & B.

Nearby

MOOTA, 5m NE on A595

Hotel:
★★ *Moota,* CA13 0QD, ☎ Aspatria (0965) 20681, AC AM BA DI, 42 rm. ℗ ⫢ ⁂ ⚲ ₺ ▣ ♫ £36. Rest. ♦ ♪ ₺ £9.

Inn or Pub:
La'al Moota, ☎ Aspatria (0965) 204 14 ℗ ⫢ ⁂ ⚲ ₺ Sandwiches, bar meals. £2.75.

WORKINGTON, 9m W on A66

Hotel:
★★★★ *Cumberland Arms,* Belle Isle Street, CA14 2XQ, ☎ (0900) 64401, AC AM BA DI, 29 rm. ℗ ₺ ❀ £30. Rest. ♦ ♪ ₺ £7.

Ambleside, 8; Ulverston, 17; London, 278 m
pop. 1,713 ☎ 053 94   Cumbria A2

The grey slate village of Coniston lies on the NW bank of Coniston Water, dramatically set below the towering crags of the Old Man of Coniston and overlooking the thickly wooded, rounded hills of the E lakeshore. Before slate quarrying, the area was known for mining and there are 18thC miners' cot-

tages above the village and many old smelting sites around the lake. It is now a popular vacation centre.

▶ In churchyard of **St. Andrew's**, restored church of 1819 built on site of 16thC chapel, is large decorated cross marking tomb of John Ruskin (1819-1900), closely associated with the area. ▶ N of church is small **Ruskin Museum**, with personal mementos of writer, artist and critic; also pictures of Donald Campbell's fatal attempt at world's water speed record on Coniston Water in 1967 (*Easter-Oct.: daily, 10-dusk*). ▶ To S, by lake shore, **Coniston Hall**, 1915 farmhouse reconstructed from 16thC ruins (*private*). ▶ Glorious beauty spot of **Tarn House★** (*2m N*), with charming ornamental lake. ▶ **Coniston Water★**, peaceful lake over 5m long. Renovated 19thC steam yacht *Gondola* provides trips down lake to **Peel Island**, setting of Arthur Ransome's *Swallows and Amazons* stories. Shore is accessible from various points off major road on W shore; picnic areas at **Brown Howe** near foot of lake. ▶ **Brantwood** (*2¹/₂m on E shore*): much-altered 18thC cottage where Ruskin lived 1872-1900, with large collection of Ruskin pictures and personal belongings; also local history, set in 250-acre estate (*15 Mar.-15 Nov.: daily, 11-5.30; winter: Wed.-Sun., 11-4*). ▶ From Coniston village rough footpath ascends past old copper mines and slate quarries to summit of **Old Man of Coniston** (2,631 ft.); tarns in mountain's high coves; above **Goats Water** is rock-climbing precipice of **Dow Crag**.

Nearby

▶ **Hawkshead★** (*4m E*), quaint village of old courts and narrow cobbled streets with 17thC timber-framed buildings; 15thC **church** contains effigies of parents of Archbishop Sandys of York (1517-88), who founded nearby **grammar school**, rebuilt 1675, restored; attended by Wordsworth (1778-83) and including desk carved with his initials. ▶ **Hawkshead Courthouse** (*1/2m N*), 15thC gatehouse remaining from manorial buildings belonging to Furness Abbey (→Barrow; *Apr.-Oct.: daily, 10-5; apply National Trust Centre, Hawkshead*). ▶ At **Colthouse** (*¹/₂m E*) is Green End cottage where Wordsworth lodged (*private*) and 17thC **Quaker Meeting House**. ▶ To S: **Esthwaite Water**, placid lake (1¹/₂m long and ¹/₂m wide), with roads running by beautiful woodlands. ▶ Near lower end of lake, **Near Sawrey**, with simple 17thC farm cottage, **Hill Top**, preserved home of children's author, Beatrix Potter (→; *Apr.-Oct.: Mon.-Thu. Sat., 10-5.30, Sun., 2-5.30; last admissions 5 or dusk*). ▶ **Grizedale Forest**, extensive forestry commission plantation between Coniston and Esthwaite Waters (*signed entry points*); herds of wild red and roe deer. Outbuildings of demolished Grizedale Hall in central clearing form information centre including wildlife museum; concerts in 'Theatre in the Forest'. ▶ **Dunnerdale★** (*W*), beautiful isolated valley of R. Duddon; from **Duddon Bridge** (*1m W of Broughton-in-Furness*), steep narrow roads run through woodlands E of river (more direct) or W (twisting round rocks) to **Ulpha** (*3m N of Broughton*). ▶ Valley widens as road crosses river and climbs through wooded crags to tiny **Seathwaite**: small 19thC church set in mountainous scenery. ▶ **Wallowbarrow Crag**, challenging rock-climbing area, rises on W. ▶ Continuing through increasingly steep and narrow upper valley, road reaches **Wrynose Pass**, where R. Duddon rises, leading E to Ambleside (→) or W to Eskdale and Ravenglass (→). □

Practical information

CONISTON
ⅈ 16 Yewdale Road, ☎ 41533.

Hotels:
★★ **Sun Inn**, LA21 8HQ, ☎ (0966) 41248, AC BA, 11 rm. ℙ ≼ ⑳ £48. Rest. ♦ ♪ Cl. Jan.-Feb. £12.50.
★ **Yewdale**, Yewdale Road, LA21 8LU, ☎ (0966) 41280, AC BA, 6 rm. ℙ £30. Rest. ♦ ♪ & £7.

Inns or Pubs:
Crown Hotel (Hartleys), ☎ (0966) 41243, AC AM BA DI ℙ ⑳ ⚄ 7 rm. Bar meals. £5.50.

Farmers Arms (Scottish Newcastle), Lowick Green, nr. Ulverston, ☎ (0229) 86 376, AC AM BA DI ℙ ≼ ⑳ ⚄ & 11 rm. Bar snacks and meals. £6.

⚠ *Park Coppice C.C.S* (300 pl), ☎ (0966) 41555.

Recommended
Craft workshops: *Fellware Studio Pottery Crafts*, Brocklebank Ground, ☎ (0966) 41449, domestic and decorative stoneware.
Guesthouses: *Shepherds Villa*, Tilberthwaite Avenue, ☎ (053 94) 41337, £19 B. & B; *Sunny Bank Mill*, Sunny Bank, ☎ (053 94) 41300, £40 B. & B.

Nearby

BLAWITH, 10m S on A5084

Hotel:
★★ **Highfield Country**, LA12 8EG, ☎ Lowick Bridge (022 985) 238, AC BA, 11 rm. ℙ ≼ ⑳ ⚄ & ⚂ £50. Rest. ♦ ♪ & Cl. 1st 2 wks. Jan. £11.

HAWKSHEAD, 4m E
ⅈ Brown Cow Laithe ☎ (096 66) 525.

Hotels:
★★★ **Field Head House**, Outgate, LA22 0PY, ☎ (096 66) 240, Tx 64117, AM BA DI, 8 rm. ℙ ≼ ⑳ ⚄ & ♪ ⚂ £75. Rest. ♦ ♪ & Cl. 7 Jan. - 7 Feb. Homegrown vegetables. £13.
★ **Highfield House**, Hawkshead Hill, LA22 0PN, ☎ (096 66) 344, 11 rm. ℙ ≼ ⑳ ⚄ £32. Rest. ♦ Cl. 22-26 Dec., 5-29 Jan. Homemade desserts - figgy pudding, Cumberland Rum Nicky. £8.
● **Tarn Haws**, Hawkshead Hill, ☎ (09666) 330, AC AM BA DI, 15 rm. ℙ ≼ ⑳ ⚄ ⌷ ⚁ £66. Rest. ♦ Cl. 12 Jan.-13 Feb. £15.

Inns or Pubs:
Drunken Duck, Barngates, ☎ (096 66) 347 ℙ ≼ ⚄ & ⚘ 6 rm. Bar snacks and à la carte menu. £6.
Queens Head (Harleys of Ulverston), ☎ (096 66) 271, AC AM BA DI ⚄ & ⚘ 9 rm. Homemade bar meals and à la carte menu. £5.50.

Recommended
Farmhouse: *Force Hill Farm*, ☎ (022 984) 205, quiet 50-acre farm, £25 B. & B.
Guesthouse: *High Crossings*, Sunny Brow, ☎ (096 66) 484, superb views. £23 B. & B.

OXEN PARK, 5m E

Inn or Pub:
Manor House (Hartleys), ☎ Greenodd (022 986) 345 ℙ ≼ ⑳ ⚄ & Sandwiches and full dinners. £5.

SETHWAITHE, 5 1/2m

Inn or Pub:
Newfield Inn, ☎ Broughton (065) 76 208 ℙ ≼ ⑳ ⚄ Bar snacks, salads and steaks. £3.50.

SPARKBRIDGE, 14m S on A5084

Hotel:
★ **Bridgefield House**, LA12 8DA, ☎ Lowick Bridge (02 85) 239, AC AM DI, 5 rm. ℙ ≼ ⑳ ⚄ £40. Rest. ● ♦ Dinner only. Booking essential. £16.

EDEN VALLEY

The green and peaceful valley of the R. Eden, with winding lanes and attractive red sandstone villages, runs down the E side of Cumbria. Several charming old towns, including Appleby (→), lie in the broad, unexplored area of Eden Vale.

▶ Following river N on B6259, narrow, steep-sided **Mallerstang Valley** with Wild Boar Fell to E and High Seat to W (both over 2,000 ft.); village of **Outhgill** has ancient church restored in 17thC by Lady Anne Clifford; N, on knoll above river, romantic ruins of **Pendragon Castle**, legendary home of King Arthur's father Uther Pendragon.

▶ Continuing N by village of Nateby, where moorland road (B6270) runs E to Swaledale in Yorkshire (→): **Kirkby Stephen★** (*10m S of Appleby*), pleasant old market town with 17th-19thC houses; large restored **church of St. Stephen**, traces of Saxon and Norman origins, with long stately nave (mainly 13thC), impressive early-16thC tower and interesting monuments, including Saxon devil and battered effigy of 1st Lord Wharton (d. 1568). ▶ **Crosby Garrett** (*3m W of Kirkby*), hamlet with partly Anglo-Saxon **church of St. Andrew★**, perched on a hill, close to sites of prehistoric burial mounds. ▶ N of Kirkby Stephen, valley broadens into lovely Eden Vale. **Brough★** (*4m N of Kirkby*), built on site of Roman fort, has majestic ruins of Norman **castle**, including part of 11thC wall and much of 17thC restorations by Lady Anne Clifford; extensive **views** (*15 Mar.-15 Oct.: Mon.-Sat., 9.30-6.30, Sun., 2-6.30. 15 Oct.-15 Mar.: Mon.-Sat., 9.30-4, Sun., 2-4*). **St. Michael's Church** (mainly 14th-16thC) retains Norman work and fragments of 15thC glass. ▶ Major town of Eden Valley, **Appleby** (→ *8m NW Brough*). ▶ Continuing through fertile countryside with lakeland fells to W and Pennines rising to E **Kirkby Thore** (*13m NW of Brough*), village on site of Roman cavalry fort of Bravoniacum. ▶ **Temple Sowerby** (*15m NW of Brough*): 17thC-18thC buildings round large village green; just N is **Acorn Bank★**, red sandstone 16thC manor-house; delightful herb garden (*Mar.-Oct.: daily, 10-5.30*). 12thC village of **Milburn** (*3m E of Temple Sowerby*), with large green including a maypole set in base of an old cross. **Knock** (2,780 ft.) rises steeply to E, with **Milburn Forest** nature reserve stretching N (*access via Dufton near Appleby*). ▶ **Edenhall** (*4m NE of Penrith*) with tiny restored Saxon church set apart in glorious countryside; interior with 15thC brasses of Sir William Stapleton and his wife. ▶ Beyond hillside hamlet of **Little Salkeld** with restored old watermill, is prehistoric stone circle of **Long Meg and Her Daughters★** (*1¹⁄₂m N of Edenhall*), largest in country after Stonehenge and inspiration to Wordsworth; Long Meg, 18 ft. high and 15 ft. round, stands alone facing her four 'daughters' in magnificent setting. ▶ Beyond, in wooded countryside, tiny village of **Glassonby**: isolated medieval church with Saxon remnants. ▶ **Great Salkeld** (*6¹⁄₂m NE of Penrith*), attractive village possessing ancient **church★** with massive 14thC defensive tower, fine Norman doorway and Roman altar in porch. ▶ Crossing river at Lazonby over old 4-arched bridge (B6413): **Kirkoswald**, charming village with several 18thC houses and remnants of 12thC castle set against background of Pennines. ▶ From Kirkoswald minor road climbs to **Armathwaite★** (*4¹⁄₂m NW of Kirkoswald*), delightful little village in wooded hollow with tiny 17thC chapel and castle in romantic position by river; upstream is serene stretch of walking country, **Nunnery Walks**. □

GRANGE-OVER-SANDS

Windermere, 15; Lancaster, 25; London, 260 m
pop. 3,864 ☎ 044 84   Cumbria B3

Pleasant 19thC holiday resort on the Cartmel peninsula with a promenade overlooking Morecambe Bay where numerous birds feed on the tidal flats.

Nearby

▶ **Cartmel** (*2m W*), charming old village with many 17th-19thC houses, dominated by beautiful 12thC priory church★ with unusual diagonally set tower (13th, 15thC); lovely nave and several interesting medieval and later monuments. Only other remains of Augustinian priory founded 1188 is simple, picturesque **gatehouse** (14thC), Cavendish Street, with art exhibitions in upper floor (*Apr.-Oct., daily*). **1658 Art Gallery**, Grammar School Road, houses collection of Michael Gibbon woodcarvings (*open most days*). ▶ **Holker Hall★** (*4m W, ¹⁄₂m N of Cark*): early 17thC hall with later additions set in 120-acre deer park; elegant interior with 18thC furniture, paintings and books; also **Lakeland Motor Museum** (*Easter Sun.-Oct.: Mon.-Fri., Sun., 10.30-4.30 (park 10.30-6); cl. Sat.*).

▶ **Arnside**, on E bank of Kent estuary leading into Morecambe Bay, pleasant holiday resort developed from old fishing port in 19thC. To S is **Arnside Knott** (571 ft.; fine **views**) and ruined **Arnside Tower**, 15thC pele tower built against Scottish raids. □

Practical information _____

GRANGE-OVER-SANDS
ⓘ Victoria Hall, Main Street, ☎ (044 84) 4026.

Hotels:
★★★ *Cumbria Grand* (Heritage), Lindale Road, LA11 6EN, ☎ (044 84) 2331, Tx 966331, AC AM BA DI, 120 rm. ℗ ≼ ∭ ◷ ♨ ⚊ ℗ £59. Rest. ♦ ⅃ ⅋ Sirloin of beef with blackcurrant and peppercorn sauce. £9.
● ★★ *Graythwaite Manor*, Fernhill Road, LA11 7JE, ☎ (044 84) 2001, AC BA, 24 rm. ℗ ≼ ∭ ⚊ ⅋ ♨ £44. Rest. ♦ ⅃ Roast duckling with apricot and brandy sauce. £10.
★★ *Netherwood*, Lindale Road, LA11 6ET, ☎ (044 84) 2552, 23 rm. ℗ ≼ ∭ ⅋ £40. Rest. ♦ ⅃ £8.
⚞ at Ayside, *Oak Head C.P.* (6 pl), ☎ (0448) 3147.

Recommended
Golf course: Meathop Road, ☎ (044 84) 3180; Grange Fell, Fell Road, ☎ (044 84) 2536.

Nearby

BEETHAM, 9m E on A6

Inn or Pub:
Wheatsheaf, ☎ Milnthorpe (04482) 2123 ℗ ⚊ ⅋ 8 rm. Bar snack and full à la carte. £4.50.

CARTMEL, 3m W

Hotel:
★★ *Aynsome Manor*, LA11 6HH, ☎ (044 854) 276, AC AM BA, 13 rm. ℗ ≼ ∭ ⚊ ⅃ ⅋ 12thC manor house associated with the founder of Cartmel Priory. £60. Rest. ● ♦ Cl. 1st 3 wks Jan. £12.50.

Restaurant:
● ♦ *Uplands*, Haggs Lane, ☎ (044 854) 248, AC AM ℗ ≼ ∭ ⅃ ⅋ ♨ Cl. Jan.-mid-Feb., Mon. lunch. 4 rm. No children under 10. Book. £16.

Inn or Pub:
Cavendish Arms Hotel (Bass), Cavendish Street, ☎ (044 854) 240, AC ℗ ⚊ ⅋ 5 rm. Bar snacks. £4.50.

HEVERSHAM, 15m E on A6

Hotel:
★★ *Bluebell*, Princes Way, LA7 7EE, ☎ Milnthorpe (044 82) 3159, AC AM BA, 28 rm. ℗ ⅋ £42. Rest. ♦ ⅃ ⅋ Cl. 25-26 Dec. £11.

WITHERSLACK, 6m N off A590

Hotel:
● ★★ *Old Vicarage*, LA11 6RS, ☎ (044 852) 381, AC AM BA DI, 7 rm. ℗ ≼ ∭ ⚊ £60. Rest. ● ♦ ⅃ Cl. 1 wk. Christmas. £15.50.

GRASMERE★★★

Keswick, 13; Windermere, 9; London, 274 m
pop. 1,029 ☎ 096 65   Cumbria A2

The wood-fringed lake and green dale of Grasmere, set between the Langdale Pikes and the Fairfield range are famed for their beauty and associated with writers, particularly William Wordsworth who lived around Grasmere for much of his life. Only a mile long and ¹⁄₂ m wide, the lake remains unspoiled. In summer the traditional Grasmere Sports Day is held, as well as a rush-bearing ceremony like that in nearby Ambleside (→).

▶ To E, at Town End, is **Dove Cottage★**, home of Wordsworth, and later of writer Thomas De Quincey: simple,

stone-floored rooms and in barn, museum with Wordsworth manuscripts and other material (*Mar., Oct., Christmas/New Year.: Mon.-Sat., 10-4 (4.30), Sun., 11-4 (4.30); Apr.-Sep.: Mon.-Sat., 9.30-5 (5.30), Sun., 11-5 (5.30)*). ▶ To W is **Allan Bank** (*private*), where Wordsworth lived 1808-11, and **Old Parsonage**, his home till 1813. In churchyard of much altered late-Norman church of **St. Oswald** containing memorial to Wordsworth, are simple graves of William, Mary and Dorothy Wordsworth, alongside that of poet Hartley Coleridge, son of more famous poet Samuel Taylor Coleridge. ▶ Fine views of lake from **Wishing Gate**, S of Dove Cottage, and **Loughrigg Terrace**★

Nearby

▶ Area offers spendid walks and climbs of varying difficulty, including common route to Helvellyn.▶ To NE: **Tongue Ghyll Force** ($2^1/_2 m$), small waterfall on slopes of **Fairfield** (2,863 ft.); a route to summit via **Alcock Tarn** near Dove Cottage, also **Greatrigg Man** (2,513 ft.). ▶ From **Grisedale Tarn**, NW of Fairfield, zigzag ascent via **Dollywaggon Pike** (2,810 ft.) to **Helvellyn**★ (3,113 ft.), with steep rounded slopes on W of range and deep craggy valleys on E including dramatically sited **Red Tarn**. Further N, range is wild and more open, dropping past Dod peaks into bleak moors of Matterdale and Threlkeld Common W of Keswick (→). ▶ To NW: **Easedale** reached by Goody Bridge, to 'white' waterfall of **Sour Milk Ghyll** ($2^1/_2 m$) and **Easedale Tarn**★ (915 ft.); path N climbs **Helm Crag** (1299 ft.), marked by strangely shaped crags. ▶ To SE, on A591: **Rydal Water**★★ (*1m*), smallest of all the lakes, fringed by reeds with crags of Nab Scar rising to N and Loughrigg Fell to S; at E end is good viewpoint from rocky wooded knoll, **Wordsworth's Seat**; just off road to N, little village of **Rydal**. At top of lane is **Rydal Mount**★, home of Wordsworth from 1813 till his death in 1850: family portraits and furniture (*Mar.-Oct.: daily, 10-5.30; Nov.-mid-Jan.: daily, 10-12.30, 2-4; cl. mid-Jan.-Feb.*). Just below is **church** (1824), with Dora's field behind it, the poet's gift to his daughter. Nearby is **Rydal Hall** (17thC with 19thC alterations), former home of local Le Flemming family and now conference centre. W of village, on N bank of lake, is **Nab Cottage**, early 18thC farmhouse, home of De Quincey in 1806 and Hartley Coleridge from 1840-49. Footbridge from village leads along most of S bank of Rydal Water. ▶ To W, scenic minor road following W bank of Grasmere Lake, leads into attractive **Elterwater**★ on B5343; from here beautiful **Langdales** can be explored (→Ambleside). □

Practical information

GRASMERE
ⓘ Red Bank Road, ☎ (096 65) 245.

Hotels:
● ★★★ **Michaels Nook**, LA22 9RP, ☎ (096 65) 496, Tx 65329, AM, 11 rm. P ⟨ ⨇ ⊾ ⟩ ⌧ £140. Rest. ● ◆ ⊾ Breast of wild duck with blackcurrants. £26.
★★★ **Gold Rill**, Langdale Road, LA22 9PU, ☎ (096 65) 486, AC AM BA DI, 16 rm. P ⟨ ⨇ ⊾ ⊾ ⟩ £78. Rest. ◆ ⊾ Cl. Nov.-Mar. Homemade soups. £11.50.
★★★ **Prince of Wales** (Mount Charlotte), Keswick Road, LA22 9PR, ☎ (096 65) 666, Tx 65364, AC AM BA DI, 81 rm. P ⟨ ⨇ ⊾ Cl. Rest. ◆ ♪ £10.
★★★ **Wordsworth**, LA22 9SW, ☎ (096 65) 592, Tx 65329, AC AM BA DI, 35 rm. P ⟨ ⨇ ⊾ ⊾ ⟩ ⌧ £84. Rest. ◆ ⊾ Collops of local venison, crystallized daffodils and fresias. £18.
● ★★ **Oak Bank**, Broadgate, LA22 9TA, ☎ (096 65) 217, AC BA, 14 rm. P ⟨ ⨇ ⊾ £40. Rest. ◆ ♪ Cl. Jan. £9.
● ★★ **White Moss House**, Rydal Water, LA22 9SE, ☎ (096 65) 295, 7 rm. P ⟨ ⨇ ⟩ £65. Rest. ● ◆ ♪ Cl. mid-Nov.-mid-Mar. Local mallard with claret and damson sauce. £17.50.
★★ **Rothay Garden**, Broadgate, LA22 9RH, ☎ (096 65) 334, AC AM BA, 6 rm. P ⟨ ⨇ ⊾ £45. Rest. ◆ ♪ Cl. Dec.-mid-Feb. Herdwick lamb parcels. £12.50.
● ★ **Grasmere Broadgate**, LA22 9TA, ☎ (096 65) 277, AC BA, 12 rm. P ⟨ ⨇ ⊾ £40. Rest. ◆ Cl. mid-Nov.-Mar. Cumberland ham with Madeira sauce. £12.

★ **Rothay Lodge**, White Bridge, LA22 9RH, ☎ (096 65) 341, 6 rm. P ⟨ ⨇ ⊾ ⊾ ⟩ £27. Rest. ◆ ⊾ Cl. Christmas, Tue. dinner. Traditional English home cooking. £7.

Nearby

ELTERWATER, 2 1/2m S on B5343

Hotel:
★ **Britannia**, LA22 9HP, ☎ Langdale (096 67) 210, Tx 8950511, AC BA, 10 rm. P ⟨ ⨇ 16thC inn adjoining the village green. £33. Rest. ◆ ⊾ Cl. Christmas, Nov. - Feb. Rest. open Sat. only. Marinaded local venison, fresh Scottish salmon. £10.

RYDAL, 1 1/2m N on A591

Hotel:
★★ **Glen Rothay**, LA22 9LR, ☎ (0966) 32524, AC AM BA DI, 11 rm. P ⟨ ⨇ 17thC inn with Wordsworthian associations. £45. Rest. ◆ ♪ Cl. 2 wks. Dec., 3 wks. Jan. £12.50.

Recommended
Guesthouse: *Foxghyll*, Under Loughrigg, ☎ (053 94) 33292, £22 B. & B.

KENDAL

Penrith, 32; Lancaster, 22; London, 250 m
pop. 23,710 ☎ 0539   Cumbria B2

This old, busy market town is known for its woolens, shoes, snuff and, more recently, mint cake. Situated on the R. Kent, it has been an important centre since Roman times. It serves as the S gateway to the Lake District and has a good museum devoted to Lakeland life.

▶ Scanty remains of **castle**, begun late 11thC, include 13thC curtain wall with towers. Katharine Parr, sixth wife of Henry VIII, was born here 1512; her prayer-book is kept in Town Hall. ▶ **Castle Dairy**, Wildman Street, is 14thC hall-house restored 1564; ▶ **Holy Trinity** 13thC parish church on ancient site (heavily restored), with 13thC coffin lid in Bellingham Chapel, 15thC black marble font, some 15thC stained glass and fragment of 9thC cross-shaft; nearby is old **grammar school**, founded 1525. ▶ **Abbot Hall**, elegant 18thC house reputedly by Carr of York, in riverside setting with garden landscaped in 1759, is now **art gallery** (18thC rooms and modern galleries containing paintings, sculpture, furniture and pottery) and **museum of Lakeland Life and Industry**★; reconstructed farm parlour and bedroom, costume, printing, weaving, local industries, farming (*Mon.-Fri., 10.30-5.30 (10.30-5 Museum), Sat., Sun., 2-5*). ▶ **Museum of Archaeology & Natural History**, Station Road (*Mon.-Fri., 10.30-5, Sat., 2-5; cl. Sun.*). ▶ **Scout Scar** (713 ft.), to SW, gives fine views over town.

Nearby

▶ **Sizergh Castle**★ ($3^1/_2 m$ S): impressive 14thC pele tower, with Tudor great hall, 18thC, containing much fine early Elizabethan woodwork; home of local Strickland family for 700 years: English and French furniture, china, family and Stuart portraits (*Apr.-Oct.: Mon., Wed., Thu. Sun., 2-5.30; 5.15 last admission*). ▶ **Levens Hall**★★ (*5m* S), Elizabethan mansion evolved from pele tower, with extraordinary **topiary garden** laid out 1692 (*Easter Sun.-Sep.: Sun.-Thu., 11-5, steam collection 2-5; cl. Fri. Sat.*). ▶ **Sedbergh** (*8m* E), old market centre in beautiful mountain setting; some 17th and 18thC buildings including library (1716), former premises of **Sedbergh School** founded 1525, and St. Andrew's parish **church**, largely 13thC on much older site. ▶ **Quaker Meeting House** (*1m SW*) of 1675 and on **Firbank Fell** to NW with tiny village of Firbank, is memorial rock where George Fox preached in 1652. ▶ **Longsleddale** (*3m NW*), secluded valley following course of R. Sprint, with broadleaf woodlands and craggy wild scenery by hamlet of **Sadgill**, where winding road ends; tracks across high fells lead N past small waterfalls to **Haweswater**, E to Wet Sleddale Reservoir

and W to Kentmere (→below). ▶ Continuing N, A6 begins long, steep climb up **Shap Fells** (1034 ft. at summit), descending past pink granite cliffs to **Shap** (*12m*), bleak village of mainly-18thC grey stone houses; restored church including Norman work; nearby are several prehistoric sites and, 1m W, in valley of R. Lowther, scanty ruins (mainly-16thC tower) of **Shap Abbey**, founded late 12thC. At **Keld** (*1m SW*) is plain little 15th-16thC chapel. ▶ **Staveley** (*5m NW*) village with 19thC church containing beautiful stained glass by Edward Burne-Jones. ▶ Branch road N follows narrow curving valley of R. Kent, to village of **Kentmere** (*4m*): restored 16thC church including Norman work and memorial (1901) to Bernard Gilpin (1517-83), 'apostle of the North'. SW is Gilpin family home, **Kentmere Hall**, ruined 14thC pele tower with 16thC farm attached (*private*). ▶ Rugged path leads W through Garburn Pass to Troutbeck near Windermere (→). Steep path N, past **Rainsborrow Crag**, and disused quarries, leads to **Kentmere Reservoir** at head of dale. ◻

Practical information _____

KENDAL
ⓘ Town Hall, Highgate, ☎ (0539) 25758.
▓▓▓ ☎ (0539) 20397.

Hotels:
★★★ **Woolpack,** Stricklandgate, LA9 4ND, ☎ (0539) 23852, Tx 53168, AC AM BA DI, 57 rm. ⓟ & £56. Rest. ♦ £10.
● ★★ **Garden House**, Fowling Lane, LA9 6PH, ☎ (0539) 31131, AC BA, 10 rm. ⓟ ≼ ᵂᵂ ⬟ ⤫ ⤴ £44. Rest. ♦ Cl. Sun. Residents only. £10.50.

Restaurants:
♦ **Castle Dairy**, 26 Wildman Street, ☎ (0539) 21170 Cl. Sun.-Tue., Aug. £13.
♦ **Riverside**, Stramongate Bridge, ☎ (0539) 24707, AC AM BA DI ⓟ ≼ ⬟ ! ⤫ Cl. 1 Jan. Book. £11.50.

Inn or Pub:
Hare and Hounds (Vaux), Levens, ☎ (0448) 60405 ⓟ ᵂᵂ ⬟ & Sandwiches, fish and steaks. £3.75.

⚓ **Millcrest C.P.**, Millcrest (36 pl), ☎ (0539) 21075; at Endmoor, *Gatebeck C.P.* (35 pl), ☎ (044 87) 425; at Sedbergh, *Pinfold C.S.* (54 pl), ☎ (0587) 20576.

Recommended
Craft workshops: *Abbotshall Craftshop*, Kirkland, ☎ (0539) 22464; at Sedbergh, 1m E on Hawes Road, *Pennine Tweeds*, Farfield Mill, ☎ (0587) 20558, woven hats, slippers, ties, scarves, rugs, skirts, etc.
Farmhouses: *Mrs. T.A. White*, Bridge House, Garnett Bridge, ☎ Selside (053 983) 288, lake-touring country. £19; B. & B.; at Burneside, *Gateside Farm*, ☎ (0539) 22036, £18; B. & B.; *Mrs. M. Hoggarth*, Low Hindhowe Farm, ☎ (0539) 22060, peaceful location with home cooking. £17; B. & B.; *Mrs. S. Beaty*, Garnett House Farm, ☎ (0539) 24542, £18; B. & B.; at Helsington, *Low Sizergh Farm*, ☎ (053 95) 60426, 270-acre dairy farm. £19; B. & B.
Golf course: The Heights ☎ 24079.

Nearby

CARTMEL FELL, 9m SW

Inn or Pub:
Masons Arms, Strawberry Bank, ☎ Crosthwaite (044 88) 486 ⓟ ≼ ᵂᵂ ⬟ & ⤫ 4 rm. Lasagne, steak pie and vegetarian meals. £6.

CROSTHWAITE, 10m W off A5074

Hotel:
★★★ **Damson Dene Cottage**, Lyth Valley, LA8 8JE, ☎ (044 88) 676, AC AM BA, 37 rm. ⓟ ≼ ᵂᵂ & ⌂ £58. Rest. ♦ ! Cl. Jan. £10.

SHAP

Hotel:
★★**Shap Wells**, CA10 3QU, ☎ (093 16) 628, AC AM BA

DI, 92 rm. ⓟ ≼ ᵂᵂ ⬟ & ⤴ £38. Rest. ♦ ! & Cl. Jan.-mid-Feb. £8.

UNDERBARROW, 3m W off A591

Hotel:
★★ **Greenriggs**, LA8 8HF, ☎ Crosthwaite (044 88) 387, 13 rm. ⓟ ≼ ᵂᵂ ⬟ £60. Rest. ♦ Cl. Jan.-Feb. Open weekends only Nov.-Dec. Homemade soups, lamb stuffed with ham and rosemary. £12.60.

KESWICK

Cockermouth, 13; Penrith, 17; London, 296 m
pop. 4,777 ☎ 0596   Cumbria A2

Magnificently set below the dark bulk of Skiddaw close to the N shores of beautiful **Derwent Water**, Keswick is a most popular base for exploring the Lake District. It is an old market and graphite-mining centre with a 12thC parish church and traces of prehistoric settlements nearby. It was transformed in the 19thC by the arrival of the Penrith railway and its dark grey slate houses are mostly Victorian.

▶ Attractive **Moot Hall** (rebuilt 1813), now an information centre. ▶ Near pleasant park bounded by R. Greta, **Fitz Park Museum and Art Gallery** (Station Road), containing manuscripts of Lakeland poets and writers (Robert Southey, Wordsworth, Hugh Walpole), 'musical stones' and local geological and natural history collections (*Apr.-Oct.: Mon.-Sat., 10-12.30, 2-5.30; cl. Sun.*). ▶ **St. John's**, imposing 19thC church by Anthony Salvin with grave of Hugh Walpole in churchyard. ▶ **Greta Hall** (late 18thC), now part of Keswick School (1898), once home of Coleridge and Southey (*private*). To N: **St. Kentigern's parish church★**, mainly 14th-16thC with traces of Norman work; carved 14thC font, early stained glass, 12 consecration crosses and marble effigy of Southey (buried here 1843) with epitaph by Wordsworth. ▶ **Derwent Water★** ($^1/_2$*m S*), lovely lake (1m long by 3m wide and 10-60 ft. deep) with delightful walks along its shores; boat rentals at landing points near Keswick and motorboat pick-up service. ▶ Its islands include **St. Herbert's** in centre, site of hermitage of 7thC saint, disciple of St. Cuthbert of Holy Island (→Northumbria). ▶ On E bank (close to B5289), glorious views from **Friar's Crag★** (*3/4m*), wooded promontory with memorial to John Ruskin (→Coniston), also from rocky hilltop of **Castle Head** (*E of road*). Past Great Wood, **Ashness Gate** (*2m*), with landing stage and narrow scenic branch road to delightful hamlet and tarn of **Watendlath★** in Lodore Wood. ▶ **Lodore Falls★** (*3m*), close to great **Shepherd's Crag**. Here footpath follows shore of Great Bay. ▶ On W bank: beautiful woods of **Manesty Park**, site of **Brackenbury** (*private*), home of novelist Hugh Walpole (1884-1941). **Cat Bells** (1,481 ft.) rises behind; starting point for ascent at **Hawse End** (*beware derelict mines*). ▶ On W side of ridge is lovely **Newlands Valley**. ▶ **Skiddaw★** (*NE of town*, 3,053 ft.), impressive ridge of dark slate rock extending N past Skiddaw Forest; starting point for climb by Latrigg (*1$^1/_2$m*). ▶ From Threlkeld (*4m E*) or Scales (*6m E*), **Blencathra Saddleback** (2,847 ft.); spectacular **views** of St. John's Vale and surrounding fells.

Nearby

▶ **Castlerigg Stone Circle★** (*1$^1/_2$m E*), spectacular prehistoric site: 48 stones arranged in circle and small inner oblong, dramatically sited in centre of wild fells. ▶ **Threlkeld** (*4m E*), village of old stone and modern houses dominated by Blencathra to N. ▶ B5322 S runs through **St. John's Vale** with Wanthwaite Crags and Dods of Helvellyn to E and lovely views down valley towards **Thirlmere★** (*7m*), narrow lake converted by dam at foot into reservoir; forest walks and nature trails, including attractive fell walk to Harrop Tarn at SW end. To E rises **Helvellyn** (→Grasmere), with long gentle climb to ridge from **Wythburn** at SE foot of lake. ▶ To S, at foot of Derwent Water, **Borrowdale★★**, with R. Derwent running

between woodlands and soaring crags. ▶ **Grange** (*4¹/₂m S*), attractive village with **view** dominated by wooded **Castle Crag** (900 ft.) with traces of Roman fort at summit; path to **Bowder Stone** (*1m*), huge precariously balanced rock. ▶ **Rosthwaite** (*6m S*), village on Stonethwaite Beck with many walks; NE to lovely Watendale Tarn, S to Langdale and Grasmere, and across river through Johnny Wood to **Seatoller** (*7¹/₂m, on B 5289*). ▶ Road continues W through **Honister Pass★**, climbing past slate quarries on fells to Honister Hause (1,190 ft.), descends sharply through wild bleak country to green of Buttermere (→). ▶ Continuing up dale, road ends at scattered hamlet of **Seathwaite**, known for intensity of its rainfall and starting point for tough walks among complex mass of **Borrowdale Fells**. Summits all give magnificent views: **Glaramara** (2,560 ft.), highest point to W, **Grey Knotts** (2,287 ft.) to E and finely formed **Great Gable★** (2,949 ft.) to SE. Beyond, reached by rough and dramatic Sty Head Pass, is **Sca Fell** (→), highest peak in England. ▶ **Bassenthwaite Lake★** (*4m NW*), most northerly of major lakes (4m long and 3/4m wide). A66 runs beside W bank with **views** across water to Skiddaw, via man-made forest of **Thornthwaite.** ▶ By lake head, where A66 continues W to Cockermouth (→), access point at **Ouse Bridge**, with view downwater. Returning to Keswick on A591 E of lake: **Bassenthwaite** village (*off A591*): large green and rebuilt Norman **church** of St. Bega sited on lakeside; **Mire House** (*4¹/₂m N of Keswick*), 17thC manor house where Alfred Lord Tennyson was inspired to write King Arthur idylls (*grounds: daily 10.30-5.30; house: Sun., Wed., Bank Hol. Mon., 2-5*). ▶ **Whinlatter Pass** (*to W via Braithwaite*), steep climb through thick conifers of **Thornthwaite Forest;** fine **views** over Bassenthwaite from lay-by at top (1,043 ft.). On descent, path to **Spout Force Waterfall** in wooded gorge.   □

Practical information

KESWICK
ⓘ (Summer) The Moot Hall, Market Square, ☎ (0596) 72645.

Hotels:
● ★★ *Grange Country House*, Manor Brow, CA12 4BA, ☎ (0596) 72500, AC, 11 rm. 🅿 ⟨ ⋘ ⌕ ⚌ £38. Rest. ♦ ఈ Cl. Nov. £10.
● ★★ *Highfield*, The Heads, CA12 5ER, ☎ (0596) 72508, 19 rm. 🅿 ⟨ ⌕ £30. Rest. ♦ Cl. Nov.-Easter. Homemade bread, jams, rum butter, herb cheese, Cumberland Rum Nicky. £8.
★ *Chaucer House*, Ambleside Road, CA12 4DR, ☎ (0596) 72318, AC AM, 30 rm. 🅿 £32. Rest. ♦ Cl. Nov.-Easter. £7.

⚕ *Derwentwater C.S.* (250 pl), ☎ (0596) 72392; at Lorton, *Whinfell Hall C.P.*, Whinfell Hall Farm (35 pl), ☎ (090 085) 260.

Recommended
Farmhouse: at Newlands, *Birkrigg Farm*, ☎ Braithwaite (059 682) 278, 220-acre farm with good views of surrounding mountains. £18. B. & B.
Golf course: Threlkeld (4m E on A66), ☎ (0596) 83324.
Guesthouses: *Holmwood House*, The Heads, ☎ (076 87) 73301, £24 B. & B.; *Watendlath Guest House*, 15 Acorn Street, ☎ (076 87) 7416, £16 B. & B.

Nearby
APPLETHWAITE, 1 1/2m N off A591

Hotel:
● ★★★ *Underscar*, CA12 4PH, ☎ (0596) 72469, Tx 64354, AC AM DI, 19 rm. 🅿 ⟨ ⋘ ⚌ ⌇ ఐ £90. Rest. ♦ ఈ Cl. Christmas, New Year, Jan. Pike and perch pie, Elizabethan pork. £17.50.

BASSENTHWAITE, 7m N on A591

Hotels:
● ★★★ *Armathwaite*, CA12 4RE, ☎ Bassenthwaite Lake (059 681) 551, AC AM BA DI, 40 rm. 🅿 ⟨ ⋘ ⚌ ఈ 🖾 ⚘ ⌇ ఐ £76. Rest. ♦ ఈ Cl. Feb. Derwent Water duckling with port, gin and damson sauce. £18.

★★ *Castle Inn*, CA12 4RG, ☎ Bassenthwaite Lake (059 681) 401, AC AM BA DI, 22 rm. 🅿 ⟨ ⋘ ⚌ ఈ 🖾 ⚘ £50. Rest. ♦ ఈ Cl. 2 wks. Nov. £10.
● ★ *Pheasant*, CA13 9YE, ☎ Bassenthwaite Lake (059 681) 234, 20 rm. 🅿 ⋘ ⚌ ఈ ⚙ £47. Rest. ♦ ఈ Cl. Christmas. Game pie, roast local duckling. £11.
★ *Ravenstone*, CA12 4QG, ☎ Bassenthwaite Lake (059 681) 240, 12 rm. 🅿 ⟨ ⋘ ⚌ £31. Rest. ♦ Cl. Nov. - Mar. £6.50.

Restaurant:
♦ *Wythop Mill*, ☎ Bassenthwaite Lake (059 681) 394 🅿 ⚙ Cl. Feb.-Mar., Mon. Apr.-Oct., Mon.-Thu. Nov.-Jan. 1 rm. Book. £9.

Recommended
Riding school: *Robin Hood Equestrian Centre*, full instruction, riding country lanes, tracks and fells.

BRAITHWAITE, 2m W on A66

Hotel:
★★ *Middle Ruddings*, CA12 5RY, ☎ (059 682) 436, AC AM BA DI, 16 rm. 🅿 ⟨ ⋘ ⚌ ఈ ⚙ £55. Rest. ♦ ⌇ ఈ Cl. Jan.-Feb. Trout farci. £10.

⚕ *Scotgate C.C.P.* (165 pl), ☎ (059 682) 343.

MUNGRISDALE, 11m NE off A66

Hotel:
● ★ *Mill*, CA11 0XR, ☎ Threlkeld (059 683) 659, 8 rm. 🅿 ⟨ ⋘ ⚌ ⚙ £40. Rest. ♦ ⌇ Cl. Oct.-Mar. Roast pheasant with apple sauce, lemon syllabub. £10.

Recommended
Farmhouse: *Mrs. C. Weightman*, Near Howe Farm, ☎ Threlkeld (059 683) 678, quiet 350-acre farm near lakes. £20 B. & B.

PORTINSCALE, 1m W

Hotel:
★★ *Rickerby Grange*, CA12 5RH, ☎ Keswick (0596) 72344, 13 rm. 🅿 ⟨ ⋘ ⚌ £32.50. Rest. ♦ ⌇ ఈ Cl. Christmas. Homemade soups, all fresh produce. £8.

SCALES, 5 1/2m on A66

Inn or Pub:
White Horse (Jenning), ☎ Threlkeld (059 683) 241 🅿 ⟨ ⚌ ఈ ⚙ Game pies and bar meals. £5.

THORNTHWAITE, 4m NW on A66

Hotels:
★★ *Swan*, CA12 5SQ, ☎ Braithwaite (059 682) 256, AC BA, 15 rm. 🅿 ⟨ ⋘ ⚌ £34. Rest. ♦ ⌇ ఈ Cl. Nov.-Mar. £10.
★ *Ladstock*, CA12 5RZ, ☎ Braithwaite (059 682) 210, 27 rm. ⟨ ⋘ ⚌ ⚙ £36. Rest. ♦ ⌇ Cl. Nov.-Mar. Traditional English cooking. £9.

UNDER SKIDDAW, 2m N on A591

Hotels:
★ *Lyzzick Hall*, CA12 4PY, ☎ (0596) 72277, AC AM BA, 21 rm. 🅿 ⟨ ⋘ ⚌ ⚙ 🖾 £40. Rest. ♦ ⌇ ఈ £12.
★ *Red House*, CA12 4QA, ☎ (0596) 72211, 23 rm. 🅿 ⟨ ⋘ ⚌ 🖾 ⌇ £50. Rest. ♦ ఈ Cl. Dec. - Feb. £7.

KIRKBY LONSDALE

Kendal, 13; Lancaster, 16; London, 249 m pop. 1,557 ☎ 0468   Cumbria B3

A charming greystone market town on the Lancashire/Yorkshire borders, Kirkby Lonsdale is set above a bend in the R. Lune. Spanning the river is the graceful 15thC **Devil's Bridge★** (*pedestrian access only*), with three beautifully ribbed arches. Old squares and cobbled streets and central Market Square containing 17thC and Georgian houses as well as dignified Victorian buildings. Off Market Street is **Church of St. Mary the Virgin★**, retaining a sumptuously carved Norman doorway in the 15th-16thC tower and one

of the most impressive Early Norman interiors in the county; notable 17th-18thC furnishings and monuments. From churchyard, glorious **views** of Howgill and Casterton fells. ☐

Practical information

KIRKBY LONSDALE

ℹ️ The Art Store, 18 Main Street, ☎ (0468) 71603.

Hotels:

★★ *Royal Hotel*, Main Street, LA6 2AE, ☎ (0468) 71217, AC AM BA DI, 22 rm. 🅿 ≼ £38. Rest. ♦ ♪ ☕ Adelaide Room. Cl. Sun. eve. Oftlers Table. Cl. Mon., Tue. £10.

★ *The Sun Hotel*, Market Street, LA6 2AU, ☎ (0468) 71965, 9 rm. 🅿 £30. Rest. ♦ ♪ ☕ Beef Wellington. £10.

Inn or Pub:

Snooty Fox, Main Street, ☎ (0468) 71308 🅿 ⚒ 2 rm. Bar snacks and à la carte menu. £5.75.

⚊ *Woodclose C.P.* (30 pl), ☎ (0468) 71403.

Nearby

BARBON, 3m N off A683

Hotel:

★ *Barbon Inn*, LA6 2LJ, ☎ Barbon (046 836) 233, AC BA, 0 rm. 🅿 ≼ ⚒ ☕ ✪ £00. Rest. ♦ ♪ Cl. Christmas. Garlic mushrooms, smoked salmon pâté. £11.50.

CASTERTON, 1 1/2m N on A683

Hotel:

★★ *Pheasant*, LA6 2RX, ☎ Kirkby Lonsdale (0468) 71230, 10 rm. 🅿 ≼ ⚒ ☕ ☕ £34. Rest. ♦ ♪ ☕ Cl. mid-Jan.-mid-Feb. £11.

Recommended

Golf course: Sedbergh Road, ☎ (0468) 71429.

DENT, 13m NE off A683

Hotel:

★ *George Dragon*, Main Street, LA10 5QL, ☎ (058 75) 256, AC BA, 10 rm. 🅿 ≼ ☕ £28.50. Rest. ♦ ♪ Cl. Christmas. Steak and kidney pie, duck. £10.50.

Recommended

Craft workshop: *Dent Crafts Centre*, ☎ (058 75) 400, unique and one-of-a-kind gifts.

LAKE DISTRICT NATIONAL PARK

The magnificent scenic area of central Cumbria known as the Lake District is protected for public enjoyment as a National Park, the largest in Britain. It covers nearly 88,000 square miles, within which are found England's highest mountains, the Sca Fell range, and scenery of outstanding natural beauty and variety. In the W, the park includes the coastline around Ravenglass. There are countless walking opportunities, with rock climbing on the precipitous crags and nature trails in the woods and forests, where herds of red and roe deer are found. Several of the major lakes have passenger boat services, and all roads make for scenic, yet careful, driving.

The main access points to the park are Kendal and Penrith, just outside the E boundary, and Carlisle in the N. At **Brockhole**, on Windermere, is the **National Park Visitor Centre**. The National Trust has information centres at Ambleside, Hawkshead, Grasmere, Keswick and Newby Bridge, and there are Forestry Commission visitor centres at Grizedale and Whinlatter. ☐

> In preparing for your trip, consult the pages pertaining to the regions. You will find there the description of the region you wish to visit, a brief history and practical information.

PENRITH

Carlisle, 19; Kendal, 32; London, 276 m
pop. 12,086 ☎ 0768   Cumbria B2

This old market town, strategically placed on the ancient N-S highway, is close to the site of the Roman fort of Voreda and the remains of a medieval castle. In the intricate network of central streets are several historic buildings including some fine 18thC town houses.

▶ In park opposite station ruins of massive square **castle** (14th-15thC), including much of S wall and E tower. ▶ St. Andrew's **Church**, rebuilt 1720-22, with original Norman tower and dignified Georgian interior. In churchyard, 10thC 'Giant's Grave' and 'Giant's Thumb'★, three large carved crosses and hogback gravestones. ▶ Nearby, interesting buildings include old **grammar school** (1564), house dated 1563 where William and Dorothy Wordsworth went to school; imposing **mansion house** (1750) and, by Market Place, **George Hotel** (18thC, partly restored), where Bonnie Prince Charlie stayed during 1745 Jacobite rebellion; **Two Lions Inn** (16thC); **Gloucester Arms** (16thC); and in Stricklandgate, **Town Hall**, 1906 conversion of two houses attributed to Robert Adam with 18thC interior features. ▶ To NE, **Penrith Beacon**, wooded hill (937 ft.) with 19thC red sandstone tower.

Nearby

▶ **Brougham Castle**★ (1¹⁄₂m SE), impressive ruins of Clifford family fortress on bank of R. Eamont, renovated in 17thC by Lady Anne Clifford; 12thC keep (*mid-Mar.-mid-Oct.: Mon.-Sat., 9.30-6.30. Sun., 2-6.30; mid-Oct.-mid-Mar.: Mon.-Sat., 9.30-4, Sun., 2-4*). To S are traces of large Roman fort of **Brocavum**. ▶ SW, by boundary walls of demolished 19thC Brougham Hall, tiny plain **St Wilfrid's Chapel**, rebuilt 1658 by Lady Anne Clifford. ▶ Little church of **St. Ninian** (1¹⁄₂m NE of castle) also rebuilt by Lady Anne (1660), fine example of Gothic Revival. ▶ Crossing river by widened 16thC 3-arched **bridge** to village of Eamont Bridge (*2m S*), mysterious prehistoric sites of **Mayburgh** (1/4m SW), large circular bank with 9 ft.-high central stone, and **King Arthur's Round Table** (1/4 m E), with ditch enclosing 300 ft. mound, used for re-enactment of the Arthurian legends closely associated with this area. ▶ Small village of **Yanwath** (W) with **Yanwath Hall** by river: impressive 14thC pele tower with 15thC hall and kitchen, now farmhouse (*private*). ▶ **Clifton** (2m S), where Scots fought English for the last time in Bonnie Prince Charlie's 1745 rebellion. Partly-rebuilt Norman **church** with memorial of St. Cuthbert in churchyard. ▶ **Lowther**★ (3¹⁄₂m SW), former estate of Lowther family, earls of Lonsdale: spectacular shell of early 19thC **Lowther Castle** (*private*) in large wooded park. N of park, **St. Michael's Church**. Mainly-17thC exterior and fine 12th-13thC interior; many elaborate Lowther monuments. E of park are estate's model villages of **Newtown**, with dignified late 17thC houses, and late 18thC **Lowther village**. ▶ S is **Lowther Wildlife Park**, devoted to European wildlife and including wild boar, rare birds and breeds of cattle. ▶ Further W, attractive old village of **Askham** with 14thC Askham Hall, present home of Earl of Lonsdale (*private*). Traces of prehistoric settlements nearby. ▶ **Hutton-in-the-Forest**★ (6m NW), 14thC pele tower with 17thC and later additions; extensive grounds. House contains furniture of various periods (*grounds: daily from dawn to dusk; house: end May-mid-Sep.: Thu., Fri., Sun., Bank Hol. Mon.*). ▶ **Dalemain**★ (3m SW), attractive Georgian-fronted house containing period furniture and portraits. Park with deer herd, gardens and picnic area; also **museum** of Westmorland and Cumberland Yeomanry (*early Apr.-early Oct.: Mon.-Thu., Sun., 11.15-5.15*). ▶ Charming village of **Dacre** (3m W) with 14thC pele tower (*private*) and ancient **church**★ on site of Saxon monastery; partly-rebuilt Norman interior, fragments of two finely carved Saxon crosses and four mysterious stone bears in churchyard. ▶ **Greystoke** (4m W), village of old and modern houses;

imposing castle set in extensive walled grounds (*private*). To E, large restored church of **St. Andrew**, impressive example of 13thC Perpendicular style.   □

Practical information ———————————————

PENRITH
ⓘ Robinson's School, Middlegate, ☎ (0768) 67466.
🚌 ☎ (0768) 62466.

Hotels:
● ★★★ *North Lakes Gateway*, Ullswater Road, ☎ (0768) 68111, Tx 64257, AC AM BA DI, 57 rm. Ⓟ 🖵 £70. Rest. ◆ £14.
★★★ *George*, Devonshire Street, CA11 7SU, ☎ (0768) 62696, AC, 31 rm. Ⓟ £40. Rest. ◆ ♪ ₺ Cl. 25-26 Dec., 1 Jan. £10.
★★ *Round Thorn*, Beacon Edge, CA11 8SJ, ☎ (0768) 63952, AC AM BA DI, 13 rm. Ⓟ ⟨ 🕸 🔍 ₺ £27. Rest. ◆ ♪ ₺ £17.

Restaurant:
● ◆ *Passepartout*, 51 Castlegate, ☎ (0768) 65852, AC BA ♪ 🎯 Cl. 3 wks. Jan.- Feb., 25-26 Dec., Bank Hols., Sun. lunch ex. Jul., Aug. Book. £17.

Inn or Pub:
Gloucester Arms (Whitbread), Great Dockray, ☎ (0768) 62150 Ⓟ 🕸 ₺ 🎯 Bar snacks and full menu. £3.50.

🅰 Penruddock, *Beckses C.S* (33 pl), ☎ (085 33) 224.

Recommended
Bakery: *Village Bakery Foodshop*, Angel Lane, ☎ (0768) 62377, bread and cakes baked on premises; also goats milk, cheese.
Bookshop/tearoom: *Bluebell*, Three Crowns Yard, ☎ (0768) 66660.
Craft workshop: *A.J. Designs*, Market Street, Brough, ☎ (093 04) 296, exquisite jewelry.
Factory showroom: at Clifton Dykes, 2m SE on A6, *Wetheriggs Country Pottery*, ☎ (0768) 62946, suppliers of handmade pottery, handwoven wool rugs, etc.
Farmhouse: at Hutton, *Bridge End Farm*, Hutton John, ☎ Greystoke (08533) 273, quiet 14-acre farm with good views. £13 B. & B.
♥ *James and John Graham*, Market Square, ☎ (0768) 62281, gourmet provisions and wine.

Nearby

BAMPTON, 10m S

Hotel:
★ *Haweswater*, CA10 2RP, ☎ (093 13) 235, AC BA DI, 16 rm. Ⓟ 🕸 £32. Rest. ◆ £7.50.

HELTON, 3m N

Hotel:
★ *Beckfoot House*, CA10 2QB, ☎ Bampton (093 13) 241, 7 rm. Ⓟ ⟨ 🕸 🔍 £30. Rest. ◆ Cl. Dec.-Feb. £7.

MELMERBY, 9m NE on A686

Restaurant:
● ◆ *Village Bakery*, ☎ Langwathby (076 881) 515 Ⓟ ⟨ 🔍 🎯 Cl. Mon., Wed., Christmas-Mar. Lamb and apricot polo. Book. £7.50.

Inn or Pub:
Shepherd (Marstons), ☎ (076) 881 217 Ⓟ 🎯 Bar snacks, grills, salads and homemade specialities. £6.10.

TEMPLE SOWERBY, 10m E on A66

Hotel:
● ★★ *Temple Sowerby House*, CA10 1AZ, ☎ Kirkby Thore (0930) 61578, AC AM BA, 12 rm. Ⓟ 🕸 🔍 ₺ 🎯 £50. Rest. ◆ ₺ Cl. Christmas, New Year. Roast lamb with orange stuffing. £12.

If you enjoy sports, consult the pages pertaining to the regions; there you will find addresses for practicing your favorite sport.

RAVENGLASS**

Whitehaven, 18; Millom, 14; London, 297 m
☎ 065 77   Cumbria A2

This attractive single-street village straddles the silted estuary of the R. Esk. It was once the important Roman stronghold and harbour of *Glannaventa*. From Ravenglass a miniature steam **railway** runs in summer via Miterdale to beautiful Eskdale, also accessible by road.

▶ In beautiful woodlands above village (*1m E on A595*), **Muncaster Castle★**, 14thC pele tower adapted by Anthony Salvin 1862-6; magnificent rhododendron and azalea gardens; 16th-17thC furniture and English portraits (*Easter-Sep.: Tue.-Sun., 12-5 (grounds), 1.30-4.30 (castle); cl. Mon. ex. Bank Hol. Mon.*). ▶ **Waberthwaite** (*4¹/₂m S*), hamlet with simple whitewashed **church** containing fragments of 9th-10thC crosses; Sca Fell Pikes rising to NE.

Nearby

▶ **Gosforth** (*4m N*) with ancient **church** (rebuilt 19thC) containing Anglo-Saxon and Norse work; in churchyard, beautiful 10thC carved **cross★**, 15 ft. high. ▶ Village is gateway to **Wasdale** and stern, deep lake of **Wast Water★**, with huge wall of loose stones, **The Screes** (1,983 ft.), rising dramatically from E edge; towards lower edge are handsome woodlands with **views** of mountains at lake head: **Yewbarrow** (2,058 ft.) on W, **Kirk Fell** (2,630 ft.), **Great Gable** (2,949 ft.) and **Lingmell Crag** (2,649 ft.) on E. ▶ Lakeside road ends at **Wasdale Head**, set in green hollow with glorious views across water and with tiniest **church** in Cumbria. ▶ SW of lake, via minor roads and Santon Bridge: **Irton**, hamlet with fine, intricately carved 9thC **cross★** in churchyard of 19thC church. ▶ **Seascale** (*3m W of Gosforth*), small seaside town with extensive sandy beach, dominated to N by controversial Sellafield nuclear plant. ▶ **Calder Bridge** (*7m N*), small village with picturesque ruins of Cistercian **abbey** founded 1134, on river bank.

Excursion to Eskdale

▶ Take miniature railway along valley of R. Mite to Irton Road, Eskdale Green or Dalegarth stations (*7m*), or narrow winding road off A595 along S bank of R. Esk, branching N at Forge House Kennels where rough road S over **Birker Fell**, with austere little **Devoke Water** to W, leads to Dunnerdale (→Coniston). Beautiful lower and middle dale with meandering river ascends to magnificent wild scenery of Upper Eskdale, between Sca Fell range on W and Bowfell on E. ▶ At **Dalegarth**, path across river past Dalegarth Hall, ancient farmhouse, to gloriously sited 60 ft. **Stanley Force★** waterfall. ▶ **Boot**, hamlet on Whillan Beck with climb past prehistoric stone circles to Burnmoor Tarn and, by river, tiny old **chapel** of St. Catherine's; across river from Woolpack Inn, path to **Birker Force** waterfall among wooded crags. Road continues E to **Hard Knott Roman Fort** (→ Ambleside), across high fells to reach Ambleside (→).   □

Practical information ———————————————

RAVENGLASS
ⓘ Ravenglass Eskdale Railway Car Park, ☎ (065 77) 278.
🚌 ☎ Barrow-in-Furness (0229) 20805.

Hotel:
★ *Pennington Arms*, Main Street, CA18 1SD, ☎ (065 77) 222, 30 rm. Ⓟ ⟨ 🕸 🔍 ₺ £32. Rest. ◆ ♪ ₺ Local seafood. £6.

🅰 at Eskdale, *Fisherground Farm* (30 pl), ☎ (09 403) 319; at Gosforth, *Seven Acres Holiday Park* (45 pl), ☎ (094 05) 480.

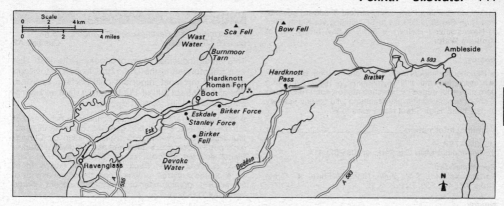

Ravenglass to Eskdale excursion

Nearby

BOOT, 10m F

Hotel:
★ *Brook House*, CA19 1TG, ☎ Eskdale (094 03) 288, 6 rm. ℗ ≮ ⌕ £27. Rest. ◆ 7 Nov. - 28 Dec. Vegetarian. £7.

CALDER BRIDGE, 9m

Inn or Pub:
Golden Fleece (Matthew Brown), ☎ Beckermet (094 684) 250 ℗ ≮ ⌕ Sandwiches, Cumberland sausage and bar meals. £3.

DRIGG, 3 1/2m N on A595

Inn or Pub:
Victoria Hotel (Jennings), ☎ Holmrook (094 04) 231 ℗ ⚏ 7 rm. Sandwiches, trout and steak. £5.

NETHER WASDALE, 11m NE off A595

Hotel:
★ *Low Wood Hall*, Wasdale Head, CA20 1ET, ☎ Wasdale (094 06) 289, 13 rm. ℗ ≮ ⚏ ⌕ ⚖ £28. Rest. ◆ ♪ Cl. Christmas, wkends. mid-Nov.-31 Jan. £6.

SEASCALE, 9m N off A595

Hotel:
★ *Scawfell*, CA20 1QU, ☎ Seascale (094 67) 28400, AC BA DI, 42 rm. ℗ ≮ ⚏ ⚉ £39. Rest. ◆ ♪ � £15.

Recommended
Golf course: Seascale, The Bank, ☎ (094 02) 28202.

WASDALE HEAD, 17m NE off A595

Hotel:
★★ *Wasdale Head*, CA20 1EX, ☎ Wasdale (094 06) 229, AC BA, 10 rm. ℗ ≮ ⚏ ⌕ £70. Rest. ◆ � Cl. mid-Nov.-28 Dec. Cumberland cooking. £11.

SCA FELL MOUNTAINS

The impressive group of mountains in the central SE Lake District, referred to as Scafell Pikes, includes England's highest summit, **Scafell Pike** (3,206 ft.). On the E edge, across the Mickledore Gap, is the separate peak known confusingly as **Sca Fell** (3,162 ft.). Formed from hard volcanic rock, the mountains are characterized by dramatic craggy outlines, towering cliffs and scree-covered slopes, and make for attractive fell-walking with magnificent views from the long summit ridges although mists can descend rapidly. The usual starting points for ascents are Wasdale, Borrowdale, Eskdale and Langdale. □

ULLSWATER***

Penrith, 6; Kendal, 31; London, 296 m
☎ 085 36   Cumbria A-B2

The curving lake of Ullswater ($7^1/_2$ m long and 1/4-3/4m wide) forms three distinct reaches with scenery of exceptional and varied beauty. From the lush green fields near Pooley Bridge at its N end through the increasingly rugged crags around Howtown to the dramatic high fells by Glenridding and Patterdale at the lake's S end. A passenger-boat service operates between Glenridding, Howtown and Pooley Bridge, and the major and minor roads running down the W and most of the E shore have access points to the lake. Surrounding fells offer magnificent walks and climbs including routes to Helvellyn, Haweswater and Ambleside.

▶ From N along W shore on A592 (leading from Penrith through to Windermere), gentle upper reach of lake runs from **Pooley Bridge**, village at head of lake, near conical wooded hill of **Dunmallet** with trace of hill fort on summit, to promontory of **Skelly Neb**, opposite Howtown and fells of Martindale. ▶ Craggy middle reach *(3 1/4m)* passes **Gowbarrow Park**, and **Fell** (1,578 ft.), with late-18thC shooting lodge, **Lyulph's Tower**, on lakeside (*private*). Track nearby leads to 65 ft. **Aira Force★** waterfall, romantically sited in wooded ravine, with smaller **High Force** above; Aira Point is associated with Wordsworth's famous 'daffodils' poem. Fells of Matterdale Common rise behind **Glencoyne Park**, with miners' cottages 'Seldom Seen' in Glencoynedale. ▶ Final reach 1 1/4m by overhanging mountains and beautiful woodlands, passes **Stybarrow Crag** with **Glencoyne Wood** stretching behind and along foot of steep **Glenridding Dodd** (1,343 ft.); splendid views across water to **Place Fell** (2,154 ft.) opposite **Glenridding**. ▶ On E shore, narrow minor road skirts lake from Pooley Bridge as far as hamlet of **Howtown**; boat services and glorious lakeside walk to Patterdale; **Hallin Fell** (1,271 ft.), overlooking Howtown on W; fine **views** from summit. ▶ Road goes S to dale head of **Martindale**, dominated by **The Nab** (1,887 ft.), with deer forest famed for its elusive Martindale red deer herd. Tiny rebuilt 17thC **church**, in solitary setting with ancient yew in churchyard. ▶ **Patterdale**, small village set in valley of Grisedale and Goldrill Becks; small **church** of St. Patrick (rebuilt 1853) containing fine tapestries by local resident Ann Macbeth (d. 1948), and nearby **St. Patrick's Well**, reputed to have healing powers. ▶ Walks and climbs in surrounding mountains include: **Helvellyn★** (3,113 ft.), ascended via Grisedale Valley or Grisedale Tarn; **St. Sunday Crag** (2,756 ft.)

to SW via Glemara Park, with **Fairfield** (2,863 ft.) beyond; and **High Street** (2,663 ft.) to SE, leading via Kidsty Pike to Haweswater (→below). ▶ 3m S is tiny, pretty lake of **Brothers Water**.

Nearby

▶ Reached by minor roads from Penrith (*10m*): **Haweswater**, converted into a huge reservoir in 1937; 1/4m long dam at N end, edged by bleached stones; road runs along E shore beside conifer plantations to wild craggy scenery at dale head. High Street range rises to W. □

Practical information _____

ULLSWATER
ⓘ Glenridding, Main Car Park, ☎ (085 32) 414.

Recommended
Farmhouse: *Mrs. S.M. Smith*, Highgate Farm, ☎ Greystoke (085 33) 339, £21; B. & B.

Nearby

GLENRIDDING, at S end of lake
ⓘ Mobile Unit, Car Park ☎ (085 32) 414.

Hotels:
● ★★★ **Ullswater**, CA11 0PA, ☎ (085 32) 444, Tx 58164, AC AM BA DI, 47 rm. ℗ ≼ ₩ ⚄ ᕗ ⚹ ♪ ⚗ £62. Rest. ♦ ᕗ £10.
★★ **Glenridding** (BW), CA11 0PB, ☎ (085 32) 228, AC AM BA DI, 45 rm. ℗ ≼ £45. Rest. ♦ Cl. mid-Jan.-mid-Feb. Fresh trout. £10.50.

HOWTOWN, 5m S of Pooley Bridge

Hotel:
★ **Howtown**, CA10 2ND, ☎ Pooley Bridge (08536) 514, 16 rm. ℗ ≼ ₩ ⚄ ⚹ £40. Rest. ♦ ᕗ Cl. Nov.-Mar. £8.

PATTERDALE, 1m S

Hotel:
★★ **Patterdale**, CA11 0NN, ☎ Glenridding (085 32) 231, AC AM, 53 rm. ℗ ≼ ₩ ⚄ ᕗ £34. Rest. ♦ ᕗ Cl. Nov.-Easter. £9.

POOLEY BRIDGE, 4m N
ⓘ The Square ☎ 530.

Hotels:
● ★★ **Sharrow Bay** (RC), Howtown Road, CA10 2LZ, ☎ (085 36) 301, 30 rm. ℗ ≼ ₩ ⚄ ᕗ ⚹ £150. Rest. ● ♦ ᕗ Cl. early Dec.-early Mar. Traditional English roast game. £27.50.
★★ **Ramsbeck**, ⚄ (085 36) 442, AC BA, 13 rm. ℗ ≼ ₩ ⚄ £45. Rest. ● ♦ ≼ Cl. Jan.-mid-Feb. £16.
★ **Sun**, CA10 2NN, ☎ Pooley Bridge (085 36) 205, 9 rm. ℗ ₩ ⚗ £27. Rest. ♦ ᕗ Local produce. £9.

⚓ Park Foot Cara C.S., Howtown Road (120 pl), ☎ (085 36) 309; Waterfoot C.P. (65 pl), ☎ (085 36) 302.

WATERMILLOCK, 2 1/2m NE

Hotels:
● ★★ **Leeming on Ullswater**, CA11 0JJ, ☎ Pooley Bridge (085 36) 622, Tx 64111, AC AM BA DI, 25 rm. ℗ ≼ ₩ ⚄ ᕗ ⚹ £86. Rest. ● ♦ ᕗ Cl. Dec.-mid-Mar. Kyle of Lochalsh scallops with leeks, medallions of veal with roquefort. £25.
● ★★ **Old Church**, CA11 0JN, ☎ Pooley Bridge (085 36) 204, 12 rm. ℗ ≼ ₩ ⚄ ♪ ⚗ £55. Rest. ♦ Cl. Nov.-Mar. Scampi with Pernod and mushrooms. £15.

⚓ Cove C.C.P., Lake Ullswater (50 pl), ☎ (085 36) 549; Knotts Hill C.P. (15 pl), ☎ (085 36) 328; Quiet C.C.P. (60 pl), ☎ (085 36) 337; Ullswater C.C.P. (155 pl), ☎ (085 36) 666.

In preparing for your trip, consult the pages pertaining to the regions. You will find there the description of the region you wish to visit, a brief history and practical information.

WHITEHAVEN

Cockermouth, 14; Ravenglass, 18; London, 325 m
pop. 29,955 ☎ 0946   Cumbria A2

This small industrial town overlooking the Irish Sea was transformed in the late 17thC from a tiny village to one of the most important coal ports in England. The simple street grid of 1680 is unchanged and merges pleasantly with modern developments.

▶ **St. James's** (1752-3), Georgian church on hill at end of attractive Queen Street; fine galleried interior with beautiful altarpiece - painting of Transfiguration by Correggio's pupil Procaccini. ▶ **Museum and art gallery** (Market Place) devoted to local history (*Mon., Tue., Thu.-Sat., 10-5; cl. Wed., Sun., Bank Hols.*). ▶ In graveyard of **St. Nicholas's** church, of which only tower remains after fire in 1971, grandmother of American President George Washington is buried.

Nearby

▶ Two other small coastal towns, once prosperous coal ports: **Workington** (*7m N*) on R. Derwent estuary, mostly 19th and 20thC buildings, and some attractive late 18thC cobbled streets round Portland Square. Traces of late 14thC castle remain in ruined **Workington Hall** (1782-1828); **St. Michael's Church** (rebuilt 18thC) includes Norman work and delightful 15thC effigy of knight and his lady. In Georgian **Parkend House** is **Helena Thompson Museum**, with costumes and applied art (*Mon.-Sat., 11-3*). ▶ **Maryport** (*13m N*), built to 18thC plan with now-disused harbour; **Maritime Museum** (Senhouse Street): local seafaring history (*Mon., Tue., Thu.-Sat., 10-12.30, 2-4.30*). ▶ To N are traces of Roman fort of *Alana*. By sandstone cliffs and lighthouse of **St. Bees Head** (426 ft.), charming old village of **St. Bees** (*4m S*) named after 7thC nunnery founded here reputedly by Irish princess St. Bega or Bee. St. Mary's parish **church**★ is portion of 12thC priory built on 7thC site; fine Norman doorway, and remarkable dragon carving, possibly 8thC, in churchyard wall. ▶ **St. Bees School**, founded 1583, includes some 16thC work. ▶ **Egremont** (*3m W*), small town with ruins of medieval castle. □

Practical information _____

WHITEHAVEN
ⓘ St. Nicholas Tower, Lowthern Street, ☎ (0946) 5678. ⬛ ☎ (0946) 2414.

Hotel:
★ **Waverley**, Tangier Street, CA28 7UX, ☎ (0946) 4337, AC BA, 24 rm. ℗ ⚹ £32. Rest. ♦ ♪ Rest. Cl. Mon. eve. £5.

Recommended
Riding school: *Kerbeck Fell Ponies*, Lamplugh, ☎ (0946) 861302.

Nearby

BECKERMET, 9m S on A595

Hotel:
★ **Royal Oak**, CA21 2XB, ☎ (094 684) 551, 8 rm. ℗ ⚄ ᕗ £45. Rest. ♦ ᕗ £8.

BRANTHWAITE, 6m

Inn or Pub:
Star (Jennings), Village Green, ☎ (0900) 2520 ℗ ≼ ₩ ᕗ Sandwiches, mixed grills and 4-course meals. £4.

DOVENBY, 6m

Inn or Pub:
Ship (Jennings), ☎ Cockermouth (0900) 822522 ℗ ≼ ₩ ⚄ 3 rm. Bar meals. £4.

LOW MORESBY, 2 1/2m N off A595

Hotel:
★★ **Roseneath**, CA28 6RX, ☎ (0946) 61572, AC BA, 10

rm. Ⓟ ⬅ ░░ ⬢ ⯎ £35. Rest. ♦ ♪ Cl. Christmas. Jugged hare. £10.

ST. BEES, 3 1/2 m S

Inn or Pub:
Manor House (Matthew Brown), Main Street, ☎ Egremont (0946) 822425, AC BA Ⓟ ░░ 8 rm. Sandwiches, steaks. £3.50.

Recommended
Golf course : ☎ (0946) 822 695.

WINDERMERE***

Keswick, 22; Kendal, 8; London, 265 m
pop. 8,575 ☎ 096 62   Cumbria AB2

The small town and popular resort of Windermere, now merged with Bowness-on-Windermere, lies close to the E shore of Windermere Lake, the largest in England. It has a wooded shoreline, several islands in its shallower middle reaches and the craggy mountains of the central Lake District rising around its N end above Ambleside (→). Roads run along both shores, and there are boat rentals and passenger steamer services. The town of Windermere developed as a resort with the arrival of the railway in the mid-19thC. It is the southern starting point to explore the lakes.

▶ **Orrest Head** (784 ft.), to N, gives glorious view of lake, also from **School Knott** to E. ▶ **Steamboat Museum**, Rayrigg Road, houses collection of historic steam and motor boats (*Apr.-mid-Nov.: Mon.-Sat., 10-5, Sun., 2-5*). ▶ Linked with town is lakeside village of **Bowness-on-Windermere** (*1m SW*) with 15thC parish **church** of St. Martin, including 15thC stained glass in E window; unusual wooden sculpture of St. Martin. Diskey Howe (300 ft.), E of church; **view**. ▶ Car ferry (*daily*) links Bowness with steep road to Hawkshead and Coniston (→). ▶ Steamers operate on the lake in summer between Lake Side, Bowness and Waterhead. ▶ On **Belle Isle**, 38-acre wooded island in middle of lake, circular house (1774) containing specially-made furniture by Gillow; portraits of Romney and de Loutherberg, set in 18thC landscaped gardens (*mid-May-Sep.: Sun.-Thu., 10.30-5; last house tour 4*). ▶ **Brockhole** (*1¹/₂ m N*): National Park visitor centre in former country house set in extensive grounds, with exhibitions on Lake District life and history (*late Mar.-early Nov.: daily from 10*). ▶ Just S is **Gummer's Howe** (1,054 ft.); fine **views** from summit. By foot of lake, **Fell Foot Country Park**: picnic areas, boat rentals and launching sites. ▶ On W side, with footpath by most of lake shore and narrow road through woodlands: **Stott Park Bobbin Mill** (*1m NW of Lake Side*), restored working mill of 1835 with original steam engine (*mid-Mar.-mid-Oct.: Mon.-Sat., 9.30-6.30, Sun., 2-6.30*). ▶ **Graythwaite Hall** (*3m further N*): 7 acre woodland gardens (*gardens only: Apr.-Jun.: daily, 10-6*). ▶ **Wray Castle** (*towards lake head*), Victorian fantasy castle (*private*); beautifully wooded grounds.

Nearby

▶ **Troutbeck** (*3m N*), hillside hamlet stretching along river with quaint 17th-18thC houses and streams running into streets; simple rebuilt **chapel** with 18thC tower. S of village is **Townend**, early 17thC farmer's house, home of Browne family for 500 years, containing original furnishings (*Apr.-Oct.: Tue.-Fri., Sun., 2-6 or dusk; cl. Sat., Mon. ex. Bank Hol. Mon.*). ▶ **Troutbeck Park** (*N*) includes farm once owned by Beatrix Potter (*private*), also traces of prehistoric settlement. From here track leads N to Roman road and High Street (2,663 ft.). ▶ **Winster** (*2¹/₂ m SE*): hamlet with old post office (1600) and beautifully-sited 19thC church; narrow road S follows lovely **Winster Valley**, branching at Bowland Bridge to run E and W of river, with **Cartmel Fell** and **Gummer's Howe** rising to W. ▶ At **Cartmel Fell** hamlet, on W road, barn-like early

16thC church of St. Anthony; delightful setting. ▶ **Lyth Valley** (*8¹/₂ m SE*), famed for its damson orchards.

Round Trip (*1 day*)

▶ Take A592 S from Windermere/Bowness along E side of lake, past Gummer's Howe to Fell Foot and Newby Bridge. ▶ Cross river (*off A590*) by fine 17thC slate **bridge** to follow winding roads through wooded country via Bouth, Colton (with rebuilt late 16thC church) and Oxen Park, joining Yeat, following beautiful SW shore of **Coniston Water** to reach Trover, dominated to NW by **Old Man of Coniston**. ▶ Take A593 S to **Broughton-in-Furness** (→Barrow-in-Furness) at head of Duddon Sands. ▶ Follow A595 W to **Duddon Bridge** (*1m*), and take twisting road N through **Duddon Valley** to Ulpha, Hall Dunnerdale and **Seathwaite**. ▶ Continue N through narrow upper valley, with **Harter Fell** (2,129 ft.) rising above woods to W, to **Cockley Beck**, where road meets **Wrynose Pass**. ▶ Climb E through steep, very narrow pass, over Furness Fells to E, leading into lovely valley of **Little Langdale** (→ Ambleside), where road meets A593. ▶ Turn r. for **Coniston** village (→), beautifully set on NW bank of Coniston Water. ▶ Take B5285 E (or minor roads skirting Tarn Hows) to old village of **Hawkshead** (*4m; → Coniston*), with Grizedale Forest stretching S, and follow wooded E shore of **Esthwaite Water** to **Near Sawrey**, where Beatrix Potter's little cottage at **Hill Top** can be visited (→Coniston). ▶ Past Far Sawrey, road reaches W shore of Windermere, where car ferry can be taken across lake to Bowness; or return by minor road S along wooded W shore, with restored **Stott Park Bobbin Mill** (*¹/₂ m N of Finsthwaite*), to Newby Bridge and N on A592 by E shore to Windermere.   ☐

Practical information ────────────

WINDERMERE
ⓘ The Gateway Centre, Victoria Street, ☎ (096 62) 6490. ▭ ☎ (096 62) 20397.

Hotels:
● ★★ *Hideaway*, Phoenix Way, LA23 1DB (B1), ☎ (096 62) 3070, 12 rm. Ⓟ ░░ ⬢ £50. Rest. ♦ ♪ Westmoreland lamb with mint. £10.
● ★★ *Miller Howe*, Rayrigg Road, LA23 1EY (B1), ☎ (096 62) 2536, AC AM DI, 13 rm. Ⓟ ⬅ ░░ ⬢ £120 incl. dinner. Rest. ● ♦ ♪ Cl. Jan.-Mar. Homemade pastries. £22.
★★ *Applegarth*, College Road, LA23 1BU (B1), ☎ (096 62) 3206, AC AM BA, 15 rm. Ⓟ ⬅ ░░ ⬢ £45. Rest. ♦ ♪ Cl. Jan.-Feb. Windermere char. £8.
★★ *Burnside*, Kendal Road, LA23 3EP (B4), ☎ (096 62) 2211, Tx 65430, AC AM BA DI, 46 rm. Ⓟ ⬅ ░░ ⬢ ⬠ ⬡ £56. Rest. ♦ ♪ ⬠ £10.
★★ *Grey Walls*, Elleray Road, LA23 1AG (B1 off. map), ☎ (096 62) 3741, AC AM DI, 15 rm. Ⓟ ░░ £36. Rest. ♦ £8.50.
★★ *Priory Country*, Rayrigg Road, LA23 1EX (B1), ☎ (096 62) 4377, AC AM BA DI, 15 rm. Ⓟ ⬅ ░░ ⬢ £70. Rest. ♦ ♪ ⬠ Cl. lunch ex. Sun., Jan. Prawn and avocado mousse. £15.
● ★ *Willowsmere*, Ambleside Road, ☎ (09662) 3575, AC AM BA DI, 14 rm. Ⓟ ░░ Cl. Nov.-Easter. £49 incl. dinner.
★ *Boston*, The Terrace, LA23 1AJ (C1), ☎ (096 62) 3654, 6 rm. Ⓟ ⬅ ⬢ £21. Rest. ♦ 27 Jun.-11 Jul., Nov.-Mar. £4.
★ *Oakthorpe*, High Street, LA23 1AF (C1), ☎ (096 62) 3547, AC BA, 20 rm. Ⓟ ⬅ £38. Rest. ♦ ♪ Cl. 24 Dec.-24 Jan. Leg of lamb steak with mint and honey sauce. £10.

Restaurant:
● ★ *Roger's*, 4 High Street (B1), ☎ (096 62) 4954, AC AM BA DI ♪ ⬢ Cl. Sun., Mon.-Sat. lunch. Shetland scallops in flaky pastry. Book. £16.

⚓ *Blakeholme*, Tower Wood (42 pl), ☎ (0448) 31417; *Fallbarrow Park*, Rayrigg Road (81 pl), ☎ (096 62) 4428; *Park Cliffe Cara*, Birks Road (252 pl), ☎ (0448) 31344; *White Cross Bay*, Troutbeck Bridge (185 pl), ☎ (096 62) 3937; at Staveley, *Ashes Lane C.C.P.*, Ashes Lane (300 pl), ☎ (0539) 821119.

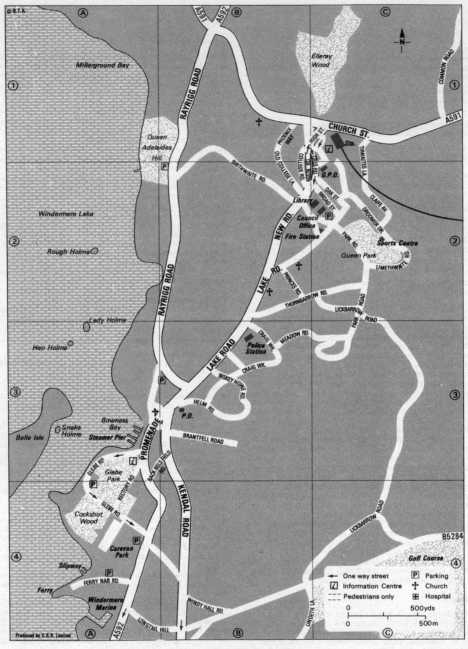

WINDERMERE

Recommended

Golf course: Cleabarrow, ☎ (096 62) 3123.

Guesthouse: *Beckmead*, 5 Park Avenue, ☎ (096 62) 2757, £19; B. & B.; *The Poplars*, Lake Road, ☎ (096 62) 2325, £23; B. & B.

Riding school: *Wynlass Beck Stables*, Cook's Corner, ☎ (096 62) 3811.

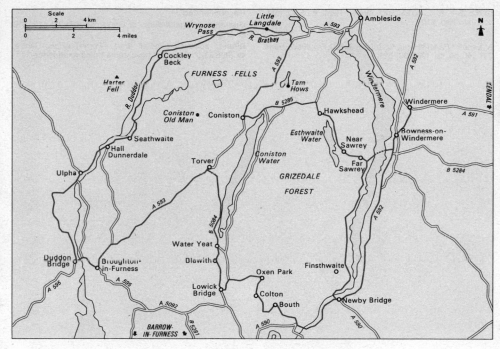

Scale
0 — 2 — 4 km
0 — 2 — 4 miles

Wrynose Pass
Little Langdale
R. Brathay
Ambleseide
A 593
N
Cockley Beck
FURNESS FELLS
Tarn Hows
Windermere
A 592
KENDAL
Harter Fell
R. Duddon
B 5285
Hawkshead
Windermere
Coniston Old Man
Coniston
Esthwaite Water
Near Sawrey
Bowness-on-Windermere
A 591
Seathwaite
Hall Dunnerdale
Torver
Coniston Water
Far Sawrey
B 5284
Ulpha
GRIZEDALE FOREST
A 593
B 5084
Water Yeat
Finsthwaite
A 592
Duddon Bridge
Broughton-in-Furness
Dlawith
Oxen Park
A 595
A 595
Lowick Bridge
Colton
A 5092
Bouth
Newby Bridge
BARROW-IN-FURNESS
B 5281
A 590
A 590

Windermere environs

Nearby

BOWNESS-ON-WINDERMERE, 1m S
ⓘ The Glebe, Bowness Bay ☎ (096 62)2895/5602.
Car rental: *Europcar,* The Belsfield Hotel, ☎ (096 62) 5910.

Hotels:
● ★★ *Lindeth Fell,* Uppers Storrs, Park Road, LA23 3JP (B4 off map), ☎ (096 62) 3286, AC AM BA DI, 15 rm. Ⓟ ₩ ⌂ ⅙ ⌕ ℘ £50. Rest. ♦ ⅙ Cl. Nov.-mid-Mar. Engllsh roasts, homemade puddings. £12.50.
● ★★ *Royal Hotel* (BW), LA23 3DB (B3), ☎ (096 62) 3045, Tx 65273 R, AC AM BA DI, 29 rm. Ⓟ ₩ ⌵ £55. Rest. ♦ ♪ £10.
★★ *Fairfield,* Brantfell Road, LA23 3AE (B3), ☎ (096 62) 6565, AC AM BA DI, 11 rm. Ⓟ ₩ ⌂ £37.50. Rest. ♦ ♪ Windermere char. £10.

Restaurants:
● ♦ *Porthole Eating House,* 3 Ash Street (B3), ☎ (096 62) 2793, AC AM BA DI Cl. Tue. lunch, Dec., Jan., part Feb. £15.
♦ *Gilpin Lodge,* Crook Road (C4 off map), ☎ (096 62) 2295, AC AM BA DI Ⓟ ₭ ₩ ⌂ ♪ Cl. 3 wks. Jan. 6 rm. Paupiette of brill with salmon mousseline. No children under 12. Book. £18.
♦ *Hedgerow Vegetarian Restaurant,* Lake Road (B3), ☎ (096 62) 5002, AC BA DI Ⓟ ♪ Cl. 2 wks. Nov. Tue.-Wed., Oct.-May. Vegetarian lasagne. £6.
♦ *Jackson's Bistro* (B3), ☎ (096 62) 6264, AC AM BA Cl. Mon., 15-31 Jan. £10.

Recommended
Craft workshops: *Craftsmen of Cumbria,* Fallbarrow Road, ☎ (096 62) 2959. Craft items, jewelry, leather, pottery, woodwork, etc.

CROOK, 2 1/2m SE on B5284
Hotel:
● ★★ *Wild Boar* (BW), LA23 3NF, ☎ (096 62) 5225, Tx 65273 W, AC AM BA DI, 38 rm. Ⓟ ₩ £66. Rest. ♦ £14.

GRIZEDALE, 4m SW
Hotel:
★ *Grizedale Lodge,* LA22 0QH, ☎ Hawkshead (096 66) 532, AC BA, 6 rm. Ⓟ ₭ ⌂ £35. Rest. ♦ ⅙ Cl. 3 Jan.-mid-Feb. Cumbrian dishes. £10.

NEWBY BRIDGE, 14m S on A592
Hotels:
● ★★★ *Whitewater,* The Lakeland Village, Backbarrow, ☎ (0448) 31133, Tx 54173, AC AM BA DI, 35 rm. Ⓟ ₭ ₩ ⌂ ⅙ ⌕ ⌂ £58. Rest. ♦ ♪ ⅙ £11.
★★ *Swan,* LA12 8NB, ☎ (0448) 31681, Tx 65108, AC AM BA DI, 36 rm. Ⓟ ₭ ₩ ⌂ ⌕ £55. Rest. ♦ ♪ Cl. 2-11 Jan. Potted char. £11.

SAWREY, 2 1/2m W by ferry
Hotel:
★ *Sawrey,* LA22 0LQ, ☎ (096 62) 3425, 18 rm. Ⓟ ₭ ₩ ⌂ ⅙ £42. Rest. ♦ ⅙ Cl. mid-Dec.-New Year. Windermere char. £9.

Inn or Pub:
Tower Bank Arms, ☎ Hawkshead (096 66) 334 Ⓟ ₭ ₩ ⌂ ⅙ ⌕ 2 rm. Homemade pies, quiches, local trout and steak. £4.90.

Recommended
Guesthouse: *West Vale,* Far Sawrey, ☎ (096 62) 2817. £25 B. & B.

TROUTBECK, 2 1/2m N on A592
Hotel:
★ *Mortal Man,* LA23 1PL, ☎ Ambleside (096 63) 33193,

12 rm. P ⸋ ⸋ ⸋ ⸋ £35 incl. dinner. Rest. ♦ ⸋ Cl. mid-Nov.-mid-Feb. £12.

⛺ *Limefitt Park* (365 pl), ☎ (0966) 32300;*Troutbeck Head C.P.* (40 pl), ☎ (085 33) 521.

Recommended

Guesthouse: *Netherdene,* ☎ Greystoke (085 33) 475. £19 B. & B.

Riding school: *Limefitt Park Pony-Trekking-Centre,* ☎ (096 63) 2564, must have some riding experience.

East Anglia

▶ East Anglia, jutting out on its own into the North Sea, is still one of the least known and most rural of English regions. It has a coastline that includes golden beaches and the liveliest of resorts, such as Great Yarmouth and Southend, but other stretches of the shoreline are hauntingly remote and beloved by birdwatchers. Inland, major towns like Cambridge and Norwich have treasures on a world-scale. Throughout the region are villages as pretty as any in Britain: with cottages half-timbered in silky grey oak (matured 500 years ago by soaking in peat bogs for a decade) or colour washed in pink (pigs' blood was formerly used).

The land has wide horizons, beloved by its most famous artist, Constable, who painted the peaceful Stour Valley; but only some East Anglian regions are as flat as outsiders accuse. Fenland, scene of an epic contest to drain wild, peaty marshes, can be explored for its wildlife reserves and springtime bulbfields on rich black reclaimed land. The Broads, a network of shallow manmade lakes and connecting rivers, is one of England's most popular and best developed tourist regions. Other regions retain a remoteness rare to discover elsewhere, such as Breckland on the Norfolk-Suffolk borders, an ancient region of sandy heath and forest, with a history reaching back to the Stone Age flint factory that can still be visited at Grimes Graves. Pre-Norman Conquest, East Anglia was the most densely populated region of Britain; in the early Middle Ages it rode on the sheep's back to a golden era of prosperity. For 700 years wool, unspun, spun or woven by Flemish weavers who came to settle, was traded worldwide, spreading such names as Worstead, Kersey and Lindsey far afield. Tiny villages have immense churches, richly adorned, as a result of that trade. Wool merchants' houses, some of them now comfortable inns, survive everywhere from that era.

When the industrial revolution came, much of the region lost its wealth to cheaper northern textile mills. The disaster had one happy outcome. Too poor to tear down medieval houses, East Anglia preserved the heritage we now see. Behind many Georgian façades, 16thC timber interiors survive intact. Today, East Anglians have one of the most fertile farm regions of the world — and more conservation-conscious farmers are replanting the hedgerows formerly swept away to make prairie-like vistas. The links across the North Sea to the Low Countries, which for centuries brought Dutch flavours to the architecture here, have always given people of the region a 'European' turn of mind. Long association with American air-bases has, since WWII, forged many links across the wider sea of the Atlantic. Some transatlantic connections go further back: Abraham Lincoln's ancestor was one of many East Anglian Nonconformists who fled for religious freedom.

For those who come here, East Anglia offers leisurely touring and explorations. They will find its broad skies are sunnier — though notably cooler and windier than elsewhere in Britain. □

 Brief regional history

Origins

400,000 years ago, Britain was still **part of the European land mass**, the Thames and the Rhine both being tributaries of a broad, northern flowing river. The first migrants to Britain — hunters and wood gatherers — therefore came by land, and there is evidence of a palaeolithic culture at Clacton in Essex where flint tools have been discovered belonging to 'Clactonian

Man'. ● After the last Ice Age the high waters of the Atlantic finally flowed into the North Sea Valley and Britain became an island. Grimes Graves, near Thetford, date from **neolithic** times. This is not a burial site but a series of hollows marking the site of one of the largest **flint mines** in Britain. Flints were excavated here and 'knapped' before being transported to customers along the ancient trackways, Peddar's Way and the Icknield Way. ● The first **Celts** came to Britain in the 2nd millennium BC and by the 1st millennium the Celtic language was in use across central and southern England. Their **Iron Age** culture (from 500 BC) is evidenced by sites such as Wandlebury Ring, an imposing hill fort, and by ramparts at Thetford.

Belgic invasions

The Belgic peoples originated in the Seine, Marne and Rhine areas and began to arrive in Britain around 100 BC. The southeast was settled by the Atrebates, Trinovantes, Catuvellauni and Cantiaci. The Trinovantes occupied much of the area of modern Essex, with the more powerful Catuvellauni farther west. The Lexden tumulus, near Colchester, is possibly the burial mound of Addedomoros, king of the Trinovantes, and contains evidence of **extensive trade** with the Roman empire. To the north, in what is now Norfolk, lived the Iceni, an indigenous people who acquired Belgic overlords. ● In AD 7 Cunobelinus (Shakespeare's Cymbeline) moved his capital to **Colchester**; the influence of his tribe was by then considerable.

The Romans

When the Romans came to Britain they made treaties with the most powerful tribes to insure safe progress through the land, and this took the form of protection in exchange for tribute. Where resistance occurred it was usually put down by force of arms. ● The Catuvellauni, however, proved more intransigent and it was only under Claudius that **Camulodunum** (Colchester) was conquered, to become in AD 49 the first Roman capital of Britain. Garrison towns were soon established across East Anglia: at Dunwich, Burgh, Caistor-by-Norwich, Tasburgh and Brancaster, linked by roads.

The Boudiccan revolt

East Anglia was not to remain peaceful for long, however, for a series of events were to follow which are among the bloodiest in Britain's history. ● In AD 60 Prasutagus, king of the Iceni, died. He had bequeathed half of his kingdom to the Emperor Nero and half to his wife, **Boudicca**, and his two daughters. In the absence of the governor, **Suetonius** Paullinus, some centurions from the governor's office, along with representatives of the provincial procurator, proceeded to claim the entire kingdom for Rome. ● When Boudicca protested she was flogged, her young daughters raped and her nobles humiliated. This outrage could not be tolerated and Boudicca assembled a **confederacy of tribes**, who, for various reasons, most of them financial, had come to distrust Rome. A great army descended upon Camulodunum, burned the town and massacred its inhabitants. Suetonius rushed to protect London, but when the commander of the 2nd Augusta legion refused to help, the town was evacuated. Boudicca sacked that city

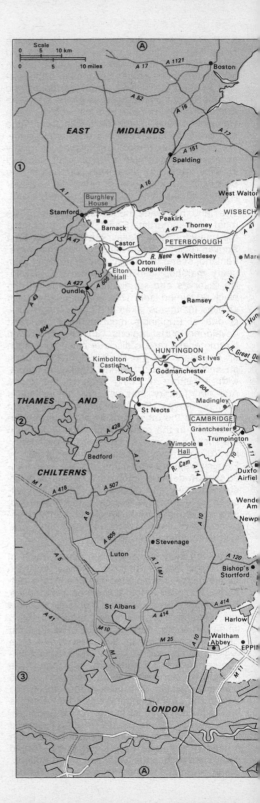

B

WELLS-NEXT-
THE-SEA
CLEY-NEXT-
THE-SEA
C

HUNSTANTON
A 149
Burnham
Market
Holkham
Hall
BLAKENEY
SHERINGHAM
CROMER
A 148
Felbrigg Hall
Mundesley

the Wash
Great
Bircham Mill
North
Creake
WALSINGHAM
HOLT
Mannington
Hall
Gardens
Happisburgh

Wolferton
Houghton
Hall
Thursford
Green
Stalham
Horsey

Sandringham
Castle Rising
FAKENHAM
Blickling Hall
Salle
AYLSHAM
Worstead
NORFOLK
NORTH
WALSHAM
Horsey

Walpole
St Peter
KING'S LYNN
A 148
Tittleshall
North
Elmham
Cawston
Great
Witchingham
Hoveton
Beeston
Hall
BROADS

Tiggenhall
St Mary
Magdalen
North Runcton
Castle Acre
A 1067
Ringland
NORWICH
Ranworth
A 149
R. Bure
Caister-
on-Sea

A 10
Narborough
SWAFFHAM
EAST
DEREHAM
A 47
South Walsham
R. Bure
GREAT
YARMOUTH

DOWNHAM
MARKET
Cockley
Cley
Oxburgh
Hall
A 1075
Hingham
R. Yare
Berney Arms
Windmill
Burgh Castle
Fritton Lake
Country Park

R. Wissey
A 134
Grimes Graves
A 11
WYMONDHAM
Caister
St Edmund
A 146
Loddon
LOWESTOFT

Washes
A 10
R. Little Ouse
THETFORD
Kilverstone
Attleborough
Rainthorpe
Hall
A 143
Oulton Broad

Mildenhall
West Stow
Park
East
Harling
Banham
Zoo
A 140
BUNGAY
BECCLES *A 146*

Wicken
Fen
Anglesey
Abbey
Bottisham
Euston
Hall
A 1066
Bressingham
DISS
Scole
R. Waveney
Suffolk
Wildlife Park

NEWMARKET
A 45
Ixworth
Norton Bird
Gardens
Fressingfield
HALESWORTH
A 12
SOUTHWOLD

Dalham
Ickworth
House
BURY
ST EDMUNDS
A 134
Wingfield
Eye
Heveningham
Hall
Laxfield
Bramfield
Blythburgh
Dunwich

A 11
Hawstead
Woolpit
A 45
Dennington
Saxtead
Mill
Bruisyard
Winery
A 1120

Kedington
A 143
STOWMARKET
Needham
Market
Helmingham
Hall
Debenham
Glemham
Hall
FRAMLINGHAM
Leiston

Cavendish
LAVENHAM
Letheringham
Tunstall
ALDEBURGH

CLARE
Haverhill
Long
Melford
Kersey
WOODBRIDGE
Butley
Priory
ORFORD

SUDBURY
Boxford
HADLEIGH
IPSWICH
Rendlesham
Sutton
Hoo
Forest
Orford
Ness

SAFFRON
WALDEN
Gainsford
End
Castle
Hedingham
Stoke-by-
Nayland
A 12
R. Orwell
R. Deben
A 45

Finchingfield
Wethersfield
A 131
R. Stout
DEDHAM
Manningtree
FELIXSTOWE

Steeple
Bumpstead
Great
Bardfield
Gosfield Hall
R. Colne
COLCHESTER
HARWICH

Great
Dunmow
Great
Saling
Coggeshall
A 120
Beth Chatto
Gardens
FRINTON-
ON-SEA
Walton-on-
the-Naze

Leaden
Roding
A 130
BRAINTREE
A 12
Copford
Rivenhall
Wivenhoe
A 133
CLACTON-
ON-SEA

CHELMSFORD
A 414
Layer
Marney
Tolleshunt
d'Arcy
St Osyth
*MERSEA
ISLAND*

Ingatestone
A 12
Margaretting
MALDON
R. Blackwater
BURNHAM-
ON-CROUCH

BRENTWOOD
A 127
A 130
Rochford
Shoeburyness

BASILDON
A 127
SOUTHEND-
ON-SEA

Grays
TILBURY
R. Thames

Dartford
SOUTH - EAST
B
C

too and proceeded then to burn Verulamium. 70,000 Romans and friends of Rome perished. ● Suetonius then drew his best forces together and faced Boudicca in battle. His attack was disciplined and highly professional. The **rebel army was defeated** and butchered — some 80,000 lost their lives. Boudicca took poison and died. Suetonius then ravaged the territories of the rebel tribes until AD 61. He was recalled to Rome after an official inquiry.

Pax Romana

The Boudiccan revolt had shown that there was a real revulsion in Britain to all things Roman; it is the achievement of the Roman administration that it was able to reverse that tendency and prove to the British aristocracy that there was much to be gained from the Roman way of life. ● From the end of the 1stC until at least the late 2ndC AD, the **Pax Romana** prevailed. Camulodunum was rebuilt along with many small towns, often based on existing settlements, such as Braughing, Water Newton, Caistor and, on the coast, Caister. ● The Romans also made attempts to drain the fens. By building **canals** which linked up the natural waterways, they improved communications. It was possible then to go by water from the fens as far as York. **Cereal growing** and **sheep rearing** were extensively practiced, grain being exported to Europe from Dunwich, Yarmouth and Brancaster. There were potteries in the Nene Valley... East Anglia was fertile, industrious and prosperous.

The Germanic invasions

In the 3rdC, Britain faced new problems from seaborne pirates and shore forts were erected at Brancaster, Burgh Castle and Bradwell to repel the invaders. ● During the next hundred years these groups of raiders had grown in strength and purpose. Waves of **Germanic people** swept across East Anglia, initially repelled by Britons. The Roman Legions withdrew to protect their interests in Gaul. Essex became occupied by **Saxons** and the old territory of the Iceni by **Angles**. ● **Roman settlements were abandoned** as were many farming areas as flood waters threatened them. The country people reverted to a more primitive way of life alongside the immigrant barbarians.

Regency lodge cottage at Hatfield Heath, Essex

The Anglo-Saxon kingdoms

By about 600 there were two Anglo-Saxon kingdoms in East Anglia: that of Essex and of East Anglia (corresponding to Norfolk and Suffolk). Great earthworks were erected, including the Devil's Ditch, which still runs for seven miles from Reach to the Stetchworth woods. The Sutton Hoo ship burial (perhaps belonging to King Raewald of East Anglia), with its jeweled sword pommels, brooches and pendants, demonstrates the skill of the Anglo-Saxon **goldsmith**.

● **Christianity** spread through the region in the early 7thC and many churches and monasteries were built, first of wood, later of stone and brick. ● **Ipswich** became an important trading centre, along with Norwich, Thetford, Dunwich and Bury St. Edmunds. Like the other powerful kingdoms of Wessex, Mercia and Northumbria, East Anglia had its law codes and councils of elders.

15th century house at Clare, Suffolk

The Danish invasions

During the 7th and 8thC a long conflict was taking place between the various Anglo-Saxon kingdoms and by 827 **Egbert of Wessex** was acknowledged overlord of Britain. The country was now united in its struggle to repel the **Danes**, but once again it was East Anglia which bore the brunt of the invasions as churches and monasteries were plundered. ● The great hero of local resistance was **King Edmund**, who refused to acknowledge Danish superiority and was slaughtered. His body was carried to Bury St. Edmunds where the saint is buried in the town named after him. ● Another patriot, celebrated in epic verse, was **Brihtnoth**, alderman of Essex, who faced the Danes under Olaf Tryggvasson. A tall, white-haired warrior, he refused a truce in exchange for gold and graciously conceded superior ground to the Danes. At the **battle of Maldon** he was killed and beheaded and the monks of Ely tenderly carried his body back to their abbey. ● The Danish 'great armies' which arrived in 865 and 892 settled East Anglia under the Danelaw and a second wave of Vikings at the end of the 10thC continued until a **Danish king**, Cnut, assumed the throne of England in 1016.

The Normans

Another hero of East Anglia resistance was **Hereward the Wake**, who established a stronghold on the Isle of Ely in 1070 and held out for many months until the

Norman blockade forced him to surrender. ● In William of Normandy's **redistribution of landholdings**, 90 Saxon landowners in Essex were deprived of their property which was given to William's Norman followers. Bishop Odo received 22 manors in Norfolk. In Suffolk 629 manors were shared out between 19 Normans. The **feudal system** of rights and obligations was then confirmed across the region. ● As in other parts of England, great castles were built at strategic places, such as Orford, Framlingham, Norwich and Castle Rising. **Peterborough** is one of Britain's finest Norman cathedrals and the cathedrals at Norwich and Ely were begun during this period, later to be extended and elaborated. Cathedrals and castles — temples of spiritual and earthly power — were the Norman contribution to the English landscape that can still be seen today.

The medieval period

The pattern of life in East Anglia during the period from the Normans until the dissolution of the monasteries under Henry VIII was similar to that of much of England. The two great landowners were the church and the aristocracy. Norfolk alone had 122 **monasteries** and these became centres of learning, while at the same time ministering to the poor and needy. The manorial system insured that the land was effectively cultivated, crops grown, animals reared. ● But East Anglia had one outstanding advantage — a **prosperous wool trade**. Flemish artisans came to the area in the 13thC, teaching the arts of spinning, weaving and dyeing to develop the manufacture of fine cloth. ● An affluent middle class, protected by the guilds, brought a third element into the social structure and towns became important as **centres of commerce**. The wool towns of Sudbury, Long Melford and Lavenham still preserve their magnificent wool churches, reflecting the prosperity of the region. The famous Paston Letters (1422-1509), written by three generations of the Pastons, a wealthy Norfolk family, contribute a wealth of information on domestic life at this period. ● During this time **Cambridge** was established as the second centre of scholarship in England. Henry III granted the first charter to the university and the first college, Peterhouse, was founded in 1284. St John's College, founded in 1511, was where Erasmus taught. King's College chapel, that masterpiece of Gothic architecture, was completed in 1515.

The Tudors

The **disestablishment of the monasteries** under Henry VIII removed at one stroke the great basis of charity that sustained and helped the poor. At first, 1,148 of the wealthiest monasteries were suppressed. All these went to 'the king and his heirs'. Dispossessed priests and monks added to the number of the poor. ● Robert Ket, a tanner from Wymondham, led the last **great peasants' revolt**, gathering his followers on Mousehold Heath, overlooking Norwich, to protest against exploitation by landowners and the enclosure of common ground. The rebellion was savagely put down by the army. ● East Anglia suffered, like the rest of England, under the **religious persecutions** of Queen Mary and Protestant nobles; priests and artisans alike were publicly burned. Under Elizabeth many Catholics fled abroad. ● However, there were new poor laws passed and a more sophisticated merchant class built houses for comfort and

for show rather than defense. Burghley House, built for William Cecil, Queen Elizabeth's treasurer, is a good example of the new grandeur and ease, with its fine painted ceilings and Renaissance paintings.

The 17th and 18thC: dissenters, engineers, innovators

After the robust splendour of Henry VIII and Queen Elizabeth, the English monarchs may have appeared supreme. The Stuart kings certainly saw themselves as divinely appointed to rule their people. But Parliament, merchants and landed gentry alike increasingly resisted such arbitrary powers. It began to be seen that the only authority for the government of men was God, and East Anglia produced the greatest Dissenter of all — **Oliver Cromwell**. ● Cromwell was born in Huntingdon and educated at the grammar school there, going on to Sydney Sussex College, Cambridge. As a Member of Parliament he supported his cousin Hampden in refusing to pay the 'ship money' levied by King Charles. (Many East Anglian ports were affected — Yarmouth, King's Lynn, Colchester and Harwich among them.) And he became increasingly involved in the building up of Parliamentary armed forces, ultimately becoming the **architect of the New Model Army**. It was at his friend John Carter's house in Yarmouth that the decision **to execute King Charles** was taken. The grounds for a **new constitution** were laid and when war broke out Cromwell led a group committed to the Puritan ethic.

15th century wooden bell tower, Blackmore, Essex

● Following the voyage of Captain Gosnold (of Grandisburgh in Suffolk) and the project to found a colony in Virginia, many groups of people set out for **North America**. One group of Puritans, led by John Winthrop of Groton, left England in 1630 with 15 ships carrying some 1,000 emigrants. This was the beginning of the Massachusetts Bay colony, of which

Winthrop was governor. In the mid-17thC George Fox founded the Society of Friends in Norwich and, a century and a half later, Thomas Paine of Thetford published *The Rights of Man*.

● So much for Dissenters. East Anglians were affected in a much more direct way by the engineering genius of **Cornelius Vermuyden**, a Dutchman. Vermuyden had negotiated with James I, Charles and Cromwell to be commissioned to investigate fen drainage. Sponsored by the Earl of Bedford, he was finally charged with the task and 30,000 acres were drained and made available for agricultural use. ● A famous agricultural pioneer was **Thomas Coke of Holkham**, who drained his land, found new ways of fertilizing it, virtually invented seed selection and a more scientific rotation of crops. His techniques provoked both admiration and consternation, for Coke offered his employees subsidies and profit sharing so that they prospered too (Holkham Hall, built by an earlier Coke, is one of the most elegant Palladian houses in England).

Paston letters

The personal correspondence of one prosperous Norfolk family has given unique insight into British daily life of the 15thC. Spanning three generations of the Paston family (who took their name from the village where they lived), the letters between various individuals provide a vivid picture of domestic life, mainly between the years 1420 and 1503, set against the nationally troubled times of the Wars of the Roses. Members of the family included Judge William Paston (1378-1444), his son John Clement, a sailor (1515-97), and Sir Robert, Earl of Yarmouth (1631-83). The letters were first published in 1787, 1789 and 1823; a more comprehensive selection was available after 1904, following the discovery of two long-lost volumes.

The 19th and 20thC

The **industrial revolution** had its effect in East Anglia as it did for most of Britain. In 1839 the main line railway from London to Brentwood opened, and was then extended to Chelmsford, Colchester, Ipswich and Harwich. Soon main lines connected London to Cambridge, Norwich and Ely and many small market towns. The region was opened up, trade increased and towns grew larger. ● **Steam trawlers** dramatically changed the fishing industry which benefited enormously, the harbours at Harwich and Lowestoft being greatly enlarged. Many villagers ceased to be agricultural labourers and took to fishing. But steam looms had the reverse effects as cottage industries collapsed under the factory system. ● The arts flourished, however, as **Constable** and **Gainsborough** gained international reputations and the Norwich and Suffolk schools also developed. ● East Anglia fortunately avoided the urban sprawl of much of industrial Britain. In the 20thC road communications improved and the coastal resorts of Hunstanton and Cromer, for example, became popular. Southend became a focus for day trips from London and sailing on the Broads attracted increasing numbers of amateur yachtsmen. ● The landscape has changed in many parts as hedges and trees have been torn out to create vastly larger fields and the 'monocultures' of grain and root crops. The old landmarks, windmills and maltings have tended to disappear. Harwich and Felixstowe have become huge container ports increasing through traffic to these points. There is a nuclear power station at Sizewell. Despite all of this, the small market towns and villages preserve their medieval charm and many of the wild coastal areas are still much the same as when the first invaders came.

Boudicca

According to one Roman writer, Queen Boudicca (also known as Boadicea) was a huge fierce woman with a mane of red hair. Whether or not she actually looked like this, she was certainly a ferocious warrior and was not afraid to stand up to the Roman invaders. Prasutagus, her husband, had been king of the Iceni tribe and was one of the British chieftains who made peace with the Romans. When he died in about AD 60, he left half his kingdom (in what is now East Anglia) to the Emperor Nero and half to his wife. However, the invaders seized all the queen's land, and were brutal not only in their treatment of Boudicca but of her daughters and subjects too. The queen retaliated by assembling at Camulodunum (Colchester) and took control of Londinium (London) and Verulamium (St. Albans) — killing as many as 70,000 Romans in the process. Nevertheless, Boudicca could not withstand all the Roman forces, and when the governor of Britain, Suetonius Paullinus, advanced with his troops against her, she was overwhelmingly defeated. Rather than suffer the humiliation of being taken prisoner she poisoned herself.

 Practical information

Information: covers counties of Cambridgeshire, Essex, Norfolk, Suffolk. *East Anglia Tourist Board*, 14 Museum Street, Ipswich, Suffolk IPL 1HU, ☎ (0473) 822922.

Weather forecast: ☎ (0223) 8092.

Ferry links: Great Yarmouth to Holland, Felixstowe to Belgium, Harwick to Scandinavia, Germany and Holland.

Self-catering cottages: *Old Hall Cottages*, c/o 28 Pensthorne House, 204 Albany Street, London NW1, ☎ (01-387) 8307; *Poplar Holidays*, Opal Cottage, Banningham, Norwich NR11 7DY, ☎ (0263) 733294; *Blakes Holidays*, Wroxham, Norwich, Norfolk NR12 8DH, ☎ (06053) 2917; *Suffolk Holiday Cottages*, The Green, Cavendish, Suffolk, ☎ (0787) 281577; *English Country Cottages*, Claypit Lane, Fakenham, Norfolk NR21 8AS, ☎ (0328) 4041.

Youth hostel: *YHA*, 40 Culver Street East, Colchester, Essex COL 1DR, ☎ (0206) 44011.

Festivals: 12-18 Jun.: *40th Aldeburgh Festival of Music and the Arts* in Aldeburgh, originally founded in 1948 by English composer Benjamin Britten.

Customs and folklores: Oct. *Colchester Oyster Feast* is held in the town hall (last Fri.). In the time of Charles II it was a time-honoured annual event. Guests are invited by the mayor, but some tickets are available at a charge, by ballot.

Scenic railway: a 3-mile run from Sheringham to Weybourne mostly parallel with the North Sea coast, designated an area of outstanding natural beauty and a tiny part of the old Midlands and Great Northern Joint Railway. Trains run every 15 min. but check the timetable. Contact: *North Norfolk Railway Co*, The Station, Sheringham, Norfolk NR26 8RA, ☎ (0263) 822045.

A changing coastline

Once a busy port, Dunwich was granted a charter by King John for the right to profit from all wrecks nearby in return for a yearly tax of 500 eels. However, the sea which made the town's living was also literally its downfall. In 1327, the sea began its onslaught: three churches and 400 houses were destroyed during a violent storm. Over the years, waves have inexorably worn away the Suffolk coastline and now all that is left of Dunwich are a few cottages and the ruins of a chapel and a leper colony. It is said that church bells can still be heard ringing beneath the waves.
East Anglia has long had to do battle with the sea. The wide open spaces of Fenland were once water-logged marshes. A drainage system had been introduced by the Romans, but by the 15thC AD this was no longer working and the land sank under water. Gradually the land was reclaimed — Viking invaders, who began raiding in the 8thC and stayed for 300 years, built embankments, dikes and water mills. Nevertheless, Fenland remained somewhat inhospitable. By the end of the 11thC, East Anglia was the most densely populated part of England (with 40-50 people per square mile), but the Fen district had few inhabitants apart from its wading birds. Intrepid individuals established isolated farmsteads, but there was not the shared open-field system which was common in other rural areas, and the land was not completely drained until the 19thC.
The once desolate Fenland and its lonely coast have given rise to a number of ghostly legends. One of the most famous concerns a huge black dog, the Black Shuck (the name comes from the Anglo-Saxon word soocca meaning 'devil'). One version of the story tells how, in the winter of 1709, a cargo ship was wrecked off the coast near Blakeney and all the crew were drowned. Among the bodies washed ashore were the captain and his black dog: ever since, whenever a disaster is about to occur, the huge dog is said to wander the coast howling for its master.

River and canal cruises: on the Norfolk Broads: five rivers — Yare, Bure, Ant, Thurne and Waveney — ideal for boating on these shallow waters, and no locks to navigate. *Blakes Holidays* (see self-catering cottages) rents cruisers, narrow boats, houseboats and sailing craft throughout the British Isles; *Blue Line Cruisers Ltd.*, Ferry View Estate, Horning, Norwich

NR12 8PT, ☎ (0692) 630128; *Hoseasons Holiday*, Sunway House, Lowestoft, Suffolk NR23 3LT, ☎ (0502) 62181/64991.

Flying: *Ipswich School of Flying Ltd*, Ipswich Airport, Nacton Road, Ipswich, Suffolk, ☎ (0473) 79510.

Gliding: *Norfolk Gliding Club*, Tibenham Airfield, Norwich, ☎ (037977) 207.

Stilton cheese

A remarkable, strong, blue-veined cheese, Stilton easily holds its own with French and Italian blue varieties. As its name indicates, it is particularly associated with the village of Stilton in Cambridgeshire. However, it is made in the district of Melton Mowbray in Leicestershire and in the surrounding counties of Derbyshire and Nottinghamshire.
Tradition has it that the cheese was made before the year 1720 in Leicestershire, and that it was sold under the name of 'Quenby cheese' to the Bell Inn at Stilton, a coaching house on the Great North Road. The Bell Inn sold so much cheese to its customers that Stilton became famous for it, and gave it the now familiar name. Notoriously difficult to make, the cheese took longer than a year to mature and had to be turned by hand each day. It used to be known as 'cream cheese' because, although hard, it came from full-cream milk. One maker, a Mrs. Musson, stated that 'Stiltons, with the exception they make no noise, are more trouble than babies'. Present-day cheese-making can be speeded artificially by the addition of cultures to the milk to encourage the development of mould which is what constitutes the blueness. Steel needles later stuck into the cheese let in air and so help the mould grow. The cheese also forms, in time, its characteristic crusty outside. Although the blue-veining is expected in this distinctive cheese, the decay process required to make it is no longer allowed to get out of hand. This was not always the case. Daniel Defoe (1660-1731) described how he sampled a cheese at the Bell Inn which was 'brought to the table with the mites and maggots round it so thick that they bring a spoon for you to eat the mites with, as you do the cheese'.
Fortunately this no longer occurs, but Stilton cheese is frequently served with a spoon — the centre being soft and creamy, and often additionally steeped in port. A traditional accompaniment to port and nuts at the end of a good meal, Stilton may also be eaten with pickles, fruit or simply bread.

Archery: *Eastern Sports Activity Holidays*, 3 Richard Avenue, Wivenhoe, Colchester CO7 9JQ, ☎ (020622) 4811; *Olympian Holiday Summer School*, Teviotdale, Long Road East, Dedham, Colchester, ☎ (0206) 322025.

Cycling: *Just Pedalling*, 9-13 Wensum Street, The Glass House, Norwich NR3 2LA, ☎ (0603) 615200.

Gymnastics: *Olympian Holiday Summer School* (see Archery).

Orienteering: *Eastern Sports Activity Holidays* (see Archery).

Snooker: *The Benbridge Hotel*, The Square, Heybridge, Maldon CM9 7LT, ☎ (0621) 57666.

Canoeing: the Norfolk Broads are ideal for amateur sailing and canoeing. *Graffham Water Residential Centre*, Perry, Huntingdon PE18 OBX, ☎ (0480) 810521; from £40 for two nights. *Academic Travel Ltd*, Briar School of English, 8 Quinton Cliff, Lowestoft NR32 4PE, ☎ (0502) 3781 or 64442 runs courses of varying lengths — 5 to 28 days.

Hunting: *Essex and Suffolk Hunt*, Church Farm, Chattisham, Ipswich, Suffolk, ☎ (0473) 87269.

Aquatic sports: Windsurfing: *Bradwell Field Studies and Sailing Centre*, Bradwell Waterside, Southminster CMO 7QY, ☎ (0621) 76256.

Sailing: *East Anglian School of Sailing*, PO Box 64, Ipswich, Suffolk IP2 8NN, ☎ (0473) 84 246; *Norfolk Cadet Sailing Club*, 55 Eastern Road, Thorpe, Norwich NR7 OUJ, ☎ (0603) 35431; *Oysterworld Sailing Holidays*, Wherry Lane, Wherry Quay, Ipswich IP4 1LG, ☎ (0473) 58900; *The Benbridge Hotel*, The Square, Heybridge, Maldon, Essex CM9 7LT, ☎ (0621) 57666; *Blackwater Yacht Charters and Sailing School*, The Old Ship, Heybridge Basin, Maldon, Essex, ☎ (0621) 55568.

 Towns and places

ALDEBURGH**

Ipswich, 26; Lowestoft, 30; London, 100 m
pop. 2,711 ☎ 072 885   Suffolk C2

A quiet, unspoiled resort. Fishing boats are hauled daily onto the long pebble beach. Aldeburgh was home to the poet George Crabbe (b. 1754) whose tale of Peter Grimes inspired composer Benjamin Britten to write his famous opera. The town annually hosts the **Aldeburgh Festival** (→) founded by Britten and singer Peter Pears.

▶ **Moot Hall**: 16thC listed building was once in the centre of town. The sea's ravages have halved the town's size.

Nearby

▶ **Thorpeness** (*2m N*):vacation village developed since 1910. **Windmill Museum** (*Easter, May, Jun., Sep.: Sat., Sun., Bank Hol. Mon.; Jul., Aug.: Tue.-Sun., 2-5*). Curious **House in Clouds** nearby is a converted water tower. ▶ **Snape** (*6m W*): village clusters near quay on the River Alde. ▶ **Tunstall Forest** (*10m W*): between **Snape** and **Orford** (→) formerly heathland, now planted with pines and firs. ▶ **Iken** (*3m W*): remote village at the head of the Alde Estuary.   □

Practical information _____

ALDEBURGH
ⓘ cinema, High Street, ☎ (072 885) 3637.

Hotels:
★★★ *Brudenell*, The Parade, IP15 5BU, ☎ (072 885) 2071, AC AM BA DI, 47 rm. Ⓟ ♪ £53. Rest. ♦ £9.50.
★★ *Uplands*, Victoria Road, IP15 5DX, ☎ (072 885) 2420, AC AM BA DI, 20 rm. Ⓟ ⊰ ▒ ⌑ ♪ £41.20. Rest. ♦ ᕋ £7.20.
★★ *White Lion*, Market Cross Place, IP15 5BJ, ☎ (072 885) 2720, AC AM BA DI, 35 rm. Ⓟ ⌑ ᕋ £45. Rest. ♦ ᕋ £8.

Inn or Pub:
Cross Keys (Adnams), Crabbe Street, ☎ (072 885) 2637 ▒ Variety of hot and cold meals, snacks. £7.

⅄ at Saxmundham, *Carlton Park C.S.* (50 pl), ☎ (0728) 3685.

Recommended
Cycle rental: *Happy Days Toy Shop*, 173 High Street, ☎ (072 885) 2638.
Golf course: Saxmundham Road, ☎ (072 885) 2890; Thorpeness, ☎ 2176.

Nearby
LEISTON, 5m N on B1122

Hotel:
★ *White Horse*, Station Road, IP16 4HD, ☎ (0728) 830694, AC BA, 9 rm. Ⓟ ▒ £29.50. Rest. ♦ ᕋ £9.

Recommended
Cycle rental: *Nunns*, 98 High Street, ☎ (0728) 830652.

AYLSHAM*

Cromer, 11; Norwich, 12; London, 126 m
☎ 0263   Norfolk C1

Fine 18thC houses surround a handsome market place. Once prosperous as a linen manufacturing town, then a famous cloth town, Aylsham was also briefly a spa. **St. Michael's**: views down nave arcades to a beautifully arched minstrels' gallery.

Nearby

▶ **Blickling** (*1m NW*) has the Jacobean redbrick mansion **Blickling Hall**★★. The house has associations with Henry VIII and his Queen Anne Boleyn, Charles II and his wife Catherine (*end Mar. - late Oct.: daily ex. Mon., Thu., 1-5*).▶ **Salle**★ (*6m SW*): dominated by mighty tower of **St. Peter and Paul** church. Queen Anne Boleyn's family lived at **Salle Moor Hall**. ▶ At **Great Witchingham** (*8m SW*) is **Norfolk Wildlife Park**: 50 acres enclose comprehensive collection of British and European mammals (*all year: daily, 10.30-6*). ▶ **Cawston**: (*4m SW*) one of the county's finest 14thC churches.   □

Practical information _____

AYLSHAM
ⓘ (0263) 73.

⅄ at North Walsham, *Scarborough Hill C.P*, Old Yarmouth Road (60 pl), ☎ (0692) 405829;at Sea palling, *Golden Beach H.C.*, Beach Road (120 pl), ☎ (069 261) 269;*Waxham Sands H.P.*, Warren Farm, Horsey (200 pl), ☎ (069 261) 325.

Recommended
Craft workshop: *Charles Matts Furniture*, Alby Crafts, ☎ (0263) 768060, handmade furniture.

Nearby
ALDBOROUGH, 6m N off A140

Restaurant:
♦ *Old Red Lion*, ☎ Cromer (0263) 761451, AC BA Ⓟ ⊰ ⌑ ▧ Cl. Sun. eve., Mon. Supreme chicken stuffed with prawns. Book. £12.20.

BLICKLING, 2m N on B1354

Hotel:
★ *Buckinghamsh Arms*, ☎ Aylsham (026 373) 2133, AC AM BA DI, 3 rm. P ⌂ 17thC inn close to the gates of Blickling Hall. £44. Rest. ♦ £13.50.

GREAT WITCHINGHAM, 12m SW off B1145

Hotel:
★★ *Lenwade House*, NR9 5QP, ☎ (0603) 872288, AC AM BA DI, 14 rm. P ⌂ ⌂ ⌂ £44.50. Rest. ♦ ᴚ £8.95.

BASILDON*

Southend-on-Sea, 11; Brentwood, 8; London, 30 m
pop. 152,301 ☎ 0268   Essex B3

The second New Town (→ Harlow) to be built in Essex, Basildon sought to give a better lifestyle to London's Eastenders.

▶ The **town centre** is the commercial, administrative and recreational focus.

Nearby

▶ **Langdon Hills** (*3m SW*) include two parkland areas: **Westley Heights** and **One Tree Hill**: open grassland and sandy heaths.   ☐

Practical information _____
BASILDON
🚊 ☎ Southend-on-Sea (0702) 611811.
Car rental: Budget, Service station, East Mayne, ☎ (0268) 282355.
Hotel:
★★★ *Crest* (Crest), Cranes Farm Road, SS14 3DG, ☎ (0268) 3955, Tx 995141, AC AM BA DI, 116 rm. P ⌂ ⌂ ⌂ £69.90. Rest. ♦ £11.50.

Recommended
Golf course: Off Sparrows Herne, Kingswood, ☎ (0268) 3532.

Nearby
BULPHAN, 10m SW off A128
Hotel:
★★★ *Olde Plough*, Brentwood Road, RM14 3ST, ☎ Grays Thurrock (0375) 891592, AC AM BA DI, 69 rm. ⌂ ⌂ ⌂ ⌂ £40. Rest. ♦ ᴚ £11.

BECCLES*

Norwich, 18; Lowestoft, 10; London, 116 m
pop. 10,677 ☎ 0502   Suffolk C2

Situated on River Waveney, in the early 19thC Beccles was a bustling port with goods passing through to Lowestoft. The Waveney forms the Suffolk-Norfolk boundary. The emphasis is on Georgian architecture.

▶ **St. Michael's Tower** stands separate from church rising 97 ft. ▶ Wander through network of old streets or passageways known as 'scores'. Several noteworthy old houses including **Roos Hall** built 1583. ▶ **Beccles District Museum**, Newgate: local history including wherry-building tools (*Apr.-Oct.: Wed., Sat., Sun., Bank Hols., 2.30-5; Nov.-Mar.: Sun., 2.30-5*).

Nearby

Sotterley (*4m SE*): **agricultural museum** with collection of agricultural and rural artifacts (*end Mar.-mid-Sep.: Sun., Bank Hols., 1-6*).   ☐

Practical information _____
BECCLES
ⓘ quay, Fen Lane, ☎ (0502) 713196.

🚊 ☎ Norwich (0603) 632055.
Hotel:
★★ *Waveney House*, Puddingmoor, NR34 9PL, ☎ (0502) 712270, AC AM BA DI, 13 rm. P ⌂ ⌂ ⌂ ⌂ £45. Rest. ♦ ᴚ £8.
Restaurant:
♦ *St. Peter's House*, Old Market, ☎ (0502) 713203. AC DA P ⌂ ⌂ ᴚ ⌂ ⌂ Cl. 2 wks. Jan., Mon.-Wed. in winter. 5 rm. Game dishes, jugged hare. Book. £14.

Recommended
Craft workshop: at Weston,*Winter Flora*, Hall Farm, ☎ (0502) 713346, dried floral arrangments.
Golf course: The Common, ☎ (0502) 712244.

Nearby
LODDON, 10m NW off A146
Hotel:
★ *Rackhams Stubbs*, Stubbs Green, NR14 6EA, ☎ (0508) 20231, 9 rm. P ⌂ ⌂ ⌂ £32. Rest. ♦ Cl. 7 Nov.-28 Feb. £8.

Recommended
Farmhouse: Rockham's Stubbs, Stubbs Green, ☎ (0508) 20231, in 200 acres, £24. B. & B.

BLAKENEY*

Hunstanton, 22; Cromer, 13; London, 124 m
pop. 1,559 ☎ 059 451   Norfolk B1

Set among marshes, a charming Norfolk coast resort with brick and flint houses. It is now open only to small boats at high tide.

▶ **Guildhall**, near the quay: only the undercroft and its 13thC brickwork remain. ▶ **St. Nicholas'** church, dating from 1220, has a beacon light that formerly guided ships safely into the harbour.

Nearby

▶ **Blakeney Point**: a coastal bird sanctuary. Access by boat from **Morston** or **Blakeney** (*all year*).   ☐

Practical information _____
Hotels:
★★★ *Blakeney*, Quayside, NR25 7NE, ☎ Cley (0263) 740797, AC AM BA DI, 52 rm. P ⌂ ⌂ ⌂ ⌂ ⌂ £60. Rest. ♦ ᴚ ᴚ £10.
★★ *Manor*, NR25 7ND, ☎ Cley (0263) 740376, 22 rm. P ⌂ ⌂ ᴚ £60. Rest. ♦ ᴚ ᴚ £10.

BLYTHBURGH

☎ 050 270   Suffolk C2

A village set at the head of the Blyth Estuary.

▶ The church of **Holy Trinity** rises dramatically from the marshes. The tower, c. 1330, remains from an earlier building. The body of the church dates from mid-15thC. A fine painted roof is the church's main feature. ▶ The **Hart Inn**: Elizabethan bedroom paneling and Stuart period stairs .   ☐

BRAINTREE*

Colchester, 15; Bishop's Stortford, 16; London, 45 m
pop. 30,975 ☎ 0376   Essex B3

A busy Essex town, once on an ancient pilgrims' route from London to **Walsingham** (→) and **Bury St. Edmunds** (→).

▶ **Braintree Heritage Centre** in market place; displays on local history (*Mon.-Sat. 10-5; Cl. Bank Hols.*). ▶ **Glazen-**

wood Gardens, Bradwell (*2m E*), acres of unusual plants in a woodland setting (*late May-early Jul.: Fri., 2-5*).

Nearby

▶ **Bocking** (*2m N*). In this village in 1816 Samuel Courtauld III set up as a silk 'throwster' and began the worldwide textile concern of the **Courtaulds** (→). Early 18thC **Post Mill** under restoration (*by appointment, tel. 0376 21421*). ▶ **Great Saling** (*5m NW*) has **Saling Hall Gardens**: a walled garden dating from 1698 (*mid-May-1 Aug., early Sep.-mid-Oct.: Wed., Thu., Fri., 2-5*). ▶ **Great Bardfield★** (*8m NW*): an attractive village set in watermeadows. **Gibraltar Mill** — dating from 1661 — towers above them. **Great Bardfield Cottage Museum**: 16thC charity cottage containing farm and domestic implements from last 100 years (*Apr.-Sep.: Sat., Sun. and Bank Hols., 2-6*). **St. Mary the Virgin** church dates from 14thC and has original stained glass. ▶ **Coggeshall** (*6m E*): an ancient wool town with remains of a 12thC Cistercian abbey. ▶ **Paycocke's House**, West Street, is a timber-framed house built c. 1500 with fine carving (*late Mar.-early Oct.: Wed., Thu., Sun., Bank Hols., 2-5.30*). ▶ **Halstead★** (*6m NE*): an attractive wool town, built on steep hill overlooking River Colne. ▶ **Gosfield Hall**, a Tudor courtyard house remodeled in 18thC (*May-Sep.: Wed., Thu., tours 2.30, 3.15, 4.15*). □

Practical information ───────────

BRAINTREE
🚃 ☎ 20774.
Hotel:
★ *Old Court*, 31 Bradford Street, CM7 6AS, ☎ (0376) 21444, AC AM BA DI, 11 rm. ▥ ⌗ ⤴ £38.50. Rest. ◆ ♪ ⴺ £7.50.

Restaurant:
● ◆ *Braintree Chinese*, 3 Rayne Road, ☎ (0376) 24319, AC AM BA DI ℗ ♪ ⌗ Cl. 25-27 Dec. Crispy duck pancake. Book. £15.

⚓ at Gosfield, *Gosfield Lake C.S.*, Church Road (150 pl), ☎ (0787) 475043.

Recommended
Golf course: King's Lane, Stisted, ☎ (0376) 24117.

Nearby

COGGESHALL, 5m E on A120
Hotel:
★★★ *White Hart*, Market End, CO6 1NH, ☎ (0376) 61654, AC AM BA DI, 18 rm. ℗ ⌗ Splendid 16thC hostelry that was once the guildhall. £65. Rest. ● ◆ ♪ ⴺ Cl. Fri. and Sun. £20.

Inns or Pubs:
Fleece (Greene King), West Street, ☎ (037) 661412 ℗ ▥ ⚫ ⴺ Bar snacks, steak and kidney pie, curry, scampi. £5.
Woolpack (Ind Coope Allsopps), 91 Church Street, ☎ (037) 661235 ℗ ◈ ▥ ⚫ ⌗ 2 rm. Homemade bar and restaurant meals. £7.

Recommended
Craft workshop: Coggeshall Pottery, 49 West Street, ☎ (0376) 61217, domestic and decorative stoneware.

EARLS COLNE, 9m NE on A604
Restaurant:
◆ *Drapers House*, High Street, ☎ (07875) 2484, AC AM BA DI ℗ ▥ ♪ ⌗ 5 rm. Breast of duck with mandarin and ginger sauce. £14.

Inns or Pubs:
Bird in Hand (Ridleys), Coggeshall Road, ☎ (078) 752557 ℗ ◈ ▥ ⚫ ⌗ Homemade dishes, filled jacket potatoes and snacks. £4.50.
Castle (Greene King), High Street, ☎ (078) 752694 ℗ ▥ ⌗ 3 rm. Bar snacks, meals lunch and eve. ex. Sun. £4.

FELSTED, 5m SE B1417
Restaurant:
◆ *Boote House*, ☎ Great Dunmow (0371) 820279, AC

AM BA DI ⚫ ⌗ Cl. 2 wks. Feb., 2 wks. Sep., Mon.-Tue., lunch Wed.-Sat., Sun. eve. 1 rm. Saddle of hare en brochette with wild mushrooms. Book. £19.

HALSTEAD, 6m N on A131
Restaurant:
◆ *Halstead Tandoori*, 73 Head Street, ☎ (0787) 476271, AC AM BA DI ⚫ ♪ ⌗ Cl. 25-26 Dec. Lamb tikka, king prawn biriani. Book. £7.50.

WETHERSFIELD, 6m NW on B1053
Restaurant:
● ◆ *Rudi's*, Village Green, ☎ Great Dunmow (0371) 850723, AM BA ℗ ▥ ⚫ ♪ Cl. Sun. eve., Mon. Seafood pancake. Book. £11.50.

BRENTWOOD*

Chelmsford, 12; Tilbury, 12; London, 25 m
pop. 73,500 ☎ 0277   Essex B3

A former coaching town, it preserves memories of a historic past amid modern developments.

▶ **Chapel of St. Thomas Martyr**, High Street: the ruins date back to 1221 when it was a pilgrims' staging post en route to Canterbury.

Nearby

▶ **Weald Country Park and Thorndon Country Park:** fishing, horse riding and visitor centre. ▶ **Billericay** (*5m E*) Norsey Wood, Outward Common Road, a medieval deer park. □

Practical information ───────────

ℹ ☎ (0245) 353 444.
🚃 ☎ Chelmsford, (0245) 353444.

Hotels:
★★★★ *Brentwood Moat*, London Road, CM14 4NR, ☎ (0277) 225252, Tx 995182, AC AM BA DI, 37 rm. ℗ ▥ ⚫ ⌗ £66. Rest. ◆ ♪ ⴺ £18.
★★ *Post House*, Brook Street, CM14 5NF, ☎ (0277) 210888, Tx 995379, AC AM BA DI, 120 rm. ℗ ▥ ⴺ ⌕ £70. Rest. ◆ ♪ ⴺ £12.50.

Recommended
Golf course: Ingrave Road, ☎ (0277) 218850; Ongar Road, ☎ 73179.

BUNGAY*

Norwich, 15; Lowestoft, 15; London, 115 m
pop. 4,106 ☎ 0986   Suffolk C2

A town of mainly Georgian houses, sited on rising ground above a loop of the **River Waveney** (views); Bungay's **castle ruins** are the surviving twin towers and massive flint walls of a Norman castle (*daily*). Fine towers distinguish the churches of **Holy Trinity** and **St. Mary**. Octagonal **market cross** was once a whipping post.

Nearby

▶ **Norfolk and Suffolk Aviation Museum**, Flixton Buck (*3 m SW*): aviation memorabilia (*Apr., May, Sep., Oct.: Sun., Bank Hols., 10-5.; Jun.: Tue., Wed., Thu., 7-9, Sun., 10-9; Jul., Aug.: Tue., 7-9, Wed.-Thu., 10-5, 7-9, Sun. and Bank Hols., 10-9*). ▶ **The Otter Trust★** Earsham (*3m SW*): conservation and breeding centre for the British otter (*Apr.-Oct.: 10.30-6*). □

In preparing for your trip, consult the pages pertaining to the regions. You will find there the description of the region you wish to visit, a brief history and practical information.

Practical information

BUNGAY

Hotel:
★ **King's Head**, Market Place, NR35 1AF, ☎ (0986) 3583, AC AM BA, 13 rm. P £30. Rest. ♦ ♪ ఉ £9.

Restaurant:
♦ **Brownes**, 20 Earshaw Street, ☎ (0986) 2545, AC BA Cl. Sun., Mon., lunch, 2 wks. Sep. £16.

⚓ Outney Meadow C.P., Broad Street (14 pl), ☎ (0986) 2338.

Recommended
Craft workshop: Henry Watson's Potteries Ltd., Wattisfield, ☎ (0359) 51239, wide variety of domestic terracotta pottery;Nursey Son Ltd., Upper Olland Street, ☎ (0986) 2821, sheepskin clothing; at Wicklewood,Locality Arts Ltd., Coign House, Hackford Road, ☎ (0953) 602186, gifts, trays, cheese-boards, table mats.
Golf course: Bungay Waveney, Outney Common (on A144), ☎ (0986) 23.
♥ at Thornham Magna,The Suffolk Spice and Herb Company, Thornham Herb Garden, ☎ Mellis 510, produces herb teas,seeds,spices,skin and hair products.

Nearby

HARLESTON, 7m SW off A143

Hotel:
★★ **Swan**, The Thoroughfare, IP20 9AS, ☎ (0379) 852221, AC BA, 10 rm. P £32. Rest. ♦ ♪ £6.

⚓ Waveney Valley Lake, Wortwell (30 pl), ☎ (098 686) 530.

Recommended
Millhouse Pottery, 1 Station Road, ☎ (0379) 852556.

MENDHAM, 2m E

Hotel:
★ **Sir Alfred Munnings**, Studio Corner, IP20 9NH, ☎ Harleston (0379) 852358, AC AM BA DI, 14 rm. P ⟨ ⚄ ▭ £28. Rest. ♦ ♪ ఉ £11.

BURNHAM-ON-CROUCH*

Colchester, 27; Chelmsford, 21; London, 52 m
pop. 6,268 ☎ 0621 **Essex B3**

This boating centre on the Crouch Estuary is known as the 'Cowes of the East Coast' with many major yacht clubs maintaining premises here. Burnham Week is last week in Aug.

▶ **St. Mary's church** (1m N) has a Purbeck marble font, c. 1200. ▶ **Museum of local history:** the land and sea connections of the 'Dengie Hundred' (mid-Mar.-late Dec.: Wed., Sat., 11-4, Sun. and Bank Hols., 2-4.30; late Aug.: daily, 11-4).

Nearby

▶ **Wallasea Island** (1m S across estuary) is the Essex yacht marina. **Dengie Peninsula** (10m N): ▶ church of **St. Peter-on-the-Wall** (2m) dates back to 654. ☐

Practical information

🚂 ☎ Southend-on-Sea (0702) 611811.

Hotel:
★ **Olde White Harte**, The Quay, CM0 8AS, ☎ Maldon (0621) 782106, 15 rm. P ⟨ ⚄ Fine Georgian inn that is famous among yachtsmen throughout the country. £33.50. Rest. ♦ ♪ ఉ £6.55.

Restaurants:
♦ **Boozles**, 4 Station Road, ☎ Maldon (0621)783167, AC BA Cl. Mon., Sun dinner. £12.
♦ **Contented Sole**, 80 High Street, ☎ Maldon (0621)

782139 ⚓ ⛳ Cl. Christmas, Bank Hols., 2 wks. Jul., Sun.-Mon. £15.

⚓ Silver Road C.P., 5 Silver Road (30 pl), ☎ (0621) 782934.

Recommended
Golf course: Ferry Lane, Creeksea, ☎ (0621) 782282.

BURY ST. EDMUNDS**

Newmarket, 15; Ipswich, 29; London, 82 m
pop. 32,890 ☎ 0284 **Suffolk B2**

The heart of the ancient market town, laid out in the 1060s and 70s on a Roman grid-pattern, is rich in fine historic buildings.

▶ **The abbey** ★ was one of Europe's greatest; shrine of the martyred King Edmund. ▶ **The abbey gate**, 1327, richly decorated in canopied niches, survives on. ▶ **Angel Hill**. Note fine Georgian buildings; **Angel Hotel** retains 13thC undercroft. ▶ At **Angel Corner** is the **Gershom Parkington collection** of **clocks and watches** (Mar.-Oct.: Mon.-Sat., 10-1 & 2-5; Nov.-Feb.: Mon.-Sat., 10-1 & 2-4). ▶ **The Athenaeum** designed by Francis Ickworth, architect of Ickworth (→) ▶ **Churchgate St.** and **Abbeygate St.** have fine Georgian shops and houses. ▶ In **Market Cross** is **art gallery** designed by Robert Adam where lunchtime and evening concerts are performed (Tue.-Sat.: 10.30-4.30). ▶ **Moyses' Hall**, Cornhill, is 12thC Norman domestic building turned into local museum (Mar.-Oct.: Mon.-Sat., 10-1 & 2-5; Nov.-Feb.: Mon.-Sat., 10-1 & 2-4; Cl. Sun., Good Fri., Easter Sat., May Day, Bank Hols.). ▶ **Suffolk Regiment Museum, Gibraltar Barracks**, Risbygate Street: military historical exhibits (Mon.-Fri.: 10-12 & 2-4; Cl. Bank Hols.). ▶ **National Roller Skating Centre**, at Rollerbury, Station Hill (open daily).

Nearby

▶ **Ickworth★** (3m SW): magnificent Palladian house with Regency and 18thC furniture (end Mar.-end Apr.: Sat. & Sun.; May-Sep.: daily — ex Mon. & Thu. — Oct.: Sat. & Sun., 1.30-5.30; park open dawn to dusk). ▶ **Horringer** (3m SW): pretty village with green. ▶ **Woolpit** (8m E) named after wolves, pit in the vicinity. ▶ **Hawstead** (4m SW): church has two Norman doorways and many memorials. ▶ **Ampton**, with **Little and Great Livermore** (5m N) on edge of Breckland (→), with 'Seven Hills' barrows and a park backing onto lake. ▶ **Almshouses** date from 1693. **Church** has Cocket chantry and fine Charles I royal arms. ▶ **Hessett** (5m SE): pleasant village surrounding **St. Ethelbert's Church★**, one of Suffolk's finest late medieval buildings. ▶ **Bardwell** (10m NE): **Bardwell Church**; one window memorializes Sir William Bardwell, died 1434. ▶ **Ixworth Thorpe** (6m NE) is a small village on River Thet. ▶ **Stowlandtoft** (7m NE) has a fine, lofty **church** with good Flemish carving in chancel. ▶ **West Stow Anglo-Saxon Village** (7m NW): replica of Anglo-Saxon village in **West Stow Country Park★** (daily: 9-dusk). ☐

Practical information

BURY ST. EDMUNDS
🛈 abbey gardens, Angel Hill, ☎ (0284) 64667.
🚂 ☎ 3947.
Car rental: Budget, Cecil Larter, Out Risbygate, ☎ (0284) 701345/6.

Hotels:
● ★★★★ **Angel**, Angel Hill, IP33 1LT, ☎ (0284) 3926, Tx 81630, AC AM BA DI, 37 rm. P ⛳ ♪ £75. Rest.
● ♦ £10.
★★★ **Priory**, Tollgate Lane, IP32 6EH, ☎ (0284) 66181, AC AM BA, 17 rm. ⟨ ∭ ⚄ ఉ ♪ £48. Rest. ♦ ♪ ఉ £7.50.
★★ **Suffolk**, Butter Market, IP33 1DC ☎ (0284) 3995, AC AM BA DI, 41 rm. P £60. Rest. ♦ ఉ £9.

Restaurants:
♦ **Bradleys**, St. Andrews Street S, ☎ (0284) 703825, BA

P ⌖ Cl. Sun., Mon., 2 wks. Christmas. Boned quail stuffed with chicken mousseline. Book. £21.
♦ *Chalice*, 28-29 Cannon Street, ☎ (0284) 4855 P ⌂ ⌖
♪ & Cl. 1 wk. Dec., Bank Hols., Sun., Mon. Vegetarian and wholefood dishes. £9.

Recommended
Craft workshop: at Barrow, *Pottery*, 27 The Green, ☎ (0284) 810961, handmade domestic stoneware pots.
Golf course: Tutt Hill, ☎ (0284) 5979; Lark Valley, Fornham St. Martin, ☎ (0284) 63426.
Guesthouse: *Trafalga Villa*, 6 Springfields Road, ☎ (0284) 2416, £19, B. & B.
Riding school: *Linkwood Riding Centre*, Bradfield St. George, ☎ (0284) 86390.

Nearby

BRADFIELD COMBUST, 6m SE on A134

Restaurant:
● ♦ *Bradfield House*, Subbury Road, ☎ Sicklesmere (028 486) 301, BA DI P ⌂ ⌖ ⌖ Cl. Sun. eve., Mon. Steak, kidney and oyster pudding. Book. £16.

IXWORTH, 7m NE on A143

Restaurant:
● ♦ *Theobalds*, 68 High Street, ☎ Pakenham (0359) 31707 AC BA ⌂ ♪ ⌖ Cl. 1 wk. Jan., Mon., Sun. eve., Sat. lunch. Book. £15.

CAMBRIDGE**

Huntingdon, 15; Bishop's Stortford, 26; London, 54 m
pop. 103,000 ☎ 0223   Cambridgeshire A2

The cool, grey-stone university town of Cambridge is best seen from the **Backs** — one-time common lands that now border the river Cam. Cambridge's first students came from Oxford in 1284 when **Peterhouse College** was founded. But the Romans were here in the year 100: their name for Cambridge was Camboritum. Though most colleges date from the Middle Ages, modern architectural examples include **Churchill College**, Madingley Road, built in 1961-68. The **Scott Polar Research Institute** has been a centre of North and South polar research since 1934; exhibition area.

▶ Cambridge University is a federation of 31 individual colleges. In general, the quadrangles, the chapels and, on occasion, the refectory halls and libraries are open.
▶ **King's College★** (on Parade), founded by Henry VI in 1441. The detached **King's Chapel★★★**, begun in 1446, is known as 'the finest flower of late Gothic in Europe'. Spectacular **fan vaulting★★★** adorns the lofty interior. Exquisite stained-glass **windows** survive the wreckage of the Reformation. ▶ **St. John's College★★** received its charter in 1511 from Lady Margaret Beaufort.

Trinity College★ (next to St. John's); the largest in Cambridge, founded by Henry VIII. The **Great Court** is the world's largest college courtyard. ▶ **Queen's College★★**, reached by a **wooden bridge** over the Cam, is one of the finest surviving examples of 15th and 16thC architecture.
▶ **Magdalene College** (pronounced Maudlin); the shorthand diaries of the vivid 17thC diarist, Samuel Pepys, are lodged here at his request. ▶ **Jesus College**, founded 1496, has a traditional association with Welsh students. ▶ **Sydney Sussex College**, founded in 1589 on the site of a Franciscan monastery and much restored in the 19thC Gothic **style**, was the college of Oliver Cromwell. ▶ **Christ's College**, founded 1505, has charming **gardens**, open to the public. The rooms of the poet Milton are preserved. ▶ **Corpus Christi**, founded 1352, was the college of Christopher Marlowe. ▶ **Pembroke College** is one of the largest in Cambridge; founded in 1346 by the Countess of Pembroke. ▶ **Great St. Mary's Church**, the university church, was the site of many events in the history of the Church in Cambridge. **Galleries** inside date from the 18thC. ▶ **Round Church**, Church of the Holy Sepulchre, has an unusual, circular Norman nave. ▶ **Senate House;**

the university's governing body gathers in 18thC setting of James Gibbs' classical building. ▶ **Churchill College**, dating from 1959 and ▶ **New Hall** from 1954. ▶ The **Fitzwilliam Museum★★**, Trumpington Street, has extensive Egyptian, Greek, Roman and English pottery collections. Paintings include works by Titian, Rembrandt and Turner (*Tue.-Sat.: lower galleries — antiquities — 10-2, upper galleries — paintings — 2-5; Sun.: all galleries, 2.15-5*). ▶ **Cambridge and County Folk Museum★**, Castle Street; has tools of many local trades, Fenland folklore, toys, Victorian kitchen (*Tue.-Sat.: 10.30-5; Sun.: 2.30-4.30*). ▶ **University Museum of Archaeology and Anthropology★**, Downing Street, has extensive collections relating to world prehistory and the archaeology of the Cambridge region (*Mon.-Fri.: 2-4; Sat.: 10-12.30*).

Nearby

▶ **Grantchester★** (*2m SE*): riverside village that forever recalls a Rupert Brooke poem. ▶ **Trumpington** (*2m S*) village set beside the river. Trumpington has a much restored 14thC **church**. The brass of Sir Roger de Trumpington is its greatest treasure. ▶ **Wimpole Hall★★** (*7m SW*). The house dates from the 17thC but major additions include Soane's Yellow Dining Room. ▶ **Anglesey Abbey★** (*6m NE*). The house dates from 1600 and is built on the site of an Augustinian abbey. A water mill in the grounds has been restored to working order (*abbey and garden: end Mar.-end Apr.: Sat., Sun., Easter Mon.; Apr.-end Oct.: Wed.-Sun. and Bank Hol. Mon., 1.30-5.30; garden only: end Mar.-end Jun.: Wed.-Sun.; end Jun.-end Oct.: 1.30-5.30 daily; Lode Mill: end Mar.-early Oct.: Sat., Sun., Bank Hol. Mon., 1.30-5.30*). ▶ **Bottisham** (*3m E*): one of Cambridgeshire's distinctive village colleges; church has fine 14thC work.

Cambridge Villages Round Trip

Exploring the farmland and villages of southern Cambridge and the Suffolk boundaries reveals a landscape that borders on fenland and recalls a pre-Roman past.

▶ Leave **Cambridge** in direction Newmarket (→). ▶ **Lode**: thatched cottages and thatched village hall are near **Anglesey Abbey** with its fine gardens. ▶ **Swaffham Bulbeck**: thatch and cream cottages and an interesting chalk church. ▶ **Stetchworth**: Fenland town, now a quiet village. Nearby, for walkers, is the colossal 7m earthwork of the **Devil's Ditch**, 60 ft. high. ▶ **Dullingham**: where a Roman farmer once lived. ▶ **Westley Waterless**: the little church has one of the finest brasses in England. ▶ **Weston Colville**: the famous brasses here are of Robert Leverer, 1427, and Abraham Gates 1636. ▶ **Balsham**, the highest spot in Cambridgeshire, 400 ft. above sea level. The massively buttressed church has fine brasses and a rood loft. ▶ **Great Abington** by the tranquil River Granta; nearby, an ancient Roman road and the Bronze Age Brent Ditch. ▶ **Little Abington**: thatched cottages and timbered houses by the Granta. ▶ **Wandlebury Ring**: ancient earthwork with fine views across Cambridge. ▶ **Great Shelford.** ▶ **Grantchester**: riverside village within walking distance of Cambridge; undying associations with poet Rupert Brooke. □

Practical information ⎯⎯⎯⎯⎯⎯⎯⎯⎯⎯

CAMBRIDGE
ℹ Wheeler Street, ☎ (0223) 322640.
✈ Cambridge Airport, ☎ (0223) 61133.
🚌 ☎ 311999.
Car rental: Europcar, Holland Motors, 315/349 Mill Road; ☎ (0223) 248198 (rail/drive).

Hotels:
★★★★ *Garden House* (B.W.H.), Granta Place off Mill Lane, CB2 1RT (B3), ☎ (0223) 63421, Tx 81463, AC AM BA DI, 117 rm. P ⌖ ⌂ ⌖ £70. Rest. ● ♦ ♪ £12.
★★★ *University Arms* (INH), Regent Street, CB2 1AD (B3), ☎ (0223) 351241, Tx 817311, AC AM BA DI, 115 rm. P ⌖ ⌂ & £52. Rest. ♦ ♪ & £10.
★★ *Arundel House*, 53 Chesterton Road, CB4 3AN (B1), ☎ (0223) 67701, AC AM BA, 72 rm. P ⌖ ⌖ ♪ £46. Rest. ♦ £8.55.

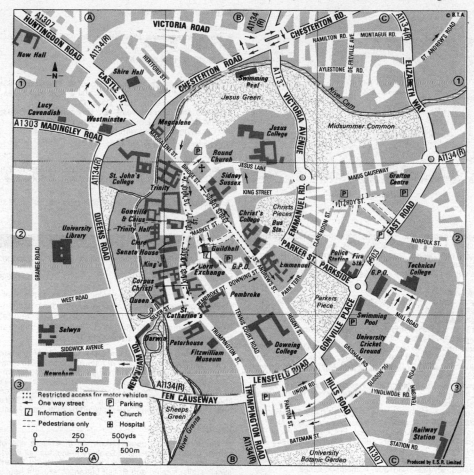

CAMBRIDGE

Restaurants:
♦ *Hobbs Pavilion*, Park Terrace (B2), ☎ (0223) 67480 ⊰ ♨ ♪ ⊗ Cl. Easter, Christmas, mid-Aug.-mid-Sep., Sun., Mon. Sweet and savoury pancakes. £6.
♦ *Jean Louis*, 15 Magdalene Street (A1), ☎ (0223) 315232, AC AM BA DI ♨ ⊗ Cl. Mon., 25-27 Dec., 1 Jan., Easter. Escalope of veal with lobster and hollandaise sauce. Book. £13.
♦ *Peking*, 21 Burleigh Street (C2), ☎ (0223) 354755 ♨ ⊗ Cl. 2 wks. Christmas, Mon. Book. £12.
♦ *Xanadu*, 7A Jesus Lane (A-B1), ☎ (0223) 311678, AC AM BA DI ♨ ⊗ Cl. 25 Dec.-1 Jan., Sun., Easter Mon. Book. £16.50.

Inns or Pubs:
Cambridge Arms (Greene King), King Street (B2), ☎ (0223) 359650 ♨ ὅ Homemade goulash, chili, daily specials, fish. £4.50.
Cambridge Blue, 85 Gwydir Street (C3 off map), ☎ (0223) 323241 P ♨ ♨ Cold buffet, barbecues in summer. £4.50.
Eagle (Greene King), Bene't Street (B3), ☎ (0223) 353782, AM ♨ Cold buffet, daily specials. £3.95.

Free Press (Greene King), Prospect Row (C2), ☎ (0223) 368337 ♨ ♨ Salads, quiches, soups. £4.
Spade Becket (Tolly Cobbold), Thompsons Lane (B1), ☎ (0223) 311701 ⊰ ♨ ὅ Lasagne, chili, steaks, salad bar, afternoon tea. £5.

⛺ at Comberton, *Highfield Farm C.S.*, Long Road (100 pl), ☎ (022 026) 2308;at Great Shelford, *Great Shelford C.C.S.*, 212 Cambridge Road (100 pl), ☎ (0223) 841185;at Longstanton, *Toad Acre C.P.*, Mill Lane (24 pl), ☎ (0353) 720661.

Recommended
Antique shops: *Jess Applin Antiques*, 8 Lensfield Road, ☎ (0223) 315168, furniture;*John Beazor Sons Ltd.*, 78-80 Regent Street, ☎ (0223) 355178, clocks and furniture;*Malcom G., Clark*, 3 Pembroke Street, ☎ (0223) 357117, furniture;*Webster-Speakman*, 79 Regent Street, ☎ (0223) 315048, clocks and furniture.
Bakery: *Fitzbillies*, 50 Regent Street, ☎ (0223) 64451, wide range of breads, sponges, fruit cakes, fresh creams.
Craft workshops: at Houghton, Alice Green Crafts, Monument House, Thicket Road, ☎ (0480) 300977, Venetian-style Flower Jewelry, toys and sweaters *Barretts*, 2 St. Mary's Passage, ☎ (0223) 66711, well-known china,

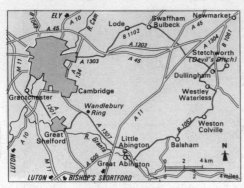

Cambridge villages

crystal, cutlery and giftware; *Midsummer Glassmakers*, Auckland Road, ☎ (0223) 316464, hand-designed glass, sculptural pieces and enamels; *Primavera*, 10 Kings Parade, ☎ (0223) 357708, ceramics, glass, jewelry; at Oakington, *Mark Bury's Workshop*, 53 Longstanton Road, ☎ (022 023) 2401, glass engraving, stone carving and lettering.
Cycle rental: *Cambridge Cycle Hire*, 118 Mill Road, ☎ (0223) 314333.
Golf course: Cambridgeshire Hotel, Bar Hill, 6m NE by A1303, ☎ (0954) 80555; at Shelford Bottom, The Gog Magog, ☎ 247626.
Guesthouse: *Cristinas*, 47 St. Andrews Road, ☎ (0223) 65855, £23 B. & B.; at Hildersham, *Lynne Hartland*, The Watermill, ☎ (0223) 891520, mill house on River Granta, £23 B. & B.
Jewelers: *Churchfarm Workshops*, 4 Church Farm, Hatley St. George, modern designer jewelry made in gold, silver and niobium.
Retail store: *Etcetera China Shops*, 17 Rose Crescent, ☎ (0223) 350001, English fine bone china and crystal.
♥ at Over, *Little Lead Soldiers*, 11A Over Industrial Par, Long Stanton Road, ☎ (0954) 30690, small lead military figures.
♥ *Felstar Estate Wines*, The Vineyards, Crick's Green, Felsted, ☎ (0245) 361504, homemade wines.

Nearby

ARRINGTON, 12m SW on A14

Hotel:
★ *Hardwicke Arms*, SG8 0AH, ☎ Cambridge (0223) 207243, AC BA, 8 rm. ℗ £30. Rest. ♦ ♪ ♿ £8.50.

BAR HILL, 5m NW on A604

Hotel:
★★ *Cambridgeshire Moat* (Q.M.H.), Huntingdon Road, CB3 8EU, ☎ Crafts Hill (0954) 80555, Tx 817141, AC AM BA DI, 100 rm. ℗ ⅏ ♿ ⊡ ⌖ ✧ £59. Rest. ● ♦ ♪ ♿ £11.

FOWLMERE, 10m S on B1368

Restaurants:
♦ *Swan House Inn*, High Street, ☎ (076 382) 444, AC AM BA DI ℗ ⅏ ♖ Cl. 25-26 Dec. Duck in honey and walnuts. Book. £11.50.
♦ *Chequers Inn*, High Street, ☎ (076 382) 369, AC AM BA DI ℗ ⅏ ♖ Cl. 25-26 Dec. Rack of lamb, escalopes of venison with wild mushrooms. Book. £23.

HORNINGSEA, 3m NE off A45

Inn or Pub:
Plough Fleece (Greene King), ☎ (0223) 860795 ℗ ⅏ ♿ Extensive range of homemade meals incl. Elizabethan rabbit. £7.

MADINGLEY, 5m W on A45

Restaurant:
♦ *Three Horseshoes*, High Street, ☎ (0954) 210221, AC AM BA DI ℗ ⅏ ♖ ♖ £17.

MELBOURN, 11m S on A10

Restaurants:
● ♦ *Pink Geranium*, 25 Station Road, ☎ Royston (0763) 60215, AC AM BA ℗ ⅏ ♖ ♖ Cl. last 2 wks. Aug., Sun., Mon., Sat. lunch, Bank Hols. Book. £15.
♦ *Sheen Mill*, Station Road, ☎ Royston (0763) 61393, AC AM BA DI ℗ ⌖ ⅏ ♖ ♪ ♖ Cl. Sun. eve., Bank Hols. 7 rm. Escalope of turkey with stem ginger. Book. £16.

WATERBEACH, 5m N off A10

Hotel:
★ *Bridge*, Clayhithe, CB5 9HZ, ☎ Cambridge (0223) 8602521, AC AM BA DI, 28 rm. ℗ ⌖ ⅏ ♿ £36. Rest. ♦ ♪ £9.

⚓ *Landbeach Marina Pk*, Ely Road (650 pl), ☎ (0223) 860019.

CHELMSFORD*

Bishop's Stortford, 18; Southend-on-Sea, 20; London, 33 m
pop. 58,974 ☎ 0245   Essex B3

County town of Essex; originally a Roman settlement, Caesaromagus, Chelmsford was an important administrative seat until 13thC. Later a modest market town until coming of railways in 1843. It was the first town to adopt electric street lighting.

▶ **Chelmsford Essex Museum**, Oaklands Park, Moulsham Street: permanent collection of natural history, Victoriana, local industry, medals (*Mon.-Fri.: 10-5.; Sun.: 2-5*). ▶ **Chelmsford Cathedral**: 15thC church became cathedral of See of Essex in 1914. Recently renovated upper floor houses library (*Mon.-Fri.: 10-4; eves. by arrangement*). ▶ **Shire hall**, fine 18thC building now replaced by new county hall.

Nearby

▶ **Danbury** (*5m E*): **country park** set in 41-acre site of former pleasure gardens of Danbury mansions (*all year*). ▶ At **South Woodham Ferrers** (*8m SE*) **Butterfly Safari**: swallowtails, foreign and British butterflies in plant house (*May-Sep.: Sun., Bank Hols., 1-5*).   □

Practical information _____

CHELMSFORD
🚉 ☎ (0245) 353444.
Car rental: Europcar, Jones Ltd, 372 Baddow Road, ☎ (0245) 355718.

Hotels:
★★★ *South Lodge*, 196 New London Road, CM2 0AR, ☎ (0245) 264564, Tx 99452, AC AM BA DI, 41 rm. ℗ ⌖ ♿ ♪ £58. Rest. ♦ ♪ ♿ £9.50.
★★ *Boswell House*, Springfield Road, CM2 6LF, ☎ (0245) 287587, AC AM BA DI, 13 rm. ℗ ♿ £37. Rest. ♦ ♪ ♿ £6.

Restaurant:
♦ *Melissa Wholefood*, 21 Broomfield Road, ☎ (0245) 353009 ℗ ♿ ♖ Cl. Bank Hols., Sun. Vegetarian, everything homemade. Book. £8.

Inn or Pub:
Endeavour (Grays), 351 Springfield Road, ☎ (024) 557717 Homemade bar food, chili, vegetarian dishes. £6.

Nearby

GREAT BADDOW, 1m S off A130

Hotel:
★★★ *Pontland Park*, West Hanningfield Road, CM2 8HR,

☎ Chelmsford (0245) 76444, Tx 995411, AC AM BA DI, 8 rm. P ⟨ ⬭ ⬭ ⓗ ⬭ ⬭ ⬭ £80. Rest. ♦ ⓗ £15.

GREAT WALTHAM, 4m N

Restaurant:
♦ *Windmill*, ☎ Chelmsford (0245) 360292, AC BA P Cl. Sun., Sat. lunch, Bank Hols. £16.

HIGH EASTER, 10m NW off A1000

Restaurant:
♦ *Punch Bowl*, ☎ Good Easter (024 531) 222, AC AM BA DI P ⬭ ♪ ⬭ Cl. Sun. dinner, Mon., lunch Tue.-Sat. Poached salmon with cucumber sauce. Book. £19.50.

RIVENHALL END, 11m N on A12

Hotel:
★★ *Rivenhall Motor Inn*, Rivenhall End, Witham, CM8 3BH, ☎ (0376) 516969, AC AM BA DI, 43 rm. P £39. Rest. ♦ ♪ Cl. 25-27 Dec. and 1 Jan. £8.50.

ROXWELL, 4m W off A1060

Restaurant:
♦ *Farmhouse Feast*, The Street, ☎ (0245 48) 583, AC BA P ⬭ ⬭ ♪ ⓗ ⬭ Cl. 1 wk. Jan., 2 wks. Jun., Sun., Mon. All food homemade, vegetarian dishes. Book. £13.

STOCK, 5m S on B1007

Inn or Pub:
The Bakers Arms (Trumans), ☎ (0277) 840423, BA P ⬭ ⓗ 2 rm. Bar snacks and basket meals, eve. restaurant Mon.-Sat. Sun. lunch. £12.

CLACTON-ON-SEA*

Harwich, 16; Colchester, 15; London, 71 m
pop. 39,618 ☎ 0255   Essex C3

South-facing resort with 7 miles of gently sloping sandy beaches.

▶ Major entertainment centre at ▶ **Clacton Pier** (*mid-Oct.-Apr.*). Funfair, including roller coaster; **Ocean Marine Show**; rides suitable for younger children (*May-mid-Sep.: daily, 10-6; end Sep.-Easter: Sat., Sun. only*).

Nearby

▶ **St. Osyth's Priory** (*3m W*): 13thC ruins with 15thC **gatehouse**. ▶ Opposite priory is parish **church**★ of St. Peter and St. Paul with glorious 16thC beamed roof. ▶ **Brightlingsea** (*8m W*) fishing town at mouth of River Colne. Yachting centre, also pleasure craft to hire. ▶ **Holland-on-Sea** (*2m NE*): sandy beaches.   □

Practical information

CLACTON-ON-SEA
ⓘ 23 Pier Avenue, ☎ (0255) 423400 (summer only).
🚂 ☎ 422178.
Car rental: Budget, Carlton Garage, 65 High Street, ☎ (0255) 420444.

Hotel:
★★ *Royal*, Marine Parade, CO15, ☎ (0255) 421215, AM BA DI, 60 rm. P ⟨ ⓗ ✈ ⓗ £49. Rest. ♦ ♪ £9.

⚠ at Jaywick, *Tower C.P.* (150 pl), ☎ (0255) 820372.

Recommended
Golf course: West Road, ☎ (0255) 421919.

Nearby

BRIGHTLINGSEA, 8m W on B1029

Restaurant:
♦ *Jacobe's Hall*, High Street, ☎ (020 630) 2113, AC AM BA DI P ⬭ ⬭ Cl. Sun., Tue., Bank Hols., Mon. Lobster thermidor, Dublin Bay prawns au gratin. Book. £15.

HOLLAND-ON-SEA, 2m E off B1032

Hotel:
★★★ *Kings Cliff*, 55 Kings Parade, CO15 5JB, ☎ (0255) 812343, AC BA, 15 rm. P ⟨ ⬭ ⓗ ⬭ £45. Rest. ● ♦ ♪ £7.50.

CLARE*

Cambridge, 27; Chelmsford, 21; London, 63 m
☎ 0787   Suffolk B2

Attractive wool town with 13thC **castle ruins** on 11thC mound. Clare exported cloth to Spain in the 15thC. It gave its name to Clare College, Cambridge (→).

▶ **Nethergate Street** is the oldest part of the town; **Cliftons** is a Tudor building with fine chimneys; 16thC **Nethergate House**, now a hotel. The **priory** dates from 1248 as the first English Augustinian foundation (*walled wild gardens: daily, 10-6*). The **church** has a fine 13thC tower, a fan-vaulted south porch and 17thC gallery. Some glass survives, but the church was destroyed by William Dowsing, the Reformation iconoclast, who claimed to have destroyed 1000 superstitious images here. ▶ **Ancient House Museum**: 15thC **priest's house** contains local history (*end Mar.-Oct.: Wed-Sat., 2.30-4.30, Sun., 11-12.30*). ▶ **Cavendish** (*3m E*): wide **village green** is the setting for a **fine church** and thatched cottages. ▶ **Cavendish Manor Vineyards**, Nether Hall Manor, offer wine tasting and a museum of local wine production all year (*Mon.-Sun.: 11-5*). ▶ **Sue Ryder Foundation Museum** shows the history of the foundation's work for the aged and international rescue besides the war-time background of its founder (*all year: Mon.-Sat., 10-5.30, Sun., 10-11 12.15-5.30*). ▶ **Stoke-by-Clare** (*3m W*), a pleasant village on the open Stour valley. The 14thC **church** has a tiny pulpit and one of the last wall paintings made prior to the Reformation. The picture, a **Doom**, shows the last judgment. **Stoke College**, now a school, is a former priory founded 1090, connected to a college of secular priests in 1415; later the home of a notorious 18thC miser, John Elwes. ▶ **Kedington** (*5m W*): sometimes called the 'Westminster Abbey' of Suffolk, the church is one of the finest in the country with 1000 years of history in its crowded interior. Earliest is a 10thC **stone crucifix** showing Christ as on a living tree. The **chancel** is 13thC. The 15thC **nave** has box pews of varying sizes, the most decorative being the **Barnardiston pew** of the family that was long the most important in Suffolk. Their pew faces a 17thC **three decker pulpit**. At the west end of the church is an 18thC **gallery** for orchestra and singers.   □

Practical information

Hotel:
★★ *Bell*, CO10 8NN, ☎ (0787) 277741, AC AM BA DI, 20 rm. P ⓗ 16thC half-timbered posting house with carved beamed ceilings and open fires. £42. Rest. ♦ ♪ ⓗ £10.

Inns or Pubs:
Seafarer, Nethergate Street, ☎ (0787) 277449, AM BA P ⬭ ⬭ Seafood, Mexican dishes, curries, steak. £3.50.
Swan Inn (Greene King), 4 High Street, ☎ (0787) 278030 P ⬭ Daily specials at lunch, à la carte eve. menu. £4.

CLEY-NEXT-THE-SEA*

Hunstanton, 19; Cromer, 12; London, 125 m
☎ 0263   Norfolk B1

Formerly a thriving port on the Glaven Estuary, its harbour has now disappeared.

▶ 18thC **customs house** and the **quay** remain near ancient ▶ **Cley Mill**. ▶ **The Hall**, 18thC, stands on high ground to the east. ▶ **Church**★ has lofty nave and great 15thC windows.

Nearby

▶ **Glandford** (*2 m S*); in village of flint and brick houses is the **Shell Museum**; the work of Sir Alfred Jodrell, an explorer. ▶ **Cley Marshes** (Norfolk Naturalists' Trust) (*1m N*): freshwater attracts many birds (*Access permits from visitor centre.*) ▶ **Cley Visitor Centre** overlooks the Cley Marsh Reserve from high ground (*Apr.-Oct.: Tue.-Sun., 10-5*). Has displays on conservation and local history. ▶ **St. Nicholas church**, Salthouse: fine example of late 15thC architecture.   □

Practical information _____

Recommended
Craft workshop: Made in Cley, High Street, ☎ (0263) 740143, full range of domestic stoneware and jewelry.

COLCHESTER**

Ipswich, 19; Chelmsford, 23; London, 52 m
pop. 87,476 ☎ 0206   Essex B2

England's oldest recorded town, Colchester is now a thriving regional centre. The medieval town plan remains intact inside the Roman walls.

▶ **The castle** is the surviving keep of a great fortress dating from the 1060s. **Roman vaults** survive underneath; castle houses **Colchester and Essex Museum** which records the Roman history of the town (*Apr.-Sep.: Mon.-Sat., 10-5, Sun., 2-5; Oct.-Mar.: Mon.-Fri., 10-5, Sat., 10-4*). ▶ **The Hollytrees** in the High Street: a house built in 1718 now contains local history displays (*Mon.-Sat.: 10-1, 2-5*). ▶ **Minories Art Gallery**, High Street: permanent collection and changing exhibitions in two Georgian houses; walled garden (*Tue.-Sat.: 11-5; Sun., 2-6*). ▶ **St. Botolph's Priory**, Priory Street: remains dating from 12thC. ▶ **Scheregate**: picturesque postern gateway. ▶ **Dutch quarter**: town's most distinctive area founded by Dutch Nonconformists and Quakers.

Nearby

▶ **Bourne Mill**: 16thC fishing lodge, converted into a water mill, maintained in working order (*all Mar.-early Oct.: Sat., Sun., Bank Hol. Mon.; Jul.-Sep.: Tue., 2-5*). ▶ Elmstead Market is the site of the **Beth Chatto Gardens★** (*all year: Mon.-Fri.; mid.-Mar.-Nov.: Sat. also*). ▶ **Stour Valley Railway Centre**, Chappel Station: collection of vintage railway locomotives (*all year: Mon.-Fri., 10-5, Sat., Sun., 11-5.30; steam days Mar.-Oct.: first Sun. in month and Bank Hols.*).   □

Practical information _____

COLCHESTER
ⓘ Queen Street, ☎ (0206) 46379/712233.
🚃 ☎ (0206) 564777.
Car rental: Europcar, Crescent Garage, Pownall Crescent, ☎ (0206) 45676 (rail/drive).
Hotels:
★★★ *George* (Q.M.H.), High Street, CO1 1TD, ☎ (0206) 578494, Tx 25971, AC AM BA DI, 47 rm. ℗ ⌿ £50. Rest. ● ◆ ≀ £9.
★★ *King's Ford Park*, Layer Road, CO2 0HS, ☎ (0206) 34301, Tx 9875629, AC AM BA DI, 15 rm. ℗ ⌣ ⚶ 🍸 ⌿ Regency house situated in a woodland park. £55. Rest. ◆ ≀ £8.50.
★ *Rose and Crown*, East Gates, CO1 2TZ, ☎ (0206) 866617, AC AM BA DI, 28 rm. ℗ ⚶ ⌿ £48. Rest. ◆ ≀ ⚶ £10.

Restaurants:
◆ *Bistro Nine*, 9 North Hill, ☎ (0206) 576466, AC BA ⅋ Cl. Sun., Mon., 1 wk. after Christmas. French country cooking, vegetarian dishes, all homemade. Book. £11.
◆ *Honeypot*, 3 St. Johns Street, ☎ (0206) 561676, AC

AM BA DI ⚶ ≀ ⅋ Cl. Sun., Mon. lunch. Caribbean curry, Mexican pancakes. Book. £10.

Inn or Pub:
Odd One Out, 28 Mersea Road, ☎ (0206) 578140 Bar snacks.

⚸ *Colchester C.C.P.*, Cymbeline Way (185 pl), ☎ (0206) 45551.

Recommended
Antique shops: *Partner Puxon*, 7/16 North Hill, ☎ (0206) 573317, furniture; *Kelvedon Antiques*, 90 High Street, Kelvedon, ☎ (0376) 70557, clocks, furniture; *Ivor and Joan Weiss*, 16 High Street, Kelvedon, ☎ (0376) 71525, paintings.
Golf course: Birch Grove, Layer Road, Kingford, ☎ (020 634) 276.

Nearby

CHAPPEL, **7m W on A604**

Restaurant:
◆ *Swan Inn*, ☎ Earls Colne (078 75) 2353, AC BA ℗ ⚶ ⚶ ≀ ⚶ ⅋ Cl. Christmas. Seafood special, poached skate. £9.

MARKS TEY, **10m W on A12/A120**

Hotel:
★★★★ *Marks Tey*, CO6 1DU, ☎ Colchester (0206) 210001, Tx 987176, AC AM BA DI, 108 rm. ⚶ ⌿ £49. Rest. ◆ ≀ ⚶ £8.45.

Oyster fishing

One aspect of Britain highly prized by the Roman invaders was its plentiful supplies of oysters. The southeast coast has long provided good fattening grounds for these shellfish, and the citizens of Colchester (once the Roman capital of England) have had rights to the valuable oyster beds on the estuary of the River Colne ever since the time of Richard I.
To celebrate this, the town holds an Oyster Feast every year in the month of October. The Mayor, Aldermen and Councillors process around the town and then return to the Town Hall for the banquet which is attended by up to 400 guests. The previous month, on the first day of September, another ceremony marks the opening of the oyster season which then runs until April (hence the idea that oysters cannot be eaten during any month without an 'R' in it). On this day the Mayor, accompanied by Councillors and Fishery Board representatives, inspects the Colne oyster grounds. The party sets off from Brightlingsea in a fishing boat and travels across the estuary to Pyefleet Creek. There the Town Clerk reads out the 1256 proclamation of fishing rights, then the assembled company drinks the Queen's health in gin and eats gingerbread. Finally, the Mayor casts a trawling net into the water to bring up the first oysters of the new season.

CONSTABLE AND GAINSBOROUGH C.

Thomas Gainsborough (born 1727 in Sudbury →) and John Constable (born 1776 in East Bergholt →) retained life-long associations with the landscape of the tranquil **river Stour**.

▶ **Gainsborough House** in Sudbury (→) includes many fine portraits of his Suffolk period in addition to a collection of 18thC china and furniture (*all year: Easter-Sep.: Tue.-Sat., 10-5, Sun. & Bank Hol. Mon., 2-5; Oct.-Apr.: Tue.-Sat., 10-4, Sun. & Bank Hol. Mon., 2-4*). At **East Bergholt**,

Constable's studio was at **Moss Cottage** (not open to the public). The artist's first and unhappy schooling was as a boarder at the **grammar school** in Lavenham. He later attended **Dedham School**. ▶ The Stour is the thread that binds the area. The barges in Constable's paintings were drawn by horse to Sudbury. ▶ **Christchurch Mansion** near Ipswich town centre contains the most important collection of Constable and Gainsborough works outside London. ☐

CROMER*

Fakenham, 21; Great Yarmouth, 31; London, 132 m
pop. 5,376 ☎ 0263   Norfolk C1

Small Norfolk coastal town, Cromer reached its height of popularity at the turn of the century when the railway arrived. **Pier pavilion** provides summer programmes of entertainment.

▶ **Cromer church** on cliff top; 160-ft. tower is among Norfolk's highest and once served as a lighthouse. ▶ **Cromer Zoo**: 5 acres (*daily*). ▶ **Cromer Museum**, East Cottages, Tucker Street: late Victorian fisherman's cottage displaying history, geology and natural history of the Cromer area (*Mon.: 10-1, 2-5; Tue.-Sat.: 10-5; Sun.: 2-5*). ▶ **Lifeboat Museum**: models, pictures, photographs (*May Sep.: daily, 10-5 or by appointment*). ▶ **'Lifeboat Ruby, Arthur Read'** can be viewed at the **Lifeboat House** on the pier (*same times as museum*).

Nearby

▶ **Felbrigg Hall**★ (*3m SW*), one of the finest 17thC country houses in Norfolk (*late Mar.-late Oct.: wkend. and Bank Hols.; May-Sep.: Sat.-Mon., Wed., Thu., 1.30-5.30*). ▶ **Alby Lace Museum and Study Centre** (*5m S*): museum of lace in a craft centre complex (*early Mar.-early Dec.: Tue.-Fri. Sun., 10-5*). ☐

Practical information _____
CROMER
ⓘ town hall, Prince of Wales Road, ☎ (0263) 512497.
🚂 ☎ Norwich (0603) 632055.
Hotels:
★★ *Cliff House*, Overstrand Road, NR27 0AL, ☎ (0263) 514094, AC AM BA, 27 rm. Ⓟ ⅏ ♿ £56. Rest. ♦ £9.
★★ *Hotel de Paris*, Jetty Cliff, NR27 9HG, ☎ (0263) 513141, 55 rm. ⅍ ◈ ♿ ⌁ £43. Rest. ♦ ⌁ ♿ Cl. 1 Nov.-28 Feb. £5.50.
★ *West Parade Hotel*, 5 Runton Road, NR27 9AR, ☎ (0263) 512443, 29 rm. Ⓟ ⅍ £27. Rest. ♦ ♿ Cl. late Oct.-mid-Apr. £8.

⚠ *Forest Park C.S.*, Northrepps Road (456 pl) ☎ (0263) 513290;*Seacroft C.P.*, Runton Road (120 pl) ☎ (0263) 511722;at Trimingham, *Woodland C.P.* (140 pl) ☎ (026 379) 301.
Recommended
Cycle rental: *Trevor Medland*, 6 Brook Street, ☎ (0263) 512537.
Farmhouse: at Trimingham, *Beacon Farm*, Coast Road, ☎ (026 379) 675. £24 B. & B.
Golf course: Royal Cromer, 145 Overstrand Road, ☎ (0263) 512884.
Guesthouses: at Roughton, *Roughton Lodge Guest House*, Norwich Road, ☎ (0263) 761296, £20 B. & B.; *The Grove Guest House*, 95 Overstrand Road, ☎ (0263) 512412, Georgian house surrounded by 3 acres of grounds, £21 B. & B.
♥ Nick Deans, Lake Cottage, Hall Road, ☎ (026 377) 423, wood, stone and bronze carvings.

Be advised that hotels and restaurants in this Guide have perhaps changed addresses; prices indicated are also subject to modifications.

Nearby

NORTHREPPS, 3m SE

Restaurant:
♦ *Northrepps Cottage*, ☎ Overstrand (026 378) 202, AC BA Ⓟ Cl. Mon., Tue. (Sep.-May), 2 wks. Oct. £11.75.

THORPE MARKET, 4m S on A149

Hotel:
★★ *Elderton Lodge*, NR11 8TZ, ☎ Southrepps (026 379) 547, AC, 9 rm. Ⓟ ⅍ ⅏ ⌁ ♧ £42. Rest. ♦ ⌁ £10.

DEDHAM**

Ipswich, 11; Colchester, 8; London, 60 m
pop. 1,905 ☎ 0206   Essex B2

Stour riverside village has associations with artists John Constable and Sir Alfred Munnings. Built along one main street and rich in attractive buildings, mainly Georgian fronted, Dedham preserves its atmosphere.

▶ Two schools founded in the 18thC are among Dedham's fine buildings: ▶ the **grammar school,** and the **English school**, 1735. ▶ **St Mary's** church has splendid tower of knapped flint.

Nearby

▶ **Manningtree**: pleasant town at head of the Stour Estuary, merges with Mistley. ▶ **Flatford Mill** (→): much visited site of a famous Constable painting. ☐

Practical information _____
DEDHAM
ⓘ Dedham Vale Countryside Centre, Duchy Barn, The Drift, ☎ (0206) 323447.
🚂 Manningtree, ☎ Ipswich (0473) 690744.
Hotels:
● ★★★ *Maison Talbooth*, CO7 6HN, ☎ Colchester (0206) 322367, AC AM BA DI, 10 rm. Ⓟ ⅍ ♿ ⌖ ⌁ Early Victorian country mansion standing in extensive grounds overlooking the Dedham Vale. £110. Rest. ● ♦ £25.
★★ *Dedham Vale*, Stratford Road, CO7 6HW, ☎ Colchester (0206) 322273, AC AM BA DI, 6 rm. Ⓟ ⅍ ⅏ ♿ £80. Rest. ♦ ⌁ £20.
● ★ *Dedham Hall*, CO7 6AD, ☎ Colchester (0206) 323027, 10 rm. Ⓟ ⅍ ⅏ ♿ ⌖ £42. Rest. ♦ Cl. Wed. eve. £10.50.

Restaurant:
● ♦ *Le Talbooth*, Gun Hill, ☎ Colchester (0206) 323150, AC AM BA DI Ⓟ £24.
Recommended
Golf course: Leavenheath, Stoke-by-Nayland, Keepers Lane, ☎ 262836.

Nearby

CATTAWADE, 5m E on A137

Restaurant:
● ♦ *Bucks*, The Street, ☎ Colchester (0206) 392571, AC AM BA DI Ⓟ ⅍ ⅏ ♿ ⌁ ⌖ Cl. Sun. eve. Crab and lobster. Book. £16.

EAST BERGHOLT, 3m N off A12

Restaurant:
♦ *Fountain House*, The Street, ☎ Colchester (0206) 298232, AC BA Ⓟ ♿ ⌁ ⌖ Cl. 2 wks. Jan., Sun. eve., Mon. Chicken in puff pastry, chocolate fondue. Book. £11.

Inn or Pub:
Royal Oak (The Dickey) (Greene King), East End, ☎ Colchester (0206) 299221 Ⓟ ⅏ ♿ ♿ Bar snacks. £4.

⚠ *The Grange C.C.P.*, East End (145 pl), ☎ (0206) 298567.

DISS*

Norwich, 21; Ipswich, 26; London, 101 m
pop. 5,463 ☎ 0379   Norfolk B2

Modest but pleasant market town takes its name from
Saxon word meaning ditch or moat. The original town
was built around a 6 1/2-acre lake, **The Mere.**

▶ Good examples of Tudor, Georgian and Victorian buildings. ▶ **St. Mary's** church dominates **market square.**

Nearby
▶ **Bressingham Hall Gardens** (*4m W*): over 5000 hardy
perennials, on 6-acre site. Also collection of steam engines and rolling stock (*early May-end Sep.: Sun., Thu.,
11.30-6; late May-early Sep.: 11.30-5.30, Wed. also in
Aug.*). ▶ At Wingfield★ (*7m SE*) **Wingfield Castle**: moated
and walled castle, 14thC seat of powerful De La Poles.
Inside walls, visit the scented garden and **Tudor Manor
House** (*Easter-end Oct.: Sat., Sun., Bank Hol. Mon., 2-6*).
▶ **Wingfield College** (*7m SE*): intimate surroundings of
former Wingfield Manor House, founded in 1362. **Church**
houses tombs of Dukes of Suffolk. Arts and Music festival annually (*Easter-end Sep.: Sat., Sun., Bank Hol. Mon.,
2-6*). ▶ **Banham Zoo Monkey Sanctuary** (*6m NW*): includes camels, sea lions and flamingoes (*daily: 10-dusk*).□

Practical information ────────────────
DISS
▒▒▒ ☎ Norwich (0603) 632055.

Restaurant:
♦ *Salisbury House*, 84 Victoria Road, ☎ (0379) 4738 P
Cl. Sun.- Mon., 2 wks. Christmas, 1 wk. spring, 1 wk.
autumn, lunch. No children under 14. £16.50.

Inn or Pub:
Greyhound (Norwich), St. Nicolas Street, ☎ (037) 951613
P ⋘ ✿ Homemade bar meals, snacks, steaks. £5.50.

⅄ *Banham Zoo*, The Grove (28 pl), ☎ (095 387) 476;at
Roydon, *Roydon C.P.*, Godfrey Davis Park Homes
(130 pl), ☎ (0279 79) 2133;at Wortham, *Honeypot C.C.P.*,
Honeypot Farm (32 pl), ☎ (037 983) 312.

Recommended
Craft workshops: *Edwin Turner*, Home Farm, Gislingham,
Eye, ☎ (037 983) 280, reproduction furniture; *Pauline A.
Bracegirdle Pottery*, Lodge Cottage, Back Street, Gisling-
ham, ☎ (0449) 781470, domestic and decorative earthen-
ware and ceramics; *Morey Woodwork and Furniture*, 34
Croft Lane, ☎ (0379) 51798, woodwork.
Golf course: Stuston, ☎ code 2847.
Farmhouses: at Fersfield, *Strenneth Farmhouse*, Old Air-
field Road, ☎ (037 988) 8182, £23 B. & B.; at South
Lopham, *Maltings Farm*, Norton Road, ☎ (037 988) 201,
£21 B. & B.
Guesthouse: at Gariboldisham, Inglenenk Guest House,
Hofton Road, ☎ (095 381) 541, £25 B. & B.
♥ at Wilby, Church Pottery, Wilby Road, ☎ (037 984) 253,
woodcarved sculptures.

Nearby
BROCKDISH, 5m E on A143
Restaurant:
● ♦ *Sheriff House*, ☎ Hoxne (037 975) 316, AC BA P
✿ Cl. Wed. Breast of chicken with king prawns and truf-
fles. Pheasant in cognac with cream sauce and raisins.
Book. £15.

BROME, 2m S off A140
Hotels:
★★★ *Brome Grange*, Broom Eye, IP23 8AP, ☎ Eye
(0379) 870456, AC AM BA DI, 22 rm. P ⋘ ♿ ⌿ £40. Rest.
♦ ⌁ ♿ £9.
★★ *Oaksmere*, IP23 8AJ, ☎ (0379) 870326, AC AM BA
DI, 5 rm. P ≼ ⋘ ◈ £49.50. Rest. ♦ £8.

REDGRAVE, 4m W on B1113

Inn or Pub:
Cross Keys, ☎ Diss (0379) 898510, AC BA P ≼ ⋘ ◈ ♿
Restaurant meals, steak, gammon. £5.50.

SCOLE, 2m E on A140

Hotel:
★★ *Scole Inn* (B.W.H.), IP21 4DR, ☎ Diss (0379) 740481,
AC AM BA DI, 20 rm. P Coaching inn built in 1655 and
one of the most imposing in England. £50. Rest. ♦ ⌁
♿ £9.

DOWNHAM MARKET*

King's Lynn, 11; Ely, 19; London, 93 m
pop. 4,678 ☎ 0366   Norfolk B1

Attractive small town, once renowned for its butter,
sited on the edge of Fenland (→).

Nearby
▶ At **Denver** (*1m S*), a hamlet occupied since Roman times,
is the Denver Sluice, a key part of the Fenland drainage,
constructed by the Dutch engineer Vermuyden in 1652.
▶ **Denver Mill**: a 6-storey tower mill of 1865, with granary,
steam mill and original equipment.   □

Practical information ────────────────
▒▒▒ ☎ King's Lynn (0553) 772021.

Hotel:
★★ *Castle*, High Street, PE38 9HF, ☎ (0366) 382157, AC
AM BA DI, 14 rm. P £33. Rest. ♦ ⌁ £9.

⅄ at Stowbridge, *Woodlakes C.P.*, Holme Road (90 pl)
☎ (0553) 810414;at Whittington, *Grange Farm C.S.* (25
pl), ☎ (0366) 500307.

Recommended
Golf course: Ryston Park, Ely Road, Denver, ☎
382133.

EAST DEREHAM*

King's Lynn, 27; Norwich, 16; London, 109 m
pop. 12,364 ☎ 0362   Norfolk B1

▶ The poet William Cowper (1731-1800) is buried in
St. Nicholas church, fine Perpendicular. Bishop 'Bloody'
Bonner, who burnt non-conformists, lived in **Bishop Bonner Cottages.** 16thC thatched buildings now museum of
local archaeology and agriculture (*daily in summer*).

Nearby
▶ **North Elmham** (*5m N*): now a small village, it has a
large, ruined Anglo-Saxon **cathedral.**   □

Practical information ────────────────
EAST DEREHAM

Hotel:
★★ *Kings Head*, Norwich Street, NR19 1AD, ☎ Dereham (0362) 3842, AC AM BA DI, 17 rm. P ⌁ ⌿ 17thC inn
with walled garden and bowling green. £36. Rest. ● ♦
⌁ ♿ £9.95.

⅄ *Dereham Touring C.P.*, Norwich Road (55 pl), ☎
(0362) 4619.

Recommended
Golf course: Quebec Road, ☎ (0362) 5900.

Nearby
ELSING, 5m NE

Inn or Pub:
Mermaid Inn, Church Street, ☎ Swanton Morley (0362)
83640 P ⋘ ◌ ✿ Home-cooked lunches, grills. £5.

SHIPDHAM, 8m S on A1075

Hotel:
★★ ***Shipdham Place***, IP25 7LX, ☎ Dereham (0362) 820303, 9 rm. 🅿 ♨ 🐕 £55. Rest. ● ♦ £21.

ELY**

King's Lynn, 30; Cambridge, 16; London, 74 m
pop. 10,268 ☎ 0353 Cambridgeshire B2

It took Normans until 1071 to break down Ely's resistance to conquest. Ely (the name means 'Island of Eels') has one of the world's first **cathedrals**. Once an island isolated in marshland, Ely is now the centre for exploring The Fenland (→).

▶ The **cathedral**★★★ took 268 years to build starting from 1083. It is based on the site of a Benedictine abbey founded in 673. ▶ **The Holy Chapel** (1321) with beautiful carvings and tracery. Around the cathedral the **college buildings** include **Kings School**, founded by King Alfred the Great. **Cromwell House**, now a vicarage, was his residence 1626-1647. ▶ **Stained Glass Museum** in the cathedral: examples of stained glass and a history of the craft (*Mar.-Oct.: Mon-Fri., 10.30-4, Sun., 12-3, Sat., Bank Hols., 10.30-4*). ▶ **Riverside Walk** leads past old houses and **Maltings Public Hall**.

Nearby

▶ **Haddenham Farmland Museum** (*7m SE*) has a collection of agricultural implements and local bygones (*first Sun. each month, 2-dusk*). ☐

Practical information

ELY
ℹ public library, Palace Green, ☎ (0353) 2062.
🚆 ☎ (0353) 2908.

Hotel:
★★★ ***Lamb*** (Q.M.H.), Lynn Road, CB7 4EJ, ☎ (0353) 3574, AC AM BA DI, 32 rm. 🅿 ⚘ 🏠 £46. Rest. ♦ ♪ ♿ £7.50.

Restaurants:
● ♦ ***Old Fire Engine House***, 25 St. Mary's Street, ☎ (0353) 2582 🅿 ♨ ✗ Cl. 24 Dec.-7 Jan., Bank Hols., Sun. eve. Jugged hare, pike in white wine. Book. £11.50.
♦ ***Peking Duck***, 26 Fore Hill, ☎ (0353) 2948, AM 🐕 ♪ ✗ Cl. 25-26 Dec., Bank Hols., Mon., Tue. lunch. Lemon chicken, Peking duck. Book. £15.

Recommended
Golf course: Ely City, Cambridge Road, ☎ (0353) 2751/3317.

EPPING*

Harlow, 7; Woodford, 7; London, 20 m
pop. 11,688 ☎ 0378 Essex A3

A busy little town built around the long High Street that once marked the edge of 6000-acre **Epping Forest**.

▶ **High Beech**, in the heart of the forest, is the Epping Forest conservation centre.

Nearby

▶ **Ongar** (*5m E*) is the start of a 45m walk, St. Peter's Way, to Bradwell (→). **Blake Hall Gardens**, Ongar: a Japanese garden and picnic areas (*Apr.-Sep.: 10-6; Oct.-Mar.: 10-5*). ▶ **Greensted Saxon Church** (*4m NW*) is the only surviving Saxon log-built church c. 850. ▶ **The Rodings** (*5m N*): a group of villages along the Roding Valley. ▶ **Harlow** (*6m N*), established as a New Town in 1947 around the village of Old Harlow, was designed by Sir Frederick Gibberd. ▶ **Harlow Museum**: local and natural history exhibits are housed in Georgian manor house (*Mon., Wed., Fri.-Sun.: 10-5; Tue., Thu.: 10-9*). ☐

Practical information

EPPING
🚆 Harlow Mill, Harlow Town, ☎ Harlow (0279) 27091.
🚌 Epping, ☎ (01) 222 1234.
Car rental: Europcar, Harlow Coachworks, River Way, Templefields Estate; ☎ Harlow (0279) 39555.

Inn or Pub:
Forest Gate, Bell Common, ☎ (0378) 72312 🅿 ♨ 🐕 ♿ Bar snacks, homemade soup in winter. £2.

⛺ *Debden Hse Campsite*, Debden Green, Loughton (225 pl), ☎ (01) 508 9435.

Recommended
Golf course: Canon's Brook, Elizabeth Way, ☎ Harlow (0279) 21482; Theydon Bois, Theydon Road, ☎ (037 881) 3054.

Nearby

ABRIDGE, 4m S

Restaurant:
♦ ***Roding***, Market Place, ☎ Theydon Bois (037 881) 3030, AC AM BA DI 🅿 Cl. Mon., Sat. lunch, Sun. dinner, 26 Dec.-early Jan. £22.

HARLOW, 10m N on A414
ℹ ☎ (0223) 311999.

Hotel:
★★★ ***Green Man*** (T.H.F.), Mulberry Green, CM17 0ET, ☎ (0279) 442521, Tx 817972, AC AM BA DI, 55 rm. 🅿 ♨ £57. Rest. ♦ ♪ £10.50.

Inn or Pub:
Willow Beauty (Greene King), Hoddings Road, ☎ (027) 937328 🅿 ♨ ♿ Bar food, specials, eve. restaurant. £10.

NORTH WEALD BASSET, 3m NE on B181

Restaurant:
♦ ***Wo Ping Chinese***, 60-62 High Road, ☎ North Weald (037 882) 3815, AC AM BA DI 🅿 🐕 ♪ ✗ Cl. 25-26 Dec. Crab with ginger and spring onions. Book. £12.

OLD HARLOW, 1m N

Hotel:
★★★★ ***Churchgate Manor***, Churchgate Street, CM17 0JT, ☎ (0279) 20246, AC AM BA, 72 rm. 🅿 ⚘ ♨ 🐕 ♿ 🖼 🏠 £61. Rest. ● ♦ ♪ £10.

WALTHAM ABBEY, 6m W on A121

Restaurant:
♦ ***Blunk's***, 20 Market Square, ☎ Lea Valley (0992) 712352, AC AM BA DI 🅿 🐕 ♪ ✗ Moules marinières, trout, sole. Book. £25.

FAKENHAM*

King's Lynn, 21; Norwich, 27; London, 110 m
pop. 37,323 ☎ 0328 Norfolk B1

A pleasant market town dominated by the fine tower of its **church**. **Two Georgian inns** are features of the market place.

Nearby

▶ The **Thursford Collection** (*6m NE*) is the world's largest collection of steam locomotives (*end Mar.-end Oct.: daily, 2-5.30; Mar., Nov.: Sun, 2-5*). ☐

Practical information

ℹ Red Lion House, 37 Saturday Market Place, ☎ (0328) 51981.

Nearby

GUIST, 5m SE on A1067

Restaurant:
● ♦ *Tollbridge*, Dereham Road, ☎ Foulsham (036 284) 359, BA ℙ ⋘ ⋒ ⚘ Cl. 3 wks. Jan., 1st wk. Oct., Sun., Mon. Local crayfish and pike, breast of goose with lime sauce. Book. £17.

FELIXSTOWE*

Ipswich, 12; Colchester, 30; London, 90 m
pop. 21,560 ☎ 0394   Suffolk C2

A sheltered resort town on the Suffolk coast, Felixstowe is between the estuaries of the **Deben** and **Orwell**. It has a **leisure centre** with 3 swimming pools, seafront **gardens** along a 2-mile promenade and a pier. Felixstowe is now Britain's largest container port.

▶ **Felixstowe Ravelin Block Landguard Fort Museum:** 18thC building with displays on history of landguard fort. □

Practical information _____

ⓘ Undercliff Road West, ☎ (0394) 276770/282126.
🚃 ☎ Ipswich, (0473) 690744.
🚢 P. and O., ☎ (0394) 604802;.

Hotels:
★★★ *Orwell Moat House* (Q.M.H.), Hamilton Road, IP11 7DX, ☎ (0394) 285511, AC AM BA DI, 60 rm. ℙ ⋘ 🕭 ⌇ £65. Rest. ♦ ♪ £9.
★★ *Ordnance*, 1 Undercliff Road, IP11 8AN, ☎ (0394) 273427, AC AM BA DI, 11 rm. ℙ ⚘ £35. Rest. ♦ ♪ £10.

⚑ *Felixstowe Beach C.P.*, Walton Avenue (400 pl), ☎ (0394) 283393;*Suffolk Sands C.P.*, Carr Road (120 pl), ☎ (039 42) 73434.

Recommended
Golf course: Felixstowe Ferry, Ferry Road, ☎ (0394) 286834.

FENLAND*

A unique English landscape, scene of an unending quiet struggle between man and water. True fenland — grazed in summer, flooded in winter — now survives mainly in the Ouse Washes, a long strip of 4689 acres bounded by the Bedford rivers.

The Romans were the first to attempt and fail to drain the fens. Success began in the 17thC when a Dutch engineer Cornelius Vermuyden cut the 21m Old and New Bedford Rivers. Boating holidays on the Great Ouse lead to Bedford (→), Huntingdon (→), Ely (→) and Cambridge (→).

▶ **Wicken Fen**★ is the nation's oldest nature reserve of 600 undrained acres. Viewing hides and displays in reception area (*all year ex. Christmas Day*).▶ **Welches Dam**, on the Ouse Washes; the RSPB maintains public hides here plus information centre (*all year*).▶ **Welney Wildfowl Refuge**, near March. Numerous hides and a large observatory are maintained by the Wildfowl Trust and overlook 800 acres of the Ouse Washes (*daily: 10-5*).   □

FRAMLINGHAM**

Diss, 8; Ipswich, 19; London, 98 m
pop. 2,130 ☎ 0728   Suffolk C2

A small market town, Framlingham has one of the finest **ruined castles** in England.

▶ The **church**, with a 100 ft. tower, has a chancel specially built for the finest tombs in Suffolk. The church interior is a richly impressive memorial to the Howards, Dukes of Norfolk, who owned the castle for generations. ▶ The **castle**★★ has its outer walls and 13 square **towers**. Built on a Saxon site in the 1190s, the castle is mainly limestone. Sir Robert Hitcham, after purchasing the site in 1635, had all except the stonework of the castle pulled down — he established a poorhouse, almshouses and school instead. The **poorhouse**, 1729, survives within the castle keep.

Nearby

▶ **Dennington** (*3m N*): **church** crowded with treasures that include carved medieval benches and Georgian box pews; **stone chancel** is fancifully decorated. ▶ **Letheringham** (*4m S*): a ravished **priory**, pillaged **church**, **woodland** on the site of 3 ancient houses are among the ghosts of a village sited on the Upper Deben River. The **water mill** and **gardens** containing a variety of wildfowl are open to view. ▶ **Badingham** (*4m NE*): in the **church** fine example of a single hammer - beam roof from 1506 and a font on which scenes depicting the Seven Sacraments are carved. ▶ **Saxtead** (*2m W*) has a **Suffolk Post Windmill** on the green; open to view. ▶ **Bruisyard Vineyard and Winery** (*4m NE*) produces an estate-bottled wine from 10 acres of vines (*May-mid-Oct.: 10.30-5*). ▶ **Laxfield** (*6m N*): 16thC **guildhall** houses the **Laxfield and District Museum**, containing farm tools, archaeological and natural history, cottage kitchen and village shop display, an observation bee hive (*late May-early Oct.: Sat., Sun., 2-5; Jul., Aug.: Wed., 2-5*). ▶ In **St. Jacobs Hall** is **Jacob's Farm Childrens' Museum** (*Apr.-Oct.: Tue., Thu., Sun.; Nov.-Mar.: Sun., 10-5*).   □

Practical information _____

FRAMLINGHAM
🚃 Saxmundham, ☎ Ipswich (0473) 690744.

Hotel:
★★ *Crown* (T.H.F.), Market Hill, IP13 9AN, ☎ (0728) 723521, AC AM BA DI, 17 rm. ℙ £65.50. Rest. ♦ £9.

Restaurant:
♦ *Market Place*, 18 Market Hill, ☎ (0728) 724275, AC BA Cl. Sun., Mon., 3 wks. Jan. £12.
Guesthouse: at Hacheston, *Mr and Mrs Ardley*, Queens Cottage, thatched cottage build in 1450, £23 B. & B.

Nearby

BRANDESTON, 4m SW

Inn or Pub:
Queens Head (Adnams), ☎ Earl Soham (072 882) 307 ℙ ⋘ ⋒ 3 rm. Home-cooked food, bar snacks. £5.

Recommended
Craft workshop: Hector Moore, The Forge, ☎ (072 882) 354, blacksmith and metal works.

CAMPSEA ASH, 6m SE on B1078

Restaurant:
♦ *Old Rectory*, ☎ Wickham Market (0728) 746524, AM BA DI ℙ ⋘ ⋒ 🕭 6 rm. Sea bream stuffed with fennel, roast saddle of hare with sloe sauce. £12.50.

SAXTEAD GREEN, 2m W on B1119

Inn or Pub:
Volunteer (Tolly Cobbold), ☎ (072) 882289 ℙ ⋘ ⋒ 🕭 ⚘ Bar snacks, specials, grills in eve., salmon, steaks. £3.

FRINTON-ON-SEA*

Clacton-on-Sea, 8; Colchester, 16; London, 72 m
pop. 14,651 ☎ 025 56   Essex C3

This quiet Essex resort retains its charms: wide, tree-lined streets that lead down to the **seafront**. The beach is gently sloping and sandy with deck chairs and changing cabins.

Nearby

▶ **Walton-on-Naze** (*3m N*) is a traditional resort, livelier than Frinton. □

Practical information ──────────────

FRINTON-ON-SEA

══ ☎ (025 56) 4164.

Hotels:
★★ **Maplin**, The Esplanade, CO13 9EL, ☎ (025 56) 3832, AC AM BA DI, 12 rm. ℙ ▱ ⌿ £52. Rest. ♦ Cl. Jan. £12.
★★ **Rock**, The Esplanade, CO13, ☎ (025 56) 5173, AC AM BA DI, 6 rm. ℙ ⋞ ⌕ ⌿ £46. Rest. ♦ ⌗ £8.50.

Recommended
Golf course: The Esplanade, ☎ (025 56) 4618.

Nearby

THORPE-LE-SOKEN, 5m W on B1033

Restaurant:
♦ **Thorpe Lodge**, Landermere Road, ☎ Clacton-on-Sea (0255) 861509, AC BA DI ℙ rms. £15.50.

GREAT YARMOUTH

Cromer, 35; Lowestoft, 10; London, 128 m
pop. 54,777 ☎ 0493   Norfolk C1

This Norfolk coastal town is a major point of entry to the **Norfolk Broads** (→) and a thriving **port**. Yarmouth won its title 'great' in 1272, with a charter granted by Henry III. For centuries its main industry was herring fishing. The **Herring Fair**, held annually under a right granted by Edward the Confessor, survived 600 years.

▶ **The Rows** narrow alleys, in the oldest part of the market area, are the town's most distinctive feature. ▶ **St. Nicholas** church dates from the 12thC. Nearby stands the **Fisherman's Hospital**, founded 1702. ▶ **Marine Parade** lines a long sandy beach; **Great Yarmouth Pleasure Beach** has over 30 rides and funfair attractions. **The Marina Centre** on Marine Parade has a 25-metre pool with 'tropical' beach and waves. ▶ **Old Merchant's House** has 17thC paneled rooms and ornate plaster ceilings. ▶ **Tollhouse Museum**: a medieval building, one of England's oldest municipal buildings.

Nearby

▶ **Caister-on-Sea** (*4m N*): a seaside village with traces of the original Roman settlement. ▶ **Caister Castle**: a ruined, moated castle. Sir John Fastolf, the model for Shakespeare's Falstaff, lived here; then the great Paston family. ▶ **Gorleston**, a suburb of Great Yarmouth, is quieter than its neighbour. Flat, sandy beach with pebbles. ▶ **Burgh Castle**★ (*3 m W*); remains of a Roman fort overlook River Waveney (*daily: dawn to dusk*). □

Practical information ──────────────

GREAT YARMOUTH
ⓘ 1 South Quay, ☎ (0493) 846345; Marine Parade, ☎ (0493) 842195.
══ Norwich ☎ (0603) 632055.
══ Norfolk Line ☎ (0493) 856133.
Car rental: Avis, Airfield Service Station, Yarmouth Road, Caister-on-Sea, ☎ (0493) 51050, ☎ (0493) 50556 (rail/drive).

Hotels:
★★★★ **Sandringham**, 74-75 Marine Parade, NR30 2DH, ☎ (0493) 852427, Tx 975037, AC AM BA DI, 24 rm. ⋞ £50. Rest. ♦ ⌗ £10.
★★★ **Carlton**, Marine Parade, NR30 3JE, ☎ (0493) 855234, Tx 975642, AC AM BA DI, 94 rm. ℙ ⋞ ⌕ £50.50. Rest. ♦ ⌗ £9.
★★★ **Star** (QMH), 24 Hall Quay, NR31 NR3, ☎

(0493)842294, Tx 975080, AC AM BA DI, 42 rm. ℙ ⋞ ⌕ £45. Rest. ♦ ⌗ ⌕ £6.
● ★★ **Imperial**, North Drive, NR30 1EQ, ☎ (0493) 851113, AC AM BA DI, 41 rm. ℙ ⋞ ⌕ ⌿ £45. Rest. ♦ ⌗ £12.
★★ **Burlington**, North Drive, NR30 1EG, ☎ (0493) 844568, AC BA, 32 rm. ℙ ⋞ ⌕ ⊛ ▱ £38. Rest. ♦ ⌗ ⌕ Cl. Nov.-Feb. £9.

Inn or Pub:
Allens (Adnams), 2 Greyfriars Way, ☎ (0493) 856758, AC AM BA ⌕ ⊛ Bar snacks. £2.

⚘ *Seashore H.C.*, North Denes (230 pl), ☎ (0493) 851131;*Vauxhall H.P.*, 80 Acle New Road (392 pl), ☎ (0493) 857231; at Belton, *Wild Duck C.C.S.*, Howards Common (150 pl), ☎ (0493) 780268; at Burgh Castle, *Burgh Castle Marina*, Butt Lane (60 pl), ☎ (0493) 780331; at Caister-on-Sea, *Grasmere C.P.*, 7 Bultitudes Loke, Yarmouth Road (46 pl), ☎ (0493) 720382; at Hemsby, *Newport C.P.* (90 pl), ☎ (0493) 730404; at Oby, *Bureside H.P.*, Boundary Farm (55 pl), ☎ (049 377) 233; at Ormesby St. Margaret, *California Cliffs CP* (40 pl), ☎ (0493) 730584; at Scratby, *Scratby Hall C.P.* (108 pl), ☎ (0493) 730283.

Recommended
Cycle rental: *Lawford Cycles*, 224 Northgate Street, ☎ (0493) 2741.
Farmhouse. at Burgh Castle, *Macleod's, Church Farm*, ☎ (0493) 780251, fort of Burgh Castle is in the farm, £20 B. & B.
Golf course: Gorleston, Warren Road, ☎ (0493) 661911; Beach House, Caister-on-Sea, ☎ (0493) 728699.

Nearby

ROLLESBY, 9m S on A149

Hotel:
★ **Old Court House**, Court Road, NR29 5HG, ☎ Fleggburgh (049 377) 865, 8 rm. ℙ ⌕ ▱ ♤ £25. Rest. ♦ Cl. 15 Nov.-5 Feb. £4.

WINTERTON-ON-SEA, 9m N on B1159

Hotel:
Fisherman's Return, The Lane, NR29 4BN, ☎ (049 376) 305, 4 rm. Traditional 17thC inn set just behind the dunes. £26. Rest. ♦ Cl. Christmas £6.40.

HADLEIGH*

Ipswich, 9; Sudbury, 12; London, 73 m
pop. 5,858 ☎ 047 32   Suffolk B2

An attractive **market town**, Hadleigh was a royal Viking town that became, in the 14thC, the most prosperous wool town in the country.

▶ Note in walking down the High Street **No.44**: good example of pargetting (decorative plasterwork); **Nos.62-66**, well-restored Charles II houses; **No.33** good Georgian; **Nos.108-110** dated 1649 with courtyard. **Church Street** leads to three remarkable buildings: the **flint church**, 14thC, the brick **deanery tower**, 1495, and the half-timbered **guildhall**, 1430.

Nearby

▶ **Wolves Wood** (*1m NE*): mixed woodland, maintained by the RSPB. □

Practical information ──────────────
══ ☎ Colchester (0206) 564777.

Hotel:
★★ **Edgehill**, 2 High Street, IP7 5AH, ☎ (0473) 822458, 6 rm. ℙ £34. Rest. ♦ £17.50.

Restaurants:
● ♦ **Weaver's**, 25 High Street, ☎ (0473) 827247, AC BA ▨ ⌗ ⊛ Cl. 25 Dec.-1 Jan., Sun., Mon. Guinea fowl pie, rack of lamb. Book. £11.

♦ *Spinning Wheel*, 117-119 High Street, ☎ (0473) 822175, AC AM BA DI ♪ ✶ Cl. 26 Dec. Book. £15.
♦ *Taviton's*, 103 High Street, ☎ (0473) 822820, AC BA P Cl. Mon. £13.50.

Recommended
Antique shops: *Randolph*, 97-99 High Street, ☎ (0473) 823789, furniture; *Gordon Sutcliffe*, 105 High Street, ☎ (0473) 823464, furniture.
Farmhouse: at Hitcham, *Wetherden Hall*, ☎ Bildeston (0449) 740412, £20 B. & B.

HALESWORTH*

Lowestoft, 21; Ipswich, 24; London, 111 m
pop. 3,927 ☎ 098 67   Suffolk C2

Attractive small town. A market has been held since 1222 in **market place** with notable timber-framed late Tudor building; nearby an ornamental **Gothic house** facing the **church**.

▶ **Almshouses** dated 1686 alongside the churchyard are now library and gallery.▶ **Brewery House**, restored 1970, was home of famous botanists William Jackson Hooker and son Joseph Dalton Hooker.

Nearby

▶ **Fressingfield** (*10m W*): fine old manor houses and village buildings include **Ufford's Hall**, the former guildhall. The **church** is enriched by a hammer - beam roof and fine 15thC carved bench ends. On one bench are the initials A.P.: Chaucer's grandaughter, Alice de la Pole. ▶ **Heveningham Hall★** (*5m SW*) is the finest Palladian building in Suffolk, designed by Sir Robert Taylor, architect to King George III.   □

Practical information ─────────

🚂 ☎ Ipswich (0473) 690744.

Nearby

BLYFORD, 2 1/2m E on B1123

Inn or Pub:
Queen's Head (Adnams), ☎ Blythburgh (050) 270404 P ⋸ ₩ 🔍 ♿ ✶ Bar snacks, homemade curry, pizza, pâtés. £2.95.

FRESSINGFIELD, 10m W on B1116

Restaurant:
● ♦ *Fox and Goose*, ☎ (037 986) 247, AC AM BA DI P 🔍 ✶ Cl. 23-26 Dec., 26 Jan.-9 Feb., Tue., Sun. dinner Nov.-Mar. Book. £22.

SIBTON, 5m S

Inn or Pub:
White Horse, Halesworth Road, ☎ Peasenhall (072 879) 337 P ₩ 🔍 3 rm. Bar snacks, steak, fish. £4.50.

YOXFORD, 7m S off A12

Restaurant:
♦ *Jacey's*, Blythburgh House, High Street, ☎ (072 877) 298, AC AM BA 🔍 ♪ ✶ Cl. 26 Dec., Sun., Mon. lunch. Goose breast with fruit stuffing. Book. £13.50.

HARWICH

Colchester, 20; Ipswich, 26; London, 76 m
pop. 17,245 ☎ 0255   Essex C2

This seafaring town on the northern tip of the Essex coast is a·point of departure for North Sea ferries (at Parkeston Quay, *2m W on River Stour*). Harwich was headquarters of the king's navy in the 17thC, when Samuel Pepys was the town's M.P. ▶ **Old Harwich**, a conservation area, retains the gridiron pattern of streets laid down in the Middle Ages. ▶ At the

Navyard Wharf, site of old naval yard, a list records the men-of-war built here 1660-1827.▶ At **Harwich Green** stands a unique manually operated treadwheel crane. The **Redoubt** nearby is a Martello Tower fortress.

Nearby

▶ **Dovercourt** (*1m S*), a holiday suburb of Harwich, once an ancient settlement included in the Domesday Book. ▶ **All Saints** church has Norman traces.▶ **Great Oakley** (*6m SW*) and **Little Oakley** (*4m SW*): two villages with well-sited **churches**. ▶ **Skipper's Island** is a 160-acre reserve of the Essex Naturalists Trust.   □

Practical information ─────────

HARWICH
ⓘ Parkeston Quay, ☎ (0255) 506139 (summer only).
🚢 DFDS Seaways, ☎ (0255) 554681; Sealink ☎ (0255) 507022.
Car rental: Hertz, Willhire Ltd, Vines Service Station, Main Road, ☎ (0255) 504744.

Hotel:
★ *Park*, Main Road, CO12 3LD, ☎ (0255) 503307, BA DI, 10 rm. P ⋸ £25. Rest. ♦ ♪ ♿ £5.

Restaurant:
♦ *Pier*, The Quay, ☎ (0255) 503363, AC AM BA DI P ⋸ ♪ ✶ Cl. Christmas. Lobster, salmon, trout. Book. £16.50.

🍴 at Bradfield, *Strangers Home Inn*, The Street (255 pl) ☎ (025 587) 304;at Harwich and Dovercourt, *Dovercourt C.P.*, Low Road (140 pl), ☎ (0255) 503433.

Nearby

DOVERCOURT, 1m SW

Hotel:
★★★ *Tower*, Main Road, CO12 3PJ, ☎ Harwich (0255) 504952, AC AM BA DI, 16 rm. P ⋸ ₩ ♿ £45. Rest. ♦ ♪ ♿ Cl. Christmas and Boxing Day. £12.

WIX CROSS, 6m W on A120

Inn or Pub:
Waggon at Wix, ☎ (025 587) 279 P ⋸ ₩ 🔍 ♿ Bar snacks, home-cooked food, steaks and salads. £5.50.

Recommended
Golf course: Parkeston Road, ☎ (025 55) 3616.

HOLT*

Cromer, 9; Fakenham, 12; London, 123 m
pop. 2,502 ☎ 0263 (71)   Norfolk B1

A neat Georgian market town of colour-washed houses with ancient **school house** founded 1555, rebuilt 1858 in a Gothic style. The **church**, restored by William Butterfield in the 19thC, has a fine east window.

▶ **Kelling Park Aviaries** has large collection of birds, owls and a rich variety of flowers (*daily: 10-8*).

Nearby

▶ **Letheringsett** village (*1m W*) on the River Glaven with 1818 iron bridge. The **church** has 11thC round tower. ▶ **Glavenside** (*2m W*) has 4 acres of splendid gardens (*Jan.-Mar.: 10-4; Apr.-Oct.: 9-6; Nov.-Dec.: 10-4*).   □

Practical information ─────────

Hotels:
★★ *Kelling Park*, Weybourne Road, Kelling, NR25 7ER, ☎ (0263) 712235, Tx 975148, 7 rm. ⋸ ₩ 🔍 ♪ ♨ £42. Rest. ♦ ♪ £8.95.
★ *Lawns*, 26 Station Road, NR25 6BS, ☎ (0263) 713390, 12 rm. P ⋸ ₩ 🔍 ♿ £39. Rest. ♦ ♪ ♿ £9.

Recommended
Craft workshops: at Erpingham, *Alby Crafts*, Cromer Road, ☎ (0263) 761590, work of over 300 craftsmen.
♥ Larners, 10 Market Place, ☎ (0263) 712323, over ninety kinds of cheese, plus freshly ground coffee.

HORNING

Great Yarmouth, 17; Norwich, 11; London, 122 m
pop. 1,033 ☎ 0692   Norfolk C1

A mile-long street of thatched houses runs along the north bank of River Bure at this popular broadland boating centre. Boathouses, Edwardian villas and plentiful moorings. River ferry is on site of a crossing in use for 1000 years.   □

Practical Information _____

HORNING

Hotels:
★★ *Petersfield House*, Lower Street, NR12 8PF, ☎ (0692) 630741, AC AM BA DI, 16 rm. ℗ ⚏ ⚑ ♨ £42. Rest. ♦ ♪ ♿ £10.
★ *Swan*, NR12 8AA, ☎ (0692) 630316, AC AM BA, 11 rm. ℗ ⚞ ⚏ ⚑ £45. Rest. ♦ £9.

Nearby

NEATISHEAD

Hotel:
★★ *Barton Angler Lodge*, Instead Road, NR12 8XP, ☎ Horning (0692) 630740, AC AM BA DI, 7 rm. ℗ ⚞ ⚏ ⚑ £50. Rest. ♦ ♪ Cl. Sun. £17.

Recommended
Guesthouse: *Regency Guest House*, Post Office Stores, ☎ (0692) 630233, £21 B. & B.

HUNSTANTON*

Cromer, 40; King's Lynn, 16; London, 138 m
pop. 3,990 ☎ 048 53   Norfolk B1

The only East Anglian seaside resort that faces west, the striped cliffs, made of successive layers of carr stone, red chalk and white chalk are the town's landmark. Popular with boating and water skiing enthusiasts, it is a base for exploring the north Norfolk coast.

► **Old Hunstanton** (*2m N*) is at the mouth of the Wash and has a fine sandy beach. **Hunstanton Hall:** 16thC residence of the Le Strange family who arrived with the invasion in 1066. ► At **Heacham** (*2m S*) is Caley Mill, where Norfolk lavender is grown and processed. The mill can be toured (*Easter-Sep.: daily, 10-6; Oct.-Easter: — shop and lavender plants only — Mon.-Fri., 9-5*).

Nearby

► At **Sandringham**★★ (*8m S*) is **Sandringham House**, vast Victorian mansion built by Edward, Prince of Wales in 1870; an official residence of H.M. The Queen. Some rooms are open to the public as are the grounds (*Apr.-Sep.: Mon.-Thu., 10.30-4.45, Sun., 11.30-4.45; house and grounds closed 21 Jul.-9 Aug.*). ► **Wolferton** (*9m S*): the **railway station** nearby has been preserved, with royal waiting rooms and relics. ► **Holme-next-the-Sea** (*3m NE*) is a long, unspoilt sandy beach and has a 400-acre nature reserve.   □

Practical information _____

HUNSTANTON

ℹ The Green, ☎ (048 53) 2610.
🚂 ☎ King's Lynn, (0553) 772021.

⚓ *Searles H.C.*, South Beach (290 pl), ☎ (048 53) 34211;at Heacham, *Heacham Beach C.P.*, South Beach Road (20 pl), ☎ (0485) 70270.

Nearby

BRANCASTLE STAITHE, 8m E on Coast Road

Inn or Pub:
Jolly Sailors, ▣ (0485) 210314, AC BA DI ℗ ⚞ ⚏ ⚑ Bar snacks and restaurant menu, Staithe mussels, local game and fish. £12.

Recommended
Cycle hire: *North Norfolk Cycle Hire*, The Dial House, The Harbour, ☎ (0485) 210719.

DERSINGHAM, 5m S

Inn or Pub:
Feathers (Bass Charrington), Manor Road, ☎ Dersington (402 07) 0485, AC BA ℗ ⚏ ⚑ 6 rm. Salads, basket meals, sandwiches, ploughmans. £4.75.

OLD HUNSTANTON, 1/2m S on A149

Hotels:
★★ *Caley Hall*, PE36 6HH, ☎ (048 53) 33486, BA, 25 rm. ⚑ ♿ £39. Rest. ♦ ♪ ♿ Cl. Sun. eve. £8.50.
★★ *Lodge*, Hunstanton Road, PE36 6HX, ☎ (048 53) 2896, AC BA, 15 rm. ▣ ⚏ ♨ £40. Rest. ♦ ♪ ♿ £8.
★★ *Le Strange Arms* (CNS), Golf Course Road, PE36 6JJ, ☎ (048 53) 2810, AC AM BA DI, 30 rm. ℗ ⚞ ⚏ ⚜ ♪♫ £53. Rest. ♦ ♪ £10.
★ *Linksway*, Golf Course Road, PE36 6JE, ☎ Hunstanton (048 53) 2209, 9 rm. ℗ ⚞ ⚏ ⚑ ⚜ ▨ ♩ £44 (incl. dinner). Rest. ♦ ♪ Cl. 15 Nov.-28 Feb.

Recommended
Golf course: Old Hunstanton, ☎ (048 53) 2811.

TITCHWELL, 9m E on A149

Hotel:
★★ *Titchwell Manor* (B.W.H.), PE31 8BB, ☎ Brancaster (0485) 210221, AC AM BA DI, 10 rm. ⚞ ⚏ ⚑ ♩ ♨ £45. Rest. ♦ £10.

HUNTINGDON*

Peterborough, 18; Cambridge, 16; London, 61 m
pop. 18,205 ☎ 0480   Cambridgeshire A2

Oliver Cromwell was born in this quiet town at the western edge of Fenland (→).

► The **Cromwell Museum**, in his former grammar school includes portraits and relics of the Cromwell family and the Puritan revolution of 1640-1660 (*Jan.-Mar.: Tue.-Fri., 2-5, Sat., 11-1, 2-4, Sun., 2-4; Apr.-Oct.: Tue.-Fri., 11-1, 2-5, Sat., Sun., 11-1, 2-4; Nov.-Dec.: Tue.-Fri., 2-5, Sat., 11-1, 2-4, Sun., 2-4; Cl. Bank Hols.*).

Nearby

► Buckden (*5m SW*): **Buckden Palace**, restored parts of the ancient palace of Bishops of Lincoln. Gardens (*daily: 10-6*).► **Godmanchester** (*1m S*): Roman-founded town; thatched houses surround **St. Mary's church**, 13th-15thC. ► **Island Hall** is a mid-18thC mansion with fine paneled rooms (*early Jun.: Sun.; Jul.-Sep.: Wed., Sun., 2.30-5.30*). ► **Hinchingbrooke House** (*3/4m W*) is a 13thC Benedictine nunnery connected to a Tudor mansion in the 16thC (*Apr.-Aug.: Sun. and Bank Hol. Mon., 2-5*). ► **Kimbolton Castle**★ (*8m SW*) is a Tudor house; mural paintings by Pellegrini and an Adam gatehouse (*Easter Sun., Mon., Bank Hols., Sun. end Jul.-end Aug: 2-6*). ► **St. Ives★** (*5m E*): bridging the River Ouse. A miniature **chapel** on the **15thC bridge** is one of only 3 in Britain.   □

Practical information _____

HUNTINGDON
ℹ library, Princes Street, ☎ (0480) 425831 (summer) / 425801 (winter).

▦▦ ☎ 54468.

Hotels:
★★ *George* (T.H.F.), George Street, PE18 6AB, ☎ (0480) 53096, AC AM BA DI, 25 rm. P 17thC posting house with a picturesque galleried courtyard. £58. Rest. ♦ £10.
★★ *Old Bridge* (Poste), High Street, PE18 6TQ, ☎ (0480) 52681, Tx 32706, AC AM BA DI, 22 rm. P ⁂ ⁑ ♩ £65. Rest. ♦ £15.

⅄ *Quiet Waters C.P.*, Hemingford Abbots (20 pl), ☎ (0480) 63405;at Grafham, *Old Manor C.P.*, Church Lane (66 pl), ☎ (0480) 810264; at Willingham, *Alwyn C.C.P.*, Over Road (90 pl), ☎ (0954) 60977; *Roseberry T.P.*, Eairth Road (80 pl), ☎ (0954) 60346.

Recommended
Golf course: Ramsey, Abbey Terrace, ☎ (0487) 812600.

Nearby

BRAMPTON, 1m W on A604

Hotel:
★★★ *Brampton* (Kingsmead), A1 Roundabout, PE18 8NH, ☎ Huntingdon (0480) 810434, AC AM BA DI, 17 rm. P ⁂ £63. Rest. ♦ ♩ ⅋ £9.

BUCKDEN, 3m S off A1

Hotel:
★ *George*, High Street, PE19 9XA, ☎ Huntingdon (0480) 810307, Tx 32394, AC AM BA DI, 12 rm. P ⁂ Traditional 16thC coaching inn on the old North Road. £47.50. Rest. ♦ ♩ £14.

GODMANCHESTER, 1m S on B1043

Hotel:
★ *Black Bull*, Post Street, PE18 8AQ, ☎ Huntingdon (0480) 53310, 9 rm. P ⁂ £28. Rest. ♦ ♩ ⅋ £12.

ELSWORTH, 7m SE

Restaurant:
● ♦ *Meadow Farm*, Broad End, ☎ Elsworth (095 47) 413, AC AM BA P ⁂ ⁑ ⅋ Cl. 1 wk. Dec., Apr., Aug., Oct., Sun., Mon., lunch by arrangement only. Book. £14.

Inn or Pub:
George Dragon (Tolly Cobbold), ☎ (095 47) 236, AC AM DI P ⁂ ⁑ ⅋ Bar meals, steaks, fish, daily specials, à la carte menu. £7.

ELTISLEY, 9m S on A45

Hotel:
★ *Leeds Arms*, The Green, PE19 4TG, ☎ Croxton (048 087) 283, AC BA, 10 rm. P ⁑ ⅋ 18thC coaching inn overlooking the village green. £37.50. Rest. ♦ ♩ ⅋ £9.

FEN DRAYTON, 6 1/2m SE on A604

Inn or Pub:
Three Tuns (Greene King), ☎ Swavesey (0954) 30242 P ⁂ ⅋ Bar meals ex. Sun. eve., barbecues Sun. eve. in summer. £6.

KEYSTON, 10m W

Restaurant:
♦ *Pheasant Inn*, Village Loop Road, ☎ Bythorn (080 14) 241, AC AM BA DI P Cl. 3 days Christmas. £14.50.

KIMBOLTON, 9m SW on A45

Restaurant:
♦ *La Côte d'Or*, High Street, ☎ Huntingdon (0480) 861587, AC BA P ⁑ ⁂ ⅋ Cl. Christmas, 1 Jan., Tue., Sun. eve. Gigot d'agneau. No children under 6. Book. £19.50.

NEEDINGWORTH, 2m E on A1123

Hotel:
Pike and Eel, Overcote Lane, PE17 3TW, ☎ St.Ives (0480) 63336, AC AM BA DI, 12 rm. P ⁑ ⁂ ⅋ Inn with lawns going down to the River Ouse. £39. Rest. ♦ ♩ ⅋ Cl. 24-25 Dec., 1 Jan. £15.

ST. IVES, 7m E off A1123

Hotel:
★★ *Slepe Hall*, Ramsey Road, PE17 4RB, ☎ (0480) 63122, AC AM BA DI, 14 rm. P £50. Rest. ♦ ♩ ⅋ Cl. 25-26 Dec. £10.50.

Recommended
Craft workshops: *Engraved Glass*, 20 East Street, ☎ (0480) 61065, engraved glassware, crystals, trophies, souvenirs and gifts; *L'Bidi Studio*, 40 The Broadway, ☎ (0480) 810545, hand-painted silks, scarves, tops, cushions and cards.
Golf course: ☎ (0480) 64459.

ST. NEOTS, 9m S

Restaurant:
♦ *Chequers*, St. Mary's Street, ☎ Huntingdon (0480) 72116, AC AM BA DI P ⁑ ⅋ Cl. 25 Dec. eve. 9 rm. Veal in brandy with mushroom sauce. Book. £20.

Recommended
Golf course: Crosshall Road, ☎ (0480) 72363.

⅄ *St. Neots C.S.*, Rush Meadow (180 pl), ☎ (0480) 74404.

SWAVESEY, 11 1/2m SE on A604

Inn or Pub:
Trinity Foot (Whitbread), ☎ (0954) 30315 P ⁂ ⅋ Home-cooked food, oysters, Scotch salmon, crab salad, local beef, English lamb. £10.

IPSWICH★★

Norwich, 40; Colchester, 19; London, 76 m
pop. 129,661 ☎ 0473   Suffolk C2

Ipswich is the thriving county town of Suffolk and one of the oldest towns in England, dating back to Anglo-Saxon 10thC. Designated a heritage town, it boasts a wealth of medieval buildings including a dozen such churches.

▶ **Christchurch Mansion★**, a Tudor mansion in the central part of Ipswich, is set in a park; rooms furnished in style of 16th-19thC. ▶ **Wolsey Memorial Art Gallery** opened in 1931, attached to the mansion, presents many works by Gainsborough, Constable and other Suffolk artists (*all year: Mon.-Sat., 10-5, dusk in winter, Sun., 2.30-4.30, dusk in winter; open some Bank Hols.*). ▶ Signposted, mile-long **Town Trail** will take you through the old town. At **Corn Hill** is the Anglo-Saxon market place. ▶ Walk down Tavern Street to the **Great White House Hotel**, described by Dickens in the Pickwick Papers: one of the hotel's notable visitors was George II in 1737. Walk down Tower Street to the Church of St. Mary: the town's main civic church. **St. Lawrence:** grand tower begun in 1431 and rebuilt with flushwork in 1882 by architect Frederick Baines. ▶ Near the **Buttermarket** is the **ancient house**, built 1567, which boasts a splendid example of **pargetting**, decorative plasterwork for which the region is famed. ▶ **Wolsey's Gateway** is all that remains of the college founded in 1526 by Cardinal Wolsey. ▶ **Ipswich Museum** (High Street): replicas of treasures found at the burial sites of Sutton Hoo and Mildenhall (*all year: Mon.-Sat., ex. Bank Hols.*).

Nearby

▶ The **Rosarium**, Claydon (*4m NW*): over 400 varieties in garden dedicated to old and rare roses. Also 18thC **lime kiln** in grounds. ▶ **Otley Hall**, (*8m NE*): moated 15thC hall with superb English domestic architecture. Set in 10 acres of informal grounds (*Easter Sun., Bank Hols.: 2-6*). ▶ **Helmingham Hall Gardens★** (*10m N*): a variety of gardens and safari rides in deer park (*early May-late Sep.: Sun., 2-6*).   □

Practical information _____

IPSWICH

ℹ town hall, Princes Street, ☎ (0473)58070.

🚂 ☎ 690744.

Car rental: Europcar, R.E. Cattermole Ltd, West End Road, ☎ (0473) 211067.

Hotels:

● ★★★ *Belstead Brook*, Belstead Road, IP2 0HD, ☎ (0473) 684241, Tx 987674, AC AM BA DI, 33 rm. ℙ ⬜ ⌂ 🍽 Elizabethan manor house in 7 acres of garden and parkland. £49. Rest. ♦ £12.

● ★★★ *Marlborough*, 73 Henley Road, IP1 3SP, ☎ (0473) 57677, Tx 81630, AC AM BA DI, 22 rm. ℙ ⬜ ⌂ ⌄ £80. Rest. ● ♦♦ £20.

★★ *Crown and Anchor*, Westgate Street, IP1 3EQ, ☎ (0473) 58506, AC AM BA DI, 55 rm. ℙ £48. Rest. ♦ ♪ £9.

★★ *Post House* (T.H.F.), London Road, IP2 0UA, ☎ (0473) 212313, Tx 987150, AC AM BA DI, 118 rm. ℙ ⬜ ⌂ ⌂ ⬜ £52. Rest. ♦ ♪ ⌂ £11.

Restaurants:

● ♦ *Singing Chef*, 200 St. Helen's Street, ☎ (0473) 55236, AC BA DI ℙ ⬜ ♪ ⌂ 🍽 Cl. last 2 wks. Aug., Sun., Mon. Book. £12.

♦ *Kwok's Rendezvous*, 23 St. Nicholas Street, ☎ (0473) 56833, AM DI ℙ ♪ ⌂ 🍽 Cl. Sun., 2 wks. Feb. Crispy duck. Book. £15.

♦ *Rajasthan*, 0 Orwell Place, ☎ (0473) 51397, AC AM BA DI ⬜ ♪ 🍽 Cl. 25-26 Dec. Book. £12.50.

Inns or Pubs:

Arboretum (Tolly Cobbold), High Street, ☎ (0473) 723355 ℙ ⌂ Bar snacks and specials.

Thrasher (Greene King), Nacton Road, ☎ (0473) 73355 ℙ ⬜ ⌂ 🍽 Bar snacks and meals, specials on Thu.-Fri. £3.

Recommended

Cycle rental: *The Bicycle Doctor,* 18 Bartholomew Street, ☎ (0473) 59853.

Farmhouse: at Witnesham, *Cowslip Farm,* ☎ (047 385) 267, £23 B. & B.

Riding school: at Swilland, *Newton Hall Equitation Centre,* ☎ (047 385) 616.

♥ at Kersey, River House Potter, The Street, ☎ (0473) 822092, handmade tableware, vases, lamps, bowls, garden pots.

Nearby

HINTLESHAM, 5m W on A1071

Hotel:

★★★ *Hintlesham Hall*, IP8 3NS, ☎ (047 387) 268, AC AM BA DI, 10 rm. ℙ ≷ ⬜ ⌂ ⌨ ⌂ No children under 10. £70. Rest. ● ♦ £20.

PIN MILL, 7m SE off B1465

Inn or Pub:

Butt Oyster (Tolly Cobbold), ☎ Woolverstone (047 384) 764 ℙ ≷ ⬜ 🍽 Home-cooked food. £3.50.

KING'S LYNN ★★

Cromer, 42; Peterborough, 35; London, 104 m
pop. 37,323 ☎ 0553
Norfolk B1

An ancient and busy port on the River Ouse, the town is rich in medieval architecture, relics of sea trade with Germany, the Low Countries and Baltic ports. **The Customs House** (1683), with its statue of Charles II, is a handsome building and the town's distinctive landmark.

▶ The **Corn Exchange** dates from 1854. ▶ **St. Nicholas Street**, leading from the market square, contains fine medieval houses. **St. Nicholas Chapel**, mainly 15thC, is the setting for the annual Kings Lynn Festival. ▶ **King Street** has **St. George's Guildhall**, built 1406 and the largest surviving medieval guildhall in England. Also a

museum of local history, and **Medieval Merchant's House**. ▶ In **Kings Staithe Square** is **Bank House**, with statue of Charles I in a niche. ▶ **Queen Street** continuing from King Street has many fine houses, including **Clifton House** and **Thoresby College**, built 1500 for priests of the Trinity Guild. ▶ In the **Saturday market place** is the huge **St. Margaret's** Church, 230 ft. long, founded 12thC. ▶ The **town hall** adjoins the **guildhall**, built for the guild of the Holy Trinity in 1421. The regalia on display in the guildhall include King John's cup — dating from 1340 — and King John's sword. ▶ **Nelson Street**, many fine old houses including **Hampton Court**, 15thC. ▶ The **museum** in Market Street has extensive collection of local history (*Mon.-Sat.: 10-5*). ▶ The **South Gate**, built 1520, is the only surviving town gate. ▶ **Red Mount** Chapel, set in **The Walk**, dates from 1485.

Nearby

▶ The **Wiggenhalls** (*4m S*) a group of four villages by the River Ouse: each has a remarkable church. ▶ **Wiggenhall St. Germans**; 15thC benches with fine carvings. Nearby is red brick **Fitton Hall**. ▶ **Wiggenhall St. Mary the Virgin** also has fine carved benches, described as the best in the country. ▶ **Wiggenhall St. Mary Magdalen★** has 18thC box pews, 17thC panelling and 15thC glass. ▶ **Terrington St. Clement** (*4m N*): church of barnack stone sometimes called 'the cathedral of the marshland'. Its massive tower was a refuge for villagers in floods of 1613 and 1670. ▶ **Walpole St. Peter** (*9m W*): one of the very finest churches in the Norfolk marshlands. ▶ **Castle Rising★** (*4m NE*). Massive, Norman, square-built **castle**, reached by decorated doorway and fine 12thC hall keep, dominates this small village. The **church**, 12thC, has been restored, but the **Hospital of the Holy and Undivided Trinity** opposite is intact from its foundation in 1614 as an almshouse. ▶ At **Houghton** is **Houghton Hall★**, built by Sir Robert Walpole in the 1730s (*Easter Sun.-end Sep.: Sun., Thu. & Bank Hols., 12-5.30*). The **village**, rebuilt in the 18thC, has pairs of cottages in avenues of limes. ▶ **North Runcton** (*5m S*): fine classical **church**, built 1713, has Ionic columns. □

Practical information _____

ℹ The Old Gaol House, Saturday Market Place, ☎ (0553) 763044.

🚂 ☎ 772021.

Car rental: Europcar, Swan Street Motors, Hardwick Road, ☎ (0553) 775005.

Hotels:

★★★ *Duke's Head* (T.H.F.), Tuesday Market Place, ☎ (0553) 774996, Tx 817349, AC BA AM DI, 72 rms ℙ £65. Rest. ♦ £12.

★★ *Stuart House*, Goodwins Road, ☎ (0553) 2169, Tx 817209, AC AM BA, 21 rms, ℙ ⬜ £35. Rest. ♦ ♪ Cl. 24 Dec.-2 Jan. £8.

Recommended

Craft workshops: at Snettisham, *Snettisham Studio,* 1 Lynn Road, ☎ (485) 41167, and hand-spun garments, toys and patchwork; at Wiggenhall St. Germans, *Jean Rowden,* Riverside crafts, Lynn Road, ☎ (055 385) 424, handpainted china and porcelain items.

Golf: Castle Rising, ☎ (0553) 654.

Guesthouses: *Havanna guesthouse,* 117 Gaywood Road, ☎ (0553) 772331 £21 B. & B.; at Terrington St. Clement, *Homelands,* 79 Sutton Road, ☎ (0553) 828401. £20 B. & B.

Nearby

GRIMSTON, 12m E on B1153

Hotel:

★★ *Longham Hall Country House*, ☎ (0485) 600250, Tx 817209, AC AM BA DI, 11 rms. ℙ ≷ ⬜ ⌂ ⌨ ⬜ ⌂ No children under 12. £65. Rest. ● ♦ £17.50.

Send us your comments and suggestions; we will use them in the next edition.

TOTTENHILL, 8m S on A10

Hotel:
★★*Oakwood House,* ☎ (0553) 810256, AC AM BA DI, 11 rms, P ▦ £31.

LAVENHAM**

Bury St. Edmunds, 11; Colchester, 22; London, 66 m
pop. 1,658 ☎ 0787   Suffolk B2

Lavenham is the most complete surviving example of a medieval town.

▶ The central focus is the **market place** atop the hill with
▶ **guildhall**: early 16thC timber-framed building with exhibition on woolen industry through the ages (*end Mar.-Oct.: daily, 11-1, 2-5.30*). ▶ The **priory** (Water Street): former Benedictine house, now owned privately (*Easter wkend., May-end Sep.: daily ex. Sun., 2-5.30; Sun. of Bank Hol. wkend. and in Aug.*). ▶ **Swan Hotel:** superb 14thC coaching inn. ▶ **Church of Sts. Peter and Paul:** 140-ft. square tower; fine example of many similar 'cloth' churches in East Anglia.

Nearby

▶ **Monks Eleigh** (*3m E*) one of a cluster of villages in the Brett Valley. Monks Eleigh has good timber-framed and thatched houses. ▶ **Lindsey** (*5m SE*): village name given to woolen cloth made here in medieval times. ▶ **Kersey**★ (*7m SE*). Colour-washed and thatched period houses cluster on hillsides. **Church** with fine Perpendicular tower dominates top of village.   □

Practical information ———————————————

Hotels:
★★ *Swan* (T.H.F.), High Street, CO10 9QA, ☎ (0787) 247477, AC AM BA DI, 48 rm. P ▦ � £70. Rest. ♦ ♪ £12.50.
★ *Angel*, Market Place, CO10 9QZ, ☎ (0787) 247388, 5 rm. P ▦ ⌕ ✻ £25. Rest. ♦ ♪ £7.

LOWESTOFT*

Norwich, 28; Ipswich, 41; London, 120 m
pop. 59,430 ☎ 0502   Suffolk C1

A lively resort and commercial fishing port, Lowestoft is also the nearest base to **Oulton Broad**★, one of England's finest inland waters. The **fishing harbour** remains the centre of Old Lowestoft. The lighthouses are the earliest recorded on English shores. Narrow streets known as **'scores'** run past curing houses for Lowestoft kippers.

▶ **Resort area**, South Town, has a fine sandy beach.
▶ **Pleasurewood Hills**, American theme park, includes 3/4 m scenic railway (*May-Sep.: 10-6*). ▶ **Lowestoft and East Suffolk Maritime Museum:** models of fishing boats and examples of fishing gear (*early May-end Sep.: 10-5*).
▶ **Royal Naval Patrol Service Museum:** model ships, documents and uniforms (*May-Oct.: 10-12, 2-4.30*).

Nearby

▶ **Somerleyton** (*5m NW*) redbrick estate cottages cluster round green of this village built for **Somerleyton Hall**, originally a Jacobean house in attractive gardens (*Mar.-Sep.: Thu., Sun., Bank Hol. Mon; Tue. and Wed. in Jul., Aug.: 2-5.30*). ▶ **Suffolk Wildlife and Country Park**★ (*4m S*) Kessingland (*all year: daily, 10-6 or one hour before dusk*). ▶ **Herringfleet** (*8m NW*): a small village on the River Waveney has round, towered Norman church and, nearby, a thatched barn, once the refectory of an Augustinian priory. ▶ **St. Olave's Priory** has early 14thC undercroft and vaulted brick ceiling.   □

Practical information ———————————————

LOWESTOFT
ℹ esplanade, ☎ (0502) 65989.
▥▥ ☎ Norwich (0603) 632055.
Car rental: Europcar, Wrights Motors Ltd, 67-77 London Road South, ☎ (0502) 516982.

Hotels:
★★ *Rockville House*, 6 Pakefield Road, NR33 0HS, ☎ (0502) 81011, AC BA, 8 rm. ✻ £27.50. Rest. ♦ £5.
★★ *Victoria*, Kirkley Cliff, NR33 0BZ, ☎ (0502) 4433, AC AM BA DI, 50 rm. P ⌕ ▦ ⌕ ♿ ▣ £45. Rest. ♦ ♪ ♿ £9.

⅄ at Kessingland, *Heathland Beach C.P.*, London Road (30 pl), ☎ (0502) 740337; *Kessington Beach H.V*, Kessingland Beach (90 pl), ☎ (0502) 740636; at Pakefield, *Beech Farm Cara Ltd*, Arbor Lane (120 pl), ☎ (0502) 2794.

Recommended
Craft workshop: Earth Pottery, 94 Norwich Road, ☎ (052 16) 702, plant pots, kitchenware, lamps, candle holders.
Cycle rental: Seaside Hire Services, 329 Whapload Road, ☎ (0502) 64759.

Nearby

CARLTON COLEVILLE, 5m SW off A1117

Hotel:
★★★ *Hedley House Park*, Chapel Road, NR33 8BL, ☎ Lowestoft (0502) 60772, Tx 975592, AC AM BA DI, 17 rm. P ▦ ⌕ ♪ £39. Rest. ♦ ♪ £5.80.

Recommended
Golf course: Rookery Park, Beccles Road, ☎ (0502) 60380.

OULTON BROAD

Hotel:
★★★ *Wherry*, Bridge Road, NR32 3LN, ☎ Lowestoft (0502) 516 845, AC AM BA DI, 23 rm. P ⌕ ▦ £40. Rest. ♦ ♪ ♿ £15.

Recommended
♥ The Cheese Shop, 74 Beccles Road, ☎ (0502) 64664, over 200 varieties of cheeses and general delicatessen.

MALDON*

Colchester, 16; Chelmsford, 9; London, 42 m
pop. 15,250 ☎ 0621   Essex B3

The town was given a royal charter in 1171; the lanes and 'chases' that run between the main streets are one of the town's distinctive features. Maldon is the home port of the traditional Thames sailing barges. The reclamation of sea salt is a local industry.

▶ 15thC **Moot Hall**, originally the corner tower of an uncompleted mansion and the 17thC **Plume Library**. ▶ In High Street, **All Saints church**, 13thC, has a distinctive triangular west tower. ▶ **Maldon Museum**, High Street, has items of local interest and a changing programme of exhibitions. ▶ **St. Mary the Virgin**, 12thC church, where a beacon-bearing landmark for sailors once stood. ▶ The **Jaguar Motor Museum**, Mill Lane: collection of Jaguar cars (*all year: Wed.-Sun., 10-6*).

Nearby

▶ **Blackwater Estuary**, a major yachting and water sports centre.   □

Practical information ———————————————

MALDON
ℹ 2 High Street, ☎ (0621) 56503.

Hotel:
★★ *Blue Boar* (T.H.F.), Silver Street, CM9 7QE, ☎ (0621) 52681, AC AM BA DI, 23 rm. P £50. Rest. ♦ £10.

Restaurant:
♦ *Francine's*, 1A High Street, ☎ (0621) 56605, AC BA ℗ ⌘ Cl. 2 wks. Aug., 1 wk. Christmas, 1 wk. spring, Sun., Mon. lunch by reserv. only. Haddock en croûte with spinach and fresh sorrel sauce. Book. £15.

Recommended
Golf course: Three Rivers, Stow Road, Purleigh, ☎ (0621) 828631; Manifold, Colchester Road, Tolleshunt d'Arcy, ☎ (0621) 860410; Warren, Woodham Walter, ☎ (0621) 3258.
♥ Shuttlewood Studios, Friars Walk, Friars Lane, ☎ (0621) 55349, designer Knitwear.
Craft workshop: Coggeshall Pottery, 49 West Street, ☎ (0376) 61217; Domestic and decorative stoneware.

Nearby

HEYBRIDGE, 2 1/2m N on B1026

Hotel:
★★ *Benbridge,* The Square, CM9 7LT, ☎ Maldon (0621) 57666, AC AM BA DI, 14 rm. ℗ £32. Rest. ♦ ⌘ J £20.

MERSEA ISLAND

Lies between the mouths of the Rivers Colne and Blackwater. An ancient causeway, the **Strood**, is the crossing point. In the 10thC Mersea Island was a fortified base of the Danes. ▶ **Mersea Island Museum**, West Mersea, has displays of local history and fishing industry. ☐

Practical information _____

Nearby

WEST MERSEA

Hotel:
★★ *Blackwater*, 20-22 Church Road, CO5 8QH, ☎ Colchester (0206) 383338, AC AM, 7 rm. ℗ ⌘ ℗ £32. Rest. ● ♦ J & Cl. 5-21 Jan. Rest. Cl. Tue. lunch and Sun. dinner. £12.

⚊ *Waldergraves Farm* (60 pl), ☎ (0206) 382898.

NEWMARKET**

Bury St. Edmunds, 15; Cambridge, 12; London, 64 m
pop. 15,851 ☎ 0638   Suffolk B2

Newmarket is the capital of horse racing in England and it possesses a unique and exciting atmosphere.

▶ **The Heath** has been the scene of racing since the nobles of James I introduced racing to England. ▶ The **Rowley Mile Racecourse**: the name derives from Charles II's hack, Old Rowley. Charles' favourite, Nell Gwynne, lived at the **Nell Gwynne Cottage**, 5 Palace Street, which escaped the widespread fire of 1683. ▶ The **Devil's Dyke**, a massive ancient earthwork, traditionally offers a free view of race meetings. ▶ **Tattersalls**, an auction ring near the station: annual bloodstock sales. ▶ **Newmarket National Horse Racing Museum** housed in Regency building; five galleries record the development of horse racing (late Mar.-early Dec.: Tue., Sat., Bank Hol. Mon., 10-5, Sun., 2-5; Aug.: Mon.-Sat., 10-5, Sun., 2-5).

Nearby

▶ At **Dalham** (*6m E*): **Dalham Hall**, a redbrick mansion on the highest point in Suffolk, was built at the start of the 18thC. ▶ **Bottisham** (*6m W*): a large village dominated by a 13thC **church**. ☐

Practical information _____

NEWMARKET
ℹ ☎ Bury St. Edmunds (0284) 3947.

Hotels:
★★★ *Newmarket Moat* (Q.M.H.), Moulton Road, CB8 8DY, ☎ (0638) 667171, AC AM BA DI, 49 rm. ℗ & J £52. Rest. ♦ J £10.
★★ *White Hart*, High Street, CB8 8JP, ☎ (0638) 663051, AC AM BA DI, 21 rm. ℗ £48. Rest. ♦ J £8.

⚊ at Burwell, *Riverside C.C.S.*, 26-30 North Street (100 pl), ☎ (0638) 741547.

Recommended
Golf course: Links, Cambridge Road, ☎ (0638) 663000; Royal Worlington, ☎ (0638) 712216.
Riding school: at Exning, Cairns Livery Stables, North End, ☎ (063 877) 671, self-catering accommodation.

Nearby

BARTON MILLS, 1m E on A11

Hotel:
★★ *Bull*, IP28 6AF, ☎ Newmarket (0638) 713230, AC AM BA DI, 16 rm. £45. Rest. ♦ J Cl. Sun. eve. £12.

MILDENHALL, 9m NW on A1101

Hotels:
★★ *Bell* (B.W.H.), High Street, IP28 7EA, ☎ (0638) 717272, AC AM BA DI, 18 rm. ℗ £38. Rest. ♦ J & £9.
★★ *Riverside*, Mill Street, IP28 7DP, ☎ (0638) 717274, AC AM DI, 19 rm. ℗ ≋ ⚈ & £35. Rest. ♦ J & £8.

SIX MILE BOTTOM, 8m SW on A1304

Hotel:
● ★★ *Swynford Paddocks*, CB8 0UE, ☎ (0638 70) 234, Tx 817438, AC AM BA DI, 15 rm. ℗ ≋ ⚈ ⚲ ⌘ House with large gardens that was once the home of Lord Byron's half-sister Augusta Leigh. £70. Rest. ♦ J & £16.

Newmarket races

Newmarket developed as the primary racing town after James I built a palace there for his hawking and hunting activities. In 1619 the first horse race took place on Newmarket Heath. Later in the same century King Charles II, took part in the races himself. By 1752 the town was sufficiently important as a racing centre for a governing body of British racing, the Jockey Club, which had been based in a London inn, to move its headquarters there.
Nowadays the town is home to over 1,500 racehorses, 40 training stables, two racecourses and 35 stud farms. Each year over 4,000 horses are sold there for millions of pounds. The best-known races held annually are the One Thousand and Two Thousand Guineas (which take place in the spring) and the Cesarewich and Cambridgeshire (run in the autumn). Although the town of Newmarket is in Suffolk, the racecourse itself is actually over the county boundary in Cambridgeshire.

NORTH WALSHAM*

Cromer, 9; Great Yarmouth, 21; London, 125 m
pop. 7,929 ☎ 0692   Norfolk C1

A prosperous town in the medieval wool weaving period, now a small centre with fine Georgian architecture. The interior of **North Walsham Church** has a monument to Sir William Paston (d.1608), who founded the Paston Grammar School in 1606 where Horatio Nelson was a student.

Nearby

▶ **Worstead** (*3m SE*): a village that gives its name to a strong cloth. Weavers' houses in the village. The **church** with tower 109 ft. high; fine details. Tracery in east window is 14thC. A notable figure in the southernmost section is St. Uncumber, who miraculously grew a beard to prevent her father forcing her into marriage. □

Practical information ───────────────

NORTH WALSHAM

🚃 ☎ Norwich (0603) 632055.

Hotel:
★ **Scarborough Hill**, Yarmouth Road, NR28 9NA, ☎ (0692) 402151, AC AM BA DI, 18 rm. ℗ ≮ ⫰ ℚ £36. Rest. ◆ ♪ £10.

Recommended
Craft workshops: Folgate Road, *Laundry Loke Ind. Est.,* ☎ (0692) 404417, quality glass drinking glasses, bells, plates, ashtrays; at Felmingham; *Belaugh Pottery,* Church Road, ☎ (0692) 403967, hand-thrown stoneware, domestic and decorative; *Sutton Windmill Pottery,* Church Road, ☎ (0692) 80595, practical domestic stoneware pottery; *Cat Pottery,* 1 Grammar School Road, ☎ (0692) 402962, life-size pottery of cats, heads, skulls.
Golf course: Mundesley, Links Road, ☎ (0263) 720095.

Nearby

KNAPTON, **7m N on B1145**

Hotel:
★★★ **Knapton Hall**, NR28 0SB, ☎ Mundesley (0263) 720405, AC AM BA, 8 rm. ℗ ≮ ⫰ ℚ ⫸ ⊡ £44. Rest. ◆ ♪ £17.

MUNDESLEY, **10m N on B1145**

Hotel:
★ **Continental** (M.C.H.), Cromer Road, NR11 8DB, ☎ (0263) 720271, AC AM BA DI, 44 rm. ≮ ⫰ ℚ ⊡ ⤻ £34. Rest. ◆ ♪ ⅙ Cl. 1 Nov.-end Mar. £17.50.

NORWICH✶✶

Cromer, 23; Ipswich, 40; London, 114 m
pop. 122,000 ☎ 0603   Norfolk C1

Ten centuries of traditions and historic associations await the traveler in Norwich, England's second largest city and one of spires dominated by a medieval cathedral.

▶ **Tombland** — a Georgian square that takes its name from a Saxon word, toom, meaning open-air market. At either end of this square are points of access to the **cathedral close**, once monastic, now a collection of medieval houses. **Bishop's palace** is now part of King Edward VI School. Founded by Bishop Salmon in 1316, it counts among its celebrated pupils Horatio, Lord Nelson and Norwich's linguist and writer John Cotman. The great Norman cathedral was begun in 1096 to house the See of East Anglia. Although a fire in 1463 destroyed much of the Norman roofing, the cathedral has survived. ▶ The **castle museum.** After the Conquest a wooden moated castle was built, replaced with present stone keep in 12thC; opened as a museum in 1894 (*Mon.-Sat.: 10-5; Sun., 2-5*). Other **museums** include **Strangers' Hall**, medieval merchant house (*Mon.-Sat.: 10-5*); **the Bridewell Museum,** in a former prison, has social and industrial exhibits; **Colman's Mustard Museum**, Bridewell Alley, tells the story of a distinctive local product (*daily: 9-5.30*). Norwich once possessed 69 churches. Today, 33 of the medieval churches survive within the old city. Of particular importance is ▶ **St. Peter Mancroft,** built between 1430-1455. ▶ **Market place** has been in operation since 14thC. ▶ **City gates**: early fortifications were a simple ditch and bank with River Wensum as main natural defense. Traces of walls remain, but gates demolished in early 19thC. ▶ **River Wensum:** beauty spots along the riverside include ▶ **Pulls Ferry,**

15thC watergate. ▶ The **guildhall**: 600-year-old flint building, now a magistrate's court.

Nearby

▶ **Caistor St. Edmunds** (*3m SE*) was the site of the Roman *Venta Icenorum*, one of Britain's most important Roman centres. ▶ **Ringland** (*8m NW*): village dominated by 15thC church. ▶ **Ranworth** (*10m NE*): pine church with superb wood screen. ▶ **Hales Hall** (*14m SE*): 15thC manor built by attorney general to Henry VII, Sir James Hobart. Recently restored; gardens and Tudor barn with craft displays (*Mar., spring and summer Bank Hols.*).

North Norfolk Coast and Broads Round Trip

One of Britain's most popular tourist areas, Norfolk's Broadland offers safe boating, rich wildlife and quiet villages along the 200 miles of tranquil rivers and 10,000 acres of the Broads. Created by man-made excavation, the Broads are shallow (9-12 ft. deep) rivers, the three main ones being the Bure, Yare and Waveney. All three enter the estuary of Breydon Water and flow to the sea at Great Yarmouth (→). Boats are for hire by the day or week. The region was once one of the most densely populated in England, and its capital, Norwich, the third largest city. Wildlife includes the rare Bittern, the 'Norfolk Hawker', a dragonfly chosen by the Broads authority as its symbol. Fishermen know the Broads yield massive pike, up to 40 lbs, and the predatory zander up to 30 inches in length. Water authority rod and line licenses are required.

▶ **Cromer**, famed for its crabs, is the only sizeable town between here and Great Yarmouth (→). ▶ **Mundesley:** solidly old-fashioned seaside resort. ▶ **Paston** was home to the family whose Paston letters are a key document of life in the Middle Ages. ▶ **Happisburgh**, pronounced 'Haisboro': a lofty church dominates a churchyard. ▶ **Horsey** stands on a point where the sea is only 2m from the Broads; **Horsey Mere** is one of the most remote and lovely of all. ▶ **Somerton**: Broadland village with 14thC church and pleasant 1 1/2 m walk to **Winterton-on-Sea.** ▶ **Martham**: fine Georgian houses in village lying 1m S of **Martham Broad** (nature reserve). ▶ **Acle**: pleasant market town near the River Bure. ▶ **South Walsham**: south of **South Walsham Broad**, with a pleasant walk by Fleet Dyke to the River Bure. **Fairhaven Garden Trust** has rare primulas and rhododendrons. ▶ **Coltishall**: quiet village near River Bure. ▶ **Worstead**: grand church built on the wealth from a famous cloth made here in the Middle Ages. □

Practical information ───────────────

NORWICH
ⓘ guildhall, Goal Street, ☎ (0603) 666071.
✈ (3 1/2m N off A140), ☎ 411923.
🚃 ☎ 632055.
Car rental: Europcar, ☎ 22002 (rail/drive), Norwich Airport, ☎ 400280.

Hotels:
★★★ **Arlington** (B.W.), 10 Arlington Lane, Newmarket Road, NR2 2DA (A3), ☎ (0603) 617841, Tx 975392, AC AM BA DI, 41 rm. ℗ ℚ ⅙ £56. Rest. ◆ ♪ £13.
★★★ **Caistor Hall**, Caistor St. Edmund, NR14 8QN (A3 off map), ☎ Framingham Earl (0603) 624406, 21 rm. ℗ ≮ ⫰ ℚ ⊡ ⤻ ℚ £40. Rest. ◆ ♪ £8.50.
★★★ **Maid's Head** (Q.M.H.), Tombland, NR3 1LB (B1), ☎ (0603) 628821, Tx 975080, AC AM BA DI, 82 rm. ℗ ≮ £55. Rest. ◆ ♪ £9.
★★★ **Nelson**, Prince of Wales Road, NR1 1DX (C2), ☎ (0603) 628612, Tx 975203, AC AM BA DI, 94 rm. ℗ ≮ ⅙ ⫸ £53.50. Rest. ◆ ♪ £9.
★★ **Post House** (T.H.F.), Ipswich Road, NR4 6EP (A3), ☎ (0603) 56431, Tx 975106, AC AM BA DI, 120 rm. ℗ ⫰ ⅙ ⊡ £60. Rest. ◆ ♪ ⅙ £10.

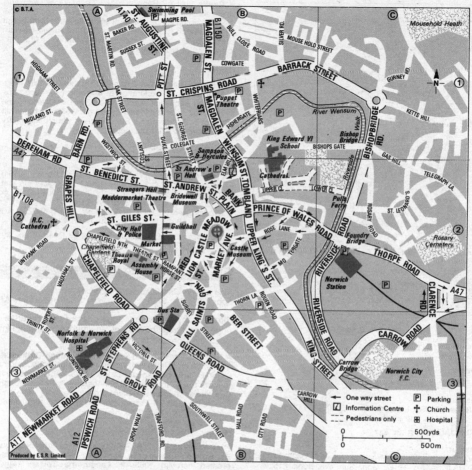

NORWICH

★ *Beeches*, 2-6 Earlham Road, NR2 3DB (A2), ☎ (0603) 621167, BA AC, 22 rm. ℗ & ⚬ £35. Rest. ◆ ⚬ & £6.
★ *Castle*, Castle Meadow, NR1 3PZ (B2), ☎ (0603) 611511, Tx 975582, AC AM BA DI, 79 rm. £38. Rest. ◆ ⚬ £10.

Restaurants:
● ◆ *Marco's*, 17 Potter Gate (A2), ☎ (0603) 624044, AC AM BA DI ⚬ Cl. Aug., Sun., Mon. Fresh pasta, local game, lobster. Book. £25.
◆ *Brasted's*, 8-10 St. Andrew's Hill (B2), ☎ (0603) 625949, AC AM BA ℗ ⚬ ⚬ ⚬ Cl. Sat. lunch., Sun. dinner, 1 wk. after Easter, last 2 wks. Jul. Pigeon breast on French salad with walnut oil and pine kernels. Book. £14.
◆ *Green's Seafood*, 82 Upper St. Giles Street (A2), ☎ (0603) 623733, AC BA ⚬ ⚬ ⚬ Cl. 25 Dec.-1 Jan., Bank Hols., Sun. Book. £12.50.

Inns or Pubs:
Adam & Eve (Norwich), Bishopgate (C1), ☎ (0603) 667423 ℗ ⚬ ⚬ Homemade soups and specials, snacks and menu. £4.
Ferryboat (Greene King), King Street (B-C3), ☎ (0603) 613553 ℗ ⚬ & ⚬ A la carte restaurant menu. £4.50.

Rosary Tavern, 95 Rosary Road (C2), ☎ (0603) 666287 £4.
Sir Garnet Wolseley (Courage Tenancy), 36 Market Place (A2), ☎ (0603) 615892 ⚬ ⚬ 2 rm. Traditional homemade pub food. £3.

Recommended
Antique shops: Arthur Brettand Sons Ltd., 42 St. Giles Street, ☎ (0603) 28171, furniture; *Henry Levine and Co.*, 55 London Street, ☎ (0603) 28709, jewelry and silver; *Mandell's Gallery*, Elm Hill, ☎ (0603) 26892, painting.
Craft workshops: at Trowse, *Le Dieu Pottery*, ☎ (0603) 24067, unusual handmade pottery; *Lenham Potter*, 215 Wroxham Road, ☎ (0603) 419065, semi-porcelain dogs, cats, goats, horses.
Cycle rental: *Dodgers*, 68 Trinity Street, ☎ (0603) 622499.
Guesthouse: *Barton Lodge*, 148 Earlham Road, ☎ (0603) 54874, £26 B. & B.
♥ *The Mustard Shop*, 3, Bridwell Alley, ☎ (0603) 27889, produces 18 different varieties of mustard.
Golf course: Barnham Broom Hotel (*7m W off A47*), ☎ (060 545) 393.

The arrow (→) is a reference to another entry.

Norfolk Broads

Nearby

BLOFIELD, 7 1/2m E by A47

Restaurant:
♦ *Hobson's*, Fox Lane, ☎ Norwich (0603) 713787, AC Ⓟ Cl. Sun., Mon. and lunch. £12.

BRUNDALL, 6m E off A47

Restaurant:
♦ *Old Beams*, 39 The Street, ☎ Norwich (0603) 712215, AC BA Ⓟ ◭ ♪ ⚕ ⅋ Cl. Mon., Sun. eve. Book. £15.

DRAYTON, 4m NW on A1067

Hotel:
★★ *Stower Grange*, School Road, ☎ Norwich (0603) 860210, AC BA DI, 10 rm. Ⓟ ⚕ £40. Rest. ♦ £11.

Restaurant:
♦ *Drayton Wood*, Drayton High Road, ☎ Norwich (0603) 409451, AC AM BA DI Ⓟ ⁓ ◭ ♪ ⅋ Cl. 24-31 Dec., Sun eve. 4 rm. Book. £16.

SPROWSTON, 3m N on A1151

Hotel:
★★★ *Sprowston Hall* (Compass), Wroxham Road, NR7 8RP, ☎ (0603) 410871, AC AM BA DI, 40 rm. Ⓟ ⚔ ⁓ ◭ ⅋ ♪ £50. Rest. ♦ £8.

ORFORD*

Norwich, 48; Ipswich, 20; London, 100 m
pop. 665 ☎ 039 94   Suffolk C2

Small Suffolk coastal town, a great port in Elizabethan times, now separated from the sea by a 10m shingle bank along the Ore and Alde Rivers. Orford, with a market square and large castle overlooking the coast, also has a fine church.

▶ **Castle** built by Henry II, 1165-71; massive keep survives, constructed of stone dredged from the sea bed. The roof commands wide **views** of shore towards **Aldeburgh** (→). ▶ **Church** has a finely decorated but ruined Norman chancel to E; spacious interior; was setting for first performances of works by Benjamin Britten.

Nearby

▶ **Dunwich Underwater Exploration Exhibition** tells progress of sub-aqua exploration of **Dunwich** (→), once capital of East Anglia (*all year: daily, 11.30-5*). ▶ **Orford Ness**: shingle spit now dominated by atomic weapons research station. ▶ **Rendlesham**: St. Gregory's church has lofty nave; nearby is a fine old rectory.   ☐

Practical information _____

Hotels:
● ★ *King's Head*, Front Street, IP12 2LW, ☎ (0394) 450271, DI, 5 rm. Ⓟ ◭ ⚕ ♪ ⅋ 13thC smugglers inn that derives its name from King Henry III. £27.50. Rest. ♦ ⚕ Cl. Mon. and Sun. dinner and Jan. £15.
★ *Crown Castle* (T.H.F.), IP12 2LJ, ☎ (0394) 450205, AC AM BA DI, 19 rm. Ⓟ ⚔ ⁓ ◭ £50. Rest. ♦ £9.

⚠ at Hollesley, *Maple Leaf C.P.*, Lodge Road (9 pl) ☎ (0394) 411202.

PETERBOROUGH**

King's Lynn, 35; Kettering, 28; London, 82 m
pop. 138,365 ☎ 0733   Cambridgeshire A1

Situated on the western edge of the Fens, Peterborough has been the site of an important settlement since the Iron and Bronze Ages.

▶ The focal point of the city is **Peterborough Cathedral**, one of the most important Norman buildings in the country (→). ▶ In **cathedral square** is the 17thC **Buttercross** built to mark the restoration of the monarchy. ▶ **Peterborough City Museum and Art Gallery**, Priestgate; note bone and marquetry work of French prisoners during Napoleonic wars (*Oct.-Apr.: Sat., 12-5; May-Sep.: Tue.-Sat., 10-5*).

Nearby

▶ **Langthorpe** (*2m SW*): village annex of Peterborough. St. Botolph's was once in nearby Westwold, but re-erected here in 1263. ▶ **Langthorpe Tower**: 14thC fortification added to 13thC rural manor house (*daily: Wed.-Sat., Tue., Sun.*). ▶ **Orton Longueville** (*2m SW*): village with fine period houses. ▶ In **Church of Holy Trinity**, 1275, 16thC wall painting of St. Christopher. ▶ **Burghley House★★** (*18m W*): Elizabethan, built from 1552-1587 by William Cecil; contains a huge collection of over 700 works of art (*Easter - Oct.: daily, 11-5, Sun., 2-5*). ▶ **March** (*18m E*): established in Saxon times, March takes its name from the word for boundary — it is situated on the boundary of the East Angles and the Middle Angles. ▶ **Church of St. Wendreda★**: 15thC, breathtaking double hammer - beam roof with flight of 200 wide-winged angels carved out of oak. Thriving town is traversed by River Nene. ▶ **Nene Valley Railway**: regular steam trains operate to Orton Mere. Round trip of 12m. (*Apr.-mid.-Oct.: wkend; 1st 3 wkend in Dec.; Wed., Thu. in Jun., Jul., Aug.*).   ☐

Practical information _____

PETERBOROUGH
ⓘ town hall, Bridge Street, ☎ (0733) 63141/317336; central library, Broadway, ☎ (0733) 48343/43146.
🚌 ☎ (0733) 68181.
Car rental: Europcar, Westside Service Station, Bourges Boulevard, ☎ (0733) 64523 (rail/drive).

Hotel:
★★★ *Bull*, Westgate, PE1 1RB, ☎ (0733) 61364, AC AM BA DI, 112 rm. Ⓟ £49. Rest. ♦ ♪ £9.

Recommended
Craft workshops: at Stilton, *Chestnut Country Crafts,* 90 North Street, ☎ (0733) 240636, stationery, toys, pottery, flower work, wooden items; at Fotheringhay, *Fotheringhay Forge,* ☎ (083 26) 323, hand-crafted fire canopies, baskets.
Golf course: Milton Ferry, ☎ (073 121) 489/793.

Nearby
MARCH, 10m SW

Inn or Pub:
White Horse, 42 West End, ☎ (035) 423054.

THORPE WOOD, 2m W on A47

Hotel:
★★★ *Peterborough Moat* (Q.M.H.), PE3 6SG, ☎ (0733) 260000, Tx 32708, AC AM BA DI, 98 rm. ℗ ⚇ ᗱ ♪ ᗺ £60. Rest. ♦ ♪ ᗱ £11.

WANSFORD, 8m W on A47

Hotels:
★★★ *Sibson House,* Great North Road, PE8 6ND, ☎ Stamford (0780) 782227, AC AM BA DI, 11 rm. ℗ ⪡ ⚇ £44. Rest. ♦ ♪ £9.
● ★★ *Haycock* (Poste), PE8 6JA, ☎ Stamford (0780) 782223, Tx 32710, AC AM BA DI, 28 rm. ℗ ⚇ ᗺ £55. Rest. ♦ £18.

WHITTLESEY, 7m SE on A605

Restaurant:
♦ *Falcon,* Paradise Lane, ☎ Peterborough (0733) 203247, AC AM BA DI ℗ ᗺ Cl. eves., 25-26 Dec., 1 Jan. eve. 8 rm. Duckling with blackcurrant, vegetarian dishes. Book. £12.

Inn or Pub:
Boat Inn (Elgoods), 2 Ramsey Road, ☎ Peterborough (0733) 202488 ℗ ⪡ ⚇ ᗺ ᗱ 4 rm. Bar snacks. £7.

Recommended
Craft workshop: *The Craft Shop,* 6 St. Mary's Street, ☎ (0733) 203620, miniature figurines and military subjects.

SAFFRON WALDEN**

Cambridge, 15; Bishop's Stortford, 12; London, 46 m
pop. 11,879 ☎ 0799   Essex B2

Ancient market town. In the largest parish **church** in Essex is a carved memorial to the saffron flower. The saffron crocus (still cultivated) was used as a dye and as a medicine — the town changed its name from Chepyng Walden in 1513. A rare **earth maze,** a turf-cut series of circles, is on the common and many fine timbered buildings survive.

▶ **St. Mary the Virgin church,** one of England's finest Perpendicular period churches. In the grounds are the flint remains of a **Norman castle.** ▶ The **museum,** Museum Street, founded 1834: collections of natural history archaeology, local history (*Oct.-Mar.: Mon.-Sat., 11-4, Sun., 2.30-5; Apr.-Sep.: Mon.-Sat., 11-5, Sun. and Bank Hols., 2.30-5*). ▶ **Castle Street,** fine old buildings. ▶ In the **market place,** the **corn exchange** dates from 1847; narrow streets, **The Rows,** are called after market traders. ▶ **Audley End House** (*2m W*). Though now largely demolished, this famous house, begun in 1603, stands on the site of Walden Abbey (*Apr.-Sep.: daily ex. Mon., 1-5.30*). □

Practical information ─────────────
SAFFRON WALDEN
ⓘ corn exchange, Market Square, ☎ (0799) 24282.
🚃 Andley End, ☎ (0799) 40431.

Hotel:
★★ *Saffron,* 10-18 High Street, CB10 1AZ, ☎ (0799) 22676, Tx 81653, AC BA, 18 rm. ℗ ⚇ £30. Rest. ● ♦ ♪ Cl. 25-30 Dec. £15.

Restaurant:
♦ *Old Hoops,* 15 King Street, ☎ (0799) 22813, AC BA DI ⚉ ♪ Cl. 25-30 Dec., Sat. lunch, Sun. 21 rm. Venison, lobster. Book. £12.

Recommended
Craft workshop: Castle Hedingham Pottery, 37 St. James Street, ☎ (0787) 60036, handmade domestic stoneware and pots.
Farmhouse: at Duddenhoe End, *Rockells Farm,* ☎ Royston (0763) 838053, £22 B. & B.
Golf course: Windmill Hill, ☎ 22786/27728.

Nearby
GREAT CHESTERFORD, 5m N on A184

Hotel:
★★ *Crown House,* CB10 1NS, ☎ Saffron Walden (0799) 30515, AC AM BA, 17 rm. ℗ ᗱ One of the original Georgian coaching inns on the road from London to Newmarket. £38. Rest. ♦ ♪ £11.

SHERINGHAM*

Cromer, 4; Fakenham, 18; London, 128 m
pop. 6,861 ☎ 0263   Norfolk C1

A traditional Norfolk coastal resort, it retains flint-built fishermens' cottages and a living seafaring tradition. The town was developed when its railhead arrived in the 19thC. Entertainments include a promenade, carnival in August, lifeboat museum.

▶ **Sheringham Hall** (*1 1/2m W*): Regency dwelling of 1812 in a fine park designed by Humphrey Repton (*by appointment only*). ▶ **North Norfolk Railway:** historic locomotives and rolling stock; steam-drawn rides in summer (*end Mar.-end Sep.: daily, 10-5*). ▶ **Norfolk Shire Horse Centre** (*2m E*): Suffolk and Shire horses at work and on display. □

Practical information ─────────────
SHERINGHAM
ⓘ Station Approach, ☎ (0263) 824329.
🚃 ☎ Norwich (0603) 632055.

Hotel:
★★ *Beaumaris,* South Street, NR26 8LL, ☎ (0263) 822370, AC BA, 25 rm. ℗ ᗱ £40. Rest. ♦ ᗱ £10.

⚓ *Snafell C.P.,* Holway Road (10 pl), ☎ (0263) 823198.

Nearby
WEST RUNTON, 2m E on A149

Hotel:
● ★★★★ *Links Country Park,* NR27 9QH, ☎ (026 375) 691, AC AM BA, 34 rm. ⚇ ᗺ ᗱ ♪ ᗺ £55. Rest. ♦ ♪ ᗱ £10.

Restaurant:
♦ *Mirabelle,* 7 Station Road, ☎ (026 375) 396, AC AM BA DI ℗ ᗺ Cl. 1st 2 wks. Nov., Mon., Sun. eve. (Oct.-May). Book. £17.

Recommended
Golf course: Links Country Park, ☎ (026 375) 691/822038.

WEYBOURNE, 4m W on A149

Hotel:
● ★★ *Maltings* (Consort), NR25 7SY, ☎ (026 370) 731, Tx 57515, AC AM BA DI, 24 rm. ℗ ⚇ ᗺ £47. Rest. ♦ ♪ £12.

Restaurant:
♦ *Gasche's Swiss,* The Street, ☎ (026 370) 220, AC AM BA DI ℗ ⚇ ᗺ Cl. Mon., Sun. eve., Christmas. Filet mignon cottage, fish risotto. Book. £18.

⚓ *Kelling Heath C.* (285 pl), ☎ (026 370) 224.

SOUTHEND-ON-SEA*

Chelmsford, 20; Brentwood, 21; London, 39 m
pop. 155,720 ☎ 0702   Essex B3

Traditionally a major seaside playground for Londoners, this cheerful Essex resort, 36m from the metropolis, has 7m of seafront.

▶ **Pier** is the world's longest pleasure pier and offers excellent fishing. ▶ **The Kursall** major entertainment centre (*daily in summer, weekends in Oct.*). ▶ **Southend Central Museum and Planetarium**, Victoria Avenue: includes local history displays (*Mon., 1-5, Tue.-Sat.: 10-5*). ▶ **Prittlewell Priory Museum**, Victoria Avenue: visit the remains of a 12thC **priory** now a museum of local history (*Tue.-Sat.: 10-1 & 2-5*). ▶ At **Southchruch Hall**, Park Lane, is a 14thC timber-framed manor house with Tudor additions (*Tue.-Sat.: 10-1 & 2-5*).

Nearby

▶ **Rochford★** (*4m N*) is an ancient market town at the head of the River Roach. **South St.** has fine Georgian and half-timbered houses. ▶ **St. Andrew's Church** has an early Tudor brick tower. ▶ **Rochford Hall**, remains of a 16thC mansion, reputedly the birthplace of Anne Boleyn, second queen to Henry VIII. ▶ **Hadleigh Castle** (*6m W*), founded in 1231 and rebuilt 1359-1370 for Edward III, features in a major painting by Constable. It overlooks fields and woodland along the Thames Estuary.   □

Practical information _____

SOUTHEND-ON-SEA
ℹ️ civic centre, Victoria Avenue, ☎ (0702) 355122; High Street, Precinct ☎ (0702) 355120.
✈ ☎ 40201 (2m N off A127).
▰▰▰ ☎ (0702) 611811.
Car rental: Europcar, SMACS, 160 Priory Crescent, ☎ (0702) 351351, Airport, ☎ (0702) 351351.
Hotels:
★★★★*Roslin,* Thorpe Esplanade, SS1 3BG, ☎ (0702) 586375, Tx 99450, AC AM BA DI, 44 rm. ℙ ≶ ⑳ £38. Rest. ♦ ♪ £8.
★*Cocklehurst Farm,* Eastwood Bury Lane, SS1, ☎ (0702) 520456, 9 rm. ℙ ⑳ £28.75. Rest. £6.50.
Restaurant:
♦ *Schulers,* 161 Eastern Esplanade, ☎ (0702) 610172, AC AM BA DI ℙ ≶ ♪ ♿ ⑳ Cl. 2 wks. Aug.- Sep., Mon., Sun. eve. Scallops and monkfish in wine sauce between layers of puff pastry. £13.50.
Recommended
Cycle rental: M. J. Thake, 18 Arterial Road, ☎ (0702) 529754.
Golf course: Thorpe Hall, Thorpe Bay, Thorpe Hall Avenue, ☎ (0702) 58220; Leigh-on-Sea, Belfairs Park, Eastwood Road North, ☎ (0702) 520322.

Nearby

ROCHFORD, 3m N on B1013
Restaurant:
♦ *Renoufs,* 1 South Street, ☎ (0702) 544393, AC AM BA DI ♪ ♿ Cl. 1st 3 wks. Jan. 2 wks. Jun., 1st 3 wks. Aug. Sat. lunch, Sun., Mon. Shellfish £15.

WESTCLIFFE-ON-SEA, 1m W on Coast.
Restaurant:
♦ *Alvaro's,* 32-34 St. Helen's Road, ☎ Southend-on-Sea (0702) 335840, AC BA ♪ ♿ Cl. Christmas 3 wks Aug., Mon., Sat. lunch. £20.

SOUTHWOLD*

Lowestoft, 13; Ipswich, 35; London, 111 m
pop. 3,756 ☎ 0502   Suffolk C2

Clifftop town on the Suffolk coast, Southwold was a quietly fashionable Victorian bathing resort. Trade with Holland led to a clear Dutch influence upon many of the town's buildings.

▶ The Perpendicular **church★** is one of the most splendid in East Suffolk. ▶ **Southwold Museum**, in Dutch gabled house: exhibition on the old Southwold railway and the battle of Sole Bay (*late May-end Sep.: daily, 2.20-4.30*). ▶ **Southwold Lifeboat Museum**: models and relics (*late May-end Sep.: 2.30-4.30*). ▶ Southwold **Sailors' Reading Room** on the cliff has maritime relics (*all year daily: 9-5*).

Nearby

▶ **Wenhaston** (*5m W*): village on high ground above River Blyth. A rare medieval painting was revealed when rain washed away its coat of whitewash. ▶ **Dunwich** (*4m SW*): now a small village, Dunwich was once a major medieval town, destroyed by the encroaching sea. ▶ **Dunwich Museum** chronicles the history of the town since Roman times (*Mar., Apr., May, Oct.: wkend; Jun., Jul., Sep.: Tue., Thu., Sat., Sun.; Aug.: daily, 2-4.30*).   □

Practical information _____

SOUTHWOLD
ℹ️ town hall, High Street, ☎ (0502) 722366.
Hotels:
★★ *Crown,* High Street, IP18 6DP, ☎ (0502) 722275, Tx 97223, AC AM BA, 11 rm. ℙ £36. Rest. ♦ £12.50.
★★ *Pier Avenue,* IP18, ☎ (0502) 722632, AC AM BA, 13 rm. ℙ ⌿ £35. Rest. ♦ ♪ £10.
Restaurant:
♦ *Dutch Barn,* Ferry Road, ☎ (0502) 723172, AC AM BA ℙ ⑳ ♿ ♪ Cl. 2 wks. Jan., Sun. eve., Mon. Local turbot in Noilly Prat and cream sauce. Book. £9.95.
Inn or Pub:
Southwold Arms (Adnams), High Street, ☎ (0502) 722099 ≶ ⑳ ♿ 2 rm. Fish, steaks, bar snacks. £4.

⅄ at Dunwich, *Cliff House*, Minsmere Road (95 pl), ☎ (072 873) 282.
Recommended
Golf course: The Common, ☎ (0502) 723234.

Nearby

WALBERSWICK, 1m S across river
Hotel:
★★ *Anchor,* IP18 6UA, ☎ Southwold (0502) 722112, Tx 97223, AC AM BA DI, 14 rm. ℙ ≶ ⑳ ♿ £36.50. Rest. ♦ ♿ £8.
Restaurant:
♦ *Potter's Wheel,* The Green, ☎ (0502) 724468, AC ≶ ⑳ ♿ ♪ Cl. Nov.-Mar., Tue. Venison, chocolate roulade. Book. £10.
Inn or Pub:
Bell (Adnams), ☎ Southwold (0502) 723109, AC BA ℙ ≶ ⑳ ♿ ♿ 3 rm. Hot and cold bar food. £4.

WRENTHAM, 5m N on A12
Restaurant:
♦ *Quiggins,* 2 High Street, ☎ (050 275) 397, AC AM BA ℙ ♿ ♪ ♿ Cl. 1st 2 wks. Jan., Sun. dinner, Mon. Beef and oyster pie. Book. £14.

Looking for a locality? Consult the index at the back of the book.

Send us your comments and suggestions; we will use them in the next edition.

STOWMARKET*

Norwich, 36; Ipswich, 12; London, 89 m
pop. 10,913 ☎ 0449   Suffolk B2

A busy market town, formerly a centre of the woolen trade and once the county town of Suffolk.

▶ The Museum of East Anglian Life: varied and developing 30-acre riverside site with important re-erected buildings: the **Eastbridge windpump**; **Alton Water Mill**, restored to working order; **Boby building**, a massive Victorian engineering workshop. Also steam traction engines and a working Suffolk Punch horse (*end Mar.-end Oct.: Mon.-Sat., 11-5, Sun., 12-5; Jun.-Aug.: Sun, 12-6*).

Nearby

▶ **Needham Market** (*4m SE*): pleasant Georgian housefronts in small town along the Ipswich road. The famous 15thC church rises abruptly from the roadside. ▶ **Haughley Park** (*3m NW*): motte and bailey castle in a village. The mellow brick house of the royal manor and park date from 1625. ▶ **Debenham**★ (*10m NE*): small town with fine **church**, mostly 15thC, on hilltop. **Crows Hill** is moated survivor of 1744 fire.   ☐

Practical information

STOWMARKET
🚌 ☎ Ipswich (0473) 690744.

Hotel:
★ *Cedars*, Needham Road, IP14 2AJ, ☎ (0449) 612668, AC AM BA, 15 rm. P ⁂ ⌂ & £38. Rest. ♦ ♪ Cl. 25-31 Dec. £9.

Recommended
Farmhouse: at Mendlesham Green, *Cherry Tree Farm,* ☎ (0449) 766376, £22 B. & B.
Golf course: Lower Road, Onehouse, ☎ 3473.

Nearby

HAUGHLEY, 3m NW off A45

Restaurant:
♦ *Old Counting House*, ☎ Stowmarket (0449) 673617, AC BA P ⌂ ⁑ Cl. Bank Hols., Sat. lunch, Sun. Fillet steak stuffed with mushrooms and pâté. Book. £13.

Inn or Pub:
Railway Tavern, Station Road, ☎ Stowmarket (0449) 673577 P ⁂ ⌂ & Bar snacks and lunchtime specials. £4.25.

NEEDHAM MARKET, 5m SE on B1113

Hotel:
★★ *Limes*, High Street, IP6 8DQ, ☎ (0449) 720305, AC AM DI, 11 rm. P ♪ £52. Rest. ♦ ♪ & Cl. Christmas. £10.

STONHAM, 5m E on A140

Restaurant:
● ♦ *Mr Underhill's*, ☎ Stowmarket (0449) 711206, BA P ⁑ ⁂ ⌂ & ⁑ Cl. Bank Hols., Sun., Mon. 1 rm. Iced mango and papaya soup, fillet of beef with green peppercorn Bearnaise. Book. £17.50.

Recommended
Craft workshop: *Brook Craft Market*, Ascot House, Norwich Road, ☎ (0449) 711495, assorted craft goods, corn dollies, pottery, toys, mobiles.

SUDBURY**

Bury St. Edmunds, 16; Chelmsford, 25; London, 59 m
pop. 17,723 ☎ 0787   Suffolk B2

Busy market town on the River Stour that gained prosperity through wool and weaving.

▶ **Market Hill** is the main centre, dominated by **St. Peter's church**. ▶ **Gainsborough House**, is the only home of

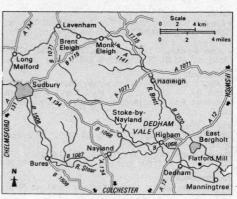

Suffolk wool towns

major artist open as a museum (*Tue.-Sat.: 10-12.30, 2-5; Sun · 3-5*) ▶ Fine **corn exchange** is now public library. ▶ **Quay Theatre** is converted 1791 principal warehouse of the Stour Navigation Company. ▶ **Valley Walk** follows track of disused railway from Sudbury to Long Melford.

Nearby

▶ **Long Melford**★ (*2m N*) almost entirely built along a 3m High Street that reaches Melford's green — crowned by one of England's finest churches, measuring 245 ft. ▶ **Melford Hall**: its turrets and topiarian grounds overlook the green; the building has recently been dated from the early 1500s. In grounds, Elizabethan **garden house**, or gazebo (*end Mar.-end Sep.: Wed., Thu., Sun., Bank Hol. Mon., 2-6*). ▶ **Kentwell Hall** was the home of the Clopton family, builders of Long Melford church. The mellow, red-brick moated mansion is still a home. ▶ **Acton** (*2m E*): in church one of the country's finest military brasses, dating from 1302, depicts Sir Robert de Bures.

Suffolk Wool Towns

Ancient wool towns of mid-Suffolk; Constable's countryside along the River Stour.

▶ **Sudbury** (→) market town was the original of Eatanswill in Charles Dickens' novel Pickwick Papers (*Thu., Sat.*). It has watermeadows by the Stour and artist Gainsborough's birthplace. ▶ **Long Melford**, centre of the antique trade, has several good restaurants. ▶ **Lavenham** (→) fine wool town with superb guildhall, many half-timbered buildings and towering church. ▶ **Brent Eleigh**: fine mural in the village church near the River Brett. ▶ **Monk's Eleigh**: cast iron village pump, with inscription, on small triangular green. ▶ **Hadleigh**: busy market town with many delightful buildings and handsome church spire. ▶ **East Bergholt**: Constable's birthplace on the River Stour with scenes of his paintings. ▶ **Flatford Mill** and **Willy Lot's cottage** nearby. ▶ **Manningtree** and **Mistley** on southern shore of Stour Estuary. ▶ **Dedham**: (→) fine houses on a handsome square in village rich in associations with Constable. ▶ **Higham**: at the meeting place of the Stour and Brett Rivers. ▶ **Stoke-by-Nayland**: hilltop village with landmark brick tower of a mighty 'wool church' often painted by Constable; fine timbered buildings. ▶ **Nayland**: old weavers' cottages and houses on a loop of the Stour; one of Suffolk's best kept villages. ▶ **Bures**: quiet village around its bridge over the Stour. Pleasant walk of 1m NE to ancient St. Stephen's Chapel.   ☐

Practical information

SUDBURY
ⓘ library, Market Hill, ☎ (0787) 72092.
🚌 ☎ Ipswich (0473) 690744.

Hotels:
★★★ *Mill* (Consort), Walnut Tree Lane, CO10 0BD, ☎ (0787) 75544, Tx 987623, AC AM BA DI, 46 rm. ℗ ⊀ ⌕ £50. Rest. ♦ ⌁ £9.
★ *Four Swans*, 10 North Street, CO10 6RB, ☎ (0787) 78103, AC AM BA DI, 17 rm. ℗ ⅙ £40. Rest. ♦ ⌁ ⅙ £10.

Restaurant:
♦ *Ford's Bistro*, 47 Gainsborough Street, ☎ (0787) 74298, BA ⅌ Cl. Sun., 1 wk. Mar., 2 wks. Aug., 1 wk. Christmas. Fish soup, mussels, vegetarian dishes. Book. £7.50.

Inns or Pubs:
Ship Star, Friars Street, ☎ (0787) 792 69 ℗ ⅏ ⅌ Snacks and meals. £4.
Swan (Greene King), Henny Street, ☎ Twinstead (078 729) 238 ℗ ⊀ ⅏ ⌕ Bar food and à la carte menu. £7.70.

Recommended
Golf course: Newton Green, Sudbury Road, ☎ (0787) 77501.

Nearby

BOXFORD, 7 1/2m E

Inn or Pub:
Fleece (Tolly Cobbold), Broad Street, ☎ (0787) 210247 ℗ ⅏ ⌕ Homemade pies, à la carte menu. £6.

Recommended
Gallery: *Laurimore*, Swan Street, ☎ (0787) 210138.

CAVENDISH, 3m W on A1092

Restaurant:
♦ *Alfonso*, The Green, ☎ Sudbury (0787) 280372, AC AM DI ℗ ⊀ ⅏ ⌕ ⌁ ⅌ Cl. Sun. eve., Mon. lunch. Homemade pasta. Book. £15.

Inn or Pub:
The George Inn (Norwich), The Green, ☎ Glemsford (0787) 280248 ℗ ⊀ ⅏ ⌕ 3 rm. Lunches and bar snacks, eve. menu: steak, gammon, duck. £5.

GLEMSFORD, 3m NW on B1065

Restaurant:
● ♦ *Weeks*, 31 Egremont Street, ☎ Sudbury (0787) 281573 ℗ ⅌ Cl. 24-31 Dec., Bank Hols., Sun., Mon. lunch. Book. £17.

LONG MELFORD, 3m N on A134

Hotels:
● ★★ *Bull* (T.H.F.), CO10 9JG, ☎ Sudbury (0787) 78494, AC AM BA DI, 27 rm. ℗ £63. Rest. ♦ £11.
★★ *Crown*, Hall Street, CO10 9JL, ☎ Sudbury (0787) 77666, AC AM BA DI, 13 rm. ℗ ⅙ £35. Rest. ♦ ⌁ ⅙ £9.

Restaurants:
● ♦ *Chimneys*, Hall Street, ☎ (0787) 79806, AC BA ℗ Cl. Mon., Sun. dinner. £19.
♦ *Countrymen*, Hall Street, ☎ Sudbury (0787) 79951, AC BA ℗ ⅏ ⌁ ⅙ ⅌ Cl. 1 wk. Feb., 1 wk. Oct., Sun. eve., Mon. Book. £12.

Inns or Pubs:
Swan, Hall Street, ☎ Sudbury (0787) 787840 £7.

SWAFFHAM*

King's Lynn, 15; Norwich, 25; London, 92 m
pop. 4,742 ☎ 0760   Norfolk B1

Once known as the Montpellier of England, the market town's Georgian and Queen Anne buildings surround a fine 1454 church.

▶ **Oakleigh House** and garden: Elizabethan with Georgian façade (*Apr.-Sep.: Thu., Sun. and Bank Hols., 2-5*).

Nearby

▶ **Cockley Cley** (*3m SW*): reconstructed campsite of the Iceni tribe with museum. ▶ **Oxburgh** (*7m SW*): 15thC moat-ed, redbrick fortified manor, **Oxburgh Hall★**, its splendid 80 ft. gatehouse includes back spiral staircase. Mary Queen of Scots was imprisoned here (*end Mar.-end Apr.: Sat., Sun., 1.30-5.30; Bank Hol. Mon., 11-5.30; May-end Sep.: daily ex. Thu., Fri, 1.30-5.30, Bank Hol. Mon., 11-5.30; early-mid- Oct.: Sat., Sun., 1.30-5.30*). □

Practical information ————————————————

SWAFFHAM

Hotel:
★★ *George*, Station Street, PE37 7LJ, ☎ (0760) 21238, AC AM BA DI, 32 rm. ℗ ⅌ ⌁ £40. Rest. ♦ ⌁ ⅙ £8.

Recommended
Craft workshop: at Methwold, *Philip Isern*, 1 Old Feltwell Road, ☎ (0366) 728573, gold and silver jewelry.
Golf course: Cley Road, ☎ (0760) 21611.

Nearby

LITTLE DUNHAM, 6m NE off A47

Hotel:
★★ *Granary*, PE32 2DF, ☎ Fakeham (0328) 701310, AC AM BA DI, 14 rm. ⊀ ⅏ ⌕ ▭ ⌁⁀ ⌁ ⌓ £33. Rest. ♦ ⌁ ⅙ £13.

THAXTED**

Saffron Walden, 8; Chelmsford, 23; London, 48 m
pop. 2,177 ☎ 0371   Essex B2

Established in Saxon times, Thaxted owed its medieval security to its cutlery and weaving industries.

▶ **Church** of St. John the Baptist, Our Lady and St. Laurence dates from between 1310 and 1510; often referred to as 'the cathedral of Essex'▶ Walk down cobbled street to **Town Street**, at top of which is the 15thC **guildhall** with **museum of local history** (*May-Sep.: Sat., Sun., Bank Hols., 2-6*). ▶ **John Webb's Windmill**, lone survivor of Thaxted's five former windmills, houses bygones exhibition (*May-Sep.: Sat., Sun., Bank Hols., 2-6*).

Nearby

▶ **Finchingfield★** (*6m NE*) is one of the prettiest villages in England. Long timber-framed **guildhall** built c. 1500; open to public; exhibits of local interest. ▶ On hill above village is the **Church of St. John** with a square Norman tower. ▶ **Spains Hall Gardens**: 16thC brick and stone manor house; gardens open (*May-late Jul.: Sun., 2-5 and Bank Hols. in May; house open by appointment*). ▶ **Great Dunmow★** (*5m S*) once a staging post on the Roman road of Stane Street. □

Practical information ————————————————

THAXTED
▭▭▭ Stansted, ☎ Cambridge (0223) 31199.

Restaurant:
♦ *Recorder's*, 17 Town Street, ☎ (0371) 830438, AC AM BA DI ⅏ ⌁ ⅌ Cl. Sun. eve., Mon. Dover sole in champagne sauce. £15.

Recommended
Antique shops: *Turpin's Antiques*, 4 Stoney Lane, ☎ (0371) 830495, furniture and metalwork.
Craft workshop: at Stanstead, *Quendon Pottery and Crafts*, Cambridge Road, Quendon, English baskets, pottery, painting, prints, glass.
Farmhouse: *Armigers*, ☎ (0371) 830618, £25 B. & B.

Nearby

BROXTED, 3m SW on B1051

Restaurant:
♦ *Whitehall*, Church End, ☎ Bishop's Stortford (0279) 850603, AC AM BA ℗ ⊀ ⅏ ⌕ ⅌ Cl. 3 wks. Jan., Sun.

eve., Mon. to non-residents. 4 rm. Maigret duck breast in port wine sauce. Book. £26.

GREAT BARDFIELD, 3m SE

Restaurant:
♦ ***Corn Dolly***, High Street, ☎ Great Dunmow (0371) 810554, AC AM BA DI Cl. Mon., Tue., Sun. dinner, Bank Hols. £17.

GREAT DUNMOW, 10m S on B184

Hotel:
★★ ***Saracen's Head*** (THF), High Street, CM6 1AG, ☎ (0371) 3901, AC AM BA DI, 24 rm. Ⓟ ♘ ♿ £106. Rest. ♦ £10.

Restaurant:
● ♦ ***Starr***, Market Place, ☎ (0371) 4321, AC BA DI Ⓟ ♪ ✗ Cl. 3 wks. Aug., 2 wks. Christmas, Sat. lunch, Sun. eve. Duck breast with kumquat sauce. £21.

The Dunmow flitch trial

Every year on Whit Monday, a mock trial is staged at Dunmow in Essex. A flitch (or side) of bacon is awarded to the married couple who can prove they have lived together for a year and a day without quarelling or regretting their union. At the trial, which is presided over by a judge, the couples are questioned about their marriage, and the verdict is given by a jury of six women and six men — all of them unmarried.
The custom, which is very old, dates from the time of Henry III and was begun by Robert Fitzwalter. The first record of an award was in 1445 to a couple who had never had a cross word owing to the fact that the husband, a sailor, had not seen his wife from the day of their marriage until the day of the trial. In fact the trial was taken seriously, and few couples were actually found worthy of awards. If they were, they were not only given a flitch but were carried together through the streets in a single chair. There have been times when the custom lapsed. Until the 18thC, only the man could apply to be awarded the flitch — suggesting that if the husband was satisfied then the marriage must be happy. This is no longer the case.

THETFORD*

Norwich, 29; Newmarket, 19; London, 83 m
pop. 19,591 ☎ 0842 Norfolk B2

This ancient town with Saxon remains has successfully combined industrial growth with its historic past. In Saxon times it was the capital of East Anglia. In the Middle Ages it had 20 parish churches and 5 monasteries.

▶ Ruins of **Thetford Priory**: founded 1104 by Norman soldier John Bigod (*Mon.-Fri.: 9.30-4, Sat., Sun., Bank Hols.: 9.30-6.30*). ▶ Ruins of **12thC Augustinian Priory of The Holy Sepulchre**, Brandon Road. ▶ Vestiges of the former Dominican monastery, the Blackfriars (founded 1340), and a Benedictine abbey, St. George. ▶ **Castle** built in 8thC but only Norman mound survives, surrounded by Iron Age ramparts. ▶ **Ancient House Museum**, White Hart Street: 15thC building; archaeology, stamps, natural history and geology collections, Saxon pottery (*Mon.-Sat.: 10-5, Sun.: 2-5; Cl. Mon., 1-2*). ▶ **Guildhall** has paintings of Norfolk and Suffolk formerly owned by Duleep Singh, Maharajah who was exiled to England after Sikh wars in 1813.

Nearby

▶ **Kilverstone** (*1m NE*): **Kilverstone Wildlife Park**: Over 50 acres of parkland with collection of animals. ▶ **Eliston** (*3m SE*): present site dates from 17thC when whole village moved from original position because it blocked the view from **Eliston Hall** (*4m SE*), home of Dukes of Grafton. **Collection** of 17th and 18thC **paintings**★ by Van Dyck, Lely and Stubbs. 17thC **church**, close to hall, was not moved when village transferred. Little Ouse River passes through the grounds (*early Jun.-late Sep.: Thu., 2.30-5.30*). ▶ **Warren Lodge** (*2m N*): visit the ruins of a 15thC hunting lodge. ▶ **Grimes Graves**★, Weeting (*2 3/4m N*): 4000-year-old flint mines excavated in 1875; intricate network of pits and shafts open to public. ▶ **Mildenhall** (*14m SW*): small Georgian town with market cross. **Mildenhall District Museum**, King Street: local history, RAF history and the story of the Mildenhall Treasure — a wealth of 4thC Roman silverware found in 1946, now housed in British Museum. ▶ **Church** has large N porch; note small shot and arrowheads embedded in woodwork dating from defense against attack by Cromwell's supporters. □

Practical information

THETFORD
ℹ Ancient House Museum, 21 White Hart Street, ☎ (0842) 2599.
🚌 ☎ Bury St. Edmunds (0284) 3947.

Hotels:
★★★ ***Bell*** (T.H.F.), King Street, IP24 2AZ, ☎ (0842) 4455, Tx 818868, AC AM BA DI, 46 rm. Ⓟ £50. Rest. ♦ £10.50.
★★ ***Thomas Paine*** (B.W.), White Hart Street, IP24 1AA, ☎ (0842) 5631, AC AM BA DI, 14 rm. Ⓟ £38.50. Rest. ♦ ♪ £10.

Restaurant:
♦ ***President***, St. Nicholas Street, ☎ (0842) 2133, AC AM BA DI Ⓟ ♨ ♪ ♿ ✗ Cl. 26 Dec.-2 Jan., last 2 wks. Aug., Sat. lunch, Sun. Black cherry duckling, schnitzel. Book. £10.

⛺ at East Harling, *The Dower House C.P.*, West Harling (200 pl), ☎ (0953) 717314.

Recommended
Golf course: Brandon Road, ☎ (0842) 2169.

Nearby

BRANDON, 9m NW on B1107

Hotel:
★★ ***Brandon House***, Bridge Street, IP27 0AX, ☎ Thetford (0842) 810171, AC AM BA DI, 15 rm. Ⓟ ♨ £43. Rest. ♦ ♪ £11.

Grimes Graves

Over 4,000 years ago, towards the end of the neolithic period, people began digging for flint to use in making tools. The most notable English flint mines were in Norfolk, near Thetford, and covered roughly 34 acres of land. Here there were about 360 shafts (each up to 40 feet deep), sunk into the ground, with galleries cut subsequently. Although most of these are now hard to distinguish, two have been preserved together with tools employed at the time. Reindeer antlers served to dig out the flint. One of the shafts, which can be visited, contains a phallus and a shrine to the Earth Mother. These fertility symbols might well have been used as offerings intended to increase the supplies of flint yielded by the mines.
Centuries after the mines were abandoned, they came to be regarded with superstition by local people. At a time when Christianity was new to Britain, the earlier pagan sacred sites were said to be haunted by the devil. Grim was a Scandinavian word for devil, and the old mines were said to be his burial place.

TILBURY*

Southend, 20; Dagenham, 10; London, 24 m
pop. 11,430 ☎ 037 52   Essex B3

Busy docks and town on northern side of Thames Estuary. The docks were developed in the 1880s.

▶ **Thurrock Local History Museum** has exhibits on domestic and social history (*Mon.-Fri.: 2-8; Sat.: 10-5*). ▶ **Tilbury Fort**, built 1682, is a large coastal fort with double moat and triumphal arch (*mid-Mar.-mid.-Oct.: daily, 10-6; mid-Oct.-mid-Mar.: Mon.-Sat., 10-3.30, Sun., 2-3.30*). ▶ **Coalhouse Fort**, East Tilbury: fine example of Victorian armoured casement fort (*last Sun. each month: 1-5*). ☐

Practical information

TILBURY

▰▰ ☎ (01) 283 7171.
▰▰ Baltic Shipping Co.

Recommended
Golf course: Orsett, Brentwood Road, ☎ (0375) 891352.

Nearby

NORTH STIFFORD, 6m NW on A1012

Hotel:
★★★ *Stifford Moat House* (Q.M.H.), High Road, RM16 1UE, ☎ Grays Thurrock (0375) 371451, Tx 966227, AC AM BA DI, 64 rm. ℙ ⧼ ⚬ & ⌇ ⌕ £55. Rest. ♦ ♪ & £11.

WALSINGHAM*

Sheringham, 21; Fakenham, 6; London, 123 m
☎ 032 872   Norfolk B1

There are important religious buildings at both **Great** and **Little Walsingham**, but it is the latter that was for centuries the most important place of pilgrimage in England. It became known as 'England's Nazareth'. The site began as a shrine built during the reign of Edward the Confessor by the lady of the manor after a vision of the Virgin Mary. King Henry VIII later confiscated and burnt the image of the Virgin. Though little remains of **Walsingham Abbey**, the abbey gardens still exist and a **Holy House** was built mid-20thC.

▶ **Little Walsingham** parish church contains a fine **seven sacrament font**. ▶ **Great Walsingham**: 14thC church with beautiful tracery in windows. ▶ **Walsingham Shirehall Museum**: history of pilgrimage, shown in the setting of a Georgian courtroom (*end Mar.-Sep.: daily, 11-1, 2-4; Oct.: wkend only, 11-1, 2-4*).

Nearby

▶ **Binham** (*NE*): flint-built village with picturesque ruins of priory, founded 11thC. ☐

Practical information

Nearby

GREAT SNORING, 3m S

Hotel:
★★ *Old Rectory*, NR21 0HP, ☎ Walsingham (032 872) 597, AM DI, 6 rm. ℙ ⧼ ⧼ ⚬ ⌇ £48. Rest. ♦ £11.

LITTLE WALSINGHAM, 1m S on B1105

ℹ shirehall museum, Common Place, Little Walsingham, ☎ (032 872) 510.

Hotel:
★ *Black Lion*, Friday Market Place, NR22 60B, ☎ (032 872) 235, AC AM BA, 25 rm. ⚬ Probably the oldest of

the hostelries serving the medieval pilgrims to the shrine of Our Lady Of Walsingham. £29.50. Rest. ♦ ♪ & £9.

WELLS-NEXT-THE-SEA*

Hunstanton, 16; Cromer, 21; London, 120 m
pop. 2,337 ☎ 0328   Norfolk B1

Old-fashioned fishing port which keeps a small fleet of whelk and shrimp boats in the harbour. Flint cottages and Georgian houses line the streets. The **Wells Centre** in a converted granary is the focus of local entertainment. The **Buttlands** is a long green at the centre of the town.

Walsingham - place of pilgrimage

During the 15thC, Walsingham was the second most important centre for pilgrims in England. Whilst the first, Canterbury, was devoted to St. Thomas Becket, Walsingham was primarily associated with the Virgin Mary. The practice of pilgrimages had grown up in the Middles Ages, when bones and relics of Christian saints were believed to have healing powers. They were kept in special shrines, and people would travel miles on foot or horseback to visit them.
Walsingham's shrine was built in 1061, after Lady Richeld had been instructed by a vision to do so. All sorts of people, including monarchs, came to the village up until the 16thC. Then, with the Reformation and Dissolution of Monasteries, the Catholic priory fell into disuse. However, pilgrimages were revived at the end of the 19thC, and a new shrine was completed in 1937. While devout Roman Catholics once again flock to the village, modern skeptics have cast doubt on the so-called miraculous effects of annual pilgrimages. Such visits always took place in spring or summer, so apparent cures might simply have been the result of fresh food and the invigorating effect of the journey.

▶ **Wells Walsingham Light Railway** is the longest 10 3/4 inch gauge railway in Britain, with an 8 m return journey (*end Mar.-Sep.*). ▶ **Holkham** (*2m W*) is the home of 'Coke of Norfolk': 18thC agricultural reformer, Thomas William Coke, who transformed a sandy wasteland into fertile pastures. ▶ The **Hall★★**, severely Palladian: extensive collection of tapestries, statues, pictures and bygones collection (*end May-end Sep.: Sun., Mon., Thu.; Jul.-end Aug.: Sun., Mon., Wed., Thu., 1.30-5; Bank Hols., 11.30-5*). ▶ **Holkham Park Gardens**: 6 acre walled garden designed by Samuel Wyatt in the 1780s. ▶ The **Burnhams**: cluster of seaside villages. ▶ **Burnham Thorpe** was the birthplace of Horatio Nelson, victor of Trafalgar, born 1758, of whom the church has relics. ▶ **Burnham Market**, centre of the Burnhams; wide, Georgian main street. ▶ **Burnham Deepdale**: font in church is carved with local scenes. ▶ **Stiffkey**: coastal village, sited in the valley of the Stiffkey River. ▶ Ancient, undisturbed **salt marshes** nearby are rich in sea aster and sea lavender. ☐

Practical information

WELLS-NEXT-THE-SEA
ℹ Wells Centre, Staithe Street, ☎ (0328) 710885.

Hotel:
★★ *Crown* (Minotel), The Buttlands, NR23 1EX, ☎ Fakenham (0328) 710209, AC AM BA DI, 15 rm. ℙ ⚬ £37.50. Rest. ♦ ♪ & £11.50.

Recommended
Craft workshop: at Maryland, *Burnham Potter*, Old Station, ☎ (0328) 710847, domestic, gift and garden pottery.

Golf course: Royal West Norfolk, Brancaster, ☎ (0485) 210223.

Nearby

BURNHAM MARKET, 6m W off A149

Restaurant:
♦ *Fishes*, Market Place, ☎ Fakenham (0328) 738588, AC AM BA DI ⚲ ⚘ Cl. Christmas, 3 wks. Jan.-Mar., Sun. eve. in winter, Mon. Own smoked fish and meat, local shellfish. Book. £15.

Recommended
Craft workshop: *Manor Farm Pottery*, North Street, ☎ (0328) 738570, earthenware casting works.

HOLKHAM, 2m W on A149

Hotel:
★ *Victoria*, NR23 1RG, ☎ Fakenham (0328) 710469, 8 rm. P ⚲ ⚌ ⚲ £32. Rest. ♦ ⚹ £9.

WISBECH*

King's Lynn, 14; Ely, 22; London, 106 m
pop. 22,932 ☎ 0945   Cambridgeshire A1

Known as the 'capital of the Fens', the town came to elegant Georgian prosperity when drainage turned the surrounding fenland into the richest of agricultural resources. Trade, reaching across the North Sea to Baltic and Low Countries, brought a distinctive foreign style to the town.

▶ **The Brinks, North** and **South**, line the river with handsome Georgian houses. ▶ **Peckover House**: splendid merchant house on North Brink, built 1722; fine Victorian garden has unusual trees (*end Mar.-end Apr.: wkend, Bank Hol. Mon.; May-end Sep.: daily ex. Thu., Fri.; early Oct.: wkend, 2-5.30; Cl. Good Fri.*). ▶ **Wisbech and Fenland Museum★**, tells history of Fenland (*Tue.-Sat.: 10-4*). ▶ **Welle Manor Hall**, Upwell (*5m SE*): ecclesiastical fortified medieval manor house; two towers remaining; dates from 1202 (*all year: first Sun. in each month, 2.30-5*).   □

Practical information _____

ⓘ district library, Ely Place, ☎ (0945) 583263/64009.
⚎ March, ☎ Peterborough (0733) 68181.

Hotel:
★★ *White Lion*, 5 South Brink, PE13 1JD, ☎ (0945) 584813, AC AM BA DI, 18 rm. P ⚹ £42. Rest. ♦ ⚲ ⚹ £9.

Inns or Pubs:
Hare & Hounds (Elgoods), 4 North Brink, ☎ (0945) 583607, AC BA P ⚲ ⚌ ⚲ ⚘ 3 rm. £3.
Kings Head (Elgoods), Old Market, ☎ (094) 565402 ⚌ ⚘ Bar snacks and meals. £4.

Recommended
Antique shop: *Peter A. Crofts*, Briar Patch, High Road, ☎ (0945) 584614, furniture, jewelry, pottery, porcelain and silver.

WOODBRIDGE*

Lowestoft, 12; Ipswich, 9; London, 81 m
pop. 9,697 ☎ 039 43   Suffolk C2

With quayside along the River Deben, Woodbridge is a peaceful sailing centre.

▶ The **shire hall** dates from 1575 with Dutch gable additions. ▶ **Gloves Yard**: 16thC timbered cottages, once the working homes of the local glove-makers. ▶ A rare **mill★** powered by the tide has been restored. ▶ Lofty spire of **St. Mary's**, 108 ft. high, crowns a building of Perpendicular style. ▶ **Woodbridge Museum★** on Market Hill illustrates history of the region (*early Apr.-late Oct.: Thu., Fri., Sat., 11-4; Sun., Bank Hols.: 2.30-4.30*).

Nearby

▶ **Rendlesham** (*2m NE*): the earliest beginnings of East Anglia in this small village in the coastal woodlands of **Rendlesham Forest**.   □

Practical information _____

WOODBRIDGE
⚎ ☎ Ipswich (0473) 690744.

Hotels:
● ★★ *Seckford Hall*, IP13 6NU, ☎ (0394) 385678, Tx 987446, AC AM BA DI, 24 rm. P ⚲ ⚌ ⚲ Elizabethan manor, containing some fine paneled rooms, beamed ceilings and great stone fireplaces. £56. Rest. ♦ ⚹ £16.50.
★★ *Melton Grange*, IP12 1EX, ☎ (039 43) 4147, AC AM BA DI, 37 rm. P ⚲ ⚌ ⚲ ⚹ ⚲ Beautiful country mansion set in its own parkland and woods £47. Rest. ♦ ⚹ £9.
★ *Crown* (T.H.F.), Thorofare, IP12 1AD, ☎ (039 43) 4242, AC AM BA DI, 18 rm. P £64. Rest. ♦ £10.

Restaurants:
● ♦ *Royal Bengal*, 6 Quay Street, ☎ (0394) 37983, AC AM BA DI P ⚲ ⚲ ⚲ ⚘ Cl. Christmas. Tandoori dishes. Book. £9.
♦ *Wine Bar*, 17 Thorofare, ☎ (0394) 32557 P ⚲ ⚘ Cl. Sun., Mon. Game, vegetarian dishes. £7.

Inn or Pub.
Olde Bell Steelyard (Greene King), New Street, ☎ (0394) 2933 P ⚲ ⚌ ⚲ Pork marsala, beef goulash, salads. £7.

Recommended
Antique shops: *David Gibbins*, 21 Market Hill, ☎ (039 43) 3531, furniture, metalwork, pottery and porcelain; *Anthony Gordon Voss*, 16 Market Hill, ☎ (039 43) 5830, clocks and furniture.
Golf course: Bromeswell Heath, ☎ (039 43) 2038.

Nearby

SHOTTISHAM, 7m SE on B1083

Hotel:
★ *Wood Hall*, IP12 3ET, ☎ (0394) 411283, AC AM BA DI, 19 rm. P ⚌ ⚍ ⚲ ⚲ Tudor house in large grounds. £35. Rest. ♦ £12.

WYMONDHAM*

Norwich, 9; Thetford, 20; London, 110 m
pop. 9,088 ☎ 0953   Norfolk B1

Pronounced 'Windam', this town is rich in timbered houses and has a market cross of 1617. Wymondham Church was formerly part of a great abbey.

Nearby

▶ **Attleborough** (*6m SW*) is a small town with an unusual church. ▶ **Breccles Hall** has attractive stream and water gardens. ▶ **Hingham** (*4m W*): Queen Anne and Georgian houses.   □

Practical information _____

WYMONDHAM
⚎ ☎ Norwich, (0603) 632055.

Hotels:
★★ *Abbey*, 10 Church Street, NR18 0PH, ☎ (0953) 602148, AC AM BA DI, 31 rm. P ⚲ ⚹ £31. Rest. ♦ £7.
★★ *Sinclair*, 28 Market Street, NR18 0BB, ☎ (0953) 606721, AC AM BA, 12 rm. P ⚌ ⚘ £38. Rest. ♦ ⚲ ⚹ £9.

Restaurant:
● ♦ *Adlards*, 16 Damgate Street, ☎ (0953) 603533 ⚘ Cl. Sun., Mon., lunch not served. Vension en croûte with cranberry and pepper sauce, local duck with kumquat sauce. Book. £17.

Nearby

BUNWELL, 7m S on B1113

Hotel:
● ★★ ***Bunwell Manor***, Bunwell Street, NR16 1QU, ☎ (095 389) 317, AC AM BA, 12 rm. [P] ♿ £38.50. Rest. ♦ ♪ ♿ £10.

HETHERSETT, 3m NE on A11

Hotel:
★★★ ***Park Farm***, NR9 3DL, ☎ Norwich (0603) 810264, AC AM BA DI, 22 rm. [P] ♿ £47.50. Rest. ♦ ♪ ♿ £10.

Inn or Pub:
Kings Head (Norwich), ☎ (0603) 810206 [P] ♿ Prawn ham, salt beef, quiche salads, beef stew dumplings, beef pudding in cloth. £4.

▶ This area has a countryside of most diversified and attractive scenery. Five counties contained within the region have a rich historical past to offer, prehistoric remains, Roman roads, ancient churches of considerable architectural interest, great castles, fine Elizabethan houses and palatial stately homes and an industrial past of lead and coal mining and cotton spinning mills.

The northern extent of the region has the lovely countryside of Derbyshire, where the landscape has several district areas. The solitary landscape of the Dark Peak, enjoyed by walkers and climbers, and in contrast the White Peak with its limestone plateau dissected by rivers and their tributaries, creating the famous and picturesque deeply wooded Derbyshire dales, is a paradise for ramblers. Linear villages lie adjacent to windy moors, others in valleys surrounded by trees. The southern countryside has gentler scenery as around Derby, with the east the industrial belt, mainly collieries. On the eastern side of the region is the rich agricultural land of the Lincolnshire Fens. Here man's control of the sea through construction of drainage dykes, has reclaimed the land creating a flat expansive landscape with typical straight fenland roads and unbroken vistas, apart from beautiful church spires breaking the skyline. Not all of Lincolnshire is flat, for the gently rising ground changes the landscape some 10 miles inland from the holiday resort coast to the range of rolling chalk hills of the Wolds. Between these two counties lies Nottinghamshire, with the ancient woodlands of Sherwood. Once a royal hunting forest of oak and silver birch, it is linked with the legend of Robin Hood and his Merry Men, and is an important area of natural history and conservation. The rural countryside has evidence of its two wealth-creating industries, rich farmland on the surface and below coal mining. Below is Leicestershire with its contrast of woodlands and harsh granite outcrops of Charnwood Forest and gentle countryside of its eastern side. Here at Rutland Water is the country's largest man-made lake, housing a nature reserve. Lying in the southern part of the region is Northamptonshire with its typical gently undulating farmland dotted with many villages and fine historical houses.

The attractions of the region are as diverse as the landscape. Popular Lincolnshire coastal resorts are noted for safe sandy beaches and family entertainment. Attractive inland water features — man-made reservoirs such as Rutland Water, Pitsford Water or Goyt Valley — offer sailing, windsurfing, trout fishing or pleasant waterside walks. There are subterranean splendours such as the Derbyshire show caverns. Rivers, an important

East● Midlands

feature, as well as canals constructed originally for industrial use, offer a variety of trips and leisure facilities. Walk or drive through unspoilt countryside or experience the beginnings of industrialization. There are impressive houses of different character like the Classical 17thC architecture of Chatsworth, full of priceless treasures, and Newstead Abbey, once home of the romantic poet Lord Byron. The excitement of wildlife parks, the tranquility of English Gardens, both grand and small, beautiful churches and important castles and museums with local festivals and fairs characterize this area. Throughout the region the tourist can experience the old and new living harmoniously side by side. □

Fox-hunting

Hunting deer was traditionally the sport of kings, but as deer became scarce, fox-hunting developed as the gentleman's pastime. An expensive hobby - requiring the upkeep of horses and packs of hounds - it could only be pursued by rich and expert riders. Attacked in recent years by campaigners against bloodsports, hunting still has a devoted following - and the number of inns in the country with such names as The Fox and Hounds shows how important a part hunting has played in English rural life. From 1 November until April each year, riders in their hunting 'pinks' (bright scarlet coats) gather for the various 'meets' across the country. The most famous of these take place in Leicestershire.

This area was developed as a hunting territory during the 1770s when there were still miles of unfenced countryside. However, much of the British landscape was rapidly changing as heathland was cleared and large open spaces were divided into smaller fields for more profitable farming. These were enclosed by dry stone walls or, more usually, hedges and fences, to create the 'patchwork quilt' effect which became typical of the English countryside. In order to make the fences and hedges, many woodlands and forests were pulled down. The immediate effect of this on hunting was to destroy the natural gorse patches where foxes hid and bred. It also created obstacles for riders going across the country. However, huntsmen soon came to regard the hedges and ditches as exciting challenges. At the same time artificial gorse covers or 'coverts' were planted to encourage foxes. Leicestershire's famous hunts include the Cottesmore, the Belvoir and the best-known, the Quorn. This was named after the Quorndon pack of hounds from Quorndon Hall, the residence of a legendary hunter, Mr Meynell, and of successive Masters of the Quorn Hunt.

 Brief regional history

Origins

This history begins in Derbyshire where, on the west-facing escarpment of the ravine called Creswell Crags, have been found the **most ancient human dwellings in** the country. In Pin Hole cavern a piece of bone was discovered in 1928 on which is engraved the figure of a dancing man, masked with an animal's head, and dating from the **upper palaeolithic** period. From **neolithic** times, on the same limestone plateau, several dozen barrows, or burial mounds, have been identified. ● The stone circle at Arbor Low comprises some forty recumbent stones in a circle 50 yards across, surrounded by a ditch. This is a **Bronze Age** site, as is the 'Nine Ladies' group of standing stones on Stanton Moor. There are neolithic and Bronze Age sites in Nottinghamshire, Leicestershire and the Lincolnshire uplands, but the region was at this time sparsely populated. ● The **Iron-Age Celts** of Lincolnshire traded their wares as far afield as Central Europe and in Leicestershire at two Iron-Age camps at Burrough-on-the-Hill and Breedon. The Coritani people inhabited the East Midlands in the centuries preceding the Roman invasion, while the powerful Brigantes occupied Derbyshire, their territory extending northwards along the Pennine range.

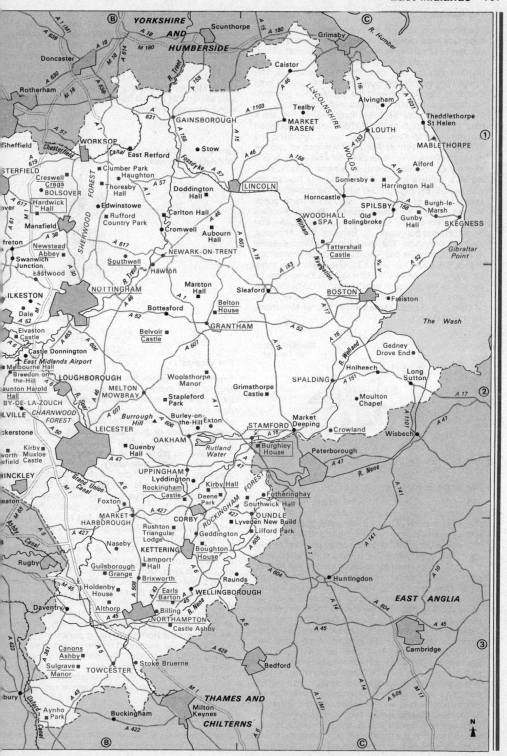

The Romans

The Roman presence in the region is evidenced by an important **road network**. Watling Street, leading from London to Cheshire, forms the western border of Leicestershire, while Ermine Street, further east, linked London with Lincoln, York and Hadrian's Wall. The Fosse Way, running obliquely across the country from Exeter to Lincoln, followed the course of a prehistoric ridgeway. Roman engineers also constructed Car Dyke, a waterway 56 miles long, linking the Nene near Peterborough to the Witham near Lincoln, and the waterway to York was completed by joining the Witham to the Trent at Torksey by means of another canal, the Foss Dyke. ● **Lincoln** became in AD 71 one of the four colonial capitals of Roman Britain, serving as a fortress for the 9th Legion. The Roman city was built on the high ground where the cathedral now stands. Parts of the Roman wall, an arch, a public fountain, baths and kilns survive. ● The Romans exploited the natural resources of the area, like iron from Scunthorpe, stone at Barnack and Ancaster, lead in Derbyshire. The early forts on Ermine Street at Great Casterton and Ancaster became prosperous towns. Leicester, too, was a Roman settlement, located where the Fosse Way crossed the River Soar on the site of the capital of the Coritani. In Derbyshire the Romans built in the lowlands at Little Chester, north of Derby, at Buxton (**Arnemetiae**) and at **Melamdra**, west of Glossop.

Norman church at Tixover

The Anglo-Saxons

The region was invaded by the **Anglo-Saxons** from the 5thC, who penetrated deep into the East Midlands, making use of Roman roads and the excellent navigable rivers, like the Trent and the Witham. There is evidence of Teutonic settlement near Leicester dating from before the Roman withdrawal. ● By the 6thC, **Leicestershire** became part of the Midland state of Mercia under the rule of Penda, with his capital at Tamworth. In 653 Penda's son Peada married the daughter of Oswy, king of Northumbria, on the understanding that he embrace the Christian religion. He brought four missionaries to Repton in that year, establishing a monastery and making **Repton** the new capital of Mercia. The mausoleum of the great Mercian kings was later built over by the Danes, and again in the 12thC as an Augustinian priory. It was rediscovered only in 1779, when a workman, digging in the chancel of the church fell through into the hidden crypt below and this fascinating survival of late Saxon architecture was revealed. By the latter part of the 8thC **Mercia** was at height of its power under Offa, reaching northwards to the Northumbrian frontier and west to the Welsh marches. **Lindsey**, the old northern division of Lincolnshire, was for a time a buffer zone between Northumbria and Mercia, changing hands seven times between 627 and 678. By 677 Lincoln became a bishopric, independent of the neighbouring bishopric of Northumbria (at York) and Mercia (at Linchfield). Northamptonshire possesses two outstanding Anglo-Saxon churches - at Earl's Barton and Brixworth. Breedon-on-the-Hill in Leicestershire had a Mercian monastery founded in 675, set within the ramparts of the old Iron-Age fort, and from which stone carvings survive.

Late 15th - century spire of Louth in Lincolnshire

The Vikings

Towards the end of the 9thC the political order of Anglo-Saxon Britain was dramatically disrupted by the marauding armies from Scandinavia, who ranged over the Midlands, plundering the monasteries and seeking tribute. Their ships could be rowed up any river with three or four feet of water, which made it difficult for local rulers to organize defenses. ● Coming up the Trent **in 874 they ravaged Repton** and destroyed its monastery. The Humber was an important entry point from which to attack the main targets of Northumbria and East Anglia. Lincolnshire again became a buffer zone as the Danes passed between the two target areas, destroying Bardney and Crowland. They built a fort at Torksey, from which they attacked Mercia, setting up a puppet king, Ceolwulf. ● By 870 they were masters of Northumbria and Mercia. The **Treaty of Wedmore** (878) was an agreement made between Alfred of Wessex and the Danish king, Guthrum, whereby England was divided between them along the **line of Watling Street**. East of the line was the Danelaw, which was administrated by the five boroughs of Derby, Leicester, Nottingham, Lincoln and Stamford. This area was one of the most heavily Scandinavian parts of Britain, the area around Horncastle being particularly densely populated, as is evidenced by the place-names, often ending in *by* or *thorpe*. The disbanded Danish soldiers were all given land to settle and farm as their own. They were free men, emerging as the yeomen of Tudor England, fiercely individualistic and intolerant of authoritarian rule.

The Norman and medieval periods

The Normans took over an economic and social order that had evolved since the settlement of the Midlands

by the Anglo-Saxons. They followed their customary procedure of **confiscating private lands** held by the English and handing them over their compatriots. In Lincolnshire, of 66 manors only two remained in English hands. ● William I built royal castles at Lincoln and Stamford. Lincoln cathedral was consecrated in 1092. In Derbyshire two royal forests were created at High Peak and Duffield Frith, guarded by the castles of Peveril and Duffield. This was a **great castle-building period** - there were 20 in Leicestershire and 30 in Lincolnshire by the Middle Ages. Lincolnshire also possessed 51 monastic houses, second only to Yorkshire. Northampton was a favourite meeting place for Norman and Plantagenet parliaments. ● The 12th and 13thC saw Lincolnshire's greatest **prosperity** when the peasants 'lived off the backs of their sheep'. Lincoln at this time was the second city of the realm, while one-third of all British **wool** was exported through Boston from the Midland clippings of three million sheep. Aaron, the Jew of Lincoln, was Henry II's greatest creditor, and the city possessed no less than 48 parish churches. ● The 14thC was a period of **decline**. High taxation during the French wars and the Black Death were contributing factors. Cloth-making at Lincoln and Stamford (the famous Lincoln 'greens' and 'scarlets') moved to Yorkshire and East Anglia. Lincoln gradually sank back to become a remote country town. ● **The East Midlands witnessed several important battles.** King Stephen was captured at the battle of Lincoln in 1141. During the civil wars of John's reign (1199-1216) Lincoln was taken by the king, who died at Newark in the same year. During the Wars of the Roses, the Yorkist Earl at Warwick took Henry VI prisoner at the battle of Northampton and marched on London, and the final and decisive battle of Bosworth was fought here when Henry Tudor defeated and killed Richard III to become, as Henry VII, the first Tudor monarch.

The Civil Wars and Nonconformity

The East Midlands mainly supported the **Parliamentarians** though there were isolated Royalist pockets. The area saw much of the action of the Civil Wars, as opposing forces passed through. ● It was at Nottingham in 1642 that Charles I raised his standard, like some feudal baron, in the presence of a handful of onlookers. ● At Winceby, just outside Hornscastle, Parliamentary forces defeated the Royalists in 1643. Newark, an important Royalist stronghold, withstood three sieges. ● And at **Naseby** in 1645 the most decisive battle was fought, when Cromwell and Sir Thomas Fairfax routed the Royalist army under Prince Rupert. ● For centuries the East Midlands, touching the same spring of dissension, had been a **centre of Nonconformity**, the cradle of English 'separatism'. At least four Calvinist groups originated in south Lincolnshire in the days of the Commonwealth, with a Baptist group at Epworth as early as 1623. In the north were a number of prominent Quaker families. John Wesley, the founder of Methodism, was born at Epworth in 1703.

Industrial life

The East Midland coalfield is effectively the southern half of one great **coalfield** which extends without a break into Yorkshire. There were open-cast fields in Derbyshire; in western and central Nottinghamshire it lies concealed, while farther east are the deepest pits.

Coal has been mined here since Tudor times, and Wollaton Hall, near Nottingham, was built in the 1580s for Sir Francis Willoughby, one of the first industrialists, with coal money. ● **Ironstone** deposits run almost continuously from the Humber into Northamptonshire and on into Oxfordshire, the biggest iron workings being around Scunthorpe and Corby ● The specialist textile trades of the region are **hosiery** and **knitwear**, the stocking-frame having been invented by William Lee, a Nottinghamshire parson, in 1589. Leicester became the largest centre for the knitwear industry, with Nottingham close behind. Nottingham also became a great **lace** producer in the 19thC, reaching a peak of production in 1910. ● At Northampton, boots and shoes have been the staple industry for centuries; it provided boots for Cromwell's men and for the Duke of Wellington's army in the Peninsular Wars. In 1719, silk 'throwing', that is, spinning by machine, was introduced at Derby from Italy. In Derbyshire, at Cromford, is Arkwright's original mill, where he installed his water-driven cotton-spinning frame in 1771. And in Derby in 1750 the manufacture of porcelain began, named *Crown Derby* by permission of George III. The city is also the birthplace of Rolls-Royce.

The 'Boat' public house at Stoke Bruerne, Northamptonshire

Well-dressing

Until the comparatively recent introduction of running water in all homes, wells were a major source of water. In the country, especially, they were regarded with great respect. Before Christian times in Britain and in other parts of the world spirits were thought to live in wells, and sacrifices were made to these water gods in order to keep them happy. Wells in various places in Britain, particularly Derbyshire, are now often associated with the time of the Black Death when 14thC England was devastated by an outbreak of deadly plague. In the town of Tissington, where there are five wells, the water remained pure and the townspeople survived - though half the population of Derbyshire perished. Less than 300 years later, when the county was suffering from drought, Tissington's wells continued to supply water. Dressing wells is an annual ceremony here, commemorating their importance in the town's history. The dressing or decorating consists of pressing flowers, leaves and other natural objects into frames of soft clay mounted above the well. In this way elaborate pictures, accompanied by religious texts, are created. Tissington's well-dressing takes place at Ascension time (usually in May), but in other parts of the country the practice may occur any time between the months of April and August.

Luddites

The Industrial Revolution brought many benefits to Britain in terms of increased productivity, trade and wealth, as well as vastly improved transport systems. However, while it created new kinds of jobs, it threatened the livelihoods of many workers. Some people lost their jobs; others, now working with machines in factories, were forced to accept lower rates of pay than they had earned when working from home. This insecurity, combined with the effects of raising food prices and resentment against wealthy employers, resulted in growing unrest.

The situation came to a head in March 1811. In Nottinghamshire, the hosiery industry, which employed much of the working population, was in difficulties. Following unemployment and reduced wages, the framework-knitters were very frustrated. Trouble broke out at the village of Arnold where workers smashed 63 power knitting-frames in one night. The men became known as Luddites after their leader who had assumed the name of Ned or General Ludd; and violence spread through the East Midlands and farther north, continuing until October 1816 (although there were sporadic outbreaks until 1840). By that time at least 1,000 stocking frames had been destroyed, together with a number of lace machines; and in the northern textile factories, weavers and finishers had broken up the new power looms and frames. Over 10,000 soldiers and police had been employed to control the mobs, and there were a number of deaths and injuries. But not everyone was against the Luddities: in the House of Lords the poet Lord Byron made a famous speech in their defense.

 Practical information

Information: covers counties of Derbyshire, Leicestershire, Lincolnshire, Northamptonshire, and Nottinghamshire. *East Midlands Tourist Board*, Exchequergate, Lincoln, Lincolnshire LN2 1PZ, ☎ (0522) 31521/3 - written and telephone enquiries only.

Weather forecast: ☎ (0602) 8091.

Self-catering cottages: *Stubbs Cottages*, CV Stubbs and Sons, Manor Warren Farm, Welton-le-Wold, Louth, Lincolnshire LN11 0QX, ☎ (0507) 604207; *Bulwick Park Cottages*, Bulwick Hall, Corby, Northamptonshire NN17 3DZ, ☎ (0780) 85245.

Youth hostel: *YHA*, 38 Bank Road, Matlock, Derbyshire DE4 3NF, ☎ (0629) 4666.

Festivals: **4-11 Jul.**: *International Organ Festival* in St. Albans, staged in the medieval abbey.

Customs and folklore: *Well-dressing* is the custom of decorating the wells and springs of Derbyshire with flowers and greenery, usually in Jul. and Aug., occasionally during Whitsun. **May**: Ashford, Etwall, Middleton, Monyash, Tissington, and Wirksworth; **Jun.**: Bakewell, Hope, Litton, Rowsley, Tideswell, Wyaston

and Youlgreave; **Jul.**: Buxton, Eyam Glapwell, Heath, Holmewood, Pilsley, and Wormhill; **Sep.**: Hartington. *Corby Pole Fair* on Whit Mon., is an old village fete featuring the roasting of an ox and climbing a greasy pole.

Other events: **30 Jul.-1 Aug.**: *Country Landowner's Association Game Fair* in Chatsworth House, a stately home near Bakewell, Derbyshire - includes shooting, fishing, gundog trials, archery, falconry, exhibitions and competitions. **30-31Aug.**: *Medieval Jousting Tournament* in Belvoir Castle, Belvoir, Leicestershire.

Scenic railway: Nene Valley Railway runs 6 miles between Rugby, Northampton and Peterborough through the pastoral water meadows of the valley of the R. Nene. Scandinavian trains are used. Contact: *Nene Valley Railway*, Wansford Station, Stibbington, Peterborough, Northants, ☎ (0780) 782854.

River and canal cruises: horse-drawn cruisers and narrow boats for rent from *Cromford Canal Society*, Old Wharf, Mill Lane, Cromford, Matlock, Derbyshire DE4 3RQ, ☎ (0629) 823727; *Anglo Welsh Waterway Holidays*, Canal Basin, Lelcester Road Market, Harborough, Leicester LE16 7BJ, ☎ (0858) 66910 - narrow boats and cruisers for rent on the Grand Union Canal and Great River.

Gliding and hang gliding: *Derbyshire and Lancashire Gliding Club*, Camphill, Great Hucklow, Buxton SK17 8RD, ☎ (0298) 871270; *Peak School of Hang Gliding*, 16 Lower Green, Findern DE6 6AD, ☎ (0283) 43879.

Parachuting: *Lincoln Parachute Centre*, Sturgate Airfield, Upton, Gainsborough DN21 5PA, ☎ (0427) 83 620.

Archery: *Anglian Sports Promotions*, Childrens Holiday, Dept.17, Willoughton Road, Skegness, ☎ (0754) 67840.

Caving and potholing: *Buxton Activity Centre*, Manchester Road, Buxton SK17 6ST, ☎ (0298) 2284.

Climbing: *Buxton Activity Centre* (→ above).

Motor racing: *Crossroads Hotel*, High Street, Weedon NN7 4PX, ☎ (0327) 40354.

Orienteering holidays: *Frontier Camp Action Centres*, Welford Avenue, Irthlingborough NN9 5XA, ☎ (0933) 651718.

Canoeing and sailing: *Whitehall Centre for Open Country Pursuits*, Long Hill, Buxton SK17 6SX, ☎ (0298) 3260.

Hunting: *Belvoir Hunt*, Manor House, Claypole, Newark, Nottinghamshire NG23 5BA, ☎ (0636) 84 487.

Partridge and pheasant shoots: *John German Estate Offices*, Ashby-de-la-Zouch, Leicestershire, ☎ (0530) 412821.

Aquatic sports: waterskiing and windsurfing: *Action Sports*, 24 Windermere Avenue, North Hykeham, Lincoln LN6 8UG, ☎ (0522) 687648; *National Water-*

sports Centre, Adbolton Lane, Holme Pierrepont, Nottingham NG12 2LU, ☎ (0602) 866301.

Rambling and hiking: *Lord Winston's Walking Tours*, East Wing, The Manor, Moreton, Pinkney, Daventry NN11 6SJ, ☎ (0295) 76342; *Peak Walks*, Ash Lea,

10 Rainbow Road, Macclesfield SK10 2PF, ☎ (0625) 612291; *Peak National Park Centre*, Losehill Hall, Castleton, Derbyshire S30 2WB, ☎ (0433) 20373.

Golf: Thonock, Lincolnshire (18-hole); North Shore Hotel and Country Club, Skegness (18-hole).

 # Towns and places

ASHBOURNE

Derby, 13; Stoke-on-Trent, 24; London, 139 m
pop. 5,755 ☎ 0335   Derbyshire A1

Market town lying on edge of Peak District National Park (→), it has unique Shrovetide football game and delicious gingerbread.

▶ 13thC parish church of **St. Oswald**★ contains stained-glass windows and monuments to local families, notably marble tomb of Penelope Boothby. **Old Grammar School**, founded by Queen Elizabeth I 1585. Both in **Church Street**: Georgian houses.

Nearby

▶ **Tissington**★ (*5m N*): attractive village of the White Peak (→). Small Norman **church** houses richly carved stone coffin lid, one of the most interesting Anglo-Saxon pieces in England. **Tissington Trail**★ on site of old **Hartington Railway**; picnic site and trail of level walking N from Ashbourne; good starting point for walks into **Dove Dale**★★ (→) with impressive lock structures, native flora. □

Practical information

ASHBOURNE
🛈 13 The Market Place ☎ (0335) 43666.

Recommended
Farmhouse: at Weston Underwood, *Parkview Farm*, ☎ (0335) 60352, large garden. £19 B. & B.
Golf course: Clifton (1 1/2m S on A515) ☎ (0335) 42078.
♥ pastry *Ashbourne Gingerbread*, 26 St. John Street, ☎ (0335) 43227; *Cannon Craft*, Sundial Farm, Brailsford, ☎ (0335) 60480, model 19C cannons, field guns.

Nearby

ALSOP EN LE DALE, 7m N off A515

Hotel:
★ *New Inns*, Buxton Road, DE6 1EX, ☎ (033 527) 203, AC DI, 13 rm. ℗ ≶ ▩ ◿ ♨ £32. Rest. ♦ ♪ £9.

BRASSINGTON, 6 1/2m NE off B5035

Inn or Pub:
Olde Gate (Marston Thompson), ☎ Carsington (062 985) 448 ℗ ≶ ▩ ◿ Beef cooked in butter, fish, salads. £6.

FENNY BENTLEY, 3m N on A515

Hotel:
★★ *Bentley Brook*, DE6 1LF, ☎ (033 529) 278, AC, 9 rm. ℗ ▩ ◡ £38. Rest. ♦ ♪ £12.

HARTINGTON, 10m N off A515

Hotels:
★ *Charles Cotton*, The Square, SK17 0AL, ☎ (029 884) 229, 10 rm. ℗ ≶ ▩ 14thC inn with fishing in the River Dove. £24. Rest. ♦ ♪ ᵴ Local trout. £7.
★ *Minton House*, Market Place, SK17 0AL, ☎ (029 884) 368, 8 rm. ≶ ▩ £25. Rest. ♦ ♪ ᵴ £8.

Inn or Pub:
Jug & Glass, ☎ (029 884) 224 ℗ ≶ ▩ ◿ ᵴ ♨ 2 rm. Bar snacks, lunch, eve. meals. £4.50.

KNOCKERDOWN, 4 1/2m NE of B5035

Inn or Pub:
Knockerdown Inn (Marston Thompson), ☎ Carsington (062 985) 209 ℗ ▩ ◿ Lunch and eve. meals, steaks, homemade specials. £5.

THORPE, 2m N off A515

Hotels:
★★★ *Izaak Walton*, Dovedale, DE6 2AY, ☎ (033 529) 278, Tx 377106, AC AM BA DI, 33 rm. ℗ ▩ ◿ ᵴ Rest. ♦ ♪ ᵴ £12.
★★ *Peveril of the Peak* (THF), DE6 2AW, ☎ (033 529) 333, AC AM BA DI, 41 rm. ≶ ▩ ◿ ⤳ £65. Rest. ♦ £11.

ASHBY-DE-LA-ZOUCH*

Derby, 15; Leicester, 17; London, 111 m
pop. 10,633 ☎ 0530   Leicestershire AB2

Named after the Norman La Zouch family who bought Ashby Manor in 1160, it became briefly a spa town in 19thC. The wide market street has Elizabethan half-timbered houses blending well with later Georgian and modern buildings.

▶ **Castle ruins**: Norman manor fortified 15thC, dismantled by Cromwell in Civil War has underground passages. Famous as setting for tournament in Sir Walter Scott's novel, *Ivanhoe* (*mid-Mar.-mid-Oct.*: *Mon.-Sat. 9.30-6.30, Sun. 2-6.30; mid-Oct.-mid-Mar.*: *Mon.-Sat. 9.30-4, Sun. 2-4.*). ▶ Near castle ruins church of **St. Helen**; E window incorporating heraldic glass from castle chapel and 'finger pillory' once used to punish anyone interrupting sermon.

Nearby

▶ **Staunton Harold Hall** (*5m NE*) existed in Saxon times, present building Jacobean with elegant 18thC Palladian façade. ▶ **Staunton Harold Church**, built in Cromwellian times, retains original 17thC cushions and hangings with fine painted ceiling. Beautiful setting of lake and wooded park. ▶ Old cottages of **Osgathorpe** (*5m S*) grouped around 14thC church; **Gracedieu Priory** (*1m NE*) founded 1240; walls, two towers and chapel visible. ▶ **Breedon-on-the-Hill** (*6m N*), on site of Iron Age hill fort. **13thC church** contains magnificent Saxon sculptures. Extensive **views** over valley of River Trent. ▶ **Calke Abbey**★ (*5m NE*), an early 18thC house, at present being restored, in a fine landscaped setting (*park open all year.*) □

Practical information

ASHBY-DE-LA-ZOUCH
🛈 13-15 Lower Church Street, ☎ (0530) 415603.

Hotel:
★★★ *Royal Osprey*, Station Road, LE6 5GP, ☎ (0530) 412833, Tx 341629, AC AM BA DI, 31 rm. ℗ ▩ £60. Rest. ♦ ♪ Cl. lunch Sat. £11.50.

Restaurant:
♦ *La Zouch*, 2 Kilwardby Street, ☎ (0530) 412536, AC AM BA DI Cl. Sun. dinner, Mon., 1-8 Jan., 1-8 Jul. £11.

Nearby

MEASHAM, 4m S on A453

Hotel:
★★ **Measham Inn**, Tamworth Road, DE12 7DY, ☎ (0530) 70095, Tx 34610, AC AM BA DI, 32 rm. ⚹ £40. Rest. ♦ ♪ Cl. lunch Mon., Wed., Sat. £7.

BAKEWELL**

Buxton, 12; Chesterfield, 13; London, 154 m
pop. 3,839 ☎ 062 981   Derbyshire A1

In the central region of the Peak District with picturesque limestone dales and outcrops of gritstone rocks. Administrative centre for the Peak District National Park(→). Famous for trout fishing and 'Bakewell Tart'(→).

▶ In centre of town: **Old Market Hall** houses Information Centre for National Park. ▶ 14thC church of **All Saints★** has medieval monuments, also important Saxon fragments. ▶ Nearby **Old House Museum★**: restored 16thC buildings with original wattle and daub interiors. Collection includes Arkwright cotton machinery (*Apr.-Oct.: daily 2.30-5*) ▶ Two bridges span River Wye, five-arched 14thC bridge and further upstream medieval packhorse bridge, rebuilt 17thC.

Nearby

▶ **Bakewell** is a good centre for visiting the **Peak** and two important houses in area. **Haddon Hall★★★** (*2m SE*), a little-altered medieval house set around two courtyards, stands on bluff overlooking river. Chapel built 11thC by William Peveril. Banqueting Hall, 1350, has oak paneling, minstrel's gallery and 400-year-old long table. Old Kitchen with great fireplaces, ovens and many items as used in Middle Ages. Long gallery, 1590, has heraldic glass and paneled walls. Interesting furniture, tapestries and paintings. ▶ Terraced rose gardens (*end Mar.-Sep.: Tue.-Sun. 11-6; cl. Sun., Mon. in Jul. and Aug. Bank Hols. Sun. and Mon., 11-6.*) ▶ **Chatsworth★★★** (*4m E*), built by Talman for 1st Duke of Devonshire late 17th-early 18thC, to replace Elizabethan house built by 'Bess of Hardwick'. Known as 'Palace of the Peak', house has Palladian exterior, with incomparable works of art; State Rooms with ceilings painted by Verrio and Laguerre; masterpiece of illusionist painting by Thornhill in Sabine room. Paintings and drawings by Rembrandt, Velasquez, Van Dyck, Inigo Jones, Palladio, Zoffany and Reynolds. Important sculpture collection formed by 6th Duke; superb furniture, tapestries, china and plate collected over fifteen generations. Gardens laid out by 'Capability' Brown; famous **Emperor Fountain**, highest gravity-fed fountain in the world; cascades and aqueduct. For children: farmyard and adventure playground (*Easter-Oct: daily; house 11.30-4.30, garden 11.30-5*). ▶ Estate village of **Edensor** visible from house, designed by Joseph Paxton in 1838-42. ▶ Area contains some of deepest and richest lead mines in Peak. Near **Sheldon** (*4m W*) are remains of **Magpie Mine**; engine house with chimneys, mainshaft and cage and reconstructed horse gin. ▶ Situated SW of Bakewell is **Arbor Low**, huge stone circle built by Beaker people. ▶ **Stanton Moor** (*8m S*) has many circles and seventy Bronze Age barrows; best known circle is **Nine Ladies**. ▶ At Birchover is **Rowter Rocks**: caves, rooms, steps, armchairs etc. carved from rocks in 17thC as retreat for local vicar. ▶ **Eyam★** (*5m N*) is famous Peak District village. Vicar William Mompesson in 1665 successfully isolated village to stop spread of the plague (→). **Church** contains engraved book displaying names of plague victims.   ▯

Practical information _____

BAKEWELL
ⓘ Old Market Hall, Bridge Street, ☎ (062 981) 3227.

Plague village

The pretty village of Eyam is celebrated for its brave inhabitants during the Great Plague which swept London in 1665. The plague reached the village probably by means of an infected box of clothing sent from London. The Rector, William Mompesson, managed to persuade his parishioners not to spread the disease further by isolating themselves from the outside world rather than running away. They did so, and five in every six villagers died — including Mompesson's wife — but the plague was contained. The villagers' courage is still honoured in an open-air service which is held every year on the last Sunday in August.

Hotel:
● ★★ **Milford House**, Mill Street, DE4 1DA, ☎ (062 981) 2130, 11 rm. ℗ ⚹ ₩ ℚ Cl. Jan.-Feb. £40. Rest. ♦ ⚹ Cl. to non-residents lunch (ex. Sun.). £8.50.

Restaurant:
● ♦ **Fischer's**, Woodhouse, Bath Street, ☎ (062 981) 2687, AC AM BA DI ℗ ₩ ℚ ⚹ ❀ Cl. Christmas, 25 Aug.-8 Sep., Sun. eve., Mon., Sat. lunch. Fillet of lamb with sorrel sauce. No children under 11. Book. £25.

⅄ **Greenhills C.P.**, Crow Hill Lane (100 pl), ☎ (062 981) 3467.

Recommended
Antique shop: *Chappell, K., Antiques & Fine Art*, King Street, ☎ (062 981) 2487, furniture, metalwork.
♥ **tearoom:** *Old Bakewell Pudding Shop*, The Square, ☎ (062 981) 2193, homemade cakes, puddings, savouries.

Nearby

ASHFORD-IN-THE-WATER, 2m NW on A6

Hotel:
★★★ **Riverside**, Fennel Street, DE4 1QF, ☎ (062 981) 4275, AC AM BA, 4 rm. ℗ ⚹ ₩ ℚ £55. Rest. ♦ ⚹ Dinner only, Sun. lunch. £16.

BASLOW, 4m NE on A619

Hotels:
● ★★★ **Cavendish**, DE4 1SP, ☎ (024 688) 2311, Tx 547150, AC AM BA DI, 23 rm. ℗ ⚹ ₩ ℚ £70. Rest. ♦ Terrine of freshwater fish, rabbit with basil sauce in a pastry case. £18.
★ **Wheatsheaf**, Netherend, DE4 1SR, ☎ (024 688) 2240, 23 rm. ℗ ₩ ℚ ⚹ £30. Rest. ♦ ♪ ⚹ £7.

Recommended
Farmhouse: *Cross Farm*, Bubnell Lane, ☎ (024 688) 2230, near National Park. No more than 1 child. £32 B. & B.

BRETTON, 10m NW off A623

Inn or Pub:
Barrel (Bass Charrington), ☎ (0433) 308 56 ℗ ⚹ ₩ ℚ ⚹ Bar snacks, salads, soups. £4.

EYAM, 7m N off A623

Restaurant:
♦ *Miners Arms*, Water Lane, ☎ Hope Valley (0433) 30853 ℗ ₩ ℚ ♪ ❀ Cl. Mon. to non-residents, Sun. dinner, 25-26 Dec. 7 rm. Book. £12.

FOOLOW, 9m NW off A623

Inn or Pub:
Lazy Landlord, ☎ (0433) 308 73 ℗ ₩ ℚ ⚹ ❀ 2 rm. Bar meals, fillet steak, pork in honey. £5.

GREAT LONGSTONE, 1m N off A6020

Hotel:
● ★★ **Croft**, DE4 1TF, ☎ (062 987) 278, AC BA, 8 rm. ℗ ₩ ℚ ⚹ ♪ Cl. Jan. £50. Rest. ♦ ♪ Cl. Mon.-Wed. £10.50.

GRINDLEFORD, 6m N on B6001

Hotel:
★★★ *Maynard Arms*, Main Road, S30 1HP, ☎ (0433) 30621, AC AM BA DI, 13 rm. ℗ ⌖ ♨ ⛲ ♫ Victorian hotel in the Peak National Park. £45. Rest. ♦ ♪ Venison and black cherry pie. 10.50.

HASSOP, 2m N on B6001

Hotel:
★★★ *Hassop Hall*, DE4 1NS, ☎ (062 987) 488, Tx 37126, AC AM BA DI, 12 rm. ℗ ⌖ ♨ ⛲ £55. Rest. ● ♦ ⅃ Cl. lunch Mon., dinner Sun. £15.

ROWSLEY, 4m SE on A6

Hotel:
● ★★ *Peacock* (Embassy), Bakewell Road, Matlock, DE4 2EB, ☎ (0629) 733518, AC AM BA DI, 20 rm. ℗ ♨ ♫ Country house built in 1652, later used as Dower House to nearby Haddon Hall. £62.50. Rest. ♦ Guinea fowl in red wine sauce. £17.

BOLSOVER

Chesterfield, 6; Mansfield, 10; London, 143 m
☎ 0246   Derbyshire A1

The town stands high on an escarpment. It once sustained many large collieries, now confined to only a few working pits.

▶ Imposing **Bolsover Castle★** dates from Norman times, substantially enlarged early 17thC. Jacobean keep, with turrets and battlements is decorative rather than defensive. Beautiful paneled rooms: fireplaces of special note. 1630s Riding School building now houses Spanish-type Riding School (*15 Mar.-15 Oct.: Mon.-Sat., 9.30-6.30, Sun. 2-6.30; Apr.-Sep., Sun. from 9.30; 16 Oct.-14 Mar.: Mon.-Sat., 9.30-4, Sun. 2-4; cl. 24-26 Dec., 1 Jan.*). ▶ Close by is **parish church**, rebuilt 19thC after a fire, but Cavendish Chapel 1624 and family monuments survive.

Nearby

▶ Favourite local beauty spot, to NW, is **Cresswell Crags★★** (→), wooded limestone gorge with natural caves, once prehistoric dwellings. ▶ **Pleasley Vale Riverside Leisure Area** has pleasant walk along River Medan, forming part of a **Nature Trail** and **Reserve**. Vale was centre for spinning silk and cotton, making extensive use of river.   □

Practical information

BOLSOVER

ℹ Library, Church Street, ☎ (0246) 823179.
🚃 Alfreton and Mansfield Parkway, ☎ Sheffield (0742) 726411.

Nearby

WARSOP, 8m E on A60

Inn or Pub:
Hare & Hounds, Church Street, ☎ Mansfield (0623) 842440. £4.

BOSTON*

Skegness, 23; Lincoln, 34; London, 118 m
pop. 27,077 ☎ 0205   Lincolnshire C2

Old seaport on River Witham opening to the Wash, in fenland country. From 13thC traded in wool and wines with Europe. Founded by St. Botolph, a monk who in 7thC erected his monastery on an island rising above the then level of the fenland.

▶ 14thC church of St. **Botolph★★** has beautiful high medieval lantern tower nicknamed 'The Stump', so high it

has been used as navigational aid by ships in Wash. Good example of Perpendicular style, several fine brasses and medieval stalls with misericords. Cross river on St. Botolph's Footbridge to Irby Place for splendid view of Stump. ▶ **Guildhall★** in South Square, built 1450 now museum, has cells where, in 1607, Pilgrim Fathers were imprisoned during unsuccessful attempt to sail to America and Holland. American town of Boston derives name from here (*daily 9.30-12, 1.30-4.30; ex. Sat., Oct.-Apr.*). **Fydell House** adjoining Guildhall is fine example of Queen Anne architecture. ▶ **Pescod Hall**, Mitre Lane, built 15thC once home of wool merchant, now warehouses. ▶ **Maud Foster Windmill★★**, over 150 years old, fine example of five-sails (or 'sweeps') Lincolnshire mill. Boston's many water ways or 'drains' (man-made watercourses typical of fen country), provide facilities for coarse-fishing and boating. Many fine old warehouses. Numerous bulb fields to S.

Nearby

▶ A few m E is **Freiston Shore★★** on the Wash, salt-marsh, sand and mud flats. (*Parking in front of old sea embankment*). At high tide these undisturbed marshes offer a variety of birdlife, some rare.   □

Practical information ────────

ℹ Assembly Rooms, Market Place, ☎ (0205) 55050.
🚃 ☎ (0205) 63281.

Hotels:
★★★ *New England*, 49 Wide Bargate, PE21 6SH, ☎ (0205) 65255, Tx 858875, AC AM BA DI, 25 rm. ℗ & ♫ £50. Rest. ♦ ♪ & £10.
★ *Burton House*, Wainfleet Road, PE21 9RW, ☎ (0205) 62307, AC AM BA, 6 rm. ℗ ♨ £38. Rest. ♦ ♪ Cl. dinner Sun.-Mon. £10.
★ *White Hart* (BI), 1-5 High Street, PE21 85H, ☎ (0205) 64877, AC AM BA DI, 31 rm. ℗ ♫ £45. Rest. ♦ ♪ £8.

Inn or Pub:
Town Pump, Craythorne Lane, ☎ (0205) 685 94 & Bar food, specials, pies, lasagne. £3.

Å at Hubbert's Bridge, *Orchards C.P.*, Frampton Lane (30 pl), ☎ (020 579) 328.

Recommended
Craft workshops: *Wrangle Potter*, Main Road, Wrangle, ☎ (0205) 870013, handmade pottery, stoneware, porcelain.
Golf course: Cowbridge, Horncastle Road (2m N on B1183) ☎ (04463) 62306.
Guesthouse: at Sutterton, *Georgian House*, Station Road, ☎ (020 586) 763, 18thC Georgian house near medieval church. £23 B. & B.

BUXTON**

Macclesfield, 12; Stoke-on-Trent, 22; London, 159 m
pop. 20,316 ☎ 0298   Derbyshire A1

An old spa town known to the Romans, it is still possible to drink the pleasant tasting waters. The highest town in England, surrounded by hills, on the edge of the Peak District National Park (→).

▶ **The Crescent★**, opposite the town's hot springs, was built late 18thC by 5th Duke of Devonshire. Elegant semi-circular building of three hotels with Assembly Room above and shops below, designed by John Carr of York, as rival to Royal Crescent at Bath. ▶ The warm blue spa water from seven springs can be seen at **St. Anne's Well**, old pump room now information centre. ▶ At rear of Crescent, **Devonshire Hospital**, originally stabling, with enormous slate-covered roof built 1881 to cover circular exercise area and **Pavilion Gardens Octagon,★** laid out 1870s. Set in 23 acres of landscaped parkland, offering leisure pool and Conservatory with variety of native and exotic plants. Recently restored Edwardian Opera House is worth a visit. ▶ Nearby **Church of St. John★** designed by

Wyatville, 1811, in Tuscan style. ▶ In the town is **Poole's Cavern Country Park**★: picnic site and tours of historic caverns. Also **Corbar Woods**★ with splendid hilltop views.

Nearby

▶ 6m N is busy industrial town of **Chapel-en-le-Frith**, lying near rugged gritstone moorland. Town's name means 'chapel in the forest', originating from when it was part of Royal Forest of the Peak. In vicinity of **18thC church**, originally built by foresters 1225, where stone cross and stocks. ▶ NW of Buxton is **Goyt Valley**★★, with two large reservoirs surrounded by wood and moorland. The beautiful countryside is rich in native flowers and birds. Accessible by road, with car parks and picnic sites in and around valley. Starting from **Errwood Hall** car park is a **nature trail**★ best enjoyed on foot. ▶ To W, on road to Macclesfield, is highest inn in England at 1690ft., **The Cat and Fiddle**. Superb views over Goyt Valley. Walk from here to Dane Bower or into Goyt Valley. ▶ To E are limestone dales and villages. Drive to **Tideswell** (*5m NE*) along **River Wye**, through picturesque **Wye Dale**★★ (→), **Miller's Dale**★★ (→) and **Tideswell Dale**★★ (→). Tideswell is surrounded on high ground by remains of lead mines and, in limestone dales, cotton mills. This small market town has **14thC church**★★ known as the 'Cathedral of the Peak'. Inside are brasses, monuments and magnificent stained-glass windows; black oak chancel stalls with misericords are 600 years old. Town has summer well-dressing ceremony. 1m S of village is start of a **nature trail**★ which includes a **basalt quarry**, cotton mills, like **Litton Mill**. 1m E, walking beside lovely **River Wye**★ you reach **Cressbrook Mill**. Of interest is Gothic-styled **apprentice house** built by Arkwright, 1779. **Ravens Tor**★, just W of Litton Mill in **Miller's Dale** (→), is a huge limestone rock overhanging the road. ▶ Village of **Taddington** (*5m SE*), with its dry valley of **Taddington Dale**★★, leads to foot of beautiful **Monsal Dale**★★ (→). Here panoramic views down to the Wye and majestic **railway viaduct**★ of Buxton to Bakewell (→) line, built 1860s.   □

Practical information ────────────

BUXTON
ⓘ The Crescent ☎ (0298) 5106.
▨▧ ☎ (0298) 2101.

Hotels:
★★★ *Lee Wood* (B.W.), 13 Manchester Road, SK17 6TQ, ☎ (0298) 3002, Tx 669848, AC AM BA DI, 42 rm. Ⓟ ⑊ ⚐ £50. Rest. ♦ ♪ Cl. 24-28 Dec. £11.50.
★★★ *Palace* (Heritage), Palace Road, SK17 6AG, ☎ 0298) 2001, Tx 668169, AC AM BA DI, 122 rm. Ⓟ ⑊ ▭ ⚐ £60. Rest. ♦ ♪ £10.
● ★★ *Grove*, Grove Parade, SK17 6QJ, ☎ (0298) 3804. AC AM BA DI, 21 rm. £32. Rest. ♦ ♪ Vegetarian dishes. £9.
★★ *Old Hall*, The Square, SK17 6BD, ☎ (0298) 2841, AC AM BA, 36 rm. Ⓟ ⚐ ♪ ⚐ £36. Rest. ♦ & £9.
★ *Hartington*, 18 Broad Walk, SK17 6JR, ☎ (0298) 2638, AC, 17 rm. Ⓟ ✿ £32. Rest. ♦ ♪ Cl. 24 Dec.-3 Jan. and lunch. £6.

Restaurant:
♦ *Nathaniels*, 35 High Street, ☎ (0298) 78388, AC AM BA DI ♪ ✿ Cl. 2 wks. Nov., Mon., Sun. eve. Prawn and salmon mousse, venison. Book. £13.

⚘ ⚲ *Newhaven C.C.P.*, Newhaven (100 pl), ☎ (029 884) 300.

Recommended
Farmhouse: *Mr and Mrs. D. Smith*, Hawthorn Farm, Fairfield Road, ☎ (0298) 3230, a 16thC farmhouse. £20 B. & B.
Golf course: Cavendish, Gadley Lane, ☎ (0298) 3494; Buxton and High Peak, Fairfield, ☎ (0298) 3453.
Guesthouse: *Lynstone Guest House*, 3 Grange Road, ☎ (0298) 77043, homey atmosphere in quiet Victorian house. £17 B. & B.
Riding school: *Northfield Farm*, Quanford, ☎ (0298) 2543.

Nearby

CHAPEL-EN-LE-FRITH, 5m N on A6

Hotel:
★ *Kings Arms*, Market Place, SK12 6EN, ☎ (0298) 812105, AC AM BA DI, 11 rm. Ⓟ ⚐ 17thC coaching inn. £23. Rest. ♦ ♪ Cl. 25 Dec.-1 Jan. £10.

CHINLEY, 2m NW of on B6062

Inn or Pub:
Old Hall Inn, ☎ (0663) 505 29, AC AM BA DI Ⓟ ⑊ ⚐ ⚐ & 8 rm. Bar meals and snacks, à la carte menu in restaurant. £8.

HURDLOW TOWN, 7m SE on A515

Inn or Pub:
Bull i'th' Thorn (Robinsons), Asbourne Road, ☎ Longnor (029 883) 348 Ⓟ ⑊ ⚐ & ✿ Bar meals, steaks, scampi. £4.

LITTLE HUCKLOW, 11m NE off B6049

Inn or Pub:
Old Bull's Head, ☎ (0298) 871 097 Ⓟ ⑊ ⚐ ⚐ & ✿ Bar snacks and coffee.

LITTON, 8m E off B6049

Restaurant:
♦ *Red Lion Inn*, ☎ (0298) 871458, AC Ⓟ ⑊ ⚐ ♪ & ✿ Cl. lunch Mon.- Fri., Sun.-Mon. eve. Duckling with orange and whisky sauce. Book. £8.50.

LONGNOR, 6m

Restaurant:
♦ *Ye Old Cheshire Cheese*, High Street, ☎ (029 883) 218, AC AM BA Ⓟ ✿ Cl. Sun. dinner and Mon. £20.

TADDINGTON, 5m E off A6

Restaurant:
♦ *Waterloo*, ☎ Buxton (0298) 85230, AC AM BA DI Ⓟ ⑊ ⚐ ⚐ ♪ & ✿ Cl. Sun., Mon. dinner. Scampi Wellington. Book. £13.

⚲ *Cottage Farm C.P.*, Blackwell in the Peak (30 pl), ☎ (029 885) 330.

TIDESWELL, 8m NE on B6049

Inn or Pub:
Anchor Inn (Frederic Adisimson), Four Lane Ends, ☎ (0298) 871 371, AC Ⓟ ⑊ ⚐ ⚐ & Bar and restaurant meals. £6.50.

CHARNWOOD FOREST★★★

Leicestershire B2

Containing some of the oldest rock formations in the country (pre-Cambrian), the diverse landscape offers contrasting scenery of high crags, woodland, heath, granite hills and valleys with man-made lakes and reservoirs. Once densely wooded, in medieval times monks cleared areas to build their abbeys. The oldest industry is quarrying for granite - since pre-Norman times.

▶ Offering attractive and peaceful walks, **Bradgate Park**★★ (→) covering 850 acres within the forest, not a formal park but stretches of open heathland, rocky hills and woods with red and fallow deer. Start at thatched and timbered village of **Newtown Linford**, entering alongside stream or near **'Old John'**, 18thC folly on 700 ft. high hill giving extensive views. Below folly, **Bradgate House**★, now in ruins, once home of Lady Jane Grey. ▶ **Swithland Wood**★★ (→) close by has ancient trees, remnant of medieval oak woods. Also lakes, craters of long-closed slate quarries, and reservoirs attracting a variety of birdlife.

Nearby

A short tour by car from **Ashby-de-la-Zouch** (→) through **Bardon** to **Copt Oak**. Here take footpath 1 m long to **Bardon Hill**, highest point in Charnwood Forest at 912 ft., with views over forest. From **Copt Oak** continue to Woodhouse Eaves. Road 1m E leads to car park from which summit of **Beacon Hill**★ (818 ft.) can be reached. Stark summit contrasts with spectacular views of gentler scenery below. Continue on from **Woodhouse Eaves** through **Swithland** with interesting medieval church, NE to **Mountsorrel** set on granite hill. From old quarries fine views across **Soar Valley.** From **Mountsorrel** make for **Cropston**, pretty thatched cottage village. Viewing **Bradgate Park** on your right, on to busy **Anstey**, with medieval packhorse bridge. Following through area of **Bradgate Park** to **Newtown Linford** then N back to **Ashby-de-la-Zouch.** □

CHESTERFIELD

Sheffield, 12; Derby, 23; London, 150 m
pop. 73,352 ☎ 0246 Derbyshire A-B1

Once a Roman fort, later a busy medieval market town. In the late 18thC James Brindley designed and built the canal connecting the town to the River Trent. By early 19thC the town became a centre for the surrounding mining district, following the building of the railways in 1840s. It is still important for coal and iron.

▶ **The Victorian Market Hall** overlooks canvas-topped stalls in the large open market place. ▶ Opposite the Hall is **The Shambles**★, the butcher's quarter of medieval times, with its network of alleyways. Walk through the Shambles to Church Way and 13thC parish church of **St. Mary and All Saints**★ whose famous 'crooked spire' dominates the skyline. ▶ George Stephenson, the great railway pioneer who built the railway through the town, lived in **Tapton House.** ▶ Further N at **Wittington** is the thatched-roofed **Revolution House,** where in 1688 conspirators plotted to overthrow James II and invite William and Mary to the throne.

Nearby

▶ **Hardwick Hall**★★★ (*8m SE*), one of the handsomest houses of the Elizabethan period, is inextricably linked with the name of its builder, Bess of Hardwick. Born at Hardwick of modest country gentry, Bess returned some sixty years and four husbands later as Countess of Shrewsbury, one of the richest women in England. A fanatical house-builder, she bought her old home from a bankrupt brother and set about building a new dwelling on the site, Hardwick Old Hall. But in 1590 Lord Shrewsbury died and Bess had total control of his vast fortune. She spent the next thirteen years building her grandest house, Hardwick Hall (close to the Old Hall, now in ruins). Designed by Robert Smythson, its immense windows are the house's most famous feature. The ground floor rooms are low and dark, rooms above more spacious while great rooms on third floor are immense and brilliantly lit. Magnificent plaster and carved alabaster fireplaces and one of the most important collections of contemporary embroidery in Britain (*29 Mar.-Oct.: Wed., Thu., Sat., Sun., Bank. Hols. Mon., 1-5.30 or sunset if earlier; cl. Good Fri. Garden daily during season 12-5.30*). ▶ **Ashover** to the S, lies in area once important for lead mining. Its fine parish church of **All Saints**★ has many interesting brasses and a large early 16thC alabaster tomb to Thomas Babington, his wife and fifteen children. □

Practical information

CHESTERFIELD

ℹ Peacock Information and Heritage Centre, Low Pavement, ☎ (0246) 207777.
🚆 ☎ Sheffield (0742) 26411.
Car rental: *Europcar*, Birmingham Road Wilson Servicentre Ltd, ☎ (0246) 74577.

Hotel:
★★★ ***Chesterfield*** (B.W.), Malkin Street, S41 7UA, ☎ (0246) 71141, Tx 547492, AC AM BA DI, 61 rm. [P] ♿ £55. Rest. ♦ ♪ £9.

Inn or Pub:
Walton Hotel (Homel), St. Augustines Road, ☎ (0246) 324 80 [P] ♨ ♿ ✗ Curry, trout, quiches, £3.

Recommended
Golf course: Walton (S off A632), ☎ (0246) 79256.

Nearby

APPERKNOWLE, 5m N off A61

Inn or Pub:
Yellow Lion, High Street, ☎ Dronfield (0246) 413 181 [P] ☼ ♨ ✎ Bar snacks and meals. £4.

CLOWNE, 8m E off A619

Hotel:
★★ ***Van Dyk***, Worksop Road, S43 4TD, ☎ (0246) 810219, AC AM BA, 16 rm. [P] ✎ £48. Rest. ♦ ♪ Cl. dinner Sun. £10.

DRONFIELD, 6m N on A61

Hotel:
★★★ ***Manor***, 10-15 High Street, S18 6PY, ☎ (0246) 413971, AC AM BA, 10 rm. [P] ✎ £35. Rest. ♦ ♪ Cl. dinner Sun., lunch Mon. 26 Dec.-31 Jan. £11.

Inn or Pub:
Blue Stoops (Wards), High Street, ☎ (0246) 412 110 [P] ✎ ✗ Bar snacks and meals, fish, pies. £3.

NEWBOLD, 1m NW on B6051

Hotel:
★★ ***Olde House***, S40 4RN, ☎ (0246) 74321, AC AM BA DI, 12 rm. [P] ♿ ✓ £45. Rest. ♦ ♪ Derbyshire lamb. £12.50.

RENISHAW, 6m NE on A616

Hotel:
★★★ ***Sitwell Arms***, Station Road, S31 9WE, ☎ (0246) 435226, Tx 547303, AC AM BA DI, 31 rm. [P] £51. Rest. ♦ ♪ ♿ Cl. Sat. lunch, 24-25 Dec. eve., 1 Jan. £11.

SPINKHILL, 9m NE on A616

Inn or Pub:
Angel (Tetleys), ☎ Eckington (0246) 432 315 [P] ♨ ✎ 3 rm. Bar snacks, salads and carvery. £3.

SUTTON-CUM-DUCKMANTON, 3m E on A632

Inn or Pub:
Arkwright Arms, Bolsover Street, ☎ (0246) 32053 [P] ☼ ♨ ✎ ✗ Homemade soups, beefburgers, apple pie. £3.50.

COALVILLE

Leicester, 12; Derby, 22; London, 104 m
☎ 0530 Leicestershire B2

Grew up around the coal-mining industry, it lies on edge of Charnwood Forest (→).

▶ **Donington-le-Heath** manor house, built around **1280**, is one of the oldest surviving dwelling houses in England. It has 16th and 17thC oak furniture and pleasant herb garden (*Easter-Sep.: Wed.-Sun., also Bank Hols. Mon., Tue. following, 2-6*).

Nearby

▶ Coalfields, served by canals and railways, have geographically influenced this area and **Swannington Open Air Museum**★ (*3m NW*) illustrates coal-mining heritage and where in 1832 George Stephenson built railway to Leicester (→; *access by arrangement*). ▶ **Moira Furnace**★ (*8m NW*), early 19thC blast furnace, best preserved in Europe, with industrial heritage trail around village of **Moira** (*daily from May*). □

Practical information ───────────

ⓘ Coalville Library, High Street, ☎ (0530) 35951/2.

Nearby

AGAR NOOK, 1 1/2m

Inn or Pub:
Davy Lamp (Wlvrhmpton Dudley), Belgrave Close, ☎ (0530) 811 955 ℗ ＆ Bar snacks. £2.

CORBY*

Northampton, 14; Leicester, 25; London, 84 m
☎ 053 63   Northamptonshire B2-3

The modern new town grew around expanding steel industry. Attempt to blend the new low-rise development with tracts of woodland, relics of the great Rockingham Forest (→). There are neighbouring ironstone villages of great charm, like Rockingham, Deene and Apethorpe.

Nearby

▶ **Rockingham Castle★★★** (*2m N*), built by William the Conqueror, stands on high ground with spectacular views. An Elizabethan house sits within massive 12thC walls and there is a medley of other buildings dating from 13th-19thC; occupied by Cromwell's Roundheads (special exhibition on Civil War; *Easter Sun.-Sep.: 2-6 Sun., Thu., and Bank Hols. Mon. and Tue.; Tue. in Aug.*). ▶ **Deene Park** (*5m NE*) is a 16th and 17thC transformation of a medieval manor house with extensive 19thC additions. The Tudor part, built round a courtyard, has the Great Hall (completed 1550) with splendid hammerbeam roof, and chimneypiece. In the house are relics of James Thomas Brudenell, 7th earl of Cardigan and leader of the Charge of the Light Brigade (*30-31 Mar., 4, 5, 25, 26 May, Sun. in Jun., 2-5, park from 1.*). ▶ Just over the hill from Deene is **Kirby Hall** built in 16thC altered in 17thC by Inigo Jones, and abandoned late 18thC. Now a romantic ruin, rich in architectural detail with fine carvings and 17thC gardens (*15 Mar.-15 Oct.: 9.30-6.30 Mon.-Sat., 2-6.30 Sun., Apr.-Sep., Sun. from 9.30.; 16 Oct.-14 Mar.: 9.30-4 Tue.-Sat., 2-4 Sun; cl. 24-26 Dec., 1 Jan.*).   □

Practical information ───────────

CORBY
ⓘ Civic Centre, George Street, ☎ 0536 202551.
▆▆▆ ☎ Kettering (0536) 521445.

Inn or Pub:
Knights Lodge (Everards), Tower Hill Road, ☎ Great Oakley (0536) 742 602 ℗ ⋙ ＆ ⊘ Bar snacks, lunch, restaurant Thu.-Sat. eve. £7.

Recommended
Craft workshops: *East Carlton Craft Workshops*, Old Coach House, ☎ (0536) 770977.
Golf course: Priors Hall Golf Club, Stamford Road, Weldon, ☎ (0536) .

Nearby

COTTINGHAM, 3m W

Hotel:
Hunting Lodge, ☎ Rockingham (0536) 771370, AC AM BA DI, 8 rm. ℗ £40. Rest. ♦ Cl. 25-26 Dec. £12.

DAVENTRY

Northampton, 12; Coventry, 18; London, 76
☎ 0327   Northamptonshire B3

The history of Daventry goes back to Iron-Age times : earthworks on **Barough Hill**, E of town, attest to this. The Royalist army of Charles I camped around the hill

before the Battle of Naseby. Attractive market place and Hall.   □

Pratical information ───────────

Nearby

BRAUSTON, 2m N

Hotel :
★★*Boatman London*, NN11 7HB, ☎ (0788) 89313, AC BA, 10 rm. ℗ ⋙ ⟋ £38. Rest. ♦ ♪ Cl. Sat. and Sun. dinner in winter. £10.

CRICK, 7m N off A5

Hotel :
★★*Post House* (T.H.F.), NN6 7XR, ☎ (0788) 822101, Tx 311107, AC AM BA DI, 96 rm ℗ ⋙ £65. Rest. ♦ ♪ £10.

DERBY*

Nottingham, 16; Chesterfield, 23; London, 128 m
pop. 218,026 ☎ 0332   Derbyshire AB2

County cathedral city, with a history dating back to Roman times, greatly influenced by the Danes, an ancient trading and market centre on the River Derwent. Famous for its Crown Derby porcelain, railway works and Rolls-Royce.

▶ The city has graceful parks and gardens, including Britain's first 'public park', the **Arboretum**, opened 1840, sited behind the Royal Crown Derby Factory. ▶ Parish church of **All Saints★** became a cathedral 1927. Rebuilt in 18thC by James Gibbs, it retains 16thC tower. Inside superb carved and gilded monument 'Bess of Hardwick' (→), who died 1607. Exquisite iron chancel screen, work of Robert Bakewell, a local ironsmith. ▶ Churches of interest are **St. Mary's-on-the-Bridge** dating from 14thC, one of five surviving churches built on a river bridge. Close by **St. Mary's Roman Catholic★**, first large parish church by A.W.N. Pugin, completed 1839. ▶ In the early 18thC, Daniel Defoe witnessed the birth of the factory system and described seeing a 'throwing mill' sited by the Derwent, close to St. Mary's Bridge. Mill threw silk, first English factory to mass produce goods. **The Industrial Museum★★★**, off Full Street, is housed in the **Silk Mill**. First floor gallery has displays illustrating Derbyshire industries past and present, including lead and coal mining, limestone quarrying, ceramics, brick making, textiles. On ground floor, **Rolls-Royce** aero engine collection. Famous firm established in Derby 1908. Exhibits show history of flying and aircraft as well as aero engine development (*Tue.-Fri., 10-5, Sat., 10-4.45; cl. Sun., Mon., and Bank Hols.*). ▶ A large employer of labour from mid-18thC is celebrated Royal Crown Derby Porcelain Company, as it is now known. The factory's **Museum★** in Osmaston Road has fine collection of Derby china and Royal Crown Derby china, dating from 1756 (*Mon.-Fri., 9-12.30, 1.30-4; cl. May Bank Hols. for 1 wk., Christmas*). ▶ **Derby City Museum and Art Gallery★★** houses local history exhibits and a superb collection of paintings, watercolours and drawings by local 18thC artist Joseph Wright (*Tue.-Sat., 10-5; cl. Sun., Christmas Day, Boxing Day, Good Fri. and Bank Hols. Mon., Tue.*)

Nearby

▶ **Kedleston Hall** (*4m NW*) is one of the finest examples of the work of Robert Adam in the country. Built 1760-70 on site of original medieval manor house, it is home of the Curzon family. Magnificent state rooms contain contemporary furniture and important collection of Old Masters; famous Roman Hall is unique. Marquis Curzon, while Viceroy of India 1898-1905, collected silver, ivories and works of art, now housed in Indian Museum. In the park is a **12thC church** (*open Easter Sun., Mon., Tue., except 6 May. Hall and museum 1-5.30; church, park and gardens 12-6*). ▶ **Elvaston Castle Country Park and Working Estate Museum★★** is just outside the city to SE. The

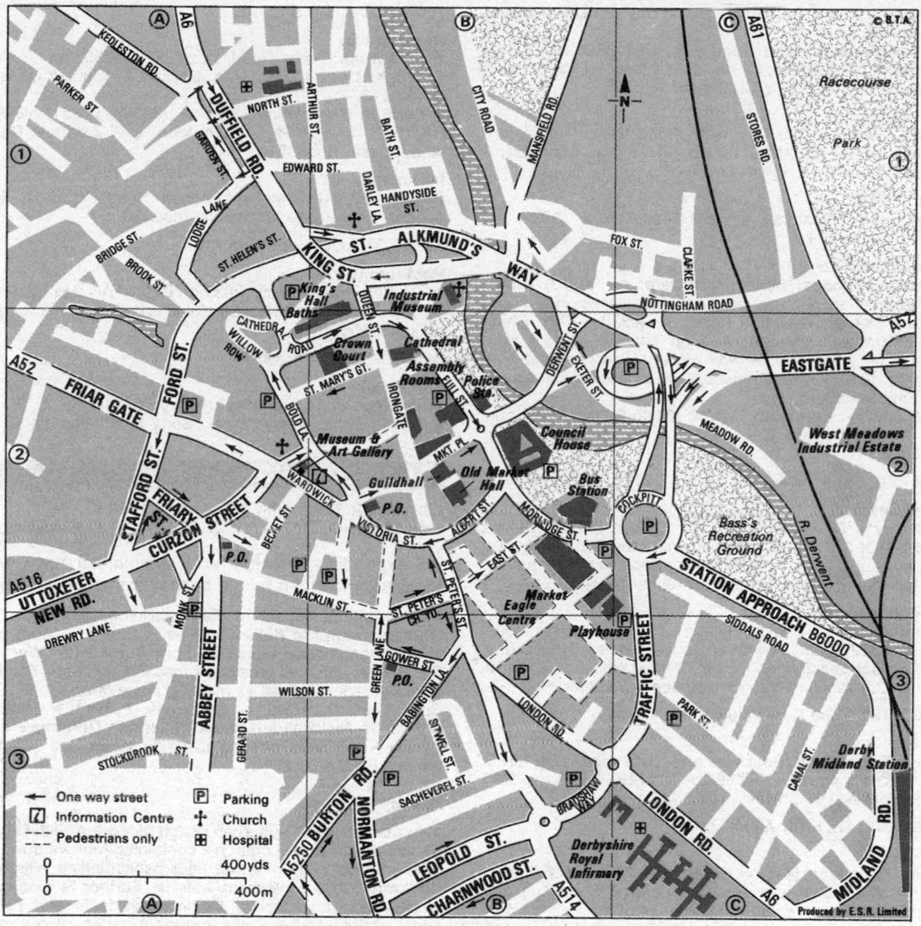

DERBY

extensive grounds are open all year as a Country Park, with serpentine lake, topiary gardens, grottoes, picnic areas and nature trail. The **Working Estate Museum**★ comprises estate buildings and workshops (*28 Mar.-31 Oct.: Wed.-Sat. 1-5, Sun. and Bank Hols. 10-6; other times by prior arrangement*). **Castle**★ itself is closed, but is fine early 19thC castellated Gothic style building, to designs of James Wyatt. ▶ The **Midland Railway Centre**★ Swanwick Junction near Ripley (*9m NE*), is a working museum portraying history of the line (*Mar.-Oct., Sat.-Sun., 10-6; other times by prior arrangement*). ▶ In attractive village of **Sudbury**, with its mellow red-brick buildings and gabled cottages is **Sudbury Hall**★★★ (*11m W*), a Charles II house with a series of rooms decorated by outstanding artists and craftsmen: ceilings painted by Laguerre, carvings by Grinling Gibbons and exceptional plasterwork (*29 Mar.-31 Oct., Wed.-Sun., and Bank Hols. Mon., 1-5.30; cl. Good Fri.*). In the former servants' wing is the **Museum of Childhood**★★ (special events for visitors; *Apr.-Oct., Wed.-Sun., and Bank Hol. Mon., 1-5.30 or sunset; cl. Good Fri.*). ▶ **Repton** (→Swadlincote)▶ At **Castle Donington**★★(*6m SE*) is a motor racing circuit with museum of racing cars, world's largest collection. □

Practical information

DERBY

ℹ Central Library,The Wardwick ☎ (0332) 31111 ext. 2185/6; ☎ (0332) 46124 (Sat. and eve. only).
✈ East Midlands Airport, Castle Donnington (12m SE off A6), ☎ (0332) 810621.
🚆 ☎ (0332) 32051.
Car rental: *Europcar*, Midlands Road, rail/drive ☎ 366061.

Hotels:

★★★ ***International*** (Consort), 228 Burton Road (B3), DE3 6AD, ☎ (0332) 369321, AC AM BA DI, 44 rm. Ⓟ ♿ £55. Rest. ♦ ♪ ♿ £10.

★★ ***Aston Court***, Midland Road (C3), DE1 2SL, ☎ (0332) 42716, AC AM BA DI, 78 rm. Ⓟ ♿ £35. Rest. ♦ ♪ Cl. Sun. dinner. £7.

★★ ***Clarendon*** (Midland), Midland Road (C3), DE1 2SB, ☎ (0332) 365235, AC AM BA DI, 48 rm. Ⓟ £38. Rest. ♦ ♪ Cl. Sat., Sun. lunch. £6.

★★ ***Gables***, 119 London Road (C3), DE1 2AR, ☎ (0332) 40633, AC AM BA, 76 rm. Ⓟ ♿ £50. Rest. ♦ ♪ Cl. Christmas. £8.

★★ ***Kedleston***, Kedleston Road (A1 off map), DE6 4JD, ☎ (0332) 559202, AC AM BA DI, 14 rm. Ⓟ ♿ £40.

Rest. ♦ ♪ Cl. Sun. dinner. Medallions of beef in Stilton sauce. £9.
★★ ***Midland***, Midland Road (C3), DE1 2SQ, ☎ (0332) 45894, AC AM BA DI, 62 rm. Ⓟ Oldest railway hotel in world. £45. Rest. ♦ ♪ Cl. Christmas. £10.

Restaurant:
♦ ***La Gondola***, 220 Osmaston Road (B3 off map), ☎ (0332) 32895, AC AM DI Ⓟ ♪ ♿ Cl. Sun. eve. Saltimbocca. Book. £12.

Inn or Pub:
Alexandra (Shipstons), Siddal's Road (C3), ☎ (0332) 365 337 Ⓟ Bar snacks.

Recommended
Craft workshops: *Denby Tableware*, ☎ (0773) 43641, handmade stoneware, cups, plates, vases etc; *Royal Crown Derby*, Osmaston Road, ☎ (0332) 47051, China tableware and giftware; at High Lane West, 8m from Derby on A609, *Bottle Kiln Pottery Gallery*, West Hallam, ☎ (0602) 329442, unusual and distinctive salt glazed ceramic sculpture.
Golf course: Kedleston Park ☎ (0332) 840035.

Nearby

BELPER, 7m N on A6

Restaurant:
♦ ***Remy's***, 84 Bridge Street, ☎ Belper (077 382) 2246, AM BA DI Ⓟ ♪ Cl. Sun. eve., Mon.-Sat. lunch, last 2 wks. Aug., 1 wk. Jan. Mignons of pork with orange and juniper berry sauce. No children under 8. Book. £17.

Recommended
Farmhouse : *Chevin Green Farm,* Chevin Road, ☎ (077 382) 2328, view over Derwent Valley, £29 B. & B.
Riding school: *Belper Riding Centre*, Whitehouse Farm, ☎ (0629) 2253, instruction courses in summer.

DRAYCOTT, 3m E on A6005

Hotel:
★★★ ***Tudor Court*** (Best Western), Gypsy Lane, DE7 3PB, ☎ (033 17) 4581, Tx 341995, AC AM BA DI, 30 rm. Ⓟ £55. Rest. ♦ ♪ £10.

INGLEBY, 8m S off A514

Inn or Pub:
John Thompson, Melbourne, ☎ (033) 286 2469 Ⓟ ♿ Roast beef and Yorkshire pudding Sun., Tue.-Sat. sandwiches only, cold buffet Mon. £4.50.

KIRK LANGLEY, 3m W on A52

Hotel:
★★ ***Meynell Arms***, Ashbourne Road, DE6 4NF, ☎ (033 124) 515, AC AM BA DI, 10 rm. Ⓟ £40. Rest. ♦ ♪ Cl. 25-26 Dec. Steak and kidney pie. £9.

MACKWORTH, 1/2m NW on A52

Hotel:
★★★ ***Mackworth***, Ashbourne Road, DE3 4LY, ☎ (033 124) 324, AC AM BA DI Ⓟ ♿ £41.50. Rest. ♦ ♪ £8.

MAKENEY, 5m N off A6

Inn or Pub:
Hollybush, Hollybush Lane, ☎ (0332) 841 729 Ⓟ Sandwiches. £2.

MORLEY, 1m N off A608

Hotel:
★★ ***Breadsall***, Priory Moor Road, DE7 6DL (B1), ☎ (0332) 832235, AC AM BA DI, 28 rm. Ⓟ £60. Rest. ♦ ♪ £12.

Recommended
Golf course: Breadsall Priory, ☎ (0332) 832235.

PASTURE HILL, 2 1/2m SW on A5250

Hotel:
★★★ ***Crest***, Littleover, DE3 7BA (B3 off map), ☎ (0332) 514933, AC AM BA DI, 66 rm. Ⓟ ♿ £70. Rest. ♦ ♪ Cl. Sat. lunch. £12.

SHARDLOW, 6m S on A6

Restaurants:
♦ ***La Marina***, Derby Road, ☎ (0332) 792553 Ⓟ ♪ Cl. 25-26 Dec., 1 Jan., Mon. English and Italian cuisine. Book. £13.
♦ ***Lady in Grey***, Wilne Lane, ☎ (0332) 792331, AC AM BA DI Ⓟ ♪ ♿ Cl. Sun.-Mon. eve. Zarzuela Catalana, paella. Book. £10.

Inn or Pub:
Dog & Duck (Marstons), London Road Ⓟ Bar snacks, homemade lunches, curries. £3.

SHELTON LOCK, 4m S on A514

Restaurant:
♦ ***Golden Pheasant***, ☎ (0332) 700112, AC AM BA DI Ⓟ ♪ ♿ Cl. Christmas. Steaks, chicken with champagne sauce. £9.50.

WILSON, 9m S off A453

Inn or Pub:
Bulls Head (Ind Coope), ☎ (033) 162 644 Ⓟ ♿ Hot and cold dishes every day ex. Sun., Mon. eves. £4.50.

GAINSBOROUGH

Lincoln, 19; Doncaster, 21; London, 149 m
pop. 20,326 ☎ 0427 Lincolnshire B1

An expanding industrial and commercial town with triple-arched stone bridge spanning the River Trent.

▶ One of the largest medieval buildings in England is **Gainsborough Old Hall★★** in Parnell Street, a 15thC and 16thC manorhouse rebuilt by Lord Burgh after Wars of the Roses with well-preserved medieval kitchen. The Pilgrim Fathers used hall as meeting place (*Mon.-Sat., 10-5; Sun., Easter-Oct. 2-5; cl. Christmas, 1 Jan.*). ▶ Minutes walk from Guildhall are **Witton Riverside Gardens★** bordering River Trent offering riverside views and scented garden for the blind.

Nearby

▶ Immediately N is suburban village of **Morton**, with Dutch-gabled buildings and **church★** containing four windows by Burne-Jones. High riverside floor banks linking village to **Walkerith** offer a pleasant walk. ▶ Further N extensive **woodland,** with Forestry Commission trails and picnic sites. ▶ **Stow** to the S has important parish church, predominantly 11thC but with Saxon doorway. To the E of Stow is remote hamlet of **Coates** with attractive medieval church of **St. Edith★**; fine family pew, rood screen. □

Practical information

GAINSBOROUGH
ⓘ Trinity Centre, Trinity Street, ☎ (0427) 617242.
Central, Green Road ☎ Retford (0777) 702491.

Hotel:
★★ ***Hickman Hill***, Cox's Hill, DN21 1HH, ☎ (0427) 3639, AC BA, 8 rm. Ⓟ £40.50. Rest. ♦ ♪ ♿ Devonshire pork casserole. £12.

Recommended
Golf course: Thonock (1m E), ☎ (0427) 2793.

Nearby

BLYTON, 4 1/2m NE on A159

Inn or Pub:
Black Horse (Bass Charrington), 93 High Street, ☎ Laughton (042 782) 277 Ⓟ ♿ Homemade pies, bar snacks. £5.

CLAYWORTH, 5m W off A631

Hotel:
★★★ ***Royston Manor***, St. Peters Lane, Retford, DN22 9AA, ☎ (0777) 817484, AC AM BA DI, 12 rm. Ⓟ ♿ £40. Rest. ♦ ♪ Cl. Sun. dinner. £10.

SCAFTWORTH VILLAGE, 11m W off A631

Inn or Pub:
King William, ☎ Doncaster (0302) 710 292 ℗ ⊞ ⬩ ⬩ ✆
Homemade pies and casseroles and freshly made salads.
£5.50.

STOW, 7m SE on B1241

Inn or Pub:
Cross Keys Inn, Stow Park Road, ☎ (0427) 788 014,
AC ℗ ≼ ⊞ ⬩ ⬩ ✆ Bar meals and à la carte restaurant
menu, Sun. lunch. £6.

WALKERINGHAM, 4m NW off A631

Hotel:
★★ *Brickmakers Arms*, Fountain Hill Road, ☎ (0427)
890375, AC AM BA, 9 rm. ℗ ⊞ ⬩ ⬩ ⬩ £28.50. Rest. ◆
♪ Cl. Sat. lunch Sun. dinner. Lobster victoria. £9.

GLOSSOP★★

Sheffield, 24; Manchester, 14; London, 174 m
pop. 25,339 ☎ 045 74   Derbyshire A1

Lies in the hills on the edge of the moorland. The
countryside contains the Dark Peak (→), a vast
region of rugged open moorland, within the Peak District National Park (→) This area has special appeal
to experienced walkers and climbers. A cotton spinning town, Glossop retains much from the Industrial
Revolution. It has the 'old town' of narrow streets
and 17thC stone buildings, and the 'new town' built
mid-19thC.

Nearby

▶ The Dark Peak (→) has two masses, **Kinder Scout**★★★
(→, 2088 ft.) and **Bleaklow**★★★ (→, 2060 ft.). To view the
dramatic scenery, take **Snake Pass**★★, a road SE from
town, winding upwards between the two masses and
on to **Ladybower**★★ (→) reservoir. Summit of the road
(1680 ft.) has a car park from where footpaths are clearly
marked into moors. Not for the inexperienced walker.
You can visit **Doctor's Gate**★, the **Roman Road** a quarter
mile off **Bleaklow** (→) side of road. Or, less rigorous, visit
Snake Inn on side and explore area around lower slopes
of Kinder Scout (→). Drive on to **Ladybower** (→) reservoir, to **Alport Dale**, where footpath up to **Alport Castle**★
offers a short gentle walk. ▶ Quiet town of **Hayfield** (4m
S) with good hill walks to **Kinder Scout** (→). Gentler walk
is 2¹/₂ m **Sett Valley Trail**★★ to **New Mills**: picnic spots at
the **Torrs**★★ and **Parkland, High Lea Hall**★★.   □

Practical information _____

GLOSSOP
ⓘ Station Forecourt, Norfolk Street, ☎ (045 74) 5920.
▰▰▰ ☎ Sheffield (0742) 726411.

Inn or Pub:
Crown Inn (Samuel Smith), Victoria Street, ☎ (0777) 817
206, AC BA ℗ ⊞ ⬩ ✆ Sandwiches, bar snacks, steaks
and à la carte restaurant menu. £12.

Recommended
Golf course: Glossop District, Sheffield Road, ☎ (0742)
3117.

◆**Nearby**
BIRCH VALE, 6m S on A6015

Inn or Pub:
Sycamore, ☎ New Mills (0663) 427 15, AC AM BA ℗ ≼
⊞ ⬩ ⬩ ✆ 1 rm. Fish, steaks, vegetarian dishes, barbecue. £10.

HAYFIELD, 5m S on A624

Hotel:
★ *Sportmans*, Kinder Road, SK12 5LE, ☎ (0663) 42118,
AM BA ℗ ⬩ ⬩ £29. Rest. ◆ ♪ ⬩ Cl. winter lunches. £8.

LITTLE HAYFIELD, 4m S on A624

Inn or Pub:
Lantern Pike (Webster Wilsons), ☎ New Mills (0663) 441
02, AC BA ℗ ≼ ⊞ ⬩ ✆ 4 rm. Bar snacks and lunches,
eve. meals. £3.50.

GRANTHAM★

Lincoln, 24; Nottingham, 24; London, 110 m
pop. 30,700 ☎ 0476   Lincolnshire B2

A prosperous market town, standing amidst the limestone hills of Lincolnshire by the River Witham, it is
the administrative capital and industrial centre of a
rich agricultural area. Prime Minister Margaret Thatcher was born here.

▶ At town centre is parish church of **St. Wulframf** with
beautiful 14thC tower and spire; houses 16thC chained
library. ▶ Opposite is 15thC **grammar school**, now King's
School; amongst old pupils, Sir Isaac Newton. On **St.
Peter's Hill** is famous statue to Newton, erected 1858.
▶ Near church is **Grantham House**, home of Hall family,
dating from 14thC (*Apr.-Sep.: Wed. pm by written appt.
only*). ▶ Some fine old coaching inns like **Angel and
Royal Hotel**★ had many royal visitors, earliest King John
who held court in 13thC before Magna Carta. ▶ Charles
Dickens stayed at the elegant late 18thC **George Hotel**★.

Nearby

▶ **Belton House**★★★ (*3m N*): fine example of Restoration
architecture, built in honey-coloured stone in late 17thC
from designs by Sir Christopher Wren, altered 1777 by
James Wyatt. Carvings by Grinling Gibbons and exquisite chapel in cedarwood is set in extensive landscaped
park (*Apr.-Oct.: Wed.-Sun. and Bank Hol. Mons. 1-5.30*).
▶ **Allington Manor House** (*5m N*), notable for Dutch
gables and interesting staircase. ▶ **Woolsthorpe
Manor**★★ (*7m S*) is small 17thC stone farmhouse, birthplace of Sir Isaac Newton. He lived here during plague
year (1665-6) and discovered theory of gravity, tradition
has it, whilst sitting under tree in the orchard (*Apr.-Oct.:
Sun.-Thu., 1.30-6*). ▶ **Belvoir Castle**★★★ (*7m SW*), home
of the Dukes of Rutland since 16thC. Originally Norman,
castle was destroyed during Civil Wars of 15th and 17thC,
and by fire in early 19thC. Present building dates from
1816, rebuilt by James Wyatt as mock medieval castle. Art
treasures include Gobelins tapestries, paintings by Holbein, Poussin, Rubens and Reynolds. Magnificent views
of Vale of Belvoir. Castle hosts special events including jousting tournaments. Famous **Belvoir foxhound**,
first bred nearby in 18thC, took name from castle (*22
Mar.-14 Oct., ex. 9-12 Jul.: Tue., Thu., Sat., 12-6, Sun.
12-7; Bank Hol. Mons. 11-7; Good Fri. only 12-6; Sun.
during Oct. 2-6*). ▶ At Bottesford, 5m N of Belvoir in
church of St. Mary, are monuments to the eight earls of
Rutland, those of 7th and 8th earl by Grinling Gibbons.
▶ **Grimsthorpe Castle** (*6 m SE*) has some 13thC features,
to which a Tudor building was added around a courtyard.
In 1722 Sir John Vanbrugh began to transform Grimsthorpe for the 1st and 2nd dukes of Ancaster; his work
never completed but the great N front and forecourt are
by him with hall and state rooms behind. ▶ **Sleaford** (*6m
SE*) is a pleasant market town in the centre of rich
farming countryside. **Parish church of St. Denys** has
some fine stone carving in the Decorated style and important N window of great flowing design. The **maltings** should
also be seen - a massive square tower with eight
detached pavilions, completed 1905.   □

Practical information _____

GRANTHAM
ⓘ The Museum, St. Peters Hill, ☎ (0476) 66444.
▰▰▰ ☎ (0476) 64135.

Hotels:
★★★ *George* (B.W.), High Street, NG31 6NN, ☎ (0476)

63286, Tx 378121, AC AM BA DI, 46 rm. ℗ £50. Rest. ♦
♪ ♿ Fresh salmon steak. £11.
★★★ *Kings,* North Parade, NG31 8AU, ☎ (0476) 65881,
AC AM BA DI, 17 rm. ℗ ♉ ♿ £37. Rest. ♦ ♪ ♿ Cream of
stilton and port wine soup. £9.
★★ *Angel Royal* (T.H.F.), High Street, NG31 6PN, ☎
(0476) 65816, AC AM BA DI, 28 rm. ℗ £64.50. Rest. ♦
Venison medallions in cream and whiskey. £10.

Restaurant:
♦ *Premier,* 2-6 North Parade, ☎ (0476) 77855, AC AM
BA DI ℗ Cl. Mon., Tue. lunch, Sun. dinner. £17.

⚴ at Folkingham, *Low Farm Touring Park,* Spring Lane
(50 pl), ☎ (052 97) 322.

Recommended
Craft workshops: *Barratt Swann,* Hardigate, Cropwell
Butler, ☎ (060 73) 2642, furniture; *Millfield Pottery,* Ever-
ton, ☎ (0777) 817723, handmade stoneware and porce-
lain.
Farmhouse: at Barkestone-le-Vale, *Mrs. Sylvia Smart,*
The Paddocks, ☎ (0949) 42208, 150-acres near Belvoir
Castle £18 B. & B.; at Redmile, *Marjorie and Peter Need,*
Peacock Farm, ☎ (0949) 42475, old farmhouse standing
in beautiful vale of Belvoir £23 B. & B.
Golf course: Belton Park, Belton Lane, Londonthorpe
Road, ☎ (0476) 63355/67399.
♥ *Catlin Bros.,* 11 High Street, ☎ (0476) 65428, huge
range of bread and cakes incl. wholemeal and organic.

Nearby
ASWARBY, 4m S off A15

Hotel:
★★ *Tally Ho,* NG34 8SA, ☎ (052 95) 205, 6 rm. ℗ ♨ ♉
♿ £28. Rest. ♦ ♪ ♿ Bar and restaurant meals, fresh
trout. £8.

BARKSTON, 6m N on A607

Restaurant:
♦ *Barkston House,* ☎ Loveden (0400) 50555, AC AM
BA DI ℗ ≮ ♨ ♉ ♉ Cl. 25-31 Dec., Sun.-Mon. eve., Sat.
lunch, Bank Hols. 2 rm. Farmhouse ragout of lamb.
Book. £13.

BARROWBY, 2m W off A52

Inn or Pub:
White Swan (Whitbread), High Road, ☎ (0476) 2375 ℗ ≮
♨ ♉ Lunch, eve. meals, steak, scampi. £5.

BOTTESFORD, 8m W

Restaurant:
♦ *Thatch,* 26 High Street, ☎ Bottesford (0949) 42330,
AC AM BA DI ℗ Cl. Sun. £15.

CAYTHORPE, 9m N on A607

Inn or Pub:
Red Lion, 62 High Street, ☎ Loveden (0400) 172 632, AC
BA ℗ ♨ ♉ 4 rm. Bar snacks and restaurant meals. £5.

CORBY GLEN, 9m SE on A151

Inn or Pub:
Woodhouse Arms, ☎ (047) 684316 ℗ ≮ ♨ ♉ ♿ Grills
and bar snacks and Sun. roast. £7.

EDENHAM, 13m SE on A151

Inn or Pub:
Five Bells (Melbournes), ☎ (0677) 832235 ℗ ♨ ♿ ♉ Bar
meals, homemade pies. £5.50.

GRIMSTHORPE, 13m SE on A151

Hotel:
★★ *Black Horse,* PE10 0LY, ☎ (077 832) 247, AC AM
BA, 4 rm. ℗ ≮ ♉ ♿ A stone-built coaching inn dating from
1759. £50. Rest. ● ♦ ♿ Cl. Christmas. Sun. £12.

KNIPTON, 5m SW off A607

Hotel:
★ *Red House,* NG32 1RH, ☎ (0476) 870352, 8 rm. ℗ ≮
♨ ♉ ♉ £22. Rest. ♦ ♪ Cl. Mon. ex. Bank Hols. £8.

OLD SOMERBY, 3m SE on A1176

Inn or Pub:
Fox & Hounds, ☎ Grantham (0476) 641 31 ℗ ♨ ♉ ♿
♉ Bar snacks, restaurant specials, seafood. £10.

SLEAFORD, 4m NE on A15
🚃 ☎ 302733.

Hotels:
★★ *White Hart,* Southgate, NG34 7RY, ☎ (0529) 302612,
AC AM BA DI, 16 rm. ℗ £35. Rest. ♦ ♪ Cl. Sun. dinner. £7.
★ *Carre Arms,* Mareham. Lane, NG34 7JP, ☎ (0529)
303156, AC BA DI, 14 rm. ℗ £36. Rest. ♦ ♪ ♿ Cl. Sun.
dinner. £10.

Inn or Pub:
Waggon Horses (William Stones), Eastgate, ☎ (0529)
303388 ℗ ♉ Chicken, gammon, scampi, beefburgers,
salads. £4.

WILSFORD, 5m W off A153

Inn or Pub:
Plough Inn, Main Road, ☎ Wilsford (0400) 303 04 ℗ ♨
♉ ♉ 2 rm. Meat and seafood dishes with salads. £3.50.

HINCKLEY

Nuneaton, 5; Leicester, 13; London, 95 m
pop. 29,325 ☎ 0455   Leicestershire A-B2

The traditional town industries of hosiery, knitwear,
and footwear co-exist with various modern light
industries.

▶ See the Framework Knitters Cottages in Bond Street,
group of 16thC thatched cottages opposite Aitkins hosiery
factory founded in 1722.

Nearby

▶ **Market Bosworth Light Railway★** at Shackerston Sta-
tion (*9m N*): enjoy trip on steam-hauled trains and visit
Railway Museum. ▶ **Battlefield of Bosworth Ambion Hill
Farm★★★,** Sutton Cheney (*5m N*), scene of one of the
country's most important battles in 1485, which ended in
Yorkist Richard III being killed, and Lancastrian claimant
Henry Tudor, being crowned Henry VII. Visit Battlefield
Centre and see 15thC come alive with armoured knights
facing new technology of the gun (*3 Apr.-27 Oct.:
Mon.-Sat. 2-5.30, Sun. and Bank Hols. Mon., also Good
Fri. 1-6*).   □

Practical information _____

HINCKLEY
ⓘ Hinckley Library, Lancaster Road, ☎ (0455)
30852/635106.
🚃 ☎ Leicester (0533) 29811.

Hotel:
★★★ *Hinckley Island* (B.W.), Watling Street, ☎ (0455)
631122, AC AM BA DI, 61 rm. ℗ ♨ ♿ ♪ £54. Rest. ♦
♪ £12.

Inn or Pub:
Black Horse (Marstons), Upper Bond Street, ☎ (0455)
637 613 ℗ Bar snacks.

Recommended
Golf course: Leicester Road (1m NE on A47), ☎ (0455)
615124.

Nearby
BARLESTONE, 8m N off A447

Inn or Pub:
Jolly Toper (Banes), Main Street, ☎ (0455) 290 454 ℗ ♨
♉ ♉ Bar snacks, chicken, scampi and chips. £4.

BURBAGE, 1m SE

Hotel:
★★ *Sketchley Grange*, Sketchley Lane, LE10 3HU, ☎ (0455) 634251, AC AM BA DI, 10 rm. P ⌇ ▥ ⌂ ⌘ £40. Rest. ♦ ♪ ⌖ Cl. Sun. Dinner only. £10.

DESFORD, 7m NE off A47

Inn or Pub:
Olde Lancaster Inn (Everards), Station Road, ☎ (045) 572 589, AC BA P ▥ Homemade pies, à la carte menu. £4.

SIBSON, 7m NW on A444

Hotel:
★★ *Millers*, Nuneaton, CV13 6LB, ☎ (0827) 880223, AC AM BA DI, 12 rm. P ▥ ⌘ Cl. Christmas. £42. Rest. ♦ ♪ Cl. Sat., Mon. lunch, Sun. dinner. Game and vegetarian dishes. £14.

ILKESTON

Derby, 11; Nottingham, 8; London, 126 m
☎ 0602   Derbyshire B2

Busy market and industrial town in the Erewash Valley, with coalfields to the N. Of interest is the **parish church** with its beautiful 14thC screen.

Nearby

▶ On road SW is **Cat and Fiddle Windmill**★, last remaining working **windmill** in Derbyshire. From here fine views of **Dale Abbey**, 3/4 m S. The lovely village of **Dale**★ lies in what was once part of **Dale Moor**. Here are the ruins of the **Abbey of St. Mary**★, and 12thC hermitage. ▶ 3m W on hillside, interesting buildings surround the 15thC **church**; in churchyard, unusual mausoleum to well-known local family, the **Sacheverell-Batemans**. ▶ 1m further on towards Derby (→) is **Breadsall**, an old farming village with 14thC **Old Hall** standing opposite the **church** with 14thC spire. Good views of **Derwent Valley**★. □

Practical information ──────────────

ⓘ The Library, Market Place, ☎ (0602) 301104.

Inn or Pub:
Durham Ox (Wards of Sheffield), Owham Street, ☎ (0602) 324 570 P ▥ ⌖ 2 rm. Bar meals and sandwiches.

Recommended
Craft workshops: *Chris Aston Pottery*, 4 High Street, Elkesley, ☎ (077 783) 391, handmade stoneware.

KETTERING

Northampton, 14; Stamford, 22; London, 77 m
pop. 44,758 ☎ 0536   Northamptonshire B3

Expanding commercial and industrial town surrounded by farmland and areas of woodland, relics of the large forests which once covered this area. Kettering lies in a line of boot- and shoe-making towns stretching the length of Northamptonshire.

▶ The **parish church** has impressive 15thC tower and spire, and overlooks the Market Square with the 17thC **manor house** and **Sawyer's Almshouses** dating from 1688.

Nearby

▶ **Boughton House**★★★ (*5m N*), home of the Duke of Buccleuch and Queensberry, originally a monastic building, acquired by family's ancestors, the Montagues, in 1528 and enlarged around seven courtyards. 1st Duke of Montague had been Ambassador at court of Louis XIV and was greatly influenced by Versailles when enlarging the house 1695 in the French style. Exceptional col-

lection of Louis XIV and XV furniture, baroque ceiling by Cheron, fine tapestries and world famous armoury; paintings by El Greco and Murillo. Splendid avenues planted by the 2nd Duke, 'Planter John' (*2-31 Aug.: daily ex. Fri.; grounds from 12.30, house 2-6*). ▶ **Rushton Triangular Lodge**★★ (*5 m N*), strange creation of Sir Thomas Tresham, begun in 1593, it symbolizes the Holy Trinity; Tresham was imprisoned many times for his religious beliefs (*15 Mar.-15 Oct.: Mon.-Sat., 9.30-6.30, Sun. 2-6.30; 16 Oct.-14 Mar. Mon.-Sat., 9.30-4; Sun. 2-4; winter closed Wed., some Thu., 24-26 Dec., 1 Jan.*). ▶ **Geddington**★ (*5m NE*) has medieval packhorse bridge over the River Ise and an unspoilt village centre. In square is Eleanor Cross, one of three remaining crosses erected by Edward I 1290, commemorating death of his queen, Eleanor of Castille. □

Practical information ──────────────

KETTERING
ⓘ Coach House, Sheep Street, ☎ (0536) 82143.
▥▥ ☎ (0536) 521445.
Car rental: *Europcar*, Chrysler Garages Ltd, Bayes Street; ☎ (0536) 510381.

Inn or Pub:
Talbot (Marstons), Meadow Road, ☎ (0536) 514 565 ▥ 4 rm. Sandwiches and meals. £3.

Recommended
Cycle rental: *Lawes*, Market Street, ☎ (0536) 510313.
Golf course: Headlands, ☎ (0536) 512074.

Nearby

ROTHWELL, 4m NW on A6

Hotel:
★ *Rothwell House*, Bridge Street, ☎ (0536) 710747, BA DI, 12 rm. P ⌀ ♪ £25. Rest. ♦ Cl. Sat. and Sun. eve. £6.50.

Inn or Pub:
Red Lion (Charles Wells), Market Square, ☎ (0536) 710 409, AC BA P ⌇⌂ ⌘ 6 rm. Bar and restaurant meals. £3.

LEICESTER*

Coventry, 24; Derby, 29; London, 97 m
pop. 277,300 ☎ 0533   Leicestershire B2

The county town and university city, sited on the R. Soar and Grand Union Canal. The Romans established a town here, followed by the Saxons, Danes and Normans. Traditional industries are hosiery and footwear, with light engineering introduced this century.

▶ The Victorian **clocktower** marks the centre of the city. ▶ Church of **St. Martin's**★ Peacock Lane, early-English to Perpendicular styles, given status of cathedral 1920. ▶ **Guildhall**★, originally medieval, present building Tudor. ▶ **Castle**★★★, Castle Gardens, St. Nicholas Circle, only mound remains of castle built by William I. Became home of Earls of Leicester including Simon de Montfort. See statue to Richard III in castle gardens. ▶ Church of **St. Mary de Castro**, Castle Street, is Norman, enlarged 12thC to serve as castle chapel. Alongside is **Rupert's Gateway**. ▶ The **Magazine**★, The Newarke, Newarke St.: 14thC gateway now museum of **Leicestershire Regiment**. ▶ **Newarke Houses Museum**★★, The Newarke, museum of social history. (*Mon.-Thu., Sat. 10-5.30. Sun. 2-5.30; cl. 25-26 Dec. and Good Fri.*). ▶ **Jewry Wall and Museum of Archaeology**, St. Nicholas Circle, site of Roman Baths and Forum, the wall is largest upright Roman structure in Britain (*same hours as above*). ▶ **Wygston House**★, Applegate, is mainly 15thC with 18thC façade, now costume museum (*same hours as above*). ▶ **Museum and Art Gallery**★★, situated in 'New Walk', promenade planted in 1785 leading from city centre to Victoria Park accessible only on foot. Three centuries of British paintings, collection of important German art

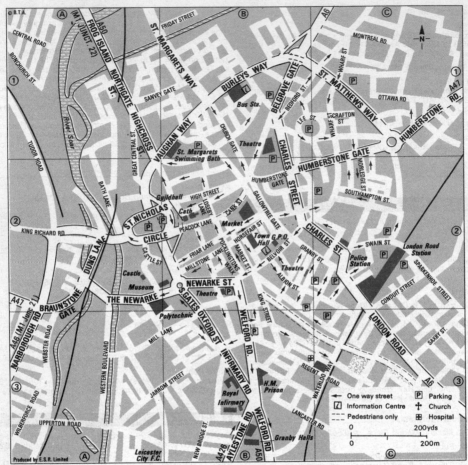

LEICESTER

(*same hours as above*). ▶ **War Memorial**★ of 1923 by Lutyens in Victoria Park. ▶ **Leicester Museum of Technology**★★, Abbey Pumping Station, Corporation Road, Industrial heritage museum for E Midlands. ▶ The wool industry developed late 14thC and markets established in **Highcross Street** and area around **Corn Exchange**. ▶ **Belgrave Hall**, Thurcaston Road, is Georgian house now period museum, interesting displays of agricultural equipment (*same hours as above*).

Nearby

▶ **Bradgate Park**★ (→) and **Swithland Woods**★ (→; *7m NE*) are open spaces of moorlands and woods within **Charnwood Forest**★★ (→). ▶ **Kirby Muxloe Castle** (*6m W*), built 1480-84 for Lord Hastings, has gatehouse and one tower remaining of brick-built castle (*15 Mar.-15 Oct.: Mon.-Sat., 9.30-6.30, Sun. 2-6.30; 16 Oct.-14 Mar.: Mon.-Sat., 9.30-4, Sun. 2-4; cl. winter on Wed. and some Thu., 24-26 Dec., 1 Jan.*). ▶ **Quenby Hall** (*5m E*) imposing example of Jacobean domestic architecture. □

Practical information

LEICESTER

ℹ️ 12 Bishop Street, ☎ (0533) 556699.
✈ East Midlands Airport (22m NW via M1), ☎ (0332) 810621.
🚌 ☎ (0533) 29811.
Car rental: *Europcar*, 186 Welford Road, ☎ (0533) 709611-2, rail/drive.

Hotels:
★★★★ *Eaton Brays* (VIR), Abbey Street (B1), LE1 3TE, ☎ (0533) 50666, Tx 342434, AC AM BA DI, 72 rm. P £52. Rest. ♦ ♪ Cl. Sun. £8.
★★★ *Belmont* (B.W.), De Montfort Street (C3), LE1 7GR, ☎ (0533) 544773, Tx 34619, AC AM BA DI, 61 rm. P & £58. Rest. ♦ & Cl. 27-30 Dec. Sat. lunch. £11.
★★ *Grand* (Embassy), Granby Street (B2), LE1 6ES, ☎ (0533) 555599, AC AM BA DI, 93 rm. P & £60. Rest. ♦ Cl. 25 Dec. £9.

Restaurants:
♦ *Water Margin*, 76-78 High Street (B2), ☎ (0533) 56422, AC AM BA DI Cantonese. £20.

♦ *White Horse*, Scraptoft Lane (A2 off map), ☎ (0533) 415951, AC AM BA DI P Cl. Sat. lunch, Sun. dinner. £12.

Inn or Pub:
Tom Hoskins (Hoskins), 13 Beaumanor Road (A1 off map), ☎ (0533) 681 160 P ⋙ ◬ ☍ ⅋ Hot and cold meals. £4.

Recommended
Craft workshops: *Dosworth Crafts*, 23 Main Street, Market Bosworth, ☎ (0455) 290869, belts, purses, bags, and bellows.
Cycle rental: *Leedhams*, 3/5 Narborough Road, ☎ (0533) 549356.
Golf course: Evington Lane, ☎ (0533) 738825.

Nearby

BRAUNSTON LANE EAST, 2 1/2m SW on A4

Hotel:
★★ *Post House* (T.H.F.), LE3 2FW, ☎ (0533) 896688, AC AM BA DI, 172 rm. P ☍ £63.50. Rest. ♦ ⅃ ☍ Cl. Sat. lunch. £10.

COSSINGTON, 6m N off A6

Restaurant:
♦ *Cossington Mill*, ☎ Sileby (050 981) 2205, AC BA P ≼ ⋙ ◬ ⅃ ☍ ⅋ Cl. Sat. lunch. Sun eve. Homemade soups, carbonade of beef. Book. £9.

ENDERBY, 5m SW on M1 Ext. 21

Inn or Pub:
Plough Inn, Mill Hill, ☎ Leicester (0533) 863 307 P ⋙ ⅋ 8 rm. Bar snacks, à la carte restaurant menu, Sun. lunch. £3.50.

GLEN PARVA, 3m SW on A426

Restaurant:
♦ *Manor*, The Ford, Little Glen Road, ☎ (0533) 774604, AO AM BA P Cl. Sun., Sat. lunch. £14.

HUNGARTON, 9m E off A47

Inn or Pub:
Black Boy (Mitchells Butlers), ☎ (053 750) 601 P ≼ ⋙ ◬ ⅋ Bar snacks and grills. £3.

ILLSTON-ON-THE-HILL, 10 SE off A47

Inn or Pub:
Fox & Goose (Everards), Main Street, ☎ (9455) 340 P ≼ ◬ Bar snacks, game pies. £3.

LEICESTER FOREST EAST, 3m W on A47

Hotel:
★★★ *Leicester Forest* (Q.M.H.), Hinckley Road, LE3 3GH, ☎ (0533) 394661, AC AM BA DI, 31 rm. P ⋙ ☍ £46. Rest. ♦ ⅃ Cl. 24-31 Dec. £10.

NARBOROUGH, 6m SW on A46

Hotel:
★★ *Charnwood*, 48 Leicester Road, LE9 5DF, ☎ (0533) 862212, AC AM BA, 20 rm. P ≼ ⋙ ⅋ £36. Rest. ♦ ☍ Cl. 26 Dec.-1 Jan. Sun. dinner. £8.

NEWTON LINFORD, 6m NW on B5327

Hotel:
★★ *Johnscliffe*, 73 Main Street, LE6 0AF, ☎ (0530) 242228, AC AM BA, 8 rm. P ≼ ⋙ ◬ ⅃ ☍ £39. Rest. ♦ ⅃ ☍ Cl. 1-5 Jan., 26-30 Dec. Homemade soups. £9.

OADBY, 2 1/2m SE on A6

Hotel:
★★★ *Leicestershire Moat* (Q.M.H.), Wigston Road, LE2 5QE, ☎ (0533) 719441, AC AM BA DI, 29 rm. P ⋙ ◬ ☍ £50. Rest. ♦ ⅃ ☍ £12.

Restaurant:
♦ *La Maison*, Glen Rise, ☎ Great Glen (053 759) 2308, AC AM BA P ⋙ ◬ ⅃ ⅋ Cl. Sun., Mon. Sole aux crevettes. Book. £12.

ROTHLEY, 1/2m W on B5328

Hotel:
● ★★★ *Rothley Court* (B.W.), Westfield Lane, LE7 7LG, ☎ (0533) 374141, AC AM BA DI, 34 rm. ≼ ⋙ ◬ ☍ ⅍ Elizabethan mansion set in 6 acres of landscaped grounds, birthplace of Thomas Macaulay. £65. Rest. ♦ ⅃ ☍ Cl. Sat. lunch. £18.

Restaurant:
♦ *Red Lion Inn*, ☎ Leicester (0533) 302488, AC AM BA DI P ⋙ ◬ ⅃ ☍ ⅋ Charnwood Forest pheasant with apples, sour cream and Calvados. Book. £10.

Recommended
Golf course: Rothley Park, Westfield Lane, ☎ (0533) 302019.

SOUTH CROXTON, 9m NE off A47

Inn or Pub:
Golden Fleece, Main Street, ☎ Melton Mowbray (0664) 840 275 P ⋙ ◬ ☍ Bar meals. £3.30.

Recommended
Craft workshops: *Zion House Potter*, 93 Main Street, ☎ (0664) 840363, stoneware pots, dishes.

THRUSSINGTON, 8m NE off A607

Inn or Pub:
Blue Lion (Ind. Coope), Rearsby Road, ☎ Rearsby (066 474) 266, BA P ≼ ⋙ ◬ 1 rm. Steaks, curry, trout, pizza. £3.50.

WHETSTONE, 4m S on A426

Restaurant:
♦ *Old Vicarage*, 123 Enderby Road, ☎ Leicester (0533) 771195 P ◬ ⅃ ⅋ Cl. Bank Hols., Sun., Sat. lunch. Medallions d'agneau. Book. £12.50.

LINCOLN★★

Grantham, 24; Grimsby, 38; London, 141 m
pop. 79,980 ☎ 0522   Lincolnshire B-C1

The old and beautiful city of Lincoln lies on the banks of the River Witham and rises on a slope of the high limestone plateau. At the top and dominating the town is the magnificent triple-towered cathedral. The Romans settled here at the junction of two great routes, Ermine Street and Fosse Way. Given status of a city of the highest rank (*Lindum Colonia*), Lincoln became centre of important agricultural region with the Romans draining the Fens. Then came under Saxon, Danish (who made town important commercial centre) and Norman influence. The waterways were used later in the Middle Ages to transport wool from the midland counties to Lincoln for export to Flanders. Today Lincoln's agricultural industry co-exists with its manufacturing and specialist engineering trades.

▶ The oldest part of the city is N of the river surrounding the **castle**, which has unusual mounds, built 1068 by William the Conqueror, and the Gothic **cathedral**. The **castle★★★** has three interesting towers, including 19thC observatory tower and wall walk, also unique prisoners' chapel (*Apr.-Oct.: Mon.-Sat. 10-6; 5 in Oct., Sun. 11-6, 5 in Oct.; Nov.-Mar., Mon.-Sat. 10-4*). The **cathedral★★★** is superb example of Early English architecture. Original Norman Cathedral of late 11thC was damaged in an earthquake in 1185 and its rebuilding undertaken by Bishop Hugh (St. Hugh) of Lincoln. Early English cathedral was built in two phases - first 1192-1250, second 1256-80; to first belongs whole structure, apart from E end and an innovation which was to be of European significance; the vaulting of the crossing and SE transept (1192-1200) introduces longitudinal ridge rib which has effect of opening out the individual bays to produce a more spacious perspective (the 'crazy vault'). Second phase is represented by famous Angel Choir with its exquisite stone carvings,

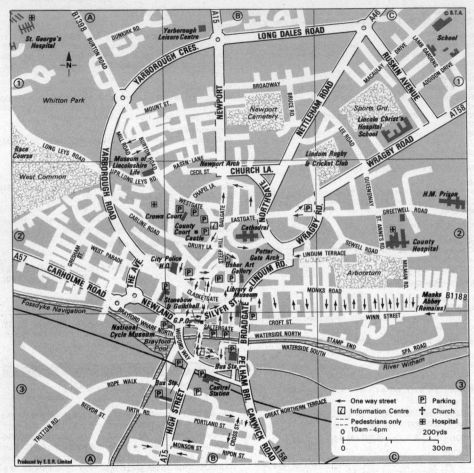

LINCOLN

which extends earlier building eastwards, providing a new great E window; two rose windows light N and S transepts, the 'Dean's Eye' and the 'Bishop's Eye', latter filled with elaborate flowing tracery of 1330s. Choirstalls are exceptionally fine, with intricately carved canopies and misericords (*summer wkdays 7.15-8; Sun. 7.15-6*). ▶ Lincoln has wealth of medieval houses near the cathedral. Cobbled street of **Steep Hill★★** descending from **Castle Square** has number of 16thC timber-framed buildings; important examples of Norman domestic architecture, like the famous **Jew's House★** built 12thC. ▶ In **High Street★★**, outstanding examples of timber-framed houses of 14th-16thC, like **Cardinal's Hat★**, late 15thC, named after Cardinal Wolsey who became Bishop of Lincoln 1514; also the **Stonebow** and **Guildhall**. ▶ Continuing down High Street, cross over river on 12thC **High Bridge★★**, Norman vaulted bridge, oldest in England, still carrying buildings with 16thC timber-framed houses. To W, river opens to **Brayford Pool**, once Roman inland port, now important waterborne commercial centre; linked with River Trent by Fossdyke Canal, cut in Roman times. ▶ **Torksey Lock★** near junction of Fossdyke and River Trent is leisure centre for extensive waterways of area,

favourite haunt of anglers. ▶ **Newport Arch★**, built 3rdC AD, only Roman gateway in Britain still used by traffic. ▶ Three major museums: **Usher Gallery★★**, Lindum Road: relics of 19thC poet Alfred Lord Tennyson, important Usher collection of watches, miniatures, porcelain and enamels (*Mon.-Sat., 10-5.30, Sun. 2.30-5*); ▶ **Museum of Lincolnshire Life★**, Old Barracks, Barton Road (*Mon.-Sat., 10-5, Sun. 2-5*). Just behind museum in **Mill Road** is restored **Ellis' Windmill★**, sole survivor of line of nine mills on the Lincoln Edge (*open*); ▶ **City and County Museum**, in Broadgate, housed in 13thC Greyfriars, earliest surviving church of Franciscan Order (*Mon.-Sat., 10-5.30, Sun., 2.30-5.00*).

Nearby

▶ **Doddington Hall★** (*5m SW*), Elizabethan mansion designed by Robert Smythson: elegant Georgian rooms with fine furniture and pictures; grounds include walled gardens and maze (*May-Sep., daily incl. Bank Hol. Mon. 2-6*). ▶ **Auborn Hall** (*7m SW*), attractive 16thC manor house with interesting carved oak staircase.   □

Practical information

LINCOLN
ℹ️ 9 Castle Hill ☎ (0522) 29828; 21 The Cornhill, ☎ (0522) 32151 ext 504/505.
Car rental: *Europcar,* Hartford Motors Ltd, Wragby Road, ☎ (0522) 31947.

Hotels:
★★★ *Eastgate Post House* (T.H.F.), Eastgate (B2), LN2 1PN, ☎ (0522) 20341, Tx 56316, AC AM BA DI, 71 rm. ℗ ⦿ ♨ £70. Rest. ♦ ♪ ♨ £10.
★★★ *White Hart* (T.H.F.), Bailgate (B2), LN1 3AR, ☎ (0522) 26222, AC AM BA DI, 49 rm. ℗ ✗ £72. Rest. ♦ ♪ Lincolnshire rabbit pasty. £15.
★★ *Duke William,* 44 Bailgate (B2), LN1 3AP, ☎ (0522) 33351, AC AM BA DI, 11 rm. ℗ ✿ £40. Rest. ♦ Cl. Mon. Christmas. £8.
★★ *D'Isney Place,* Eastgate (B2), LN2 4AA, ☎ (0522) 38881, AC AM BA DI, 17 rm. ℗ ⦿ £46.
★★ *Hillcrest,* 15 Lindum Terrace (B2), LN2 5RT, ☎ (0522) 26341, AC BA, 15 rm. ℗ ⧊ ⦿ ⦾ £35. Rest. ♦ Cl. Sun. lunch, dinner. £10.

Restaurants:
● ♦ *Wig and Mitre,* 29 Steep Hill (B2), ☎ (0522) 35190, AC AM BA DI Sautéed pigeon breasts with pine kernels. £9.50.
♦ *Harvey's,* 1 Exchequer Gate, Castle Square (B2), ☎ (0522) 21886, AC BA ⧊ ✿ Cl. 1-5 Jan., Sun.-Sat. lunch. Barbados entrecote. Book. £13.50.
♦ *White's,* 15 The Strait (B2), ☎ (0522) 24851, AC AM BA Cl. Mon., 2 wks. after New Year. £25.

Inns or Pubs:
Cornhill Vaults, Cornhill (B2), ☎ (0522) 35113 ✿ Bar snacks, homemade soups and pates, vegetarian dishes. £3.50.
Jolly Brewer, Broadgate (A2-3), ☎ (0522) 228 583 ℗ ⦿ ♨ ✿ Homemade pies and bar snacks. £2.50.
Victoria, Union Road (A2), ☎ (0522) 360 48 ⧊ ♨ Lasagne, vegetarian dishes, bar snacks and curries. £2.

⚓ at Fiskerton, *Shortferry C.P.,* Ferry Road (30 pl), ☎ (0526) 398021; at Metheringham, *White Horse Inn H.P.* (12 pl), ☎ (0526) 398341.

Recommended
Antique shop: *Hansord, David J.,* 32 Steep Hill, ☎ (0522) 30044, clocks, furniture and scientific instruments.
Farmhouse: at Sturton-by-Stow, *Sheila Bradshaw,* The Village Farm, ☎ (0427) 788 309, 400 acres in centre of village. £22 B. & B.
Golf course: Torksey ☎ (042 771) 210; Carholme, Carholme Road, ☎ (0522) 23725.
Guesthouse: *Mr and Mrs Bridge,* Mayfield, 213 Yarborough Road, ☎ (0522) 33732, £20 B. & B.; *Ridgeways,* 243 Burton Road, ☎ (0522) 46878, £25 B. & B.; at Sudbrooke, *Mr and Mrs Bowditch,* Oak Cottage, Nettleham Lane, ☎ (0522) 751705, quiet garden cottage. £20 B. & B.

Nearby

BRANSTON, 2m SE on B1188

Hotel:
★★ *Moor Lodge,* LN4 1HU, ☎ (0522) 791366, Tx 56396, AC AM BA DI, 25 rm. ℗ ⧊ ♨ £45. Rest. ♦ ♪ ♨ Cl. Sat. lunch. £9.

COLEBY, 5m S off A607

Inn or Pub:
Bell Inn (Melbournes), Far Lane, ☎ Lincoln (0522) 810 240, AC BA DI ℗ ⧊ ✿ Cold carvery and steaks. £6.50.

DUNHOLME, 5m N on A46

Hotel:
★★ *Four Seasons,* Scothern Lane, LN3 2QP, ☎ (0673) 60108, AC AM BA, 12 rm. ℗ ⦿ ⧊ ♨ ✿ ♪ £38. Rest. ♦ ♪ £8.

LINCOLNSHIRE WOLDS★★★

Lincolnshire

216 square miles of Lincolnshire Wolds have been designated as an area of outstanding natural beauty. The roads wind through tranquil and unspoilt countryside of rounded hills, deep wooded valleys, broad plateaus with small market towns and villages. The stretch of Bluestone Heath Road, in the heart of the Wolds, runs SE along the line of a prehistoric track from Welton-Le-Wold to just above South Ormsby. Free of villages, typical wolds landscape, route offers specific viewpoints, i.e. at Belchford. Around Somersby (→), Bag Enderby and Harrington (→), the gently undulating, well wooded countryside of the southern wolds contrasts with the chalky plateaus of the higher wolds. This is Tennyson country. Somersby is the birthplace of the 19thC poet Alfred, Lord Tennyson, and much of his inspiration came from the Wolds. Viewed from the flat expanse of the Fens, the rising chalk uplands appear majestic, although highest point is barely 550 ft. This area is lightly populated, fine sheep-rearing country, intensively farmed for wheat and peas. □

LOUGHBOROUGH★

Leicester, 11; Nottingham, 15; London, 114 m
pop. 49,081 ☎ 0509   Leicestershire B2

Lies in the Soar Valley on the Grand Union Canal. A country township mentioned in the Domesday Book, market town in Middle Ages, and present day town of diverse trades, well known for its hosiery, engineering and pharmaceutical industries. A multi-racial community fostered by its university and colleges. Bell casting at John Taylor's foundry has supplied bells for churches world-wide for over a century.

▶ Old Loughborough lies around **All Saints,** its parish church, with Church Gate's narrow shopping street close

Lincolnshire wolds

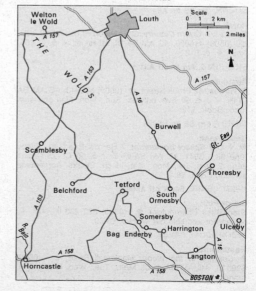

by leading to the **Market Place** with the **Town Hall** looking down on the twice-weekly market. ▶ **Carillon Tower** of 47 bells in Queen's Park is only municipal carillon in Britain, a memorial to dead of both World Wars. ▶ SE of town, **Great Central Steam Trust** at Great Central Station offers trips on old steam locomotives.

Nearby

▶ Granite has been quarried in the area for centuries. **Mountsorrel** has cottages in local brick, roofed with thatch of Swithland slate. High on the granite hill, panoramic views over **Soar Valley★** or quiet canalside walks. ▶ **Quorn** village is home of famous Quorn Hunt. ▶ **Prestwold Hall** (*3m E*; *by written appt.*), 1840 house and garden, with 18thC French and English furniture and marbled plasterwork.   □

Practical information ────────────

LOUGHBOROUGH
ⓘ John Storer House, Wards End ☎ (0509) 230131.
▅▅▅ ☎ Leicester (0533) 29811.

Hotel:
★★ *Cedars*, Cedar Road, LE11 2AB, ☎ (0509) 214459, 37 rm. ℙ ▥ ⌂ ▤ £38. Rest. ♦ ♪ Cl. Sat. lunch, Sun. dinner and 26-28 Dec. £12.

Restaurant:
♦ *Roger Burdell*, 11-12 Sparrow Hill, ☎ (0509) 231813, AC AM BA DI ♪ ⅋ Cl. Sun. eve., Mon. lunch., Bank Hols. Leicestershire sirloin with mushroom, onion and Madeira sauce. Book. £19.

Inn or Pub:
Boat (Marstons), Meadow Lane, ☎ (0509) 214 578 ℙ ▥ ⌂ Bar snacks and lunch. £3.50.

Recommended
Golf course: Longcliffe, Snell's Nook Lane, Nanpantan, ☎ (0509) 239129.
Riding school: *School of National Equitation*, Bunny Hill Top, Costock, ☎ (050 982) 2366.

Nearby
KEGWORTH, 11m NW on A6

Hotel:
★★★ *Yew Lodge*, 33 Packington Hill, DE7 2DF, ☎ (05097) 2518, AC AM BA DI, 54 rm. ℙ ⌂ ♿ £44. Rest. ♦ ♪ ♿ £10.

QUORN, 3m SE on A6

Hotel:
● ★★★★ *Quorn Country*, Charnwood House, LE12 8BB, ☎ (0509) 415050, AC AM BA DI, 19 rm. ℙ ▥ ♿ ⚲ £65. Rest. ♦ ♿ £12.

SHEPSHED, 4m W off A512

Restaurant:
♦ *Turtles*, 42 Brook Street, ☎ (0509) 502843, AC AM BA DI ℙ ⌂ ♪ ♿ ⅋ Eve. only ex. Sun., Mon. Fish and seafood. Book. £12.

SILEBY, 6m SE on B5328

Restaurant:
● ♦ *Old School Restaurant*, 7 Barrow Road, ☎ Sileby (050 981) 3941, AC AM BA ℙ ⌂ ♪ ♿ ⅋ Cl. 25 Dec.-1 Jan., 2 wks. Jul., Mon., Sat. lunch. Steaks, homemade sweets. Book. £8.

WEST LEAKE, 6m N off A6006

Inn or Pub:
Star (Bass Charrington), ☎ (0509) 822 233 ℙ ⑂ ▥ ⌂ Mixed hot and cold bar snacks. £3.50.

WOODHOUSE EAVES, 3m S

Restaurant:
♦ *Cottage in the Wood*, Maplewell Road, ☎ (0509) 890318, AC AM BA ℙ Cl. Mon., Tue., Wed. lunch, Sun. dinner. £13.

WYMESWOLD, 5m NE on A6006

Inn or Pub:
Windmill Inn (Home), Brook Street, ☎ (0509) 881 074 ℙ ▥ ⌂ ⅋ Bar snacks, trout, scampi, gammon. £4.

LOUTH

Grimsby, 17; Skyness, 21; London, 151 m
pop. 13,019 ☎ 0507   Lincolnshire C1

A flourishing market town of narrow winding streets, with busy market place. The attractive red brick is a distinctive feature of the town.

▶ Well-preserved Georgian buildings particularly in **Westgate**. Parish church of **St. James**, completed mid-15thC, has soaring spire of Ancaster stone. It is featured in Turner's painting 'Horse Fair at Louth'. ▶ The **Old Grammar School** had the Tennyson brothers as pupils. ▶ On the edge of town is **Hubbard Hill★** natural park and woodland.

Nearby

▶ **Little Cawthorpe Manor** (*3m E*) is interesting 17thC house with Dutch gables. ▶ 5m NE is **Alvingham★** with its water mill where you can see how corn was milled in 18thC.   □

Practical information ────────────

LOUTH

Hotel:
★★ *Priory*, Eastgate, LN11 9AJ, ☎ (0507) 602930, AC BA, 12 rm. ℙ ▥ ⌂ ⅋ ⚲ £45. Rest. ♦ Cl. Sun. £8.

Restaurant:
♦ *Mr Chips*, 17-21 Aswell Street, ☎ (0507) 603756 ℙ ⌂ ♿ Cl. 25-26 Dec., 1 Jan., Sun. Fish and chips. £3.

▲ at North Somercotes, *Lakeside Holiday Park* (400 pl), ☎ (050 785) 315.

Recommended
Farmhouse: at Swinhope, *Hoe Hill*, ☎ (047 283) 206, old farmhouse in Lincolnshire Wolds. £20 B. & B.
Golf course: Crowtree Lane, ☎ (0507) 603681.

Nearby
TETFORD, 8m S off A16

Hotel:
★ *White Hart*, LN96QQ, ☎ (065 883) 255, AC BA, 6 rm. ℙ ▥ ⌂ ⅋ 16thC coaching inn in the Lincolnshire Wolds. Cl. Christmas. £24. Rest. ♦ ♪ Cl. dinner Sun., Mon. £10.

TETNEY LOCK, 13m NE off A1031

Inn or Pub:
Crown & Anchor (Bass North), nr. Grimsby, ☎ Marsh Chapel (047 286) 291 ℙ ⑂ ⌂ ♿ Basket meals, soup, scampi. £3.

MABLETHORPE★★

Louth, 15; Skegness, 18m
☎ 0521   Lincolnshire C1

Lively seaside resort in the centre of Lincolnshire holiday coast with stretches of flat golden sands and safe shallow bathing.

Nearby

▶ Sandy dunes stretch S to **Sutton-on-Sea**. Here are launch facilities for small boats or sailboard. ▶ N on the coast is **Theddlethorpe St. Helen**, where grass-covered dunes are an important **Nature Reserve★★**. From **Gibraltar Point★★** (→) to the **Humber**, miles of flat sand-dunes with marshland behind. Vast expanses of ridged sand and mud at low tide. ▶ **Alford** to SW is marshland town with

gentle slopes of Wolds to W: five-sailed **windmill★** built early 19thC; thatched Elizabethan manor in town centre now houses **folk museum** (*6 May-26 Sep.: Mon.-Fri., 10.30-1, 2-4.30.*)   ☐

Practical information

MABLETHORPE

ℹ️ The Dunes Family Entertainment Centre, Central Promenade, ☎ (0521) 72496.

⚠ *Camping Club Site*, Highfield, 120 Church Lane (105 pl), ☎ (052 13) 2374; *Golden Sands Est.*, Quebec Road (450 pl), ☎ (0521) 77871.

Nearby

SUTTON-ON-SEA, 2m S on A52

Hotels:
★★★ *Grange and Links*, Sea Lane, Sandilands, LN12 2RA, ☎ (0521) 413 34, AC AM BA DI, 16 rm. Ⓟ ⋙ ⚓ ⚲ ♨ £44. Rest. ♦ £10.
★ *Bacchus*, High Street, LN12 2EY, ☎ (0521) 41204, AC BA AM, 22 rm. Ⓟ ⋙ £32. Rest. ♦ ♩ Cl. dinner 7-8. £7.

Recommended
Golf course: Sandilands Golf Club, ☎ (0521) 414432.

MANSFIELD

Nottingham, 15; Chesterfield, 12; London, 143 m
pop. 58,949 ☎ 0623   Nottinghamshire B1

Astride River Mann, Mansfield is a market and industrial town of hosiery mills and collieries. On the edge of Sherwood Forest (→), careful planting of conifers has helped transform legacy of colliery slag heaps to pleasant landscaped scenery.

▶ **Railway viaduct** is of interest, as is **local history museum** (*Mon-Fri. 10-6.*).

Nearby

▶ Good centre for touring **Sherwood Forest★★★** (→) area with its three main centres of interest: **Sherwood Forest Country Park** (→), **Rufford Park** (→) and **Cresswell Crags** (→).   ☐

Practical information
🚌 Alfreton and Mansfield Parkway, ☎ Derby (0332) 32051.

Recommended
Riding school: *Bakersfield Equestrian Centre*, Park Hall Road, Mansfield Woodhouse, ☎ (0623) 3897, partially experienced and experienced, elementary instruction.

MARKET HARBOROUGH

Leicester, 15; Northampton, 18; London, 83 m
pop. 15,852 ☎ 0858   Leicestershire B2-3

Lies in traditional English fox hunting country of gated roads and lanes meandering past farms and hamlets. A rich agricultural area, it has held a market since 1204.

▶ Its most famous building is former **Grammar School★**, timber-framed, with open ground floor used for weekly butter market. First floor level used as school founded 1614. Once a great coaching centre, several old inns survive. **The Three Swans** has magnificent 18thC wrought-iron sign.

Nearby

▶ **Foxton★★** (*2m N*), typical village of area, with Foxton Moor once favourite hunting ground of Lords of Manor. Situated on the Grand Union Canal, ¹/₂m W of village, is famous staircase of 10 locks built 1812 descending over

75 ft. ▶ **Naseby Battle and Farm Museum★★★** (*6m SW*): miniature layout of Naseby Battlefield, with battle relics. During 17thC Civil War Market Harborough was plundered by Royalist Prince Rupert. Charles I made town his headquarters 1645 and held council of war before the Battle of Naseby.   ☐

Practical information

MARKET HARBOROUGH
ℹ️ Pen Lloyd Library, Adam and Eve Street, ☎ (0858) 62649/62699.
🚌 ☎ Leicester (0533) 29811.

Hotels:
★★ *Three Swans*, High Street, LE16 7NJ, ☎ (0858) 66644, AC AM BA DI, 18 rm. Ⓟ 14thC inn, said to be one of the most famous in country. £48. Rest. ♦ ♩ £12.
★ *Angel*, High Street, LE16 7NL, ☎ (0858) 63123, AC AM BA DI, 20 rm. Ⓟ £35. Rest. ♦ ♩ Cl. Sun. dinner..

Recommended
Antique shop: *Hoffman, J.E.*, Owsley House, Ashley, ☎ (0858) 8315, clocks.
Craft workshops: at Little Bowden, *Quorn Pottery*, 46-48 Scotland Road, ☎ (0858) 31537, post-box teapots, teapot clocks, lightbulb cruets and candles.
Golf course: Okendon Road (1m S on A500), ☎ (0858) 63684.
♥ *Spencer's Cheese Shop*, 13 Church Street, ☎ (0858) 65729, pork pies, cheese, bread.

Nearby

EAST LANGTON, 4m N by A6

Restaurant:
♦ *Bell Inn*, Main Street, ☎ East Langton (085 884) 567, AC BA Ⓟ Cl. Sun. dinner. £12.

HUSBANDS BOSWORTH, 6m SW on A427

Restaurant:
♦ *Fernie Lodge*, Berridge's Lane, ☎ Market Harborough (0858) 880551, AC BA Ⓟ ⋙ ⚓ ♩ ⚱ ❀ Cl. Sat.-Mon. lunch, Sun. eve. Smoked Stemborough Mill trout. Book. £12.

MARSTON TRUSSELL, 2m W off A427

Hotel:
★★ *Sun Inn*, Main Street, LE16 9TY, ☎ (0858) 65531, AC AM BA DI, 10 rm. Ⓟ ⚓ £40. Rest. ♦ ♩ £13.

WELFORD, 8 1/2m SW on A50

Inn or Pub:
Shoulder Of Mutton (Manns), 12 High Street, ☎ (085 881) 375, BA Ⓟ ⋙ ⚱ Homemade pies, curry, seafood dishes. £5.

MARKET RASEN

Lincoln, 16; Louth, 14; London, 158 m
pop. 3,050 ☎ 0673   Lincolnshire C1

Old market town on the River Rase has pleasant blend of architectural styles and well-known racecourse.

Nearby

▶ **Tealby★** (*4m E*): the **church**, with massive late Norman tower, dominates this attractive village at foot of Lincolnshire Wolds (→). Derelict **Bayons Manor**, built early 19thC, stands in deer park to S of village. ▶ Join long-distance footpath **'The Viking Way'★**, which extends 130m from Humber Bridge to Oakham (→) in Leicestershire. Taking name from the many settlements established by invading Vikings in 9thC, footpath is marked by a special Viking helmet symbol. ▶ **Caistor★** (*6m N*) was an Iron-Age hill fort before becoming a Roman settlement: traces of Roman Wall and a well survive; parish church has a Saxon W tower and windows.   ☐

Practical information

MARKET RASEN

🚌 ☎ Lincoln (0522) 39502.

Hotel:
★★ *Limes*, Gainsborough Road, LN8 3JN, ☎ (0673) 842357, AC AM BA DI, 17 rm. ℙ 𝄢 ☽ ⅋ £40. Rest. ♦ ♪ Cl. Sat. lunch dinner, 25 Dec.- 1 Jan. £12.

Restaurant:
♦ *Carafe*, 5 King Street, ☎ (0673) 843427, AC AM DI Cl. Sun., Mon., 2 wks. Aug., 2 wks. after Christmas. £15.

⚲ *Walesby Woodlands C.P.*, Walesby Grange (50 pl), ☎ (0673) 843285.

Recommended
Golf course: Legsby Road (off A631), ☎ (0673) 842416.

Nearby

SIXHILLS, 3m E off A631

Hotel:
★ *Durham Ox*, 846 Fosseway, LE14 3PD, ☎ (0509) 880240, Tx 341995, AC AM BA DI ℙ ⅋ £32.50. Rest. ♦ ♪ ☽ Cl. Christmas. £8.

MATLOCK★★

Derby, 18; Chesterfield, 11; London, 148 m
pop. 13,706 ☎ 0629   Derbyshire A1

On the edge of the Peak District National Park (→) and surrounded by beautiful woodland and hilly scenery, Matlock is a popular inland tourist resort and spa, lying along the dramatic Derwent limestone gorge.

▶ Dominating area at **Matlock Dale** is 350 ft. peak of **High Tor★**. ▶ **Heights of Abraham★★★**, high over **Matlock Bath,** are reached by spectacular cable car ride. Ride travels over **River Derwent Valley** and up **Long Tor escarpment** through woods. Visit **Great Rutland Cavern Nestus Mine★★**, where atmosphere of a working Derbyshire lead mine is recreated; also **Great Masson Cavern★★**, its passages revealing veins of calcite and fluorspar. The 35 acres of landscape woodland can be explored on foot following marked trail, with picnic/play area and **Victorian Prospect Tower★** to climb for superb views (*Easter-Oct., daily 10-5, later in high season; Nov.-Mar.: Sat., Sun. 10-4*). ▶ The Peak District's main industry for 2000 years has been lead mining. **The Peak District Mining Museum★★** at **Matlock Bath** illustrates all facets of industry: experience working conditions by climbing shafts and operating pumps (*mid-Feb.-mid-Nov.: Mon.-Sun., 11-4; cl. Christmas Day*). ▶ For conducted underground visit, **Temple Mine★**, a few m from museum, offers view of old lead and fluorspar workings of 1920s and 30s (*Easter-Oct.: daily 11-4 or longer; Nov.-Easter: wkends only 2-4; cl. Christmas Day*). ▶ Medicinal Springs and Baths have long been the attraction of the site and at original **thermal bath,** at Matlock Bath, is **Matlock Bath Aquarium★** housing freshwater fish in over 40 aquaria (*Easter-Sep., daily 11-5.30; also winter wkends.*). ▶ High on the hillside, above Matlock to SE are ruins of 19thC **Riber Castle** with **Wildlife Park★★★**: collection of European birds and animals, with successful breeding of rare livestock, including world's largest collection of lynx (*10-4 winter, 5 summer; cl. Christmas Day*). ▶ Families with young children should visit **Gulliver's Kingdom★★★** and **Royal Cave★★★**, wooded hillside theme park with Dinosaur Trail, Junior Fun Fair, Model Village and Railways.

Nearby

▶ 2m S is **Cromford**, known as birthplace of Industrial Revolution, where world's first successful waterpowered cotton spinning mill was built by Richard Arkwright 1771. Restored original mill at **Arkwright's Cromford Mill★★** (*Wed.-Fri., 10-4.30, Sun.11-5*) ▶ Further S is

Wirksworth★, centre for lead mining since Roman times where limestone is still quarried. It holds an industrial court dating back to 13thC and the standard measure for lead miners - a brass dish made 1513. Town has its traditional summer well-dressing ceremony. ▶ **Crich** (*6m SE*), hilltop village where in disused quarry is **National Tramway Museum★★**: travel on vintage horse-drawn, steam and electric trams in unique period street and within route overlooking Derwent Valley (*28 Mar.-6 Apr., then wkends and Bank Hols. to end Oct., 10.30-6.30, Mon.-Thu; 6 May-25 Sep., and Fri., 25 Jul.-Aug., 10-5.30*). ▶ **Youlgreave★★** (*9m NW*), picturesque old lead mining village, on the edge of **Bradford Dale**: restored **church★**, battlemented and gargoyled, has fine 12th and 15thC workmanship; Cockayne monument is of interest, also 19thC Burne-Jones window in 14thC chancel. Lovely scenery by **River Lathkill** at **Conksbury Bridge★★** close by. ▶ **Lea Gardens** (*3 m SE*), in woodland setting: hybrid and specie rhododendrons and azaleas, covering 3 acres.   ☐

Practical information

MATLOCK

ⅈ The Pavilion, ☎ (0629) 55082.
🚌 Matlock, Matlock Bath, ☎ Derby (0332) 32051.

Hotels:
★★★ *New Bath* (T.H.F.), New Bath Road, DE4 3PX, ☎ (0629) 3275, AC AM BA DI, 56 rm. ℙ 𝄢 ⌱ ♨ £65. Rest. ♦ ♪ ☽ £10.50.
● ★★ *Riber Hall*, DE4 5JU, ☎ (0629) 2795, AC AM BA DI, 11 rm. ℙ ⊰ 𝄢 ⅋ ♨ Elizabethan manor house in 4 acres of grounds with delightful walled garden. £80. Rest. ♦ £20.

Inn or Pub:
White Lion (Home), Starkholmes Road, ☎ (0629) 2511 ℙ ⊰ 𝄢 𝄢 Bar snacks and homemade meals. £3.50.

⚲ at Kirk Ireton, *Blackwall Plantation*, Blackwall (150 pl), ☎ (0335) 70903.

Recommended
Craft workshops: *Cargo Leathergoods*, The Old Workshop, North Street, Cromford, ☎ (062 982) 4574, hand-made leather goods; *Denby Seconds Shop*, 44 North Parade, ☎ 56408, handmade stoneware.
Farmhouse: *Farley Farm*, Farley, ☎ (0629) 2533, £19 B. & B.; at Aldwark, *Tithe Farm*, Grange Mill, ☎ (062 985) 263, homemade baked goods and fresh produce. £20 B. & B.
Golf course: Chesterfield Road (1m NE on A632), ☎ (0629) 2191.
Riding school: at Tansley, *Knabbhall Equestrian Centre*, Hopkin Farm, ☎ (0629) 2253.

Nearby

CRICH, 6m SE off A6

Inn or Pub:
Cliff Inn (Kimberley), Cromford Road, ☎ Ambergate (077 385) 2444 ℙ ⊰ 𝄢 Bar snacks incl. trout dishes. £3.

Recommended
Craft workshops: *Crich Pottery*, Market Place, ☎ (077 385) 3171, hand-thrown stoneware, bowls, punch sets, jugs, teapots.

DARLEY DALE, 2m N off A6

Hotels:
★★ *Red House*, Old Road, DE4 5JU, ☎ (0629) 734854, AC AM BA DI, 7 rm. ℙ ⅋ 𝄢 ⅋ £40. Rest. ♦ ♪ £6.
★ *Whitworth*, Dale Road North, DE4 2EQ, ☎ (0629) 733568, AC BA, 7 rm. ℙ ♨ £26. Rest. ♦ ♪ ☽ £8.

LEA, 2m SE

Restaurant:
♦ *Coach House*, ☎ Dethick (062 984) 346 ℙ Cl. Sun. dinner. £11.50.

Recommended
♥ ice cream: *The Coach House*, homemade Jersey ice cream.

STONE EDGE, 5m NE off A632

Inn or Pub:
Red Lion, ☎ Chesterfield (0246) 506 142, AC AM BA DI Ⓟ ← ⋘ ⚲ ఊ ⌘ Full à la carte menu, table d'hote in French restaurant. Full range of meals in bar. £7.

WINSTER, 5m W on B5056

Inn or Pub:
Miners Standard, Top Bank, ☎ (062 988) 279 Ⓟ ← ⋘ ⚲ ఊ Bar snacks. £3.

WOOLEY MOOR, 5m E off A61

Inn or Pub:
White Horse, White Horse Lane, ☎ Chesterfield (0246) 590 319 Ⓟ ← ⋘ ← ఊ Homemade dishes ex. Sun. £4.25.

MELTON MOWBRAY

Leicester, 15; Grantham, 16; London, 111 m
pop. 23,379 ☎ 0664   · Leicestershire B2

Old market town famous for Stilton cheese, pork pies and as centre for hunting the fox. Rich pasture land surrounds the town in the valley of the River Eye.

▶ Streets radiate from the Market Place with many interesting historic buildings like **Anne of Cleves House★** dating from 1384, given by Henry VIII to his discarded Queen 1541. ▶ Beautiful church of **St. Mary the Virgin★** begun 1170, completed 1532. ▶ Riverside walks in **Egerton Park. Melton Carnegie Museum★**, Thorpe End, has displays on Stilton cheese and Melton pies.

Nearby

▶ Picnic areas at **Burrough-on-the-Hill** (*5m S*). ▶ **Stapleford Park★** (*4m E*) is Tudor mansion with unique collection of Victorian Staffordshire pottery figures.   ☐

Melton Mowbray pies

The old market town and hunting centre of Melton Mowbray has long been famous for its pork pies. Rich crusty pastry made with lard and flour encloses pork meat surrounded by a layer of succulent jelly; ideal for serving with tea, lunch or on picnics. First known in Leicestershire at the beginning of the last century, Melton Mowbray pies are said to have become popular because of the town's association with hunting. With their firm crust and solid centre, they were ideal traveling fare. They would neither collapse in the hand, nor be too easily squashed in riders, saddlebags, and they were substantial enough to provide nourishment for hours of energetic riding.

Practical information ───────────

MELTON MOWBRAY
ⓘ Melton Carnegie Museum, Thorpe End ☎ (0664) 69946.
🚌 ☎ Leicester (0533) 29811.

Hotels:
★★★★ *Harboro'* (Anchor), Burton Street, LE13 1AF, ☎ (0664) 60121, Tx 341713, AC AM BA DI, 28 rm. Ⓟ £50. Rest. ♦ ♪ £10.
★★ *Sysonby Knoll*, Ashfordby Road, LE13 0HP, ☎ (0664) 63563, AC BA, 21 rm. Ⓟ ← ఊ ▣ ⋘ £32. Rest. ♦ ♪ ఊ £7.

Recommended
Farmhouse: *Manor House*, Saxelby, ☎ (0664) 812269, 125 acres with cows, sheep and home-cooking. £19 B. & B.
Golf course: Thorpe Arnold, ☎ (0664) 62118.

Nearby
OLD DALBY, **14m NE off A46**

Inn or Pub:
Crown, ☎ (0664) 823 139 Ⓟ ← ⋘ ⚲ ఊ Full range of bar and restaurant meals. £7.

NEWARK-ON-TRENT

Lincoln, 17; Nottingham, 20; London, 125 m
pop. 33,143 ☎ 0636   Nottinghamshire B2

Market and industrial town by River Trent, retaining much of its historic past.

▶ Central area with medieval street pattern has large cobbled market place dominated by 18thC **Town Hall** built by John Carr of York. ▶ In Appletongate, is **Municipal Museum** (*10-1, 2-5 Mon.-Sat., 10-1 Thu., Apr.-Sep. 2-5 Sun.*). ▶ Parish church of **St. Mary Magdalene** in Church Street with soaring Perpendicular spire, 16thC choir stalls and rood screen. ▶ Walk down Kirkgate towards Town Wharf near river, pass attractive **Ossington Coffee Palace** built 1882. ▶ Opposite is **Newark Castle★★★**, well-preserved remains of 12thC castle, where King John died 1216. Finest surviving Norman Gatehouse in the country. Important Royalist stronghold in Civil War, withstanding three sieges. Exhibition in SW tower, dungeon and undercroft (*Apr.-Sep.: 2-5 Tue., Wed., Fri., Sat., Sun., 2-6; Oct.-Mar. by appt. Gardens all year daily 9-dusk*). ▶ From castle take Riverside Walk to **Millgate Folk Museum★★** with printers workshop demonstrating traditional methods on 19thC machines (*10-12, 1-5 Mon.-Fri., Apr.-Sep. 2-6, Sat. Sun.; other times by appt.*). ▶ Nearby is **Town Wharf** and **Cuckstool Wharf**, where riverboat trips can be taken. ▶ NE at **Winthorpe** is **Newark Air Museum★★**, largest privately owned collection of aircraft: includes a Vulcan, Hastings and Mark 3 Shackleton (*Apr. Oct.: 10-5 Mon.-Fri., 10-1 Sat., 10-6 Sun.; Nov. Mar.: 10-dusk Sun.; other times by appt.*).

Nearby

▶ **Hawton** (*3m SW*) is small village once important base for Cromwell's men during Civil War. Church of **All Saints★★** famed for 14thC Easter Sepulchre. ▶ **Cromwell** (*6m N*) has in **Old Rectory Vina Cooke Collection of Dolls and Bygone Childhood★** (*appt. advisable*). ▶ **Carlton Hall** (*7m N*) is 18thC house on site of former manor. Fine 'flying' staircase of 41 steps with balustrade. (*Apr.-Oct. written appt. only*). ▶ **Southwell** (*8m W*) is small market town close to Sherwood Forest★★★ (→). Famous for its 12th-14thC **minster★★**, raised to cathedral status in 1884. Chapter House contains remarkable group of stone carvings, known as 'The Leaves of Southwell', which date from 13thC, representing the very English foliage of oak, hawthorn and maple. Twin towers, flanking W façade, date from early 12thC (*daily 8-5.30 summer wkdays, dusk winter wkdays; 8-7 wkends*). ▶ Opposite is 15thC coaching inn, **Saracen's Head**, where Charles I stayed before his surrender to Scots 1646.   ☐

Practical information ───────────

NEWARK-ON-TRENT
ⓘ The Ossington, Beast Market Hill, ☎ (0636) 78962.
🚌 ☎ (0636) 704431.

Hotels:
★★ *Grange*, 73 London Road, NG24 1RZ, ☎ (0636) 70339, AC BA, 9 rm. Ⓟ ▣ ⚲ £36. Rest. ♦ ♪ Cl. Christmas New Year. Homemade pâté and soups. £8.
★★ *Robin Hood* (Anchor), Lombard Street, NG2 41XB, ☎ (0636) 703858, Tx 858875, AC AM BA DI, 20 rm. Ⓟ ఊ £50. Rest. ♦ ♪ £12.
★ *South Parade*, 117-119 Balderton Gate, NG24 1RY, ☎ (0636) 703008, 18 rm. Ⓟ ⚲ £28. Rest. ♦ ♪ £6.

Restaurant:
♦ *Gannets*, 35 Castlegate, ☎ (0636) 702066 ← ⋘ ♪ ⌘ Cl. Christmas. Poachers roll, spicy lentil pie. £3.50.

Recommended
Golf course: Coddington (4m E on A17), ☎ (063 684) 282.

Nearby

HOVERINGHAM, 1m SW off A612

Inn or Pub:
Marquis of Granby, Main Street, ☎ Nottingham (0602) 663 080 ℗ ⌖ ⌕ 4 rm. Bar meals incl. homemade soups and seafood dishes. £5.

SOUTHWELL, 8m W on A612

Hotel:
★★★ *Saracens* (Anchor), Market Place Head, NG25 0HE, ☎ (0636) 812701, Tx 377201, AC AM BA DI, 27 rm. ℗ ⌖ 16thC coaching inn with genuine period features. £53. Rest. ♦ ⌙ Cl. Sat. lunch, 27-29 Dec. £11.

Restaurant:
♦ *Leo's*, 12 King Street, ☎ (0636) 812119, AC AM BA DI ⌙ ⌖ Cl. Sun., Mon. Warm salad of pigeon breast. £20.

SUTTON-ON-TRENT, 8m N off A1

Hotel:
★★ *Old England*, Newark Road, NG26 9QA, ☎ (0636) 821216, 10 rm. ℗ ⌖ £38. Rest. ♦ Cl. Christmas. £10.

UPTON, 5m W on A612

Inn or Pub:
Cross & Keys, Main Street, ☎ (0636) 813 269 ℗ ⌖

⌖ ⌕ & Full range of bar snacks and homecooked hot & cold food. £5.50.

NORTHAMPTON**

Kettering, 14; Bedford, 21; London, 67 m
pop. 154,172 ☎ 0604   Northamptonshire B3

Busy county town on the River Nene, a good touring centre for the surrounding unspoilt countryside of secluded villages and historic houses. Once the most important medieval stronghold in the Midlands, little remains of the old town, but the cobbled Market Square survives, housing one of the largest markets in England. Famous for the manufacture of footwear, the town's shoemakers, during the 17thC Civil War, supplied Cromwell's Parliamentarians with 1500 pairs, free of charge. Angered by this, Charles II destroyed the castle and town walls.

▶ Spaciously planned town with sports/leisure centre at **Weston Favell** and the new **Derngate** entertainments and exhibition complex. ▶ Fine walks along the Nene and **Grand Union Canal**★ alongside R. Nene is attractive point to hire boat. ▶ Wealth of parks and gardens, notably **Abington Park** with **Abington Museum**★★, an 18thC house with medieval hall, once home of Shakespeare's granddaughter; mainly devoted to decorative arts and Northampton's past (*Mon.-Sat., 10-12.30, 2-6; Apr.-Sep. 2.30-5; cl. Good Fri., 24-26 Dec.*). ▶ **Delapré Park**★★ with Elizabethan garden and **Delaprée Abbey**, house built on site of former nunnery founded in 1145, now contains county records. ▶ **Central Museum and Art Gallery**★★ in Guildhall Road opposite the Royal Theatre has magnificent collection of shoes through the ages (*Mon.-Sat., 10-6; cl. Good Fri., 24-26 Dec.*). ▶ **The Museum of Leathercraft**★ in Bridge Street exhibits leather from ancient Egypt to present day (*Mon.-Sat., 10-1, 2-5.30; cl. Sun. and Good Fri.*). ▶ Interesting churches, particularly to N in Sheep Street, church of the **Holy Sepulchre**★★, built to commemorate the First Crusade, one of England's best surviving round churches dating from 12thC and modeled on the Holy Sepulchre, Jerusalem. **St. Matthew's**★★ Kettering Road, houses Henry Moore's 'Madonna and Child' and Graham Sutherland's 'Crucifixion'.

Nearby

▶ Facilities offered for inland cruising at **Billing Aquadrome**★★★ (*4m E*), based on five lakes in area of woodland and open space in Nene Valley, with caravan site, providing safe boating, water-sports and fishing (*21 Mar.-12 Oct., daily.*). ▶ **Althorp**★★★ (*6m NW*), family home of Princess of Wales, built by Sir John Spencer 1508 with major alterations by Henry Holland in late 18thC. Superb collection of works of art: fine French and English furniture, English and Continental porcelain, portraits by Rubens, Van Dyck, Lely, Gainsborough and Reynolds (*daily: gates open 1.20, house 1.30-5.30; Aug., Bank Hols., 11-6*). ▶ **Holdenby House**★★ (*6m NW*) has remains of one of largest Elizabethan gardens in Britain with original entrance arches, terraces and ponds (*gardens open Apr.-Sep., Sun. and Bank Hols. Mon. 2-6; also Thu. in Jul. and Aug., 2-6*). ▶ **Lamport Hall**★★, (*8m N*), present house mainly 17th and 18thC. Wooded gardens, parkland and nature trail; first Alpine garden in England. (*Easter-Sep., Sun., and Bank Hols. Mon. also Thu. in Jul. and Aug., 2.15-5.15.*). ▶ **Castle Ashby**★★(*8m E*), Elizabethan house, built 1574 with Inigo Jones front, 1635. Charming English garden with lakes and waterfalls, variety of wildfowl (*gardens open all year daily 10-6; house 6 Jul.-25 Aug., 2-5*). ▶ **Guilsborough Grange Wildlife Park**★★★ (*10m N*): over 400 animals and birds of 70 varieties (*daily 10-7 or dusk*). ▶ **Brixworth** (*7m N*) village has perhaps finest Anglo-Saxon church in the country, **All Saints**★★, dating from c. 680 and its fabric using Roman bricks from surrounding settlements. ▶ **Earls Barton** (*7m E*) has church of **All Saints**★★ with celebrated Anglo-Saxon tower. □

Northampton shoe trade

As an important area for cattle-rearing (with a well-established cattle market), Northampton had one of the major raw materials necessary for the manufacture of leather goods - hide. Another, the wherewithal for tanning or treating the leather, was found in the oak bark plentifully supplied by forests in the area. Northampton's first recorded footwear order was for 10,000 pairs of soldiers boots in 1642. In 1853 Thomas Crick of Leicester, which (together with Norwich and Strafford) was also an important shoe-making town, invented a practical method of riveting soles to uppers; by the end of the 19thC, England had developed a considerable trade in exporting footwear. Although mineral salts came to replace bark as tanning agents, and the Midlands could no longer supply all the necessary raw leather, the area remained a centre for the shoe industry. After the First World War there was increasing competition from cheaper imported footwear, and from the development of synthetic leather substitutes.

Practical information _____

NORTHAMPTON
ⓘ 21 St. Giles Street, ☎ (0604) 22677.
▭▭ ☎ Rugby (0788) 60116.
Car rental: *Budget,* London Road, ☎ (0604) 62841.

Hotels:
★★★★ *Northampton Moat House* (Q.M.H.), Silver Street, NN1 2TA, ☎ (0604) 22441, Tx 31142, AC AM BA DI, 137 rm. & £65. Rest. ♦ ⌙ & Cl. 25 Dec. dinner, Sat. lunch. Duck with wild woodland fruits. £9.
★★★ *Angel* (Q.M.H.), Bridge Street, NN1 1NH, ☎ (0604) 21661, AC AM BA DI, 44 rm. ℗ £50. Rest. ♦ ⌙ £7.
★★ *Grand*, Gold Street, NN1 1RE, ☎ (0604) 250511, Tx 311198, AC AM BA DI, 68 rm. ℗ £48. Rest. ♦ £7.

Restaurants:
◆ *Ca d'Oro*, 334 Wellingborough Road, ☎ (0604) 32660, AC AM BA DI Cl. Sat. lunch, Sun. £19.
◆ *Napoleon's Bistro*, 9-11 Welford Road, ☎ (0604) 713899, AC AM BA DI Cl. Sat. lunch, Sun. £14.
◆ *Royal Bengal*, 39-41 Bridge Street, ☎ (0604) 38617 ℙ ⫯ ⚴ ♪ ℀ Cl. Christmas. £16.50.
◆ *Vineyard*, 7 Derngate, ☎ (0604) 33978. AC AM BA DI Cl. Sun. £16.

⚓ at Sywell, *Overstone Solarium*, Ecton Lane (150 pl), ☎ (0604) 45255.

Recommended
Craft workshops: *Brixworth Pottery*, Beech Hill, Church Street, Brixworth, ☎ (0604) 880758, homemade ceramics; *Bugbrooke*, The Old Wharf Inn, Bugbrooke, ☎ (0604) 831893, handmade wool, felt hangings and woven tapestries.
Cycle rental: *Lawes*, St. Giles Square, ☎ (0604) 39383.
Golf course: Delaprée Park Golf Club, Eagle Drive ☎ (0604) 64036; Northamptonshire Country, Church Brampton, ☎ (0604) 843025.
Riding school: *Chapmans Close Riding Establishment*, Weedon Road, Nether Heyford, ☎ (0327) 41859, elementary instruction.

Nearby

ASHBY ST. LEDGERS, 15m NW off A361

Inn or Pub:
Old Coach House, ☎ (0758) 890349, AC BA ℙ ⫯ ▦ ⚴ 6 rm. Bar snacks and à la carte restaurant. £6.50.

BEDFORD, 1 1/2m E on A428

Inn or Pub:
Britannia (Manns/Hamden Hosts), Bedford Road, ☎ (0604) 301 437, AC BA ℙ ⫯ ▦ ⚴ ௲ Bar meals with daily specials. £3.

BRAUNSTON, 16m NW off A45

Inn or Pub:
Old Plough (Ind Coope), 482 High Street, ☎ Rugby (0788) 890 000 ℙ ▦ ⚴ Salads, hot meals, sandwiches. £5.

CASTLE ASHBY, 5m E off A428

Hotel:
★★★ *Falcon*, NN7 1LG, ☎ (060 129) 200, Tx 312207, AC AM BA, 14 rm. ℙ ▦ ⚴ £47. Rest. ◆ ♪ Local venison. £15.

HORTON, 6m SE on B526

Restaurant:
● ◆ *French Partridge*, Newport Pagnell Road, ☎ (0604) 870033 ℙ ▦ ⚴ ℀ Cl. lunch, Sun., Mon., 3 wks. Jul.-Aug., 2 wks. Christmas, 2 wks. Easter. Veal escalope with green peppercorns, cream and brandy sauce. £16.

KILSBY, 16m NW on A5

Restaurant:
◆ *Hunt House*, Main Road, ☎ Crick (0788) 823282, AC AM BA DI ℙ ⫯ ⚴ ௲ ℀ Cl. Sun., Mon. Stuffed quail in filo pastry. Book. £15.50.

ROADE, 6m S off A508

Restaurant:
● ◆ *Roadhouse*, 16-18 High Street, ☎ (0604) 863372, AC AM BA ℙ ℀ Cl. Sat. lunch, Sun., Mon. 3 rm. Roulade of spinach with beurre blanc sauce. Book. £15.

WEEDON, 8m W on A45

Hotel:
★★ *Crossroads* (B.W.), High Street, NN7 4PX, ☎ (0327) 40354, Tx 312311, AC AM BA DI, 50 rm. ℙ ⫯ ▦ ℀ ௶ £50. Rest. ◆ ♪ Roast duck with blackcurrant and apple sauce. £12.

WESTON FAVELL, 1m E off A4500

Hotel:
★★★ *Westone Moat House* (Q.M.H.), Ashley Way, NN3

3EA, ☎ (0604) 406262, Tx 312587, AC AM BA DI, 66 rm. ℙ ▦ ⚴ ௲ £50. Rest. ◆ ௲ Cl. 25-31 Dec. £10.

NOTTINGHAM**

Derby, 16; Newark-on-Trent, 20; London, 128 m
pop. 277,800 ☎ 0602   Nottinghamshire B2

Ancient and modern county and university town, standing in the Trent Valley. Famous for lace, hosiery, bicycles, tobacco, engineering and home to the massive Boots pharmaceuticals organization created by Jesse Boot from one small shop in the city. Its folk hero, Robin Hood, was England's most popular outlaw.

▶ The centre with historic Old Market Square has impressive 1929 **Council House**★ with dome; Little John, massive hour bell of the clock housing inside four frescoes, one depicting Robin Hood. ▶ Area known as the **Lace Market**★, probably named mid-19thC, was site of earliest settlement; thriving commercial centre under Anglo-Saxon, Danish and Norman rule and residential area in 17thC and early 18thC. From late 18thC, cotton mills appeared and back-to-back housing for mill workers. Nottingham's lace machines appeared early 19thC. Success of the trade encouraged growth of warehouses. In **Broadway**, the street and imposing **warehouses**★ were laid out by T.C. Hine; in **Storey Street**, elaborately decorated the **Adams warehouse**★, also by Hine. ▶ **Nottingham Castle and Museum**★★★, on edge of city centre, is a 17thC ducal palace, perched on a 130ft. rock, site of William the Conqueror's castle and later medieval royal castle. This was administrative centre, home of the High Sheriffs who watched over royal hunting forests of Sherwood and the High Peak. Present building houses a museum: paintings from all periods - from Picasso to local artists such as Bonington and Thomas and Paul Sandby; see especially Turner's *Nottingham Castle from the R. Leen*, 1830; permanent exhibitions of ceramics, silver and glass and medieval alabaster carvings for which Nottingham is famous (*Apr.-Sep.: 10-5.45; Oct.-Mar.: 10-4.45; cl. Christmas Day*). ▶ **Brewhouse Yard**★, below Castle Rock, originally housed watermill, dovecote and brewhouse for castle, then in 16thC became hideout for thieves and by early 17thC retreat for religious dissenters. **Museum**★ is housed in group of five restored houses and displays local history (*daily 10-12, 1-5; cl. Christmas Day*). **Trip to Jerusalem** dating from 1199, popular inn where it is said Crusaders stopped for refreshments. ▶ In **Castle Gate** nearby are three elegant late 18thC buildings housing the **Costume and Textiles Museum**★★: unique 1632 Eyre Map tapestries of Nottinghamshire; also displays of hand- and machine-made lace (*daily 10-5; cl. Christmas Day*). At top end of **Castle Gate**, the 15thC reconstructed timber-framed building known as **Severns** housing the **Lace Centre**★★ (*daily 10-5, 4 Jan.-Feb., cl. 25-26 Dec.*). ▶ City has many man-made caves, tunnelled hundreds of years ago, used then for brewing, tanning and pottery making. See **Mortimer's Hole**★, a passage 100 yds long below Castle (*tours summer daily; Sun. at 2, 3, 4; in winter 2, 3*). ▶ Before leaving castle area stop at **Castle Gatehouse**, main surviving part of the medieval castle, for special display on romantic legend of Robin Hood. ▶ City is an important sports venue, home to famous Trent Bridge Cricket ground and **National Water Sports Centre at Holme Pierrepoint**★★★ (*2m E*), 270-acre park with nature reserve and 3.5m water sport course (*daily during daylight hours*). Nearby is **Holme Pierrepoint Hall**, fine brick crenellated early Tudor family manor house. Adjoining **church** has examples of Nottinghamshire alabaster monuments. (*Easter Sun.-Tue., Jun.-Aug.: Tue., Thu., Fri., Sun. 2-6*). ▶ **Wollaton Hall**★★ (*3m W*), important example of Elizabethan domestic architecture, built by Sir Francis Willoughby 1580-88, now houses **City of Nottingham Natural History Museum**★ (*Apr.-Sep.: 10-7 Mon.-Sat., Sun. 2-5; Oct.-Mar.: 10-dusk, Mon.-Sat., Sun. 1.30-4.30; cl. Christmas Day*). In 18thC stable block is **Nottingham Industrial**

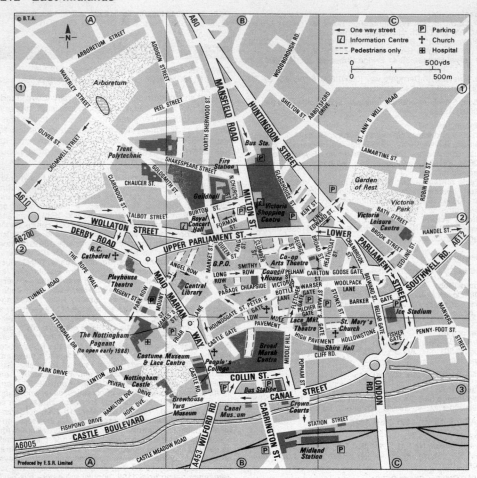

NOTTINGHAM

Museum housing most comprehensive collection of lace machines in the world (*Apr.-Sep.: 10-6 Mon.-Sat., Sun. 2-6; Oct.-Mar.: 10-4.30 Thu.-Sat., Sun. 1.30-4.30; cl. Christmas Day*).

Nearby

▶ **Thrumpton Hall** (*7m S*), Jacobean home of the Seymour family, has a particularly fine staircase and relics of Lord Byron (*by prior appt.*). ▶ To NW is the coalfield belt with its horizon of pit-head machinery. **Eastwood★** (*8¹/₂ m NW*) lies near the River Erewash in hilly countryside. Famous writer D.H. Lawrence born here 1885 and featured area in many novels; his birthplace, **8a Victoria Street★★**, now museum (*daily 10-5; cl. 24 Dec.-1 Jan.*). For Lawrence enthusiasts, visit **28 Garden Road★★**, later family home with ground floor furnished as described in his book *Sons and Lovers* (*open to public*). ▶ **Newstead Abbey★★★** (*11m N*): beautiful lakes and gardens surround the ruined abbey and grand country house. Originally an Augustinian priory founded 1170, converted to country home in 16thC by Byron family; once home of romantic poet Lord Byron, who sold Abbey 1817 because of mounting debts. Neo-Gothic restoration of 19thC

undertaken by a subsequent owner. For enthusiasts of Byron's life and works, Newstead is a treasure trove of important memorabilia (*Good Fri.-Sep., 2-6 incl. Sun. and Bank Hols. Tours out of season by appt.*). Byron, who died in Greece 1824, is buried at **Hucknall Torkard** Church to the S.
□

Practical information ———————————

NOTTINGHAM

ⓘ 18 Milton Street, ☎ (0602) 470661; Castle Gatehouse, Nottingham Castle, Castle Road, ☎ 470661.
✈ East Midlands Airport, Castle Donnington (15m SW off A453), ☎ (0332) 810621.
🚉 ☎ (0602) 476151.
Car rental: *Europcar*, 10/14 Marks Street; rail/drive ☎ (0602) 581644.

Hotels:
● ★★★★ *Savoy*, 296 Mansfield Road, NG5 2BT (B2), ☎ (0602) 602621, Tx 377429, AC AM BA DI, 182 rm. Ⓟ ⑤ ⑨ £48. Rest. ♦ ♪ ⑤ £8.
● ★★★ *Waltons*, North Lodge, The Park, NG7 1AG (A3),

D. H. Lawrence

Much of Lawrence's work is set in the area of the Nottinghamshire coalfields, around the town of Eastwood where he was born in 1885. David Herbert was the son of a miner, but he was not a physically strong child and his mother encouraged him to develop his intellectual gifts. He went to Nottingham University and then became a schoolteacher. However, after the success of his first novel, The White Peacock, he devoted himself to writing for a living. He traveled in Europe, had an affair with a married German aristocrat and subsequently married her. Lawrence and Frieda returned to England when World War I broke out, but they met with much hostility in the Cornish village where they settled. In 1915 Lawrence was prosecuted for obscenity following the publication of his novel The Rainbow; and his frank treatment of human sexuality again got him into trouble when Lady Chatterley's Lover appeared in 1928. This novel became the subject of a famous obscenity trial in 1959-60. This marked a turning point in British attitudes to censorship; and the unexpurgated version of Lady Chatterley was finally published in the UK. Lawrence's popular reputation has tended to be one of notoriety which is unfortunate since he was really concerned in exploring the most profound human emotions rather than in depicting lurid sex. Nevertheless, he is ranked among the most influencial 20thC writers - a fine poet as well as a novelist.

☎ (0602) 475215, AC AM BA, 9 rm. ℗ ⌂ ▭ £50. Rest. ♦ ♪ Cl. Sun. dinner. £12.

★★★ *Albany* (THF), St. James's Street, NG1 6BN (B2), ☎ (0602) 470131, Tx 37211, AC AM BA DI, 152 rm. ♣ £72. Rest. ♦ ♪ ♣ £12.

★★ *George*, George Street, N61 3BP (B2), ☎ (0602) 475641, Tx 378150, AC AM BA DI, 75 rm. ⌘ £45. Rest. ♦ ♪ ♣ Cl. Sun., Christmas. £9.

★ *Flying Horse* (Berni), Poultry, NG1 2HX, ☎ (0602) 502831, AC AM BA DI, 58 rm. ℗ ⌘ £38. Rest. ♦ ♪ Cl. 25-26 Dec. £10.

Restaurants:

♦ *Ben Bowers*, 128 Derby Road (A2), ☎ (0602) 413388, AC AM BA DI ℗ ♪ ♣ ⌘ Cl. 25-26 Dec., Sun., lunch Sat., Bank Hols. Fondue bourguignonne. Book. £9.

♦ *Chand*, 26 Mansfield Road (B1), ☎ (0602) 474103, AC AM BA DI ♪ ⌘ Cl. Christmas. Indian. Book. £7.

♦ *La Grenouille*, 32 Lenton Boulevard (A2), ☎ Plumtree (0602) 411088 ℗ ♪ ⌘ Cl. Christmas, Bank Hols., 2 wks. summer. Cuisses de grenouille, escargots provençale. Book. £14.

♦ *Le Tetard*, 10 Pilcher Gate (B2), ☎ (0602) 598253, AC AM BA DI ⌂ ♪ ⌘ Cl. Sun. Apr.-Sep., Sun. eve. Oct.-Mar. Book. £13.

♦ *Moulin Rouge*, Trinity Square, ☎ (0602) 472845.

♦ *Pagoda*, 31-33 Greyfriar Gate (B2), ☎ (0602) 501105, AC AM BA DI ♪ ♣ ⌘ Cl. Christmas. Fillet steak Cantonese style. Book. £8.50.

♦ *Rhinegold*, King John Chambers, Fletcher Gate (B2), ☎ (0602) 501294, AC AM BA Cl. Bank Hols. £11.

♦ *Something Special*, 103 Derby Road, Canning Circus (A2), ☎ (0602) 412139, AC AM BA DI ℗ ⌂ ♪ ♣ ⌘ Cl. Sat. lunch., Sun. Escalope de carpe royale. Book. £14.

♦ *Staropolska*, King John's Arcade, 13-15 Bridlesmith Gate (B2), ☎ (0602) 502672, AC DI ♪ ⌘ Cl. Sun., Mon. eve. Polish dishes. Book. £10.

♦ *Trattoria Conti*, 14-16 Wheeler Gate (B2), ☎ (0602) 474056, AC AM BA DI ℗ ⌂ ♪ ⌘ Cl. Bank Hols., 28 Jul.-25 Aug., Sun. Fillet of chicken breast stuffed with ham and cheese. £12.

⚓ *Holme Pierrepont C.C.P.*, Sports Centre, Adbolton Lane (360 pl), ☎ (0602) 821212.

Recommended

Farmhouse: *Ivy House Farm*, Hawksworth, ☎ (0949) 50361, £23 B. & B.

Golf course: Nottinghamshire, Hollinwell, Kirby-in-Ashfield, ☎ (0623) 753225; Wollaton Park, ☎ (0602) 787574.

Manor house: at Langar, *Langar Hall*, ☎ (0949) 60559, £40 B. & B.

Nearby

ARNOLD, 4m N off A60

Hotel:
★★ *Bestwood Lodge* (Consort), Bestwood Lodge Drive, NG5 8NE, ☎ (0602) 203011, Tx 575 151, AC AM BA DI, 36 rm. ♣ ⌘ ⌂ £37.50. Rest. ♦ ♪ £8.

BAGTHORPE, 12m NW off A608

Inn or Pub:
Dixies Arms (Home), School Lane, ☎ (0773) 810 505 ℗ ♣ ⌘ ⌂ ♣ Large range of cold snacks. £2.

BEESTON, 2 1/2m SW off A52

Restaurant:
● ♦ *Les Artistes Gourmands*, 61 Wollaton Road, ☎ (0602) 228288, AC AM BA DI ⌘ ⌂ ♪ ⌘ Cl. 2 wks. Jan., 1 wk. Aug., Sat. lunch. Salmon fillets with passion fruit sauce. Book. £15.

CALVERTON, 7m N off A614

Inn or Pub:
Admiral Rodney (Home), Main Street, ☎ (0602) 652 264 ℗ ⌘ ⌂ Homemade pies and vegetarian bar meals. £3.50.

CAYTHORPE, 8m NE off A6097

Inn or Pub:
Old Volunteer (Hardy Hansons), ☎ (0602) 663 205 ℗ ♣ ⌘ ⌂ ♣ Chili con carne, chicken with pineapple. £6.

GUNTHORPE, 8m NE on A6097

Restaurant:
♦ *Mr Toad's*, Riverfront, ☎ (0602) 663409 ℗ ⌘ ⌂ ♣ ⌘ Cl. Mon.-Tue., Sun. eve., Jan.-Feb., Christmas. Vegetarian. Book. £10.

KIMBERLEY, 5m NW on A610

Inn or Pub:
Nelson Railway (Hardy Hansons), Station Road, ☎ (0602) 382 177 ℗ ⌘ ⌂ ♣ 2 rm. Bar snacks and main dishes with puddings. £3.

LONG EATON

ⓘ Library, Tamworth Road, ☎ 735426.
🚃 ☎ Derby (0332) 32051.

Hotel:
★★ *Novotel* (Novotel), Bostocks Lane, M1 exit 25, NG10 4EP, ☎ (0602) 720106, Tx 377585, AC AM BA DI, 109 rm. ℗ ⌘ ♣ ▭ £50. Rest. ♦ ♪ £12.

LOWDHAM, 7m NE off A612

Hotel:
★★ *Springfield Inn*, Old Epperstone Road, ☎ (0602) 663387, AC AM DI, 10 rm. ℗ ♣ ⌘ ⌂ £35. Rest. ♦ ♪ Cl. Christmas. £8.

PLUMTREE, 5m S on A606

Restaurant:
● ♦ *Perkins Bar Bistro*, Old Railway Station, ☎ (06077) 3695, AC AM ℗ ⌘ ⌂ ♪ ⌘ Cl. Christmas, 1 wk. Sep., Sun.-Mon. Blanquette d'agneau. Book. £11.

RAVENSHEAD, 11m N off A60

Inn or Pub:
Little John (Mansfield), Main Road, ☎ (0623) 792670 ℗ ⌘ ⌂ ♣ Bar snacks, homemade pies, barbecue, cold buffets, steak and roast dishes. £6.

Recommended
Craft workshops: *Longdale Rural Craft*, Longdale Lane, ☎ (0623) 7948581, leatherwork, pokerwork, pottery, model making.

SOUTH NORMANTON, 14m N off M11

Hotel:
★★★★ *Swallow*, Carter Lane East, M1 exit 28, DE55 2EH, ☎ (0773) 812000, Tx 377264, AC AM BA DI, 123 rm. P ⓑ ⌂ £60. Rest. ♦ ↕ ⓑ £10.50.

TOTON, 4m SW

Restaurant:
♦ *Grange Farm*, ☎ (0602) 729426, AC BA P Cl. Sun., Mon. lunch, Bank Hols., 24-26 Dec., 1 Jan. £12.

UNDERWOOD, 11m NW off M1

Hotel:
★ *Hole-in-the-Wall*, Main Road, NG16 5GQ, ☎ (0773) 713936, 19 rm. P ⌂ ⅋ £27.50. Rest. ♦ ↕ ⓑ £6.

OAKHAM**

Stamford, 11; Corby, 13; London, 101 m
pop. 7,914 ☎ 0572   Leicestershire B2

Formerly the capital of Rutland, once smallest county in England. The old Market Place has medieval Butter Cross, with five-hole stocks still in position, but many old houses were replaced in mid-19thC. The High Street has red and blue brick houses, the bricks made in the local kiln founded 17thC.

▶ Interesting 12th-15thC **church** restored by Sir Gilbert Scott in 19thC. ▶ The original **Grammar School** founded in 1587 stands in churchyard. ▶ All that remains of **Oakham Castle★★**, built 1190, is the banqueting hall, like a church, with nave and aisles and beautifully carved capitals. ▶ **Rutland County Museum**, Catmos Street, houses exhibits relating to history of Rutland. ▶ Late 17thC house of **Burley-on-the-Hill** (*2m NE*) has fine gardens.

Nearby

▶ **Rutland Water★★★** to SE, largest man-made lake in Europe, with 27 m of shoreline: picnic sites, sailing, windsurfing, cycling, trout fishing and nature reserve. **Normanton Church**, all that's left of great Rutland estate, has become best-known landmark, with early 19thC tower and portico; built to replace medieval church, now houses county's first Water Museum; four car parks and picnic areas: S side near village of **Edith Weston**. NE side nearest to village of **Empingham**. N, village of **Whitwell** and highest point **Barnsdale** area. On shallow end to W is **Nature Reserve** containing hides for viewing birdlife (*Good Fri.-Oct.: Sat., Sun. and Bank Hols.*). ▶ **Exton★** (*8m NE*), pretty village with church containing nine splendid monuments, particularly by Grinling Gibbons (1686) and Nollekens (1766).   □

Practical information ———————————

OAKHAM
ⓘ Oakham Library, Catmos Street, ☎ (0572) 2918.
🚌 ☎ Leicester (0533) 29811.

Hotels:
★★★ *Crown* (B.W.), 16 High Street, LE15 6AP, ☎ (0572) 3631, AC AM BA DI, 25 rm. P £42. Rest. ♦ Cl. to non. res. 24-25 Dec. £12.50.
★ *George*, Market Place, LE15 6DT, ☎ (0572) 56971, AC AM BA DI, 19 rm. P ⓑ ⅋ £42. Rest. ♦ ↕ £9.

Recommended
Cycle rental: *Rutland Water Cycle Hire*, Whitwell Car Park, Rutland Water, ☎ (078 086) 705.

Looking for a locality? Consult the index at the back of the book.

Nearby

COTTESMORE, 4m NE on B668

Inn or Pub:
Sun Inn (Everards), ☎ (0532) 812 321 P ⅋ ₩ ⌂ ⓑ ⅋ Extensive range of bar meals with salads. £5.

EXTON, 6m NE off A606

Inn or Pub:
Fox & Hounds (Melbourns), ☎ Oakham (0572) 812 403 P ⅋ ₩ ⌂ ⓑ 3 rm. Extensive range of meals incl. trout and duckling. £5.

HAMBLETON, 1m E off A606

Hotel:
● ★★ *Hambleton Hall*, LE15 8TH, ☎ (0572) 56991, AC AM BA DI, 15 rm. P ⅋ ₩ ⌂ ⓑ ⌀ ☼ £99. Rest. ● ♦ ⓑ Scottish lobster with sauces. £30.

LANGHAM, 2m NW on A606

Restaurant:
♦ *Noel Arms*, Bridge Street, ☎ (0572) 2931, AC AM BA DI P ⌂ ↕ Steaks, fish pie. £9.25.

⚑ *Ranksborough Hall* (100 pl), ☎ (0572) 2984.

OUNDLE

Peterborough, 13; Northampton, 28; London, 83 m
pop. 3,255 ☎ 0832   Northamptonshire C2-3

Well-preserved stone-built town set in a loop of River Nene. Its Early English church spire is a landmark for miles around.

▶ The former **White Lion Inn** dates from 1641. ▶ The façade of the 17thC **Talbot Inn** was built out of stone from Fotheringay Castle.

Nearby

▶ To E is **Ashton** with thatched cottages around the village green. ▶ To N, **Fotheringay★**, with site of **castle**, now demolished, where Mary Queen of Scots was executed 1587. The **church★★** contains tombs of Richard II and Richard III of England and Edward Duke of York killed at Agincourt 1415. ▶ **Southwick Hall** (*1/2m NW*), 14thC manor house with Elizabethan and Georgian additions (*Easter, May, Spring and Aug. Bank Hols., Sun., Mon., also Sun. 13 Apr., 29 Jun., 27 Jul., Wed., 28 May-20 Aug. 2.30-5*). ▶ **Lyveden New Bield** (*4m SW*), roofless house built by Sir Thomas Tresham in 1594, shaped like a cross to symbolize the Passion (*daily*). ▶ **Lilford Park★★★** towards **Thrapston** has acres of grassland and woodland containing a wide variety of birds and farm animals (*Easter-Oct., daily 10-6*).   □

Practical information ———————————

OUNDLE
ⓘ Market Place, ☎ (0832) 74333.

Hotel:
★★ *Talbot* (Anchor), New Street, PE8 4EA, ☎ (0832) 73621, Tx 32364, AC AM BA DI, 39 rm. P ₩ ⓑ £52. Rest. ♦ ↕ £10.

Restaurant:
● ♦ *Tyrrells*, 6-8 New Street, ☎ (0832) 72347, AC AM BA ↕ ⓑ ⅋ Cl. Sun. eve., Mon. Book. £12.

Recommended
Golf course: Benefield Road (1m W on A427), ☎ (0832) 73267.

Nearby

FOTHERINGAY, 3m N

Restaurant:
♦ *Falcon Inn*, Main Street, ☎ Cotterstock (083 26) 254 P ₩ ⌂ ⓑ Cl. 25-30 Dec., Mon. Rabbit cooked in cider with apples and walnuts. Book. £7.

NASSINGTON, 3m NE

Restaurant:
♦ **Black Horse Inn**, 2 Fotheringhay Road, ☎ Stamford (0780) 782324, AC AM BA DI ℗ ▦ £11.

THRAPSTON, 7m SW on A605

Hotel:
★★ **Bridge**, Bridge Street, NN14 4JB, ☎ (080 12) 2128, AC AM BA DI, 18 rm. ℗ £30. Rest. ♦ ♪ ♿ £11.

WADENHOE, 6m S off A605

Inn or Pub:
Kings Head, ☎ Clopton (08015) 222 ℗ ♦ ▦ ♨ ✂ Huntingdon fidgit pie and cold salads. £3.

PEAK DISTRICT NATIONAL PARK★★★

Derbyshire A1

542 sq. miles of National Park, the area is divided into the White Peak and Dark Peak. The White Peak is the central and S area of a limestone plateau, dissected by rivers with steep-sided wooded dales. The distinctive white stone walls criss-crossing the green pastures, dramatic rocks and cliffs are other characteristics of the area. The limestone dales are well-known beauty spots. The Dark Peak lying on the NE and NW margins of this limestone plateau is a complete contrast: rugged open moorland of gritstone and shale, and miles of dark stone walls. High, peat-covered summits, and strange gritstone edges that stretch for miles give the area its rather forbidding character. The highest part is Kinder Scout (→) at 2088 ft., and the region has a special appeal to experienced walkers and climbers.

▶ The S area of the Dark Peak (→) has walking areas of Hope and Edale Valleys, separated by the ridge between Lose Hill and Mam Tor. ▶ Below impressive Mam Tor is **Castleton★**, a small village with four show caves and rare **Blue John** stone, a purplish stone used for decoration. **Cave Dale** is a deep dry gorge approached via footpath off the market place, from where an impressive view of the ruined Norman **Peveril Castle★★** can be seen. This area is dotted with lead workings and natural caves. **Peak Cavern** is a true cave. **Blue John Mine★★** descends steeply with many steps. **Speedewell Cavern★★**: an old lead

mine designed 1774, where you can travel underground by boat on a canal. This cavern is at the deep dry gorge of **Winnats Pass★★**. **Teak Cliff Cavern★★★** (3/4m W) is approached via short footpath from car park, giving spectacular views over **Hope Valley★★** (→). The caves hollowed out by underground rivers during many centuries were discovered by mining operations in 18thC. The many chambers are magnificent. Apart from seeing richest deposits of beautiful Blue John stone, still being mined, you will see **'Fossil Cave'** with fossilized shells and deep down the finest chamber, **'The Dream Cave'**, with its hundreds of stalactites. ▶ **Edale**, the other side of Mam Tor, is where the **Pennine Way★★★** (→) begins its 250m path N. Also a gentler route up onto **Kinder Scout** (→) via **Jacob's Ladder★★**. In winter there is skiing on the SE slopes. For horseback riders, **trekking centre** using hills and moors around **Edale Valley**. ▶ **River Derwent Valley★★** is a distinctive feature of area. An escarpment of gritstone rock runs length of the valley. The outcrops or edges dominate the skyline of the upper Derwent, supplying footpaths for ramblers and superb viewpoints. Many bridges were constructed at crossing points along old packhorse routes. Derwent village bridge, built in Middle Ages, now re-erected at **Slippery Stones**, reached via footpath above **Howden Reservoir**. Together with **Ladybower** (→) and **Derwent, Howden** makes up the three large reservoirs. A road on W side of reservoirs leads to **Derwent Dale**. To penetrate further up valley from here you must walk, bike or use minibus service. ▶ 4m below Ladybower is **Hathersage★★**, surrounded by rugged heather-covered moorland. At **Padley Wood**, S of town, is Burbage Brook, bubbling white as it descends steep-sided valley. In **churchyard**, gravestone of Little John, friend of Robin Hood. N of village is **Stanage Edge★★**, longest gritstone edge in Derbyshire, accessible by car and with footpath underneath and along the top. W of village, footpaths criss-cross over **Offerton Moor**. ▶ The River Wye, with its deeply cut valley, flows through a number of dales. Most beautiful part lies from **Monsal Dale★★** through **Miller's Dale★★**, Chee Dale to **Wye Dale★★**. Many tributary valleys exist, mostly dry valleys of **Deep Dale, Tideswell Dale, Cressbrook Dale** (→) and **Taddington Dale** (→). The gradual erosion of rivers has left in some dales stone pinnacles and caves, as in Deep Dale. Wonderful area to enjoy native flowers and birds. ▶ Perhaps the most famous of the Derbyshire Dales is **Dove Dale★★** (→), 2m stretch on River Dove, known as 'Little Switzerland', with excellent viewpoint at **Sharplow Point★★** called 'Lover's Leap'. □

Practical information _____

🚃 Hathersage, Hope, New Mills Central, ☎ Sheffield (0742) 726411.

BAMFORD, 12m NW of Bakewell

Hotels:
★★ **Marquis of Granby**, Hathersage Road, S30 2BH, ☎ (0433) 51206, 7 rm. ♦ ♨ £34. Rest. ♦ ♪ ♿ Cl. Sun.-Mon. £10.
★★ **Rising Sun**, S30 2AL, ☎ (0433) 51323, AC AM BA, 13 rm. ℗ ▦ ♫ £42. Rest. ♦ ♪ ♿ £8.

Inn or Pub:
Derwent Hotel, Main Road, ☎ Hope Valley (0433) 513 95, AC AM BA DI ℗ ♦ ▦ 10 rm. Homecooked pies, vegetarian dishes and grills. £5.50.

CASTLETON, 15 1/2m SE of Glossop

Inn or Pub:
Bull's Head Hotel (Robinsons), Cross Street, ☎ (0433) 20256 ℗ ♦ ▦ ♿ 5 rm. Wide choice of bar foods. £3.50.

EDALE, 5m NW

Inn or Pub:
Cheshire Cheese, Edale Road, ☎ (0433) 20381 ℗ ♦ ▦ ♿ 6 rm. Homemade pies, fish dishes. £5.

Northern Peak district

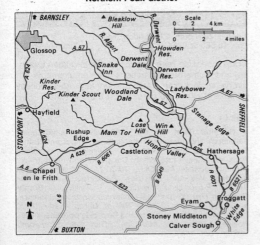

HATHERSAGE, 10m N of Bakewell on B6001

Hotels:
★★★ *Hathersage* (B.W.), Main Road, ☎ (0433) 50259, AC AM BA DI, 14 rm. ℙ £54. Rest. ♦ ♪ £10.
★★ *George*, Main Road, S30 1BB, ☎ (0433) 50436, AC AM BA, 18 rm. ℙ ⚘ ⚘ 16thC coaching inn. £50. Rest. ♦ ⚘ Charlotte prawns. £10.

Inn or Pub:
Plough (Stone/Bass Charr.), Leadmill Bridge, ☎ (0433) 50319 ℙ ⚘ ⚘ Sandwiches, ploughmans' lunches.

HOPE, 12m W of Bakewell

Hotel:
★★★ *Poachers Arms*, Castelton Road, S30 2RD, ☎ (0433) 20380, AC AM BA DI, 7 rm. ℙ ⚘ £45. Rest. ♦ Cl. 25-26 Dec. All game in season. £10.

⚘ *Laneside C.P.*, Laneside Farm (45 pl), ☎ (0433) 20214.

ROCKINGHAM FOREST★★

Leicestershire B2

Rich undulating farmland and tracts of woodland stretching from the Welland Valley to the Nene in the S and between Stamford and Northampton. Used as royal forests from the time of the Norman kings, this area is ideal for walking, using the miles of public footpaths through woodlands like Grafton Park Wood (*NE of Kettering*), Kingswood (Corby), Wakerley Wood (*NE of Corby*) and country parks like East Carlton Countryside Park (*W of Corby*). Traditional family activities and entertainments from steam trains at Nene Valley Steam and Railway, Wansford Station (*S of Stamford*) to many historic houses (→ centres: Corby, Kettering, Oundle and Stamford). □

SHERWOOD FOREST★★★

Nottinghamshire B1

Once a medieval royal hunting forest controlled and protected for the benefit of the kings who hunted game, the area covered not only woodlands of oak and birch, but leafy glades and even open farmland. The ordinary people suffered greatly from the harsh forest laws and cruelty of the kings' men. Out of this grew the legend of Robin Hood, protector of the poor. From the mid-17thC, when the forests ceased to be under royal control, the oak woods began to be cleared, some of the rich agricultural land exposed becoming the estates of noblemen. The area in the N is known sometimes as 'The Dukeries' since, in the 18thC, ducal estates were established, the finest being Clumber Park (→). Three major centres offer different attractions.

▶ In heart of forest is **Sherwood Forest Country Park★★**, 450 acres of ancient oak woodland, the largest in Europe. The **Visitor Centre**, near the attractive wooded village of **Edwinstowe**, has many activities. There are many marked walks and footpaths through the dense bracken and ancient oaks, passing the gnarled old Major Oak, the largest in the forest with a circumference of 30ft., said to have sheltered Robin Hood. Nature trail for the visually handicapped. ▶ Nearby is **Rufford★★** with ruined 12thC Cistercian abbey (*not open to public*) and beautiful **Country Park** of woodland, parkland and lake; rare breeds of sheep in meadow area. The Craft Centre includes a gallery with demonstrations (*Jan.-Feb.: 11-4.30 Sat., Sun. only; Mar.: 11-5 Mon.-Sun.; Apr.: 11-5 Tue.-Sun and Bank Hols. Mon.; May, Jun., Sep.: Tue.-Sat. 11-5, Sun. 11-6.30 also Bank Hols. Mon.; Jul.-Aug.: Mon.-Sat. 11-5, Sun. 11-6.30; Oct.-Dec.: Mon.-Sun. 11-4.30*). ▶ For a change of

scenery, on the N edge of forest is **Creswell Crags★★**, a narrow limestone gorge which contains prehistoric cave dwellings once used by woolly rhinoceros, bison and bears and colonized by Neanderthal and Stone Age man. **Visitors Centre**, just before entrance to gorge, has exhibitions explaining history of area; woodland path leads to picturesque gorge and lake (*May-Sep.: 9.30-7; winter 9.30-4, Mon.-Wed., Sat., Sun. 2-4; cl. 25-26 Dec.*). □

Practical information _____

EDWINSTOWE

ⓘ Sherwood Forest Visitor Centre, ☎ (0623) 823202.

⚘ *Sherwood Forest C.P.* (110 pl), ☎ (0623) 823132.

Recommended
Craft workshops: *Church Farm Craft Workshops*, Mansfield Road, ☎ (0623) 824243.

Robin Hood

Still a familiar figure to most British people, Robin Hood was first mentioned in texts written in the 14thC. We cannot be sure whether he really existed, but he is said to have lived in Nottinghamshire's Sherwood Forest during the 12thC at the time of Richard I. According to legend, he was a sworn enemy of the Sheriff of Nottingham, and lived as an outlaw in the forest with a band of 'merry men' who included such characters as Little John (a giant of a man), Friar Tuck and Will Scarlet. His sweetheart was Maid Marion.
It is possible that in real life this now mythological figure was actually Robert Fitz-Ooth, Earl of Huntingdon. Certainly he was said to be the champion of the poor and oppressed, and a gallant protector of women. A skillful archer, he attacked and robbed the rich, then distributed his booty among the poor.
Many plays were performed for hundreds of years on the theme of the Robin Hood legend; and in Derbyshire several places are connected with his name. His most famous companion, Little John, is said to be buried in Hathersage. Indeed, when his supposed grave was opened in 1784, an enormous thigh bone was found: it measured 32 inches and would have belonged to a man seven feet tall.

SKEGNESS★

Boston, 23; Louth, 21; London, 140 m
pop. 13,580 ☎ 0754   Lincolnshire C1

Bracing seaside resort on E coast with golden beaches and numerous attractions and amusements for everyone, including traditional donkey rides; holiday camp and extensive gardens on the seafront.

Nearby

▶ **Gibraltar Point** (*4m S*): 1,500 acres of sand-dunes, saltmarsh and freshwater habitats, an important **Nature Reserve and Field Centre★★** studying bird migration. Area stretches S into Wash. Car parks and many tracks through dunes (*May-Oct.: 10.30-1, 2-5, also 6-dusk Jul.-Aug.; Nov.-Apr.: Sat., Sun., Bank Hols., Easter Week 10.30-1, 2-5 or dusk if earlier*). ▶ The village of **Burgh-le-Marsh** (*7m W*) has well-preserved working **windmill★**. ▶ **Gunby Hall★★** (*2 ¹/₂ m NW of Burgh*): early 18thC house with English furniture and Reynolds portraits; walled flower gardens (*29 Mar.-Sep., Thu. 2-6; other days written appt. only*). □

Practical information

SKEGNESS
ⓘ Embassy Centre, Grand Parade ☎ (0754) 4821.
🚞 ☎ (0754) 4186.

Hotel:
★★★ *County*, North Parade, PE25 2UB, ☎ (0754) 2461, AC AM BA DI, 44 rm. ℗ ⊰ க் £44. Rest. ♦ ♪ க் £8.

⚓ *Richmond Drive C.P.*, Richmond Drive (200 pl), ☎ (0754) 2097; at Ingoldmells, *Coastfield C.P.*, Roman Bank, Vickers Point (12 pl), ☎ (0754) 72592.

Recommended
Craft workshops: *Heather & Michel Ducos*, Commercial Road, Alford, ☎ (052 12) 3342, domestic and decorative stone-ware.
Golf course: North Shore, North Shore Road, ☎ (0754) 3298.

Nearby

BURGH-LE-MARSH, 4m W on A158

Inn or Pub:
White Hart Hotel, High Street, ☎ (0754) 810 321, AM ℗ 5 rm. Bar snacks and à la carte menu. £10.

SEACROFT, 2m S

Hotel:
★★ *Vine*, Vine Road, PE25 3DB, ☎ (0754) 3018, AC AM BA DI, 20 rm. ℗ ⅏ £44. Rest. ♦ ♪ க் £9.

Recommended
Golf course: ☎ Leeds (0532) 3020.

SPALDING*

Peterborough, 20; Stamford, 19; London, 102 m
pop. 18,182 ☎ 0775   Lincolnshire C2

Spalding lies in fen country, only just above sea level, on the River Welland. The drainage of the fens, started by the Romans and completed in 17thC and 18thC, produced some of the most fertile farming land in this country. Now cultivated and noted for its bulbfields, known as capital of 'Tulipland'.

▶ **Parish church** of SS. Mary and Nicholas, 13thC, has fine hammerbeam roof with carved wooden angels. Other churches (19thC) all house flower festivals in May. ▶ **The Museum**, Broad Street (*by appt. only*), houses collection from 'The Gentleman's Society', famous antiquarian society founded early 18thC, boasting famous early member Sir Isaac Newton. ▶ **Ayscoughfee Hall and Gardens** dates from 15thC, greatly restored, showing Dutch influence; museum of British Birds (*daily*). ▶ **Springfield Gardens**★ has 25 acres of show gardens planted with spring flowering bulbs and shrubs (*28 Mar.-Sep., 10-6*); famous 'Flower Parade' through Spalding in May.

Nearby

▶ Many marshland villages and towns. Few miles N is **Surfleet**, attractive village with leaning church tower and small sailing centre on banks of River Glen. ▶ **Moulton** (*4m E*) has pleasant village green and 12thC church with crocketed spire. Nearby early 19thC **Moulton Mill**★ is eight storeys high, one of the tallest in England. To the S is **Moulton Chapel**★, small community with unusual octagonal church dating from early 18thC in Dutch style. ▶ **Holbeach** (*8m E*): market town since 13thC, 14thC parish church has W tower with broach spire ringed by gargoyle-like animal carvings. Parish stretches E across fenland with scattered villages and extensive marshes to sea embankments. ▶ **Long Sutton** (*12m E*): 13thC **church** of St. Mary has spire constructed of timber and covered with lead, also features double-storeyed monks' cell with 14thC vaulting. Further E is **Sutton Bridge** beside River Nene, a port until last century: interesting 19thC housing, wharves and warehouses by river and late 19thC swing-

bridge. ▶ **Gedney Drove End**★ with main street running parallel with seawall is closest village to shoreline. Near embanked shores of Wash, typical fen country, winds sweeping across flat marshy levels, partly used as nature reserve, peaceful haven for wildfowl. ▶ **Crowland** (*10m S*), typical example of fenland settlement which originally stood on island amidst marshes; now nestles beside partly ruined 12thC **Norman Abbey** - N aisle now parish church - within flood embankments. Interesting 14thC triangular **bridge**★ once spanning three streams, now on dry land.   □

Practical information

SPALDING
ⓘ Ayscoughfee Hall, Churchgate, ☎ (0755) 5468.
🚞 ☎ (0755) 2371.

Hotels:
★★★ *Woodlands*, 80 Pinchbeck Road, PE11 1QF, ☎ (0775) 69933, AC AM BA DI, 6 rm. ℗ ⅏ ♨ £42. Rest. ♦ ♪ £10.

★★ *Dembleby*, Broad Street, PE11 1TB, ☎ (0775) 67060, AC AM BA DI, 8 rm. ℗ ⅏ ⅋ £37. Rest. ♦ ♪ Cl. Sat. lunch, Sun. dinner. £9.

★ *Red Lion*, Market Place, PE11 1SU, ☎ (0755) 2869, AC AM BA DI, 31 rm. ℗ க் £32. Rest. ♦ ♪ Cl. Sun. dinner. £5.

Nearby

BOURNE, 12m W on A151

Hotel:
★★ *Angel*, North Street, ☎ (0778) 422346, AC BA, 12 rm. ℗ ⅋ £35. Rest. ♦ ♪ க் £10.

HOLBEACH, 8m E on A151

Inn or Pub:
Bell (Good Sons), High Street, ☎ (0406) 23223 6 rm. Homecooked bar meals and à la carte menu £4.

⚓ *Matapos Touring Park*, Main Street, Fleet Hargate (60 pl), ☎ (0406) 22910; *Whapole Manor C.P.*, Whapole Manor, Saracens Head (20 pl), ☎ (0406) 22837.

LONG SUTTON, 14m E on A17

Inn or Pub:
Bull (Bass Charrington), Market Place, ☎ Holbeach (0406) 362 258 ℗ 8 rm. Bar snacks and 3-course meals. £3.50.

RIPPINGALE, 5m N of Bourne off A15

Inn or Pub:
Bull (Melbourns), High Street, ☎ Dowsby (077 835) 652 ℗ ⊰ ⅏ ♨ க் Steak and various dishes in sauces. £7.

TOFT, 3m SW on A6121

Hotel:
★★ *Toft*, Main Road, PE10 0JT, ☎ (077 833) 614, BA, 22 rm. ℗ ⅏ ♨ க் ⅋ £35. Rest. ♦ ♪ க் Cl. Sun. dinner. £7.

SPILSBY

Skegness, 12; Boston, 16; London, 134 m
☎ 0790   Lincolnshire C1

A small friendly market town lying between, to the N the Lincolnshire Wolds (→), to the S the fenlands and tulip fields and to the E the coast only 10 miles away. Names of towns and villages in the Wolds give evidence of the Danish invaders: many end with 'by', Danish for 'settlement' and 'thorpe' meaning 'farm'. Spilsby has been a busy market centre since 14thC for the outlying villages and farms.

▶ The parish church of **St. James** dominates the main crossroads; interesting 14th-16thC tombs and memorials to the Willoughby family who had close associations with the town. Church also has monuments to Spilsby's most famous son, Capt. Sir John Franklin, arctic explorer; his

bronze statue stands in **market place** and plaque on **High Street** bakery marks birthplace.

Nearby

▶ Spilsby is an ideal centre for touring the Wolds and coast. 8m NW is the little village of **Somersby★★** (→), birthplace of the 19thC poet Alfred, Lord Tennyson. This southern part of the Wolds is known as Tennyson country. Rectory where he was born now a private house. At **Stockwith Mill** (→) relax by Tennyson's 'Brook'. Close by is village of **Harrington** with **Harrington Hall★★**, present building dating from 17thC, original medieval house mentioned in Domesday Book (*Easter-Oct.: Thu., 2-5; also 30 Mar., 4, 11, 25 May, 6 Jul. 2-6*). ▶ SW, attractive Wold village of **Old Bolingbroke**: mounds mark site of castle, birthplace in 1367 of Henry IV. In Civil War, a major battle took place at nearby Winceby. The castle was pulled down by Cromwell's men after victory. □

Practical information

ⓘ Council Offices, 41b High Street, ☎ (0790) 52301.

Restaurant:

♦ *Buttercross*, 18 Lower Market Street, ☎ (0790) 53147 ⌂ ♪ ♿ Cl. Christmas, 2 wks. Jun., Tue., Sun. Garlic roasted leg of lamb stuffed with apricots. Book. £10.

STAMFORD*

Peterborough, 4; Spalding, 19; London, 90 m
pop. 16,127 ☎ 0780   Lincolnshire B-C2

Handsome country town, known for its stone-built houses and churches with Collyweston slate roofs. It has five medieval churches, Tudor houses and Georgian mansions, untouched by the industrial age. Once important Roman crossing point, has been under Saxon, Danish (who made it capital of the Fens) and Norman influence. Stamford was prosperous wool centre from 12thC.

▶ Town has unique conformity - **St. Martin's★★** area (S of river) has 18thC High Street, architecturally finest in country. ▶ 15thC **St. Martin's★★** Church with high tower, late Perpendicular, has tombs of Cecil family, especially Lord Burghley, Queen Elizabeth I's Lord Treasurer, builder of Burghley House. ▶ In St. Paul's Street, **Stamford School** with 13thC gateway of Brasenose College. ▶ **Browne's Hospital** in Broad Street, founded by wealthy wool merchant late 15thC, outstanding example of medieval almshouses. ▶ **Stamford Museum★**, Broad Street: display of Stamford Ware Pottery, earliest glazed wares produced since Roman Times: also features techniques used by Collyweston slaters (*May-Sep.: 10-5 Tue.-Sat., Sun. 2-5; Oct.-Apr.: 10-12.30, 1.30-5 Tue.-Sat.; open Bank Hols. Mon.; cl. 25-26 Dec., Good Fri.*). ▶ To E on Priory Road is Benedictine priory of **St. Leonard's.**

Nearby

▶ **Market Deeping** (*16m NE*) has a number of fine old houses, a 12th-13thC parish church and a **rectory★**, continuously inhabited since 13thC, and originally refectory of an abbey. □

Practical information

STAMFORD
ⓘ Museum, Broad Street, ☎ (0780) 55611.
▦▦ ☎ (0780) 63332.

Hotels:

● ★★★ *George* (Poste), St. Martin's, PE9 2LB, ☎ (0780) 55171, Tx 32578, AC AM BA DI, 48 rm. ⓟ ⌂ £75. Rest. ● ♦ ♿ £20.
★★ *Garden House*, 42 High Street, St. Martin's, PE9 2LP, ☎ (0780) 63359, AC BA, 21 rm. ⓟ ⌂ ♿ £45. Rest. ♦ ♪ £12.50.
★★ *Lady Anne's*, 37-38 High Street, St. Martin's, PE9

Local heavyweight

For many years Daniel Lambert of Stamford had the reputation of being the heaviest man who ever lived in England. Since his death only two heavier British males have been recorded, the last dying in 1984.
Daniel Lambert was born in 1770 and, just before his death at the age of 39, he weighed 52 stone 11 lbs (1,370 lbs) and was 5 feet 11 inches tall. Making the most of his huge size, Mr Lambert exhibited himself in London in the year 1806. People were invited to pay an admission fee of one shilling (five pence) to come and see him in his lodgings at Picadilly. At present a life-size model of this giant can be seen in Stamford Museum clad in a suit of clothes which actually belonged to him. When Lambert suddenly died while staying at the Bull and Swan in the High Street, it was necessary to knock down a wall of the ground floor room he had occupied (he was unable to climb stairs) in order to remove the body for burial. The enormous coffin was mounted on wheels and rolled down a specially-constructed slope to the grave in St. Martin's churchyard.

2LJ, ☎ (0780) 53175, Tx 32376, AC AM BA DI, 27 rm. ⓟ ⌂ ♿ £44. Rest. ♦ ♿ Cl. 28-30 Dec. £9.

Restaurants:

♦ *Candlesticks*, 1 Church Lane, ☎ (0780) 64033, AC BA ⓟ ⌂ ♪ ♿ ⊛ Cl. Mon., Tue., Sat. lunch. 4 rm. Sauté de veau Marengo. £9.50.
♦ *The Courtyard*, 18a Maiden Lane, ☎ (0780) 51505, AC AM BA DI ⌂ ♪ ♿ ⊛ Cl. Sun. eve., Mon., Christmas, 1 Jan. £17.

Inn or Pub:

Hurdler (Everards), 93 New Cross Road, ☎ (0780) 634 28 ⓟ ⌂ ⌂ ♿ Hot and cold snacks. £3.50.

Recommended

Golf course: Luffenham Heath, Ketton ☎ 720205; Burghley Park, St. Martins ☎ 2100.

Nearby

MARKET DEEPING 7m E on A16

Hotel:

★ *Deeping Stage Inn*, 16 Market Place, PE6 8EA, ☎ (0778) 343234, AM BA DI, 8 rm. ⓟ ⌂ ⊛ Georgian coaching inn. £30. Rest. ♦ £6.

SOUTH LUFFENHAM 6m SW on A6121

Inn or Pub:

Boot & Shoe, 10 The Street, ☎ (0780) 720 177 ⓟ ⌂ ⌂ ♿ 4 rm. Bar snacks. £7.50.

STRETTON 7m NW on A1

Inn or Pub:

Jackson Stops, ☎ (078 081) 237 ⓟ ⌂ ⌂ ⊛ Homemade and vegetarian dishes. £4.75.

Recommended

Riding School: *Stretton Riding Centre*, Manor Bungalow Farm, ☎ (078 081) 323.

SWADLINCOTE

Burton-upon-Trent, 6; Derby, 14; London, 116 m
☎ 0283   Derbyshire A2

This large industrial town is made up of three settlements: Swadlincote, Church Gresley and Newhall. During the 19thC collieries, brickworks and potteries were established, although coal and clay were being mined in the late 18thC. Bottle-shaped kilns were

once a distinct feature of the skyline. Today only one colliery is operating and the stocks of stoneware pipes seen covering the landscape are evidence of the surviving pottery industry.

▶ The centre of the town has been redeveloped in recent years, providing new shops and civic amenities. The **parish church** at Church Gresley is on the site of a 12thC Augustinian priory. There is a life-size figure of Sir Thomas Gresley, died 1699.

Nearby

▶ 6m NE is the market gardening town of Melbourne, derived from Mel-bourne meaning the Mill by the Stream. Thomas Cook, founder of the famous worldwide travel agency, was born here and in the High Street can be seen cottages and a Mission Hall built at his expense in the late 19thC. The 12thC parish church is a fine example of Norman architecture. E of church is **Melbourne Hall★**, once home of Lord Melbourne and Lady Caroline Lamb. The Hall, built 12thC, enlarged 17thC, houses important collection of paintings including works by Rembrandt and Gainsborough. The gardens, started in 1699, are in the Dutch formal style by an English landscape designer, Henry Wise. The early 18thC wrought-iron pergola, known as the 'bird cage', is a celebrated work by Robert Bakewell *(Jun.-Oct.: Wed., 2-6; gardens Apr.-Sep., Wed., Sat., Sun., Bank Hols. Mon. 2-6).* ▶ **Repton** *(10m N)* with its spacious High Street and old market cross has interesting and recent archaeological excavations, near the grounds of its famous and ancient **public school**. Unearthed was a Viking fortified camp, the first to be definitely identified and firmly dated to AD 874-5. Parish church of **St. Wystan★★** is a fine example of Saxon work. ▶ As a contrast to the rural villages, **Shardlow**, 9m NE, is one of only two surviving almost complete inland ports. Lying in low meadows at confluence of Derwent and Trent crossed by Trent and Mersey Canal, development began in late 18thC when engineer James Bridley built canal. Here wharves, side cuts, warehouses and docks were built to service the canal community for its sail making and boat building. Clock warehouse, built 1780, has been restored to house **canal museum.** Many buildings like Broughton House, attributed to 'Capability' Brown, are listed as of architectural or historical interest. ☐

TOWCESTER

Northampton, 9; Buckingham, 10; London, 64 m
pop. 5,010 ☎ 0327   Northamptonshire B3

Built on site of Roman station, known today for its racecourse, the town has mainly Victorian buildings, some Georgian.

▶ **The Saracen's Head Inn** is described by Dickens in *Pickwick Papers.* ▶ Interesting chained books in the 13thC church of **St. Lawrence.** ▶ **Silverstone** motor racing circuit to SW hosts British Grand Prix (odd-numbered years).

Nearby

▶ **Stoke Bruerne★**, to E, is village of thatched roofs in wooded hillside surroundings with its locks, Boat Inn and Waterways Museum, situated on one of England's major canal routes. **Waterways Museum★★**, alongside **Grand Union**, has fascinating exhibits covering 200 years of working boatpeople's life *(Easter-Oct.: daily 10-6. incl. Bank Hols.; Oct.-Easter: Tue.-Sun. 10-4; cl. 25, 26 Dec.).* Canal towpath through double-arched bridge slopes down beside flight of 14 locks. In the opposite direction, towpath leads to **Blisworth Tunnel**, one of longest built and still in use. Before steam tugs, boats were 'legged' through tunnels by men strapped to boats on tunnel side, walking the boats through. ▶ **Stoke Park Pavilions★**, outside village, are pavilions and colonnades attributed to Inigo Jones, all that remains of a country house built in 17thC *(Jun. Sun., Jul., Aug. Sat., Sun. and Bank Hols.,*

2-6; other times by appt.). ▶ **Sulgrave Manor★★** *(11m SW)* home of Elizabethan ancestors of George Washington. Washington Coat of Arms (three mullets and two bars) seen in main doorway is said to have inspired 'Stars and Stripes' of American national flag *(Feb.-Dec. daily ex. Wed., 10.30-1, 2-5.30 Oct.- Mar., cl. Jan.).* ▶ **Canons Ashby** *(10m NW)* carefully restored 16thC manor house, home of the poet John Dryden: Elizabethan wall paintings and Jacobean plasterwork; medieval priory church, 70-acre park *(29 Mar.-Oct., Wed.-Sun. and Bank Hols. Mon., 1-5.30 or dusk; cl. Good Fri.).* ▶ **Aynho Park★★** *(15m SE)*, manor-house built in stages from Jacobean times to 19thC; interiors by Sir John Soane *(May-Sep., Wed. and Thur., 2-5).* ▶ At Kings Sutton, just N of Aynho, the parish church of **St. Peter** possesses a soaring and richly ornamented spire. ▶ The history of Daventry *(12 m NE)* goes back to Iron-Age times. Earthworks on **Borough Hill★** E of the town testify to this. The Royalist army of Charles I camped round the hill before Battle of Naseby. Town has an attractive market place, and Hall. ☐

Practical information

TOWCESTER

Inn or Pub:
Saracen's Head (Charles Wells), Watling Street, ☎ (0327) 50 414, AC AM BA DI Ⓟ ⌛ 12 rm. A la carte menu. £8.

Recommended
Antique shop: *Cameron, Malcolm*, The Antique Galleries, Watling Street, ☎ (032 733) 238, furniture; *Reindeer Antiques Ltd.*, 43 Watling Street, Potterspury, ☎ (0908) 542407, clocks, furniture, metalwork and paintings.
Golf course: Woodlands, Farthingstone, ☎ (032 736) 291.
Guesthouse: *Mandalay House*, Watling Street, ☎ (0327) 50784, £21 B. & B.
♥ *Pickwick Shop*, 197 Watling Street West, ☎ (0327) 50692, the birthplace of the Towcester cheesecake.

Nearby

CHACOMBE, 13m W off B4525

Inn or Pub:
George the Dragon, Silver Street, ☎ Banbury (0295) 710 602, AC BA DI Ⓟ ⌛ ⌛ ♿ Wide range of food and bar snacks. £4.50.

COSGROVE, 8m SE off A508

Inn or Pub:
Navigation Inn, Trupp Wharf, ☎ Milton Keynes (0908) 543 156 Ⓟ ⌛ ⌛ ♿ Hot and cold buffet counter and bar meals. £6.

CULWORTH, 9m W off B4525

Hotel:
★ *Paddock*, High Street, OX17 2BE, ☎ (029 576) 491, 7 rm. Ⓟ ⌛ ⌛ ⌛ £25. Rest. ♦ Cl. Christmas. £6.

EYDON, 10m W off B4525

Inn or Pub:
Royal Oak, Lime Avenue, ☎ Byfield (0327) 615 26 Ⓟ ⌛ ⌛ 2 rm. Bar snacks and 3-course meals. £10.

GAYTON, 4m N

Inn or Pub:
Queen Victoria, ☎ (0604) 858 438, AM BA Ⓟ ⌛ ⌛ ♿ Hot and cold bar meals incl. sirloin steaks. £10.50.

GREATWORTH, 10m W off A43

Inn or Pub:
The Inn (Hook Norton), Chapel Road, ☎ Banbury (0295) 711 503 Ⓟ ⌛ ⌛ ♿ Grills and bar snacks. £5.

STOKE BRUERNE, 4m E off A508

Restaurant:
● ♦ *The Butty*, 5 Canalside, ☎ Roade (0604) 863654, AC BA Ⓟ ⌛ ⌛ ⌛ Cl. 2 wks. Aug., 1 wk. winter., Sun.-Mon., Sat. lunch. Italian dishes. Book. £15.

Inn or Pub:
The Boat Inn, ☎ (0604) 862 428, AC AM BA DI ⓟ ⫱ ⌂
⌞ Homemade dishes and bar snacks. £6.

SULGRAVE, 9m W off B4525

Hotel:
★★ *Thatched*, Banbury, OX17 2SE, ☎ (029 576) 232, AC
AM BA DI, 7 rm. ⓟ ⌂ ⌞ £40. Rest. ♦ ⌶ Cl. 25 Dec. din-
ner. £9.

THORPE MANDEVILLE, 10m W on B4525

Restaurant:
♦ *Three Conies*, ☎ Banbury (0295) 711025, AC BA ⓟ
⌂ ⌞ ⅋ Cl. Sun.-Mon. eve. 2 rm. Chicken supreme
with green peppercorns, lime, brandy and cream sauce.
£14.50.

UPPINGHAM

Oakham, 6; Leicester, 19; London, 91 m
pop. 3,493 ☎ 0572   Leicestershire B2

Small market town with long High Street displaying
pleasant houses dating from late 16th and early
19thC, mostly shops. Its well-known public school,
founded in 16thC, is still housed in its original buildings around courtyards and quadrangles.

Nearby

▶ **Lyddington** (*2m S*), attractive village of ironstone houses. Just N of village green is **Bede House★** and its
13thC market cross. Originally palace of Bishops of Lincoln, in 1602 became almshouses. Fine hall with beautiful
early 16thC wooden ceiling.   □

Practical information ─────────────────────
UPPINGHAM

Hotel:
★★★ *Falcon* (Inter), Market Place, LE15 9PY, ☎ (0572)
823535, AC AM BA DI, 25 rm. ⓟ ⌂ £52. Rest. ♦ ⌶
⌶ £12.50.

Restaurant:
● ♦ *Lake Isle*, 16 High Street East,, ☎ (0572) 822951,
AC AM BA DI ⌂ Cl. 2 wks. Feb., 2 wks. Sep.-Oct., Sun.
eve., Mon., Bank Hols. 5 rm. Book. £14.

Recommended
▼ tearoom: *M.C.S. Baines and Son*, 5 High Street, ☎
(0572) 823317, full range of bread, cakes, confectionery.

Nearby

HALLATON, 7m W off A47

Inn or Pub:
Bewicke Arms, ☎ (085 889) 217 ⓟ ⫱ ⌂ ⌞ ⅋ Full menu
7 days a week and bar snacks. £5.

LYDDINGTON, 1m S off A6003

Hotel:
★★ *Marquess of Exeter*, 52 Main Street, LE15 9LT, ☎
(0572) 822477, AC AM BA DI, 15 rm. ⓟ ⌞ ⌶ ⅋ £50. Rest.
♦ ⌶ ⌶ £8.

PRESTON, 1 1/2m N on A6003

Inn or Pub:
Fox & Hounds, Cross Lane, ☎ Manton (057 285) 492 ⫱
⌂ ⌞ ⅋ Homemade rolls, hot and cold bar meals incl.
vegetarian, traditional Sun. lunch. £8.

SKEFFINGTON, 9m W on A47

Inn or Pub:
Fox & Hounds (Davenports), Uppingham Road, ☎
Billesdon (053 755) 250 ⓟ ⫱ ⌂ ⌶ ⅋ Fresh fish dishes
and vegetarian. £5.

WING, 3m N off A6003

Inn or Pub:
Kings Arms, Top Street, ☎ Manton (057 285) 315, BA ⓟ
⌞ ⌶ Hot and cold bar snacks, à la carte menu in restau-
rant. £5.

WELLINGBOROUGH

Kettering, 8; Northampton, 10; London, 69 m
pop. 47,709 ☎ 0933   Northamptonshire B3

A busy market and light industrial town, with shoemak-
ing its principal industry. There are some attractive
17thC buildings relating to its earlier reputation as a
spa, though its significant development was 19thC.

▶ The parish church of **All Hallows★** is mainly 13th
and 14thC, with some spirited misericords and fine carved
bosses; 15thC wall paintings depict the Seven Deadly Sins and the Three Quick and the Three Dead; also
one of the best collections of modern stained glass in the
country including work by John Piper.

Nearby

▶ 10m NE is the village of Raunds with its splendid parish
church of **St. Mary★**. Early English broach spire is particularly well proportioned. Tower has a 15thC clock dial,
stone faced with twenty-four discs of the hours; fine E
window of c. 1275, and medieval wall paintings.   □

Practical information ─────────────────────
WELLINGBOROUGH
⊞ ☎ Kettering (0536) 521445.

Hotels:
★★ *High View*, 156 Midland Road, NN8 1NGT, ☎ (0933)
78733, AC AM BA DI, 15 rm. ⓟ £31. Rest. ♦ ⌶ Cl. Christmas. £7.50.
★★ *Hind* (Q.M.H.), Sheep Street, NN8 1BY, ☎ (0933)
222827, AC AM BA DI, 32 rm. ⓟ £50. Rest. ♦ ⌶ ⌶ Cl. 26
Dec. £9.

Inn or Pub:
Vivian Arms (Charles Wells), Knox Road, ☎ (0933) 223
660 ⓟ ⌂ ⌞ ⌶ Hot pies and toasted sandwiches. £2.

Recommended
Golf course: Gt. Harrowden Hall (2m N on A509),
☎ (0536) 67723.

Nearby

RUSHDEN, 6m E off A45

Hotel:
★ *Westward*, Shirley Road, NN10 9BY, ☎ (0933) 312376,
26 rm. ⓟ ⌞ ⌶ ⌸ £34. Rest. ♦ ⌶ ⌶ Cl. 23 Dec.-2 Jan. £8.

WOODHALL SPA

Boston, 19; Lincoln, 19; London, 136 m
pop. 2,526 ☎ 0526   Lincolnshire C1

Small tranquil town, has Victorian pump room and
bathing facilities utilizing the beneficial spring water
first found in early 19thC. Surrounded by pine and
birch woods, the woodland walks are particularly
attractive. The town has many sports activities, and a
championship golf course is one of the major attractions.

▶ At **Town Moor** there is a romantic ruined tower, thought
to be Cromwell's hunting tower.

Nearby

▶ **Tattershall Castle★★★** (*3¹/₂ m SE*), earliest surviving
brick-built building in England, a fortified mid-15thC castle
with moat (*29 Mar.-Oct.: 11-6.30 Mon.-Sat., 1-6.30 Sun.;*

Nov-28 Mar.: 12-6, 1-6.30 Sun.; cl. 25, 26 Dec.). ▶ **Horncastle** *(7m NE)* is a busy market town serving a mainly agricultural area. Fragments of wall from the Roman town *(Banovallum)* survive. There are some pleasant old brick houses and inns. □

Practical information

WOODHALL SPA
ℹ Jubilee Park, Stixwould Road, ☎ (0526) 52448.

Hotels:
★★★ *Golf* (Quality), Broadway, LN10 6SG, ☎ (0526) 53535, AC AM BA DI, 51 rm. ℙ ⏣ ⓖ ⌓ ⏴ £50. Rest. ◆ ⌓ ⓖ £9.
★★★ *Petwood* (Consort), Stixwould Road, CN10 6QF, ☎ (0526) 52411, AC AM BA DI, 30 rm. ℙ ⏣ ⏣ £55. Rest. ◆ Trout and grouse. £10.
★ *Dower House*, Manor Estate, LN10 6PY, ☎ (0526) 52588, AC AM BA, 7 rm. ℙ ⏣ ⏣ £40. Rest. ◆ ⌓ ⓖ Cl. Sun. dinner. £10.

⚑ *Bainland Park*, Horncastle Road (100 pl), ☎ (0526) 52903.

Recommended
Antique shop: *Best, James Ltd.*, The Broadway, ☎ (0526) 52513, prints, furniture, glass, jewelry, pottery and silver.
Golf course: ☎ (0526) 52511.
♥ gifts: *Fulbeck Heath Craft Centre*, Ryland Grange Cottage, Fulbeck Heath, ☎ (0400) 61563, hand-carved wooden items, painted ceramics and soft toys.

Nearby

HORNCASTLE, 8m NE on A158

Restaurant:
◆ *Magpies*, 73-75 East Street, ☎ Horncastle (065 82) · 7004, AC ⏣ ⌓ ⏣ Cl. 3 wks. Aug., Sun. eve., Mon., lunches by arrangement only. Book. £12.

Inn or Pub:
Red Lion (Shipstone), Bull Ring, ☎ (065) 823 338 ℙ ⏣ 4 rm. Lunchtime homemade dishes. £3.

TIMBERLAND, 6m W off B1191

Hotel:
★ *Penny Farthing*, Station Road, ☎ (052 67) 359, AC BA DI, 7 rm. ⏣ ⏣ £26. Rest. ◆ ⓖ £10.

WORKSOP

Mansfield, 14; Sheffield, 17; London, 156 m
pop. 36,382 ☎ 0909   Nottinghamshire B1

The market town of Worksop grew up within Sherwood Forest (→) and is known as the gateway to 'The Dukeries'.

▶ Blending of Georgian buildings and Victorian industrial architecture. The town's most notable building are the **Priory Church of Our Ladys and St. Cuthbert** and **Gatehouse** off Retford Road. Church has Norman nave; Lady Chapel is Early English; huge S door is made of yew wood from Sherwood Forest. The 14thC **Gatehouse** has a double archway and its upper room houses county's first elementary school, 1628.

Nearby

▶ Excellent touring centre for the **Sherwood Forest**★★★ (→) area. ▶ **Clumber Park**★★ *(4 ¹⁄₂m SE)* is a fine example of 18thC, created for the Dukes of Newcastle, now covering nearly 4000 acres of parkland. Two-mile

long double avenue of lime trees known as 'Dukes Drive' planted early 19thC; beautiful lake with Classical bridge and estate village of Hardwicke, with steep-pitched Tudor roofs and huge chimney stacks. In the grounds exquisite **Clumber Chapel**, a masterpiece of late Victorian Gothic revival by G.F. Bodley *(daily)*. ▶ **Thoresby Hall** *(8m S)* is the only mansion in the Dukeries still occupied by the original owners; present neo-Tudor house, built by Salvin in late 19thC, stands in large parkland with pleasant riverside walk and deer park *(Easter Sun. and Mon., Sun. and Bank Hol Mon. in May, Jun.-Aug.; house 1-5; grounds 11-6)*. ▶ Worksop is on the edge of the Midlands coalfield. Coal mining is an important contribution to the local economy and the **National Mining Museum**★★★ at **Lound Hall, Haughton** *(10 m SE)* illustrates the history of British coal mining; simulated underground galleries, nearly two m long, vividly illustrate conditions for mineworkers underground *(Tue.-Sat. 10.30-5.30, Sun. 2-5.30; cl. dusk in winter)*. ▶ **Babworth** and **Scrooby** near **East Retford**, were once homes of the Pilgrim Fathers. ▶ 2m NW of **Retford** between villages of **Sutton** and **Lound**, is the **Westlands Waterfowl Reserve**★. These shallow lagoons, left by gravel workings, provide perfect habitat for the indigenous wildfowl and resting place for migratory species. □

Practical information

WORKSOP
ℹ Queen's Buildings, Potter Street, ☎ (0909) 475531.
🚃 ☎ Sheffield (0742) 26411.

Inn or Pub:
White Lion, Park Street, ☎ (0909) 478 125 ℙ ⏣ ⏣ ⏣
Snacks, quiches, beef venision. £3.

⚑ *Clumber Park Camp*, The Walled Garden (60 pl), ☎ (0909) 482303; at Tuxford, *Green Acres C.P.*, Lincoln Road (75 pl), ☎ (0777) 870264.

Recommended
Craft workshops: *The Gallery*, The Pottery, Tickhill Road, Harworth, ☎ (0302) 743838, porcelain stoneware, paintings and prints.
Golf course: Lindrick, ☎ (0909) 475282; Windmill Lane, ☎ (0909) 2696.

Nearby

BARNBY MOOR, 6m NE off A634

Hotel:
★★★ *Ye Olde Bell* (T.H.F.), DN22 8QS, ☎ (0777) 705121, AC AM BA DI, 58 rm. ℙ ⏣ ⏣ ⏣ £61.50. Rest. ◆ £10.

BLYTH, 7m N on A6045

Hotel:
★ *Angel*, S81 8HG, ☎ (090976) 213, 6 rm. ℙ ⏣ ⏣ £25. Rest. ◆ ⌓ Stuffed plaice with prawns. £6.

Recommended
♥ stained glass: *Nornay Originals*, Bawtry Road, ☎ (090 976) 205, Tiffany-style lamps.

OLLERTON, 8m SE on A614

Hotel:
★ *Hop Pole*, Main Street, NG22 9AD, ☎ (0623) 822573, AC AM BA, 12 rm. ℙ ⏣ 17thC coaching inn near the centre of Sherwood Forest. £40. Rest. ◆ ⌓ £7.

RETFORD, 7 1/2m NE
ℹ Town Hall, The Square, ☎ (0777) 706741.

Inn or Pub:
Market Hotel, Westcarr Road, ☎ (0777) 703 278, AC BA ℙ ⏣ Bar snacks and restaurant menu. £8.

Heart of England

▶ Since the name of William Shakespeare stands at the centre of Britain's cultural heritage, it would seem logical to regard Stratford-upon-Avon as standing, if not precisely in terms of geography, at the centre of this region, truly at the very heart of England. This historic town lies in the Vale of Evesham, an area given over intensively to vegetable and fruit production, with especially delicious plums in season. South of the Vale and extending south-west into Avon are the Cotswold Hills, dotted with small villages, still medieval, built of golden Cotswold stone. There, too, are the famous 'wool churches' endowed by the rich woolstaplers of medieval times. To the west, the region shares a common border with Wales, where stretches of Offa's Dyke can still be seen, along with the ruins of the castles of the Marcher lords. Between the Cotswolds and the mountains of Wales are the beautiful valleys of the Severn and the Wye; the cathedral towns of Gloucester, Worcester and Shrewsbury all lie on the Severn, Hereford on the Wye. On the Wye too is Tintern Abbey, one of the most romantic of ruins. The fashion for taking the waters led to the development of spa towns, like Malvern and Cheltenham.

Northward the region presents a very different picture, for it was Birmingham and the Black Country, the Potteries and Coalbrookdale that saw the dawn of the industrial revolution and its massive growth. The vast conurbation of Birmingham dominates the centre of England. Further north in Staffordshire, are the pottery towns, some of the typical bottle kilns still surviving. In the Severn Gorge is Coalbrookdale, where coke smelting began, and Ironbridge, now a working museum of the industrial age. Many famous writers and artists came to Coalbrookdale at the end of the 18thC, attracted by the 'romantic' sight of furnaces belching out flames into a graceful river setting. At the extreme north of Staffordshire, the moors rise to join the Peak District National Park in Derbyshire. This is fine walking country, and magnificent walks can also be enjoyed all along the border with Wales, and particularly at Wenlock Edge.

This region possesses monuments of every period in British history from Bronze Age megaliths to witnesses of the more recent industrial past and, in between, some of the grandest castles, the finest cathedrals and prettiest market towns.   □

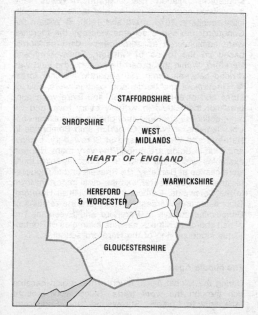

STAFFORDSHIRE

SHROPSHIRE

WEST MIDLANDS

HEART OF ENGLAND

WARWICKSHIRE

HEREFORD & WORCESTER

GLOUCESTERSHIRE

The Princes in the Tower

One of English history's unsolved mysteries is the murder of young King Edward V and his brother, Richard Duke of York.
Born in the troubled period of the Wars of the Roses, the two boys were sons of Edward IV of the House of York. When the king died in 1483, Edward, aged thirteen, and his younger brother Richard were living in Ludlow, Shropshire. Their uncle, Earl Rivers, set out to take the future king to London. Another uncle, however, their father's brother Richard, Duke of Gloucester, intercepted Earl Rivers and took charge of the boy himself. Edward, and later his brother Richard were housed in the Tower of London. Richard of Gloucester was crowned King of England and the two boys were never seen again.
In 1676, bones were discovered below some stairs in the Tower of London and these were assumed to be the remains of the young princes. They were buried in the Henry VII Chapel in Westminster Abbey, but in later years there was some doubt that these bones really did belong to the princes. Moreover, the long-held belief that Richard III arranged for their murder was challenged. Some people now believe that, in fact, Henry VII, who became king after defeating Richard in battle in 1485, was the guilty party.

● *Brief regional history*

Prehistory

The earliest evidence of human settlement is found in southern Hereford and Worcester, dating from Palaeolithic times. **King Arthur's Cave** was excavated in 1871, when the bones of numerous extinct animals were found - mammoth, woolly rhinoceros, hyena, bison and bear. ● From the Neolithic period come the Cotswold-Severn chambered tombs in the Gloucestershire area, like the barrows of Belas Knap and Hetty Pegler's Tump, roofed by massive stones. In Staffordshire are the Devil's Ring and Finger, near the Salop border, and the long, low burial mounds in the north-east, near the Derbyshire border. ● Bronze Age remains include chambered mounds near Ludlow and the stone circles on Stapely Hill, Salop. Iron Age hill forts are plentiful in the region: at Bury Ditches, Hopesay Burrow Camp, Caer Caradoc, the Wrekin and Old Oswestry in Salop; at Berry Ring near Stafford and Bury Bark, near Stone. There are seventeen forts along the Cotswold escarpment, such as that at Crickley Hill. The **Herefordshire Beacon** in the Malvern Hills is one of the finest contour forts in Britain. ● Before the arrival of the Romans, Belgic tribes had arrived in the area, establishing an important settlement at Bagendon in Gloucestershire on territory occupied by the Celtic Dobunni. Further north, along the Welsh border, lived the Cornovii.

The Romans

After the Claudian invasion **Caratacus**, son of the Catuvellauni leader Cunobelinus, retreated across Britain towards the Welsh marches, becoming in AD 51 the leader of the Ordovices. The famous Roman victory over the Ordovices is recorded by Tacitus; afterwards Caratacus was taken to Rome but was pardoned for his bravery and dignity. ● A legionary base was established at Wroxeter (*Virconium Cornoviorum*) in the 60s, but this was later abandoned, being replaced by the more permanent military bases at Chester and Caerleon. **Worxeter** subsequently grew to become a substantial town, enclosing an area of 180 acres. Gloucester (*Glevum*) was one of the first three *colonia* in Britain, along with Lincoln and Colchester, cities of the highest rank. **Cirencester (***Coronium***)** lay at the junction of the Fosse Way, Ermine Street and Akeman Street and was a regional capital

Mid-12th century stone porch of Kilpeck Church, Herefordshire

by the time of Diocletian (284-305), the second largest city in Britain. ● There were the usual *forum, basilica*, temples, bath houses and shops, but, exceptionally, many fine town houses of great luxury with colonnaded frontages, mosaics and imported marbles. In Gloucestershire, too, were many fine country villas.

Saxons and Danes

In early Saxon times Gloucestershire, Hereford and Worcester were occupied by the Hwicca tribe. They spread north into Warwickshire along the line of the Avon. ● From the 7th until the 9th century, most of the region formed part of the powerful kingdom of Mercia. Peada, son of Penda, was baptized a Christian in 650 and founded a monastery at Lichfield, moving his political capital to Tamworth. Under the famous **Offa** (757-96) the Mercian territory reached across Britain to East Anglia and north to the Humber. Offa's Dyke, the most extensive linear earthwork in Britain, runs for over a hundred miles from the mouth of the Wye to the Dee. ● The **monastic movement** was strong in Worcestershire, the monks also beginning fruit and vegetable production in the Vale of Evesham at this time. Hereford was an episcopal see by the late 7th century. The cathedral church of Worcester and the Gloucester and Evesham abbeys were among the largest landowners in the Cotswolds. ● At the end of the 9th century, the region was ravaged by the Danes, but regained for Mercia by Ethelfleda, Lady of Mercians in the 10th century. Edward the Elder (870-924) divided the Anglo-Saxon land of Mercia into shires and **Shrewsbury** became a mint town.

Norman castles and cathedrals

The impact of the Normans on the Welsh border landscape would be hard to exaggerate. When the Normans came the area had very few towns and only a scattered population. The geography of Wales made it a difficult country to control and there were significant revolts in 1075, 1088 and 1100. ● William the Conqueror devised a scheme whereby the marches were administered as **semi-independent earldoms**, based on the towns of Chester, Shrewsbury and Hereford. Within this broad framework, the land was divided between some 150 separate marcher lords. ● Throughout the borderland castles were built of stone and of earth and timber, and there were hundreds of them, built in virtually every town and village, acting as strategic strongholds for political control. Remains at Wilton, Goodrich amd Pembridge in Hereford and Worcester and at Shrewsbury, Ludlow and Clun in Salop are among the very many Norman examples which still exist. In Gloucestershire there were castles at Berkeley, St. Briavels and at Gloucester itself. ● **Cirencester** was the most important town in the Cotswolds. Cathedrals were built at Hereford, Gloucester and Worcester. There are the remains of Benedictine abbeys at Pershore and Evesham. The parish church at Kilpeck has fine examples of Romanesque stone carving of the Hereford school.

The Middle Ages

During the Middle Ages, much of the region became rich through the **wool trade**. Salop wool brought prosperity to Ludlow, Shrewsbury and Bridgnorth.

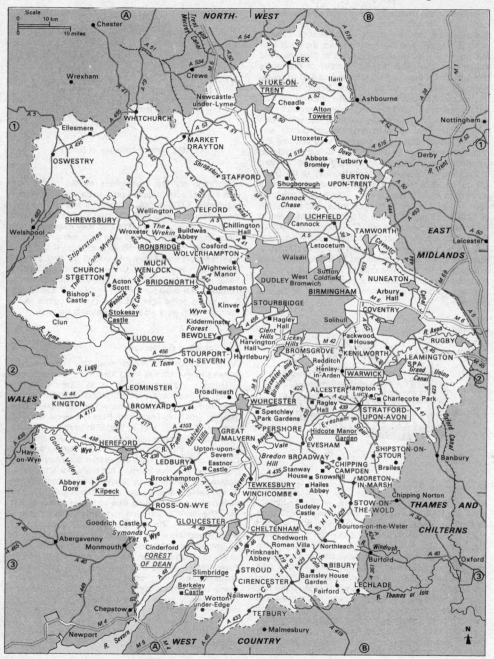

Shrewsbury became the market for a large area, including much of north Wales. But it was **Gloucestershire** that became the chief centre. In 1279 the parish of Blockley, for example, was assessed as having enough pasture to feed 800 sheep. Twenty years later the number had grown to 1,162 and by 1383 to 2,065.

● The graziers and wool traders became powerful merchants, endowing the great **wool churches** that were built or remodeled in the Perpendicular style from the 1370s - churches like Cirencester, Northleach, Chipping Campden, Fairford, Winchcombe, Lechlade and Chedworth. Fairford is famous for

its stained glass, made for the church by Flower Barnard, the King's master glasspainter. ● In Warwickshire the two major administrative centres were at Warwick and Kenilworth, where the great castles grew up. The Beauchamp earls of Warwick lived at Warwick, the most famous member of the family being **Warwick the Kingmaker**, who featured so prominently in the Wars of the Roses. Simon de Montford owned **Kenilworth**, and after his death at the battle of Evesham in 1265 the castle was besieged by the king's forces for six months before it fell, with much loss of life. This castle's most famous owner was John of Gaunt, Duke of Lancaster, who became the greatest landowner in Britain, his Beaufort children becoming the ancestors of Edward IV and Richard III and of every sovereign from Henry VII to the present queen. ● In the Middle Ages, **Tewkesbury** was a place of much importance. King John spent Christmas here in 1204, Henry III made a truce with the Welsh in 1236 and King Alexander of Scotland came here to do homage to Edward I. In 1471, during the Wars of the Roses, the great battle took place at the southern end of the town between Queen Margaret's Lancastrian forces and the Yorkists led by Edward IV. It was a total rout for the Lancastrians and in the dreadful slaughter which followed Margaret's son, the young Prince of Wales, was killed by Edward IV beside the abbey.

16th century cottages at Bibury

celebration for the bicentenary of the poet's birth with illuminations, feasts and a wide variety of entertainments. 2,000 people attended a ball and all-night masquerade. It was perhaps then that the tradesmen of Stratford began to realize that they needed to take steps to accommodate the ever increasing number of literary pilgrims. ● In 1858 Shakespeare's birthplace was restored and today it is visited by over 250,000 people annually. A new Gothic theatre was built in 1869, replaced in 1932 by the **Shakespeare Memorial Theatre**. The town has grown in size and has recently acquired some light industry, but the centre of the town is much as it was in Shakespeare's time.

Late 15th century open-hall house at Stottesdon in Salop

Shakespeare

One of the most famous dates in British history must be **1564** when William Shakespeare was born at **Stratford-upon-Avon**. His father was a glover and wool dealer who became an alderman of the town and high bailiff. William left school early because his father ran into financial difficulties and at the age of eighteen married Anne Hathaway, who lived a mile from his home and was pregnant. He seems to have left Stratford in about 1586 and within eight years had made a name for himself in London as a poet and playwright. He worked for an acting company called the King's Men which performed continuously in London from 1594-1613. By the time he was in his early thirties, William was able to help his father financially and in 1597 he bought **New Place**, one of the largest houses in Stratford. He probably retired to New Place in 1610, dying of a fever in 1616, and was buried in the chancel of Holy Trinity church. ● Shakespeare's influence on the growth of Stratford did not become significant until the later 18th century, although it was famous as his birthplace within a few years of his death. In 1643 Queen Henrietta Maria stayed at the house of Elizabeth Hall, Shakespeare's grand-daughter. In 1764 David Garrick organized a magnificent

The Industrial Revolution

While much of the land is rural, this region was to witness some of the most important developments in Britain's industrial revolution. In Stuart times, the Forest of Dean was producing coal, iron and timber. Coal and iron have been mined on the upper Trent around Stoke-on-Trent and Burslem since the 13th century. ● But it was in the 18th century that dramatic developments began to occur. In 1707 the pioneer British industrialist, Abraham Darby, went to Coalbrookdale where he acquired a blast furnace and developed his new method for the coke smelting of iron ore. Abraham Darby II was using a steam engine by the early 1740s. By the 1750s the Shropshire coalfield became the **leading iron-producing area of Britain**. The world's first cast-iron bridge was erected at Ironbridge in 1779, the first iron-built boat in 1787. ● **Coalport** was the creation of William Reynolds, an immensely influential Shropshire ironmaster. It lay at the junction between the Shropshire canal and the River Severn and it was here that Reynolds brought china manufacturing, chain making and boat building. Many of the monuments of the industrial revolution have recently been brought together at the working museum of Ironbridge.

The Potteries

The six towns of the North Staffordshire potteries are Burslem, Hanley, Longton, Turnstall, Fenton and Stoke. Pottery had been of regional importance in the 1680s. Burslem was the largest settlement in medieval times and was the first to industrialize, for by about 1710 it contained 43 pot-banks, or potteries, out of 52 in the whole district. Technical improvements were already well under way in the first half of the 18th century and it only required the coming of

the canals to open up the market nationally. By 1750 there were important potteries at Hanley, Shelton, Stoke and Turnstall. ● Men like **Josiah Wedgwood** and the master potters, Wood, Adams and Spode, raised the quality and the range of products. Wedgwood built a garden village at Etruria for himself and his workers, which must have possessed great charm but is now sadly demolished. The townscapes were dominated by the bottle kilns, some of which still survive, particularly at Longton where they have been restored under a preservation trust.

The Black Country

Most people who live in the Black Country still feel that they belong to separate communities rather than a single conurbation, even if the outsider may not be able to recognize where one town begins and another ends. The area earned its dreadful name in the 19th century when collieries and blast furnaces filled the air with smoke and grime - a scene that was 'black by day and red by night'. Walsall, Wednesbury, Wolverhampton and Dudley all retain a strong identity, but the main colliery towns before 1850 were smaller settlements, like Bilston, Tipton, Coseley, Sedgley, West Bromwich and Rowley Regis, which grew up in a haphazard fashion. ● Alongside coal and iron, many **specialist industries** flourished. Wolverhampton and Willenhall made locks and keys, Wednesbury tubes for guns and for piping. Cradley made nails. The glass industry developed in the Stour Valley, particularly after the Stourbridge Canal was opened in 1776; indeed canals were the making of the Black Country as a whole.

Birmingham

Birmingham is **Britain's second city** and one of the principal manufacturing and commercial centres in the country. But whereas the towns of the Black Country grew outwards to meet each other and become a great conurbation, Birmingham was a single town which grew into a great city. ● In the 16th century

this was still a small place but already with a reputation for ironfounding. During the Civil Wars, Birmingham workshops produced 1,500 swords for the Parliamentarians. ● But it was in the 18th century that the city found itself at the centre of that phenomenon which was the **industrial revolution**, pioneering new techniques of production and engineering. The astonishing rise of Birmingham owes much to a group of brilliant and imaginative local citizens, many of whom were members of a philosophical and scientific association known as the Lunar Society. Among them were the engineer, **James Watt**, the pioneer of steam engine production, Matthew Boulton, the chemist, Joseph Priestley and the printer, John Baskerville. Boulton's Soho Manufactury, established in 1761, developed and marketed Watt's steam engines for industrial use and these became famous throughout Europe. The metal and gun trades also began in the 18th century and, at the other end of the scale, Birmingham produced brass trinkets and jewelry for a world market, which became known as the 'toy trade'. ● Despite bad housing, Birmingham became well-known in the late 19th century for its enlightened attitude to urban problems. Known in Victorian times as the **'workshop of the world'** it remains a city of very many trades. Still mainly concerned with engineering, the largest single industry is that of motor vehicle production located at the newly automated plant at Longbridge.

Shakespeare

The town of Stratford-upon-Avon has long been devoted to the memory of William Shakespeare. It is perhaps appropriate that the best-known of English writers was born in the very heart of England.

William Shakespeare's life was not well recorded by his contemporaries, but it is generally agreed that he was born in Stratford in 1564, and educated at the town's free grammar school. He married Anne Hathaway in 1582, may have spent more time teaching, then went to London where he became involved in the theatre, acting in the King's company of players at theatres including the Globe and the Blackfriars. His earliest known play (Henry IV) was performed in 1590-1, and his subsequent output was prodigious. Not only did he write 37 five-act plays — both tragedies and comedies — he also published collections of sonnets, poems, plus two long works in verse, Venus and Adonis and The Rape of Lucrece, which were dedicated to his patron, the Earl of Southampton. His dramatic work was often set beyond the shores of England such as Hamlet, Julius Caesar, Two Gentlemen of Verona, Romeo and Juliet and the last play, The Tempest (where the action takes place on an imaginary island).

Shakespeare's universal appeal may be accounted for by the extraordinary range of expression in his plays — his writing encompasses vulgar language as well as fine rhetoric, tragedies contain comic elements, and gravediggers and porters rub shoulders with gentlewomen and dukes. Interpretations of his dramas have varied greatly in the centuries succeeding his death in 1616 but his popularity has never waned. He is believed to have spent most of the last five years of his life in Stratford and is buried in Stratford church.

19th century bottle kilns at Longton, Staffordshire

Oak-apple Day

In 1651, after defeat by Cromwell's forces at the Battle of Worcester, the young Charles (later to become King Charles II) fled with some of his officers meaning to escape abroad.
Before he could leave the country, however, he was forced to go into hiding. His first place of sanctuary was a large oak tree near the battlefield, where the prince hid for a day while the Roundheads searched for fugitives close by. When Charles eventually returned to England from exile and was crowned King of England at the Restoration of 1660, the oak became a symbol to the British people. Loyalists would wear a sprig of oak in their hats on 29 May - which was both the date of the Restoration and of King Charles's birthday, and became known as Oak-apple Day.
The famous Boscobel Oak, which hid the King, is no longer in existence but saplings were planted from its acorns in the Botanic Gardens in Chelsea and in Hyde Park, London; a fragment of the original tree, made into a small tray, can be seen in the Bodleian Library, Oxford.

 Practical information

Information: covers counties of Gloucester, Hereford and Worcester, Shropshire, Staffordshire, Warwickshire and West Midlands. *Heart of England Tourist Board*, 2/4 Trinity Street, Worcester WR1 2PW, ☎ (0905) 613132.

Weather forecast: ☎ (0522) 8091/0452 8091.

Self-catering cottages: *Cottage Holidays*, Sling Cottage, Upper Bentley, Redditch, Worcestershire, ☎ (0527) 401740. *Country Farm Holidays*, Shaw Mews, Worcester, WR1 3QQ, ☎ (0905) 613744. *Heart of England Cottages*, Iveson House, Ampney St. Peter, Cirencester, ☎ (0285) 87217.

Youth hostelling: *YHA*, 38 Bank Road, Matlock, Derbyshire DE4 3NF, ☎ (0629) 4666.

Festivals: Mar.-Jan.: *Shakespeare Theatre Season*, a season of plays performed by the world-renowned theatre company. **27 Jul.-15 Aug.**: *Coventry Mystery Plays* in the cathedral ruins, Coventry, the story of the life of Christ told in amusing, moving, reverent and robust theatre. **4-19 Jul.**: *Cheltenham International Festival*, music classics, jazz, folk singing, modern British composers. **3-18 Oct.**: *Cheltenham Festival of Literature*.

Customs and folklore: May: a medieval *Cheese Rolling Ceremony* (on the first Sunday) in Randwick, Gloucestershire: three cheeses are blessed and rolled around the church three times - one is then cut up and distributed to all those present. *Endon Well Dressing* on Spring Bank Hols. (see East Midlands for details of the tradition). **Sep.**: *Abbots Bromley Horn Dance*, Staffordshire, held the first Monday after first Sunday after 4 Sep.

Other events: 17-20 Apr.: *Devizes to Westminster International Canoe Race* along the River Thames;

6-9 Jul.: *Royal International Agricultural Show*, Stoneleigh, Kenilworth, Warwickshire.

Scenic railway: The Severn Valley railway trip is the closest to an original steam train journey in Britain; it runs 13 miles from Bridgnorth, astride the river Severn, south to Bewdley, and Kidderminster, at least three times daily in each direction; special Sunday lunch dining trains. Contact: *Severn Valley Railway Co. Ltd.*, Railway Station, Bewdley, Worcestershire DY12 1BG, ☎ (0299) 403816.

Walking: *The Curious Wayfarer*, Fern Villa, 6a Christchurch Villas, Malvern Road, Cheltenham, Gloucestershire GL50 2NT, ☎ (0242) 525409; *Greenscape UK*, Amberley, Wickham Close, Wickhamford, Worcestershire WR11 6SE, ☎ (0386) 832507.

River and canal cruises: *Noseasons Holidays Ltd.*, Sunway House, Lowestoft, Suffolk NR23 3LT, ☎ (0502) 62211; *Avondale Cruisers*, 69 Burford Road, Evesham, Worcestershire, ☎ (0386) 2759.

Archery: *PGL Young Adventure Ltd.*, Station Street, Ross-on-Wye, Herefordshire HR9 7AH, ☎ (0989) 65556.

Canoeing: weekly courses run at the *Severn Bank Centre*, Minsterworth GL2 8JH, ☎ (045275) 357; enquire here or at Minsterworth TIC. Three outdoor centres in Hereford and Worcester including *PGL Young Adventure Ltd.*, 108 Station Street, Ross-on-Wye, ☎ (0989) 4211 - sailing and canoeing courses for children.

Cider

The word 'cider' comes from the Latin sicera *meaning 'strong drink' ; and cider (from apples), along with mead (made from fermented honey) and perry (from pears), is one of Britain's oldest alcoholic drinks. Both cider and perry were introduced to this country from northern France by the Norman conquerors during the 11thC. Normandy, like Britain and other northern European regions, had a climate that was too cold for vine growing. The inhabitants therefore concentrated on making intoxicating brews from more hardy crops. They discovered that the juice of apples, when they had been squashed in wooden presses, and then left to ferment for a year or two, would make a very pleasing drink. The first apples used were similar to what we call crab apples, and the south and southeastern parts of England were initially the cider-making districts. When the small red acidic apples now used were first cultivated during the 17thC, however, production moved to the heart of England and the West Country.*
The county of Hereford has long been famous for its cider. As long ago as 1677, one Andrew Yarrenton wrote that the county 'hath the best of wool, the best of cider, the best of fruit, the best of wheat, and the best rivers'. Devon, however, is also justly proud of its cider (there often called 'scrumpy'). In general Devon cider is dry whereas that from Herefordshire is sweeter. This traditional drink can vary considerably : it may be sweet, semi-sweet or very dry (rough); cloudy, clear or fizzy; and its alcoholic content can range from virtually non-existent to highly potent.

Climbing and mountaineering: *Tops Holidays*, The Activity Centre, Hope under Dinmore, Leominster, Herefordshire HR6 OPW, ☎ (0568) 611412.

Field sports: *Avon and Airlie Sporting Ltd.*, Avon, Chippenham, Wiltshire, ☎ (024974) 225.

Flying: *Mortimers Cross Inn*, Mortimers Cross, Leominster, Herefordshire HR6 9PD, ☎ (056881) 238.

Gliding: *Amberley Inn*, Amberley, Stroud GL5 5AF, ☎ (045387) 2565.

Golfing : Cirencester, Gloucestershire (18-hole); Belmont, Herefordshire (18-hole); Ross-on-Wye, Herefordshire (18-hole); Hawkstone Park Hotel, Weston-under-Redcastle, Shropshire (18-hole); Belfry Hotel, Wishaw (18-hole).

Edward Elgar

One of Britain's most famous composers was largely self-taught - though he was the son of an organist and music teacher, and did have violin lessons. He was born at Broadheath, near Worcester and, after leaving school, worked at a lawyer's office in order to support himself while he studied and composed music. In 1899, his Enigma Variations were first performed. Still the most frequently played of Elgar's music, this work consists of fourteen variations on a theme - the different style of each reflecting the different personalities of fourteen friends. Following the publication and performance of Enigma and of the choral work The Dream of Gerontius the next year, Elgar became recognized as the leading English composer. Indeed, his rise to prominence marked a revival in British music which had seen no composers of international standing since the time of Purcell in the 17thC. In his wake came Vaughan Williams, Holst and Britten.
After the Elgar Festival, which took place in London in 1904, the composer was knighted, made Master of the King's Music in 1924 and awarded a number of honorary degrees.

Shropshire soul cakes

All Souls Day on 2 November was the day when the Roman Catholic Church prayed for the souls of dead people in purgatory, and the custom arose of sending 'soul cakes' to friends and family of a dead person. However, in time 'souling' consisted of simply going from house to house begging for sweets or money. Until the middle of the last century, special soul cakes were baked for All Souls Day. These are still a Shropshire specialty, and are a kind of spiced bun made from butter, flour, sugar, milk, eggs and yeast. In some parts of Shropshire and Cheshire children still go around the houses collecting money. As they do so they sing souling songs like this one from Market Drayton :

Soul, soul, for a soul cake! I pray, good missis, for a soul cake! An apple or pear, a plum or a cherry, any good thing to make us merry.

And in certain Cheshire villages a Soul Caking play is performed.

Hunting: ideal countryside in the Cotswolds. *Cotswold Hunt*, Kenelm, Oakridge Lynch, Stroud, Gloucestershire, ☎ (028576) 206; *Warwickshire Hunt*, Old Pumphouse Cottage, Avon Dassett, Leamington Spa, Warwickshire, ☎ (029589) 317.

Parachuting: *Gainsborough House Hotel*, Bewdley Hill, Kidderminster, Worcestershire DYLL 6BS, ☎ (0562) 754041; *Mortimers Cross Inn* (see above).

Sailing and cruising: *PGL Young Adventure Ltd.* (one week sailing holidays for families), 2-5 Market Place, Ross-on-Wye, Herefordshire HR9 5LD, ☎ (0989) 65556.

Skiing: *Roger Drummond Outdoor Services*, South View, 8 Severn Bank, Shrewsbury SYL 2JD, ☎ (0743) 65022.

Windsurfing: *Cove House*, Ashton Keynes SN6 6NS, ☎ (0285) 861221.

 Towns and places ═══════

ALCESTER*

Worcester, 18; Stratford-upon-Avon, 8; London,104 m pop. 5,207 ☎ 0789 Warwickshire B2

This town would once have lain in the Forest of Arden (→). A thoroughfare - on Roman Ryknild Street - then a market town, it possesses a variety of fine buildings.

▶ **Town Hall**, 1641, ornately timbered and supported on sturdy stone columns. ▶ In **Butter Street**, **Church Street** and **Henley Street** good examples of Tudor, Georgian and Regency houses.

Nearby

▶ Little remains of Shakespeare's Forest of Arden today.
▶ **Oversley Wood** (*1 ¹/₂ m SE*) is a protected scrap of ancient woodland; nature trail of particular interest to birdwatchers. ▶ **Bidford on Avon** (*5m S*) has buildings stripped with gold and bluish stone, notably the **Old Falcon**. ▶ On road S to Cleeve Prior is a great 15thC 8-arched stone bridge over the River Avon. ▶ **Ragley Hall★** (*2m SW*) outstanding Palladian residence. Built for Lord Conway in 1680, designed by Robert Hooke. Treasures include paintings by Reynolds and Rubens, opulent Baroque plasterwork, English and French furniture, porcelain and silver (*Apr., May & Sep.: daily ex. Mon. & Fri., 1.30-5.30; Bank Hols: 12-5.30*). Park laid out by Capability Brown; adventure trails and picnic spots (*all year: daily ex. Mon. & Fri., 11-6; Jul., Aug. daily*). ▶ **Coughton Court** (*2m N*) is an Elizabethan manor, from 1409-1946 property of Throckmorton family, renowned for their fierce Catholic allegiance. House contains many relics of its eventful history and some remarkable tapestries and paintings (*Apr.-Oct.: Sat. & Sun., 2-5; May-Sep.: Wed.-Sun., also Bank Hols., 2-6*). ☐

> Don't forget to consult the Practical Holiday Guide: it can help in solving many problems.

Practical information

ALCESTER

Hotel:
★★ *Cherrytrees*, Stratford Road, B49 6LN, ☎ (0789) 762505, AC BA, 22 rm. P ≼ ▥ ⌁ ⧫ £35. Rest. ◆ ♪ ⧫ Cl. dinner 25-26 Dec. £8.

Restaurant:
◆ *Rossini*, 50 Birmingham Road, ☎ Stratford-upon-Avon (0789) 762764, AC AM BA DI P Cl. 3 wks. mid-summer, Sun. £12.

Recommended
Cycle rental: at Conway, *Norman Pillinger Cycles*, 9 Hertford Road.
Farmhouse: at Sambourne, *Sambourne Hall Farm*, Wike Lane, Redditch, ☎ (052 785) 2151, £22; double B. & B.

Nearby
BIDFORD-ON-AVON, 3m S off A439

Hotel:
★★ *White Lion*, High Street, B50 4BQ, ☎ Bidford-on-Avon (0789) 773309, AC AM, 15 rm. P ≼ £40. Rest. ◆ ♪ £12.

BEWDLEY*

Birmingham, 19; Worcester, 17; London, 144 m
pop. 8,696 ☎ 0299   Hereford & Worcester A2

A small yet gracious town, with an air of tranquillity created by the slow flowing River Severn. Evidence of Bewdley's past role as a river port can be found along its quays and narrow side streets.

▶ **Severn Valley Steam Railway** has a station here with carriage and wagon workshops. Route follows river N to **Bridgnorth** (→) and S to **Kidderminster** (→). ▶ **The Old Shambles** is now site of splendid museum: exhibitions of traditional local trades and crafts include charcoal burning and rope-making (*Mar.-Nov.: Mon.-Sat., 10-5.30, Sun., 2-5.30*). ▶ **West Midlands Safari Park** has large collection of exotic species (*Mar.-Nov: daily*). □

Practical information

ℹ️ library, Load Street, ☎ 403303.

Hotel:
★ *Black Boy*, Kidderminster Road, DY12 1AG, ☎ (0299) 402119, AC AM BA, 25 rm. P £39. Rest. ◆ Cl. 25-26 Dec. £9.

Restaurant:
◆ *Bailiffs House*, 68 High Street, ☎ (0299) 402691, AC AM BA DI P ♪ ✑ Cl. Sat. lunch, Sun eve., Mon. Book. £16.50.

Recommended
Riding school: at Cleobury Mortimer, *The Mounts*, Crumps Brook, Hereford, ☎ (074 636) 677, at Woverley, *Lea Castle Riding School*, ☎ (0562) 850611.

BIBURY*

Cirencester, 7; Oxford, 30; London, 86 m
pop. 603 ☎ 028 574   Gloucestershire B3

Low-roofed cottages and the shallow, sparkling River Coln make this village a small jewel, with many visitors in summer.

▶ The cottages of Arlington Row formed a sheep house in 14thC. In 17thC it was converted into homes for workers at nearby Arlington Mill, now a museum: corn-grinding machinery in working order, Victoriana, contemporary craft exhibitions and trout pool (*Mar.-Oct.: daily, 10.30-7,*

dusk if earlier; Nov.-Feb.: wkends only*). ▶ **Bibury Trout Farm** (*daily in summer*). □

Practical information

Hotels:
● ★★ *Swan*, GL7 5NW, ☎ (028 574) 204, AC BA, 24 rm. P ≼ ▥ Former coaching inn built of Cotswold stone with riverside gardens in 1720. £52.50. Rest. ◆ ≼ ⧫ Fresh Bibury trout. £14.50.
★★ *Bibury Court*, GL7 5NT, ☎ (028 574) 337, AC AM BA DI, 16 rm. P ▥ ⌁ By the side of the river, a fine Jacobean mansion built in 1633, standing in its own grounds. £45. Rest. ◆ Cl. lunch Christmas. £15.

Inn or Pub:
Catherine Wheel (Courage), ☎ (028 574) 250, 2 rm P ▥ . Homemade soup, local trout, steak, prawns in garlic butter. £4.

BIRMINGHAM**

Stratford-upon-Avon, 29; Worcester, 28; London, 105 m
pop. 1,013,995 ☎ 021   West Midlands B2

Birmingham is Britain's second largest city and lies at the heart of the Midlands. It has long held a reputation for industrial and manufacturing excellence and was the main supplier of arms and armour to the Parliamentarian cause during the Civil War. Fine guns are still made in the city. Its great era of civic and industrial pride was the 19thC and some grand buildings of this time remain. Birmingham has an astonishing multi-level network of roads, ring roads (beltways), flyovers and underpasses which carry much of the freight that 100 years ago came into the city by canal. This is a vital modern city with excellent cultural facilities: fine museums, galleries, theatre (Birmingham Repertory) and music (Birmingham Symphony Orchestra), as well as some delightful suburbs and green open spaces.

▶ **Cathedral of St. Philip**★★ (off Colmore Row), a rarity: handsome early 18thC English Baroque, interior with restrained white and gold plasterwork, beautiful **stained glass**★★ by Edward Burne-Jones in E & W windows. ▶ **St. Martin's Church** (Bull Ring), Birmingham's mother church: oldest part is 13thC; S transept window again Burne-Jones; 14thC monuments to de Birmingham family. ▶ **St. Chad's Cathedral**, fine early work (1839-41) of A.W.N. Pugin; 15thC German statues in reredos; 16thC carved oak pulpit; 15thC stalls from Cologne. ▶ **Town hall**★: splendid Classical building of Corinthian order inspired by Roman Temple of Castor and Pollux; often venue for concerts by Birmingham Symphony Orchestra. ▶ **Museum and art gallery**★★ (Victoria Square) houses one of best art collections outside London particularly **pre-Raphaelites**; Sir Edward Burne-Jones (native of Birmingham) well represented; also Canaletto, Bellini, Botticelli, Rembrandt, Turner, Pissarro, Constable; modern collection includes Augustus John, Stanley Spencer, Lowry; sculpture by Renoir, Rodin, Epstein, Henry Moore. Also domestic, near Eastern and S American archaeology; natural history (*wkdays: 10-6, Sun.: 2-5.30*). ▶ **Museum of Science and Industry**★ (Newhall Street); homage is paid to Birmingham's engineering skills; turbines, beam engines, steam pumps; motor cars and motorcycles ancient and modern; guns and small arms from city's long gun-making tradition (*Mon.-Fri.: 10-5, Sat. 10-5.30, Sun. 2-5.30*). ▶ **Ikon Gallery** devoted to contemporary art, particularly local. ▶ **Gas Street Basin:** begin an exploration of the Birmingham Canal Navigations from here where colourful narrow boats are often moored. Long rises of locks and attractive bridges can be seen along the several towpath routes. All paths and bridges are being restored as part of Birmingham's industrial archaeology project. ▶ **Edgbaston** (1 ½ m SW city centre): sedate suburb with attractive Regency and Victorian houses; **Botanic Gardens** (Westbourne

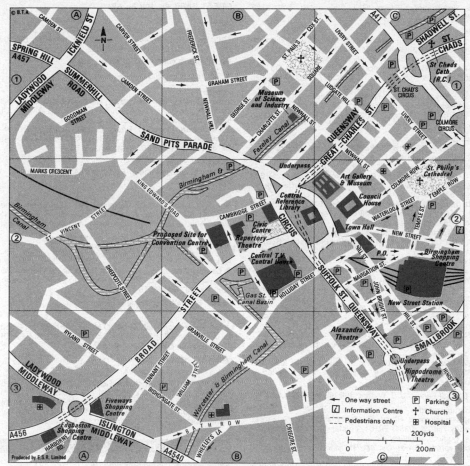

BIRMINGHAM

Road) has delightful glasshouses with orchids, hibiscus, water lilies and bromeliads; rose and alpine gardens (*daily: 9-8 or dusk, opens 10 Sun.*). ▶ **Barber Institute of Fine Arts**★★ (University of Birmingham campus, *Mon.-Fri.: 10-5 by request at door*), city's second splendid art collection: Italian Renaissance bronzes, drawings and miniatures; sculpture including works by Rodin, Barye, Degas; ivory, enamels, gold and silver; large collection European masters.

Nearby

▶ **Aston Hall** (*2 1/2 m N*): a Jacobean mansion with splendid oak-paneled long gallery lined with tapestries, lavish strapwork ceiling (*Feb.-Nov.: Mon.-Sat., 10-5, Sun. 2-5*).
▶ **Asbury Cottage** (Great Barr, *3 m NE centre West Bromwich*): Francis Asbury, 1st Bishop of American Methodist Church lived here 1746-71; furnished in authentic 18thC manner (*daily Mon.-Fri.: 2-4; Bank Hols.*). ▶ **Oak House** (Oak Road, *1/2 m from centre West Bromwich*): Tudor timber-framed house with unusual lantern tower; 16th - 18thC furniture (*Apr.-Sep.: Mon.-Sat., 10-8, Sun., 2.30-8; Oct.-Mar.: Mon.-Sat., 10-4; closed Thu. 10-1 all year*).
▶ **Bournville** (*4 m SW city centre*): garden city suburb of

Birmingham built by Quaker Cadbury family, main local employers, to improve living conditions for their chocolate-factory employees; model for many later garden city developments. ▶ SE of Bournville, Kings Norton has **Serbian Orthodox Church of St. Lazer,** built 1965-8 to design of Serbian architect; lavish **interior** with frescos.
▶ At **Redditch** (*14m S city centre*) is the **National Needle Museum**★ housed in only remaining water-powered needle mill in the world (**Forge Mill**). Adjacent, excavated remains of **Bordesley Abbey,** 12thC Cistercian monastery with finds on display (*Apr.-Oct.: Mon.-Fri., 11-4.30, Sat., 1-5, Sun. & Bank Hols., 11.30-5*). ☐

Practical information ―――――――――

BIRMINGHAM
🛈 2 City Arcade (C2), ☎ 643 2514; Birmingham Airport, ☎ 767 5511.
✈ Birmingham (6 1/2m E by A45), ☎ 767 7153.
🚇 New, Moor and International Street, ☎ 643 2711.
🚌 ☎ 622 4373.
Car rental: Europcar, New Street Rail Station, ☎ 643 1430 (rail/drive); Airport Arrivals Hall, ☎ 742 6507; Monaco House, Bristol Street, ☎ 622 5311-6/780 2414 (rail/drive);

Avis, International Street Rail Station, ☎ 742 6183 (rail/drive).

Hotels:
★★★★ *Albany* (T.F.), Smallbrook, Queensway, Birmingham, B5 4EW(C3), ☎ (021) 643 8171, Tx 337031, AC AM BA DI, 254 rm. ♿ ⊠ £53. Rest. ♦ ♪ ♿ Cl. Sun. £9.
★★★ *Grand* (Q.M.H.), Colmore Row, Birmingham, B3 2DA (Cl off map), ☎ (021) 236 7951, Tx 338174, AC AM BA DI, 184 rm. ♿ £55. Rest. ♦ ♪ ♿ Cl. Christmas. £9.
★★★ *Royal Angus Thistle* (Thistle), St. Chads, Queensway, B4 6HY(Cl), ☎ (021) 236 4211, Tx 336889, AC AM BA DI, 139 rm. P ♿ £63. Rest. ♦ ♪ ♿ Cl. lunch Sat. £10.95.

Restaurants:
● ♦ *Chung Ying*, 16-18 Wrottesley Street (C3), ☎ (021) 622 5669, AC AM BA DI ♪ ✖ Cl. Christmas. Dim-sum, char siu. Book. £8.
● ♦ *Ho Tung*, 308 Bull Ring Centre (C2), ☎ (021) 643 0033, AC AM BA DI P ♪ ✖ Peking stuffed duck. Book. £7.
♦ *Dynasty*, 93-103 Hurst St (C3), ☎ (021) 622 5306, AC AM BA DI P ♪ ♿ ✖ Cl. 25-26 Dec. Fresh sea bass steamed in black bean sauce. £7.
♦ *La Capanna*, Hurst Street (C3), ☎ (021) 622 2287, AC AM BA DI. Cl. Sun., Jul.-10 Aug. Popular Italian Restaurant . £10.
♦ *Lorenzo's*, Park Street (C2), ☎ (021) 643 0541, AC AM BA DI. Cl. Sun., Sat. and Mon. lunch, Bank Hols. £17.
♦ *Maharaja*, 23-25 Hurst Street (C2), ☎ (021) 622 2641, AC AM BA DI ♪ ♿ Cl. 2 wks. Jul., Sun. Chicken kebab. £8.
♦ *New Happy Gathering*, 43-45 Station Street (C2), ☎ (021) 643 1859, AC AM BA DI. Cl. 3 days Christmas. Cantonese menu. £9.
♦ *Rajdoot*, 12-22 Albert Street (C2), ☎ (021) 643 8805, AC AM BA DI P ♪ ♿ ✖ Cl. 24-25 Dec., Bank Hols., Sun. lunch. Book. £12.
♦ *Wild Oats*, 5 Raddlebarn Road, Selly Oak, ☎ (021) 471 2459 ♪ ♿ ✖ Cl. Christmas, 1 Jan., Sun.-Mon. Vegetarian. Book. £5.

⚖ *Chapel Lane C.C.S*, Wythall, (96 pl), ☎ (0564) 826483.

Recommended
Crafts workshop: *Royal Brierley Crystal*, North Street, Brierley Hill, ☎ (0384) 70161, crystal glasses, decanters, jugs, goblets, pitchers, etc.
Cycle rental: *Tower Cycles*, 91 Aston Street, ☎ (021) 359 2938.
Factory showroom: at Halesowen, 8m W of Birmingham off A956, *Regency Crystal Limited*, Unit 2, Maypole Fields, Cradley, ☎ 68348, Regency crystal manufacturers.
Golf course: Pype Hayes, Eachelhurst Road, Walmley, ☎ 361104; Warley, Lightwoods Hill, ☎ 429 2440.

Nearby
BIRMINGHAM AIRPORT, 8m E

Hotel:
★★★ *Excelsior* (Trusthouse Forte), Coventry Road, Elmdon, B26 3QW, ☎ (021) 743 8141, Tx 338005, AC AM BA DI, 141 rm. P £62. Rest. ♦ ♪ £11.

EDGBASTON, 1 1/2 m S

Hotels:
● ★★★ *Plough Harrow* (Crest), Hagley Road, B16 8LS, ☎ (021) 454 4111, Tx 338074, AC AM BA DI, 44 rm. P ♪ £75. Rest. ● ♦ ♪ ♿ Cl. 26 Dec., dinner 1 Jan. £33.
★★ *Hagley Court*, 229 Hagley Road, B16 9RP, ☎ (021) 454 6514, AC BA, 25 rm. P ✖ £30. Rest. ♦ ♪ ♿ Cl. Christmas. £8.

Restaurants:
♦ *Pinocchio's*, 8 Chad Square, ☎ (021) 454 8672, AC AM BA DI P Cl. Sun. Italian. £18.
♦ *Sloan's*, 27-29 Chad Square, Hawthorne Road, ☎ (021) 455 7719, AC AM BA DI P ♪ ✖ Cl. Bank Hols., Sun. Lobster with herb sauce. Book. £18.

Recommended
Golf course: Church Road, ☎ 454 1736.

GREAT BARR, 6m NW on A34

Hotel:
★★ *Post House* (Trusthouse Forte), Chapel Lane, B43 7BG, ☎ (021) 357 7444, Tx 338497, AC AM BA DI, 204 rm. P ♿ ♿ ⊠ £50. Rest. ♦ ♿ £12.50.

NATIONAL EXHIBITION CENTRE, 9m E

ⓘ ☎ 780 4141.

Hotels:
★★★★ *Birmingham Metropole*, Blackfirs Lane, Bickenhill, B40 1PP, ☎ (021) 780 4242, Tx 336129, AC AM BA DI, 500 rm. P ≼ ♿ ♪ £75. Rest. ♦ ♪ ♿ £10.
★★★ *Arden*, Coventry Road, Bickenhill, B92 0EH, ☎ Hampton-in-Arden (067 55) 3221, Tx 337766, AC AM BA DI, 46 rm. P ♿ £39.50. Rest. ♦ ♪ ♿ £8.

SOLIHULL, 10m S on A45
ⓘ Central Library, Homer Road ☎ 704 6965.
🚃 ☎ 643 2711.

Restaurant:
● ♦ *Liaison French Cuisine*, 761 Old Lode Lane, ☎ (021) 743 3993, AC AM BA DI P ♿ ♪ ♿ ✖ Cl. Christmas., Aug. Guinea fowl with Armagnac sauce and fresh chervil. Book. £13.

SUTTON COLDFIELD, 7m N on A4151

Restaurant:
♦ *Le Bon Viveur*, 65 Birmingham Road, ☎ (021) 355 5836, AC AM BA DI P ♪ ♿ ✖ Cl. 3 wks. Aug., Sun.-Mon. Lobster soufflé. Book. £16.

WEST BROMWICH, 7m NW on A41

Hotel:
★★★ *West Bromwich Moat* (Q.M.H.), Birmingham Road, B70 6RS, ☎ (021) 553 6111, Tx 336232, AC AM BA DI, 181 rm. P ♿ ♿ £61. Rest. ♦ ♪ ♿ £10.

WISHAW, 10m NE off A446

Hotel:
★★★ *Belfry* (De Vere), Sutton Coldfield, B76 9PR, ☎ Curdworth (0675) 70301, Tx 338848, AC AM BA DI, 170 rm. P ≼ ♿ ♿ ⊠ ▱ ♪ Country manor overlooking two championship golf courses. £85. Rest. ♦ ♪ ♿ Cl. lunch Sat. Roast duck with blackcurrant and fig sauce. £17.50.

BRIDGNORTH★★

Shrewsbury, 21; Kidderminster, 14; London, 147 m
pop. 10,332 ☎ 074 62   *Shropshire A2*

Two towns in one: High Town is built on a sandstone ridge overlooking the Severn, linked to Low Town by a steep road, flights of winding steps and, most novel, a funicular railway.

Immediately noticeable, timbered **town hall** in **High Street**, traffic passing through its stone supports. Further on, **North Gate**, much restored, relic of town walls. ▶ **East Castle Street** rivals **High Street** with its elegant buildings. Graceful, French-influenced **Church of St. Mary Magdalene**, designed by engineer Thomas Telford (→), begun 1792. ▶ Norman **Keep** is all that remains of **castle**; dates from pre-Conquest times, but demolished by Parliamentarians during Civil War. **Castle grounds** now a park with views★ across Severn. ▶ **St. Leonard's Church** stands in a little close of pretty houses, a mixture of styles and periods. ▶ **Cartway** was once main road linking two parts of town. Halfway up is **Bishop Percy's House**, 1580, sumptuously timbered. From this road, **caves** in the sandstone can be seen, used as hermitages until Victorian times. ▶ In **Low Town**, remnants of wharf with attractive riverside houses.

Nearby

▶ **Severn Valley Railway** has its N terminus at Bridgnorth Station. Steam trains follow River Severn to **Kidderminster via Bewdley** (→). Main locomotive depot also here

(services: regular intervals daily Mar.-early Sep.; wkends Mar.-Oct., also Dec.). ▶ **The Midland Motor Museum** *(2m S)* specializes in sports, racing cars and motor cycles, with nearly 90 vehicles on display *(daily: Jun.-Aug., 10-6, Nov.-Feb., 10-dusk; Mar., May, Sep. & Oct., Mon.-Fri., 10-5, Sun. & Bank Hols., 10-6).* ▶ **Quatford** *(2 ¹/₂ m SE)* has splendid sham castle on sandstone cliff, built 1830. ▶ Near Quatt *(4m SE)* is Dudmaston, mainly 10thC house, containing important modern paintings and sculpture by Matisse, Henry Moore and Barbara Hepworth. Grounds, with lakeside garden *(Apr.-end Sep.: Wed. & Sun., 2.30-6).* ▶ **Acton Round Hall** *(6 m W):* fine 18thC manor-house *(early May-late Sep.: 2.30-5.30).* □

Practical information

BRIDGNORTH
ⓘ library, Listley Street, ☎ 3358.

Hotels:
★ *Croft*, St. Mary's Street, WV16 4DW, ☎ (074 62) 2416, AC BA, 7 rm. ♨ £30.
★ *Severn Arms*, Underhill Street, WV16 4BB, ☎ (074 62) 4616, 10 rm. ∉ ✓ £23. Rest. ♦ ♪ £6.

Restaurant:
♦ *The Old Colonial Restaurant*, 3 Bridge Street, Low Town, ☎ (07462) 66510, AC AM BA DI P ⌂ ♪ ⌇ King prawn bhuna. Book. £5.50.

Inn or Pub:
Railwayman's Arms, 7 Valley Railway, Bridgnorth Station, ☎ (074 62) 4361 P ∉ ∰ ♨ Bar snacks.

Recommended
Farmhouse: *Charleotte Farm*, Cleobury North, ☎ (074 633) 238. £20 double; B. & B.
Golf course: Stanley Lane, ☎ 3315.

Nearby

SHIPLEY, 7m E on A454

Restaurant:
♦ *Thornescroft*, Bridgnorth Road, ☎ Pattingham (0902) 700253, AC AM BA DI P ∰ ♨ ✵ Cl. Christmas, 1 Jan., 10-27 Aug., Sun.-Mon. Seafood, raspberry pavlova. Book. £9.50.

WORFIELD, 3m E off A454

Hotel:
★★ *Old Vicarage*, WV15 5JZ, ☎ (074 64) 498, Tx 35438, AC AM BA DI, 10 rm. P ∉ ∰ ♨ ✓ ♫ £46. Rest. ♦ ♪ £13.

BROADWAY*

Stratford-upon-Avon, 15; Oxford, 37; London, 95 m
pop. 3,000 ☎ 0386   Hereford & Worcester B2

Georgian, Stuart and Tudor buildings of great individual beauty blend harmoniously in this outstanding village on the fringe of the Vale of Evesham.

▶ Long **High Street** is lined with fine buildings, grandest being **Lygon Arms Hotel**, formerly a manor house, thought to have sheltered both Charles I and Cromwell during Civil War.

Nearby

▶ **Fish Hill** *(1 ¹/₂ m E)* climbs steeply up the Cotswold Escarpment. At summit is **Broadway Tower Country Park,** with its principal feature **Broadway Tower.** Superb views from this 18thC folly over many counties, also exhibitions *(Apr.-Oct.: daily, 10-6).* ▶ **Stanway** *(5 m SW)* is a quiet hamlet set in parkland, in which stands a lovely Jacobean manor, **Stanway House:** gatehouse by Inigo Jones and immense 14thC tithe barn *(Jun.-Aug.: Tue.-Thu., 2-5).* ▶ **Stanton** *(1 ¹/₂ m N of Stanway)* is a peaceful village tucked below Shenbarrow Hill. ▶ **Snowshill Manor** *(3m S)* is a Tudor house with terraced garden, once home of Catherine Parr, wife of Henry VIII; unique collection of

craftsmanship including musical instruments, clocks and toys *(Apr. Oct.: Sat., Sun. & Easter Sat.-Mon., 11-1, 2-6).* ▶ **Buckland Rectory** *(2m SW)* is the oldest medieval parsonage in the country still in use; magnificent medieval great hall, with open timber roof *(May-Sep.: Mon., 11-4; Fri. also in Aug.).* □

Practical information

BROADWAY
ⓘ Cotswold Court, ☎ 852937.

Hotels:
● ★★★ *Lygon Arms* (Prestige), WR12 7DU, ☎ (0386) 852255, Tx 338260, AC AM BA DI, 64 rm. P ∰ ♨ ⌇ £95. Rest. ● ♦ ♨ £17.50.
● ★★ *Collin House*, Collin Lane, WR12 7PB, ☎ (0386) 858354, AC BA, 7 rm. P ∉ ∰ ♨ ✵ ⌂ No children under 6. £32. Rest. ● ♦ ♨ Cl. 24-26 Dec. £13.

Restaurant:
♦ *Hunters Lodge*, High Street, ☎ (0386) 853247, AC AM BA DI P ∰ ♨ ♨ ✵ Cl. 2 wks. Feb., 2wks. Aug., Sun. eve., Mon. Hunters' game pie. Book. £15.

Inn or Pub:
Crown Trumpet (Whitbread), Church Street, ☎ (0386) 853202, 3 rm. P ∉ ∰ ♨ Home-made pies, salads and ploughman's lunch. £4.50.

▲ *Leedons Park*, Childswickham Road, (325 pl) ☎ (0386) 852423.

Recommended
Antique shop: *Ewart, Gavina*, 60-62 High Street, ☎ (0386) 853371, glass, maps, pottery, porcelain and silver; *Keil, H.W. Ltd.*, Tudor House, ☎ (0386) 852408, architectural items, carpets and furniture.
Cycle rental: *Broadway Cycle Hire*, 39 High Street.
Farmhouses: *Manor Farm*, Wormington, ☎ (038 673) 302. £24 double; B. & B.; *Millbrook Farm*, Murcot, ☎ (0386) 830416. Pleasant view. £22 double; B. & B.

Nearby

BUCKLAND, 1m SW off A46

Hotel:
● ★★★ *Buckland Manor*, Nr Broadway, Worcsay, WR12 7LY, ☎ Broadway (0386) 852626, AC AM BA DI, 11 rm. P ∉ ∰ ♨ ✵ ⌂ ⌇ £105. Rest. ● ♦ Cl. mid-Jan.-mid-Feb. £20.

WILLERSEYHILL, 2m by A44

Hotel:
● ★★★ *Dormy House*, WR12 7LF, ☎ (0386) 852711, Tx 338275, AC AM BA DI, 50 rm. P ∉ ∰ ♨ ✵ ⌇ £80. Rest. ♦ Cl. Christmas. £20.

Recommended
Golf course: Willersey Hill ☎ 853683.

BROMSGROVE*

Birmingham, 14; Worcester, 8; London,124 m
pop. 38,000 ☎ 0527   Hereford & Worcester B2

Nail-making was the staple industry of this busy market town for 300 years until machines took over. The bronze gates of Buckingham Palace (→) were made here.

▶ **Church of St. John the Baptist** stands high on hill, reached by long flight of steps, with tall 14thC tower and spire. Fine alabaster monuments, interesting tombs in churchyard, 200-year-old lime trees.

Nearby

▶ **Beacon Hill** *(3m N)* at 1000 ft. is the highest point of **Lickey Hills**, commanding views. ▶ The open-air **Avoncroft Museum of Buildings** *(2m SW)* has a remarkable collection of buildings rescued from dereliction. Exhibits

include 1946 'prefab', working forge, windmill and cockpit theatre (*Mar., Jun.-Jul., Aug. & Nov.: daily, 11-5.30; Apr., May, Sep. & Oct.: Cl. Mon. ex. Bank Hols.*). ▶ **Harvington Hall** (*3m NW*) is a lovely moated 16thC manor, once home of John Wall, one of last in England to be martyred for his Catholic faith. Built in 1697 manor abounds in trapdoors, hidden passages and priest holes; Georgian chapel in garden (*Feb., Mar., Oct. & Nov.: daily, ex. Mon., 2-6 or dusk; Easter Sun.-end Sep.: Sun., 2-6, wkdays ex. Mon., 11.30-1 & 2-6, open Bank Hols., cl. following Fri.*).　　□

Practical information

BROMSGROVE
ⓘ 47-49 Worcester Road, ☎ 31809.
▱▱ ☎ Worcester (0905) 27211.

Hotel:
★ *Forest Inn*, 290 Birmingham Road, B61 0ER, ☎ (0527) 72063, AC, 8 rm. ℗ Former coaching inn just outside the town. £28. Rest. ◆ ♪ Cl. Christmas. £7.

Restaurant:
● ◆ *Grafton Manor*, Grafton Lane, ☎ (0527) 31525, AC AM BA DI, 8 rm. ℗ ⌇ ⋙ ◠ ⚘ Cl. lunch Mon.-Sat. 8 rm. Gravlax. Book. £19.50.

Recommended
Bed and breakfast: c/o Mrs P. Jones, 238A Birmingham Road, Liekey End, ☎ (0527) 76270. £15 double; B. & B. **Craft workshops:** *Daub and Wattle Ltd.*, Windsor Street, ☎ (0527) 79979, original ceramic gifts; *Staffordshire Peak Arts Centre*, The Old School, Cauldon Lowe, ☎ (053 86) 431, at Hamstall Ridware, *Ridware Arts Centre*, Hamstall Hall, ☎ (088 922) 351.

Nearby

BELBROUGHTON, 6m NW on B4188

Restaurants:
● ◆ *Bell Inn*, Bell End, ☎ (0652) 730232, AC AM BA ℗ ⋙ ◠ ♪ & Cl. 1st wk. Jan., Mon., Sat. lunch, Sun. eve. Rabbit with sweet chestnut and cognac sauce. Book. £14.50.
◆ *Freshman's*, Church Hill, ☎ (0562) 730467, AC DI BA ℗ ⋙ ◠ ♪ & ⚘ Cl. Sat. lunch, Sun.-Mon. Lamb Wellington. Book (eve.). £16.

BROMYARD*

Leominster, 11; Worcester, 14; London, 127 m
pop. 3,100 ☎ 0885　　　　　　　Hereford & Worcester A2

Surrounded by rich farmland, with delightful walking country NE on the Bromyard Downs, the River Frome flows through this small market town. There are many black-and-white buildings and an interesting Norman church.

Nearby

▶ At **Lower Brockhampton** (*2 m E*) is pretty timbered manor, c. 1400, almost entirely surrounded by a moat, with detached gatehouse (*Easter Sat.-end Oct.: Wed.-Sat. Bank Hol. Mon., 10-1, 2-6, Sun., 10-1*).　　□

Practical information

ⓘ council offices, 1 Rowberry Street, ☎ 82341.

Restaurant:
◆ *Old Penny*, High Street, ☎ (0885) 83227, AC AM BA £10.

Recommended
Craft workshop: at Hanbury, *Jinney Ring Craft Centre*, ☎ (052 784) 272.
Riding school: *Hanburies Riding Centre*, Bishop Frome, ☎ (0562) 850611.

BURTON-UPON-TRENT* ▶

Derby, 11; Lichfield, 11; London, 127 m
pop. 59,040 ☎ 0283　　　　　　　Staffordshire B1

The administrative and industrial centre of East Stafford, large and thriving, this town was granted a charter by King John in 1200. Burton is best known for its long association with the brewing industry. Signs of this activity are still in evidence, the rich smell of malt, hops and yeast pervading the streets of solid, Victorian buildings.

▶ **R. Trent** is a vital influence on life of town. Purity of its water, drawn from great depths upstream, was responsible for development of brewing. **Trent Washlands** now form a large area of semi-natural parkland. ▶ **Town hall** has three distinct parts, earliest c. 1882 and latest c. 1938. Central section with clock-tower is high Victorian Gothic, c. 1893. ▶ **Bass Museum and Shire Horse Stables** (Horninglow Street) tells history of brewing. Among exhibits are fully-functioning miniature brewery and truck shaped like large beer bottle. Also home of four magnificent Shire horses who, arrayed in brass and leather, drew brewer's drays to inns (*daily, 11-4.30. Tours of the modern brewery by arrangement* ☎ 0283 45301 ext. 2242). ▶ **St. Modwen's church** stands on site where Anglo-Saxon nobleman Wulfric Spot founded an abbey in 1004. Cromwell's army dealt the death-blow to this abbey by letting off two barrels of gunpowder within it. Present church contains relics of its predecessor: 15thC font and 16thC coffer.

Nearby

▶ **Abbots Bromley**★ (*10m W*) is reached through what remains of **Needwood Forest** (→). Lovely town with ancient church, hexagonal butter cross, black-and-white cottages, a green and five old inns along main street. Once an important stopping place for coaches traveling from Manchester to Birmingham, famous now for Horn Dance which takes place every September (→). ▶ **Hoar Cross** (*7m W*), pretty village with beautiful late 19thC **Church of the Holy Angels** by Bodley, somewhat sombre without, within lavishly decorated. Adjoining church is **Hoar Cross Hall**, built 19thC Jacobean style; collection of Victorian costume and textiles, including work by William Morris; private chapel also by Bodley, 20 acres of wooded grounds. ▶ **Uttoxeter** is chiefly known for racecourse. Unspoiled town with weekly street and livestock market (*Wed.*) held since 1252. In market square is **Johnson Memorial** to Dr. Johnson , whose father kept a bookstall here. ▶ **Tutbury** (*4 1/2 m NW*), bordering Dove, is historic little town once lying at centre of Mercian kingdom (→), on an important crossing point of river. **High Street** has some attractive old buildings, notably black-and-white inn, **Dog and Partridge**. Castle has lain in ruins since it was destroyed by Parliamentarians 1646. It has had an eventful history, once being prison for Mary Queen of Scots. Tutbury has a good Norman **church**★; notable W door and splendid nave with stout Norman pillars. ▶ In an old Georgian **corn mill** is sheepskin shop, selling products manufactured here. Crystal glass is also made in Tutbury; two shops sell fine glassware.　　□

Practical information

BURTON-UPON-TRENT
ⓘ town hall, King Edward Square, ☎ 45454.
Car rental: Avis, 8 Dale Street, ☎ 38632 (rail/drive).

Inns or Pubs:
Burton Bridge Brewery (Burton Bridge), 24 Bridge Street, ☎ (0283) 36596 ℗ Cold bar food.
Coopers Tavern (Bass), Cross Street, ☎ (0283) 32551. Snacks.

Recommended
Craft workshop: *Maggie B. Knitwear*, 56 Oak Road, ☎ (028 371) 2703, machine-knitted garments.

Golf course: Ashby Road East (3m SE on A50), ☎ 44551.

Nearby

BRANSTON, 2m SW on A5121

Hotel:
★★★ *Riverside Inn*, Riverside Drive, DE14 3EP, ☎ Burton-on-Trent (0283) 63117, AC BA, 22 rm. ℙ ⅢⅢ ↙ £38.50. Rest. ◆ ♪ & £9. ☎ (0283) 511234.

Recommended
Golf course: Burton Road, ☎ 43207.

NEWTON SOLNEY, 3m NE by A50 on B5008

Hotel:
★★ *Newton Park* (Embassy), DE15 0SS, ☎ Burton-on-Trent (0283) 703568, AC AM BA DI, 26 rm. ℙ ⅢⅢ An old stone house, covered with creepers. Set in over 4 acres (1.62 hec.) of gardens. £40. Rest. ● ◆ £9.

RANGEMOOR, 3m W off B5017

Hotel:
★ *Needwood Manor*, Tatenhill Common, DE13 9RS, ☎ Barton (028 371) 2932, AC BA, 10 rm. ℙ ⅄ ⅢⅢ ⅏ £43. Rest. ◆ £11.

ROLLESTON-ON-DOVE, 2m NW off A50

Hotel:
● ★★★ *Brookhouse Inn*, Brookside, DE13 9BD, ☎ Burton-on-Trent (0283) 814188, Tx 913001, AC AM BA DI, 16 rm. ℙ ⅢⅢ ⅄ ↙ Inn converted from William and Mary period farmhouse. £55. Rest. ◆ & Cl. Sun., Bank Hols., 25 Dec.-7 Jan. £14.

TUTBURY, 3m N on A50

Hotel:
● ★★★ *Olde Dog Partridge*, High Street, DE13 9LS, ☎ Burton-on-Trent (0283) 813030, AC AM BA, 18 rm. ℙ ⅄ ⅢⅢ ⅄ Half-timbered inn built in the mid-15thC. £50. Rest. ◆ ♪ Cl. Sun.-Mon., lunch Sat. Salmon and venison. £14.50.

CHEADLE

Staffordshire B1

Among gentle hills and moorland, this little market town is identifiable from afar by the lofty spire of Pugin's remarkable Roman Catholic **Church of St. Giles★**.

▶ Built 1841-46, interior is richly and colourfully decorated with metalwork, glass, stenciled walls, patterned tiles.

Nearby

▶ **Hawksmoor Nature Reserve** (*2m NE*) opened 1927: 250-acres of marsh, moor and woodland; many unusual trees; rich in bird life; nature trails. ▶ At Ipstones (*4¹/₂ m N*) is **Moorland Farm Park** with over 50 rare British farm animals, including local Tamworth pigs (*Apr.-Oct.: daily, 10.30-5.30*). ▶ **Alton** (*4 m E*) in Churnet Valley has a romantic setting developed by the 15th and 16th Earls of Shrewsbury, who transformed bare hillside with extravagant Gothic mansion and magnificent ornamental gardens. **House,** partially demolished, preserves a splendid silhouette. Note **chapel:** ceiling by Pugin. ▶ Large grounds contain **pleasure park; gardens** with many fountains and ornaments. Complex known as **Alton Towers** (*Easter-Oct.: daily*). ☐

Practical information _____

Hotel:
★ *Royal Oak*, High Street, ST10 1AN, ☎ (0538) 753116, BA, 6 rm. ℙ £25. Rest. ◆ ♪ £4.

Recommended
Bed and breakfast: *The Grange*, Oakamoor Road, ☎ (0538) 754093. £22 double; B. & B.

Farmhouse: at Oakamoor, *Old Furnace Farm*, Breendale, ☎ (0538) 702442. £14 double; B. & B.
⋏ *Hales Hall C.C.P.*, Oakmore Road, ST10 1BU (30 pl.), ☎ (0538) 753305.

CHELTENHAM*

Gloucester, 8; Oxford, 43; London, 101 m
pop. 85,000 ☎ 0242   Gloucestershire B3

The discovery of health-giving spring waters here led to the transformation from Cotswold village to elegant Regency spa town, enjoying the patronage of George III.

▶ In Pitville Park (*N of town centre*) stand **Pitville Pump Rooms★**; one of Cheltenham's grandest Regency buildings, 1825. Contains a **Gallery of Fashion:** costume and accessories 1760s to present; also displays outlining town's history (*Apr.-Oct.: Tue.-Sun., 10.30-5; Nov.-Mar.: Tue.-Sat., 10.30-5*). ▶ **Art Gallery and Museum:** excellent paintings, particularly 17thC Dutch; English glass, ceramics and furniture; arts and crafts; metalwork and jewelry; local folklore; geology and archaeology (*Mon. Sat.: 10-5.30; cl. Bank Hols.*). ▶ **Gustav Holst Birthplace Museum:** small Regency house where the composer was born, now museum devoted to his life and music (*Tue.-Fri.: 12-5.30; Sat.: 11-5.30*). ▶ **Church of St. Mary** is only medieval church in Cheltenham. ▶ **All Saints** (Pitville), by John Middleton who came to town in 1860 and quickly built five churches; this his best. ▶ Among Cheltenham's many parks are **Imperial Gardens** and **Pitville Park.** ▶ Good Regency architecture in **Promenade** and **Montpellier Walk** (notice caryatids).

Nearby

▶ **Elkstone Church** (*6m S*) is one of best Norman churches in area: note carved door in 14thC S porch, interior with vaulted roof. ▶ There is good hilly countryside to explore around Cheltenham; **Leckhampton Hill** (*just S of town*) is easily accessible; splendid **views** and rock formation known as Devil's Chimney. ▶ Steep climb to **Birdlip** on crest of **Birdlip Hill;** view over Vale of Gloucester. ☐

Practical information _____

CHELTENHAM
ⓘ municipal offices, Promenade (B2), ☎ 522878.
🚌 ☎ Gloucester (0452) 29501.
🚃 (B1), ☎ 58411.
Car-rental: Avis, ☎ (0452) 64214/5 (rail/drive); Budget, Haines Strange Ltd., 53 Albion Street, ☎ 35222.

Hotels:
★★★ *Queen's* (T.F.), The Promenade, GL50 1NN (B2), ☎ (0242) 514724, Tx 43381, AC AM BA DI, 77 rm. ℙ & £60. Rest. ◆ ♪ & £12.
★★ *Wyastone*, Parabola Road, GL50 3BG (B3), ☎ (0242) 516654, AC AM BA DI, 13 rm. ℙ ⅏ £55. Rest. ◆ £10.
★ *Regency House*, 50 Clarence Square, GL50 4JR (B1), ☎ (0242) 582718, 8 rm. ℙ ⅄ £30. Rest. ◆ ♪ Cl. 24-25 Dec. and 1 Jan. £7.

Restaurants:
● ◆ *La Ciboulette*, 24-26 Suffolk Road (B3), ☎ (0242) 573449, AC AM BA ♪ & ⅏ Cl. Christmas, Easter, 3 wks. Aug., Sun.-Mon. French cuisine, fish, game. Book. £18.
◆ *Chives*, 226 Bath Road (B2), ☎ (0242) 516676, AC BA ℙ ⅢⅢ ♪ & ⅏ Cl. Bank Hols., Sun., Mon.-Thu. eve. Mediterranean casserole, home-made soups and puddings. Book. £14.50.
◆ *Mayflower*, 32 Clarence Street (B2), ☎ (0242) 522426, AM DI ♪ ⅏ Cl. Christmas. Szechuan bird's nest soup. Book. £16.
◆ *Number Twelve*, 12 Suffolk Parade (A3), ☎ (0242) 584544, AM AC DI. Cl. Sun. dinner, Mon. and Bank Hols. £12.
◆ *Rajvooj Tandoori*, 1 Albion Street (B2), ☎ (0242) 524288, AC AM DI BA. Cl. Christmas Day. £8.50.

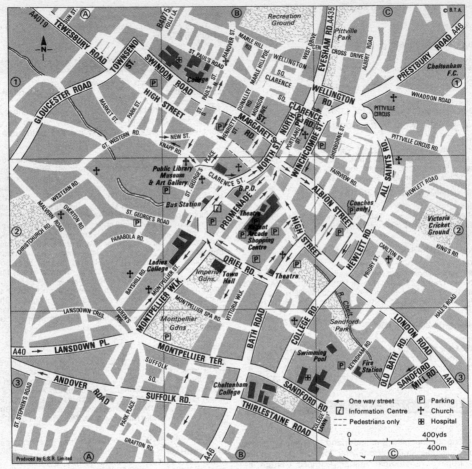

CHELTENHAM

🏕 *Beggars Roost C.C.S.*, Bamfulong Lane, Staverton, (25 pl), ☎ (0452) 712705; *Long Willows Camp*, Station Road, Woodmancote, (30 pl), ☎ (024 267) 4113.

Recommended
Antique shop: *Curtis, George*, 14 Suffolk Parade, ☎ (0242) 513828, clocks; *Keil, H.W. Ltd.*, 129-131 The Promenade, ☎ (0242) 22509, carpets and furniture; *Martin Co. Ltd.*, 19 The Promenade, ☎ (0242) 22821, jewelry and silver; *Scott Cooper Ltd.*, 52 The Promenade, ☎ (0242) 22580, jewelry and silver.
Cycle rental: *A. Williams Co.*, 8-14 Portland Street.
Golf course: Cotswold Hills, Ullenwood, ☎ 515264.

Nearby

CLEEVE HILL, 4m NE on A46

Hotel:
★★★ *Rising Sun* (Whitbread Coaching), GL52 3PX, ☎ Bishops Cleeve (024 267) 6281, AC AM BA DI, 25 rm. P ⬅ 🕸 🦢 🏊 🎵 £46. Rest. ♦ ♪ £10.

Restaurant:
♦ *Malvern View*, ☎ Bishops Cleeve (024 267) 2017, AC

BA, 7 rm. P ⬅ 🕸 🦢 🏊 Cl. Christmas, New Year lunch, res. only Sun. eve. *Carré d'agneau en croûte*. Book. £14.50.

GOLDEN VALLEY, 1 1/2 m W off A40

Hotel:
★★★ *Golden Valley Thistle*, Gloucester Road, GL51 0TS, ☎ (0242) 32691, Tx 43410, AC AM BA DI, 99 rm. P 🕸 🦢 ♪ £68. Rest. ♦ ♪ Cl. Christmas. £12.

PRESTBURY, 1m NE on A46

Hotel:
● ★★ *Prestbury House*, The Burgage, GL52 3DN, ☎ (0242) 529533, 10 rm. P 🕸 🦢 ⅃ £46. Rest. ♦ Cl. 1-14 Aug., Christmas and Bank Hols. £13.

SHURDINGTON, 2 1/2 m S off A46

Hotel:
● ★★★ *Greenway*, GL51 5UG, ☎ (0242) 862352, Tx 437216, AC AM BA DI, 12 rm. P ⬅ 🕸 🦢 🏊 No children under 7. £100. Rest. ● ♦ ⅃ Cl. Sun. and lunch Sat., Bank Hols. £20.

SOUTHAM, 3m NE on A46

Hotel:
★★★ **De La Bere** (B.W.), GL52 3NH, ☎ (0242) 37771, Tx 43232, AC AM BA DI, 35 rm. ℗ ⋜ ⬚ 🍴 ♪ ⏰ Tudor manor built in 1485. £74. Rest. ◆ £12.
Farmhouse: *Ham Hill Farm*, ☎ (0242) 584415, £18 double B. & B.

CHIPPING CAMPDEN*

Stratford-upon-Avon, 12; Oxford, 36; London, 96 m
pop. 1,936 ☎ 0386   Gloucestershire B2

A town made rich through wool in medieval times, Chipping Campden's many beautiful buildings have been carefully preserved, making this a favourite Cots-wold centre.

▶ While earlier fragments survive, the **church**★ is mainly Perpendicular and one of the loveliest of 'wool' churches; pinnacled tower, soaring nave. Sir Baptist Hicks bought the manor in 1610 and endowed church and town gen-erously. His **monument** is in **Noel Chapel**; fine **brasses** to Sir William Grevil and his wife, below high altar. ▶ Stone **market hall**, 1627, bearing Hicks coat-of-arms; arched and timber-roofed on stone columns. ▶ **Woolstaplers Hall**, late 14thC: one room with splendid oak roof and stone oriel window; houses local **museum** (*Easter-Sep.: daily*). ▶ **Almshouses** in Church Street in dignified Cotswold vernacular style, also built by Hicks. ▶ **Camp-den Car Collection**: notable cars 1927-63, particularly Jaguars, all in working order (*Apr.-Sep.: daily*).

Nearby

▶ **Dover's Hill** (*l m SE*): superb view over Vale of Evesham and Midlands Plain from N edge of Cotswolds. Cotswold Olympics held here 1605-1851; sporting pursuits includ-ed cudgel-playing, wrestling and shin-kicking. Hill is also most northerly point of **Cotswold Way Paths**★, 95m in all and definitely best way to experience Cotswolds. Small sections may be undertaken along its length for excellent **views**, but it takes 7-10 days to walk entire length to Bath (→). ▶ **Kiftsgate Court** (*3 m NE*): **views** from garden containing many unusual plants, old-fashioned roses, tree peonies. (*Easter Sun.-end Sep.: Wed., Thu. & Sun., 2-6, also Bank Hols., 2-6*). ▶ **Hidcote Manor Garden**★ (*4 m NE*): a unique sequence of small gardens enclosed by walls and hedges; great variety of roses, shrubs and plants all collected and laid out this century (*Easter Sat.-end Oct.: daily ex. Tue. & Fri., 11-8*).   □

Practical information

CHIPPING CAMPDEN
ℹ Woolstaplers Hall Museum, High Street, ☎ 840289.

Hotels:
★★ **Noel Arms**, High Street, GL55 6AT, ☎ Evesham (0386) 840317, AC BA, 19 rm. ℗ ᵭ ⬚ 14thC inn situated in the centre of an attractive old wool town. £45.50. Rest. ◆ £11.50.
★ **King's Arms**, High Street, GL55 6AW, ☎ Evesham (0386) 840256, AC BA, 15 rm. ℗ ⋜ ⬚ ◬ £48. Rest. ◆ £13.50.

Nearby

BROAD CAMPDEN, 1m S

Hotel:
● ★ **Malt House**, GL55 6UU, ☎ Evesham (0386) 840295, AC, 5 rm. ℗ ⬚ ◬ ⊗ £48. Rest. ◆ Cl. dinner Sun. and Christmas. £15.

MICKLETON, 2m N on B4081

Hotel:
★★★ **Three Ways** (Inter), Chapel Lane, GL55 6SB, ☎ (038 677) 231, AC AM BA DI, 37 rm. ℗ ◬ ᵭ £50. Rest. ◆ ♪ ᵭ £11.

CHURCH STRETTON*

Shrewsbury, 13; Leominster, 27; London, 174 m
pop. 3,890 ☎ 0694   Shropshire A2

A little town in hill country that flowered as a health resort in late 18th0 early 19thC. Now a good centre for the healthy visitor, with excellent walking, golf, hang gliding and horseback riding.

▶ **St. Lawrence Church**: Norman and Early English; ancient Sheila-na-gig (fertility symbol) carved above N doorway.

Nearby

▶ **Acton Scott Working Farm Museum** (*2m S*): Shire horse working demonstration, rare breeds (*Apr.-Oct.: daily*). ▶ Two picturesque villages close to Church Stret-ton: **Minton** (*2 ¹/₂ m SW*) with cottages around a village green and **Little Stretton** (*1 m S*), timbered houses and 20thC church with thatched roof. ▶ **Wilderhope Manor**: late 16thC limestone house; good plaster ceilings, views over Corve Dale, circular walk through wooded grounds (*Apr.-Sep.: Wed. & Sat., 2-4.30; Oct.-Mar.: Sat., 2-4.30*). ▶ W of Stretton rises **Long Mynd**✦: beautiful bracken-clothed moorland with sheep and wild ponies, spectac-ular **views**. ▶ In **Carding Mill Valley**, information centre and shop (*Apr.-Sep.: daily; wkends in Oct.*). ▶ **The Stiper-stones** rises further W; here too excellent walking country, picnic spots and views over River Severn and mountains of Wales.

Shropshire Hills Round Trip★

▶ The sheep farming, high moorland landscape around Church Stretton is most unexpected so close to large Midlands towns. England seems to have claimed a little of Wales in a finger-like protrusion W of Stretton. Grazed by Clun Forest sheep and haunt of buzzards and kestrels, this is upland country to be explored at a leisurely pace. ▶ Leave Stretton going N to **Leebotwood** (*3m*): attractive village with 13thC church among trees; turn l. here, 3 ¹/₂ m NE to **Acton Burnell**★: ruined fortified medieval manor or 'castle', built 1284-93; attractive **church**, medieval **tiles** in N transept, **brass** on tomb of Sir Richard Lee. ▶ Route then drops S for 4 ¹/₂ m passing moorland peaks of **Caer Caradoc** and **Hope Bowdler Hill** to W; on to **Longville-in-the-Dale** in **Ape Dale** and below **Wenlock Edge**. ▶ Follow minor road that climbs over Edge, passing **Wilderhope Manor** (→), then dropping into Corve Dale. Turn r. to fol-low course of River Corve SW; **Brown Clee Hill** rises to

The Shropshire hills

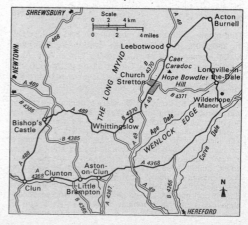

S. ▶ Pass through **Diddlebury** (interesting Saxon/Norman church), proceed W to **Aston-on-Clun**: attractive buildings in lovely setting; see Kangaroo Inn with little stone Round House adjacent. ▶ Continue W through **Little Brampton** to **Clunton**, one of peaceful Clun Valley villages, largest of which is **Clun★** itself (*2m W*): ancient border outpost that has seen much raiding across Welsh border. **Museum** in town hall; mound above river only remains of Norman stronghold; large Norman **church**, 18thC lych-gate. ▶ Route then turns N, parallel with **Offa's Dyke** (→) to W. ▶ **Bishop's Castle★**: another border settlement with castle remains, built in Norman times when the land was bequeathed to Bishop of Hereford. 18thC brick **town hall** with cupola; in cobbled lane is **House of Crutches**, upper storey supported by timber posts. ▶ N of town bear r. to meet A489. Follow WSW, the **Long Mynd** (→) rises to N. Turn l. for **Whittingslow** at S edge of Long Mynd. Return to Stretton on A49.

Practical information

CHURCH STRETTON
ⓘ Church Street, ☎ 722535.
▐▬▬ ☎ Shrewsbury (0743) 64041.

Inn or Pub:
Kings Arms (Shrewsbury), High Sreet, ☎ (0694) 722807 ⧓ Lunch and eve. ex. Tue. Home-made ploughman's lunch, quiches. £4.

Recommended
Golf course: Links Road (1/2m off A49) ☎ 722281.

Nearby

ALL STRETTON, 1m N on B4370

Hotel:
★★ *Stretton Hall*, SY6 6HG, ☎ (0694) 723224, AC AM BA DI, 12 rm. P ⧓ ∰ ◿ ⚘ £44. Rest. ◆ ♪ £10.50.

Recommended
Bed and breakfast: *Dudgeley Mill*, ☎ (0694) 723461. £25 double; B. & B.
Riding school: *The Green Farm*, Wentnor, ☎ (058 861) 394.

LITTLE STRETTON, 2m S on B4370

Hotel:
★ *Mynd House*, Ludlow Road, SY6 6RB, ☎ (0694) 722212, AC BA, 13 rm. P ⧓ ∰ ◿ £38. Rest. ◆ ♪ Cl. mid-Dec.-end Jan. £8.

Inn or Pub:
Ragleth, Ludlow Road, ☎ (0694) 722711 P ⧓ ∰ ◿ ఉ Home-made lasagne and steaks. £8.

CIRENCESTER*

Gloucester, 19; Swindon, 15; London, 98 m
pop. 16,100 ☎ 0285   Gloucestershire B3

This small Cotswold town was in the 2nd century BC the most important town, after London, in all Britain. A vital Roman administrative centre, Fosse Way, Akeman Street and Ermine Street all pass through the town centre. In the Middle Ages it grew rich through the wool trade.

▶ **Church of St. John the Baptist★★** dominates **market square** (note ancient market cross); 15thC Perpendicular like other 'wool' churches, it is on an even grander scale: S **porch** is 3-storeyed, interior fan-vaulted. **Tower** built with money given by Crown in gratitude to townspeople for successfully beheading rebel Earls Kent and Salisbury in 1399. **Nave** filled with light from lofty clerestory windows; beautiful medieval **glass** in E and W windows; fine **brasses** of many local wool merchants; unusual pre-Reformation gilded pulpit; superb church plate: Anne Boleyn cup may be viewed. ▶ Relics of Roman occupation on display in **Corinium Museum★** (Park Street): superb **mosaics**, also displays recounting Cirencester's

history (*Apr.-Sep.: Mon.-Sat., 10-5.30, Sun., 2-5.30; Oct.-Mar.: Tue.-Sat., 10-5, Sun., 2-5*). **Cirencester Park:** 300 acres belonging to **Cirencester House**; 5m avenue of chestnuts, good walks, model farm, children's playground (*wkends in summer*), polo matches most Sundays in summer. ▶ Querns earthworks, SW of town, site of Roman **amphitheatre**.

Nearby

▶ **Chedworth Roman Villa★** (*6m N*): well-preserved house, pavements, hypocaust; small museum (*Mar.-Oct.: Tue.-Sun., Bank Hols. Mon., 11-6 or sunset; Nov.-early Dec. & Feb.: Wed.-Sun., 11- 4*). ▶ **Northleach** (*10m NE*): ranked with Cirencester in Middle Ages: lovely village with beautiful 'wool' **church★**. Outstanding **brasses** of wool merchants: note how feet of merchants rest on sheep, wool sacks. ▶ **Cotswold Countryside Collection:** splendid museum of agricultural history housed in old Northleach 'House of Correction' (*Easter-end Sep.: daily, 10-5.30, Sun., 2-5.30*). ▶ **Barnsley House** (*4 m NE*) has exceptional **18thC Knot-garden**, lime and laburnum walks, vegetable garden, with Doric temple (*Mon.-Fri.: 10-6 (or dusk); first Sun. in May, Jun. & Jul.*).

Practical information

CIRENCESTER
ⓘ Corn Hall, Market Place, ☎ 4180.

Hotels:
● ★★★ *King's Head* (B.W.), Market Place, GL7 2NR, ☎ (0285) 3322, Tx 43470, AC AM BA DI, 70 rm. P ఉ ◿ £56. Rest. ◆ Cl. 27-30 Dec. £11.
★★★ *Fleece* (Fine Inn), Market Place, GL7 4NZ, ☎ (0285) 68507, Tx 437287, AC AM BA DI, 19 rm. P ⬙ Comfortable Tudor inn. £50. Rest. ◆ ♪ £13.
★★ *Corinium Court*, Gloucester Street, GL7 2DG, ☎ (0285) 4499, AC AM BA DI, 9 rm. P ∰ ◿ £48. Rest. ◆ ♪ £13.

Restaurant:
◆ *Rajdoot Tandoori*, 35 Castle Street, ☎ (0285) 2651, AC AM BA DI ♪ ⬙ £6.

Inn or Pub:
Drillmans Arms (Archers), Gloucester Road, (A417), ☎ Stratton (0285) 3892, AM BA DI, 1 rm. P ఉ Home-made dishes and à la carte meals with large choice of vegetables. £6.

⋏ *Cotswold Cara Park*, Broadway Lane, South Cerney, (304 pl.), ☎ (0285) 860216.

Recommended
Antique shops: *Stokes, William H.*, Roberts House, Siddington, ☎ (0285) 67101, furniture; *Thornborough Galleries*, 28 Gloucester Street, ☎ (0285) 2055, carpets and fabrics.
Bed and breakfast: at South Cerney, *Abalus House*, 6 Trunchard Gardens, ☎ (0285) 860999. £19 double.
Craft workshop: *Cirencester Workshops*, Brewery Court, ☎ (0285) 61566.
Golf course: Cheltenham Road, Bagendon (on A435) ☎ (0285) 2465.

Nearby

STRATTON, 1 1/4m NW on A417

Hotel:
● ★★ *Stratton House*, Gloucester Road, GL7 2LE, ☎ (0285) 61761, AC AM BA DI, 26 rm. P ⧓ ∰ ◿ ఉ ◿ £47. Rest. ◆ ఉ Bibury trout. £10.

COVENTRY*

Leicester, 24; Oxford, 45; London, 97 m
pop. 340,100 ☎ 0203   West Midlands B2

Coventry grew steadily from the first minor settlement around a 7thC Anglo-Saxon convent, through a major cloth-trading phase, to become a key industrial

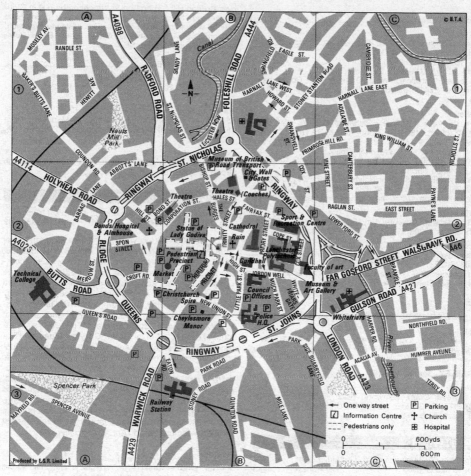

COVENTRY

city from the 18thC on, particularly associated with motorcars, bicycles and sewing machines. In November 1940 the city was devastated by aerial bombardment. From the ruins arose a vital modern city and superb modern **cathedral**★★★.

▶ Cathedral stands in city centre, at r. angles to Gothic **old cathedral** ruins, left with medieval tower and spire intact. Modern building of pale red sandstone (Basil Spence) consecrated 1962. Beside broad steps leading to porch, Epstein's sculpture, *St. Michael and Lucifer*★. ▶ Interior filled with coloured light from many stained-glass windows: golden glass in **Chapel of Unity** (Margaret Traherne), **baptistery window** of intense colour (John Piper); before it stands **font** of uncarved rock from Bethlehem. Circular **Guild Chapel** has clear glass windows affording **views** of city; **Crown of Thorns** placed centrally (Geoffrey Clark); **Chapel of Christ Servant** contains map showing sites and names of Coventry's industrial plants; **lectern** superb bronze eagle (Elizabeth Frink). **Tapestry**★ above high altar by Graham Sutherland: Christ in Majesty. Whites, greys, yellows and deep reds on still green background; diminutive figure of Man between Christ's feet. ▶ **Holy Trinity** (facing shopping precinct), most important

of Coventry's medieval remnants: tall spired, Perpendicular building; 13thC vaulted N porch; lantern tower (George Gilbert Scott removed bells and belfry 1854) with painted wood roof; 15thC painted nave roof, light blue with gold stars; carved misericords brought here from **Whitefriars** (remains in Whitefriar's Street), a Carmelite monastery founded 1342, badly damaged 1940. ▶ **Priory Row** (facing cathedral courtyard) has early 16thC timbered houses; no. 11 is handsome early 18thC. ▶ **Ford's Hospital** (Greyfriar's Lane), built 1529: timber-framed with carved gables. ▶ **St. Mary's Hall** (Bayley Lane), built as guildhall 1340 and still intact: stained glass, minstrel's gallery, late 14thC tapestry depicting Assumption of the Virgin Mary. ▶ **Art gallery and museum** (Jordan Wall): archaeology, natural and industrial history, Graham Sutherland's sketches for cathedral tapestry, British landscape paintings (*daily ex. Sun. am*). ▶ **Museum of British Road Transport** (St. Agnes Lane) has vintage and classic motorcycles and cars: Triumph, Daimler, Jaguar, Riley. ▶ In Broadgate Street, a **statue** of Lady Godiva (→) enacting her legendary ride and a **clock** showing the same with Peeping Tom who peeps obligingly every hour.   □

The arrow (→) is a reference to another entry.

Practical information

COVENTRY
ℹ central library, Smithford Way (B2), ☎ 20084.
✈ Coventry Airport, ☎ 301717.
🚆 (B3), ☎ 555211.
🚌 (B2), $23116.
Car-rental: Europcar, West Orchard (off Corporation Street), ☎ 27477, (rail/drive); Henlys, Kempas Highway, ☎ 410076.

Hotels:
★★★ ***De Vere*** (De Vere), Cathedral Square, CV1 5RP (B2), ☎ (0203) 51851, Tx 31380, AC AM BA DI, 215 rm. Ⓟ ♿ £9.50. Rest. ♦ ♪ £63.
★★★ ***Hylands***, 153 Warwick Road, CV3 6AU (A3), ☎ (0203) 501600, AC AM BA DI, 56 rm. Ⓟ £45. Rest. ♦ ♪ ♿ Cl. lunch Sat. £9.
★ ***Trinity House***, 28 Lower Holyhead Road, CV1 3AU(A2), ☎ (0203) 555654, 8 rm. Ⓟ ✗ £24. Rest. ● ♦ ♪ Cl. Christmas, lunch, Sun. Home-made soups and desserts. £8.

Restaurant:
♦ ***Grandstand***, Coventry City FC, King Richard Street, Highfield, ☎ (0203) 27053, AC BA Ⓟ Cl. eve. £8.95.

Recommended
Farmhouse: at Meriden, *Woodlands Farm*, Back Lane, ☎ (0676) 22317. £20 double; B. & B.
Golf course: The Grange, Copsewood (3m E on A428), ☎ 451 465; Finham Park, ☎ 414152.

Nearby

BALSALL COMMON, 7m W by A4023 on B4101

Hotel:
● ★★ ***Haigs***, 273 Kenilworth Road, CV7 7EL, ☎ Berkswell (0676) 33004, AC AM BA DI, 14 rm. Ⓟ ✗ No children under 4. £40. Rest. ♦ Cl. 26 Dec.-4 Jan. £8.

KERESLEY, 3m N off B4098

Hotel:
★★★ ***Royal Court***, Tamworth Road, CV7 8JG, ☎ (020 333) 4171, Tx 312549, AC AM BA DI, 99 rm. ♨ ♿ ✗ ⛳ £50. Rest. ♦ ♿ £11.

DROITWICH

Worcester, 7; Birmingham, 20; London, 120 m
pop. 18,025 ☎ 0905 Hereford & Worcester

Unique in Britain, Droitwich developed as a natural brine spa. The waters, believed to have curative properties, may still be sampled today.

▶ **Droitwich Lido Park:** open-air swimming pool filled with brine waters, but diluted from 2 $^1/_2$ pounds per gallon that occurs naturally. ▶ Several timbered buildings, notably **Raven Hotel**, St. Andrew's Street. ▶ **Sacred Heart Church,** modeled on a Roman court of justice, has interior filled with Venetian glass **mosaics,** telling the story of St. Richard, a 13thC Bishop of Chichester born in Droitwich. ▶ **Droitwich Heritage Centre** traces town's development from saltings to thriving Victorian spa town (*Mon.-Sat.: 10-5, cl. Sun. & Bank Hols.*).

Nearby

▶ **Ombersley** (*2 $^1/_2$ m W*), with timbered cottages and old inns. Parish church stands in grounds of **Ombersley Court,** 1720 (*not open*). ▶ **Salwarpe** (*1m W*): village where **Droitwich-Worcester Canal** separates Norman **church** from black-and-white **Salwarpe Court** (*not open*). ▶ **Clack's Farm** (*6m W*): gardens of great range and interest (*spring to autumn, some wkends*). ▶ **Hanbury Hall** (*3 $^1/_2$ m E*): Wren-style country house with finely painted ceiling and staircase by Sir James Thornhill (*May-Sep.: Wed.-Sun. and Bank Hols. Mon., 2-6; Apr.-Oct., Sat. & Sun., 2-5*). ▶ **Wychavon Way** is a 40 m marked path from **Holt Fleet** W of Droitwich, through **Vale of Evesham** (→) over **Bredon Hill** (→) and on to **Winchcombe** (→) in Gloucestershire. Short stretches through lovely countryside may be walked from Holt Fleet or Ombersley to Droitwich, or from Droitwich to **Shernal Green, Shell, Earl's Common** or **Flyford Flavell** to SE. □

Practical information

ℹ Heritage Centre, Heritage Way, ☎ 774312.
🚆 Droitwich Spa, ☎ Worcester (0905) 27211.

Hotel:
★★★ ***Chateau Impney***, WR9 0BN, ☎ (0905) 774411, Tx 336673, AC AM BA DI, 67 rm. Ⓟ ♨ ⛳ Mansion built in 1875 in the style of a 16thC French castle. £80. Rest. ♦ ♪ £20.

Recommended
Farmhouse: at Hanbury, *Little Lodge Farm*, Broughton Green, ☎ (052 784) 305. £24 double; B. & B.

DUDLEY*

Wolverhampton, 6; Birmingham, 10; London, 116 m
pop. 187,228 ☎ 0384 West Midlands B2

▶ **Dudley Castle** crowning a hill has Norman keep; from top, extensive **views** over industrial landscape; 14thC gatehouse and parts of curtain wall. ▶ Incorporating parts of the castle ruins, **Dudley Zoo:** large range of species, some housed in buildings designed by Messrs. Tecton, responsible for London Zoo (*daily 10-dusk*). ▶ **Dudley Museum and Art Gallery:** fossils from surrounding area; Oriental art and ceramics; Brooke Robinson Collection of 17th-19thC's paintings. (*Tue.-Fri. 10-5*). ▶ **Black Country Museum** (Tipton Road): open-air museum devoted to rich industrial heritage of area; operating tramway and authentic trams; reconstructed turn-of-century street with hardware shop, chemist, pub (selling local ale), workers' cottages; Dudley Canal flows through museum; trips on narrow boats through Dudley Canal Tunnel (longest navigable canal tunnel in Britain); nail-making, chain-making and other local industries of recent past regularly demonstrated (*Apr.-Dec.: daily*).

Nearby

▶ **The Wren's Nest** (*41m NW*) is a National Nature Reserve; particularly interesting geology. □

Practical information

DUDLEY
ℹ 39 Churchill Precinct, ☎ 50333.
🚆 Sandwell Dudley, ☎ Birmingham (021) 643 2711.

Hotels:
★★ ***Station***, Castle Hill, DY1 4RA, ☎ (0384) 53418, AC AM BA, 29 rm. Ⓟ ♿ £36. Rest. ♦ ♪ ♿ Cl. Christmas. £9.
★ ***Ward Arms***, Birmingham Road, DY1 4RN, ☎ (0384) 52723, AC AM BA, 12 rm. Ⓟ £30. Rest. ♦ ♪ ♿ £5.

Recommended
Golf course: Himley Hall Park, ☎ (0902) 895207.

Nearby

OLDBURY, 3m E on A457

Restaurant:
● ♦ ***Jonathan's***, 16 Wolverhampton Road, Quinton, ☎ 021-429 3757, AC AM BA DI Ⓟ ♨ ♪ ✗ Cl. 26-27 Dec. Victorian dishes, Chipstead churdles. Book. £14.

In preparing for your trip, consult the pages pertaining to the regions. You will find there the description of the region you wish to visit, a brief history and practical information.

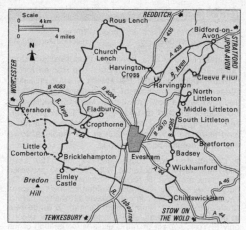

Vale of Evesham village

EVESHAM*

Worcester, 16; Oxford, 36; London, 99 m
pop. 15,069 ☎ 0386   Hereford & Worcester B2

The town takes its name from Eove, a swineherd who experienced a vision of Our Lady, prompting the foundation of an abbey in 714. It became a place of pilgrimage after the death of Simon de Montfort at the Battle of Evesham in 1265. Slain during a ferocious storm, this 'people's hero' was laid to rest beneath the Abbey's high altar. Evesham's modern prosperity derives from fruit growing and market gardening.

▶ Abbey is no more destroyed — during Dissolution. Fine **bell tower**★ survives, completed 1539. There are 13 bells; the carillon is heard every 3 hours. ▶ In the **Abbey Precinct** which stretches to river bank are two **churches**: All Saints and St. Lawrence. ▶ **Norman gateway** links Precinct with market place. ▶ **Almonry**, 14thC half-timbered, is now the information centre and museum (*Easter-Sep.: daily ex. Mon. & Wed.*). ▶ Round House, restored 15thC merchant's house, and town hall (1856) stand in **market place**. ▶ **Dresden House**: elegant Georgian house (1692) is in High Street.

Vale of Evesham Village Tour★

In spring the vale is clothed in blossom, with frequent glimpses of bullfinches growing fat on stolen buds from the apple and plum orchards. From spring to late autumn, stalls beside the road sell fresh produce from the fields and sometimes local pickles, preserves and brews of cider too.

▶ Take A44 W out of Evesham; after 3 $^1/_2$ m turn r. to **Cropthorne; church** has Norman features; black-and-white cottages overlook River Avon. ▶ Continue through village, then l., 1m to **Fladbury**★; **church** with Norman tower similar to Cropthorne; fine brasses within. 17thC **rectory, mill** by the lock used continuously from Domesday to 1930. ▶ Continue N, after 2m turn r., then l., and so N to **Rous Lench**: picturesque timbered **court**, village green. ▶ Turn SE again to **Church Lench** (1 $^1/_2$ m).▶ Continue on same twisting road to **Harvington Cross** and **Harvington** a little further on: charming 15th-16thC cottages. Turn l. towards Stratford (→), turning r. at **Bidford-on-Avon** (→ Alcester). r. again after 3/4m, turning sharply from the straight Roman route of **Ryknild Street** which lies ahead but is now the minor road. ▶ One mile to **Cleeve Prior**, its village green flanked by stone cottages; **church**

has Norman features. ▶ Detouring l. through **North Littleton, Middle Littleton**★ with beautiful composition of **church**, 17thC **manor house** and large **tithe barn** (*daily, 9-6*) then through **South Littleton**.▶ Under railway, turn l. to **Bretforton**★. Timber, thatch, brick and stone, here are all manner of cottages. The medieval **Fleece Inn** with its crooked black-and-white walls stands in square, still a functioning inn. **St. Leonard's church** of great interest; note also **Gothic Bretforton Hall**, Strawberry Hill. ▶ S to **Badsey**: part-Norman **church** and some fine houses. ▶ Continue S through **Wickhamford**: noteworthy church **interior**, adjacent picturesque **manor**.▶ Meet A44, turn l., then r. after 3/4m; 1m S to **Childswickham**; on the fringe of the vale, stone and timbered cottages, Badsey Brook, village green and **church**. ▶ Turning W traverse the vale, crossing A435, seeing **Bredon Hill**.▶ Continue 6 $^1/_2$ m to **Elmley Castle**★; no longer a castle, but many half-timbered houses and an interesting church. Footpath access to Bredon Hill. ▶ N through **Bricklehampton**, or NW through **Little Comberton** to meet A44 once more. From here l. to **Pershore** (→), or r. to return N to Evesham. ☐

Practical information ────────────

ℹ️ Almonry Museum, Abbey Gate, ☎ 6944.
🚌 ☎ Worcester (0905) 27211.

Hotels:
● ★★★ *Evesham*, Cooper's Lane, WR11 6DA, ☎ (0386) 49111, Tx 339342, AC AM BA DI, 34 rm. 🅿️ 🎠 🏊 £60. Rest. ● ◆ & Cl. 25-26 Dec. £12.50.
★★★ *Northwick Arms*, Waterside, WR11 6BT, ☎ (0386) 40322, AC AM BA, 25 rm. 🅿️ £43. Rest. ◆ ♪ £9.
★★ *Waterside*, 56 Waterside, WR11 6JZ, ☎ (0386) 2420, AC AM BA, 13 rm. 🅿️ £40. Rest. ◆ ♪ Cl. 24 Dec.-1 Jan. £8.50.

⚓ *Small Moors Hol. Park*, Anchor Lane, Harvington, (18 pl), ☎ 870446;*The Ranch C.P.*, Station Road, Honeybourne, (120 pl), ☎ (0386) 830744.

Recommended
Bed and breakfast: *Dayleen Guest House*, 16 Broadway Road, ☎ (0386) 6676. £25 double; B. & B.
Golf course: Craycombe Links, Fladbury, ☎ 860395.
Riding school: *Moyfield Riding School*, South Littleton, ☎ (0386) 830207, novice to experienced, full instruction.
♥ *The Basket Maker*, Main Street, South Littleton, ☎ (0386) 830504, traditional willow and cane baskets.

FOREST OF DEAN*

A3

This enchanting area of ancient deciduous forest is bounded on the S and E by the broadening Severn and by the Wye to the W. The traditional inhabitants - 'Foresters' - still adhere to certain rites and privileges set down in ancient times; their presence here and that of the Romans before them has lent the forest a distinct cultural history. Its natural history too is rich and varied, and the best way to discover this is to travel on foot, along a network of footpaths and marked trails.

▶ **Cinderford** is the largest town in the forest; evidence of ancient iron and coal workings, pretty 19thC church.▶ 2m S at **Soudley** is **Dean Heritage Museum Trust** (Camp Mill): the 'Free-Miners', charcoal burning and many of the forest's traditions explained and demonstrated. Also smallholding, craft workshops, picnic site, book and souvenir shops (*Apr.-Sep.: daily, 10-6; Nov.-Dec., 10-5*).▶ **Little Dean Hall** ($^1/_2$ m SE Cinderford): manor of Lords of Dene; oldest Saxon remnants can be seen in cellar; Roman temple excavated in grounds, also ancient forest trees in gardens (*Apr.-Oct.: daily, 2-6, Bank Hols., 11-6*). ▶ **Littledean** itself commands splendid views S across Severn; evidence of Roman roads that served mines; 14thC **Church of St. Ethelbert** with wagon roofs and interesting carvings in forest stone on churchyard grave-

stones. ▶ **Mitcheldean** (*3 1/2 m N Cinderford*): attractive northernmost village of forest with old mining connections; part 14th-15thC parish **church★**; nave has wagon roof with many bosses; roof in N aisle lavishly carved; 15thC wall painting of Last Judgment. ▶ 5m S Cinderford: **Blakeney**; village on SE borders of forest, set on a wooded slope with colour-washed houses; **views** over Severn Valley. ▶ At **Lydney** (*2 1/2 m SW Blakeney*), **Lydney Park** has wooded gardens with azaleas and other flowering shrubs; lake, daffodils and magnolias in April (*spring and early summer: Sun. & Wed., Bank Hols.*). ▶ 3/4m N Lydney: **Dean Forest Railway** (Norchard Steam Centre), the remaining 4m stretch of steam railway network that served whole forest; steam train rides, museum, gift shop, restaurant (*special steam open days: Sun., Jun.-Sep.; other days, check locally*). ▶ **Bream** (*2 1/2 m NW Lydney*): attractive little village of colour-washed houses; Roman scowles (mineworkings) can be seen in surrounding woodland. ▶ **Parkend** (*1 1/2 m N Bream*) is still an active coal-mining village inhabited by Free Miners, independent of nationalized industry. **Cannop Ponds** are just N of village. ▶ **St. Briavels★** (*3 1/2 m W Bream*): village gazing down over River Wye from elevated position; 13thC castle remains (now housing youth hostel) affording spectacular views across forest; **church** with good Norman and Early English features. ▶ **Clearwell Caves** at **Clearwell** (*2m N St. Briavels*): caverns where iron was mined in ancient times may be explored, also mining implements and geological exhibition, picnic area (*Mar.-Oct.: daily, 10-5*). ▶ **Clearwell Castle** is flamboyant 18thC Gothic. ▶ Traveling N, 1m S Coleford is **'Puzzle Wood'**: part of Lambsquay Wood with network of woodland paths around ancient iron working (*Easter - end. Oct.: 11-7., cl. Mon. ex. Bank Hols.*) ▶ **Coleford** is an attractive small town, again with a mining history. ▶ **English Bicknor** (*3m NE Coleford*): **Church of St. Mary** has fine Norman interior; nave has wagon roof, carved arcades and pier capitals, early 14thC stone effigies. 1/2m SW Coleford is **Newland**; its **church★** known as 'Cathedral of the Forest', owing to its grand proportions and 'close' of handsome houses. Spacious 13th - 14thC interior, 13th - 14thC monuments. In S chancel note **miner's brass**: figure of medieval miner wielding a pick and holding a candlestick in his mouth, surmounting a knight's helmet. ▶ **West Dean** in the heart of the forest is the site of 17thC **Speech House**, now an inn but still used for Forester's Court held 10 times per year. ▶ Adjacent picnic site is at beginning of **Speech House Trail**: marked path through ancient part of forest, some splendid old hollies among oaks. □

Practical information

FOREST OF DEAN

⛺ *Braceland Campsite*, Braceland Drive, Christchurch, Coleford, (750 pl), ☎ (0594) 33376.

Recommended
Cycle rental: at Christchurch, Christchurch Camp Site, nr. Coleford, ☎ (0594) 34882.

Nearby

CLEARWELL, 6m SW of Cinderford off B4231

Hotel:
★★ ***Wyndham Arms***, GL16 8JT, ☎ Dean (0594) 33666, AC, 5 rm. Ⓟ ♨ ⛰ £53. Rest. ♦ ♿ Cl. 25-26 Dec. £14.50.

COLEFORD, 4m W of Cinderford on B4226

Hotels:
★ ***Speech House*** (T.F.), GL16 7EL, ☎ Dean (0594) 22607, AC AM BA DI, 13 rm. Ⓟ ❀ ♨ ⛰ Historic hotel, originally built in 1676 as a court house. £60. Rest. ♦ ♿ £10.
★ ***Bell's Club***, Lords Hill, GL16 8BD, ☎ Dean (0594) 32583, AC BA, 32 rm. Ⓟ ♨ ⛰ ♿ ↗ ⛳ £32. Rest. ♦ ♪ ♿ Cl. Christmas. £7.50.

GLOUCESTER★★

Tewkesbury, 11; Bristol, 38; London, 109 m
pop. 106,526 ☎ 0452 Gloucestershire A3

Gloucester today is a thriving commercial city and, rather surprisingly, an inland port. The Roman fort of *Glevum* which guarded the lowest Severn crossing; Gleawcester in the time of Alfred the Great, a fortified town with its own royal mint. Here too William the Conqueror elected to undertake the Domesday survey. During the Civil War the city held out against a long siege by Royalists. Much of the medieval town was later demolished in revenge.

▶ **Cathedral★★** was consecrated 15 July 1100. Lofty mid-15thC **tower** is crowned with pinnacles, patterned with blank arcading. ▶ **Nave** is dominated, like Tewkesbury Abbey (→), by enormous Norman columns; graceful vaulting of 1242, N aisle only retains rib-vaulted ceiling. **Choir** built 1337-77, Norman crypt beneath. **E window★★** at time of building was largest in the world, now second only to York; subject of 14thC glass is Coronation of the Virgin; heraldic devices of families who fought at Crécy (1346) also shown. **Lady Chapel** finished 1500; two fan-vaulted **chantry chapels**. ▶ In N ambulatory **tomb★★** of Edward II: effigy of Purbeck marble, canopy of fine Painswick limestone wonderfully carved, the king's head borne up by angels. **Chapter house** retains Norman barrel roof. **Cloisters★★** exquisitely fan-vaulted; E walk earliest, 1351-77, and model for St. George's Chapel, Windsor. Off S walk is **library,** 14thC: beautiful roof, 10thC manuscripts. ▶ Adjoining cathedral is a **brass rubbing centre:** materials provided, replicas of cathedral brasses (*Jul.-Aug: Mon.-Sat., 10-5, Sun., 2-5*). ▶ **Blackfriars** (Ladybellgate Street): remains of Dominican friary founded 1239 (*Apr.-Sep.: Mon.-Sat., 9.30-6.30, Sun. 2-6.30*). ▶ **Gloucester City East Gate** (Eastgate Street): Roman and medieval defensive gates, underground exhibition chamber (*May-Sep.: Wed. & Fri., 2-5, Sat. 10-12, 2-5*). ▶ **Museum and art gallery** (Brunswick Road): changing art exhibitions; freshwater aquarium and beehive, Roman mosaics and sculpture, English landscape painting and antique furniture (*Mon.-Sat., 10-5, cl. Bank Hols.*). ▶ **House of the Tailor of Gloucester**: the authentic house now selling Beatrix Potter books and trinkets; exhibition of manuscripts of her books and miniature working models of her characters. (*Mon.-Sat.: 9.30-5.30*). ▶ **Gloucester Regimental Museum** (Commercial Road) (*Mon.-Fri.: 10-5*). ▶ **Gloucester Docks:** attractively restored area; 19thC warehouses, tours given. ▶ **Robert Opie Collections★** (Albert Warehouse): museum devoted to history of consumerism: 'The Pack-Age'; vast array of bottles, packets, boxes and tins from Victorian to present (*Tue.-Sun.: 10-6, open Bank Hols.*). ▶ **Gloucester Antique Centre,** another restored warehouse with large collection of antiques presented in Victorian-style arcade (*Mon.-Fri.: 9-5; Sat.: 9-4.30; Sun.: 1-4.30*).

Nearby

▶ **Prinknash Abbey★** (*4m SE*): 14th - 16thC Benedictine monastery and new building in parkland; monks make and sell Prinknash pottery characterized by pewter-like lustrous glaze. In grounds: Prinknash Bird Park; also otters and pets corner. ▶ Near **Great Witcombe** (*6m E*) is **Crickley Hill** Country Park: beechwood, views, site of neolithic and Iron Age forts, nature trails (*all year*). ▶ In Great Witcombe: **Roman villa**; courtyard type (*any reasonable time, key available at bottom of drive to villa*). ▶ **Ashleworth tithe barn** (*6m N*): late 15thC limestone barn, stone slate roof and great supporting timbers (*daily: 9-6 or dusk*). ▶ **Elmore Court** (*4m SW*): 16thC house with Georgian wing; fine Elizabethan staircase (*first Sun. in month May-Sep.*). ▶ **Westbury Court Garden** (*9m SW*): formal Dutch water garden laid out 1696-1705 (*Easter Sat.-Oct.: Wed.-Sun. & Bank Hol. Mon., 11-6*). ▶ Westbury-on-Severn also has interesting parish **church:** 13thC detached tower and 14thC spire with wooden shingles.

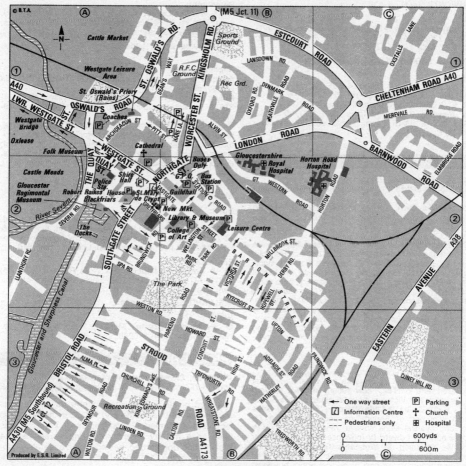

GLOUCESTER

▶ **Frampton Court** (*near Frampton- on-Severn, 7m SW*): Georgian house with fine interior; botanical paintings from 'Frampton Flora' gardens with orangery and 17thC dovecote (*by appt.* ☎ 0452 740267). □

Practical information

GLOUCESTER
ℹ️ St. Michael's Tower, The Cross (A2), ☎ 421188.
🚂 (B2), ☎ 29501.
🚌 (B2), ☎ 29030.
Car rental: Europcar, Watts Truck Centre Ltd., Mercia Road, ☎ 28248 (rail/drive).

Hotel:
★★ *Fleece*, 19 Westgate Street, GL1 2NR (A1-2), ☎ (0452) 22762, AC BA, 40 rm. Ⓟ & £35. Rest. ♦ ⅃ & £5.

Restaurant:
♦ *College Green*, 7-11 College Street (B2), ☎ (0452) 20739, AC AM. Cl. Mon. eve., Tue.-Sun., Bank Hols. £12.

Recommended
Craft workshops: *Colin Squire and Janice Williams*, Sheldon Cottage, The Bottoms, ☎ (0452) 740639, hand-woven rugs, decorative hangings, embroidered articles. *Dean Heritage Museum Trust*, Camp Hill, Soudley, ☎ (0594) 22170, pottery, engraved glass, pokerwork, leather goods, knitwear.
Delicatessen: at 1m W of city on N side of A40, *Over Farm Market*, Over, ☎ (0452) 21014, wide range of local produce, wholefoods, herbs etc.
Factory showroom: at Cranham, 6m NE of Stroud off A46, *Prinknash Pottery*, Prinknash Abbey, ☎ (90452) 812239, numerous patterns and decorative motif pottery.
Farmhouse: at Tirley, *Tow Street Farm*, ☎ (045 278) 442. £20 double; B. & B.
Golf course: Gloucester Golf & Country Club, Matson Lane, ☎ 25653.

Nearby

BARNWOOD, 1m E

Hotel:
★★★ *Crest* (Crest), Crest Way, GL4 7RX, ☎ (0452) 613311, Tx 437273, AC AM BA DI, 100 rm. Ⓟ ⚡ & ⅃ £97. Rest. ♦ ⅃ & £12.

TWIGWORTH, 1m N on A38

Hotel:
★★ *Twigworth Lodge*, A38 Tewkesbury Road, GL2 9PG, ☎ (0452) 730266, AC AM BA DI, 12 rm. P ▩ ♤ ▭ £40. Rest. ◆ ♪ ♿ £9.

UPTON ST. LEONARDS, 4m on B4073

Hotels:
★★ *Tara* (B.W.), Upton Hill, GL4 8DE, ☎ (0452) 67412, Tx 449848, AC AM BA DI, 24 rm. P ⁂ ▩ ♤ ⌁ ▭ £60. Rest. ◆ ♪ Chicken and broccoli terrine. £13.
★★★ *Bowden*, Bond End Lane, GL4 8ED, ☎ (0452) 614121, AC AM BA DI, 24 rm. P ⁂ ▩ ♤ £48. Rest. ◆ ♪ Cl. 25-26 Dec. £8.

GREAT MALVERN*

Worcester, 8; Hereford, 22; London, 126 m
pop. 30,153 ☎ 068 45   Hereford & Worcester A2

A former spa town, spruce Victorian colour-washed houses sit against the rising hills looking over the Vale of Evesham.

▶ The splendid, ornate tower of the **priory church**★ is a principal feature of Malvern. Founded 11thC as a Benedictine priory, piers and arches of **nave** are Norman, incorporated into 15thC remodeling. Screen walls of chancel are covered with **tiles** made in the monastery, here mid - 15thC with over 100 different patterns. Oak **choir stalls** have carved **misericords** depicting labours of the months; superb 15thC **stained glass**★, **clerestory** and **E and W windows**. ▶ **Gatehouse** is all that survives of monastery. ▶ **St. Anne's Well**, on hillside above town: the spring water 'famous for containing nothing at all' may be tasted here.

Nearby

▶ **Malvern Wells** (*2m S*): the pure spa waters were first discovered here in 17thC; now suburb of Great Malvern with Regency and Victorian houses; **church** has a S window by Burne-Jones. ▶ **Little Malvern** (*3/4m W*): **St. Giles Church** was part of Benedictine priory founded 1171; tower and chancel alone survive, rest is late 15thC. W window portrays Edward IV (now headless) and Eleanor Woodville his queen. **St. Wulstan's Church** is where the composer Elgar and his family are buried. ▶ **Little Malvern Court** incorporates part of original priory buildings, but mainly 15thC. Used as a hideout during years of Catholic persecution; concealed rooms, staircases (*mid-Apr. - mid-Jul.: Wed. & Thu., 2.30-5*). ▶ **West Malvern** (*3/4m W*), reached through rocky gap in the hills, superb views over wooded, rolling landscape of Herefordshire.   □

Practical information

GREAT MALVERN
ℹ Winter Gardens, Grange Road, ☎ 892289.
🚃 Great Malvern and Malvern Link, ☎ Worcester (0905) 272 11.

Hotels:
★★★ *Foley Arms* (Best Western), 14 Worcester Road, WR14 4QS, ☎ (068 45) 3397, Tx 437269, AC AM BA DI, 26 rm. P ▩ £54. Rest. ◆ Cl. 25-29 Dec. £9.
● ★★ *Cotford*, 51 Graham Road, WR14 2JW, ☎ (068 45) 2427, AC BA, 14 rm. P ⁂ ▩ ♤ £38. Rest. ◆ ♪ Cl. 25 - 26 Dec. £10.
★★ *Essington*, Hollywell Road, WR14 4LQ, ☎ (068 45) 61177, AC BA, 10 rm. P ⁂ ▩ ♤ £44. Rest. ◆ £12.
★★ *Mount Pleasant*, Belle Vue Terrace, WR14 4PZ, ☎ (068 45) 61837, AC AM BA DI, 14 rm. P ⁂ ▩ ⌁ No children under 8. £50. Rest. ◆ ♪ Cl. 24-26 Dec. £12.
★ *Bredon*, 34 Worcester Road, WR14 4AA, ☎ (068 45) 5323, AC AM BA, 9 rm. P ⁂ £40.
★ *Malvern Hills*, British Camp, Wynds Point, WR13 6TW, ☎ Colwall (0684) 40237, AC AM DI, 13 rm. P ▩ £40. Rest. ◆ £9.50.

Restaurant:
● ◆ *Walmer Lodge*, 49 Abbey Road, ☎ (068 45) 4139, 8 rm. P ⁂ ▩ ♤ ⌁ No children under 14. Cl. Christmas, Sun. Salmon, crab and shrimp soup. Book. £12.50.

⚓ *Riverside C. P.*, Little Clevelode, (75 pl), ☎ (0684) 310475.

Recommended
Antique shop: *Lewis, Gerald*, Brooks House, Stiffords Bridge, clocks and furniture.
Riding school: *Avenue Riding Centre*, Welland, ☎ (0684) 310731, novice to experienced, western style riding available.
♥ *Boehm of Malvern England Ltd.*, Tanhouse Lane, ☎ (0886) 32111, elegant Boehm porcelain, wooden sculptures of animals; *Midsummer Weavers*, The Old School, Henley Castle, ☎ (0684) 310045, hand-woven fabrics, domestic looms and other local crafts.

Nearby

MALVERN WELLS, 3m S on A449

Hotel:
● ★★ *Cottage in the Wood* (Consort), Holywell Road, WR14 4LG, ☎ (068 45) 3487, AC BA, 20 rm. P ⁂ ▩ ♤ ♿ ⌁ Georgian Dower house surrounded by 7 acres of woodland. £90. Rest. ◆ Cl. 23-28 Dec. Local salmon. £16.

Restaurant:
● ◆ *Croque-en-Bouche*, 211 Wells Road, ☎ (068 45) 65612, AC ⁂ ⌁ Cl. Sun.-Tue., lunch. Medallions of venison. Book. £20.

WELLAND, 4m S on B4208

Hotel:
● ★★ *Holdfast Cottage*, Marlbank Road, WR13 6NA, ☎ Hanley Swan (0684) 310288, 9 rm. P ♤ £45.

HEREFORD**

Worcester, 25; Abergavenny, 24; London, 139m
pop. 48,277 ☎ 0432   Hereford & Worcester A2

Hereford is still an important centre for the famous red-and-white beef cattle and for cider. Its history is long and embattled; Saxon capital of West Mercia, used as a military base by the English against the Welsh, then bombarded, besieged and eventually captured during the Civil War. Today Hereford is an agricultural town with a placid air, set in lovely countryside.

▶ **Cathedral**★ bears marks of its troubled past. Oldest remaining parts are Norman, but it was founded by Saxon King Offa (→ Offa's Dyke). Norman **nave** is intact, with its great circular piers; delightful 13thC **Lady Chapel**, with cathedral's oldest **stained glass** in SW window. ▶ Two chantry chapels: **Audley Chapel** (note painted screen) and **Bishop Stanbury's Chapel**. Fine **misericords** in chancel; carved figures include a mermaid, a griffin and a goat apparently playing a lute. ▶ Above E aisle is the **Mappa Mundi**★: remarkable world map drawn on vellum in 1280. **Chained library**★★ contains 1,400 books and 227 manuscripts. ▶ **City museum and art gallery** (Broad Street): local natural history including 'live' beekeeping display; geology and archaeology; gallery: porcelain, silver, glass; 19thC watercolours and local artists (*Tue., Wed. & Fri.: 10-6; Thu. 10-5; Sat. (summer): 10-5; Sat. (winter): 10-4*). ▶ **Museum of Cider** (Pomona Place): great wooden presses, regular displays by a cooper and 'King Offa Distillery', history and craft of cider-making explained (*Jun.-Sep.: 10-5 daily; cl. Tue. in Apr., May-Oct.; Nov.-Mar., pre-booked parties only*). ▶ **Old House** (High Town): Jacobean house furnished in 17thC manner throughout (*Mon.: 10-1, Tue.-Fri.: 10-1, 2-5.; Sat.: 10-1, 2-5.30; winter Sat.: 10-1*). ▶ **All Saints** (High Street): late 13th - early 14thC church with canopied **choir stalls**, **misericords**; excellent **chained library** of 300 volumes in S chapel; Hereford claims two of only seven such libraries

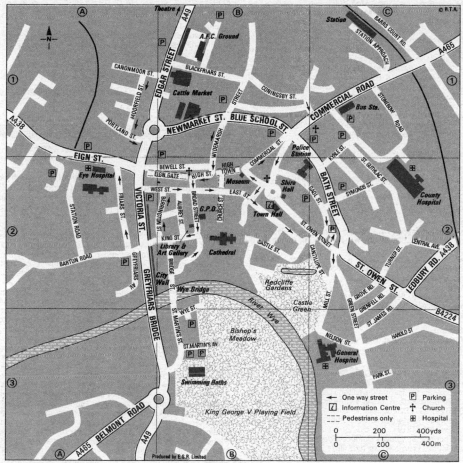

HEREFORD

in England. ▶ **Churchill Gardens Museum** (Venns Lane): 'Roaring Meg', the cannon that destroyed Goodrich Castle is here, as are fine collections of 18th and 19thC costume and furniture, also Victorian nursery, butler's pantry and parlour. Exhibition of work by Brian Hatton, local artist killed in WWII (*summer: Tue.-Sun., 2-5.; winter: Tue.-Sat., 2-5*). ▶ **St. John Coningsby Chapel and Museum** (Widemarsh Street): former hospice founded by Sir Thomas Coningsby in 1614, now restored as medieval museum; history of Order of St. John of Jerusalem and the Coningsby Pensioners (*Easter-Oct.: daily, 2-5 ex. Mon. & Fri.*). ▶ Adjacent ruins of **Blackfriars**, now in **Blackfriars' Gardens** with England's only surviving example of 14thC **preaching cross** (*daily*). ▶ **Bulmer Railway Centre** (Whitecross Road): home of GWR steam locomotive 'King George IV' and other restored engines, including Bulmer Cider Train (*wkends Apr.-Sep.; occasional steam open days*). ▶ **Wye Bridge** (*S of town*) spans the river in imposing style. Built 1490 it has 6 arches. Though often wrecked and repaired, 4 arches are original. ▶ Fragments of 13thC **city walls** in Victoria Street and West Street.

Nearby

▶ **Herefordshire Waterworks Museum** (Ledbury Road, town outskirts) houses Broomy Hill engines: magnificent steam pumping engines in Victorian pumping house (*daily: 2-5.; regular working exhibits in summer, daily mid-Jul. - end Aug.*). ▶ **Kilpeck** (*9m SW*) has one of the finest small Norman **churches★** in England, its rich strange decoration excellently preserved; **S doorway** is carved with Tree of Life, dragons, birds, a phoenix and an angel; many bizarre or delightful decorative figures on exterior. Inside, two chancel arches richly carved in different style. Note unusual **W windows** and **holy water stoup.** ▶ **Kentchurch Court** (*14 m SW*): 14thC fortified manor rebuilt by Nash in late 18thC; gateway and NW tower surviving medieval portions (*May-Sep.: daily*). ▶ **Abbey Dore** (*13m SW*): **St. Mary's**, formerly Cistercian Dore Abbey; founded 1137, destroyed at the Dissolution, restored as parish church by John Abelin 17thC; 13thC **clerestory** and **tiles** in chancel, 17thC **glass** and **carved oak screen.** ▶ **Abbey Dore Court Garden★**: delightful river, herb, walled and rock gardens (*mid-Mar. - end Oct.: daily, 10.30-6.30*). ▶ **Brobury Garden and Gallery** (*11 m W*): terraced and rock gardens on banks of River Wye. 19th and 20thC watercolours in

house (*garden, Jun.-Sep.: Mon.-Sat., 9-4.30; gallery, all year: Mon.-Sat., 9-4.30*). ▶ **Moccas Court** (*13m W*), standing in parkland near Wye; designed by Adam, in 1775. Classical brick house with fine interior, gardens, picnicking (*Apr.-Sep.: Thu. 2-6*). In park is beautiful Norman church of St. Michael. ▶ At Swainshill (*5m W*) is **The Weir**, garden known for spring displays; views over Wye and into Wales (*Easter-early May: daily ex. Sat., 2-6; mid-May - end Oct.: Wed. & Bank Hol. Mon., 2-6*). ▶ **Dinmore Manor** (*6 m N*) has 14thC chapel and cloisters; gardens with 1930s water garden and grotto (*daily*). ▶ Abbey Dore lies towards S end of **Golden Valley**, an area of beautiful wooded, hilly countryside. To W rise **Black Mountains** (→); a little river follows valley, running beside several villages including **Eywas Harold** and **Bacton**.　☐

Practical information ―――――――――――

HEREFORD
ℹ️ Shire hall, 1A St. Owen Street (B2), ☎ 268430.
🚌 (C1), ☎ 56201.
Car rental: Europcar, RF Brown Son Ltd., Whitecross Road, ☎ 275720.

Hotels:
★★★ **Green Dragon** (T.F.), Broad Street, HR4 9BG (B2), ☎ (0432) 272506, Tx 35491, AC AM BA DI, 88 rm. 🅿 & £60. Rest. ♦ & £11.50.
★★★ **Hereford Moat House** (Queens Moat), Belmont Road, HR2 7BP (A3), ☎ (0432) 54301, AC AM BA DI, 32 rm. 🅿 ⁂ & ⌿ £55. Rest. ♦ ⁑ & Cl. lunch Sat., 26-30 Dec. £9.
★★ **Graftonbury**, Grafton Lane, Hereford, HR2 8BN (B3 off map), ☎ (0432) 56411, AC AM BA DI, 41 rm. 🅿 ∈ ⁂ ⌕ & ◫ ⌿ £37. Rest. ♦ ⁑ Local salmon. £9.

Restaurant:
♦ **Effy's**, 96 East Street (B2), ☎ (0432) 59754, AC AM DI. Cl. Sun., Bank Hols.

Recommended
Craft workshop: *Baobab*, The Cots, Westhope, Canon Pyon, ☎ (043 271) 204, furniture and other woodworks.
Farmhouses: at Tarrington,Wilton Oaks, ☎ (0432 79) 212. £20 double; B. & B.; at Wormbridge, *Duffryn Farm*, ☎ (098121) 217. £20 double; B. & B.
Golf course: Herefordshire Golf Club, Ravens Causeway, Wormsley, ☎ 71219.
Riding school: *Longtown Outdoor Education Centre*, The Court House, Longtown, ☎ (087 387) 225.
♥ *Hereford Cider Museum*, Cider Mills, Ryelands Street, ☎ (0432) 54207, this museum is a showcase for cider and cider makers. *Craft Inn*, at Peterchurch, High Street, ☎ (098 16) 651, this workshop has dried and pressed flower pictures.

Nearby

FOWNHOPE, 3m SE on B4224

Hotel:
★★ **Green Man**, HR1 4PE, ☎ (043 277) 243, 12 rm. 🅿 ∈ ⁂ Half-timbered 15thC inn situated in the Wye Valley. £31. Rest. ♦ ⁑ £9.

Inn or Pub:
Forge Ferry, Ferry Lane, ☎ (0432) 77391 🅿 ∈ ⁂ ⌕ & Home-made dishes. £5.50.

Recommended
Guesthouse: *The Bowens Farmhouse*, ☎ (043 277) 430. £30 double; B. & B.

LUGWARDINE, 2m E on A438

Hotel:
★ **Longworth Hall**, HR1 4DF, ☎ (0432) 850223, Tx 8955503, AC BA, 16 rm. 🅿 ∈ ⁂ ⌕ & £40. Rest. ♦ & £10.50.

MUCH BIRCH, 6m S on A49

Hotel:
★★ **Pilgrim** (Inter Hotel), HR2 8HJ, ☎ Golden Valley

(0981) 540742, AC AM BA DI, 19 rm. 🅿 ∈ ⁂ ⌕ & ⌀ £65. Rest. ♦ & Cl. 29 Dec.-6 Jan. Wye salmon. £13.

Recommended
Crafts workshop: *Cottage Clocks*, Bryn Garth Cottage, Much Birch, ☎ (0981) 540419, attractive wall-clocks in a variety of wood and handpainted.

STRETTON SUGWAS, 3m NW on A480

Hotel:
★ **Priory**, HR4 7AR, ☎ Hereford (0432) 760264, AC BA, 8 rm. 🅿 ⁂ £14.

IRONBRIDGE**

Shrewsbury, 16; Birmingham, 26; London, 156 m
pop. 2,477 ☎ 095 245　　　　　　Shropshire A1

Now given over to a superb **working museum★** of industrial heritage (while it, with neighbour **Coalbrookdale**, is still living and working), Ironbridge in its dramatic gorge setting is one of the touchstones of English history and industrial development.

▶ Central and symbolic feature is the **Iron Bridge★**. This elegant structure was the first of its kind in the world, cast 1779. ▶ Inside **tollhouse** is information centre, shop and exhibition telling how bridge came to be built. ▶ Within walking distance and clearly signposted is **Severn Warehouse**: restored 1840s warehouse and wharf; audio-visual program and exhibition on Ironbridge Gorge. ▶ **Coalbrookdale Museum of Iron** and the **Old Furnace**: show production techniques and uses of iron from earliest times; also Abraham Darby's pioneering blast furnace that enabled iron ore to be smelted using coke. ▶ In **long warehouse** adjacent is **Elton Gallery**: fascinating collection of paintings, tickets, timetables relating to steam trains and railways; changing exhibitions on art of Industrial Revolution. ▶ Turning r. from bridge: **Bedlam Furnaces**, constructed 1757, painted by Philip de Loutherbourg in 1801. ▶ **Jackfield Works and Tile Museum**: in late 19thC these were two of world's largest decorative tileworks; beautiful tiles displayed, 1850s - 1960s. ▶ **Coalport China Works Museum**: restored as museum with workshops and kilns; historic china displayed, modern Coalport for sale. ▶ Above the works: **Hay Inclined Plane** at top of **Tar Tunnel** (*summer*); plane was ingenious method for hauling boats from Severn to Coalport Canal. ▶ **Blists Hill Open-Air Museum**: houses, shops, pub, steam locomotive, foundry, candle factory, all faithfully restored to show what daily working life was like here in late 19thC (*daily: 10-6 in summer, 5 in winter*).☐

Practical information ―――――――――――

ℹ️ Iron Bridge Tollhouse, Telford, ☎ (0952) 882753.

Hotel:
★ **Tontine**, The Square, TF8 7AL, ☎ (095 245) 2127, AC BA, 11 rm. 🅿 £28. Rest. ♦ ⁑ & £8.50.

Inn or Pub:
Shakespeare (Wellington), High Street, Coalport, Telford, ☎ (0592) 580675 🅿 ∈ ⁂ ⌕ & ✂ Range of hot and cold food. £3.

Recommended
Farmhouse: at Shifnal, Suttonhill Farm, ☎ Norton (095 271) 217. £20 double; B. & B.

KENILWORTH*

Coventry, 5; Warwick, 5; London, 103 m
pop. 18,782 ☎ 0926　　　　　　Warwickshire B2

This site was settled in ancient times and its fortunes grew along with its great **castle** and **abbey**. The abbey was abandoned during the Dissolution, the castle dismantled after the Civil War.

▶ **Castle**★ is now a splendid ruin. Founded 1112 as a wooden Norman fortress, extended and enriched into great Tudor castle where Elizabeth I was lavishly entertained by Robert Dudley. Remains of Norman **keep** with walls 20 ft. thick, **John of Gaunt's Chapel** and great hall, Robert Dudley's **gatehouse** and **stables** (*mid-Mar. - mid-Oct.: 9.30-6.30; mid-Oct. - mid-Mar.: 9.30-4; open Sun. Apr.-Sep.: 9.30, otherwise 2*). ▶ Scant remains of once wealthy **Abbey of St. Mary**: 14thC **abbey gatehouse** and **abbey barn.** ▶ **Little Virginia** is name reputedly given to these thatched almshouses by Sir Walter Raleigh on his return from New World; he is believed to have planted first potatoes in England here.

Nearby

▶ **Stoneleigh Abbey** (*3 m E*): originally a small Cistercian abbey founded 1155, extended and altered after Dissolution to huge Georgian residence. State rooms with rich plasterwork; **grounds** with miniature steam railway (*Sun. & Bank Hols.*), ponds, woodland, picnicking (*Easter Sun.-end Sep.: Sun., Mon. & Thu.; grounds, 11.30 - 5.30; house, 1-5.30*). ▶ **Stoneleigh** itself has 16thC **almshouses** and fine Norman parish **church.** ▶ **Baddesley Chilton** (*7m W*); 14thC moated manor, Queen Anne bridge, Georgian stables, 120-acre grounds. (*Easter - end Sep.: Wed.-Sun. Bank Hol. Mon., 2-6; Oct: Sat. Sun., 2-6*). □

Practical information

KENILWORTH

ⓘ library, 11 Smalley Place, ☎ 52595.

Hotels:

★★★ ***De Montfort*** (De Vere), The Square, CV8 1ED, ☎ (0926) 55944, Tx 311012, AC AM BA DI, 96 rm. 🄿 £80. Rest. ♦ ♪ Cl. lunch Sat. Kebab of lamb. £11.

★★★ ***Kenilworth Moat Hse*** (Queens Moat), Chesford Bridge, CV8 2LN, ☎ (0926) 58331, AC AM BA DI, 48 rm. 🄿 ♿ £56. Rest. ♦ ♪ ♿ £11.

Restaurants:

● ♦ ***Diments***, 121-123 Warwick Road, ☎ (0926) 53763, AC AM BA DI 🄿 ♪ ✈ Cl. 3 wks. Aug., Sun.-Mon., Sat. lunch. *Magret de canard aux baies de cassis*. Book. £13.50.

● ♦ ***Restaurant Bosquet***, 97A Warwick Road, ☎ (0926) 52463, AC AM ✈ Cl. 1st wk. Aug., last 2 wks. Jul., Sun.-Mon. French cuisine. Book. £13.

♦ ***Ana's Bistro***, 121-123 Warwick Road, ☎ (0926) 53763, AM AC DI 🄿 Cl. Sun., Mon., 1 wk Easter, first 3wks. Aug., Bank Hols. £9.

♦ ***Ristorante Portofino***, 14 Talisman Square, ☎ (0926) 57186, AC AM BA DI 🄿 ♪ ✈ Cl. Sun. Book. £8.

♦ ***Romano's***, 60 Waverley Road, ☎ (0926) 57473, AC BA 🄿 ♪ ✈ Cl. Sun., Aug. Home-made cannelloni and lasagne. Book. £15.

Recommended

Cycle rental: *Mike Vaughan*, 3 High Street.
Farmhouse: at Meer end, *Malt House Farm*, Meer End Road, ☎ (0676) 33490. £19 double; B. & B.
Golf course: Crew Lane (on A452), ☎ 54296.

Nearby

LEEK WOOTON, 3m S off A46

Hotel:

★★ ***Wootton Court***, CV35 7QU, ☎ Warwick (0926) 495196, AC AM BA DI, 13 rm. 🄿 ⚘ ♨ ♪ £34. Rest. ♦ Cl. Christmas. £6.

KINGTON*

Hereford, 21; Leominster, 13; London, 150m
pop. 2,067 ☎ 0544 Hereford & Worcester A2

A small but important sheep market town, lying at the foot of Hergest Ridge. Its proximity to the Welsh border, sense of remoteness and great age contribute to a luminous air reflected in the many mysterious tales connected with the area.

▶ **St. Mary's Church** above town: 13thC chancel, **tomb** with alabaster effigies of Thomas Vaughan (d. 1469) and his wife Ellen who earned name 'Gethin' (Terrible) by cunningly shooting an arrow through heart of her brother's murderer while taking part in an archery tournament. Her husband's ghost could only be laid to rest after having been lured into a snuff box, then tossed into Hergest Pool.

Nearby

▶ **Hergest Ridge** offers fine walking; views over **Radnor Hills** and **Forest** in Wales. ▶ **Offa's Dyke Path** passes over ridge; particularly good stretch on **Rushock Hill** and **Bradnop Wood** to N. ▶ **Cymmau Farmhouse** (*4m SW*): timber-framed, stone-tiled farmhouse of 17thC (*Bank Hols. in spring and summer; Sat., Sun. & Mon., 2-6; other times by appt.*). ▶ **Hergest Croft Gardens** (*1/2 m W*): 50 acres including kitchen and Edwardian gardens; wood with azaleas and rhododendrons (*end Apr. - Sep.: daily; Oct.: Sun., 1.30-6.30*). □

Practical information

KINGTON

ⓘ 2 Mill Street, ☎ 230202.

Recommended

Golf course: Bradnor Hill (off B4355), ☎ 230340.

Nearby

BREDWARDINE, 7m S on B4352

Hotel:

★★ ***Red Lion***, HR3 6BU, ☎ Moccas (098 17) 303, AC AM BA DI, 10 rm. 🄿 ♨ £45. Rest. ♦ ♪ Cl. Nov. - Mar. £12.

WHITNEY-ON-WYE, 8m S on A438

Restaurant:

● ♦ ***Rhydspence Inn***, ☎ Clifford (049 73) 262, AC AM BA, 6 rm. 🄿 ⚘ ♨ ♪ ✈ Rib of beef, jugged hare. Book. £9.

LEAMINGTON SPA*

Coventry, 8; Warwick, 2; London, 96 m
pop. 56,538 ☎ 0926 Warwickshire B2

The curative mineral waters, first discovered in 1586, are still used today in a modern treatment centre. The town's heyday as a spa was early - mid-19th century, reflected in Regency and Victorian crescents and terraces.

▶ **Royal Pump Room** bordering River Leam, Tuscan-built colonnade (1814) survives; the waters may be taken here. ▶ **Jephson Gardens** (opposite Pump Room): lakes, fountains, displays of spring and summer flowers. ▶ **Art gallery and museum**: porcelain; glass; modern paintings include works by Sutherland, Lowry, Spencer (*Mon.-Sat.*). ▶ Regency architecture in **Landsdowne Crescent, Landsdowne Circus** (Nathaniel Hawthorne lived at no.10); villas in **Newbold Terrace** thought to be by John Nash.

Nearby

▶ **Farnborough Hall** (*14m SE*): mid-18thC stone mansion with rococo detailing, plasterwork; **grounds** with terraced walk, series of lakes, 18thC temples, **views** over Edgehill (→) from terrace (*Apr.-end Sep.: Wed., Sat., May Bank Hols., Sun. & Mon., 2-6; terrace walk only: Thu., Fri. & Sun., 2-6*). ▶ **Marton** (*7m NE*), village with black-and-white thatched cottages and **Museum of Country Bygones:** farm implements and egg gender detector (*Easter-end Oct.: daily, 10-8*). □

Practical information ———————————

LEAMINGTON SPA

ⓘ Jephson Lodge, Jephson Gardens, The Parade, ☎ 311470.

▦ ☎ Rugby (0788) 60116.

Car rental: Avis, Leamington Spa Rail Station, Old Warwick Road, ☎ 28484 (rail/drive).

Hotels:

★★★ *Blackdown*, Sandy Lane, CV32 6RD, ☎ (0926) 24761, AC AM BA DI, 11 rm. ℗ ⫷ ▥ ⟃ £60. Rest. ♦ ⌡ ㅎ £14.

★★ *Abbacourt*, 40 Kenilworth Road, CV32 6JF, ☎ (0926) 311158, AC AM BA DI, 21 rm. ℗ ▥ ㅎ £52. Rest. ♦ ⌡ ㅎ £13.

★★ *Beech Lodge*, 28 Warwick New Road, CV32 5JJ, ☎ (0926) 22227, AC BA, 12 rm. ℗ No children under 4. £48. Rest. ♦ ⌡ ㅎ Cl. Christmas. £10.

Restaurant:

♦ *Rainbow Vegetarian Restaurant*, 9 Regent Place, ☎ (0926) 311056 ▥ ⟃ ⌡ ⫻ Cl. 15-22 Aug., Sun , Tue. and Wed eve. *Aubergine farcie*. Book. £7.

Recommended

Farmhouses: at Radford Semele, *Sharmer Farm*, Fosse Way, ☎ (0926) 612448. £19 double; B. & B.; at Hunningham, *R. L. Hancock*, Snowford Hall, ☎ (0926) 632297. £24 double; B. & B.

Golf course: Leamington Country, Golf Lane Whitnash, ☎ 25961.

Nearby

BISHOPS TACHBROOK, 2m S off A452

Hotel:

● ★★★ *Mallory Court* (R.C.), Harbury Lane, Tachbrook Mallory, CV33 9QB, ☎ Leamington Spa (0926) 30214, Tx 317294, AC AM BA, 9 rm. ℗ ⫷ ▥ ⟃ ⫻ Converted manor house in 10 acres of landscaped gardens. No children under 12. £105. Rest. ● ♦ Cl. 26 Dec. - 1 Jan. £32.

PRINCETHORPE, 8m NE on B4453

Hotel:

★★ *Woodhouse*, Leamington Road, CV23 9PZ, ☎ Marton (0926) 632303, AC AM DI, 22 rm. ℗ ⫷ ▥ ⟃ ▭ ⫻ £50. Rest. ♦ ⌡ ㅎ Cl. 25 - 26 Dec. £12.

LECHLADE*

Cirencester, 11; Oxford, 21; London, 77 m
☎ 0367　　　　　　　　　　　Gloucestershire B3

A pretty town on the E edge of Gloucestershire and the highest navigable point on the Thames, marked by 18thC Halfpenny Bridge.

▶ **St. Lawrences's Church**, 15thC 'wool' church: light, spacious interior; chancel roof with carved and painted bosses.

Nearby

▶ **Fairford** (*4m W*) has a splendid, late Perpendicular 'wool' **church★** known for 28 beautiful **windows** with untouched 15thC stained glass; woodwork is superb and rare in Gloucestershire.　　　　　　　　□

Practical information ———————————

Nearby

FAIRFORD, 4m W on A417

Hotel:

★★ *Hyperion*, London Street, GL7 4AH, ☎ Cirencester (0285) 712349, AC AM BA DI, 23 rm. ℗ ▥ ⫷ ㅎ £45. Rest. ♦ ⌡ ㅎ £12.

LEDBURY*

Hereford, 15; Gloucester, 16; London, 120m
pop. 4,985 ☎ 0531　　　　　Hereford & Worcester A2

A lovely town sheltered by the Malverns, it is surrounded by low hills, woodland, pasture and hopfields.

▶ In market place stands 17thC timbered **market hall**, held aloft on 16 stout timber columns. ▶ Leading from here to church is **Church Lane★**; narrow and cobbled, lined with timbered houses with overhanging upper storeys. ▶ **Church** is very fine: Norman remnants; detached bell-tower with 200 ft **spire**; 19thC **glass** by Kempe in **N Chapel**, which has excellent monument of 13thC priest at prayer; other fine **monuments** to local families. ▶ **High Street** has several inns, particularly **The Feather** with beautiful 16thC timbering. ▶ Surpassing even The Feathers; **Ledbury Park** at crossroads, built c. 1600. ▶ Facing market hall: **St. Katharine's Hospital**, named after local saint, founded 1232. ▶ **Old grammar school**, 1500, now Heritage Centre (*May-Oct.: daily*).

Nearby

▶ **Eastnor★** (*2m E*) has 19thC castle, surrounded by deer park with many rare trees; castle contains collection of paintings, tapestries, armour and furniture (*Sun. & Bank Hols. Mon. in spring & summer*). ▶ **Much Marcle** (*4m SW*) has two fine houses: Homme House, part 16thC with Georgian E front (*not open*), and Hellens; Jacobean manor incorporating 13thC building; **great hall** has stone table at which Edward, the Black Prince, once dined (*Easter-Oct.: Wed., Sat. & Sun., 2-6, or by appt.*).　　　　□

Practical information ———————————

LEDBURY

ⓘ St.Katherines, High Street, ☎ 2461.

▦ ☎ Hereford (0432) 266534.

Hotel:

★★ *Feathers*, High Street, HR8 1DS, ☎ (0531) 5266, AC AM DI, 11 rm. ℗ Famous old inn in the centre of town with an attractive half-timbered façade. £51. Rest. ♦ ⌡ £9.

Recommended

Craft workshops: *Collection*, 13 The Southend, ☎ (0531) 4641, pottery, basketry, jewelry, glassware, woodwork prints; *Ledbury Craft Centre*, 1 High Street, ☎ (0531) 4661, knitcraft, china-painting, patchwork; at Newent, 10m SW of Ledbury off M50, *Cowdy Glass Workshop*, Culver Street, ☎ (0531) 821173, handmade coloured glassware.

Nearby

BROOMSBERROW HEATH, 2m S off A417

Hotel:

★★ *Grove House*, HR8 1PE, ☎ Broomsberrow (053 181) 584, 3 rm. ℗ ▥ ⟃ ⫻ ⟁ £40. Rest. ♦ £13.50.

HOPE END, 3m N off A449

Hotel:

● ★ *Hope End*, HR8 1JQ, ☎ (0531) 3613, AC BA, 7 rm. ℗ ▥ ⟃ ⫻ No children under 4. £70. Rest. ● ♦ Cl. dinner Mon. - Tue. end Nov. - end Feb. £19.

LEEK*

Buxton, 13; Stoke-on-Trent, 10; London, 161 m
pop. 19,598 ☎ 0538　　　　　　　Staffordshire B1

This town belongs more to the North than the Midlands with its 19thC mills and houses of dark stone. It is small, relatively unspoiled and surrounded by inspiring moorland country.

▶ Many good civic and industrial buildings, including **Brindley Mill** (1752), a water-powered corn mill, restored to working order (*Mon. & Fri.-Bank Hols.; Jul. & Aug.: Mon., Tue. & Thu.*). ▶ **Nicholson Institute** contains library and art gallery (*Mon.-Wed. & Fri.: 10-7; Thu.-Sat.; 10-1*).

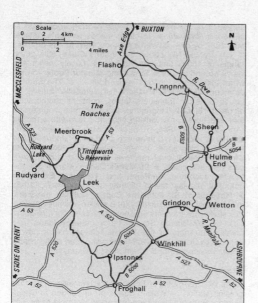

North Staffordshire moors

Nearby

▶ **Cheddleton** (*4 m S*) is perched on a hill, gazing down on the **River Churnet**. **Church of St. Edward** has fine Victorian decoration and stained glass by Morris, Burne-Jones, Madox Brown. ▶ **North Staffordshire Steam Railway Centre** based around picturesque station (*daily May-Sep.; Sun. & Bank Hols., 12-5*). ▶ **Cheddleton Flint Mill**, 1756-65, has twin water wheels that drive flint grinding-pans. Flints, brought here by canal from Kent and Sussex, were ground for use in ceramics industry in nearby Potteries (→). Collection of mill machinery, including model steam engine. ▶ **Ilam** (*13m SE*) sits in beautiful Manifold Valley (→). **Church**, ancient but restored, has a powerfully carved Norman font; also a sentimental but imposing monument to David Pike-Watts, leaning from his couch to bless his daughter and grandchildren. In churchyard are two Saxon crosses. ▶ **Ilam Hall Country Park**: 84 acres of wooded countryside. River Manifold re-appears here, having vanished underground at **Beeston Tor** (*4m N*); nature trail, picnicking (*Apr.-Oct.: daily, 10-6; Nov.-Mar.: Sat. & Sun., 10-5*).

North Staffordshire Moors

▶ Take A520 S from Leek, branching l. after 1 ¹/₂ m to **Ipstones**, village atop windswept moor. ▶ S to **Froghall** on the **River Churnet** and **Caldon Canal**; good picnic spot. ▶ N through hamlet of **Foxt**, crossing A523 to **Winkhill** and NE to **Grindon** on the high moors, visible far away by its narrow church spire. ▶ Down into the **Manifold Valley** and N to isolated **Wetton**; explore environs on foot. ▶ ¹/₂ m SW is **Thor's Cave**, inhabited in ancient times, overlooking river. N across B054 via **Hulme End** to **Sheen**, high on shoulder of Sheen Hill (1,247 ft.). ▶ Continue NW above river to **Longnor**, in **Dovedale**. Tiny market town, alone on moors: stone buildings, including market hall (1873). ▶ Continue N, then 2nd left W along **Dove Valley**, S on A53, then W to **Flash**, reputedly the highest village in England. 1 ¹/₂ m N is **Axe Edge** and border with Derbyshire. S on A53, passing **The Roaches** to the W, rocks like jagged teeth against the sky; highest is **Five Clouds** (1,500 ft.); **Hen Cloud** stands in isolation. Further on, also W are **Ramshaw Rocks**. ▶ Continue S to Leek or NW to

Meerbrook at head of **Tittesworth Reservoir**; NW 1 ¹/₂ m then dropping S to meet A523 before turning W to **Rudyard**, on a wooded valley side next to **Rudyard Lake**, where many water sports take place. ▶ SE to Leek, 2 ¹/₂ m. □

Practical information

LEEK
ⓘ market place, ☎ 399181.

Hotel:
★★ *Jester*, 81 Mill Street, ST13 8EU, ☎ (0538) 383997, 14 rm. Ⓟ £35. Rest. ♦ Cl. 26 - 27 Dec. £11.

Recommended
Craft workshop: Wesleyan House, Alstonefield, ☎ (033 527) 249, oak furniture.
Farmhouse: at Rudyard, *Fairboroughs Farm*, ☎ Rushton Spencer (02606) 341. £16 double; B. & B.
Golf course: Birchall (1/2m S on A520), ☎ 382226.
Riding school: *Moorlands Trail Riding*, The Mill, Winkhill, ☎ Waterhouse 638.

Nearby

ONECOTE, 5m E on B5053

Inn or Pub:
Jervis Arms, ☎ (0538) 206 Ⓟ ≋ ▥ ⚄ ✧ Home-cooked meats and steaks, vegetarian and children's meals. £3.

Recommended
Farmhouse: Pethill Bank, Bottonhouse, ☎ (05388) 555/27. £20 double: B. & B.

WATERHOUSES, 8m SE on A523

Restaurant:
● ♦ *Old Beams*, Leek Road, ☎ (053 86) 254, AC AM BA DI, 2 rm. Ⓟ ≋ ▥ ⚄ ✧ Cl. Sun.-Mon., 1st 2 wks. Jan., 1 wk. Oct. Rabbit stuffed with calf's sweetbreads and truffles. Book. £6.

LEOMINSTER*

Shrewsbury, 29; Hereford, 13; London, 142 m
pop. 8,637 ☎ 0568   Hereford & Worcester A2

Once reckoned to produce the finest wool in the world, 'Lemster Ore'. Leominster is a small agricultural town with lush surrounding countryside.

▶ **Old town hall**, now Grange Court: timber-framed, rich decorative carving. ▶ **Priory church** of St. Peter and St. Paul, established in Norman times on site of earlier Saxon church: unusual Norman features, particularly W doorway with wonderful carving and early pointed arch; N aisle contains ducking-stool. ▶ **Leominster and District Folk Museum** relates agricultural history of area; farming tools, traditional smocks (*Apr.-Oct.: daily; Nov.-Mar.: wkends only*).

Nearby

▶ **Weobly** (*8 ¹/₂ m SW*) abounds in black-and-white houses. ▶ **Eardisland** (*4m W*), village on the River Arrow, rich in timber-framed houses; note **Staick House** by bridge. ▶ **Burton Court**: 18thC house with 14thC great hall; displays of oriental costume and working model fairground (*Whitsun.-mid-Sep.: Wed., Thu., Sat., Sun. & Bank Hol. Mon., 2.30-6*). ▶ **Pembridge** (*4m W Eardisland*): village with early 16thC **market house**, interesting **church** with detached bell tower, notice great supporting timbers inside. ▶ **Croft Castle★** (*5m NW*): ancient Welsh border 'castle' (fortified house) with four corner towers. Interior exceptionally 18thC rococo. ▶ ¹/₂ m avenue of chestnuts. Access to **Croft Ambrey** Iron Age fort via footpath (*Easter wkend Apr.-Oct.: Sat. Sun., 2-5; May-Sep.: Wed.-Sun. & Bank Hol. Mon., 2-6*). ▶ **Berrington Hall★**(*3m N*): superb 18thC Neoclassical house by Henry Holland: exquisite ornamental plasterwork and painted ceilings, grand central staircase. Over 400 acres of parkland, work

of omnipresent Capability Brown (*open as Croft Castle; teas*). ▶ **Shobdon** (*9m W*): remarkable church, plain exterior belies astonishing Gothic interior; white, ornate, stucco-paneled, enormous pulpit. ▶ **Mortimer's Cross Mill** (*¹/₂ m NW*): 18thC watermill, designed to be operated by one man; used commercially until 1940s (*Apr.-Sep.: Thu. only, 12-5*). □

Practical information

LEOMINSTER
ⓘ School Lane, ☎ 2291/6460.
▰▰ ☎ Hereford (0432) 266534.

Hotels:
★★ **Talbot** (B.W.), West Street, HR6 8EP, ☎ (0568) 2121, AC AM BA DI, 30 rm. Ⓟ ⌘ £46. Rest. ◆ ♪ £13.
★ **Royal Oak**, South Street, HR6 8JA, ☎ (0568) 2610, AC AM BA DI, 17 rm. Ⓟ 18thC coaching inn whose fine Regency lounge has a minstrels' gallery. £42. Rest. ◆ £9.

Inn or Pub:
Royal Oak, South Street, ☎ (0568) 2610, 20 rm. Ⓟ ♿ Full à la carte menu. £4.50.

Recommended
Bed and breakfast: *Lopper Hall*, South Street, ☎ (0568) 611622. £24 double; B. & B.
Golf course: Ford Bridge (3m N on A49), ☎ 2863.
Riding school: *Meadow Bank Riding Stables*, Meadow Bank, Hamnish, ☎ (056 882) 267.
♥ *Kimmerton's Chocolatiers*, 22 Drapers Lane, ☎ (0568) 2746, hand-made chocolates, fudge, and ice cream. *Sloane Carpets*, Unit 5, Southern Avenue, ☎ (0568) 5863, hand-made rugs and carpet squares.

Nearby

STOKE PRIOR, 2m SE

Restaurant:
◆ **Wheelbarrow Castle**, ☎ Leominster (0568) 2219, AC AM BA, 3 rm. Ⓟ ♪ £14.

WEOBLEY, 8m SW off A4112

Hotel:
★★★ **Red Lion**, HR4 8SE, ☎ (0544) 318220, AC AM BA DI, 7 rm. Ⓟ 14thC half-timbered building situated in the centre of the village. £41. Rest. ◆ ♿ £14.

LICHFIELD**

Stafford, 17; Birmingham, 20; London, 124 m
pop. 25,408 ☎ 0543/05432   Staffordshire B1

St. Chad, early Bishop of Mercia, came to seek solitude in Lichfield when it was a remote and marshy settlement in the heavily wooded Midlands. He founded the city, and by 700 there was a shrine to him here. The cathedral, 'mother church' of the Midlands, still dominates this lovely town.

▶ **Cathedral**★ was restored 18th and 19thC after an embattled history. Under Henry VIII it lost shrine to St. Chad; besieged twice during Civil War, it lost a spire. It now has **3 towers** surmounted by spires, widely known as 'Ladies of the Vale'. The **W front**★ is sumptuous with row upon row of statues and arcades. **Nave** survives from 13thC. In **Lady Chapel**★, begun 1320, 16thC Flemish stained glass, brought here 1802. Among many **monuments** are busts of Samuel Johnson and David Garrick, by Westmacott (1793) in S transept; two eminent sons of Lichfield, Garrick learned Greek from Johnson when latter was schoolmaster here. Two monuments by Francis Chantrey: kneeling figure of Bishop Ryder in N chancel, tranquil 'Sleeping Children' in S chancel aisle. In N transept is Epstein's bust of Bishop Woods (1953). Note also brass and iron **pulpit** by Gilbert Scott. ▶ **Chapter house**, used as a library, is octagonal, with vaulted roof ascending from a central column; houses a very great treasure, the exquisite 8thC illuminated **Gospel of St. Chad**★, pre-

served here for over 1,000 years (*written application to cathedral librarian*). ▶ In **close** stands **bishop's palace**, built 1687 by one of Wren's masons. Next to it is **deanery** (1704). Behind NW corner lies **Vicar's Close**, little quadrangle of 16thC timbered houses. ▶ Lovely walks and views around and over **Stowe** and **Minster Pools,** formed when marshes or 'moggs' were drained. ▶ The **Samuel Johnson Birthplace Museum** (Breadmarket Street), in house built by Johnson's father, contains memorabilia of great 18thC lexicographer, including manuscripts, letters and books, his walking stick and favourite armchair (*Apr.-Oct.: Mon.-Sat., 10-5 or 4; May-Sep.: also Sun., 2.30-5*). In **Market Square** are statues of Johnson and friend and biographer James Boswell. ▶ **Guildhall** (Bore Street) is rebuilt over medieval dungeons; prison exercise yard still visible. ▶ **St. Mary's Centre** (Market Square) houses **Lichfield Heritage and Treasury Exhibition:** colourful display telling history of town (*daily, 10-5*). ▶ **Hospital of St. John the Baptist Outside the Bars**: immediately recognizable by its 8 ancient chimney stacks, this shelter for travelers was once Norman priory, re-opened 1495 by Bishop Smyth. Tudor gateway leads to a small quadrangle of fine houses; **chapel** has a new E window by John Piper (1984) (*hospital open daily; chapel open, services Sun.: 8-10 am most weekdays*).

Nearby

▶ At Wall (*2m SW*) is **Letocetum**★, remains of Roman posting station on Watling Street, great London to Chester road. Bath house is best-preserved example of its kind in Britain; part of hostel may also be seen. Small museum displays finds, including coins, urns (*Apr.-Sep.: 9.30-6.30, Sun., 2-6.30; Oct.-Mar.: 9.30-4.30, Sun., 2-4.30*). ▶ **Museum of Staffordshire Regiment** (*3m SE*): uniforms, badges, weapons, medals telling history of regiment (*Mon.-Fri.: 9-4.30; cl. Bank Hols.*). ▶ **Hanch Hall** (*3 ¹/₂ m NW*) has architectural styles from Tudor to Victorian; striking Queen Anne façade; rich strapwork staircase; Elizabethan cellars with secret passage; collections of teapots, dolls, needlework, costume (*Apr.-Sep.: Sun., Bank Hol. Mon. & Tue. following 2-6; Jun.-Sep.: Tue.-Thu. & Sat., 2-6*). ▶ **Ridware Arts Centre** (*7 ¹/₂ m NW*): group of old buildings housing craft studios, contemporary art and pottery displays, also farm animals (*Mar.-Dec.: Tue.-Sun., 10.30-5.30, Bank Hols.; Jan.-Mar.: wkends only*). Part-Norman **church of St. Michael** adjacent. ▶ **Cannock Chase** (*6-12m NW*), some 25m of woodland and lowland heath. At **Brocton Coppice**, a few great oaks remain, thick across Staffordshire when Plantagenet kings hunted here; good viewpoints throughout chase including **Castle Ring** and **Coppice Hill**, from where the Clee Hills in Salop may be seen; bird and animal life rich and various. □

Practical information

LICHFIELD
ⓘ Donegal House, Bore Street, ☎ 252109.
▰▰ Lichfield Trent and City Valley, ☎ Birmingham (021) 6432711.

Hotels:
★★ **George** (Embassy), Bird Street, WS13 6PR, ☎ (0543) 414822, AC AM BA DI, 42 rm. Ⓟ £50. Rest. ◆ ♿ £10.50.
★ **Hollies Club**, Hollies Avenue, Cannock, WS11 1DW, ☎ Cannock (054 35) 3151, AC AM BA DI, 7 rm. Ⓟ ♨ ♿ ⌘ £30. Rest. ◆ ♨ ♪ Cl. lunch Sat., dinner Sun. £9.

Restaurant:
◆ **Thrales**, 40-44 Tamworth Street, ☎ (0543) 255091 Ⓟ ♿ ⌘ Cl. Sun. French cuisine, fish, game. Book. £12.50.

Recommended
Golf course: Whittington Barracks, Tamworth Road (on A51), ☎ 432317.
Riding school: *Gartmore Riding School*, Hall Lane, Hammerwich, ☎ (054 36) 6117.

Be advised that hotels and restaurants in this Guide have perhaps changed addresses; prices indicated are also subject to modifications.

Nearby

ARMITAGE, 2m E of Rugeley on A513

Restaurant:
◆ *Old Farmhouse*, ☎ (0543) 490353, AC AM BA DI ℗ ⑈
⌕ ᵭ ⌧ Cl. Sun. eve., Mon. Pigeon in red wine sauce
with black cherries. Book. £12.

CANNOCK, 8m E on A6100

Hotel:
★★★ *Roman Way*, Watling Street, Hatherton, WS11 1SH,
☎ (054 35) 72121, AC AM BA DI, 24 rm. ℗ ⌕ ᵭ £45. Rest.
◆ ♪ ᵭ Cl. dinner Christmas. £13.

RUGELEY, 8m N on A51

Hotel:
★ *Cedar Tree*, Main Road, WS15 1DY, ☎ (088 94) 4241,
AC AM BA DI, 25 rm. ℗ ⑈ ⌧ £35. Rest. ◆ ♪ ᵭ £7.

⚑ *Silvertrees Cara Pk.*, Stafford Brook Road, Penkridge
Bank, (30 pl), ☎ (088 94) 2185.

LUDLOW**

Shrewsbury, 35; Leominster, 11; London, 168 m
pop. 7,496 ☎ 0584   Shropshire A2

This gracious town was planned on a medieval grid
pattern, having earlier developed as an adjunct to
the massive castle. Its medieval wealth was earned
from wool, glove-making and malting. Superb domestic architecture attests to this wealth, from medieval
stone through black-and-white timbering to handsome
Georgian façades.

▶ **Ludlow Castle**★★ was founded 1085 on site high above
Corve and Teme; extensive outer bailey but no central
keep; inner bailey has deep moat; highly unusual circular **chapel** with zig-zag decoration and 16thC **great hall.**
This Norman border stronghold developed into an important Tudor **seat of government** (*daily*). ▶ **Church of St.
Lawrence**★ has impressive 135 ft. Perpendicular tower;
15thC interior, finely carved medieval misericords in choir.
▶ **Butter Cross** at centre of town and Classical town hall
(1743-4). ▶ Adjacent **museum of local history** (*Apr.-Sep.:
wkdays; Jun.-Aug.: daily*). ▶ **Broad Street**★: wide thoroughfare with raised pavements and a long sweep of Georgian façades, descending to 13thC **Broad Gate**, the only
remaining medieval city gate. ▶ **Lower Broad Street** drops
to **Ludford Bridge**, 15thC 3-arched stone bridge. ▶ Of
many buildings worth perusal: **The Feathers**★ (Bull Ring),
richly ornamented timbered inn of 1603. ▶ In churchyard,
The Reader's House, medieval house with 17thC black-
and-white 3-storeyed porch. ▶ 15thC **guildhall** (Mill
Street): attractive Gothic Revival doorway of 1768. ▶ **Rose
and Crown Inn** (behind Butter Cross), a hostelry since
16thC with timbered courtyard.

Nearby

▶ **Stokesay Castle**★★ (*7 ¹/₂ m NW*), one of the earliest
(with Acton Burnell) and complete English fortified houses, in beautiful moated setting: two squat towers, great
hall★ (*Mar.-Oct.: daily ex. Tue.; Nov.: daily ex. Mon. &
Tue.*). ▶ **Tenbury Wells** (*10m SE*): this little town had
brief flowering after brine springs were discovered here in
1839. Now a peaceful Teme-side market town with some
good Georgian and timbered buildings and an old
3-arched bridge.   □

Practical information _____

LUDLOW
ℹ Castle Street, ☎ 3857.
🚂 ☎ Hereford (0432) 266534.

Hotels:
● ★★★ *Feathers*, Bull Ring, SY8 1AA, ☎ (0584) 5261,
Tx 35637, AC AM BA DI, 37 rm. ℗ ♪ £80. Rest. ●
◆ £14.50.

★★ *Angel* (Consort), Broad Street, SY8 1NG, ☎ (0584)
2581, AC AM BA DI, 17 rm. ℗ ⌧ £51. Rest. ◆ £10.
★★ *Overton Grange*, SY8 4AD, ☎ (0584) 3500, AC AM BA
DI, 17 rm. ℗ ⌕ ⑈ ⌕ £49. Rest. ◆ ♪ ᵭ £10.

Restaurants:
◆ *Dinham Weir Restaurant*, Dinham Bridge, ☎ (0584)
4431, AC BA DI ℗ ⌕ ⑈ ⌕ ♪ ᵭ ⌧ Cl. Out. eve. Duck with
port and blackcurrant sauce. Book. £12.
◆ *Penny Anthony*, 5 Church Street, ☎ (0584) 3282, AM
BA DI ⌧ Cl. Dec.-Jan., Sun. Terrine of scallops. £11.

Inn or Pub:
Church Inn, Church Street, ☎ (0584) 2174, 7 rm ⌧ Bar
snacks and home-cooked meals. £6.

Recommended
Antique shop: Cave, R.G. Sons Ltd., 17 Broad Street,
☎ (0584) 3568, clocks, furniture and metalwork; *Edwards,
Martin*, 23 Bull Ring, ☎ (0584) 5124, furniture and silver;
Rumens, Olivia, The Gallery, 30 Corve Street, ☎ (0584)
3952, paintings; *Smith, Paul*, 10 Church Street, ☎ (0584)
2666, furniture; *Woolston, Stanley*, 29 Broad Street,
☎ (0584) 3554, furniture, carpets and paintings.
Farmhouse: at Little Hereford, *Lower Upton Farm*, ☎ (058
472) 322, 160-acre mixed farm. £16 double; B. & B.
Golf course: Bromfield, ☎ 77285.
♥ at Oakamoor, *Dot Merry*, 10-11 The Square, ☎ (0538)
702744, artist specializing in domestic animal portraiture.

Nearby

CLUN, 12m NW on B4368

Hotel:
★ *Sun Inn*, High Street, SY7 8JB, ☎ (058 84) 559, AC, 9
rm. ℗ ⌕ ⌧ £35. Rest. ◆ ♪ £9.

Restaurant:
◆ *Old Post Office*, 9 The Square, ☎ (05884) 687. Cl. Sun.;
Mon., lunch not served Nov.-Mar., Feb. £14.

Recommended
Crafts workshop: Riversdale Studio, Buffalo Lane, ☎ (058
84) 521, hand-printed original designs.

DIDDLEBURY, 8m N on B365

Hotel:
★ *Glebe Farm*, SY7 9DH, ☎ Munsdale (058 476) 221, 8
rm. ℗ ⑈ ⌕ ⌧ ⌕ £38. Rest. ◆ Cl. 1 Nov. - 1 Mar. early
Jun. £10.

HOPTON WAFERS, 9m E off A4117

Restaurant:
◆ *Crown Inn*, ☎ Cleobury Mortimer (0299) 270372, AC
BA ℗ ⑈ Cl. Mon., Sun. eve. Stilton soup, ice cream. £13.

LLANFAIR WATERDINE, 8m SW off B4355

Restaurant:
◆ *Red Lion Inn*, ☎ Knighton (0547) 528214, AC BA,
4 rm. ℗ ⌕ ⑈ ⌕ ⌧ Guinea fowl in red wine sauce.
Book. £10.50.

TENBURY WELLS, 17m SE on A4112

Hotel:
★ *Swan*, WR15 8AH, ☎ Ludlow (0584) 810422, AC BA, 9
rm. ℗ ⌕ ⑈ ⌕ £20. Rest. ◆ £6.

MALVERN HILLS

This range of hills is a mere 9m in length, the highest
peak reaching only 1,394 ft., yet it possesses considerable grandeur. Site of ancient hill forts and historical boundary between Herefordshire and Worcestershire, the hills have worked powerfully on the imagi-
nation of poets, artists and musicians.

▶ Well-signposted 45m 'Elgar Route' is a good way to
explore hills and environs by car. ▶ Many access points
and parking places, some with café or picnicking facilities on both E & W sides of hills. Paths which interweave

on Malverns are well trodden and climbs gentle; hard-surfaced track up to Worcestershire Beacon (*suitable for wheelchairs and strollers but not motor vehicles*). ▶ Of twenty separate summits, **Worcestershire Beacon** (1,394 ft.) is highest; **Herefordshire Beacon** (1,370 ft.) comes next. **Chase End Hill** tends to be less crowded; **views★** from any point along ridge are magnificent. ▶ Looking NE, **Worcester Cathedral** is visible. To the E, the distinctive copper roof makes **Pershore Abbey** stand out from plain. **Bredon Hill** swells upward from vale, an ideal place for an Iron Age hill fort. SSE on a clear day, Gloucester Cathedral is visible. Looking W, the landscape is markedly dissimilar. Herefordshire, historically divided from Worcestershire by Malverns, stretches with wooded hills to Welsh border. On horizon, dark shapes of **Black Mountains** in Wales. ▫

MARKET DRAYTON*

Stoke-on-Trent, 17; Shrewsbury, 20; London, 161 m
pop. 9,003 ☎ 0630   Shropshire A1

A small market town in flat land bordering the River Tern and **Shropshire Union Canal,** it has an attractive sprinkling of black-and-white buildings and 14thC church.

Nearby

▶ **Hodnet Hall Gardens** (5½ m SW): lakes and ponds, mature trees, kitchen garden, year-long colour from shrubs and flowers, tearooms, gift shop (*end Mar.-Sep.: wkdays, 2-5, Sun. & Bank Hols., 12-6*). ▫

Practical information

MARKET DRAYTON

Hotel:
★★ *Corbet Arms*, High Street, TF9 1PY, ☎ (0630) 2037, AC AM BA DI, 12 rm. P £45. Rest. ♦ ♪ & £9.50.

Recommended
Golf course: Sutton, ☎ 2266.

Nearby

TERN HILL, 3m SE on A53

Hotel:
★ *Tern Hill Hall*, TF9 3PU, ☎ (063 083) 310, AC AM BA DI, 11 rm. P ≤ 𝓌 ◿ ⅀ £33. Rest. ♦ ♪ £10.50.

MORETON-IN-MARSH*

Worcester, 29; Oxford, 28; London, 86 m
pop. 2,545 ☎ 0608   Gloucestershire B2

A dignified small Cotswold town whose main street is part of the Roman Fosse Way, lined with handsome stone houses and inns. The 17thC curfew bell still hangs in 16thC **Curfew Tower.**

Nearby

▶ **Four Shires Stone** (1 ½ m E), 18thC monument inscribed on sides facing each of the four counties that meet here: Gloucestershire, Oxfordshire, Warwickshire and Worcestershire (now Hereford and Worcester). ▶ **Sezincote Garden** (1 ½ m W): mature trees and oriental water gardens by Repton and Daniell surrounding exotic early 19thC Indian-style **house** by S.P. Cockerell (*garden, all year ex. Dec.: Thu., Fri. & Bank Hol. Mon., 2-6 or dusk; house, May-Sep.: Thu. & Fri., 2.30-6*). ▶ **Bourton-on-the-Hill** (1 ½ m W): village, with **church** of Norman origin, mainly 15thC interior. **Bourton House**, bottom of hill, 18thC house with signs of earlier 16thC building; sturdy 16thC **tithe barn** E of house. ▶ **Batsford Park Arboretum** (1 ½ m NW): many hundreds of different trees, native and exotic, in tranquil parkland (*Apr.-Oct.: daily, 10-5*). ▫

Practical information

MORETON-IN-MARSH
ⓘ council offices, High Street, ☎ 50881.
🚌 ☎ 50330.

Hotels:
● ★★★ *Manor House*, High Street, GL56 0LJ, ☎ (0608) 50501, Tx 837151, AC AM BA DI, 38 rm. P 𝓌 & ⅀ ▱ ⚲ 17thC manor house in 2-acre garden. No children under 12. £58. Rest. ♦ & £14.
★★ *Redesdale Arms*, GL56 0AW, ☎ (0608) 50308, AC AM DI, 15 rm. P 𝓌 & ⅀ ⚲ Former coaching inn built in 18thC on the ancient Roman Fosse Way. £50. Rest. ♦ ♪ & £10.

Inn or Pub:
Wellington (Hook Norton), London Road, ☎ (0608) 50936 P 𝓌 ◿ ⚲ Bar snacks.

Recommended
Antique shop: *Sampson, Anthony*, Dale House, High Street, ☎ (0608) 50763, furniture.
Craft workshop: at Burton-on-the-Water, *Chestnut Gallery*, High Street, ☎ (0451) 20017, selection of a wide variety of crafts.
Farmhouse: *Old Farm*, ☎ (0608) 50394. £18 double; B. & B.

Nearby

BLOCKLEY, 3 1/2m NW on B4479

Restaurant:
♦ *Lower Brook House*, Lower Street, ☎ (0386) 700286, AC, 8 rm. P ≤ 𝓌 ◿ & ⚲ Cl. Jan. Roast rack of English lamb. Book. £14.50.

Inn or Pub:
Crown, High Street, ☎ (0386) 700245, AC AM BA DI 15 rm. P ≤ 𝓌 ◿ Sandwiches, ploughman's lunch, chili con carne, filet steak and Dover sole. £8.

Recommended
Antique shop: *Aldbury Antiques*, High Street, ☎ (0386) 700280, pottery and porcelain.

MUCH WENLOCK*

Shrewsbury, 13; Kidderminster, 20; London, 157 m
pop. 2,535 ☎ 0952   Shropshire A2

The heart of this little town is not red sandstone and brick as is customary in this part of Shropshire, but a gentle grey.

▶ **Wenlock Priory** was the reason for the town's growth in Middle Ages. Founded by St. Milburga in 680, twice demolished, finally restored 1080 when it became Cluniac priory. Part of W front and walls of chapter house with decorative arcades remain (*mid-Mar. - mid-Oct.: 9.30-6.30; mid-Oct. - mid Mar.: 9.30-4; open Sun., 2.30 all year*). ▶ Nearby is 15thC **Prior's Lodge.** ▶ **Holy Trinity Church,** part Norman; two storeyed 13thC porch; decorative stone carving. ▶ **Guildhall:** splendid building still in use; timbered, on oak posts; (*Apr.-Sep.: wkdays ex. Wed.*). ▶ **Much Wenlock Museum:** history of town and environs (*Apr.-Oct.: daily ex. Sun.*).

Nearby

▶ **Wenlock Edge** stretches SW of town; good bird watching, walking and **views.** ▶ **Shipton Hall** (*7m SW*): Elizabethan manor of local grey limestone; fine interior. Georgian stables with cupola; medieval dovecote in grounds (*May-Sep.: Thu., also Sun. in Jul. & Aug., Bank Hols., Sun. & Mon., 2.30-5.30*). ▶ **Buildwas Abbey** (3 ¹/₂ m NW): remarkably complete remains of Cistercian abbey founded 1135. 180 ft. long with stout Norman columns; parts of crypt, sacristy and tower preserved (*mid-Mar. - mid-Oct.: 9.30-6.30; mid-Oct. - mid-Mar.: 9.30-4; Sun. at 2 all year*). ▶ **Benthall Hall** (*4m NE*); 16thC stone house; star-shaped brick chimneys; 17thC carved oak staircase;

decorative plasterwork; attractive garden (*Easter Sat. - end Sep.: Tue., Wed., Sat. & Bank Hol. Mon., 2-6*). ☐

Practical information _____

ⓘ The Guildhall, Wilmore Street, ☎ 727509.

Hotel:
★ *Gaskell Arms*, Bourton Road, ☎ (0952) 727212, AC ◨A DI, 11 rm. ℗ ⋘ ⋙ £41. Rest. ♦ £10.

Inn or Pub:
George Dragon, High Street, ☎ (0952) 727312 ℗ ḙ. Home-cooked lunch and evening meals, vegetarian menu, lamb curry, duck. £4.50.

Recommended
Coffee shop: *Scott's*, 5 High Street, ☎ (0952) 727596.

NUNEATON*

Leicester, 18; Coventry, 9; London, 101 m
pop. 60,377 ☎ 0203   Warwickshire B2

Now a large, busy town of the West Midlands, its site was settled in ancient times (Etone in Domesday survey) and it prospered as a coal-mining centre as early as the 14thC.

Nearby

▶ **Arbury Hall**★ (*2m SW*): large Elizabethan house extensively Gothicized in 18thC; interior has remarkable plasterwork in imitation of fan-vaulting, 'like petrified lacework' according to George Eliot. 17thC stable block houses collection vintage bicycles and motorcycles; grounds with lakes, woodlands, roses and spring bulbs (*Easter-end Sep.: Sun.; also Tue. & Wed. in Jul. & Aug.; hall: 2-5; gardens: 1-6*). ▶ **Hartsmill Hayes Country Park:** 136 acres with walks, picnic sites and viewpoints; **St. Lawrence's Wood** and **The Hayes:** areas of managed mixed woodland (*dawn-dusk*). ☐

Practical information _____

ⓘ public library, Church Street, ☎ 384027.
▰▰ ☎ Rugby (0788) 60116.

Hotels:
★★ *Chase*, Higham Lane, CV11 6AG, ☎ (0203) 383406, AC AM BA, 28 rm. ℗ ⋘ ⋙ £40. Rest. ♦ ♪ Cl. lunch Sat. £8.
★ *Drachenfels*, 25 Attleborough Road, GD11 482, ☎ (0203) 383030, AC ℗ ⋘ £22. Rest. ♦ ⚓♪ḙ £6.

Recommended
Craft workshops: *Old Post Office Pottery Gallery*, 11 The Crescent, Brinklow, ☎ (0788) 832210, local potters display, stoneware, earthenware and ceramics; *Pailton Pottery*, 12 Lutterworth Road, ☎ (0788) 832064, a large selection of kitchenware and tableware; at Grendon, *Carter Pottery*, Highfields Farm, ☎ (082 77) 3307, hand-thrown stoneware.
Golf course: Golf Drive, Whiteston, ☎ 38328.

OSWESTRY*

Wrexham, 16; Shrewsbury, 19; London, 181 m
pop. 13,200 ☎ 0691   Shropshire A1

Like so many English towns that seem now to epitomize picturesque tranquillity, Oswestry has seen destruction and bitter fighting many times throughout its long past. Burned down twice - by the English in 1215 and by the Welsh in 1233 - it was described during the Civil War by Cromwell's commander Thomas Myddleton as 'a very strong town...the key that lets us in to Wales'; Oswestry has paid dearly for its position so close to the Welsh-English border. W of the town lies beautiful hill country stretching into Wales, and E is a wide, flat plain dotted with **meres,** known as Shropshire's Lake District.

▶ Oswestry's Norman **castle** was finally demolished by Cromwell's troops after having withstood numerous previous attacks; fragments of 12thC walls remain. ▶ **Llwyd Mansion** (Bailey Street), 1604, timber-framed, bearing double headed eagle, symbol of Roman Empire, arms granted to Llwyd family. ▶ **Croeswylan Stone** (Cross of Weeping; Morda Road) marks place outside city walls where markets were held, 1559, when plague afflicted the town.

Nearby

▶ **Old Oswestry**★: excellent example of Iron Age hill fort; 7 ramparts covering 40 acres, it stands 100 ft. above surroundings; believed to have been completed and abandoned before Roman invasion (43 AD) (*all year*). ▶ **Old racecourse** (*2 $1/2$ m W*) on common land high above plain commands superb views★; course was in use from 18thC to 1848. ▶ **Whittington Castle** (*3m E*): stone border fortress of Norman origin; gatehouse with 2 round towers is most complete part; remains of 5 other towers, only one still standing. ▶ Near Nescliffe (*9 $1/2$ m SE*) and visible from A5 is **Kynaston's Cave**, long series of steps approach cave where highwayman Humphrey Kynaston had his hideout. ▶ **Llanymynech** (*6m S*): the Welsh/English border runs through the village pub; village itself is below **Llanymynech Hill** riddled with shafts and caves of Roman zinc, lead and copper mines. **Offa's Dyke** (→) runs across top of hill, good walks and **view.** ▶ **Llanyblodwel** (*6m SW*): bizarre **church** designed by incumbent Rev. John Parker 1847-50; peculiar semi-detached octagonal tower and spire with swelling outline, interior of odd proportions, walls covered with hand-painted texts. ▶ **The Shropshire Meres: Ellesmere** (*9m NE*) is the centre of this district of 9 lakes, carved out of Shropshire Plain in last Ice Age; perfect area for boating, bird watching; largest lake, **The Mere,** has a heronry. Ellesmere **church** has lovely chancel chapel roof. ☐

Practical information _____

OSWESTRY
ⓘ library, Arthur Street, ☎ 0662753; Mile End Service Area, ☎ 465151.

Hotel:
★★ *Wynnstay* (T.F.), Church Street, SY11 2SZ, ☎ (0691) 655261, AC AM BA DI, 31 rm. ℗ ⋘ ⚓ £55. Rest. ♦ ḙ Salmon in puff pastry. £10.

Restaurant:
♦ *Good Companion Wine Bar*, 10 Beatrice Street, ☎ (0691) 655768, AM DI ♪ḙ ⋙ Cl. Sun., Mon. lunch. Peppered steak, lasagne verdi. £9.50.

Inn or Pub:
Golden Lion (Marstons), Upper Church Street, ☎ (0691) 653747 ℗ ⋘ ⋙ Snacks at lunchtime.

⚓ *Cranberry Moss C.C.S.*, Kinnerley, (60 pl), ☎ (074 381) 444; *Fernwood Caravan Pk.*, Lyneal, Ellesmere, (50 pl), ☎ (094 875) 221.

Recommended
Farmhouse: at Whittington, *Perry Farm*, ☎ (0691) 230. £20 double; B. & B.
Golf course: Aston Park, ☎ 221.
Riding School: *Penycoed Riding Holidays*, Llynclys Hill, ☎ (0691) 830608.

Nearby

ELLESMERE, 8m NE on A495

Hotel:
★★ *Grange*, Grange Road, SY12 9DE, ☎ (069 171) 3495, AC BA DI, 16 rm. ℗ ⋘ ⚓ḙ ♪ £45. Rest. ♦ ♪ Cl. 27 Dec. - 4 Jan. £12.

Recommended
Riding School: *Forge Farm Riding Centre*, Perthy, ☎ Ellesmere 2500, basic and elementary instruction.

MORDA, 1 1/2m S on A483

Hotel:
● ★★ *Sweeney Hall*, SY10 9EU, ☎ (0691) 652450, AC BA, 8 rm. ℙ ░ ♦ £40. Rest. ♦ ♪ £9.

RHYDYCROESAU, 3m W on B4580

Hotel:
★ *Pen-y-Dyffryn*, SY10 7DT, ☎ (0691) 653700, 6 rm. ℙ ♦ ░ ♦ ♦ ♦ £45. Rest. ♦ ♪ ♦ Cl. Mon., dinner Sun. £10.

PERSHORE*

Worcester, 9; Gloucester, 22; London, 102 m
pop. 6,850 ☎ 0386   Hereford & Worcester B2

At the centre of a fruit-growing region, Pershore has two wide and elegant streets and a fine abbey. A dessert plum takes its name from the town.

▶ **Abbey** of local limestone stands solid and dignified in grassy surroundings. Nave, transept and crossing are Norman; buttressed **lantern tower**★ is early 14thC; superb vaulted **roof**★. ▶ Entering Pershore from E, road crosses solid 14thC six-arched **bridge** over Avon.

Nearby

▶ **Bredon Hill**★ (*5m SE*). This lovely outcrop of Cotswold stone is visible from far away; site of Iron Age hill fort, now 'Parson's Folly', crowns the hill, magnificent views. ▶ **Bredon** village (*8 1/2 m S*) has great charm: the 14thC **tithe barn** is of inspiring proportions (*Wed. & Thu.: 2-6.; Sat. & Sun.:, 10-6 or sunset*). ▶ **Bredon Springs** Garden (*8m SW, nr. Ashton under Hill*): 1 1/2 acres in lovely setting (*Apr.-Oct.: Sat., Sun., Wed., Thu. & Bank Hol. Mon. & Tue., 10-dusk*). ▶ **Wick** (*1m E*): church has wagon roof; **Wick Manor** looks every inch Elizabethan, timber-framed, but dates from 1924, a picturesque fake.   ☐

Practical information _____

PERSHORE
ⓘ 37 High Street, ☎ 554711.
▰▰ ☎ Worcester (0905) 27211.

Hotel:
★ *Manor House*, Bridge Street, WR10 1AX, ☎ (0386) 552713, AC AM BA DI, 8 rm. ℙ £32. Rest. ♦ Cl. Christmas day. £9.

Restaurant:
♦ *Zhivago's*, 22 Bridge Street, ☎ (0386) 553828, AC AM BA DI. Cl. Mon., dinner Sun., 3-24 Aug. £15.

Recommended
♥ *Jennie Hill Gallery of Local Arts*, 86 High Street, ☎ (0386) 553969, it has jewelry, glass, pottery, woodwork, metal sculpture.

Nearby

WYRE PIDDLE, 1m NE on B4083

Hotel:
● ★★ *Avonside*, Main Road, WR10 2JB, ☎ (0386) 552654, AC, 7 rm. ℙ ♦ ░ ▱ No children under 7. £50. Rest. ♦ ♪ Cl. Dec. - Feb. £13.

ROSS-ON-WYE*

Hereford, 15; Gloucester, 17; London, 124 m
pop. 8,281 ☎ 0989   Hereford & Worcester A3

Ross stands on a promontory looking over the Wye as it broadens and meanders southward. The surrounding landscape is one of gentle beauty, wooded and quiet enough to be a refuge for a rich variety of wild animals and plants.

▶ The influence of John Kyrle, 'The Man of Ross', (1637-1724) is seen and felt everywhere. A modest man, philanthropic on a grand scale, he engaged in early 'town planning' and the results were very fortunate for Ross. His house is no. 34 in the triangular **market place**, now shops; his bust over one of them. His delightful **garden and summer house** to rear may be visited (*by application at chemist shop, J.F. Hart*). ▶ **Market House**, 1660-74, raised on arcaded columns, is made of local red sandstone. ▶ **The Prospect** near church is a walled public garden funded by Kyrle; elegant gates and **views** over town and countryside. ▶ **Wilton Bridge:** built 1597, 6 stone arches span the Wye; large sundial mounted on central parapet. ▶ **St. Mary's Church;** 208 ft. spire; interior has lovely stained glass and many monuments including one to John Kyrle mounted in N wall of sanctuary.

Nearby

▶ **Symond's Yat**★ (*6m SW*) or 'gate' affords superb **views** over Wye Valley far below. Climb from river to **Yat Rock** is steep but well worn. ▶ **Brockhampton-by-Ross** (*5m N*) possesses a rare, successful modern church★; built 1901-2 by W.R. Lethaby, follower of William Morris; interior contains tapestry by Burne-Jones. Note thatched **lychgate** in churchyard. ▶ **Falconry Centre** at Newent (*9 m W*): free-flying hawks; aviaries for nesting, breeding and rearing chicks; eagles and buzzards fly in regular displays; also falconry museum, picnic area, shop (*Mar.-Oct.: daily 10.30-5.30; Cl. Tue.*). ▶ **Goodrich Castle**★ (*5 m SW*): magnificent 12th-14thC ruins on rocky hill overlooking Wye, demolished in Civil War by Cromwell's army with aid of 'Roaring Meg', a cannon able to fire 200 lb. cannon balls (*all year: daily*). ▶ **Wye Valley Visitor Centre** at Whitchurch (*7m SW*): tropical butterflies in glasshouse garden; a maze and museum of mazes; craft workshops; church of St. Dubricious next to Wye; garden centre (*Easter - end Oct.: daily, 11-5.30*).   ☐

Practical information _____

ROSS-ON-WYE
ⓘ 20 Broad Street, ☎ 62768.

Hotels:
● ★★★★ *Chase* (Q.M.H.), Gloucester Road, HR9 5LH, ☎ (0989) 63161, AC AM BA DI, 40 rm. ℙ ░ ♪ Georgian country house, situated in 11 acres of garden with broad lawns and a lake. £67. Rest. ♦ Hereford veal. £16.
★★ *Orles Barn*, Wilton, HR9 6AE, ☎ (0989) 62155, AC AM BA DI, 8 rm. ℙ ♦ ░ ♦ ♦ ▱ £37. Rest. ♦ ♪ Cl. dinner Sun. & Nov. - Feb. £8.50.
★★ *Rosswyn*, High Street, HR9 5BZ, ☎ (0989) 62733, AC BA, 9 rm. ░ £34. Rest. ♦ ♪ £12.
★★ *Royal* (T.F.), Palace Pound, HR9 5HZ, ☎ (0989) 65105, AC AM BA DI, 30 rm. ℙ ♦ ░ ♦ £66. Rest. ♦ £11.50.

Restaurants:
♦ *Meader's*, 1 Copse Cross Street, ☎ (0989) 62803 ♪ ░ Cl. 25-26 Dec., Sun., Mon. eve. Hungarian and vegetarian dishes. Book. £8.50.
♦ *Walford House Hotel*, Walford Road, ☎ (0989) 63829, AC AM BA DI ℙ ♦ ░ ♦ ♦ ░ *Magret de canard aux poireaux*. Book. £16.50.

Recommended
Cycle rental: *Little and Hall*, 48 Broad Street, ☎ (0989) 62639.
Farmhouse: *Aberhall Farm*, St. Owen's Bross, ☎ Harewood End (098987) 256. £20 double; B. & B.
Golf course: Two Park, Gorsley, ☎ 822667.

Nearby

HAREWOOD END, 4m W on A49

Hotel:
● ★★★ *Pengethley* (Best Western), HR9 6LL, ☎ Hare-

wood End (0989) 87211, AC AM BA DI, 20 rm. P ⧉ ☷ ⌕ ᕯ ⊡ ↙ ᾧ £100. Rest. ● ◆ ♪ ⅍ £25.

PENCRAIG, 3m SW on A40

Hotel:

★★ *Pencraig Court*, HR9 6HR, ☎ Llangarron (0989) 84306, AC AM BA, 11 rm. P ⧉ ☷ ⌕ ⬦ £42. Rest. ◆ Cl. Nov. - Mar. Salmon poached in wine £12.

SYMONDS YAT, 6m SW off A40

Hotels:

★★ *Royal*, HR9 6JL, ☎ (0600) 890238, AM, 23 rm. P ⧉ ☷ ⌕ ⬦ Ⴂ £44. Rest. ◆ ♪ £13.

★★ *Wye Rapids*, HR9 6BL, ☎ (0600) 890366, AC AM BA DI, 15 rm. P ⧉ ☷ ⌕ £45. Rest. ◆ ♪ Cl. Nov. - Feb. £10.

★ *Paddocks*, HR9 6BL, ☎ (0600) 890246, 27 rm. P ⧉ ☷ ⌕ ↗ £36. Rest. ◆ ♪ ⅍ Cl. Nov. - Mar. £11.50.

Restaurant:

◆ *The Gallery Restaurant*, Wayside, ☎ (0600) 890408, AC AM BA P ☷ ♪ ⅍ ⬦ Cl. 1st 2 wks. Nov., Sun. Game dishes, fish. £22.50.

Inn or Pub:

Wye Knot, Symonds Yat West, ☎ (0600) 890501, AC AM BA P ⧉ ☷ ⌕ Wide range of bar meals. £10.

⚑ *Symonds Yat East*, HR9 6JL (7 pl), ☎ (0600) 890129.

WHITCHURCH, 7m SW on A49

Hotel:

★ *Portland Guest Hse*, HR9 6DB, ☎ Symonds Yat (0600) 890757, BA, 8 rm. P ⧉ ☷ £23. Rest. ◆ ♪ Cl. Jan. £6.

WILTON, 1m W on A40

Hotel:

★★ *Castle Lodge*, HR9 6AD, ☎ (0989) 62234, AC BA, 10 rm. P ⧉ ☷ ⌕ ↙ £36. Rest. ◆ ♪ Cl. Christmas and 1-3 Jan. £10.

RUGBY*

Coventry, 12; Northampton, 22; London, 81 m
pop. 59,039 ☎ 0788   Warwickshire B2

A large industrial town where the traditional employments are railway engineering and light industry. Famous for its venerable public school; also the birthplace of the game of the same name(→). □

Practical information _____

RUGBY

Ⓘ library, St. Matthews Street, ☎ 2687.
▬▬ ☎ 60116.
Car rental: Europcar, ☎ (0203) 27477 (rail/drive).

Hotel:

★★★ *Brownsover Hall*, Old Leicester Road, Brownsover Old Vil, CV21 1HU, ☎ (0788) 73131, Tx 311794, AC AM BA DI, 15 rm. P ⧉ ☷ ⌕ ↙ ᾧ Victorian mansion designed by Sir George Gilbert Scott. £60. Rest. ◆ ♪ £10.

Restaurant:

◆ *Andalucia*, 10 Henry Street, ☎ (0788) 76404, AC AM BA DI P ⬦ ♪ ⅍ ⬦ Cl. Sun. eve. Paella, kebabs. Book. £10.

Recommended

Cycle rental: *Thorntons Cycle Centre*, 100/102 Cambridge Street, ☎ (0788) 72440.
Farmhouse: *Lawford Hill Farm*, Lawford Heath Lane, Long Lawford, ☎ (0788) 2001. £20 double; B. & B.
Golf course: Clifton Road, ☎ 75134.
♥ *Shaheen Pan Sweet Ctr.*, 88 Craven Road, ☎ (0788) 68181, wide range of Indian confections, cakes, breads and kulfi.

Nearby

CLIFTON-U-DUNSMORE, 1m NE on B5414

Hotel:

★★★ *Clifton Court*, Lilbourne Road, CV23 0BB, ☎ (0788)

65033, AC BA, 14 rm. P ⧉ ☷ ⌕ ❀ £60. Rest. ◆ ♪ Cl. 25 - 31 Dec. £9.

DUNCHURCH, 3m S on A426

Hotel:

● ★★★ *Dun Cow*, The Green, CV22 6NJ, ☎ (0788) 810233, Tx 312242, AC AM BA DI, 22 rm, P ⅍ Fine traditional coaching inn of the 17thC. £60. Rest. ◆ ♪ £10.50.

STRETTON-UNDER-FOSSE, 5m NW on A427

Hotel:

★ *Ashton Lodge*, CV23 0PJ, ☎ (0788) 832278, AC AM DI, 11 rm. P ⧉ ☷ ⌕ £40. Rest. ◆ ♪ Cl. Christmas. £13.50.

SHIPSTON-ON-STOUR*

Stratford-upon-Avon, 11; Oxford, 31; London, 89 m
pop. 3,072 ☎ 0608   Warwickshire B2

Small town on the banks of the Stour in the pastoral region known as Feldon. It grew rich as a wool and sheep-trading centre and retains a wealthy country town atmosphere.

Nearby

▶ **Edge Hill** (*8m NE*): this wooded ridge shelters site of the first major battle of Civil War in October 1642 when the Royalists claimed victory. Excellent views from ridge over park-like landscape. ▶ **Upton House** (*1m S of Edge Hill*), in splendid gardens and grounds with lakes. Classical house with 15thC fragments; collections of paintings, Brussels tapestries, English and European porcelain, 18thC furniture (*Apr. - end Sep.: Mon.-Thu., 2-6; some wkends in summer*). ▶ **Honington Hall** (*1m N*): charming brick house of 1685 with busts of emperors over ground-floor windows; 18thC plasterwork and octagonal salon. (*late spring - late summer: Wed. & Bank Hol. Mon., 2.30-5.30*). ▶ **Honington Church** is a fine, mainly Classical building of 1680 with elegant interior: box pews, Tuscan arcades, rich marble monuments, carved pulpit and stalls. □

Practical information _____

SHIPSTON-ON-STOUR

Hotels:

★★ *Old Mill*, CV36 4AW, ☎ (0608) 61880, AC AM BA DI, 5 rm. P ⧉ ☷ ⌕ £55. Rest. ◆ ♪ Cl. dinner Sun. £18.50.
★ *Bell Inn*, Sheep Street, CV36 4AF, ☎ (0608) 61880, AC AM BA DI, 8 rm. P ⬦ ↙ ᾧ £38. Rest. ◆ ♪ ⅍ Local game. £7.
★ *White Bear*, High Street, CV36 4AJ, ☎ (0608) 61558, AC AM BA DI, 9 rm. P £50. Rest. ◆ ♪ Cl. Christmas. £13.50.

Nearby

LOWER BRAILES, 4m E on B4035

Restaurant:

◆ *Feldon House*, ☎ Brailes (060 885) 580, 3 rm. P ☷ ⌕ Lovage soup, wild salmon with leek sauce, home-made ice cream. Book. £14.50.

SHREWSBURY**

Wrexham, 31; Telford, 12; London, 150 m
pop. 87,300 ☎ 0743   Shropshire B1

On a hill enclosed by the Severn, there is only one approach to the town that does not involve crossing the river, a narrow gap some 300 yards wide. Thus it is a perfect defensive site, which explains its foundation by those who lived at *Viroconium*, but feared for their safety when the Roman soldiers marched away for good. Essentially a medieval town with much

Tudor expansion, there are many crooked streets and narrow alleyways.

► **St. Mary's church**: tall sandstone spire a distinctive feature of Shrewsbury's skyline; good 13thC nave arcades; 15thC nave roof with carved bosses, figures include a pig and a pelican. E chancel has **Jesse window**★ of glowing colours. In N chancel windows and centre window of S aisle: 16thC stained glass from Cologne brought here in 19thC, also some 15thC glass from Herchenrode (→). ► **St. Chad's**: late 18thC church by George Steuart; porticoed W tower with dome, circular nave. ► **Rowley's House** (Barker Street): sturdy timber-framed building, now museum exhibiting Roman finds from **Wroxeter** (→) (*daily ex. Sun.: 10-5*). ► **Clive House** (College Hill): mid-18thC house where Lord Clive once lived, now **museum** of 1st Queen's Dragoon Guards, also recounts Shrewsbury's history and has Shropshire pottery (*Mon.-Sat.: 10-5*). ► **Coleham Pumping Station** (Coleham Head): Victorian building with two huge beam engines (*Whitsun. - mid-Sep.: daily, ex. Mon.*). ► **Castle** is positioned in narrow gap where loop of Severn almost encloses town; first castle built pre-Domesday, extended thereafter, finally (as Royalist stronghold) dismantled after Civil War. Thomas Telford restored run-down building 1790 as a private house; now regimental **museum** for 4 Shropshire regiments (*Easter-Oct.: daily, 11-5; Nov.-Easter: Mon.-Sat., 10-4*). ► Good remaining stretch of **town walls**. ► Shrewsbury has a wealth of interesting buildings. ► **Bear Steps**: worn covered steps lead from Fish Street up to St. Alkmund's Place flanked by ancient timbered cottages. ► **Abbot's house** in **Butcher's Row** (rich in timbered buildings), 1450; wide timber sills at ground level are where medieval shopkeepers displayed their goods. ► **Old market hall**, supported on stone columns, 1596. ► **Ireland's Mansion** (corner of High Street), built 1575 by wealthy wool merchant Robert Ireland. ► Explore also **Grope Lane, Gullet Passage** and **Wyle Cop.**

Nearby

► **Viroconium, Wroxeter**★ (*5m SE*): important 2ndC Roman town that covered 180 acres. It survived for nearly 200 years, being dismantled to provide building stone for Anglo-Saxon Shrewsbury. Impressive remains of large wall separating **bath complex** from exercise yards. **Museum** displays finds, illuminates continuing excavations on site (*mid-Mar. - mid-Oct.: 9.30-6.30; mid-Oct. - mid-Mar.: 9.30-4; Sun.: Apr.-Sep. opens 9.30, otherwise at 2*). ► **Attingham Park**★ (*4m SE*): grand house by George Steuart, 1783; famous painted boudoir, staircase and picture gallery by Nash, collection of Regency silver, deer park and grounds bordering River Tern laid out by Repton (*Easter-end Sep.: Sat.-Wed., 2-5.30; Bank Hol. Mon.: 11.30-5.30*). ► **Adcote** (*7m NW*): 1879 by Norman Shaw; hall designed on Elizabethan lines with minstrels' gallery (*all year by appt.*). ► **Haughmond Abbey** (*4m NE*): Augustinian abbey founded 1135, after Dissolution became private home. Church demolished 1539, but Abbot's lodging is peaceful country house; remains of 12thC chapter house with carved Norman **doorways**, small **museum** with 14thC statue of Virgin and Child (*mid-Mar. - mid-Oct.: 9.30-6.30; mid-Oct. - mid-Mar.: 9.30-4; Sun.: 2 all year*). ► **Butterfly World** (*Yockleton, 7m W*): tropical butterfly house, collection of exotic insects (*early Apr.-end Oct.: 10-6 daily*). ► **Condover** (*3m S*): parish **church** contains large and varied collection of **monuments**, including Sir Thomas Cholmondeley by G.F. Watts and Roger Owen and wife by Roubiliac.   □

Practical information _____

SHREWSBURY
ℹ The Square, ☎ 50761.
🚂 ☎ 64041.
Car rental: Europcar, St. Michaels, Honkmoore Street, ☎ 59623 (rail/drive).

Hotels:
★★★ *Ainsworth Radbrook*, Radbrook Road, SY3 9BQ, ☎ (0743) 4861, AC AM BA DI, 48 rm. 🄿 ⅏ ♿ ↲ 🕭 Manor

house and ancestral home of the Clan McPherson, standing in 4 acres of grounds. £50. Rest. ♦ £8.
★★★ *Prince Rupert* (Consort), Butcher Row, SY1 1UQ, ☎ (0743) 52461, Tx 35100, AC AM BA DI, 70 rm. 🄿 🄦 ⚅ £62. Rest. ♦ ♪ £11.
★ *Beauchamp*, The Mount, SY3 8PJ, ☎ (0743) 3230, AC AM BA DI, 27 rm. 🄿 ⅏ 🄦 ♿ £40. Rest. ♦ ♪ £8.
★ *Britannia*, Mardol, SY1 1TU, ☎ (0743) 231246, Tx 629462, AC AM BA DI, 25 rm. 🄿 ⚅ £36. Rest. ♦ £7.
★ *Sandford House*, St. Julian Friars, SY1 1XL, ☎ (0743) 3829, 10 rm. 🄿 £25. Rest. ♦ £5.95.

Restaurants:
♦ *Delany's*, St. Julian's Craft Centre, St. Alkmond's Square, ☎ (0743) 60602 🄦 ♪ Cl. Bank Hols., eve., Sun. Cauliflower paprikash. Book. £3.
♦ *Old Police House*, Castle Court, Castle Street, ☎ (0743) 60668, AC BA 🄦 ♪ ⚅ Cl. 25-26 Dec., Easter Mon., Sun. Muscovy duck in damson sauce. Book. £11.50.

Recommended
Bakery: *T.O. Williams*, 12 Mount Pleasant Road, Harlescott, ☎ (0743) 53757, bread, cakes and local produce.
Farmhouse: at Bomere Heath, *Grange Farm*, ☎ (0939) 290234. £16 double; B. & B.
Golf course: Hawkstone Park Hotel, Weston-under-Redcastle, ☎ (093 924) 611; Condover, ☎ 722955.
Riding schools: at Baschurch, *P.G.L. Adventure Centre*, Boreaton Park, ☎ (0939) 260551.

🏇 *Prescott Riding Centre*, ☎ (0939) 260712.

Nearby

DORRINGTON, 7m S on A49
Restaurant:
● ♦ *Country Friends*, ☎ (074 373) 707, AM BA DI 🄿 ⅏ ♪ ⚅ Cl. lunch Mon., Sun. Duck with bacon and walnuts. Book. £11.50.

HALFWAY HOUSE, 10m W on A458
Inn or Pub:
Halfway House (Burtonwood), ☎ (0743) 78387 🄿 ⚅ ⅏ 🄦 ♿ From steaks to local gammon, trout and cheese rolls. £4.50.

NESSCLIFFE, 8m NW on A5
Hotel:
★ *Nesscliffe*, SY4 1DB, ☎ (0743) 81253, 5 rm. 🄿 ⚅ ⅏ £23. Rest. ♦ ♪ £15.

Restaurant:
♦ *Old Three Pigeons*, ☎ (074 381) 279, AM AC BA DI. £10.

SHELTON CORNER, 1m W on A458
Hotel:
★ *Crossroads*, SY3 8DL, ☎ (0743) 62235, 8 rm. 🄿 ⚅ ⅏ £20. Rest. ♦ ♪ £6.

STAFFORD*

Stoke-on-Trent, 18; Birmingham, 28; London, 141 m
pop. 54, 530 ☎ 0785   Staffordshire A1

An important centre in medieval times, Stafford today is an interesting county town with narrow streets and striking public buildings. Shoes have been made here since the 18thC.

► **St. Mary's church** in central Stafford is a large impressive building with 13thC octagonal tower; interior is light and spacious, extensively restored by Gilbert Scott 1840s but with earlier features including unusual Norman **font** with crouching beasts and figures as supports; Izaak Walton (→) was baptized here: his **bust** in N aisle is inscribed 'Izaak Walton, Piscator'. ► L. of churchyard is **Church Lane**, leading to **Mill Street** with 17thC **almshouses**. College stands in a little open court around a chapel founded 1660. ► In **Greengate Street** is **High House**, richly timbered, dated 1555; Charles I and Prince

Rupert stayed here while recruiting soldiers 1642, en route to the Battle of Shrewsbury. ► In same street, good Norman **church** of St. Chad: note **font**. ► **Shire Hall** in market square is a grand, late Georgian building (1795) by John Harvey. ► **County buildings**, Martin Street, (1893) brick-and-stone baroque. ► **William Salt Library** in 18thC town house, has extensive collection of books, deeds, drawings and engravings relating to Staffordshire's history, made by local banker William Salt, opened 1874 (*Tue.-Thu., 9.30-12.45 & 1.45-5; Fri.: 9.30-12.45 & 1.45-4.30; Sat., 9.30-1; closed Bank Hols.*).

Nearby

► **Shugborough★** (5^1/$_2$ m SE): magnificent country seat of Earls of Lichfield, begun 1693 with much added since, most spectacularly the great **portico** by Samuel Wyatt (1794). **Interior** is opulently furnished and decorated: Louis XV and Louis XVI **furniture★**; 18th and 19thC glass and silver; paintings by Sir George Hayter, Nicholas Dall, Reni, Reynolds. **Setting★** of house is spectacular: 900 acres of parkland containing garden **monuments★**, including the **Arch of Hadrian** and **Doric temple**; stable block houses **Staffordshire County Museum**: displays of agricultural and industrial heritage. **Shugborough Park Farm** is an agricultural museum with rare breeds of livestock (*house, gardens, museum and farm-mid-Mar. - Oct.: Tue.-Fri., 10.30-5.30, Sat. & Sun., 2-5.30, Bank Hols., 10-5.30; Oct. - Mar.: museum farm only, Tue.-Fri., 10.30-4.30; Sun., 2-4.30*). ► At **Shallowford** (6 ^{1}/$_2$ m S) is **Izaak Walton's Cottage**, half-timbered, with the River Fleece flowing close by; small museum (*Apr.-Sep.: Wed.-Sun; Oct.-Mar.: Sat. & Sun.*). ► **Pillaton Old Hall** (4 ^{1}/$_2$ m S): 15thC gatehouse, wing and chapel remain of this mellow brick mansion. **Chapel** of St. Moowena, rebuilt 1488, contains rare carved wooden figure of saint, perhaps late 13thC. ► **Eccleshall** (7m NW) is a small town with handsome William and Mary house among **castle ruins**: wooded grounds with moated garden; inside, paintings, porcelain and 18thC work (*Easter-Sep.: Sun., Tue. & Thu., 2-5.30; Bank Hols., 11-5.30*). ► **Mill Meece Pumping Station** (3 m N of Eccleshall): steam-powered water pumping station standing on river (*Sat. & Sun.*). □

Practical information

ⓘ Ancient High House, Greengate Street, ☎ 40204. 🚃 ☎ 211377.
Car rental: Europcar, Davies Motors, Lichfield Road, ☎ 51115.

Hotels:
★★★ *Tillington Hall* (De Vere), Eccleshall Road, ST16 1JJ, ☎ (0785) 53531, Tx 36566, AC AM BA DI, 93 rm. 🅿 ♿ 🌣 £58. Rest. ♦ ♪ Cl. lunch Sat. £9.
★★ *Abbey*, 65-68 Lichfield Road, ST17 4LW, ☎ (0785) 58531, BA, 21 rm. 🅿 ♒ £35. Rest. ♦ ♪ Cl. lunch Sun., Christmas. Venison and stuffed trout. £9.
★★ *Albridge*, 73 Wolverhampton Road, ST17 4AW, ☎ (0785) 54100, AC AM BA DI, 21 rm. 🅿 £36.50. Rest. ♦ ♪ Cl. 26 Dec. £9.
★★ *Swan* (Berni Inn), 46 Greengate Street, ST16 2JA, ☎ (0785) 58142, AC AM BA DI, 32 rm. 🅿 ♒ ♒ £45. Rest. ♦ ♪ ♿ Cl. Christmas. £12.

Recommended
Art gallery: *Stafford Art Gallery*, The Green, ☎ (0785) 57303.
Golf course: Brocton Hall, (4m SE), ☎ 661901.

STOKE-ON-TRENT★★

Manchester, 46; Birmingham, 43; London, 161 m
pop. 257,200 ☎ 0782   Staffordshire B1

Stoke is 'The Potteries'; first five and since 1910 six towns in one: Burslem, Hanley, Longton, Tunstall, Fenton and Stoke. The manufacture of fine ceramics has been the city's lifeblood since the 18thC, though there is evidence that local coal mined in the 13thC

was used to fire potter's kilns. From these small origins a great industry grew and thrives still.

► **City Museum and Art Gallery★★** (Hanley): excellent displays including archaeology, social and natural history, decorative and fine arts and **ceramics★**, both local and foreign (*Mon.-Sat., 10.30-5, Sun., 2-5*). ► **Ford Green Hall** (2 ^{1}/$_2$ m N of Hanley on B5051): part of City Museum; lovely timber-framed house with Georgian additions housing little local museum (*Mon., Wed., Thu., Sat.: 10-12.30; 2-5, Sun., 2-5*). ► In Etruria (outer Hanley) is **Shirley's Bone and Flint Mill**, built 1856 to prepare these materials for use in pottery industry (*opening 1987*). ► In Longton is splendid **Gladstone Pottery Museum★**. This was a busy, unmodernized 'potbank' until closure mid-1960s. Four restored **bottle ovens**; small workshops; frequent potters' demonstrations; working museum producing traditional cream-ware glazes, floral china jewelry; gift and tea shops (*Mon.-Sat., 10.30-5.30, Sun., 2-6*). ► In Tunstall is the **Chatterley Whitfield Mining Museum★**; tour mine, once largest in N Staffordshire, steam winding-engine, railway locomotives and coal wagons (*daily ex. Mon*). ► **Moorcroft Pottery** (*between Hanley and Burslem*) has restored bottle kiln and exhibition of the pottery's history (*Mon.-Fri., 10-4. Sat, 9.30-12.30*) ► In Burslem, 'Mother of the Potteries', is the **Wedgwood Memorial Institute**, imposing brick building with terra-cotta reliefs depicting months of year; statue of Josiah Wedgwood above porch; museum, library and gallery.

All the great potteries associated with Stoke have either excellent museums and/or factory tours and factory shops. Factory tours must normally be booked in advance and minimum numbers are often required. Check local tourist information. ► **Wedgwood Visitor Centre★** (*Barlaston, 5m S Stoke*): museum, cinema, demonstration hall, shop (*Mon.-Fri., 9-5, Sat., 10-4; Apr.-Oct. only: closed Sun.*). ► **Coalport**: demonstrations of traditional pottery skills at the **Craft Centre** (Park Street, Fenton; *Mon.-Thur., 9.30-4.30, Fri., 9.30-12.30*). ► **Minton Museum and Shop** (London Road, Stoke; *Mon.-Fri., 9-12.30, 1.30-4.30*). ► **Sir Henry Doulton Gallery**, also shop and factory (Nile Street, Burslem; *Mon.-Fri., 9-12.30, 1.30-4.15*). ► **John Beswick** (Barford Street, Longton): factory and shop. ► **Spode** (Church Street, Stoke): shop and factory.

Nearby

► **Foxfield Steam Railway** (*6m SE*): locomotive museum: round-trips by steam train on preserved line (*trips: Sun. & Bank Hols., Apr.-Sep.*). ► **Newcastle-under-Lyme** (*3m W*): not one of the Potteries although close by; many buildings of interest and a good museum and art gallery in Brampton Park. ► **Trentham Gardens** (*5m S*): 700 acres of landscaped grounds with Italian, rose and rock gardens; swimming, boating and miniature railway (*daily*). ► **Whitmore Hall** (*7m SW*): fine brick façade of 1696 conceals timber-framed house of earlier date; early 17thC stables (*May-Aug.: Tue. & Wed., 2-5.30*). ► **Dorothy Clive Garden** (*9m W*): woodland and water garden; spring bulbs, roses and azaleas in 7 landscaped acres (*Mar.-Nov.: daily, 11-7.30*). ► **Mow Cop** (*9m N*), straddling border with Cheshire, a great hill over 1,000 ft. high; from summit **views** across Cheshire Plain and E over moors; just across border castle-like **folly**, built 1754 solely to ornament rocky landscape. □

Practical information

STOKE-ON-TRENT
ⓘ 1 Glebe Street, ☎ 411222.
🚃 ☎ 411411.
Car rental: Europcar, Snows Garage Ltd., Leek Road, Hanley, ☎ 262856 (rail/drive).

Hotel:
★★★ *North Stafford* (T.F.), Station Road, ST4 2AE, ☎ (0782) 48501, Tx 36287, AC AM BA DI, 69 rm. 🅿 £59.50. Rest. ♦ ♪ £11.

▲ *Trentham Gardens Ltd.*, Stone Road, Trentham, ST4 8AX (200 pl), ☎ (0782) 657341.

Recommended

Art centre: *Staffordshire Peak Arts*, The Old School, Cauldon Lowe, ☎ (053 86) 431.

Craft shops: *Royal Doulton*, Minton, London Road, ☎ (0782) 47771, a large variety of china, crystal and giftware; *Spode Ltd.*, Spode Seconds Shop, Church Street, ☎ (0782) 46011, fine bone china, stone china and imperial earthenware.

Craft showroom: at Longton, *Waterford-Aynley China Reject Shop*, 25 Uttoxeter Road, ☎ (0782) 319216, wide range of bone china tableware.

Craft workshops: *Coalport and Crown Staffordshire*, King Street, Fenton, ☎ (0782) 49174, elegant bone china tableware, giftware, delicate flowers; *Renaissance International Ltd.*, Dewsbury Road, Fenton Industrial Estate, ☎ (0782) 413518, hand-painted figurines; *Staffordshire Potteries Ltd.*, Meir Park, ☎ (0782) 315251, home-produced kilncraft tableware and stoneware; at Barlaston, *Josiah Wedgwood and Sons Ltd.*, Wedgwood Visitor Centre, ☎ (0782) 1393218, huge selection of china products; at Longton, *Healacraft China Ltd.*, New Park Works, Weston Coyney Road, ☎ (0782) 332621, fine bone china flowers and various small gift items; *John Beswick Ltd.*, Barford, ☎ (0782) 3304, animal studies and character figures in china and porcelain; *Royal Grafton*, Malborough Road, ☎ (0782) 315667, inexpensive bone china tableware and accessory pieces; *Staffordshire Crystal Ltd.*, Gladstone Museum Centre, Uttoxeter Road, ☎ (0782) 334194, handcut and sandblasted crystal pieces.

Cycle rentals: *Roy Swinnerton*, 69 Victoria Road, Fenton; at Waterhouse, *Waterhouse*, Brown End Farm.

Golf courses: Greenway Hall, Stanley Road, Stockton Brook, ☎ 502204.

Riding school: *Mow Cop Riding Centre*, Cop Machins Farm, Mow Lane, Mow Cop, ☎ (0782) 514502.

♥ *G.Leese*, Oatcake Shop, 134 Chell Street, ☎ (0782) 261899, long-established bakery famous for oatcakes; at Waterhouse, *Lindy's Kitchen*, The Old School, Cauldon Lowe, ☎ (053 876) 431, coffee, teas, home-made cake, wholefood lunches.

Nearby

ALTON, 12m SE

Hotel:

★ *Bulls Head*, High Street, ST10 4AQ, ☎ Oakmoor (0538) 702307, BA, 6 rm. ℗ ⚘ An 18thC inn with exposed beams and stonework. This friendly inn offers real ale and homecooking. £35.

Restaurant:

♦ *Wild Duck Inn*, New Road, ☎ Oakamoor (0538) 702218 ℗ Cl. Mon., Sun. dinner. £10.

BURSLEM, 2m N on A50

Hotel:

★ *George*, Swan Square, ST6 2AE, ☎ (0782) 84021, AC AM BA DI, 38 rm. ℗ £45. Rest. ♦ ♪ £8.

Recommended

Craft shop: *Bottle Oven and Seconds Shop*, Sanbach Road, Cobridge, ☎ (0782) 24323, producers of ceramic art and all hand-painted; *Royal Doulton*, Nile Street, Burslem, ☎ (0782) 84271, sculptural ceramic works of art.

HANLEY, 1m NE on A50

Hotel:

★★★ *Stakis Grand*, ST1 5NB, ☎ (0782) 22361, Tx 778704, AC AM BA DI, 93 rm. ℗ £55. Rest. ♦ ♪ £10.

Recommended

Craft workshops: *Johnson Brothers Work Shop*, Hanley, Lichfield Street, ☎ (0782) 263934, china tableware; *Masons Ironstone Factory*, Hanley, Broad Street, ☎ (0782) 264354, ironstone tableware and giftware;

NEWCASTLE-UNDER-LYME, 12m W on A50

ⓘ reference library, Ironmarket, ☎ 618125.

Car rental: Europcar, Appleyard Staffordshire Ltd., London Road, ☎ 633954.

Hotels:

● ★★★ *Deansfield*, 98 Lancaster Road, ST5 1DS, ☎ (0782) 619040, Tx 669581, AC AM BA DI, 11 rm. ℗ ⚘ ⋘ ⚘ ⚘ £36. Rest. ♦ £8.

★★ *Post House* (T.F.), Clayton Road, ST5 4DL, ☎ (0782) 625151, Tx 36531, AC AM BA DI, 126 rm. ℗ ⚘ ⋘ ⚘ £55. Rest. ♦ Cl. lunch Sat. £11.

★★ *Thomas Forshaw*, Liverpool Road, Cross Heath, ST5 9DX, ☎ (0782) 612431, Tx 36681, AC AM BA DI, 75 rm. ℗ ⚘ ♪ £50. Rest. ♦ ♪ £10.50.

Recommended

Crafts workshops: *Portmeirion Potteries Ltd.*, 25 George Street, ☎ (0782) 615192, hand-made pottery; *The Potteries Centre at Keele*, M6 Motorway Services Area, Keele, ☎ (0782) 638783, first and second quality tableware in china, porcelain.

Golf: Municipal, Keel Road, ☎ 627596; Whitmore Road, ☎ 616583.

STONE, 8m S on A34

Hotels:

★★★ *Crown*, High Street, ST15 8AS, ☎ (0785) 813535, AC AM BA DI, 29 rm. ℗ ⚘ ⚘ £37. Rest. ♦ ♪ Cl. dinner Christmas. £8.50.

★★ *Stone House*, ST15 0BQ, ☎ (0785) 815531, AC AM BA DI, 17 rm. ℗ ⚘ ⚘ ⚘ ⚘ ♪ £45. Rest. ♦ ⚘ £10.

Restaurant:

♦ *La Casserole*, 6 Oulton Road, ☎ (0785) 814232 Cl. Sun. and Mon., 15-28 Feb., 23 Aug.-1 Sep.

SWYNNERTON, 3m W off A51

Hotel:

★ *Fitzherbert Arms*, ST15 0RA, ☎ (078 135) 542, AC AM BA DI, 12 rm. ℗ ⚘ ⚘ £25. Rest. ♦ ♪ ⚘ £7.25.

STOURBRIDGE*

Birmingham, 14; Kidderminster, 7; London, 141 m
pop. 55,136 ☎ 0384   West Midlands B2

Stourbridge, on the fringes of both the industrial Black Country and agricultural Worcestershire, is famous for its glass. A thriving country town, it serves the rural area to the W.

Nearby

▶ Stourbridge grew along with its glass industry. At **Wordsley** (*1m N*), Stuart crystal is still made; factory tours, shop and café (*tours: Mon.-Fri., 10, 11.15, 2, 3.15, last tour not offered Fri.*). ▶ **Redhouse Cone and Museum:** one of only 4 remaining glass-making cones in Britain; glass-making demonstrations and other local crafts, **glass museum** (*daily*). ▶ **Hagley Hall** (*1 1/2 m SE*): grand Palladian mansion built 1754-60 by Sanderson Miller for the 1st Baron Lyttelton; fine rococo interior; extensive grounds and deer park; restaurant (*Bank Hols. from Easter; daily, Jul.-Aug. ex. Sat. 2-5*). ▶ **Kinver** (*4 1/2 m W*): large village of brick and whitewash. **St. Peter's church** stands prominently on hill above town; in modern N aisle (completed 1976), clear glass panels have been let into the wall; **views** across fields and hills; note brass of Sir Edward Grey in Grey Chapel, with his two wives, seven sons and ten daughters. ▶ **Kinver Edge** above church: large area of open ground with sweeping views across Wyre Forest (→); **Staffordshire Way** has its southerly terminus here. It is a 93m marked path that travels N through Cannock Chase (→), Abbots Bromley (→), Trent Valley ending at Mow Cop (→) in N Stafford. Short stretches can be undertaken from Kinver Edge; Kinver itself is networked with footpaths and there are many good walks beside the canal and rivers Severn and Stour. ▶ **Clent** (*4m S*), at foot of **Clent Hills**, now a country park just beyond urban Birmingham. ▶ **St. Kenelm's Chapel** on E side of Clent is said to be the site of young Saxon saint's burial. □

Practical information

STOURBRIDGE
🚌 Town and Junction, ☎ Birmingham (021) 643 2711.
Car rental: Budget, Jessups Ltd., Apex House, Hagley Road, ☎ 375737.

Hotel:
★ *Talbot*, High Street, DY8 1DW, ☎ (0384) 394350, AC AM DA, 22 rm. £41. Rest. ♦ ♪ £8.

Recommended
Crystal workshops: at Wordsley, 1m N of Stourbridge on A491, *Stuart Crystal*, Redhouse Glassworks, ☎ (0384) 71161, crystal seconds; *Tudor Crystal Factory Shop*, Junction Road, ☎ (038 43) 4805, full lead crystal tableware and accessory pieces.
Glass showroom: at 2m N of Stourbridge off A41, *Webb Corbett Royal Doulton Crystal*, Coalbourne Hill, Amblecote, ☎ (038 43) 29528, crystal glasses, bowls, bells, vases, candlesticks.
Glass workshop: at 2m N of Stourbridge off A491, *Thomas Webb Crystal*, King William Street, Amblecote, ☎ (0384) 392521, glassware, decanters, bowls, glasses, goblets, vases.

Nearby

KINGSWINFORD, 3m N on A491

Hotel:
★ *Summerhill House*, Swindon Road, DY6 9XA, ☎ (0384) 295254, AC AM BA, 10 rm. P ♻ £38. Rest. ♦ ♪ Salmon and pheasant. £7.

STOURPORT-ON-SEVERN*

Kidderminster, 4; Worcester, 12; London, 150 m
pop. 19,054 ☎ 029 93   Hereford & Worcester A2

At the confluence of the Severn, Stour and Staffordshire and Worcestershire Canal, Stourport is England's only example of a purpose-built 18thC canal port.

▶ Large **canal basin** and early 19thC **warehouse** remain, former often filled with brightly coloured craft. ▶ Fine cast-iron **bridge** (1870) links Stourport with **Areley Kings** across Severn. ▶ (*1m SE of Areley*) series of **caves** cut into sandstone used as hermitage.

Nearby
▶ **Hartlebury Castle** (*2m E*), seat of Bishops of Worcester for more than 1,000 years. Original moated building begun early 13thC, later fortified, substantially destroyed in Civil War, rebuilt 17thC and 18thC; 15thC **great hall**; **Bishop Hurd's library** of 1782, rococo **salon**. **County museum** housed in N Wing (*state rooms, Easter Sun.-Sep.: 1st Sun. in month; Easter-end Aug.: every Wed; Bank Hols.: 2-5; county museum, Mar.-Oct.: Mon.-Fri., 2-5, Sun., 2-6; Bank Hols., 11-5*). □

Practical information

STOURPORT-ON-SEVERN
ℹ library, County Buildings, Worcester Street, ☎ 2866.

Hotels:
★★ *Stourport Moat Hse*, 35 Hartlebury Road, DY13 9LT, ☎ (029 93) 77333, Tx 9335494, AC AM BA DI, 42 rm. P ♻ ⚒ ♻ ⬛ ♪ ♩ Former country home set in 23 acres of garden. £48. Rest. ♦ ♪ & £12.
★ *Oakleigh*, 17 York Street, DY13 9EE, ☎ (029 93) 77568, 8 rm. P ⚒ & ♻ £28.

Restaurant:
♦ *Severn Tandoori*, 11 Bridge Street, ☎ (029 93) 3090, AM BA DI P ♪ & ♻ Cl. 25-26 Dec. East Indian dishes. Book. £6.

Nearby

ABBERLEY, 5m SW off A451

Hotel:
● ★★★★ *Elms* (Prestige), WR6 6AT, ☎ Great Witley (029 921) 666, Tx 337105, AC AM BA DI, 27 rm. P ♻ ⚒ ♻ & ♻ ♪ Country house built in 1710, standing in 12 acres of superb gardens. £71. Rest. ● ♦ ♪ £19.

STONE, 8m S on A34

Hotel:
★★★★ *Stone Manor*, DY10 4PJ, ☎ Chaddesley Corbett (056 283) 555, Tx 335661, AC AM BA DI, 23 rm. P ♻ ⚒ ♻ Converted Georgian manorhouse with 25 acres of woodland. £55. Rest. ♦ ♪ & Salmon. £15.

STOW-ON-THE-WOLD*

Worcester, 33; Oxford, 30; London, 86 m
pop. 1,596 ☎ 0451   Gloucestershire B3

The highest Cotswold town, Stow-on-the-Wold has an important medieval sheep market, as is demonstrated by the size of the market square.

▶ In square are medieval **market cross**, and wooden **stocks**. At W end is **St. Edward's church**, endowed by wool merchants; foundation is Norman, much added-to and rebuilt. Declared a ruin after acting as prison to 1,000 of Cromwell's captives during Civil War, restored 1680s, 1847.

Nearby
▶ **Bourton-on-the-Water**★ (*4 1/2 m SW*) is a showpiece village. The infant Windrush flows through it, crossed by footbridges with lawns on either side. ▶ **Model village** in authentic store; tiny hedges and trees; miniature Windrush with working water-wheel (*daily*). ▶ **Birdland:** 3 1/2 -acre garden with many exotic species; emphasis on conservation (*daily*). ▶ **Beautiful Butterflies Ltd.**, also an insect zoo (*daily*). ▶ **Cotswold Motor Museum** recreates 1920s village bicycle shop; vintage pedal cars, antique baby carriages, dolls' prams; vintage caravans (trailers); hundreds of 19th - 20thC enamel advertisement panels (*daily*). Adjacent in **old mill** is exhibition of past village life; photo-

North Cotswold villages

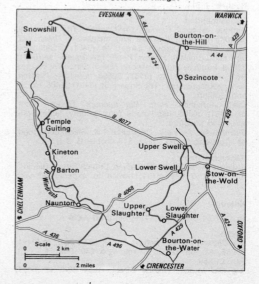

graphic history of Bourton; Edwardian shop, period toys, model reconstruction of working mill (*daily*). ▶ At **Guiting Power** (*6m SW*) is **Cotswold Farm Park★**: extensive collection of rare farm breeds; pony-trap rides. (*Apr.-Sep.: daily*).

North Cotswold Villages Round Trip

The area around Stow has some of the loveliest villages and countryside of the Cotswolds; many pleasant lanes with wildflowers, shallow streams and stone walls. The landscape is gentle, undramatic and immensely pleasing.

▶ Leave Stow on B407; after 1m reaching **Upper Swell** and l. to **Lower Swell**; through both villages runs the River Dikler; former has lovely 18thC manor, and church in latter has superb Norman carving. ▶ S to **Upper Slaughter** and **Lower Slaughter**, both animated by little River Eye. $1/_2$ m S is Bourton-on-the Water (→). ▶ NW, crossing B4068 to **Naunton**, strung along Windrush Valley. **Church** has superb **pulpit**; carved stone c. 1400, decorated with tracery and canopied panels. ▶ Follow Windrush N, to **Barton**: 18thC Barton House, fine Cotswold building. ▶ N again to **Kineton** with 17thC farmhouses. ▶ **Temple Guiting**, thus named as holy place of Knights Templars, last village in Windrush Valley before one turns r. then soon l. again, crossing B404, climbing N, through beautiful countryside to reach **Snowshill**, stone cottages and lovely **manor** (*open to public*). ▶ ESE through charming landscape, staying high on wolds to **Bourton-on-the-Hill** (→). ▶ Down to **Sezincote**: beautiful garden surrounding extravagant Indian-style house (→). Return to Stow on A424 (*4m*). □

Practical information

STOW-ON-THE-WOLD
ⓘ the library, St. Edwards Hall, The Square, ☎ 30352.

Hotels:
● ★★ *Unicorn Crest* (Crest), Sheep Street, GL54 1HQ, ☎ (0451) 30257, AC AM BA DI, 20 rm. ℗ ≼ ⌇ £51.50. Rest. ♦ ♪ £12.
★★ *Grapevine*, Sheep Street, GL54 1AU, ☎ (0451) 30344, AC BA, 19 rm. ≼ ⅏ £55. Rest. ♦ ♪ Cl. Christmas - 12 Jan. £9.
★ *Brookside*, Riverside, GL54 2BS, ☎ (0451) 20371, AC AM BA DI, 10 rm. ℗ ≼ ⌇ £48. Rest. ♦ ♪ ᵫ £10.50.
★ *Royalist*, Digbeth Street, GL54 1BN, ☎ (0451) 30670, AC AM BA DI, 12 rm. ℗ ⅏ No children under 5. The oldest hotel in Stow, originally built in the 10thC. £40. Rest. ♦ ♪ £11.

Recommended
Antique shops: *Clarke, Christopher*, The Fossway, ☎ (0451) 30476, furniture and metalwork; *Greenwold, Lynn*, Digbeth, Digbeth Street, ☎ (0451) 30398, pottery and porcelain; *Hockin, Keith*, The Square, ☎ (0451) 31058, furniture and metalwork; *Nutter, Simon W.*, Wraggs Row, Fosse Way, ☎ (0451) 30658, furniture; *Preston, Antony Antiques Ltd.*, The Square, ☎ (0451) 31406, clocks and furniture.
Craft workshop: *Hart Villa Interiors*, Sheep Street, ☎ (0451) 30392, hand-made rugs, pottery, lamps, pictures and sculpture.
Farmhouse: *Fairview*, Oddington Hill, Bledington Road, ☎ Cotswold (0451) 30279. £18 double; B. & B.

Recommended:
Riding school: *Cromwell Stables*, Church Street, Bledington, ☎ (060 871) 8191, novice to experienced with full instruction.

Nearby
BOURTON-ON-THE-WATER, 4m S off A429

Hotels:
★★ *Chester House*, Victoria Street, GL54 2BU, ☎ (0451) 20286, AC AM BA DI, 22 rm. ⌇ ᵫ £40. Rest. ♦ ♪ Cl. Jan. £10.50.
★★ *Old Manse*, Victoria Street, GL54 2BX, ☎ (0451) 20642, AC BA, 10 rm. ℗ ⅏ No children under 5. £45. Rest. ♦ ♪ ᵫ Cl. mid-Jan. £10.

Restaurant:
● ♦ *Rose Tree*, Riverside, ☎ (0451) 20635, AC AM BA DI ≼ ⅏ ♪ ⅏ Cl. lunch Oct.-Apr., mid-Jan.-mid-Feb., Sun.-Mon. eve. Fillet of English lamb with madeira and basil. Book. £10.

Recommended
Craft workshop: *Bourton Pottery*, Clayton Row, functional and decorative pottery pieces.
Riding school: *Long Distance Riding Centre*, Fossway, ☎ (0451) 20358, novice to experienced with full instruction.
♥ *The Cotswold Perfumery Ltd.*, Victoria Street, ☎ (0451) 20698, fragrance in the form of cologne, bath oil or bubble bath.

LOWER SLAUGHTER, 1m N

Hotel:
● ★★★ *Manor* (Best Western), GL54 2HP, ☎ (0451) 20456, Tx 437287, AC AM BA DI, 21 rm. ℗ ≼ ⅏ ⌇ ⅏ ⅏ No children under 8. Medieval Cotswold manor house, set in 14 acres of gardens and woodlands. £80. Rest. ♦ ♪ £17.

LOWER SWELL, 1m W on B4086

Hotel:
● ★★ *Old Farmhouse*, GL54 1LF, ☎ (0451) 30232, AC BA, 13 rm. ℗ ⅏ ⌇ £44. Rest. ♦ ᵫ Cl. 23 Dec. - 23 Jan. £11.

Inn or Pub:
Golden Ball (Donnington), ☎ (0451) 30247 ℗ ≼ ⅏ ⌇ ⅏ Bar meals with home-made pies and pâtés. £9.50.

UPPER SLAUGHTER, 1 1/2m NW

Hotel:
● ★★ *Lords of the Manor*, GL54 2JD, ☎ (0451) 20243, Tx 83147, AC AM BA DI, 15 rm. ℗ ≼ ⅏ ᵫ ⅏ No children under 2. £85. Rest. ♦ ♪ Cl. 1 - 14 Jan. £17.

STRATFORD-UPON-AVON***

Birmingham, 22; Oxford, 38; London, 96 m
pop. 20,941 ☎ 0789   Warwickshire B2

Apart from London, Stratford is probably Britain's most famous town, for here in April 1564, William Shakespeare was born, and here he is buried. Even if the all-pervasive Shakespearian connections were absent, this remains a lovely riverside town with fine architecture of many periods in placid lowland country.

▶ **Shakespeare's Birthplace** (Henley Street), containing Shakespearian artifacts and costume exhibition. **New Place** (Chapel Street): house that Shakespeare bought in his prosperity, then reckoned to be finest house in Stratford; only foundations remain. Rev. Francis Gastren bought property 1753, later cut down the mulberry tree planted by poet to avoid showing it to visitors, then demolished New Place because of a squabble over rates; lovely grounds preserved as Elizabethan 'knot garden'. **Hall's Croft:** Shakespeare's daughter Susannah lived here after her marriage to Dr. John Hall. **Anne Hathaway's cottage** (at Shottery 1m W), stoutly thatched, where Anne Hathaway lived before her marriage to Shakespeare (*all Trust properties open Apr.-Oct.: wkdays, 9-6 (9-5 Oct.); Sun., 10-6 (10-5 Oct.); Nov.-Mar.: wkdays only, 9-4.30; Anne Hathaway's cottage also open Nov.-Mar.: Sun., 1.30-4.30*). ▶ Shakespeare is buried in **Holy Trinity Church★**; notice Gothic **organ case**, hammerbeam roof and 16thC carved misericords and monuments in Clopton Chapel; Shakespeare's tomb and those of his daughter Susannah and her husband are in chancel. **Royal Shakespeare Theatre** built 1932, designed by Elizabeth Scott, with gardens bordering the Avon; guided tours backstage and of adjoining **gallery** (*daily: 1.30, 5.30*).

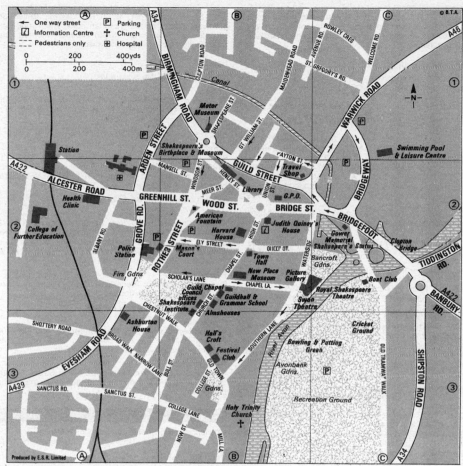

STRATFORD-UPON-AVON

Gallery has fascinating collection of theatre paintings, portraits, costumes and props, sound recordings of famous past productions (*daily: 9-6; Sun., 12-5*). ▶ **Harvard House** (High Street, 1596): this timber-framed house was home of Katherine and Robert Harvard whose son John founded Harvard University, USA (*Apr.-Oct.: Mon.-Sat., 9-1 & 2-6, Sun., 2-6; Nov.-Mar.: Thu.-Sat., 10-1 & 2-4*). ▶ **Grammar school**: early 15thC building where Shakespeare was educated (*during school hols.*). ▶ **Arms and Armour Museum** (Poets Arbour, Sheep Street): collection of weapons from pocket pistols to cannons ranging over 600 years (*daily ex. Sun.: 10-6*). ▶ **Garrick Inn**, named after famous actor who began Shakespeare Festival 18thC. ▶ **Stratford Butterfly Farm** (Tramway Walk): many exotic species in glasshouse with pools and tropical plants (*daily*). ▶ **Stratford Motor Museum**: vintage cars and appropriate fashionable dress from early days of motoring (*Apr.-Oct.: daily, 9.30-6; Nov.-Mar.: 10-4*). ▶ **Brass rubbing centre** (Summer House, Avonbank Gardens): reproduction brasses; equipment and instruction provided (*daily: 10-6; winter: Sat., Sun., 10-4*).

Nearby

▶ **Clopton Bridge**: 15thC stone bridge with 14 arches. ▶ **Mary Arden's House**, Wilmcote (*3 m NW*) pale-timbered farmhouse, childhood home of Shakespeare's mother; farm buildings contain collection of old Warwickshire farm implements; country crafts (*Apr.-Oct.: wkdays, 9-6, Sun., 10-6; Nov.-Mar.: wkdays only, 9-4.30*). ▶ **Charlecote Park** (supposed scene of youthful Shakespeare's poaching exploits, and his apprehension by Sir Thomas Lucy; seat of locally powerful Lucy family since 1247. Beautiful Elizabethan house with characteristic tall chimney stacks; 18thC additions include drawing room and billiard room by Gibson; objects and pictures from Beckford's Fonthill Abbey. Gardens and deer park (*Easter Sat.-Tue.: 11-5; Apr.: Sat. & Sun., 11-5; May-end Sep.: daily ex. Mon. & Thu. & Bank Hol. Mon., 11-6; Oct.: Sat. & Sun., 11-5*). ▶ **Hampton Lucy** (*4m NE*) in Avon Valley with Georgian Gothic **church**, 1822-6, designed by Rickman and Hutchinson; apsidal **chancel** with fine stone vaulting added 1856 by G. Gilbert Scott. ▶ **Wootton Warren** (*7m NW*) on River Alne and Stratford-upon-Avon Canal: half-timbered and whitewashed cottages; interesting **church**: many periods represented from 11thC (lower part of

tower) through 12thC (nave), 14thC (nave, wall painting, S chapel) to 16th & 18thC tombs. ▶ **Henley in Arden** has a long High Street and market square with numerous attractive buildings including 15thC **guildhall** and 17th and 18thC coaching inns. □

Practical information

STRATFORD-UPON-AVON
ⓘ Judith Shakespeare's House, 1 High Street, ☎ 293127.
▒▒▒ (A1), ☎ Rugby (0788) 60116.
Car rental: Europcar, F Guyer Sons, Rother Street (B2), ☎ 69107; Avis, ☎ (0926) 28484 (rail/drive).

Hotels:
★★★★ *Moat House Intl* (Q.M.H.), Bridgefoot, CV37 6YR (C2), ☎ (0789) 67511, Tx 311127, AC AM BA DI, 249 rm. P ⫷ ⑳ & ⌡ £70. Rest. ♦ ♪ & £14.50.
● ★★★ *Welcombe*, Warwick Road, CV37 0NR (C1), ☎ (0789) 295252, Tx 31347, AC AM BA DI, 84 rm. P ⫷ ⑳ ⚲ & ⌡ ⌅ Victorian baronial-style house, standing in 150-acres, with its own golf course. £90. Rest. ♦ & Cl. 29 Dec. - 3 Jan. £20.
★★★ *Arden*, Waterside, CV37 6BA (B2), ☎ (0789) 294949, Tx 311726, AC AM BA DI, 59 rm. P ⫷ ⑳ ⌡ £58. Rest. ♦ £10.
★★★ *Falcon* (Q.M.H.), Chapel Street, CV37 6HA (B2), ☎ (0789) 205777, Tx 312522, AC AM BA DI, 73 rm. P ⌡ £64. Rest. ♦ ♪ & £10.50.
★★★ *Grosvenor House* (B.W.), Warwick Road, CV37 6YT (C1), ☎ (0789) 69213, Tx 311699, AC AM BA DI, 57 rm. P ⑳ ⚯ £52. Rest. ♦ ♪ & Cl. 24 - 28 Dec. £13.50.
★★★ *Shakespeare* (T.F.), Chapel Street, CV37 6ER (B2), ☎ (0789) 294771, Tx 311181, AC AM BA DI, 66 rm. P ⚲ & £75. Rest. ♦ ♪ & £17.50.
● ★★ *Stratford House*, Sheep Street, CV37 6EF (B2), ☎ (0789) 68288, Tx 312522, AC AM BA DI, 9 rm. & £54. Rest. ♦ Cl. Jan. £14.
★★ *Dukes*, Payton Street, CV37 6UA (B1-B2), ☎ (0789) 69300, AC BA, 20 rm. P ⑳ ⚲ ⚯ ⌡ ⑫ £50. Rest. ♦ Cl. 25 - 30 Dec. Stuffed trout. £9.

Restaurants:
● ♦ *Bunburys*, 3 Greenhill Street (B2), ☎ (0789) 293563, AC AM BA DI ⑳ ♪ ⚯ Cl. Mon. Venison. Book. £14.
♦ *Dbut*, 21-23 Sheep Street (B2), ☎ (0789) 293546, AC AM BA DI. Cl. Sun. £14.
♦ *Giovanni*, 8 Ely Street (B2), ☎ (0789) 297999, AC AM BA ♪ & ⚯ Cl. Bank Hols., Sun. Book. £10.50.
♦ *Marlowe's*, 18 High Street (B2), ☎ (0789) 204999, AC AM BA DI P ⚯ Cl. last 2 wks. Jan. Drunken duck marinaded in gin, red wine, lemon juice and juniper berries. Book. £5.
♦ *Rumours*, 10 Henley Street (B2), ☎ (0789) 204297, AC AM BA DI ♪ ⚯ No children under 8. Cl. 1st wk. Jan. Wild mushroom cocktail (with pine kernels and herbs in filo pastry). Book. £15.

⚑ *Avon P.*, Warwick Road, (90 pl), ☎ (0789) 293438; *Dodwell P.*, Evesham Road, (50 pl), ☎ (0789) 204957; *Island Meadow C.P.*, The Mill House, Aston Cantlow, (15 pl), ☎ (078 981) 273.

Recommended
Bed and breakfast: at Oxhill, Nolands Farm, ☎ (0926) 640309. £15 double; B. & B.
Craft centre: *Centre Arts*, Studio1, Henley Street, ☎ (0789) 68731, hand-made products, wood carvings, toys, puzzles, cards.
Craft workshops: *Craft Factory*, Main Street, Middle Tysoe, ☎ (029 588) 705, traditional English clothes, toys, dolls, gifts, souvenirs; *Stratford-upon-Avon Pottery*, Firs Farmhouse, Lower Quinton, ☎ (0789) 720703, domestic stoneware, mugs, vases, honey-pots, goblets.
Cycle rental: *Knotts*, 15 Western Road.
Farmhouses: at Dorsington, *Church Farm*, ☎ (0789) 720471. £20 double; B. & B.; at Loxley, ☎ (0789) 840478. £30 double; B. & B.
Golf course: Tiddington Road, ☎ 205749.
♥ *Arbour Antiques Ltd.*, Poet's Arbour, Sheep Street, ☎ (0789) 293453, arms, armour and metalwork; *Scoops*, 26 Henley Street, ☎ (0789) 68758, first-and second-

quality glassware, crystal and china; *The Little Gallery Ltd.*, 37 Henley Street, ☎ (0789) 293742, British gift products, Tudor houses, Victorian dolls; *The Tappit Hen*, 57 Henley Street, ☎ (0789) 69933, modern and reproduction hand-cast pewter pieces.

Nearby

ALDERMINSTER, 4m S on A34
Hotel:
● ★★★★ *Ettington Park*, CV37 8BS, ☎ (0789) 740740, Tx 311825, AC AM BA DI, 49 rm. P ⫷ ⑳ ⚲ & ⚯ ▱ ⌆ ⌡ ⑫ £90. Rest. ● ♦ & £24.

BILLESLEY, 4m on A422
Hotel:
★★★ *Billesley Manor*, B49 6NF, ☎ (0789) 763737, Tx 312599, AC AM BA DI, 28 rm. P ⫷ ⑳ ⚲ & ⚯ ▱ Fine old manorhouse, first mentioned in 1066, set in 11 acres of grounds. £70. Rest. ● ♦ ♪ £17.

ETTINGTON, 4m SE on A422
Hotel:
● ★★ *Chase Country Hse*, Banbury Road, CV37 7NZ, ☎ (0789) 740000, AC AM BA, 11 rm. ⑳ ⚲ ⚯ No children under 8. Secluded country house, standing in 14 acres of ground and surrounded by farmland. £51.50. Rest. ● ♦ ♪ Cl. dinner Sun., Christmas. £15.

Recommended
Bed and breakfast: *Houndshill House*, Banbury Road, ☎ (0789) 740267. £30 double; B. & B.

HENLEY-IN-ARDEN, 8m N on A34
Restaurant:
♦ *Le Filbert Cottage*, 64 High Street, ☎ (056 42) 2700, AC AM BA DI ⫷ ⚲ ♪ ⚯ Cl. Sun., Bank Hols., Mon. *Bisque de crabe, veau zurichoise*. £16.50.

Recommended
Craft workshop: *Torquil Pottery*, 81 High Street, Solihull, ☎ (056 42) 2174, a wide range of stoneware and porcelain pottery.

STROUD*

Cheltenham, 14; Bristol, 32; London, 109 m
pop. 20,930 ☎ 04536/0453   Gloucestershire A3

This town of steep, narrow streets was in the late 18th - early 19thC an important centre for the production of broadcloth and the dyeing trade: 'Stroudwater Scarlets' were famous for their use in military uniforms.

▶ **Stroudwater Canal,** entering Severn at Framilode, was constructed 1779 to transport raw wool to town, take finished cloth away. ▶ **St. Lawrence Church,** rebuilt 19thC with 14thC tower. ▶ **All Saints** (uplands) early 20thC in Early English manner. ▶ **Congregational Chapel** (1835-7), in grand Classical style. ▶ **Stroud Subscription Rooms** by same architect. ▶ **Museum:** local history and archaeology.

Nearby

▶ Walk across **Minchinhampton Common** (*SE of town*) to **Minchinhampton** for wonderful views. ▶ **Haresfield Beacon** to **Frocester Hill** (*3m SW*): both offering lovely walks. ▶ Near **Nympsfield** (*3m S*), village on Stroudwater Hills is **Hetty Pegler's Trunk,** impressive chambered long barrow (*key from cottage on Uley-Stroud Road*). ▶ **Painswick★** (*3¹/₂ m N*), town where Cotswold stone is very pale; many fine houses of wealthy 17th and 18thC clothiers. **Misorden Park Gardens** (*8m NE*): Tudor manor with terraced garden, yew hedges, rose garden, spectacular spring colours (*early Apr. - late Sep.: Wed., Thu., 10-4.30*). ▶ **Owlpen Manor★** (*nr. Oursley, 8m SW*): beautiful Tudor house; 17thC gazebo, early 18thC corn mill and 15thC barn; church rebuilt 19thC on site of earlier one; remarkable group of buildings; 18thC terraced gardens (*wkdays Apr.-Sep.: written appt. necessary*). ▶ **Slimbridge★★** (*9m*

W): headquarters of the Wildfowl Trust; huge collection of captive wildfowl, notably flocks of white-fronted geese in winter and Bewick's Swans; hides; also tropical birds and waterfowl; cafés; shops (daily). ▶ **Berkeley Castle**★★ (11m SW): perfectly preserved castle built 1153, where Edward II was murdered 1327. Norman keep, great hall, dungeon, state rooms with splendid paintings and tapestries, **gardens** and **deer park**, butterfly house in summer.□

Practical information

STROUD

ⓘ council offices, High Street, ☎ 4252.

▰▰▰ ☎ Gloucester (0452) 29501.

Hotels:

★★ **London**, 30 London Road, GL5 2AJ, ☎ (045 36) 79992, AC BA DI, 10 rm. ℗ ✕ No children under 6. £40. Rest. ◆ ♪ Cl. Sun. £12.

★ **Downfield**, 134 Cainscross Road, GL5 4HN, ☎ (045.36) 4496, 23 rm. ℗ ♿ £28. Rest. ◆ ♿ Cl. Christmas. £7.

⚠ The Tudor Arms C.C.P., Shepherd's Patch, Slimbridge, (75 pl), ☎ (045 389) 483.

Recommended

Dennis French Woodware, The Craft Shop, Brimscombe Hill, Brimscombe, ☎ (0453) 883054, woodware.

Golf course: Stinchcombe Hill, Dursley, ☎ (0453) 2015.

♥ West of England Woollen Mills, Frome Hall, Chestnut Lane, ☎ (045 36) 77301, a wide range of suitings and fabrics in pure wool.

Nearby

AMBERLEY, 2m S off A46

Hotel:

★★ **Amberley Inn** (B.W.), GL5 5AF, ☎ (045 387) 2565, AC AM BA, 15 rm. ℗ ≮ ⚲ ♪ ⚫ £47. Rest. ◆ £11.50.

BERKELEY, 4m SW off A38

Hotels:

★★ **Old Schoolhouse**, Canonbury Street, GL13 9BG, ☎ Dursley (0453) 811711, AC BA, 7 rm ℗ ≮ ✕ £40. Rest. ◆ ♿ Cl. Christmas. Halibut with lime and ginger butter. £14.

★★ **Prince of Wales**, GL13 9HD, ☎ Dursley (0453) 810474, AC AM BA DI, 7 rm. ℗ ▥ This traditional Victorian inn is an ideal 'stopping-off' point for a journey N or W. £38. Rest. ◆ £9.50.

Recommended

Craft workshop: Berkeley Saddlery, 12 High Street, Berkeley, ☎ (0453) 811821, new bridle work and general leather goods.

CHALFORD, 4m E off A419

Hotel:

★★ **Springfield House**, London Road, GL6 8NW, ☎ Brimscombe (0453) 883555, AC AM BA DI, 7 rm. ℗ ≮ ▥ ⚲ ♪ £47.50. Rest. ◆ ♿ Cl. 1 - 14 Jan. £11.50.

MINCHINHAMPTON, 3m SE off A419

Hotel:

● ★★★ **Burleigh Court**, GL5 2PF, ☎ Brimscombe (0453) 883804, AC AM BA, 12 rm. ℗ ≮ ▥ ⚲ ✕ £45. Rest. ◆ ♿ Cl. 24 - 31 Dec. £12.50.

Recommended

Bed and breakfast: at Nailsworth, Orchard Close, Springhill, ☎ (045 383) 2503. £22 double.

PAINSWICK, 3m N on A46

Hotel:

● ★★ **Painswick**, Kemps Lane, GL6 6YB, ☎ (0452) 812160, Tx 43605, AC AM BA DI, 15 rm. ℗ ≮ ▥ ⚲ ♪ £60. Rest. ◆ ♿ £15.

Recommended

Antique shop: Hamand Antiques, Friday Street, Painswick, ☎ (0452) 812310, furniture, oriental ceramics, metalwork, pottery, porcelain.

RODBOROUGH COMMON, 2m S off A46

Hotel:

★★★ **Bear of Rodborough**(Anchor), GL5 5DE, ☎

Amberley (045 387) 3522, Tx 437130, AC AM BA DI, 48 rm. ℗ ≮ ▥ ♿ ♪ £55. Rest. ◆ ♿ £12.50.

⚠ Rodborough Fort C.C., Rodborough, (40 pl), ☎ (045 36) 3478.

STONEHOUSE, 2m W on A419

Hotel:

★★★ **Stonehouse Court**, Bristol Road, GL10 3RA, ☎ (045 382) 5155, Tx 437244, AC AM BA DI, 23 rm. ℗ ≮ ▥ ♿ ♿ ✕ ♪ ⚲ £54. Rest. ◆ ♿ Cl. 25 Dec. - 12 Jan. Fish and game. £16.

TAMWORTH*

Nottingham, 35; Birmingham, 17; London, 124 m
pop. 63,260 ☎ 0827   Staffordshire B1

An ancient town standing on the rivers Tame and Anker, it was early capital of Saxon Mercia. King Offa lived here, enclosing the town with a defensive ditch and establishing a royal mint.

▶ **Castle**★ has circular Norman keep, on a mound that is probably 10thC, part of a fortress founded by Ethelfleda, daughter of Alfred the Great, who defeated the Danes here in 913. Later additions include Tudor **hall** squeezed inside keep, housing **museum:** coins minted at Tamworth (daily ex. Fri.: 10-5.30; Sun.: 2-5.30). ▶ **St. Editha's Church** has remarkable **double-spiral staircase** in SW turret; reredos by Gilbert Scott, stained glass by Burne-Jones, Madox Brown and William Morris. Ornate 18thC Ferrers monument. ▶ **Town hall**, 1701, raised on columns with arched windows crowned with a cupola.

Nearby

▶ **Drayton Manor Park and Zoo** (Fazeley, 1 ¹/₂ m S): 160 acres of parkland with open-plan zoo and amusement park, lakes and picnicking. ▶ Highly unusual **church of St. Chad** at Hopwas (2m NW), 1881, mixes domestic black and-white timbering with ecclesiastical forms.   □

Practical information

TAMWORTH

ⓘ Marmion House, Lichfield Street, ☎ 64222.

▰▰▰ ☎ Coventry (0203) 555211.

Hotel:

★★★ **Castle**, Ladybank, B79 7NB, ☎ (0827) 57181, AC AM BA, 25 rm. ⚲ £40. Rest. ◆ ♿ £8.

Inn or Pub:

Bulls Head (Marstons), Watling Street, ☎ (0827) 287 820 ℗ Snacks and cooked meals. £4.50.

⚠ Drayton Manor P., Fazeley, (75 pl), ☎ (0827) 287979.

Recommended

Golf course: Eagle Drive, ☎ 53850.

Nearby

ATHERSTONE, 7m SE on A5

Hotels:

★ **Chapel House**, Friars Gate, CV9 1EY, ☎ (082 77) 66238, AC BA DI, 10 rm. ▥ ⚲ ✕ ▭ £35. Rest. ◆ ♪ ♿ Cl. 24 Dec. - 2 Jan., Aug. £15.50.

★ **Old Red Lion**, Long Street, CV9 1BB, ☎ (082 77) 3156, Tx 342817, AC AM BA DI, 10 rm. ⚲ £33. Rest. ◆ ♿ Cl. 25 - 26 Dec. £10.

TELFORD*

Shrewsbury, 12; Birmingham, 33; London, 152 m
pop. 100,000 ☎ 0952   Shropshire A1

Telford is a new town, begun in 1963 and named after the great engineer and architect, Thomas Telford (→), so active in Shropshire. It is light industrial town that is planned to house 150,000 people by the late 80s.

Nearby

▶ **The Wrekin:** this striking hill rears up from flat land beside the Severn; good walking and views from summit. ▶ **Ruins of Linesham Abbey** (*2m NE*), founded 1148; adopted as a stronghold during Civil War, which contributed to its ruination (*Apr.-Sep.: Mon.-Sat., 9.30-6.30, Sun., 2-6.30*). ▶ **Weston Park**★ (*3 ¹/₂ m SE nr. Shifnal*): graceful Restoration mansion designed by Lady Wilbraham, 1671. Gobelin and Aubusson **tapestries;** collection of **paintings** by Van Dyck, Gainsborough, Lely, Holbein; 19thC orangery; terraced gardens; extensive grounds by Capability Brown with lakes, woods and fallow deer; other attractions include pottery, miniature railway, butterfly farm (*Easter-end Sep.: wkends mid-Jul. - end Aug. daily*). **Church of St Andrew** adjoins house: carved pulpit c. 1701; numerous monuments to Wilbraham and Bradford ancestors. ▶ **Shifnal** is an old town, principally Georgian, owing to a fire 1591; Norman churches, a sprinkling of black-and-white houses that survived fire. ▶ **Newport** (*6m NE*): small town with attractive main street.　□

Practical information

TELFORD

▨▨▨　☎ Wolverhampton (0902) 59545.
Car rental: Europcar, George Oakley & Co., Park Street, ☎ 460147, Shipnal.

Hotel:
★ **Hillview**, Cold Hatton, TF6 6QB, ☎ Great Bolas (095 283) 577, AC, 6 rm. ℗ ⚒ ⚑ ⚹ £27.50. Rest. ♦ ♪ ⚹ £7.

Recommended
Farmhouses: at Shawbury, *New Farm*, ☎ (0939) 250358. £20 double; B. & B.; at Wrockwardine, *Wrockwardine Farm*, ☎ (0952) 42278. £18 double; B. & B.
Golf course: Wrekin, Ercall Woods (off A5), ☎ 44032.
Riding school: Lilleshall Riding Livery Stables, Child Pit Farm, Lilleshall, ☎ Telford 607166.

Nearby

DONNINGTON, 2m N on A518

Hotel:
★★ **White House**, Wellington Road, TF2 8NG, ☎ (0952) 604276, AC BA, 10 rm. ℗ ⚒ ⚑ ⚹ £40. Rest. ♦ ♪ ⚹ £12.

NEWPORT, 2m NE
ℹ 9 St. Mary's Street, ☎ 814109.

Hotel:
★★ **Royal Victoria**, St. Mary's Street, TF10 7BJ, ☎ (0952) 810831, AC AM BA, 22 rm. ℗ A pleasant Georgian inn overlooking a garden. Queen Victoria is reputed to have stayed here. £33. Rest. ♦ £8.50.

SUTTON HILL, 3m S off A442

Hotel:
★★★ **Telford**, Great Hay, TF7 4DT, ☎ (0952) 585642, Tx 35481, AC AM BA DI, 58 rm. ℗ ⚒ ⚑ ⚒ £58. Rest. ♦ ♪ £9.50.

WELLINGTON, 2m W on A5061
ℹ 9 Walker Street, ☎ 48295.
▨▨▨　☎ Shrewsbury (0743) 64041.

Hotels:
★★★ **Buckatree Hall** (B.W.), The Wrekin, TF6 5AL, ☎ (0952) 51821, Tx 35701, AC AM BA DI, 37 rm. ℗ ⚒ Country house standing in 10 acres of woodland. £41. Rest. ♦ £8.50.
★ **Charlton Arms**, Church Street, TF1 1DG, ☎ (0952) 51351, Tx 629064, AC AM BA DI, 27 rm. ℗ £48. Rest. ♦ ♪ £10.

TETBURY*

Cirencester, 11; Bristol, 29; London, 106 m
pop. 4,467 ☎ 0666　　　　　　　Gloucestershire B3

Tetbury is a low-lying, South Cotswold market town with fine 18thC buildings and handsome market hall.

▶ **St. Mary's church** is early Gothic Revival style, completed 1781. ▶ **Market hall**, built 1655: stone building supported on Tuscan columns; stone slate roof, cupola with weathervane of gilded dolphins. ▶ **The Chipping** was original market place. From NE corner flight of stone steps leads to old burial ground (now cattle market); **cottages** beside steps, 1690.

Nearby

▶ **Westonbirt Arboretum,**★ founded 1829: rare trees in 116 acres (*daily: Apr.-Oct.*). ▶ **Chavenage House** (*2m N*): Elizabethan manor with 16th & 17thC tapestries and furniture; fine medieval **barn.** (*Easter; May-Sep.: Thu., Sun., Bank Hols., 2-5*). ▶ **Wotton-Under-Edge**★ (*8m W*): pleasant town of narrow streets; Cotswold Way Path (→) passes through Wotton. Climb section just N of town to **Nibley Knoll** for superb **view**★ over Severn Vale to Black Mountains. Also, monument to William Tyndale, first translator of Bible into English. ▶ **Kingswood Abbey Gatehouse** (*1m S of Wotton*) only remains of Kingswood Abbey (*mid-Mar. - mid-Oct.: daily, 10-6; end Oct. - mid-Mar.: daily, 10-4*). ▶ **Newark Park** (*1 ¹/₂ m E of Wotton*): hunting lodge remodeled 1790s by James Wyatt. Built of stones from Abbey (demolished 1540); magnificent situation on cliff edge and woodland garden. (*Apr., May, Aug. & Sep.: Wed. & Thu., 2-5*).　□

Practical information

TETBURY
ℹ Old Court House, 63 Long Street, ☎ 53552.

Hotels:
● ★★★ **Close** (Prestige), 8 Long Street, GL8 8AG, ☎ (0666) 52272, Tx 43232, AC AM BA DI, 12 rm. ℗ ⚒ ⚒ £60. Rest. ♦ £16.
● ★★★ **Snooty Fox** (B.W.), Market Place, GL8 8DD, ☎ (0666) 52436, Tx 449848, AC AM BA DI, 12 rm. ⚒ Traditional Cotswold stone coaching inn in the market square. £70. Rest. ♦ ♪ £16.50.

Restaurants:
♦ **Gentle Gardener**, Long Street, ☎ (0666) 52884, AC AM BA DI. 9 rm. ℗ ⚒ ♪ ⚒ Lamb and eggplant charlotte. Book. £12.50.
♦ **Hubbits**, 7 New Church Street, ☎ (0666) 53306, AC AM BA ♪ ⚒ Cl. 2 wks. Jan., Sun eve., Mon. Lemon sole with dill, prawns and cream, vegetarian dishes. Book. £11.

Recommended
Antique shops: Bolam, George S., Oak House, 1 The Chipping, ☎ (066) 52211, furniture, pottery, porcelain and paintings; *Bristow, J. M. Antiques*, 28 Long Street, ☎ (0666) 52222, clocks and furniture; *Marsh Jasper*, 3 The Chipping, ☎ (0666) 52832, furniture.
Art gallery: *Long Street Gallery*, 50 Long Street, ☎ (0666) 53722.
▼ **Dairy:** *House of Cheese*, 13 Church Street, ☎ (0666) 522865, sells a wide selection of British and continental cheeses.

Nearby

BEVERSTONE, 2m S off A442

Hotel:
● ★★★ **Calcot Manor**, GL8 8YJ, ☎ Leighterton (066 689) 335, AC AM BA DI, 7 rm. ℗ ⚒ ⚒ ⚑ ⚒ ⚒ ╱ ⚒ £75. Rest. ● ♦ ⚒ Cl. 7 - 14 Jan. £18.

WESTONBIRT, 2m SW on A433

Hotel:
● ★★ **Hare and Hounds** (B.W.), GL8 8QL, ☎ (066 688) 233, AC AM BA, 27 rm. ℗ ⚒ ╱⚒ £53. Rest. ♦ £12.

TEWKESBURY**

Worcester, 15; Gloucester, 11; London, 110 m
pop. 9,454 ☎ 0684　　　　　　　Gloucestershire B2

A town that has successfully preserved many of its attractive historic buildings. The Severn and Avon merge here.

▶ **Abbey church★** is Tewkesbury's great glory. Consecrated 1121; **tower** and **nave** are Norman architecture of the first order. **W front★** has 65 ft. Norman **arch;** inside, 14 massive Norman columns support 14thC vaulted **roof.** Three **chantry chapels: chapel of Robert Fitz Hamon★** (N of altar), founder of the abbey: beautiful fan-vaulting; **Trinity Chapel** (S of altar), built for Edward Despencer similar to Fitz Hamon Chapel, with effigy of the knight kneeling at prayer; splendid **Beauchamp Chapel** (N of altar), erected 1422 by Isabel Despencer, Countess of Warwick, to her first husband. Two storeys, each finely vaulted. Exquisite 14thC **stained glass** in choir. ▶ **Tewkesbury Museum** (Barton Street) housed in two ancient timbered houses, also information centre; learn here about the bloody Battle of Tewkesbury, 1471 (*Easter-end Sep.: daily*). ▶ **Abbey Cottages:** originally 23 shops, built 1430. ▶ **John Moore Museum** (41 Abbey Cottages) is devoted to this writer (*Easter-Oct.: Tue.-Sat.*). ▶ **Little museum** (no. 45) has part of solid oak staircase and a smoke apron; simply furnished to suggest how medieval tradesmen lived. ▶ **Old Baptist Chapel Court** (Church Street): one of the oldest Nonconformist chapels in the country; some original features, 17thC furnishings. ▶ **House of Nodding Gables** (High Street), formerly ticket-office for stagecoaches. ▶ **Lilley's Alley** (off Church Street) has cottage with pronounced over hang; medieval cruck-framed barn at end. ▶ **Old Hat Shop:** 17thC timber-framed with Beadle's hat mounted outside. ▶ **Black Bear Inn:** founded 1308, believed to be oldest inn in Gloucestershire. ▶ **King John's Bridge** over Avon, built 1197. ▶ **Mythe Bridge** over Severn: 170 ft. span, built by Telford, 1824.

Nearby

▶ **Upton-upon-Severn** (*6m N*), riverside town with unusual landmark: 18thC cupola crowning medieval tower, once attached to parish church, known locally as 'The Pepperpot', now a **heritage centre** (*Easter Sep.: daily*). ▶ **Deerhurst** (*4m SW*): Anglo-Saxon **priory church★**; 9thC carved font, 8thC Virgin and Child sculpture in W porch. ▶ **Odda's Chapel** (*SW of priory*): remarkable Saxon relic, built into later timbered orchard farmhouse; inscribed stone dug up in nearby orchard informs that chapel was built by Earl Odda to his brother Aelfric, dedicated 12 April 1056 (stone in Ashmolean Museum, Oxford). ▶ **Priory gardens** at Kemerton (*6m NE*): 4 acres of gardens with stream, fern and sunken garden (*May-Sep.: every Thu., occasional Sun. in summer*). ☐

Practical information _____

TEWKESBURY

ⓘ museum, 64 Barton Street, ☎ 295027.

Hotels:
● ★★★ *Bell* (B.W.), 52 Church Street, GL20 5SA, ☎ (0684) 293293, Tx 43535, AC AM BA, 25 rm. ℗ ᴊ 𝄞 Historic Elizabethan black-and-white timbered inn, formerly a guest house of Tewkesbury Abbey. £50. Rest. ♦ ♪ £12.
★★★ *Tewkesbury Park*, Lincoln Green Lane, GL20 7DN, ☎ (0684) 295405, Tx 43563, AC AM BA DI, 52 rm. ℗ 𝄞 ∭ ⌇ ♪ £59. Rest. ♦ ♪ Cl. lunch Sat. £13.
● ★★ *Tudor House*, 51 High Street, GL20 5BH, ☎ (0684) 297755, AC AM BA DI, 16 rm. ℗ ∭ 𝄇 £50. Rest. ♦ ♪ £9.50.
★ *Royal Hop Pole*(Crest), Church Street, GL20 5RT, ☎ (0684) 293236, Tx 437176, AC AM BA DI, 29 rm. ℗ ∭ 15thC coaching inn, with Dickensian associations, which stands in the centre of the town. £72. Rest. ♦ ♪ ᴅ £12.

Inn or Pub:
Berkeley Arms (Wadworth), Church Street, ☎ (0684) 294034, 3 rm. ⌇ Hot and cold bar meals. £2.

⚲ *Abbey Cara Club Site*, Gander Lane, (170 pl), ☎ (0684) 294035.

Recommended
Farmhouse: at Longdon, *The Moat House*, ☎ Birtsmorton (068481) 313. £21 double; B. & B.

Golf course: Tewkesbury Park Hotel, Lincoln Green Lane, ☎ 295405.
Silk showroom: *Beckford Silk*, The Old Vicarage, ☎ (0386) 881507, silk ties, scarves.

Nearby
CORSE LAWN, Gm OW on D4211

Restaurant:
● ♦ *Corse Lawn House*, Gloucestershire, ☎ Tirley (045 278) 479, AC AM BA DI, 10 rm. ℗ 𝄞 ∭ ⌇ & ☞ Cl. Sun. eve. Scallops in shellfish sauce, veal and Noilly Prat. Book. £18.

UPTON-UPON-SEVERN, 6m N on A4104
ⓘ The Pepperpot, Church Street, ☎ (068 46) 4200.

Hotels:
★★ *White Lion*, High Street, WR8 0HJ, ☎ (068 46) 2551, AC BA DI AC, 10 rm. ℗ 18thC coaching inn featured in Fielding's *Tom Jones*. £50. Rest. ♦ ♪ & Cl. Christmas. £11.
★ *Pool House*, Hanley Road, WR8 0PA, ☎ (068 46) 2151, AC AM, 9 rm. ℗ 𝄞 ∭ ☞ £30.

Recommended
Farmhouse: Ryall House Farm, ☎ (06846) 2649. £23 double; B. & B.

WARWICK★★★

Birmingham, 21; Banbury, 20; London, 91 m
pop. 21,701 ☎ 0926   Warwickshire B2

County town set on rocky foundations high above the Avon. Founded in Saxon times, it grew strong under the protection of the great **castle** of the Earls of Warwick. Most of the town was rebuilt after major fire in 1694, but there are some splendid medieval remnants.

▶ First defenses on site of **castle★★** erected by Ethelfleda, daughter of King Alfred, 916; enlarged and fortified over next two centuries; most of present castle is work of Beauchamp family beginning mid-14thC. Magnificent **state rooms** with rich furnishing and paintings by Van Dyck, Raphael, Rubens, Holbein; in private apartments, a royal weekend party of 1898 is recreated by Madame Tussaud. Towers, armoury, dungeons, landscaped grounds with woodland walks bordering the Avon (*Nov.-Feb.: 10-4.30; Mar.-Oct.: 10-5.30*). ▶ **Collegiate church of St. Mary★★**, rebuilt after fire of 1649, but with original 12thC crypt; 14thC chapter house and chancel, early 18thC nave and tower. Superb **Beauchamp Chapel★★★**, 1443-64, with splendid **monument** to Richard Beauchamp, Earl of Warwick (d. 1439): gilded brass effigy on Purbeck marble, he is armoured with griffin and bear at his feet; on either side, tombs of Ambrose Dudley, Earl of Warwick (d. 1589) and Robert Dudley, Earl of Leicester (d. 1588). Rich stone vaulting, 15thC stained glass with saintly figures including Thomas à Becket, magnificent Gothic **reredos**. Other tombs include Thomas Dudley and wife with joined hands (in chancel), Duke Greville, Lord Brooke in chapter house: counselor to Queen Elizabeth I and highly accomplished poet. ▶ **Lord Leycester Hospital** (Jury Street), 1383, untouched by fire; built over **W Gate** by Guild of the Holy Trinity of Our Lady, a very powerful force in pre-Dissolution Warwick. Transformed 1571 by Robert Dudley into almshouses and hospital for elderly and poor. **Guildhall** (now museum); **Chaplains Hall** (Queen's Own Hussars Regimental Museum): restored 11thC **chapel** and **brethrens' kitchen** (*Mon.-Sat.: 10-5.30 summer, 10-4 winter*). ▶ 17thC **market hall** now home to **museum:** all aspects of history of Warwickshire including its geology, wildlife (*Apr.-Oct. daily, ex. Sun.*). ▶ **Oken House**, built by great benefactor of Warwick, Thomas Oken (d. 1573), now contains **Joy Robinson Doll Museum** (*daily*). ▶ **Eastgate:** earthern entry through city walls, 15thC structure with St. Peter's Chapel above built by Henry VI. **St. John's House** (Coten End, 1626-66) on site of 12thC travelers' 'hospital'; now **museum** of costume and Warwickshire by-

gones. (May-Sep.: Tue.-Sat., Bank Hol. Mon., also Sun. pm). ▶ **Court House** (Fury Street) 1775, one of finest post-fire houses with impressive Neoclassical façade. ▶ **St. Nicholas Park** (off Banbury Road): attractive park with open-air pool, tennis facilities and riverside walks, small boats for hire; excellent views of castle from river.

Nearby

▶ **Packwood House★** (7m NW): many-gabled, timbered Elizabethan manor, enlarged mid-17thC and restored this century; contains Flemish tapestries, 17thC Flemish glass and other fine needlework. Formal Carolean **garden** with gazebos and trimmed yews, laid out 17thC representing Sermon on the Mount: multitude, twelve apostles and four evangelists; greatest yew represents Christ (Easter-end Sep.: Wed.-Sun. & Bank Hol. Mon., 2-6; Oct.: Sat. & Sun., 2.-5). **Guy's Cliffe** (just N on Warwick-Kenilworth Road): 10thC Earl Guy, slayer of dragons and Danish giants is said to have lived in cave hermitage here. Ruined Palladian mansion adjacent was built in 1751, gothicized early 19thC. Pillar opposite old Saxon mill (now restaurant) near river marks place where Piers Gaveston, favourite of Edward II, was executed in 1312. □

Practical information

WARWICK
ℹ court house, Jury Street, ☎ 492212.
🚃 ☎ Rugby (0788) 60116.

Hotels:
★★★ **Lord Leycester** (Consort), 17 Jury Street, CV34 4EJ, ☎ (0926) 491481, Tx 41363, AC AM BA DI, 48 rm. ℗ £48. Rest. ♦ ⅃ £10.50.
★★ **Warwick Arms**, High Street, CV34 4AT, ☎ (0926) 492759, AC AM BA DI, 29 rm. ℗ £46. Rest. ♦ ⅃ & Cl. 25 Dec. - 1 Jan. £10.50.
★ **Crown**, Coventry Road, CV34 4NT, ☎ (0926) 492087, AC BA, 14 rm. ℗ £35. Rest. ♦ ⅃ & Cl. Christmas. £10.
★ **Woolpack** (Toby), Market Place, CV34 4SD, ☎ (0926) 496191, AC AM BA DI, 30 rm. ◈ £36. Rest. ♦ ⅃ Cl. Christmas, New Year Day £7.50.

Restaurants:
● ♦ **Randolph's**, Coten End, ☎ (0926) 491292, AC BA ◈ Cl. Christmas., lunch. Everything home-made, light French style cooking. Book. £18.
● ♦ **Westgate Arms**, Bowling Green Street, ☎ (0926) 492362, AC AM BA DI, 10 rm. ℗ ⌁ ⋙ ⌁ Cl. Sun., 25-26 Dec., Bank Hols. Mon. Chicken à l'homard. Book. £14.
♦ **Aylesford**, 1 High Street, ☎ (0926) 492799, AM AC DI, Cl. Mon. dinner, Sun., 1 wk. at Christmas and Bank Hols. £18.

Inn or Pub:
Seven Star (Courage), ☎ (0926) 492658 ℗ ⋙ Extensive range of home-made dishes. £3.

Recommended
Crafts workshop: Warwick Gallery Craft Shop, 12-14 Smith Street, ☎ (0296) 495880, all hand-made goods: pottery, prints, silk-screen prints.
Farmhouse: at Wellesbourne, Little Hill Farm, ☎ Stratford-upon-Avon (0789) 840261. £18 double; B. & B.

Nearby

BARFORD, 2m S on A429
Hotel:
★★ **Glebe**, Church Street, CV35 8BS, ☎ (0926) 624218, AC AM BA DI, 13 rm. ℗ ⋙ ⌁ ◈ £45.50. Rest. ♦ ⅃ Cl. 1 - 7 Jan. £11.50.

FARNBOROUGH, 12m SE off A423
Inn or Pub:
Butchers Arms, ☎ (029 589) 615, AC DI ℗ ⌁ ⋙ ⌁ Extensive range of dishes. £5.50.

HASELEY, 4m NW on A41
Hotel:
★★ **Haseley House**, CV35 7HF, ☎ Haseley Knob (092

687) 227, AC AM BA DI, 20 rm. ℗ ⋙ ⌁ ♫ £44. Rest. ♦ ⅃ & Cl. lunch Mon. - Sat., Christmas. £16.

HENLEY-IN-ARDEN, 5m W
Restaurant:
♦ **Othello**, 148 High Street, ☎ (05642) 3089, AC AM BA DI. Cl. Sun. £17.50.

LONGBRIDGE, 11/2m on A46
Hotel:
★★ **Ladbroke** (Ladbroke), CV34 6RE, ☎ (0926) 499555, Tx 312468, AC AM BA DI, 127 rm. ℗ ⋙ & ▭ £78. Rest. ♦ ⅃ & Cl. lunch Sat. £12.

WHITCHURCH*

Chester, 22; Telford, 22; London, 171 m
pop. 7,246 ☎ 0948   Shropshire A1

The 14thC church, which replaced the 10thC one built by Ethelfleda, King Alfred's daughter, collapsed entirely shortly after the congregation had left evensong on 31 July 1711. This had been the 'White Church' from which the town's name is derived. The present restrained 18thC tower is a visible landmark far across the flat surrounding land.

▶ **St. Alkmund's Church** has high, noble interior; below stone slab in porch is heart of John Talbot, first Earl of Shrewsbury, carried home at his request, when killed in action (aged 80) fighting forces of Joan of Arc, 1453. □

Practical information

WHITCHURCH
ℹ civic centre, High Street, ☎ 4577.
🚃 ☎ Shrewsbury (0743) 64041.

Hotel:
★★ **Hollies**, Chester Road, SY13 1LZ, ☎ (0948) 2184, AC AM BA DI, 15 rm. ℗ ⌁ & £28. Rest. ♦ ⅃ & £7.

Recommended
Golf course: Hill Valley, Terrick Road (off A41), ☎ 3031.

Nearby

DODINGTON, 2m S on A41
Hotel:
★★ **Dodington Lodge**, SY13 1EN, ☎ (0948) 2539, AC BA DI, 9 rm. ℗ ⋙ & £32. Rest. ♦ ⅃ & £10.

REDBROOK
Hotel:
★★ **Redbrook Hunting Lodge**, Wrexham Road, ☎ Redbrook Maelor (094 873) 204, AC AM DI, 11 rm. ℗ ⋙ ◈ £35. Rest. ♦ £9.

WESTON-UNDER-REDCASTLE, 8m S on A49
Hotel:
★★★ **Hawkstone Park** (Best Western), SY4 5UY, ☎ Lee Brockhurst (093 924) 611, AC AM BA DI, 59 rm. ℗ ⌁ ⋙ ⌁ & ⌁ ⅃ £53. Rest. ♦ ⅃ & £8.50.

WINCHCOMBE*

Gloucester, 15; Cheltenham, 7; London, 101 m
pop. 4,754 ☎ 0242   Gloucestershire B2

A good town for observing the beauty of Cotswold stone slate roofs and fine Cotswold vernacular architecture. Once the site of a great Benedictine abbey destroyed at the Dissolution.

▶ **St. Peter's** is one of Cotswold's 15thC 'wool' churches; many extraordinary carved heads on exterior. ▶ Two groups of almshouses: one 16thC, the **Chandos Alms-houses**, the other 1865 by Sir Gilbert Scott, the **Sudeley Almshouses**.

Nearby

▶ **Hailes Abbey** (*2m NE*): extensive remains of abbey founded 1246 by Richard, younger brother of Edward III. His son Edmund brought a phial to abbey said to contain Christ's blood; thus Hailes became a place of pilgrimage until Dissolution. Good **museum** of archaeological finds (*mid-Mar. - Oct.: 9.30-6.30; mid-Oct. - mid-Mar.: 9.30-4; Sun · Apr.-Sep. opens 9.30, other times at 2*). ▶ **Belas Knap Long Barrow** (*2m S*): 178 ft long neolithic chambered long barrow; excavations have exposed more than 30 human skeletons. ▶ **Sudeley Castle**★: 15thC castle with eventful history reconstructed by Sir Gilbert Scott in 1858; medieval castle was home of Katherine Parr, sixth wife of Henry VIII; 'history of falconry' displays; collection of antique toys; paintings including Rubens, Van Dyck and Constable; lovely Elizabethan-style garden★ (*daily Apr.-Oct.: 12-5*). ▶ Winchcombe is S terminus of **Wychavon Way** footpath (→ Droitwich). ☐

Practical information ――――――――――――――
ℹ town hall, High Street, ☎ 602925.

Restaurant:
● ♦ *Corner Cupboard Inn*, Gloucester Street, ☎ (0242) 602303 ℙ ᨏ ♪ ᕷ ᠖ Cl. lunch, Sun.-Mon. Book. £12.50.

Inn or Pub:
Bell (Donnington), Grotton Road, ☎ (0242) 602205 ℙ ᠖ ᨏ
ᕦ ᠖ Bar meals.

WOLVERHAMPTON*

Telford, 21; Birmingham, 15; London, 132 m
pop. 256,000 ☎ 0902   West Midlands B2

Busy industrial centre of the Black Country, its traditional industry, still commercially practiced, is that of making locks and keys.

▶ **Museum and art gallery**★, Lichfield Street, houses a fine collection of paintings by Turner, Gainsborough and Romney; modern collection includes work by Andy Warhol (*daily ex. Sun.*). ▶ **Museum** at **Bilston** (*3m E*) displays local pottery, history of iron and steel industry and Bilston enamels (*daily ex. Sun.*). ▶ **Bantock House Museum** (*1m W town centre*) has examples of Royal Worcester and Wedgwood and superb collections of japanning and enamel work (*daily*). ▶ **West Park** with boating lake and splendid Victorian glass house. ▶ **St. Peter's Church** of red sandstone stands at centre of town: 15thC carved stone **pulpit, monuments**, 16th and 17thC German and Flemish **stained glass** in chancel, Anglo-Saxon cross in gardens.

Nearby

▶ **Wightwick Manor** (*3m W*), built 1887 in Jacobean style, has much work by Pre-Raphaelites: paintings by Burne-Jones, Millais, Madox Brown and Rossetti; wallpapers, textiles and tapestries by William Morris; tiles by de Morgan and stained glass by Kempe; landscaped gardens and lake (*Thu., Sat., Bank Hols., 2.30-5.30 ex. Feb.*). ▶ **Moseley Old Hall** (*4m N*): Elizabethan manor with priest-holes and secret passages. Refuge of Charles I after defeat at Battle of Worcester. Reconstruction of 17thC garden with plants of that time (*Apr.-Oct.: Wed., Sat. Sun., 2-6 or dusk; Mar. & Nov.: Sun., 2-6*). ▶ **Chillington Hall** (*8m NW*): Georgian house incorporating 16thC elements, E front by Sir John Soane. Note early 18thC **staircase** and Soane's **salon**; grounds with wooded walks and lake: Greek temple, dovecote and small elegant bridges (*Easter, then May-Sep.: Thu., 2.30-5.30; Aug.: Sun., 2.30-5.30*). ▶ **Boscobel House** (*8m NW*): grounds contained oak tree that hid future Charles II after Battle of Worcester; house 1600 (*mid-Mar. - mid.-Oct.: 9.30-6.30; Oct.-Mar.: 9.30-4; open Sun. Apr.-Sep. at 9.30, otherwise 2*). ▶ **Whiteladies Priory** (*1m SW of Boscobel House*): ruins of late Norman nunnery. ▶ **Aerospace Museum** at Cosford (*8m NW*) displays many historic aircraft, missiles and aero engines, also model aircraft. Picnic spots (*daily 10-4; cl. wkends Nov.-Mar.*). ▶ **Tong** (*10m NW*): 15thC **church tower**; has a square base that becomes octagonal. ☐

Practical information ――――――――――――――
WOLVERHAMPTON
ℹ 16 Queen's Arcade, Mander Centre, ☎ 714571.
Car rental: Europcar, 75-77 Bilston Road, ☎ 53544 (rail/drive).

Hotels:
★★★ *Goldthorn*, Penn Road, WV3 0ER, ☎ (0902) 29216, Tx 339816, AC AM BA DI, 86 rm. ℙ £45. Rest. ♦ ♪ ᕷ Cl. 25 - 26 Dec. £12.
★★★ *Park Hall* (Embassy), Park Drive, Goldthorn Park, WV4 5AJ, ☎ (0902) 331121, AC AM BA DI, 57 rm. ℙ ᨏ ᕦ £55. Rest. ♦ ♪ Cl. 24 - 26 Dec. £9.50.
★★★ *York*, 138-140 Tettenhall Road, WV6 0BQ, ☎ (0902) 758211, AC AM BA DI, 15 rm. ℙ ᕷ £44. Rest. ♦ ♪ ᕷ Cl. Christmas. £12.

Recommended
Golf course: Patshull Park Hotel, Burnhill Green, ☎ 700100.
Riding school: *Brookfield Riding Livery Centre*, Shareshill, ☎ (0902) 414090: at Codsall, *Barn Farm Riding Stables*, Gunstone, Codall.

Nearby

ALDRIDGE, 10m E on A454

Hotel:
★★★ *Fairlawns* (Consort), 178 Little Aston Road, WS9 0NU, ☎ (0922) 55122, Tx 339873, AC AM BA DI, 30 rm. ℙ ᕷ ᨏ ᕦ ᕷ £43. Rest. ♦ ♪ ᕷ Cl. lunch Sat. £11.

WALSALL, 8m E

Hotels:
● ★★★ *Barons Court* (Best Western), A461 Walsall-Lichfield Road, WS9 9AH, ☎ Brownhills (0543) 376543, Tx 333061, AC AM BA DI, 76 rm. ℙ ᕷ ᠖ £50. Rest. ♦ ♪ ᕷ £11.
★★ *Crest Hotel* (Crest), Birmingham Road, WS5 3AB, ☎ (0922) 33555, Tx 335479, AC AM BA DI, 100 rm. ℙ £60. Rest. ♦ £8.50.

Restaurant:
♦ *L'Auchel*, 196C Walsall Wood Road, Lazy Hill, Aldridge, ☎ (0922) 57322, AC AM DI. Cl. Sun., lunch not served Mon. and Sat. £10.50.

WORCESTER**

Birmingham, 29; Gloucester, 25; London, 118 m
pop. 75,466 ☎ 0905   Hereford & Worcester B2

'The Faithful City', so called for its loyalty to King Charles even after the decisive Royalist defeat at the Battle of Worcester (1651); also renowned for its beautiful cathedral, fine porcelain and piquant sauce.

▶ **Cathedral**★★★: site probably first used as a place of worship in late 7thC; present building begun 1084. Exterior now almost entirely mid-Victorian restoration work; best-preserved part of Norman building is **crypt** built by St. Wulfstan (1084-92); also Norman/Transitional **chapter house** with ten sides, roof supported by a single central pillar; this is earliest of a type unique to Britain. Fire 1202 destroyed almost all Wulfstan's building; greater part of cathedral fabric is of later date. Interior of gracious proportions and unity of style, particularly **chancel**; **Lady Chapel** (begun 1224) splendid with Purbeck marble, detailed sculpture; beasts and religious scenes in spandrels; **monument** to Charlotte Digby by Chantrey. S of high altar, **Prince Arthur's Chantry**★★: elder brother of Henry VIII, died 1502. Ornate yet delicate, beautiful vaulting and reredos, tomb-chest of Prince. **Choir stalls** by George Gilbert Scott with thirty-seven 14thC **misericords**★ carved with beasts, labours of the seasons and biblical scenes. Worcester was King John's favourite city. His **tomb** stands in chancel below high altar, original coffin lid (1230); Purbeck marble **effigy**★ of King surmounts tomb. In N transept: Roubiliac's rococo monument (1746) to Bishop Hough; 15thC **Beauchamp Tomb** near· N door, woman's head rests upon a swan. ▶ **Cloister** is 13th

- 14thC taking nearly a century to build, finely vaulted. Remains of Benedictine monastary in cathedral gardens and around **College Green.** Off S cloister walk is **refectory,** now King's School hall; Norman doorway onto College Green. A few visible remains of **Guestern Hall** off S transept; considered unsafe and demolished 1862. **Edgar Tower,** the monastery gatehouse, is complete. ▶ **Cathedral gardens** reach down to Severn. ▶ **Guildhall** (High Street) now tourist information centre: splendid 18thC building; grand **Assembly Room** with painted ceiling, portraits (*weekdays*). ▶ **Greyfriars** (Friar Street), now **Tudor House Museum:** 15thC half-timbered building, probably first guest hall for Franciscan friary; exhibitions of domestic Worcester life from Elizabethan times; period rooms include Edwardian schoolroom and nursery, kitchen c. 1900, gardens (*Mon.-Sat. ex. Thu. 10.30-5*). ▶ **City museum and art gallery** (Foregate Street): local geology, natural history, costume, 19thC pharmacy, 19thC oil paintings and watercolours (*Mon-Wed., Fri.: 9.30-6; Sat.: 9.30-5*). ▶ **The Commandery★** was Hospital of Wulfstan, founded 1085; present building 15thC timber-framed, in 1545 became home of Wylde family, loyal to Stuarts in Civil War. Galleried **great hall;** early 16thC religious wall paintings in room on first floor where the sick were nursed by monks, now a fascinating **Civil War Centre:** audio-visual program, weapons, period rooms. Also antique porcelain, doll-making displays, reconstructed workshop demonstrating crafts from Worcester's past: cooper, cobbler, blacksmith, glovemaker (*Mon.-Sat.: 10.30-5; Sat.: 2-5*). ▶ **Dyson Perrins Museum★:** superb collection of Royal Worcester porcelain including first piece made by company 1751; rare services made for royal family and European monarchs (*Mon.-Fri., 10-5*). ▶ **Royal Porcelain Works** may be toured to see craftsmen at work (*tours start 9.55 & 2 Mon.-Fri.; reserve:* ☎ 0905-23221).

Nearby

▶ **Lower Broadheath** (*3¹/₂ m NW*) is the cottage where Sir Edward Elgar was born; now a **museum★** devoted to the composer with musical scores, concert programs, letters, press-clippings and photographs (*May-Sep.: daily, 10.30-6; Oct.-mid-Jan.: 1.30-4.30; mid-Feb.-end Apr.: 1.30-4.30; cl. Wed. all year*). ▶ **Spetchley Park** (*3m E*): beautiful gardens and deer park, rare plants and shrubs, garden centre (*end Mar.-end Sep.: daily ex. Sat., 11-5; Sun.: 2-5.30; Bank Hol. Mon.: 11-5.30*). ▶ **Great Witley** has an astonishing white and gold, Italianate rococo parish **church★;** painted ceiling and windows were brought here from Duke of Chandos' demolished palace of Canons, Middlesex (1747); painted ceiling by Antonio Bellacci; what appears to be stucco is in fact papier mâché. Huge monument in S transept to Lord Foley (by Rysbrack). ▶ **Witley Court,** Foley home, burned down 1937, now in ruins. ▶ N of **Abberley Hill** lies Italianate **Abberley Court** (*12m NW*); built 1846: five principal rooms in ornate mid-Victorian style (*open some pms in summer*). ▶ Two splendid **dovecotes** at **Hawford** (*3m N*), 16thC half-timbered (*9-6 or dusk*) and **Wichenford,** 17thC half-timbered (*open as Hawford*). □

Practical information _____

WORCESTER
ⓘ guildhall, High Street, ☎ 23471.
🚉 ☎ 27211.
Car rental: Europcar, Peter Cooper Garage Services Ltd, Redhill Filling; Station, London Road Shrub Hill Rail Station, ☎ 354096 (rail/drive).

Hotels:
★★★ **Giffard** (T.F.), High Street, WR1 2QR, ☎ (0905) 27155, Tx 338869, AC AM BA DI, 104 rm. ♿ £60. Rest. ♦ ♪ ♿ £10.
● ★★ **Ye Olde Talbot** (Whitbread), Friar Street, WR1

2NA, ☎ (0905) 23573, AC AM BA DI, 17 rm. ⌘ £40. Rest. ♦ ♪ Cl. Christmas. £9.
● ★ **Park House,** 12 Droitwich Road, WR3 7LJ, ☎ (0905) 21816, 6 rm. ℗ ♿ £22. Rest. ♦ ♪ ♿ Cl. Christmas. £8.
★ **Diglis,** Riverside, WR1 2NF, ☎ (0905) 353518, AC AM BA DI, 15 rm. ♿ £40.50. Rest. ♦ £7.

Restaurants:
● ♦ **Brown's,** The Old Cornmill, South Quay, ☎ (0905) 26263, AC AM BA ♿ ♿ ⌘ Cl. Christmas, Bank Hols., Sat. lunch, Sun. Local salmon from the Severn and Wye rivers. Book. £18.
♦ **King Charles 11,** New Street, ☎ (0905) 22449, AC AM BA DI ♪ ♿ Cl. Bank Hols., Sun. Beef Wellington, saddle of lamb. Book. £16.
♦ **Purbani Tandoori,** 27 The Tything, ☎ (0905) 27402, AC AM BA DI ℗ ♿ ♪ ♿ ⌘ Tandoori mixed grill. £7.

Recommended
Cycle rental: *Foregate Street Station,* Refreshment Room, Platform, Foregate Street Station, ☎ (0905) 613501.
Farmhouse: at Shelsley Beauchamp, *Church House Farm,* ☎ (08865) 393. £19 double; B. & B.
Golf course: Worcester Golf Country Club, Boughton Park, ☎ 422555.
Riding school: *Foxworth Farm,* Stitchins Hill, Leigh Sinton, ☎ (0886) 32532.
♥ *Natural Break,* 4 The Hopmarket, ☎ (0905) 26654, restaurant and shop offering health food.

Nearby

WARNDON, 2m NE

Restaurant:
♦ **The Haywain,** Tolladine Road, ☎ (0905) 58615, AC AM BA ℗ ♿ ⋙ ♿ ♪ ♿ ⌘ Cl. Mon., Sat. lunch, Sun. eve. Book. £9.

WYRE FOREST

A precious remainder of the ancient forest of middle England, cleared for ship-building and as raw material for timber-framed buildings, then as fuel for the industrial furnaces that roared throughout the Midlands in the 18th and 19thC. Now in the care of the Forestry Commission, a combination of natural deciduous woodland and conifer plantation supports a rich mixture of bird, animal and plant life, including the rare Kentish Glory moth. Good centres from which to explore the area: **Bewdley** (→), **Stourport-on-Severn** (→), **Stourbridge** (→) and **Bridgnorth** (→).

▶ **Wyre Forest Visitor Centre** (Callow Hill, *on Bewdley-Ludlow Road*): picnic area, information on forest crafts and wildlife, walks, trails and views.

Nearby

▶ **Kidderminster:** long a centre of carpet manufacture; **museum** (Exchange Street) relates its history (*daily ex. Wed., Sun. & Bank Hols.*). ▶ **Stone House Cottage Gardens** (*2m SE*): sheltered garden with rare shrubs (*Mar.-Nov.: Wed.-Fri. & Sat., 10-6; some Sun. in summer*). ▶ **Cleobury Mortimer** (*W of forest on Bewdley-Ludlow Road*): it is claimed William Langland, author of Piers Plowman, was born here; E window in **church** is a memorial to him. ▶ **Mawley Hall** (*1m S*): grand 18thC brick house, elegant interior plasterwork (*by written app. only*). ▶ **Kinlet** (*N of forest, 3 ¹/₂ m NE Cleobury Mortimer*): mainly Norman church and monuments. Surrounding area good for walks, picnics and exploring forest. □

Northern Ireland

▶ The grandeur of the coastline and the rural tranquillity of the countryside, together with the commercial bustle of the urban areas and the tangible evidence of the province's past, make Northern Ireland a restful place to visit.

Its 5,000 square miles (roughly the size of Yorkshire) possess the most varied scenery and geology in the United Kingdom. Nowhere is one far from hills or mountains which are served by a good network of minor roads. The coast offers huge sandy beaches as well as soaring cliffs and fjord-type inlets. The unusual cliff formations at the renowned Giant's Causeway are formed by the basalt lava that underlies a large area of the province.

Northern Ireland is much less densely populated than the rest of the United Kingdom with farming playing an important part in the economy. The rural communities retain strong regional identities and even on a short visit the traveler can detect variations in accents, customs and culture.

The ancient province of Ulster comprises nine counties. Only six of these counties make up present day 'Northern Ireland'. These six counties - Antrim, Down, Armagh, Tyrone, Londonderry and Fermanagh - became part of the United Kingdom in 1920 and its devolved Parliament at Stormont, near Belfast, was opened by George V in 1921. Since 1972 Parliament has been suspended. Northern Ireland is now represented at Westminster and the European Parliament.

The foundation of Northern Ireland's association with Great Britain was laid with the 'Plantation'. This was a policy practiced from Tudor times onwards to encourage English and Scottish merchants to settle in the province. The legacy of the Scottish Planters can be heard in the accents of Antrim while the London Guilds left their mark in names such as Londonderry and Draperstown.

Many monuments bear witness to the events that have shaped Northern Ireland's history from Stone Age and St. Patrick's grave sites to Norman castles and the present vacant house of Parliament. In beautiful country, a naturalist's paradise, communities with ancestors and families scattered worldwide retain old traditions and hospitality which make a visit a rewarding experience.

Pipes and drums

It would be hard to spend much time in Ulster without hearing the sound of bands — pipe bands, flute bands, accordion bands, brass bands — on bandstands, concert platforms and, of course, in the many parades. The most celebrated are seen on 12 July when about 120 bands appear on the streets of Belfast and approximately 20 smaller parades take place in other parts of the province.

'The Twelfth', as it is known, marks the victory of the Protestant William of Orange over Catholic James II at the famous Battle of the Boyne in 1690. Shortly after the Orange Order was established by Protestant settlers in Northern Ireland to give them a sense of solidarity in a predominantly Catholic country. It quickly became an integral part of Ulster's social and political life, and by the present century two-thirds of Protestant men were members of the order and used Orange halls as their social centres. Besides wielding great political power, the order has long been associated with exuberant parades: the Orangemen wear bowler hats and sashes, carry banners to commemorate the Boyne victory and play rousing music. The Belfast parades terminate at Finaghy Field, outside the city, where the marchers hear speeches by politicians and churchmen. A month later, on 12 August, the Orangemen celebrate the day in 1688 when the Apprentice Boys of Londonderry slammed the gates of the walled city against James's army.

The Lambeg drums carried on parade play an important part in the celebrations. Made by hand and painted in brilliant colours, they are enormous and weigh over 30 lbs. Not surprisingly, the noise they make is also huge - in Ulster it is referred to as 'blattering'.

 ## Brief regional history

Prehistory

The earliest settlement in Ireland dates from the **mesolithic period**. These seem to have been mainly in the north, and flintwork artifacts have been found along the coast of Antrim and Down. At Mountsandel, excavations have revealed the post holes of round huts dating from 6650 BC. ● Neolithic farmers arrived in about 3000 BC. These types of megalithic long barrows exist in Ireland: the 'court tomb', so called because the burial chamber is preceded by an open space, or court; the 'portal tombs', and the 'passage tombs'. Grave goods, such as beads, pendants and pins have been found near these sites. Passage tombs, such as the Giant's Ring, south of Belfast are

scattered all over the north. ● Throughout the **Bronze Age**, Ireland had a flourishing metal industry, and fine objects made of gold, copper and bronze were exported to Britain and to Europe. The **stone circles** at Beaghmore date from this period. ● The first Celtic settlers arrived about 600 BC and brought with them the Gaelic language and the knowledge of iron working. It was these settlers who were to develop the cultural tradition which still exists in Ireland today and which was only to have its first serious setback with the Anglo-Norman invasion. Ulster was, in many ways, the strongest and most fully Celtic of all the regions of Ireland. The earliest examples of pagan Celtic art are from the north-east, where the Celts established a bridgehead. Ulster remained the most obstinately Gaelic of the provinces and the last champion of Irish independence under the 'Great Earl', Hugh O'Neill, in the 16thC.

The Celtic state

At the beginning of the Christian era, Ireland was divided into five kingdoms, or *tuatha*. These were Ulster, Meath, Leinster, Munster and Connacht. At first, Ulster seems to have been dominant, but by the time of **Niall of Nine Hostages** (early 5thC) power had passed to Meath. The kings were supported by an aristocracy, whose lands and rights were minutely defined by law. There were no towns, but massive **stone forts** in which lived whole communities. Such a one was Emain Macha, near Armagh, where a great earthwork still stands, marking the site of the ancient palace of the kings of Ulster, destroyed by tribes from Connacht in 450.

Randalstown Presbyterian church, c. 1798

Christianity

The first certain date is AD 431, when **St. Germanus**, bishop of Auxerre, sought the approval of Pope Celestine I to send Palladius to Ireland. Missionary history, however, is dominated by the career of **St. Patrick**, who traditionally converted all of Ireland but in fact concentrated on the north and west. He is supposed to have started his mission at Saul, near Downpatrick, and he established his cathedral at Armagh. By the end of the 6thC the missionary church of Ireland was extremely active, sending monks as far afield as the Rhineland, but, more significantly for British history, sending St. Columba to Iona. The Irish monasteries became important centres of scholarship, where classical authors as well as the writings of the Early Fathers were studied. Many monasteries were built on islands or peninsulas such as Devenish in lower Lough Erne and Nendrum on Mahee Island

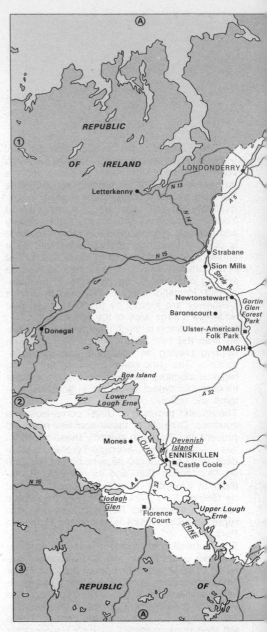

in Strangford Lough. To the 6th-9thC belong the ruined churches at Killevy and St. John's Point and the high crosses at Arboe, Tynan and Devenish.

The Norse invasions

The first recorded appearance of Norsemen in Ireland was in 795. After that they increased their raids, undertaking a full-scale invasion of the north in the 840s. From the 870s they ruled Dublin and in the early

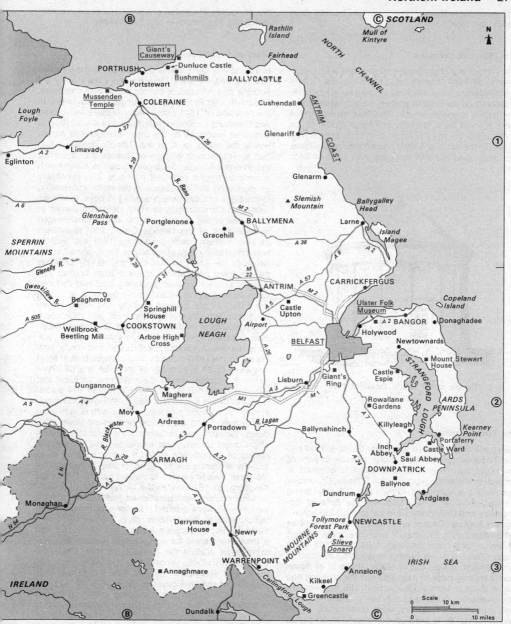

10thC extended their power in the south. Under **Brian Boru**, the Scandinavians were defeated at the Battle of Contarf in 1041 and Boru became the first High King of all Ireland.

The Normans

By the mid-12thC Ireland had collapsed into **anarchy** as one high king after another sought supremacy. A number of Anglo-Norman knights, in particular the Earl of Pembroke, known as 'Strongbow', crossed to Ireland ostensibly in the king's name. ● In 1171 Henry II arrived with a sizable army, officially to reform a degenerate church, in fact to clip the wings of his over-zealous barons. Leinster was granted to Strongbow, Ulster to John de Courcy, while the king himself took Dublin. De Courcy invaded Ulster, defeating Mac Dunlevy in 1177. He built a massive castle at Carrickfergus and further strongholds at Newry, Donaghadee, Dromore and Coleraine. From the Norman period

also date two well-preserved Cistercian houses, Grey Abbey and Inch.

The 13th-15th centuries

The Dominicans, Franciscans, Carmelites and Augustinians all built friaries in Ireland in the 13thC. Meanwhile the administration of the country became organized on an **English pattern** - a jury system was introduced, coinage struck. The first market towns grew up with fairs, markets and trade guilds. In the south of the country the Anglo-Irish lords predominated, while the north and west shared their still-continuing Gaelic customs and language with parts of Scotland.

Temple of the Winds, Downhill, 1783

The Tudor plantations

Henry VIII determined to assimilate Gaelic Ireland into the Tudor state. In 1541, under various threats of recriminations, he was formally offered the throne in Ireland. In Ulster the Savages, the O'Neills, O'Donnels and Maguires submitted, O'Neill and O'Donnel being created earls. ● Under Elizabeth the **Acts of Supremacy and Uniformity** were passed in 1560 enforcing the Anglican Church on Ireland. There were **three rebellions** during Elizabeth's reign, the most serious of which took place between 1594 and 1603 when Hugh O'Neill with his brother-in-law Maguire tried to drive English troops out of Ulster. **Philip III of Spain** sent a military force to help him, and the rebellion had some support from Pope Clement VIII. It eventually and inevitably failed, and the earl's lands, together with those of his followers, were confiscated. O'Neill fled to Rome. ● In the Tudor and early Stuart period it was considered expedient to 'plant' Ireland with colonies of Englishmen to redress the somewhat uneven balance of sympathy for the monarchy. After the 'Flight of the Earls', their lands in Ulster were made into English-style counties under the names Armagh, Cavan, Coleraine, Donegal, Fermanagh and Tyrone.● In 1610 Scottish and English settlers were invited to settle the confiscated lands. Most of the new arrivals came from Presbyterian Lowland Scotland and they brought their tenantry and labourers with them. The city of London was also involved in the plantations - Derry was renamed Londonderry and the city guilds of London are commemorated in settlements like Draperstown and Salterstown.

Wars and rebellions

In Ireland the 'Old English' descended from the Anglo-Norman settlers were Catholic and closely involved with the descendants of the old Gaelic Irish chieftains. The north was Protestant and largely Presbyterian. In the rebellion of 1641 many Ulster settlers were killed and Cromwell's ruthless subjugation of the south was largely in response to the often exaggerated atrocities in the north. ● After the Catholic **James II** had fled to France and **William of Orange** had assumed the throne of England, James landed in Ireland with a body of troops provided by Louis XIV, eventually encountering stiff resistance in the north, culminating in the siege of Derry which lasted 105 days. ● William landed at Carrickfergus in 1690, defeating James at the Battle of the Boyne, a battle still commemorated by members of the Orange Order. Irish resistance to King William continued but by 1701 the country was effectively conquered, power being placed in the hands of the Anglican 'Ascendancy'. ● By 1774 the penals laws preventing Catholics from holding any political position or from acquiring land had reduced Catholic holdings in Ireland to five per cent. ● During the 18thC Ulster became wealthy and influential as the textile industry, particularly linen, was developed, and agricultural methods improved. But many Ulstermen resented their treatment, as second-class citizens, by the Anglican 'Ascendancy' and many emigrated to the United States. It is claimed that at least one-third of all presidents of the USA are of Ulster descent, notable among them Andrew Jackson and Woodrow Wilson. ● After the union of the parliaments of Great Britain and Ireland following the rebellion of 1801, Ulster's economic links with Britain were strengthened and the radical movement slowly died down. Belfast grew to become the largest industrial city. Cotton spinning was introduced in 1777 and the revival of shipbuilding added a further impetus to its growth. ● During the struggles for Irish independence Northern Ireland elected to remain part of the United Kingdom. In 1920 under the Government of Ireland Act the country was **partitioned** and two equal Irish parliaments were created - **Ulster and Ireland**, both subordinate to Westminster. ● In the troubled years since Partition, Northern Ireland has developed into a **Protestant state** for a Protestant people, with discrimination against the Catholic minority. Since the 1960s that Catholic minority has become increasingly vocal and violence in the province led to the **suspension of regional government** in 1972. ● At present, while a British peace-keeping military presence is maintained, the British government is seeking to involve the Irish government in a closer collaboration with the north, despite resistance from Unionist quarters.

 Practical information

Information: *Northern Ireland Tourist Board,* River House, 48 High Street, Belfast BT1 2DS, ☎ (0232) 231221.

Weather forecast: ☎ (0232) 8091.

Railway station: Central Station, East Bridge Street, Belfast, ☎ (0232) 230310.

Sealink car ferries, UK to Northern Ireland: ☎ (01) 834 8122 Mon-Sat., 7.30am - 7.30pm.

Sealink boat train information: from Fishguard, Holyhead, Stranraer and Heysham (Isle of Man): ☎ (01) 834 2345.

B + I Line Services: ☎ (01) 734 4681. Liverpool office: ☎ (051) 227 2131.

Ferry links: Liverpool, ☎ (051) 922 6234; Scotland: Stranraer, ☎ (0776) 2262 and Cairnryan, ☎ (05812) 276; Isle of Man, ☎ (0624) 23344 and the Continent.

Youth hostel: *YHA Northern Ireland*, 56 Bradbury Place, Belfast BT7 1RU, ☎ (0232) 324733.

Festivals: **Jun.-Jul.**: *Fiddlestone Festival* of Belleek, County Fermanagh (gathering of traditional Irish fiddlers); **19-26 Nov. 1988**: *25th Belfast Festival of Art* at Queen's University.

Customs and folklore: **12 Jul.**: *Battle of the Boyne celebrations* throughout Northern Ireland - biggest parade in Belfast; **Aug.**: *Ould Lammas Fair*, Ballycastle, County Antrim, one of Ireland's oldest fairs, origin uncertain; **Sat. before Christmas week**: *Closing of the Gates Ceremony*, Londonderry, County Londonderry, burning effigy of traitor Lieutenant-Colonel Robert Lundy, military governor of Londonderry in 1688.

Other events: **17-21 Apr.**: *Circuit of Ireland International Motor rally*, starting and finishing in Belfast; **19-22 May**: *Royal Ulster Agricultural Society 120th annual show and industrial exhibition*, the showgrounds, Balmoral, Belfast; *Belfast International Rose Trials*, Sir Thomas and Lady Dixon Park, Upper Malone, Belfast.

Scenic railway: Shane's Castle Light Railway is the only remaining narrow-gauge steam-operated railway in Ireland. It opened in 1971, 2 steam engines running from the outskirts of Antrim to the ruins of Old Shane's Castle - 1.5 miles in a 3-foot gauge, much of the journey in a nature reserve. Contact: *Shane's Castle Railway*, Shane's Castle, Antrim, ☎ Antrim 62216.

Aquatic sports: sailing, windsurfing and waterskiing: *Craigavon Watersports Centre*, Craigavon Lake, Portadown, Craigavon, ☎ (0762) 42669/41199.

Canoeing: *Craigavon Watersports Centre* (→ above).

Deer stalking: Mr J. McCurdy, Forest Service, Dept. of Agriculture, Belfast BT4 35B, ☎ (0232) 650111 ext. 268.

Golf: Co. Antrim: Ballymena (9-hole), Balmoral (18-hole), Carrickfergus (18-hole), Dunmurry (18-hole), Portstewart (18-hole), Royal Portrush (18-hole); Co. Armagh: Craigavon (18-hole); Co. Down: Bangor (18-hole), Royal County Down (18-hole), Warreb (18-hole); Co. Tyrone: Dungannon (18-hole), Killymoon (18-hole).

Hunting: *East Down Hunt*, 16 Church Hill, Newcastle, County Down BT33 0JU, ☎ (03967) 23217.

Parachuting and parascending: *Wild Geese School of Adventure Training*, 27 Drumeil Road, Aghadowey, Coleraine BT51 4BB, ☎ (026585) 669.

River and canal cruises: *Blakes Holidays*, Wroxham, Norwich NR12 8DH, ☎ (06053) 3221.

Sailing and cruising: *Strangford Yacht Charter*, Killinchy, County Down, ☎ (0238) 541186; *Ulster Cruising School*, The Marina, Carrickfergus, Antrim, ☎ (09603) 68818/65407.

Linen

Ireland's damp climate has proved ideal for two major crops, potatoes and flax - both of which were introduced from abroad. Cloth has been made from flax since prehistoric times in various parts of the world: the flax plant (which also provides linseed oil) produces a fibre which cannot be rivaled for its strength and long-lasting qualities. Normally buff-coloured, though the best quality is creamy white, the fibre can be woven into a very strong cloth which may be bleached pure white. This linen cloth is also very good at absorbing moisture and conducting heat away from the body - so is very suitable for clothes worn in hot climates, as well as for articles like sheets and dish cloths which are subjected to prolonged use. The flax fibre is also made into twine and canvas.

During the 17thC French Huguenots escaped religious persecution in France and came to live in Northern Ireland. The settlers brought flax and their skill in making it into cloth with them. The new crop soon became an important one for farmers in the north, and although there were as yet no textile factories, the fibre was spun and woven into fabric in cottages and farmhouses throughout the province. By 1727 linen was the third-largest export, and when the agriculturalist Arthur Young visited Ulster in the 1770s he complained that it was 'a whole province peopled by weavers'. As the century progressed the Industrial Revolution brought mechanized production - by the 1790s flax could be spun on a machine rather than laboriously by hand. Belfast, whose trade with Britain had come to depend to a great extent on the linen industry, exchanged its linen cloth and livestock products for flaxseed, bleaching materials and coal, iron and timber. Many of the surrounding towns and villages developed because of the textile industry (cotton cloth was also being produced); and the town of Londonderry became noted for its shirt making. By the outset of the 20thC, Belfast was a major world centre for linen and for its other important industry, shipbuilding. However, since then both industries have declined significantly. Flax is no longer considered an economic crop and has to be imported; man-made and other fibres have proved more popular in recent years, and in general Ulster's spinning and weaving industries have dwindled. By the 1960s linen production employed less than 15,000 people - less than a third of 1927's labour force. On the other hand, the textile trade of Northern Ireland is still thriving; finishing techniques such as bleaching, dying and printing are important to the industry of the province, and Derry is still a shirt-making centre.

Towns and places

Larne, 17; Ballymena, 11; Belfast, 23 m
☎ 084 94   Antrim C2

An expanding town with new industries, linked to Belfast by motorway, Antrim preserves its past.

▶ A little to the N of Antrim stands one of the finest specimens of the round towers in the N of Ireland; it is 95 ft. high, tapers upwards, diminishing from 52 ft. in circumference at the base to 36 ft. near the top. The door is 12 ft. from the ground and is square. Over the entrance there is a device in open stonework, resembling a Maltese cross, which would strengthen the idea of the towers having been erected within the Christian period. Some archaeologists say the tower was built in the 7thC at the same time as the two near Tuam by Goban Saer, a celebrated architect of that age. ▶ Extending along the shore are the grounds of the ruined **Antrim Castle** and the new **Antrim Forum**, a large recreational centre. **Massereene** is a scenic golf course along the shore. ▶ **Shane's Castle** was originally built in the 16thC, rebuilt by Nash in the 18thC, by Lanyon in the 19thC, and finally burned down in the 1920's. A steam train now runs on a 3-ft. gauge through the woods and along the shore (*Mar.-May: Sun., Bank Hols.; Jul.-Aug.: Tue., Wed., Thu.*). There are hides for observing the Lough's plentiful birdlife.

Nearby

▶ **Castle Upton** at Templepatrick (*5m E*), 17thC manor house remodeled by Robert Adam who also designed the mausoleum. Art gallery near stable courtyard (*Mon., Sun., 11-6; house : May, Jun. by appt. only*).   □

Practical information ————————

ANTRIM

Recommended
Antique shop: *New Abbey Antiques*, Caragh Lodge, Glen Road, Newtownabbey, ☎ (0231) 62036, furniture, jewelry, paintings, pottery and silver.

Nearby

DUNADRY, 4m NE on M2

Hotel:
Dunadry Inn, 2 Islandreagh Drive, BT41 2HA, ☎ Templepatrick (084 94) 32474, Tx 747245, AC AM BA DI, 64 rm. P ≮ ⚋ ⚭ ⚫ 🏊 ⌿ £65. Rest. ♦ ⚘ & Cl. 24-26 Dec. Lobster, salmon. £16.

Antrim

This has been called the most scenic coast in Ireland . The 24m road running NW from Larne to Cushendall hugs the coastline. The main road then veers inland and minor roads lead through the most northerly of the 9 Antrim glens. From S to N these are Glenarm, Glencoy, Glenariff, Ballyeamon, Glenaan, Glencorp, Glendun, Glenesk and Glentassie. The glens were caused by rivers rising in the SW running down to the sea and where coastal villages grew. Until 150 years ago they were even more isolated due to the lack of a proper road. The glens each have a character of their own but all share tranquillity and beauty.

▶ **Ballygalley Head** (*3m N of Larne*) is a 250 ft. high promontory overlooking the sea. ▶ A little further on **Ballygalley Castle** beside the beach is a 17thC Plantation fortified house (now a hotel). ▶ **Glenarm** has the oldest vil-

lage. The turreted castle bears a resemblance to the Tower of London: the building was started in the 17thC; later additions; now the seat of the Earl of Antrim. The surrounding forest has fine walks and waterfalls. ▶ **Carnlough**, a resort at the foot of Glencoy, has a pretty harbour and a good pebble beach. ▶ At **Garron Point** the coast falls away more abruptly. A road left leads to **Garron Tower** (now a school) built by the Marchioness of Londonderry in 1848. ▶ **Red Bay**, named for the predominant sandstone, encloses the famed **Glenariff** which is warmed by the Gulf Stream. The village of **Waterfoot** stands at the outflow of the glen. Up the glen, abounding in wildflowers, are two fine waterfalls, **Ess-na-larach**, and **Ess-na-crub**, in a wooded ravine. ▶ **Cushendall★** is a small resort at the head of three glens offering diverse activities such as boating and fishing; popular with antiquarians, botanists and geologists. ▶ **Ossian's Grave**, reputed resting place of the pagan warrior and poet, is marked by a half circle of stones and lies NW of the village, accessible by footpath. ▶ The red **Turnley's Tower** was built in 1809 . Centre of the Glens of Antrim *feis* (competitive festivals of music and dancing) in Jul. ▶ **Cushendun★**, at the foot of **Glendun**, is off the main Antrim coast road. Its cottages and village and beach are protected by the National Trust. The River Dun is noted for its salmon and sea trout. ▶ Further N the scenery becomes more rugged. ▶ Following the minor seaward road from Cushendun, take the winding road down to the beach at **Murlough Bay**. ▶ **Fairhead**, which shelters this bay, is a basalt promontory over 600 ft. high. **Views** of Scotland, about 13m away. ▶ Two small lakes on the headland were probably Bronze Age refuges. One has a small artificial island on it and spears found here are now in the Ulster Museum.   □

Practical information ————————

⚏ at Cushendun, *Cushendun C.P.*, 14 Glendun Road (74 pl), ☎ (026 674) 254; at Glenariff, *Glenariff Forest Park*, 98 Glenariff Road (60 pl), ☎ (030 588) 232.

Nearby

BALLYGALLY

Hotel:
Halfway, 352 Coast Road, BT40 2RA, ☎ (0574) 83265, AC, 13 rm. P ≮ ⚋ ⌿ £19. Rest. ♦ ⚘ £7.

CARNLOUGH

Hotel:
● *Londonderry Arms*, Harbour Road, BT44 0EU, ☎ (0574) 85255, AC AM BA DI, 12 rm. P ≮ ⚋ ⚭ An 18thC coaching inn built by Lady Londonderry, Sir Winston Churchill's great-grandmother. £33.50. Rest. ♦ ⚘ & £10.50.

CUSHENDALL
⚏ Chapel Road, ☎ (026 67) 71415.

Hotel:
Thornlea, 6 Coast Road, BT44 0RU, ☎ Ballymena (0266) 71223, AC AM BA DI, 15 rm. P ≮ ⚱ £28.50. Rest. ♦ ⚘ £13.

⚏ *Glenville C.P.*, 20 Layde Road (6 pl), ☎ (0266) 71520.

Down C2

Low hills cover the fertile Ards Peninsula, a tongue of land about 19m long separated by Strangford Lough from the mainland. At the S end of the Lough, a narrow entrance guarded by the towns of Portaferry and Strangford admits the fierce tidal currents which give the Lough its Viking name (Violent Fjord). The sea-

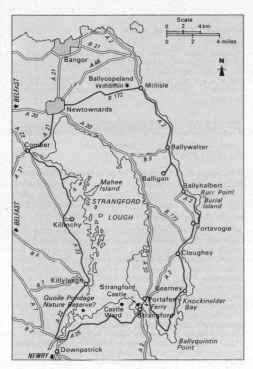

Ards Peninsula

ward side of the Peninsula has many fine beaches and fishing harbours.

▶ **Movilla Abbey** (*1m E of Newtownards*), founded in the 13thC; arcade and square tower date from 17thC. ▶ Nearby, the once famed **Grey Abbey★**, the ruins of which alone remain, was built in 1193 by **Africa**, wife of the Norman knight **John de Courcy**, and daughter of **Godfred**, king of the Isle of Man, for a community of Cistercian monks. The extent and character of the remains give evidence of its former splendor, the stately windows of Gothic structure showing a beauty of design and richness of art, though the structure is now overgrown with ivy and crumbling. The abbey was destroyed in the great rebellion of 1641 and was partly restored in 1685 by the first Lord Montgomery, into whose hands it had fallen (*daily ex. Mon.*). ▶ From **Scrabo Hill Tower** (*Jun.-Sep., 12-5.30 ex. Mon.*), weather permitting, **views** of the Mourne Mountains, Dundonald and Belfast. ▶ Nearby is **Kempe Stones**, dolmen with large capstone still in place.

Round trip from Newtownards

▶ **Newtownards**: fine Georgian town hall and good shopping centre with nearby airfield for pleasure flights. ▶ On road to **Millisle**, a small coastal resort at the head of miles of beaches, is **Ballycopeland Windmill**, the only working windmill in Ireland (*Apr.-Sep.: until 7; Oct.-Mar.: Sat., Sun. until 4; closed Mon.*). ▶ The coastal road leads S to **Ballywalter** with harbour and village. Inland is **Balligan** with a little church dating from 1704. ▶ At **Ballyhalbert** the main road turns inland but at the end of the beach is **Burr Point** and **Burial Island**, ancient site and most easterly spot in Ireland. ▶ **Portavogie**, a fishing village with modern harbour. ▶ **Cloughey** is a small resort with beaches and dunes. An unclassified road leads S to **Kearney**, a restored fishing village, and on to **Knockinelder Bay**. **Bally-**

quintin Point is the southernmost point of the peninsula. ▶ Turning sharply NW the road comes to **Portaferry★** with pleasant waterfront; a car ferry crosses the narrows to Strangford (*every 1/2 hour, 7.30-10.30*). ▶ Magnificent **views** up and down the lough; **Strangford Castle** overlooks the harbour. ▶ **Castle** (*1m W*) has grounds leading down to the Lough side. ▶ Continue by **Quoile Pondage National Nature Reserve** and turn sharply left on to A22 to **Killyleagh**, birthplace of Sir Hans Soane, founder of the British Museum. The castle was originally built by John de Courcy and was reconstructed in the mid-19thC. ▶ A detour from **Killinchy** leads to **Mahee Island** via **Comber**; return to **Newtownards**. ☐

Practical information

✈ at Ballyhalbert, *Ballyhalbert C.P.*, Shore Road (46 pl), ☎ (024 77) 58426; at Ballywalter, *Ballyferris C.P.*, Whitechurch Road (50 pl), ☎ (024 77) 58244; *Rockmore C.P.*, 69 Whitechurch Road (17 pl), ☎ (0247) 861428; *Rosebank C.P.*, 199 Whitechurch Road (6 pl), ☎ (02477) 58211; *Sandy Cove C.P.*, 194 Whitechurch Road (18 pl), ☎ (024 77) 58200.

CLOUGHEY

Hotel:
Roadhouse, 204-208 Main Road, BT22 1JA, ☎ Portavogie (024 77) 71500, AC BA, 11 rm. P ⫤ ⪽ ⪫ £38. Rest. ♦ ⫯ Cl. Christmas. £8.50.

KILLINCHY

Restaurant:
♦ **Balloo House**, 1 Comber Road, ☎ (0238) 541210, AC BA DI P ⫤ ▨ ⪽ ⫯ & Cl. Christmas. Book. £11.

NEWTOWNARDS

Hotel:
Strangford Arms, 92 Church Street, BT23 4AL, ☎ (0247) 814141, AC AM BA DI, 36 rm. P ⪽ ⪫ £54. Rest. ♦ ⫯ & Cl. 20-21 Apr. and Christmas. £11.50.

PORTAFERRY

Hotel:
Portaferry, 10 The Strand, BT22 1PE, ☎ (024 77) 28231, AC AM BA DI, 5 rm. P ⫤ ⪽ ⪫ ⫐ An attractive family-run old inn opposite the ferry terminal at the S end of Strangford Lough. £32. Rest. ♦ ⫯ Cl. Christmas. £14.

ARMAGH*

Newry, 16; Omagh, 39; Belfast, 32 m
☎ 0861   Armagh B2

Armagh, the county, is named after the city. The name goes back long before St. Patrick to pagan times and comes from **Ard-Macha** - Macha's height - Macha being a semi-mythical heroine, founder of the palace of Emania, 300 BC. The surface for the most part is flat, but Slieve Gullion (1,893 ft.) rises abruptly from the plain and commands a view scarcely exceeded by any other mountain in Ireland. Near the top is a small lake celebrated in legend and on the summit is a great stone cairn. The town of Armagh is the metropolitan see of all Ireland; the see was founded by St. Patrick c. 457. After the Anglo-Norman invasion in the 13thC, the question of ecclesiastical supremacy was bitterly fought between the Irish incumbents of St. Patrick's see, and the Archbishops of Dublin, who upheld the English interest. These bishops took the title of 'Primate of Ireland' so those of Armagh took that of 'Primate of all Ireland'. During Reformation, the Catholics were forced to go into hiding and the Protestants took possession of the ancient cathedral, but the Protestant bishops of both sees still claim the distinctive title. At the time of Catholic emancipation the cathedral was not returned to the Catholics and they even-

tually built the present twin-spired church on the other side of the city.

▶ Around the Mall, the large recreational area (once the city's racecourse), much of Francis Johnstone's work can be seen in the imposing Georgian houses. The schoolhouse on the E side is now a **county museum** and art gallery: natural and local history exhibitions, Victorian doll collection (*Mon.-Sat., 10-5*). ▶ In **Sovereign's House** is the Royal Irish Fusiliers Regimental Museum (*Mon.-Fri., 10-4.30*). ▶ **The Astronomy Centre** comprises an observatory (founded in 1791), a planetarium and Hall of Astronomy: simulations of 'Voyager', shuttle from the U.S. space program (*daily ex. Sun.*).

Nearby

▶ On the Callan River, 3m N of Armagh, is **Bellanaboy**, or the **Yellow Ford** where, in 1598, a great battle was fought in which Hugh O'Neill, Earl of Tyrone, defeated Sir Henry Bagenal, and Bagenal himself and 1,300 of his men were killed. The ford has however lost its old name. ▶ 3m to the W of Armagh are the ruins of the **Palace of Emania**. ▶ Other towns of importance are **Lurgan**, in the NE corner, a neat and thriving city, **Portadown**, on the Upper Bann, **Tanderagee**, on the Cusher River with **Tanderagee Castle** crowning the hill over it, **Markethill**, a flourishing little town near **Gosford Castle** and **Charlemont**, on the Blackwater, commanding a pass across the river. The old castle is now occupied by the military. □

The Palace of Emania

The Palace of Emania is one of the most important sights in Northern Ireland. It was the residence of the kings of Ulster from 300 BC to AD 332 and was situated about 3 miles W of the present city of Armagh. The remains of this old royal residence are still there, and consist of a great circular rath, or rampart of earth, with a deep fosse, enclosing 11 acres, within which are two smaller forts. For some reason Emania is now generally called Navan Fort and appears as such on maps. The Gaelic name is Eamhuin, pronounced Aven, latinized Emania; when the 'n' of the Gaelic article 'an' is placed before Aven (or Eamhuin), the sound represented is Navan. In the 1stC AD, the palace was the residence and training place of the militia called the Red Branch Knights under the Ulster king Conor Mac Nessa. They lived in and took their name from one of the houses, called Craobn-ruadh (pronounced Creeve-roe) and the house has left its name on the adjacent town of Creeverce. The finest part of ancient Irish romantic literature has reference to the Red Branch Knights and their exploits. Their chief heroes were the great Cuchullin, the Achilles of Irish legend, the sons of Usna with one of whom Deirdre of the Sorrows fell in love, and Queen Naeve who led an army against the mighty Cuchullin. All of them appear in Irish poetry, most notably in the works of W. B. Yeats.

Practical information ⎯⎯⎯⎯⎯⎯⎯⎯⎯

ARMAGH
ⓘ library headquarters, Charlemont Gardens, ☎ (0861) 7561.

Hotel:
Ballinahinch House, Richhill, BT61 9NA, ☎ Richhill (0762) 870081, 6 rm. ⋹ ⌕ ⌽ ⛁ £18.50. Rest. ◆ ⌇ Cl. Oct.-Mar. £10.

⼊ at Lurgan, *Kinnegoe C.P.*, Kinnegoe Mamra (60 pl), ☎ (076 22) 5366.

Nearby

CRAIGAVON, 13m NE on A3

Hotels:
Seagoe, Upper Church Lane, BT53 5QS, ☎ Portadown (0762) 333076, AC AM BA DI, 38 rm. ℗ ⌨ ら ⚘ £47. Rest. ◆ ⌇ ら Cl. Christmas. Duckling. £10.50.
Silverwood, Kiln Road, BT66 6NF, ☎ (0762) 27722, AC AM BA DI, 28 rm. ℗ ⋹ ⌕ ら ⚘ ⌒ £34.50. Rest. ◆ ⌇ ら £8.50.

BALLYCASTLE*

Larne, 40; Ballymena, 28; Belfast, 60 m
pop. 3,284 ☎ 026 57   Antrim B1

A vacation resort popular for golf, fishing and walking, Ballycastle is the venue for a *feis* in June and the Ould Lammas Fair in August. Horse trading takes place and stalls sell local specialities such as dulse (dried edible seaweed) and Yellowman (confectionery).

▶ The town is set back from the harbour; there is a **memorial** to Guglielmo Marconi, who tested his invention, 'the wireless', here in 1898. On the mountainside, **Ballycastle Forest** and **Ballypatrick Forest**: picnicking areas, nature trails and scenic drives. Right of the golf links is **Bonmargy Friary**, the remains of an early 16thC Franciscan priory. The MacDonnells, who became the Earls of Antrim, are buried here. ▶ **Rathlin Island★**, with its precipitous white coastline, can be reached by motorboat from Ballycastle. It has much of interest for the botanist, ornithologist and geologist. Near the E lighthouse on the island is the cave where, in 1306, the fugitive Scottish king Robert Bruce is said to have watched a spider persevere with its web, encouraging Bruce's own endeavours, ending with his triumph at Bannockburn. The cave can be visited by boat. ▶ **Carrick-a-rede ropebridge★** connects an isolated basalt stack to the mainland over a 60 ft. chasm. It is now made of planks and wire, but is still thrilling for the visitor and gives salmon fisherman access to their fisheries (*May-Sep.*). ▶ Beautiful **views** can be seen from nearby **Ballintoy** reached by a winding road. □

Practical information ⎯⎯⎯⎯⎯⎯⎯⎯⎯

ⓘ 7 Mary Street, ☎ (026 57) 62024.

Hotel:
★ **Antrim Arms**, 75 Castle Street, BT54 6AS, ☎ (026 57) 62284, 16 rm. ℗ ⌒ A 200-yr.-old inn. £29.50. Rest. ◆ ⌇ Cl. 25-26 Dec. £12.50.

Recommended
Golf course: ☎ (02657) 62536.
Riding school: *Loughaveema Trekking Centre*, 61 Ballyvennayht Road, ☎ (026 57) 62576.

BALLYMENA*

Londonderry, 52; Larne, 21; Belfast, 25 m
pop. 28,166 ☎ 0266   Antrim B1

Antrim's county town stands in a fertile and prosperous farming region. It owes its past prosperity to the linen and tobacco trades.

Nearby

▶ NE is **Newtown Crommelin**, named after the French Huguenot weaver Louis Crommelin who, with other religious refugees, came here in the late 17thC. This influx did much to harness the latent local skills and turn linen into a booming industry. Less than 100 years ago this area used its water power for spinning, weaving and beetling mills, giving Irish linen a worldwide reputation. ▶ Another group taking refuge here were the Moravians, settling at **Gracehill** in 1746. The little community, built around a green, still looks much as it did in the 18thC. The

Moravians made their living by clock and lace making, and men and women lived and were buried separately. ▶ The Cistercian abbey at **Portglenone**, which straddles the Bann, was founded in 1951 (the first abbey founded since the Reformation). The order modernized a Georgian mansion, which contains fireplaces from the ruined **Ballyscullion Palace**, built by the eccentric Earl of Bristol and Bishop of Derry on the N shore of the nearby **Lough Beg. Portglenone Forest** has nature trails, a bluebell wood and rhododendrons. ▶ **Broughshane** is celebrated for its connections with daffodils. An impressive daffodil garden can be seen at the New University at Coleraine (→; *bulbs can be bought in late Aug.*). ▶ **Slemish Mountain** (*7m NE*) is an extinct volcanic mountain and place of pilgrimage on 17 Mar., St. Patrick's Day. Ireland's patron saint is reputed to have been a swineherd on the mountainside. Near the peak is a parking lot and picnic spot. □

Practical information

ⓘ 2 Ballymoney Road, ☎ (0266) 46043.

Hotel:
★★★ ***Adair Arms***, Ballymoney Road, BT43 5BS, ☎ (0266) 3674, AC AM BA DI, 42 rm. Ⓟ £44. Rest. ♦ £13.

Recommended
Golf course: Broughshane, 2m E on A42, ☎ (0266) 861207.

BANGOR*

Lisburn, 18; Newtownards, 5; Belfast, 15 m
☎ 0247 Down C2

Bangor (the name comes from Bane-Choraidh, 'the White Choir') is a large resort overlooking Belfast Lough with over 3 miles of sea front and surrounding parks and woodland. In former days it was one of the most celebrated religious establishments in Ireland, a famous seat of learning and a 'city of the saints'. St. Comhgall founded an abbey here in 552, the fragments of which still exist, and laid the foundation of the great school to which students from all parts of Europe came. Its seminary, directed by St. Carthagus, supplied King Alfred, in England, with his professors when he founded Oxford. In 818 the Norsemen descended on the establishment and slew more than 1,000 of the 3,000 monks that resided there. Bangor was part of the O'Neill dominion and the remains of a castle, still in good condition, stand on the quay. The town is now residential with a large villa population from neighbouring Belfast.

▶ **Bangor Castle**, in a beautiful setting, was built mid-19thC in English manor house style and is now the town hall. The former stable and laundry now house a visitors' centre with local and natural history collections and audio-visual shows (*11-4.30, cl. Mon. & Sun.*). ▶ **Bangor Bay** has three piers; inner pier dominated by a stone tower (or custom house) built in the 16thC. ▶ On the opposite side of the bay are the **marine gardens** and **Pickie Pool**, a large open-air swimming pool. ▶ A path along the shore W from the gardens leads around the coast to **Strinland's Glen** and **Connor Park.**

Nearby

▶ **Groomsport:** village with sandy beach and harbour. ▶ The **Copeland Islands** can be seen here and visited by boat from Bangor. One of the islands has an important bird observatory and seal haunt. ▶ **Donaghadee** is a good boating centre and was once Northern Ireland's principal port. ▶ **Helen's Bay** to the W has fine beaches and **Crawfordsburn Country Park.** The park is a wooded ravine offering riverside walks and facilities for camping and boating. ▶ **Cultra Manor,** housing the **Ulster Folk and Transport Museum** (*May-Sep.: Mon.-Sat., 11-6; Sun., 2-6 Oct.-Apr.: Mon.-Sat., 11-5; Sun., 2-5*), is in an 180-acre park with a number of old buildings from different regions of Ireland. A small village with church, flax mill, weaver's house, well-equipped school house and furnished cottages can be seen. Demonstrations of weaving, spinning and thatching in summer. The galleries illustrate domestic and agricultural life in bygone days. Also housed in Cultra Manor is a **transport museum** displaying items such as a dog-cart, pony-traps, monoplanes and a merchant schooner. The bicycle collection is notable. □

Practical information

BANGOR
ⓘ 34 Quay Street, ☎ (0247) 454069.

Hotels:
★★ ***Ballyholme***, 256-262 Seacliff Road, BT20 5HT, ☎ (0247) 472807, AC AM BA, 35 rm. Ⓟ £34. Rest. ♦ ♪ £8.50.
★ ***The Sands***, 10-12 Seacliff Road, BT20 5EY, ☎ (0247) 473696, AC AM BA DI, 12 rm. Ⓟ £40. Rest. ♦ ♪ Cl. 25-26 Dec., 1 Jan. £9.50.
Winston, 19 Queen's Parade, BT20 3BJ, ☎ (0247) 454575, AC AM BA DI, 46 rm. Ⓟ £36.50. Rest. ♦ ♪ Cl. 25-26 Dec. £9.50.

⛺ at Millisle, *Seaview C.P.*, 1 Donaghadee Road (27 pl), ☎ (0247) 861248; at Moira, *Woburn C.P.*, Main Street (15 pl), ☎ (0846) 611516.

Nearby

CRAIGAVAD, 5m W on A2

Hotel:
Culloden, 142 Bangor Road, BT18 0EX, ☎ Holywood (023 17) 5223, Tx 74617, AC AM BA DI, 76 rm. Ⓟ Set in 12 acres of beautiful gardens and woodland. £78. Rest. ♦ ♪ £9.50.

CRAWFORDSBURN, 3m NW

Hotel:
Old Inn, 15 Main Street, BT19 1JH, ☎ Helen's Bay (0247) 853255, AC AM BA DI, 21 rm. Ⓟ A coaching inn built in 1614 and used by smugglers. £59.50. Rest. ♦ ♪ Cl. Christmas, 1 Jan. £9.50.

BELFAST**

Lisburn, 7; Ballymena, 33 m
pop. 329,958 ☎ 0232 Antrim C2

The capital of Northern Ireland and its most important commercial and industrial centre is beautifully situated, with unspoiled hills and high cliffs to the N and W that form a natural amphitheatre. To the E the River Lagan flows into Belfast Lough and the Irish Sea. The lough accommodates world renowned shipyards and several harbours which service ships from all over the world. The city grew rapidly from the 17th to the 19thC through its expertise and success in the linen and tobacco industries, together with the marine-dependent trades, such as rope making and engineering. The excellent central shopping area is for pedestrians only.

▶ **The City Hall** opened just after the turn of the century, one of the last of the grand Victorian buildings testifying to the city's affluence. Built from Portland stone, it dominates **Donegall Square** at the centre of the city. More interesting architecturally are the varied works of the Irish architect Charles Lanyon. ▶ The **custom house** standing in **Queen's Square** overlooks **Donegall Quay**. Lanyon designed it in Italianate style and the carved pediment has figures representing peace, manufacture, commerce and industry. ▶ The nearby **Sinclair Seamen's Church** in **Corporation Square** has an interesting interior. The pulpit is fashioned like a ship's prow, and the organ decorated with nautical clocks and port and starboard lights. ▶ In

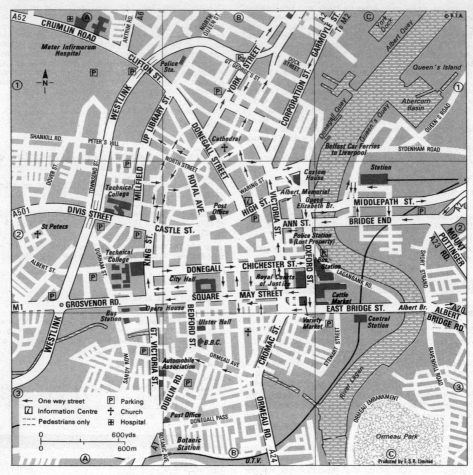

BELFAST

Queen's University to the S of the city, Lanyon used a Tudor style with mellow brickwork and mullioned windows. In **Great Victoria Street**, W of city centre: **The Grand Opera House★** recently restored, with lavish gilt interior. ▶ **The Crown Liquor Saloon** still sells drinks and has a magnificent ornate interior. ▶ Further S is the **Ulster Museum★** (*Mon.-Fri., 10-5; Sat., 1-5; Sun., 2-5*), partially rebuilt and extended in the 1970s: Irish art and furniture, glass, silver, ceramics and costume, excellent industrial archaeology section, contemporary international art collection and natural history section. The most spectacular display is the 'Girona Treasure', found 1968 off the Antrim coast in a 16thC Spanish ship: cannon, coins and jewelry. Note the golden salamander brooch with embedded rubies. ▶ **The Botanic Gardens** in which the museum stands have a remarkable palm house (*Mon.-Fri., 10-4; Sat., Sun., 2-4*).

Nearby

▶ **Lagan Valley Regional Park**: 9m of canal towpath towards Lisburn. ▶ **Lady Dixon Park** has 20,000 rose bushes; international rose trials held in the summer; children's play area. ▶ The **Giants Ring★** (*1m S of Shaw's*

Bridge, between the Lagan and Ballylesson*): largest prehistoric earthwork in Ireland, over 600 ft. in diameter with 12 ft. banked circle with five upright stones in the middle. A neolithic site, the stones were probably an ancient grave. ▶ The N suburbs have two hilly and scenic parks, **Hazlewood** and **Bellevue**, former demesne of the 19thC Belfast Castle. ▶ The former contains the city **Zoo** (*Mar.-Oct.: 9-6.; Nov.-Feb.: 10-3.30*). ▶ **Cave Hill** towers behind these two parks and a walk to **McArt's Fort** (1,100 ft.), an ancient volcanic crater, is rewarded by a view over Belfast and the lough. ▶ **Stormont** to the E, former Northern Ireland Parliament Building is set in 300 acres. ▶ **Hillsborough**, to the S: Georgian houses, some now antique shops. ▶ **Hillsborough Fort** in the park on the S side, built c. 1650 by Colonel Arthur Hill to protect the Dublin to Carrickfergus road; later made a royal garrison by Charles II (*Apr.-Sep.: Tue.-Sat., 10-6, Sun., 2-6; Oct.-Mar.: Tue.-Sat., 10-4, Sun., 2-4*). □

Practical information ────────────

BELFAST
ⓘ 52 High Street, ☎ (0232) 246609; Belfast Airport, Aldegrove, ☎ (08494) 53444.

✈ Belfast Airport, 12m NW on M2, ☎ (0232) 2292710.
⛴ Liverpool and Isle of Man, ☎ (0232) 226800.
Car rental: Europcar, G.M.G. Garages Ltd., 176-184
Shore Road, ☎ (0232) 772203; Avis, ☎ (0232) 2400404,
rail/drive.

Hotels:
★★★ *Drumkeen*, Upper Galwally, BT8 4TL (B2), ☎ (0232)
645321, AC BA, 28 rm. P ⏣ ✸ £52.50. Rest. ♦ £9.50.
★★★ *Stormont*, 587 Upper Newtownards Road, BT4 3LP
(C2 off map), ☎ (0232) 658621, AC AM BA DI, 67 rm. P
✸ £63. Rest. ♦ Cl. Christmas. £9.50.
★★★ *Wellington Park*, 21 Malone Road, BT9 6RW (A2 off
map), ☎ (0232) 661232, Tx 747052, AC AM BA DI, 52
rm. P ⌿ £64. Rest. ♦ £10.
Forum, Great Victoria Street, BT2 7AP (A3), ☎ (0232)
245161, Tx 74491, AC AM BA DI, 200 rm. P ✸ ⌿ £80.
Rest. ♦ £9.50.

Restaurant:
♦ *Strand*, 12 Stranmillis Road (B1 off map), ☎ (0232)
682266, AC AM BA DI P ⌕ ♨ ✸ Cl. 12-13 Jul., Sun. 2
rm. Book. £10.50.

Inn or Pub:
King's Head, Lisburn Road (off A3), ☎ (0232) 600455,
AC BA P ♿ ✸ Table d'hôte restaurant. £8.

Recommended
Craft Workshop: *Belfast Pottery*, Rosebank Enterprise
Park, Flax Street, Crumlin Road, ☎ (0232) 752672,
Irish pottery.
Golf course: Balmoral, Lisburn Road, ☎ (0232) 668540.

Nearby

DUNMURRY, 5 1/2m SW on A1

Hotel:
Conway (T.H.F.), Kingsway, BT17 9ES, ☎ (0232) 612101,
Tx 74281, AC AM BA DI, 76 rm. P ⏣ ▱ ♨ £66. Rest.
♦ £9.50.

GLENGORMLEY, 6m on NW by A8 on B56

Restaurant:
♦ *Sleepy Hollow*, 15 Kiln Road, ☎ (023 13) 44042, AC
AM BA DI P Cl. Sun.-Tue., lunch. £15.75.

NEWTOWNABBEY, 4m NE on M2

Hotels:
★★★ *Glenavna House*, 588 Shore Road, BT37 0SN, ☎
Whiteabbey (0231) 64461, AC AM BA, 19 rm. P ⏣ Coun-
try mansion standing in 11 acres of parkland. £44. Rest.
♦ £9.50.
Chimney Corner, 630 Antrim Road, BT36 8RH, ☎ Glen-
gormley (023 13) 44925, Tx 748158, AC AM BA DI, 63 rm.
P ⏣ ✸ ⌿ £52.50. Rest. ♦ £10.50.

⚓ *Jordanstown Lough*, Shore Road (6 pl), ☎ (0231)
63133.

CARRICKFERGUS*

Ballymena, 38; Larne, 12; Belfast, 10 m
pop. 17,633 ☎ 09603   Antrim C2

An ancient town around the harbour and castle.

▶ The castle is the finest surviving Norman castle in Ire-
land and was used as a military base up to 1928. ▶ It
houses a **museum** displaying the history of former Irish
cavalry regiments (*Apr.-Sep.: Mon.-Sat., 10-6, Sun., 2-6;
Oct.-Mar.: 10-4, Sun., 2-4*). ▶ The parish church of **St.
Nicholas**, reconstructed 1614, contains a monument to Sir
Arthur Chichester, first Governor of Ulster, and a 16thC
Flemish glass window representing the baptism of Christ.

Nearby

▶ **Whitehead**, at the foot of **Island Magee Peninsula**,
is a resort with promenade, golf courses and other
facilities. From the Whitehead excursion station, steam
express trains leave for Portrush and special seasonal

and summer vintage steam train events also take place
here. **Island Magee** is a 7m-long peninsula connected at
the S end by road and the N end by a ferry service from
Ferris's Bay to **Larne** (*daily: 7.30-5.30, passengers only*).
▶ Along the E are precipitous cliffs known as the **Gob-
bins. Browns Bay** in the N has a sandy beach. ▶ **Larne**
is a resort popular with those visiting the glens. The shortest crossing between Scotland and Ireland leaves from
here to Stranraer. ▶ At the entrance to the harbour, a
92 ft. **round tower** commemorates James Chaine, M.P.,
'Father of the Port'. ▶ On a promontory at the S end of
the town, known as the **Curran**, stands the ruined **Older-
fleet Castle**. Thousands of flint implements have been
found on this small site indicating a neolithic manufacturing centre.   □

Practical information _____

ℹ️ Town Hall and Castle Green, ☎ (096 03) 63604 (summer only).

Hotels:
★ *Dobbins Inn*, 6-8 High Street, BT38 9HG, ☎ (096 03)
63905, AC BA, 13 rm. ⌿ ♘ A 17thC inn with many secret
passages, believed to be haunted. £45. Rest. ♦ £8.50.
Dolphin, 16 Marine Parade, Whitehead, BT38 9QD, ☎
(096 03) 72481, 22 rm. P ✸ £50. Rest. ♦ .

Recommended
Golf course: 35 North Road, ☎ (09603) 63713.

LARNE on A2

ℹ️ Council Offices, Victoria Road, ☎ (0574) 72313.
Car rental: *Europcar, G.M.G.* Garages Ltd., 96-98
Glenarm Road, ☎ (0574) 79360.

Hotel:
Magheramorne House (Consort/Hospitality), 59 Shore
Road, BT40 3HW, ☎ (0574) 79444, AC AM BA DI, 23 rm,
P ⚞ ⏣ ⌕ ♿ ⌿ ♘ A 19thC Gothic-style house situated
in 43 acres. £45. Rest. ♦ ♨ ♿ Rainbow trout. £11.

⚓ *Curran C.P.*, 131 Curran Road (29 pl), ☎ (0574) 73797.

COLERAINE*

Londonderry, 30; Ballymena, 27; Belfast, 50 m
pop. 15,967 ☎ 0265   Londonderry B1

There are two songs in Ireland about this market town
on the Bann River - one about 'Kitty of Coleraine'
and another about 'Coleraine'. But the town has other
reasons for its fame. Swift (1667-1745) lived here for
a time as did Lever (1806-1872), the Irish novelist,
remembered for such fine books as *Harry Lorrequer*
and *Charles O'Malley*. The MacDonnells of Antrim
acquired much land here after the flight of the earls
and, as with Derry, the London companies took over
the whole district from James I. 4m to the W is the
huge fortress of Dun Ceithern, where the legendary
Heroes of the Red Branch - 2nd and 4thC fighting
men of Ulster, are reputed to have lived when not at
Emain (Navan Fort). 1m above Coleraine is the great
fort or mound, one of the largest in the country, now
called Mount Sandel but called Dundavan in ancient
times and the residence of 'Niall of the brilliant
deeds', in the pre-Christian era. King Conchubar, of
the great Deirdre story, is said to have sailed down
the river to stay here.   □

Practical information _____

COLERAINE

ℹ️ swimming pool, Main Street, ☎ (0265) 848258 (summer only).
Car rental: *Avis*, ☎ (0265) 3654, rail/drive.

⚓ *Marina C.P.*, Portstewart Road (8 pl), ☎ (0265) 4768; at Castlerock, *Castlerock*, 24 Sea Road (87 pl), ☎ (026 584) 8381.

Recommended
Golf course: Castlerock, 5m W, ☎ (026 584) 314.

Nearby
AGHADOWEY, 11m S by A37 on A29

Hotel:
Greenhill House, 24 Greenhill Road, BT51 4EU, ☎ (026 585) 241, AC, 7 rm. Ⓟ ⬜ ⬜ ⬜ £24. Rest. ♦ Cl. Nov.-Mar. £8.

BLACKHILL, 8m SE by A29

Restaurant:
♦ *MacDuffs*, 112 Killeague Road, ☎ Aghadowey (026 585) 433 Ⓟ ⬜ ⬜ ⬜ Cl. Sun., Mon., 25-26 Dec., lunch. £11.50.

COOKSTOWN*

Omagh, 28; Portadown, 27; Belfast, 31 m
☎ 064 87   Tyrone B2

Founded by planter Alan Cook, this market town has an exceptionally long and broad main street.

Nearby
▶ Two buildings by John Nash can be seen at Killymoon to the S of the town and Lissan Rectory (*2m NE*) ▶ Evidence of ancient associations of the area are at **Beaghmore**, a large area of stone circles, cairns and alignments. ▶ **Tullahogue Fort** is a hilltop inauguration site of the O'Neills, Chiefs of Ulster from 12th to 17thC, the last inauguration being in 1595. ▶ Their principal seat was **Dungannon★**, but its castle was burned in the early 17thC to prevent its capture by Planters. ▶ Well worth a visit is the **Tyrone Crystal Factory** at Dungannon: glass blowing and cutting and finishing of very fine lead crystal glasses, decanters and vases (*Mon.-Thu.; Fri., am only*). ▶ Near **Moneymore**, the Draper's company town, is **Springhill House**. It is a good example of a 17thC fortified manor house; costume museum (*Apr.-Sep., 2-6 ex. Tue.*). ▶ The **Wellbrook Beetling Mill** (*4m W*) is a water-powered 18thC mill (*Apr., May, Sep.: Sat., Sun., 2-6; Jun.-Aug.: daily ex. Tue.*). ▶ Close by are **Drum Manor** remains and Forest Park, with delightful butterfly garden. There is also a fine shrub collection and a special garden for the blind.   □

Practical information

ⓘ Town Hall, Burn Road, ☎ (06487) 63359/63441.

Hotels:
★ **Glenavon House**, 52 Drum Road, BT80 8JQ, ☎ (064 87) 64949, AC BA, 20 rm. Ⓟ ⌡ £35.
★ **Greenvale**, 57 Drum Road, BT80 8JQ, ☎ (064 87) 62243, 11 rm. Ⓟ ⬜ ⬜ £33.

Recommended
Golf course: Moyola Park, Shanemullagh Castledawson, ☎ (0648) 68392.
♥ glassware: at Dungannon,*Tyrone Crystal*, Oaks Road, ☎ (086 87) 25335.

DOWNPATRICK*

Newry, 26; Bangor, 27; Belfast, 22 m
pop. 8,245 ☎ 0396   Down C2

Downpatrick, county capital, takes its name from St. Patrick and down (*dun* in Irish), where the famous cathedral stands. The present **Downpatrick Cathedral** is built on the site of an older cathedral, one of the most ancient edifices in Ireland, which was destroyed by the Danes and in which, it is said, the

Dungannon, an historic city

Dungannon (Geanan's Fort) was the earliest seat of the O'Neills and continued in their possession until 1607. The O' Neill castle stood upon a hill crowning the town, but was destroyed by Gerald, ninth Earl of Kildare, and scarcely a trace of it remains. Because of the warlike tendencies of the O'Neills, it was exposed to the constant vicissitudes of war. It was here that Shane the Proud held sway for years and was virtual ruler of Ulster, until his treacherous assassination at the instigation of the English lord deputy. This historic locality was also the scene of many of the exploits of Hugh O'Neill and Sir Phelim O'Neill, the leader of the insurrection of 1641. In the parish church of Dungannon, the delegates (Protestant) of the Irish volunteers of 1782 met and issued their declaration that only the king, lords and commons of Ireland possessed the right to make laws for Ireland. Today in Dungannon there are manufacturers of linen goods, glass, fabrics, earthenware firebricks, and tiles as well as a trade in corn and flax and a large cattle and pig market.

remains of St. Patrick, St. Bridget and St. Columbkill were buried. A cathedral was erected on the site by Malachy O'Morgair, Bishop of Down, in 1140, and was burned during the war of Edward Bruce, restored in 1412 and again burned by Lord Deputy De Grey in 1538. In 1790 the present structure was erected on its ruins; it has a lofty square tower at the left end, embattled and pinnacled, giving the cathedral, which stands on a hill, a massive and imposing appearance. The interior is richly ornamented. In the town below is a wide Georgian mall where the St. Patrick Heritage Centre in the gatehouse of 18thC jail can be visited (*Tue.-Fri., 11-6, Sat., 2-6*).

Nearby
▶ At **Wells of Struell** ($1/2m$ E): 17thC bathhouse; pilgrims have visited these wells in the hope of a cure for eye ailments. ▶ The remains of the 12thC **Saul Abbey★** and replica church commemorate St. Patrick's arrival in Down for his first missionary journey, and the possible place of his death in 461. ▶ Footpath leads up **Slieve Patrick** to a large granite monument of the saint looking across the lough. ▶ At the foot of Strangford Lough is **Castle Ward★**. The 600 acre grounds contain a formal garden, parkland, sawmills and ornamental lake with wildfowl; also Palladian temple and Victorian laundry (*Apr.-Sep., 2-6, ex. Fri.*). Close by are two earlier castles, **Old Castle Ward**, **Andley's Castle** and a double-horned cairn. ▶ On the coast, entered from Downpatrick by **Ardtole** with its ruined medieval church, is the small fishing village of **Ardglass**, at one time a sizable trading centre with numerous fortified warehouses. The best-preserved of these is **Jordans Castle** which houses a small museum. Near Saintfield (*10m NW*) are **Rowallane Gardens** with azaleas, rhododendrons, rock gardens and an informal wall garden (*Apr., Jul.-Oct.: Mon.-Fri., 9-6, Sat., Sun., 2-6;. Nov.-Mar.: Fri., 9-4.30*).   □

Practical information

DOWNPATRICK
🚢 to Portaferry.

Hotel:
★★★ **Abbey Lodge**, 38 Belfast Road, BT30 9AV, ☎ (0396) 4511, AC AM BA DI, 21 rm. Ⓟ ⬜ £32. Rest. ♦ £10.50.

⚓ *Silver Bay C.P.*, 15 Ardminnan Road, Cloughey (13 pl), ☎ (024 77) 71321; at Ardglass, *Corney Island C.P.*, Killop Road (6 pl), ☎ (0396) 841448; at Castle Ward, *Castle Ward Estate* (19 pl), ☎ (039 686) 204.

Recommended
Golf course: Ardglass Golf Club, Castle Place, Ardglass, ☎ (0396) 841755.

Nearby

BALLYNAHINCH, 15m NW by A25 on A24

Restaurant:
♦ **Woodlands**, 29 Spa Road, ☎ (0238) 562650, AC BA DI ℙ ≼ ♨ ♤ ♪ ఉ ⊗ Cl. Sun.-Wed., lunch. Local seafood. Book. £15.

ENNISKILLEN*

Sligo, 42; Londonderry, 59; Belfast, 87 m
pop. 10,429 ☎ 0365   Fermanagh A2

Enniskillen is the assize town of the county of Fermanagh, one of the two counties, among the six administered by the British in Northern Ireland, which has a large Catholic majority. The other is Tyrone. Fermanagh takes its name from *Fir Monach*, or men of Manach, the ancestors of the people of the county who settled here in the 3thC. Enniskillen is built on an island formed by two branches of the River Erne, and is connected to mainland by bridges. In Irish it is called *Inis-Cethlenn*, or island of Kethlenda, wife of a mythical chieftain. The town and surrounding country was originally a stronghold of the Maguires, until James I gave it to one Cole whose descendants still possess a major portion of it. Enniskillen has always been regarded as having an important military position commanding the route from Ulster to Connaught. The ancient Maguire Castle is presently used as a British military barracks.

Nearby

▶ Take the A4 SE by **Castle Coole**, with its lovely gardens, and through **Clodagh Glen**, where there are large limestone **caves** (*underground boat trip through stalagmites and stalactites*), through **Lisbellaw** (*10m*) to **Maguiresbridge** (*9m*), a village on the Colebrooke river; here leave the A4 and turn S to **Lisnaskea** (*1 1/2 m*), which was once the inauguration place of the Maguires. Leave the town by the same road and arrive, after 1/2m to a side road which branches off NE, and after some 3m, through signposted country lanes, reach **Belleisle**, in Upper Lough Erne. Belleisle formerly belonged to the MacManus who named **BallyMacmanus** (bally - *baile* in Irish - with which so many Irish place names begin, means town or burgh) Belleisle is memorable as having been the residence of the great Irish scholar, **Cahal Maguire**, dean of Cloger who, in the 15thC, compiled the *Annals of Ulster*, a valuable historical work. ▶ From Belleisle take the main road N for 8m, along the l. bank of the Erne River and the Lough this time, passing Lough Barry and Lough Laragh to Enniskillen. ▶ Leave Enniskillen traveling W, on the W course of the A4, which goes on (8m) to **Belcoo** and the border with County Cavan, leaving on its **Belmore Mountain** (1,312 ft.), a beauty spot with splendid cliffs and ancient monuments. ▶ After leaving on the A4 W, instead of going on to Belcoo, after 3m, take a side road N to **Derrygonnelly** which is reached after 6m; 2m S of this town is **Knockmore Cliff** (919 ft.), a precipitous and conspicuous rock; continue N from Derrygonnelly for 5m to the famous 16thC **Tully Castle** on a promontory that juts into the lake; it has a keep, is turreted at the angles, and is surrounded by an outer wall. The castle was erected as a stronghold by some of the first Scottish settlers in Ireland, however, it was captured and destroyed by Rory, brother of Lord Maguire, and sixty of its inmates were killed. It was never rebuilt. The

ruins of another castle, **Monea**, of the same period, are a few miles to the SE. Return S to Enniskillen 8m along the lough, passing **Tully Bay**, in the midst of beautiful surroundings. ▶ 2m N of Enniskillen are some remarkable **crannoges** or artificial island habitations.

▶ **Devenish Island** (*3m*): this island in Lough Erne is one of the most interesting spots in Ireland to the tourist and antiquarian. It contains several ancient remains, among them the **monastic house of St. Molaisse**, who died in 563, and a **round tower**. The establishment, several times plundered by the Danes, was rebuilt about 1130 as a small quadrangular structure and though it stood in its original form until the beginning of the 19thC, little remains. The round tower is considered one of the most perfect in Ireland and is in an excellent state of preservation. With the cone, it is 74 ft. high and 48 ft. in circumference. The **sculptures** on it are curious and artistically executed.   □

Practical information _____

ENNISKILLEN
ⓘ Lakeland Vistor Centre, Shore Road, ☎ (0365) 23110/25050.

Hotels:
★★★ *Killyhevlin* (Consort), Dublin Road, BT74 6HQ, ☎ (0365) 23481, AC AM BA DI, 23 rm. ℙ ≼ ♨ £54.50. Rest. ♦ £12.50.
★★ *Fort Lodge*, 72 Forthill Street, BT74 6AJ, ☎ (0365) 23275, 12 rm. ℙ ⊗ £34. Rest. ♦ £10.

Recommended
Craft Workshop: at Belleek, *Belleek China*, ☎ (036 565) 501, pottery and china.
Golf course: Castlecoole, ☎ (0365) 25250.

Nearby

IRVINESTOWN, 10m N on A32

Hotel:
Mahon's, Mill Street, BT74 9XX, ☎ (036 56) 21656, AC BA, 21 rm. ℙ £31.50. Rest. ♦ £8.

LISNASKEA, 10m SE by A4 on A34

Hotel:
★ *Ortine*, Main Street, ☎ (036 57) 21206, AC BA, 20 rm. ℙ ♨ £28.50. Rest. ♦ £7.50.

⚓ *Share Centre*, Smiths, Strand (34 pl), ☎ (036 57) 22122.

LONDONDERRY*

Buncrana, 13; Coleraine, 20; Belfast, 70 m
pop. 62,697 ☎ 0504   Londonderry A1

It was in Derry (the oak grove) that St. Columba founded a monastery, in the 6thC, in a beautiful position on a hillside by a broad river leading into the wide estuary of Lough Foyle and the Atlantic Ocean. The prefix 'London' was added in the early 17thC when James I granted the city and surrounding areas to colonists or Planters financed by the guilds of London. The city walls are renowned for the two 17thC sieges they withstood. The second siege (1688-9), lasting 105 days and costing thousands of lives, was relieved only by ships sent by William of Orange.

▶ The heart of the city lies within these **walls**, which are 18 ft. thick and 1m around - the only unbroken city walls in the British Isles. Old cannons face outwards and it is possible to walk around the wall (*guided tours available*).
▶ Four main streets radiate from '**the Diamond**' to four old gateways - **Bishop's Gate, Ferryquay Gate, Shipquay Gate** and **Butcher's Gate**; three more gates were added later. ▶ **St. Columba's Cathedral** is a good example of Gothic with some 19thC additions. ▶ Just outside the walls is the **Guildhall** (*9-4, Mon.-Fri.*), completed 1890 and

modeled on its London counterpart. Fine stained-glass windows illustrate the city's history.

Nearby

▶ **Ballygarnet Field** (*5m NE*): a memorial marks the spot where the first woman to fly the Atlantic, Amelia Earhart, landed her plane in 1932. ▶ Following the road E by the shore of Lough Foyle is **Eglinton**, established by the Grocer's Guild, with an English-type green and two oak trees which came from Windsor Great Park. ▶ Nearby **Muff Glen** offers walks by the stream. ▶ At **Ballykelly** a fortified house was erected by the Fishmonger's Guild. ▶ In **Limavady**, Jane Ross, who noted down the melody of the 'Londonderry Air' from a strolling musician, is commemorated. ▶ The six-arch bridge over the river lies near the attractive **Roe Valley Country Park**. Old mills and bleaching greens can be seen - reminders of the local linen industry that was dependent on river power. There is a visitor's centre and camping and caravan facilities.   □

Practical information ⸻⸻⸻⸻

LONDONDERRY
ℹ️ Foyle Street, ☎ (0504) 267284.
✈ Eglington Airport, 6m E, ☎ (0504) 810784.
Car rental: Hertz, Desmond Motors Ltd., 173 Strand Road, ☎ (0504) 260420.

Hotels:
★★★★ *Everglades* (Consort/Hospitality), Prehen Road, BT47 2PA, ☎ (0504) 46722, Tx 748005, AC AM BA DI, 38 rm. ℗ & ✿ £68. Rest. ♦ Cl. 25-26 Dec. £10.50.
★★★ *White Horse Inn*, 68 Clooney Road, BT47 3PA, ☎ Campsie (0504) 860606, AC AM BA DI, 44 rm. ℗ ✿ £42. Rest. ♦ £11.50.

⚓ at Limavady, *Roe Valley*, 41 Leap Road (15 pl), ☎ (05047) 62074; at Magilligan, *Benone C.P.*, Benone Avenue (40 pl), ☎ (050 47) 50324.

Recommended
Golf course: City of Derry, Prehen Londonderry, ☎ (0504) 42610.

Nearby

STRABANE, 14m SW on A5
ℹ️ Lifford Road, ☎ (0504) 883735.

Hotel:
★★★ *Fir Trees Lodge*, Melmont Road, BT82 9JT, ☎ (0504) 883003, AC AM BA DI, 26 rm. ℗ ✿ ↙ £34. Rest. ♦ £10.50.

Recommended
Golf course: Ballycolman, ☎ (0504) 882271.

LOUGH ERNE

Omagh, 19; Londonderry, 30; Belfast, 85 m
☎ 0365   Fermanagh A2-3

Upper and Lower Lough Erne belong almost exclusively to Fermanagh and stretch through nearly the whole length of the county; they can vie with lakes in any other part of the world for the quiet and gentle beauty of their scenery and they possess hundreds of islands. There are shrines around the lakes with relics of their early Christian past.

▶ The River Erne rising in the Republic has a navigable course of over 50m, passing through lakes and rivers in Fermanagh until it passes again over the meandering border to flow into Donegal Bay at Ballyshannon in the Republic. In Ulster, the waterway is divided into the Lower and Upper loughs. ▶ The Lower Lough, 18m long, lies in a basin gouged out by ancient glaciers giving a depth of 77 ft. below sea level and a spectacular viewpoint on the N shore from a limestone scarp at the Cliffs of Magho. ▶ The shallower Upper Lough is really a series of flood islands with a maze of waterways. ▶ The water level of

the Upper Lough is controlled by a dam at Portora, and the Lower Lough for use by the Hydro-Electric Power Station at Ballyshannon in the Republic. ▶ The area is a paradise for those who enjoy the outdoor life in beautiful and tranquil surroundings, especially fishermen and sailors. Roach, perch, bream, rudd and eels are plentiful. (The nearby smaller loughs of Melvin and Macnean bordering on the Republic are also renowned for catches.) Cruising boats and other craft can be easily rented and the loughs have many jetties, small marinas and waterside shops.   □

LOUGH NEAGH

Armagh, 12; Londonderry, 38; Belfast, 13 m
                                          Antrim B2

The largest lake in the British Isles with 65m of shoreline. It lies in the central lowlands only 40 ft. above sea level with a sedgy and wooded shoreline, beaches and little harbours. Fishing is popular, with abundant rudd, roach, perch, pyke and eels, and game fish are also found in the linking rivers of Bann, Main, Sixmilewater, Ballinderry and Moyota.

Nearby

▶ Where the River Bann leaves Lough Neagh there is a busy eel fishery at **Toombridge** (*visits by appt.*). The eels used to swim upriver from Coleraine, but are now transported by tanker to the lough, where they grow to maturity. ▶ Cruises around the lough can be made from the marina at **Sixmilewater** (*Jul.-Aug.*). ▶ **Oxford Island** (actually a peninsula) on the S shore offers many activities - a nature trail, a centre with an exhibition and children's natural history library, observation hides, boating, bathing and picnicking. There is a marina. ▶ **Maghery**, at the mouth of the Blackwater, also has a marina. The river is one of Ireland's most popular canoeing venues. ▶ **Mountjoy Castle**, 17thC ruin, overlooks the lough in the NW corner. ▶ High cross at **Arboe★** (on the shore W of Cookstown): Early Christian wheel-headed stone cross with sculpted scenes from the life of Christ and the Old Testament decorating all its surfaces.   □

Practical information ⸻⸻⸻⸻

MAGHERA

Hotel:
Glenburn, Glen Road, BT46 5JP, ☎ (0648) 42203, 4 rm. ℗ ✿ ↗ £50. Rest. ♦ £10.

The MOURNE MOUNTAINS

Warrenpoint, 10; Armagh, 23; Belfast, 28 m
☎ 06937   Down C3

These mountains were formed by the action of rivers and glaciers on a mass of granite. There are also some areas of slate on Slieve Binnian (*slieve* means 'mountain' in Irish) and the low Mournes. Within a 25m circuit fifteen summits rise to over 2,000ft. A road circumvents them, but only Spelga Pass goes through part of the range. The 'Wilderness', as the central area is called, is perfect for the walker, with streams, heather and rocks. Two large reservoirs in the Silent Valley supply Belfast's water. High drystone walls enclose the reservoirs and link all the principal peaks of the range. A coastal road goes around the foot of the Mourne range from Newcastle to Rostrevor. The first section the mountains 'sweep down to the sea' but towards the mouth of Carlingford Lough there are a succession of beaches. ▶ The fishing village of Annalong has a harbour and working cornmill, with an exhibition of water-power technology (*Easter-May:*

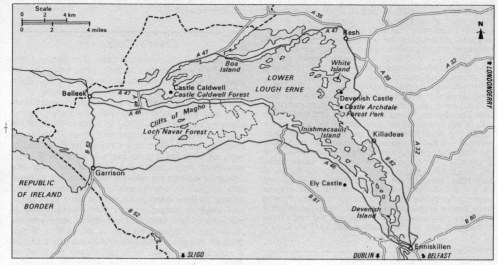

Lower lough Erne

wkends; *Jun.-Aug.: Mon.-Sat., 11-6, Sun., 2-6).* From Kilkeel (→) a road branches into the mountain range leading to **Spelga Pass**. □

NEWCASTLE*

Newry, 18; Bangor, 37; Belfast, 31 m
pop. 6,246 ☎ 039 67   Down C3

A beautifully situated seaside resort at the base of Slieve Donard with a 5m beach, recreation grounds and good walks. On the promenade is a fountain commemorating Percy French, the author of the famous 'Mountains of Mourne' song.

Nearby

▶ S of town at **Bloody Bridge** picnic site: path ascends the Mourne range to **Slieve Donard**★ (2796 ft.); magnificent **views**, picnicking, camping and caravanning. A natural history exhibition highlights the plants and animals found in the wooded glens and special pony-trekking routes have been laid out. ▶ **Castlewellan Forest Park** *(4m N of Tollymore)* has a long lake, fine gardens and an arboretum. ▶ **Dundrum** *(5m N)*: John de Courcey's dramatically sited castle *(keep open Apr.-Sep.: Tue.-Sat., 10-7, Sun., 2-7; Oct.-Mar.: Sat., 10-4, Sun., 2-4).* ▶ At **Slidderyford** *(1m N of Newcastle)*, a near-perfect dolmen and at **Legananny** *(7m SW of Ballynahinch)*, at the foot of Slieve Croob, is the distinctive and much-photographed tripod dolmen. □

Practical information

NEWCASTLE
ℹ️ The Newcastle Centre, Central Promenade, ☎ (03967) 22222.

Hotels:
★★★ ***Burrendale*** (Consort/Hospitality), Castlewellan Road, BT33 0JZ, ☎ (039 67) 22599, AC BA DI, 30 rm. 🅿 ⌗ ☒ ⏛ 🕭 £36.50. Rest. ♦ £13.50.
★★★ ***Slieve Donard***, Downs Road, BT33 0IJ, ☎ (039 67) 23681, AC AM BA DI, 106 rm. 🅿 ⌗ ☒ ⏛ 🕭 £63. Rest. ♦ £13.

⚲ *Lazy B J C.S.*, Dundrum Road (60 pl), ☎ (039 67) 23533; *Tollymore Forest Park*, 176 Tullbrannigan Road (95 pl), ☎ (039 67) 22428; at Annalong, *Annalong Marine Park*, Main Street (44 pl), ☎ (039 676) 68101.

Recommended
Riding Schools: at Castlewellan, *Mount Pleasant Trekking Centre*, 15 Bannanstown Road, ☎ (039 67) 78651, trekking with escort through 14,000-acre forest and park; *Newcastle Riding Centre*, 35 Carnacavill Road, ☎ (039 67) 22694, riding instruction with tuition in stable management.

Nearby

KILKEEL, 11m SW on A2
ℹ️ Caravan, Town Centre, ☎ (069 37) 63092.

Hotel:
Kilmorey Arms, 41 Greencastle Street, ☎ (069 37) 62220, BA DI, 6 rm. ⌗ ⏛ £64. Rest. ♦ £12.

⚲ *Chesnutt C.P.*, Grange Road (15 pl), ☎ (069 37) 62653; *Silvertove C.P.*, 98 Leestone Road (15 pl), ☎ (069 37) 63136.

OMAGH*

Londonderry, 36; Dundalk, 61; Belfast, 70 m
pop. 14,627 ☎ 0662   Tyrone A2

Omagh is the assize town of **County Tyrone**, its largest towns being Strabane and Dungannon. The name comes from **Tir Eoghain** (pronounced Tir Owen) and means the land of Owen but this ancient principality was the inheritence of the O'Neills until the Plantation. Omagh stands on a hill at the base of which is the confluence of the Camowen and Drumragh rivers. To its S is the picturesque town of Fintona, W of which, on one of the headstreams of the Owenreagh, is Dromore.

Nearby

▶ **Ulster American Folk Park**★ *(3m N, Apr.-Sep.: Mon.-Sat., 11-6.30, Sun., Bank Hols., 11.30-7; Sep.-Mar.: 10.30-5).* The showpiece is the ancestral homestead of

the Mellon family of Pittsburgh U.S.A., with reconstructions of bygone rural life of Ulster and the new 'pioneer' life to which many Irish men and women sailed. ▶ The American connection can also be seen at **Dergalt**, near Strabane, the house of the grandfather of the 28th U.S. President, Woodrow Wilson (*open all year - call at farm*). ▶ To the NW of Omagh is **Newtownstewart** named after William Stewart, ancestor of the Lords of Mountjoy. James II retreated this way after the siege of Derry. ▶ **Harry Avery's Castle** is a conspicuous ruin 1/2m SW of Newtownstewart. ▶ **Baronscourt**, a little further SW situated in a valley below the peak of Betsy Bell, is seat of the Dukes of Abercorn. It was built in early 18thC and altered later in the century by Sir John Soane and again in the 19thC. The estate includes fine gardens and three lakes; neolithic and Early Christian finds have been made here (*gardens only open*). ▶ **Gortin Glen Forest Park★**, E of Strule River, has magnificent drives, deer, nature tracks and an exhibition hall. ▶ 25m N of Omagh on the A5, is **Sion Mills**, with its linen works and garden village and then, a further 5m N, **Strabane**, on the River Mourne where John Dunlap was apprenticed at Gray's Printing Shop before emigrating to America. He issued the first American daily paper in 1771 and was the first printer of the Declaration of Independence (*daily ex. Thu., Sun.*).□

Practical information ────────────

ⓘ 1 Market Street, ☎ (0662) 478312.

Hotel:
★★ *Royal Arms* (Consort), 51-53 High Street, BT78 1BA, ☎ (0662) 3262, AC BA, 21 rm. ℗ ⋘ ⌡ ♨ £34. Rest. ♦ £6.50.

Å at Mountfield Omagh, *Mountfield C.P.* (4 pl), ☎ (0662) 45321.

Recommended
Golf course: Newtownstewart Golf Club, 38 Golf Course Road, ☎ (06626) 61204.

PORTRUSH*

Coleraine, 5; Ballymena, 31; Belfast, 68 m
pop. 5,114 ☎ 0265   Antrim B1

An important vacation centre with many facilities situated on a promontory with bays and beaches on either side. It benefits from the Gulf Stream which maintains an equable sea temperature.

Nearby

▶ **The Giant's Causeway★** has fascinated visitors for centuries. A 5m circular walk will show the full extent of this extraordinary coastline. The hexagonal basalt columns look almost man-made where they form stepping stones into the sea. Elsewhere the tallest columns are 40ft. high. They were formed over 60,000,000 yrs. ago by molten basalt surfacing from a fault line stretching from the Antrim coast to Skye in Scotland. An audio-visual theatre at the **Visitor's Centre** gives the facts and the 'Giant' legends. ▶ **Dunseverick Castle** (*4m NE of Bushmills*) was situated at the end of an ancient route where the Celts crossed to and from Scotland. One wall of the castle now remains on the cliff edge. ▶ **Dunluce Castle★** (*4m E of Portrush*) is a spectacularly-placed ruin built on sheer rock jutting in to the sea (*Apr.-Sep.: Mon.-Sat., 10-7, Sun., 2-7; Oct.-Mar.: Tue.-Sat., 10-4, Sun., 2-4*) At one time it was the seat of the Marquis of Antrim. In 1639 part of the castle, including the kitchens, subsided into the huge cave below. The mainland buildings were erected after this date and thereafter fell into decay. ▶ At **Devrock**, off the main Portrush to Ballymoney road, is Ireland's only safari park; also an indoor theatre, children's amusements, café and picnicking. ▶ 2m inland from the causeway is **Bushmills★**, celebrated for its whiskey distilling since 1609. The very popular tours may

need advance reservations (*1hr tours every am and mid-pm wkdays, ex. Fri.*).   □

─────────────────────────

Giant's Causeway

It is said that thousands of years ago Scotland and Ireland were connected by land; even today only 13 miles of sea separate the most southwesterly point of Scotland from the northeastern tip of Ulster.
Along the north coast of County Antrim between Portrush and Ballycastle the basalt cliffs known as the Giant's Causeway are similar to some of those of the Scottish Hebrides. They consist of about 37,000 stone columns, mostly 20 ft. but some as much as 400 ft. high, which make a great pathway up to 40 ft. wide stretching from behind the edge of the cliffs and disappearing into the sea. Because they are so regularly shaped, mostly in hexagons and polygons, they appear to have been laid down by some giant hand; and there is indeed a story that the causeway is the work of Finn McCool, the mythical Ulster warrior. According to legend, he was in love with a female giant on the island of Staffa in the Hebrides and built a path across the sea to bring her back to his home. Many of the rock formations within the causeway have also been given fanciful names like the Wishing Well, Giant's Organ and Lord Antrim's Parlour. Nevertheless, there has long been a scientific explanation for this extraordinary natural phenomenon: it is the result of volcanic action about 30 million years ago, and is composed of lava flow which solidified as it cooled on entering the sea.
The strange sight of the Giant's Causeway has attracted visitors for hundreds of years, and the first descriptive account of it appeared at the end of the 17thC. Visitors included one Chevalier de la Tocnaye who made his way to the edge of the cliff on horseback - sensibly equipped with an umbrella - and was enchanted with the view. Dr. Samuel Johnson was less enthralled when he made the trip in the 18thC; but, not surprisingly, he had found the two-week journey on packhorse somewhat of an ordeal, for until the 1830s there was no proper coast road. However intrepid early travelers had one compensation: the last resting point before the causeway happened to be at Bushmills. There they were able to restore themselves with the finest whiskey brewed in the world's oldest legal distillery - still thriving today.

─────────────────────────

Practical information ────────────

PORTRUSH
ⓘ Town Hall.

Hotels:
★★ *Northern Counties*, BT56 8BN, ☎ (0265) 823755, AC AM BA DI, 88 rm. ▭ ⌡ £32.50. Rest. ♦ £9.50.
★★ *Skerry Bhan*, 3-5 Lansdowne Crescent, BT56 8AY, ☎ (0265) 822328, 42 rm. ⅋ £26. Rest. ♦ £7.50.

Restaurant:
● ♦ *Ramore*, The Harbour, ☎ (0265) 824313 ℗ ⋦ ⋟ ♿ ⅋ Cl. 2wks. end Jan., Sun.-Mon., lunch. Book. £13.50.

Å *Carrick Dhu C.P.*, 12 Ballyreagh Road (57 pl), ☎ (0265) 823712; *Margoth C.P.*, 126 Dunluce Road (70 pl), ☎ (0265) 822531; *Portrush C.P.*, Loguestown Road (65 pl), ☎ (0265) 823537.

Recommended
Golf course: Royal Portrush, Bushmills Road, ☎ (0265) 822311.

Nearby

PORTBALLINTRAE, 5m NE on A2
ⓘ Beach Road, ☎ (026 57) 31672.

Hotels:
★★ *Bayview*, 2 Bayhead Road, BT57 8RZ, ☎ Bushmills (026 57) 31453, AC BA, 16 rm. Ⓟ ≪ ⌖ ⌿ £36.50. Rest. ◆ £10.50.
★★ *Beach*, 61 Beach Road, BT57 8RT, ☎ Bushmills (026 57) 31214, AC BA, 28 rm. Ⓟ ⌖ ⌿ ⌕ £38. Rest. ◆ £9.50.

⚠ *Ballintrea C.P.*, 60 Ballaghmore Road (31 pl), ☎ (026 57) 31478.

PORTSTEWART, 2 1/2m NE on A2
ⓘ Town Hall, The Crescent, ☎ (026 583) 2286.

Hotel:
★ *Windsor*, 8 The Promenade, BT55 7AD, ☎ (026 583) 2523, 28 rm. Ⓟ ⌖ £24. Rest. ◆ Cl. Jan. - Mar. £8.

⚠ *Juniper Hill C.P.*, 70 Ballyreagh Road (75 pl), ☎ (026 583) 2023; *Portstewart*, 80 Mill Road (57 pl), ☎ (026 583) 3092.

Recommended
Golf course: Portstewart Golf Club, 117 Strand Road, ☎ (026 583) 2015.

The SPERRIN MOUNTAINS

Omagh, 15; Londonderry, 17; Belfast, 48 m
☎ 0504   B1-2

This range contrasts in every way with Down's Mourne Mountains. About 40m across, it has gentle contours and is at its highest at Mount Sawel (2240 ft.). A good network of roads gives access to a wide variety of scenery. One of many pleasant drives can be taken through the **Glenelly Valley**, with its trout-filled river, then by a switchback road through **Barnes Gap** to join the equally beautiful **Owenkillen Valley**.

▶ At the NE end of the range the Belfast to Derry route crosses wilder country of the **Glenshane Pass**. Stone circles, standing stones and cairns all bear witness to early occupation of this region, which is now sparsely populated; farming and forestry are the main industries. ▶ There are twelve forest parks, most with camping and caravan facilities. ▶ The surrounding towns of Draperstown, Cookstown and Newtownstewart have their roots in the 'Plantation' period.   □

STRANGFORD LOUGH

Ballymena, 30; Newcastle, 20; Belfast, 7 m
☎ 039 686   Down C2

The characteristic *drumlins* (Irish for 'ridge') of County Down form little islands in the Strangford Lough.

▶ One of the largest islands on the W side is **Mahee Island**, linked to the mainland by a causeway. Excavated ruins at **Nendrum Castle** include part of a round tower and three concentric walls. The foundation is thought to be 7thC. Objects such as writing blocks and a bell found in a 1920s excavation are now in the Ulster Museum (→). The neighbouring tower houses were erected by Planters from the 16th to early 17thC. ▶ The foreshore of the lough is a nature reserve with 130 species of birds, some from the observatory at **Castle Espie★** where there is a natural history exhibition and café (*Wed.-Sat., 10-5*). The most spectacular of the many species of fish caught here is the huge skate. ▶ Freshwater fishing takes place at the extreme end of the Lough, where a flood barrier protects **Quoile Pondage** from salt water. Reed beds, grasslands and mud flats now make it an ideal bird refuge and National Nature Reserve. ▶ **Inch Abbey**, one of County Down's four Cistercian abbeys, stands in the Quoile marshes and can be reached by causeway (*Apr.-Sep., 10-7; Sun., 2-7*).□

WARREN POINT

Newtownards, 38; Armagh, 28; Belfast, 35 m
☎ 06937   Down C3

A pleasant resort with a tree-lined promenade, public gardens and yacht marina. Excursion boats cross the Carlingford Lough to Omeath in the Republic.

Nearby ·

▶ **Narrow Water Castle**, once a stronghold protecting the mouth of Newry River, is a landmark NW of the resort. ▶ **Rostrevor** enjoys a mild climate. Short walks can be made from here to the ruins of the Early Christian **Kilbroney Church, St. Bridget's Wells** and **Fairy Glen**. ▶ **Kilkeel** has several miles of sand and shingle beaches and is a busy fishing harbour. The quarrying and dressing of Mourne granite also takes place here. ▶ **Greencastle** is a conspicuous feature at the mouth of Carlingford Lough. ▶ **Newry** lies at the head of the Lough on the border of County Down and County Armagh. It heads the oldest stretch of inland navigation canals in the British Isles. The name Newry derives from a 'yew tree' reputed to have been planted by St. Patrick and still flourishing 700 years later. ▶ **Bessbrook** (*13m NW*) is a garden village founded in the 19thC to house workers from the local linen spinning mills. ▶ **Derrymore House** (*open by appt. with National Trust*) is an unusual 18thC thatched manor house. Near the border with the Republic, **Slieve Gullion** (*5m SW of Newry*): views of both Belfast and Dublin on a clear day. There are also beautiful forest drives and caravan and picnic facilities. Two Stone Age cairns and the **Kilnasaggart Cross** pillar, possibly Ireland's oldest Christian monument, can be seen in the area.   □

Practical information _____

ⓘ Boating Pool, ☎ (06937) 72256.

⚠ at Rostrevor, *Kilbroney C.P.* (70 pl), ☎ (069 37) 38134.

Isle of Man

The Isle of Man lies off the NW coast of England, within sight of Ireland, England, Scotland and Wales; a country in its own right, with its own laws, government, police force, health and education facilities funded by its own taxes and revenues. As can be expected from its geographical location, its historical ties are many. Originally, the island was most influenced by Gaelic (both Irish and Scottish) culture, but in the 11thC was conquered by the Norsemen or Vikings along with the Scottish Isles. At this stage, the Parliamentary structure was formed which has endured to the present day, giving the Isle of Man the oldest continuous legislature known.

The climate is generally temperate, without extremes of cold in the winter or heat in the summer owing mainly to its maritime situation and also to the waters of the Gulf Stream which wash its shores. The island's one hundred miles of coastline range from rugged cliffs to sandy beaches and the land rises from the sea to a height of 2,036 ft. at its highest point on the summit of Snaefell. □

 ## Brief regional history

Prehistory

The earliest evidence of human settlement on the island dates from the **mesolithic period**. Flint tools have been found at a number of sites, mostly in coastal areas. ● **Neolithic farmers** reached here in about 3000 B.C. and some important archaeological remains survive. The Meayll Circle is unique in the British Isles, with six pairs of burial chambers, preceded by a forecourt marked by eight standing stones. King Orry's Grave is another huge long barrow. Other sites are the Cloven Stones at Baldrine, the stone circle at Ballakelly and the Giant's Grave at Liaghtny-Foawr. The island was colonized by the Beaker People in about 1800 B.C., some of whose bronze axes and pottery survive. ● Most significant for the Isle of Man's history was the arrival of the **Celts** in about 200 B.C. There are hill-forts on the South Barrule, at Chapel Hill, Balladoole, at Cronk Sumark, Sulby, Castleward and Bradden. Celtic round houses have been excavated at Ballacaigen, the largest of them 90 ft. in diameter, and other houses have been found at Clos-ny-Challagh.

The Celtic Church

There is no evidence of Roman occupation of the island, so the Celtic way of life and the Gaelic language continued uninterrupted. Traditionally, **Christianity** reached here in 447 when St. Patrick sent his disciple Germanus to be the first bishop. **St. Ninian**, who died in 432, is also supposed to have visited the island and one life of St. Patrick says that he was shipwrecked here before his mission to Ireland. Other Irish missionaries were St. Maughold and St. Brigid. St. Columba had a considerable influence upon the Manx Church. ● It is clear that Christianity was firmly established by the 6th century, for the ruins of many small **chapels**, or *keeils*, have been found — simple rectangular chambers on stone foundations. Over 170 **Manx crosses** have also survived, dating from A.D. 650 onwards, the stone slabs intricately carved with typical Celtic interlace ornament.

The Scandinavian invasions

From about 790 **Viking raiders** began to arrive in the Irish Sea to plunder and finally to settle the Isle of Man.● From 990-1079 the island was a possession

of the **Earls of Orkney**. ● In 1079 **Godred Crovan**, perhaps the benign 'King Orry' of Manx legend, invaded the island and ruled here until 1095. He established the 'Kingdom of Man and the Isles' in which Man and the Hebrides were united and he initiated a system of government based on the **House of Keys** (or representatives). The island was divided into six administrative divisions, or 'shealdings'. His descendants ruled the island, for the most part peaceably, until by the **Treaty of Perth** in 1266, Norway handed the Isle of Man over to the kings of Scotland. There are three Norse ship burials on the island and a number of Norse crosses survive, carved with scenes from Scandinavian mythology.

The 13th and 14th centuries

Alexander of Scotland ruled the island from 1266-90. Under Edward I of England the Isle of Man passed into English hands. ● In 1313 Robert the Bruce claimed the lordship, overthrowing the English garrison at Castle Rushan. ● Edward III granted the Lordship to Sir William Montacute, who sold it to the Earl of Wiltshire. ● It then passed to the Earl of Northumberland and finally in 1405 to Sir John Stanley, his heirs and successors.

The Stanley family and the Dukes of Atholl

The **Stanleys** ruled the Isle of Man from 1405-1736, though few members of the family actually visited the island. During the **Civil Wars** the area supported Charles I and the island was fortified. ● Under Bishop **Thomas Wilson** (born 1663) much was achieved for the islanders' welfare — grammar schools were built and libraries provided for each parish. Wilson also took the first steps towards providing a literature in the Manx language, although insisting that the children should read English at school. ● The **Dukes of Atholl** acquired the governorship in 1737, but under the unpopular 4th duke, the island was purchased by the British government in 1828 for £417. Since that time the Isle of Man has been a **Crown dependency**, still maintaining its ancient Tynwald Court and the House of Keys and a measure of independence, particularly with regard to taxation and customs duties.

 Practical information

Information: *Isle of Man Tourist Board*, 7-13 Victoria Street, Douglas, ☎ (0624) 4323 winter, 4328 summer.

Weather forecast: ☎ (061) 246 8091.

Sealink car ferries: ☎ (01) 834 8122 Mon.-Sat., 8a.m. - 7.15p.m.; ferry links: to Britain and Northern Ireland.

Youth hostelling: YHA, 12 Wynnstay Road, Colwyn Bay, Clwyd LL29 8NB, ☎ (0492) 31406.

Scenic railway: a vintage transport system runs almost continuously for 30 miles up the eastern shoreline. The Manx electric railway runs from Derby Castle stables in Douglas on a round trip through Peel and Ramsey. You can change tram trains at Laxey and take one which climbs Snaefell Mountain, from which a view of five countries is visible on a clear day. Contact: *Manx Electric Railway*, Derby Castle Station, Douglas, ☎ (0624) 4549.

Motorcycling: *International TT Motorcycle Races*, 30 May, 1, 3, 5 Jun.

 Towns and places

CASTLETOWN

Douglas, 10; Peel, 11; Ramsey, 22m
pop. 3,141 ☎ 0624   Isle of Man

Ancient capital of the island, its name derives from Castle Rushen dating from *c.* 1200 A.D. The original castle was the residence of the last Norse King of Man who died 1266. The major additions are mainly 17thC (*Open daily 10-7, admission charge*).

Nearby

▶ **Ballasalla** (*2m N*) is the site of Rushen Abbey; once chief monastic settlement on the island, a 12thC Cistercian foundation where the Chronicles of Man were written, now in British Museum. ▶ **Silverdale**; Manx National Park with boating lake and amusements for children; picnic area.   □

Practical information _____

CASTLETOWN
ⓘ Commissioner's Office, Parliament Square, ☎ (0624) 823518.

Inns or Pubs:
Castle Arms (Okells), Quayside, ☎ (0624) 823242 ⊀ & ⊗ Sandwiches at lunch. £3.
Victoria Hotel, Malew Street, ☎ (0624) 823 529 Bar snacks and meals. £2-£5.

Recommended
Cycle rental: *Castletown Cycles*, 6 Arbory Street, ☎ (0624) 823587.
Golf course: Fort Island, 2m E, ☎ (0624) 822201.

Nearby

BALLASALLA

Restaurant:
♦ *La Rosette*, ☎ (0624) 822940 ⊿ ♪ ⊗ Cl. 2 wks. end Jan., Sun., Mon. lunch. Charming little French restaurant. Cosy and well furnished. Book. £13.

Recommended
Craft workshop: *Shebeg Gallery*, ☎ (0624) 823497, mat and glazed porcelain figurines.

> Be advised that hotels and restaurants in this Guide have perhaps changed addresses; prices indicated are also subject to modifications.

DOUGLAS

Peel, 10; Castletown, 10; Ramsey, 12m
pop. 19,944 ☎ 0624   Isle of Man

Developed mainly in the 1820s, with the coming of the steamer, as a playground for North of England vacationers, Douglas is almost totally tourist oriented. Nearly two miles of wide promenade front the sandy bay which is lined with a theatre, several dance halls, a casino and many other entertainments.

▶ The House of Keys contains the King's Chamber and the Tynwald Court; **devoted mainly to Manx** archaeology, Manx artists, poets and folk history (*Mon. -Fri., 10-5*). ▶ **Manx electric railway**; opened 1893, travels 17 1/2m to Ramsey and connects at **Laxey** with the broader-gauge line to the summit of **Snaefell**. ▶ **The Tower of refuge** erected 1832 to mark the dangerous rocks in Douglas Bay and provide refuge for anyone wrecked upon them. The tower was built by Sir William Hillary who founded an Institution for the Preservation of Lives and Property from Shipwreck, which later became the Royal National Lifeboat Institution.

Nearby

▶ **Kirk Braddan church** dates from 1773 on site of 13thC church. Many crosses and grave stones bear witness to the intermingling of the Celtic and Norse races, some being in memory of Celtic parents and spouses and inscribed in Norse. The graveyard also has The Rev. Robert Brown's memorial, the father of the Manx poet The Rev. T. E. Brown.   □

Practical information ───────────────

ⓘ 13 Victoria Street, ☎ (0624) 74323; public library, 10 Elm Tree Road, at Onchan, ☎ (0624) 22311.
✈ Ronaldsway Airport, 7m SW, ☎ (0624) 823311.
⛴ To Heysham, Liverpool, Belfast, Dublin, Fleetwood.

Hotels:
★★★ *Palace* (Consort), Central Promenade, ☎ (0624) 74521, Tx 627742, AC AM BA DI, 135 rm. Ⓟ ⋞ ❀ 」 ♫ £58.50. Rest. ♦ £8.25.
★★★ *Sefton*, Harris Promenade, ☎ (0624) 26011, Tx 627519, AC AM BA DI, 80 rm. Ⓟ ⋞ ढ ❀ 🖾 ♫ £40. Rest. ♦ £8.
★ *Woodbourne*, Alexander Drive, ☎ (0624) 21766, BA, 12 rm. No shower. £25. Rest. ♦ Cl. Oct.-20 May. £7.50.

Restaurants:
♦ *Boncompte's*, King Edward Road, Onchan, ☎ (0624) 75626, AC BA DI ⋞ Cl. Sun., Sat. for lunch. Well-prepared food accompanied by a good wine list. £12.
♦ *L'Expérience*, Summerhill, ☎ (0624) 23103, AC BA DI Ⓟ ⋞ ♪ ढ ❀ Cl. Tue., Sun. lunch. Book. £11.

⚐ at Hillberry, 1/2m W, *Glen Dhoo Int. Farm* (90 pl), ☎ (0624) 21254.

Recommended
Cycle rental: *Callow Cycle Hire*, 9 Castle Mona Shops, ☎ (0624) 75340.
Golf course: Pulrose Park, 1m from Douglas Pier, ☎ (0624) 5952; Howstrake at Onchan, 1m N, ☎ (0624) 24299; Douglas Golf, Pullrose Road, ☎ (0624) 75952.
♥ *The Granary*, 50 Strand Street, ☎ (0624) 29599, handmade preservative-free wholemeal bread.

LAXEY

Peel, 12; Douglas, 6; Ramsey, 7m
☎ 0624   Isle of Man

Laxey, on the main Douglas to Ramsey road, has a small harbour connected to more modern parts of the town by Garwick Glen. 'Lady Isabella', the great water wheel at Laxey is the largest of its kind in the world

with a diameter of 72 1/2 ft. Built 1854 to pump water from the mines at rate of 250 gallons per minute from a depth of 200 fathoms, it had fallen into disrepair by 1940 but has been restored.

Nearby

▶ **'King Orry's Grave'**; burial place of a group of New Stone Age people *c.* 1700 B. C. ▶ From Douglas an alternative route north leads over excellent mountain road to Snaefell (2,036 ft.) and affords magnificent **view**. From the summit, west to **Sulby Glen** and the Tholt-Y-Will Glens with excellent wood, hill and stream walks.   □

Practical information ───────────────

Inn or Pub:
Mines Tavern (Okells), Electric Railway Station, ☎ (0624) 781484 Ⓟ ⋞ ▩ ♤ ढ ❀ Bar snacks at lunch. £4-£5.
⚐ *Laxey Commissioners*, Quarry Road (40 pl), ☎ (0624) 781241.

Recommended
♥ *St. Georges Woollen Mills Ltd.*, St. Georges Mills, ☎ (0624) 781395, manx tweeds and tartans woven on premises.

PEEL

Douglas, 10; Castletown, 10; Ramsey, 15m
☎ 0624   Isle of Man

The main town of the W of the island is an active fishing port, an archaeological site of interest and a resort. The beach is sandy and safe. The harbour serves a fishing fleet mainly concerned with herrings for kippering, for which the Isle of Man is famous, and another local delicacy 'Queenies', small scallops.

Nearby

▶ On **St. Patrick's Isle** is 11thC **Peel Castle** of which the **Cathedral of St. Germans** forms part. Archaeological digs are still in progress on this site. ▶ **St. Johns** (*2 1/2m E*), site of **Tynwald Hill** where the annual Tynwald Ceremony is held. ▶ S towards the sea again, the road passes through **South Barrule** and the **Round Table**. ▶ **Port Erin**, an unspoilt village. The sandy beach slopes gently and good bathing, boating and windsurfing are available. 1m S lies the Calf of Man separated from the mainland by the Calf Sound and accessible by boat trip; a bird sanctuary with many indigenous and migrant species. ▶ **Cregneash Folk Museum**: a preserved Manx crofting village with weaver's shed, a turner's shop and village smithy.   □

Practical information ───────────────

PEEL

⚐ *Peal C.P.*, Derby Road (100 pl), ☎ (0624) 842341.

Recommended
Craft workshop: at St. John's, 2m SE,*St. John's Crystal Ltd.*, Tynwald Mills, ☎ (062 471) 256, decorative and functional crystal glassware.
Golf course: Rheast Lane, ☎ (0624) 842227.
♥ *Tynwald Woolen Mills Ltd.*, ☎ (062 471) 213, elegant fabric, rugs, kilts, jackets, coats, sweaters.

Nearby

PORT ERIN

Restaurant:
♦ *Molyneux's Seaford*, ☎ (0624) 833633, AC ⋞ Well-prepared fish. Cl. lunch. £13.50.

Inn or Pub:
Station Hotel (Helen Brearley), Station Road, ☎ (0624)

832236, AC BA Ⓟ ⚡ 🏊 22 rm. A la carte eve., lunch (ex. Sun.). £3.50.

RAMSEY

Laxey, 7; Douglas, 12; Peel, 15m
☎ 0624   Isle of Man

Capital of the N of the island. The bay has 10m of sand and shingle beach from Ramsey Head to the Point of Ayre. The river and harbour divide the town which has attractive narrow streets. ▶ A swing bridge gives access to Mooragh Park with 9-hole golf course, lake and amusements. ▶ The **harbour** has two 360 ft. piers. ▶ **Grove Rural Life Museum** (*May.-Sep.: daily*). ▶ **Thor Cross** (*4m N*) at Bride; ancient monument liberally carved with figures depicting various legends of Thor. ▶ At Andreas is **Thorwald's Cross** later dated; represents the coming of Christian ideals. ▶ On road to Peel; **Ballaugh**, a pleasant village built on reclaimed land known as the Curraghs, a favourite spot of botanists and bird lovers. ▶ **Curraghs Wildlife Park**; 26 acres of nature reserve containing many rare species of deer, birds and other animals in their natural habitat.   ☐

Practical information _____

RAMSEY

Restaurant:
♦ *Harbour Bistro*, East Street, ☎ (0624) 814182 ♪ ♿ ⚿ Cl. 2 wks. end Jan., Nov. Casserole of guinea fowl with avocado and grapes. Book. £10.

Recommended
Cycle rental: *John Mead*, 37 Parliament Street, ☎ (0624) 813092.

Nearby

ANDREAS, 4m NW

Restaurant:
♦ *Grosvenor*, Kirk Andreas, ☎ (062 488) 576, AC BA Cl. Tue. and Sun. dinner, Oct. £8.50.

Northumbria

▶ Some of the most unspoiled and strikingly beautiful country in England Is found in the remote expanses of Northumberland and Durham which, together with the heavily populated industrial conurbations on the Tees, Tyne and Wear estuaries, make up the north-eastern region of Northumbria. It stretches from the Yorkshire boundary to the Scottish border, between the North Sea coastline of sandy beaches, cliffs and coves, through gentle pastoral scenery and increasingly lonely river valleys, to the wild mountainous moors and rounded folle of the Pennines and Cheviot Hills on the west and north-west.

For centuries this was powerful border territory and it is rich in reminders of the past. There are the remarkably well-preserved remains of Hadrian's Wall lying in glorious scenery by the South Tyne Valley; many medieval castles, monasteries and churches; the ancient city of Durham with its magnificent Norman cathedral; and off the coast in the far north, beautiful Holy Island, home of the Irish missionaries who made the Anglo-Saxon kingdom of Northumbria famous as the northern centre of early Christianity.

Interesting in a very different way is the northeast's industrial heritage. The heavily built-up towns of Tees-side, Wearside and Tyneside have an impressive legacy as world centres of mining, shipping and engineering, with many museums and industrial sites, and the region's attractive major city of Newcastle-upon-Tyne has some fine Victorian public buildings as well as being a lively cultural, shopping and entertainment centre. Seaside resorts and long stretches of unspoiled coastline are rarely far away, while inland roads follow river valleys through colliery villages and market towns into increasingly remote countryside. Each river valley has its distinctive scenic character, from the pastoral beauty of the Derwent, Wear and Tees in Durham, the high moors and steep woodlands of the Allendales and Tyne valleys on the west, to the lonely hills and forests of Redesdale and Coquetdale in Northumberland, which form part of the magnificently wild expanse of Northumberland National Park. ☐

The Jarrow 'Crusade'

The period known as the Depression during the 1930s was a time of mass unemployment and great hardship among workers in areas where industry was in decline. Such regions included villages in Durham county, South Wales and Lancashire where almost all adult men could be out of work. When Jarrow's shipyards closed down, two-thirds of its working population became permanently unemployed and it was known as 'the town that was murdered'. In 1934, the government classified Tyneside, South Wales, West Cumberland (now Cumbria) and Scotland as 'depressed areas' but its injection of a £2 million grant did little to revive flagging industries, and a total of only 12,000 new jobs was created by new industries started near Gateshead and in South Wales in 1937.

As the employment situation grew more desperate, there was increasing unrest. A National Unemployed Workers Movement was started, and the Communist Party gained support. Groups of unemployed men from depressed areas marched to London. The first of these marches set out from Jarrow in 1936. Although demonstrations in London did not prove very effective, the men gained considerable sympathy as they walked through the countryside. In places along the route, soup kitchens were established to feed them, and they were given beds and shelter in local schools.

In recent years of national unemployment, the northeast has once again been one of the areas where most jobs have been lost.

NORTHUMBERLAND

TYNE AND WEAR

NORTHUMBRIA

DURHAM

CLEVELAND

Brief regional history

Prehistory

The earliest settlements of Northumbria date from the mesolithic period around 5000-3000 BC. ● Barrows and cairns from the **neolithic** period have also been discovered but these are scarce. The first significant evidence is of the **Beaker people** who arrived from across the North Sea in about 1800 BC. We know very little about their settlements, more about their funerary practices, for they placed their dead in stone cists in the ground, along with the typical Beaker pottery which gives this people their name. Many Beaker cists have been found in the moors near Chillingham. At a later date, burial gave way to cremation - cinerary urns date from about 1000 BC. ● Evidence of the Bronze Age is slight, but there was considerable activity during the **Iron Age** from 500 BC with many defensive hill forts being built, the largest of which is Yeavering Bell, where 130 wooden huts were enclosed within stone ramparts.

Bastle house,
Millbridge

Roman Northumbria

The Roman occupation of Britain took a generation to reach the Tyne. Under **Agricola** a whole network of roads and forts were built. A line of garrisons linked the Forth Clyde isthmus, Stanegate joined Carlisle with Corbridge and Dere Street was built north of York. ● **Hadrian's Wall**, Britain's best-known Roman remain, was constructed between 122 and 128 with the purpose of controlling the frontier and preventing raids from the north, with forts on the wall line. Twenty years after it was finished, the wall was abandoned in favour of the reoccupation of southern Scotland and a new barrier, the **Antonine Wall**, was made. This however only lasted for twenty years, after which the Romans withdrew to Hadrian's Wall which remained the northern frontier for the remainder of the occupation. There were sixteen forts in all, with milecastles every mile. In its prime the wall was manned by up to 15,000 troops, around whose camps clustered civilian settlements, providing artisan labour. Housesteads is perhaps the most dramatically sited of the forts, while Chesters is the best preserved.

The Anglo-Saxons

After the departure of the Romans, the region was controlled by a number of small British kingdoms. The **Votadini** groups held Northumbria until the mid-6thC when Angles, already established in Yorkshire, began to arrive at the coast. ● In about 547 Ida and his followers reached **Bamburgh** and settled there. With the accession of Aethelfrith, his kingdom of Bernicia

extended from the Tyne to the Forth with Bamburgh as capital. Further south the kingdom of Deira covered the Yorkshire wolds and continued northwards to the Tees. Between the two was uninhabited forest and marshland. In 605 King Aethelfrith seized **Deira** and the united kingdoms formed the most powerful Anglo-Saxon state for 80 years. ● **Paulinus**, who had accompanied Augustine on his mission to Britain, was invited north by the Christian wife of King Edward of Deira and preached at Yeavering, it is said, for thirty-six days, baptizing several thousand Northumbrians in the River Glen. Later, at the invitation of Oswald of Northumbria, **Aidan** brought the first Celtic monks from Iona to Lindisfarne. ● The period which followed was the golden age of Anglo-Saxon **monasticism**. The monasteries at Lindisfarne and those founded a little later by Benedict Biscop at Monkwearmouth and Jarrow became centres of learning with an international reputation. Bede's *Ecclesiastical History of the British People* was completed at Jarrow in 731. There were great libraries there and at Hexham. ● The greatest glory of Anglo-Saxon art, the **Lindisfarne Gospels**, were illuminated between 689 and 721 with their unique blend of Celtic, Saxon and Mediterranean decorative elements.

The Danish invasions

The first Danish pirates arrived in 793, sacking Lindisfarne, and a year later Jarrow fell into their hands. The body and relics of St. Cuthbert, that holiest of men, were carried by his followers from place to place for seven years until they settled at **Chester-le-Street**. A hundred years later his remains were taken to Durham. ● By 876 the Danelaw had separated the northern kingdom from the other Anglo-Saxon kingdoms in the West Midlands and Wessex. After the last Scandinavian ruler was expelled from York in 944 the area of Northumberland, along with Durham, became an **earldom** within the kingdom of England.

The Normans

Following the Norman conquest, **William I** and his son Rufus sought to continue to rule Northumbria through the earldom, but this policy proved unsuccessful. ● A whole succession of **rebellions** resulted in a devastation of the northern lands in 1080. After Robert Mowbray's rebellion, when he was besieged in Bamburgh Castle, the earldom was suppressed, its lands taken by the king. This 'harrying of the north' made parts of Durham a desert - *hoc est wasta* says the Domesday survey - and it was some considerable time before the area was repopulated. ● In the usual fashion, the lands of Northumberland and Durham were parceled out among William's followers. **Durham Castle** was built by him after his return from Scotland in 1072 as a stronghold for his agents. ● There followed, between 1093 and 1133, the creation of Durham Cathedral, one of the most perfect and historically interesting buildings in Europe, and possessing the earliest **rib-vaults** in the West. The combination of cathedral, castle and monastery, perched high on a rock overlooking the river Wear, creates an unforgettable impression.

Medieval Northumbria

In 1074 William I had made the bishops of Durham earls of that area. In the late 12thC Durham became

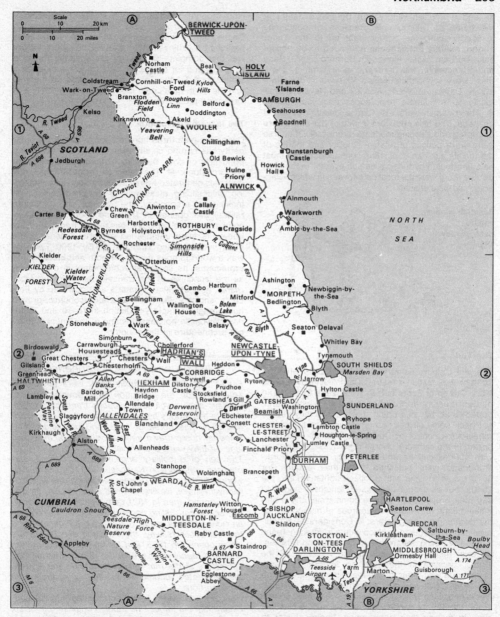

the **County Palatine** and during the Middle Ages the bishops ruled like kings. They could administer law, issue pardons, mint coins and create boroughs by charter. Bishop Puiset, en route for the Third Crusade, had his galley furnished with a silver throne with cutlery to match. ● As the power of the bishops grew, so did that of certain noble families and in particular the **Nevilles** and the **Percies**. It was they who put Bolingbroke on the throne in 1399 and these families were heavily involved in British politics in the 15thC. ● From 1461-64 Northumberland was the focus of the **Wars of the Roses** with Edward IV defeat-

ing the Lancastrians at Percy's Cross and Hexham, besieging Bamburgh and Dunstanburgh castles. ● The **Anglo-Scottish wars** during the period 1330-1490 comprise a detailed succession of battles, raids and truces. Edward I was defeated at Bannockburn while almost a century later, the English under Henry VIII routed the army of James IV at Flodden Field. Northumbria was the target of the powerful **Douglas** family and there was great rivalry between the Douglases and the Percies, culminating in a Scots raid on Durham in 1388, the subsequent personal combat between Hotspur and Douglas at Newcas-

tle and a Scottish victory (but Douglas's death) at the battle of Otterburn. ● Because of continuing insecurity along the border right up to the Tudor period, **military fortifications** continued to be necessary. Durham Castle, along with Barnard Castle, Raby and Brancepeth, are Durham's most famous examples, while in Northumberland Warkworth, Dunstanburgh, Bamburgh, Wark, Alnwick and Newcastle still testify to the area's remoteness and vulnerability. ● The Scottish wars also had a deleterious effect on trade. The hide and wool trades of the north were disrupted and shipping made hazardous. ● Of course there were periods of relative stability and the life of the mainly agrarian population continued for the most part unaffected by these dramatic events. In times of trouble there were the local pele towers in which villagers could take shelter.

Beamish winding engine, near Stanley, 1855

The Tudors

The last Catholic rising took place in 1569 when an attempt was made to restore Catholicism by making **Mary Queen of Scots** heir to Elizabeth's throne. The northern earls, Northumberland and Westmorland, hoped that by supporting the cause they would get back some of their former power. For a time the rebels took control of Durham and mass was celebrated in the cathedral. Fierce repercussions followed with 400 executions and the Percy earls of Northumberland were banished from their estates for 60 years. ● Trouble with Scotland continued into the 1540s, but as danger decreased, landlords began to see their properties in a more commercial and profit-making light, rather than as sources of manpower for the declining border musters. ● Considerable agricultural improvements took place with a marked increase in sheep farming. Meanwhile in Durham and Newcastle **coal mining**, which had begun as early as the 13thC, became in the 16th an important source of revenue with fleets of tall-masted colliers carrying coal south. Salt was sent to Yarmouth for the curing of herrings and Newcastle became the main source in the country for window glass. The middle classes, slow in making their appearance, began at last to exercise some influence.

The Civil War

The first event as far as the north was concerned came when a Scottish Presbyterian army, in revolt against Charles I's imposition of a prayer book on the Scottish Church, crossed the border in 1640 and occupied Newcastle after defeating the king's forces at Newburn. In 1642 the king sent fresh forces to Newcastle, securing it as a royalist town. In 1643 Parliament's Solemn League and Covenant with Scot-

land brought Scottish troops to the Parliamentary side. Royalist troops were besieged in **Tynemouth Castle**, finally surrendering after the walls were breached by mines and artillery. The Scots victory was then complete. ● The war damaged the Tyneside economy and for a time the coal trade remained at a standstill. ● By the 1650s recovery was on the way and the north-east could look forward to stability and increasing prosperity.

The industrial revolution

During the past three hundred years, Durham's prosperity has sprung chiefly from mining and quarrying, principally of coal, but also of lead, clay, limestone and ironstone. ● The need to process these raw materials generated **heavy industry** such as engineering, shipbuilding, glass-making and chemicals. Steel-making was a specialty. The Stockton and Darlington railway was opened in 1825 and soon other railway companies were providing passenger transport. New ironworks were established at various centres, the most famous being **Consett**. ● By 1900 Tyneside was a world famous centre for both **shipbuilding** and **armaments**. Its crowning achievement is often seen as the launching of the transatlantic liner, the *Mauritania*, built by Swan Hunter's and powered by Parson's engines. ● The Victorian economic growth had brought a rapid population increase and Victorian Newcastle possesses some of the finest **municipal architecture** in the country.

George and Robert Stephenson

Father and son, the Stephensons were largely responsible for the invention and development of railways as a revolutionary public transport system. Prior to this, goods had been carried slowly and laboriously by packhorse or boat, and people too had relied on horse-drawn vehicles, ships - or their own legs - if they wanted to travel.

The son of a colliery engine-keeper, George Stephenson was born in Newcastle in 1781 and at first worked in the mines. Largely self-taught, he was brilliantly inventive. He first devised a safety lamp for use underground, then in 1821 demonstrated his locomotive engine for pulling coal trucks. This ran at 6 miles an hour. He was made responsible for constructing the first public railway, the Stockton and Darlington, which opened in 1825, and for the subsequent Liverpool and Manchester (1830). In 1829, he astonished spectators at the trial run of his engine, the Rocket: the celebrated locomotive reached a speed of 30 miles an hour.

George's son Robert benefited from more formal education than his father - he studied engineering for six months at Edinburgh University. After working in his father's engine works, he turned his attention to designing railway bridges. One of his most famous, the Brittania 'tube' bridge over the Menai Straits in North Wales, used more than 2 million rivets to hold its steel plates together. Despite this, there were fears that the bridge would not be strong enough to bear the repeated weight of locomotive trains with their cargoes and passengers. Consequently, to test its strength, three of the heaviest available steam engines were chained together on the day of the inauguration, The bridge held.

Border country

Until 1707, when the Act of Union was passed, Scotland had remained largely independent of England - although from the beginning of the 17thC both kingdoms had been ruled by one sovereign. Even today, their churches, and legal and educational systems differ in many respects, and since 1927 there has been an active Scottish Nationalist Party - the more fervent nationalists have campaigned for home rule. Nevertheless, relations between the two countries have remained harmonious ever since the mid-18thC.
It was not always so. When they occupied England nearly two thousand years ago, the Romans built a wall 73 miles long, to keep the fierce Scots out. Throughout the medieval period, there was continued fighting - particularly in the border areas between the two countries. There were frequent raids from both sides, and the border itself wavered. The town of Berwick-upon-Tweed, situated 57 miles from Edinburgh, 63 miles from Newcastle and over 300 miles from London, changed hands thirteen times between the 12th and the 15thC until it was eventually made part of England in 1482. Its walled fortifications were among the last to be built - evidence of the fact that it had to be able to defend itself against marauders even as late as the 16thC. Elsewhere fortified houses known as 'pele towers' were constructed throughout Northumbria and the southern counties of Scotland. These would have sheltered the local people and their animals when they were threatened by raiders.
Nowadays, Border inhabitants celebrate their differences rather than fighting over them. At the town of Norham-on-Tweed, 7 miles from Berwick, fishermen from both sides of the border meet on 14 February each year for the ancient blessing ceremony which marks the opening of the fishing season at 11.45 pm.

 Practical information

Information: covers the counties of Cleveland, Durham, Northumberland and Tyne and Wear. *Northumbria Tourist Board*, 9 Osborne Terrace, Jesmond, Newcastle-upon-Tyne NE2 1NT, ☎ (0632) 817744.

Weather forecast: ☎ (0632) 8091.

The sanctuary knocker

In English medieval law, fugitives from justice had the right to claim sanctuary in a church. Once inside, they could not be harmed nor even arrested. At Durham Cathedral the great door would be opened once the runaway had knocked and tolled the sanctuary bell. Even if he only had the massive iron knocker within his grasp, the fugitive was considered to be under the protection of the church. But in order to be granted sanctuary, he had to confess his crime to the clergy, give up all his weapons and pay a fee. Then he must swear to leave the country within nine days. This he did wearing a white robe and carrying a cross so that everyone would know he been given refuge by the church, and thus he was protected from arrest and injury.

Ferry link: Newcastle-upon-Tyne to Scandinavia.

Self-catering cottages: *'Keyholes'*, Dunstansteads, Embleton, Alnwick, ☎ (066576) 221; *Stotsfold Hall*, Steel, Hexham, ☎ (0434) 73270.

Youth hostelling: YHA, 57 Whitby Avenue, Guisborough, Cleveland TS14 7NA, ☎ (0287) 35831.

Festivals: May 9-17: *Ashington Festival* in Northumberland: art, entertainment and sporting events.

Customs and folklore: 14 Feb.: at midnight the Vicar of Norham *Blesses the Nets* of salmon fishers at the start of the fishing season. **May:** Berwick on Tweed *May Fair* (on the last Fri.), dating back at least as far as 1302. **Boxing Day:** *Greatham Sword Dance* on the village green is a dance, winter tradition, and remnant of pre-Christian faith. **31 Dec.:** for the *Flaming Tar Barrels Ceremony* in Allendale Town, 'guizers' carry blazing tar barrels on their heads to the market place where there is an unlit bonfire; after walking around it they hurl their headgear in and so set fire to it.

National park: Northumberland: *Information Centre*, Eastburn, South Park, Hexham, ☎ (0434) 5555.

Canoeing: *Reivers of Tarset*, Forest Lodge, Comb, Greenhaugh, ☎ (0660) 40245, run 6 night-courses. Also run windsurfing courses.

Climbing and moutaineering holidays: *North of England Adventure Training Ltd.*, Former School House, Craster NE66 3TW, ☎ (066576) 551.

Fishing holidays: *Chevy Sport Ltd.*, Blagdon House, Smith Square, Cramlington NE23 6QL, ☎ (0670) 713210.

Gliding holidays: *Northumbria Gliding Club*, Hedley on the Hill, Chopwell, Newcastle-on-Tyne, ☎ (0207) 561286.

Golfing: Hobson, nr. Durham (18-hole); Hexham (18-hole); Foxton Hall (18-hole); Alnmouth Village (9-hole).

Microlighting holidays: *Northumbria Microlights*, Warden House, 49 Perry Park Road, Tynemouth, ☎ (0632) 580982.

Orienteering holidays: *Northumbria Calvert Trust Kielder Adventure Centre*, Low Cranecleugh, Kielder Water, Hexham NE48 IBS, ☎ (0660) 50232.

Sailing and cruising holidays: *Northumbrian Sea Sports*, The Wamses, Beadnell, ☎ (06683) 289.

Skiing holidays: *Consett and District YMCA*, Parliament Street, Consett DH8 5DH, ☎ (0207) 502680.

Fishing holidays: *Chevy Sport Ltd.*, Blagdon House, Smith Square, Cramlington NE23 6QL, ☎ (0670) 713210.

Hunting: *College Valley and North Northumberland Hunt*, Allenby House, Berwick-upon-Tweed, ☎ (0289) 86545.

Towns and places ══════════

ALLENDALES*

Northumberland A2

The dales of East and West Allen Rivers, lying between the South Tyne Valley and Weardale are of great natural beauty. Thickly wooded valleys slope steeply to the water's edge and high moorland, dotted with burns, stretches beyond as the rivers move through the North Pennines. Along the River Allen, S of Bardon Mill on the Tyne, the river and hill scenery is particularly beautiful and the woodland of **Allen Banks** is the home of roe deer and red squirrels. In the winter the moorland roads can be bleak and hazardous, but in the spring and summer the Allendales make fine walking, picnicking and touring country, rich in animal and birdlife.

Excursion (round trip)

▶ Start from **Haydon Bridge**, a small unpretentious town at crossing of South Tyne River close to Hadrian's Wall (→) or Hexham (→), with original medieval village of Haydon, 1/4m N. ▶ In 1m **Langley Castle** (14thC, restored and now a restaurant); across fells by **Emertley Hill** (1,033 ft.) to Catton (*3m*). ▶ Along steep wooded valley of East Allen River up to **Allendale Town** (*4¹/₂ m*), pleasant little resort with vacation amenities; good walks; skiing nearby in winter. ▶ Climbing on through Allendale Common scattered with ruins of old lead mines, to village of **Allenheads** (*9m*), former centre of lead mining industry and a local ski resort. Weardale (→) is reached from here via road E to Rookhope/Stanhope or by continuing S to Cowshill. ▶ Returning from Allenheads via delightfully named **Dirt Pot**, cross high moors, with **Killhope Law** (2,207 ft.) to S. ▶ **Coalcleugh** (*11m*), former mining village high above sea level. ▶ Descend secluded valley of West Allen River, through Ninebanks (*16¹/₂m*), with ruined pele tower. ▶ Divert to **Whitfield** (*18m*), a hamlet with two churches. ▶ Meeting of East and West Allen Rivers at Cupola Bridge, visible from hairpin bends on road. ▶ Footpath to scanty ruins of **Steward Pele** and through 194-acre **Allen**

Allendales

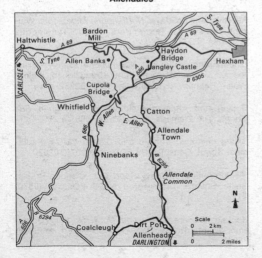

Banks, with lovely river walks, beech and oak woods and picnic sites accessible from road at **Plankey Mill**, **Ridley Hall** and **Bardon Mill** (*24m*): busy village on South Tyne just S of Roman fort of **Vindolanda** (→Hadrian's Wall), from which A69 runs E back to Haydon Bridge and Hexham (→) or W to Haltwhistle (→).   □

Practical information

ALLENDALE TOWN, on E Allen R.

Hotel:
★ *Hotspur*, NE47 9BW, ☎ (043 483) 355, 6 rm. Ⓟ 🔍 ⚡ £25. Rest. ◆ ⎔ & Local game dishes, fresh salmon. £5.

ALNWICK**

Newcastle-upon-Tyne, 33; Berwick-upon-Tweed, 30; London, 307 m
pop. 6,972 ☎ 0665   Northumberland B1

An attractive ancient town, Alnwick is a commercial centre with a busy market, fine 18thC houses and interesting old buildings. It was the capital of the earls of Northumberland, the Percy family, whose magnificent **castle** lies on a slope to the River Aln at the N end of the town.

▶ From S: **Denwick Bridge** (18thC), designed by John Adam, and Percy Tenantry Column (1816), topped by the Percy lion, probably erected in gratitude for rent reductions by 2nd Duke of Northumberland. ▶ At town entrance, **Hotspur Gate** (15thC), only surviving remnant of medieval walls. ▶ Notable buildings around market place include **Northumberland Hall** (1826) and the **Shambles**, the medieval meat market. ▶ From N: **Lion Bridge** (1773), also by John Adam; views of castle opposite. ▶ Near castle are **Pottergate Tower** (1768) and **St. Michael's Church** (14th-15thC) with traces of Norman origins and containing fine 14thC Flemish chest. ▶ **Alnwick Castle★**, splendid example of medieval fortification, with central keep and massive encircling wall (12thC, strengthened 1309-15 when towers were added); largely rebuilt in 19thC by Anthony Salvin; retains impressive gatehouse (c. 1440) preceded by a barbican; inner 14thC gatehouse above original dungeon. Sumptuous 19thC interior houses fine collections of paintings (Titian, Canaletto and Van Dyck); furniture, silver, Meissen china, manuscripts, and British and Roman antiquities (*5 May-Oct.: daily ex. Sat., 1-5*).

Nearby

▶ **Hulne Park** (*3m NW*): 2000-acre castle estate landscaped by Capability Brown, with remains of 14thC gateway of Alnwick Abbey, founded 1147, and beautiful ruins of Hulne Priory★, very early example of an English Carmelite friary (c. 1240); curtain wall, tower (1488) and parts of remarkably long, aisleless church remain. **Brislee Tower** (*1m S of priory*), designed by John Adam in 1781; fine view. ▶ **Callaly Castle★**; (*10m W, near Whittingham*): 17thC mansion built round 13thC pele tower with Georgian and Victorian additions, set in beautiful countryside; 18thC salon is particularly fine (*4 May-6 Jun. 6 Jul.-15 Sep.: Sat., Sun. Bank Hols., 2.15-5.30*). ▶ **Howick Hall** (*6m NE*): lovely flower, shrub and rhododendron gardens (*Apr.-Sep.: daily, 2-7*). ▶ **Craster** (*8m NE*), tiny fishing village famous for its kippers. ▶ **Dunstanburgh Castle★** (*9m NE*): dramatic ruins of 14thC gatehouse, towers and curtain wall set on extensive promontory overlooking sea cliffs to N (*mid-Mar.-mid-Oct.: Mon.-Sat., 9.30-6.30, Sun., 2-6.30; mid-Oct.-mid-Mar.: Mon.-Wed. Sat., 9.30-4, Sun., 2-4; also Good Fri.*). ▶ **Alnmouth** (*4m SE*): pleasant seaside resort with good beach. ▶ **Warkworth** (*3m S of Alnmouth*): attractive small town on **River Coquet** crossed by 14thC bridge (now pedestrians only), dominated by magnificent ruins

of **Warkworth Castle**★ (12th-15thC), including the keep and dungeon, towers, gatehouse and great hall (*Apr.-Oct.: daily, Sun. pm only*); **St. Laurence's Church**, by market place: has a beautiful Norman interior. ▶ **Amble** (*2m further S*), coal-exporting town with sandy beach; offshore is **Coquet Island**, breeding ground for eider ducks, with a lighthouse built on remnants of a 12thC monastery. □

Practical information

ALNWICK
ℹ️ The Shambles, Northumberland Hall, ☎ (0665) 603129.
🚂 Alnmouth, ☎ Tyneside (091) 232 6262.

Hotels:
★★ **White Swan** (Swallow), Bondgate Within, NE66 1TD, ☎ (0665) 602109, Tx 53168, AC AM BA DI, 41 rm. ℙ ♪ £60. Rest. ♦ ♪ £10.50.
★ **Hotspur**, Bondgate Without, NE66 1PR, ☎ (0665) 602924, AC BA, 28 rm. ℙ ⌕ £50. Rest. ♦ ♪ ⌕ Cl. 25-26 Dec. Poached salmon steak with prawn sauce. £10.

Inn or Pub:
Oddfellows Arms, Narrowgate, ☎ 602695.

⚓ **Dunstan Hill C.C.S.**, Dunstan Hill, Craster (160 pl), ☎ (066 576) 310; *Proctors Stead C.S.*, Proctors Stead, Craster (20 pl), ☎ (066 576) 613.

Recommended
Craft workshops: *Breamish Valley Pottery*, Branton West Side, Powburn, ☎ (066 578) 263, hand-thrown domestic stoneware; *Shilbottle Glass Studio*, West End, ☎ (066 575) 521, free-blown hand-finished glassware with engraving.
Cycle rental: *Marine House*, Marine House Private Hotel, 1 Marine Road, ☎ (0665) 830349.
Farmhouse: at Eglingham, *West Ditehburn*, ☎ (066 578) 337. £24 double; B. & B.
Golf course: Swansfield Park, ☎ (0665) 602632.

Nearby
ALNMOUTH, 3m E off A1068
Hotels:
★★ **Saddle**, 24-25 Northumberland Street, NE66 2RA, ☎ (0665) 830476, AC BA DI, 9 rm. ℙ ♪ ⌕ £30. Rest. ♦ ♪ ⌕ Cl. Christmas. £12.
★ **Schooner**, Northumberland Street, NE66 2RS, ☎ (0665) 830216, AC AM BA DI, 21 rm. ℙ ⌕ ♪ ⌕ £37. Rest. ♦ ⌕ ♪ ⌕ Fresh salmon. £13.

Recommended
Golf course: Alnmouth Village, Marine Road, ☎ (0665) 830370.

BAMBURGH*

Berwick-upon-Tweed, 20; Alnwick, 17; London, 325 m
pop. 567 ☎ 066 84   Northumberland B1

This small coastal resort, once the capital of a Saxon kingdom, is dominated by its huge castle perched spectacularly on an outcrop of almost vertical rock, visible for many miles around. The village also has a fine church and a museum devoted to local heroine Grace Darling.

▶ The **castle**★, much restored in 19thC and now partly private residences, retains its magnificent keep (c. 1164) with original Norman arch and houses a collection of armour, paintings and tapestries (*May-Oct.: daily ex. Sat., 1-5*). ▶ The large parish **church of St. Aidan**★ (late 12th-13thC): beautiful chancel with original lancet windows; interesting memorials including a 14thC knight's effigy. ▶ **Grace Darling Museum**, near church, with memorabilia (*Apr.-mid-Oct.: daily 11-6, 7 Jun.-Aug.*).

Nearby
▶ Via market town of Belford and Al, **Kyloe Hills** (*10m NE*), woodlands with extensive views to Cheviot Hills and

sea. Off A1 is **Beal** (*3m NW*), leading to Holy Island (→). ▶ Along B1340 coast road: **Seahouses** (*4m S*), herring-fishing port and vacation resort with long stretch of sands to N beside protected area of **St. Aidan's Dunes**. ▶ Trips leave Seahouses harbour for the **Farne Islands**★, a nature reserve for numerous species of seabirds and for grey seals. Landing is restricted to Staple Island and Inner Farne, on which is tiny restored 14thC **chapel** built on site of hermit's cell of St. Cuthbert (*Apr.-Oct.: daily*). ▶ **Beadnell** (*2m further S*), centre of vacation area, with splendid sands of **Beadnell Bay** and good sailing; 18thC lime kilns by tiny harbour. ▶ **Newton Links**, beautiful 4m stretch of protected coastline from Beadnell Bay S to Dunstanburgh Castle. (→). □

Practical information

BAMBURGH
Hotels:
● ★★ **Lord Crewe Arms**, Front Street, NE69 7BL, ☎ (066 84) 243, 27 rm. ℙ ⌕ ⌕ £45. Rest. ♦ Cl. Nov.-Mar. Poached salmon with lobster sauce. £12.
★★ **Victoria**, Front Street, NE69 7BP, ☎ (066 84) 431, AC AM DI, 25 rm. ℙ £35. Rest. ♦ ⌕ ⌕ £10.
★ **Mizen Head**, Lucker Road, NE69 7BS, ☎ (066 84) 254, 17 rm. ℙ 📺 ⌕ 📺 £28. Rest. ♦ £7.

⚓ **Annstead C.C. S.**, Beadnell (150 pl), ☎ (0665) 720586; *Bradford Kaims C.P.*, P.O. Box 62 (80 pl), ☎ (066 83) 432.

Recommended
Golf course: Bamburgh Castle, ☎ (066 84) 378.

Nearby
BELFORD, 4m W on A1
Hotel:
★★ **Blue Bell** (Swallow), Market Place, NE70 7NE, ☎ (066 83) 543, Tx 53168, AC AM BA DI, 15 rm. ℙ ⌕ 📺 ⌕ ♪ Late Georgian coaching inn with attractive gardens. £52. Rest. ♦ ⌕ Venison. £10.

SEAHOUSES, 3m SE on B1340
ℹ️ 16 Main Street, ☎ 720424.

Hotels:
★★ **Beach House**, Seafront, NE68 7SR, ☎ (0665) 720337, AC BA, 14 rm. ℙ ⌕ 📺 ⌕ ⌕ £44. Rest. ♦ ♪ Cl. mid-Nov.-Mar. Clootie dumpling with rum sauce. £10.50.
★★ **Olde Ship**, NE68 7RD, ☎ (0665) 720200, 9 rm. ℙ Small inn overlooking the sea. £35. Rest. ♦ ♪ Cl. Dec.-Feb. Northumbrian beef stovies, clootie dumpling. £7.50.

Inn or Pub:
Warenford Lodge, Warenford (5m SW), ☎ (066 83) 453.

⚓ *Seafield Park C.P.*, Seafield Park (20 pl), ☎ (0665) 720628.

Recommended
Golf course: Beadnell Road, ☎ (0665) 720794.
Guesthouse: Rowena, 99 Main Street, ☎ 720471. £18 double; B. & B.

BARNARD CASTLE*

Darlington, 15; Bishop Auckland, 14; London, 254 m
pop. 6,075 ☎ 0833   Durham A3

This small, grey stone market town set in peaceful countryside on the N bank of the River Tees is named after the **castle** built by Bernard de Balliol in the late 12thC, the ruins of which remain. The succession of steep roads that run down to the river are known collectively as **The Bank**. To the E of the town is the magnificent **Bowes Museum**.
▶ Approaching from S, road crosses a ribbed bridge (1569, rebuilt after 1771). ▶ In town centre is octagonal **market cross** (1747), formerly the town hall, and opposite it the parish **church**, thoroughly restored but with some

Norman features. The **King's Head** in the large market place is where Charles Dickens stayed in 1838 when working on *Nicholas Nickleby*. ▶ Just below market cross is the Tudor **Blagraves House** and further down are elegant Georgian houses at **Thorngate**. ▶ Perched on a craggy cliff top covering 6$^1/_2$ acres on the E of the town are the **castle** ruins, which include a massive circular keep (14thC) with a window displaying the boar emblem of Richard III (*mid-Mar.-mid-Oct.: Mon.-Sat., 2.30-6.30, Sun., 2-6.30; mid-Oct.-mid-Mar.: Mon.-Sat., 9.30-4, Sun., 2-4*). ▶ The **Bowes Museum★**, Newgate: an astonishing 19thC building modeled on a French Renaissance château; contains major collections of European art from the late medieval period to the 19thC: paintings by Goya, El Greco, Tiepolo, Boucher and Gainsborough; tapestries, furniture, porcelain, glass, jewelry, sculpture, metalwork, as well as a children's gallery, music room and costume collection (*May-Sep.: Mon.-Sat., 10-5.30, Sun., 2-5; Oct., Mar., Apr.: Mon.-Sat., 10-5, Sun., 2-5; Nov.-Feb.: Mon.-Sat., 10-4, Sun., 2-4*).

Nearby

▶ **Egglestone Abbey** (*1m E*), picturesque ruins of a monastery founded in late 12thC, with walks along the wooded river bank (*open daily, ex. Sun. am*). ▶ **Staindrop** (*6m NE*), attractive mainly 18thC village with a large church (11thC-14thC) containing remarkable alabaster monuments to the powerful local Neville and Vane families. To the N of the village is their splendid family seat, **Raby Castle★** (14thC with 18th and 19thC alterations), set in walled gardens within a park where deer herds roam; it includes a gateway, keep and huge Barons' Hall, an opulent drawing room, portraits and 19thC French furniture. Outside, a collection of horse-drawn carriages and fire engines (*Easter and Bank Hols.: Sat.-Tue.; mid-Apr.-Jun.: Wed. Sun.; Jul.-Sep.: Mon.-Fri. Sun.; castle, 2-5, park gardens, 1-5.30*).   □

Practical information

BARNARD CASTLE
ℹ️ 43 Galgate, ☎ (0833) 38481.

Hotel:
★ **Raby Arms**, 17 Market Place, DL12 8NF, ☎ Teesdale (0833) 37105, 4 rm. Ⓟ £18. Rest. ♦ £5.

Restaurant:
♦ **Blagraves House**, 30-32 The Bank, ☎ Teesdale 37668, AC AM BA Ⓟ ☷ ♧ ⚭ Cl. Sun., Mon. Book. £16.

Inn or Pub:
Old Well, 21 The Bank, ☎ (0833) 37529.

⚓ *Thorpe Hall*, Wycliffe (12 pl), ☎ 27230.

Recommended
Golf course: Marwood (3/4m N on B6278), ☎ (0833) 38355.
Riding school: *Park House Farm Riding Centre*, Baldersdale, ☎ (0833) 50474.
♥ **Tearoom:** *Market Place*, 29 Market Place, ☎ (0833) 37049.

Nearby

GRETA BRIDGE, 5m SE on A66

Hotel:
★ **Morrit Arms**, Rowkeby, DL12 9SE, ☎ Teesdale (0833) 27232, AC BA DI AM, 23 rm. Ⓟ ⚶ ☷ ♧ ◡ £46. Rest. ♦ ᕯ £12.

BERWICK-UPON-TWEED**

Alnwick, 30; Dunbar, 28; London, 336 m
pop. 12,772 ☎ 0289   Northumberland A1

A small and ancient seaport of extraordinary charm, Berwick stands in a key border position at the mouth of the Scottish River Tweed. By 1482 it had changed hands between Scotland and England thirteen times

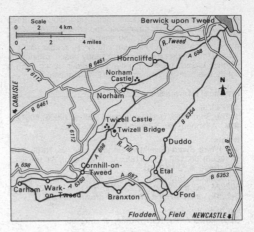

South Tweed valley

and over the following centuries became a semi-independent English outpost. It retains a sense of its long and checkered history, with splendid Elizabethan ramparts enclosing many Georgian houses and other historic buildings, laid out on an early street pattern. Inland runs the long, peaceful valley of the River Tweed, marking the Scottish border. Southwards, over the river and through the suburb of Tweedmouth, is Berwick's seaside resort of **Spittal** with sandy beaches stretching far down the NE coast.

▶ The remarkably well-preserved **Elizabethan walls★**, begun in 1558 and based on an Italian plan, are one of the finest examples in Europe of the new system of fortification designed to withstand gunpowder; from **Meg's Mount**, one of the defensive bastions, a 2m walk along the top of the ramparts; good views. ▶ Traces remain of the earlier **walls** of Edward I (13thC), particularly to the W of the town near the scanty ruins of **Berwick Castle** (13thC) and the impressive **Royal Border Bridge★** (1847-50), a curving railway viaduct with twenty-eight arches, designed by Robert Stephenson. ▶ In the town centre is the **Town Hall** (18thC), with a tower and spire. Beyond it are **Ravensdowne Barracks** (1717-21), attributed to Vanbrugh and now housing a military museum, and the parish **church of Holy Trinity** (c. 1650), with an elegant, partly-altered Puritan interior.

Excursion along South Tweed Valley

▶ Leaving on A698 over Royal Tweed Bridge (1928) and branching N (*in 3m*) to Horncliffe: **Union Chain Bridge** (*5m, off to r.*), first suspension bridge in country, built 1820, in beautiful pastoral setting. ▶ Through pleasant village of Horncliffe to **Norham★** (*6$^1/_2$ m*), ancient village with much-restored church containing a fine Norman chancel; also massive **castle★**, built in 12thC for the bishops of Durham and retaining its Norman keep (*mid-Mar.-mid-Oct.: Mon.-Sat., 9.30-6.30, Sun., 2-6.30; mid-Oct.-mid-Mar.: Mon.-Sat., 9.30-4, Sun., 2-4*). ▶ Rejoining A698, **Twizell Bridge** (*10m*), built c. 1450, a single arch spanning ravine with picturesque ruins of **Twizell Castle** (late 18thC) close by. ▶ **Cornhill-on-Tweed** (*13m*), pleasant residential town, on road to Scotland via Coldstream, on opposite side of river. ▶ **Wark-on-Tweed** (*15$^1/_2$ m W on B6350*) has traces of its once formidable 12thC castle; **Carham** (*17m*) and Scottish border, with sites of prehistoric camps in hills to S. ▶ S from Cornhill (*off A697*) **Branxton** village (*4m*) and site of Battle of **Flodden Field★**, where King James IV of Scotland and much of his army were killed in 1513 fighting the English. ▶ **Ford** (*5m E of Branxton on B6353*): 19thC

'model' village set on a promontory overlooking Flodden Hill and the Cheviots beyond, with an imposing restored 13th-14thC castle (*not open*) and in **Lady Waterford Hall**, the old village school, a collection of late-19thC water-colours by Lady Waterford, a Pre-Raphaelite follower.
► B6354 NE (*7m SW of Berwick*) leads past restored **Heatherslaw Mill**, one of the oldest water driven flour mills, via **Etal** and **Duddo**, both with scanty ruins of castles and near Duddo, traces of prehistoric stone circle.□

Practical information _____

BERWICK-UPON-TWEED
ⓘ Castlegate Car Park, ☎ (0289) 307187.

Hotels:
★★★★ **King's Arms**, Hide Hill, TD15 1EJ, ☎ (0289) 307454, Tx 8811232, AC AM BA DI, 37 rm. ∰ ♿ ⌧ ♺ £52. Rest. ♦ ♪ ♿ Local fish. £11.50.
★ **Castle Hotel**, Castlegate, TD15 1LF, ☎ (0289) 306471, AC AM BA DI, 16 rm. £28. Rest. ♦ ♪ ♿ £5.

⚠ Ord House C.P., East Ord, (60 pl), ☎ 305288.

Recommended
Cycle rental: *Chapels Cycle Hire*, 17A Bridge Street, ☎ (0289) 306295.
Golf course: *Goswick*, ☎ (0289) 87266.
Guesthouse: at Norham, *Dromore House*, 12 Pedwell Way, ☎ (0289) 82313. £17 double; B. & B.

Nearby

CORNHILL-ON-TWEED

Hotels:
★★ **Collingwood Arms**, TD12 4UH, ☎ Coldstream (0890) 2424, AC BA, 20 rm. ℗ ≼ ∰ ♿ ⌧ ♺ Handsome Georgian coaching inn on the route to Scotland. £38. Rest. ♦ ♪ Tweed salmon. £9.95.
★ **Tillmouth Park**, TD12 4UU, ☎ Coldstream (0890) 2255, AC AM BA DI, 16 rm. ℗ ≼ ∰ ♺ ♺ 19thC manor house situated in 2 1/2 acres of garden. Fishing facilities available (salmon, trout). £30. Rest. ♦ Tweed salmon. £12.95.

BISHOP AUCKLAND

Darlington, 13; Durham, 12; London, 255 m
pop. 32,572 ☎ 0388   Durham B3

Set high above the River Wear, Bishop Auckland is a small industrial town with a busy market. Bishops of Durham have had a residence here since the 12thC and the grounds of the palace, **Auckland Castle**, are open as a public **park**.

► The park has lawns, woods, streams and, in the NE corner, an 18thC deer shelter. The castle (mainly 18thC) is private but the fine chapel (from 1660) and 14thC hall, gothicized by James Wyatt in 1795, are sometimes open (*Sun., Mon. Wed., 2-5 in summer*). The parish **church** of St. Andrew's, to the S of the town, is thought to be the largest in the county and dates from the 13thC.

Nearby

► At **Escombe** (*3m W*) is a small Saxon **church★**, one of the two oldest in England, and virtually unaltered since its construction in the 7thC; many of its stones came from the nearby Roman fort of Vinovia (Binchester). ► **Witton Park** (*5m W, near Witton-le-Wear*), a leisure park surrounding the extensively restored Witton Castle, dating from 1410 (*daily*). ► **Hamsterley Forest** (*8 m W*), has been made into a large recreation area with a 4¹/₂ m forest drive, nature trails and picnic facilities. ► At **Shildon** (*2m SE*), the cottage home of railway pioneer Timothy Hackworth, contemporary of George Stephenson (*Apr.-Sep.: Wed.-Sun.*)   □

┌───┐
│ Send us your comments and suggestions; we will │
│ use them in the next edition.   │
└───┘

Practical information _____

BISHOP AUCKLAND
🚍 ☎ Darlington (0325) 355111.

Hotel:
★★ **Kings Arms**, 36 Market Place, DL14 7NX, ☎ (0388) 001290, AC AM BA DI, 14 rm. ℗ ≼ ⌧ £36. Rest. ♦ ≼ ♺ ♪ Cl. 25 Dec.-1 Jan. £10.

Recommended
Craft workshop: *Spinstercraft*, Dans Castle, Tow Law, ☎ (0388) 730016, selection from several local craftpeople, toys, knitwear.
Golf course: High Plains, ☎ (0388) 602198.
Riding schools: *Hamsterley Riding School*, Hamsterley, ☎ (0388) 328; *West Hoppyland Trekking Centre*, Hamsterley, ☎ (0388) 617.

Nearby

NEW COUNDON, 2m NE on A689

Hotel:
★★ **Park Head**, DL14 8QE, ☎ (0388) 661727, AC BA DI, 12 rm. ℗ ≼ ♺ ♿ £30. Rest. ♦ ♪ Cl. Christmas. £7.

RUSHYFORD, 6m E on A689

Hotel:
★★★★ **Eden Arms** (Swallow), DL17 0LL, ☎ Bishop Auckland (0388) 720541, Tx 53168, AC AM BA DI, 51 rm. ℗ ≼ ∰ ♿ ⌧ ⌧ ♺ £50. Rest. ♦ ♿ £10.

SHILDON, 3m SE off A6072

Restaurant:
● ♦ *Rajah Tandoori*, 100 Main Street, ☎ (0388) 773563, AC AM BA DI ℗ ≼ ⌧ Cl. Christmas, Sun. lunch. Book. £8.

WEST AUCKLAND, 4m SW on A688

Hotel:
★★ **Old Manor House**, DL9 9HH, ☎ Bishop Auckland (0388) 832504, AC AM DI, 15 rm. ℗ ∰ ⌧ ⌧ ♺ £46. Rest. ♦ ♪ ♿ Braised duckling. £10.

Inn or Pub:
Blacksmiths Arms, Spring Gardens, ☎ (0388) 832618.

CHESTER-LE-STREET

Newcastle-upon-Tyne, 8; Durham, 8; London, 268 m
pop. 20,520 ☎ 0385   Durham B2

The busy colliery town of Chester-le-Street now shows little sign of its illustrious history. Once a Roman fortress on the main military road from York to Hadrian's Wall, it became the centre of northern Christianity in the 10thC when the monks fleeing from Holy Island (→) with the body of St. Cuthbert found a resting place here from 882-995.

► The parish **church of St. Mary and St. Cuthbert**, built on the site of the wooden Saxon one, is 13th-14thC with later alterations. It is notable for its graceful 156 ft. spire (c.1400), the anchorage built onto the tower's N wall and the line of effigies (mostly Elizabethan imitations) of the Lumley family, whose ancestral home is nearby.

Nearby

► **Lumley Castle** (*1m E*), impressive example of a late 14thC castle with courtyard and four-square battlements, standing high in wooded parkland; later alterations include fine early 18thC interiors by John Vanbrugh. It is now a hotel specializing in medieval banquets. ► **Lambton Castle and Pleasure Park** (*1m NE*), the large estate of the Lambtons, earls of Durham, whose history goes back to the 13thC, has been converted into a safari park with picnic areas, an amusement park and entertainments within the castle (19thC), dramatically sited above the River Wear (*daily, Mar.-Oct.*). ► At Beamish (*4m W*) **North of England Open Air Museum★**: local buildings, including shops, colliery, pit cottages and a station with working steam

engines. All has been rebuilt in 200 acres of countryside to show aspects of life around 1900 (*mid-Apr-mid-Sep.: daily, 10-6; Oct.-Mar.: Tue.-Sun., 10-5*).

Practical information _____

CHESTER-LE-STREET
☎ Newcastle-upon-Tyne (091) 232 6262.

Hotel:
★★★ *Lumley Castle* (Consort), DH3 4NX, ☎ 891111, Tx 537433, AC AM BA DI, 50 rm. ⒫ ∰ ♤ ♪ Stately 13thC castle dominating parkland area. £62. Rest. ♦ ♤ ♪ ♭ Cl. 25-26 Dec. Lumley special steak. £11.50.

Recommended
Golf course: Lumley Park, ☎ (0385) 883218; South Moor Golf Club, The Middles, Craghead, Stanley, ☎ (0297) 32848.

Nearby

SHOTLEY BRIDGE, 14m W on A693

Hotel:
★ *Crown & Crossed Swords*, DH8 0HU, ☎ Consett (0207) 502006, 7 rm. ⒫ ♤ £24. Rest. ♦ ♪ Local trout. £6.

TANTOBIE, 8m W off A693

Hotel:
★ *Oak Tree*, DH9 9RF, ☎ (0207) 235445, 5 rm. ⒫ ♢ ♤ ♭ ♪ ♧ £28. Rest. ♦ ♭ Venison. £16.

CORBRIDGE**

Newcastle-upon-Tyne, 19; Durham, 30; London, 284 m
pop. 2,757 ☎ 043 471   Northumberland A2

A small stone-built town in a beautiful setting on the N bank of the Tyne, Corbridge was a strategic crossing point in Roman times and the site of the large fort of *Corstopitum*. Today, Corbridge is entered from the S over a handsome seven arched bridge built in the 17thC. As well as its Roman fort, the town has many historic buildings, including a 13thC priest's house - now used as the Information Centre. It is an attractive base from which to explore nearby Hadrian's Wall (→).

► The parish **church of St. Andrew**, rebuilt in the 13thC, has an early Saxon **tower** incorporating a complete Roman arch taken from nearby *Corstopitum*. ► The excavated site of this large fort, **Corbridge Roman Station★** (¹⁄₂m NW of the town), shows shops, temples, houses and granaries, and the museum's rich collection of finds includes the outstanding 3rdC sculpture known as the Corbridge Lion (*mid-Mar.-mid-Oct.: Mon.-Sat., 9.30-6.30, Sun., 2-6.30; mid-Oct.-mid-Mar.: Mon.-Sat., 9.30-4, Sun., 2-4*).

Nearby

► Close to the edge of **Devil's Water**, the tributary of the Tyne whose steep wooded banks are a haven for wildlife, are the remains of **Dilston Castle** (*1m SW*), left uncompleted after its owner, the last earl of Derwentwater, was executed for his part in the 1715 Jacobite rebellion. ► **Aydon Castle** (1¹⁄₂m NE): good example of an early 14thC fortified manor-house. ► The road along the S bank of the Tyne leads through the village of Riding Mill to **Stocksfield** (*3m SE*); **National Tractor and Farm Museum**, Newton, devoted to agricultural life, with working machinery and farm animals (*daily, 10-5*). ► Opposite Stocksfield, beautifully set on the N bank of the Tyne, is the village of **Bywell**, with two fine churches: **St. Andrew's** (10th-13thC with a Saxon tower) and **St. Peter's** (mainly 13thC). ► Also **castle**, a 15thC tower house, and the hall, converted by James Paine in 1760 (*not open to the public*).

Practical information _____

CORBRIDGE
ⓘ Vicar's Pele, Market Place, ☎ (043 471) 2815.
☎ Newcastle-upon-Tyne (091) 232 6262.

Hotels:
★ *Angel*, Main Street, NE45 5LA, ☎ (043 471) 2119, AC AM BA DI, 6 rm. ⒫ 16thC Tudor Inn. £25. Rest. ♦ ♪ ♭ Cl. Sun. dinner. £5.50.
★ *Riverside*, Main Street, NE45 5LE, ☎ (043 471) 2942, 11 rm. ≼ ♤ ♭ £27. Rest. ♦ ♤ ♭ Cl. Sun. dinner only. Fresh salmon and trout in season. £9.

Inn or Pub:
Wheatsheaf Hotel, Watling Street, ☎ (043 471) 2020.

Recommended
Golf course: Stocksfield, New Ridley Road, ☎ (0661) 843041.
♥ *The Corbridge Larder*, Heron House, Hill Street, ☎ (043 471) 294, the Burt's delicatessen, best known for its cheese counter.

Nearby

FARNLEY, 1/2m S on A695

Restaurant:
♦ *Ramblers Country House*, Tinklers Bank, ☎ (043 471) 2424, AC AM BA DI ⒫ ∰ ♤ ♭ ♨ Cl. lunch Sun., Mon. Pheasant in sour cream and blackcurrant sauce. Book. £15.

DARLINGTON

Middlesbrough, 16; Newcastle-upon-Tyne, 36; London, 244 m
pop. 85,519 ☎ 0325   Durham B3

This industrial town on the small River Skerne still has traces of its history as a medieval market town and 18thC textile centre but its greatest claim to fame is its link with the early railway.

► George Stephenson's original steam engine *Locomotion No.1* can be seen, along with other historic engines and railways exhibits, in **North Road Station Museum** (*Apr.-Sep., Mon.-Sat., 10-6, Sun., 2-5; Oct.-Mar., Mon.-Sat., 10-4, Sun., 2-4*). ► On the E edge of the town centre, with its mix of old and new buildings, is the large grey stone **Church of St. Cuthbert★**, dating from the late 12thC and an important example of Early English architecture. ► Off the market place is **Darlington Museum**, Tubwell Row: collections of local and natural history (*Mon.-Fri., 10-1 & 2-6, Thur. only, 10-1, Sat., 10-1 & 2-5.30, cl. Sun.*). Nearby **art gallery and library**, Crown Street, includes a tourist information centre (*Mon.-Fri., 10-8, Sat., 10-5.30, cl. Sun.*).

Practical information _____

DARLINGTON
ⓘ District Library, Crown Street, ☎ (0325) 469858.
✈ Tees-side Airport (6m E off A67) ☎ (0325) 332811.
Car rental: *Europcar*, 53 Duke Street, ☎ (0325) 460771-2; rail/drive, ☎ (0325) 488037.

Hotels:
★★★ *King's Head* (Swallow), Priestgate, DL1 1NW, ☎ (0325) 380222, Tx 587112, AC AM BA DI, 86 rm. ⒫ ♭ £45. Rest. ♦ ≼ ♤ ♪ ♭ Oriental peppers. £9.
★★★ *St. George* (M.C.H.), Tees-side Airport, DL2 1RH, ☎ Dinsdale (0325) 332631, Tx 58664, AC AM BA DI, 58 rm. ⒫ £44. Rest. ♦ £9.50.

Restaurants:
♦ *Bishop's House*, 38 Coniscliffe Road, ☎ (0325) 28666, AC BA ♪ ♨ Cl. Christmas, Jan. Book. £12.
♦ *Victor's*, 84 Victoria Road, ☎ (0325) 480818, AC AM BA DI ♪ ♨ Cl. Sun. lunch, Mon. Sorbets. Book. £12.

Inn or Pub:
Pennyweight, Bakehouse Hill, ☎ (0325) 464244.

Recommended

Golf courses: Haughton Grange (off B1256), ☎ (0325) 463936; Dinsdale Spa, Middleton-St.-George (3m E on A67), ☎ 332222.

Nearby

BLACKWELL GRANGE, 1 1/2m S on A167

Hotel:

★★★ *Blackwell Grange* (Q.M.H.), DL3 8QH, ☎ (0325) 460111, Tx 587272, AC AM BA DI, 98 rm. ⓟ ≼ ⅏ ⚄ � ∴ ⅃ ⚄ 17thC mansion set in 6 1/2 acres of parkland. £52. Rest. ◆ ⅃ ⚄ Durham lamb chop. £9.50.

COATHAM MUNDEVILLE, 5m N off A167

Hotel:

★★★ *Hallgarth Country*, DL1 3LU, ☎ Aycliffe (0325) 313333, AC AM BA DI, 20 rm. ⓟ ≼ ⅏ ⚄ ⅃ ⚄ Elegantly converted Georgian house surrounded by 56 acres of garden and woodlands. £58. Rest. ● ◆ ⅃ Cl. 22 Dec.-2 Jan., Mayday Bank Hol. Mrs. Crocker's beef and red wine pie. £12.50.

HEADLAM, 9m NW off A67

Hotel:

★★ *Headlam*, Gainford, DL2 3HA, ☎ (0325) 730238, AC DA, 13 rm. ⓟ ≼ ⅏ ⚄ ⚄ ∴ Part Jacobean manor house with 3 acres of gardens. £40. Rest. ◆ ≼ ⚄ ⅃ Cl. Sun. and 25 Dec.-1 Jan. £11.

NEASHAM, 3m SE

Hotel:

★★ *Newbus Arms*, Newbus Arms, DL2 1PE, ☎ Darlington (0325) 721071, Tx 58664, AC AM BA DI, 15 rm. ⓟ ≼ ⅏ ⚄ £70. Rest. ● ◆ ≼ ⚄ Roast quail stuffed with chestnuts with peach sauce. £18.

DURHAM***

Newcastle-upon-Tyne, 16; Darlington, 20; London, 262 m
pop. 26,422 ☎ 0385/091   Durham B2

The ancient and beautiful city of Durham is dramatically sited on a high rocky peninsula of the River Wear, its magnificent cathedral and castle towering over it. Durham's importance began in the late 10thC when monks bearing St. Cuthbert's body settled on the steep wooded promontory, building a wooden cathedral to house the saint's coffin. This almost impregnable site became a wealthy place of pilgrimage and a key northern stronghold for the Norman conquerors. Bishops of Durham were given princely independence and from the 11thC, when the present cathedral and castle were begun, a succession of powerful prince-bishops left their individual marks on Durham's architecture and history. Today's busy university city includes numerous interesting buildings and churches in its winding streets and alleyways and around the cobbled market place. Skirting them is the river, with old bridges connecting with the wooded riverside path, which provides beautiful walks and views.

▶ The **cathedral**★, regarded as the finest Norman cathedral in western Europe, was built in 40 years (1093-1133). Its imposing exterior, with a central tower over 200 ft. high, was partly altered in 1795, including the N doorway where the grotesquely shaped **knocker** (12thC) gave fugitives protection from the law (original now in cathedral museum). Inside, massive piers and decorated columns line the **nave**, below the first example in Europe of stone-ribbed vaulting, the splendidly proportioned interior giving an impression of immense size. In contrast are the graceful **Galilee Chapel** at the W end (added 1175, with later alterations), containing the tomb of the Venerable Bede, whose remains were brought here in 1020 from Jarrow

(→); and at the E end the light-filled **Chapel of the Nine Altars** (mid-13thC). Other glories include the stone-carved **Neville Screen** (c. 1375), behind which is St. Cuthbert's tomb; the **bishop's throne** - supposedly the highest in Christendom - incorporating Bishop Hatfield's 14thC tomb; the 17thC **choirstalls** and font cover. In the S transept is an early 16thC astronomical clock and near the much restored cloisters is the monks' dormitory (c. 1400), now the library and **Treasury Museum**, containing St. Cuthbert's relics, church plate, manuscripts and other cathedral treasures (*Mon.-Sat., 10-4.30, Sun., 2-4.30*).

▶ Opposite, across Palace Green, is the splendid **castle**★ of the bishops of Durham, dating to 1072 with various impressive alterations over the centuries, and used since 1837 by the university. Parts open to the public include the **kitchen**, with huge fireplaces of c. 1500; **great hall**, dating from 1300; **Bishop Tunstall's Gallery** (16thC) and **chapel** containing delightful misericords and reached by a remarkable black oak staircase (1662); the 12thC **Constable's Hall**, below which is the magnificent, perfectly preserved Norman **doorway**; and the beautiful, restored Norman **chapel** (*Apr., Jul.-Sep.: Mon.-Sat., 10-12 2-4.30; other months: Mon., Wed., Sat., 2-4*). ▶ **Palace Green** is lined with old buildings, mainly 15th and 17thC; notable are **Bishop Cosin's Hall** (17thC) and the **almshouses** founded by him, **Abbey House** (early 18thC), and the old **grammar school** (1661). To the E run charming, mainly 18thC cobbled streets of **North** and **South Bailey**, leading down to elegant **Prebends Bridge** (1772), the old **Fulling Mill** and, upstream, **Framwellgate Bridge** (12thC, rebuilt), giving fine views. ▶ Interesting buildings in the **market place** include the **Town Hall** (rebuilt 1851), **St. Nicholas Church** with its elegant spire (rebuilt 1857-8) and the large, copper-plated equestrian **statue** of 3rd Lord Londonderry. Nearby is **Saddler Street**, Durham's historic theatre-land, and across **Elvet Bridge** (dating to 12thC) attractive mainly 18thC **Old Elvet** with Royal County Hotel. New Elvet, passing **Kingsbridge** footbridge by Ove Arup (1963), leads to Hallgarth Street, with 15thC tithe-barns by the prison and **St. Oswald's Church**, basically 12thC; window by Ford Maddox Brown. ▶ To NW, near County Hall, is **Durham Light Infantry Museum and Arts Centre**, devoted to the regiment's 200-yr. history; exhibitions of arts and crafts in upper galleries (*Tue.-Sat., 10-5, Sun., 2-5; open Bank Hols.*). ▶ **Gulbenkian Museum of Oriental Art and Archaeology**★, Elvet Hill, has well-displayed collections from all periods and cultures of the Orient, including Egyptian antiquities and Chinese pottery and porcelain (*Mon.-Fri., 9.30-1, Sat., 9.30-12 2.15-5, Sun., 2.15-5; cl. wkends Bank Hols. Nov.-Feb.*).

Nearby

▶ **Finchale Priory**★ (*5m N*): romantic ruins of 13th-14thC priory on site of early 12thC hermitage of St. Godric, whose stone tomb is in the chapel; beautiful setting with riverside walks (*mid-Mar.-mid-Oct.: Mon.-Sat., 9.30-6.30, Sun., 2-6.30; mid-Oct.-mid-Mar.: Mon.-Sat., 9.30-4, Sun., 2-4*). ▶ **Brancepeth** (*4m SW*): with magnificent castle (mainly rebuilt 19thC) belonging to powerful Neville family until 1569 (*not open*); in the grounds is **St. Brandon Church** (12th-14thC), containing Neville monuments and fine 17thC woodwork. ▶ **Lanchester** (*8m NW*): attractive village dating to Roman times; **All Saints Church** (12th-13thC) has fine chancel, some 13thC stained glass and a Roman altar stone from fort of **Longovicium** whose remains are 1/4m SW. ▢

Practical information _____

. **DURHAM**

ⓘ Market Place (B2), ☎ (091) 3843720.

🚌 ☎ (091) 43737.

🚆 (A2), ☎ (091) 3843322.

Hotels:

★★★★ *Royal County* (Swallow), Old Elvet (B2), DH1 3JN, ☎ (091) 66821, Tx 538238, AC AM BA DI, 119 rm. ≼ ⚄ ⅃ £58. Rest. ◆ ⅃ Local salmon. £11.

★★★ *Three Tuns* (Swallow), New Elvet (B2), DH1 3AQ,

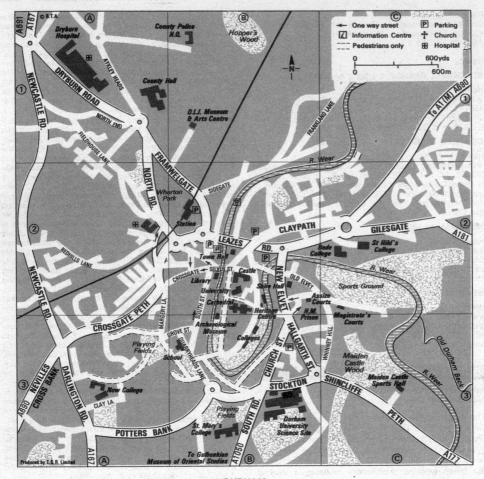

DURHAM

☎ (091) 64326, Tx 538238, AC AM BA DI, 54 rm. Ⓟ
♩ £55. Rest. ♦ 㐧 Cl. Christmas. £10.

Restaurant:
♦ *Undercroft Restaurant*, The College, Durham Cathedral
(B3), ☎ (091) 3863721 㐧 Cl. 25-26 Dec., Good Fri. Home-
made quiches. £6.

Inn or Pub:
Stonebridge, Nevilles Cross (A3), ☎ (091) 3869591.

⋏ *Coal Hole C.P.*, West Sherburn (25 pl), ☎ (091)
3863394: at Castleside, *Allensford P.C.S.*, *Allensford*
(44 pl.), ☎ (0207) 509522; *Manor P.C.S.*, Broadmeadows,
Ripon Burn (36 pl), ☎ (0207) 501000.

Recommended
Craft workshop: *Pickering Nook Craft Centre*, Consett
Road, Burnopfield, ☎ (0308) 897141, over 100 artists and
craftspeople display their works.
Farmhouse: at Brancepeth, *Stokeley Farm*, Oakeshaw,
Brook, ☎ (0388) 746443. £17 double; B. & B.
Golf courses: Brancepeth Castle Golf Club, Brancepeth,
☎ (091) 780075; Durham City, Littleburn, Langley Moor,
☎ (091) 780806.

Nearby
BOWBURN, 4m SE on A177

Hotel:
★★ *Bowburn Hall*, DH6 5NT, ☎ Coxhoe (0385) 770311,
Tx 537681, AC AM BA DI, 20 rm. Ⓟ ⋞ ⁂ ⟅ £40. Rest. ♦
Local salmon. £10.50.

⋏*The Grange C.C.S.*, Meadow Lane (60 pl), ☎ (091)
384 4778.

CROXDALE, 3m S on A167

Hotel:
★★★ *Bridge*, DH1 3SP, ☎ (0385) 780524, Tx 538156, AC
AM BA DI, 49 rm. Ⓟ £42. Rest. ♦ ⟅ £11.

Inn or Pub:
Coach Horses, Butchers Race, ☎ (091) 3814484.

Be advised that hotels and restaurants in this Guide
have perhaps changed addresses; prices indicated
are also subject to modifications.

GATESHEAD

Newcastle-upon-Tyne, 16; Durham, 19; London, 273 m
pop. 91,429 ☎ 0632/091   Tyne & Wear B2

A sprawling town of industrial and modern estates, Gateshead has its own proud history of shipbuilding and engineering.

▶ The rebuilt Norman **church of St. Mary's**, on the river bank, has some fine 17thC woodwork. ▶ Near the large Saltwell Park in the city centre is **Shipley Art Gallery**, which has collections of British and continental paintings and modern British crafts (*Mon.-Fri., 10-5.30, Sat., 10-4.30, Sun., 2-5; Bank Hols., 10-5.30*).

Nearby

▶ **Ryton** (*6m W*), reached via Winlaton and Blaydon, is an attractive colliery village on the riverside with a 13thC **church** with 17thC wood carving. ▶ SW from Blaydon along the lower Derwent Valley, the A694 passes **Axwell Park** and on the opposite bank **Derwent Walk**, a 10m pedestrian way along the disused railway line from Swalwell to Consett; rich in animal and birdlife. ▶ The road and walk pass Winlaton and **Winlaton Mill** (*3m*), known for its ironworks, and at **Rowland's Gill** (*6m*) a side road (or pathway) leads to Burnopfield and the **Gibside Chapel★**, beautiful example of Georgian architecture designed by James Paine in 1760 and later used as a mausoleum for the Bowes family; the approach is by a terrace with an avenue of oaks (*Apr.-Sep.: Wed., Sat., Sun., Good Fri., Bank Hols.: 2-5; Oct.: Wed., Sat., Sun., 2-5; otherwise by appt.*). ▶ The A694 continues along the Derwent Valley to **Ebchester** (*10m*), site of the Roman fort of *Vincomara* with 10 acres of beautiful riverside walks.   ▯

Practical information

ⓘ Central Library, Prince Consort Road; ☎ (091) 4773478/9.

▭ (metro), ☎ 232 6262.

Hotel:
★★★ *Five Bridges* (Swallow), High West Street, NE8 1PE, ☎ Tyneside (091) 477 1105, Tx 53534, AC AM BA DI, 10 rm. ℗ ও £55. Rest. ◆ ♪ £10.50.

⚐ *Derwent Park C.C.S.*, Rowlands Gill (55 pl), ☎ 3863394.

Recommended
Golf courses: Tynemouth, Spital Dene, ☎ (0632) 574578.

HADRIAN'S WALL***

A2

The great wall ordered by Emperor Hadrian c. 120 runs for 73m from Bowness in Cumbria in the W to Wallsend-on-Tyne in the E. Up to 10 ft. thick and 15-16 ft. high topped by a 6 ft. parapet, it served as a military barrier. Along it were milecastles housing small garrisons, with look-out turrets in between, and sixteen forts, permanent military towns with native settlements alongside. A steep defensive ditch ran along the N side and a military road along the S side, parallel with a flat-bottomed ditch - the Vallum. Over the centuries parts of the wall have disappeared but traces of it can be seen throughout most of its length and particularly fine sections remain between Cholerford and Gilsland, easily reached from Corbridge, Hexham, Haydon Bridge or Haltwhistle. Walks and drives along the wall give splendid views of the surrounding countryside.

▶ From the E (*A69*) **Benwell** (*2m from Newcastle centre*): remains of small temple and Vallum gateway; **Den-**

ton Burn (*3m*): well-preserved turret; **Heddon-on-the-Wall** (*7m*): good section of wall. ▶ Following from here on B6318 or Military Way (built by General Wade after 1745 Jacobite rebellion, using ruins of Hadrian's Wall). ▶ **Rudchester** (*8¹/₂ m*), site of *Vindovala* fort. ▶ **Halton Chesters** (*15m*), site of *Onnum* fort. Large Roman fort at Corbridge (→)(*2¹/₂ m S on 468*). ▶ Continuing on B6001 (*21m*) **Chollerford**, N of Hexham (→): well-preserved turret on **Brunton Bank** and (*in ¹/₂ m*) large cavalry fort of *Cilurnum*, **Chesters★**, with excavated baths and good Roman collections in John Clayton **museum** (*mid-Mar.-mid-Oct.: Mon.-Sat., 9.30-6.30, Sun., 2-6.30 (Apr.-Sep., 9.30-6.30); mid-Oct.-mid-Mar.: Mon.-Sat., 9.30-4, Sun., 2-4; cl. Christmas, New Year*). ▶ **Carrawburgh** (*25 m*), site of *Brocolita* fort and bull-cult Temple of Mithras and Well of Coventina, Celtic goddess (*open: as Chesters*). ▶ **Housesteads** (*30 m*)⚐: excavated fort of *Vercovicium*, best preserved on wall, with small museum (*open: as Chesters*) and spectacular views; walks and rock climbing to N and (*¹/₂m W*) good example of turret at **Sewingshields**. ▶ **Chesterholm★** (*¹/₂m S on road to Bardon Mill*): well-preserved fort of *Vindolanda* with civilian settlement and museum (*open: as Chesters*). ▶ **Once Brewed Inn** (*32¹/₂m*): information centre, near Crag Lough and Winshields Crag (1,230 ft.), highest point of wall, and (*34m*) **Cawfields**, milecastle with picnic site. ▶ **Great Chesters** (*36m*): fort of *Aesica*, with splendid views and walks by **Nine Nicks of Thirlwall**. ▶ **Walltown Crags** (*38m*): good stretch of wall. ▶ **Carvoran** (*39m S*): site of earlier fort (c. 80), close to Greenhead where roads and wall converge. ▶ **Gilsland** (*42m*): 1m W of village, Harrow's Scar milecastle and remnants of Willowford Bridge. ▶ **Birdoswald★**, (*2m SW, in Cumbria, leaving B6318*): large cavalry fort of **Camboglanna**, with view of Irthing Valley. The wall continues through Cumbria (→).   ▯

HALTWHISTLE

Hexham, 16; Carlisle, 22; London, 303 m
pop. 3,522 ☎ 0498   Northumberland A2

A small industrial town of grey-stone houses set on a steep bank very close to Hadrian's Wall and several Roman forts, with the beautiful South Tyne Valley to its south. The 13thC restored parish **church** of Holy Cross has an impressive Early English interior.

Nearby

▶ **Blenkinsopp Hall** (*1m W on A69*), early 19thC house with attractive gardens (*occasionally open in spring and summer*) and ruins of 14thC **Blenkinsopp Castle** (*2m*), with fragments of Roman Maiden Way close by. ▶ **Greenhead** (*3m W*), village at crossing point of Roman roads, with early 19thC church and ¹/₂m N, romantic shell of **Thirlwall Castle** (14thC) and **Nine Nicks of Thirlwall**, a group of crags. ▶ **Gilsland** (*4¹/₂m*), village at edge of Northumberland divided by Hadrian's Wall (→).

Excursion down South Tyne valley

▶ Leaving on road SW, follow river bank past ruins of **Bellister Castle** (16th-17thC) to Rowfoot, near which is **Featherstone Castle** (*3m*), Victorian with 14thC tower (*not usually open*). ▶ Past **Plenmeller Common** down to **Lambley** (*5m*), centre for valley walks and close to Pennine Way footpath (→), with 13-arched Victorian railway **viaduct** spanning river. ▶ A689 to Knarsdale and Slaggyford (*10m*) passes **Knarsdale Forest** and Common to W and Whitfield Moor and **Williamston Fell** (*1,582 ft.*) to E. ▶ Continuing S: **Kirkhaugh** (*13m*), with church (1868) containing Saxon cross in churchyard on opposite river bank below **Kip**

Law (*1,540 ft.*), past site of Roman fort ($^1/_2$m to W) and over Cumbrian border to Alston (→).

Practical information _____

ⓘ Sycamore Street, ☎ 20351.
▨▨▨ ☎ Newcastle-upon-Tyne (091) 232 6262.
⚠ Seldom Seen C.P. (20 pl), ☎ (0498) 20571.

Recommended
Farmhouse: White Craig Farm, Shield Hill, ☎ 20565, £20 double; B. & B.

HARTLEPOOL

Middlesbrough, 10; Bishop Auckland, 23; London, 260 m
pop. 91,749 ☎ 0429   Cleveland B3

The ancient port of Hartlepool was overwhelmed by the industrial development of West Hartlepool in the 19thC, since when the town has been almost entirely rebuilt. Its shipyards have closed down and North Sea oil rather than coal has become the main export.

▶ Traces of the history of 'Old' Hartlepool, on the **Heugh headland** NE of the docks, remain in the stretch of medieval wall by the harbour and in **St. Hilda's Church★**, built 1185-1215 on the site of a 7thC Saxon convent, restored at various times since. ▶ **Gray Museum and Art Gallery**, Clarence Road, has collections of 19th and 20thC paintings and oriental antiquities; displays of local and natural history (*Mon.-Sat., 10-5.30, Sun., 3-5*). ▶ The **Maritime Museum**, Northgate, is devoted to Hartlepool's fishing, shipbuilding and engineering industries (*Mon.-Sat., 10-5*). ▶ S is the seaside suburb of **Seaton Carew**, with a good stretch of sandy beach and views to the Tees estuary.

Practical information _____

HARTLEPOOL
ⓘ Civic Centre, Victoria Road, ☎ 66522 ext 375.
✈ Tees-side (20m SW), ☎ Dinsdale (0325) 332811.
▨▨▨ ☎ Middlesbrough (0642) 225535.

Hotel:
★★ **Grand,** Swainson Street, TS24 8AA, ☎ 266345, AC, AM BA DI, 44 rm. ℗ ᜒ £55. Rest. ♦ ⌕ ♪ ᜒ Cl. Sun. lunch. £8.
⚠ *Crimdon P.,* Blackhall Rocks (100 pl), ☎ (0429) 267801.

Recommended
Golf course: Seaton Carew, Tees Road (on A178), ☎ 66249; Castle Eden & Peterlee Golf Club, ☎ 836220; Hart Warren ☎ 4398.

HEXHAM★★

Newcastle-upon-Tyne, 23; Carlisle, 38; London, 287 m
pop. 9,630 ☎ 0434   Northumberland A2

An old yet lively town overlooking the River Tyne, Hexham is a good base from which to explore nearby Hadrian's Wall and the surrounding countryside. Ancient buildings are clustered round the busy market place and line the town's long main street. The grounds of the magnificent abbey form part of the public park leading up to the grassy hilltop of the **Seal**; good views.

▶ The **abbey church★★** dates from 674, and the Saxon crypt survives almost intact, built largely from stones taken from the Roman fort at Corbridge (→). The beautiful and very long transept (1190-1230) is an excellent example of Early English architecture. The church contains many treasures, including a Saxon bishop's stone chair, the Acca Cross (c. 740), a Roman soldier's tombstone, 15thC portraits of Hexham bishops

and medieval misericords. Among scanty remains of monastic buildings are the lavatorium and 12thC gateway. ▶ Off the market place are: **Moot Hall**, a tower house of c. 1400, now a library; **Manor Office** (1330), a medieval prison (now Tourist Information Centre); the former **grammar school** (1684) and the colonnaded 18thC **Shambles**.

Excursion S to Derwent Reservoir

▶ A trip through wooded valleys and farmland, forests and high moors to the Derwent lakeside. Leaving Hexham by B6306: **Linnels Bridge** (*2m*), rebuilt in 1698. ▶ **Dipton Wood** (*2$^1/_2$m*) and Devil's Water, whose banks were site of bloody battles of Hexham in 1463 and 1464. ▶ The road climbs from the valley past **Slaley Forest** and into moorland before a sudden drop into **Blanchland★** (*12m*), serene 18thC village on secluded river banks with remains of **abbey** church (14thC tower and N transept). **Lord Crewe Arms** also incorporates fragments of monastic buildings. ▶ **Derwent Reservoir★** (*1m*), a 3$^1/_2$m long lake, with picnic areas and Pows Hill bird and nature reserve around it.

Excursion N into North Tynedale and Wark Forest

▶ A journey up the remote North Tyne Valley, crossing Hadrian's Wall and moving into the vast stretch of high moorland and thick forests of Northumberland National Park. ▶ Cross the river over 18thC bridge. ▶ **Wall** (*3m*): village with 19thC church and large green, close to Hadrian's Wall (→). ▶ Just before crossroads (*4m*), footpath to **Brunton Bank**, with well-preserved **Roman turret** and 18thC chapel on site of Battle of Heavenfield (634) where Northumbrian King Oswald defeated West Britons. ▶ Over narrow five-arched **bridge** (18thC), near remnants of the Roman bridge, into **Chollerford**, close by the Roman fort of **Chesters** (→Hadrian's Wall). ▶ **Simonburn** (*8m*): pleasant village, with much restored 13thC church containing local family monuments, once serving largest parish in England. ▶ Side road just past Nunwick House (18thC) and Park (*private*) leads (*in 3m*) to **Ravensheugh Crags** (840 ft.), with glorious views of wooded valley, and the **Goatstones**, a small prehistoric site. ▶ Returning to B6320, road to I. forms Border Forest Park boundary leading into **Wark Forest.** ▶ **Stonehaugh**, modern foresters' village close to Pennine Way, long-distance footpath (→Derbyshire), with picnic area, forest walks and forest drive (*6m*) along Wark Burn to **Wark** village, once a local capital, with remains of a Norman castle. ▶ **Houxty** (*1m*), with views SE over **Chipchase Castle**: 14thC pele tower with fine Jacobean additions (*not open*). ▶ Road and Pennine Way lead down to **Bellingham★** (*15m*), tiny market town, capital of North Tynedale, with **church★**, remarkable for its stone-vaulted nave (17thC). ▶ **Hareshaw Linn** (1$^1/_2$ m N of town): 30 ft. waterfall reached through wooded glen. ▶ Road continues over wild moorland by **Hareshaw Head** (1,020 ft.) to Otterburn in Redesdale (→) or road W goes further up North Tyne Valley, passing ruins of Dally Castle (13thC), into National Park and Kielder Forest (→).   ☐

Practical information _____

HEXHAM
ⓘ Manor Office, Hallgate, ☎ (0434) 605225.
▨▨▨ ☎ Newcastle-upon-Tyne (091) 232 6262.

Hotels:
● ★★ **County**, Priestpopple, NE46 1PS, ☎ (0434) 602030, AC AM BA, 10 rm. ℗ ☺ £36. Rest. ♦ ⌕ ♪ £11.
★★ **Beaumont**, Beaumont Street, NE46 3LZ, ☎ (0434) 602331, AC AM BA DI, 21 rm. £38. Rest. ♦ ⌕ ⌕ ♪ Cl. 26 Dec., 1 Jan. Guinea fowl chasseur. £10.
★★ **Royal** (Consort), Priestpopple, NE46 1PQ, ☎ (0434) 602270, Tx 57515, AC AM BA DI, 25 rm. ℗ ⌗ £41. Rest. ♦ ♪ £9.

Restaurant:
♦ **Pine Kitchen**, Battlehill, ☎ (0434) 606688, AC AM BA DI ♪ ᜒ ✿ Cl. Tue. dinner. Book. £9.

⚐ *Causey Hill C.P.*, Causey Hill (50 pl), ☎ (0434) 602834; *Hexham Racecourse C.C.S.* (120 pl), ☎ (0434) 606847; *Lowgate C.P.*, Lowgate (10 pl), ☎ (0434) 602827.

Recommended
Farmhouse: *Thistlerigg Farm*, High Worden, ☎ (0434) 602041, close to Northumbria National Park, £18 double B. & B.; at Stocksfild-on-tyne, *Wheelbirks Jersey Farm*, ☎ (0661) 843378, £22 double B. & B.
Golf course: Spital Park ☎ (0434) 603072.
Guesthouse: *Kitty Frisk House*, Corbridge Road, ☎ (0434) 606850, £23 double B. & B.
♥ *Bordercraft*, 4 Market Street, ☎ (0434) 83508, Handmade fashion knitwear, jewelry, pottery, glass.

Nearby
BLANCHLAND, 15m S on B6306
Hotel:
● ★★ *Lord Crewe Arms*, DH8 9SP, ☎ (043 475) 251, 15 rm. ℗ ⚘ 🕮 £50. Rest. ♦ Cl. Jan. Rack of lamb in mint and honey. £11.50.

CHOLLERFORD, 7m N off A6079
Hotel:
★★★ *George* (Swallow), NE46 4EW, ☎ Humshaugh (0434) 81 611, Tx 53168, AC AM DA DI, 54 rm. ℗ ⚘ 🕮 ⚐ £60. Rest. ♦ Cl. New year. Venison, salmon and trout. £11.

HAYDON BRIDGE, 7m W on A69
Hotel:
★★ *Anchor* (Exec Hotel), John Martin Street, NE47 6AB, ☎ (0434) 84 227, AC AM BA DI, 10 rm. ℗ ⚘ ⚐ ♪ 🕮 Former coaching inn dating from the 15thC, on the banks of the River South Tyne. £32. Rest. ♦ Steak and kidney pie. £8.

Restaurant:
● ♦ *General Havelock Inn*, Ratcliffe Road, ☎ (043484) 376 ℗ ⚘ 🕮 ⚐ Cl. 1-15 Jan., Easter, 1st wk. Sep., Sun.-Tue. Book. £13.

WALL, 5 m N on A6079
Hotel:
★ *Hadrian*, NE46 4EE, ☎ Humshaugh (0434)81 232, 9 rm. ℗ ⚘ 🕮 ⚐ Inn built in 1740 with stones taken from Hadrian's Wall. £30. Rest. ♦ ♪ Monkfish and smoked salmon terrine. £9.

HOLY ISLAND OR LINDISFARNE**

pop. 190   Northumberland A1

Reached from **Beal** by a 3m causeway which is covered at high tide (*times listed or available from tourist centres*), Holy Island is steeped in history and is of outstanding natural beauty. It was settled in the early 7thC by monks from Iona led by St. Aidan (d. 651) and later St. Cuthbert (d. 687), who spread Christianity throughout the north. The monastery produced the glorious Lindisfarne Gospels (c. 700; now in British Museum). Viking invasions forced the monks to flee in 875, but the Benedictines founded a new monastery on the island in 1082, of which the ruins remain.

▶ Next to tiny village, with 12th-13thC parish **church**, are beautiful Norman ruins of the **priory**★, with a small museum containing a few relics and a facsimile of the Lindisfarne Gospels (*mid-Mar.-mid-Oct.: Mon.-Sat., 9.30-6.30, Sun., 2-6.30 (Apr.-Sep., 9.30-6.30), mid-Oct.-mid-Mar.: Mon.-Sat., 9.30-4, Sun., 2-4*). ▶ To E of village, on steep rock giving superb views, small 16thC **castle**★ converted by Edwin Lutyens in 1903 (*Apr.-Sep.: 11-5 daily ex. Fri. but open Good Fri.; Oct.: Sat. Sun. only, 2-5*). ▶ On limestone cliffs and sand-dunes in N, **nature reserve** for numerous seabirds; seals can often be seen offshore.□

KIELDER FOREST*

A2

This huge man-made forest area, part of the Border Forest Park, includes the recently created 7m-long artificial lake of Kielder Water. Numerous walks and drives lead through the forest, which is rich in wildlife and scattered with remains of prehistoric settlements.

▶ At **Kielder Water's**★ N end is Kielder Viaduct (1867), a fine example of railway architecture. Beside the water are picnic and camping sites, adventure playgrounds and other facilities, including fishing lets. ▶ The castle (1775) in **Kielder** village, on N, houses the Information Centre and a 12m forest drive (*toll*) runs from here to Byrness by Redesdale Forest. ▶ The Kielder **stone**, a 20 ft. sandstone block, marks the W boundary with Cumbria.   □

MIDDLESBROUGH

Darlington, 16; Sunderland, 28; London, 250 m
pop. 149,770 ☎ 0642   Cleveland B3

Middlesbrough, once a tiny village on the S bank of the River Tees, is now the heart of the large conurbation of Tees-side that includes Thornaby, Stockton (→), Billingham and Redcar (→). The town was born in the 1830s with the extension of the Stockton-Darlington Railway and grew dramatically, thriving iron and steel industries quickly following coal and shipbuilding. The massive **Transporter Bridge** (1911) is a monument to Tees-side engineering (also responsible for Sydney Harbour Bridge). New light industries have partly replaced the declining traditional ones, and the town, known for its well-kept parks, has a totally redeveloped centre with a large shopping precinct.

▶ **Dorman Museum and Art Gallery**, Linthorpe Road, has collections of local and regional history and pottery, and of contemporary British art (*Mon.-Fri., 10-6, Sat., 10-5, cl. Sun.*).

Nearby

▶ At Coulby Newham (*3m S*), **Newham Grange Leisure Farm**, a lively working farm including pets' corners and an agricultural museum; period shops (*Apr.-Oct.: 10-6 daily*). ▶ **Marton** (*2m SE*): **Captain Cook Birthplace Museum**★, Stewart Park, devoted to the life of the world explorer born here in 1728 (*10-6 or dusk in winter, Mon.-Sat.; cl. Sun.*). ▶ Ormesby (*3m SE*): **Ormesby Hall**★, mid-18thC house containing lovely plasterwork and with a small garden, set in an extensive private estate (*Apr.-Oct.: 2-6, Wed., Sat., Sun., Bank Hols*). ▶ **Kirkleatham**★ (*4m E*): outstanding among the village's interesting buildings is the **Sir William Turner Hospital** (1742; *daily till dusk*). ▶ Guisborough★ (*5m E*), attractive market town at the foot of the Cleveland Hills which developed around a magnificent 12thC **priory**, of which the massive gatehouse and E wall remain (*mid-Mar.-mid-Oct.: Mon.-Sat., 9.30-6.30, Sun., 2-6.30; mid-Oct.-mid-Mar.: Mon.-Sat., 9.30-4, Sun., 2-4*).   □

Practical information

ℹ 125 Albert Road, ☎ (0642) 245432 ext. 3580; 243425. ✈ Tees-side (13m SW), ☎ Dinsdale (0325) 332811. ➡ ☎ (0642) 225535.
Car rental: *Europcar*, Dutton Forshaw North East, Longlands roundabout (rail/drive), ☎ (0642) 244744.

Hotels:
★★★★ *Ladbroke Dragonara*, Fry Street, TS1 1JH, ☎ (0642) 248133, Tx 58266, AC AM BA DI, 144 rm. ℗ ♿ £53. Rest. ♦ ♪ ♿ Game dishes. £11.
★★★ *Baltimore*, 250 Marton Road, TS4 2EZ, ☎ (0642)

224111, Tx 58517, AC AM BA DI, 31 rm. P ✺ £40. Rest.
♦ ♪ £7.

Restaurant:
♦ *East Ocean Seafood Restaurant*, 34 Borough Road,
☎ (0642) 218655, AC AM BA DI ♪ & ✺ Cl. 25-26 Dec.
Dar Beano (Chinese fondu). £8.50.

Recommended
Golf courses: Brass Castle Lane, ☎ (0642)
311515/316430; Middlesbrough Municipal, Ladgate Lane,
☎ (0642) 315533.

MIDDLETON-IN-TEESDALE*

Barnard Castle, 10; Bishop Auckland, 20; London, 267 m
pop. 1,132 ☎ 0833   Durham A3

This peaceful little town was once the centre of a
flourishing lead-mining industry. Beautiful countryside
lies on all sides, and Middleton is a good base from
which to explore the rugged country of Upper Teesdale.

Nearby
▶ Going NW on the B6277, the road at first follows the
valley of the Tees, with woods and meadows giving way
to increasingly wild and barren moorland as it climbs up
through the Pennines into Cumbria. ▶ In 5m, past Newbiggin, a footpath opposite the High Force Hotel leads to
High Force★, an awesome 70 ft. waterfall dropping over
a basalt cliff into a wooded glen. ▶ By Langdon Beck (*a
further 3m*) a long walking track goes SW to the biggest
waterfall in England, **Cauldron Snout★**, a 200 yd. long
series of cascades. Nearby is the Cow Green Reservoir, the NW boundary of the **Teesdale Nature Reserve**
with many rare plants and good rambling country. ▶ From
Langdon Beck, the road W climbs steeply to cross the
bleak Pennine mountains into Cumbria and Alston (→) or
branches N over wild fell country to St. John's Chapel in
Weardale (→).   ☐

Practical information _____

MIDDLETON-IN-TEESDALE
ⓘ 1 Market Place, ☎ (0833) 40806.

Hotel:
● ★ *Teesdale*, DL12 0QG, ☎ Teesdale (0833) 40264,
BA, 14 rm. P £19.50. Rest. ♦ ♪ £10.

Nearby
EGGLESTON, 4m E on B6278

Restaurant:
♦ *Three Tuns Inn*, nr. Barnard Castle, ☎ Teesdale (0833)
50289 P ≼ ♨ ⌕ ✺ Cl. Mon., Sun. eve. Christmas. Homemade soups, pâté, cottage pie. Book. £10.

ROMALDKIRK, 4m SE on B6277

Hotel:
● ★★★ *Rose Crown* (B.W.), DL12 9EB, ☎ Tees-
dale (0833) 0213, AC AM BA DI, 15 rm. P ⌕ & ♪ ◿ £50.
Rest. ♦ & Fillet of red mullet in butter and nutmeg. £15.

MORPETH

Newcastle-upon-Tyne, 17; Alnwick, 19; London, 291 m
pop. 14,301 ☎ 0670   Northumberland B2

A market town built on a bend of the River Wansbeck,
Morpeth has the remains of a castle★ and an impressive parish church★, with some surviving old houses
in Oldgate near the market-place.

▶ **Town Hall**, Bridge Street, was designed in 1714 by John
Vanbrugh and rebuilt 1870. ▶ In Oldgate is 15thC **town
belfry**.

Nearby
▶ **Mitford** village (*2m W*), ancestral home of renowned
Mitford family, with ruins of 12thC castle and rebuilt Norman church. ▶ **Meldon Park** (*7m W*): house built by John
Dobson in 1832 with attractive gardens (*end May-end
Jun.: daily 2-5, Aug. Bank Hols.*). ▶ **Hartburn** (*8m W*), with
Norman church rebuilt in 13thC. ▶ **Cambo** (*12m W*): 18thC
'model' village where Capability Brown went to school,
associated with **Wallington House★** (*1m S*), built in 1688,
with 18thC alterations and great hall added 19thC. Set in
100 acres of woodlands and lakes, with glorious **garden** and fuchsia conservatory, the house has exceptional 18th-19thC interior, containing fine porcelain, furniture
and pictures (*grounds: all year; house: Apr.-Sep.: daily
ex. Tue., 2-6; Oct.: Wed., Sat. Sun., 2-5*). ▶ To E (*A197*)
Ashington (*3¹/₂ m*), large mining town with modernized
centre and many leisure facilities in 2m - long Wansbeck
Riverside Park. ▶ **Newbiggin-by-the-Sea** (*6m*): holiday
resort; St. Bartholomew's Church has 13thC interior
and 14thC spire. ▶ **Bedlington** (*4m SE*), a mining village,
with attractive old buildings in main street, famous for
its annual miners' gala and breed of curly-haired terriers.
▶ **Blyth** (*9m SE*), former coal and ship-building port with
seaside leisure facilities. The old town centre is in
Northumberland Street, North Blyth.   ☐

Practical information _____

MORPETH
ⓘ The Chantry, Bridge Street, ☎ (0670) 511323.
▭▭ ☎ Newcastle-upon-Tyne (091) 232 6262.

Restaurant:
● ♦ *La Brasserie*, 59 Bridge Street, ☎ (0670) 56200, AC
AM BA DI P ≼ ✺ Cl. Bank Hols., Mon., Sun. eve. Chicken
tempura with walnut sauce. £13.

⚓ at Ashington, *Wansbeck Riverside*, Green Lane (44 pl),
☎ (0670) 812323.

Recommended
Cycle rental: *Glenbar Hire Ltd*, Coopies Lane, ☎ (0670)
55076, Please give advanced notice.
Golf course: The Common, ☎ (0670) 519980.
Guesthouse: *Aaron House*, 73 Newgate Street, ☎ (0670)
55837, on the banks of the river Wansbeck. £22 double
B. & B.
♥ *Spindles* of Harbottle, Lightpipe Hall, Harbottle,
☎ (0669) 50243, wood-turned items, spinning wheels and
looms; *Chantry Silver*, The Chantry, Chantry Place, (0670)
☎ 58584, Silver jewelry of all descriptions and precious stones.

Nearby
LONGHORSLEY, 6m N on A697

Hotel:
● ★★★★ *Linden Hall* (Prestige), NE65 8XF, ☎ Norpeth
(0670) 56611 Tx 538224, AC AM BA DI, 45 rm. P ♨ &
& ♪° ◿ Georgian country house set in extensive grounds.
£62.50. Rest. ♦ ♪ & Smoked stuffed salmon. £18.50.

NEWCASTLE-UPON-TYNE***

Durham, 19; Darlington, 36; London, 274 m
pop. 199,064 ☎ 0632/091   Tyne & Wear B2

The chief city of Northumbria, Newcastle is the largest industrial, commercial and shopping centre of
the north-east. It lies on the N bank of the Tyne about
9m from the river mouth, an important defensive position against the Scots in the Middle Ages, when the
'new' castle was built. The remains of the castle are
found among other historic buildings in the old part of
the city by the riverside, close to the cathedral
and the Tyne, Swing and High-Level bridges, three
of Newcastle's several impressive bridges. Thriving
industries based on coal, ship-building and railways
transformed the town in the 19thC, when the digni-

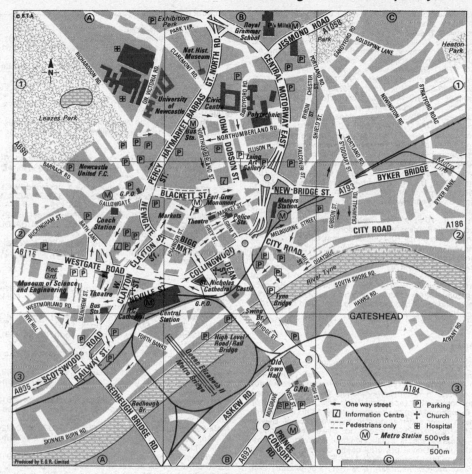

NEWCASTLE-ON-TYNE

fied stone buildings and streets of a new city centre, one of the best-planned in England, were laid out by Newcastle architect and builders John Dobson, Richard Grainger and John Clayton. Complex modern developments, including a huge new shopping precinct have again changed the city's character. Open spaces, including the Town Moor and the large park of Jesmond Dene, lie on the city's outskirts.

▶ To S, near riverside: remains of 12thC **castle★** with splendid **keep** built by Henry II (*Apr.-Sep.: Mon.-Fri., Sun., 10-5; Oct.-Mar.: Mon.-Fri, Sun., 10-4; cl. Sat.*); **Black Gate**, remarkable barbican-gatehouse added 1247, housing the world's only **bagpipe museum** (*Mon.-Fri., Sun. 10-5; cl. Sat.*); and beautiful Norman **chapel** (*Mon., 2-4, Tue.-Sat., 10-4.30, 3.30 Oct.-Mar.*). ▶ Nearby is **St. Nicholas Cathedral**, St. Nicholas Street, rebuilt in mid-14thC and extensively restored in 19thC; glorious 194 ft. lantern spire (c. 1450) tops the W tower and Early English interior includes a tiny barrel-vaulted crypt (14thC); monuments and furnishings. ▶ Notable old buildings close to steep steps and winding narrow lanes by Quayside; **Guildhall** (1658, with additions by Dobson 1823), inside which is great

hall with hammer-beam roof and Merchant Adventurers' Court with fine chimneypiece; **Moot Hall** (1810); handsome 16th-17thC houses in **Sandhill; Customs House** (1776, restored in 19thC); **Trinity House** (1721); and **All Saints Church**, a graceful Georgian building on a hilltop▶ Further E is **Keelmen's Hospital**, built by the coal-ferriers themselves in 1701. Also, standing among remnants of old town walls, medieval **Sallyport** or **Wall Knot Tower** and **Corner Tower**. Nearby, on City Road, is **John G. Joicey Museum** of local history, housed in beautifully restored 17thC Holy Jesus Hospital (*Mon.-Fri., 10-5.30, Sat., 10-4.30; cl. Sun.*).▶ W, near Dobson's splendid **Central Station** (1850), are the **Roman Catholic Cathedral** designed by Pugin in 1844 with slender spire added 1872; **St. John's Church** (14th-15thC) with fine 17thC pulpit; **Assembly Rooms** of c. 1775 in splendid style of Nash; remains of **Blackfriars monastery** founded 1239, including refectory and cloister; **St. Andrew's Church** (12thC); and stretching S from this churchyard, fragments of the old town walls.▶ In town centre: vast modern **Swan House** roundabout incorporating replica of old **Royal Arcade** shopping area leading to intricate network of traffic flows and pedestrian-only areas. Elegant Victorian build-

ings, including magnificent covered **Grainger's Markets**, line many streets, of which the finest is curving **Grey Street** with **Theatre Royal**, and at top the **Grey Monument** (1838), 135 ft. high Doric column with statue of Prime Minister Earl Grey. ► Off New Bridge Street is **Laing Art Gallery★** with collections of British watercolours and oils from 17thC (including works of John Martin), ceramics, silver, textiles and glass (*Mon.-Fri., 10-5.30, Sat., 10-4.30, Sun., 2.30-5.30; Bank Hols, 10-5.30*). Affiliated to it is **Plummer Tower**, 18thC hall converted from fragment of 13thC wall (*occasionally open*). ► To W of centre is **Museum of Science and Engineering**, West Blandford Street (*Mon.-Fri., 10-5.30, Sat., 10-4.30; cl. Sun.*). ► To N of centre: Dobson's **St. Thomas's Church** (1825) on a large green opposite impressive **Civic Centre** (1960-68), designed by George Kenyon on semi-monastic plan, with 250 ft. central tower, arcaded cloister and large pool. To E and W extend modern buldings of Polytechnic and University. ► In University Quadrangle is **Museum of Antiquities★**, Dept. of Archaeology, with prehistoric, Roman, Anglo-Saxon and medieval antiquities, mainly from Northumberland and including Roman reconstructions (*Mon.-Fri., 10-5*). ► Also **Greek Museum**, Dept. of Classics, Percy Building, with collections of Greek and Etruscan art (*Mon.-Fri., 10-4.30*); ► **Hatton Gallery**, Dept. of Fine Art, with permanent collection of paintings and frequent loan exhibitions (*Mon.-Fri., 10-5, Sat., 10-4 during term*). ► In University's Dept. of Mining Engineering, Queen Victoria Road, is **museum** devoted to history of mining (*Mon.-Fri., 9-5*). ► Beyond University is **Hancock Museum**, Barras Bridge, containing natural history displays and an ethnographical section (*Mon.-Sat., 10-5, Sun., (Easter-Sep.), 2-5*).

Nearby

► Through heavily industrialized suburbs of Elswick and Scotswood to **Newburn** (*6m W*), with 13thC church and, off A69, **Wylam-on-Tyne** (*9m*), where river park walk leads to cottage in which railway pioneer George Stephenson was born in 1781 (*Apr.-Oct.: Wed., Thur., Sat., Sun., 2-5*). ► **Ovingham** (*11m*) has restored mainly 13thC church with Saxon tower and memorial to engraver Thomas Bewick (1753-1828); road continues to Bywell (→Corbridge). ► Across Tyne is small industrial town of **Prudhoe**, with ruins of once powerful **castle** on spur overlooking the river (*mid-Mar.-mid-Oct.: Mon.-Sat., 9.30-6.30, Sun., 2-6.30; mid-Oct.-mid-Mar.: Mon.-Sat., 9.30-4, Sun., 2-4*). ► W on A69 to Hadrian's Wall (→). ► Crossing Town Moor and passing Gosforth Park to E: **Ponteland** (*7¹/₂m NW on A696*), now residential village with Church of St. Mary dating to 12thC, retaining Norman tower; and '**Blackbird**', 17thC manor house incorporating 14thC pele tower. ► **Belsay** (*14m NW*): reproduction of 1830s Italian village with ruins of **castle** (14thC pele tower) in grounds of Belsay Hall, built in 1810 (*private*). ► **Bolam Lake** (*3m N*), created by John Dobson, and **Country Park**; Bolam village (*4m N*) has church mainly dating to 12thC with well-preserved Saxon tower. ► E, through industrial and residential Wallsend: ► **North Shields**, fishing town retaining old fish quay and some Georgian and Victorian houses among modern developments. ► **Tynemouth**, Newcastle's coastal resort with fine stretch of sandy beach and, on the rocky headland, ruins of 11thC Benedictine **priory** and **castle**; 14thC gatehouse, parts of presbytery and 15thC chantry chapel with splendid roof bosses remain (*mid-Mar.-mid-Oct.: Mon.-Sat., 9.30-6.30, Sun., 2-6.30; mid-Oct.-mid-Mar.: Mon.-Sat., 9.30-4, Sun., 2-4*)► **Whitley Bay** (*3m N*), popular NE resort with extensive beaches, amusement parks and holiday facilities. ► Further up coast is harbour of **Seaton Sluice**, with picturesque cottages, and 1m inland, **Seaton Delaval Hall★**; a masterpiece by John Vanbrugh built 1720-29. Parts open to public are: inhabited W wing: fine furniture, portraits and ceramics; central block; stables in E wing and gardens where tiny 14thC church retains original Norman chancel and includes memorials to Delaval family (*May-Sep.: Wed., Sun., Bank Hols, 2-6*).   □

Practical information _____

NEWCASTLE-UPON-TYNE
ⓘ Central Library, Princess Square, ☎ (091)261 0691; Blackfriars Tourist Centre, Monk Street, ☎ (091) 261 5367.
✈ (5m NW off A696), ☎ (091) 2860966; Newcastle Airport, Woolsington, ☎ (091) 271 1929.
▭ Central, ☎ (091) 232 6262.
▭ (A2); ☎ (091) 261 6177.
⚓ Norway Line, ☎ (091) 585555; DFDS Seaways, ☎ (091) 2575655.
Car rental: *Europcar*, 90 Westmorland Road and Newcastle Airport, ☎ (091) 2865070; rail/drive, ☎ (091) 610772.

Hotels:
★★★ *Hospitality Inn* (M.C.), Osborne Road, Jesmond (B-C1 off map), NE2 2AT , ☎ (091) 281 4961, Tx 53636, AC AM BA DI, 68 rm. ℙ ◄ £53. Rest. ♦ ♪ ♭ £9.
★★★ *Imperial* (Swallow), Jesmond Road, Jesmond (B-C1 off map), NE2 1PR, ☎ (091) 281 5511, Tx 537972, AC AM BA DI, 13 rm. ℙ ♭ ▭ £54. Rest. ♦ ♪ ♭ £10.
★★★ *Newcastle Crest* (Crest), New Bridge Street (B1-2), NE1 8BS, ☎ (091) 232 6191, Tx 53467, AC AM BA DI, 180 rm. ℙ ◄ ◄ ♭ £66.50. Rest. ♦ ♪ ♭ £12.50.
★★★ *Royal Station* (Crest), Neville Street (A2), NE99 1DW, ☎ Tyneside (091) 232 0781, Tx 53681, AC AM BA DI, 131 rm. ℙ ♭ £60. Rest. ♦ ♪ £10.25.

Restaurants:
● ♦ *Fisherman's Lodge*, Jesmond Dene, ☎ Tyneside (091) 2813281, AC AM BA DI ℙ ◄ ▨ ◄ ♪ ⚘ Cl. Bank Hols., Sat. lunch, Sun. Seafood. Book. £15.50.
● ♦ *Rupali*, 6 Bigg Market (B2), ☎ (0632) 328629, AC AM BA DI ♪ ⚘ Cl. Sun. lunch. Book. £6.
● ♦ *Sachins*, Old Hawthorn Inn, Forth Banks (A3), ☎ (0632) 619035, AC AM BA DI ℙ ◄ ♪ ⚘ Cl. 25-26 Dec., Easter, lunch Bank Hols., Sun. Punjabi cuisine, chicken jalfrezi. Book. £11.
♦ *Jade Garden*, 53, Stowell Street (A2), ☎ (091) 2615889, AC AM BA DI ℙ ♪ ⚘ Cl. Christmas, 1 Jan. Popular Cantonese restaurant. Book. £9.50.
♦ *Le Roussillon*, 52-54 St. Andrews Street (A2), ☎ (091) 2611341, AC AM BA DI ℙ ♪ ⚘ Cl. Sun., Sat. lunch. Lobster terrine. Book. £17.
♦ *Michelangelo*, 25 King Street, Quayside (B2), ☎ (0632) 614415, AC AM BA DI ℙ ♪ ♭ ⚘ Cl. Bank Hols., Sun. Book. £11.50.
♦ *Ristorante Roma*, 22 Collingwood Street (B2), ☎ (091) 2320612, AC AM BA ◄ ♪ ♭ ⚘ Cl. Sun. lunch. Book. £12.
♦ *The Super Natural*, 2 Princess Square (B2), ☎ (0632) 612730 ℙ ♭ Cl. Sun., Bank Hols. Vegetarian dishes, Mexican bean pot. £1.50.

Recommended
Cycle rental: *Glenbar Hire Ltd*, 217 Jesmond Road, Jesmond, ☎ (0632) 815376.
Golf courses: Hobson, Burnopfield, ☎ (0207) 70941; Arcot Hall, Dudley, Cramlington, ☎ (091) 2362794.
Riding school: *Lincoln Riding Centre*, High Pit Farm, East Cramlington, ☎ (0632) 736171, riding for the disabled.

Nearby

HIGH GOSFORTH PARK, 4 1/2m N off A6125

Hotel:
● ★★★★ *Gosforth Park* (Thistle), NE3 5HN, ☎ (091 236) 4111, Tx 53655, AC AM BA DI, 178 rm. ℙ ▨ ◄ ♭ ▭ ♪ £83. Rest. ♦ ♪ ♭ £16.
▲▲*Newcastle Race course* (90 pl) ☎ (091 236) 3258.

Recommended
Golf course: Northumberland, ☎ (091 236) 2009.

SEATON BURN, 6m N off A6125

Hotel:
★★★★ *Holiday Inn*, Great North Road, NE13 6BT, ☎ (091 236) 5432, Tx 53271, AC AM BA DI, 150 rm. ℙ ◄ ▨ ◄ ♭ ▭ £65. Rest. ♦ ♪ ♭ Kielder game casserole. £15.

WALLSEND, 2m N on A6125

Hotel:

★★★ *Newcastle Moat House*, Coast Road, NE28 9NH, ☎ (091 262) 8989, Tx 53853, AC AM BA DI, 172 rm. ℙ ⌁ ⌁ ㅎ £55. Rest. ♦ ♪ ㅎ £10.

WOOLSINGTON, 7m NW on A696

Hotel:

★★★ *Stakis Airport* (Stakis), Airport, NE13 8DJ, ☎ Ponteland (0661) 24911, Tx 537121, AC AM BA DI, 100 rm. ℙ ㅎ £50. Rest. ♦ ♪ ㅎ £9.

NORTHUMBERLAND NATIONAL PARK

A1

This huge area of remote hills and moorland stretches for 40m down the W part of Northumberland, from the NE slopes of the Cheviot Hills to Hadrian's Wall, taking in the Simonside Hills by Rothbury on the E. Adjoining it to the SW is the Border Forest Park, including Kielder Forest (→), making a total of 574 sq. m of country for public enjoyment. No roads run the length of the park, which falls naturally into five separate regions that are accessible from towns and villages on the outskirts (→Wooler, Rothbury, Otterburn in Redesdale and Corbridge, Hexham and Haltwhistle). Each region has a distinctive beautiful landscape and all offer glorious walks, including sections of the Pennine Way (→), with scenic drives and leisure facilities in the central areas.

▶ To the N, reached from Wooler (→), Cornhill-on-Tweed (→Berwick) or Rothbury (→), are the bare, grass-covered **Cheviot Hills**, their ridge forming the Scottish/Northumbrian border. They make splendid rambling country and are the home of wild goats, hares, foxes and many species of birds, particularly curlews; on the lower slopes graze Cheviot, Blackface and cross-breed sheep. Several river valleys cut into the hills, including the particularly beautiful **Harthorpe** and **Breamish** valleys, the latter with an Information Centre at **Ingram**.▶ The River Coquet Valley runs E into Rothbury (→), where the nearby **Coquetdale** and heathery **Simonside Hills** (adjoining Harwood Forest) form a second region.▶ Further SW are the upper valleys of the **River Rede** (easily reached from Otterburn in Redesdale→) and the **North Tyne**, past Bellingham (→Hexham). Beyond them **Kielder Forest** and **Wark Forest** stretch across to the Cumbrian border.▶ The fifth and southernmost region includes the particularly good stretch of **Hadrian's Wall** (→) between Gilsland and Chollerford, conveniently reached from Hexham (→).   □

PENNINE WAY

A3

Almost a quarter of this 250m long footpath from Edale in Derbyshire to Kirk Yetholm over the Scottish border falls within Northumbria. It follows old drovers' roads and miners' tracks, bridgeways and a few Roman roads through the wild and bleak mountain chains of the Pennines and Cheviot Hills, occasionally twisting E or W into more gentle wooded and river country. To cover its full length and tackle the rugged N reaches needs experience in walking and climbing, but short walks and strolls giving wonderful views are possible along many sections of the way, particularly around Hadrian's Wall and the S parts.

▶ In Durham the path moves up the beautiful **Tees Valley** by Middleton-in-Teesdale (→) and **High Force** and **Cauldron Snout** waterfalls, before swinging W through the **Lune Forest** into Cumbria, past **Cross Fell** (2,930 ft.), the highest peak in the Pennines, and down to Alston. From

here the path moves up the secluded **South Tyne Valley** (→Haltwhistle), crossing into Northumberland and taking in 8m of dramatic scenery along **Hadrian's Wall** E of Greenhead, with an Information Centre at **Once Brewed**. From here the path weaves in and out of the Border Forest and National Parks to reach **Bellingham** in North Tynedale in 10m (→Hexham). Open moorland surrounds most of the 18m section to **Byrness**, with an Information Centre, in Redesdale (→). The last and toughest 28m section climbs along the Scottish border ridge of the **Cheviots** (1,300-2,500 ft.), through spectacular and largely unsignposted country, before dropping down to Kirk Yetholm.   □

PETERLEE

Middlesbrough, 16; Sunderland, 11; London, 263 m
pop. 22,765 ☎ 0783   Durham B2

A new town founded in 1950 and named after a much respected local pit worker who rose to become President of the Miners' Federation. Peterlee has an attractive shopping centre, three churches of distinguished modern architecture and plenty of green spaces among its sprawling industrial and housing estates.

▶ On the S outskirts is **Castle Eden Dene**, a 4m stretch of woodland along a ravine created at the end of the Ice Age, which is a haven for wildlife, particularly birds and butterflies, and kept by the town corporation as a nature reserve (*not always open to the public*).   □

Practical information _____

ℹ 20 Upper Chare, ☎ (0783) 586 4450.

Hotel:

★★★ *Norseman*, Bede Way, SR8 1BU, ☎ Sunderland (0783) 862161, AC AM BA DI, 26 rm. ℙ ㅎ £32. Rest. ♦ Lobster. £7.50.

REDCAR

Middlesbrough, 10; Whitley, 26; London, 258 m
pop. 84,931 ☎ 0642   Cleveland B3

A popular seaside resort and the playground for its large Tees-side neighbour Middlesbrough (→), Redcar has a long stretch of sandy beach from which two outcrops of rock, Saltscar and Redcar, run out to sea.

▶ The town's leisure attractions include a race course as well as three large parks and the usual vacation entertainments. On the long promenade are a huge indoor amusement park, the Coatham Amusement Park, and the maritime **Zetland Museum** (*Mon.-Sat., 10-5.30; cl. Sun.*), named after its main exhibit, the world's oldest lifeboat. Built in 1800, for nearly 90 years it helped rescue sailors shipwrecked in the treacherous shallows around the Tees estuary.

Nearby

▶ **Saltburn-by-the-Sea** (3½ m S), a popular resort built in Victorian times on the cliffs that rise here in contrast to the flat coastline to the N; its Italian gardens were laid out in the 1860s. ▶ Continuing S, the road passes **Boulby Head**, where the cliffs, rich in fossils, reach the highest point (679 ft.) on the E coast, and crosses the Yorkshire boundary at Staithes (→).   □

Practical information _____

REDCAR
ℹ Regent Cinema Building, Newcomen Terrace, ☎ (0642) 471921.
🚂 British Steel, Central, East, ☎ Middlesbrough (0642) 225 535.

Hotel:
★★ *Newbigging*, Queen Street, TS10 1BE, ☎ Cleveland (0642) 482059, AM DI BA DI, 25 rm. P £28.

Inn or Pub:
Yorkshire Coble, West Dyke Road, ☎ (0642) 482071.

Recommended
Golf course: Cleveland, Coatham (SW on A174), ☎ (0642) 483693.

Nearby

GUISBOROUGH, 10m S on A171

Hotel:
★ *Fox*, 10 Bow Street, TS14 6BP, ☎ (0287) 32958, AC AM, 7 rm. P £25. Rest. ♦ ↕ & Cl. Christmas. £6.50.

Inn or Pub:
Anchor Inn, Belmangate, ☎ (0287) 32715.

LOFTUS, 16m

Hotel:
★★ *Grinkle Park*, Grinkle, Easington, TS13 4UB, ☎ Guisborough (0287) 40515, AC BA, 20 rm. P ≼ ₩ ⟐ ℘ ↲ ⟐ Victorian mansion surrounded by formal gardens and parkland £65. Rest. ♦ Local game from the estate. £12.

REDESDALE

The River Rede stretching from Otterburn to the Cheviot Hills runs through the wild fell country and thick woods of Northumberland National Park and Redesdale Forest, a scenic area rich in bird and animal life.

▶ **Otterburn**★, attractive village and holiday area with good walks and fishing; by river is disused early 19thC **mill** where Otterburn tweeds were produced. The **Percy Cross** (³/₄m N) commemorates Battle of Otterburn in 1388 when the Scots defeated the Northumbrian Percies. ▶ Along river valley: **Elishaw** (3m N) is start of National Park area, with moors stretching E and W. **Rochester** (6m N), old hamlet (to r.) is built from ruins of 1st-3rdC Roman fort of **Bremenium**. ▶ From **Redesdale Camp** (7m) line of Roman Dere Street goes NW, past remains of Roman camps and on to earthworks at **Chew Green** Roman camp, with superb views of Cheviots and Coquet Valley; branch road left returns to A68 above Byrness (area part of army artillery range and access limited). ▶ **Byrness** (12m), small foresters' village with 18thC church and Information Centre for **Redesdale Forest**★; walks, forest drives, camping and picnic sites; E starting point for nature drive (toll) to Kielder Forest (→). ▶ A68 continues N past Castcleugh Reservoir and climbs steeply through Cheviots to Scottish border at **Carter Bar** (1,371 ft.), with panoramic view to Firth of Forth.

Practical information

Nearby

BYRNESS, 10 m NW on A68

Hotel:
★ *Byrness,* Otterburn, ☎ Otterburn (0830) 20231, 6 rm P ≼ ₩ ⟐ £23. Rest. ♦ £7.25.

KNOWESGATE, 10m SE on A696

Hotel:
★★ *Knowesgate* (Inter), Kirkwhelpington, NE19 2SH, ☎ Otterburn (0830) 40261, AC AM BA DI, 16 rm. P ≼ ₩ & ⟐ £48. Rest. ♦ ↕ £12.

OTTERBURN, 23m N of Hexham on A696

Hotels:
★★ *Percy Arms* (Consort), NE 19 1NR, ☎ (0830) 20261, AC AM BA DI, 30 rm. P ≼ ₩ ⟐ & ⟐ £50. Rest. ♦ & Cl. 26 Dec.-2 Jan. Northumberland lamb, local salmon. £12.
★ *Otterburn Hall*, NE19 1HE, ☎ (0830) 20663, BA AC,

48 rm. P ≼ ₩ ⟐ & ⋇ ℘ £40. Rest. ♦ & Cl. Jan. Local salmon, trout and venison. £7.
★ *Otterburn Tower*, NE19 1NP, ☎ (0830) 20620, AC AM BA DI, 15 rm. P ≼ ₩ ⟐ Jacobean border castle. £37.50. Rest. ♦ ↕ Traditional country cooking, game £9.50.

ROCHESTER, 5m NW on A68

Hotel:
★ *Redesdale Arms*, NE19 1TA, ☎ Otterburn (0830) 20668, AC AM, 11 rm. P ≼ ⟐ £25. Rest. ↕ Home made steak and kidney pie. £6.

ROTHBURY*

Alnwick, 12; Morpeth, 15; London, 306 m
pop. 1,694 ☎ 0669   Northumberland A1

This picturesque old market town on the sloping N bank of the River Coquet is surrounded by beautiful countryside. Rothbury Forest runs to its N and S, with the Simonside Hills and Coquetdale close by and the Cheviot Hills and National Park within easy reach.

▶ Near the busy centre is **All Saints' Church** (13thC, restored) with a font incorporating a fine Saxon cross (c. 800).

Nearby

▶ **Cragside**★ (¹/₂ m E, B6341): extraordinary 19thC mansion, the first house in the world to be lit by electricity, built by Norman Shaw for Lord Armstrong; interior has original furniture and Pre-Raphaelite paintings; extensive **park** is famed for its trees, rhododendrons and lakes (park: Apr.-Sep.: daily, 10.30-6; Oct.: daily, 10.30-5; Nov.-Mar.: Sat. Sun., 10.30-4; house: Apr.-Sep.: daily ex. Mon. but open Bank Hols., 2-6; Oct.: Wed., Sat. Sun., 2-5). ▶ **Brinkburn Priory** (5m E, B6344): skillfully restored 12th-13thC Augustinian abbey in peaceful setting. ▶ To S: **Simonside Hills**, adjoining Harwood Forest to SW, beautiful heather-clad hillsides offering good walks and climbing, with splendid views from crests of **Simonside** (1,408 ft.), **Ravensheugh** (1,384 ft.) and highest peak of **Tosson Hill** (1,444 ft.); prehistoric sites at **Tosson Burgh** (748 ft.) and **Lordenshaw** (879 ft.); nature trails and forest walks to W and S. ▶ To W and N along beautiful **Coquet River Valley**★. ▶ **Holystone** (7m), with Lady's Well, associated with St. Ninian (daily, till dusk), and nearby the **Five Kings** standing stones. ▶ **Harbottle** (9m): attractive village with remains of 12thC castle; paths lead up to Harbottle Hills on W. ▶ **Alwinton** (10¹/₂ m), with distinctive church built on a slope; many traces of Roman and prehistoric camps in area. ▶ To W is **Kidland Forest** and Upper Coquetdale leading over to **Chew Green Roman camp** (→Redesdale); area is restricted because of Redesdale Artillery Range. ▶ To N lie the rounded and grass-covered **Cheviot Hills**, beautiful walking country with fine views. Road continues through Netherton and back to Rothbury or on to join A697 N to Wooler (→).   □

Practical information

ROTHBURY

Hotels:
★★ *Coquet Vale*, Station Road, NE65 7QZ, ☎ (0669) 20305, AC BA, 9 rm. P £34. Rest. ♦ ↕ & Northumberland roast beef. £9.
★ *Queens Head*, Townfoot, NE65 7SR, ☎ (0669) 20470, AC AM BA DI, 6 rm. P £22. Rest. ♦ £6.

Restaurant:
♦ *Angler's Arms*, Weldon Bridge, ☎ (066 570) 655, AM BA P £11.

Recommended
Golf course: race course, ☎ (0669) 20718.

> Looking for a locality? Consult the index at the back of the book.

Nearby

LONGFRAMLINGTON, 5m E

Restaurant:
♦ ***Besom Barn***, ☎ (066 570) 627, AC AM BA DI Ⓟ ⚘ ♨ ⛱ ♪ ♿ ⛔ Cl. Sun. eve., 1 Jan., Christmas, Mon. lunch, 4 rm. Griddled boned pork loin in a calvados and cream sauce. Book. £14.

POWBURN, 2m N on A697

Hotel:
● ★★ ***Breamish House***, NE66 4LL, ☎ (066 578) 266, 10 rm. Ⓟ ⚘ ♨ ⛱ ⛔ No children under 12 years. £42.50. Rest. ● ♦ ♿ Cl. Jan. Homemade soups and sweets. £14.

SOUTH SHIELDS

Sunderland, 8; Newcastle-upon-Tyne, 10; London, 273 m
pop. 86,488 ☎ 0632/91 Tyne & Wear B2

The shipbuilding port and seaside resort of South Shields is built around the S headland of the Tyne estuary, with dockyards along its W river front and a long stretch of smooth beach on its E seafront. In Roman times it was an important supply base and guarded the entrance to the Tyne.

▶ On the Lawe, the N point of the heavily built-up town, is the excavated 3rdC **Arbeia Roman fort**, Baring Street; its museum has finds from the large site including the Regina tombstone showing a woman with her sewing and jewel box (*Easter-Sep.: Mon.-Fri., 10-5.30, Sat., 10-4, Sun., 2-5; Oct.-Apr.: Mon.-Thur., 10-4, Fri., 10-3, Sat., 10-12, cl.Sun.*). ▶ **Museum and art gallery**, Ocean Road, is devoted to local history (*Mon.-Fri., 10-5.30, Sat., 10-4.30, Sun., 2-5*).

Nearby

▶ **Jarrow** (*3½ m W*): this industrial town, linked by the Tyne tunnel to the N side of the river, was made famous in the 1930s by the hunger march of its unemployed shipyard workers to Parliament (→). Hidden away, E of the rebuilt modern centre, is **St. Paul's Church★**, with an 11thC tower and a chancel dating to 684 when the great monastery of St. Paul's was founded here. This was where the Venerable Bede lived and worked for over 50 years, producing his great *Ecclesiastical History of the English People*. The monastery's history is told in the nearby **Bede Monastery Museum**, Jarrow Hall (*Apr.-Oct.: Tue.-Sat., 10-5.30, Sun., 2.30-5.30; Nov.-Mar.: Tue.-Sat., 11-4.30, Sun., 2.30-5.30; cl. Mon. ex. Bank Hols.*). □

Practical information

SOUTH SHIELDS
ⓘ South Foreshore, ☎ (091) 4557411/4568841.
🚆 (metro), ☎ (091) 232 6262.

Hotels:
★★★ ***Sea***, Sea Road, NE33 2LD, ☎ (091) 456 6227, AC AM BA DI, 29 rm. Ⓟ ⚘ ⛳ £39.50. Rest. ♦ ♪ Cl. 26 Dec. £10.50.
★ ***New Crown***, Mowbray Road, NE33 3NG, ☎ (091) 455 34722, AC AM BA DI, 11 rm. Ⓟ ⚘ ⛱ £34. Rest. ♦ ♪ Trout and crab. £7.

Inn or Pub:
Ship Royal, 1 Ocean Road, ☎ (0632) 560782.

Recommended
Golf course: Hillcrest, Cleadon Hills, ☎ (0632) 568942; Whitburn Golf Club, Lizard Lane, ☎ (091) 329 2144.

Nearby

TYNEMOUTH, via Tyne Tunnel

Hotel:
★★ ***Park***, Grand Parade, NE30 4JQ, ☎ (091) 257 1406, AC AM BA DI, 27 rm. Ⓟ ⚘ ⛱ £36. Rest. ♦ ♪ Cl. 25 Dec.-1 Jan. Dover sole and estouffade. £9.50.

Recommended
♥ *Holly House Gallery*, 14 Front Street, ☎ (0632) 592753.

WHITLEY BAY, 2m N on A193
ⓘ Central Promenade, ☎ (091) 252 4494

Hotel:
★ ***Cavendish***, 52 Esplanade, NE26 2AS, ☎ (091) 253 3010, AC AM BA, 11 rm. Ⓟ ♿ £25. Rest. ♦ ♪ ♿ Cl. Sun. dinner. Fresh lobster. £8.

Recommended
Golf course: Claremont Road, ☎ (091) 2520180.

STOCKTON-ON-TEES

Middlesbrough, 4; Darlington, 13; London, 249 m
pop. 154,585 ☎ 0642 Cleveland B3

After the opening in 1825 of the Stockton-Darlington railway line, carrying the world's first passenger train, the old port of Stockton expanded rapidly, and the town's buildings, including numerous churches, are mainly 18th and 19thC, interspersed with modern developments and plentiful open spaces. **Norton**, the northern and oldest part of the town, retains a prosperous village atmosphere.

▶ The open-air market, established in 1310, is still held in the remarkably wide High Street (*Wed., Sat.*). ▶ To the S, on the road to the attractive historic market town of **Yarm**, is **Preston Hall**, a social history museum with a reconstructed period street in working order; large park includes zoo and recreational areas (*Mon.-Sat., 10-5.30, Sun., 2-5.30*). □

Practical information

STOCKTON-ON-TEES
✈ Tees-side (7m SW off A67), ☎ Dinsdale (0325) 332811.
🚆 ☎ Middlesbrough (0642) 225535.
Car rental: *Avis*, John Street, ☎ (0642) 672521.

Hotels:
★★★ ***Swallow*** (Swallow), 10 John Walker Square, High Street, TS18 1AQ, ☎ (0642) 679721, Tx 587895, AC AM BA DI, 126 rm. Ⓟ ♿ £80. Rest. ♦ ♪ £10.50.
★ ***Stonyroyd***, 187 Oxbridge Lane, TS18 4JB, ☎ (0642) 607734, 13 rm. Ⓟ ♨ ⛱ £30. Rest. ♦ ♪ ♿ £8.

Inn or Pub:
Green Dragon, Finkle Street, ☎ (0642) 672798.

Nearby

BILLINGHAM, 3m N off A19

Hotel:
★★ ***Billingham Arms***, Town Square, TS23 2HD, ☎ (0642) 553661, Tx 587746, AC AM BA DI, 63 rm. Ⓟ ♿ ⛳ £49. Rest. ♦ ♿ Cl. Sat. lunch. Cl. 24-25 Dec. £11.

Recommended
Golf course: Sandy Lane, ☎ (0642) 554494.

EAGLESCLIFFE, 1m on A135

Hotel:
● ★★ ***Parkmore*** (B.W.), 636 Yarm Road, TS16 0DH, ☎ (0642) 786815, AC AM BA DI, 39 rm. Ⓟ ♨ ⛱ £37. Rest. ♦ ♪ ♿ £11.

Inn or Pub:
Pot & Glass, Church Road, ☎ (0642) 780145.

Recommended
Golf course: Yarm Road (3m S on A19), ☎ (0642) 780098.

THORNABY, 1m W on A1032

Hotel:
★★★ ***Golden Eagle***, Trenchard Avenue, TS17 6BR,

☎ (0642) 766511, Tx 587565, AC AM BA DI, 57 rm. ℗ ⚡ ⚓ ⚲ £34.50. Rest. ♦ ⚲ £9.

SUNDERLAND

Newcastle, 12; Durham, 14; London, 272 m
pop. 195,064 ☎ 0783   Tyne & Wear B2

This industrial seaport at the mouth of the River Wear is the most important town in the north-east after Newcastle. It was once a big coal-exporting port and among the greatest shipbuilding centres in the world. A trace of the Saxon history of **Monkwearmouth**, the northern part of the town, is left in St. Peter's Church, now isolated among modern developments. The town has several museums and attractive sandy beaches at the suburb resorts of Roker and Seaburn, beyond the dock area to the N.

▶ The Saxon porch and the tower at the W end of **St. Peter's Church★**, Monkwearmouth, survive from the monastery founded here in 674, which became renowned for its learning. The Venerable Bede lived here for a short time as a boy before moving to the fellow-monastery at Jarrow (→). ▶ The **Museum and art gallery**, Borough Road, has collections of natural and local history, English silver, pottery and glass (for which Sunderland is noted), as well as 19th and 20thC paintings (*Mon.-Fri., 10-5.30, Sat., 10-4, Sun., 2-5*). ▶ **Grindon Close Museum**, Grindon Lane, shows local life in the early 20thC in reconstructed rooms and shop interiors (*Mon., Wed., Fri., 9-12, 1-6; Tue., 9.30-12, 1-5; Sat., 9.30-12.15, 1.15-4; Sun., (Jun.-Sep.) 2-5; cl. Thu.*). ▶ **Monkwearmouth Station**, North Bridge Street: fine example of 19thC railway architecture, now a transport museum which includes rolling stock and the restored Victorian railway booking office (*Mon.-Fri., 10-5.30; Sat., 10-4.30; Sun., 2-5; Bank Hols., 10-5.30*).

Nearby

▶ **Ryhope** (*3m S*): old **pumping station** turned into a working industrial museum (*Easter-Sep.: Sat., Sun. only*). ▶ **Hylton Castle** (*3/4m W*); a fortified tower house of c. 1400 emblazoned with heraldic shields, including one of the Washington family (*mid-Mar.-mid-Oct.: Mon.-Sat., 9.30-6.30, Sun., 2-6; mid-Oct.-mid-Mar.: Mon.-Sat., 9.30-4, Sun., 2-4*). ▶ **Washington** (*5 m W*): just before the entrance to the 'new town' is the **Waterfowl Park** bird sanctuary (*Mon.-Sat., 9.30-6; Sun., 12-6.30*) and in the old village **Washington Old Hall★**, early 17thC manor incorporating portions of the 12thC house that was the home from 1183 to 1613 of the ancestors of America's first president, George Washington. It contains period furniture, Delftware and Washington family relics (*Apr.-Oct.: daily ex. Fri., 11-5; Nov.-Feb.: Sat., Sun., 2-4; Mar.: Sat., Sun., 11-5*). ▶ Along coast road, **Marsden Bay** (*3m N*), with a man-made grotto (now a pub/restaurant) cut in the cliffside and a bird sanctuary on the offshore rock. ▶ Visible from many directions: **Penshaw Monument** (*4m E*) on Penshaw Hill, a copy of a Greek Doric temple built in 1884 in honour of Lord Lambton (→ Chester-le-Street). □

Practical information _____

SUNDERLAND
ℹ The Walkway, Crowtree Leisure Centre, Crowtree Road, ☎ (0783) 650960/650990.
🚏 ☎ Newcastle-upon-Tyne (091) 232 6262.
Car rental: *Europcar*, Minories Ltd., Newcastle Road, ☎ (0783) 492701.

Hotel:
★★★ *Seaburn* (Swallow), Queen's Parade, SR6 8DB, ☎ (0783) 292041, Tx 53168, AC AM BA DI, 82 rm. ℗ ⚲ £55. Rest. ♦ ⚲ Cl. lunch Sat. Local salmon. £8.50.

Inn or Pub:
Saltgrass, 36 Ayres Quay, Deptford, ☎ (0783) 657229.

Recommended
Cycle rental: *Glenbar Hire Ltd*, 223 Hylton Road, ☎ (0783) 40389.
Golf course: Wearside, Coxgreen, ☎ (0783) 342518.

Nearby
WASHINGTON, 2m W off A1231
Hotels:
★★★ *George Washington* (Consort), Stone Cellar Road, District 12, NE37 1PH, ☎ (091) 4172626, Tx 537143, AC AM BA DI, 70 rm. ℗ ♨ ⚓ ⚲ ▭ ⤴ £63. Rest. ♦ ♪ ⚲ Steak and kidney pie. £12.50.
★★ *Post House* (T.F.), Emerson District 5, NE37 1LB, ☎ (091) 4162264, Tx 537574, AC AM BA DI, 138 rm. ℗ ⚲ £60. Rest. ♦ ♪ ⚲ Smoked craster haddock. £10.

WEARDALE

☎ 0956   A2

The remote upper valley of the River Wear was once the hunting preserve of the bishops of Durham and important for its lead mines, the ruins of which can often be seen among the heather and streams. The rugged and varied landscape makes for scenic driving and good walking.

Nearby

▶ From the agricultural town of **Wolsingham** (*12m W of Bishop Auckland* →), where the Wear spreads its banks, follow the river valley W. ▶ **Frosterley** (*3m*), a village famous for its 'marble' - crystallized limestone - found in Durham Cathedral and many local churches. ▶ **Stanhope** (*5¹/₂ m*): attractive old market and quarrying town, main centre for walks over the moors, dotted here with burns and linns (small waterfalls); **church**, dating from the 13thC, has some medieval glass and, in its churchyard, a fossilized tree stump believed to be 250 million years old. ▶ Villages of **Eastgate** and **Westgate** (*9m, 12m*), once the borders of the Bishop of Durham's hunting park and centres for walking. ▶ **St. John's Chapel** (*14m*), a charming village with many waterfalls in the vicinity and **Chapel Fell** (2,284 ft.) rising to the S; from here, a high moorland road branches off S to Langdon Beck and Teesdale (→Middleton-in-Teesdale). ▶ Climbing further into the Pennines, the road passes, to SW, Burnhope Reservoir and beyond it, **Burnhope Seat** (2,448 ft.), the highest point in County Durham. ▶ Just before Nenthead and the Cumbrian border (*20m*) is **Killhope Wheel**, a large restored mill-wheel of the 1860s that helped power the valley's lead mines; picnic areas give splendid views of the wild Pennine landscape, which continues as the road goes on to Alston in Cumbria (→).   □

WOOLER*

Berwick-upon-Tweed, 22; Morpeth, 32; London, 323 m
pop. 1,925 ☎ 0668   Northumberland A1

This small market town on a main route to Scotland lies at the NE edge of the Cheviot Hills and the Northumberland National Park (→) and is a good base to explore the peaceful surrounding countryside, with opportunities for fishing and walking. It stands on a bluff overlooking Millfield Plain, the wide valley of the River Till, where a lake existed in prehistoric times; in the nearby hills are many traces of prehistoric settlements.

Nearby

▶ To SE: **Chillingham★** (*6m*), with a largely Norman parish church containing sumptuous 15thC tomb of Sir Ralph Grey and his wife, first owners of the now ruined castle nearby; in the extensive park roam the Chillingham **wild**

white cattle★, purest surviving descendants of the prehistoric ox, which have interbred here since the early 13thC when the park was walled in (*approachable only by guided walk*; Apr.-Oct.: Mon., Wed.-Sat., 10-12 & 2-5, Sun., 2-5; open Bank Hols.). ▶ To E of park (*1m*), **Ros Castle**, steep hill with sweeping views and traces of Iron Age camp. ▶ **Old Bewick** (*2m S*): hamlet with little 12thC church outside it and to E late prehistoric cliff fort giving fine views. ▶ To W (A697), past site of Battle of Homildon Hill (1402) where English defeated Scots' to **Akeld** and (*B6351*) along valley of River Glen to **Yeavering** (*3¹⁄₂ m*): **Yeavering Bell★** (*1m S*), Iron Age hillfort (1,182 ft.) with splendid views and beside it excavated 7thC Saxon palace of **Gefrin**. ▶ **Kirknewton** (*1m further*), substantially built border-village with church containing carving of Virgin and Magi - the latter apparently wearing kilts. Continuing W and SW, roads cross Scottish border around beautiful walking country of N Cheviots. ▶ **Doddington** (*3m N*), lying under steep slopes of Dod Law (654 ft.) with views of surrounding hills and walks across moorland; restored 13thC church has a W-facing altar. ▶ 5m NW of village, via side road to Fenton, **Roughting Linn**, waterfall in thick woods with mysterious cup-and ring-marked rocks nearby, dating from Bronze Age, and to W an Iron Age fort, **Ford** (*2m N; → Berwick*). ☐

Practical information

ⓘ Bus Station Car Park, High Street, ☎ (0668) 81602.

Hotels:
★★ *Tankerville Arms*, Cottage Road, NE71 6AD, ☎ (0668) 81581, 17 rm. Ⓟ ≶ ₩ ⌕ £37. Rest. ◆ ♪ ᵶ £9.
★ *Black Bull*, High Street, NE71 6BY, ☎ (0668) 81309, 11 rm. Ⓟ ≶ ᵶ ⌕ £28. Rest. ◆ ♪ ᵶ Home made steak pies and desserts. £4.
★ *Ryecroft*, 28 Ryecroft Way, NE71 6AB, ☎ (0668) 81459, AC BA, 11 rm. Ⓟ ≶ ⌕ £32. Rest. ◆ Cl. 1st 2wks.Nov. Game pie. £10.

Recommended
Craft workshops: at Etal, *Errol Hut Smithy Workshop*, Letham Hill, ☎ (089 082) 317, ornamental wrought-iron work and woodwork.
Guesthouse: *Loreto*, 1 Ryecroft Way, ☎ (0668) 81350, £21 double B. & B.

▶ This is a region of marked contrasts in countryside, town and city, in history and personality. One of the most densely populated areas in Britain, it includes sprawling urban and industrial developments, dominated by the two huge conurbations of Manchester and Liverpool. But countryside fringes and stretches far beyond the urban areas and is remarkably varied: bare moors, wooded hills and river valleys, rich pastureland, marshlands, sandy beaches. Amidst this landscape are found small market towns, coastal resorts, rural and industrial villages, isolated hamlets and farmsteads. Historically the region offers much of interest. There are prehistoric and Roman sites, many old half-timbered halls and churches, landscaped country parks and mansions, while the wealthy legacy of the Industrial Revolution includes not only masterpieces of engineering and civic architecture but also museums and art galleries rivalled only by London.

The county of Cheshire, in the south, became known for its salt mines and silk manufacture, and is still famed for its cheese. Much of it is pleasantly rural, with small urban and suburban developments and no big towns. The attractive capital, the Roman city of Chester close to the Dee estuary on the west, is remarkable for its medieval streets lined with 'black-and-white' buildings — characteristic of Cheshire generally. In the east, wild hilly scenery gives way to the rolling uplands of the central plain and the woods of Delamere Forest, dotted with meres or lakes full of wildlife.

In sharp contrast are the closely built-up towns of southern Lancashire and the important commercial and cultural centres of Manchester and Liverpool. Here was the birthplace of the Industrial Revolution and the cloth-manufacturing centre of the world, still evident in old cotton and wool mills, canals, railways, docks, coal mines, as well as in chapels and churches, handsome Victorian public buildings and notable art collections. Many sites have been restored, including Liverpool's splendid docklands, to make lively museums of social, engineering and industrial history.

Moors rise behind the towns and villages set in the Pennine foothills of the eastern border, while to the west is the flat expanse of the Fylde between the Mersey and Ribble estuaries and the long sandy Lancashire coastline with genteel and brash holiday resorts. Beautiful countryside extends through much of Northern Lancashire, where the historic capital of Lancaster lies, including the high moorland of the Forest of Bowland between the isolated Lune Valley in the far north and Ribblesdale by Clitheroe. ☐

North ● West

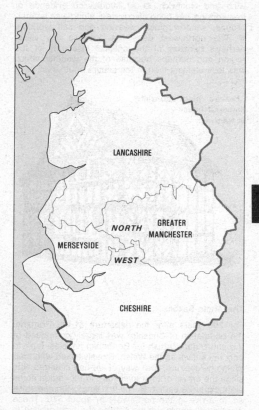

LANCASHIRE

GREATER MANCHESTER

NORTH

MERSEYSIDE

WEST

CHESHIRE

Pace-egging

Egg rolling or pace-egging takes place every Easter Monday afternoon in Preston when children roll brightly-coloured hard-boiled eggs down the grassy slopes at Avenham Park. It also happens in Scarborough and Barton-upon-Humber.

Eggs have long been given as presents at Easter time, for they were seen as symbols of new life or resurrection. In fact, the custom of giving eggs dyed in their shells was a Christian adaptation of an old pagan festival. The practice of rolling them down a hill is also said to commemorate the stone being rolled away from the tomb of Christ.

Brief regional history

The Romans

Although the Claudian invasion began in AD 43, it was not until AD 60 that Paulinus marched north-west against Anglesea, perhaps using Chester as a base. ● **Chester** remained strategically important throughout the Roman occupation, principally as a base from which to monitor events in Wales and to keep the Ordovices under control. It grew into a large garrison town, linked by road to Carlisle and York. Manchester, Ribchester and Overburgh had small garrisons and there were settlements at Wilderspool, Northwich and Nantwich. ● At Middlewich evidence of **ironworking** has been discovered, along with leather, bronze, window glass, weaving and salt working. ● The north-west does not possess any villas, perhaps because of the political insecurity of the region and perhaps because of the weather which was less clement than in the secure south-east.

Cheshire 'black-and-white' timbered house at Nantwich

The Anglo-Saxons

For 200 years after the departure of the Romans, the population of Cheshire was largely comprised of the short, **dark British** (or Brythonic) peoples, later to become known as the Welsh. Closely linked with their Welsh neighbours, their way of life had changed little since the arrival of their ancestors in the region some eight centuries earlier. ● The first **Anglo-Saxons** started to arrive in the north-west in about 570. These were small family groups settling the high ground in the Lune and Ribble areas. They had traveled from Yorkshire, Northumberland and Durham across the Pennines. In 600 a second wave came, also apparently peacefully. ● But with the rise to power of Aethelfrith of Northumbria came war. A substantial Northumbrian force defeated the Britons at the **battle of Chester** in 615, and, according to Bede, slaughtered many of the inhabitants. The area of Cheshire then came under the control of **Mercia**, which in the 8th century became the most powerful kingdom in Britain. ● The north-west was not significantly affected by the Danish invasions, but they had invaders of their own, the **Norse-Irish** from Ireland and the Isle of Man who came as settlers and became successful traders. The great stone crosses of the Wirral were made by them.

The Norman Conquest and the Middle Ages

The Norman Conquest of 1066, carried out so swiftly and efficiently, did not at once subdue all of the country. The north-east rebelled and so did Chester and Shrewsbury. In the winter of 1069-70 William marched across the Pennines, laying waste the manors in his path and destroying Macclesfield and Stockport. This was standard and effective Norman practice. ● The king gave the land between the Ribble and the Mersey to Roger of Poitou, who founded the first Benedictine abbey at **Lancaster**. He later rebelled and his confiscated lands were granted to Stephen of Blois, a grandson of the Conqueror. ● On his accession in 1189 Richard I granted the honour of Lancaster to his brother John, who became king ten years later. It subsequently passed to Edmund, Henry III's youngest son and then to Thomas, earl of Lancaster who was executed by Edward III. The fourth earl, Henry of Lancaster was rewarded in 1351 for his bravery in the Hundred Years War by having his Lancashire estate created County Palatine and himself made duke. The title later passed to John of Gaunt. ● Yet in spite of its continuing royal connections, Lancaster was not a rich county in the Middle Ages, being badly affected by the Scottish wars and the protracted Wars of the Roses. Under the Tudors the economic climate improved and this period saw the building of some of the finest half-timbered houses in the country. Cheshire became absorbed into England with the **Act of Union** with Wales, sending its first members to Parliament in 1543. ● During the Civil Wars much of Lancashire and Cheshire were Royalist, though **Manchester** and **Liverpool** supported Parliament. And it was the growth of these two towns which was to transform the face of the region.

Manchester

Manchester is one of the great regional cities of Britain, dominating the north-west. In many ways it can be seen as the first of a generation of vast **industrial** cities to be created in the western world during the past 250 years. In 1717 it was just a market town, but by 1851 its **textile industry** had made it a huge manufacturing centre with over 300,000 inhabitants. By 1911 the population had grown to 2,350,000. ● A Roman fort, a Norman barony, by the 16th century Manchester had become a flourishing market for the **cloth trade**, exporting goods via London to Europe. ● In 1620 the industrial era began with the weaving of 'fustian', a cloth with a linen warp but a cotton weft. ● From the 1770s the textile industry was to start its rapid growth. In 1762 the first wholly artificial canal had opened, linking Salford with Runcorn, instigated by the duke of Bridgewater and built by the great **James Brindley**. By 1776 it linked Manchester with the Mersey and Liverpool, so serving the requirements of the burgeoning cotton industry. ● Until the industrial revolution, the spinning wheel, invented in India and introduced into Europe in the Middle Ages, was still the fastest way to make a continuous thread or yarn. In cottage-industry days, women (or 'spinsters') were in charge of the spinning, weaving being regarded as man's work. The loom would be installed in an upstairs room, with a long window to give good light. ● In 1770 James Hargreaves' **spinning 'jenny'** was patented, which operated a number of spindles simultaneously. Sir

Richard Arkwright produced a better machine, capable of making stronger yarn. Then a third machine, **Samuel Crompton's 'mule'** vastly increased productivity, making it possible for a single operator to work more than 1,000 spindles at once. ● The spinning machines were run on water power until Watt's steam engine offered a more reliable source of power. The first **power-driven machine** loom was patented in 1785 by Edmund Cartwright. Manchester's first cotton mill was built in the early 1780s and by 1800 the city was said to be 'steam mad'. ● By 1830 there were 99 cotton-spinning mills. In that year also the Liverpool and Manchester **railway** opened. By the mid-century cotton had almost entirely replaced the manufacture of wool and linen in the Lancashire mills. ● The second half of the century was to see both growth and diversification. Manchester became less important as the source of manufacture than as the **financial centre** of the cotton trade. At the Royal Exchange, yarn and cloth for the entire trade were bought and sold. Many specialist kinds of engineering grew up — steam engines, locomotives, armaments and machine tools were all made here. And the opening of the Manchester Ship Canal in 1894 made this the fourth port in Britain. A city of wealth and vitality, with a powerful merchant class, Manchester has the first **civic university**, an internationally influential newspaper, and an outstanding symphony orchestra. ● The Local Government Act of 1972 created the metropolitan **county of Greater Manchester**, comprising Bolton, Bury, Oldham, Rochdale, Salford, Stockport, Tameside, Trafford and Wigan. ● The economic depression of the 1970s reflected the decline in the staple industries and attempts are again being made to diversify in the highly specialized weaving towns such as Burnley and Blackburn by attracting light engineering to the vacant mills.

Late 17th-century farmhouse at Heapey

Liverpool

Liverpool, although granted a charter by King John in 1207, had by 1660 a population of only 2,000. Overshadowed in medieval times by the port of Chester, the balance tilted in Liverpool's favour when the **River Dee** at Chester started to silt up. ● During the early part of the 17th century most of the shipping trade was local, and particularly with **Ireland**. The Irish trade, however, was adversely affected by Cromwell's punitive campaign, and under the Restoration navigation laws that were designed to regulate imports provided a further threat. The Irish were obliged to sell elsewhere and Liverpool to seek new markets. ● On

15 September 1666 the *Antelope* set sail for Barbados, laden with linen cloth, shoes, nails and coal. In August 1667 she returned safe and sound and filled to the brim with sugar, the first ship to make the Atlantic crossing from Liverpool and back. ● This highly profitable voyage stimulated others and ten years later six ships regularly plied between Liverpool and the West Indies. The enterprising **Allyn Smith** built a sugar refinery at Liverpool and made his fortune. Soon trade in tobacco became even more lucrative. Much of Liverpool's trade in the 18th century derived from privateering, whenever any war justified this, and many rich cargoes were brought home. ● A more reliable source of revenue was the **African trade**, and that meant slaving. In 1770 the *Liverpool Merchant* carried 220 blacks from Africa to Barbados where they were sold for over £4,000. Soon special ships were built, designed for speed so as to keep the maximum cargo alive. Ships would set off for Africa laden with clothes, shoes, spirits and household goods which were bartered for slaves on the Guinea coast. The captain would then take his new cargo to Barbados, reloading with sugar and molasses. This 'infamous triangle' became increasingly unacceptable and the abolition of the slave trade in **1807** finally ended it. ● But this did not deter the Liverpool businessmen, for in the 19th century they were catering to markets much further afield — in South America and the Far East. From five docks in the 18th century, Liverpool had ninety-eight by the mid-19th century and when the **Gladstone dock** opened in 1927 it could accommodate the largest ships in the world, including the new passenger liners. ● Now the teeming quaysides are empty and most of the warehouses have gone. Liverpool, like Manchester, is experiencing a period of readjustment.
● In **Cheshire**, too, new industries have been developed at Crewe, the old railway centre; at Sandbach, with its manufacture of chemicals and at Nantwich with light industry. **Chester**, the gateway to North Wales, preserves its ancient dignity, with its city walls, castle and cathedral standing on a site chosen by the Romans two thousand years ago.

Salt mining

Since Roman times salt had been obtained from evaporated seawater. Used as both an essential means of preserving food and of enhancing its flavour, it was a valuable commodity and therefore highly prized. In large medieval households the silver salt cellar was placed in the centre of the long table where family and guests ate their meals. Important people sat between this and the head of the table ("above" the salt); less important guests were placed on the other side of it ("below" the salt). Hence a person spoken of as being "above the salt" was regarded as distinguished.
Inland saltwater springs were discovered in Cheshire during the Middle Ages, and the salt was transported along roads which became known as "saltways". In the late 17thC, rock salt was extracted from the ground, and this mining became a major local industry, with the salt later sent by canal to Liverpool for processing. In some areas the continued mining has led to subsidence and flooding; nowadays the salt is largely extracted from natural brine.

The cotton industry

Cotton manufacture was a major British industry during the last century, and Lancashire was its centre. Prior to the 17thC, wool, linen and silk clothes were made here, but when supplies of cotton "wool" began to be imported from abroad, the new cloth made from it quickly became popular for rich people's clothing and furnishings.

At first its manufacture was carried out in the form of a "cottage" industry — always working from home, the spinners would spin the raw cotton into thread before it was taken to weavers who would turn it into lengths of cloth ready for dying and making up into garments. A number of inventions between 1760 and 1820 turned what had been hand craft into a mechanized process. This made cotton cloth more plentiful and cheaper, and contributed largely to the growth of towns such as Manchester and Preston where the spinners and weavers, operating the new machines, were now gathered in factories. In the hundred years from 1777, Preston's population grew from 6,000 to 90,000. The region was particularly suited to cotton manufacture because of the abundant water supply around the Pennine valleys — the new power looms and spinning machines were driven by water. Later, when steam gradually replaced water as a source of power, cotton mills were sited nearer the central Lancashire coalfield. By 1850, many different types of cotton fabric were being manufactured from imported raw cotton. The finished cloth was then sold on the home market and exported to America, Europe, Africa and even India which had provided the raw material. After 1913, however, British cotton cloth was rivalled by cheaper fabric from the rapidly developing Indian textile industry. Moreover, the invention of man-made fabrics on a major scale from the mid-1950s meant that there were many cheap and versatile alternatives to cotton.

 Practical information

Information: covers counties of Cheshire, Greater Manchester, Derbyshire, Merseyside and the High Peak District of Derbyshire. *North West Tourist Board*, The Last Drop Village, Bromley Cross, Bolton, Lancashire BL7 9PZ, ☎ (0204) 591511.

Weather forecast: ☎ (061246) 8091.

Ferry link: Liverpool to Isle of Man and Northern Ireland.

Youth hostelling: *YHA Regional Office*, 38 Bank Road, Matlock, Derbyshire DEA 3NF, ☎ (0629) 4666.

Festivals: 8-15 Jul.: *Shrewsbury International Music Festival*: a non-competitive festival open to any music and dance groups.

Customs and folklore: on Easter Saturday: the *Britannia Coconutters* (or Nutters) dance through Bacup, their faces blackened, wearing black jerseys, red and white kilts, white stockings and white turbans with coloured feathers on their heads.

Bridgewater Canal

Legend has it that the Duke of Bridgewater, to distract himself from an unhappy love affair, turned his attention to developing his estates. These included large coal deposits at Worsley, seven miles from Manchester. Owing to the poor roads and the difficulties of navigating the rivers in the area, it was considered an uneconomic proposition to attempt mining the coal here as it would prove costly to transport. However, the Duke decided to employ the services of engineer James Brindley to build a canal between Worsley and Manchester.

The Bridgewater Canal, opened in 1761 to great acclaim, was not the first in Britain (the Romans had constructed waterways, and the Exeter Ship Canal was built in 1544) but it signified the beginning of a new age of transport. Brindley wanted to keep the water as level as possible and accordingly included locks and an aqueduct to overcome the problem of carrying the canal up or down hill. His ideas inspired later engineers such as Telford and Rennie, other waterways were soon constructed around England, and by the 1820s the country's canals stretched some 3,000 miles.

Britain's canal age brought many changes: at a time when roads were often little better than muddy tracks, transporting bulky or fragile cargo by packhorse was slow and expensive. Now not only coal but other goods such as breakable pottery, heavy clay and flint could be sent far afield. Canals were also responsible for important developments in the appearance of the English landscape. In addition to constructions such as aqueducts, tunnels, locks and embankments, canals brought water to places which had few rivers or lakes — with a consequent variation in plant and animal life.

The last major canal to be built was also in the Northwest region. This was the Manchester Ship (1891) which provided a sufficiently deep channel for large ships to sail inland to Manchester. By this time, however, canals had been superseded by railways as the major transport system across the country. The horsedrawn barge was much slower than steam locomotives. As competition increased, boatmen's wages were reduced, and men with families could no longer afford lodgings on shore. Instead their boats became their homes. Over the years their long wooden "narrow boats" evolved a distinctive style, with brightly painted flower and castle scenes decorating them. Canals now are valued for their picturesque qualities rather than their commercial usefulness. However, they play a significant role in the tourist and leisure markets, with diesel-powered boats cruising alongside the traditional wooden barges.

Other events: 2-4 Apr.: *Grand National* horse race at Aintree, Britain's premier and most famous steeplechase; **Oct.**: *Blackpool Illuminations*, a five mile spectacle of lighting along the promenade.

River and canal cruises: *NV-Way Cruisers*, Preston Street, Carnforth, Lancashire, ☎ (0524) 734457; *Preston Hire Cruisers*, Moons Bridge, Wharf, Hollawforthlane, Woodplumpton, Lancashire, ☎ (0772) 632823.

Cheshire cheese

Dairy produce has always been an important part of the British diet, and cheese-making was a superb way of preserving milk. The oldest of the native cheeses is Cheshire. This was referred to in the 11thC Domesday Book but, according to tradition, it had existed hundreds of years before, prior to the Roman conquest.

Cheshire cheese is either creamy white or apricot in colour, with a crumbly texture and a distinctive tangy flavour — this is owing to the salty pastures on which the Cheshire cattle graze.

With the benefit of Roman expertise, dairy food production increased and "Cheshire" cheese was made not only in that county but in parts of North Wales, the Midlands, and Shropshire; and local families established reputations for particularly fine cheesemaking. During the 17thC when people in other parts of the country wanted to imitate the Cheshire taste, some even went to the lengths of transporting Cheshire soil to different areas. The most flourishing period for Cheshire cheese was the late 18thC, when all the servants on the farms around the county helped the manufacturing, and their produce would be sold at towns such as Nantwich and Chester where there were special cheese fairs. With the advent of canals, the cheese could be transported to different parts of the country, and railways meant that its production was no longer confined to farmhouses. Instead the fresh milk could be sent to large factories; the first of these was set up in 1875. Cheshire cheese can be served in many ways: cooked in various dishes, grilled on toast, eaten simply with bread and pickles — or even with sweet biscuits, cake or fruit which contrast deliciously with its salty flavour.

Sailing and cruising holidays: *Morecambe Adventure Sailing Trips*, 7 Burlington Avenue, Morecambe, Lancashire LA5 4XL, ☎ (0524) 415718.

Golfing: *Moorside Hotel*, Mudhurst Lane, Higher Disley (9- and 18-hole); *Blackwood*, nr. Blackpool (18-hole); *Royal Lytham*, Lancashire (18-hole).

Hunting: *Boxing Day Meet* at The Cross, Malpas, 11 am; grouse, pheasant, duck, rough shooting, deer stalking: *A C Sporting Services*, Hornby Castle, Estate Office, Hornby, Lancaster, ☎ (0468) 21291.

 Towns and places

BIRKENHEAD*

Liverpool, 12; Chester, 16; London, 208 m
pop. 123,907 ☎ 051   Merseyside A2

This industrial town on the Mersey estuary opposite Liverpool was little more than a hamlet and ruined medieval priory in the early 19thC. It changed dramatically with the opening of shipyards and docks and its prosperity is reflected in the Classical **Town Hall** (1883-7) and other Victorian public buildings. Effectively, Birkenhead is now part of Liverpool particularly since the opening of the Mersey Tunnel in 1934.

▶ **Williamson Art Gallery Museum** (Slatey Road): collections of local and maritime history, 18th and 19thC British watercolours and Liverpool porcelain (*Mon.-Sat., 10-5, Sun., 2-5; closed Bank Hols.*). ▶ Near **St.Mary's Church** (1821 with later additions), remains of 12thC **Priory** with chapter house (now chapel); ruined refectory and crypt. ▶ Beautiful **Birkenhead Park** laid out 1843-7 by Joseph Paxton.

Nearby

▶ **Wallasey** (*3 m N*), seaside holiday area with pleasant suburbs on NE tip of peninsula. ▶ **New Brighton** (at Mersey mouth) day-tripper resort with sandy beach and amusement parks on long promenade. ▶ Near **Moreton** is former **Leasowe Castle** (now convalescent home), erected 1593 for Earl of Derby. ▶ **Hoylake** (*8 m NW*), at mouth of Dee estuary, and **West Kirby** (*2 m S of Hoylake*): twin resorts with sandy beaches and views across to Welsh mountains. ▶ Continuing S along coastal valley, **Thursta-**ston on edge of **Wirral Country Park;** protected heathland with fine walks. ▶ **Neston** and to S hamlet of **Ness:** childhood cottage of Nelson's mistress Lady Hamilton (1763-1815) and splendid **Ness Gardens★:** sweeping lawns and fine specimen trees and shrubs, rocks, water, heather and terraced gardens, roses and herbs; Visitor Centre and views across Dee estuary (*daily, 9-dusk*). ▶ **Port Sunlight** (*3 m S*), beautifully preserved 'model' village and factory (1888) of 'Sunlight' soap magnate and benefactor Lord Leverhulme; **Heritage Centre** (Greendale Road) shows village's history (*Easter-Oct.: Mon.-Fri., 12-4. Wk ends & Bank Hols., 2-4*); **Lady Lever Art Gallery** (1914-22), contains outstanding collections of English 18thC furniture and Lord Syet's bequest of 18th and 19thC British paintings; Chinese porcelain, Wedgwood, antique sculpture (*Mon.-Sat., 10-5, Sun., 2-5*). ▶ **Ellesmere Port** (*9 m S*), industrial port at junction of Shropshire Union and Manchester Ship Canals; working **Boat Museum★** on canal including historic canal and river boats, steam engines and exhibitions (*daily, 10-5, 4 in winter*). ☐

Practical information

BIRKENHEAD

ⓘ Central Library, Borough Road, ☎ (051) 652 6106.
🚂 B. North, B. Park, ☎ (051) 709 9696.
Car rental: Europcar, New Hall Service Station, New Chester Road, ☎ (051) 327 7226.

Recommended
Golf course: Royal Liverpool, Meols Drive, Hoylake, ☎ (051) 632 3101; Caldy, Links Hey Road, ☎ (051) 625 5660; Heswall, Cottage Lane, ☎ (051) 342 1237.

Nearby

BROMBOROUGH, 5m S off A41

Hotel:
★★ *Dibbinsdale*, Dibbinsdale Road, L63 0HJ, ☎ Bromborough (051) 334 5171, AC AM BA DI, 25 rm. P 🅿 ⚛ £42.50. Rest. ♦ ⌡ £9.

HESWALL, 6m SW on A540

Restaurant:
● ♦ *Les Bougies*, Les Bougies, 106 Telegraph Road, ☎ (051) 342 6673, AC BA P ▥ ⌡ ⚛ Cl. Aug., Sun. dinner only. Book. £11.

MORETON, 1m W on A551

Hotel:
★★★★ *Leasowe Castle*, Leasowe Road, Wallasey and New Brighton, L46 3RF, ☎ (051) 606 9191, Tx 627189, AC AM BA DI, 46 rm. P ≪ ▥ 🅿 ⅄ ⚛ £70.50. Rest. ♦ ⌡ ⅄Tx. £7.

NEW BRIGHTON, 2m NE Wall on A554
ℹ The Bathing Pool, Marine Parade, ☎ (051) 638 7144. 🚇 ☎ (051) 709 9696.

Inn or Pub:
Magazine (Bass), Magazine Brow, ☎ (051 630) 3081 P ≪ 🅿 ⚛ Bar snacks, 3-course lunches. £2.50.

OXTON, 1m SW on A552

Hotel:
★★★ *Bowler Hat* (Distinctive), 2 Talbot Road, L43 2HH, ☎ (051) 652 4931, Tx 628761, AC AM BA DI, 32 rm. ▥ ⅄ £52. Rest. ♦ ⌡ ⅄Tx. £12.

Restaurant:
♦ *Beadles*, 15 Rosemount, ☎ (051) 653 9010 ⌡ ⚛ Cl. Aug., Sun., Mon., lunch. Book. £13.

PARKGATE, 10m on B5134

Hotel:
★★★ *Ship*, L64 6SA, ☎ (051) 336 3931, Tx 858875, AC AM BA DI, 26 rm. £48. Rest. ♦ £10.

Restaurants:
♦ *Mr Chow's*, The Parade, ☎ Liverpool (051) 336 2385, AC AM BA DI Chinese. £16.
♦ *The Bistro*, 1 The Parade, ☎ (051) 336 4187, AC AM BA DI P ≪ ▥ 🅿 ⌡ ⅄ ⚛ Venison, pan-fried shark, aux fines herbes. £9.

THORNTON HOUGH, 6m S on B5136

Hotel:
★★★ *Thornton Hall*, Neston Road, L63 1JF, ☎ (051) 336 3938, AC AM BA DI, 38 rm. P ≪ ▥ 🅿 ⅄ ⚛ £49. Rest. ♦ ⌡ ⅄ £9.

WALLASEY, 3m NW off M53

Hotel:
★★ *Belvidere*, 85-89 Seabank Road, L45 7PB, ☎ (051) 639 8145, 24 rm. P £30. Rest. ♦ ⌡ ⅄ £7.

BLACKBURN*

Preston, 11; Burnley, 11; London, 219 m
pop. 109,564 ☎ 0254   Lancashire B2

A hilly industrial town that developed from the late 18thC into one of the greatest cotton-producers in the world. Its centre has been extensively rebuilt with a large shopping precinct and indoor market, as well as a cathedral rebuilt from the 19thC parish church.

▶ **Lewis Textile Museum**★ (Exchange Street): history of spinning and weaving industry with working models of machines including Hargreaves' Spinning Jenny and Crompton's mule (*Mon.-Sat., 9.30-5*). ▶ **Cathedral**, till 1926 St. Mary's Parish Church (1820-6, reconstructed 1831). ▶ **Museum and Art Gallery** (Museum Street): collections of local history, coins, Japanese prints, ceramics,

ethnography and natural history, plus East Lancashire Regiment collections (*Mon.-Sat., 9.30-5*). ▶ Major parks include **Corporation Park** (1857) with lakes and leisure facilities; **Griffin Park**, containing former mansion of Griffin House; and **Whitton Park**, ancestral home of local Fielden family, with nature trail through woodlands and Visitor Centre in former stables; displays of agricultural machinery and natural history room (*Thur.-Sat., 1-5. Sun. Bank Hols., 11-5. Also Mon.-Wed. during school hols., 1-5*).

Nearby

▶ **Ribchester**★ (*3 m N*), attractive village overlooking meadows and woodland by River Ribble, with 18thC **bridge** and medieval **church** standing on site of large 1st-2ndC Roman cavalry **fort** of Bremetennacum; **museum** containing Roman finds adjoining excavated granaries (*Feb.-Nov.: daily 2-5; Jun.-Aug.: 11.30-5*). ▶ In remote setting at **Stydd** (*1/₂ m NE*), small mainly 12thC **church** of St. Saviour's with beautifully preserved doorway and, nearby, little group of **almshouses** (1728). ▶ **Darwen** (*3 m S*), town with cotton-weaving history, surrounded by moorland and retaining several old mills including 300 ft. **India Mill** chimney (1859-67); **Sunnyhurst Wood Centre** in park; displays of local history and temporary exhibitions (*Tue., Thur., Sat. & Sun., 2-4.30*). ▶ **Turton Tower**★ (*5m S*): 15thC pele tower with Elizabethan farmhouse attached, set in 8 acres of grounds; interior includes period furniture, paintings, weapons and local history room (*Sat.-Wed., 12-6*). On nearby Turton Heights are remains of prehistoric stone circle. ▶ **Accrington** (*7 m E*), former cotton town also known for brick manufacture, with modernized centre; in **Haworth Park** overlooking moors is **Art Gallery** containing fine collection of Tiffany glass plus English watercolours and European paintings (*daily ex. Fri., 2-5*). ☐

Practical information _____

BLACKBURN
ℹ Town Hall, ☎ (0254) 53277/55201 ext. 248/214. 🚇 ☎ (0254) 662 537.

Hotel:
★★ *White House*, Wellington Street, St.Johns, BB1 8AF, ☎ (0254) 51151, AC AM BA DI, 12 rm. P ▥ ⅄ ⅃ £32. Rest. ♦ ⅄ £7.

Restaurant:
♦ *Lovin' Spoonful*, 76 King William Street, ☎ (0254) 675505 🅿 ⌡ ⚛ Cl. Mon., eves. Vegetarian dishes. £4.50.

Recommended
Golf course: Pleasington, Blackburn (3m W off A59), ☎ (0254) 22177.
♥ *Sanderson*, 453 Whalley New Road, ☎ (0254) 54807, Family-run bakery offering wide range of bread, cakes etc.

Nearby

BALDERSTONE, 5m NW off A59

Inn or Pub:
Myerscough (Robinsons), ☎ (0254) 812222 P ≪ ▥ 🅿 ⅄ ⚛ Bar snacks and meals, home-made soup, steak and kidney pie. £5.50.

BILLINGTON, 6m NE off A59

Restaurant:
● ♦ *Foxfields*, Whalley Road, ☎ Whalley (025482) 2556, AC AM BA DI P ≪ ▥ 🅿 ⌡ ⚛ Cl. 25-26 Dec., Bank Hols., Mon. Game, seafood. No children under 8. Book. £17.

CLAYTON-LE-MOORS, 5m NE on A678

Hotel:
★★★ *Dunkenhalgh*, Blackburn Road, BB5 5JP, ☎ (0254) 398021, Tx 63282, AC AM BA DI, 54 rm. P ≪ ▥ 🅿 ⅃ ⅆ £50. Rest. ♦ ⌡Tx. £10.

DARWEN, 5m S on A666

Hotel:
★★★ *Whitehall*, Park Road, BB3 2JU, ☎ (0254) 71595, AC BA DI AM, 18 rm. P ⪡ ♨ ⪦ ⊠ £50. Rest. ♦ ♪ £11.

Inn or Pub:
Old Rosins, Pickup Bank, ☎ (0254) 771264, AM BA P ♨ ⪦ ❀ Home cooked bar meals and a la carte restaurant. £4.

GREAT HARWOOD, 6m NE off A678

Restaurant:
♦ *Tiffany*, Tiffany, 79 Church Street, ☎ (0254) 889528, AC ♪ ዽ ❀ Cl. 25-26 Dec., 1-2 Jan., Mon. Book. £18.

LANGHO, 5m NE

Restaurant:
♦ *Northcote Manor*, Northcote Road, ☎ Blackburn (0254) 40555, AC AM BA DI P Cl. Mon. 25-26 Dec. and 1 Jan. £15.

LIVESEY, 3m S off A666

Inn or Pub:
Black Bull (Thwaits), Brokenstones Road, Tockholes, ☎ (0254) 664771 P ⪡ ♨ ⪦ ዽ ❀ Steak pie, black pudding and bar snacks. £3.50.

PLEASINGTON, 4m SW off A674

Inn or Pub:
Butlers Arms (Brown), ☎ Blackburn (0254) 21561 P ⪡ ♨ ⪦ Bar snacks and 3 course meals. £4.

BLACKPOOL*

Preston, 16; Lancaster, 26; London, 228 m
pop. 146,297 ☎ 0253   Lancashire A1

This large seaside resort, developed in the 1850s, is famed for its 7 m stretch of sands, 3 piers and numerous holiday entertainments centering on the wide promenade and **Blackpool Tower.** There are also parks and flower gardens, golf courses, swimming pools, an ice-rink, casinos and discos, and the Blackpool Illuminations (*Sep.-Oct.*). The promenade continues for 18 m, reaching the nearby resorts of Fleetwood (→) and Lytham St.Anne's (→).

▶ Attractions include enormous amusement park of **Pleasure Beach, Coral Island** and **Sandcastle** indoor leisure centres, **Splashland** waterslide and **Blackpool Zoo**, set in 32 acres with picnic areas and a miniature railway (*daily from 10*). ▶ **All Hallows Church**, at Bispham (*3 m*), was rebuilt in 20thC but includes Norman work in doorway.

Nearby

▶ **Poulton-le-Fylde** (*3 m NE*), small market town with old market cross and **St.Chad's Church** (rebuilt 1752-3) retaining 17thC tower and furnishings in galleried interior. ☐

Practical information —————

BLACKPOOL
ℹ 1 Clifton Street, ☎ (0253) 1623; 25212 (weekdays only); 87a Coronation Street, ☎ (0253) 21891.
✈ 5m S off A584, ☎ (0253) 43061.
🚌 B.North, ☎ (0253) 935 9439, B.South, ☎ (0253) 6772 59439.
🚃 (A2) ☎ (0253) 20051.
⛴ Isle of Man Steampacket Co., ☎ (0524) 53802.
Car rental: Europcar, T.H. Bennett Motors Ltd, Church Street, ☎ (0253) 20332; Avis, rail/drive, ☎ (0253) 37771.

Hotels:
★★★★ *Imperial* (Quality), North Promenade, FY1 2HB (A1 off map), ☎ (0253) 23971, Tx 677376, AC AM BA DI, 159 rm. P ⪡ ⊠ ♪ £68. Rest. ♦ ♪Tx. £10.
★★★ *Cliffs*, Queen's Promenade, FY2 9SG (A1 off map), ☎ (0253) 52388, AC AM BA, 168 rm. £55. Rest. ♦ £8.

★★★ *Pembroke* (Metropole), North Promenade, FY1 2JQ (A1 off map), ☎ (0253) 23434, Tx 677469, AC AM BA DI, 201 rm. P ⪡ ዽ ⊠ £62.50. Rest. ♦ ♪ ዽTx. £9.
● ★★ *Sunray*, 42 Knowle Avenue, FY2 9TQ (A1), ☎ (0253) 51937, 9 rm. P £32. Rest. ♦ £7.
★★ *Headlands*, New South Promenade, FY4 1NJ (A3), ☎ (0253) 41179, AC BA, 50 rm. P ⪡ £35. Rest. ♦ £9.
★★ *Warwick* (B.W.), 603 New South Promenade, FY4 1NG (A3), ☎ (0253) 42192, AC AM BA DI, 52 rm. P ⪡ ⊠ £25. Rest. ♦ ♪ ዽ £7.
★ *Kimberley*, New South Promenade, FY4 1NQ (A3 off map), ☎ (0253) 41184, AC BA, 60 rm. P ⪡ £33. Rest. ♦ ♪ ዽ £5.

Restaurants:
♦ *Danish Kitchen*, 295 Church Street (B1), ☎ (0253) 24291 P ዽ Cl. 24-26 Dec., Sun. Pies, quiches, flans, cakes. £3.
♦ *Jasmine Cottage*, 52 Coronation Street (A1), ☎ (0253) 25303, AC BA ♪ ዽ ❀ Cl. 25-26 Dec. £6.
♦ *White Tower*, Balmoral Road, Promenade (A1), ☎ (0253) 46710, AC AM BA DI P ⪡ ♪ ❀ Cl. Jan., Sun. eve., Mon. Leg of lamb with whisky and chestnut sauce. Book. £9.50.

Inns or Pubs:
New Mariners, 8 Norbreck Rd (A1 off map), ☎ Norbeck (0253) 51154 P ⪡ ♨ ❀ Bar snacks and meals. £3.
Ramsden Arms (Tetley Walker), Talbot Road (A1), ☎ (0253) 23215 P ⪡ ዽ 6 rm. Varying menu. £3.50.

⚓ *Gillet Farm C.C.P.*, Peel Road, Peel (95 pl), ☎ (0253) 61676;*Pipers Height C.P.*, Peel Road, Peel (118 pl), ☎ (0253) 63767.

Recommended
at Marton,*Coronation Rock Company Ltd*, 11 Cherry Tree Road North, ☎ (0253) 62366, rock and novelty candy.
Golf course: North Shore, Devonshire Road, ☎ 51017; Blackpool Park, Stanley Park, ☎ 33960.
♥ *Venetian Glass Company Ltd*, Squires Gate Lane, ☎ (0253) 403950, animals, figures, etc. in brown glass.

Nearby

ELSWICK, 7m E on B5269

Inn or Pub:
Ship (Bonnington), High Street, ☎ (0995) 70131 P ♨ ⪦ ዽ Bar snacks.

LITTLE SINGLETON, 6m NE on B5260

Hotel:
★★ *Mains Hall*, 86 Mains Lane (A 585), FY6 7LE, ☎ Poulton-le-Fylde (0253) 885130, 7 rm. P ⪡ ♨ ⪦ £30.

THORNTON-LE-FYLDE, 4m N off A688

Restaurant:
● ♦ *River House*, Skipool Creek, ☎ (0253) 883497, AC AM P ⪡ ♨ ⪦ ♪ 4 rm. Crayfish, salmon, grouse. Book. £16.

BOLTON*

Blackburn, 13; Manchester, 11; London, 205 m
pop. 143,960 ☎ 0204   Greater Manchester B2

Before it became one of the great cotton towns of the Industrial Revolution, Bolton was already a medieval textile centre. Engineering and chemical works superseded cotton and today's industrial town includes large converted mills, attractive 18thC houses and several museums.

▶ In centre (1939): **Museum Art Gallery** (Le Mans Crescent): archaeology, local industrial and natural history, geology and Egyptology; 18thC watercolours, sculpture and ceramics (*Mon., Tue., Thur. & Fri., 9.30-5.30, Sat., 10-5; closed Wed., Sun. & Bank Hols.*). ▶ Imposing **Town Hall** (1873); 19thC bronze **statue** (Nelson Square) of Samuel Crompton (1753-1827) who invented spinning

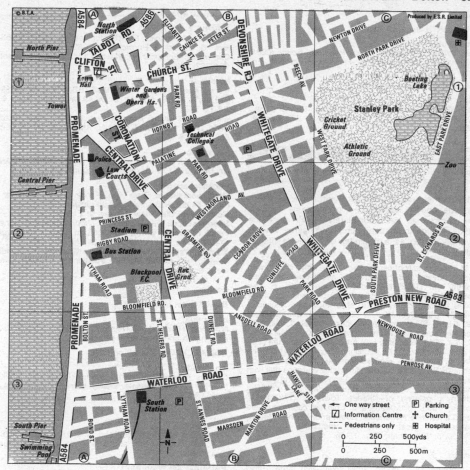

BLACKPOOL

mule in Bolton; ▶ **St.Peter's Church** (rebuilt 19thC): traces of Norman work, part of Anglo-Saxon cross and in churchyard Crompton's grave. ▶ **Local History Museum** (St.George's Street); social history of region (*Mon.-Sat., 10-12, 1-5; closed Sun. & Bank Hols.*). ▶ At **Tonge Moor** (*2 m N*): **Textile Museum:** early textile machines including Crompton's mule (*Mon. & Thur., 2-7.30, Tue. & Fri., 9.30-5.30, Sat., 9.30-12.30; closed Wed., Sun. & Bank Hols.*). ▶ **Hall i'th' Wood★**, restored, largely 16thC timber-framed manor-house with period furnishings and Crompton relics (*Apr.-Sep.: Mon.-Wed., Fri. & Sat., 10-6, Sun. 2-6; Oct.-Mar.: Mon.-Wed., Fri. & Sat., 10-5*)▶ **Smithills Hall★** (*2¹/₂ m NW*), timber-framed house dating from 14thC, with early 15thC great hall, oak paneling and 16th-17thC furnishings; grounds include nature trail and trailside museum (*hours as for Hall i'th'Wood*).

Nearby

▶ **Lostock** (*3 m*) with 16thC **gatehouse** of demolished hall. ▶ **Rivington,** moorland village with small 16th-17thC **church** with detached bell tower and charming Unitarian **chapel** (1703) including original box pews; beautiful 400-acre **Lever Park** (*S*), with 18thC **Rivington Hall** and restored **syet barn,** set on slope of **Rivington Pike** (1191 ft) with fine views from summit. ☐

Practical information _____

BOLTON
ⓘ Town Hall, ☎ (0204) 22311 ext.384174.
▬▬ ☎ Manchester, (061) 832 8353.
Car rental: Europcar, Long Causeway Sce Station, ☎ (0204) 78772.

Hotel:
★★★ *Pack Horse* (De Vere), 1 Nelson Square, Bradshawgate, BL1 1DP, ☎ (0204) 27261, Tx 635168, AC AM BA DI, 74 rm. ⎣ £52. Rest. ♦ ♪ ⎣Tx. £10.

Inn or Pub:
York (Burtonwood), 112 Newport Street, ☎ (0204) 383892 Ⓟ ▓ Snacks, basket meals and 3-course lunches. £2.50.

Recommended
Golf course: Links Road, ☎ (0204) 42336; Bolton Lostock, Lostock Park, ☎ (0204) 43067.

Nearby

AINSWORTH, 3m E off A58

Inn or Pub:
Duke William (Whitbread), Wells Road, ☎ Bolton (0204) 24726 ℗ 🕮 ⌕ ❀ Lunch Mon.-Fri., eve. meals Wed., Fri-Sat. £3.50.

EGERTON, 3 1/2m N on A666

Hotel:
★★★ *Egerton House*, Blackburn Road, BL7 9PL, ☎ (0204) 57171, AC AM DI, 27 rm. ℗ ⚡ 🕮 ⌕ ⏚ £58. Rest. ♦ ⌙ £10.

BURNLEY*

Clitheroe, 12; Manchester, 24; London, 220 m
pop. 76,365 ☎ 0282   Lancashire B2

An industrial town close to the South Pennines, Burnley was one of Lancashire's great textile centres. The centre has been completely rebuilt since the 1950s, though the parish church and nearby Towneley Hall remain as a reminder of Burnley's medieval past.

▶ **St. Peter's**, to N of centre: large early 16thC church with 15thC tower and 18th-19thC alterations, including carved font (1532) and Towneley memorials. ▶ **Tow House Museum** (Manchester Road) on banks of canal: textile heritage centre set in area known as 'Weavers' Triangle' (*Apr.-Oct.: Wed. & Sun., 2-4*). ▶ **Queen Street Mill** (Harle Syke): re-opened steam-powered mill, with working original looms (*Easter-Sep.: Thur.-Mon., 10.30-4.30*). ▶ **Towneley Hall Art Gallery & Museum** (*1¹/₂ m SE*): Towneley family mansion dating from 14thC, with 16th, 17th & 19thC modifications, set in large **park** on banks of River Calder; note impressive entrance hall with plasterwork by Vassali (1792), Elizabethan long gallery, fine collections of period furniture, paintings including Zoffany's painting of Charles Towneley (1737-1805), ivories, 18thC glassware and Chinese ceramics; also **East Lancashire Regimental Room** and, in Brew House, **museum of local crafts and industries** (*Mon.-Fri., 10-5.30, 5.15 in winter; Sun., 12-5*).

Nearby

▶ **Padiham** (*2¹/₂ m W*), small town with large 19thC **church of St.Leonard's** in centre, containing finely carved 16thC font from Whalley Abbey (→Clitheroe). ▶ Nearby is **Gawthorpe Hall★**, early 17thC manor-house (restored 1850) set in landscaped gardens by river; minstrel gallery; Jacobean long gallery; Kay-Shuttleworth collections of embroidery, lace and costumes; Ryder collection of early European furniture; **craft gallery** in coach house (*house: mid-Mar.-Oct.: Wed., Sat., Sun., Bank Hols, Good Fri.; also Tue. in Jul. & Aug., 2-6; craft gallery: daily ex. Mon., 2-5; garden: mid-Mar.-mid-Oct.: daily, 10-6*). ▶ **Nelson** (*4 m N*), 19thC cotton town with large **parks**, early 19thC **church of St. Paul's**; in **St.Mary's** (19thC), William Morris/Edward Burne-Jones stained glass (1919). ▶ Open moorland stretches W, with floodlit **Pendle Heritage Centre** in restored 17thC manor-houses at **Barrowford** (*1 m N*), including small local history museum (*Apr.-Nov.: Sat. & Sun., Tue.-Thur. & Bank Hol. Mon., 2-4.30*). ▶ Old textile centre of **Colne** (*2 m*): largely 16thC St.Bartholomew's **Church** dating from Norman times and, **British in India Museum** (Sun Street); paintings, photographs and memorabilia of era of British rule in India (*May-Sep.: Sat. & Sun., 2-5*). ▶ To E: moorland stretches into Yorkshire, with old Roman Road, **Long Causeway**, leading over hills; fine climb on **Worsthorne Moor** (1400 ft) with Towneley's old home of **Hurstwood Hall** (*3¹/₂ m*) on edge of moor close to 16thC **Spenser Hall**, childhood home of poet Edmund Spenser. ▶ To NE, close to Nelson and Colne, high unspoilt moors of **Forest of Trawden** extending into Yorkshire's **Haworth Moor,** with fine views of Calder valleys.   □

Practical information

BURNLEY
ℹ Burnley Mechanics, Manchester Road, ☎ (0282) 30055.
🚂 B. Central, B. Barracks, ☎ (0282) 25421.
Car rental: Europcar, D. Kitchen Ltd, Trafalgar Street, ☎ (0282) 54262.

Hotels:
★★★★ *Keirby* (Virani), Keirby Walk, BB11 2DH, ☎ (0282) 27611, Tx 63119, AC AM BA DI, 49 rm. ℗ £40. Rest. ♦ ⌙ ♿Tx. £7.
★★ *Rosehill House*, Rosehill Avenue, Manchester Road, BB11 2PW, ☎ (0282) 53831, AC AM BA, 20 rm. ℗ 🕮 ♿ £38. Rest. ♦ ⌙ ♿ £8.

Inn or Pub:
Coal Clough House (Greenall), ☎ (0282) 28800, AC AM BA DI ℗ 🕮 ⌕ ❀ Bar snacks, 3-course meals. £6.

Recommended
Craft workshops: *Slate Age*, Fence Gate, Fence, ☎ (0282) 66952, Hand-crafted slate giftware.
Golf course: Glen View Burnley, ☎ 21045.
Riding school: *Fence Riding School*, Cuckstool Lane, Fence in Pendle, ☎ (0282) 63586; at Bacup,*Old Clough Stables*, New Row, Weir Cillage, ☎ (0706) 876862.
♥ *Doug Moore*, Lower Park Marina, Kelbrook Rd, Barnoldswick, ☎ (0282) 815883, traditionally painted chandlery, brassware.

Nearby

BLACKO, 7m N on A682

Inn or Pub:
Moorcock (Thwaits), ☎ Nelson (0282) 64186 ℗ ⚡ 🕮 ⌕ 2 rm. English and continental dishes. £3.

HOLME CHAPEL, 4m SE on A646

Inn or Pub:
Queens (Brutonwood), 412 Burnley Road, ☎ (0282) 36712 ⚡ ⌕ ♿ Bar meals, steaks, curries, chicken chasseur. £3.50.

MERECLOUGH, 3m SE off A646

Inn or Pub:
Kettledrum, 302 Red Lees Road, ☎ Burnley (0282) 34282 ℗ ⌕ ⚡ Snacks, lunch and a la carte eve. meals (ex. Thu.). £4.50.

PADIHAM, 4m W on A671

Restaurant:
♦ *Sam's Bistro*, 35 Burnley Road, ☎ (0282) 71358, AC BA ℗ 🕮 ⌙ ❀ 2 rm. Salmon in pastry with smoked oysters. Book. £7.

READ, 5m W on A671

Restaurant:
♦ *Belvedere*, ☎ Padiham (0282) 72250, BA ℗ ⚡ 🕮 ⌕ ♿ ❀ Cl. Mon., Sat.-Sun. lunch. Italian dishes. £10.

REEDLEY, 5m N off A56

Hotel:
★★★ *Oaks*, Colne Road, Pendle, BB10 2LF, ☎ (0282) 414141, Tx 635309, AC AM BA DI, 32 rm. ⚡ 🕮 ▭ £56. Rest. ♦ ⌙ £15.

BURY*

Blackburn, 17; Manchester, 9; London, 206 m
pop. 67,529 ☎ 0706   Greater Manchester B2

Industrial town known in the 19thC for yarn manufacture and textile printing. The birthplace of John Kay (1704-64), inventor of the flying shuttle, and Robert Peel. Few traces of Bury's medieval past remain but the centre has some imposing Victorian and 20thC public buildings.

▶ In centre: church of **St. Mary's** (originally medieval, rebuilt 19thC); **Art Gallery & Museum** (1899-1901; Silver Street): Wrigley collection of 19thC paintings, watercolours, engravings and local history (*Mon.-Fri., 10-6, Sat., 10-5*); **Town Hall** (1954); in Market Place, **statue** of Robert Peel (1852); **Derby Hall** and **Athenaeum** (both mid-19thC) (Market Street). ▶ **Castle Armoury** (Castle Street), picturesque 19thC building on site of medieval castle.

Nearby

▶ **Edenfield** (*5 m N*), village of stone houses set in high moorland. ▶ **Rawtenstall** (→) and **Forest of Rossendale**.□

Practical information _____

BURY

▦ ☎ Manchester, (061) 832 8353.

Hotels:
★★ *Bolholt*, off Walshaw Road, BL8 1PS, ☎ (061) 764 5239, BA, 36 rm. ℗ ≼ ▥ ◿ & ⋌ £40. Rest. ♦ ↕ & £12.
★ *Woolfield House*, Wash Lane, BL9 7DH, ☎ (061) 764 3446, 13 rm. ℗ & ⅋ £35. Rest. ♦ ↕ & £8.

Recommended
Farmhouse: at Hawkshaw,*Leo Farm Livery Stables*, Redisher Lane, ☎ (020 488) 3668, £23 double B. B.

Nearby

BIRTLE, 2 1/2m NE off B6222

Hotel:
★★★ *Normandie*, Elbut Lane, BL9 6UT, ☎ (061) 764 3869, AC AM BA DI, 17 rm. ℗ ≼ ▥ & ⅋ Cl. 26 Dec.-4 Jan.; £46. Rest.● ♦ ↕ & Cl. 4 Jan., Sat. and Sun. lunch. Nouvelle cuisine. caneton rôti aux kumquats et cognac. £22.

CHEESDEN, 6m NW on A680

Inn or Pub:
Owd Betts (Greenhall), Edenfield Road, Rochdale, ☎ (0706) 49904 ℗ ≼▥ Bar snacks, steaks, Lancashire hotpot. £4.

LITTLEBOROUGH, 5m NE on A58

Hotel:
★ *Sun*, 96 Featherstall Road, OL15 8NY, ☎ (0706) 78957, AC AM BA DI, 8 rm. ℗ ⅋ £18. Rest. ♦ £5.

MILNROW, 2m E on A640

Restaurant:
♦ *Moorcock*, Huddersfield Road, ☎ Saddleworth (045 77) 2659, AC AM BA DI ℗ ≼▥ ↕ & ⅋ Cl. Mon., Sat. lunch, Sun. eve. Drunken shrimps. Book. £9.

ROCHDALE, 7m E on A58

Restaurant:
♦ *One Eleven*, 111 Yorkshire Street, ☎ (0706) 344901, AC AM BA DI ℗ ↕ ⅋ Cl. 3 wks. from 21 Jun., 1 wk. Sep. Book. £12.50.

Inn or Pub:
Cemetery, 470 Bury Road, ☎ (0706) 43214 ℗▥ Jacket potatoes. £2.
Yew Tree (Smiths), ☎ (0706) 49742, AC BA ℗▦ ⅋ Bar snacks, à la carte menu, carvery. £12.

Recommended
Golf course: Bacup (A671), Bankside Lane, ☎ (0706) 3170.

CHESTER***

Birkenhead, 16; Nantwich, 21; London, 182 m
pop. 77,270 ☎ 0244   Cheshire A3

Set close to the Welsh border, the ancient county town of Chester was one of the most important Roman military bases in Britain. It flourished in the Middle Ages as a key border town and trading port and still looks remarkably medieval. Enclosed within the old city walls are narrow streets of black-and-white timbered houses and inns, as well as a medieval cathedral.

▶ **City Walls★**, mostly medieval and exceptionally well-preserved, of red sandstone 12-40 ft high; walkway along top (2 m) gives fine views. ▶ **King Charles' Tower** (NE corner), from which Charles I watched defeat of his army at Battle of Rowton Moor 1645, includes **museum** with displays on Civil War (*Apr.-Oct.: Mon.-Fri., 1-5, Sat., 2-5, Sun., 2-5.30; Nov.-Mar.: Sat., 1-4.30 or dusk, Sun., 2-4.30 or dusk*). ▶ In Eastgate, Westgate, Bridge and Northgate Streets, **Rows★**: arcades forming continuous passages along lst floor of houses, and now lined with shops, several of which have medieval crypts. **British Heritage Centre** includes reconstructions of Rows in Victorian times. ▶ Notable buildings on Watergate Street include: richly carved **Bishop Lloyd's House** (1615), **Custom House Inn** (1637), **Trinity Church** (1865) and **Stanley Palace** (1591). ▶ In Northgate Street: new **shopping precinct** and **market** next to Town Hall (1869). ▶ **Abbey Gateway** (14th-15thC) leads to **Cathedral★** (12th-16thC, heavily restored); on site of 11thC abbey, with traces of original Norman church; simple interior includes Lady Chapel (1250-75) and 13th-14thC choir with carved **stalls★** including fine misericords. Off cloisters are **chapter house** (13thC), Norman **undercroft** and **St.Anselm's Chapel** (12thC). ▶ **Grosvenor Museum** (Grosvenor Street): Roman finds from Chester, plus natural history, art and folk life (*Mon.-Sat., 10.30-5, Sun., 2-5*). ▶ **St.Mary on the Hill** (14th-16thC): fine Tudor roof, 17thC effigies, medieval glass; now exhibition and study centre (*Mon.-Fri., 2-4.30*). ▶ **Castle**, entirely rebuilt 1793-1820: splendid Classical buildings, incorporating **Agricola Tower** and 12thC stone-vaulted **chapel** from original 11thC castle, now houses **Military Museum**. ▶ Near **Bridge Gate** (1782), picturesque 7-arched **Dee Bridge** (14thC, widened 1826), and fine single-arched **Grosvenor Bridge** (1826). ▶ Outside walls: large, excavated **Roman amphitheatre** able to seat 8,000 spectators, with **Roman gardens** beside it, including a **hypocaust** and reconstructed medieval **High Cross**. ▶ Nearby is partly-ruined **St. John's**, with Norman nave of original 11thC church and Saxon cross fragments. ▶ **Grosvenor Park**, with riverside walks. ▶ **Zoo★** (*2 m N*), with over 3,000 animals in 100 acres of natural enclosures (*daily, 10 - dusk*).

Nearby

▶ **Shotwick** (*5 m NW*), once important Welsh border village: medieval **church** topped with tower (ca. 1500) and interior with twin naves containing Georgian woodwork and 14thC stained glass. ▶ **Tarvin** (*5 m E*): medieval **church** containing fine 14thC woodwork. ▶ Conifer woods and ponds of **Delamere Forest** (*E; →Northwich*). ▶ **Tarporley** (*11 m SE*), set in pretty countryside, with some attractive 16th-18thC houses in centre and medieval **church** altered over centuries; fine medieval furnishings. ▶ **Bunbury**: 18th 19thC houses, restored **church** with partly 14thC tower and traceried E window, containing fine effigy of Sir Hugh Calveley (builder of 14thC church) and 16thC effigy of Sir George Beeston. ▶ Remains of 13thC **Beeston Castle★** (EH) lie on crag above, giving sweeping views; small **museum** shows history of castle; nearby is convincingly medieval 19thC **Peckforton Castle** by Salvin (*private*).   □

Practical information _____

CHESTER
ⓘ Town Hall, Northgate Street (A2), ☎ (0244) 40144 ext. 2111/2250; Chester Visitor Centre, Vicar's Lane (B2), ☎ (0244) 313126.
▦ (C1), ☎ (0244) 40170.
Car rental: Europcar, Hoole Road Service Station, Hoole, rail/drive; ☎ (0244) 312893.

Hotels:
● ★★★★ *Chester Grosvenor* (Prestige), Eastgate Street,

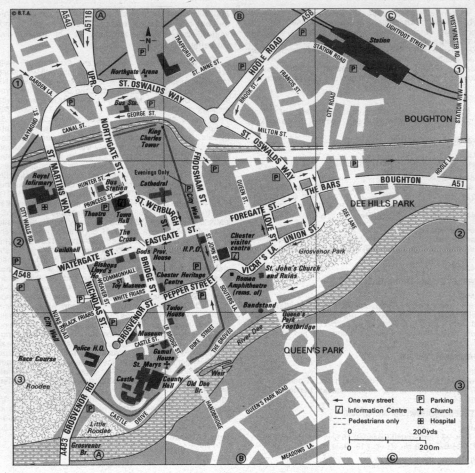

CHESTER

CH1 1LT (A-B2), ☎ (0244) 24024, Tx 61240, AC AM BA DI, 108 rm. P ⅙ ♩ £99. Rest. ● ♦ ⅙Tx. £16.
● ★★★★ *Mollington Banastre* (B.W.), Parkgate Road, CH1 6NF (A1 off map), ☎ (0244) 851471, Tx 61686, AC AM BA DI, 70 rm. P ⚌ ⚓ ⅙ ⊠ ⚄ ⅃ ⚗ £65. Rest. ♦ ⅃ ⅙Tx. £13.50.
★★★ *Abbots Well* (Embassy), Whitchurch Road, Cristleton, CH3 5QL (C2 off map), ☎ (0244) 332121, Tx 61561, AC AM BA DI, 127 rm. P ⚮ ⚌ ⚓ ⅙ £60. Rest. ♦ ⅃ ⅙Tx. £12.
★★★ *Plantation Inn*, Liverpool Road, CH2 1AG (A1 off map), ☎ (0244) 374100, Tx 61263, AC AM BA DI, 93 rm. P ⅙ ♩ £55. Rest. ♦ ⅃ ⅙Tx. £14.
★★★ *Queen* (T.H.F.), City Road, CH1 3AH (C1), ☎ (0244) 28341, Tx 617101, AC AM BA DI, 91 rm. P ⅙ £49. Rest. ♦ ⅃ ⅙Tx. £10.
★★★ *Rowton Hall* (Consort), Rowton Lane, CH3 6AD (C2 off map), ☎ (0244) 335262, Tx 61556, AC AM BA DI, 42 rm. P ⚮ ⚌ ⅃ ⅙ Stately 17thC manor-house situated on the site of the Battle of Rowton Moor. £52. Rest. ♦ ⅃ ⅙Tx. £9.
★★ *City Walls*, City Walls Road, 14 Stanley Place, CH1 2LU (A2), ☎ (0244) 313416, AC BA AM, 17 rm. P £33. Rest. ♦ ⅃ ⅙ £10.

★★ *Dene*, Hoole Road, CH2 3ND (B1), ☎ (0244) 21165, 47 rm. P ⚌ ♩ £45. Rest. ♦ ⅃ £7.
★★ *Green Bough*, 60 Hoole Road, CH2 3NL (B1 off map), ☎ (0244) 26241, AC BA, 11 rm. P ⚘ £32. Rest. ♦ £8.

Restaurants:
♦ *Abbey Green*, Abbey Green, off Northgate Street (A2), ☎ (0244) 313251, AC P ⚌ ⚓ ⅃ ⅙ Cl. Sun., Mon. dinner. Book. £9.50.
♦ *Pippa's In Town*, 58 Watergate Street (A2), ☎ (0244) 313721, AC AM DI BA £15.

⚐ *Chester Southerly CP*, Balderton Lane, Marlston-cum-Lache (95 pl), ☎ (0829) 270791.

Recommended
Craft workshops: at Burwardsley, 11m SE off A41, *Cheshire Candle Workshops Ltd.*, ☎ (0829) 70401, hand-sculpted candles.
Farmhouse: at Bickley, *Yew Tree Farm*, ☎ (082 922) 262, £18 double B. B.
Golf course: Vicars Cross, Littleton (2 1/2m E on A56), ☎ (0244) 335174.
Guesthouse: *Roslyn Guest House*, 8 Chester Street, nr. Saltney, ☎ (0244) 672306, £18 double B. B.

Nearby

BARTON, 11m S on A534

Inn or Pub:
Cock o' Barton, ☎ (082 925) 277 P ⫣ ⏧ ⫦ Large choice of hot meals, snacks and salads. £5.50.

Recommended
Farmhouse: *Millhey Farm*, Malpas, ☎ (082 925) 431, £16 double B. & B.

FARNDON, 9m S on B5130

Inn or Pub:
Greyhound (Greenall), High Street, ☎ (0829) 270244 P ⫣ ⏧ ⫦ ⅍ 4 rm. River Dee salmon, pies, vegetarian meals. £6.50.

Recommended
Craft workshops: *Barn Studios*, Top Farm Centre, High Street, ☎ (0829) 270020, 6 local craftsmen displaying their works.

LITTLE BARROW, 6m NE off AS1

Inn or Pub:
Railway (Greenall), Station Lane, ☎ (0244) 301145 P ⫣ ⏧ ⫦ ⅍ ⬥ Large selection of steaks, fish, pies. £5.

PUDDINGTON, 8m NW off A540

Hotel:
★★ *Craxton Wood*, Parkgate Road, L66 9PB, ☎ (051) 339 4717, AC AM BA DI, 14 rm. P ⫣ ⏧ ⫦ ⅍ £58. Rest. ● ⬥ ♪ ⅍ £17.

Restaurant:
⬥ *Craxton Wood*, Craxton Wood, Parkgate Road, ☎ 051-3394717, AC AM BA DI P ⫣ ⏧ ⫦ ♪ ⬥ Cl. Bank Hols., last 2 wks Aug., Sun. 14 rm. Book. £17.

WILLINGTON, 8m E off A51

Hotel:
● ★★ *Willington Hall*, CW6 0NB, ☎ Kelsall (0829) 52321, AC AM BA DI, 10 rm. P ⫣ ⏧ ⫦ ♪ £50. Rest. ⬥ £10.

CHORLEY*

Preston, 9; Manchester, 22; London, 204 m
pop. 54,775 ☎ 0257   Lancashire A2

A hilly industrial town on the W edge of rising moorland, with a rebuilt centre and modern estates mixed with old cotton mills and housing, including a few attractive Georgian terraces.

▶ Restored **St. Laurence's** Church, with 15thC tower, includes 2 medieval **fonts**, relics of St. Laurence (brought here in 15thC) and carved wood Standish **pew.**▶ Among several 19thC churches, **St. Georges's** (1822-5): galleried interior with delicate iron columns. ▶ **Astley Hall★:** impressive Elizabethan mansion set beside lake and sweeping lawns; **Art Gallery and Museum:** period furniture, glass, pottery and paintings (*Apr.-Sep.: daily 12-5.30; Oct.-Mar.: Mon.-Fri., 12-3.30, Sat., 10-3.30, Sun., 11-3.30*).

Nearby

▶ **Leyland** (*7 m NW*); a few early 19thC houses; medieval **St. Andrew's** Church (partly rebuilt); **British Commercial Vehicle Museum** (King Street); from horse-drawn and early steam wagons to petrol and recent vehicles (*Apr.-Sep.: Tue.-Sun., 10-5. Oct., Nov.: Sat., Sun. only 10-5*).   □

Practical information

CHORLEY
🚌 ☎ (0257) 62616.

Inn or Pub:
Railway (Matthew Brown), ☎ (025 72) 62632 P ⫣ ⏧ ⫦ ⬥ Bar snacks, salmon, Sunday lunch. £2.50.

Recommended
Golf course: fall o' th' Hill, Heath Charnock (on A673), ☎ (821) 480263.

Nearby

CHARNOCK RICHARD, 1m N on A49

Hotels:
★★★ *Park Hall*, Park Hall Road, PR7 5LP, ☎ Eccleston (0257) 452090, Tx 677604, AC AM BA DI, 117 rm. P ⫣ ⏧ ⅍ ⬿ ⬚ ♪ ⅃ ⬱ £50. Rest. ⬥ ♪ ⅍Tx. £12.
★★ *Travelodge* (Trusthouse Forte), Mill Lane, PR7 5LR, ☎ Coppull (0257) 791746, Tx 67315, AC AM BA DI, 103 rm. P ⏧ ⫦ ⅍ £40. Rest. ⬥ ♪ ⅍Tx. £6.

WITTLE-LE-WOODS, 4m N off A6711

Hotel:
● ★★★ *Shawhill Golf Club*, Preston Road, PR6 7PP, ☎ Chorley (025 72) 69221, AC AM BA DI, 22 rm. P ⫣ ⏧ ⫦ ⅍ ⅃ £60. Rest. ⬥ ♪ ⅍ £10.

CLITHEROE*

Preston, 18; Burnley, 12; London, 227 m
pop. 13,552 ☎ 0200   Lancashire B1

This historic market town is set on a hillside below the shell of a Norman keep, built on a steep limestone rock. Although partly industrialized, Clitheroe retains much of its former charm, with pleasant streets of stone-built houses overlooking the woods and meadows of the Ribble Valley.

▶ **Castle** remains consist of 9ft- thick walls of 12thC keep, supposedly smallest in country; hilltop site gives fine views. **Castle Museum** (Castle House): displays of local history, archaeology and geology (*Easter-Oct.: 2-4.30*). ▶ **St.Mary Magdalene** (rebuilt 1828-29) dates from Norman times and retains 15thC tower and a few interesting old furnishings. ▶ **Low Moor**, to W: early 19thC **mill** and mill houses near fine 5-arched **Eadsforth Bridge** over Ribble.

Nearby

▶ To E rises **Pendles Hill** (1827 ft), giving fine views from summit; after a vision here in 1652, George Fox founded Quaker movement. ▶ **Browsholme Hall** (*5 m NW*), Tudor mansion with Elizabethan front and Queen Anne and Regency additions, home of Parker family, Bowbearers of Forest of Bowland (→); interior includes portraits and period furniture (*Easter Sat. & following wk., late May Bank Hol. wk end; Sat. in Jun., Jul. & Aug.; summer Bank Hol. & preceding wk: 2-5*). ▶ **Sawley Abbey** (*3 m NE*): scanty remains in meadows by riverside of Cistercian abbey founded 1147. ▶ **Whalley★** (*6 m S*), attractive old town by Calder River; ancient **church** of St.Mary, with 3 Anglo-Saxon crosses in churchyard, includes Norman and 13thC work, 15thC tower and much fine woodwork. Ruins of 13thC Cistercian **abbey**, include 14th-15thC gatehouses and traces of 14thC church and cloister. ▶ **Great Milton** (*2 m NW of Whalley*): medieval **All Hallows Church:** largely 13thC interior with many 15th-17thC furnishings and splendid alabaster, marble and stone monuments (16th-18thC) of Shireburn family in Elizabethan **chapel.** ▶ Further NW is **Stonyhurst College**, RC boys' school founded by Jesuits in 1593 and transferred here in 1794, situated at Elizabethan mansion of Sir Richard Shireburn.   □

Practical information

CLITHEROE
ℹ Council Offices, Church Walk, ☎ (0200) 25566.

Hotel:
★ *White Lion*, Market Place, BB7 2BZ, ☎ (0200) 26955, 6 rm. P ⅃ £23. Rest. ⬥ ♪ ⅍ £5.

Inn or Pub:
Hodder Bridge, ☎ Stonyhurst (028 486) 216, AC BA Ⓟ ⪜
⠿ ⟐ 4 rm. Bar snacks and meals, carvery restaurant. £4.

⚲ *Clitheroe C.C.C.*, Edisford Road (150 pl), ☎ (0200)
25294.

Recommended
Farmhouse: *Lower Standen Farm*, Whalley Road,
☎ (0200) 24176, £19 double B. & B.
Golf course: Clitheroe, ☎ (0200) 22618.

Nearby

BOLTON-BY-BOWLAND, 7m NE off A59

Hotel:
● ★★★ *Harrop Fold Country Farmhouse*, Harrop Fold,
BB7 4PJ, ☎ Bolton-by-Bowland (0200) 7600, AC BA, 8
rm. Ⓟ ⪜ ⠿ ⟐ ⚘ ⤴ ⟐ £40. Rest. ◆ £10.

WHITEWELL, 6m NW off B6478

Hotel:
★★ *Inn at Whitewell*, Forest of Bowland, BB7 3AT,
☎ Dunsop Bridge (020 08) 222, AC AM BA DI, 12 rm. Ⓟ
⪜ ⟐ £43. Rest. ◆ £10.

CONGLETON*

Macclesfield, 8; Stoke-on-Trent, 13; London, 170 m
pop. 23,482 ☎ 0260   Cheshire B3

An attractive market town, Congleton has a history
dating from Norman times. Silk and cotton mills grew
up in the 18thC, with yarn manufacture continuing into
the 20thC. A few early mills and 17thC timber-framed
buildings survive.

▶ Early 19thC houses around parish church of **St. Peter**
(1740); fine box pews and large central pulpit in unaltered
galleried interior. ▶ Below is narrow High Street with Victorian Gothic style **Town Hall** (1864-66).

Nearby

▶ **Macclesfield Canal** (→Macclesfield) passes E of town
with, to S, 'roving' **bridges** and lock complex near **Bosley**
(*5 m NE*). ▶ At **North Rode** (*4 m NE*) is massive 20-arched
railway **viaduct** (1849) designed by Robert Stephenson.
▶ **Sandback** (*7 m W*), old market and former salt-mining
town, with winding streets and, in cobbled market place,
2 tall carved **Saxon cross shafts** (8thC, reassembled).
▶ **Astbury** (*1 m S*), with a few old cottages around
remarkable 14th-15thC **church★**: beautiful 15thC beamed
roofs and Jacobean furnishings. ▶ **Little Moreton Hall★** (*4
m;*): magnificent example of black-and-white half-timbered house (1559-89); moat, carved gables, Elizabethan
wood-and plasterwork, chapel and great hall: also knot
garden (*Mar. & Oct.: Sat., Sun., 2-5.30 or dusk; Apr.-Sep.:
daily ex. Tue. & Good Fri., 2-5.30*).   □

Practical information _____

CONGLETON
ⓘ Town Hall, High Street, ☎ (0260) 271095.

Restaurant:
◆ *Oddfellows*, 20 Rood Hill, ☎ (0260) 270243, AM ⠿ ⟐
⟐ ⚘ Cl. 25-26 Dec., 1 Jan., Bank Hols. Book. £10.

Recommended
Golf course: Biddulph Road, ☎ (0260) 3540.

Nearby

ASTBURY, 1m S off A34

Hotel:
★ *Egerton Arms*, ☎ Congleton (0260) 273946, BA, 7 rm.
Ⓟ ⠿ ⟐ ⟐ ⤴ ⟐ £30. Rest. ◆ ⟐ ⟐ Cl. 25 Dec. £9.

BRERETON GREEN, 5m W on A50

Inn or Pub:
Bear's Head, ☎ Holmes Chapel (0477) 35251, AC AM BA
DI Ⓟ ⪜ ⠿ ⟐ ⟐ ⚘ 21 rm. Bar snacks, lunches, a la carte
restaurant. £7.50.

GOOSTREY, 8m NW off A535

Inn or Pub:
Crown Marstons (Marstons), 111 Main Road, ☎ Holmes
Chapel (0477) 32128, AC Ⓟ ⪜ ⠿ ⟐ ⚘ 2 rm. Bar snacks,
restaurant. £5.50.

HOLMES CHAPEL, 5m NW on A50

Hotels:
★★★ *Old Vicarage*, Knutsford Road, CW4 7DE, ☎ (0477)
32041, AC AM BA DI, 8 rm. Ⓟ ⪜ ⠿ ⚘ ⟐ £45. Rest. ◆
⟐ ⟐ £12.50.
★★ *Holly Lodge*, 70 London Road, CW4 7AS, ☎ (0477)
37033, AC AM BA DI, 34 rm. Ⓟ ⠿ ⟐ £40. Rest. ◆ ⟐
⟐ £10.

Inn or Pub:
Swan (Smith), Station Road, ☎ (0477) 32259 Ⓟ ⠿ ⚘ 2
rm. Home-made pies, casseroles, salads. £3.50.

MOW COP, 6m S off A34

Inn or Pub:
Chesire View (Marstons), Station Road, ☎ (0782) 514211,
AC BA Ⓟ ⪜ ⠿ ⟐ ⚘ Bar meals, cottage pie, salads.
£1.50.

SANDBACH, 6m off A534
ⓘ Motorway Service Area, M6 Northbound ☎ (0260)
760460.
🚂 ☎ Crewe (0270) 255245.

Hotel:
● ★★★ *Chimney House* (Whitbread), Congleton Road,
CW11 0SF, ☎ (093 67) 4141, Tx 666971, AC AM BA, 52
rm. Ⓟ ⪜ ⠿ ⟐ £55. Rest. ◆ ⟐ ⟐Tx. £10.

SWETTENHAM, 7m NW

Inn or Pub:
Swettenham Arms, ☎ Holmes Chapel (0477) 71283 Ⓟ ⠿
⚘ Rest.excl. Sun eve. £6.

FLEETWOOD*

Blackpool, 9; Preston, 23; London, 239 m
pop. 27,899 ☎ 039 17   Lancashire A1

A seaside resort and fishing port planned in the
mid-19thC by Sir Peter Hesketh Fleetwood. Its long
stretch of sandy beach and wide promenade gives
fine views and entertainment include yachting and
wind surfing, boating lakes, amusement parks and a
leisure centre. A passenger ferry connects Fleetwood
with the seaside village of **Knott End** across the river
mouth and the promenade runs South to Thornton
Cleveleys and on to Blackpool (→).

▶ The town retains a few neo-Classical buildings in
Queen's Terrace and the curved **North Euston Hotel.**
▶ **Rossall School**, on cliffside, includes traces of
17th-18thC work in the interior. ▶ **Fleetwood Museum**
(Dock Street): small maritime museum devoted to fishing
and town's history (*Easter-Oct.: daily ex. Wed., 2-5*).

Nearby

▶ **Thornton Cleveleys** (*3 m S*), sister resort of Fleetwood,
developed in 19th-20thC from two former villages; fine
sand and family holiday entertainment on and around promenade; impressive 70ft high brick **windmill** built in 1794.□

Practical information _____

FLEETWOOD
ⓘ Marine Hall, Esplanade, ☎ (039 17) 71141.

Hotel:
★★★ *North Euston*, The Esplanade, FY7 6BN, ☎ (039 17) 6525, AC AM BA DI, 57 rm. P ⩫ £41. Rest. ♦ ⌁ ⅍ Cl. 25 Dec. £10.

⚐ *Kneps Farm C.P.*, River Road, Thornton (65 pl), ☎ (0253) 823632; *Carr Royd Leisure*, Sower Carr Lane, Hambleton (25 pl), ☎ (0253) 700222; at Pilling, *Fold House C.P.*, Head Dyke Lane (10 pl), ☎ (039 130) 267.

Recommended
Golf course: The Fleetwood, Princes Way, ☎ (039 17) 3661.

FOREST OF BOWLAND*

B1

The fells and moorland of the Forest of Bowland are now the heart of a designated area of outstanding natural beauty which covers 310 square miles and includes the **Lune Valley** (→) in N, **Beacon Fell Country Park** in SW and **Pendle Hill** near Clitheroe (→) to SE.

Round trip from Lancaster through Trough of Bowland (56 m, halfday).

▶ From Lancaster (→), road crosses River Conder (1¹/₂ m) and follows fells via **Brow Top** and **Lee** (7 m), with nearby **Abbeystead reservoir.** ▶ From **Marston** to **Sykes** (13 m) beautiful scenic drive on high narrow moorland road through **Trough of Bowland★**, past **Whins Brow** (1561 ft). ▶ Woodlands extend N of **Dunsop Bridge**, in river valley, and road follows river, crossing line of Roman road just before village of **Newton** (18 m), with 18thC **Friends Meeting House.** ▶ **Slaidburn★** 20 m, charming amber-stoned village giving wonderful views of fells; **church** (mainly 15thC): 3-decker pulpit. To N lies large expanse of **Gisburn Forest.** ▶ Crossing River Hodder, follow road S along slopes of Easington Fell (1300 ft) to **Meanly** (24 m) and through open moorland to **Cow Ark,** then via **Bashall Eaves** and **Walker Fold**, set in wooded pastureland. ▶ **Chipping** (30 m), market centre sited close to the fells; many 17thC stone houses and restored **church** retaining some 13th-14thC work in interior. Nearby are traces of neolithic settlements: N of **Bleasdale** (41 m)

is site of early Bronze Age wooden circle. ▶ To S lies **Beacon Fell Country Park** and road skirts Bleasdale Moors to N, passing scattered farmsteads between villages of **Oakenclough** (46 m) and **Street** (49 m) before joining up with major roads into Lancaster (56 m). □

Practical information

CHIPPING, 7m W off B6243

Hotel:
★★ *Gibbon Bridge*, Moss Lane, PR3 2TQ, ☎ (099 56) 456, AC BA, 7 rm. P ⩫ ⚒ ⚑ ⌁ ⅏ £30. Rest. ♦ ⅍ £8.

GISBURN, 10m NE on A682

Hotel:
★★★ *Stirk House* (Consort), BB7 4LJ, ☎ (020 05) 581, Tx 635238, AC AM BA DI, 52 rm. P ⩫ ⚑ ☒ ⅃ £49. Rest. ♦ ⅍Tx. £10.

SLAIDBURN, 8m N on B6478

Hotels:
● ★★ *Parrock Head Farm*, Woodhouse Lane, BB7 3AH, ☎ Slaidburn (020 06) 614, AM, 8 rm. P ⩫ ⚒ ⚑ £37. Rest. ● ♦ £12.
★★ *Hark to Bounty*, BB7 3ER, ☎ Slaidburn (020 06) 246, Tx 635165, AC AM DA DI, 8 rm. P ⩫ ⚑ Ancient inn, dating back to the 13thC, set in the heart of the forest of Bowland. £28. Rest. ♦ ⅍ ⅍Tx. £10.

Recommended
Farmhouse: *Hammerton Hall*, ☎ (020 06) 676, £18 double B. & B. 58-acre mixed livestock farm.

KNUTSFORD*

Manchester, 17; Macclesfield, 12; London, 178 m
pop. 13,628 ☎ 0565   *Cheshire B3*

An attractive old market town with winding streets. 18thC houses set on a hill, and 19th-20thC villas.

▶ Knutsford was the 'Cranford' of novelist Mrs Gaskell (1810-65); she is buried beside small brick-built **Unitarian Chapel** (1689) and nearby in King Street is **Gaskell Memorial Tower.** ▶ **King's Coffee House** (1907, also King Street): extraordinary white stone fantasy of R.H. Wyatt.

Nearby

▶ **Tatton Park★** (2 m N): 1000-acre deer park with lakes, historical nature trails, 1930s working farm, and 50-acre garden that forms setting for fine **house** (1788-1820) by Samuel and Lewis Wyatt; collections of pictures, furniture, china, glass and silverware; also in park is restored 15thC **Old Hall** (Apr.-mid-May, Sep. & Oct.: park: Mon.-Sat., 11-6 (pedestrians 9-7), Sun. & Bank Hols., 10-6. Garden: Mon.-Sat., 11.30-5, Sun. & Bank Hols., 10.30-5.30. House: Mon.-Sat., 10-4, Sun. & Bank Hols., 1-5. Farm: daily, 12-4. Mid-May-Aug.: park: Mon.-Sat., 10.30-7 (Pedestrians 9-8), Sun. & Bank Hols., 10-7. Old Hall: tours Apr.-Oct.: Mon.-Sat., 12-4 (Jul. & Aug., 12-5), Sun. & Bank Hols., 12-5; Nov.-Mar.: park: 11-dusk (pedestrians: 9-dusk); house, Old Hall & farm closed ex. Sun. in Nov. & Mar.). ▶ **Peover Hall★** (3¹/₂ m S), 16thC house with later additions; 17thC **stables**, large **garden** set in 18thC landscaped **park** (May-Sep.: Mon. ex. Bank Hols., 2.30-5. Thur., 2-5 stables and garden only). ▶ In park, dominated by Hall, is **Over Peover Church**, rebuilt in 1811 but retaining earlier chapels with Mainwaring family monuments (medieval & 17thC). ▶ **Lower Peover** (2 m W): rare example of black-and- white timbered **church** (13thC, restored) with massive stone tower (ca. 1500) and much fine Jacobean woodwork. ▶ **Mobberley** with late medieval **church** (ca. 1500). ▶ **Wilmslow**, old village, now a suburb of Manchester; a few old houses, modern shopping precinct and restored 15th-16thC **church** by R. Bollin. ▶ **Styal Country Park** (1¹/₂ m N) and **Quarry Bank Mill★**: almost complete cotton mill colony of Industrial Revolution; model village, chapels, school, shop and Apprentices' House, and in mill (1784) working **museum**

From Lancaster through Trough of Bowland

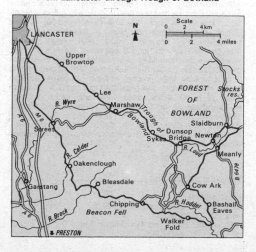

set in park with woodlands and access to pretty Bollin Valley (*park: all year during daylight hours; mill complex: Apr.-May: Tue.-Sun. & Bank Hols. 11-5; Jun.-Sep.: daily, 11-5, Oct.-Mar: Tue.-Sun., 11-4*). □

Practical information

KNUTSFORD
ⓘ Council Offices, Toft Road, ☎ (0565) 2611.
🚆 ☎ Manchester, (061) 832 8353.

Hotels:
★★ ***Angel***, 96 King Street, WA16 6HQ, ☎ Knutsford (0565) 52627, AC AM BA DI, 12 rm. Ⓟ ⊗ ⌂ Handsome Georgian building on the main street. £30. Rest. ♦ ♪ £11.
★★ ***Royal George*** (Berni), King Street, WA16 6EE, ☎ (0565) 4151, AC AM BA DI, 31 rm. Ⓟ ♿ ⊗ ⌂ £48. Rest. ♦ ♪ ♿ £6.

Restaurants:
● ♦ ***La Belle Epoque***, 60 King Street, ☎ (0565) 3060, AC AM BA DI Ⓟ ⩪ ⌂ ♪ ⊗ Cl. 1 wk. Jan., Sun. 5 rm. Book. £25.
♦ ***David's Place***, 10 Princess Street, ☎ (0565) 3356, AC AM BA Cl. Sun. £15.

Recommended
Antique Shop: *Wisehall, Michael*, Minshull Gallery, 7 Minshull Street, ☎ (0565) 4901, Furniture and metalwork.
Golf course: Mere, 4m E of M6, jct.19, ☎ (0565) 830155; Mereheath Lane, ☎ (0565) 3355.

Nearby

BUCKLOW HILL, 4m N on A556

Hotels:
● ★★★★ ***Cotton's***, Manchester Road, WA16 0SU, ☎ (0565) 50333, Tx 669931, AC AM BA DI, 62 rm. Ⓟ ♿ ▭ ⌂ £63. Rest. ♦ ♪ ♿ £10.
★★★ ***Swan*** (De Vere), Chester Road, WA16 6RD, ☎ (0565) 830295, Tx 666911, AC AM BA DI, 70 rm. Ⓟ ♿ £60. Rest. ♦ ♪ ♿ Tx. £10.

LOWER PEOVER, 3 1/2m S by A50

Restaurant:
♦ ***Bells of Peover***, The Cobbles, ☎ (056581) 2269 Ⓟ ⩪ £14.

MOBBERLEY, 2m E on B5085

Inn or Pub:
Chapel House (Boddingtons), Pepper Street, ☎ (056587) 2391 Ⓟ ⩪ ⌂ ♿ ⊗ Bar meals, sandwiches. £1.50.

PLUMLEY, 4m SW off A556

Inn or Pub:
Golden Pheasant (Lees), Plumley Moor Road, ☎ Lower Peover (056581) 226, AC AM BA DI Ⓟ ✻ ⩪ ⌂ ♿ ⊗ 10 rm. 3-course meals. £5.
Smoker (Robinson), ☎ Lower Peover (233 81) 2405 Ⓟ ⩪ ⌂ ♿ ⊗ Bar snacks and restaurant. £8.50.

TABLEY, 2m NW on A556, M6 Ex. 19

Inn or Pub:
Windmill (Robinson), Chester Road, ☎ Knutsford (0565) 2650 Ⓟ ⩪ ♿ ⊗ Hot meals, salads and bar snacks. £4.

LANCASTER**

Morecambe, 4; Preston, 23; London, 234 m
pop. 45,126 ☎ 0524 Lancashire A1

The historic town of Lancaster is situated on the River Lune estuary within easy reach of Morecambe Bay and the Lune Valley (→) and Forest of Bowland (→). Its impressive castle and ancient church of St.Mary stand high above the town, which largely dates from the 18thC when Lancaster briefly prospered as a port.

▶ On Castle Hill above the river with extensive views: **castle**, dating from medieval times and remodeled 18th-19thC, with massive gatehouse (ca. 1400) (*not open to public*) and **keep** (11thC, rebuilt 16thC) including small **museum** of prison equipment in Hadrian's Tower; **Shire Hall** (18thC, in splendid Gothic style) has carved stone ceiling (*Easter-Oct.: Mon.-Sat., 10.30-12, 2-3.30*). ▶ Close by is **St.Mary's Church★**, largely 14th-15thC; fine chancel and restored 18thC tower; originally part of Benedictine priory founded in 1094 on Roman-Saxon site, it includes traces of Roman basilica, small Saxon doorway and exquisitely carved oak **stalls★** (14thC). ▶ **Period Cottage** (15 Castle Hill): recreated artisan's home (*May-Sep.: Mon., Tue., Thu. & Sat. pm*). ▶ **Judges' Lodgings** (1675; Church Street), housing **Museum of Childhood;** also Town House containing furniture by Gillow of Lancaster (*Easter-Oct.: Apr. & Oct.: Mon.-Fri., 2-5; May & Jun.: Mon.-Sat., 2-5; Jul.-Sep.: Mon.-Fri., 10-1, 2-5, Sat., 2-5*). ▶ On river front: **St. George's Quay** with fine Georgian warehouses and an old **Customs House** (1764); small **Maritime Museum** devoted to local sea-trading and fishing history (*Apr.-Oct.: daily 11-5; Nov.-Mar.: daily 2-5*). ▶ River is spanned by impressive stone **canal viaduct** and 5-arched **Skerton Bridge** (both late 18thC). ▶ In old centre to SE, **City Museum** (Market Square), porticoed former Town Hall (18thC) containing collections of local history plus **Museum of King's Own Royal Regiment** (*Mon.-Fri., 10-5, Sat., 10-3*). ▶ New **Town Hall** (Dalton Square), built 1906-9, in front of which is large **Victoria Memorial** (1907) by Herbert Hampton with bronze statues of 19thC worthies. ▶ Nearby, to E, is **St. Peter's** RC Cathedral (1857-59), with elaborate 240 ft. spire. ▶ **Hornsea Pottery** (Wyresdale Road) set in gardens with adventure playground and children's farmyard, gives factory tours (*daily 10-5*). ▶ Topping hill of **Williamson Park,** laid out 19thC, is 150 ft. high **Ashton Memorial** (1906-09), Baroque-style monument to Lord Ashton's wife; views across Morecambe Bay and towards Lakeland mountains. ▶ At Bailrigg (*3 m S*) is extensive campus of **Lancaster University,** designed 1963-64.

Nearby

▶ **Carnforth** (*6 m N*), small town with **Steamtown Railway Museum** that includes *Flying Scotsman* steam locomotive (*Easter-Oct.: daily 9-5; Nov.-Easter: daily 10-4; closed Xmas*). ▶ **Warton** (*7 m N*); medieval **church** incorporating arms of President George Washington's ancestors in 15thC tower; nearby are ruins of 14thC **Rectory** (*mid-Mar.-mid-Oct.: Mon.-Sat., 9.30-6.30, Sun., 2-6.30. Mid-Oct.-mid-Mar.: Mon.-Sat., 9.30-4, Sun., 2-4*). ▶ Through pleasant old village of **Yealand Conyers** with 17thC **Friends Meeting House** to **Leighton Hall★** (*9 m N*): home of Gillow family dating from 12thC, restored 18thC with neo-Gothic façade (1800); interior contains Gillow furniture; falconry displays held in extensive grounds (*May-Sep.: Tue.-Fri. & Sun., 2-4.30/5 (falconry 3.30). Closed Sat. & Mon. ex. Bank Hol. Mon.*). ▶ **Silverdale** (*1 m W*), pleasant little seaside resort with views across Morecambe Bay and huge **Breakstone,** Ice Age boulder; woodlands and low-lying 'mosses' stretching to Arnside over Cumbrian border are designated area of outstanding natural beauty, with national wildfowl refuge of **Leighton Moss,** nature walks and protected cliff paths. ▶ **Glasson Dock** (*4 m S*), 18thC dock with busy yachting basin. ▶ **Thurnham** (*6 m S*); thatched cottages and historic **Thurnham Hall,** 16thC with 19thC Gothic front set in gardens (*Apr.-Sep.: Mon.-Fri. & Sun., 2-5. Closed Sat.*). ▶ Beside sandy beach are scanty ruins of **Cockersand Abbey** (founded 1190; *1 m W*) including chapter house. □

Practical information

LANCASTER
ⓘ 7 Dalton Square, ☎ (0524) 32878.
🚆 ☎ (0524) 32333.
Car rental: Europcar, Rix Manor Ltd, 88 King Street, ☎ (0524) 36767/32233.

Inns or Pubs:
Howe Ghyll (Mitchells), Green Lane, ☎ (0524) 32011 �Ⓟ ⌂
🍴 ᵬ Bar snacks, 3-course meals at lunch. £4.50.
Stonewell Tavern (Thwaits), Lower Church Street,
☎ (0524) 33209 Ⓟ ᵬ Large selection of home-cooked
food. £4.
Water Witch (Yates), Canal Side, ☎ (0524) 63828 Ⓟ ⌂ ⌂
🍴 ⌣ Jacket potatoes, steak, lunch and dinner. £4.50.

⚑ *Robinsons Caravans*, Claylands Farm, Cabus (32 pl),
☎ (0524) 791242;at Bentham, *Riverside C.P.*, Wenning
Avenue (30 pl), ☎ (0468) 61272.

Recommended
Bed and Breakfast: at Hest bank,*Tennessee*, 62 Coas-
tal Road, ☎ (0524) 822741, Overlooking Morecombe Bay.
£18 double B. & B.
Craft workshops: *Hornsea Pottery Co. Ltd*, Wryesdale
Road, ☎ (0524) 68444, Large selection of giftware and
pottery cookware; at Low Bentham, *Bentham Pottery*,
Oysterber Farm, ☎ (0468) 61567, unique individually-
made pottery.
Farmhouse: at Bolton-le-Sands, *Thwaite End Farm*, A6
Road, ☎ (0524) 732551, £22 double B. & B.
Golf course: Ashton Hall, Ashton (3m S on A588),
☎ (0524) 751247; Lansil, Caton Road. ☎ (0524) 39269
Guesthouse: *Mrs M. Houghton*, 3 Edenbreck, Sunnyside
Lane, ☎ (0524) 32464, £24 double B. & B.

Nearby

BAY HORSE, 6m S off A6

Hotel:
★ *Foxholes*, Oakenclough Road, LA2 9DB, ☎ Forton
(0524) 791237, 10 rm. Ⓟ ⌂ ⌂ 🍴 ⌣ £28. Rest. ♦ ♪ ᵬ £9.

SILVERDALE, 12m N off A6/M6

Hotel:
★ *Silverdale*, Shore Road, LA5 0TP, ☎ (0524) 701206,
AC, 9 rm. Ⓟ ⌂ 🍴 £25. Rest. ♦ ♪ ᵬ £8.

Recommended
♥ *Wolf House Gallery*, Jenny Browns Point, Gibraltar,
☎ (0524) 701405, One offs: pottery, wooden sculpture
and paintings.

SLYNE, 2m N on A6

Inn or Pub:
Slyne Lodge, ☎ Hest Bank (0524) 823 389, AC Ⓟ ⌂ ᵬ
⌣ 13 rm. Bar meals, steaks. £5.50.

WATERSIDE PARK, 3m NE off A683

Hotel:
★★★ *Post House* (T.H.F.), Caton Road, LA1 3RA,
☎ (0524) 65999, Tx 65363, AC AM BA DI, 117 rm. Ⓟ ⌂
⌂ 🍴 ᵬ ☒ ⌐ £70. Rest. ♦ ♪ ᵬTx. £11.50.

LIVERPOOL **

Preston, 30; Chester, 25; London, 198 m
pop. 538,809 ☎ 051   Merseyside A2

Set on the mouth of the Mersey estuary, this major
English city developed with the opening of its first
dock in 1715. It became established as the country's
chief transatlantic port in the 19th to 20thC, and the
docklands stretch for 7 m. Little trace of Liverpool's
medieval past remains and radical replanning in
recent times includes a new centre and the entrance
to the Mersey Tunnel, although many impressive
19thC buildings remain.

▶ In centre: **St.George's Hall★** (1839; Lime Street) large,
fine Classical building with concert hall off tunnel-vaulted
Great Hall. ▶ To S large new St. John's shopping precinct. ▶ Castle Street includes at N end **Town Hall★**
(1749-54) by John Wood the Elder, several impressive
bank buildings, and at S end, Derby Square, site of
medieval castle, with Queen Victoria **monument** (1902-06)

by Westmacott. ▶ **Cotton Exchange** (1906; Old Hall
Street), in Renaissance style with double colonnade.
▶ **Bluecoat School** (1716-17) and **Bluecoat Chambers**
(both School Lane), attractive Queen Anne building situated on cobbled quadrangle (*Mon.-Sat., 10-5*)▶ Further
S is **Beatle City** (Seal Street), light and sound 'museum'
devoted to Beatles era. ▶ In William Brown Street, **Ses-
sions House** (1882-84) among Classical 19thC buildings:
▶ **Walker Art Gallery★**: splendid collection of European
14th-20thC paintings (*Mon.-Sat., 10-5, Sun., 2-5*.) ▶ **Merseyside County Museum★**: displays from fine Joseph
Mayer collection, plus natural and local history, with land
transport gallery; Planetarium (*closed Mon.*); and King's
Regiment Museum (*Mon.-Sat., 10-5, Sun., 2-5. Closed
Xmas, New Year, Good Fri.*). ▶ **Pierhead,** covering large
waterfront site and including magnificent 5-storeyed
Albert Dock warehouses (1841-45). ▶ **Merseyside Maritime Museum★**, next to **Albert Dock Village** (shops and
restaurants), includes quayside trail, old sailing vessels
and exhibitions in 19thC Classical dock buildings (*daily
10.30-5.30*). ▶ Overlooking Pierhead, with views of Mersey, is rebuilt parish church of **St. Nicholas** (1952).
▶ Opposite is dock entrance to **Mersey Tunnel** (1925-34),
$3^1/_2$ m long roadway beneath river linking Liverpool to
Birkenhead. ▶ To E of centre, in 'woot end': **Anglican cathedral★** (1904-78; St. James's Mount) built of red
sandstone by Giles Gilbert Scott, with magnificent 331 ft
tower and vast rectangular central space with high arches
and beautiful vaulting. ▶ Georgian streets lie to N and E.
▶ **RC cathedral★** (1962-67; Mount Pleasant): impressive
building (Frederick Gibberd), with pinnacled glass-paneled
tower and huge open interior brilliantly lit by abstract
stained glass (John Piper and Patrick Reyntiens), the
massive brick **crypt** (1933-58) was designed in Renaissance style by Edwin Lutyens. ▶ **University** buildings
(mainly 1950s on) spread to N and E, with original Victorian
building (1890) on Brownlow Hill; University **Art Gallery**
(Abercromby Square) contains paintings, furniture, porcelain and silver (*Mon., Tue. & Thur., 12-2, Wed. & Fri., 12-4.
Closed Aug. & Bank Hols.*). ▶ Outer districts E: **Wavertree,** with fine Georgian church of **Holy Trinity** (1794, restored). ▶ **Toxteth,** including remarkable almost entirely
iron church of St.Michael in the Hamlet (1814-15▶ **Child-
wall** with only medieval **church** in Liverpool. ▶ Outer districts S: **Prince's Park** landscaped by Paxton (1842) and
larger **Sefton Park** including lake, with nearby **St. Agnes**
Church (1883) of red brick. ▶ Just E, at Mossley Hill,
is **Sudley Art Gallery★** containing mainly English 18th
& 19thC paintings and sculpture (*Mon.-Sat., 10-5, Sun.,
2-5*). ▶ Other notable churches include **St. Anne's** (1837),
Aigburth, of red sandstone, and **All Hallows** (1872-76),
Allerton, with tall pinnacled tower. ▶ **Speke Hall★** (*7 m S*),
splendid example of half-timbered house, Jacobean
plasterwork in Great Parlour and priest holes, with furniture and tapestries; set in Victorian gardens with walks in
woodland (*Apr.-Sep.: Mon.-Sat., 10-5 (4 last admission),
Sun., 2-7 (6); Oct.-Mar.: Mon.-Sat., 10-5 (4), Sun., 2-5 (4);
closed Xmas, New Year, Good Fri.*). ▶ Outer districts N &
NE: **Stanley Park** (1867-70) and nearby **Newsham Park.**
▶ **Croxteth Hall & Country Park★** (*5 m NE*), ancestral
home of Earls of Sefton, with house (mainly 18th-19thC,
dating to 16thC) including paintings and costumes set in
500-acre wooded park with gardens, working farm, heritage centre, miniature railway (*park: all year daily; hall,
farm & garden: Good Fri.-Sep.: daily, 11-5; farm & Heritage Centre open winter*). ▶ **Sefton** (*7 m N*): 16thC
St.Helen's Church with large 14thC tower, containing
16thC woodwork and 13th-16thC monuments of
Molyneux family.   □

Practical information _____

LIVERPOOL
ⓘ 29 Lime Street (C1), ☎ (051) 709 3631; Atlantic Pavilion, Albert Dock (A2), ☎ (051) 708 8854.
✈ (6m SE off A561), ☎ (051) 494 0066.
🚆 (C1) ☎ (051) 709 9696.
🚆 (C2) ☎ (051) 709 6481.
⛴ B & I Line, ☎ (051) 227 3131, Belfast Car Ferries,
☎ (051) 922 6234.

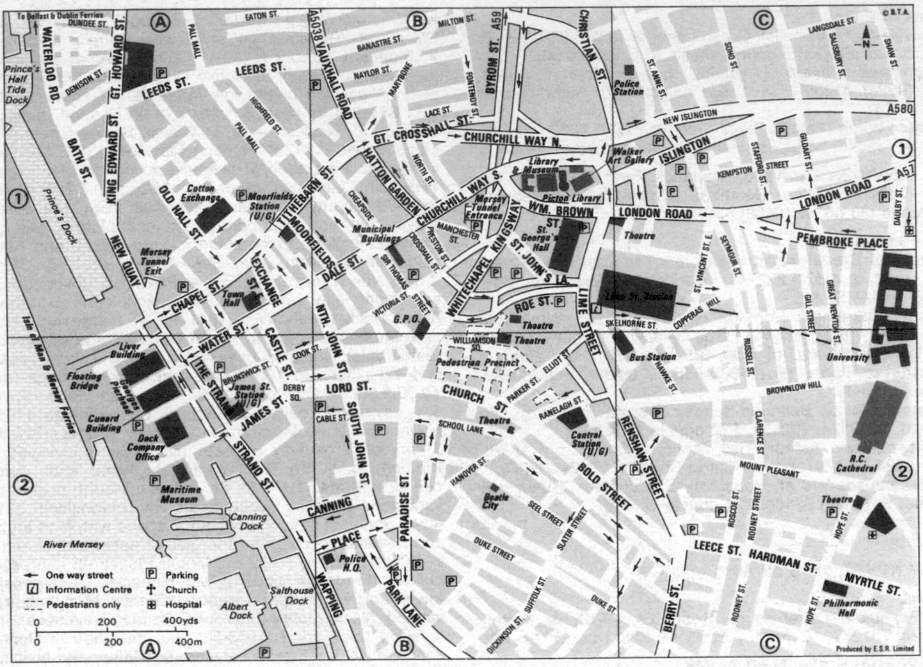

LIVERPOOL

Car rental: Europcar, St. Vincent Street, ☎ (051) 708 9150; Lime St. Rail Station; rail/drive, ☎ (051) 709 6570; Airport, Terminal Building.

Hotels:

★★★★ ***Atlantic Tower*** (Thistle), Chapel Street, L3 9RE (A1), ☎ (051) 227 4444, Tx 627070, AC AM BA DI, 226 rm. Ⓟ ☼ ♿ £71. Rest. ♦ ♪ ♿Tx. £10.

★★★★ ***Liverpool Moat House***, Paradise Street, L1 8JD (B2), ☎ (051) 709 0181, Tx 627270, AC AM BA DI, 260 rm. Ⓟ ♿ ▭ £60. Rest. ♦ ♪ ♿Tx. £7.75.

★★★ ***Britannia Adelphi*** (Britannia), Ranelagh Place, L3 5UL (C2), ☎ (051) 709 7200, Tx 629644, AC AM BA DI, 344 rm. Ⓟ ♿ ▭ £70. Rest. ♦ ♪ ♿Tx. £9.

★★ ***Bradford***, Tithebarne Street, L2 2EW (A1), ☎ (051) 236 8782, Tx 627657, AC AM BA DI, 43 rm. Ⓟ £35. Rest. ♦ ♪ ♿Tx. £5.95.

★★ ***Caribbean***, Seddon Road 2 1/2m SE off A561, L19 2LJ (C2 off map), ☎ (051) 427 2711, BA, 37 rm. Ⓟ ☼ ⚒ ✓ £28. Rest. ♦ ♪ ♿ £6.

★★ ***Grange***, Holmefield Road, Aigburth, L19 3PG (C2 off map), ☎ (051) 427 2950, AC AM BA DI, 25 rm. Ⓟ ♨ £40. Rest. ♦ £10.

★★ ***Shaftesbury***, Mount Pleasant, L3 5SA (C2), ☎ (051) 709 4421, AC AM BA DI, 67 rm. ⚒ £32. Rest. ♦ £6.

Restaurants:

● ♦ ***Far East Restaurant***, 27 Berry Street (A2), ☎ (051) 709 3141, AC AM BA DI Ⓟ ♪ ⚒ Cl. 25-26 Dec. Cantonese dishes. Book. £5.

● ♦ ***The Armadillo***, The Armadillo, 20 Matthew Street (B2), ☎ (051) 236 4123, AC BA ♪ Cl. Christmas, Sun.-Mon. £14.

♦ ***Beaujolais***, 50 Seel Street (B2), ☎ (051) 709 1327, AC AM DI BA ♪ ⚒ Cl. Sun. lunch. Book. £14.

♦ ***Churchill's***, Churchill House, Tithebarn Street (A1), ☎ (051) 227 3877, AC AM BA DI Ⓟ ♪ ⚒ Cl. Bank Hols., Sat lunch, Sun. Book. £11.

♦ ***Elham***, 95 Renshaw Street (C2), ☎ (051) 709 1589, AC AM BA DI Cl. lunch. Arabic cuisine.

♦ ***Jenny's Seafood***, Old Ropery, Fenwick Street (A2), ☎ (051) 236 0332, AC AM BA DI ♪ ⚒ Cl. 25 Dec.-1 Jan. Bank Hols., Sun. £12.

♦ ***La Grande Bouffe***, 48a Castle Street (A2), ☎ (051) 236 3375, AC AM BA Ⓟ ♪ ⚒ Cl. 25 Dec., Bank Hols., Sat. lunch, Sun., Mon. eve. Book. £14.

♦ ***Lau's***, Rankin Hall, 44 Ullet Road (C2), ☎ (051) 734 3930, AC AM BA DI Ⓟ Cl. Sun., 25-26 Dec £9.50.

♦ ***Ristorante del Secolo***, first floor, 36-40 Stanley Street (A2), ☎ (051) 236 4004, AM DI AC BA Sat. and Sun. 1-15 Aug. Italian. £15.

Recommended

Bakery: *Dafnas Cheesecake Factory*, 240 Smithdown Road, Wavertree, ☎ (051) 773 7808, a local bakery using traditional methods.

Golf course: Chidwall, Naylors Road, Gateacre, ☎ (051) 487 9982; Formby, Golf Road, ☎ (070 48) 72164; West Derby, Yew Tree Lane, ☎ (051) 228 1540.

Nearby

AIGBURTH, 3m S

Restaurant:

♦ ***L'Alouette***, 2 Lark Lane, ☎ Liverpool (051) 7272142, AC BA Sat. lunch and Mon. £15.

BLUNDELLSANDS, 9m N off A565

Hotel:

★★ ***Blundellsands*** (Whitbread), Serpentine, L23 6TE, ☎ (051) 924 6515, AC AM BA DI, 39 rm. Ⓟ £45. Rest. ♦ ♪ ♿ £10.

KNOWLSLEY, 4 1/2m NE on B5194

Hotel:

★★ ***Cherry Tree*** (Crest), East Lancs Road, L34 9HA,

☎ Liverpool (051) 546 7531, Tx 629769, AC AM BA DI, 50 rm. ℗ & £46. Rest. ♦ ♪ &Tx. £8.50.

NETHERTON, 5m N off A5036

Hotel:
★★★ *Park* (G.W.), Park Lane West, Bootle, L30 3SU, ☎ (051) 525 7555, Tx 629772, AC AM BA DI, 60 rm. ℗ & £47. Rest. ♦ ♪ &Tx. £8.

LUNE VALLEY*

A1

The peaceful valley of the winding River Lune runs E from Lancaster through beautiful countryside, in which there are opportunities for secluded walks.

Round trip from Lancaster along Lune Valley

▶ From Lancaster follow A683 and/or branch roads: **Halton** (2¹/₂m off A683), village on N bank of river: ancient **church** (rebuilt 19thC); 15thC **Halton cross** (early 11thC) carved with Norse legends. ▶ In 1m beautiful wooded ravine of **Crook of Lune★**, with lovely view and footpaths by river below village of **Caton** (4 m): its church, at nearby Brookhouse, retains fine Norman doorway and medieval tower. ▶ **Claughton** (6 m) has oldest dated bell in England (1296) in its rebuilt **church**, close to 17thC farmhouse that was wing of Tudor Hall. ▶ Continuing on A683, branch road leads to pretty village of **Wray**, 1 m SE of **Hornby** (9 m) on bank of River Wenning: unusual twisted octagonal tower (16thC) of restored **church**, containing Anglo-Saxon cross fragments, built by Sir Edward Stanley. His family **castle**, rebuilt 19thC around impressive medieval keep (*private*), provides part of view from **Loyne Bridge** on road to **Gressingham** (1m N). Here, stream flows into Lune from hillside village, with church (mainly 18thC) retaining fine Norman doorway and Saxon cross fragments. ▶ Returning to A683, hilly climb leads to **Melling** (11 m) and **Tunstall** (13 m), where attractive unrestored **church** (mainly 15thC) includes Roman altar stone and medieval stained glass; Brontë sisters worshipped here (Charlotte wrote of it in *Jane Eyre*) when pupils at Vicar of Tunstall's school in **Cowan Bridge** (2 m NE), plain house by bridge (*private*). From Tunstall, avenue of limes leads to **Thurland Castle**, rebuilt 19thC from 15thC ruins and retaining fine moat (*private*). ▶ Road continues across Cumbrian border to Kirkby Lonsdale (→). ▶ On N bank of river, following B6254 W from Kirkby Lonsdale: **Whittington** (1¹/₂m), village with 17thC cottages and restored medieval **church** giving lovely views across valley, overlooking 19thC Tudor mansion of **Whittington Hall**. ▶ **Arkholme** (4¹/₂m), with pretty village street; medieval **church** by river and, high above valley, rebuilt Elizabethan mansion of **Storrs Hall** (*private*). Branch road (1 m) leads via **Gressingham** to **Hornby** on A683 (above) or return to Lancaster on B6254 and A6 via **Carnforth**. □

Practical information ─────────────

CATON, 3 1/2m NE off A683

Hotel:
★ *Ship*, Lancaster Road, LA2 9QJ, ☎ Caton (0524) 770265, 3 rm. ℗ ⅍ £18.90. Rest. ♦ £5.

Recommended
Craft workshops: *The Lunesdale Pottery*, Farrier's Yard, ☎ (0524) 770284, contemporary stoneware pieces.

HORNBY, 6m NE on A683

Hotel:
★★ *Castle*, Main Street, LA2 8JT, ☎ (0468) 21204, AM BA AC, 13 rm. ℗ ≼ ⚲ & ♪ ⚬ £36. Rest. ♦ ♪ & £10.

MELLING, 10m NE on A683

Hotel:
★★ *Melling Hall*, Hornby, via Carnforth, LA6 2RA, ☎ Hornby (0468) 21298, AC AM BA, 13 rm. ℗ ⚲ ⚬ ♪ £30. Rest. ♦ ♪ & £10.

LYTHAM ST. ANNES*

Blackpool, 7; Preston, 14; London, 230 m
pop. 39,599 ☎ 0253   Lancashire A2

This pleasant seaside resort stretches along nearly 7 miles of shore from Lytham, to St. Anne's below Blackpool (→). Lytham began to develop as a dignified resort in the late 18thC and includes some Regency and early Victorian houses; St. Anne's was built from 1875 by wealthy cotton magnates. Apart from the promenade and pier, the resort is known for its parks and flower gardens.

▶ At Lytham, attractions include **Fairhaven Lake**, on seafront, with sailing, boating and water-skiing facilities, and **Nature Reserve** (Clifton Drive N) for flora and fauna. ▶ Near main street and market place is **Lytham Hall**, an impressive mansion rebuilt in 1757-64 with elaborate plaster ceilings (*sometimes open*). ▶ **Motive Power Museum** (Dock Road) houses collection of steam locomotives from 1890, diesel and aero engines and vintage cars (*May-Oct.: daily*). □

Practical information ─────────────

LYTHAM ST. ANNES
🄸 St. Anne's Square, ☎ (0253) 721222/725610.
🚃 ☎ Preston (0772) 59439.

Hotels:
★★★ *Chadwick*, South Promenade, FY8 1NP, ☎ (0253) 720061, AC AM BA DI, 70 rm. ℗ ≼ & ⌷ £32. Rest. ♦ ♪ & £8.
★★★ *Fernlea*, 15 South Promenade, FY8 1LU, ☎ (0253) 726726, Tx 677150, AC AM BA DI, 95 rm. ℗ ≼ & ⚲ ⌷ £45. Rest. ♦ ♪ &Tx. £10.
★★★ *St.Ives* (Consort), 7 South Promenade, FY8 1LS, ☎ (0253) 720011, AC DI, 73 rm. ℗ ≼ ⌷ £36. Rest. ♦ ♪ & £8.
● ★★ *Grand*, South Promenade, FY8 1NB, ☎ (0253) 721288, Tx 67481, AC AM BA DI, 40 rm. ℗ ≼ £52. Rest. ♦ ♪ &Tx. £10.
★★ *Lindum*, 63-67 South Promenade, FY8 1LZ, ☎ (0253) 721534, AC AM BA, 80 rm. ℗ ≼ £30. Rest. ♦ ♪ £7.

Restaurants:
● ♦ *C'est La Vie*, South Promenade, ☎ (0253) 725871, AC BA ℗ ⨇ ♪ & ⚲ Cl. 25-28 Dec. 84 rm. Book. £12.
♦ *Bennett's Bistro*, 15 Park Street, FY8 5LU, ☎ (0253) 739265 ℗ ♪ ⚲ Cl. Sun.-Mon. Book. £12.

⚲ *Eastham Hall C.P.*, Saltcoates Road (250 pl), ☎ (0253) 737907.

Recommended
Golf course: Fairhaven, Lytham Hall Park, Ansdell (off A584), ☎ (0253) 736741; Royal Lytham and St. Annes, Links Gate, ☎ (0253) 724206.

MACCLESFIELD*

Manchester, 18; Congleton, 8; London, 178 m
pop. 47,525 ☎ 0625   Cheshire B3

Set on the edge of the Southern Pennines, Macclesfield developed in the 18thC as the centre of the silk industry, which continued into the 20thC. A few early mills remain, and narrow streets on the medieval pattern lead up to the parish church, with some fine Georgian buildings around the Classical **Town Hall** (1823) in the Market Place. To the E is **Macclesfield Forest**.

▶ **St.Michael's**, rebuilt 13thC parish church, contains many large medieval tombs of local Savage family. ▶ In **West Park** is **Museum & Art Gallery** (Prestbury Road) with Egyptian collection, local history (*Easter-Sep.: Tue.-Sun., 2-4.30; Oct.-Easter: Sat. & Sun., 2-4.30; open Bank Hols.*). ▶ **Christ Church** (1775; Catherine Street) has monument

in galleried interior to Charles Roe, founder of silk industry; large **Sunday School** (1813; Roe Street) is planned as silk heritage centre.

Nearby

▶ **Nether Alderley Mill** (*6 m NW*): restored 15thC water mill with working machinery (*Apr.-Jun. & Oct.: Wed., Sun. & Bank Hol. Mons., 2-5.30 or dusk; Jul.-Sep.: daily ex. Mon. but open Bank Hol. Mons., 2-5.30.*) In village, large medieval **church** with later alterations includes Stanley family monuments. ▶ **Over Alderley** (*W*): **Hare Hill Garden** walled garden set in parkland (*Apr.-Oct.: Wed., Thur., Sun. & Bank Hol. Mons., 2-5.30*). ▶ **Prestbury** (*3 m N*), now smart commuter suburb with well-preserved pretty village centre including Norman chapel in churchyard of **St. Peter's** (13th-15thC, restored) and half-timbered **priest's house.** ▶ **Adlington Hall** (*5 m N*): Elizabethan timbered house with 15thC Great Hall (*Good Fri.-Sep.: Sun. & Bank Hols., plus Wed. & Sat. in Aug., 2-5.30*). ▶ **Capesthorne Hall**★ (*8 m W*): early 18thC house with later alterations set in park overlooking woods and lake; home of Bromley Davenport family since Norman times; also attractive Georgian chapel and gardens (*Apr.: Sun. only; May-Jun.: Wed., Sat. & Sun; Jul.-Sep.: Tue.-Thur., Sat. & Sun.: 12-6; house 2-5*). ▶ **Jodrell Bank** (*SW*), 250 ft. radio telescope built in 1952-66 with visitor centre including working models, planetarium and garden (*mid-Mar.-Oct.: daily 10.30-5.30; Nov.-mid-Mar.: wkends, 2-5*). ▶ **Gawsworth Hall**★ (*4 m SW*), furnished Tudor timber-framed manor house with tilting ground, set among trees and ornamental pools; home of Mary Fitton (d.1620), supposed 'dark lady' of Shakespeare's sonnets (*late Mar.-late Oct.: daily, 2-6*). Nearby, originally part of 15thC manor, are **church** and **rectory** with medieval great hall. ▶ Further E, in lovely countryside between Macclesfield and Congleton, runs **Macclesfield Canal** (completed 1831), fine piece of engineering designed by Thomas Telford. □

Practical information

MACCLESFIELD
ⓘ Town Hall, Market Place, ☎ (0625) 21955 ext. 115/114.
🚃 ☎ Manchester (061) 832 8353.

Hotel:
★ **Ellesmere**, 311 Buxton Road, SK11 7ES, ☎ (0625) 23791, AC AM BA, 9 rm. P 🕭 ♨ ✓ £30. Rest. ♦ , £9.

Restaurants:
♦ **Da Topo Gigio**, 15 Church Street, ☎ (0625) 22231, AC AM BA Cl. Sun., Mon. and Aug. £9.
♦ **Harlequin's**, 68a Chestergate, ☎ (0625) 32657, AC BA 𝍫 ♪ 🕭 ✽ Cl. 25 Dec., Bank Hols., Sun. Book. £7.50.
♦ **Oliver's Bistro**, 101 Chestergate, ☎ (0625) 32003, AC AM BA French. £8.

Inns or Pubs:
Bull's Head (Tetley), Market Place, ☎ (0625) 25871 P ✽ 15 rm. Bar snacks and specials. £5.
Cat & Fiddle (Robinson), ☎ (0298) 3364 P ⦓ Sandwich, 3-course meals ex. Mon eve. £5.

Recommended
Golf course: The Hollins, ☎ (0625) 23227.

Nearby

ALDERLEY EDGE, 5m NW on A34

Hotels:
★★ **De Trafford Arms** (G.W.), London Road, SK9 7AA, ☎ (0625) 583881, Tx 629462, AC AM BA DI, 37 rm. P ♨ 🕭 £56. Rest. ♦ ♪ 🕭Tx. £8.50.
★★ **Milverton House**, Wilmslow Road, SK9 7QL, ☎ Alderley Edge (0625) 583615, AC, 16 rm. P ⦓ 𝍫 ♨ £35. Rest. ♦ 🕭 £7.50.

Restaurants:
♦ **Octobers Bistro**, 47 London Road, ☎ (0625) 583942, AC BA P ♪ ✽ Cl. Sun., lunch. Book. £11.50.
♦ **Mandarin**, 2 The Parade, ☎ (0625) 584434, AM P 𝍫 ♨ ♪ 🕭 ✽ Cl. 25-26 Dec., Mon. £10.50.

BOLLINGTON, 4m N on B5091

Hotel:
★★★★ **Belgrade** (Consort-Bell), Jackson Lane, Kerridge, SK10 5BE, ☎ (0625) 73246, Tx 667217, AC AM BA DI, 64 rm. P ⦓ 𝍫 ✽ £40. Rest. ♦ ♪Tx. £10.

LANGLEY, 3m SE off A523

Inn or Pub:
Hanging Gate, Higher Sutton, ☎ (026 05) 2238 P ⦓𝍫 ♨ ✽ Bar snacks, 3-course meals, trout, game pie. £5.50.
Leather's Smithy (Tetley), Clarke Lane, Langley, ☎ (026 05) 2313 P ⦓ 𝍫 ♨ 🕭 Full range of food. £4.

MOTTRAM ST. ANDREW, 2m N off A538

Hotel:
★★★ **Mottram Hall** (De Vere), SK10 4QT, ☎ Prestbury (0625) 828135, Tx 668181, AC AM BA DI, 71 rm. P ⦓𝍫 🕭 ♨ ✏ Georgian country house standing in 120 acres of parkland, including ornamental gardens and lake. £70. Rest. ♦ ♪ 🕭Tx. £15.

NETHER ALDERLEY, 2m S on A34

Restaurant:
♦ **Wizard Country**, Macclesfield Road, ☎ (0625) 584 000, AC AM BA DI P ⦓ 𝍫 ♨ ♪ 🕭 ✽ Cl. Mon., Sun. eve. Mon.-Sat. lunch. Seafood pancakes. £11.

PRESTBURY, 4m N on A538

Hotel:
★★ **Bridge**, The Village, SK10 4DQ, ☎ (0625) 829326, AC AM BA DI, 6 rm. P 𝍫 ✽ £55. Rest. ● ♦ ♪ 🕭 £12.

Restaurants:
♦ **Gallery**, The Village, ☎ (0625) 829466, AC 𝍫 ✽ Cl. Aug., Sun.-Mon. Book. £7.
♦ **Legh Arms**, The Village, ☎ (0625) 829130, AC AM BA DI P ♨ ♪ 🕭 ✽ Cl. 25 Dec. eve. Book. £12.50.
♦ **White House**, ☎ (0625) 829376, AC AM DI P £10.

Recommended
Artizana, The Cillage, ☎ (0625) 827582.

RAINOW, 3m NE on A5082

Inn or Pub:
Highwayman (Thwaits), ☎ (0625) 73245 P ⦓ 𝍫 ♨ Bar snacks. £4.50.

WILDBOARCLOUGH, 9m SE off A54

Inn or Pub:
Crag Inn, ☎ (026 07) 239 P ⦓ 𝍫 ♨ ✽ Extensive bar food and a la carte restaurant. £6.

WINCLE, 5m SE off A54

Hotel:
★★ **Fourways Diner**, Clenlow Cross, SK11 0QL, ☎ (026 07) 228, AC BA, 7 rm. P ⦓ 𝍫 ♨ 🝙 £33. Rest. ♦ ♪ £7.

MANCHESTER**

Bolton, 11; Stockport, 6; London, 184 m
pop. 451,000 ☎ 061   Greater Manchester A2

Manchester is the commercial, entertainment and cultural centre of a huge sprawling conurbation. Set on the River Irwell it was known for weaving in medieval times and in the 18th-19thC grew into the industrial capital of the cotton industry, associated with the radical reform movement as well as factories, slums and riots. With the opening of the Manchester Ship Canal in 1894, it also became a major inland port. There is little trace of the city's long history among the vast modern development schemes but the centre includes some splendid 19thC public buildings and a few Georgian enclaves.

▶ Centre: Gothic **Town Hall** (1867-76; extended 1938 Albert Square) by Alfred Waterhouse, including great hall with hammerbeam roof (*tours*). ▶ **City Art Gallery**★

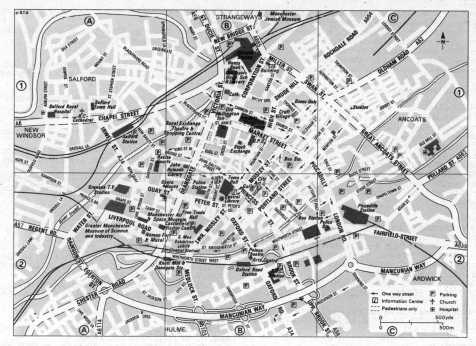

MANCHESTER

(Mosley Street) housed in splendid Classical building (1825-29) by Charles Barry: outstanding collections of European paintings, drawings, sculpture and decorative arts; adjoining **Athenaeum** (1837 Princess Street) houses **Gallery of Modern Art** with collections from 1900 (Mon.-Sat., 10-6). ▶ **Central Reference Library** (1934). ▶ **Free Trade Hall** (1856, restored after bomb damage 1940; Peter Street): splendid Renaissance building, home of city's Halle Orchestra. ▶ **John Rylands Library** (1890-99, in fine Gothic style), including early printed books, fine bindings and rare engravings among collections. ▶ To N of Town Hall, with extensive shopping area and modern developments: **St. Ann's** (1709-12), dignified Wren-style church with galleried interior, fine font (1711) and Carracci's *Descent from the Cross*; attractive St. Ann's Square has **statue** of Cobden (1867). ▶ **Royal Exchange** (Cross and Market Streets), large block built 1914-21 as a cotton exchange, now theatre complex, with 16thC half-timbered pub nearby. ▶ To NW, facing river, small **cathedral★** (mainly 15th-16thC, restored): interior includes choir **stalls★** (1505-09) with quaint misericords and 18thC ironwork and brass of Warden Huntingdon (d.1458); paintings (1963) by Carel Weight over entrance to octagonal **chapter house** (1485) and Eric Gill sculpture (1933). ▶ Beyond is **Cheltham's Hospital★** (1422), fine collegiate buildings (now school) including splendid 17thC **library**.

Outer districts

▶ SE of centre: **University** district with late 19thC and modern buildings. In Oxford Road: ▶ **Manchester Museum**, devoted mainly to natural history and archaeology (Mon.-Sat., 10-5); ▶ **Whitworth Art Gallery★**, with distinguished collections of watercolours, drawings, paintings and sculpture; also important textile collection (Mon.-Sat., 10-5, Thur., 10-9). ▶ In Liverpool Road: **Science Industry Museum**, housed in world's first passenger railway station, has working exhibits showing story of power, plus Liverpool/Manchester railway exhibition (daily, 10.30-5). ▶ **Air & Space Museum** includes historic aircraft and space artifacts (daily, 10-5). ▶ Opposite is **Castleford Urban Heritage Park**. ▶ **Rusholme** (2 m S): **Platt Hall**, Georgian country house of 1760s containing **English Costume Gallery**, with extensive collection of clothes and accessories from 17thC to present (Apr.-Sep.: Tue.-Fri., 10-6). ▶ **Didsbury** (5 m S), smart suburb with attractive park and early 17thC stone church of **St. James** containing 17th-18thC monuments; nearby is **Fletcher Moss**, parsonage with **heritage museum** devoted to local history and regional artists including L.S. Lowry (spring and summer, apply locally). ▶ **Northenden** (7 m S): 16thC half-timbered **Wythenshawe Hall** (→Stockport). ▶ N of centre: **Cheetham** (3¹/₂ m NW), with elegant, unaltered Gothic church of **St. Luke** (1839). **Transport Museum** (Boyle Street): collection of large vehicles (Apr.-Oct.: Wed., Sat., Sun. & Bank Hols., 10-5)▶ **Prestwich: Heaton Hall★** (6 m N) : magnificent house designed in 1722 with sumptuous interior decorations and period furniture and paintings (spring summer, apply locally).

Nearby

▶ **Salford** (W), separated from Manchester only by narrow Irwell, old industrial town, mostly rebuilt. Notable buildings include: **St. John's RC Cathedral** (1855); **St. Philip's** church (1825) by Robert Smirke; Classical **Town Hall** (1825-27). By **Peel Park** is **Museum & Art Gallery**, with regional paintings including large L.S. Lowry collection (Mon.-Fri., 10-5, Sun., 2-5). **Ordsall Hall** (Taylorson Street): 15th-17thC timbered house now housing local history **museum** (Mon.-Fri., 10-5, Sun., 2-5). **Mining Museum** (Buile Hill Park) includes reproductions of mines (Mon.-Fri., 10-12.30, 1.30-5, Sun., 2-5). ▶ **Eccles** (W), former cotton town noted for its 'cakes', has restored 15th-16thC church, **St. Mary's**, with fine 15thC nave roof,

some 17thC monuments. **Monks Hall** (Wellington Road) dating to 16thC is **museum** containing toys and industrial machines (*Mon.-Fri., 10-5, Sun., 2-5*). ▶ **Middleton** (*N*), old textile town near hills towards Rochdale, has interesting turn-of-the-century buildings by Edgar Wood and a large medieval **church** set on a hill, **St.Leonard's**, with traces of Norman work, 16th-17thC woodwork and monuments. ☐

Practical information

MANCHESTER

ⓘ Town Hall Extension, Lloyd Street, ☎ (061) 234 3157/8; Manchester Inter. Airport, Inter. Arrivals Hall, ☎ (061) 436 3344.

✈ Manchester international Airport (10m off A5103), ☎ (061) 489 3000.

▦ Picadilly (C2), Victoria (B1), ☎ (061) 832 8353.

▭ (B2) ☎ 2286400/2287800.

Car rental: Europcar, Piccadilly Plaza, York Street, ☎ (061) 8324114; Manchester Airport, ☎ (061) 436 2200437 6161.

Hotels:
★★★★ *Piccadilly* (Embassy), P.O. Box 107, Piccadilly, M60 1QR (B1), ☎ (061) 236 8414, Tx 668765, AC AM BA DI, 255 rm. ℗ £90. Rest. ♦ ♪ &Tx. £11.50.

★★★ *Britannia* (Britannia), Portland Street, M1 3LA (B2), ☎ (061) 228 2288, Tx 665007, AC AM BA DI, 362 rm. ℗ ⌂ ⌐ £67. Rest. ♦ ♪Tx. £12.

★★★ *Grand* (T.H.F.), Aytoun Street, M1 3DR (B2), ☎ (061) 236 9559, Tx 667580, AC AM BA DI, 140 rm. ℗ £67.50. Rest. ♦ Tx. £9.

★★ *Simpson's*, 122 Withington Road, M16 8FB (A2), ☎ (061) 226 2235, Tx 667822, AC AM BA DI, 40 rm. ℗ ⌐ £32. Rest. ♦ ♪ &Tx. £7.

Restaurants:
● ♦ *Armenian Taverna*, 3 Princess Street (B2), ☎ (061) 834 9025, AC AM BA DI ⟨ ◻ ♪ Cl. Sat. Book. £8.50.

● ♦ *Connaught*, 60 George Street (B2), ☎ (061) 236 0191, AC AM BA DI ℗ ♪ & ℅ Cl. 25 Dec. £13.

● ♦ *Hong Kong*, 47 Faulkner Street (B2), ☎ (061) 236 0565, AC AM BA DI ℗ ♪ ℅ Cl. 24-25 Dec. Book. £11.

● ♦ *Moss Nook*, Ringway Road, Manchester Airport, ☎ (061) 437 4778, AC AM BA DI ℗ ▦ ℅ Cl. 2 wks Dec.-Jan. Book. £18.50.

● ♦ *Mr Kuks*, 55a Mosley Street (B1), ☎ (061) 236 0659, AM BA AC DI ♪ ℅ Cl. Mon., 25 Dec. £8.

♦ *Assam Gourmet*, 17a Bloom Street (A1), ☎ (061) 236 6836, AM AC DI Cl. 25-26 Dec., 1 Jan., Good Fri., Bank Hols. lunch. Indian. £10.

♦ *Gaylord*, Marriot's Court, Spring Gardens, Amethyst House (B1), ☎ (061) 832 6037, AC AM BA DI ℗ ♪ & Cl. 25 Dec.-1 Jan. Book. £9.50.

♦ *Isola Bella*, 6 Booth St (B2), ☎ (061) 236 6417, AC BA DI ♪ ℅ Cl. Bank Hols., lunch. Book. £15.

♦ *Kathmandu Tandoori*, 44 Sackville Street (B2), ☎ (061) 236 4684, AC AM BA DI ℗ ♪ & ℅ Cl. 25-26 Dec., Bank Hols. lunch. Book. £6.

♦ *Leen Hong*, 35 George Street (B2), ☎ (061) 228 0926, AC AM BA DI Cl. Mon. Japanese. £15.

♦ *Market*, 30 Edge Street (B2), ☎ (061) 834 3743, AC AM ℗ ♪ ℅ Cl. Aug., Sun.-Mon. lunch. Book. £11.

♦ *Mina Japan*, 63 George Street (B2), ☎ (061) 228 2598, AC AM BA DI Cl. Mon. Japanese. £15.

♦ *On the Eighth Day*, 109 Oxford Road, All Saints (B2), ☎ (061) 273 1850 ▦ ♪ & Cl. Sun., 25 Dec-1 Jan. Vegetarian dishes. £4.

♦ *Rajdoot*, St.James House, South King's Street (A1), ☎ (061) 834 2176, AC AM BA DI ♪ ℅ Cl. Sun. lunch, Bank Hols. lunch. Book. £9.

♦ *Sam's Chop House*, Back Pool Fold, Chapel Walks (A1), ☎ (061) 834 1526, AC AM BA DI ℅ Cl. Bank Hols., Sat., Sun. eve. Book. £8.

♦ *Tandoor*, 34 Charlotte Street (B2), ☎ (061) 236 1085, AC AM BA DI ♪ ℅ Cl. 25-26 Dec., Bank Hols. lunch, 1 Jan. lunch, Sun. lunch. Indian dishes. Book. £10.

♦ *Terrazza*, 14 Nicholas Street (B1), ☎ (061) 236 4033, AC AM BA DI ℗ ♪ ℅ Cl. Mon., Bank Hols. Sun. Book. £9.

♦ *Truffles*, 63 Bridge Street (A1), ☎ (061) 832 9393, AC

AM BA DI ♪ ℅ Cl. Bank Hols., 2 wks Aug., Sun.-Mon. Book. £17.

♦ *Woo Sang*, 19 George Street (B2), ☎ (061) 236 3697, AC AM BA DI Cantonese. £15.

Inns or Pubs:
Britons Protection, 50 Great Bridgewater Street (B2), ☎ (061) 236 5895, AC ▦ & ℅ Snacks and restaurant menu. £6.

⚓ *Holly Bank C.P.*, Warburton Bridge Road, Rixton (40 pl), ☎ (061) 775 2842.

Recommended
Antique shop: *Koopman, E. C. T., Son Ltd*, 4 John Dalton Street, ☎ (061) 834 2420, jewelry and silver.
Delicatessen: at Alderley Edge, *Alderley Cheese Wedge*, 16 London Road, ☎ (0625) 583728, over a hundred varieties of cheeses.
Golf course: The Dales, Ashbourne Grove Stand, ☎ (061) 766 2388; Swinton Park, East Lancashire Road, Swinton, ☎ (061) 794 1785.

Nearby

ALTRINCHAM, 8m SW on A56

Hotels:
★★★ *Cresta Court* (B.W.), Church Street, WA14 4DP, ☎ (061) 928 8017, Tx 667242, AC AM BA DI, 139 rm. ℗ & £49.50. Rest. ♦ ♪ &Tx. £9.

★★★ *Pelican* (GW), Manchester Road, West Timperley, WA14 5NH, ☎ (061) 962 7414, AC AM BA DI, 50 rm. ℗ & £49. Rest. ♦ ♪ & £8.

Restaurants:
♦ *Hilal*, 351 Stockport Road, Timperley, ☎ (061) 980 4090, AC BA ℗ Cl. 25-26 Dec. £9.50.

♦ *Le Bon Viveur*, Wood Lane, Timperley, ☎ (061) 904 0266, AM BA DI. ℗ Cl. public hols. ex. Christmas, Sat. lunch. £18.

♦ *Nutcracker*, 43 Oxford Road, ☎ (061) 928 4399 ℗ ℅ Cl. Bank Hols., Sun., Wed. eve. Vegetarian dishes. £5.

ASHTON-UNDER-LYNE, 6m E off A635

Hotel:
★★ *York House*, York Place, off Richmond Street, OL6 7TX, ☎ (061) 330 5899, AC AM BA DI, 24 rm. ℗ £45. Rest. ♦ ♪ £10.

Recommended
Antique shop: *Kenworthy's Ltd*, 226 Stamford Street, ☎ (061) 3303043, Jewelry and silver.

BOWDON, 11m SW on A56

Hotels:
● ★★★ *Bowdon*, Langham Road, Manchester Airport (Ringway), WA14 2HT (B2 off map), ☎ (061) 928 7121, Tx 668208, AC AM BA DI, 41 rm. ◻ £50. Rest. ♦ ♪Tx. £10.

★★★ *Bowdon Croft*, Green Walk, WA14 2SN, ☎ (061) 928 1718, AM AC BA DI, 8 rm. ℗ ⟨ ▦ ◻ ℅ £51. Rest. ♦ & £11.

FALLOWFIELD, 3m S on B5093

Hotel:
★★★ *Willow Bank*, 340 Wilmslow Road, MI4 6AF (B2 off map), ☎ (061) 224 0461, Tx 668222, AC AM BA DI, 123 rm. ℗ £40. Rest. ♦ ♪Tx. £10.

HALE BARNES, 3m SE on A538

Hotel:
★★★ *Four Seasons*, Hale Road, WA15 8XW, ☎ (061) 904 0301, Tx 665492, AC AM BA DI, 48 rm. ℗ & £80. Rest. ♦ ♪ &Tx. £11.

HALE, 11m SE on A538

Hotel:
★★ *Ashley* (De Vere), Ashley Road, WA15 9SF, ☎ (061) 928 3794, Tx 669406, AC AM BA DI, 49 rm. ℗ ◻ £55. Rest. ♦ ♪Tx. £9.

LEVENSHULME, 3m SE on A6

Restaurant:
♦ *That Cafe*, 1031 Stockport Road, ☎ (061) 432 4672, AC AM BA ♪ ✵ Cl. Sun. eve., Mon. eve., Tue.-Sat. lunch. Book. £12.

RUSHOLME, 2m OE on A04

Restaurant:
♦ *Casa Espana*, 100 Wilmslow Road, ☎ (061) 224 6826, AC AM BA DI ℗ ♪ ✵ Cl. Sun. Book. £12.

SALE, 4m SW off A56

Hotel:
★★★ *Amblehurst Private*, 44 Washway Road, M33 1QZ, ☎ Manchester (061) 973 8800, Tx 668871, AC AM DI, 10 rm. ℗ ⬛ £42. Rest. ♦ ♪Tx. £10.

SALFORD, 3m N off M62

Hotel:
★★ *Beaucliffe*, 254 Eccles Old Road, M6 8ES (A1 off map), ☎ (061) 789 5092, AC AM BA DI, 21 rm. ℗ ⅋ £42. Rest. ♦ ♪ ⅋ £8.

Inn or Pub:
Mark Addy, Stanley Street, ☎ (061) 832 4080 ℗ ⋞ ⬛ 50 varieties of cheese, 9 pates. £2.

Recommended
Golf course: *Brackley Municipal*, Walken, ☎ (061) 790 6076.

WYTENSHAWE, 2m E off M56

Hotel:
★★★ *Excelsior* (T.H.F.), Ringway Road, Manchester Airport, M22 5NS (B2 off map), ☎ (061) 437 5811, Tx 668721, AC AM BA DI, 308 rm. ℗ ⅋ ▣ £62. Rest. ♦ ⅋Tx. £10.

MORECAMBE*

Lancaster, 4; Preston, 27; London, 241 m
pop. 41,432 ☎ 0524   Lancashire A1

This popular holiday resort looks across Morecambe Bay towards the Cumbrian mountains. Originally a group of villages, of which a few 17thC houses remain, it developed with the coming of the railway in 1848. Good beaches, five miles of promenades, a pier, parks and gardens are among the resort's attractions, which also include **Marineland oceanarium**, Morecambe **Leisure Park** and illuminations (*Aug.-Oct.*).

▶ **Heysham**, to S, has similar holiday attractions, including **Leisure Park** and **harbour.** Its old **church**, next to 17th-18thC cottages on edge of bay, includes Anglo-Saxon and Norman work. On clifftop above church, giving splendid views, is plain little Saxon **chapel** named after St.Patrick who supposedly landed here with missionaries from Ireland; nearby are tombs cut into rock. ▶ At **Middleton** (*1 m SE*) is 15thC **church** overlooking park, with wooden bell-chamber and interesting woodwork, brasses and stained-glass windows. ▶ **Overton**: largely Norman **church** isolated in field. Beyond, to SW, lies **Sunderland Point**, cut off from mainland except at low tide.   □

Practical information _____

MORECAMBE
ⓘ Marine Road Central, ☎ (0524) 414110.
▰▰▰ ☎ Lancaster, (0524) 32333.

Hotels:
★★★ *Midland*, Marine Road, LA4 4BZ, ☎ (0524) 417180, AC AM BA DI, 46 rm. ℗ ⅋ £60. Rest. ♦ ♪ ⅋ £10.
★★★ *Strathmore* (Consort), Marine Road East, LA4 5AP, ☎ (0524) 421234, Tx 57515, AC AM BA DI, 55 rm. ℗ ⋞ ⅋ ✵ £46. Rest. ♦ ♪ ⅋Tx. £7.

⚓ *Broadfields C.P.*, 276 Oxcliffe Road (58 pl), ☎ (0524) 410278;*Holgates C.P.*, Cove Road, Silverdale (50 pl), ☎ (0524) 701508;*Sandside Farm C.C.S.*, St.Michaels Lane, Bolton-le-Sands (10 pl), ☎ (0524) 822311.

Recommended
Golf course: *The Club House, Bare (5m from M6)*, ☎ (0524) 412841.

Nearby

CARNFORTH, 6 1/2m N off A6/M6

Hotel:
★★ *Royal Station*, Market Street, LA5 9BT, ☎ (0524) 732033, AM BA DI, 12 rm. ℗ £33. Rest. ♦ ♪ ⅋ £9.

HEST BANK, 2 1/2m NE on A5105

Inn or Pub:
Hest Bank (Boddingtons), Hest Bank Lane, ☎ (0524) 824339 ℗ ⋞ ⬛ ⌕ ⅋ ✵ 3-course meals Mon.-Fri. £4.

HEATON-WITH-OXCLIFFE, 4m S off B5273

Inn or Pub:
Golden Ball (Snatchems, Mitchells), Lancaster Road, ☎ (0524) 63317 ℗ ⋞ ⬛ ⌕ Bar snacks, local salmon. £3.50.

NANTWICH*

Chester, 2; Stocke-on-Trent, 14; London, 165 m
pop. 11,867 ☎ 0270   Cheshire B3

An old market town, Nantwich was known from Roman times for its salt mines and remained a centre of communications after the salt trade declined. Its parish church and outline of streets remain from medieval times and the town has a pleasant mix of Tudor, Georgian and Victorian architecture, 20thC developments. To the E is the 19thC railway town of Crewe.

▶ **St.Mary's**, in centre, is mainly 14th-15thC and contains much medieval stone and wood carving, including vaulted stone roof and choir **stalls** and misericords. ▶ **Welsh Row**, beyond bridge (1803), includes many fine old buildings, and on outskirts **Churche's Mansion** (Hospital Street), 16thC half-timbered house (*Apr.-Oct.: daily, 10-5*). ▶ **Museum** (Pillory Street) shows local history (*Mon. & Tue., Thur.-Sat., 10.30-4.30*).

Nearby

▶ **Dorfold Hall** (*1 m W*), Jacobean country house (*Apr.-Oct.: Tue. & Bank Hol. Mons., 2-5*). ▶ Nearby village of **Acton** has medieval **church** restored over centuries, retaining 13thC work and, among monuments, 14th and early 17thC effigies of Mainwarings and Wilbrahams families. ▶ S of **Faddiley** (*4 m W*) is small restored 17thC **Woodhey Chapel** (*Apr.-Oct.: Sat. & Bank Hol. Mons., 2-5*). ▶ Continuing W, A534 runs by sharp slopes of **Peckforton** and **Bickerton Hills** through beautiful border country with remains of castles crossing into Wales by 14thC **bridge** spanning River Dee at **Farndon** (*17 m W*); nearby is **Stretton Mill**, restored water-powered corn mill dating from 16thC (*Easter-Sep.: Tue.-Sun. & Bank Hols., 2-6*). ▶ **Cholmondeley Castle Gardens** (*9 m W*), park of large early 19thC castle (*private*) with lakeside picnic area, old chapel and farm with rare animal breeds (*Easter-Sep.: Sun. & Bank Hols., 12-6*). ▶ **Malpas** (*5 m SW*), village with 18thC houses overlooked by medieval **church** (14thC with 15th and 16thC additions; mound behind church is site of castle that once commanded Welsh border route.   □

Practical information _____

NANTWICH
ⓘ Beam Street, ☎ (0270) 623914.
▰▰▰ ☎ Crewe, (0270) 255245.

Hotel:
★ **Lamb**, Hospital Street, CW5 5RH, ☎ (0270) 625286, AC BA, 16 rm. P ⌘ £36. Rest. ♦ ♪ £10.

Restaurants:
♦ **Churche's Mansion**, 150 Hopital Street, ☎ (0270) 625933, AC AM DI BA P ⌘ Cl. Christmas.
♦ **Jade House**, 12a Love Lane, ☎ (0270) 626456, AC BA ⌘ ♪ Cl. 24-25 Dec. Book. £8.
♦ **Peter Cellers Steak House**, 1-3 Pillory Street, ☎ (0270) 629349. £10.

Nearby

AUDLEM, 7m S on A529

Inn or Pub:
Bridge (Marstons), 12 Shropshire Street, ☎ (0270) 811267 P ⌘ ⌘ Hot and cold meals, Sun. lunch. £3.50.

CREWE, 4m NE on A534
⌐ Market Hall, Earle Street, ☎ (0270) 583191.
▨▨ ☎ (0270) 255245.
Car-rental: Europcar, Crew Arms Motor Co, Station Approach, Crewe Road; rail/drive ☎ (0270) 256421-2.

Hotel:
★★★ **Crewe Arms** (Embassy), Nantwich Road, CW1 1DW, ☎ (0270) 213204, AC AM BA DI, 35 rm. P £50. Rest. ♦ ♪ ⌘ £8.

Recommended
Golf course: Fields Road, Haslington, ☎ (0270) 585032.

MALPAS, 14m W

Restaurant:
♦ **Market House**, Church Street, ☎ (0948) 860400, AC BA ⌘ Cl. Sun. dinner, Mon., 2 wks in Aug. £13.

MARBURY, 8m SW off A530

Inn or Pub:
Swan (Shewsbury), ☎ (0948) 3715 P ⌘ ⌘ ⌘ Home-made specials, steaks, salads. £5.50.

SPURSTOW, 8m NW on A49

Restaurant:
♦ **Rembrandt**, Whitchurch Road, ☎ Bunbury (0829) 260281, AC AM BA DI P ⌘ ♪ ⌘ Cl. 24 Dec., Mon. Book. £11.

WORLESTON, 2 1/2m N on A54

Hotel:
● ★★★ **Rookery Hall** (Prestige), CW5 6DQ, ☎ (0270) 626866, Tx 367169, AC AM BA DI, 11 rm. P ⌘ ⌘ ⌘ ⌘ £120. Rest. ● ♦ Tx. £25.

NORTHWICH*

Chester, 18; Manchester, 24; London, 176 m
pop. 17,126 ☎ 0606   Cheshire B3

The centre of Cheshire's once rich salt-mining industry, Northwich grew rapidly in the 18th-19thC. Subsidence damaged the town, which has a restored medieval parish **church** among otherwise 19thC buildings and modern developments.

▶ **St. Helen's**, Whitton: large, restored church (mainly 15thC) set on hill, with splendid 16thC nave and chancel roof. ▶ **Salt Museum** (London Road) shows history of Cheshire's salt industry (*daily ex. Mon., 2-5 (10-5 Jul. & Aug.); closed Sun. Oct.-Easter*).

Nearby

▶ **Anderton Boat Lift**★ (*1$^{1}/_{2}$ m NW*), remarkable piece of engineering designed 1875 to raise barges from River Weaver to **Trent & Mersey Canal.** ▶ **Great Budworth** (*3 m N*): imposing 14th-15thC **church** on hill above village; interior includes fine 16thC roof and medieval stalls. ▶ **Arley Hall Gardens**★ (*2 m NE*): Victorian mansion including chapel by Anthony Salvin; charming gardens of great variety,

woodland walk and farm animals (*Apr.-Sep.: Tue.-Sun. & Bank Hol. Mons., 2-5, gardens 5.30; Jul. & Aug., 12-5/5.30*). ▶ **Vale Royal Abbey**, Whitegate (*3$^{1}/_{2}$ m SW*), 16thC house built on site of Cistercian abbey founded in 1277, set in grounds (*Sat., Sun. & Bank Hol. Mons., 11-4. Closed 25th Dec.*). ▶ Extending 12 m NW towards Mersey Estuary is **Delamere Forest**★, with walks and drives among hills and pinewoods dotted with ponds (meres); on high point of **Eddisbury Hill** (567 ft) above Delamere village (*8 m*) is reconstructed Saxon fort.   □

Practical information _____

NORTHWICH
▨▨▨ ☎ Manchester (061) 832 8353.

Hotel:
★★★ **Woodpecker** (GW), London Rd, CW9 8EG, ☎ (0606) 45524, Tx 629462, AC AM BA DI, 34 rm. P ⌘ £48. Rest. ♦ ♪ ⌘ Cl. Christmas.

Recommended
Golf course: Delamere Forest (N off A556), ☎ (0606) 882807; Sandiway, ☎ (0606) 883247.

Nearby

GREAT BUDWORTH, 3m N off A559

Inn or Pub:
George & Dragon (Tetley), High Street, ☎ Comberbach (0606) 891317, AC P ⌘ ⌘ ⌘ Lunches, restaurant Wed-Sun eve. £3.50.

HARTFORD, 2m SW off A559

Hotel:
★★★★ **Hartford Hall** (Consort), School Lane, CW8 1PW, ☎ Northwich (0606) 75711, AC AM BA DI, 21 rm. P ⌘ ⌘ ⌘ ⌘ £55. Rest. ♦ ♪ ⌘ £11.

LITTLE LEIGH, 3 1/2m NW off A533

Inn or Pub:
Holly Bush (Greenall), ☎ (0606) 853196 P ⌘ ⌘ ⌘ Sandwiches and pies. £4.

OLDHAM*

Burnley, 21; Manchester, 7; London, 197 m
pop. 107,095 ☎ 061   Greater Manchester B2

The industrial revolution transformed Oldham from a hillside village into an important cotton-spinning centre. Much of the town has been redeveloped, with a new shopping and Civic Centre alongside 19thC buildings. Alexandra Park provides some green space and the local specialities of black pudding, tripe and muffins can be bought in Tommyfield open market.
▶ **Art Gallery** (Union Street): collections of paintings, ceramics and glass, and oriental objets d'art (*Mon., Wed.-Fri., 10-5; Tue., 10-1; Sat., 10-4*). ▶ **Local Interest Centre** (Greaves Street); exhibitions on local themes (*hours as above*).

Nearby

▶ **Ashton-under-Lyne** (*4 m S*), 19thC cotton town with restored medieval parish **church** of St. Michael containing magnificent stained glass, ca. 1500. ▶ **Uppermill** (*5 m E*), with **Saddleworth Museum & Art Gallery** (High Street), former woollen mill alongside Huddersfield Narrow Canal: local history (*daily, 2-5*). ▶ Road ascends moors via **Delph**, old cloth-making village with some weavers' stone houses and cobbled streets, reaching summit of Standedge (1471 ft) on Yorkshire border. ▶ **Rochdale** (*7 m N*), once prosperous mill town beside moors. ▶ **Town Hall** (1866), Victorian Gothic building with 190ft tower and lavishly decorated interior (*tours*), set in public gardens with **statue** of John Bright. On hill above giving fine views, restored medieval **church** of St.Chad with partly 13thC interior. ▶ **Art Gallery** (Esplanade) containing British 18th-20thC paintings (*Mon., Tue., Thu. & Fri., 10-5;*

Wed., 1-5; Sat., 10-5; Sun., 2.30-5); ▶ **Museum** (Sparrow Lane): 18thC vicarage with displays of local history and rural industries including reconstructed interiors and John Bright memorabilia (*Mon.-Fri., 12-5; Sat., 10-1, 2-5; closed Sun. & public hols.*).▶ In Toad Lane is original store of Rochdale Co-operative Pioneers, opened 1844, now **museum** containing material associated with co-operative movement (*Tue.-Sat., 10-12, 2-4*). ▶ **Healey Dell** nature reserve (*2¹⁄₂ m N of Rochdale*), with nature trail set in wooded moorland valley. ▶ **Littleborough** (*3 m E*), small town with many stone buildings including heritage centre in **Coach House** showing Pennine local history (*Sun.-Fri., 2-5; Sat., 10-5*); nearby, to S, is **Hollingworth Lake Country Park** with sailing, boat rentals and nature reserve. ▶ A58 continues climb into moors, close to well-preserved stretch of **Roman road** that runs across the Yorkshire border. □

Practical information ————————————

OLDHAM
ⓘ Local Studies Library, 84 Union Street, ☎ (061) 678 4654.
▰▰ O. Mumps, O. Werneth, ☎ (061) 832 8353.
Car rental: Europcar, Volksmater Ltd, 151-157 Huddersfield Road, ☎ (061) 63337098.

Hotel:
★★★★ **Belgrade** (Consort-Bell), Manchester Street, OL8 1UZ, ☎ (061) 624 0555, Tx 667782, AC AM BA DI, 135 rm. ℗ ✖ £46. Rest. ◆ ♪ ⅃Tx. £10.75.

Inn or Pub:
Bulls Head (Bass), Grains Bar, ☎ (061 624) 1759 ℗ ⸮ ⚲ Bar snacks, full a la carte menu. £3.

⅄ at Littleborough, *Hollingworth Lake CP*, Rakewood (20 pl), ☎ (0706) 78661.

Recommended
Golf course: Stamford, Huddersfield Road, Stalybridge, ☎ (045 75) 2126.
❦: *J. Bradbury Co.*, Alexandra Craft Centre, Uppermill, Dam Head, ☎ (045 77) 5984, craft centre filled with china, pottery, wooden items etc.

Nearby

CHADDERTON, 1m W on A627

Hotel:
★★★ **Bower** (De Vere), Hollinwood Avenue, OL9 8DE, ☎ (061) 682 7254, Tx 666883, AC AM BA DI, 66 rm. ℗ ⚿ ⅃ £75. Rest. ◆ ♪Tx. £11.50.

DELPH, 6m NE on A62

Hotel:
★★★ **Cottage**, Huddersfield Road, OL3 5LX, ☎ Saddleworth (045 77) 4297, AC AM BA DI, 7 rm. ℗ ⸮ ⚿ ⚲ ▣ ⚉ £49.95. Rest. ◆ ♪ £14.38.

SCOUTHEAD, 3m E on A62

Inn or Pub:
Three Crowns (Webster), 955 Huddersfield Road, ☎ (061) 624 1766 ℗ ⸮ ⅃ ⚿ Bar snacks, full meals. £4.50.

UPPERMILL, 4m E on A670

Inn or Pub:
Cross Keys (Leesan), Running Hill Gate, ☎ (045 77) 4626 ℗ ⸮ ⚿ Bar snacks, 3-course meals. £3.50.

ORMSKIRK*

Preston,17; Liverpool, 13; London, 205 m
pop. 27,753 ☎ 0695   Lancashire A2

This old market town has been largely rebuilt but the **church** of St. Peter & St. Paul is medieval, and has an unusual 15thC tower and spire set side by side; in the Derby Chapel are 15th-16thC tombs of the Earls of Derby.

Nearby

▶ **Burscough** (*2¹⁄₂ m N*), to NW at **Martin Mere**, 45-acre **Wildfowl Trust.** ▶ **Rufford Old Hall★** (*7 m N*): half-timbered 15thC hall set in gardens and containing 17thC furniture, tapestries, 16thC arms and armour; wings include **museum** of Lancashire village life in 18th-19thC (*Apr.-Oct. daily ex. Fri., 2-5.30, gardens. 11-5*). ▶ In **Rufford** village is small, typically Victorian brick and stone **church** (1869) with memorials from earlier church. ▶ **Aughton** (*1¹⁄₂ m S*): **church** of St.Michael (mainly 15th-16thC) has 14thC spire rising from octagonal tower, and a few interesting 17th-18thC monuments plus part of Anglo-Saxon cross (9th-10thC). □

Practical information ————————————

ORMSKIRK
▰▰ ☎ Liverpool (051) 709 9696.

Inn or Pub:
Buck i'th' Vine (Walker), Burscough Street, ☎ (0695) 72647 ℗ ⚿ ✖ ⅃ Bar snacks and homemade specials, chili, pizza, pies. £3.
⅄ *Abbey Farm*, Blythe Lane (35 pl), ☎ (0695) 72686.

Recommended
Antique shop: *Webster, E.W. Antiques*, Wash Farm, Bickerstaffe, ☎ (0695) 24322, furniture and metalwork.
Golf course: Cranes Lane, Lathom, ☎ (0695) 72112.

PRESTON*

Lancaster, 23; Manchester, 32; London, 213 m
pop. 143,734 ☎ 0772   Lancashire A2

An industrial, commercial and shopping centre, Preston is set on the Ribble with docks built in the late 19thC. The town was transformed by the Industrial Revolution, when it became an important engineering and cotton-weaving centre. It retains an attractive Georgian quarter, old mills and many Victorian churches among extensive recent rebuilding. There are several parks and imposing 19th and 20thC public buildings.

▶ In or near centre: pedestrians-only St.George's shopping precinct (1964) between **Fishergate** and **Friargate**, the town's principal modern streets. ▶ S of Fishergate, around **Winckley Square**, are pleasant late-Georgian houses. ▶ Market Place is dominated by **Harris Museum and Art Gallery★**, built 1882-93 in Classical style and containing collections of fine and decorative arts and natural history (*Mon.-Fri., 10-5*). ▶ Parish church of **St.John's** (Church Street), rebuilt 19thC with tall partly 16thC steeple. ▶ **St.Paul's** (1823-25, Park Road), stone-built in Gothic style with largely original, well-preserved interior. ▶ Outside centre: **St.Walburghe's** RC church (Weston Street) built 1850-54 by Joseph Hansom (designer of hansom cab). ▶ **Fulwood Barracks** (Watling Street Road), fine stone building of 1842-48, housing **Museum** of Queen's Lancashire Regiment (*Mon.-Fri., 8.30-12.30, 2-4.30*).

Nearby

▶ **Walton-le-Dale** and Higher Walton (*3 m SE*), with partly 16thC **church** of St.Leonard above Ribble, containing monuments. ▶ **Hoghton Tower★** (*6 m SE*), dramatic 16thC fortified mansion set on hill, with walled gardens and banqueting hall; interior includes collection of antique dolls and doll's houses (*Easter Sat., Sun. & Mon.; Sun., Easter - Oct., plus Sat. in Jul. & Aug. & Bank Hols.; 2-5*). ▶ **Samlesbury** (*3 m E*), village with 16thC **church** of St.Leonard in attractive setting near Ribble, containing fine monument (1801) by Kendrick. ▶ **Samlesbury Hall** (*2¹⁄₂ m further*): timber-framed manor-house, with 15thC beamed hall; also collection of furniture and changing exhibitions (*Tue.-Sun., 11.30-5, 4 in winter; closed Mon.*). ▶ **Woodplumpton** (*45 m NW*), village in Fylde countryside with attractive creamy-

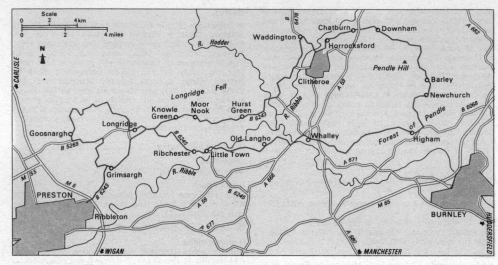

Ribble valley and forest of Pendle

pink stone **church** of St.Anne (15thC, largely rebuilt 1748). ▶ **Garstang** (*7 m N*), small market town on Lancaster Canal and River Wyre, with some attractive 18thC buildings. ▶ 1 m S, at **Churchtown,** is Garstang's ancient parish **church** of St.Helen's, with 15thC tower and 13thC stonework in interior. ▶ **Beacon Fell Country Park**★ (*8 m NNE*): 185 acres of conifer woods and moorland with picnic areas, woodland walks and fine views from summit (873 ft); part of Forest of Bowland (→).

Ribble Valley and Forest of Pendle round trip (¹/₂ 1 day)

▶ Beautiful drive through valley of River Ribble, moving into remote fells near Yorkshire border and returning via **Pendle Hill** and **Forest of Pendle.**

▶ From Preston via district of **Ribbleton** (B6243), branching (*2 m*) to B5269: **Goosnargh** (*5 m*), attractive little village, grouped round **church** dating to early 16thC and Bushell Hospital, founded 1735. ▶ **Longridge** (*7 m*), in wooded countryside at edge of **Longridge Fell** (over 1150 ft). ▶ B6243 skirts Fell — sweeping views from **Jeffrey Hill** and **Kemple End** — via **Knowle Green, Moor Nook** and **Hurst Green** (*10 m*), village set deep below hillside. ▶ Crossing river and branching left: **Waddington** (*16 m, on B6478*), village in moorland setting with **Old Hall** dating to 15thC, home of Waddington family, and **church** (rebuilt 1901) retaining some 15thC work. ▶ Descending to valley, in 3m, historic market and cotton town of **Clitheroe** (→), with ruin of Norman **keep** high above attractive streets. ▶ From here skirt N edge of **Pendle Hill**, with glorious views from summit (1827 ft) via pleasant stone-built villages of **Horrocksford, Chatburn** and **Downham** (*21 m*), with restored **church** retaining 15thC tower and attractive interior, and large rebuilt **Downham Hall** dating to 16thC. ▶ Following E side of hill: **Barley** (*25 m*); **Newchurch,** where **church** perched on hillside includes 18thC galleried interior; and into high moorland of **Forest of Pendle** around **Higham** (*28 m, on A6068*). ▶ **Whalley** (*32 m*): ruins of 13thC **abbey** by River Calder and medieval **church**★. ▶ **Langho** (*35 m*): two villages, with plain 16thC church incorporating stones from Whalley Abbey lying 3/4 m NW of new (19thC) church. ▶ Branching right: **Ribchester** (*40 m B6245*), attractive village with medieval church, excavated granaries and **museum** containing Roman remains. ▶ Continuing on B6245 and branching left onto B6243: **Grimsargh** (*46 m*), with rebuilt 19thC **church** containing brass of William Cross (d.1827) and wife Ellen, overlook-ing meadows by riverside. From there return to Preston (*50 m*). □

Practical information _____

PRESTON
ⓘ Town Hall, Lancaster Road, ☎ 53731/54881 ext. 6103. ▰▰▰ ☎ 59439.
Car rental: Europcar, Dutton Foreshaw Ltd, Corporation Street, ☎ 59014/59034.

Restaurant:
♦ **Tiggis,** 38 Guildhall Street, ☎ (0772) 58527, AC BA ♪ ❀ Cl. Sun. £7.

Inn or Pub:
The Olde Blue Bell (Smith), 116 Church Street, ☎ (0772) 51280 ℗ ♿ ❀ 3 rm. Home-made specials, steaks, grills, salads. £2.

Recommended
Golf course: Penwortham, Blundell Lane (SW off A59), ☎ (0772) 744630; Fulwood Hall Lane, Fulwood, ☎ (0772) 700011.

Nearby

BARTLE, 3m NW off M55

Hotel:
★★★ **Bartle Hall,** Lea Lane, PR4 0HA, ☎ Preston (0772) 690506, AC AM BA DI, 12 rm. ℗ ♿ 〰 ◷ ❀ ▱ ⌐ £45. Rest. ♦ ♪ ♿ £9.

Inn or Pub:
Sitting Goose (Thwaits), Sidgreaves Lane, ☎ Catforth (0772) 690344, AC ℗ ♿ 〰 ◷ ♿ Home roasts, bar snacks. £2.

BARTON, 6m N on A6

Hotel:
★★★ **Barton Grange** (B.W.), Garstang Road, PR3 5AA, ☎ Broughton (0772) 862551, Tx 67392, AC AM BA DI, 68 rm. ℗ 〰 ▱ ♩ £52.50. Rest. ♦ ♪Tx. £10.

BROUGHTON, 4m N on B411

Hotel:
★★★ **Broughton Park,** 418 Garstang Road, PR3 5JB, ☎ (0772) 864087, Tx 67180, AC AM BA DI, 98 rm. ℗ ♿ 〰 ◷ ♿ ▱ £50. Rest. ♦ ♪ ♿ £10.50.

CATFORTH, 7m NW off B5269

Inn or Pub:
Running Pump (Robinsons), Catforth Road, ☎ (609) 265
Ⓟ 🕭 ⅏ 🍴 ⅙ ⅏ Snacks and home cooking using local
produce. £4.

CATTERALL, 9m N on B6430

Hotel:
★★★ *Pickerings Country House*, Garstang Road, PR3
0HA, ☎ Garstang (099 52) 2133, AC BA DI, 3 rm. Ⓟ ⅏ 🕭
⅏ 🥂 🍴 £40. Rest. ♦ ≀ £13.

CLAYTON-LE-WOODS, 6m S on B5256

Hotel:
★★★ *Pines*, nr Chorley, PR6 7ED, ☎ Preston (0772)
38551, Tx 677584, AC AM BA DI, 25 rm. Ⓟ ⅏ ⅙ ⅏
£53.15. Rest. ♦ ≀ ⅙Tx. £12.50.

GOOSNARGH, 6m N off B5269

Restaurant:
♦ *Horns*, ☎ Broughton (0772) 865230, AC AM BA DI Ⓟ
🕭 ≀ ⅏ Cl. Mon. Book. £9.50.

Recommended
Farmhouse: *Eaves Green Farm*, Eaves Green Lane,
☎ (0772) 865455, £19 double B. B.

LONGBRIDGE, 6m NE on B6243

Restaurant:
♦ *Corporation Arms*, Lower Road, ☎ (077 478) 2644, AC
AM BA Ⓟ 🕭 ⅏ 🕭 ≀ ⅙ ⅏ Cl. 25 Dec. Book. £10.

RIBCHESTER, 9m NE on B5245

Inn or Pub:
White Bull (Whitbread), Church Street, ☎ (025 484) 303 Ⓟ
⅏ 🕭 ⅙ ⅏ Snacks and 3-course meals, steaks, salads.
£6.

SAMLESBURY, 5m E off A59

Hotel:
★★★ *Trafalgar* (Consort), Preston New Road, PR5 0UL,
☎ Samlesbury (077 477) 351, Tx 677362, AC AM BA DI,
80 rm. Ⓟ ⅙ 🖃 £55. Rest. ♦ ≀ ⅙Tx. £7.

THORNLEY, 7m NE off B6243

Hotel:
★ *Blackmoss*, Longridge, PR3 2TB, ☎ (077 478) 3148,
AC AM DI, 10 rm. Ⓟ ⅏ ⅏ 🕭 ⅙ ⅏ 🖃 ⅔ £46. Rest. ♦
⅙ £15.

RAWTENSTALL*

Burnley, 7; Manchester, 18; London, 214 m
pop. 22,231 ☎ 0706   Lancashire B2

Rawtenstall is the centre of a chain of overgrown
industrial villages along the Rossendale Valley.
Modern rebuilding mixes with old mills, coal mines
and many 19thC churches and chapels.

▶ In **Whitaker Park**, set on hillside, is small **Rossendale Museum** containing displays of traditional Lancashire
industries, fine arts and natural history (*Mon.-Fri., 1-5
(also 6-7.30 Wed., Apr.-Sep.), Sat., 10-12, Sun. (Apr.-Oct.
only) 3-5*). ▶ To N at **Crawshaw Booth**: large late 19thC
church of St. John's with impressive tower, and **Friends'
Meeting House** of 1716; and by **Goodshaw** (*2 m*), 18thC
Baptist **Chapel** (*mid- Mar.-mid- Oct.: Mon.-Sat., 9.30-6.30,
Sun., 2-6.30; mid-Oct.-mid-Mar.: Mon.-Sat., 9.30-4, Sun.,
2-4*). ▶ **Bacup** (*3 m E*) includes **Natural History Society's
Museum** (*Yorkshire Street; Thur., 7.30-10*). ▶ **Haslingden**
(*W*): St. James' **Church** (1780, enlarged 1827) containing
early 16thC font. ▶ **Helmshore** (*4 m S of Haslingden*)
where **Textile Museums**★ (Holcombe Road) show
development of Lancashire textile industry; ▶ N of valley
stretches high moorland of **Forest of Rossendale**, with
fine walks and views on 45-mile **Rossendale Way**.
▶ To S Rossendale Fells extend across Yorkshire

border to Rochdale (→), with more good fell-walking and
high point of **Whittle Hill** (1534 ft).   □

Practical information _____

ℹ 41-45 Kay Street, ☎ (0706) 217777 ext.245.

Recommended
Golf course: Rossendale, Ewood Lane, Head, Haslingden,
☎ (0706) 213056.

Nearby
RAMSBOTTOM, 2m S off A676

Hotel:
★★★ *Old Mill*, Springwood, BL0 9OS, ☎ Springwood
(070) 82 2991, AC AM BA DI, 17 rm. Ⓟ ⅙ ⅏ 🕭 ⅙ £49.
Rest. ♦ ≀ ⅙ £10.   .

RUNCORN*

Liverpool, 14; Chester, 17; London, 193 m
pop. 63,995 ☎ 0928   Cheshire A3

This chemical manufacturing town at the head of the
Mersey estuary is part of a large new development
scheme. The impressive iron **railway bridge** (1864-68)
and **road bridge** (1956-61) span the Manchester Ship
Canal and the Mersey to link Runcorn with Widnes.

▶ Excavated remains of **Norton Priory**★ (*3 m E*), in extensive woodland gardens; **museum** shows monastic life
and crafts (*Mar.-Oct.: Mon.-Fri., 12-5; Sat. & Sun., 12-6.
Nov.-Feb.: daily, 12-4; cl. 25 Dec.*).

Nearby
▶ Across Mersey estuary: **Widnes**, 19thC industrial town
on St.Helen's Canal; facing riverside promenade is majestic redstone church of **St. Mary** (1908-10); at **Farnworth**
(*N*), is well-restored ancient red sandstone church,
St.Luke's. ▶ **Hale** (*W*), village attractively sited on estuary
with **lighthouse** and renovated 18thC **church** retaining
medieval tower. ▶ **Halewood** (*N*), industrial district with
19thC **church** includes much stained glass by William
Morris (1870s).   □

Practical information _____
RUNCORN
ℹ 57/61 Church Street, ☎ (0928) 76776.
🚂 ☎ Liverpool (051) 709 9696.

Hotel:
★ *Panorama*, Castle Road, Halton, WA7 2BE, ☎ (092 85)
64772, AC AM BA DI, 14 rm. Ⓟ ⅏ ⅏ £27. Rest. ♦ ≀
⅙ £5.75.

Recommended
Golf course: Clifton Road (off A558), ☎ (0928) 72093.

Nearby
DARESBURY, 4m S on B5356

Hotel:
★★★ *Lord Daresbury* (De Vere), Chester Road, WA4 4BB,
☎ Warrington (0925) 67331, Tx 629330, AC AM BA DI,
141 rm. Ⓟ ⅙ ⅏ 🕭 ⅙ 🖃 £85. Rest. ♦ ≀ ⅙Tx. £10.

FRODSHAM, 5m S on A56

Hotel:
★★ *Old Hall*, Main Street, WA6 7AB, ☎ (0928) 32052, AC
AM BA DI, 25 rm. Ⓟ 🕭 ⅙ 🖃 £44. Rest. ♦ ⅙ £10.

WIDNES, 1m N on A533
ℹ Municipal Buildings, Kingsway ☎ (0928) 424 2061.
🚂 ☎ (0928) 709 9696.

Hotel:
★★★ *Hill Crest*, 75 Cronton Lane, WA8 9AR, ☎ (051) 424
1616, Tx 627098, AC AM BA DI, 46 rm. Ⓟ ⅙ £38.50. Rest.
♦ ≀ ⅙ £12.

Recommended
Golf course: Dunalk Road, ☎ (0928) 424 6230; Highfield Road ☎ (0928) 424 2995.

ST. HELEN'S*

Liverpool, 12; Wigan, 9; London, 196 m
pop. 98,769 ☎ 0744   Merseyside A2

This industrial town is the centre of the British glass industry, founded here in the late 18thC. Until recent pit closures it was also the centre of the South Lancashire coal industry. Much of the town has been rebuilt since its rapid growth in the 19thC, though the scanty ruins of a 15thC abbey remain in **Windleshaw RC cemetery**.

▶ **Museum & Art Gallery** (College Street); natural and local history (*Mon.-Fri., 10-5, Sat., 10-1*). ▶ To SW of centre: **Pilkington Glass Works** (Prescot Road) with **museum★** showing evolution of glass-making techniques (*Mon.-Fri., 10-5, Sat., Sun. & Bank Hols., 2-4.30*).

Nearby

▶ **Windle Hall** (*5 m NE across Lancashire border*): 3-acre walled garden surrounded by lawns and woodland (*Jul.-early Sep.: Sun. only, 2-6*). ▶ **Prescot** (*5 m SW*): **museum** (Church Street) devoted to town's clock-and watch-making industry (*Tue.-Sat., 10-5, Sun., 2-5; closed Mon. ex. Bank Hol. Mons.*); old parish **church** with 18thC tower; in Vicarage Place is Victorian RC **Church of Our Lady** by Joseph Hansom. ▶ NW of Prescot: **Knowsley Safari Park** (*daily*) in grounds of **Knowsley Hall**, home of the Earls of Derby, dating to 14thC. ▶ **Rainhill** (*SE*): a few old farmhouses and 19thC mansions, **St. Bartholomew's** RC church, built in 1840 in fine Classical style. □

Practical information

🚃 ☎ Wigan (0942) 42231.

Recommended
Golf course: Grange Park, Toll Bar, Prescott Road (1m SW on A58), ☎ (0744) 26318.

Nearby

NEWTON-LEWILLWS, 4m E off A49/M6

Hotel:
★★ *Post House* (Trusthouse Forte), Lodge Lane, Haydock, WA12 0JG, ☎ Wigan (0942) 717878, Tx 677672, AC AM BA DI, 98 rm. P & £70. Rest. ♦ ♪ &Tx. £9.

SOUTHPORT*

Manchester, 38; Liverpool, 20; London, 220 m
pop. 88,596 ☎ 0704   Merseyside A2

A pleasant seaside resort and residential town with a promenade fronting nearly 7 m of sandy beach.

▶ Holiday attractions around promenade include **Pleasureland** amusement park, **model village** and live entertainment at **Theatre and Floral Hall** Complex; Princes Park houses 4-acre **zoo** (*daily from 10*). ▶ **Lord Street**, lined with well-built 19thC public buildings and shops, includes **Atkinson Art Gallery:** collections of British art, English glass, Chinese porcelain (*Mon.-Wed. & Fri., 10-5, Thur. & Sat., 10-1*). ▶ Nearby are **Holy Trinity** (Manchester Road), Edwardian church of red brick and white stone and **Hesketh Park**, laid out 1864-68 with lake▶ At **Churchtown**, old centre 1 m N with attractive 18th and early 19thC houses by village green; **Botanic Gardens** with boating lake and **museum** devoted to natural and local history (*May-Sep.: Tue.-Sat., 10-6, Sun., 2-5. Oct.-Apr.: Tue.-Sat., 10-5, Sun., 2-5; closed Mon. ex. Bank Hol. Mon. when closed following Fri.*); ▶ **St.Cuthbert**, old parish church with tower and spire, contains early 18thC **woodcarving** from demolished St. Peter's, Liverpool; ▶ **Meols**

Hall, 17thC house containing pictures, furniture and china (*Apr.-Sep.: Thur. & Bank Hol. Mons., 2-5*).

Nearby

▶ To S, via fine stretch of coastland with **nature reserve** at **Ainsdale** (*3 m*). ▶ **Formby** (*7¹/₂ m*), former fishing village now cut off from sea. Georgian church of **St.Peter** near sandhills and 19thC **St. Luke's**, on ancient site, including worn Norman font. **Formby Hall** (16th-17thC, restored), is nearby. ▶ **Halsall** (*5 m SE*), village with notable medieval **church** (partly restored 19thC); beautifully carved late 15thC **stalls** plus some old stained glass. By church is old **Grammar School**, founded 1593. ▶ **Tarleton** (*6 m NE*), big village by River Douglas, spanned by old 3-arched bridge and canal bridge, with a few 17th-18thC houses among newer developments and plain brick church of **St. Mary** (1719 with stone turret and cupola of thin tower added 1824), including square pews and cast-iron stove in simple galleried interior. □

Practical information

SOUTHPORT
ℹ Cambridge Arcade, ☎ (0704) 33133/40404.

Hotels:
★★★★ *Prince of Wales* (Quality), Lord Street, PR8 1JS, ☎ (0704) 36688, Tx 67415, AC AM BA DI, 101 rm. P ▨ & £72. Rest. ♦ ♪ &Tx. £8.
★★★ *Royal Clifton*, Promenade, PR8 1RB, ☎ (0704) 33771, Tx 677191, AC AM BA DI, 115 rm. P ⊰ & ⊠ £60. Rest. ♦ ♪ &Tx. £9.
★★★ *Scarisbrick*, 239 Lord Street, PR8 1NZ, ☎ (0704) 43000, Tx 67107, AC AM BA DI, 60 rm. P & £60. Rest. ♦ ♪ &Tx. £9.
● ★★ *Ambassador*, 13 Bath Street, PR9 0DP, ☎ (0704) 30459, BA, 8 rm. P £30. Rest. ♦ ♪ £5.
★★ *Bold*, 583 Lord Street, PR9 0BE, ☎ (0704) 32578, AC AM BA DI, 24 rm. P £39. Rest. ♦ ♪ £8.

Restaurants:
♦ *La Terrasse*, 1st floor, 180 Lord Street, ☎ (0704) 30995, AC AM BA DI Cl. Sun. dinner, Mon., Tue. and 1st 2 wks Sep. £11.
♦ *Squires*, 78-80 King Street, ☎ (0704) 30046, AC AM BA DI Cl. Sun. £15.

Recommended
Golf courses: Park Road, ☎ (0704) 35286; Hesketh, Cockle Dick's Lane off Cambridge Road, ☎ (0704) 36897; Bradshaws Lane, Ainsdale, ☎ (0704) 78000.

Nearby

FORMBY, 5m S off A565

Hotel:
★★★ *Tree Tops*, Southport Old Road, L37 0AB, ☎ (0704) 874649, AC AM BA DI, 11 rm. P ⊰ ▨ ⚲ & ⚛ ⊠ ⏌ ⚬ £48. Rest. ♦ ♪ £15.

MERE BROW, 7m E on A565

Restaurant:
♦ *Crab & Lobster*, Legh Arms, ☎ Hesketh Bank (077 473) 2734 P ⚲ ♪ & ⚛ Cl. Christmas, Jan., Mon.-Sun., lunches. Home-made sweets. Book. £14.

STOCKPORT*

Manchester, 6; Macclesfield, 12; London, 193 m
pop. 135,489 ☎ 061   Greater Manchester B2

Stockport is built on the slopes of a narrow valley of the River Mersey, spanned by a 22-arched railway **viaduct** (1839-40). Below is the originally medieval town, with narrow streets rising steeply to the market place and St.Mary's parish church. In the later town above is **St.Peter's** church (1748). A few 16thC timber-framed houses and 18thC buildings have

survived, along with 19th-20thC churches and public buildings.

▶ **St.Mary's**, rebuilt 1813 by Lewis Wyatt, retains 14thC chancel. ▶ **War Memorial Art Gallery** (Wellington Road S): small collection of paintings and changing exhibitions *(Mon.-Fri., 12-5, Sat., 10-4; closed Sun. & Bank Hols.).* ▶ In **Vernon Park, museum** shows local history *(Apr.-Sep.: Mon.-Sat., 1-5; Oct.-Mar.: Mon.-Sat., 1-4. Closed Sun. & Bank Hols.).*

Nearby

▶ Attractive countryside around valleys of Rivers Etherow, Goyt and Tame, with old mill towns and villages on edge of Derbyshire moors: **Marple** *(3 m E)* with **aqueduct** (1794) of **Peak Forest Canal** 200 ft. above river; **Compstall** *(1 m N)*, model mill village with nearby **Etherow Country Park**, in wooded valley with lake, nature trails and visitor centre. ▶ **Disley** *(7 m SE)*, with rebuilt early 16thC **church** on border of **Lyme Park**★: 1300-acre deer park surrounding **Lyme Hall**, Elizabethan mansion remodeled 18thC with elaborate interior Jacobean decorations; set in extensive gardens *(park: all year 8-dusk; house: Apr.-Oct.: Tue.-Sat., 2-4.30 (4 in Oct.), Sun., Good Fri. & Bank Hol. Mons., 1-5.30, 4.30 in Oct.)*▶ **Bramhall Hall**★, Bramhall *(4 m S)*: splendid example of black-and-white timber and plaster architecture, 14th-16thC, set in 60-acre landscaped park with lakes and nature trail *(Apr.-Sep.: daily ex. Mon., 12-5; Oct.-Nov., Jan.-Mar.: daily ex. Mon., 12-4; closed Dec.; open Bank Hol. Mons.).* ▶ Via Manchester suburbs towns: **Cheadle** *(3 m W)*; 16thC St. Mary's **church** containing 16thC screen and 15thC effigies. ▶ **Wythenshawe Hall**, Northenden *(6 m W)*: 16thC timber-framed house with later additions, set in parkland; with 17thC furniture, pictures and Tudor wall paintings *(open spring & summer; apply locally)*. ▶ **Altrincham** *(9 m W)*, pleasant town known for market gardens. ▶ **Dunham Massey**★ *(3 m SW)*: early 18thC hall and park, with 17thC chapel, 18thC furniture, Huguenot silver; set in gardens and deer park, including Elizabethan mill *(Apr.-Oct.: gardens: Mon.-Thu., 12-5.30, Sat., Sun. & Bank Hol. Mons., 11-5.30; house: Mon.-Thu., 1-5, Sat., Sun. & Bank Hol. Mons., 12-4.30.).* ▶ **Warburton**: charming old **church** of St. Werburgh, partly timber-framed with 17th and 18thC stone and brick replacements. □

Practical information ――――――――――

STOCKPORT
ⓘ 9 Princes Street, ☎ (061) 480 0315.
🚌 ☎ (061) 832 8353.
Car-rental: Europcar, Wellington Vehicles Ltd, 65 Wellington Road; South, ☎ (061) 477343.

Restaurant:
♦ **Coconut Willy's**, 37 St.Petergate, ☎ Manchester (061) 480 7013, BA Ⓟ 🔍 ♪ ♿ 🍽 Cl. 1 Jan., Sun., Mon. Book. £7.50.

Inn or Pub:
Red Bull (Robinsons), 14 Middle Highgate, ☎ (061) 480 2087. Bar snacks and home-made lunches, steaks. £4.

Recommended
Craft Workshops: at Chapel-en-le-frith, *Cameron Pearson*, Sheffield Road, ☎ (0298) 2740. Manufacture of cast aluminium, brass and bronze signs.
Golf course: Hazel Grove, Buxton Road, ☎ (061) 483 3217; Offerton Road, ☎ (061) 427 2001.

Nearby

BRAMHALL, 4m S on A5102
ⓘ 13 Bramhall Lane South, ☎ (061) 440 8400.

Hotel:
★★★★ **Bramhall Moat House** (Queens), Bramhall Lane South, SK7 2EB, ☎ (061) 439 8116, AC AM BA DI, 40 rm. Ⓟ 🔍 ♿ £58. Rest. ♦ ♪ ♿ £11.

Recommended
Golf course: Ladyhom Road, ☎ (061) 439 4057.

COMPSTALL, 4m E on B6104

Inn or Pub:
George (Robinsons), Compstall Road, ☎ (061 427) 1299 Ⓟ ≼ 〰 🔍 🍽 Snacks and full meals. £3.50.

DISLEY, 6m SE on A6

Hotel:
★★★ **Moorside** (B.W.), Mudhurst Lane, Higher Disley, SK12 2BY, ☎ (066 32) 4151, Tx 665170, AC AM BA DI, 41 rm. Ⓟ 〰 ♿ ♪ 🐾 £70. Rest. ♦ ♪ ♿Tx. £12.

Restaurant:
● ♦ **The Ginnel**, 3 Buxton Old Road, ☎ (066 3) 64494, AC AM BA DI Ⓟ ♪ 🍽 Cl. 1 wk. Jan.,Tue., Sat. lunch, Mon. & Sun. eve. £12.

HANDFORTH, 1m S on A34

Hotels:
● ★★★★ **Belfry**, Stanley Road, SK9 3LD, ☎ (061) 437 0511, Tx 666358, AC AM BA DI, 96 rm. Ⓟ 〰 ♿ 🍽 ♪ £60. Rest. ● ♦ ♪ Cl. 25-26 Dec. 1, Jan. Tx. £20.
★★★ **Pinewood**, 180 Wilmslow Road, SK9 3LG, ☎ Wilmslow (0625) 529211, AC AM BA DI, 64 rm. Ⓟ ≼ 〰 🔍 ♿ £45. Rest. ♦ ♪ ♿ £10.

HAUGHTON GREEN, 3m NE on A6017

Hotel:
★★★ **Old Rectory**, Meadow Lane, Denton, M34 1GD, ☎ (061) 336 7516, Tx 668615, AC, 26 rm. Ⓟ ≼ 〰 🔍 🍽 £45. Rest. ♦ ♪Tx. £10.

HIGH LANE, 5m SE on A6

Restaurant:
♦ **Red Lion**, Buxton Road, ☎ Disley (066 32) 5227, AC AM BA DI Ⓟ ♪ ♿ 🍽 Cl. 24-25 Dec. Book. £10.

Inn or Pub:
Royal Oak (Burtonwood), Buxton Road, ☎ Disley (0663) 62380, 3 rm. Ⓟ ≼ 〰 Bar snacks and meals. £1.20.

OFFERTON, 2m S on A6

Hotel:
★★★★ **Belgrade** (Consort), 67 Dialstone Lane, SK2 6AG, ☎ 061-483 3851, Tx 667217, AC AM BA DI, 160 rm. Ⓟ 🍽 £36. Rest. ♦ ♪Tx. £10.

OVERSLEY FORD, 3m NW on A538

Hotel:
★★★ **Valley Lodge**, Altrincham Road, Wilmslow, SK9 4LR, ☎ (0625) 529201, Tx 666401, AC AM BA DI, 105 rm. Ⓟ £45. Rest. ♦ ♪Tx. £10.

ROMILEY, 3 1/2m N

Restaurant:
♦ **Waterside**, 166 Stockport Road, ☎ (061) 430 4302, AC BA Cl. Mon. £10.

WILMSLOW, 7m S on A34

Hotel:
● ★★★★ **Stanneylands**, Stanneylands Road, SK9 4EY, ☎ (0625) 525225, Tx 666 358, AC AM BA DI, 33 rm. Ⓟ ≼ 〰 🔍 ♿ 🍽 £65. Rest. ● ♦ ♿ £16.

Restaurant:
♦ **Mandarin**, Parsonage Green, ☎ (0625) 524096, BA Ⓟ 🔍 ♪ ♿ 🍽 Cl. 25-26 Dec. Pepper beef with black bean sauce. £9.50.

WARRINGTON*

Liverpool, 18; Manchester, 20; London, 184 m
pop. 81,366 ☎ 0925   Cheshire B2

This old industrial town is noted for ironworks, chemicals and soap factories and has recently been extensively redeveloped. Evidence of town's long history remains in ancient parish **church**, a few timber-framed 16th-17thC houses, some 18thC buildings

as well as in the many churches and chapels from the 18th-19thC.

▶ **Museum Art Gallery** (1857, by John Dobson; Bold Street); collections of natural history, geology; local history from prehistoric times; and in art gallery 19thC English watercolours and oils (*Mon.-Fri., 10-5.30, Sat., 10-5; closed Sun. & Bank Hols.*). ▶ **Town Hall** (1750; Sankey Street) was originally designed as Patten family mansion by James Gibbs; **Holy Trinity** Church (1760), with 19thC tower and galleried interior with box pews. ▶ **St. Elphin** parish church, restored 19thC with 281 ft. spire, retains 12th & 14thC work in crypt and chancel, ornate organ screen (1908). ▶ By modern bridge is **statue** of Oliver Cromwell. ▶ To N, at **Orford,** is **museum** of South Lancashire Regiment, Peninsula Barracks (*Mon.-Fri., 9-3*); and at **Winwick,** 14thC **St. Oswald's** Church, much renovated over centuries. On W wall, primitive stone carving known as 'Winwick pig'.

Nearby

▶ **Risley Moss Nature Park** (*5 m NE*), near Birchwood, with woodland trails (*Apr.-Sep.: Mon.-Fri., 9-6 (Visitor Centre, 9.30-4.30), Sat. & Sun., 9-8 (Visitor Centre, 9.30-5); Oct.-Mar.: Mon.-Fri., 8.30-5 (Visitor Centre, 9-4.30), Sat. & Sun., 8.30-6 (Visitor Centre, 9-5*). ▶ **Great Sankey** (*3 m W*), industrialized area including small Georgian brick **church,** with later alterations. ▶ **Grappenhall** (*3 m SE*), village with some old stone houses and **church** rebuilt 16thC. ▶ **Higher Walton** (*4 m SW*), old village with modern estates and 19thC **church** with tower; **Walton Hall** is nearby; $^{1}/_{2}$ m N is extensive Roman site. □

Practical information

WARRINGTON
ℹ 80 Sankey Street, ☎ (0925) 36501.
🚂 W. Central, W. Bank Quay, ☎ (0925) 32245.
Car rental: Europcar, C.D. Bramall Ltd, Owen Street, ☎ (0925) 573126; Avis, rail/drive, ☎ (0925) 827752.

Hotel:
★★ *Birchdale*, Birchdale Road, Appleton, WA4 5AW, ☎ (0925) 63662, 22 rm. P 👗 ⚡ £29.

Recommended
Golf course: Leigh, Kenyon Hall, Kenyon, ☎ (0925) 76 3130; Hill Warren, London Road, Appleton (3m S on A49), ☎ (0925) 61775.

Nearby

GRAPPENHALL, 1m E off A56
Hotels:
★★★ *Fir Grove*, Knutsford Old Road, WA4 2LD, ☎ (0925) 67471, Tx 628117, AC AM BA DI, 38 rm. P 👗 ⚡ £40. Rest. ♦ ♪ 👗Tx. £10.
★ *Ribblesdale*, Balmoral Road, WA4 2EB, ☎ (0925) 601197, AC BA AM, 15 rm. P 👗 ⚡ £35. Rest. ♦ ♪ £9.

HEATLEY, 7m E on A6144
Inn or Pub:
Railway (Boddingtons), Mill Lane, ☎ (092 575) 2742 P 👗 ⚡ Bar snacks and lunches. £4.

LYMM, 4m SE on A56
Hotel:
★★★ *Lymm* (De Vere), Whitbarrow Road, WA13 9AF, ☎ (0925) 752233, Tx 629455, AC AM BA DI, 69 rm. P ⚡ 👗 £59. Rest. ♦ ♪ 👗Tx. £11.

STRETTON, 3 1/2m S on A49
Hotel:
★ *Old Vicarage*, Stretton Road, WA4 4NS, ☎ Norcott Brock (0925) 73238, AC BA AM DI, 36 rm. P 👗 ⚡ ♪ £45. Rest. ♦ ♪ 👗 £10.

> If you enjoy sports, consult the pages pertaining to the regions; there you will find addresses for practicing your favorite sport.

WIGAN*

Preston, 18; Warrington, 14; London, 196 m
pop. 81,674 ☎ 0942   Greater Manchester B2

A medieval market town on the site of a Roman fort, Wigan was transformed by the Industrial Revolution into an important coal-mining, engineering and textile centre.

▶ In or near centre: **All Saints** parish church (medieval, restored 19thC); partly 13thC tower, much stained glass including Morris window (1868), Minton tiles; to S is Gothic-style **war memorial** by Giles Gilbert Scott. ▶ Near Market Place: late Georgian terraces and former medieval rectory **Wigan Hall** (1875). ▶ **Mesnes Park,** with serpentine lake. ▶ **Mab's Cross** (Standishgate) much worn ancient monument. ▶ On canalside: **Wigan Pier,** heritage centre with exhibition and concert halls (*daily, 10-5*). On W outskirts: large well-planned **Heinz factory** (1954-59).

Nearby

▶ **Haigh Hall** (1827-40; *2 m NE*), attractive house with fine plaster ceilings, now used as Wigan Library and set in public **park.** ▶ **Standish** (*4 m NW*), former market centre with large medieval church of **St. Wilfrid★** (rebuilt 16thC), with lovely paneled roofs, among other fine monuments (mainly 18th-19thC). ▶ **Hindley** (*SE*), large colliery village with attractive Georgian brick chapel, **All Saints** (1766), with galleried interior in black and gold. □

Practical information

WIGAN
🚂 W. N. Western, W. Wallgate, ☎ (0942) 42231.

Hotels:
★★★ *Brocket Arms*, Mesnes Road, WN1 2DD, ☎ (0942) 46283, Tx 628117, AC AM BA DI, 27 rm. P 👗 ⚡ £36. Rest. ♦ £9.
★★ *Holland Hall*, 6 Lafford Lane, Upholland, WN8 0QZ, ☎ (0695) 624426, AC AM BA DI, 11 rm. P 👗 ⚡ ✓ £36. Rest. ♦ £6.

Recommended
Golf courses: Haydock Park, Golborne Park, Newton-le-Willows,☎ (09252)2852; Dean Wood, Lafford Lane, Upholland (on A577),☎ (0695) 622219; Arley Hall, Haigh, ☎ (0257) 421360.
♥ *Muffin Man*, 103 Park Road, ☎ (0942) 43350, oven-baked muffins, warm cakes, meat pies and cakes.

Nearby

DALTON, 9m W off A5209
Restaurant:
♦ *Prescotts Farm*, Lees Lane, Parbold, ☎ (025 76) 4137, AC P 👗 ♪ 👗 ⚡ Cl. Sat. lunch, Mon. £10.

LEIGH, 8m SE on A578
Hotel:
★★★ *Greyhound* (Embassy), Warrington Road, WN7 3XQ, ☎ (0942) 671256, AC AM BA DI, 54 rm. P 👗 £55. Rest. ♦ ♪ 👗 £8.

STANDISH, 5m N on A49
Hotel:
★★★ *Cassinelli's Almond*, Almond Brook Road, WN6 0SR, ☎ (0257) 425588, Tx 677662, AC AM BA DI, 43 rm. P 👗 ⚡ £39. Rest. ♦ ♪ 👗Tx. £5.

Inn or Pub:
Crown, Platt Lane, ☎ Worthington (0257) 421354 P 👗 ⚡ 👗 ⚡ Daily specials, fresh vegetables, home-baked pies. £2.50.

WRIGHTINGTON, 7m NW on B5250
Restaurant:
♦ *The High Moor*, Highmoor Lane, ☎ Appley Bridge (025 75) 2364, AC AM BA DI P 👗 ⚡ ♪ 👗 ⚡ Cl. 1 wk Jan., last 2 wks Aug., Sun. eve., Sat. lunch, Mon. Book. £16.

▶ Here lie the cities of Aberdeen, Dundee, Perth and Stirling; the beautiful valleys of the Dee, Don, Findhorn, Tay and Spey; the inland resorts of Pitlochry and Callander, and the world-famous scenery of Loch Lomond and the Trossachs. Clearly, it is not an area for generalizations. It is mainly lowland in character but includes peaks of 4,000 ft. and contains what many consider to be Scotland's loveliest loch.

History and legend haunt many areas. The Trossachs and Loch Lomond were the scenes of Rob Roy's exploits. Robert the Bruce and William Wallace won victories at Bannockburn and Stirling Bridge near Stirling, a city steeped in history. The Grampian region includes the granite city of Aberdeen, the prosperous centre of the North Sea oil industry, but also interesting for its ancient cathedral, university and its museums. The fishing towns and villages of the F and N-facing coasts have their own charac ter and reflect their long histories. They include Fraserburgh, Macduff, Banff, Buckie and Lossiemouth. Elgin has a ruined cathedral. To the S is Dufftown, the centre of the whisky-distilling industry. Most of the distilleries in the area offer a tour and a dram to visitors.

But above all, this is the land of castles. The Queen spends much of the summer at Balmoral. Only its grounds are open, but visitors are welcome inside many memorable castles, such as Fyvie, Fraser, Glamis, Stirling, Craigievar, Edzell and Doune. Earlier partly-ruined castles not to be missed include Huntly, Kildrummy and Tolquhon.

The Tayside region has, naturally, the 119-m River Tay as its chief geographical feature. Its

Central and Eastern Scotland

attractions range from Scotland's most remote outpost at Rannoch, to bustling Dundee and Perth and many delightful small resorts. The early Scottish kings were crowned at Scone and there are countless reminders of the earlier Picts. Ancient abbeys stand at Arbroath and Brechin, and cathedrals at Dunblane and Dunkeld. □

French influence on Scottish cuisine

Mary Queen of Scots, like her mother, Mary of Guise, influenced southern Scottish cooking very strongly in the 16thC. Many of the strange-sounding names for classic Scottish dishes in the south have come about through generations of mispronunciation of the old French. We can still hear these odd words in the Scots language: tassie from the French tasse (cup); haggis from hachis; collops from escalope; purry from puree, and many more besides.

 # Brief regional history

Prehistory

The earliest evidence of human settlement dates from the **Mesolithic period**. These first inhabitants were hunters and fishermen, living on the west coast from Argyll down to Kirkcudbright and in the Forth Estuarary. ● **Neolithic farmers** arrived in the 2nd millennium, settling the west coast and as far north as Shetland. The huge chambered tomb at Maeshowe in Orkney was built by them and is the finest example in Europe. Skara Brae, also in Orkney, is a remarkably well preserved Stone Age village. The Beaker People settled in eastern Scotland from 1800 B.C. ushering in the Bronze Age. The great stone circles at Brodgar in Orkney and Callanish in Lewis are Bronze Age sites as are the dwellings at Jarlshof in Shetland. ● From about 700 B.C. Iron Age **Celts** arrived. Hill-forts with stone ramparts and timber frames date from the 7th

and 6th centuries B.C. and are mainly to be found in the south of the country. The dry-stone round towers, known as *brochs* are unique to Scotland. They occur in the north and are typically about 40 ft. high, with a 40 ft. diameter, tapering at the top. It is possible that the broch dwellers were intermittently at war with the fort dwellers further south. Both can be seen as ancestors of the **Picts**.

The Romans

In AD 80 **Agricola**, Governor of Britain, advanced to the Forth-Clyde line and in 84 defeated the Caledonian chieftain, Calgacus, at Mons Graupius, an unidentified site, perhaps near Huntly in Grampian. But permanent occupation of Scotland was considered too expensive in terms of men and materials and the Romans eventually made **Hadrian's Wall** their northern frontier. The **Antonine Wall** was constructed from the Forth to the Clyde from about A.D. 142 but was abandoned c.163.

The peoples of Scotland

Four different peoples occupied Scotland during the Dark Ages.● The **Picts**, literally the 'painted ones', occupied the central and eastern highlands, including Caledones, uniting into a single kingdom by the 7th century.● The **Scots**, who came from Antrim in Northern Ireland, began to raid the west coast from the 3rd century establishing the kingdom of Dál Riáta in Argyll in the 6th century.● They were **Goidelic Celts** who spoke Irish Gaelic. The Britons of Strathclyde were **Brythonic Celts** — like the Welsh, the Cornish and the people of Brittany.● The fourth element in this ethnic pattern were the **Angles**, a Germanic people who settled the east coast from the 5th century, creating in the 7th century the powerful kingdom of Northumbria which stretched from the Humber to the Forth. These four groups were ultimately to merge to form the kingdom of the Scots.

Christianity

The **Christian Church** in Scotland was founded at Whithorn by **St. Ninian** in 397. St. Columba established his monastery at Iona in 565 and was influential in converting the Picts. St. Mungo settled in Glasgow. St. Aidan introduced the Celtic Church into Northumbria in the 630s, founding the famous monastery at Lindisfarne. ● The **sculpted stones** and **crosses** are the principal remnants of the Early Christian Church in Scotland, Celtic crosses being found in the west and Northumbrian forms in the east, the supreme example being the Ruthwell Cross.

A united Scotland

Viking raids on Britain had begun in the 8th century, Iona and Lindisfarne being sacked in the 790s. During the 9th century, Caithness, Sutherland and the western and northern isles were settled by Norsemen. This threat from without gave the Scots a common enemy and drew them closer together.● Scotland and Pictland were united under **Kenneth Mac Alpin** in 843.● In 1018 **Malcolm II** defeated the Northumbrians at Carham, annexing Lothian. The death of the last King of Strathclyde in the same year gave that region to his heir, **Duncan**, grandson of Malcolm II. When Malcolm died in 1034 he handed a united Scotland to his successor. To start with the monarchy was weak and the succession uncertain. Duncan was murdered by **Macbeth** in 1040 and Macbeth by Duncan's son Malcolm Canmore in 1057. Rebellions continued until 1230.● The Norsemen were also dangerous and it was only in 1266 after the defeat of King Haakon of Norway at Largs that Scotland acquired the **Hebrides**. Orkney and Shetland remained Norse until 1472. In 1174 William the Lion was captured by the English while on a raid south of the border and forced to acknowledge English supremacy. In 1189 Scotland purchased her independence from Richard I who needed the money for his crusade. But the struggle for independence from an increasingly powerful English state was just beginning.

The Wars of Independence

In 1286 Alexander III died. His heir was his young granddaughter Margaret, 'Maid of Norway', who died in the Orkneys on her way back from Norway. Edward I of England was invited to adjudicate between the various contenders for the Scottish throne, known as the 'Competitors'. He chose **John Balliol** who was enthroned at Scone in 1292, having been forced to acknowledge Edward's overlordship. ● The Scottish barons rebelled, and allied with France, seized power. The **English** invaded, defeating the Scots at Dunbar in 1296, whereupon Balliol surrendered his kingdom. **William Wallace**, the first great hero of **Scottish nationalism**, defeated the English at Stirling Bridge in 1297 but was utterly humiliated at Falkirk. In 1305 Wallace was executed as a traitor.● **Robert Bruce**, grandson of one of the Competitors, rose in revolt in 1306 and was crowned Robert I. The Scottish strongholds were successively recovered, Edinburgh in 1314. In that year Edward II sent an expedition to relieve Stirling but was spectacularly defeated at Bannockburn. By the **Treaty of Northampton** in 1328 Edward formally recognized Scottish independence.

The House of Stewart

Robert Bruce's successor, David II, left no direct heirs and the throne passed to **Robert Stewart**, sixth hereditary High Steward of Scotland. The House of Stewart reigned in Scotland until the death of Queen Anne in 1714. But the earlier kings were constantly involved in a power struggle with the other Scottish nobles who had grown strong during the Wars of Independence. There was a **Battle of the Clans**, thirty against thirty at Perth in 1396. In 1406 James I was captured at sea by the English; later he was murdered at Perth. James II was accidentally killed by an exploding gun at Roxburgh in 1460. James III, a man of great artistic sensibility, was murdered by Scottish nobles at Sauchieburn in 1488.

● During the Middle Ages, Scotland's economy was based on **agriculture**. In the highlands and islands this was virtually subsistence farming, with cattle the only surplus. In the east and south, arable farming was dominant, while the great Border abbeys of Jedburgh, Dryburgh, Melrose and Kelso pastured vast flocks of sheep whose wool, exported through Berwick, made Scotland one of the main suppliers in western Europe. Scotland's first university, St.

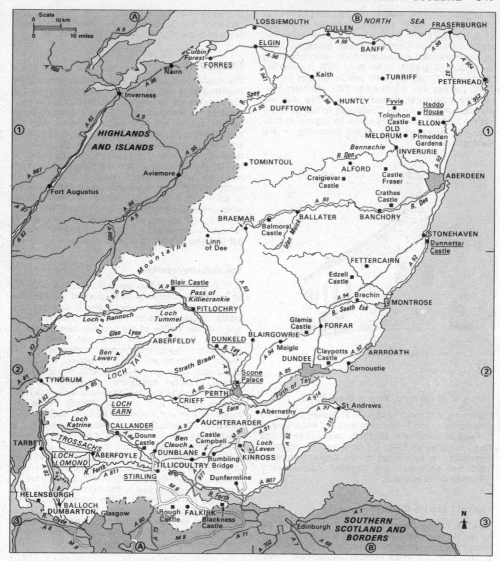

LOSSIEMOUTH   Ⓑ *NORTH SEA*   FRASERBURGH

Ⓐ

CULLEN

A 9

ELGIN   A 96   BANFF

Culbin Forest

FORRES

Nairn

Keith   TURRIFF   PETERHEAD

A 96

Spey

Inverness

DUFFTOWN   HUNTLY   Fyvie   Haddo House

Tolquhon Castle

OLD MELDRUM   Pitmedden Gardens

HIGHLANDS AND ISLANDS

A 95

A 9

Aviemore

TOMINTOUL

R. Don   Bennachie   INVERURIE

ALFORD

Castle Fraser

Craigievar Castle

ABERDEEN

Fort Augustus

Crathes Castle

R. Dee

BRAEMAR   BALLATER   BANCHORY

Balmoral Castle

Linn of Dee

Grampian Mountains

Glen Muick

A 93

STONEHAVEN

Dunnottar Castle

FETTERCAIRN

Blair Castle

Pass of Killiecrankie

PITLOCHRY

Edzell Castle

A 94   Brechin

MONTROSE

R. South Esk

Loch Rannoch   Loch Tummel

Glen Lyon

ABERFELDY

DUNKELD

R. Tay

Glamis Castle

BLAIRGOWRIE

Meigle

FORFAR

Claypotts Castle

ARBROATH

Ben Lawers

Strath Braan

A 94

DUNDEE

LOCH TAY

Carnoustie

TYNDRUM

Scone Palace

PERTH

Firth of Tay

CRIEFF

R. Earn

St Andrews

LOCH EARN

Loch Katrine

CALLANDER

AUCHTERARDER

Abernethy

A 91

TROSSACHS

Doune Castle

Ben Cleuch

Castle Campbell

A 90

Loch Leven

KINROSS

LOCH LOMOND

ABERFOYLE

DUNBLANE

Rumbling Bridge

TILLICOULTRY

Dunfermline

STIRLING

A 907

HELENSBURGH

R. Forth

BALLOCH

DUMBARTON   Glasgow

Rough Castle

FALKIRK

Blackness Castle

Edinburgh

SOUTHERN SCOTLAND AND BORDERS

R. Clyde

N

Ⓐ   Ⓑ

Andrews, was founded in 1411, Glasgow in 1451. Berwick, Perth, Dundee and Aberdeen became ports with considerable European trade.

The Auld Alliance

Under James IV, Scotland entered **international politics**. Since the time of John Balliol, Scotland had pursued a policy of friendship with **France** and in the 16th century France was surrounded by enemies. Henry VII had cautiously married his daughter Margaret to James IV, but Henry VIII was the last person to be conciliatory. ● In 1513 **James IV** agreed to support Louis XII against the **Holy League** and mounted a major campaign against England. At Flodden he was

killed, along with 10,000 of his men in a disastrous battle. James V married Madeleine of France and after her death **Mary of Lorraine**, daughter of the duc de Guise, championing the cause of **Catholicism** in the face of Henry VIII's reformation in the south. In 1542 a large Scots army invaded Cumbria but was defeated at Solway Moss. James, prostrated by the death of his young sons and by defeat in battle died a month later, only a week after the birth of his daughter, Mary.

Mary, Queen of Scots

For most Catholics, **Mary Stewart**, granddaughter of Margaret Tudor, was the legitimate heir to the throne

of England. She had married the Dauphin of France in 1558, but returned to Scotland, widowed, at the age of eighteen. By then the Parliament in Edinburgh had abolished Roman Catholicism and, prudently, Mary let the **Protestant settlement** stand, even permitting **John Knox** to preach to her.● In 1565 she married her cousin Darnley and their son James was born in 1566. Darnley was murdered in 1567 and Mary married the adventurer, **James Bothwell**. She was imprisoned at Loch Leven Castle and forced by Elisabeth to abdicate, escaped and fled to England. In 1587 she was executed for alleged complicity in the Babington Plot.

Kineff Old Kirk, Grampian

James VI of Scotland, King of Great Britain

During his long minority, **James VI** skilfully bargained with Catholics and Protestants alike and endeavoured to keep in favour with Elizabeth, with whom he had come to terms in 1586, a year before his mother's execution. He succeeded to the English throne in 1603 and from that time Scotland was smoothly governed in his absence.

Charles I and the Covenanters

Charles demonstrated a genius for annoying the Scots. He first canceled all grants of Crown property since 1540 (i.e. before the Reformation). Next he tried to impose his will on the Scottish Committee of Parliament by placing **bishops**, appointed by him, in central government. He then imposed a new **prayer book** on the Scottish kirk, provoking riots in Edinburgh. When the General Assembly met in 1638, it issued a National Covenant whereby the Church should be controlled by Presbyterians, that bishops should be abolished and the new prayer book abandoned. **War** inevitably followed. The two short 'Bishops Wars' ended with a victory for the Covenanters and the collapse of royal policy. ● In the Civil War which followed, the **Covenanters** naturally sided with Parliament. The Duke of Montrose, however, declared for the king, winning some striking victories before his defeat at Philiphaugh. Charles was utterly defeated by 1646, and it was then that the extraordinary **Engagement** between the king and certain moderate Scotsmen was entered upon, whereby the Scots agreed to help the king if he would agree to the establishment

of **Presbyterianism** in England. This led to the utter defeat of the Scots by **Oliver Cromwell** and eight years of humiliation under the Commonwealth.

The Act of Union

The departure of James II and the acceptance of the English throne by William of Orange, welcomed in England, did not find favour with the Scots. The massacre of the **MacDonalds** at Glencoe aroused public opinion against the new monarch, which was further inflamed by William's suppression of the Darien scheme, a Scottish trading company proposing to trade in Africa and the Indies, which ended in ruin.● When it became clear that Queen Anne would leave no heir, the Scots made it a condition of accepting the Hanoverian succession that the terms of union with England be revised. The **Act of Union** which followed permitted Scotland to keep her Church and her legal system and to send 16 peers and 45 MPs to Westminster. The Scottish Parliament sat for the last time in 1707.

The Jacobite rebellions

In 1715 the **Earl of Mar** led episcopalian and Catholic Highlanders to rebel in support of the Old Pretender, **James**, son of James II, also arousing considerable Lowland support. The rebels occupied Perth and met the forces of the pro-Hanoverian Duke of Argyll at Sheriffmuir. The battle was indecisive but desertions followed and Mar and the Pretender fled to France. ● The **rebellion** of 1745 received less general support, although the charismatic Prince **Charles Edward Stewart** had early successes, capturing Carlisle and marching on Derby. At Culloden his **Highlanders** were routed and the 'Bonnie Prince' escaped to Skye and thence to France.● Scotland paid dearly for her Jacobite sympathies. The losses at Culloden were considerable and the Highlands were thereafter ruthlessly policed, the wearing of the kilt forbidden. Over the next hundred years the old Highland way of life completely disappeared. New landowners, whose interests lay in the south, were increasingly happy to buy or lease great tracts of land, provided that the crofters were evicted. During the infamous 'Highland Clearances' thousands were dispossessed. Between 1760 and 1808 some 12,000 left for America and 30,000 for the colonies. By 1860 the Highlands were virtually empty.

The later 18th and 19th centuries

By the middle of the 18th century **Glasgow** had become Britain's biggest importer of **tobacco**. Linen manufacture was the chief industry and the cotton industry developed, particularly in Lanarkshire and Renfrewshire. Better transportation and the new canals helped the **mining industry**, particularly coal, while the Glaswegian James Watt's steam engine helped to industrialize the whole of Britain. Clydeside developed its shipbuilding and marine engineering.● In **Edinburgh, literature and philosophy** flourished under the Enlightenment with revival of interest in vernacular verse and the enormous popularity of **Robert Burns**. The philosopher **David Hume** and the economic theories of **Adam Smith** attracted European attention. **Painters** like Alan Ramsay and Henry Raeburn and **architects** like James Gibbs and

Robert Adam enhanced Scotland's artistic reputation. In Edinburgh the **New Town** with its elegant Neoclassical crescents and terraces earned the city its title of the 'Athens of the North'.● In 1822 William IV paid a state visit to Edinburgh. **Holyrood Palace** was refurbished for the occasion with tartans, weapons and banners, masterminded by Sir Walter Scott. Nostalgia for the old Highland way of life was further confirmed by the royal purchase of Balmoral and Queen Victoria and Prince Albert paid many visits there, engulfed in tartan and the sound of the pipes.

The 20th century

The first half of the century witnessed Scotland's gallant participation in two **world wars** and the inauguration in 1947 of the **Edinburgh Festival** which has become internationally renowned. ● More recent years have seen the exploitation of **North Sea oil**, the development of Scottish nationalism and the debate on devolution. Despite a close involvement with the south and increasingly with Europe, crossing the border is still most emphatically crossing into another country — vigorous, articulate and welcoming.

Bonnie Prince Charlie and the '45 Rebellion

Charles Edward Stewart, the Young Pretender, was born in Rome in 1720, the son of James, the exiled Stewart king, and the Princess Clementina Sobieski, daughter of King John of Poland.
At the age of 22, Charles resolved to win the British throne by force. He chose his moment well, for in 1744 Britain and France were at war, and the French were eager to help the Stewart cause. However, much of the French fleet was destroyed in a storm and the British navy had been alerted by spies. Charles arrived at Eriskay in Aug. 1745, and his Scottish supporters urged him to abandon the rising. 'But I am come home,' he insisted, and within a week he had rallied an army of some 2,000 Highlanders.
The rising looked strong enough at first, and by September the prince rode into Perth wearing tartan trimmed with gold. The Highlanders captured Edinburgh with ease, by rushing one of the city gates as it opened to let a coach out. The city surrendered almost without resistance. There followed a victory for Charles at Prestonpans, and from there he invaded England.
At this juncture the English were alarmed and began to muster all forces to counter the prince and his rebel soldiers. When the Jacobites reached Derby, there was a run on the banks in London, and George II prepared to flee to Hanover. Charles' officers insisted on a return at this point, having learned that the Duke of Cumberland was on his way with a huge army to put down the rebellion. Charles retired to the Highlands before Cumberland's advance, but was finally vanquished at Culloden on April 16th. Bonnie Prince Charlie was forced to flee, and wandered through the Highlands with a price of £30,000 on his head before escaping to France. He died, a disillusioned drunkard, in Rome in 1788.

● *Practical information*

Information: *Helensburgh Tourist Office*, The Clock Tower, Strathclyde, ☎ (0436) 2642; *Greater Glasgow Tourist Board,* 35-39, St Vincent place Glasgow GI 2ER ☎ (041) 227 4894. *City of Dundee Tourist Board,* City Chambers, Dundee DD1 3BY ☎ (382) 23141. City of Aberdeen Tourist Board, St. Nicholas house, Broad Street, Aberdeen, AB9 1DE ☎ (224) 632727.

Weather forecast: ☎ (0382) 8091.

Ferry links to the Shetland Isles.

Self-catering cottages: *Ardblair Castle Cottages*, Ardblair Castle, Blairgowrie, Perthshire, ☎ (0250) 3155; *Aberfeldy Country Cottages*, Moness Farm, Aberfeldy, Perthshire PH15 2DY, ☎ (0887) 20851; *Mountquhanle Holiday Homes, Cupar, Fife KY15 4QJ, ☎ (082624) 252.

Youth hostelling: *Scottish YHA,* 7 Glebe Crescent, Stirling FK8 2JA, ☎ (0786) 2821.

Festivals: **12 - 21 Feb.**: *St. Andrews Festival;* **May - Oct.**: *Pitlochry Festival Theatre Season;* **20 - 31 May**: *Perth Festival of the Arts;* **5 - 15 Aug.**: *Aberdeen International Youth Festival;* **9 - 16 Oct.**: *National Gaelic Mod* (festival of Gaelic languages, literature, history, music and art) in Stirling.

Customs and folklore: *Hogmanay* (→ Scottish Borders); **11 Jan.**: *Burning of the Clavie*, Burghead, Grampian (half a whisky barrel filled with tar and wood, is lit and paraded around the village); **Jun.**: *Lanimer Day*, Lanark, Strathclyde (famous celebrations, a week of events: thousands of people on foot perambulate along the traditional paths to visit the ancient March Stones); *Riding the Marches*, in Aberdeen (procession to a pipe band); *Maggie Fair* in Garmouth on the fourth Sat. (stalls, sideshows, teas, raffle); **Aug.**: *Inverkeithing Lammas Fair*.

Other events: **Jun.**: *British Amateur Golf Championship*, Prestwick Golf Course, Prestwick St. Nicholas, Prestwick, Strathclyde; *RSAC International Scottish rally driving*, Scotland's only international motorsport event; **Aug.**: *Cowal Highland Gathering*, The Stadium, Dunoon, Strathclyde.

Aquatic sports: sailing, windsurfing and waterskiing: *Lochearnhead Water Sports Centre*, Lochearnhead, Perthshire, ☎ (05673) 330 for sports on Loch Tay; three centres in Lothian, two in Strathclyde and two in Tayside; enquire *STB*.

Archery: *Highland Adventure*, Knockshannock Lodge, Glenisla, Alyth, Perthshire PH11 8PE, ☎ (057582) 207.

Canoeing: *Lochearnhead Water Sports Centre* (→ Aquatic sports).

Climbing: *Ardenbeg*, Grant Road, Grantown-on-Spey, Morayshire PH26 3LD, ☎ (0479) 2824; *Carnoch Outdoor Centre*, Carnoch House, Glencoe, Argyll PA39 4HS, ☎ (08552) 350.

Field sports: *British Association for Shooting and Conservation,* Buchanan Home Farm, Drymen, Stirlingshire, ☎ (0360) 60840; *British Field Sports Society,* Glenmore Lodge, Old Edinburgh Road, Moffat, Dumfriesshire, ☎ (0683) 20571.

Golf: Fife: Burntisland (18-hole), Carnoustie (18-hole), Gleneagles Hotel (18-hole), Royal Aberdeen (9- and 18-hole), St. Andrew's (18-hole), Prestwick Strathclyde (18-hole); almost 100 courses in central Scotland.

Hunting: *Linlithgow and Stirlingshire Hunt,* Wester Gormyre, Torphichen, Bathgate, West Lothian, ☎ (0506) 52598.

Orienteering: *Highland Adventure* (→ Archery).

Skiing: *Carnoch Outdoor Centre* (→ Climbing).

Pigeon, clay pigeon shooting and trout fishing: *Highland Consultants,* PO Box 7, Elgin, Morayshire IV30 3LZ, ☎ (0343) 830259.

Sailing and cruising: *Yacht Corryvreckan,* Kerrera, Oban, Argyll PA34 4SX, ☎ (0631) 64371; *BorroBoats,* Dungallan Parks, Oban, Argyll PA34 4PE, ☎ (0631) 63292; *Gill Yacht Charters,* Rowancraig, Ardfern, by Lochgilphead, Argyll PA31 8QN, ☎ (08525) 257.

Walking: *C-n-Do Scotland Ltd.,* Howlands Cottage, Sauchieburn, Stirling FK7 9PZ, ☎ (0786) 812355; *Shieling Holidays,* Grantown-on-Spey PH26 3EZ, ☎ (0479) 2991 for walking tours throughout Scotland.

 Towns and places

ABERDEEN*

Edinburgh, 130; Dundee, 67 m
pop. 186,757 ☎ 0224   Grampian B1

Aberdeen, the 'Granite City', has become one of Britain's most prosperous areas as a result of the exploitation of North Sea oil, though, in fact, no oil is brought ashore here. Modern development has changed the city centre but Old Aberdeen and much of the harbour area retain their historic buildings and attractive old streets. These are the two areas of most interest. Old Aberdeen profited from the favour of Robert the Bruce, who completed Brig o' Balgownie. Its cobbled streets contain the ancient St. Machar's Cathedral and King's College.

The centre

▶ Handsome **Union Street** (built 1800-20) runs for 1m through the centre. The focal point is **Castlegate** where the fine Mercat cross stands. ▶ In **Shiprow** is Provost Ross's House built in 1593 and housing the **Aberdeen Maritime Museum** (*Mon.-Sat., 10-5*) with exhibits on the fishing industry, shipbuilding and North Sea oil and gas. ▶ On N side of Union Street is **Provost Skene's House** (*Mon.-Sat.*), furnished in period style and with a museum of civic and domestic life. ▶ Near the Town House is the 17thC **tolbooth**, the old prison (*tours by appointment*). ▶ Aberdeen's most striking building is **Marischal College**, one of the world's largest granite structures with a neo-Gothic pinnacled façade. It includes the **University Anthropological Museum** (*Mon.-Fri., 10-5, Sun. 2-5*) with a section on Scotland's prehistory. ▶ The **Kirk of St. Nicholas** (*Mon., Thu., Fri. 12-4; Sat. 10-12*) is really three churches in one. ▶ 18thC **James Dun's House** in Schoolhill stages various exhibitions. ▶ The nearby **art gallery** (*Mon.-Sat. 10-5, Thu. 10-8, Sun. 2-5*) concentrates on Scottish art; also Impressionist works.

Old Aberdeen

The original settlement was founded 1m N of the modern city, around the cathedral built by St. Machar (6thC). The present twin-spired granite **cathedral** (*open 9-5*) was built in the 15thC, the splendid heraldic ceiling being added in the 16thC. ▶ **King's College** was founded in 1495 by Bishop Elphinstone. The present 16thC building incorporates an impressive Gothic **chapel** (*Mon.-Fri. 9-5*). ▶ The **Cruickshank Botanic Gardens** (*Mon.-Fri. 9-5; May-Sep. Sat., Sun. 2-5*) include rock and water gardens▶ N of Old

Aberdeen is **Brig o'Balgownie**, the oldest (1286) bridge in Scotland and still in use. The single Gothic pointed arch is 57 ft. wide.   □

Practical information

ABERDEEN
ⓘ St. Nicholas House, Broad Street, ☎ (0224) 632727; Stonehaven Road, ☎ (0224) 873030 (summer only).
✈ Aberdeen Airport, ☎ (0224) 722331.
🚃 ☎ (0224) 582005 (motorail connection).
⛴ to Orkney and Shetland Islands (Lerwick); P. and O., ☎ (0224) 572615.
Car-rental: Europcar, 121 Causewayend, ☎ (0224) 631199; Airport counter, ☎ (0224) 770770.

Hotels:
★★★★ *Royal,* Bath Street, AB1 2HY (C2), ☎ (0224) 585152, AC AM BA DI, 43 rm. Ⓟ ♿ ⚘ £50. Rest. ♦ ♪ ♿ £17.
★★★ *Atholl,* 54 Kings Gate, AB9 2YN (C1), ☎ (0224) 323505, AC AM BA DI, 38 rm. Ⓟ ⚘ ♪ £55.50. Rest. ♦ £15.
★★★ *Caledonian Thistle,* Union Terrace, AB9 IHE (C2), ☎ (0224) 640233, Tx 73758, AC AM BA DI, 74 rm. Ⓟ ⚘ ♿ £80. Rest. ♦ ♪ ♿ £15.50.
★★★ *Station,* 78 Guild Street, AB9 2DN (C2), ☎ (0224) 587214, Tx 73161, AM BA DI, 57 rm. Ⓟ £46. Rest. ♦ ♪ £11.50.

Restaurants:
♦ *Aberdeen Rendezvous,* 218-222 George Street (C2), ☎ (0224) 633610, AC AM BA DI Chinese-Peking. £10.
♦ *Atlantis Sea Food,* 145 Crown Street (C2), ☎ (0224) 59 1403, AC AM BA DI Cl. Christmas, 1 Jan., Sun. £21.
♦ *Gerard's,* 50 Chapel Street (B2), ☎ (0224) 63 9500, AC AM BA DI ♪ ♿ Cl. Bank Hols., Sun. Book. £18.
♦ *Nargile,* 77-79 Skene Street (B2), ☎ (0224) 636093, AC AM BA DI Cl. Sun., 25 Dec.-5 Jan. Turkish food. £12.
♦ *Pinocchio,* 58-60 Justice Mill Lane (C2), ☎ (0224) 58 4599, AC AM BA DI £10.
♦ *Poldino's,* 7 Little Belmont Street (C2), ☎ (0224) 64 7777, AC AM BA DI ♿ ♪ ⚘ Cl. Christmas, 1 Jan., Sun. Book. £11.50.
♦ *Trattoria Luigi's,* 4 Bridge Street (C2), ☎ (0224) 59 0001, AC AM BA DI Cl. Sun. £14.

⚕ Hazelhead C.S. (165 pl), ☎ (0224) 642121; at Maryculter, 8m SW, *Lower Deeside C.* (45 pl), ☎ (0224) 733860.

Recommended
Antique shop: at Kinellar, *Bell,* John of Aberdeen Ltd., Balbrogie by Blackburn, ☎ (0224) 79209.
Golf course: King's Links, 19 Golf Road, ☎ (0224) 581464; St. Fittick's Road, Balnagask, ☎ (0224) 876407.

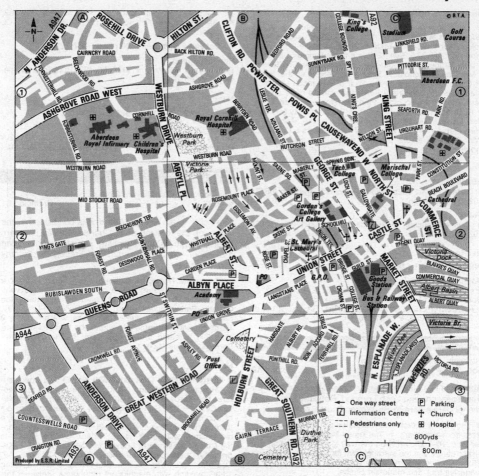

ABERDEEN

Produced by E.S.R. Limited

Nearby

ABERDEEN AIRPORT, 6m NW by A96

Hotels:
★★★★ *Holiday Inn Aberdeen*, Riverview Drive, Farburn Dyce, AB2 OA2, ☎ (0224) 770011, Tx 739651, AC AM BA DI, 154 rm. P 〰 & ⊠ 〠 £68. Rest. ♦ ♪ & £13.
★★ *Dyce Skean Dhu* (M.C.H.), Farburn Terrace, AB2 ODW, ☎ (0224) 723101, Tx 73473, AC AM BA DI, 222 rm. P & £52.50. Rest. ♦ ♪ & £9.50.

ALTENS, 3m S on A956

Hotel:
★★★★ *Skean Dhu* (M.C.H.), Souter Head Road, AB1 4LF, ☎ (0224) 877000, Tx 739631, AC AM BA DI, 222 rm. P 〈 〰 △ & ⊡ ♪ £69. Rest. ♦ ♪ & £10.50.

BANCHORY-DEVENICK, 4 1/2m SW on B9077

Hotel:
★★★ *Ardoe House*, South Deeside Road, AB1 5YP, ☎ (0224) 867355, AC AM BA DI, 21 rm. P 〈 〰 △ A baronial house set in 50 acres of grounds that include a stretch of the River Dee. £69. Rest. ♦ ♪ £23.

BUCKSBURN, 4m NW by A96

Hotel:
★★★★ *Moat House* (Q.M.H.), Old Meldrum Road, ☎ (0224) 713911, Tx 73108, AC AM BA DI, 98 rm. P ⊠ £68. Rest. ♦ £10.

ABERFELDY*

Glasgow, 73; Perth, 32; Edinburgh, 76 m
pop. 1,477 ☎ 0887   Tayside A2

Aberfeldy is a vacation resort beautifully situated on the River Tay between Pitlochry (→) and Loch Tay. Blair Castle, the Pass of Killiekrankie and many other places of historical and archaeological interest are only a short drive away.

► Splendid five-arched **bridge** over the Tay built in 1733. ► A **monument** beside bridge commemorates founding of Black Watch regiment. ► Paths and natural trail thread the lovely wooded **Birks o' Aberfeldy** with views of Moness Falls.

Nearby

▶ On opposite bank of the Tay reached by Wade Bridge★, is **Weem**, where 16thC auld kirk is used as mausoleum for the Clan Menzies. **Castle Menzies** (*Apr.-Sep.: Mon.-Sat., 10.30-5, Sun., 2-5*) is a fine example of a 16thC Z-plan fortified tower house. ▶ Ruined **Comrie Castle** was a Menzies stronghold. ▶ The ruined keep is all that is left of **Garth Castle**, built by the Wolf of Badenoch (→). ▶ A road runs through pretty **Fortingall** with its huge ancient yew tree, and then more than 20m through **Glen Lyon**. ▶ At **Bridge of Balgie** a road runs S of Loch Tay (→) past **Ben Lawers Visitor Centre** (*Jun.-Aug.: 10-5, Apr.: 11-4, May, Sep.: 11-4*) telling story of Ben Lawers★ (3,984 ft.) from Ice Age to the present; nature trail and walk up mountain.　☐

Practical information _____

ABERFELDY

ℹ️ District Tourist Association, 8 Dunkeld Street, ☎ (0887) 20276 (summer only).

Hotel:
★ **Guinach House**, Urlar Road, PH15 2ET, ☎ (0887) 20251, 7 rm. ⓟ ⫯ ⁂ ⚲ 𝄞 £46. Rest. ♦ ⫶ Cl. Oct.-Mar. £11.

Nearby

WEEM, 1m NW by B846

Hotels:
★★ **Ailean Chraggan**, ☎ (0887) 20346, 3 rm. ⓟ ⫯ ⁂ ⚲ Book. £39. Rest. ♦ ⫶ Cl. 1-3 Jan. Book. £12.
★★ **Weem**, PL15 2LB, ☎ (0887) 20381, BA DI, 12 rm. ⓟ ⫯ ⁂ ⚲ £34. Rest. ♦ ⚬ £13.50.

ABERFOYLE*

Glasgow, 27; Edinburgh, 56 m
pop. 546 ☎ 087 72　　　　　　　Central A2

Aberfoyle is a pleasant village marvelously located for the Trossachs and Loch Lomond. Rob Roy met Baillie Nichol Jarvie here in Sir Walter Scott's novel.

▶ The ruined **church** has mortsafes to preserve corpses from body-snatchers. ▶ The **David Marshall Lodge** (*Easter-Oct.: 10-4.30*), 1m N on the way to the Trossachs, is a visitor centre and the starting point for walks in the **Queen Elizabeth Forest Park** which stretches to Loch Lomond: 'waterfall trail' and mountain climbs.

Nearby

▶ The A821 to the Trossachs is known as the **Duke's Road** because the Duke of Montrose built a toll road to cater to Scott enthusiasts. The modern road climbs up to a fine **viewpoint** over the Trossachs★. ▶ Nearby is the entrance to the **Achray Forest Drive** (*10-6, charge per car*), a scenic road affording views of the Trossachs, walks and picnic places. ▶ The 15m drive★ W to the E bank of **Loch Lomond** is exceptionally beautiful. From Lochard there are fine views of **Ben Lomond**. ▶ **Kinlochard** is the base for a number of walks including one to the summit of **Ben Venue** (2,393 ft.). ▶ The road continues past Loch Chon and Loch Arklet to **Inversnaid** (→) on Loch Lomond. ▶ The **Lake of Monteith**, 3m E of Aberfoyle, is the only 'lake' in Scotland. ▶ On the Island of **Inchmahome**, reached by ferry from Port of Monteith, stands **Inchmahome Priory** (*Oct.-Mar.: 9.30-4; Apr.-Sep.: 9.30-7*); Mary Queen of Scots was given sanctuary in this 13thC priory in 1547.　☐

Practical information _____

ABERFOYLE

ℹ️ Main Street, ☎ (087 72) 352 (summer only).

Hotels:
★★★ **Covenanters Inn** (Heritage), FK8 3XB, ☎ (087 72) 347, AC AM BA, 47 rm. ⓟ ⫯ ⁂ ⚲ ⚬ 𝄞 £59. Rest. ♦ ⫶ ⚬ £12.50.

★ **Baillie Nichol** (Heritage), FK8 3SZ, ☎ (087 72) 202, AC AM BA, 37 rm. ⓟ ⫯ ⚲ ⚬ 𝄞 £52.50. Rest. ♦ ⫶ ⚬ Cl. Jan.-Mar. £11.50.

⚕ *Cobeland Campsite* (100 pl), ☎ (087 72) 392.

Recommended
Golf course: Braeval, ☎ (087 72) 493; Buchanan Castle, ☎ (0360) 60307.

Nearby

KINLOCHARD, 3m W on B829

Hotel:
★★★★ **Forest Hills**, FK8 3TL, ☎ (087 77) 277, AC AM BA DI, 17 rm. ⓟ ⫯ ⁂ ⚲ ▱ ⌁ 𝄞 ⚬ £58. Rest. ♦ ⫶ £11.50.

ALFORD*

Aberdeen, 20; Stonehaven, 25 m
☎ 0336　　　　　　　　　　　Grampian B1

The richly fertile Vale of Alford was celebrated in the verse of the dialect poet Charles Murray. Modern Alford village is an excellent centre for exploring a number of castles such as Fraser, Kildrummy and Craigievar.

▶ **Grampian Transport Museum** (*Apr.-Sep.: 11-5*) is a road and rail museum with a collection of vintage vehicles including horse-drawn and steam-driven. ▶ **Haughton Country Park** includes Alford Valley Railway (*Apr., May, Sep.: weekends 11-5, Jun.- Aug.: daily*), which runs for 2 1/2m through the battlefield where the Marquis of Montrose (→) defeated the Covenanters. ▶ **Murray Country Park** has nature trails.

Nearby

▶ **Castle Fraser★** (*May-Sep.: 2-6; 9m E*) is a spectacular example of 16th and 17thC Flemish style of architecture; fine gardens and grounds (*9.30-sunset*). ▶ **Craigievar Castle★**, 7m S (*May-Sep.: 2-6*) is a perfect example of Scottish baronial style in a delightful wooded setting; a turreted L-plan tower house built in 17thC, it has splendid plaster ceilings. ▶ Near Tarland on the B9119 is the **Culsh Pictish earth house** (*flashlight required*). ▶ **Kildrummy Castle** (*Apr.-Sep.: Mon.-Sat., 9.30-7, Sun., 2-7; Oct.-Mar.: Mon-Sat, 9.30-4, Sun., 2-4*) is an imposing 13thC building with magnificent gatehouse. Between this and the 'new' castle is **Kildrummy Castle Water Trust** (*Apr.- Oct.: 9-5*), a rock and water garden.　☐

Practical information _____

ALFORD

🚌 ☎ (0336) 2052.

⚕ *Haughton House Muni*, Montgarrie Road (135 pl), ☎ (0336) 2107.

Nearby

KILDRUMMY, 7 1/2m NW on B973

Hotel:
● ★★★ **Kildrummy Castle**, AB3 8RA, ☎ (033 65) 288, Tx 946240, AC AM BA DI, 17 rm. ⓟ ⫯ ⁂ ⚲ A 19thC mansion in 20 acres of grounds, including ruins of the original castle. £63.50. Rest. ● ♦ ⚲ Cl. 4 Jan.-13 Mar. £16.

ARBROATH*

Dundee, 16; Aberdeen, 51; Edinburgh, 72 m
pop. 23,934 ☎ 0241　　　　　　　Tayside B2

Arbroath is one of Scotland's most attractive coastal resorts. It is well known for its ancient abbey and as the home of the 'smokie', or smoked haddock.

▶ **Arbroath Abbey★** (*Apr.-Sep.: Mon.-Sat. 9.30-12.30, 1.30-7, Sun. 2-7, Oct.-Mar.: till 4*) was founded in 1178 by William the Lion; museum in restored abbot's house.
▶ **Signal Tower Museum** (*Apr.-Sep.: Mon.-Sat., 10.30-1, 2-5, Jul., Aug.: Sun., 2-5; Oct.-Mar.: Mon.-Fri., 2-5, Sat., 10.30-1, 2-7*) features local history particularly of the Bellrock Lighthouse, fishing and wildlife. ▶ **Cliffs Nature Trail,** a 3m walk, starts at NE end of the promenade.
▶ **Elliot Nature Trail** starts from Elliot Junction W of the centre.

Nearby

▶ **Carnoustie** (*7m S*) is a bustling vacation resort famous for its championship golf course. ▶ 3m NW of Carnoustie are the **Ardestie** and **Carlungie** earth houses (*Apr.-Sep.: Mon.-Sat., 9.30-7, Sun., 2-7; Oct.-Mar.: Mon.-Sat., 9.30-4, Sun., 2-4*) ▶ **Vigean's Church,** 1 1/2 N of Arbroath, has a museum of sculpted stone (*same opening times as earth houses*). ▶ **Kellie Castle** (*3m W*) dates mainly from 16thC; it incorporates a gallery for Scottish artists. ☐

Practical information _____

ARBROATH
ⓘ Market Place, ☎ (0241) 72609/76680.

Hotels:
★★★ **Letham Grange,** Colliston, ☎ Sowanbank (024 189) 373, Tx 76438, AC AM BA DI, 19 rm. ℗ ⊰ ⅏ ⌖ ⚘ ⚗ £73.50. Rest. ♦ ♪ ⅋ £15.50.
★★★ **Rosely,** Forfar Road, ☎ (0241) 76828, AC AM, 11 rm. ℗ ⅏ ⌖ £27.

Restaurants:
♦ **Carriage Room,** Meadowbank Inn, Montrose Road, ☎ (0241) 75755, AC AM BA DI ℗ ⌖ ♪ ⅋ ⚘ Cl. 2 wks Jan., Sun.-Mon., Sat. lunch. Book. £11.
♦ **The But'n'Ben,** Auchmithie, ☎ (0241) 77223 ℗ ⌖ ⅋ ⚘ Cl. Tue. Book. £9.

Recommended
Golf course: Elliot, 1m S, ☎ (0241) 72272.

Nearby

CARNOUSTIE, 7m SW on A930
ⓘ 24 High Street, ☎ (0241) 52258.

Hotels:
★★★ **Carlogie House,** Carlogie Road, ☎ (0241) 53185, AC AM BA DI, 11 rm. ℗ ⅏ ⌖ ⚘ £46. Rest. ♦ ♪ ⅋ Cl. 1-3 Jan. £10.50.
★ **Earlston,** 24 Church Street, ☎ (0241) 52352, AC AM BA DI, 17 rm. ℗ ⊰ ⚗ £35. Rest. ♦ ♪ £10.

Inn or Pub:
Station, Station Road, ☎ (0241) 524447, AC BA ℗ ⅏ ⅋ 10 rm. Variation of bar snacks, meals with homemade specials. £4.

AUCHTERARDER*

Perth, 14; Glasgow, 45; Edinburgh, 55 m
pop. 2,838 ☎ 07646   Tayside A2

Auchterarder was burnt down in 1715 by the Earl of Mar's troops. Its single street, almost 2m long, contains many antique shops to cater to visitors to the Gleneagles Hotel and its celebrated golf course.

▶ **Auchterarder Heritage Centre** (*Mon.-Fri. 10-5, weaving demonstrations 1-3*) has displays of steam power, industrial weaving and local history; knitwear and textiles shop.

Nearby

▶ **Tullibardine** Church (*3m NW*) is a collegiate chapel and mausoleum for the Earls of Perth. ▶ **Strathallan Aircraft Collection** (*Apr.-Oct.: 10-5*), 2m N, includes a Hurricane, a Mosquito and a Lancaster. ▶ **Innerpeffray Library** (*Mon.-Sat., ex. Thu., 10-1, 2-5, Sun. 2-4*), 6 m N of Auchte-

rarder, was founded in 1691; the oldest public library still in existence in Scotland: number of rare books. ☐

Practical information _____

AUCHTERARDER
ⓘ Crown Wynd, High Street, ☎ (076 46) 3450 (summer only).

Hotels:
● ★★★★ **Gleneagles,** PH3 1NF, ☎ (076 46) 2231, Tx 76105, AC AM BA DI, 254 rm. ℗ ⊰ ⅏ ⌖ ⅋ ⌗ ⏤ ⌖ ♪ £200. Rest. ♦ ♪ ⅋ £21.
★★★ **Coll Earn House,** High Street, PH3 1DF, ☎ (076 46) 3553, AC AM BA DI, 8 rm. ℗ ⅏ ⌖ £47. Rest. ♦ ♪ ⅋ £15.50.

Recommended
Golf course: Orchil Road, 1m SW, ☎ (076 46) 2804; Gleneagles, ☎ (076 46) 3543.

BALLATER*

Aberdeen, 41; Perth, 67; Edinburgh, 111 m
pop. 1,051 ☎ 0338   Grampian B1

A popular vacation resort often though briefly visited by royalty in the days when the railway from Aberdeen ended here 7m short of Balmoral. An extension of the line begun but firmly vetoed by Queen Victoria forms an attractive footpath. The surrounding river, woods and moorland make the town an ideal walking and touring centre.

▶ The **bridge** over the Dee was opened by Queen Victoria in 1885. From it there is a walk to the viewpoint of **Craig Cailleach** (1,896 ft.).

Nearby

▶ The excursion along **Glen Muick** to S is a scenic drive. The road along E bank passes the waterfall of **Linn of Muick** (*4 1/2 m*) ending at an information centre and a 3/4 m walk to Loch Muick. ▶ **Muir of Dinnet** to E is an area of moorland beautified by Loch Kinord and Loch Davan.
▶ **Aboyne** (*11m E*), well known for its Highland gathering, has walks through Glen Tanar. **Aboyne Castle** (*not open*) was built in 1801. To W of Ballater is **Abergeldie Castle** (*not open*) on S bank of the Dee, a 19thC building incorporating a 16thC tower. ☐

Practical information _____

BALLATER
ⓘ Station Square, ☎ (0338) 55306 (summer only).

Hotels:
★★★★ **Craigendarroch,** Braemar Road, AB3 5XA, ☎ (0338) 55858, Tx 739952, AC AM BA DI, 23 rm. ℗ ⊰ ⅏ ⌖ ⅋ ⚘ ⏤ ⌖ £79. Rest. ♦ ♪ ⅋ £18.
● ★★★ **Tullich Lodge,** AB3 5SB, ☎ (0338) 55406, AC AM, 10 rm. ℗ ⊰ ⅏ ⌖ A Victorian baronial house set in 6 acres of grounds with views over the country. £94. Rest. ♦ Cl. mid-Dec.-mid-Mar. £17.
● ★★ **Darroch Learg,** Braemar Road, AB3 5UX, ☎ (0338) 55443, BA, 23 rm. ℗ ⊰ ⅏ ⌖ Scottish baronial style, standing in 4 acres of garden and woodland. £42. Rest. ♦ Cl. Nov.-Jan. £12.50.
★ **Invercauld Arms,** AB3 5QJ, ☎ (0338) 55417, AC AM BA DI, 25 rm. ℗ ⊰ ⅏ ⌖ £36. Rest. ♦ ♪ £11.

Recommended
Golf course: ☎ (0338) 55567.

In preparing for your trip, consult the pages pertaining to the regions. You will find there the description of the region you wish to visit, as well as a list of sites that must be seen, a brief history and practical information.

BALLOCH*

Helensburgh, 7; Glasgow, 18; Edinburgh, 62 m
☎ 038 985   Strathclyde A3

Balloch is a resort on the River Leven, route from Loch Lomond to the Clyde. It is an excellent centre for excursions along Loch Lomond by boat and road.

▶ **Balloch Castle Country Park** (*8-dusk*), covering 200 acres on SE shore of Loch Lomond, has a visitor centre (*Apr., May, Sep.: weekends, 10-5; Jun.-Aug.: daily 10-5*) explaining the history of the Lennox stronghold of which only the mound remains. A ranger service provides guided walks; nature trail, walled garden, 19thC castle.

Nearby

▶ To NW is **Cameron House** containing collections of porcelain, furniture, paintings and whisky; mementoes of Tobias Smollett, who lived here. ▶ In the grounds is **Cameron Wildlife Park,** a drive-through reserve with adventure playground, boats and wild animals. ▶ At **Alexandra** to S, mill shops and a sheepskin factory are open to the public.   □

Practical information ──────────────────

BALLOCH
ⓘ ☎ (0389) 53533 (summer only).

Hotel:
★ *Balloch*, G83 8LQ, ☎ Alexandria (0389) 52579, AC AM BA DI, 13 rm. ℗ ⫽⩗ An 18thC coaching house, situated on the banks of the River Leven, close to Loch Lomond. £36.50. Rest. ◆ ⌡ & Cl. 1-3 Jan. £12.50.

⅄ *Tullichewan C.P.*, Old Luss Road (140 pl), ☎ (0389) 59475.

Nearby
KILLEARN, 10m E on A875

Hotel:
★ *Black Bull*, G63 9NG, ☎ (0360) 50215, AC AM BA DI, 13 rm. ℗ ⩜ ⩗ A peaceful, small, country town inn, dating from 1880 when it was a coaching inn. £39.50. Rest. ◆ ⌡ & £12.50.

BANCHORY*

Aberdeen, 17; Dundee, 55; Edinburgh, 118 m
pop. 4,683 ☎ 033 02   Grampian B1

Banchory is a pleasant sheltered town long known as a health resort. It is a convenient centre for exploring Deeside to the W as well as Aberdeen and its coast to the E.

▶ **Banchory Museum** (*Jun.-Sep.: daily ex. Thu. 2-5.20*) has an exhibition of local history. ▶ Just S of town, the Water of Feugh rushes in a series of *cascades* to join the Dee; a footbridge gives views of climbing salmon.

Nearby

Crathes Castle (*2m E; Easter, May-Sep.: Mon.-Sat., 11-6, Sun., 2-6*) seat of the Burnetts of Ley from 1323 to 1951, is an L-plan 16thC tower house: three magnificent painted ceilings; park and gardens (*daily 9.30-sunset*) have fine trees and shrubs; woodland nature trail. ▶ **Drum Castle** (*May-Sep.: daily 2-6*) at **Peterculter** is a 17thC mansion built onto a tower of 1272. ▶ **Kincardine O'Neil** (*8m W*) has the ruins of a large 13thC church.   □

Practical information ──────────────────

BANCHORY
ⓘ Dee Street Car Park, ☎ (033 02) 2000 (summer only).

Hotels:
★★★ *Burnett Arms* (Consort), 25 High Street, ☎ (033 02)

2545, Tx 739925, AC AM BA DI, 17 rm. ℗ ⫽ An old coaching inn in the centre of the town, completely modernized to offer 20thC comforts. £33.50. Rest. ◆ ⌡ & £9.50.
● ★★ *Banchory Lodge*, Dee Street, AB3 3HS, ☎ (033 02) 2625, AC AM BA DI, 25 rm. ℗ ⫽ ⩜ ⩗ ⌡ An 18thC riverside country house built on the site of an old monastery, standing in 19 acres. £53. Rest. ◆ Cl. 13 Dec.-28 Jan. £14.
● ★★ *Raemoir House*, AB3 4ED, ☎ (033 02) 2622, AC AM BA DI, 23 rm. ℗ ⫽ ⩜ ⩗ & ◡ An 18thC mansion in 70 acres of wooded grounds. £69. Rest. ◆ & £19.

Recommended
Golf course: Kinneskie, ☎ (03302) 2365; Torphins, ☎ (033 982) 493.
Craft workshop: *Ingasetter (Fragrance of Scotland)*, North Deeside Road, ☎ (033 02) 2600, wide range of fragrance soaps, aftershave, creams.

Nearby
ABOYNE, 13m W by A93

Hotels:
● ★★ *Birse Lodge*, Charleston Road, AB3 5EL, ☎ (0339) 2253, AM DI, 16 rm. ℗ ⩜ ⩗ & Victorian granite house in 3 acres of grounds near River Dee. £50. Rest. ◆ & Cl. mid-Oct.-mid-Mar. £14.
★★ *Huntley Arms* (C.N.S.), AB3 5HS, ☎ (0339) 2101, Tx 57515, AC AM BA DI, 30 rm. ℗ ⩜ ⩗ £44. Rest. ◆ ⌡ & £15.

⅄ *Drummie Hill C.P.*, Tarland (20 pl), ☎ (033 981) 388.

BANFF*

Aberdeen, 47; Inverness, 74; Edinburgh, 177 m
pop. 3,843 ☎ 026 12   Grampian B1

Banff is a royal burgh which received its charter in 1163. Little remains of the old castle which Edward I visited. Built on three terraces, Banff has several attractive streets with impressive buildings dating from the 17th, 18th and 19thC .

▶ **Duff House**★ (*Apr.-Sep.: Mon.-Sat., 9.30-7, Sun., 2-7*) is one of the finest examples of Georgian Baroque style in Britain. ▶ **Banff Museum** (*Jun.-Sep.: ex. Thu., 2-5.30*) has an exhibition of British birds as well as local exhibits. ▶ **West Buchan Railway** (*Apr., May, Sep.: weekends 11-6, Jun.-Aug.: daily, 11-8*) operates a narrow-gauge coastal railway hauled by steam and diesel. ▶ **Banff Castle** was built on the old castle site in 1750.

Nearby

▶ To E, **Macduff** is an important fishing port with several tourist facilities. ▶ Beyond it, **Gardenstown** and **Crovie** are quaint villages set on Gamrie Bay. ▶ Splendid views from nearby **Troup Head.** ▶ **Whitehills** (*3m W*) is a fishing village;▶ beyond it stand the massive ruins of **Boyne Castle.** ▶ **Portsoy** is an appealing small town famous for its serpentine marble. ▶ To SW is **Fordyce Castle,** a tower built in 1592.   □

Practical information ──────────────────

BANFF
ⓘ Collie Lodge, ☎ (02612) 2419 (summer only).

Hotels:
★★★ *Banff Springs* (Consort), Golden Knowes Road, AB4 2JE, ☎ (026 12) 2881, AC AM BA DI, 30 rm. ℗ ⫽ ⩗ ⫘ ⌡ £40. Rest. ◆ ⌡ £10.50.
★ *Carmelite House*, Low Street, AB4 1AY, ☎ (026 12) 2152, 8 rm. ℗ ⌡ £24. Rest. ◆ £6.50.

Restaurant:
◆ *The County*, 32 High Street, ☎ (026 12) 5353, AM DI ℗ ⫽ ⩜ ⩗ ⫘ 7 rm. Book. £12.

Recommended
Golf course: Duff House, The Barnyards, ☎ (026 12) 2062.

Nearby

MACDUFF, 2m E on A90

Hotels:
★★ ***Deveron House***, 25-27 Union Road, AB4 IUD, ☎ (0261) 32309, AC AM BA DI, 17 rm. 🅿 ⚘ ⛵ ⛳ £42. Rest. ♦ ♪ ♿ £8.50.
★★ ***Fife Arms*** (I.N.H./Exec Hotel), Shore Street, AB4 1UB, ☎ (0261) 32408, AC BA DI, 22 rm. 🅿 ⚘ ⛵ ⛳ £36. Rest. ♦ ♪ £9.50.

Recommended
Golf course: Royal Tarlair, ☎ (0261) 32897.
♥ *Jennie Ross Classic Knitwear*, Macduff Industrial Estate, ☎ (0261) 33035, pullover and cardigan sweaters for women.

BLAIRGOWRIE

Perth, 16; Dundee, 19; Edinburgh, 60 m
pop. 7,028 ☎ 0250 Tayside B2

In the past, a centre first of the flax, and then of the jute industry. Blairgowrie is a good touring centre for Deeside, Pitlochry and Perth.

▶ **Ardblair Castle** (*guided tours Thu. p.m. in season*), is an L-plan tower house of 16thC: exhibits relating to the Oliphants including many Jacobite relics. ▶ At **Westmill Trout Farm** (*daily 9-7*) visitors may feed or catch fish.

Nearby

▶ **Alyth** (*5m E*) has ruins of 13thC church and a folk museum (*May-Sep.: Tue-Sat., 1-5*). ▶ The **Belmont estate** has woodland walks and a nature trail. ▶ **Meigle Museum★**, (*Apr.-Sep.: Mon.-Sat., 9.30-7, Oct.-Mar.: Mon.-Sat., 9.30-4*) 3m S of Alyth, has magnificent collection of 25 carved Early Christian stones found by the churchyard. ▶ **Coupar Angus** (*5m SE*) has a tollbooth built in 1762 and remains of 12thC abbey. ▶ The **beech hedge** (*5m S*), planted in 1746, is 600 yards long and, at 85 ft. high, is thought to be the highest in the world. □

Practical information

BLAIRGOWRIE
ⓘ Wellmeadow, ☎ (0250) 2960 (summer only).

Hotels:
★★ ***Altamount House***, Coupar Angus Road, PH10 6JN, ☎ (0250) 3512, AC BA DI, 7 rm. 🅿 ⚘ ≋ ⛵ ⛳ £58. Rest. ♦ ♿ Cl. 1 wk. Oct., Jan., 14 Feb. £10.
★★ ***Muirton House***, Essendy Road, PH10 6QU, ☎ (0250) 2113, AC AM BA DI, 9 rm. 🅿 ⚘ ≋ ⛵ £45.

⛺ *Ballintuim Hotel C.P.* (30 pl), ☎ (025 086) 276.

Recommended
Golf course: Rosemount, ☎ (0250) 2383.

Nearby

ALYTH, 5m E off B926

Hotel:
★★ ***Lands of Loyal***, Loyal Road, PH11 8JQ, ☎ (082 83) 2481, AC AM BA, 14 rm. 🅿 ⚘ ≋ ⛵ ⛳ Victorian mansion with magnificent ceiling in the dining room, fine oak-paneled hall. £50. Rest. ♦ ♪ Cl. Jan.-Mar. £10.50.

BRIDGE OF CALLY, 6m NW on A93

Inn or pub:
● ★★ ***Bridge of Cally***, PH10 7JJ, ☎ (025 086) 231, DI, 9 rm. 🅿 ⚘ ≋ ⛳ A 200-year-old drovers' inn on the banks of the River Ardle surrounded by woodland. £34.50. Rest. ♦ ♪ ♿ £11.

GLENSHEE, 16m W on A94

Hotel:
● ★★ ***Dalmunzie House***, PH10 7QG, ☎ (025 085) 224, AC AM DI, 19 rm. 🅿 ⚘ ≋ ⛵ ♿ ⛳ ⛳ £54.50. Rest. ♦ ♿ Cl. 1 Nov.-20 Dec. £15.50.

KINCLAVEN, 6m O off A93

Hotel:
● ★★ ***Ballathie House***, ☎ Meikleour (025 083) 268, Tx 7273916, AC AM BA DI, 33 rm. 🅿 ⚘ ≋ ⛵ ⛳ Victorian baronial style house, in 10 acres of grounds. £63. Rest. ♦ Cl. 2 Jan.-27 Feb. £14.

KINLOCH, 2m W on A93

Hotel:
● ★★ ***Kinloch House***, PH10 6SG, ☎ Essendy (025 084) 237, AC AM DI, 13 rm. 🅿 ⚘ ≋ ⛵ £46. Rest. ● ♦ ♿ Cl. 7-28 Dec. £13.50.

BRAEMAR*

Dundee, 51; Aberdeen, 58; Edinburgh, 85 m
☎ 033 83 Grampian A-B1

Braemar has become a year-round resort with the development of ski slopes at Glen Shee to the S and Mar Lodge to the W. It is an excellent touring centre for Deeside and the Cairngorms.

▶ **Braemar Castle** (*May-Sep.: 10-6*) built by the Earl of Mar in 1628, was an important element in keeping the peace after the 1645 rising. ▶ The scanty remains of **Kindrochit Castle** date from 14thC. ▶ The **mound** where the Earl of Mar raised his standard in support of James VIII is occupied by the Invercauld Arms Hotel.

Nearby

▶ The **Linn of Dee★** (*8m W*) is favourite beauty spot where the river becomes cascades and waterfalls: walks, mountain climbs (Lochanager 3,786 ft.) and the Lairig Ghru long-distance path over the Cairngorms. ▶ To E the **Old Bridge of Dee** was built in 1752. ▶ **Balmoral Castle★**, built mid-17thC, is owned by the Queen who normally lives there for much of Aug. and Sep. Visitors allowed into grounds and ballroom with art exhibition (*May-Jul.: Mon.-Sat. 10-5*). **Crathie Church**, near the castle gates, was built in 1895. Among various royal associations is the **monument** erected by Queen Victoria to her retailer John Brown. □

Practical information

ⓘ Balnellan Road, ☎ (03383) 600 (summer only).

Hotels:
★★ ***Fife Arms***, Mar Road, AB3 5YN, ☎ (033 83) 644, AC AM BA DI, 87 rm. 🅿 ⚘ ≋ ♿ ⛳ £45. Rest. ♦ ♪ ♿ £10.
★ ***Callater Lodge***, 9 Glenshee Road, AB3 5YQ, ☎ (033 83) 275, AC BA, 9 rm. 🅿 ≋ Cl. mid-Oct.-26 Dec. £25.

Recommended
Golf course: Cluniebank Road, ☎ (03383) 618.

CALLANDER**

Perth, 41; Glasgow, 43; Edinburgh, 52 m
pop. 2,286 ☎ 0877 Central A2

Set on the River Teith and overlooked by Ben Ledi (2,873 ft.) and other impressive peaks, Callander is an ideal centre for touring the Trossachs and the Highlands. A dignified and charming town, it was the background for television's 'Dr Finlay's Casebook' and 'The Country Diary of an Edwardian Lady'.

▶ Remains of a **Roman camp** in E part of town. ▶ The **Brackling Falls** are in the pretty gorge of Kiltie Water.

Queen Victoria and Balmoral

In 1842 Queen Victoria had to postpone a holiday in Brussels owing to an illness. When she recovered, it was suggested that she might try Scotland instead. On her arrival in Edinburgh she was enchanted with the city, but became even more enamoured of the Highlands soon after this.

The Queen's Scottish doctor, Sir James Clark, recommended the climate of the Upper Deeside in particular as being beneficial for her rheumatism. Victoria took his advice, and in 1848 singled out Balmoral as a favourite place. She wrote: 'All seemed to breathe freedom and peace, to make one forget the world and its sad turmoils.' Four years later she bought Balmoral house and estate for £31,500 and Prince Albert spent considerable time rebuilding and refurbishing the house, adding flamboyant Scottish touches to the design.

Victoria made a habit of visiting the local residents, while staying at Balmoral, and regularly attended the Braemar Gathering. After Albert's death in 1861, John Brown, the son of a local farmer, became such a close friend of hers that the newspapers referred to her as 'Mrs Brown'.

As a result of the Queen's interest in all things Scottish, not only did the tartan become highly fashionable, but kilts, sporrans, and 'Celtic' jewelry became popular. No fewer than 18 separate clan societies were formed, and a mythology of piping was invented to satisfy the Scots-crazed Victorians.

Nearby

▶ 1m W, the A821 branches left to run along N bank of Loch Venachar through **Brig O' Turk** to Loch Achray, the Trossachs (→) and Loch Katrine (→). ▶ The A84 continues NW by the attractive **Falls of Leny,** through the narrow **Pass of Leny** and along E bank of lovely **Loch Lubnaig.** ▶ **Strathyre Forest Information Centre** (*May-Sep.*) gives details of many forest walks in the vicinity and has a display illustrating a working forest. ☐

Practical information

CALLANDER

ⓘ Leny Road, ☎ (0877) 30342 (summer only).

Hotels:

● ★★ *Bridgend House*, Bridge Street, FK17 8AA, ☎ (0877) 30130, AC AM BA DI, 7 rm. ℗ ≼ ∭ ⚘ £52. Rest. ♦ ♪ ♨ £10.50.

● ★★ *Lubnaig*, Leny Feus, FK17 8AS, ☎ (0877) 30376, 10 rm. ℗ ∭ ⚘ £37. Rest. ♦ ♪ Cl. mid-Nov.-Easter. £10.50.

● ★★ *Roman Camp*, Main Street, FK17 8BG, ☎ (0877) 30003, 11 rm. ℗ ≼ ∭ ⚘ Miniature chateau built in 1625 on site of Roman camp, set in 24 acres of beautiful grounds. £71. Rest. ● ♦ Cl. Dec.-Mar. £20.

⅄ *Callander H.P.*, Invertossachs Road (35 pl), ☎ (0877) 30265; *Gart C.P.*, Stirling Road (121 pl), ☎ (0877) 30002.

Recommended

Golf course: Aveland Road, ☎ (0877) 30090.

CRIEFF*

Perth, 18; Glasgow, 50; Edinburgh, 60 m
pop. 5,101 ☎ 0764   Tayside A2

Crieff is a pleasant hillside resort above the River Earn. It is a good centre for visiting Stirling, Loch Lomond and the Trossachs to the W and Perth to the E.

▶ The **stocks** and 17thC octagonal **town cross** stand by the town hall. ▶ The Celtic **Mercat cross** dates from 10thC. ▶ **Glenturret Distillery★** (*Mar.-Jun., Sep.-Oct.: Mon.-Fri., 10-12, 1.30-3.30; Jul.-Aug.: Mon.-Sat., 9.45-4; Nov.-Dec.: Mon.-Fri., 2, 2.45, 3.30*), is the oldest in Scotland: heritage centre, theatre and exhibition. ▶ **Stuart Strathearn** glass factory (*Mon.-Fri. 9-4.30*), shop. ▶ **Crieff Nature Trail** starts 1 1/2m NW at Culcrieff Farm. ▶ **Lady Mary's walk** from Taylor Park picnic area along banks of river.

Nearby

Muthill (*3 1/2m S*) is an early 19thC village: 15thC church. ▶ **Drummon Castle** (*not open*), at the end of a 1m avenue, was founded in 1491 but only the square tower is original: **the gardens** (*Apr., Sep.: Wed., Sun. 2-6; May-Aug.: daily*) have a multiple sundial dated 1630. ▶ **Muthill Museum** (*Easter, Jun.-Sep.: Tue., Thu., Sat., Sun., 2.30-5*) is a small folk museum illustrating life in the district from the 18thC. ☐

Practical information

CRIEFF

ⓘ James Square, ☎ (0764) 2578 (summer only).

Hotels:

★★ *Crieff Hydro*, PH7 3LQ, ☎ (0764) 2401, AC AM BA DI, 200 rm. ℗ ≼ ∭ ⚘ ♨ ⤿ ♪ ♫ £62. Rest. ♦ ♨ £8.

★★ *Murraypark*, Connaught Terrace, PH7 3DJ, ☎ (0764) 3731, AM BA DI, 15 rm. ℗ ≼ ∭ ⚘ £47. Rest. ♦ ♪ ♨ £14.

★ *Gwydyr House*, Comrie Road, PH7 4BP, ☎ (0764) 3277, 10 rm. ℗ ≼ ∭ ⚘ £25. Rest. ♦ ♪ ♨ Cl. Nov.-Mar. £8.

Recommended

Golf course: Perth Road, ☎ (0764) 2909; Peat Road, Muthill, ☎ (0764) 3319.

Showroom: *Perthshire Paperweights Ltd.*, Muthill Road, ☎ (0764) 2409, glass paperweights with 19thC designs; *Stuart Strathearn Ltd.*, Muthill Road, ☎ (0764) 2942, extensive selection of crystal giftware.

♥ *Dorraga Sweater Shop*, 55 King Street, ☎ (0764) 4647, hand-knit and hand-loomed sweaters.

Nearby

SMA GLEN, 5m N on A822

Hotel:

★ *Foulford Inn*, PH7 3LN, ☎ (0764) 2407, 11 rm. ℗ ≼ ∭ ⚘ ♨ beautifully situated in wild, open countryside, 19thC former droving inn. £31.50. Rest. ♦ ♨ Cl. Feb. £8.50.

CULLEN**

Banff, 12; Aberdeen, 59; Edinburgh, 189 m
pop. 1,378 ☎ 0542   Grampian B1

Cullen was built between 1820 and 1830 to replace the old town around the parish church 1 1/2m S. A splendid viaduct of the now closed railway divides Cullen into the modern town on the clifftop and the older sea town around the harbour. Gaily painted cottages, fine white 'singing' sands and the sandstone rocks called the 'Three Kings' make a delightful picture.

▶ The **market cross** in the square dates from 1696. ▶ The **auld kirk** at Old Cullen was founded in 13thC and includes a beautiful **sacrament house,** an imposing **laird's gallery** of 1602 and an ornate **monument** to Alexander Ogilvy.

Nearby

▶ To E stand the ruins of 15thC **Findlater Castle,** a fortress of the Ogilvies. ▶ **Sandend** is a charming former fishing village founded in 17thC. ▶ The ruins of **Deskford Church** (*4m S*) incorporate a finely carved **sacrament**

house. ▶ To W, the main road passes through the attractive fishing villages of **Portknockie** and **Findochty** to **Buckie**, a busy fishing town remarkable for the number of its churches. The **Maritime Museum and Peter Anson Gallery** (*Mon.-Fri., 10-8, Sat. 10-12*) is concerned with the fishing industry; the gallery has many local watercolours.□

Practical information _____

CULLEN
ⓘ 20 Seafield Street, ☎ (0542) 40757 (summer only).

Hotel:
★★ *Cullen Bay*, AB5 2XA, ☎ (0542) 40432, AM BA DI, 17 rm. ℗ ⟨ ▦ ⚲ ⫽ £55.50. Rest. ♦ ⌁ ₺ £10.50.

Recommended
Golf course: The Links, ☎ (0542) 40685.

Nearby

BUCKIE, 5m SW off A98

Hotel:
★★ *Cluny*, 2 High Street, AB5 1AL, ☎ (0542) 32922, AC AM BA DI, 16 rm. ℗ ⟨ ⫽ £38.50. Rest. ♦ ⌁ ₺ Cl. 1-3 Jan. £8.50.

DUFFTOWN

Perth, 80; Aberdeen, 40 m
☎ 0340   Grampian B1

Founded in 1817 by James Duff, Earl of Fife, Dufftown is the centre of the whisky distilling industry, and the home of seven distilleries.

▶ **Balvenie Castle** (*Apr.-Sep.: Thu.-Sat., 9.30-7, Sun., 2-7*) was originally built in 13thC by the Comys; much rebuilding in 15th and 16thC changed it into a tower-house mansion. ▶ **Mortlach Church** was probably founded in 12thC but was largely rebuilt in 19thC. ▶ **Dufftown Museum** (*open summer*) has local collections.▶ Glenfiddich Distillery (*mid-May-mid-Oct.: Mon.-Fri., 9.30-4.30, Sat. 9.30-4.30, Sun., 12-4.30*) offers guided tours and audiovisual show.

Nearby

▶ 15thC **Auchindoun Castle** (*1 1/2m SE*) has three-storey keep surrounded by Pictish earthworks. ▶ The single cast-iron span of **Craigellachie Bridge** (*4m N*) was built in 1814. **Rothes**, 3m farther N, has the remains of a castle and the Glen Grant Distillery (*Easter-Sep.: Mon.-Fri., 10-4*). ▶ To the NW **Ballindalloch** has a 16thC castle. (*May-Sep.: Sun., 2-4*). ▶ **Glenfarclas Distillery** has a visitor centre with tours (*Jul.-Sep.: Mon.-Fri., 9-4.30, Sat. 10-4*).   □

Practical information _____

Nearby

ROTHES, 10m N on A941

Hotel:
★★ *Rothes Glen*, IV33 7AH, ☎ (034 03) 254, AC AM BA DI, 16 rm. ℗ ⟨ ▦ ⚲ Scottish baronial style mansion, in 40 acres of grounds. £60.50. Rest. ♦ ₺ £19.

DUMBARTON

Glasgow, 4; Stirling, 20; Edinburgh, 50 m
☎ 0389   Central A3

A royal burgh on the N bank of the Clyde, Dumbarton was once capital of the ancient kingdom of Strathclyde. It is a large industrial town with a busy modern centre, but some old buildings have survived.

▶ **Dumbarton Castle** (*Apr.-Sep.: Mon.-Sat., 9.30-7, Sun., 2-7; Oct.-Mar.: Mon.-Sat., 9.30-4, Sun., 2-4*) is built on two

levels on a 240 ft. rock; only the 17th and 18thC fortifications have survived.

Nearby

▶ At Milton to NE, **Overtoun Nature Trail** winds for 2m through the woodlands of lovely **Overtoun Glen** including the Spardie Linn waterfall.   □

DUNBLANE*

Perth, 29; Glasgow, 33; Edinburgh, 42 m
pop. 6,783 ☎ 0786   Central A2

A small ancient town built on hills through which the winding Allan Water threads. Its cathedral, much admired by John Ruskin, cathedral close and quaint narrow streets give Dunblane its special character.

▶ The **cathedral**★ is mainly 13thC with the Gothic W front its outstanding feature. ▶ The **old bridge** was built in 1409 and the coaching inn above it was a haunt of Robert Burns. ▶ The **Ramoyle** in the centre has retained its 300-year-old narrow streets.

Nearby

▶ Near **Braco** (*5m NE*) was the Roman camp of **Ardoch**, now marked by a large-scale, complex system of earthworks. ▶ On the banks of the River Teith stands 14thC **Doune Castle**★ (*5m W; Apr.-Oct.: 10-5, Cl. Thu.*); superbly preserved and restored, it gives a vivid picture of life in a medieval stronghold. ▶ **Doune Park Gardens** are adjacent to **Doune Motor Museum** (*Apr.-Oct.: 10-5*), where 40 vintage cars are displayed in running order. ▶ **Blair Drummon Safari Park** (*early Apr.-Sep.: 10-4.30*) lies 2m S of Doune.   □

Practical information _____

DUNBLANE
ⓘ Stirling Road, ☎ (0786) 824428 (summer only).

Hotel:
★ *Stakis Dunblane*, FK15 0HG, ☎ (0786) 822551, Tx 776284, AC AM BA DI, 188 rm. ℗ ⟨ ▦ ⚲ ₺ ▱ ⚯ ⊘ £70. Rest. ♦ ⌁ ₺ £10.

Recommended
Golf course: Perth Road, ☎ (0786) 823711.
Riding school: *The Scottish School of Equitation*, Dam of Quoigs, Greenloaning, ☎ (078 688) 278, hacking, trekking, moor, farmland, covered school.

Nearby

DOUNE, 2m NW on A84

Hotel:
★★ *Woodside*, Stirling Road, FK16 6AB, ☎ (0786) 841237, AC, 14 rm. ℗ ▦ A famous 17thC coaching inn. £39. Rest. ♦ ⌁ ₺ £15.

Restaurant:
♦ *Broughton's*, Burnbank Cottages, Blairdrummond, ☎ (0786) 841897, AC ℗ ▦ ⚲ ₺ ⚯ Cl. Sun.-Mon., 4 wks. winter-spring. Venison in bilberry sauce. Book. £14.

KINBUCK, 3 1/2m N by B8033

Hotel:
● ★★ *Cromlix House* (P.O.B.), FK15 9JT, ☎ (0786) 822125, AC AM BA DI, 14 rm. ℗ ⟨ ▦ ⚲ ⊘ 19thC Scottish baronial country house with interesting tapestry and Kinndull portraits. £102. Rest. ● ♦ ₺ £26.50.

DUNDEE*

Glasgow, 83; Aberdeen, 67; Edinburgh, 63 m
pop. 172,294 ☎ 0382   Tayside B2

Dundee, Scotland's fourth-largest city set on the N shore of the Tay Estuary, is a major commercial

centre and port. It became a royal burgh about 1190 and had a checkered history, being captured at various times by Henry VIII, the Marquis of Montrose and General Monk. Dundee has a splendid position and outstanding parks.

▶ The 15thC **old steeple** surmounts the city churches, three churches under one roof. ▶ The Albert Institute in Albert Square contains the **City Museum and Art Gallery★★**, also known as the McManus Galleries (*Mon.-Sat., 10-5.30*): archaeological collections, wide range of paintings. ▶ **Barrack Street Museum** (*Mon.-Sat., 10-5.30*) has exhibits on natural history and shipping. ▶ **Camperdown Park** (*in NW*) has a zoo, adventure playground and golf museum. ▶ In Victoria Dock lies the oldest surviving British man o' war, the *Unicorn*. ▶ The **Mills Observatory** (*Apr.-Sep.: Mon.-Fri., 10-5, Sat., 2-5; Oct.-Mar.: Mon.-Fri., 3-10, Sat., 2-5*) has displays on astronomy and space exploration, as well as a small planetarium.

Nearby

▶ At **Broughty Ferry**, a seaside resort to the E, 15thC **Broughty Castle** (*Jul.-Sep.: Mon.-Thu., Sat., 10-1, 2-5.30, Sun., 2-5*) houses a museum on the whaling industry, the Tay Estuary and armour.▶ **Claypotts Castle★** (*Apr.-Sep.: Mon.-Sat., 9.30-7, Sun., 2-7; Oct.-Mar.: Mon.-Sat., 9.30-4, Sun., 2-4*) is a remarkably complete and well-preserved Z-plan tower house of the 16thC.　　　　　☐

Practical information _____

DUNDEE
ⓘ Nethergate Centre, ☎ (0382) 27723.
✈ Dundee Airport, 1 1/2m SW, ☎ (0382) 643242.
Car-rental: Europcar, St. Roques Auto Co. Ltd., 64 Ward Road, ☎ (0382) 21281.

Hotels:
★★★ *Angus Thistle*, 101 Marketgait, DD1 1QU, ☎ (0382) 26874, Tx 76456, AC AM BA DI, 58 rm. ℙ ♨ ✔ £79. Rest. ♦ ♪ ♿ £10.50.
★★ *Queen's*, Nethergate, DD1 4DU, ☎ (0382) 22515, AC AM BA DI, 60 rm. ℙ ♨ ♿ ✿ ◔ £59. Rest. ♦ ♪ ♿ £13.

Restaurants:
♦ *Raffles*, 18 Perth Road, ☎ (0382) 26344 ♿ ✿ Cl. Sun.-Mon., 2 wks. Christmas, 2 wks. Jul. Book. £9.50.
♦ *The Square Peg*, 10 Constitution Road, ☎ (0382) 28265 ℙ ✿ Cl. Bank Hols., Sun. Vegetarian dishes. Book. £6.

Recommended
Golf course: Caird Park, off Kingsway Bypass, ☎ (0382) 453606; Camperdown Park, 2m NW by A923, ☎ (0382) 645450.

Nearby
AUCHTERHOUSE, 7m NW

Hotel:
● ★★ *Old Mansion House*, DD3 0QN, ☎ (082 626) 366, AM BA DI, 6 rm. ℙ ♨ ♨ ◔ ▭ ✈ Built in the 15thC, family house in Scottish baronial style with 11 acres of grounds. £68. Rest. ♦ ♿ Cl. 1-8 Jan. £19.

DUNKELD★★

Perth, 14; Aberdeen, 88; Edinburgh, 58 m
☎ 035 02　　　　　　　　　　　Tayside A2

Dunkeld is a small ancient cathedral city on the River Tay, which in the 9thC was the ecclesiastical capital of Scotland. It is also a popular vacation resort. Its 17thC buildings, some of the finest domestic architecture in Scotland, have been carefully restored.

▶ The **cathedral** (*Apr.-Sep.: Mon.-Sat., 9.30-7, Sun., 2-7; Oct.-Mar.: closes 4*), though partly roofless, retains much of its beauty. ▶ The **choir** is used as the parish church and has the magnificent **tomb of the Wolf of Badenoch** (→). ▶ The delightful **'Little Houses'★** comprise 40 hous-

es and two shops: information centre (*Apr.-Oct.*). ▶ The elegant **bridge** over the Tay was built by Thomas Telford. ▶ The **Museum of the Scottish Horse Regiment** (*Easter week, May-Sep.: Mon.-Sat., 10-12.30, 1.30-5, Sun., 11-12.30, 1.30-5*).

Nearby

▶ The **Hermitage** (*1m N*), an 18thC folly, is the centrepiece of a woodland walk beside the **River Braan.**▶ **Loch of the Lowes** (*2m NE*) is a wildlife reserve where ospreys can be observed. ▶ In **Birnam Wood**, made famous from Shakespeare's *Macbeth*, is a walk along the Tay to the summit of Birnam Hill.　　　　　☐

Practical information _____

DUNKELD
ⓘ The Cross, ☎ (035 02) 688 (summer only).

Hotels:
★★ *Dunkeld House*, PH8 0HX, ☎ (035 02) 771, BA, 31 rm. ♨ ⌘ ♿ ✈ A 19thC mansion house, standing in 100 acres of garden on the banks of the River Tay. £78. Rest. ♦ ♿ Cl. Dec. £15.
★ *Atholl Arms*, Tayside Terrace, PH8 0AH, ☎ Bridgehead (035 02) 219, AC AM BA, 20 rm. ♨ ⌘ ♨ £40. Rest. ♦ Cl. Feb. £10.50.

⚐ *Bankfoot C.S.* (50 pl), ☎ (0738) 26178;*Erigmore House C.P.*, Birnam (200 pl), ☎ (035 02) 236.

Recommended
Craft workshops: *Jeremy Law (Scotland) Ltd.*, City Hall, Atholl Street, ☎ (035 02) 569, hand-crafted leather goods;at Killin,*Ben Ghias Workshops*, Tomorocher, ☎ (056 72) 527, hand-knit and hand-woven woolens and rugs.
Golf course: 1m N on A293, ☎ (035 02) 524.

ELGIN★★

Inverness, 39; Aberdeen, 68; Edinburgh, 198 m
pop. 18,702 ☎ 0343　　　　　　　　Grampian B1

Elgin is an old and elegant town preserving several arcaded buildings on streets laid out in the medieval pattern. The cathedral was founded in 1224 but it and much of the town were burnt by the Wolf of Badenoch (→) in 1390. It was rebuilt, but the central tower collapsed on Easter Sunday 1711. It is now a ruin though restoration work is in progress.

▶ The **cathedral★** (*Apr.-Sep.: Mon.-Sat., 9.30-7, Sun., 2-7; Oct.-Mar.: closes 4*) was regarded as the most beautiful in Scotland and still impresses with its soaring towers and stone tracery. ▶ **Little Cross** in High Street was erected in 1733. ▶ Opposite is the **Elgin Museum** (*Apr.-Sep.: Mon-Fri., 10-4, Sat., 10-12*) with collections on local history. ▶ The **column** on Lady Hill commemorates the last Duke of Gordon.

Nearby

Birnie (*3m S*) has a church built *c.* 1140, once the seat of the bishopric. ▶ Farther S is **Millbuies Park** with walks and nature trails. **Pluscarden Abbey** (*6m SW*), founded in 1230, was given in 1943 to the Benedictines who have carried out extensive restoration. ▶ Nearby is **Monaughty Forest Walk**. Lossiemouth (→) lies 6m N. **Fochabers** (*9m E*) on the River Spey is a Georgian town with a folk museum (*summer: 9.30-1, 2-6; winter: closes 5*). **Baxter's Visitor Centre** (*Apr.-Oct.: Mon.-Fri., 10-4*) is a nostalgic picture of the past with a reconstructed 'Old Shop' and guided tours of Baxter's traditional food factory. ▶ At **Spey Bay**, where the Spey flows into the sea, is **Tugnet Ice House** (*Jun.-Sep.: 10-4*) presenting an exhibition on salmon fishing and wildlife on the estuary, set in the largest ice house in Scotland.　　　　　☐

Practical information ――――――――――

ELGIN
ⓘ 17 High Street, ☎ (0343) 3388/2666.

Hotel:
★★★ *Mansion House*, The Haugh, IV30 1AW, ☎ (0343) 48811, AC AM BA DI, 12 rm. Ⓟ ≼ ᴍ ☖ ⌘ £54. Rest. ♦ ⚹ £13.50.

Restaurant:
♦ *Enrico's*, 15 Grey Friars Street, ☎ (0343) 2849, AC AM BA DI Cl. Sun. £10.

⚲ *Riverside C.P.*, West Road (47 pl), ☎ (0343) 2813.

Recommended
Golf course: Hardhillock, Birnie Road, 1m S, ☎ (0343) 2338.
♥ *Gordon and MacPhail*, 58-60 South Street, ☎ (0343) 45111, wine, spirit and grocery shop specializing in Scotch whiskies.

ELLON

Aberdeen, 17; Fraserburgh, 27; Edinburgh, 147 m
pop. 6,304 ☎ 0358   Grampian B1

Ellon, a market town and agricultural centre on the River Ythan, was once an important Pictish settlement. During the Middle Ages, justice was dispensed by the Earls of Buchan at the Moot.

▶ A monument marks the site of the Moot Hill. ▶ The **old bridge** was built in 1793. ▶ A fragment of the **old castle** is splendidly sited on a river terrace.

Nearby
▶ **Haddo House**★★ (*c. 7m NW; May-Sep.: 2-6*), is an imposing mansion built for the Earl of Aberdeen: fine furniture and historic portraits, most of the Haddo estate is a **country park** with woodland walks: visitor centre (*May-Sep.: 11-6*), with information on the park's history and its flora and fauna. ▶ To SE, across the Ythan Estuary from Newburgh, is the **Sands of Forvie Nature Reserve** where eider and tern colonies flourish among giant sand dunes and grassy cliffs. ▶ Charming **Collieston** was both a fishing and smuggling centre. ▶ Farther N is the tower of **Old Slains Castle**. ▶ The 'new' castle, 4m N, is an extensive ruin close to the landfall of the oil pipeline from the 'Forties Field'. ▶ **Bullers of Buchan** is a remarkable rock chasm amid wild cliffs.   ☐

Practical information ――――――――――
ⓘ Market Street Car Park, ☎ (0358) 20730 (summer only).

Hotels:
★★★ *Ladbroke Mercury*, ☎ (0358) 20666, Tx 739200, AC AM BA DI, 40 rm. Ⓟ ☖ ႕ £58. Rest. ♦ ⚹ ႕ £10.
★ *New Inn*, Market Street, AB4 9TD, ☎ (0358) 20425, AC AM BA DI, 12 rm. Ⓟ ≼ A 200-year-old coaching inn in which Dr. Johnson is believed to have stayed. £37. Rest. ♦ £7.

Recommended
Golf course: McDonald, ☎ (0358) 20576.

FETTERCAIRN

☎ 033 045   Grampian B2

Fettercairn, founded in the mid-18thC, is surrounded by castles and stately homes. Entrance to the village is through a turreted arch commemorating a visit by Queen Victoria and Prince Albert in 1861.

▶ The **town cross** came from the now-vanished burgh of Kincardine. ▶ **Fettercairn House** (*not open*) was built by the first Earl of Middleton.

Nearby
▶ **Edzell Castle**★ (*Apr.-Sep.: Mon.-Sat., 9.30-7, Sun., 2-7; Oct.-Mar.: close 4*), 6m SW, was a 16thC tower house, to which was added an elegant mansion; the outstanding feature is the **'Pleasance'**, a formal garden whose walls are decorated with heraldic symbols. ▶ A road runs NW for 14m along **Glen Esk**. The **Folk Museum** (*Easter-May: Sun., 2-6; Jun.-Sep.: daily*) at Tarfside depicts 19thC life in the glen. The road ends at **Lochlee Church** from which there is a path to Loch Lee (old churchyard) passing ruins of **Invermark Castle**. ▶ N of Fettercairn is **Fasque** where 19thC house is the home of the Gladstone family. ▶ To W is **Balbegno Castle** (*not open*), a 16thC tower house with a fine rib-vaulted ceiling in the great hall.   ☐

FORFAR

Dundee, 12; Aberdeen, 55; Edinburgh, 75 m
pop. 12,652 ☎ 0307   Tayside B2

Forfar is an ancient burgh, but its current charter dates from 1665 and only an old octagonal tower marks the site of the vanished castle. One of the last battles between the Picts and the Scots was fought *c.* 845 on the shore of Forfar Loch.

▶ **Forfar Museum and Art Gallery** (*Mon.-Wed., 9.30-7, Thu., Sat., 9.30-5*) has exhibits on local archaeology and the 19thC flax industry. ▶ **Lochside Country Park** round Forfar Loch has nature walks.

Nearby
Restenneth Priory (*1 1/2m NE*) was founded *c.* 710 by Nechton, King of the Picts; most of the ruin is 12thC but the tower is older. ▶ **Aberlemno sculpted stone** (*5m NE*) is a splendid Pictish stone in a churchyard; three other stones stand behind the road. ▶ **Glamis Castle**★ (*Easter weekend, May-Sep.: Sun.-Fri., 1-5*) was the childhood home of Queen Elizabeth the Queen Mother and birthplace of Princess Margaret. Parts of the early tower have walls 15 ft. thick. There are fine collections of china, tapestries and furniture. ▶ Nearby **Angus Folk Museum**★ (*May-Sep.: 12-5*) consists of six 17thC cottages furnished to give a fascinating picture of domestic and agricultural life in bygone days. ▶ To NE, **Finavon Castle** dates from 1300 but it collapsed in the 18thC. ▶ **Finavon Dovecot**, the largest dovecote in Scotland, has an exhibition on Angus dovecotes. ▶ **Kirriemuir** (*5m NW*) is J.M. Barrie's birthplace (*May-Sep.: Mon.-Sat., 10-12.30, 2-6, Sun., 2-6*).   ☐

Practical information ――――――――――

FORFAR
ⓘ The Myre, ☎ (0307) 67876.

Hotel:
★★★ *Benholm*, 78 Glamis Road, DD8 1DS, ☎ (0307) 64281, AC AM BA DI, 7 rm. Ⓟ ᴍ ☖ ⌘ £57.50. Rest. ♦ £18.

Recommended
Golf course: Cunninghill, Arbroath Road, 1m E on A932, ☎ (0307) 2120.

FORRES*

Inverness, 27; Aberdeen, 80; Edinburgh, 165 m
pop. 8,346 ☎ 0309   Grampian A1

Forres is a royal burgh whose history may go back 2,000 years. Its castle was a royal residence by the 9thC. The opening scenes of Shakespeare's *Macbeth* are set there, including the witches' 'blasted heath'.

▶ **Sueno's stone**★★ is a superbly sculpted 23 ft. stone with a wheel cross on one side and warlike scenes on the other. It is probably more than 1000-years-old. ▶ **Nelson**

Tower was built in commemoration of Nelson's victory at Trafalgar. ▶ The **Falconer Museum** (*Oct.-Mar.: 10-12.30, 1.30-4; Apr.-Sep.: 9.30-6.30*) includes collections on fossils, weapons and natural history.

Nearby

Darnaway Visitor Centre (*Jan.-mid-Sep.: 11-5*), 3 1/2m W, offers an audio visual show, guided walks and tours of the estate. ▶ **Darnaway Castle** (*tours from visitor centre, Jun.-mid-Sep.: Sun., Wed. 11-5*) is notable for 15thC Randolph's Hall with a magnificent oak ceiling. ▶ To N of Brodie Castle (→), 3m W of Forres, is the beautiful village of **Dyke**: church with three-decked pulpit for minister, precentor and penitent. ▶ To N, **Coulbin Forest** was planted to tame the shifting sands: information centre at **Cloddymoss.** ▶ **Findhorn** (*4m N*), once an important port, is now a beach resort with water sports. □

Practical information _____

ⓘ Falconer Museum, Tolbooth Street, ☎ (0309) 72938.

Hotels:
★★ **Ramnee**, Victoria Road, IV36 0BN, ☎ (0309) 72410, AC AM BA, 21 rm. Ⓟ ≼ ⌂ ⊸⊗ £43. Rest. ♦ Cl. Jan. £11.50.

⚠ at Findhorn, **Findhorn Bay C.P.** (75 pl), ☎ (0309) 30203.

FRASERBURGH*

Aberdeen, 40; Peterhead, 18 m
☎ 0346   Grampian B1

An attractive mixture of old and new, Fraserburgh was founded in 1546 by Sir Alexander Fraser. For a short time in 1575 the seat of a university, it is now a prosperous fishing port with some industrial development.

▶ On Kinnaird Head stands **Kinnaird Castle**, built by Sir Alexander Fraser in 1570. It now serves as a lighthouse, with only the central tower remaining. Between the lighthouse and the sea is the **Wine Tower**, probably a 16thC defense tower.

Nearby

▶ To SE are the scanty remains of **Inverallochy Castle** and of **Cairnbulg Castle** (*not open*). ▶ To W the cliffs are magnificent. ▶ At **Rosehearty** are the ruins of 15thC Pitsligo Castle; nearby stand the old (17thC) and new (19thC) churches of **Pitsligo**: the new contains fine carved paneling. ▶ 1m N of **New Aberdour** is St. Drostan's **well** and **chapel.** ▶ On a headland stand the picturesque ruins of **Dundarg Castle**, built in 13thC within an Iron Age fort. Farther W, **Pennan** is a delightful fishing village reminiscent of Cornwall. □

HELENSBURGH

Glasgow, 22; Edinburgh, 68 m
pop. 16,432 ☎ 0436   Strathclyde A3

Helensburgh is a popular but quiet coastal resort with some fine Victorian buildings. It was laid out by Sir James Colquhoun in the late 18thC. It was the home of John Logie Baird, the television pioneer, and of the architect Charles Rennie Mackintosh.

▶ **Helensburgh Museum** (*Mon., Thu., 10-1, 2-8, Tue., Wed., Fri., Sat., 10-1, 2-5*), contains Baird's first television set. ▶ **Hill House** (*daily 1-5*), was designed by Mackintosh in 1902. ▶ Nature trail at **Ardmore Point**, reached from the A814 between Helensburgh and Cardross. ▶ **Adam and Eve Walk** in Camsail Wood on the **Rosneath Peninsula.** □

Practical information _____

HELENSBURGH
ⓘ Pier Head Car Park, ☎ (0436) 2642 (summer only).
🚢 To Gourock, summer only (3-5 daily).

Hotel:
★★★ **Commodore**, 112 West Clyde Street, G84 8ES, ☎ (0436) 6924, AC AM BA DI, 45 rm. Ⓟ ≼ ⚹ £58.50. Rest. ♦ ♪ ⚹ £10.50.

Nearby

ARDEN, 5m NE on A82

Hotel:
★★★★ **Lomond Castle Log**, G83 8RB, ☎ (038 985) 681, Tx 776154, AC AM BA DI, 21 rm. Ⓟ ≼ ⌂ ⚲ ⊡ ⤴ ⌿ £63. Rest. ♦ ♪ £11.50.

RHU, 2m W on A814

Hotel:
★★★ **Rosslea Hall** (B.W.H.), Shore Road, G84 8NF, ☎ (0436) 820684, AC AM BA DI, 31 rm. Ⓟ ≼ ⌂ ⚲ ⚹ ⌿ ⚿ £58. Rest. ♦ ♪ ⚹ £13.

HUNTLY*

Peterhead, 40; Aberdeen, 30 m
☎ 0466   Grampian B1

Huntly, founded in the 18thC, lies in a plain surrounded by hills. It is a pleasant holiday resort and market town. Its two main streets meet in an attractive square. The palatial castle ruins dominate the town. ▶ **Huntly Castle★** (*Apr.-Sep.: Mon.-Sat., 9.30-7, Sun., 2-7; Oct.-Mar.: closes 4*) is a splendid large ruin of a 16thC palace with outstanding heraldic main doorway; behind, high on the bank of Deveron Water, is part of an earlier Norman castle. ▶ **Huntly Museum** (*Tue.-Sat., 10-12, 2- 4*) has local history displays. ▶ Castle Street runs under an arch formed by the buildings of the **Gordon Schools** founded by the Duchess of Gordon.

Nearby

▶ **Leith Hall** (*May-Sep.: daily 2-6*), 8m S, is a family mansion approached by a lovely avenue and set around a courtyard, three wings were added to the original 1650 nucleus in the 18thC. ▶ **Druminnor Castle** (*not open*), farther S, is a 16thC mansion built onto an earlier round tower. ▶ **Craig Castle** (*not open*) is a 16thC L-plan tower house with modern wings. ▶ **Keith**, 11m NW of Huntly, has a new and old town. **Milton Tower** was once part of a 15thC castle of the Ogilvies. The picturesque **Auld Brig**, one of the oldest in Scotland. Two distilleries are open to the public. □

Practical information _____

Hotel:
★★ **Castle**, AB5 4SH, ☎ (0466) 2696, AM BA DI, 24 rm. Ⓟ ≼ ⌂ ⚲ ⚹ ⌿ Georgian mansion set in 5 acres of gardens. £40.50. Rest. ♦ ⚹ £11.

INVERURIE*

Aberdeen, 12; Peterhead, 25 m
☎ 0467   Grampian B1

An ancient royal burgh, now a granite market town set in beautiful surroundings. There are several castles and many prehistoric monuments in the area.

▶ The **Bass** within the cemetery was the site of a Norman castle. To W of the Bass are four early Pictish stones. ▶ **Brandsbutt Stone** bears Pictish symbols and 8thC Ogham writing. ▶ **Keith Hall** (*not open*) is a 16th Z-plan castle. ▶ **Kinkell Church**, has a sacrament house dated 1524. ▶ **Inverurie Museum** (*Mon-Fri., 2-5, Sat., 10-12*) has archaeological displays.

Nearby

▶ To N is **Pitcaple Castle** with its two round towers dating from 15th and 16thC. ▶ The **Maiden Stone**, 1m beyond Chapel of Garioch, is a beautifully sculpted pillar of red sandstone 10 ft. high. ▶ The ridge of **Bennachie★** (→; *6 m W)* rising to 1,733 ft. has forest trails, hill walks and picnic sites. ▶ The **Picardy Stone**, 2m NW of Insch, has Pictish symbols. ▶ **Burra Castle** (*by written appointment*), 4 m NE of Inverurie, is a 17thC tower house. ▶ The church at **Kintore**, 4m S of Inverurie, has a sacrament house and an early Pictish stone. ▶ **Balbithan House** (*by appointment May, Jun., Jul.*) is a 17thC L-plan tower house with an interesting garden. □

Nearby

PITCAPLE

Hotel:
★★ *Pittodrie House*, AB5 9HS, ☎ (046 76) 202, AC AM BA DI, 14 rm. ℗ ⊀ ⚏ ⚐ ⚑ ⚒ Partly dating back to 1480, ivy-clad miniature castle in 3000 acres of grounds. £69. Rest. ♦ £21.

KINROSS*

Perth, 18; Stirling, 25; Edinburgh, 28 m
pop. 3,493 ☎ 0577   Tayside A2

The town was the old county capital, and has agricultural and woolen industries.

▶ The focal points is the 17thC **tollbooth; Kinross Museum** has many exhibits relating to local history, including displays of linen manufacturing, peat-cutting and archaeological finds (*Tue.-Sat. 1-5*). Between the town and the loch is **Kinross House★★**, one of the earliest Renaissance buildings in Scotland with a beautiful view E across Loch Leven to an island castle and **Lomond Hills**. Gardens are open to the public (*May.-Sep. 2-7*). ▶ 4m SE, on the shore of Loch Leven, is the **Vane Farm Nature Reserve**. Between end of Sep. and Apr. the area is a favourite place for wintering wildfowl (*Apr.-Oct.: daily ex. Fri. 10-5, Nov.-Mar.: Sat. & Sun. 10-4.30*). On the island in Loch Leven stands a romantic **castle★**, reached by a ferry from Kinross. The tower is 14thC with 16thC curtain wall. In 14thC English attempted to submerge castle by damming the River Leven (*Apr.-Sep.: Mon.-Sat., 9.30-7, Sun. 2-7*). ▶ 2m NE of Kincross is **Burleigh Castle**, a handsome tower dating from 1500, (*Apr.-Sep.: Mon.-Sat. 9.30-7, Sun. 2-7; Oct.-Mar.: Mon.-Sat., 9.30-4, Sun. 2-4*). □

KINROSS
ⓘ Turfhills Service Area, ☎ (0577) 63680 (summer only).

Hotels:
★★★ *Windlestrae*, The Muirs, KY13 7AS, ☎ (0577) 63217, AC AM BA DI, 18 rm. ℗ ⚏ ⚐ ⚑ £55.50. Rest. ♦ ♪ £16.
★★ *Green* (B.W.), 2 The Muirs, KY13 7AS, ☎ (0577) 63467, Tx 76684, AC AM BA DI, 45 rm. ℗ ⊀ ⚏ ⚐ ⚒ ⊠ ⚑ £54. Rest. ♦ ♪ ♿ Book. £16.

Recommended
Craft workshop: *Lochleven Mill Shop*, Lochleven Mills, ☎ (0577) 63521, superb knitwear, jewelry, handbags and Scottish souvenirs.
Golf course: Green Hotel, Beeches Park, ☎ (0577) 63467.

Nearby

CLEISH, 4m

Hotel:
★★ *Nivingston House*, KY13 7LS, ☎ Cleish Hills (057 75) 216, AC AM BA DI, 7 rm. ℗ ⊀ ⚏ ⚐ ⚑ £57.50. Rest. ♦ £16.

Don't forget to consult the Practical Holiday Guide: it can help in solving many problems.

LOCH EARN**

A2

Loch Earn is beautiful throughout its 7m length between Lochearnhead and St. Fillans. The available water sports add vitality to the tranquillity of its mountain setting. The main road runs along the N shore and a smaller more attractive road along the S.

▶ **Lochearnhead** is a touring centre with a wealth of water sport. ▶ Near **Edinample Castle** (*not open*), a fortified 16thC mansion, are the **Edinample Falls**. ▶ **St. Fillans**, a sailing and mountaineering centre off Neish Isle, was the scene of the brutal murder of a MacGregor chief by twelve sons of MacNab.

Nearby

Comrie, a delightul resort 5m E of St. Fillans, lies on the Highland Fault and suffers the greatest number of earth tremors in Britain; it is home of **Museum of Scottish Tartans** (*Easter-Sep.: Mon.-Sat., 9-5, Sun., 2-4; Oct.-Easter.: Mon.-Fri., 10-4, Sat., 10-1*). ▶ Pleasant woodland walk through **Glen Lednock** with the Devil's Cauldron Waterfall. The **obelisk** on Dunmore is to Henry Dundas, Viscount Melville. ▶ At **Balquhidder**, to W of the A84 road to Strathyre (→), are the reputed graves of Rob Roy and his family near the ruins of two ancient churches. □

Practical information

BALLQUHIDDER, 5m SW of A84

Hotel:
★★ *Ledcreich*, FK19 8PQ, ☎ Strathyre (087 74) 230, AC AM BA DI, 4 rm. ℗ ⊀ ⚏ ⚐ ⚒ ⚑ £48. Rest. ♦ ♿ £16.50.

LOCHEARNHEADH

Hotels:
★★ *Lochearnhead*, Lochside, FK19 8PU, ☎ (056 73) 229, AC AM BA DI, 14 rm. ℗ ⊀ ⚏ ⚐ ⚑ £37.50. Rest. ♦ Cl. Oct.-Feb. £16.
★ *Mansewood*, FK19 8NS, ☎ (056 73) 213, Tx 29514, 6 rm. ℗ ⊀ £32. Rest. ♦ £11.

ST. FILLANS, 7m

Hotel:
★★ *Four Seasons*, PH6 2NE, ☎ (076 485) 333, AC AM DI, 18 rm. ℗ ⊀ ⚏ ⚐ ♿ £57. Rest. ♦ ♿ Cl. Nov.-Easter. £14.

LOCH LOMOND***

A2

Loch Lomond is the largest (23m long, 5m at its widest point), most famous and one of the loveliest of Scotland's lochs. More than 30 islands, many of them with ruins, give added interest to the beautiful views afforded by the main road along its W bank and from the quieter, more rewarding road along the S part of its E bank.

Balloch (→) is the S gateway to Loch Lomond, by road or water. ▶ The A82 stays close to the W bank skirting picturesque **Luss** (→) through **Inverbeg** (*ferry to Rowardennan*) to **Tarbet** (→). ▶ **Inveruglas** is best known for its power station, but on the offshore island is a castle of the MacFarlanes. **Ardlui**, at head of loch, is starting point for ascent of Ben Vorlich (3,092 ft.). ▶ The E road from Drymen reaches the lochside at **Balmaha**. ▶ Boats run to **Inchcailloch** (nature trail), largest of the five islands that together with part of the mainland comprise the **Loch Lomond Nature Reserve**. ▶ The road meanders through the Pass of Balmaha, past picnic sites and paths to **Rowardennan**: footpath to summit of Ben Lomond. ▶ A path goes to **Inversnaid**, reached by road from Aberfoyle. ▶ The path continues N and passes **Rob Roy's**

Cave, reputed to have been the hiding place of the outlaw Robert the Bruce. □

Practical information _____

ROWARDENNAN

Hotel:
★★ *Rowardennan*, G63 0AR, ☎ Balmaha (036 087) 273, 8 rm. ℗ ≮ ▨ ☖ £37. Rest. ♦ ⌡ ¿ Cl. Nov. £10.50.

⚓ at Balmaha, *Cashell C.S.*, Forestry Commission (200 pl), ☎ (036 087) 234.

LOCH TAY*

A2

Loch Tay, one of Scotland's loveliest lochs, surrounded by mountains along its 15m length, is famous for its salmon fishing. Roads run along both banks, the narrower S one giving splendid views of Ben Lawers (3,984 ft.) across the loch.

▶ **Kenmore,** at E end, is a model village set round a green, at one end of which is the turreted entrance to Taymouth Castle (*not open*). The village bridge dates from 1774. ▶ To N of the main road along N bank is the **Ben Lawers Visitor Centre** (→). ▶ **Killin,** at the head of the loch, is a pretty vacation village. ▶ By the lochside stand the ruins of **Finlarig Castle,** the stronghold of a ruthless Campbell chief, and beside them, a beheading pit. ▶ The attractive **Falls of Dochart** are formed by the rapids of the River Dochart as it flows into the loch. The clan MacNab has its burial ground on an islet here. The 18thC **church** has a seven-sided 9thC font. □

Practical information _____

ARDEONAIG, 7m E

Hotel:
★ *Ardeonaig*, FK21 8SU, ☎ Killin (056 72) 400, Tx 76163, 14 rm. ℗ ≮ ▨ ☖ 17thC Drove inn, which attracts fishermen. £48. Rest. ♦ Cl. Nov.-Easter. £13.50.

FORTINGALL, 5m NW off A827

Hotel:
★ *Fortingall*, PH15 2NQ, ☎ Kenmore (088 73) 367, BA, 14 rm. ℗ ≮ ▨ ☖ ⚘ A small 19thC hotel in beautiful thatched village at the entrance to Glen Lyon. £38. Rest. ♦ ⌡ £10.50.

KENMORE

Hotel:
★★ *Kenmore*, The Square, ☎ (088 73) 205, Tx PH152NU, AC AM BA DI, 38 rm. ℗ ≮ ▨ ☖ ¿ ⚘ ⌿ £63. Rest. ♦ ¿ £12.50.

KILLIN, 1/2m SW on A827
🛈 Main Street, ☎ (05672) 254 (summer only).

Hotels:
★★★ *Killin* (B.W.), FK21 8TP, ☎ (056 72) 296, AC AM BA DI, 30 rm. ℗ ≮ ▨ ☖ ¿ ⌿ £46. Rest. ♦ ⌡ ¿ £10.50.
★ *Bridge of Lochay*, FK21 8TS, ☎ (056 72) 272, 17 rm. ℗ ≮ ▨ ☖ £35. Rest. ♦ Cl. 8 Nov.-11 Apr. £10.50.

Recommended
Golf course: ☎ (056 72) 312.

LOSSIEMOUTH*

Inverness, 44; Aberdeen, 73; Edinburgh, 203 m
pop. 6,650 ☎ 034 381　　　　　　Grampian A-B1

Lossiemouth is a popular resort with extensive sandy beaches and tourist facilities. It was founded as a port for Elgin (→) 5m S, expanded with the herring boom, and is still a fishing port.

▶ **Lossiemouth Fishery and Community Museum** (*Mar., Apr., Sep., Oct.: Mon.-Sat., 2-5; Jun.-Aug.: Mon.-Fri., 10-1, 2-5, 6.30-8.30, Sat., 10-1, 2-5*) depicts the fishing industry.

Nearby
▶ To S are the splendid ruins of **Spynie Palace** (*unsafe, view from outside only*), the bishop's palace notable for 15thC **David's Tower.** ▶ **Duffus Castle** to SW is a fine example of a Norman castle with moat. **Covesea Caves** (*3m W*) have smuggling associations. ▶ **Gordonstoun School** which the Duke of Edinburgh and Prince Charles attended is 1/2m away. ▶ **Burghead** is a small fishing town; **Burghead Well** is a rock chamber containing a pool of water. **Burghead Museum** (*Tue., 1.30-5, Thu., 5-8.30, Sat., 10-12*) has exhibits on the fishing industry and local history. □

Practical information _____

Hotel:
★ *Huntly House*, Stotfield Road, IV31 6QP, ☎ (034 381) 2085, AC AM BA DI, 12 rm. ℗ ≮ £30. Rest. ♦ ⌡ £4.50.

⚓ *Silver Sands Leisure*, Covesea West Beach (140 pl), ☎ (034 381) 3262.

Recommended
Golf course: Stotfield Road, Moray, ☎ (034 381) 2018.

MONTROSE

Aberdeen, 39; Dundee, 29; Edinburgh, 92 m
pop. 12,127 ☎ 0674　　　　　　　　Tayside B2

Montrose is set on a spit of land between the sea and the Montrose Basin lagoon. It is an ancient burgh, its castle having been destroyed by William Wallace in 1297. The Marquis of Montrose (→) was born at Old Montrose. The busy harbour has profited from the development of North Sea oil.

▶ **Montrose Museum and Art Gallery** (*Apr.-Sep.: Mon.-Sat., 10.30-1, 2-5, Jul., Aug.: Sun., 2-5; Oct.-Mar.: Mon.-Fri., 2-5, Sat., 10.30-1, 2-5*) contains three Pictish stones and whaling and geological exhibits. ▶ The graceful steeple on the **old church** dates from 1834. ▶ **Montrose Basin** is a bird reserve with hides.

Nearby
▶ **St. Cyrus Nature Reserve** (*4m N*) has rare plant life. ▶ **Red Castle** (*7m S*) is a red sandstone ruin probably of the 15thC replacing an earlier fortress built by William the Lion. **Brechin** (*9m W*) is notable for the small cathedral founded in 12thC, rebuilt in 1901 and now the parish church; the magnificent 87 ft. **round tower** attached to it was built *c.* 1000, one of only two such towers on the mainland (→). A fragment has survived of the **Maison Dieu** chapel founded in 1257. □

Practical information _____

🛈 212 High Street, ☎ (0674) 72000.

Hotels:
★★★ *Links* (B.W.), Mid Links, ☎ (0674) 72288, AC AM BA DI, 22 rm. ℗ ≮ ☖ ¿ ⌿ £42. Rest. ♦ ⌡ ¿ £12.
★★★ *Park*, John Street, DD10 8RJ, ☎ (0674) 73415, Tx 76367, AC AM BA DI, 59 rm. ℗ ▨ ¿ ⌿ ⚘ £50. Rest. ♦ ⌡ ¿ £10.50.

Recommended
Golf course: Medal and Broomfield, East Links Road, 1m E off A92, ☎ (0674) 72634.

Be advised that hotels and restaurants in this Guide have perhaps changed addresses; prices indicated are also subject to modifications.

OLDMELDRUM

Aberdeen, 18; Inverness, 89; Edinburgh, 143 m
pop. 1,343 ☎ 065 12   Grampian B1

In spite of modern development, Oldmeldrum has preserved its narrow medieval streets and attractive buildings in what is now a preservation area. There are splendid views of Bennachie (→) to the W.

▶ **Glengarioch Distillery** is housed in a former tannery (*guided tours Mon.-Fri., 2.30, 7.30*).

Nearby
▶ **Pitmedden Gardens**★ (*daily 9.30-dusk*), 3m E, is famous for the late 17thC **Great Garden** created by Alexander Seton, Lord Pitmedden. Highland cattle and Orkney sheep on grounds; nature trail. ▶ **Museum of Farming Life** (*May-Sep.: 11-5*). ▶ **Udny Castle** (*not open*) to the S has a battlemented keep 100 ft. high. ▶ The impressive ruins (*3m NE*) of **Tolquhon Castle**★ (*Apr.-Sep.: Mon.-Sat., 9.30-7, Sun., 2-7; Oct.-Mar.: closes 4*) are beautifully sited in a wooded dell. ▶ At **Barra Hill** (*1m SW*), the site of a Pictish fort, Robert the Bruce defeated John Comyn in the Battle of Barra in 1307. □

Practical information

Hotel:
★★ *Meldrum House*, AB5 OAE, ☎ (065 12) 2294, AM DI, 11 rm. ⓟ ▦ ♩ Country mansion, parts of which date from 13thC, with garden and woodland. £70. Rest. ◆ Cl. Dec.-Mar. £20.

PERTH**

Dundee, 22; Glasgow, 64; Edinburgh, 44 m
pop. 41,916 ☎ 0738   Tayside A2

Perth, sometimes called the 'gateway to the Highlands', was the capital of Scotland until · the mid-15thC and its history is, to a great extent, Scotland's. The country's kings from Kenneth II on were crowned at the Abbey of Scone though in 1297 the Coronation Stone was taken to London by Edward I. Bonnie Prince Charlie mustered his army at Perth for his march into England. Today, Perth is a gracious Georgian city, pleasantly situated on the banks of the Tay.

▶ At **St. John's Kirk** (founded 12thC), John Knox thundered against idolatry in 1559. ▶ The **Museum and Art Gallery** (*Mon.-Sat., 10-1, 2-5*) has history, art, natural history and archaeological collections. ▶ The **Fair Maid's House**, supposedly the home of Catherine Glover, heroine of Walter Scott's *Fair Maid of Perth*, is now a craft centre (*Mon.-Sat., 10-5*); exhibition gallery (*Mon.-Sat., 11-4, Sun., 11-5*). ▶ **Balhousie Castle**, an ancient tower house, contains the **Black Watch Museum** (*Mon.-Fri., 10-4.30 and Easter-Sep.: Sun., 2-4.30*) illustrating the history of the famous regiment.

Nearby
▶ **Huntingtower Castle** is a 15thC castellated mansion (*Apr.-Sep.: Mon.-Sat., 9.30-7, Sun., 2-7; Oct.-Mar.: closes 4*), formerly called Ruthven Castle and the scene of James VI's kidnapping by dissident nobles. ▶ 19thC **Scone Palace**★★ (*early Apr.-mid-Oct.: Mon.-Sat., 10-5.30, Sun., 2-5.30; Jul.-Aug.: Sun. 11-5.30; 2m N*), stands on the site of the ancient abbey where the early kings of Scotland were crowned; fine collections of furniture, ivories and china. ▶ Nature trail to the top of **Kinnoul Hill** reveals a breathtaking view of the city, the Tay and the foothills of the Highlands. ▶ At **Aberneth**★ (*8m SE*), once a Pictish capital, stands the 11thC **round tower** (→), 74 ft. high and one of only two such defense towers in

mainland Scotland. **Aberneth Glen Circular Walk** leads through woods to an Iron Age fort. □

Practical information

PERTH
ⓘ The Round House, Marshall Place ☎ (0738) 22900/27108.
Car-rental: Europcar, 26 Glasgow Road, ☎ (0738) 36888.

Hotels:
★★★ *Isle of Skye*, 18 Dundee Road, PH2 7AB (C2), ☎ (0738) 24471, AC AM BA DI, 44 rm. ⓟ & £52. Rest. ◆ ♩ & £10.
★★★ *Lovat*, 90-92 Glasgow Road, PH2 0LT (A2), ☎ (0738) 36555, AC AM BA DI, 35 rm. ⓟ ◿ & ⅀ £48. Rest. ◆ ♩ & £12.
★★★ *Royal George* (T.H.F.), Tay Street, PH1 5LD (C2), ☎ (0738) 24455, AC AM BA DI, 43 rm. ⓟ ⪜ ▦ ◿ £64. Rest. ◆ £10.

Restaurants:
● ◆ *Coach House*, 8 North Port (C1), ☎ (0738) 27950, AC BA Cl. 1-15 Jan., 2 wks. mid-Jul., Sun.-Mon. Fillet of lamb with a charlotte of aubergine in port sauce. Book. £16.50.
◆ *Timothy's*, 24 St. John Street (C2), ☎ (0738) 26641, AC ⓟ ♩ & ⅀ Cl. 1 wk. Christmas, Sun., Mon. Nettle soup with white wine. Book. £7.

Inn or Pub:
Old Ship Inn, 31 High Street (B2), ☎ (0738) 24929 ◿ Full range of bar snacks and meals incl. chef's speciality. £4.

Recommended
Antique shops: *Walter S. Beaton*, 75 Kinnoull Street, ☎ (0738) 28127, furniture, pottery and porcelain; *John Scott-Adie*, 16 St. John Street, ☎ (0738) 25550, paintings.
Craft workshops: *Caithness Glass, PLC*, Inveralmond Indus. Estate., Inveralmond, ☎ (0738) 37373, handblown glassware, *Perth Craft Centre*, 38 South Street, ☎ (0738) 38232, hand-made Scottish goods.
Golf course: Craigie Hill, Cherrybank , West Boundary by A9, ☎ (0738) 24377.
♥ *John Dewar Sons Ltd.*, Inveralmond, ☎ (0738) 21231, many gift items carrying Dewar name.

Nearby

GLENFARG, 8m N off M90

Hotel:
★★★ *Bein Inn*, PH2 9PY, ☎ (057 73) 216, AC BA, 14 rm. ⓟ ◿ ⅀ A former drovers inn situated in a quiet little village surrounded by the Ochill Hills. £40. Rest. ◆ ♩ £15.

SCONE, 2 1/2m NE off A94

Hotels:
★★★ *Murrayshall House*, Murrayshall, PH2 7PH, ☎ (0738) 51171, AC AM BA DI, 22 rm. ⓟ ⪜ ▦ ◿ ⅀ ◆ ◿ £48. Rest. ◆ & £10.
● ★★ *Balcraig House*, PH2 7PQ, ☎ (0738) 51123, AC AM BA DI, 10 rm. ⓟ ⪜ ▦ ◿ ⅀ ♪ ♩ ◿ £80. Rest. ● ◆ & £22.

⚤ *Scone Racecourse* (200 pl), ☎ (0738) 52323.

PETERHEAD

Fraserburgh, 18; Aberdeen, 35; Edinburgh, 165 m
pop. 16,804 ☎ 0779   Grampian B1

Peterhead is the most easterly of Scotland's towns and has been among its most prosperous ever since the late 18thC when it was a popular spa. Its most significant feature is its huge harbour which, in the 1820s, saw a flourishing whaling industry, at the turn of the century, a boom in herring fishing and now a prosperous fishing industry. A recent development has been the construction of oil-rig bases.

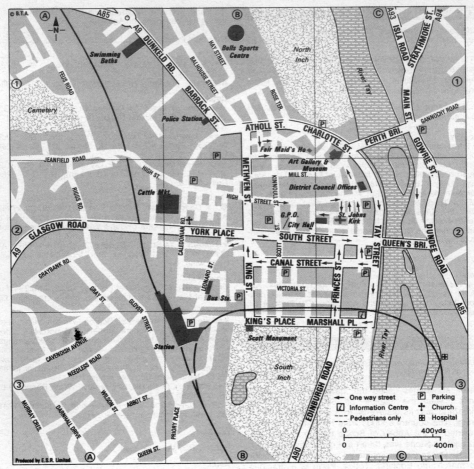

PERTH

▶ **Arbuthnot Museum and Art Gallery** (*Mon.-Fri., 10-12, 2-5, Sat. 2-5*) has exhibitions relating to the fishing industry and whaling.

Nearby

▶ Near Mintlow (*10m W*) is the 230-acre **Aden Country Park** with paths, a nature trail and the **North East of Scotland Heritage Centre** (*Easter-mid-Oct.: 1-5 or 6*).
▶ Nearby are the ruins of the Cistercian **Deer Abbey** (*Apr.-Sep.: Thu.-Sat., 9.30-7, Sun., 2-7*) founded in 1219.
▶ To the N of Peterhead are the ruins of 16thC **Inverugie Castle**. □

Practical information _____

Hotel:
● ★★★ **Waterside Inn** (C.N.S.), Fraserburgh Road, AB4 7BN, ☎ (0779) 71121, Tx 739413, AC AM BA DI, 120 rm. ℗ ⟨ ※ ♨ ↺ & £55. Rest. ♦ ♪ & £9.50.

Recommended
Golf course: Craigewan, ☎ (0779) 2149.

PITLOCHRY**

Perth, 27; Edinburgh, 71 m
pop. 2,194 ☎ 0796   Tayside A2

Pitlochry has long been one of Scotland's leading inland resorts. Set among mountains, glens and lochs, it has catered to fashionable visitors for more than 100 years, many coming for their health as well as for the beauty spots. Pitlochry has become internationally known for its drama season and concerts staged at its splendid theatre.

▶ **Festival Theatre** was founded in 1951. ▶ The power station, **dam and fish pass** (*Easter-Oct.: 9.40-5.30*) feature an exhibition on hydro electricity including an audio visual display. The 1,000 ft. fish pass allows salmon to climb from pool to pool to their spawning grounds; observation windows. ▶ The reservoir of **Loch Faskally** is a popular leisure centre (*Apr.-Sep.: dawn-dusk*)

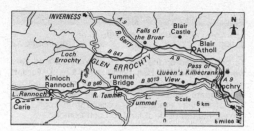

Round trip from Pitlochry

Round trip *(approx. 80m)*

▶ The A9 runs N 3m to the **Pass of Killiecrankie**, in whose wooded gorge the Jacobites routed the English; visitor centre *(Apr.-Jun., Sep.-Oct.: 10-6; Jul.-Aug.: 9.30-6)*. ▶ Outside **Blair Atholl** stands the white baronial **Blair Castle** *(Easter week, Sun., Mon. in Apr., then daily late Apr.-mid-Oct.: Mon.-Sat., 10-6, Sun., 2-6)*, the oldest part dates from 13thC; the 32 rooms contain exhibits giving a vivid picture of life between 16th and 20thC. ▶ By the entrance to the spectacular **Falls of Bruar** is the **Clan Donnachaidh Museum** *(Apr.-mid-Oct.: Mon.-Sat., 10-1, 2-5.30)* with exhibits relating to clan chiefs and clan life. ▶ The B847 branches left through **Glen Errochty** to the B846 which runs through **Kinloch Rannoch**. This whole area has many hydro-electric works but is still scenic. ▶ Roads run along both N and S banks of **Loch Rannoch** ending at the remote railway station of Rannoch. ▶ There are lovely forest walks at **Carie**. ▶ For the return journey, follow road through **Tummel Bridge**. ▶ Near E end of **Loch Tummel**★ is magnificent **Queen's view**, beloved of Queen Victoria, over lochs and mountains with **Schiehallion** (3,547 ft.) dominating the landscape: **forestry information centre** *(Easter-Sep.: 10-5.30)* and network of paths; Pitlochry is 6m away. ☐

Practical information

PITLOCHRY
ℹ 22 Atholl Road, ☎ (0796) 2215/2751.

Hotels:
★★★ *Atholl Palace* (T.H.F.), Atholl Road, PH16 5LY, ☎ (0796) 2400, Tx 76406, AC AM BA DI, 84 rm. ⓟ ⫷ ⋙ ⚄ ⌕ ⌂ ♪ Early 19thC baronial style building in 46 acres of grounds. £68.50. Rest. ♦ ♪ ⚄ £11.50.
★★★ *Castlebeigh*, 10 Knockyard Road, PH16 5HJ, ☎ (0796) 2925, AC BA, 21 rm. ⓟ ⫷ ⋙ ⚄ £41. Rest. ♦ ♪ Cl. Nov.-Mar. £10.
● ★★ *Burnside* (I.N.H.), 19 West Moulin Road, PH16 5EA, ☎ (0796) 2203, AM BA DI, 23 rm. ⓟ ⫷ ⋙ ⚄ ⌕ ♪ £43. Rest. ♦ ♪ ⚄ Cl. Nov.-Mar. £10.
★★ *Airdaniar*, 160 Atholl Road, PH16 5AR, ☎ (0796) 2266, AC BA, 10 rm. ⓟ ⫷ ⋙ ⚄ £40. Rest. ♦ Cl. Nov.-Mar £9.50.
★★ *Birchwood* (I.N.H.), 2 East Moulin Road, PH16 5DW, ☎ (0796) 2477, AC BA, 16 rm. ⓟ ⫷ ⋙ ⚄ ⌖ £42. Rest. ♦ Cl. Christmas, Jan. £10.
★★ *Craigard*, Strathview Terrace, PH16 5AZ, ☎ (0796) 2592, BA, 10 rm. ⓟ ⫷ ⋙ ♪ £37. Rest. ♦ Cl. 25 Oct.-16 Apr. £10.50.
★★ *Pine Trees*, Strathview Terrace, PH16 5QR, ☎ (0796) 2121, AC AM BA DI, 29 rm. ⓟ ⫷ ⋙ ⚄ Victorian country house, in 14 acres of gardens and woodland. £46. Rest. ♦ ♪ ⚄ Cl. Jan.-Apr. £10.50.

⚲ *Faskally Home Farm* (255 pl), ☎ (0796) 2007;*Milton of Fonab C.P.* (190 pl), ☎ (0796) 2882;at Blair Atholl, 7m N, *Blair Castle C.P.* (330 pl), ☎ (079 681) 263; at Tummel Bridge, 9m W, *Tummel Val H.P.* (110 pl), ☎ (088 24) 221.

Recommended
Golf courses: ☎ (0796) 2117; Blair Atholl, ☎ (079681) 407.

Riding schools: *Armoury Trekking Centre*, Armoury Road, ☎ (0796) 2102, trekking mountain forest;at Blair Atholl, *Blair Castle Trekking Centre*, ☎ (079 681) 263, trekking, mountains and forest.

Nearby

KILLIECRANKIE, 4m NW off A9

Hotel:
● ★★ *Killiecrankie*, PH16 5LG, ☎ (079 684) 3220, 12 rm. ⓟ ⫷ ⋙ ⚄ ⌕ £68. Rest. ● ♦ ⚄ Cl. mid-Oct.-Easter. £15.

STRATHTUMMEL, 2m N off A9

Hotel:
● ★★ *Port-an-Eilean*, PH16 5RU, ☎ Tummel Bridge (088 24) 233, 12 rm. ⓟ ⫷ ⋙ ⚄ £40. Rest. ♦ Cl. Oct.-May. £10.

STIRLING**

Falkirk, 14; Perth, 35; Edinburgh, 37 m
pop. 36,640 ☎ 0786   Central A2

Once the capital of Scotland, Stirling has a royal castle to rival Edinburgh's and many reminders of its proud history among its fine buildings. Here Mary Queen of Scots and James VI were crowned, and John Knox thundered his denunciations. William Wallace and Robert the Bruce won bloody battles near the city but Bonnie Prince Charlie failed to capture the castle.

▶ The **castle**★★, royal residence of the Stuart kings, is a splendid Renaissance building dating from the 15th and 16thC *(Oct.-Mar.: Mon.-Sat., 9.30-5.05, Sun., 12.30-4.20; Apr.-Sep.: Mon.-Sat., 9.30-6, Sun., 10.30-5.30)*. The main buildings are the **Palace**, **Parliament Hall**, the **Chapel Royal** and the **King's Old Buildings**. Within the castle is the **Museum of the Argyll and Sutherland Highlanders**. ▶ On one side of the esplanade is the **Landmark Centre** *(Mar.-Oct.: 9-6)* with audio visual display on Stirling's past. ▶ Down Castle Wynd is **Argyll's Lodging** built in 1630 as the home of the Marquis of Argyll. **Mars Wark** opposite is all that remains of the Renaissance palace built in 1572 by the Earl of Mar, Regent of Scotland. ▶ The **Church of the Holy Reude** (15thC) was divided into E and W churches until 1936. ▶ Nearby 17thC **Cowane's Hospital**, now the Guildhall, is used for exhibitions. ▶ Broad Street contains the **Mercat cross** and the **tollbooth**, where the council and court sat and prisoners were incarcerated. ▶ The **Smith Art Gallery and Museum** *(Wed.- Sat., 2-5, Sun., 10.30-5)* is in Albert Place. ▶ The **Wallace Monument** *(Feb.-Oct.)* overlooking the city on Abbey Craig has several floors with exhibitions and audio visual display.

Nearby

▶ To N at **Bridge of Allan** is the modern complex of the **Univerity of Stirling** including the MacRobert Arts Centre. ▶ **Cambuskenneth Abbey** *(Apr.-Sep.: Mon.-Sat., 9.30-7, Sun., 2-7; Oct.-Mar.: Mon.-Sat., 9.30-6, Sun., 2-4)*, 1m E, founded 12thC, was the scene of Robert the Bruce's Parliament in 1326. ▶ **Bannockburn Heritage Centre** *(Mar.-Oct.: 10-6)* stands near the site of the battle at which Robert the Bruce won Scotland's independence; an audio visual display describes the battle. ☐

Practical information

STIRLING
ℹ Dumbarton Road, ☎ (0786) 75019; Bannockburn, ☎ (0786) 815663 (summer only).
🚌 ☎ (0786) 73085 (motorail connection).
Car-rental: Europcar, Mogil Motors Ltd., Drip Road, ☎ (0786) 72164/74891.

Hotels:
★★★ *Golden Lion*, 8 King Street, FK8 1BD, ☎ (0786)

75351, Tx 777734, AC AM BA DI, 75 rm. ℙ ㊧ ⤴ £51. Rest.
♦ ♪ ㊧ £11.50.
★★ *Kings Gate*, 5 King Street, FK8 1DN, ☎ (0786) 73944,
AC AM BA DI, 15 rm. ℙ £33.50. Rest. ♦ ♪ £10.50.
★★ *Terraces* (C.N.S.), 4 Melville Terrace, FK8 2ND,
☎ (0786) 72268, AC AM BA DI, 14 rm. ℙ ⌕ £43. Rest. ♦
♪ £9.

Restaurant:
♦ *Heritage*, 16 Allan Park, ☎ (0786) 73660, AC BA DI ℙ
₩ ⌕ ♪ ㊧ Cl. Christmas, New Year. 4 rm. Book. £16.

Inn or Pub:
Barnton Bar Bistro, Barnton Street, ☎ (0786) 61698 ⅋
Variety of bar snacks and meals incl. vegetarian dishes.
£5.

▲ *Cornton C.P.* (70 pl), ☎ (0786) 74503;at Auchenbowie,
4m S, *Auchenbowie C.S.* (60 pl), ☎ (0324) 822142;at Fin-
try, 13m W, *Ross C.P.* (16 pl), ☎ (036 086) 201.

Recommended
Golf course: Queen's Road, ☎ (0786) 64098.

Nearby

AIRTH, 9m SE

Hotel:
★★★ *Airth Castle*, FK2 8JF, ☎ (032 483) 411, Tx 777975,
AM BA DI, 23 rm. ℙ ₩ ㊧ ⅋ ▱ A 14thC castle set in 54
acres of woodland overlooking the Firth of Forth.

STONEHAVEN*

Aberdeen, 16; Dundee, 51; Edinburgh, 114 m
pop. 7,834 ☎ 0569   Grampian B1

A fishing port, market centre and popular vacation
resort, Stonehaven was founded by Earl Marischal in
the early 17thC. The bridge divides the town into the
old area round the harbour and the new area.

▶ The **Tollbooth Museum** (*Mon., Wed., Fri., Sat., 10-12;
Jun.-Sep.: Thu., Sun., 2-5*), housed in the late 16thC tollbooth, first used as a storehouse, then as a prison, has
fishing and local history displays. ▶ In the High Street
stand the **Mercat cross** and the **town steeple**. ▶ On an
isolated crag to the S are the extensive and spectacular ruins of **Dunnottar Castle**★ (*Nov.-Mar.: Mon.-Sat., 9-6,
Sun., 2-5*); particularly interesting are the gatehouse, well,
drawing room and domestic rooms; in the Whigs' Vault,
167 men and women many of whom died, were
imprisoned.

Nearby

▶ **Arbuthnott House**, 10m S (*not open*), has 16th, 17th
and 18thC features. **Arbuthnott Church** dates from 13thC;
the adjoining **Arbuthnott Aisle** is a two-storey building
with a splendid knight's effigy. ▶ **Muchalls Castle** (*not
open*) is a complete L-plan laird's house of the early
17thC.   ▫

Practical information _____

ℹ️ The Square, ☎ (0569) 62806 (summer only).

Hotels:
★★★ *Commodore*, Cowie Park, ☎ (0569) 62936, Tx
739111, AC AM BA DI, 40 rm. ℙ ⧗ £52. Rest. ♦ ♪
㊧ £12.60.
★★ *County*, Arduthie Road, ☎ (0569) 64386, BA, 14 rm.
£38.50. Rest. ♦ ♪ £10.

▲ *Queen Elizabeth C.S.* (34 pl), ☎ (0569) 62001.

Recommended
Golf course: Cowie, 1m N on Aberdeen Road, ☎ (0569)
62124.

_____
Send us your comments and suggestions; we will
use them in the next edition.
_____

TARBET

Aberfoyle, 14; Callander, 21; Perth, 55 m
☎ 030 12   Strathclyde A2

Tarbet, located on the W shore of Loch Lomond, has
wonderful views of Ben Lomond (3,192 ft.). Tarbet,
or more usually Trabert, signifies an isthmus across
which boats can be dragged. In the 13thC King Haakon of Norway dragged his galleys from Loch Long
across the 2m neck of land to Loch Lomond.

Nearby

▶ To N is **Inveruglas** power station, part of the Loch Sloy
hydro-electric scheme. ▶ **Luss** (*7m S*) is one of Scotland's
prettiest villages; the church has fine oak beams and a
15thC effigy of St. Kessog; a scenic dead-end road runs 2
1/2m up **Glen Luss**. ▶ 18thC **Rossdhu House** (*not open*)
3m S of Luss, is the seat of the Colquhouns.   ▫

Practical information _____

Nearby

ARDLUI, 7m N on A82

Hotel:
★★ *Ardlui*, ☎ Inveruglas (030 14) 243, AM BA, 11 rm. ℙ ⧗
₩ Built as a shooting lodge, later converted to coaching
inn; in 9 acres of grounds by Loch Lomond. £42. Rest. ♦
㊧ £12.50.

▲ *Ardlui C.S.* (20 pl), ☎ (030 14) 243.

ARROCHAR, 2m W on A83

Hotel:
★★★ *Tarbet* (C.N.S.), Loch Lomond, G83 7DE, ☎ (030
12) 228, AC AM BA DI, 91 rm. ℙ ⧗ ㊧ ⅋ £44. Rest. ♦ ♪
㊧ Cl. Jan. £10.50.

▲ *Ardgartan C.S.*, Forestry Commission (200 pl), ☎ (030
12) 597.

LUSS, 7m S

Hotel:
★★ *Inverbeg Inn*, G83 8PD, ☎ (043 686) 678, Tx 777205,
AC BA AM DI, 14 rm. ℙ ⧗ ₩ ⌕ ㊧ Well situated on the
shores of Loch Lomond, with a private landing-stage and
boats for fishing. £52.50. Rest. ♦ ㊧ £10.50.

▲ *Luss C.C.S.* (90 pl), ☎ (043 686) 658.

TILLICOULTRY

Stirling, 10; Perth, 28; Edinburgh, 35 m
☎ 0259   Central A2

Tillicoultry was a prosperous textile-manufacturing
centre in the 19thC. It is now a residential town of
great charm, particularly attractive features being the
Murray Gardens and the Murray Clock. The summit
of Ben Cleuch (2,363 ft.) to the N is reached by way
of beautiful Tillicoultry Glen.

Nearby

▶ To the E is **Dollar**, best known for its school, 'Dollar
Academy'. ▶ On the slopes of the Ochils in wooded
Dollar Glen stands **Castle Campbell**★ (*3m E; Apr.-Sep.:
Mon.-Sat., 9.30-7, Sun., 2-7; Oct.-Mar.: Mon.-Sat., 9.30-4,
ex. Thu. pm., Fri., Sun., 2-4*), traditionally known as the
'Castle of Gloom'; the oldest part is the well-preserved
15thC tower. The Marquis of Montrose failed to capture
the castle, Oliver Cromwell burnt it. ▶ **Rumbling Bridge
Gorge**★, 1 1/2m S of Muckhart off the A823, is a favourite beauty spot where the gorge of the River Devon is
spanned by modern and ancient bridges; charming walks
include the picturesque **Devil's Mill cataract**. ▶ **Menstrie
Castle** (*May-Sep.: Wed., Sat., Sun., 2.30-5*), to the W is

the restored 16thC home of William Alexander, Lieutenant for the Plantation of Nova Scotia: Nova Scotia Commemoration Rooms. □

Practical information —————————————

TILLICOULTRY

ⓘ Clock Mill, Upper Mill Street, ☎ (0259) 52176.

⚠ at Dollar, *Riverside C.P.* (30 pl), ☎ (025 94) 2896.

Nearby

GLENDEVON, 8m NE

Hotel:
★ *Tormaukin*, FK14 7JY, ☎ (025 982) 252, AC AM, 6 rm. ℗ ⚡ ⌕ ♫ A splendid roadside inn with attractively decorated bedrooms. £40. Rest. ● ♦ ♪ ♿ Cl. Jan. £14.

TOMINTOUL

Alford, 25; Inverurie, 40; Aberdeen, 50 m
☎ 080 74   Grampian A-B1

Tomintoul lies at the N approach to the Lecht Pass linking Deeside and Speyside. It was founded by the Duke of Gordon in 1776. At 1,150 ft., it is one of Scotland's highest villages; stopping point on the Malt Whisky Trail (→).

▶ **Tomintoul Museum** (*Easter, mid-May-Sep.: 9.30-6.30*) contains a reconstruction of a farm kitchen and historic and wildlife displays. ▶ **Glenlivet Distillery**: visitor centre (*Easter-late Oct.: Mon.-Fri., 10-4*). ▶ **Tomintoul Country Walk** is a 3m circuit.

Nearby

▶ **Blairfindy Castle** in Glenlivet is a small ruined Gordon castle built in 1586. ▶ **Corgaff Castle** (*9m SE*) was a Hanoverian garrison castle built onto a 16thC tower to guard the military Lecht Road. ▶ A further 13m E, **Glenbuchat Castle** (*not open*) dates from late 16thC. The village **church** is attractive. ▶ Grantown-on-Spey (→) lies 12m W of Tomintoul. □

Practical information —————————————

Hotel:
★ *Richmond Arms*, The Square, AB3 9ET, ☎ (080 74) 209, 26 rm. ℗ ⚡ ⌕ ⌕ ♫ £28.50. Rest. ♦ ♿ £9.

Restaurant:
♦ *Glenmulliach Restaurant*, ☎ (080 74) 356, AC BA ℗ ⚡ ⌕ ⌕ ♪ Cl. Dec. £7.

Recommended
Riding School: *Tomintoul Pony Trekking Centre*, Argyle House, ☎ (080 74) 223.

TROSSACHS**

☎ 087 76   Central A2

Ever since Victorian times, the small area known as the Trossachs, variously translated as 'the place that lies athwart' or the 'bristling country', has been overwhelmingly popular with visitors. It properly refers to the short stretch of rugged countryside between Loch Achray and Loch Katrine. It displays a superb harmony between loch and hill, but that is not unique in Scotland. It was Walter Scott's novel *Rob Roy* that brought fame to the area, which is now con-

sidered to extend E as far as Callander. It was Scott's *Lady of the Lake* that celebrated Loch Katrine. The defile between the two lochs was once a rough scramble; now a winding road connects them. Loch Katrine is best appreciated from the old steamer *Sir Walter Scott*, which sails its length during summer. A track runs along the N bank (→ Aberfoyle and Callander). □

TURRIFF

Peterhead, 25; Aberdeen, 32 m
☎ 0888   Grampian B1

A busy market town built of red sandstone and surrounded by rich agricultural land. It was the scene of the 'Trot of Turriff' in 1639, the first clash of the Civil War when a party of Royalists routed the Covenanters.

▶ Of the old **church** once owned by the Knights Templar, only the choir and belfry survive.

Nearby

▶ **Fyvie Castle** (*May-Sep.: 2-5; 9m S*), is a superb and marvelously preserved example of Scottish baronial architecture. Its 150 ft. long S front has a tower house at each end and huge central gatehouse tower. It preserves the original battlemented castle of c. 1400. The outstanding interior feature is the magnificent **wheel stair**; fine collection of portraits. ▶ Two castles lie to NE of Turriff, neither open: **Delgatie Castle** is a white L-plan tower house built in 1570 on a 13thC nucleus; splendid Renaissance painted ceilings. **Craigston Castle**, built 1604-7, has impressive 17thC carved oak panels. ▶ Ruined **Eden Castle**, 4m N of Turriff, was built in 1676. ⊓

TYNDRUM

Callander, 22; Stirling, 33; Edinburgh, 70 m
☎ 083 84   Central A2

A Highland village important as a rail and road junction for the routes to Oban and Fort William.

▶ Beyond Bridge of Orchy (*6m N*) and Loch Tulla is the approach to dramatic **Glencoe** (→). A path runs from **Loch Tulla** through Glen Tulla past the ruins of **Achallader Castle**, a stronghold of the Campbells where the Glencoe Massacre was reputedly planned. ▶ **St. Fillan's Pool** (*2m E*) was used to test the madness of lunatics. ▶ There are a few remains of 14thC **Strathfillan Priory**. □

Practical information —————————————

ⓘ car park, ☎ (083 84) 246.

Hotel:
★ *Invervey*, FK20 8RY, ☎ (083 84) 219, AM BA, 17 rm. ℗ ⚡ ♿ £28.50. Rest. ♦ ♪ £9.50.

Restaurant:
♦ *Clifton Coffee House*, ☎ (083 84) 271, AC AM BA DI ℗ ♿ ⌕ Cl. Nov.-1 Apr. eve. Scottish dishes. £5.

⚠ *Pine Trees C.P.* (42 pl), ☎ (083 84) 243; at Glendochart, *Glendochart C.P.* (100 pl), ☎ (056 72) 637.

Recommended
♥ *Clifton Coffee House*, ☎ (083 84) 271, food shop stocks smoked fish, meat, pâtés.

Lochinver 427
Lochmaddy 421
Lochranza 412
Lockerbie 375
Lockerbie 375
Lockington 668
Lockmaben 375
Loddiswell 628
Loddon 155
Lode 150
Loders 605
Lofthouse 694
Loftus 310
Londesborough 701

■ **London**

Admiralty Arch 76
Albert Embankment 76
Alexandra Palace 73
All Souls Church 80
Anchor Inn 82
Apsley House 75
Asgill House 80
Athaneum 77
Bank of England 70
Banqueting House 87
Barbican 65
Battersea 68
Bear Gardens Museum 82
Belgravia 76
Berkeley Square 77
Berwick Street 77
Bethnal Green 68
Blackheath 68
Bloody Tower 84
Bloomsbury 68
Bluecoat School 85
Borough 77
British Museum 68
Broadcasting House 80
Brompton 69
Brompton Oratory 76
Buckingham Palace 69
Burlington House 79
Cafe Royal 80
Camden Passage 77
Carlton House Terrace 76
Carlyle's House 69
Charing Cross 80
Charlton House 68
Chelsea 69
Chelsea Old Church 69
Cheshire Cheese 79
Chester 80
Chiswick 70
Chiswick House 70
Christ Church 68
Church of Notre Dame de France 81
Church of Our Lady of the Assumption 81
Church of St. George the Martyr 82
Church of the Immaculate Conception 77
Church Walk 73
Churches 70
City 70
City of London Cemetery 69
Clarence House 77
Cock Tavern 79
Commonwealth Institute 75
Congress House 68
Convent of the Holy Child 78
County Hall 76
Courtauld Institute Galleries 68
Courtauld Institute of Art 78
Covent Garden 71
Cumberland 80
Dean's Yard 86
Dulwich 71
Ealing 72
Eltham Palace 68
Embankment 83
Embankment Gardens 83
Euston 80
Fenton House 83
Fulham Palace 73
Geffrye Museum 68
George and Vulture 79
George Inn 82
Greenwich 72
Greycoat School 85
Grosvenor Chapel 77
Grosvenor Square 77
Guildhall 72
Hammersmith and Fulham 72
Hampstead and Highgate 73
Hampstead Heath 73

Hampton Court 73
Hanover Square 77
Haymarket 79
Her Majesty's Theatre 79
Hertford House 86
Highgate 69
Highgate Cemetery 69
Hogarth House 70
Holborn 74
Holy Trinity 70
Hoop and Grapes 79
Horniman Museum 72
Houses of Parliament 74
Hyde Park 75
Hyde Park Corner 75
Imperial War Museum 75
Institute of Contemporary Arts 76
International Conference Centre 86
Isabella Plantation 81
Jack Straw's Castle 73
Jamaica Wine House 79
Jewish Museum 68
Keats House 73
Kensal Rise 69
Kensington 75
Kensington Palace 75
Kenwood House 73
Kew Bridge Engines Trust 70
Kew Gardens 75
Kew Green 76
Kings Cross 80
Kneller Hall 85
Knightsbridge 76
Lambeth 76
Lancaster House 77
Lauderdale House 73
Law Centre 83
Lawn Tennis Museum 87
Leadenhall 77
Leicester Square 79
Lincoln's Inn 74
London Dungeon 82
London Library 77
London Planetarium 76
London Transport Museum 71
Madame Tussaud's 76
Magpie and Stump 79
Mansion House 70
Marble Hill House 85
Marianne North Gallery 76
Mayfair 77
Methodist Central Hall 86
Michael Faraday Museum 77
Montpellier Row 85
Morden College 68
Mosque 80
Museum of Childhood 68
Museum of London 65
Musical Museum 70
National Gallery 78
National Portrait Gallery 78
National Postal Museum 70
Natural History Museum 78
New Covent Garden 77
Norman Shaw Building 86
Old Royal Observatory 72
Old Vic Theatre 76
Olde Dr Butler's Head 79
Olde Watling 79
Olde Wine Shades 79
Open Air Theatre 80
Orleans House Gallery 85
Osterley House 78
Oxford Street 78
Paddington's 80
Pall Mall 77
Palladium 81
Palm House 76
Parliament Square 86
Pembroke Lodge 81
Percival David Foundation 68
Pets' Corner 69
Petticoat Lane 77
Physic Garden 69
Piccadilly 79
Piccadilly Circus 79
Pimlico 85
Pitshanger Manor 72
Pollock's Toy Museum 68
Portobello Road 77
Public Records Office Museum 74
Punch Tavern 79
Queen Mary's Garden 80
Queen's House 72
Ranelagh Gardens 70
Ranger's House 72
Regent Street 80
Regent's Park 80
Richmond 80

Richmond Bridge 80
Richmond Theatre 80
Romney's House 73
Ronnie Scott's 81
Royal Albert Hall 75
Royal Armoury 84
Royal Exchange 70
Royal Festival Hall 81
Royal Hospital 69
Royal Mint 71
Royal Naval College 72
Royal Opera Arcade 79
Royal Opera House 71
Samuel Pepys 79
Savoy Chapel 83
Savoy Hotel 83
Sawyer's Hill 81
Science Museum 81
Senate House 68
Smith Square 86
Smithfield 77
Soho 81
South Bank Arts Centre 81
Southwark 82
Southwark Cathedral 82
Speaker's Corner 75
Spitalfields 77
Square Rigger 79
St. Alfege 72
St. Andrew Holborn 70
St. Andrew Undershaft 70
St. Andrew-by-the-Wardrobe 70
St. Bartholomew the Great 70
St. Benedict's Church 73
St. Benet 70
St. Botolph Aldgate 70
St. Botolph Without Bishopsgate 70
St. Bride 70
St. Clement Danes 83
St. Dunstan 70
St. Edmund the King 70
St. Ethelreda's Church 74
St. George's Church 68
St. George's Church 78
St. George's Hospital 76
St. George-in-the-East 87
St. Giles Cripplegate 65
St. Giles Cripplegate 70
St. Giles-in-the-Fields 81
St. Helen Bishopsgate 70
St. James Carlickhythe 70
St. James's Church 79
St. James's Palace 76
St. James's Park 82
St. John's Chapel 84
St. John's Church 86
St. John's Wood Chapel 80
St. Katherine Cree 70
St. Lawrence Jewry 70
St. Magnus the Martyr 70
St. Margaret Lothbury 70
St. Margaret Pattens 70
St. Margaret's Church 86
St. Martin Ludgate 70
St. Martin-in-the-Fields 83
St. Mary Abchurch 70
St. Mary Aldermary 70
St. Mary Magdalene 81
St. Mary Overie's Dock 82
St. Mary the Virgin 85
St. Mary Woolnoth 70
St. Mary-le-Bow 70
St. Mary-le-Strand 83
St. Michael Cornhill 70
St. Michael Paternoster 70
St. Nicholas Cole Abbey 70
St. Nicholas Parish Church 70
St. Olave 70
St. Pancras 74
St. Pancras 80
St. Pancras New Church 74
St. Pancras Old Church 74
St. Paul's Cathedral 71
St. Paul's Cathedral 82
St. Peter's Church 76
St. Peter's Church 78
St. Peter-upon-Cornhill 70
St. Sepulchre 70
St. Stephen Walbrook 70
St. Thomas's Tower 84
St. Vedast 70
Strand Aldwych 83
Strawberry Hill 85
Syon Park and House 83
Tate Gallery 83
Telecom Tower 68
Temperate House 76
Temple 83
Temple Bar 70

The Mall 76
The Museum of Mankind 79
The Spaniards Inn and Toll House 73
Theatre Royal 71
Theatre Royal 79
Tower Bridge 84
Tower Green 85
Tower of London 84
Trafalgar Square 87
Traitor's Gate 84
Trinity Almshouses 87
Trinity House 71
Twickenham 85
University College 68
Vanbrugh Castle 72
Victoria 80
Victoria 85
Victoria and Albert Museum 86
Victoria Embankment 83
Wakefield Tower 84
Waterloo 80
Waterloo Place 77
Waterlow Park 73
Wembley Stadium and Conference
Centre 86
Westminster 86
Westminster Abbey 86
Westminster Cathedral 85
White Tower 84
Whitechapel 87
Whitechapel Bell Foundry 87
Whitehall 87
Wick House 81
Williamson's Tavern 79
Wimbledon 87
Windmill Theatre 81
Zoological Gardens 80

■L (suite)

Londonderry 281
Long Crendon 540
Long Eaton 213
Long Hanborough 545
Long Marston 541
Long Melford 179
Long Mynd 237
Long Sutton 217
Long Sutton 622
Long Wittenham 517
Long Wittenham 525
Longbridge 266
Longbridge 341
Longcot 541
Longframlington 311
Longham 491
Longhorsley 306
Longleat House 621
Longnor 194
Longnor 249
Longstock 507
Longton 257
Longtown 131
Longtown 133
Looe 628
Loseley House 458
Lossiemouth 362
Lostock 323
Lostwithiel 629
Lough Erne 282
Lough Neagh 282
Loughborough 205
Loughor 575
Lound 221
Louth 206
Low Moresby 142
Low Row 693
Lowdham 213
Lower Beeding 462
Lower Bentham 679
Lower Brailes 255
Lower Broadheath 268
Lower Brockhampton 234
Lower Halstow 473
Lower Inkpen 530
Lower Parkstone 500
Lower Peover 329
Lower Slaughter 260
Lower Swell 260
Lowestoft 172
Loweswater 131
Lowther 139
Luccombe 633
Luddesdown 470
Ludlow 251

Lugwardine 246
Luing 419
Lullingstone 455
Lullington 451
Lullington 621
Lulworth Cove 493
Lumley Castle 299
Lundy Island 602
Lune Forest 309
Lune Valley 333
Lurgan 276
Luss 366
Lustleigh 609
Luton 531
Luton Hoo 531
Lybster 427
Lyddington 220
Lydford 635
Lydiard 648
Lydney 242
Lyme Park 343
Lyme Regis 629
Lyminge 462
Lymington 496
Lymm 344
Lympne Castle 462
Lympsham 657
Lympstone 619
Lyndhurst 497
Lynsted 473
Lynton and Lynmouth 630
Lytes Cary 622
Lytham St. Annes 333

■M

Mablethorpe 206
Macclesfield 333
Macduff 355
Machynlleth 578
Mackworth 198
Macpenny's 492
Madingley 160
Madron 636
Maesllyn 580
Magee Island 279
Maghera 282
Maghery 282
Mahee Island 275
Maidencombe 652
Maidenhead 531
Maidstone 464
Makeney 198
Maldon 172
Malham 667
Mallaig 417
Mallwyd 578
Malmesbury 630
Malpas 337
Maltby 670
Malton 682
Malvern Hills 251
Malvern Wells 244
Manaton 609
Manchester 334
Manderston House 380
Manifold Valley 249
Manningtree 163
Manningtree 179
Manorbier Castle 586
Mansfield 207
Manx electric railway 289
Mapledurham 538
Maplehurst 462
Mapperton 605
Marazion 636
Marbury 338
March 176
Margate 465
Markenfield Hall 686
Market Deeping 218
Market Drayton 252
Market Harborough 207
Market Rasen 207
Market Weighton 701
Markethill 276
Markington 674
Marks Tey 162
Marlborough 631
Marlow 532
Marnhull 504
Marple 343
Marsden Bay 312
Marsh Benham 534
Marsh Gibbon 523
Marshside 461

Marston Moretaine 521
Marston Trussell 207
Martham 174
Martinhoe 630
Martock 627
Marton 247
Marton 305
Marwood Hill 598
Mary Tavy 650
Maryport 142
Masham 681
Masham 682
Matlock 208
Mattingley 488
Mauchline 373
Mauleverer Chantry 678
Mawgan Porth 635
Mawnan Smith 619
Mayfield 476
Measham 192
Meavy 650
Medmenham 527
Meerbrook 249
Melbourn 160
Melbourne 219
Meldon Park 306
Melksham 604
Mellerstain House 386
Melling 333
Mellon Udrigle 406
Mells 621
Melmerby 140
Melness 426
Melrose 390
Meltham 676
Melton Mowbray 209
Menai Bridge 557
Mendham 157
Mendip Hills 632
Meonstoke 493
Meopham 470
Mercery Lane 442
Mere 632
Mere Brow 342
Mereclough 324
Merry Maidens 636
Mersea Island 173
Mersham 436
Mersham-le-Hatch 436
Merstham 469
Merthyr Cynog 560
Merthyr Tydfil 578
Mevagissey 646
Michelham 459
Mickleham 449
Mickleton 237
Middle Littleton 241
Middle Wallop 507
Middleham 682
Middleham Castle 681
Middlesbrough 305
Middlethorpe 700
Middleton 336
Middleton 337
Middleton Stoney 545
Middleton-in-Teesdale 306
Middleton-on-Sea 438
Midhurst 466
Milburn 135
Mildenhall 173
Mildenhall 181
Milford Haven 570
Milford on Sea 496
Miller's Dale 215
Millisle 275
Millom 130
Millport 389
Milngavie 384
Milnrow 325
Milton 523
Milton 581
Milton Abbas 490
Milton Abbas 615
Milton Common 541
Milton Dameral 625
Milton Keynes 533
Milton on Stour 504
Milton Regis 473
Milton Street 472
Milton Tower 360
Milverton 649
Minchinhampton 262
Minehead 632
Minffordd 567
Minstead 497
Minster Lovell 544
Minster-in-Sheppey 463
Minster-in-Thanet 466
Minton 237

Mirfield 676
Misorden Park Gardens 262
Mistley 163
Mitford 306
Mithian 646
Mobberley 329
Moccas Court 246
Mochrum 396
Modbury 639
Moelfre 557
Moffat 390
Moira Furnace 195
Mold 578
Molland 645
Moneymore 280
Monk Bretton Priory 668
Monk Fryston 690
Monk's Eleigh 179
Monks Eleigh 172
Monkton Combe 601
Monkwearmouth 312
Monmouth 579
Monsal Dale 215
Mont Orgueil (Castle of) 115
Montacute 659
Montgomery 580
Montrose 362
Moor Park House 539
Moor Top 679
Moorfoots 381
Moota 133
Morar 417
Morda 254
Morecambe 337
Moreton 320
Moreton 489
Moreton 614
Moreton-in-Marsh 252
Moretonhampstead 609
Morley 198
Morley 681
Morpeth 306
Mortehoe 626
Mortimer West End 488
Mortimer's Cross Mill 250
Morton 198
Morvern 406
Morvich 422
Morwenstow 608
Morwhellham Quay 649
Moseley Old Hall 267
Mottisfont 507
Mottram St. Andrew 334
Moulsford-on-Thames 542
Moulton 217
Moulton Hall 685
Mount Edgcumbe 638
Mount Grace Priory 684
Mountsorrel 206
Mousa Island 422
Mousehole 636
Mow Cop 257
Mow Cop 328
Much Birch 246
Much Hadham 522
Much Marcle 248
Much Wenlock 252
Muchelney 622
Muck 409
Mudeford 492
Mugdake 401
Muir of Ord 401
Muirfield 391
Muirhead 384
Muker 693
Mull (Isle of) 413
Mullion 624
Muncaster Castle 140
Mundesley 174
Mungrisdale 138
Murcott 537
Murlaggan 406
Murlough Bay 274
Musbury 598
Musselburgh 379
Myddfai 573

■ N

Nadder Valley 633
Nafferton 701
Nairn 418
Nant Peris 572
Nantwich 337
Narbeth 570
Narborough 203

Nassington 215
National Exhibition Centre 232
Naunton 260
Naworth Castle 130
Nawton 676
Nayland 179
Near Sawrey 143
Neasham 301
Neath 579
Headshead 109
Needham Market 179
Needingworth 170
Nefyn 582
Nell Gwynne Cottage 173
Nelson 324
Nenthead 127
Ness 320
Nesscliffe 256
Nether Alderley 334
Nether Alderley Mill 334
Nether Largie 417
Nether Stowey 604
Nether Wasdale 141
Nether Winchendon 519
Netherton 333
Nethy Bridge 401
Nettlecombe 605
Nettlestone 503
Nevern 564
New Abbey 375
New Alresford 509
New Brig O' Doon 373
New Brighton 320
New Coundon 299
New Denham 521
New Forest 497
New Galloway 391
New Lanark 388
New Mills 199
New Milton 492
New Quay 579
New Radnor 574
New Romney 466
Newark Park 264
Newark-on-Trent 209
Newbiggin-by-the-Sea 306
Newbold 195
Newbridge 545
Newbridge 582
Newbridge 638
Newburn 308
Newbury 533
Newby Bridge 145
Newby Hall 686
Newby Wiske 684
Newcastle 283
Newcastle 581
Newcastle Emlyn 564
Newcastle-under-Lyme 257
Newcastle-upon-Tyne 306
Newchurch 340
Newchurch 463
Newdigate 449
Newdigate 467
Newent 254
Newgale 584
Newgate Street 529
Newingreen 463
Newland 242
Newlyn 636
Newmarket 173
Newport 264
Newport Pagnell 533
Newquay 633
Newry 285
Newstead Abbey 212
Newtimber Place 462
Newton 329
Newton 495
Newton 581
Newton Abbot 650
Newton Arlosh 132
Newton Ferrers 639
Newton Linford 203
Newton Links 297
Newton Solney 235
Newton St. Cyres 617
Newton Stewart 391
Newton-Lewillws 342
Newtonmore 419
Newtown 580
Newtown Crommelin 276
Newtown Linford 194
Newtown-in-St. Martin 625
Newtownabbey 279
Newtownards 275
Newtownards 275
Newtownstewart 285
Nine Maidens 636

Ninebanks 296
Nisabost 408
Niton 505
Noke 537
Norfolk Wildlife Park 154
Norham 298
North Berwick 391
North Bovey 609
North Cadbury 658
North Downs 467
North Elmham 164
North Foreland 441
North Leigh 544
North Meadow 648
North Molton 645
North Newbald 668
North Orkshire Moors 683
North Petherton 604
North Rode 328
North Runcton 171
North Shields 308
North Stifford 182
North Stoke 542
North Uist 421
North Walsham 173
North Weald Basset 165
North Wootton 644
Northallerton 684
Northam 603
Northampton 210
Northcott Mouth 608
Northenden 343
Northiam 460
Northiam 471
Northleach 238
Northop 568
Northop Hall 579
Northrepps 163
Northumberland National Park 309
Northumbria 296
Northwich 338
Northwood 492
Norton Priory 341
Norwich 174
Noss Head 427
Noss Mayo 639
Nostell Priory 695
Nottingham 211
Nun Monkton 698
Nuneaton 253
Nunney 621
Nunnington 676
Nunnington Hall 675
Nuthurst 462
Nyetimber 438

■ O

Oadby 203
Oak House 231
Oakford 651
Oakham 214
Onkley 488
Oakley 522
Oakwell Hall 669
Oare 618
Oban 419
Ockham 458
Ockley 449
Odiham 494
Odstock 643
Offerton 343
Okehampton 635
Old Basing 487
Old Bewick 313
Old Bolingbroke 218
Old Colwyn 575
Old Dalby 209
Old Harlow 165
Old Harry Rocks 508
Old Hornsea 676
Old Hunstanton 169
Old Oswentry 253
Old Radnor 574
Old Sarum 641
Old Sodbury 612
Old Somerby 200
Old Town 643
Old Warden 522
Old Winchester Hill 493
Oldbury 240
Oldham 338
Oldmeldrum 363
Ollerton 221
Olney 534
Omagh 283

Ombersley 240
Onecote 249
Ongar 165
Onich 406
Orbost 424
Ord 423
Orford 176
Orford Ness 176
Orkney Islands 420
Ormesby 305
Ormskirk 339
Oronsy 409
Orton 129
Orton Longueville 176
Orwell 166
Osborne House 492
Osgathorpe 191
Osmington Mills 657
Osmotherley 684
Ospringe 455
Oswestry 253
Otley 681
Otley Hall 170
Otterburn 310
Otterton 619
Ottery St. Mary 625
Oulton Broad 172
Oulton Broad 172
Oundle 214
Outer Hebrides 421
Outiane 676
Outwood 469
Over Alderley 334
Oversley Ford 343
Oversley Wood 229
Overton 337
Oving 447
Ovingham 308
Ovington 510
Ower 498
Owlpen Manor 262
Owslebury 510
Oxburgh 180
Oxen Park 134
Oxford 534
Oxford Island 282
Oxted 478
Oxton 321
Oxwich 568

■ P

Packwood House 266
Padiham 324
Padstow 635
Paignton 652
Painswick 262
Painter'S Forstal 456
Paisley 392
Pandy 556
Pangbourne 538
Pant Mawr 576
Papa Westray 420
Parke 650
Parkgate 321
Parkgate 467
Parracombe 630
Paston 174
Pasture Hill 198
Patchem 441
Pateley Bridge 694
Patrington 698
Patrixbourne 444
Patterdale 141
Pattyndenne Manor 457
Paull 678
Peacehaven 468
Peak District National Park 215
Pearson Park 678
Peasmarsh 471
Peat Inn 395
Peebles 393
Peel 289
Peel Island 134
Pegwell Bay 469
Pelistry 643
Pembrey 575
Pembridge 249
Pembroke 581
Penarth 563
Pencarrow Head 621
Penclawdd 568
Pencraig 255
Pendine 572
Pendoggett 655
Pendower 654

Penegoes 578
Penielheugh 386
Peninver 414
Penmaen 568
Penmaenpool 567
Penmon 557
Penn 520
Penn St. Village 518
Pennal 578
Pennan 360
Pennarth Fawr 582
Pennine Way 309
Penrhyn Castle 558
Penrice 568
Penrith 139
Penshurst 474
Pentwyn 564
Penybont 574
Penzance 636
Peover Hall 329
Pernmill 412
Perranporth 646
Perranuthnoe 638
Pershore 254
Perth 363
Peterborough 176
Peterculter 354
Peterhead 363
Peterlee 309
Petersfield 499
Pett Bottom 445
Petworth 468
Pevensey 468
Piccott's End 526
Pickering 684
Piddletrenthide 615
Piel Island 129
Pike of Stickle 128
Pillaton 640
Pillaton Old Hall 257
Pilton 599
Pilton 644
Pin Mill 171
Pinhoe 617
Pitcaple 361
Pitlochry 364
Pitstone 541
Plankey Mill 296
Plaxtol 438
Pleasington 322
Pleasurewood Hills 172
Plockton 415
Plumley 330
Plumpton 473
Plumtree 213
Plymouth 638
Plymstock 640
Plymtree 625
Plynhimon 567
Pocklington 701
Polesden Lacey 448
Polkerris 621
Polperro 628
Polzeath 655
Pont-y-Pant 559
Pontefract 685
Ponteland 308
Ponterwyd 556
Pontrhydfendigaid 587
Pontshaen 571
Pontsticill 561
Pool 647
Pool-in-Wharfedale 674
Poole 499
Poolewe 406
Pooley Bridge 141
Porlock 633
Port Appin 420
Port Askaig 411
Port Bannatyne 412
Port Carlisle 132
Port Charlotte 411
Port Dinorwic 562
Port Ellen 411
Port Erin 289
Port Eynon 568
Port Isaac 655
Port Logan 395
Port Lympne 462
Port Mary 374
Port Talbot 581
Port William 396
Portadown 276
Portaferry 275
Portaferry 275
Portankill 395
Portavogie 275
Portballintrae 285
Portchester 502

Portelet Bay 117
Portgaverne 655
Portglenone 277
Porthcawl 581
Porthcurno 636
Porthmadog 582
Portinfer 117
Portinscale 138
Portland (Isle of) 657
Portloe 654
Portmanomack 402
Portpatrick 395
Portquin 655
Portree 423
Portree 423
Portrush 284
Portscatho 654
Portsmouth 500
Portsonachan 410
Portstewart 285
Portswood 507
Postbridge 597
Poughill 608
Poulton-le-Fylde 322
Poundisford 649
Poundisford Park 649
Poundstock 608
Powburn 311
Powderham Castle 650
Powerstock 605
Powis Castle 587
Prawle Point 640
Prescot 342
Prestatyn 583
Prestbury 236
Prestbury 334
Presteigne 574
Preston 220
Preston 339
Prestwick 393
Priddy 632
Princethorpe 248
Prinknash Abbey 242
Priors Dean 499
Privett 499
Probus 654
Prudhoe 308
Puckeridge 540
Puckley 437
Puddington 327
Puddletown 614
Puffin Island 559
Pulborough 468
Pulls Ferry 174
Purse Caundle 645
Putsborough Sands 626
Pwllheli 582
Pyrford Lock 454

■ Q

Quantock Hills 640
Quarry Bank Mill 329
Quatford 233
Queen Camel 658
Queensferry 578
Quetivel mill 120
Quorn 206
Quorn 206

■ R

Raby Castle 298
Radcot 525
Radstock 601
Raglan 587
Ragley Hall 229
Rainham 445
Rainhill 342
Rainow 334
Rammerscales 375
Ramsbotton 341
Ramsden 544
Ramsey 290
Ramsey Island 584
Ramsgate 469
Ramster 459
Rangemoor 235
Rangeworthy 607
Ranworth 174
Rathlin Island 276
Ratho 380
Raunds 220
Ravenglass 140

Ravenscar 689
Ravenscraig Castle 387
Ravenshead 213
Ravensheugh 310
Ravensheugh Crags 304
Ravenstonedale 129
Rawcliffe 671
Rawtenstall 341
Read 324
Reading 537
Readymoney Cove 621
Reay 426
Red Tarn 136
Redbourn 539
Redbrook 266
Redcar 309
Redcastle 401
Redditch 231
Redesdale 310
Redgrave 164
Reedley 324
Reeth 685
Reeth 686
Reeth 693
Reiff 427
Reigate 469
Reigate Heath 469
Remenham 528
Rendlesham 176
Renfrew 384
Renishaw 195
Repton 107
Repton 219
Retford 221
Rhandirmyn 578
Rhayader 582
Rhiw 577
Rhos-on-Sea 574
Rhosmaen 573
Rhossili 568
Rhu 360
Rhudodach 412
Rhum 409
Rhydycroesau 254
Rhyl 583
Ribchester 321
Richborough Castle 471
Richmond 685
Rickmansworth 538
Ridley Hall 296
Ridware 250
Rievaulx 675
Ringland 174
Ringwood 502
Ripley 458
Ripon 686
Rippingale 217
Ripponden 673
Rivenhall End 161
Riverhill House 472
Rivington 323
Roade 211
Robertsbridge 460
Robeston Wathen 570
Robin Hood's Bay 697
Rochbourne 494
Rochdale 325
Rochdale 338
Roche Abbey 670
Rochester 310
Rochester 469
Rochford 178
Rock 636
Rockcliffe 131
Rockcliffe 375
Rockingham Castle 196
Rockingham Forest 216
Rockley 632
Rodborough Common 263
Rodmell 473
Rogate 466
Rollesby 167
Rolleston-on-Dove 235
Rollright Stones 524
Rolvenden 477
Romaldkirk 306
Romiley 343
Romsey 503
Rosebank 388
Rosedale Abbey 683
Rosemarkie 401
Ross-on-Wye 254
Rosthwaite 131
Rosthwaite 138
Rostrevor 282
Rostrevor 285
Rothbury 310
Rother valley 477
Rotherfield Greys 527

Rotherham 687
Rotherwick 488
Rothes 357
Rothesay 412
Rothley 203
Rothwell 201
Rottingdean 440
Rottingdean 441
Rous Lench 241
Rousay 420
Rousdon 630
Rovenden 474
Rowardennan 362
Rowen 566
Rowsley 193
Roxwell 161
Royston 540
Rozel Bay 117
Ruan High Lanes 654
Rudchester 303
Rudry 562
Rudston 670
Rudyard 249
Rufford 216
Rufford 339
Rugby 251
Rugeley 251
Runcorn 341
Runcorn 341
Runfold 455
Rushden 220
Rushlake Green 437
Rusholme 335
Rusholme 337
Rushyford 299
Rusper 462
Ruswarp 697
Ruthin 583
Ruthwell 375
Rydal 136
Ryde 503
Rye 470
Rye 471
Ryhope 312
Ryton 303

■S

Saddell 402
Sadgill 138
Saffron Walden 177
Salcombe 640
Salcombe Regis 645
Sale 337
Salen 413
Salford 335
Salford Village 533
Salfords 469
Salisbury 641
Salle 154
Salle Moor Hall 154
Saltaire 669
Saltburn-by-the-Sea 309
Saltcoats 393
Saltrum House 639
Saltwood Castle 462
Salwarpe 240
Samlesbury 339
Sampford Courtenay 635
Sancreed 636
Sand Point 657
Sandbach 328
Sandbank 404
Sandbanks 500
Sandend 306
Sandford Orcas 645
Sandgate 456
Sandhurst 441
Sandown 503
Sandquay 613
Sandringham 169
Sandsend 697
Sandside 130
Sandtoft 689
Sandwich 471
Sandwood Bay 404
Sandy Mouth 608
Sandypark 610
Sanquhar 394
Sark 117
Saundersfoot 586
Saunton Sands 599
Saunton Sands 626
Savill Gardens 476
Sawbridgeworth 522
Sawrey 145

Saxtead 166
Saxtead Green 166
Sca Fell 141
Sca Fell Mountains 141
Scaftworth Village 199
Scalasaig 409
Scalby 689
Scales 138
Scarborough 687
Scarista 408
Scayne'S Hill 461
Scilly Isles 643
Scole 164
Scone 363
Scotch Corner 686
Scourie 404
Scourie 405
Scouthead 339
Scrabster 426
Scunthorpe 689
Seacroft 217
Seaford 472
Seaford Head 472
Seahouses 297
Seahouses 297
Seale 458
Seascale 140
Seathwaite 134
Seathwaite 138
Seathwaite 143
Seatoller 131
Seatoller 138
Seaton 645
Seaton Burn 308
Seaton Carew 304
Seaton Sluice 308
Seaview 495
Seaview 503
Sedbergh 136
Sedlescombe 437
Sefton 331
Seil (Island of) 419
Selborne 486
Selby 690
Selkirk 394
Selsey 447
Selworthy 633
Semley 504
Settle 690
Settle-Carlisle Railway 690
Sevenoaks 472
Sewingshields 303
Sezincote 252
Shaftesbury 504
Shaldon 650
Shaldon 651
Shalfleet 495
Shalfleet 510
Shallowford 257
Shanklin 504
Shap 137
Shapwick 623
Shardlow 198
Shardlow 219
Sharpitor 640
Shawford 510
Shebbar 625
Shedfield 493
Sheen 249
Sheerness 463
Sheffield 691
Sheldon 192
Shelton Corner 256
Shelton Lock 198
Shepherd's Crag 137
Shepperton 453
Shepshed 206
Shepton Mallet 644
Sherborne 644
Shere 458
Shere 467
Sheriff Hutton 683
Sheringham 177
Sherwood Forest 216
Shetland Islands 421
Shiel Bridge 422
Shifnal 264
Shildon 299
Shildon 299
Shillingford 542
Shin Falls 401
Shinfield 538
Shipdham 165
Shipham 610
Shipley 233
Shipley 461
Shipley 669
Shipston-on-Stour 255
Shipton 523

Shipton Gorge 605
Shipton Hall 252
Shirburn 527
Shobdon 250
Shopford 130
Shoreham-By-Sea 472
Shorne 470
Shorwell 499
Shotley Bridge 300
Shottisham 183
Shotwick 325
Shrewsbury 255
Shugborough 257
Shurdington 236
Shute Barton 598
Sibford Ferris 520
Sibford Gower 520
Sibson 201
Sibton 168
Sidbury 645
Sidmouth 645
Sileby 206
Silchester 488
Silkstone 668
Silloth 132
Silverdale 330
Simonburn 304
Simonsbath 618
Simonside Hills 309
Simonstone 696
Sissinghurst 447
Sittingbourne 473
Six Mile Bottom 173
Sixhills 208
Sixmilewater 282
Sizergh Castle 136
Skeabost Bridge 425
Skeffington 220
Skegness 216
Skelmorlie 389
Skelmorlie Aisle 389
Skelpick 426
Skelton 698
Skelton 700
Skelwith Bridge 129
Skenfrith 579
Skerray 426
Skipper's Island 168
Skipsea 670
Skipton 692
Skipton Castle 692
Skirmett 529
Skokholm Island 570
Skye 423
Slaidburn 329
Sleaford 199
Sleat 423
Sledmere House 701
Slemish Mountain 277
Slidderyford 283
Sligachan 424
Slimbridge 262
Slough 543
Slyne 331
Sma Glen 356
Smallhythe Place 474
Smarden 437
Snaefell 289
Snainton 689
Snaith 671
Snape 154
Snowdon Mountain Railway 572
Snowdonia National Park 584
Snowshill 260
Snowshill Manor 233
Soar Mill Cove 641
Solihull 232
Solva 584
Somerleyton 172
Somersby 218
Somerton 174
Somerton 622
Sompting 478
Sonning 538
Sonning-on-Thames 538
Sopley 502
Sotterley 155
South Croxton 203
South Downs 473
South Godstone 451
South Leigh 545
South Luffenham 218
South Marston 648
South Molton 645
South Normanton 214
South Ormsby 205
South Queensferry 380
South Sands 641
South Shields 311

South Stoke 541
South Tawton 635
South Uist 421
South Walsham 174
South Woodham Ferrers 160
South Zeal 635
Southam 237
Southampton 505
Southborough 476
Southbourne 491
Southease 473
Southend-on-Sea 178
Southgate 676
Southill 522
Southover Grange 463
Southport 342
Southsea 500
Southwell 209
Southwick 494
Southwold 178
Spalding 217
Sparkbridge 134
Sparkwell 639
Speldhurst 475
Speldhurst 476
Spetchely Park 268
Spilsby 217
Spinkhill 195
Spinningdale 401
Spittal 298
Sprotborough 670
Sprowston 176
Spurstow 338
St. Adhelm's 508
St. Agnes 643
St. Agnes 646
St. Aidan's Dunes 297
St. Albans 539
St. Andrews 394
St. Anne 115
St. Aubin 118
St. Austell 646
St. Bees 142
St. Boswells 381
St. Brelade's Bay 118
St. Briavels 242
St. Catherine's Island 586
St. Clears 572
St. Clement's Bay 117
St. Columb Major 634
St. Cross Hospital 509
St. David's 584
St. Endellion 655
St. Fillans 361
St. Florence 586
St. Germans 639
St. Helen's 342
St. Hélier 118
St. Ives 169
St. Ives 647
St. John 119
St. Just 636
St. Just-in-Roseland 654
St. Kew 655
St. Keyne 628
St. Laurence's 297
St. Lawrence 117
St. Lawrence 505
St. Leonard's Grange 497
St. Marg'S At Cliffe 450
St. Margaret's Island 586
St. Martin 116
St. Martin 643
St. Mary 643
St. Mary'S Bay 467
St. Mary's Loch 391
St. Mawes 654
St. Mawgan 634
St. Mellons 564
St. Michael's Mount 636
St. Michaels 539
St. Minver 655
St. Monans 373
St. Neot 603
St. Neots 170
St. Newlyn East 634
St. Olave's Priory 172
St. Peter 119
St. Peter Port 120
St. Sampson 121
St. Saviour 116
St. Saviour 117
St. Tudwal's Islands 577
Staddle Bridge 684
Staffa 413
Stafford 256
Stagsden 521
Stagsden 522
Stagshaw 128

Staindrop 298
Staines 453
Stainforth 690
Stamford 218
Standish 344
Stanford-in-the-Vale 541
Stanhope 312
Stanstead 439
Stansted 438
Stansted Park 495
Stanton 233
Stanton Harcourt 545
Stanton Moor 192
Stanway 233
Stanwick 131
Staple 477
Staveley 137
Steep Holm 657
Steeple Aston 545
Steeton 685
Stenness 420
Stetchworth 158
Stevenage 540
Steventon 488
Steventon 518
Steward Pele 296
Stewarton 387
Steyning 473
Steyning 473
Sticklepath 635
Stiffkey 182
Stirling 365
Stock 161
Stock-sub-Hamdon 658
Stockbridge 507
Stockport 342
Stocksfield 300
Stockton-on-Tees 311
Stogursey 604
Stoke 602
Stoke Bishop 607
Stoke Bruerne 219
Stoke d'Abernon 454
Stoke Fleming 613
Stoke Gabriel 653
Stoke Manderville 519
Stoke Poges 524
Stoke Prior 250
Stoke Row 528
Stoke-by-Clare 161
Stoke-by-Nayland 179
Stoke-on-Trent 257
Stokesay Castle 251
Ston Easton 656
Stone 258
Stone 448
Stone Cross 452
Stone Edge 209
Stoneacre 465
Stonehaugh 304
Stonehaven 366
Stonehenge 597
Stonehouse 263
Stoneleigh Abbey 247
Stonesfield 544
Stonham 179
Stonor 528
Stonor Park 529
Stony Stratford 533
Stopham Bridge 469
Stornoway 408
Stornoway 416
Storrington 469
Stourbridge 258
Stourhead 632
Stourport-on-Severn 259
Stow 198
Stow-on-the-Wold 259
Stowe House 523
Stowlandtoft 157
Stowmarket 179
Strabane 282
Strabane 284
Strachur 410
Strangford Lough 285
Stranraer 395
Strata Florida Abbey 587
Stratfield Saye 488
Stratford-upon-Avon 260
Strath Mailadale 426
Strath of Kildonan 426
Strathblane 384
Strathpeffer 425
Strathsteven 403
Strathtummel 365
Strathy Point 426
Stratton 238
Stratton 608
Stratton St. Margaret 648

Streatley-on-Thames 542
Street 623
Strete 613
Stretton 218
Stretton 344
Stretton Sugwas 246
Stretton-Under-Fosse 255
Stromness 420
Strone Garden 404
Strontian 418
Strood 470
Stroud 262
Stuckton 494
Studland 507
Studley Royal 686
Sturminster Newton 504
Stydd 321
Sudbury 179
Sudbury 197
Sudeley Castle 267
Suffolk Wildlife and Country Park 172
Sulby Glen 289
Sulgrave 219
Sumburgh 421
Summer Isles 427
Summercourt 634
Sunbury-on-Thames 453
Sunderland 312
Sunlight Port 320
Sunningdale 518
Surfleet 217
Sutton 221
Sutton Benger 611
Sutton Bridge 217
Sutton Coldfield 232
Sutton Courtenay 517
Sutton Hill 264
Sutton-Cum-Duckmanton 195
Sutton-on-Sea 206
Sutton-on-Sea 207
Sutton-on-the-Forest 698
Sutton-on-Trent 210
Sutton-under-Whitestonecliffe 693
Sutton-upon-Derwent 700
Swadlincote 218
Swaffham 180
Swaffham Bulbeck 158
Swainshill 246
Swalcliffe 520
Swaledale 206
Swallowfield Park 538
Swan Lake Bay 581
Swanage 507
Swannery 657
Swansea 584
Swavesey 170
Sway 496
Sweetheart Abbey 374
Swettenham 328
Swimbridge 645
Swimbrook 544
Swindon 648
Swine 678
Swithland 195
Swynnerton 258
Sydling St. Nicholas 614
Symond's Yat 254

■ T

Tabley 330
Tadcaster 697
Taddington 194
Tadworth 453
Tain 402
Tal-y-Bont 566
Tal-y-Llyn 567
Talgarth 586
Talkin 131
Talland Bay 629
Talmine 426
Talsarnau 569
Talybont 561
Talyllyn Narrow-Gauge Railway 555
Tamworth 263
Tanderagee 276
Tanera More 427
Tangmere 447
Tankerton 451
Tantallon Castle 391
Tantobie 300
Tapeley Park 602
Taplow 532
Tarbat Ness 402
Tarbert 408

Tarbert 425
Tarbet 366
Tarleton 342
Tarporley 325
Tarrant Monkton 490
Tarvin 325
Tattersalls 173
Tattershall Castle 220
Tatton Park 329
Taunton 648
Tavistock 649
Tawstock 599
Tayinloan 414
Tayinloan 425
Taynuilt 410
Tayvallich 417
Tealby 207
Tedburn St. Mary 617
Teignmouth 650
Telford 263
Telham 437
Temple Sowerby 140
Templeborough 687
Tenbury Wells 251
Tenby 586
Tenterden 473
Tern Hill 252
Tetbury 264
Tetford 206
Tetney Lock 206
Tewkesbury 264
Thakeham 469
Thame 540
Thaxted 180
The Antrim Coast 274
The Barringtons 524
The Chiltern Hills 527
The Hurlers 628
The Mourne Mountains 282
The Mumbles 585
The Needles 510
The Rodings 165
The Sperrin Mountains 285
The Tower of refuge 289
The Trundle 446
The Vyne 488
The Wiggenhalls 171
The Wren's Nest 240
Theale 538
Thetford 181
Thirsk 693
Thor Cross 290
Thoresby Hall 221
Thornaby 311
Thornbury 607
Thornbury 625
Thorne 671
Thornhill 394
Thornley 341
Thornthwaite 138
Thornton 669
Thornton Abbey 672
Thornton Cleveleys 328
Thornton Dale 685
Thornton Hough 321
Thornton-le-Fylde 322
Thorpe 191
Thorpe Mandeville 220
Thorpe Market 163
Thorpe Wood 177
Thorpe-le-Soken 167
Thorpeness 154
Thorwald's Cross 290
Thrapston 214
Thrapston 215
Threave Castle 374
Three Cocks 586
Three Crosses 568
Three Legged Cross 477
Threlkeld 137
Threshfield 695
Throwleigh 609
Thrumpton Hall 212
Thrussington 203
Thruxton 487
Thurlestone 640
Thurnham 330
Thursby 132
Thursford Collection 165
Thurso 426
Thurstaston 320
Tichborne 509
Tickhill 670
Tickton 669
Tideswell 194
Tighnabruaich 404
Tilbury 182
Tilehurst 538
Tilford 455

Tillicoultry 366
Tillington 468
Timberland 221
Tintagel 608
Tintern 565
Tintern Abbey 565
Tintinhull House 658
Tirabad 577
Tiree 409
Tiroran 413
Tisbury 633
Tissington 191
Titchfield 493
Titchwell 169
Tiverton 651
Tobermory 413
Todmorden 673
Toft 217
Tolpuddle 489
Tolpuddle 614
Tomintoul 367
Tonbridge 474
Tong 267
Tongue 426
Toombridge 282
Topsham 617
Torbryan 653
Torquay 652
Torridon 415
Torrin 423
Torrisdale Bay 426
Torrylin 412
Torteval 116
Tosson Burgh 310
Totland 510
Totnes 653
Toton 214
Tottenhill 172
Towcester 219
Traquair House 393
Tre'r-ddol 556
Trearddur Bay 571
Trebarwith 609
Trecastle 560
Trecastle 574
Trefriw 576
Trefor 557
Tregaron 587
Tregrohan 646
Tregynon 580
Trelawnyd 583
Trelissick 654
Trelowarren 624
Tremadog 582
Trent 645
Trentham Gardens 257
Trerice 634
Tresco 643
Tretower Court and Castle 566
Trevaunance Cove 646
Trevelgue Head 634
Trewint 603
Trewithen 654
Treyarnon Bay 636
Tring 541
Trongate 383
Troon 393
Trossachs 367
Trotternish 423
Trottiscliffe 438
Trotton 466
Troutbeck 143
Trowbridge 604
Trull 649
Trumpington 158
Truro 653
Tucktonia 492
Tudely 475
Tunbridge Wells 475
Tunstall 257
Tunstall 333
Turnberry 382
Turriff 367
Turton Tower 321
Turvey 534
Turville 529
Tutbury 234
Tweeddale 381
Tweedsmuir 390
Twigworth 244
Two Bridges 650
Ty Mawr 559
Tyndrum 367
Tynemouth 308
Tynemouth 311
Tywford 510
Tywyn 555

U

Uckfield 476
Udimore 471
Uffculme 651
Uffington 541
Ugbrooke House 650
Uig 423
Ullapool 426
Ullswater 141
Ulpha 134
Ulpha 143
Ulva 413
Ulverston 130
Umberleigh 599
Under Skiddaw 138
Underbarrow 137
Underwood 214
Unst 422
Uphall 389
Uppark 446
Upper Borth 556
Upper Denton 130
Upper Nidderdale 694
Upper Parkstone 500
Upper Slaughter 260
Upper Swell 260
Upper Wharfedale 695
Uppermill 338
Uppingham 220
Upsettlington 374
Upton 210
Upton House 255
Upton St. Leonards 244
Upton-upon-Severn 265
Urquhart Castle 405
Usk 587
Uttoxeter 234

V

Vale of Rheidol Steam Railway 566
Vale of the White Horse 541
Valley of the Rocks 630
Veensgarth 421
Ventnor 504
Verwood 509
Veryan 654
Vindolanda 296
Virginia Water 476
Viroconium Wroxeter 256

W

Waberthwaite 140
Waddesdon Manor 519
Waddington 340
Wadebridge 655
Wadenhoe 215
Wadhurst 476
Wakefield 695
Walberswick 178
Walberton 436
Walkeringham 199
Walkerith 198
Walkern 540
Wall 304
Wallasea Island 157
Wallasey 320
Wallasey 321
Wallcrouch 477
Wallingford 541
Wallsend 309
Walmer 448
Walmer Castle 448
Walney (Isle of) 129
Walsall 267
Walsingham 182
Waltham Abbey 165
Waltham St. Lawrence 532
Walton 130
Walton 696
Walton-in-Gordano 612
Walton-le-Dale 339
Walton-on-Naze 167
Walton-on-Thames 454
Walton-on-the-Hill 453
Wamphray 391
Wandlebury Ring 158
Wansford 177
Wantage 542
Warburton 343
Ware 528

Wareham 508
Warfield 518
Wargrave 527
Wargrave 528
Wark 304
Wark-on-Tweed 298
Warkworth 296
Warkworth Castle 297
Warminster 632
Warndon 268
Warren Point 285
Warrington 343
Warsop 193
Warton 330
Warwick 132
Warwick 265
Warwick Bridge 132
Warwick on Eden 133
Wasdale 140
Wasdale Head 141
Wash Common 534
Washaway 603
Washington 312
Washington 469
Watchet 655
Watendlath 137
Water Oakley 543
Waterbeach 160
Waterfoot 274
Waterhead 128
Waterhouses 249
Watermillock 142
Waternish 423
Waterside Park 331
Watersmeet 630
Watford 539
Wath 694
Wath-in-Nidderdale 695
Watlington 527
Watlington 542
Waverley Abbey 455
Weald (the) 477
Weardale 312
Weare Giffard 623
Weedon 211
Weem 352
Welford 207
Welland 244
Wellingborough 220
Wellington 264
Wellington 649
Wells 655
Wells-next-the-Sea 182
Welsh Highland Railway 582
Welshpool 587
Welton 678
Welton-le-Wold 205
Welwick 698
Welwyn 526
Wendover 519
Wendron 624
Wenhaston 178
Wenlock Edge 252
Wensley 696
Wensleydale 696
Wensleydale 696
Wentbridge 685
Weobly 249
Wesgate-on-Sea 466
West Auckland 299
West Baborough 640
West Bay 605
West Bexington 605
West Bromwich 232
West Byfleet 478
West Clandon 458
West Dean 242
West Green House 494
West Harptree 632
West Hoathly 451
West Ilsley 534
West Kirby 320
West Leake 206
West Malling 465
West Malling 465
West Malvern 244
West Meon 493
West Mersea 173
West Pennard 622
West Quantoxhead 640
West Runton 177
West Stoke 658
West Tarfield 686
West Taring 478
West Wemyss 387
West Wittering 447
West Witton 682
West Wycombe 529
West Wycombe 529

Westbury 656
Westbury Court Garden 242
Westcliffe-on-Sea 178
Westerham 478
Westgate 314
Westhampnett 447
Westley Waterless 158
Westnewton 132
Weston 626
Weston Bay 657
Weston Colville 158
Weston Favell 211
Weston Green 454
Weston Park 264
Weston-on-the-Green 546
Weston-Super-Mare 656
Weston-under-Redcastle 266
Westonbirt 264
Westonzoyland 604
Westport 414
Westray 420
Westwood Manor 603
Wetheral 132
Wetheral 133
Wetherby 696
Wethersfield 156
Wetton 249
Weybourne 177
Weybridge 454
Weyhill 459
Weymouth 657
Whalley 327
Whalley 040
Wheathampstead 540
Wheddon Cross 618
Wherwell 487
Whetstone 203
Whimple 617
Whippingham 492
Whipsnade 525
Whitby 697
Whitchurch 254
Whitchurch 266
Whitchurch 517
White Corriers 407
White Sheet Hill 632
Whitebridge 405
Whitebrook 579
Whitehaven 142
Whitehead 279
Whiteinch 383
Whiteladies Priory 267
Whiteness 422
Whitesand Bay 584
Whitewell 328
Whitfield 296
Whitfield 450
Whithorn 396
Whiting Bay 412
Whitland 572
Whitley Bay 308
Whitley Bay 311
Whitmore Hall 257
Whitney-on-Wye 247
Whitstable 461
Whittington 333
Whittington Castle 253
Whittington Castle 253
Whittlesey 177
Whitwell 214
Whitwell 505
Whitwell-on-the-Hill 683
Wichenford 268
Wick 254
Wick 427
Wickham 530
Widecombe-in-the-Moor 597
Widemouth Bay 608
Widnes 341
Wigan 344
Wightwick Manor 267
Wigton 132
Wigtown 396
Wildboarclough 334
Wilderhope Manor 237
Willerby 678
Willerseyhill 233
Willesley Poune 448
Williamston Fell 303
Willington 327
Willington 522
Williton 655
Wilmcote 261
Wilmington 451
Wilmington 626
Wilmslow 329
Wilmslow 343
Wilsford 200
Wilson 198

Wilton 255
Wilton 641
Wimborne Minster 508
Wimpole Hall 158
Wincanton 658
Winchcombe 266
Winchelsea 470
Winchester 509
Wincle 334
Windermere*** 143
Windle Hall 342
Windsor 542
Winestead 698
Wing 220
Wingfield Castle 164
Winkhill 249
Winkton 492
Winsford 618
Winslow 523
Winslow 523
Winster 143
Winster 209
Winterbourne 608
Winterton 689
Winterton-on-Sea 167
Winterton-on-Sea 174
Winthorpe 209
Wirksworth 208
Wisbech 183
Wishaw 232
Wisley Gardens 458
Withernsea 697
Witherslack 135
Withyham 475
Withypool 618
Witley 457
Witley 457
Witley Court 268

Witney 544
Wittington 195
Wittle-le-Woods 327
Witton Park 299
Wix Cross 168
Woburn 530
Woking 478
Wokingham 538
Wolf'S Castle 568
Wolferton 169
Wolfeton House 614
Wolsingham 312
Wolverhampton 267
Wolves Wood 167
Wooburn 521
Woodbridge 183
Woodbury Cross 598
Woodhall Spa 220
Woodhouse
Eaves 206
Woodlands 497
Woodplumpton 339
Woodstock 545
Woody Bay 630
Wookey Hole 656
Wool 508
Woolacombe 626
Wooler 312
Wooley Moor 209
Woolhampton 534
Woolpit 157
Woolsington 309
Woolsthorpe
Manor 199
Wootton Bassett 648
Wootton Warren 261
Worbarrow Bay 493
Worcester 267

Worcester Lodge 612
Worcestershire
Beacon 252
Wordsley 258
Worfield 233
Workington 133
Workington 142
Worksop 221
Worlebury Hill 657
Worleston 338
Worplesdon 458
Worstead 174
Worth 460
Worth Matravers 508
Worthing 478
Wotton 449
Wotton-under-Edge 264
Wray 333
Wrelton 685
Wrentham 178
Wrest Park 521
Wrexham 588
Wrightington 344
Wrotham 439
Wroxton 520
Wroxton St. Mary 520
Wrynose Pass 128
Wychavon Way 240
Wye 437
Wye Dale 215
Wylam-on-Tyne 308
Wymeswold 206
Wymondham 183
Wyre Forest 268
Wyre Piddle 254
Wytenshawe 337
Wythburn 137

■Y

Yalding 465
Yanwath 139
Yapton 438
Yarm 311
Yarmouth 510
Yealand Conyers 330
Yeavering 313
Yell 422
Yellow Ford 276
Yelverton 650
Yelverton 650
Yeovil 658
Yeovilton 658
Ynyslas 556
York 698
Yorkshire Dales National
Park 700
Yorkshire Dales Railway 692
Yorkshire Wolds 700
Youlgreave 208
Yoxford 168
Ystradffin 578

■Z

Zennor 636